Albert Slavin, Ed.M., CPA
Lillian L. and Harry A. Cowan, Professor of Accounting
Northeastern University

Isaac N. Reynolds, Ph.D.
Professor of Accounting
University of North Carolina at Chapel Hill

Consulting Editor
Allen B. Sanders, Ph.D., CMA
Professor of Accounting
Elon College

BASIC ACCOUNTING
THIRD EDITION

BASIC ACCOUNTING

The Dryden Press

Hinsdale, Illinois

Preface

As the title implies, *Basic Accounting* is a teachable *basic accounting* text. Its primary objective is to present the managerial and financial *uses* of accounting information as an aid to decision making, concomitantly with a presentation of fundamental accounting practice and theory. Thus the resultant effect is a balanced approach to the basic structural form, modern data collection systems, and the uses of accounting.

The book is designed for use primarily in the first-year basic accounting course. It is arranged, however, to meet several needs. For the first-year course every chapter can be used. For a graduate-level MBA survey course, all chapters, except 6 and 7, and careful deletions in certain other chapters, constitute a high-level course. For the many schools that teach only one course in elementary accounting, Chapters 1–17 and Chapter 26 provide excellent coverage of basic accounting. Several chapters are divided into sections and some include the more complex concepts in appendixes, which may be skipped without interruption of continuity. By carefully integrating the managerial uses of accounting with the traditional subject matter of financial accounting, the book provides students of business administration with the basic concepts and uses of accounting and accounting majors with a broad foundation for advanced study.

The book is divided into five parts:

1. Basic Concepts and Methodology: Service and Merchandising Businesses

2. Income Measurement and Valuation Problems Related to Sources and Uses of Invested Capital

3. Financial Reporting: Analysis and Interpretive Problems

4. Cost Accumulation, Cost Control, and Financial Planning

5. Federal Income Taxes and Contemporary Accounting Topics

Part 1 (Chapters 1–6) covers the basic accounting cycle, introduces the various ways of processing a mass of data, and includes a discussion of automatic data processing.

Part 2 (Chapters 7–16) covers an introduction to simple interest and compound interest; the accounting for cash; the measurement and control of receivables, inventory, and plant and equipment; paid-in capital, and short-term and long-term business financing and investments.

Part 3 (Chapters 17–19) covers disclosure in financial reporting, statement of changes in financial position, and price level reporting problems.

Part 4 (Chapters 20–25) introduces cost accumulation and control for general manufacturing operations, job order and process cost systems, standard costs and direct costing, responsibility accounting, cost control in managerial decisions, capital budgeting, and quantitative techniques for decision making.

Part 5 (Chapters 26–27) introduces federal income taxes and summarizes briefly some accounting topics that either are still in the development stage or are covered in more advanced courses and in current accounting literature.

In this edition we have done more than update existing material. It is a modern revision in every sense of the term. Some important new features of the third edition are discussed below.

1. A new introductory chapter that, drawing heavily on the Price Waterhouse Foundation Study Group recommendations, provides for the student a picture of the overall societal role of accounting. This chapter also provides a basic explanation of the business papers, source documents, and data-processing concepts that will be encountered in later chapters.

2. Instead of describing data-processing systems in a single chapter, the introductory conceptual material is followed by specific examples of data-processing applications throughout the text. Various systems—from unit-record equipment to direct-access computers—are used in these illustrations.

3. After the basic accounting model has been introduced, the appendix to Chapter 6 explains accounting standards and the structure of the Financial Accounting Standards Board (FASB) against the background of the AICPA's Accounting Objectives Study Group.

4. Chapter 7, a completely new chapter, brings together a discussion of simple interest and compound interest. The introduction of this material at this time will allow the student to concentrate on accounting concepts instead of interest techniques in later chapters. The interest and present value tables presented in the Appendix to the book have been expanded to allow a greater variety of examples to be used by the instructor.

5. Chapter 17, Disclosure in Financial Reporting, has been given a strong theoretical orientation; it contains many of the theory answers to reporting problems.

6. Chapter 18, Statement of Changes in Financial Position, emphasizes the provisions of APB Opinion No. 19 and both the all-financial resources and the working capital concepts. The direct T-account approach is used as the device for analyzing the needed information for the statement.

7. In light of the serious consideration of the general price level reporting problem by the FASB, Chapter 19 is updated to provide the essentials to the problem.

8. Chapters 24 and 25, Quantitative Techniques for Decision Making and Capital Budgeting Decisions (treated in one chapter in the Second Edition), contain additional decision models and techniques.

9. Chapter 27, Contemporary Accounting Topics, a new chapter, covers a wide variety of topics: valuation methods, regulatory agencies, human resources accounting, social accounting measurements, business combinations and consolidated statements, national income accounting, and other topics. These topics can be assigned at various times throughout the book. For example, the actual consolidated statements of the Burlington Industries are presented; these can be referred to while teaching Chapter 1, 2, or 3.

10. All other chapters have been updated and, where appropriate, include information from *Objectives of Financial Statements,* a Report of the Study Group on the Objectives of Financial Statements of the AICPA.

11. Many chapters have one or more appendixes. These appendixes contain information of an optional nature. Some teachers may use all or part of the material in them; others may omit the information in some of them.

12. A substantial portion of the end-of-chapter material is new. Problems similar to the time-tested problems and exercises in the previous two editions are included; many new decision problems have been added. By permission of the Institute of Management Accounting and the AICPA, CMA, and CPA, problems and questions have been added to this edition.

13. A glossary of important terms has been added to each chapter. It should serve as a good review source for the student, as well as a planning aid for the instructor.

We feel that this Third Edition has four very important characteristics.

1. *Easy teachability.* The examples are presented in a manner that proceeds from the simple to the complex. The end-of-chapter materials are well coordinated with the chapter material.

2. *Contemporary and modern coverage.* Data processing is integrated throughout the book; the theory sections are up to date and are integrated with text material; the contemporary topics chapter contains subjects that can be assigned at any time.

3. *A balance of managerial uses of accounting with the structural form of accounting.*

4. *Flexibility.* Chapter appendixes may or may not be used; Chapter 7 can be taught at any time—even during the first days of class; Chapter 14 can be moved up and taught after Chapter 5; many of the other chapters can be taught in a sequence other than that in which they appear in the book.

As in the Second Edition, the end-of-chapter material is divided into four parts: (1) questions for class discussion, (2) short exercises, (3) class demonstration problems designed for the use of the instructor, and (4) problems; some of the end-of-chapter material is identified as accounting policy decision problems, financial policy decision problems, and management policy decision problems. The demonstration problems, averaging four to a chapter, exemplify the highlights of each chapter. The questions and exercises are designed either for class discussion or for outside assignment; they test the student's understanding of the chapter contents. The problems stress both theory and practice and are graded by level of difficulty and approximate completion time.

The decision problems are also correlated to the chapter material but are set within a broader business background and furnish a specific business orientation for in-depth analysis and class discussion.

An optional self-study guide, prepared by Dr. Allen B. Sanders, not only tests the student's comprehension of the text but also reduces the amount of class time required to cover the individual chapters. Each chapter of the study guide has two basic components: (1) a concise explanation of the most important concepts in the corresponding textbook chapter, and (2) exercises interacting with the textbook and accompanied by answers.

Also available are a set of working papers, which should be sufficient for one-half the text. The set of working papers is designed in such a way that it can be used for either the first half of the text or the second half. A short practice set, *The Condominium Wholesale Furniture Company,* containing narrative and working papers, furnishes a review of the fundamentals established in Part I.

The use of color in the text, the marginal notations underscoring accounting concepts, the chapter glossaries, the wide margins, and a comprehensive index greatly enhance the usefulness of the book. The discussions and problems in the text and all the supplementary materials have been classroom-tested over a sustained period by the authors, and those in the two preceding editions by professors in schools throughout the world.

We are grateful to our colleagues and students for their help and encouragement, and are indebted to the many users of the earlier editions for their support and their constructive criticisms and comments. We hope that they and others will continue in the future, as they have done in the past, to furnish us with their invaluable suggestions. Whatever deficiencies still persist, whatever errors of omission or commission still remain are, of course, entirely attributable to the authors. We are also indebted to many individuals and organizations for their permission to use certain material created by them. These acknowledgments are shown on the following page.

Boston, Massachusetts **Albert Slavin**

Chapel Hill, North Carolina **Isaac N. Reynolds**
February 1975

Acknowledgments

We wish to express our gratitude to our many colleagues who offered valuable suggestions and criticisms many of which have been incorporated in this edition. Especially helpful were the reviews of Professors Edward Alterman, Carl E. High, and Frances Avner, New York City Community College; Allan R. Bailey, San Diego State University; Ronald Copeland, University of South Carolina; Ronald H. Eaton, Memphis State University; Ross A. Flaherty, University of Texas at Arlington; Harold L. Goldman, Los Angeles Pierce College; E. Dee Hubbard and Karl M. Skousen, Brigham Young University; Lawrence H. Malchman, Northeastern University; Johnn T. Miller, Chabot College; Charles C. Rolen, University of Tennessee at Nashville; Michael J. Scanlan, University of Missouri at Columbia; and Jane Black Stockard, CPA, Kansas State University.

We acknowledge with appreciation permission from the American Institute of Certified Public Accountants to quote from its Opinions and other pronouncements and to reprint (or to adapt) material from the Uniform CPA Examination (Copyright © 1969–1974 by the American Institute of Certified Public Accountants, Inc.); the Financial Accounting Standards Board to use material prepared by its staff; the American Accounting Association to quote from its official pronouncements; the Institute of Management Accounting to reprint (or to adapt) questions from its Certificate in Management Accounting Examinations (Copyright © 1972–1973 by the Institute of Management Accounting); Wesley T. Andrews, Jr., a Ph.D. candidate at the University of North Carolina, for the use of a case authored by him and published in the *Accounting Review;* for permission to reprint (or to adapt) certain materials credit for which is indicated individually by footnote or source note.

We appreciate the editorial suggestions of Professor Albert Gminder, Elon College; Professor Janie Council, Elon College; and Professor Henry Dauderis, Loyola University, Montreal, Canada.

We are grateful to Mr. Stephen E. Dailey, Jr., teaching assistant at Northeastern University, and to Mr. Mark Sink, an accounting major at the University of North Carolina, for their aid in preparing the Instructor's Manual.

Finally, we are especially indebted to Dr. Allen B. Sanders, Elon College, North Carolina, whose assistance in the preparation of the manuscript was all-pervasive and invaluable. Dr. Sanders has contributed immeasurably to the improvement of this edition.

Contents

Part One

Basic Concepts and Methodology:

Service and Merchandising Businesses

Accounting: Its Nature, Function, and Environment

1

"The basic objective of financial statements is to provide information useful for making economic decisions."[1] Although such accounting information is most commonly provided in terms of dollars, it is frequently supplemented by notes in narrative form.

Conceptually, accounting is the discipline that provides information on which external and internal users of the information may base decisions that result in the allocation of economic resources in society.

Concept of Accounting

How this allocation is made is illustrated by some examples of the use of accounting information by persons or groups inside the organization (internal users) and by persons or groups outside the organization (external users). Those within an organization who *produce* accounting information also *use* such information from other organizations.

The purposes of this chapter are (1) to introduce the reader to the role and scope of accounting in the modern world, (2) to describe sources from which the basic data of accounting are recorded, and (3) to provide an overview of the methods and systems by which masses of raw data are summarized and organized into useful form for decision makers. Following some examples of uses of accounting information by decision makers is a discussion of the basic media used to capture data for communication to them. Capturing large

[1] *Objectives of Financial Statements: Report of the Accounting Objectives Study Group* (New York: American Institute of Certified Public Accountants, 1973), p. 13.

amounts of information, however, does not necessarily mean that it will be useful; it must be classified and summarized into some meaningful form.

| Data Processing | The act of converting large amounts of data into useful form is known as data processing. |

The final section contains a brief description of data-processing systems. Because such a large portion of accounting routines today are performed by automated equipment, specific illustrations of data-processing applications are contained in or appended to appropriate chapters throughout this book.

As specific business papers or source documents are encountered in later chapters, it is suggested that the reader refer back to the descriptions and illustrations in this chapter. Later chapters will concentrate on accounting practices and procedures, and will provide data-processing examples to help the reader conceptualize these practices as part of the overall information system. Reference to the data-processing section of this chapter may make those examples more meaningful as devices to integrate accounting theory and accounting procedures.

HISTORICAL PERSPECTIVE

Accounting arose out of the needs of its environment. In the earliest civilizations it became necessary to develop bookkeeping methods to maintain records of grain stored in the custody of the temple priests. Later came the need for expansion of bookkeeping to include such things as tax records, payroll systems, and records of production costs. As conditions changed, accounting methods also had to change to keep pace; thus, accounting has always been a creature of its environment.

Accounting has also done much to shape the environment. In 1494, when an Italian monk named Luca Pacioli wrote a chapter in a mathematics textbook, double-entry bookkeeping was promulgated. The mechanics of the double-entry system—still with us today—provided the means by which adequate determinations could be made of the profitability of cooperative business ventures. Ability to render reports that disclosed the results of operations, the financial status of the venture as a whole, and the status of each individual member's share provided the incentive for individuals to invest in voyages for trading and exploration. Also among the primary instances of accounting's influence on the environment is the enlargement in the first half of the twentieth century of the *attest function,* the certification by independent professional accountants of the fairness of financial statements. Such independent auditors are called certified public accountants (CPAs) in the United States and chartered accountants (CAs) in Canada. The rise of the attest function of accounting has been a major factor in the willingness of millions of absentee owners to invest money in share capital, thus enabling the growth of today's large business corporations.

Accounting, therefore, is not a new discipline; it is as old as civilization itself. It has developed as a product of its environment, but has also exerted an influence on the shape of that environment. In both roles, accounting continues to expand. The following two sections will describe the nature of accounting in terms of some of its users.

PRESENT-DAY EXTERNAL USERS OF ACCOUNTING

External users are those persons or groups outside the organization for which accounting is performed. Following are examples of such external users.

1. Investors, both individual and institutional, who seek information that will allow them to evaluate and compare the financial health and economic potential of business firms. Individuals and organizations, sometimes finding themselves with excess cash for a temporary period, desire to use it in an investment that is safe, at the same time yielding the highest possible rate of return for that type of investment. Individuals buy stocks or bonds for long-term savings and for retirement plans; large institutions such as insurance companies or universities tend to accumulate cash in various funds. Both groups must keep their investments under constant review and revision. As a basis for their investment decisions, all these investors are dependent upon accounting information included in the annual reports of corporations. Figure 1-1 is an extract from such an annual report.

Figure 1-1 Extracts from an Annual Report

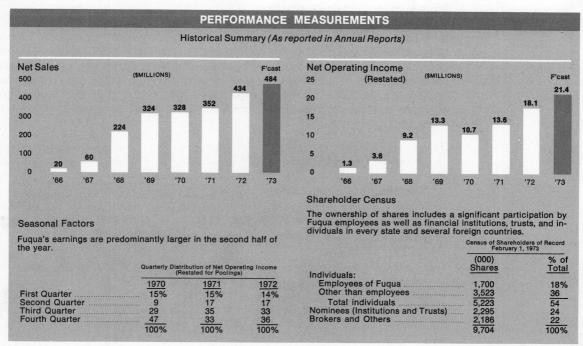

Source: Fuqua Industries, Incorporated; reproduced by permission.

2. Members of or contributors to *not-for-profit* organizations such as community funds, churches, colleges, fraternities and sororities, service clubs, and numerous other such entities need accounting reports to see how their funds are being used and to determine if the organization deserves continued support, the amount of such support, or if the support should be transferred to another group. Although cost effectiveness (that is, the extent of organizational goal attainment per dollar contributed) is only one of several factors considered by external users of information about not-for-profit agencies, it is an important criterion in the decision regarding continuation of participation and support.

3. Taxing authorities, regulatory agencies, and other governmental institutions use accounting information. Income tax returns are examples of financial reports to governmental agencies prepared with information taken directly from accounting records of individuals and businesses. The reports accompanying remittances of taxes to fund federal old age, survivor insurance, and medical-care programs and to fund unemployment compensation payments are determined from payroll accounts. Reports of collection of sales taxes as well as federal excise taxes must be based on accurate records of sales.

Important to consumers is the use of accounting reports by governmental regulatory commissions, especially those which have the authority to prescribe the rates that may be charged for services to the public. Rate setting for public utilities usually hinges on the concept of a "fair return on investment." It is not surprising, therefore, that most such regulatory agencies are authorized by law to prescribe accounting systems for, and require accounting reports from, the firms subject to their jurisdiction.

An inclusive list of other government users of accounting information is too long for our purpose. Note should be taken, however, of the national income accounting system used by the United States Department of Commerce, which compiles accounting information from all segments of the economy to determine indicators of national economic growth such as gross national product and a host of other summarized data. Such data are used by the Federal government to formulate fiscal and monetary policies in an effort to maintain a more stable economy.

PRESENT-DAY INTERNAL USERS OF ACCOUNTING

Planning and Controlling

Two of the most frequently listed functions of management are planning and controlling. *Planning* is the function that defines the goals and objectives of the organization; a major portion of planning is financial.

Budgets

Organizations of all types prepare budgets; a *budget* is simply a financial plan for a future period. Usually a budget covers a period of one year and is developed in organizational detail showing planned activity in terms of units of output of goods and services and in terms of man-hours and machine-hours, together with planned inflows and outflows of money and other resources.

Budget preparation is an important part of the planning function, and its starting point is the accounting records for the prior year.

Controlling is the function of monitoring budget execution (the day-to-day operations of the enterprise) and intervening when necessary to redirect operations toward accomplishment of plans. The primary element of the monitoring process is a group of special reports provided by the accounting system to each responsible manager. These periodic reports contain data that compare budgeted performance with actual performance, enabling the manager to exercise control. Typical is a report to the sales manager, as illustrated in Figure 1-2. It shows planned sales to date compared with actual sales to date.

Figure 1-2 Analysis of Sales

Cost Determination

Many internal decisions require details of product cost information. The determination of prices in the environment in which today's business operates is rarely an automatic result of the interaction between supply and demand. A firm may have to bid competitively against other firms for a specific job; if its bid exceeds cost plus a reasonable rate of return, it probably will not be awarded the contract. On the other hand, if the firm bids less than its cost to perform the job, it will be awarded the contract but will also incur a loss.

The Robinson-Patman Act prohibits discrimination in prices quoted to different buyers, except where it can be demonstrated that actual cost differences exist in supplying these different customers. Accurate accounting records are of critical importance if the firm is asked to defend itself against allegations of price discrimination.

Other Decisions

Managers are faced daily with capital budgeting decisions, those decisions involving a commitment of funds for replacement, overhaul, or repair of machinery, buildings, or equipment. Also, most businesses invest substantial sums in inventory, the merchandise items they intend to resell. For each inventory item carried, decisions must continually be made about the optimum quantity to be bought on the next order. Sometimes the question is one of "make or buy." In production operations, choices must be made between hiring of additional work force or use of overtime. In all these situations—as in numerous others—managers require cost data provided by the accounting system.

RELATION OF ACCOUNTING TO OTHER DISCIPLINES

From the foregoing, it can easily be seen that a close relation exists between the concepts of accounting and the concepts of other disciplines. Economics is basically a study of the processes of allocation of scarce resources. Using the monetary unit of the society as the yardstick of value measurements, accounting information is needed to evaluate alternative uses of economic resources, thereby forming the basis for ultimate allocation decisions.

Accounting has an impact on personal behavior—sometimes in a very direct way and at other times in a more subtle manner. Incentive pay systems, which depend upon accounting for measurement, are part of the reward structure of many firms with a direct effect on personal behavior. Recent behavioral science research has begun to question the impact on people of the use of accounting-based budgetary controls. Some findings suggest an adverse effect on employee motivation that leads to lower worker productivity. Attention is now being focused on environmental and social welfare aspects of our industrial and financial institutions. Questions are being raised about the true social costs of production which today's accounting systems do not measure. The current interest in research in *social accounting* serves to emphasize the relation between accounting and social welfare.

The political structure of the United States is based on a legal framework; an example is the concept of property rights. It is a legal function to define those property rights (ownership, suretyship, and other rights), but it is an accounting function to measure their value, thus enabling comparisons on which to base exchanges of property. This same measurement function of accounting creates another set of close relationships—the interdependence of accounting and *quantitative decision models.* The use of quantitative analysis together with the development of high-capacity electronic computers constitutes a revolution in the business environment, and accounting must provide the underlying information.

Accounting records constitute a history of economic events that take place in an organization. Purchases of merchandise, equipment, or services occur daily; sales of merchandise and services occur almost continually. So that the accountant will be aware of them, each such event is recorded on a basic business paper or source document. Copies of these documents are sent to the accountant to communicate the basic data to him.

Although business forms are designed with organizational letterheads and insignia and with different format, certain aspects of several of them are common to most firms. In order to understand the accounting processes, one should have a good working knowledge of the more commonly used documents. Sometimes all copies remain within the business; these are referred to in this text as *internal* forms. When copies are sent to another business or outside agency, they are referred to as *external* forms. Much time and effort is devoted by the employees of the enterprise to preparing, using, and filing these forms, which vary in shape, size, color, and content. Sometimes these forms are simply called *business papers;* the data-processing department employees usually describe them as *source documents.* A description of some of the more commonly used papers follows; their use will be described in more detail in appropriate later chapters.

Purchase requisition: an internal document used by any department to request the purchasing department to buy materials, supplies, equipment, or services. Minimum information on this form would include a clear description of the item to be purchased, quantity required, desired delivery date, and the

Figure 1-3 Purchase Requisition

ELON COLLEGE		**PURCHASE REQUEST**	DATE May 28, 1976	
QUANTITY	CATALOG NO.	DESCRIPTION		PRICE
		Services to repair one calculator,		
		Monroe model 8F-213, serial number B858110		

(ATTACH LIST IF ADDITIONAL SPACE IS NEEDED)

ORDER FROM Monroe Calculator Company   SHIP VIA   TERMS

ADDRESS   F.O.B. POINT

DELIVERY REQUIRED   DELIVER TO Room A-307   DEPT Bus. Admin.   APPROVED DEPT. HEAD

BUDGET CLASSIFICATION 1156,Supplies and Other Expense   FUNDS AVAILABLE Yes   APPROVED

BUS. MGR.

Source: Elon College

signature of the person authorized to incur charges against a department. An example is shown in Figure 1-3.

Purchase order: an external document sent by the purchasing department to a supplier or a vendor placing an order for goods or services. It is signed by one of the authorized buyers in the purchasing department and contains the vendor's stock number (if known), a description of the item, and the quantity required. It must also specify where to ship the material or render the service and the required delivery or completion date. Prices and credit terms are usually ascertained before issuance of a purchase order and are shown on the order. Figure 1-4 shows the purchase order that resulted from the purchase requisition in Figure 1-3.

Receiver's report: an internal form prepared by the receiving department to report the arrival of goods from a vendor. Basic information on this form includes date of receipt; purchase order number on which the goods were ordered; stock number, description, and quantity of each item received; condi-

Figure 1-4 Purchase Order for Services

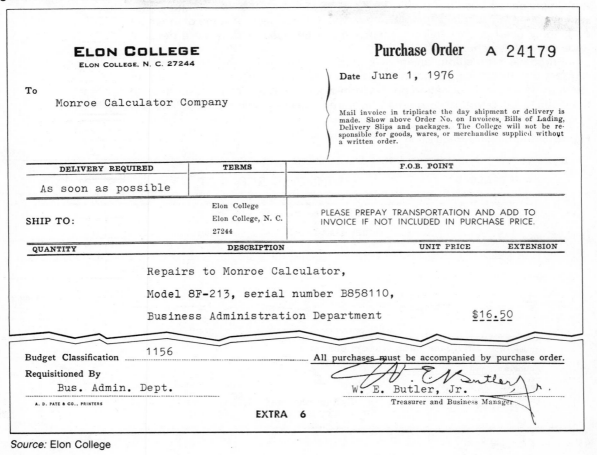

Source: Elon College

tion of the goods; and the signature of the inspector who has checked the receipt.

Invoice: an external document sometimes described as a *bill* or *dealer's bill.* It is a formal notification that goods have been shipped or services provided, and constitutes a request for payment. In addition to descriptive information (stock numbers, items, quantities, price, and other relevant information), it contains a reference to the applicable purchase order or sales order and the terms of payment. Discounts offered for prompt payment and date that payment is due must be clearly specified. An example of an invoice is shown in Figure 1-5.

Figure 1-5 Invoice

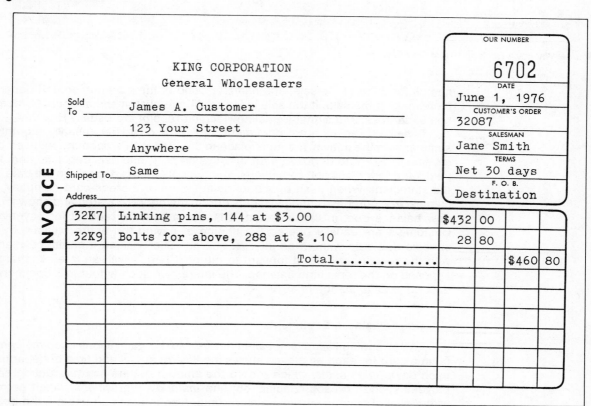

Check: a written order directing a bank to pay a specified amount of money to the order of a payee. Most major payments are made by check; a carbon copy of the check communicates the payment information to the accounting department for recording. (Figure 1-6 shows a check and check stub.)

Sales ticket: an internal document used to record an ''over-the-counter'' sale either for cash or for credit. If the sale is for cash, basic information on it includes date of sale; stock number, description, quantity, and price of each

Figure 1-6 Check and Check Stub

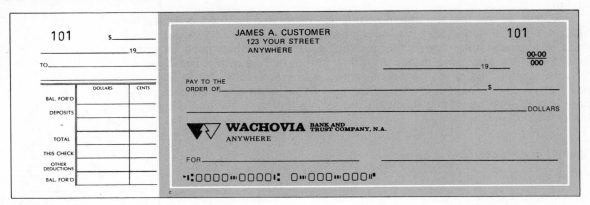

Source: Wachovia Bank and Trust Company, N. A.

item; total value of the sale; and name or code of the salesperson and department making the sale. If the sale is for credit, the customer's account number, name, address, and signature acknowledging receipt are usually required.

Statement: an external document sent to a customer (usually monthly) summarizing the activity that took place in the customer's account. As used by a bank, it is sent to depositors for information only, and lists deposits, checks paid, other additions and reductions, and the balance on deposit on the date of the statement. When used by a department store or a credit-card company, it summarizes purchases and payments during the period covered and shows the new balance due; in this instance, it is also a specific request for payment. Customers are usually offered the choice of paying the entire balance by a specific due date without an interest charge, or of making a partial payment, with the remainder carried forward to the next period with an interest charge imposed on the remaining balance. The interest on such amounts is commonly described as a finance charge.

Other Business Documents

The foregoing listing is not all-inclusive. Most organizations use *time cards* (a time card for each employee shows the time of arrival and time of departure each day); *time tickets,* which record the amount of time that production employees spend on each specific job; and *materials requisitions,* which permit withdrawal of materials from the storeroom. Also in common use are the *debit memorandum,* which informs a creditor that a business is claiming a reduction in the amount to be paid on an invoice; and the *credit memorandum,* which informs a debtor of an adjustment in his account which reduces the balance in his account. These documents are explained in more detail later.

It is current practice to purchase all forms in sets designed to meet the unique needs of the using enterprise. The firm's name and address are preprinted on the forms. Purchase orders, sales tickets, and credit memorandums are usually preprinted with a series of consecutive numbers so that all may be accounted for, thus strengthening internal control in the organization. Most forms—for example, purchase requests (a requisition), purchase orders, and sales tickets—require several copies; these are often purchased in multicopy sets with one-time carbon paper that can be torn out and discarded. When multicopy forms are used within the framework of carefully designed procedures as illustrated in Figure 1-7, the twin benefits of greater efficiency and better protection against loss by theft or carelessness (internal control) result.

DATA PROCESSING

Examples of actual applications of data-processing equipment to accounting procedures are used throughout this book, but simple illustrations of manual records make it easier for the reader to grasp basic accounting concepts. It is important to recognize, however, that these manual systems are not adequate for modern organizations.

The Basic Concept

Data are facts or measurements that describe events. The singular of data is datum. In accounting, data are expressed in quantitative terms, usually in monetary units, which in the United States and Canada are dollars and cents. The term data, however, includes nonmonetary information such as hours worked, units of material used, employees' names, and employee identification numbers. When applied to data, the term *processing* describes all the steps taken to make data useful for a specified purpose. Therefore, *data processing* is simply the activity required to capture information that measures economic events and to transform that information to a state in which it is useful for various purposes.

Types of Data Processing

It is not accurate to assume that data processing refers only to the use of sophisticated equipment. Methods of data processing are usually placed into the categories discussed below.

Manual. An individual or a very small organization may perform all data processing by manual methods. When an accounting student uses pencil and paper to work his exercises and problems, he is using data processing. In similar fashion, the total accounting system of a small business, a fraternity, or a civic organization may consist of a record of receipts and payments recorded by hand. Since, even in the largest firms, some aspects of data processing are manual, Figure 1-7 illustrates a typical procedure with several manual operations that uses some of the documents previously discussed. The circled numbers in Figure 1-7 give a key to the steps listed on page 15.
Mechanical or electromechanical. To the manual process may be added some pieces of equipment such as typewriters, adding machines and calculators, bookkeeping machines, or cash registers. The procedure illustrated in Figure 1-7 would probably use some of these items.

Figure 1-7 Purchase and Payment Procedure

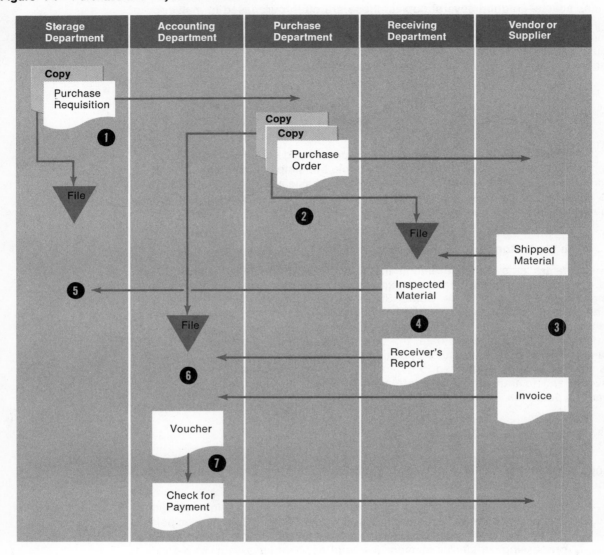

Such equipment may or may not be electrically powered, and tends to be introduced as the size of the data-processing task increases.

Electrical or unit record. The general term *electric accounting machines* (EAM) or *unit-record equipment* includes a group of specialized equipment items designed to prepare and manipulate punched cards. By means of a key punch—a hand-operated machine with a typewriter keyboard which codes data from source documents by punching holes into specific columns of a card—information that has been recorded on business papers (source documents) is transferred to decks of punched

(Ch. 1)

❶ Since the storage department requires some material, a purchase requisition is sent to the purchasing department. A copy is retained in file by storage for follow-up if the material is not received on time.

❷ The purchasing department negotiates a purchase, and sends a purchase order to the supplier. A copy to the receiving department is to be used to check for receipt of proper items and quantities. Another copy to the accounting department will be used to check the accuracy of billed prices and discount terms on the invoice.

❸ The supplier (or vendor) ships the material to the buyer's receiving department and mails an invoice direct to its accounting department.

❹ When the material is received, the receiving department checks the material against its filed copy of the purchase order, inspects the material for quality, and forwards accepted items to the storage department. A receiver's report, sent to the accounting department, shows what was received, and notes any shortage or damage.

❺ The storage department checks off items received against its file copy of the original purchase requisition, and stores the material.

❻ The accounting department matches the purchase order copy, the vendor's invoice, and the receiver's report. After the accuracy of prices, extensions, and discount is checked (with any adjustment for damage or shortage), a voucher is prepared approving payment of the invoice.

❼ The approved invoice is sent to the disbursing section of the accounting department, where a check is prepared and mailed to the vendor.

cards. It is then a simple matter for unit-record machines to sort, match, or merge these cards so that data from many original source documents can be classified more quickly and accurately than by manual or mechanical methods. An item of unit-record equipment is an *accounting machine* or *tabulator;* it is capable of reading punched cards, storing data in internal registers, and producing subtotals and a total *(summarizing).* Attached to this machine is a printer, which is capable of producing printed reports of detail and/or summary data. It can also cause a new deck of cards to be punched with updated data.

Electronic. Using a combination of internal storage of data and instructions for processing it, *electronic data-processing* (EDP) systems can process great volumes of information at very high speeds. The heart of any EDP system is a computer. Another term used to describe the computer itself is *central processing unit* (CPU). Connected by electrical cable to the CPU are two groups of devices called *input/output devices.* These machines are capable of reading punched cards, paper tape, magnetic tape, or several other types of data storage media, and of transmitting the data read therefrom into the CPU. The information is processed and the results transmitted back from the CPU to the input/output devices, which punch these results into a new (updated) deck of cards, record them on tape (or other storage media), or print them in the form of a report. The basic concept of an EDP system is contained in Figure 1-8.

Figure 1-8
An EDP System

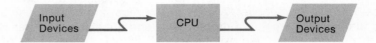

Processing Operations

Every organization has some type of data-processing system. Depending upon the size and nature of the organization, its data-processing system may range from a purely manual system through all possible combinations up to the most highly sophisticated electronic system. Regardless of the type of data processing, every system has the same basic elements in its data-processing cycle. These elements are (1) data origination, (2) data manipulation, and (3) data reporting. Although some persons would include additional elements—storage, for example—it is considered that the foregoing three are so significant as to warrant brief consideration at this point.

Data Origination

Data are usually captured for the first time when they are recorded on one of the source documents described earlier as business papers. Each sale over the counter, for example, is recorded on a sales ticket. Periodically (usually at the end of each day) all such documents are forwarded to the data-processing section. If an EAM or an EDP system is in use, the data from the documents are key-punched into cards or, in some of the newer large-scale systems, recorded directly on magnetic tape by a keyboard operation.

Data Manipulation

In this phase of the cycle certain basic steps are common to all types of data processing. Whether the following are done manually or by machine, the captured data must be (1) *classified* into groupings such as sales for credit, collections from customers, receipts of inventory items, and dozens of other categories; (2) *sorted* into sequence within categories (for example, sales on account must be placed in, customer account number sequence); (3) *calculated* and *summarized* to produce certain meaningful totals and subtotals; and finally (4) *recorded* and *stored* in an organized manner so that the data (or summaries thereof) can be retrieved and reported.

Data Reporting

Data reporting is the communication of useful and meaningful output to the several types of users of information. All organizations have a need for certain standardized reports, and the data-processing system must be designed to produce them. Typical of such reports are the annual reports of business firms containing the basic accounting statements. Each organization, however, also has its own unique needs for internal reports to all levels of management. The frequency, amount of detail reported, and number of such reports from any data-processing system depend upon the type of system used. In general, the cost/benefit concept prevails. As an organization moves away from a manual system, the ability to produce a great number and variety of reports increases, but so does the cost. The problem for each firm is to find the proper cost/benefit balance in the design of its data-processing system.

RELATION OF DATA PROCESSING TO ACCOUNTING

It is probably already obvious that any accounting system must include a data-processing system. The two are not synonymous; accounting is more than data processing, and data-processing systems exist for purposes other than accounting. Because a large portion of the work of developing and recording accounting information can be reduced to data-processing routines, accounting departments were among the first groups to recognize the usefulness of more automated types of data-processing equipment as they began to become available.

The basic principles of data-processing operations are the same regardless of the type of system employed. Accordingly, throughout this textbook accounting methods will be presented as if a manual system were in use. Although this will make it easier for the reader to understand the basic accounting concepts and methods, it must be borne in mind that only the smallest enterprises use a manual system. To help the reader make the transition to a more realistic situation, examples showing how certain accounting operations are applied to punched card unit-record systems or electronic computer systems are included in or appended to some of the later chapters.

ACCOUNTING IN BROAD PERSPECTIVE

This introductory chapter has described and illustrated the role of accounting as one of providing information, that is useful in making economic decisions, to men and women as individuals and as members of organizations. Accounting necessarily starts with the capturing of information by recording it on business papers or source documents. This process, however, is only the beginning. Having knowledge of the types of decisions to be made, the accountant must convert the raw data into a useful form and report it to decision makers—both external and internal. He must determine what classifications are meaningful, and must summarize and reduce large quantities of bits of information into manageable subtotals and totals. The accountant's competence bears directly on the quality of decisions made and, therefore, on the efficiency of distribution of economic resources.

Accounting The discipline that provides information which is useful for the making of economic decisions.

Annual Report A report containing basic accounting statements rendered by firms at the close of each business year. It is designed for external users of accounting data.

Budget A financial plan for a future period developed in organizational detail.

Business Papers The basic supporting forms on which data describing economic events are initially captured.

Central Processing Unit (CPU) The computer itself—the heart of an electronic data-processing system.

Check A written order to a bank to pay a specified amount to the order of a payee.

Controlling The management function which consists of monitoring actual versus planned activity, and taking corrective action where appropriate.

Data The plural of datum. A datum is a descriptive fact or a measurement usually expressed in quantitative terms.

Data Processing The activity required to capture data that describe economic events and transform such data into a form that is useful for specified purposes.

Electric Accounting Machines (EAM) Electrically powered equipment designed for punched card processing. (*See* Unit-Record Equipment.)

Electronic Data Processing (EDP) Data processing by electronic computer systems which are capable of receiving data in coded form, executing processing steps under control of previously prepared instructions stored in the CPU, and transmitting the results in coded or in printed form.

External Users Individuals, groups, or institutions outside the enterprise.

Internal Users Individuals or groups within the enterprise.

Invoice A formal notification to a customer that payment for goods or services is due.

Key Punch A machine with a typewriter-like keyboard used to punch data into electric accounting machine cards (punched cards).

Materials Requisition An internal form used by any department of the organization to withdraw materials or supplies from storage.

Not-for-Profit Organizations Enterprises organized for purposes other than engaging in business operations for profit. Examples include charitable groups, service and civic clubs, churches, social clubs, and numerous other nonbusiness enterprises.

Planning The function that defines the goals and objectives of an organization.

Processing Manipulation of data to transform them to a form in which they are useful for a specified purpose.

Purchase Order An external form sent from an organization to a vendor or supplier. It represents the formal placement of an order for materials or services.

Purchase Requisition An internal form used by any department of an organization requesting the purchasing agent to place an order with a vendor.

Quantitative Decision Models Mathematical formulas which, given certain items of information, are designed to compute the best choice from among a group of alternatives.

Receiver's Report An internal form reporting the receipt and inspection of materials or services from a supplier.

Sales Order A form for recording an order taken by a salesman committing the organization to supply goods or services to a customer.

Sales Ticket A form used to record over-the-counter sales.

Social Accounting A relatively new concept in which measurement of social-welfare aspects of events would be considered along with measurement of economic aspects of events.

Source Documents A term used in data processing to describe the basic business papers (see above) on which data are initially recorded.

Statement A periodic (usually monthly) summary sent to each customer listing purchases and payments and showing the balance due as of the date of the statement. It is sometimes used in lieu of an invoice.

Tabulator The piece of unit-record equipment that summarizes data punched into cards. It can produce printed reports or punch summary cards.

Unit-Record Equipment An inclusive term used to describe electric accounting machines (EAM) used for punched-card processing.

Q1-1. What is the basic role of accounting in society?

Q1-2. Why can we claim that accounting is both a product of its environment and an influence on its environment?

Q1-3. What is a CPA? a CA? Explain the relationship of each to the attest function.

Q1-4. Cite three examples of users of accounting reports who are external to the organization for which accounting is being performed.

Q1-5. What role does accounting play in the planning function of management? in the controlling function?

Q1-6. What is the relationship between accounting and economics? accounting and social welfare? accounting and law? accounting and quantitative decision models?

Q1-7. Why are business papers (source documents) necessary to an accounting system?

Q1-8. What is the relationship between accounting and data processing?

Q1-9. What elements are common to all data-processing systems (manual, mechanical, unit record, or electronic)?

ACCOUNTING:
NATURE,
FUNCTION,
ENVIRONMENT

E1-1. Complete the following chart by filling in the blanks as illustrated for a and b.

User of Accounting Information	Typical Decision Made by That User	Example of Accounting Data Useful Thereto
a. Bank loan officer	To grant or to refuse a loan application	Records of income of the applicant
b. District Director of Internal Revenue	To accept or question a taxpayer's return	Records to validate income, withholding, and deductions
c. Contributor to a charitable group		
d. Treasurer of an industrial firm		
e. Sales manager of a large firm		
f. Chairman of a church budget committee		
g. Investment manager of an insurance company		

E1-2. Listed below are some selected figures from annual reports of business firms. (Assets are things of value held by the company.)

	A Steel Producer		A Commercial Bank		An Automobile Manufacturer		A Pharmaceuticals Manufacturer		A Textiles Manufacturer		A Trading-Stamp Company	
	1973	1972	1973	1972	1973	1972	1973	1972	1973	1972	1973	1972
Total assets (in millions)	$3,919	$3,645	$3,915	$3,385	$12,954	$11,634	$1,604	$ 942	$ 310	$ 276	$ 636	$ 607
Total debt (in millions)	1,677	1,509	478	451	6,549	5,673	150	117	166	140	402	373
Total earnings for year (in millions)	207	135	327	247	906	870	139	123	10	4	30	39
Earnings per share of stock (in dollars)	4.72	3.02	2.19	2.15	9.13	8.52	1.78	1.58	1.79	.65	2.70	3.59
Dividends paid per share of stock (in dollars)	1.65	1.20	.69	.61½	3.20	2.67½	.74¼	.67½	.47½	0	3.02	3.49
Approximate market price per share of stock at time of issuance of 1973 report	$29.87		$20.75		$50.67		$31.25		$8.12		$10.12	

a. Which figures are of greatest interest to the government agency responsible for income tax collection?

b. Which company's earnings declined in 1973?

c. Which company's earnings per share showed the greatest dollar increase in 1973?

d. Which company's earnings per share showed the greatest percentage increase in 1973?

e. Does there appear to be a relationship between earnings per share and market price of a firm's stock? If so, what is the relationship?

f. Does there appear to be a relationship between dividends paid to shareholders and the market price of stock? If so, what is the relationship?

g. Does debt as a percentage of assets appear to affect market price per share? Explain.

h. Each of the financial statements from which these data came bears an independent auditor's certification. How does that knowledge affect your attitude toward these figures?

E1-3. Shown below are partial data obtained from a computer printout from the accounting records of a firm. Suggest some management decisions that might be made on the basis of this information.

Inventory File

Stock No.	Description	Avg. Units Sold per Month	Cost per Unit	Quantity On Hand	Quantity On Order	Qty. Sold Past 6 Mos.
1815	Combs, Pocket	1,122	$.08	28,500	10,000	6,730
1832	Files, Nail	833	.13	1,200	2,000	5,000
1853	Kit, First Aid	1,612	.19	1,023	1,000	9,672
1854	Lotion, After Shave	1,045	.21		1,000	6,271

E1-4. Using Figure 1-7 as a model, diagram the order and shipping procedure (receipt of a sales order, shipment of material to the customer, and preparation of the invoice) for a firm that receives orders daily by mail from its salesmen and sends an invoice immediately after each shipment.

E1-5. For a business which uses a punched-card data-processing system in its accounting department, complete the following table.

Data to Be Key-Punched into Cards	Source Document from Which Data Are Obtained
a. Daily sales over the counter on credit	_____
b. Total hours worked by an employee in a pay period	_____
c. Additions to inventory of merchandise	_____
d. Reductions of inventory by withdrawal of materials from store	_____
e. Additons to amounts owed to vendors or suppliers of goods and services	_____
f. Reductions of inventory by over-the-counter sales	_____
g. Reductions of amounts owed to vendors as a result of receipt of damaged goods	_____

ACCOUNTING:
NATURE,
FUNCTION,
ENVIRONMENT

E1-6. Match the data-processing operations in column A with the equipment to perform them in column B. (See example.)

A	B
Operation	Equipment

a. Placing a deck of punched cards into numeric sequence ___3___

b. Adding a column of figures manually _____

c. Recording newly calculated data on magnetic tape _____

d. Adding a column of figures mechanically _____

e. Summarizing a deck of punched cards and printing a report _____

f. Making a large number of calculations at high speeds under control of an internally stored program _____

g. Transferring data from source documents into punched cards _____

h. Mechanical recording of sales _____

1. Desk calculator

2. Cash register

3. Sorter

4. CPU

5. Pencil and paper

6. Key punch

7. CPU and an output device

8. Accounting machine

Note: The nature of the text material in Chapter 1 does not warrant the inclusion of demonstration problems and problems.

The Basic
Accounting Model:
Real Accounts

2

The presentation of accounting information in a meaningful format and the submission of this information to those who use it as a guide to action make it necessary that the preparer of accounting data understand rather precisely how to use the basic accounting model that has been developed over the past seven hundred years. An understanding of the basic model requires a knowledge of the boundary line of the business unit, the entity; the various components included in the model; the mathematics of the model; the mathematical operations of the elements of the accounting equation; and the underlying concepts, standards, and assumptions. The development of the basic model using only statement of financial position accounts constitutes an integrated but rather lengthy discussion. In an effort to present the unity of this initial development, this chapter discusses (1) the genesis of double-entry accounting, the accounting equation, and the statement of financial position and (2) the development of the basic accounting model using those items contained in the statement of financial position.

THE ACCOUNTING EQUATION
AND THE STATEMENT
OF FINANCIAL POSITION

THE ENTITY CONCEPT

In order to provide meaningful decision-making information about a business unit, the accountant must maintain a separate set of records for each business enterprise of an owner. The focal point of attention is not the owner but each independent unit, which has well-defined boundaries. For example, suppose that John Goodwin owns a grocery store, a hardware store, and a service station, and that he also has a car, a residence, some stocks and bonds, and other personal items of value. These are shown in graphic form below.

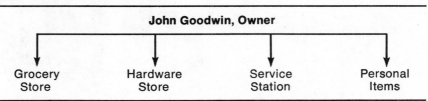

John Goodwin, Owner

| Grocery Store | Hardware Store | Service Station | Personal Items |

If the accountant's total attention is focused on John Goodwin, he may lose sight of the individual economic units. Thus, in this case, the accounting information for all Goodwin's activities lumped together is useless in making decisions for any single unit.

Business Entity

In order to accomplish the accounting objectives mentioned in the preceding paragraph, a set of records must be provided for each of the individual business units, and the focal point of attention must be the individual unit rather than the owner.

This is referred to as the *entity concept*.

ASSETS

The *assets* of a business are everything of value found in the business. The word *value* is used here in the sense of future usefulness to a continuing business enterprise; it does not necessarily indicate the cost of replacing the asset nor how much it may bring in if offered for sale. Cash, notes and accounts receivable (amounts owed to the business through transactions on credit), land, buildings, and high-grade, readily marketable stocks or bonds of other companies (*marketable securities*) are examples of assets in a business. An asset is placed on the books of the acquiring entity at its full cost even though it has not been fully paid for in cash; the amount of any debt or claim against the asset is shown as a liability.

EQUITIES: LIABILITIES AND OWNER'S EQUITY

The *equities* represent claims against, or rights in, the assets of a business. The two major classifications of individuals who have equities in a business are the *creditors* (liability holders) and the *owners*.

The *liabilities* of a business are everything owed to creditors. Liabilities represent claims of the creditors against the assets of the business unit. *Accounts payable* and *notes payable,* which are amounts owed by the business through purchases on credit, are some liabilities that a business may have. Wages owed to employees is another example.

The *owner's equity* (*capital* and *proprietorship* are alternative terms) represents the proprietor's, the partners', or the stockholders' claims against the assets of a business, or the *excess* of all assets over all liabilities.

THE ACCOUNTING EQUATION

Because equities, by definition, represent the total claims against assets, then assets must equal equities. This relationship is shown here.

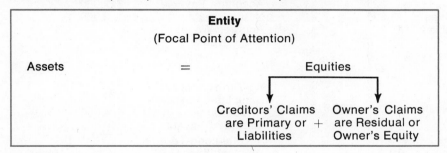

The equities of the unit are broken down into the *primary claims,* those of the creditors, and the *residual claims,* those of the owner(s). Since assets are derived primarily from these two sources, the truth of the equation is reinforced. Another source is a *gift* of assets, which increases the owner's equity.

The following equation, then, is the *basic accounting equation,* which expresses the financial position of any business entity at all times.

$$\text{Assets} = \text{Liabilities} + \text{Owner's Equity, or}$$
$$\text{Assets} = \text{Sources of Assets}$$

To add an element of preciseness, the equation is modified slightly to indicate the particular kind of business organization: *single proprietorship, partnership,* or *corporation.* For example, in a corporation the equation is

$$\text{Assets} = \text{Liabilities} + \text{Stockholders' Equity}$$

and in a partnership the equation is

$$\text{Assets} = \text{Liabilities} + \text{Partners' Equity}$$

The various forms of business organization are considered in more detail later in this chapter.

The equation may be restated for various analytical purposes in the following manner:

$$\text{Assets} - \text{Liabilities} = \text{Owner's Equity}$$

The use of this particular form of the equation is discussed later.

The term *net assets* often is used in business; it may be expressed as follows:

$$\text{Assets} - \text{Liabilities} = \text{Net Assets}$$

BASIC MODEL:
REAL ACCOUNTS

Figure 2-1 Account-Form Position Statement

ASSETS	=	LIABILITIES + STOCKHOLDERS' EQUITY

MURROW CLOTHING STORE
Statement of Financial Position
December 31, 1976

Assets			*Liabilities and Stockholders' Equity*		
Current Assets			Current Liabilities		
Cash	$ 325		Accounts Payable	$12,060	
Marketable Securities	1,900		Notes Payable	2,060	
Accounts Receivable	11,025		Accrued Wages		
Notes Receivable	2,520		Payable	970	
Merchandise Inventory	14,750		Total Current		
Prepaid Insurance	275		Liabilities		$15,090
Office Supplies	26		Long-Term Liabilities		
Store Supplies	89		Bank Loan Payable		
Total Current Assets		$30,910	(due June 1, 1981)	$ 4,000	
			Mortgage Payable	10,000	
Plant and Equipment			Total Long-Term		
Land	$ 3,000		Liabilities		14,000
Building	10,000		Total Liabilities		$29,090
Store Equipment	2,500				
Delivery Equipment	3,250		Stockholders' Equity		
Total Plant and			Capital Stock	$20,000	
Equipment		18,750	Retained Earnings	570	
			Total Stockholders'		
			Equity		20,570
			Total Liabilities and		
			Stockholders'		
Total Assets		$49,660	Equity		$49,660

The relationship expressed by the accounting equation is fundamental to the recording process. In essence, *bookkeeping* is the process of recording changes in the elements of the equation resulting from business operations.

STATEMENT OF FINANCIAL POSITION

The *statement of financial position*, or *position statement*, is an expanded expression of the accounting equation (Figure 2-1). The statement of financial position summarizes the assets, liabilities, and stockholders' equity of a business entity as of a specific time. This statement is often called a *balance sheet*, but the more descriptive term *statement of financial position* is used in this text. An *account form* of position statement with the accounting equation superimposed is shown in Figure 2-1.

A variant form of the same statement, the *report form,* is shown in Figure 2-2. Both statements are acceptable illustrations of the accounting equation.

BASIC CONCEPTS
AND
METHODOLOGY

(Ch. 2)

The heading of a statement of financial position usually contains three lines of information:

1. Name of the business
2. Name of the statement
3. Date of the statement

The date given in the example shows that it presents the financial position of the firm as of the close of business on December 31, 1976.

Figure 2-2
Report-Form Position
Statement

MURROW CLOTHING STORE
Statement of Financial Position
December 31, 1976

Assets

Current Assets		
Cash	$ 325	
Marketable Securities	1,900	
Accounts Receivable	11,025	
Notes Receivable	2,520	
Merchandise Inventory	14,750	
Prepaid Insurance	275	
Office Supplies	26	
Store Supplies	89	
Total Current Assets		$30,910
Plant and Equipment		
Land	$ 3,000	
Building	10,000	
Store Equipment	2,500	
Delivery Equipment	3,250	
Total Plant and Equipment		18,750
Total Assets		$49,660

Liabilities and Stockholders' Equity

Current Liabilities		
Accounts Payable	$12,060	
Notes Payable	2,060	
Accrued Wages Payable	970	
Total Current Liabilities		$15,090
Long-Term Liabilities		
Bank Loan Payable (due June 1, 1981)	$ 4,000	
Mortgage Payable	10,000	
Total Long-Term Liabilities		14,000
Total Liabilities		$29,090
Stockholders' Equity		
Capital Stock	$20,000	
Retained Earnings	570	
Total Stockholders' Equity		20,570
Total Liabilities and Stockholders' Equity		$49,660

BASIC MODEL:
REAL ACCOUNTS

Dollar signs are used on formal typed or printed statements at the top of each column of figures. A new column is created whenever a line is drawn for addition, subtraction, or other reasons. A double line is drawn under any amount that is the final result of a series of calculations.

Need for Classification in a Statement of Financial Position

Note that the assets and liabilities in the statement of financial position for the Murrow Clothing Store are *classified*.

A financial statement should be classified so as to be of maximum value to an analyst, banker, creditor, employee, or other interested person; it can be made more easily understandable by the manner in which the items are arranged. The kind of classifications and the order of arrangement to be shown in the statement depend on tradition, the nature of the business activity, and the expected use of the statement.

Classification of Assets—Current

Current assets consist of cash and other assets that are expected to be converted into cash or to be used in the operation of the business typically within one year. Current assets are usually listed in the order of their probable *liquidity*, or their expected conversion into cash. The current assets, listed in order of liquidity, of the Murrow Clothing Store are the following

Cash. Cash is any item that a bank will accept as a deposit and which is immediately available and acceptable as a means of payment. Cash includes coins, currency, checks, bank drafts, money orders, and demand deposits in commercial banks.

Marketable Securities. Businesses that have a temporary excess of cash on hand and want to earn interest on it may buy promises to pay issued by other companies (usually referred to as *commercial paper*) or by governmental agencies or institutions (called *notes* or *bonds*). Many finance companies, for example, sell short-term notes that will usually mature within sixty days to six months. The United States government also issues short-term Treasury notes and certificates of indebtedness that are often acquired by businesses as temporary investments of excess cash. Also, high-grade industrial bonds and stocks may be purchased as temporary investments.

Accounts Receivable. Accounts receivable represent the amounts due from customers for services rendered or for merchandise, or for any asset, sold on credit (*open account*). A business with a limited number of customers could list them individually in the statement of financial position. If the debtors are numerous, however, the individual names are eliminated and the statement shows the total amount of accounts receivable in one figure. Information about amounts due from each customer must be maintained on a separate supporting record.

Notes Receivable. A note receivable is a formal written promise by a customer to pay a fixed amount of money on demand or on a specific date. Since the note is usually transferable by endorsement to another party or to a bank, it represents an asset that can be converted readily into cash.

Merchandise Inventory. Businesses that offer products for sale must have them readily available. All the merchandise on hand at any given time is called *merchandise inventory.* Merchandise inventories are found on retail store shelves and in stockrooms or warehouses.

Prepaid Items. Prepaid items are current assets that have been acquired for purpose of consumption during the next twelve months. The items, however, that are placed on the statement of financial position have not been used up at the statement date. A physical inventory (or other methods of computing the inventory) is usually taken of these assets at the statement date so that the cost of the unconsumed portion may be shown. Some common prepaid items are described in the following paragraphs.

Prepaid Insurance. Every business must protect itself against hazards. Consequently, businesses take out insurance policies for protection. The cost of this type of protection is called an insurance premium and is paid in advance. Insurance policies commonly are issued against such hazards as fire, burglary, personal injury, business interruption, and injury to employees (workmen's compensation). The unexpired portion is listed on the statement. ✳

Office Supplies. Supplies such as stamps, stationery, and business forms required in an office are grouped under the title Office Supplies and are current assets of the business.

Store Supplies. Store supplies include wrapping paper, twine, paper bags, and similar items used in a store. They are also classified as current assets.

Assets used in the general operation of the business should not be included in the merchandise inventory.

Classification of Assets—Plant and Equipment

Plant and equipment comprises assets used over a long period in the operation of the business. These assets are customarily listed on the statement of financial position according to the degree of permanency; the most permanent item is listed first. Some typical plant and equipment assets are the following.

Land. Land is shown separately on the statement of financial position, although land and the buildings on the land are usually sold together. Land and buildings are classified separately because the buildings will deteriorate through usage, whereas the land will not.

Buildings. In order for a building to appear on the statement of financial position, it must be owned by the business or held under a long-term lease whose provisions, for all practical purposes, amount to ownership.

Store Equipment. Showcases, counters, and shelves are typical permanent items of store equipment used in selling the merchandise inventory.

Delivery Equipment. Delivery equipment consists of trucks, cars, and other types of equipment owned that are used for the delivery of products to the customer.

Other Classification Groupings

Other groupings are used for such items as long-term investments in stocks and bonds (Long-Term Investment) and for intangible plant items such as goodwill and trademarks (Intangible Assets).

Classification of Liabilities—Current

The term *current liabilities* is used principally to designate obligations whose *liquidation* (payment or settlement) is reasonably expected to require the use of current assets or the creation (substitution) of other current liabilities.[1]

All liabilities to be paid within a one-year period are classified as current. In general, current liabilities are listed on the statement of financial position in their probable order of liquidation; those that, on the average, will be paid first are shown first, those to be paid next are next, and so on. Typical current liabilities are the following

Accounts Payable. Accounts payable represent amounts owed to creditors resulting from purchases on credit (open charge account). If creditors are few, their names may be listed separately on the statement of financial position. If creditors are numerous, the statement of financial position shows only the total amount of accounts payable. Information about amounts owed to each creditor must be maintained in a separate supporting record.

Notes Payable. A note payable is a formal written promise to pay money to a creditor for value received. A *trade note payable* arises from the purchase of merchandise or services used in the course of business. A note payable to a bank arises when a company borrows money from a bank for business use. Generally these two items are *short term* and are classified as current liabilities, unless the note is for more than one year.

Accrued Liabilities. Accrued wages payable and accrued interest payable are typical *accrued liabilities,* which are debts that have accumulated because of the passage of time but that are not yet due for payment. These items are customarily placed last among the current liabilities.

Classification of Liabilities—Long Term

Debts that are not due for at least a year are called *long-term,* or *fixed,* liabilities. If part of a long-term liability is due within a year from the date of the statement of financial position, the amount of that part should be shown as current. There is no particular sequence in which long-term liabilities appear in the position statement; however, size may be one criterion.

Mortgage Payable. A mortgage payable is a debt owed by the business that is secured by a specific asset or assets. The legal document by which the debt is secured is called a *mortgage.* A business may arrange a long-term loan with a bank, for example, and give to the bank as security a mortgage on its land and building. If the business fails to meet the terms of payment of the mortgage, the bank can take necessary legal action to take possession of the asset, or to sell it and satisfy the mortgage claim from the proceeds of the sale. Any balance remaining from the sale of the asset reverts to the business.

Bonds Payable. As a means of raising funds, corporations issue *bonds,* which are long-term promises to repay funds that are borrowed. These obligations may or may not be secured by assets of the borrowing company. Many corporations have excellent credit ratings and therefore do not need to offer specific security for loans.

Owner's Equity on the Statement of Financial Position

The form of a business organization determines the manner of reporting the owner's equity on the statement of financial position. The three common

[1] AICPA, *APB Accounting Principles,* Vol. 2 (Chicago: Commerce Clearing House, Inc., 1973), p. 6011.

BASIC CONCEPTS
AND
METHODOLOGY

(Ch. 2)

forms of business organization are (1) the corporation, (2) the single proprietorship, and (3) the partnership. The ownership interest in each of these organizational forms is disclosed in a slightly different manner on the statement of financial position.

A corporation is a separate legal entity, created by a *charter* from the state in which it is organized; it is owned by several *stockholders*. Each stockholder owns a certain portion of the corporation, expressed in *shares of stock*. *Stock certificates* are issued to him as evidence of his ownership. *Capital stock* is a term describing investments by the stockholders. Shares may be issued at *par*, which is the face value decided upon by the organizers and stated in the charter, or at a *premium* or *discount*.

The primary advantage of the corporation to its owners is that the stockholders' personal assets cannot be taken by creditors to satisfy the debts of the business; only the assets of the business itself can be taken; this concept is referred to as *limited liability* of the shareholders. There are also other significant legal advantages, which will be studied in later chapters. In turn, corporations are subject to special government regulation and taxation. Because the corporate form is the most important form of business ownership today, it is stressed throughout this text. Moreover, the use of the simple form of corporate ownership accentuates the entity concept of accounting. However, in Chapters 2 and 3 the procedures applicable to the single proprietorship are presented. Corporations and partnerships are discussed in detail in later chapters.

The income, or profits, of the corporation may be distributed to the stockholders in the form of *dividends* or may be retained in the corporation. The part that is kept is referred to as *retained earnings*. Retained earnings are not a part of the capital stock, but are a part of the total stockholders' equity. They represent the accumulated undistributed earnings of the corporation—that is, the total net income of the business from the date it was organized less the total dividends paid and the total losses sustained during the same period. Retained earnings must be accounted for separately from the capital stock because of the legal restrictions placed on the original capital paid in by investors.

Corporation. The owners' equity section of a position statement for a corporation is shown as

Stockholders' Equity		
Capital Stock	$20,000	
Retained Earnings	570	
Total Stockholders' Equity		$20,570

Single Proprietorship. Many businesses are owned by individuals; they are referred to as *single proprietorships*. If a business is small and its operations are comparatively simple, the single-proprietorship form of ownership offers several advantages over the corporate form: The owner has a more direct control of the business, he does not have to report to several stockholders, and the business is not subject to the special regulations and taxes for corporations. But his personal assets can be taken as payment of the debts of the business. Careful management will, of course, minimize the chances of such an event.

BASIC MODEL:
REAL ACCOUNTS

(Ch. 2)

31

If the Murrow Clothing Store is a single proprietorship owned by Douglas Murrow, then his equity would be shown on the statement of financial position as follows:

Owner's Equity	
Douglas Murrow, Capital	$20,570

The owner's equity for the single proprietorship is listed with the name of the proprietor, followed by the word "Capital." The total owner's equity may be shown as one item, because there are no legal restrictions on withdrawals by a single proprietor as there are for the stockholders of a corporation.

Partnership. Often several individuals find it advantageous to form a business by establishing a *partnership.* In this case, the owners are the *partners* of the business. The advantages of a partnership are similar to those of a single proprietorship, with the added advantages of a greater amount of capital contributed by the several partners and the different abilities that the partners can bring to the management of the business. The primary disadvantage of the partnership is that each partner may be held personally responsible for all the debts of the business.

If Douglas Murrow and John Wells own the Murrow Clothing Store as partners, their equity would be shown on the statement of financial position as follows:[2]

Partners' Equity		
Douglas Murrow, Capital	$10,085	
John Wells, Capital	10,485	
Total Partners' Equity		$20,570

DEVELOPMENT OF THE BASIC MODEL USING ONLY POSITION STATEMENT ACCOUNTS

To obtain the data needed to prepare statements of financial position, an orderly accounting system must be developed. This chapter describes several possible systems, leading up to a discussion of the one in general use in modern business.

In this section of this chapter and in the following two chapters, *service businesses,* which sell services rather than merchandise, are used as illustrations. Service businesses are used first to illustrate the operation of an ac-

[2] For an introduction to the management studies of the statement of financial position, see the Appendix to Chapter 2.

(Ch. 2)

counting system because they do not offer the added complications of the inventories required in *merchandising businesses*.

All businesses go through an initial cycle, during which the owners pay in an investment and acquire plant and equipment prior to beginning regular operations. The transactions involved in the organization of the Whitside Realty Corporation Limited follow.[3]

1976

July 1 The Whitside Realty Corporation Limited was organized by John Whitside, Ronald Raymond, and James Baker. The charter (proper legal authorization) was received from the Secretary of State, and capital stock in the amount of $50,000 was issued at par (sold for face amount) for cash; that is, the stockholders—Whitside, Raymond, and Baker—made an investment of $50,000 in the business. Whitside invested $40,000; Raymond, $6,000; and Baker, $4,000. Issued stock certificates numbered 1001, 1002, and 1003.

5 Purchased land and building for $30,000 in cash. The land was appraised at $5,000; the building, at $25,000. Issued check No. 1.

10 Purchased furniture on account from the Jones Company for $8,000; supplier's invoice is dated July 8, 1976.

20 Paid the Jones Company $5,000 on account. Issued check No. 2.

25 The corporation found that some of the furniture was not what it wanted, so it sold the furniture, which had cost $1,800, to James Hill for $1,800 on account. Hill promised to pay this amount in 30 days; issued invoice No. 1.

31 Collected $1,000 from James Hill on account.

The following discussion is based on these transactions.

PREPARATION OF A STATEMENT OF FINANCIAL POSITION AFTER EACH TRANSACTION

Since the statement of financial position is an expanded variation of the accounting equation, it is obvious that the total of the separate sides are always equal. A possible solution to the problem of accumulating data is the preparation of a statement of financial position immediately after each transaction.

Issuance of Capital Stock

The statement of financial position shown in Figure 2-3 would be prepared after the three stockholders incorporate their business and the capital stock of $50,000 has been issued. (In this chapter, the account form of position statement is used to show the effect of each transaction on each side of the accounting equation.)

[3] The word *limited* is often used with the name of the corporation to designate the limited liability of corporate shareholders; in Canada and other commonwealths of the United Kingdom, the use of the word *limited* or *ltd.* in the corporate title is a legal requirement.

Figure 2-3
After Original
Investment

WHITSIDE REALTY CORPORATION LIMITED
Statement of Financial Position
July 1, 1976

Assets		Liabilities and Stockholders' Equity	
Current Assets		Stockholders' Equity	
(+) Cash	$50,000	(+) Capital Stock	$50,000

This transaction involves an increase of an asset, Cash, accompanied by an increase in a stockholders' equity item, Capital Stock. The plus and minus signs show the direction of change of each item in the transaction; *they would not be part* of an actual statement.

Purchase of Land and Building

A statement of financial position prepared after the land and building are purchased appears in Figure 2-4.

Figure 2-4   After Purchase of Land and Building

WHITSIDE REALTY CORPORATION LIMITED
Statement of Financial Position
July 5, 1976

Assets			Liabilities and Stockholders' Equity	
Current Assets			Stockholders' Equity	
(−) Cash		$20,000	Capital Stock	$50,000
Plant and Equipment				
(+) Land	$ 5,000			
(+) Building	25,000			
Total Plant and Equipment		30,000		
Total Assets		$50,000	Total Stockholders' Equity	$50,000

This transaction involves increases of assets, Land and Building, accompanied by a decrease of an asset, Cash, with no change occurring in the stockholders' equity.

Purchase of Furniture on Account

The statement prepared after the corporation purchased furniture on account from the Jones Company is shown in Figure 2-5.

(Ch. 2)

Figure 2-5 After Purchase of Furniture on Account

WHITSIDE REALTY CORPORATION LIMITED
Statement of Financial Position
July 10, 1976

Assets			*Liabilities and Stockholders' Equity*	
Current Assets			Current Liabilities	
Cash		$20,000	(+) Accounts Payable	$ 8,000
Plant and Equipment			Stockholders' Equity	
Land	$ 5,000		Capital Stock	50,000
Building	25,000			
(+) Furniture	8,000			
Total Plant and				
Equipment		38,000	Total Liabilities and	
Total Assets		$58,000	Stockholders' Equity	$58,000

This transaction involves an increase of an asset, Furniture, accompanied by an increase of a liability, Accounts Payable, with no change occurring in the stockholders' equity and no change in any other assets.

Payment of Accounts Payable

The statement of financial position appearing in Figure 2-6 is prepared after the corporation pays to the Jones Company on account $5,000 in cash.

The transaction reflected in this statement involves a decrease of a liability, Accounts Payable, accompanied by a decrease of an asset, Cash.

Figure 2-6 After Partial Payment of Accounts Payable

WHITSIDE REALTY CORPORATION LIMITED
Statement of Financial Position
July 20, 1976

Assets			*Liabilities and Stockholders' Equity*	
Current Assets			Current Liabilities	
(−) Cash		$15,000	(−) Accounts Payable	$ 3,000
Plant and Equipment			Stockholders' Equity	
Land	$ 5,000		Capital Stock	50,000
Building	25,000			
Furniture	8,000			
Total Plant and				
Equipment		38,000	Total Liabilities and	
Total Assets		$53,000	Stockholders' Equity	$53,000

Sale of Furniture on Account

After the corporation sells some of its furniture to James Hill on account, the statement of financial position shown in Figure 2-7 is prepared.

Figure 2-7 After Sale of Furniture on Account

WHITSIDE REALTY CORPORATION LIMITED
Statement of Financial Position
July 25, 1976

Assets			*Liabilities and Stockholders' Equity*	
Current Assets			Current Liabilities	
Cash	$15,000		Accounts Payable	$ 3,000
(+) Accounts			Stockholders' Equity	
Receivable	1,800		Capital Stock	50,000
Total Current Assets		$16,800		
Plant and Equipment				
Land	$ 5,000			
Building	25,000			
(−) Furniture	6,200			
Total Plant and				
Equipment		36,200	Total Liabilities and	
Total Assets		$53,000	Stockholders' Equity	$53,000

1. The amount of money yet to be received from James Hill is reflected as an asset, Accounts Receivable. It is a current asset because it is collectible within a year.
2. This transaction involves an increase of an asset, Accounts Receivable, accompanied by a decrease of an asset, Furniture. It is similar to the transaction of July 5 in that it consists of an exchange of one asset for another (Figure 2-4).
3. The furniture was sold at cost. If it had been sold at a price above its cost, a stockholders' equity item, Retained Earnings, would have been increased by the amount of the gain.

Collection of Accounts Receivable

After James Hill makes a payment of $1,000, the statement of financial position shown in Figure 2-8 is prepared.

As in Figure 2-7, this transaction involves an increase of an asset, Cash, accompanied by a decrease of an asset, Accounts Receivable.

The method of accumulating accounting data illustrated thus far gives the desired results of enabling a business to prepare a statement of financial position, but, in most instances, the time and expense involved would prohibit its

Figure 2-8 After Collection of Accounts Receivable

WHITSIDE REALTY CORPORATION LIMITED
Statement of Financial Position
July 31, 1976

Assets			Liabilities and Stockholders' Equity	
Current Assets			Current Liabilities	
(+) Cash	$16,000		Accounts Payable	$ 3,000
(−) Accounts			Stockholders' Equity	
Receivable	800		Capital Stock	50,000
Total Current Assets		$16,800		
Plant and Equipment				
Land	$ 5,000			
Building	25,000			
Furniture	6,200			
Total Plant and				
Equipment		36,200	Total Liabilities and	
Total Assets		$53,000	Stockholders' Equity	$53,000

use. Moreover, a statement of financial position prepared after each transaction is not needed by those who use accounting information as a guide to action. A statement of financial position prepared at the end of each month is usually sufficient.

EXPANSION OF THE ACCOUNTING EQUATION

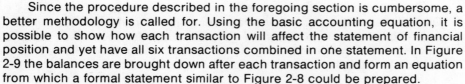

Since the procedure described in the foregoing section is cumbersome, a better methodology is called for. Using the basic accounting equation, it is possible to show how each transaction will affect the statement of financial position and yet have all six transactions combined in one statement. In Figure 2-9 the balances are brought down after each transaction and form an equation from which a formal statement similar to Figure 2-8 could be prepared.

After each transaction, the total of the Assets columns equals the total of the Liabilities and Stockholders' Equity columns. For example, after the July 25 transaction, the assets total of $53,000 = ($15,000 + $1,800 + $5,000 + $25,000 + $6,200) equals the liabilities and stockholders' equity total of $53,000 = ($3,000 + $50,000). A formal statement of financial position could be prepared from Figure 2-9 after the July 31 transaction by simply arranging the various assets, liabilities, and stockholders' equity items in the form illustrated in Figure 2-8.

Although this method tends to shorten the accounting process, it is unsuitable for most companies because it cannot easily be expanded to provide for a large number of asset and liability items. For example, it would be virtually impossible to use this procedure in a company that has fifty assets and twenty-five liabilities.

Figure 2-9 Expanded Accounting Equation

WHITSIDE REALTY CORPORATION LIMITED
Expanded Accounting Equation Revealing Financial Position
For Month Ended July 31, 1976

Date		Business Transaction	Cash	+	Accounts Receivable	+	Land	+	Building	+	Furniture	=	Accounts Payable	+	Capital Stock
							Assets					=	Liabilities	+	Stockholders' Equity
1976 July	1	Issued capital stock for $50,000 in cash.	+$50,000									=			+$50,000
	5	Purchased land and building for $30,000 in cash. Land is appraised at $5,000; building, at $25,000.	−30,000				+$5,000		+$25,000						
		Balances	$20,000	+			$5,000	+	$25,000			=			$50,000
	10	Purchased furniture on account from the Jones Company for $8,000.									+$8,000	=	+$8,000		
		Balances	$20,000	+			$5,000	+	$25,000	+	$8,000	=	$8,000	+	$50,000
	20	Paid the Jones Company $5,000 on account.	−5,000										−5,000		
		Balances	$15,000	+			$5,000	+	$25,000	+	$8,000	=	$3,000	+	$50,000
	25	Sold furniture at cost to James Hill for $1,800 on account.			+$1,800						−1,800				
		Balances	$15,000	+	$1,800	+	$5,000	+	$25,000	+	$6,200	=	$3,000	+	$50,000
	31	Collected $1,000 from James Hill on account.	+1,000		−1,000										
		Balances	$16,000	+	$ 800	+	$5,000	+	$25,000	+	$6,200	=	$3,000	+	$50,000

A SEPARATE PAGE FOR EACH COMPONENT OF THE ACCOUNTING EQUATION

One solution to the problem of data accumulation for an expanded number of assets and liabilities is to designate a separate page for each asset, liability, and stockholders' equity item. Using the six transactions of the Whitside Realty Corporation Limited, this method may be illustrated as follows:

ASSET PAGES

	Cash	Page 101
1976		
July 1	Contribution of stockholders	+$50,000
5	Purchase of land and building	− 30,000
20	Payment to Jones Company on account	− 5,000
31	Collection from James Hill	+ 1,000
	(Cash on hand $16,000)	

	Accounts Receivable	**Page 111**
1976		
July 25	Sale of furniture on account	+$1,800
31	Collection on account	− 1,000
	(Balance due $800)	

	Land	**Page 151**
1976		
July 5	Purchase of land	+$5,000

	Building	**Page 152**
1976		
July 5	Purchase of building	+$25,000

	Furniture	**Page 157**
1976		
July 10	Purchase of furniture on account	+$8,000
25	Sale of furniture at cost	− 1,800
	(Furniture on hand $6,200)	

LIABILITY PAGES

	Accounts Payable	**Page 201**
1976		
July 10	Purchase of furniture on account	$8,000
20	Payment on account	− 5,000
	(Balance due $3,000)	

STOCKHOLDERS' EQUITY PAGES

	Capital Stock	**Page 251**
1976		
July 1	Issued capital stock to three stockholders	+$50,000

A comment about the page numbering system should be made. The pages could be numbered 1, 2, 3, 4, 5, 6, 7; but if the numbers are to have a specific meaning—for example, 100–199 for assets, 200–249 for liabilities, and 250–299 for stockholders' equity items—and if expansion is contemplated (the insertion of new pages for new items), then the numbering system should be something like the one shown.

At the end of a designated period, the *balance,* or final amount, of each page may be obtained by adding the plus items and the minus items and subtracting the total of the minus items from the total of the plus items. These balances can then be arranged as a formal statement of financial position as shown in Figure 2-8.

This procedure does permit unlimited expansion, but the use of the plus and minus signs contributes to mathematical errors, and there is no economical way to run a mathematical check on the accuracy of the items contained in the accounting equation. Something else needs to be done to the system.

DIVISION OF SEPARATE PAGES INTO COLUMNS—CREATION OF ACCOUNTS

A possible solution to the problem of an accounting data accumulation system is the division of the pages, referred to in accounting as *accounts,* into two sections by drawing a line down the middle of the page and using both sides to record financial information pertaining to the particular item for which the account is maintained. The accounting equation

$$\text{Assets} = \text{Liabilities} + \text{Stockholders' Equity}$$

suggests the following arrangement: Assets appear on the left side of the equation; therefore, the left side of the account is used to record increases of assets, and the opposite side, the right side, is used to record decreases. Similarly, since liabilities and the stockholders' equity appear on the right side of the accounting equation, the right side of the account is used to record increases in liability and stockholders' equity accounts, and the opposite side, the left side, is used to record decreases.

An example of this kind of account is shown here.

			Account Title		Account Number
Date	Explanation	Amount	Date	Explanation	Amount
	Use this side to record increases in assets and decreases in liability and stockholders' equity items.			Use this side to record decreases in assets and increases in liability and stockholders' equity items.	

Again using the six transactions of the Whitside Realty Corporation Limited, the "account" feature of the accounting system is demonstrated. Before the information is placed in the accounts, each transaction is analyzed in the light of the foregoing suggestions for recording the information.

1976
July 1 The Whitside Realty Corporation Limited was organized and capital stock was issued for cash in the amount of $50,000. Cash, an asset, is

increased by $50,000, and Capital Stock, a stockholders' equity item, is likewise increased. The $50,000 is placed on the left side of the asset account, Cash, to indicate that it has been increased, and the same figure is placed on the right side of the Stockholders' Equity account to indicate that it also has been increased.

July 5 Purchased land and building for $30,000 in cash. The land was appraised at $5,000; the building, at $25,000. Both land and building are assets; thus, the $5,000 and the $25,000 are placed on the left sides of the Land and Building accounts, respectively, to reflect increases. The Cash account is decreased by $30,000; thus, this amount is placed on the right side of the Cash account.

10 Purchased furniture on account from the Jones Company for $8,000. The asset Furniture is increased by $8,000; this amount is placed on the left side of the Furniture account. A liability account, Accounts Payable, is increased by the amount due the Jones Company; $8,000 is placed on the right side of the Accounts Payable account to indicate that it has been increased.

20 Paid the Jones Company $5,000 on account. The liability Accounts Payable is decreased and the asset Cash is also decreased. The $5,000 is placed on the left side of the Accounts Payable account to record the decrease; the same figure is placed on the right side of the asset account, Cash, to reflect the decrease.

25 Sold furniture that cost $1,800 to James Hill for $1,800 on account. The asset Accounts Receivable is increased by $1,800 and the asset Furniture is decreased by $1,800. The increase in the asset Accounts Receivable is shown by placing the amount on the left side of the Accounts Receivable account; and the decrease in the asset Furniture is shown by placing the amount on the right side of the Furniture account.

31 Collected $1,000 from James Hill on account. The asset Cash is increased by $1,000; the asset Accounts Receivable is decreased by $1,000. The increase of the asset Cash is shown by placing the $1,000 on the left side of the Cash account; the decrease of the asset Accounts Receivable is shown by placing the $1,000 on the right side of the Accounts Receivable account.

These transactions would appear in the accounts as shown here.

		Cash					Acct. No. 101
Date		Explanation	Amount	Date		Explanation	Amount
1976 July	1	Issuance of Capital Stock*	50,000	1976 July	5	Purchased land and building	30,000
	31	Collection from Hill	1,000		20	Payment to Jones Co.	5,000
		16,000	51,000				35,000

* After the journal is introduced, it will be evident that explanations in ledger accounts are rarely needed.

(Ch. 2)

Accounts Receivable Acct. No. 111

Date	Explanation	Amount	Date	Explanation	Amount
1976 July 25	Sold furniture on account 800	1,800	1976 July 31	Collection on account	1,000

Land Acct. No. 151

Date	Explanation	Amount	Date	Explanation	Amount
1976 July 5	Purchased land	5,000			

Building Acct. No. 152

Date	Explanation	Amount	Date	Explanation	Amount
1976 July 5	Purchased building	25,000			

Furniture Acct. No. 157

Date	Explanation	Amount	Date	Explanation	Amount
1976 July 10	Purchased furniture on account 6,200	8,000	1976 July 25	Sold furniture on account	1,800

Accounts Payable Acct. No. 201

Date	Explanation	Amount	Date	Explanation	Amount
1976 July 20	Paid on account	5,000	1976 July 10	Purchased furniture on account 3,000	8,000

Capital Stock Acct. No. 251

Date	Explanation	Amount	Date	Explanation	Amount
			1976 July 1	Issued for cash	50,000

(Ch. 2)

After all the transactions are recorded, the accounts are *footed;* that is, each amount column containing more than one entry is totaled in small pencil figures under the last amount on each side (see the Cash account, for example). Then the balance of each account is determined by subtracting the smaller amount from the larger; the balance is placed in the Explanation column of the side with the larger amount. As a check on the accuracy of the work in relation to the accounting equation, the total of the balances on the left sides of the accounts is compared to the total of the balances on the right sides. If the totals agree, it is presumed that the accounting is correct up to this point. This listing of account balances is called a *trial balance* (illustrated in Figure 2-10). After the trial balance is prepared, a statement of financial position similar to Figure 2-8 can be prepared.

Figure 2-10
Trial Balance

WHITSIDE REALTY CORPORATION LIMITED
Trial Balance
July 31, 1976

Acct. No.	Account Title	Left-Side Balances	Right-Side Balances
101	Cash	$16,000	
111	Accounts Receivable	800	
151	Land	5,000	
152	Building	25,000	
157	Furniture	6,200	
201	Accounts Payable		$ 3,000
251	Capital Stock		50,000
	Totals	$53,000	$53,000

TOOLS OF ACCOUNTING

Before the final stage of the basic accounting methodology is discussed, the following accounting tools should be considered:

1. The T account
2. Debits and credits
3. The formal account

The T Account

The simplest form of any account is called a "T account" because of its shape. Owing to its simplicity, this form best clarifies the effects of transactions on a given account. As indicated in the preceding section, each account consists of a left side and a right side, with the title of the account written across the top.

(Ch. 2)

The left side of an account is called the *debit* side, and the right side of an account is called the *credit* side.

Account Title	
Debit (left side)	*Credit* (right side)

The terms "debit" and "credit" originally had a more specific meaning, related to *debtor* and *creditor* accounts; today they may be used as nouns, verbs, or adjectives depending on whether one is talking about an amount on the left side (*a debit*) or the right side (*a credit*), the process of placing an amount on the left side (*to debit*) or the right side (*to credit*), or the characteristics of information on the left side (*a debit entry*) or the right side (*a credit entry*).

Substituting the terms "debit" and "credit" for the longer analytical description in the preceding section, the following rules may be stated:

Debit to record:	Credit to record:
An increase of an asset	A decrease of an asset
A decrease of a liability	An increase of a liability
A decrease in the stockholders' equity	An increase in the stockholders' equity

The relationship of the rules of debit and credit to the statement of financial position and to the accounting equation may be illustrated as follows:

Assets (Property Owned by a Business)		Liabilities (Creditors' Claims to Assets)		Stockholders' Equity (Owners' Claims to Assets)	
Debit	Credit	Debit	Credit	Debit	Credit
Increase	Decrease	Decrease	Increase	Decrease	Increase

The abbreviation for credit is *Cr.;* for debit it is *Dr.*

The Formal Ledger Account

In actual business practice, the T account is expanded to a formal *ledger account.* A *ledger account* is a statistical device used for sorting accounting information into homogeneous groupings; it typically consists of two sides, with columns on each side for (1) the date, (2) an explanation, (3) the page number of the source from which the amount was transferred (called the *folio column*), and (4) the amount. A standard form of the ledger account for Cash is shown; the folio column is indicated by an F.

Cash							Acct. No. 101
Date	Explanation	F	Debit	Date	Explanation	F	Credit

A variation of the T form is the three-money-column form, with Debit, Credit, and Balance columns. After each entry, the balance of the account may be computed and entered in the Balance column. This form is useful when frequent reference is made to the balance of an account, as, for example, in the individual separate customers and creditors accounts.

A three-money-column account form is shown below.

Cash					Acct. No. 101
Date	Explanation	F	Debit	Credit	Balance

The book or other storage medium (punched cards, magnetic tape, and so forth) that contains all the accounts of a business is called the *ledger*.

DEVELOPMENT OF THE GENERAL JOURNAL AND POSTING

In the preceding sections of this chapter, the six transactions of the Whitside Realty Corporation Limited were analyzed in terms of their effect on asset, liability, and stockholders' equity accounts, and the information was entered directly into the accounts. Records can be kept in this manner; however, most businesses need more detailed information as well as a means of ensuring a properly functioning and systematic procedure for the recording of transactions. The desired additional information includes a chronological record of transactions and a complete history of each transaction recorded *in one place*. It is often necessary to view a transaction in its entirety, including reference to the underlying documents and supporting papers. Since every entry consists of at least one debit and one credit, the transaction is recorded on different ledger pages. If the ledger contains many accounts, it may be difficult to reconstruct the complete transaction.

The recording process is commonly divided into two parts:

1. *Journalizing*, or recording transactions in a book called a *journal*. The record of a transaction in the journal is called a *journal entry*.
2. *Posting*, or transferring amounts in the journal to the correct accounts in the ledger.

1. Journalizing
2. Posting

Entering Transactions in the Journal

The following entry, in the basic form of a journal, the *general journal*, shows the July 1 transaction of the Whitside Realty Corporation Limited.

GENERAL JOURNAL   Page 1

	Date 1976	Debit — Credit — Explanation	F	Debit	Credit
❶					
❷ ❸	July 1	Cash		50000 —	
❹ ❻ ❽		Capital Stock			50000 —
		To record the issuance of Capital stock to John Whitside, Ronald Raymond, and James Baker; issued stock certificates numbered 1001, 1002, 1003.			

❶ The year is written in small figures at the top of the Date column. It should be written in that position on every page of the journal.

❷ The month of the first transaction recorded on this page is entered. It is not necessary to write the month again on this page unless it changes.

❸ The date of each transaction is entered.

❹ The title of the account debited is placed in the Explanation column against the date line. In order to eliminate confusion, it is important that the account title written in the journal entry should be the exact title of the account as it appears in the ledger.

❺ The amount of the debit is entered in the Debit money column.

❻ The title of the account credited is indented approximately one inch from the Date column.

❼ The amount of the credit is entered in the Credit money column.

❽ The explanation is entered on the next line, indented an additional one inch. The explanation should contain all the essential information as well as a reference to the relevant source document from which the information was obtained—inspection report, receiver's report, check number, and so on.

In journals, ledger accounts, and trial balances, the use of two zeros or a dash in the cents column is a matter of choice. Thus, an amount may be written 2,357.00 or 2,357.—. Many accountants feel that a dash is more easily written than two zeros, and that the use of dashes facilitates the addition of the cents column.

In a statement of financial position and other statements it is preferable, for the sake of appearance, to use zeros. In the interest of space and time, the zero column will be omitted in most of the journals, ledgers, and statements that are illustrated in the remaining pages of this book.

Figure 2-11   Posting Flow Chart

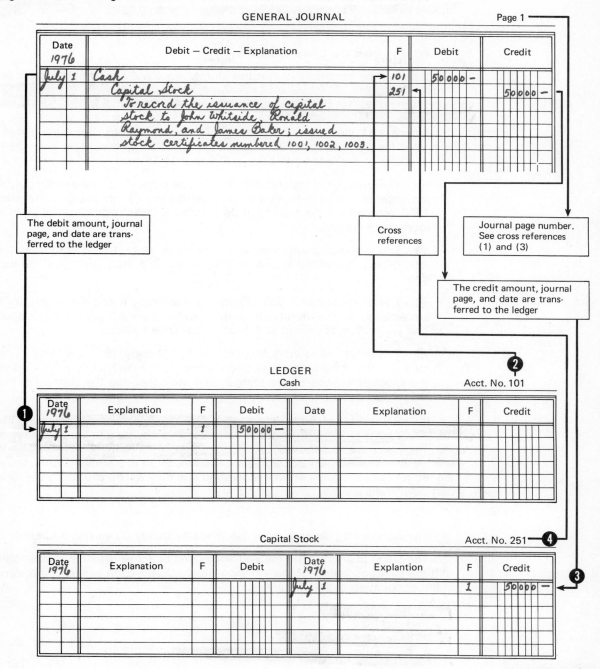

GENERAL JOURNAL   Page 1

Date 1976	Debit — Credit — Explanation	F	Debit	Credit
July 1	Cash	101	50000 —	
	Capital Stock	251		50000 —
	To record the issuance of capital stock to John Whitside, Ronald Raymond, and James Baker; issued stock certificates numbered 1001, 1002, 1003.			

The debit amount, journal page, and date are transferred to the ledger

Cross references

Journal page number. See cross references (1) and (3)

The credit amount, journal page, and date are transferred to the ledger

LEDGER
Cash   Acct. No. 101

Date 1976	Explanation	F	Debit	Date	Explanation	F	Credit
July 1		1	50000 —				

Capital Stock   Acct. No. 251

Date 1976	Explanation	F	Debit	Date 1976	Explantion	F	Credit
				July 1		1	50000 —

BASIC MODEL:
REAL ACCOUNTS

Dollar signs need not be written in journals and ledger accounts. They should be used in statements of financial position and other formal statements.

Posting from the General Journal

It should be emphasized that the journal does not *replace* the ledger account. The journal is called a *book of original entry,* because it is necessary first to journalize the transaction and then to post to the proper accounts in the ledger (the *book of final entry*).

Figure 2-11 illustrates the posting of the July 1 entry from the general journal of the corporation to its ledger. Posting normally should be done daily. Explanations of encircled numbers in Figure 2-11 follow:

❶ The debit amount, $50,000, the journal page, 1, and the date, July 1, are entered on the debit side of the Cash account in the ledger. The year, 1976, is written at the top of the Date column. Dollar signs are not used in journals or ledgers.

❷ The ledger account number for the debit entry, 101, is entered in the folio (F) column of the journal to cross-reference the journal and the ledger.

❸ The credit amount, $50,000, the journal page, 1, and the date, July 1, are entered on the credit side of the Capital Stock account in the ledger. The year, 1976, is written at the top of the Date column.

❹ The ledger account number for the credit entry, 251, is entered in the folio column of the journal to complete the cross referencing. It follows that the cross reference in the journal also indicates that the posting to the ledger has been completed.

It should be observed that explanations are not usually used in the Explanation columns of the ledger accounts. The cross reference to the journal page from which the information was recorded permits any interested person to quickly find a complete story of the transaction. Short explanations are used in the ledger accounts only when it is deemed that they will be especially useful in particular transactions.

The Accounting Sequence for the Whitside Realty Corporation Limited

The stage of accounting methodology used in actual practice is illustrated with the six transactions of the Whitside Realty Corporation Limited. The steps in the accounting sequence are:

1. Journalizing
2. Posting
3. Preparing a trial balance
4. Preparing a statement of financial position

Journalizing. The six transactions of the Whitside Realty Corporation Limited appear in the general journal as follows:

1976					
July	1	Cash	101	50,000	
		Capital Stock	251		50,000
		To record the issuance of capital stock to John Whitside, Ronald Raymond, and James Baker; issued stock certificates numbered 1001, 1002, 1003.			
	5	Land	151	5,000	
		Building	152	25,000	
		Cash	101		30,000
		To record purchase of land and building for cash; issued check No. 1.			
	10	Furniture	157	8,000	
		Accounts Payable— Jones Company	201		8,000
		To record purchase of furniture on account; supplier's invoice is dated July 10, 1976.			
	20	Accounts Payable— Jones Company	201	5,000	
		Cash	101		5,000
		To record payment on account; issued check No. 2.			
	25	Accounts Receivable—James Hill	111	1,800	
		Furniture	157		1,800
		To record credit sale of furniture at cost; invoice No. 1.			
	31	Cash	101	1,000	
		Accounts Receivable— James Hill	111		1,000
		To record collection on account.			

Posting. The transactions are posted from page 1 of the general journal to the ledger accounts shown. The cross references are entered in both the journal and the accounts.

After all the journal entries are posted, the accountant foots each account as shown in the ledger on page 50.

The system under discussion is called *double-entry accounting,* because it requires that each record of a transaction have debits and credits of equal amount. Every transaction does not necessarily have a single debit and a single

BASIC MODEL: REAL ACCOUNTS

(Ch. 2)

LEDGER

Cash   Acct. No. 101

Date					Date				
1976 July	1		1	50,000	1976 July	5		1	30,000
	31	16,000	1	1,000		20		1	5,000
				51,000					35,000

Accounts Receivable   Acct. No. 111

Date					Date				
1976 July	25	800	1	1,800	1976 July	31		1	1,000

Land   Acct. No. 151

Date					Date				
1976 July	5		1	5,000					

Building   Acct. No. 152

Date					Date				
1976 July	5		1	25,000					

Furniture   Acct. No. 157

Date					Date				
1976 July	10	6,200	1	8,000	1976 July	25		1	1,800

Accounts Payable   Acct. No. 201

Date					Date				
1976 July	20		1	5,000	1976 July	10	3,000	1	8,000

Capital Stock   Acct. No. 251

Date					Date				
					1976 July	1		1	50,000

credit. For example, the July 5 entry of the corporation involves two debits totaling $30,000 and one credit of $30,000. This is called a *compound entry*. Regardless of the number of accounts debited and credited in a single transaction, the total amount of all the debits and the total amount of all the credits in each transaction must be equal. It follows that the total of the debit and the credit balances in all the accounts must also be equal.

As stated previously, it is customary to prepare a trial balance to test the equality of the debit and credit balances in the ledger before a formal statement of financial position is prepared. The July 31, 1976, trial balance of the Whitside Realty Corporation Limited is shown below.

WHITSIDE REALTY CORPORATION LIMITED
Trial Balance
July 31, 1976

Acct. No.	Account Title	Debits	Credits
101	Cash	$16,000	
111	Accounts Receivable	800	
151	Land	5,000	
152	Building	25,000	
157	Furniture	6,200	
201	Accounts Payable		$ 3,000
251	Capital Stock		50,000
	Totals	$53,000	$53,000

The trial balance proves the equality of debits and credits, but this does not insure the accuracy of the accounts; for example, an entire transaction could be omitted, the debit and credit amounts of an entry could be identically incorrect, a wrong account could be debited or credited, or both the debit and credit amounts for a given transaction could be posted twice. If the trial balance is in balance, however, the accountant considers this strong presumptive evidence of accuracy and proceeds from that point.

The trial balance is useful to the accountant in preparing periodic financial statements. The accountant could prepare a statement of financial position directly from the accounts; but the trial balance furnishes a convenient summary of the information for the preparation of the statement of financial position.

If a trial balance does not balance, the following steps should be followed in the indicated sequence to locate the error.

1. Find the difference between the trial balance totals.
2. Examine the trial balance for balances that may be in the wrong column.
3. Re-add the trial balance columns.
4. Check the trial balance figures against those appearing in the ledger to see whether the amounts correspond and whether they have been entered in the proper columns.
5. Check the additions on each side of each ledger account and recompute the balances.
6. Check postings from journal to ledger.

BASIC MODEL:
REAL ACCOUNTS

The trial balance may not balance because of a single error. Time and effort may be saved by applying the following special tests after step 1:

1. Errors in the amount of $0.01, $0.10, $1, $10, $100, and so on, may be due to errors in addition or subtraction.
2. If the trial balance difference is divisible by 2, the error may be due to a debit amount entered as a credit amount, or vice versa.
3. If the trial balance difference is divisible by 9 or 99, the error may be due to a transposition of figures ($83.41 posted as $38.41) or a slide ($1.05 posted as $105.00).

Statement of Financial Position

The next step in the accounting sequence is the preparation of the formal statement of financial position for the Whitside Realty Corporation Limited (Figure 2-12). Note that Figure 2-12 is the same as Figure 2-8.

Figure 2-12   Formal Statement of Financial Position

WHITSIDE REALTY CORPORATION LIMITED
Statement of Financial Position
July 31, 1976

Assets			*Liabilities and Stockholders' Equity*	
Current Assets			Current Liabilities	
Cash	$16,000		Accounts Payable	$ 3,000
Accounts Receivable	800		Stockholders' Equity	
Total Current Assets		$16,800	Capital Stock	50,000
Plant and Equipment				
Land	$ 5,000			
Building	25,000			
Furniture	6,200			
Total Plant and Equipment		36,200	Total Liabilities and	
Total Assets		$53,000	Stockholders' Equity	$53,000

PROCEDURES APPLICABLE TO A SINGLE PROPRIETORSHIP

Many small service businesses are single proprietorships. Among these are professional offices conducted by doctors, lawyers, accountants, and engineers or service stations and small retail outlets. The only difference between the single-proprietorship form of business organization and that of the corporation in relation to the example of the Whitside Realty Corporation Limited is the investment by the owners. If John Whitside had created a single-proprietorship form of realty business and had invested $50,000 in cash, the following journal entry would have been made:

(Ch. 2)

```
         GENERAL JOURNAL                    Page 1
1976
July   1   Cash                              50,000
               John  Whitside,  Capital               50,000
                   To record investment by proprietor
                   to form a realty business to be
                   called the Whitside Realty Company.
```

All the other entries would be recorded in the same way regardless of the form of business organization. The statement of financial position prepared at July 31, 1976, for the Whitside Realty Company, a single proprietorship, would be similar to Figure 2-12 with the exception of the owner's equity section, which would appear as follows:

Owner's Equity
    John Whitside, Capital $50,000

CALCULATIONS FOR THE MURROW CLOTHING STORE

To provide information that will be of maximum assistance in decision making, the financial data should be in a form and manner that make them understandable, meaningful, and useful. The absolute amounts contained in the statement of financial position for the Murrow Clothing Store (see pages 26–27 for applicable financial statements for the Murrow Clothing Store) are quite useful to management, but they tell only part of the story. For example, a total current asset amount of $30,910 indicates a certain purchasing-power command over goods and services, but how adequate is this amount for the Murrow Clothing Store? The data begin to become more meaningful when they are compared with other related information of current or past years. The following relationships revealed by position statements are central to certain financial management decisions.

Current Ratio

The relationship of current assets to current liabilities gives some indication of the firm's ability to pay its current debts as they mature.

Ratio Analysis

This relationship is called the *current ratio;* it is computed by dividing the current assets by the current liabilities.

The current ratio of the Murrow Clothing Store is computed as in Figure 2-13.

Figure 2-13
Computation of the
Current Ratio

$$\frac{\text{Current Assets}}{\text{Current Liabilities}} = \frac{\$30,910}{\$15,090} = 2.05 \text{ to } 1$$

The Murrow Clothing Store has approximately $2.05 of current assets for every $1 of current liabilities. This means that even if the current assets of the company were to shrink in value by as much as 50 percent, the short-term creditors could still be paid in full.

In the past, as a rule of thumb, a current ratio of 2 to 1 was considered satisfactory. Analysts, however, generally agree that no one ratio is sufficient and that certain other factors must be considered, such as the nature of the business, the season of the year, the composition of the specific items in the current assets category, and the quality of the management of the company.

Grantors of credit emphasize the relative convertibility of the current assets into cash. To illustrate, assume that the Amber Company and the Battle Company have the following current ratios:

BASIC CONCEPTS
AND
METHODOLOGY

(Ch. 2)

	Amber Company	Battle Company
Current Assets		
Cash	$ 500	$10,000
Accounts Receivable	700	14,000
Merchandise Inventory	28,800	6,000
Total Current Assets	$30,000	$30,000
Current Liabilities		
Accounts Payable	$15,000	$15,000
Current Ratio	2:1	2:1

Although each company has a current ratio of 2 to 1, the Battle Company is apparently in a far better position to meet its obligations. The Amber Company first must sell its $28,800 merchandise inventory and then convert the resulting receivables into cash; or it can sell its inventory for cash as a single lot, probably for less than the stated value. The Battle Company has $24,000 in cash and receivables and only $6,000 in merchandise inventory to be converted. The Amber Company thus may have a favorable current ratio but may be unable to pay its current liabilities because of an unfavorable distribution of the current assets.

Acid-Test Ratio

A supplementary test of the ability of a business to meet its current obligations is the acid-test ratio, which is expressed as follows:

$$\text{Acid-Test Ratio} = \frac{\text{Quick Current Assets}}{\text{Current Liabilities}}$$

Quick current assets include only cash, readily marketable securities, and receivables. The acid-test ratio for the Murrow Clothing Store is computed as follows:

$$\frac{\text{Quick Current Assets}}{\text{Current Liabilities}} = \frac{(\$325 + \$1,900 + \$11,025 + \$2,520)}{\$15,090}$$

$$= \frac{\$15,770}{\$15,090}$$

$$= 1.05 \text{ to } 1$$

If the analyst is not satisfied with the current ratio as an indicator of liquidity, he may use the acid-test ratio, which excludes merchandise inventory and prepaid items. If the quick current assets are larger than the current liabilities (that is, if the acid-test ratio is better than 1 to 1), there is evidence of a strong short-term credit position and indication that the company is able to meet its currently maturing obligations.

BASIC MODEL:
REAL ACCOUNTS

Working Capital

A term frequently used in financial statement analysis is *working capital,* or *circulating capital.* Working capital is the difference between the current assets and the current liabilities. The working capital of the Murrow Clothing Store is

$$\text{Current Assets} - \text{Current Liabilities} = \text{Working Capital}$$
$$\$30,910 \quad - \quad \$15,090 \quad = \quad \$15,820$$

The business has an excess of $15,820 to use in operations after the current assets are converted into cash and the current liabilities are paid.

An interesting comparison may be made regarding working capital analysis, assuming the following information:

	Line	Carson Company	Dickinson Company
Current Assets	(a)	$200,000	$800,000
Current Liabilities	(b)	100,000	600,000
Working Capital	(a − b)	$100,000	$200,000
Current Ratio	(a ÷ b)	2:1	1.33:1

The Dickinson Company has twice as much working capital as the Carson Company, but its debt-paying ability is not as satisfactory. The relationship between current assets and current liabilities may be more significant than their difference.

Working capital flows through the business in a regular pattern; this flow may be diagramed as illustrated below. As funds flow into the business, the management of the Murrow Clothing Store must make decisions about when, how much, and for what purpose the funds are to be used or put back into the flow cycle. This is the point at which management must apply its skill in planning and making effective use of available working capital.

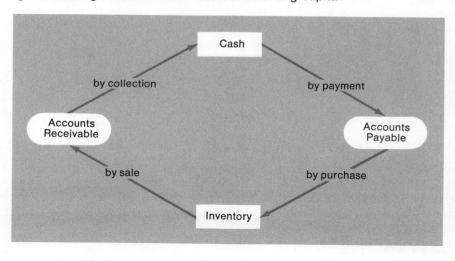

Ratio Analysis—Limitations

A particular ratio may be satisfactory under one set of circumstances and entirely unsatisfactory under another set. Ratios are generalizations and reflect conditions that exist only at a particular time. The ratios change continually with the continuing operations of the business. Sole reliance on ratio analysis may at times give a misleading indication of financial condition. Often nonfinancial information, including the quality of the employees and employee-management relations, must be analyzed in order to get a realistic picture of the financial position of the business. Understanding and correct interpretation of ratios, however, reduce the area over which subjective judgment must be exercised and thus aid the analyst in making sound decisions.

The ratios and comparisons discussed in this and subsequent chapters are valuable managerial aids, provided the user is aware of their limitations. The Murrow Clothing Store's current ratio of 2.05 to 1, computed in Figure 2-13, shows the relationship between two groups of items as of a given moment of time only. The ratio may fluctuate considerably during the course of the year. Furthermore, the ratio may have little meaning unless it is related to the entire business unit. One small section of a painting has little meaning without the rest of the picture; or if one states, for example, that Paul Clifford is an excellent student, we know very little about him. If we are told that he is twenty-two years old, is in the upper 5 percent of his class, and is president of Beta Gamma Sigma and captain of the basketball team, we know a good deal more about him. Similarly, if we state that both the Atwater Company and the Excel Company each have current ratios of 2 to 1, it does not mean too much unless the acid-test ratio and specific composition of the current assets are known.

GLOSSARY

Account A statistical device used for sorting accounting information into homogeneous groupings.

Acid-Test Ratio Quick current assets divided by current liabilities; the ratio is a measure of the immediate debt-paying ability of the firm.

Asset A thing of value held by an economic enterprise.

Balance The difference between the total of the debit amount in an account and the total of the credit amount in an account.

Compound Entry A journal entry with more than one debit account or more than one credit account.

Credit The right side of an account; the amount shown on the right side of an account; or the process of placing an amount on the right side of an account.

Current Assets Cash and other assets that are expected to be converted into cash or to be used in the operations of the business within one year.

Current Liabilities Obligations whose payment or settlement is reasonably expected to require the use of current assets or the creation of other current liabilities within a one-year period.

Current Ratio Current assets divided by current liabilities; the ratio is a measure of the short-run debt-paying ability of the firm.

Debit The left side of an account; the amount shown on the left side of an account; or the process of placing an amount on the left side of an account.

Entity Concept A term referring to the notion of placing emphasis on the business unit for purposes of accounting rather than on the owner(s) of the business.

Equities Claims against, or property rights in, the assets of a business.

Folio The cross-reference column in a journal or a ledger.

Footing The totaling of a column of figures and showing of the total in small pencil figures under the last amount in the column (also used as a noun).

Journal The book(s) of original entry for all transactions.

Journalizing The process of recording a transaction, analyzed in terms of its debits and credits, in a record of original entry, referred to as a journal.

Ledger The book that contains all the ledger accounts; or any collection of ledger accounts.

Liability An obligation of a business, or a creditors' claim against the assets of a business.

Long-Term Liability An obligation that matures after one year.

Merchandising Business A business that sells products or merchandise.

Net Assets Assets minus liabilities.

Owner's Equity The owner's or owners' claims against assets of a business. As used in this text, owner's equity implies that the business is a single proprietorship and, therefore, represents the proprietor's claims against assets of the single proprietorship.

Partners' Equity The partners' claims against the assets of a partnership business.

Plant and Equipment The tangible long-lived assets of a firm that are used in the operations of the firm and are not held for resale.

Posting The process of transferring an amount recorded in the journal to the indicated account in the ledger.

Quick Current Assets Cash plus marketable securities plus receivables.

Service Business A business that sells a service, for example, a certified public accounting firm.

Statement of Financial Position The statement that summarizes the assets, liabilities, and owner's (or owners') equity of a business unit as of a specific time.

Stockholders' Equity The stockholders' claims against the assets of a corporation.

T Account A simple form of ledger account in the shape of a T used for analyzing transactions and for teaching purposes.

Trial Balance A statement which shows the balances of all ledger accounts arranged according to whether they are debits or credits; the total of the debits must equal the total of the credits in this statement.

Working Capital Current assets minus current liabilities.

Q2-1. What is the entity concept? Identify the ways in which this concept aids the accounting function.

Q2-2. Define and give three examples of each of the following terms: (a) assets, (b) liabilities, (c) owner's equity.

Q2-3. What are current assets? Give five examples. In what order should these items be listed on the statement of financial position?

Q2-4. What is the purpose of the statement of financial position?

Q2-5. What is plant and equipment? Give five examples.

Q2-6. What are current liabilities? Give five examples.

Q2-7. State how each of the following should be computed: (a) current ratio, (b) acid-test ratio, (c) working capital. What is the major purpose of each of these ratios?

Q2-8. On December 31, 1976, the Agel Company had a current ratio of 3 to 1, and the Boston Company had a current ratio of 2 to 1. Is the Agel Company in a better financial position to pay its accounts payable when they are due than the Boston Company is? Discuss.

Q2-9. What is a business transaction? Give eight examples.

Q2-10. What is the difference between the terms *debit* and *credit*?

Q2-11. What is the function (a) of the general journal? (b) of the ledger?

Q2-12. A balanced trial balance is a correct trial balance. Discuss.

Q2-13. Robert Hanson purchased furniture on account from the Jones Company. Hanson debited the Furniture account for $800, and erroneously credited the Accounts Receivable account for $800. (a) What effect would the error have on the debit and credit totals of the trial balance taken at the end of the period? (b) What accounts in the trial balance would be incorrectly stated?

Q2-14. What does the term *ledger account* mean? Indicate two forms of the account. State the reasons and circumstances for using each form.

Q2-15. Why are the assets and liabilities classified in the statement of financial position?

Q2-16. Give an example of a transaction that would result (a) in an increase of an asset accompanied by an increase in the owner's equity; (b) in an increase of an asset accompanied by an increase of a liability; (c) in an increase of an asset accompanied by a decrease of an asset; (d) in a decrease of an asset accompanied by a decrease of a liability.

E2-1. Assume that the Chapel Hill Corporation has the following items at the end of the year:

Total Assets	$405,000
Total Long-Term Liabilities	50,500
Capital Stock	150,000
Retained Earnings	135,000
Current Assets	80,000

Compute the amount of current liabilities.

E2-2. The books of the Travis Armour Company contain the following items:

Retained Earnings	$ 75,000
Cash	45,000
Capital Stock	150,000
Accounts Receivable	9,000
Accounts Payable	6,400
Prepaid Insurance	1,600

Select the current assets and prepare in good form the Current Assets section of the statement of financial position as of December 31, 1976.

E2-3. The books of the Bunker Company contain the following items:

Cash	$ 10,500
Land	20,000
John Bunker, Capital	200,000
Building	320,000
Long-Term Notes Payable (due July 1, 1999)	100,000
Delivery Equipment	20,000
Office Supplies	2,000

Select the plant and equipment items, and prepare in good form the Plant and Equipment section of the statement of financial position as of December 31, 1976.

E2-4. The books of the Canyon Company contain the following items:

Accounts Receivable	$ 3,500
Accounts Payable	12,000
Notes Receivable	2,000
Notes Payable	4,000
Accrued Wages Payable	1,500
Retained Earnings	45,000
Bonds Payable (due July 1, 1999)	35,000

Select the current liabilities, and prepare in good form the Current Liabilities section of the statement of financial position as of December 31, 1976.

E2-5. The following condensed statement was prepared for the Durham Company as of December 31, 1976:

DURHAM COMPANY
Statement of Financial Position
December 31, 1976

Assets

Current Assets	$ 60,000
Plant and Equipment	200,000
Total Assets	$260,000

Liabilities and Stockholders' Equity

Current Liabilities	$ 15,000
Long-Term Liabilities	60,000
Total Liabilities	$ 75,000
Stockholders' Equity	185,000
Total Liabilities and Stockholders' Equity	$260,000

(a) Compute (1) the current ratio and (2) the working capital. (b) Explain the significance of each to management.

E2-6. Assume that the Durham Company (see E2-5) has the following current assets: cash, $4,000; marketable securities, $3,000; accounts receivable, $28,000; merchandise inventory, $20,000; and prepaid insurance, $5,000. Compute the acid-test ratio and explain its significance to management.

E2-7. Assume that a firm has current assets, $50,000; current liabilities, $20,000; long-term liabilities, $60,000; and stockholders' equity, $250,000 at the end of the year. Compute the amount of plant and equipment.

E2-8. The following financial information is available for the Aprile Company as of December 31, 1976:

Marketable Securities	$ 20,000
Accounts Receivable	80,000
Wages Payable	120,000
Buildings	100,000
Prepaid Insurance	2,000
Inventories	90,000
Capital Stock	100,000
Accounts Payable	65,000
Cash on Hand	4,500
Cash in Bank	210,000
Retained Earnings	?
Land	40,000
Bonds Payable	200,000

Prepare a statement of financial position for the Aprile Company as of December 31, 1976.

E2-9. The following statement of financial position was prepared by the bookkeeper of the Hudson Company:

HUDSON COMPANY
Statement of Financial Position
For the Year Ended December 31, 1976

Assets

Current Assets		
Cash	$ 4,000	
Accounts Receivable	12,000	
Building	24,000	
Merchandise Inventory	6,000	
Total Current Assets		$46,000
Plant and Equipment		
Marketable Securities	$ 6,000	
Store Equipment	3,000	
Office Supplies	200	
Delivery Equipment	2,700	
Total Plant and Equipment		11,900
Total Assets		$57,900

Liabilities and Owner's Equity

Current Liabilities		
Accounts Payable	$13,200	
Notes Payable (due June 1, 1977)	4,000	
Notes Payable (due July 1, 1999)	2,000	
Total Current Liabilities		$19,200
Long-Term Liabilities		
Mortgage Payable (due May 1, 1998)	$16,000	
Accrued Wages and Salaries Payable	500	
Total Long-Term Liabilities		16,500
Total Liabilities		$35,700
Owner's Equity		
I. M. Hudson, Capital		22,200
Total Liabilities and Assets		$57,900

List the errors in this statement.

E2-10. The following transactions were engaged in by the Calvin Corporation during the month of March 1976:

1976
March 1 Received a charter and issued all authorized capital stock at par for $200,000 in cash.

     2 Purchased land and buildings for $60,000 in cash and a 20-year mortgage payable for $40,000. The land was appraised at $30,000; the building, at $70,000.

     3 Purchased service supplies from the Rand Company for $2,000 on account.

    31 Sold a portion of the lot purchased on March 2 for its approximate cost of $5,000. The buyer, the White Sands Company, paid $3,000 in cash and issued a 90-day note for $2,000.

1. Journalize the transactions.
2. Post to formal ledger accounts. (Assign appropriate numbers to accounts.)
3. Take a trial balance.
4. Prepare a classified account-form statement of financial position.

E2-11. The Branson Corporation engaged in the following transactions during the first week of operations:

1976
June 1 Issued capital stock at par to the four incorporators for $50,000 in cash.

     3 Purchased office equipment from Black and Sons for $6,000 on account.

     5 Purchased land for a future building site at a cost of $30,000; paid $10,000 down and issued a mortgage note payable in 10 years for the balance.

Prepare a classified account-form statement of financial position after each transaction.

E2-12. The following T accounts were taken from the ledger of the Raleigh Company:

Cash

1976			1976		
Sept. 20		60,000	Sept. 23		8,000
				29	4,000
				30	32,000

Marketable Securities (U.S. Treasury Notes)

1976		
Sept. 29		4,000

Office Supplies

1976		
Sept. 23		8,000

Land

1976		
Sept. 30		10,000

Building

1976		
Sept. 30		30,000

Mortgage Payable

			1976		
			Sept. 30		8,000

Capital Stock

			1976		
			Sept. 20		60,000

Analyze these accounts and describe each transaction.

E2-13. The following statements of financial position were prepared immediately following each of three transactions engaged in by the Cimeron Company.

CIMERON COMPANY
Statement of Financial Position
July 1, 1976

Assets		Owner's Equity	
Current Assets		Owner's Equity	
Cash	$ 50,000	Thomas Cimeron, Capital	$ 50,000

CIMERON COMPANY
Statement of Financial Position
July 3, 1976

Assets			*Liabilities and Owner's Equity*	
Current Assets			Long-Term Liabilities	
Cash		$ 35,000	Mortgage Payable	$ 55,000
Plant and Equipment			Owner's Equity	
Land	$10,000		Thomas Cimeron, Capital	50,000
Building	60,000			
Total Plant and				
Equipment		70,000	Total Liabilities and	
Total Assets		$105,000	Owner's Equity	$105,000

CIMERON COMPANY
Statement of Financial Position
July 5, 1976

Assets			*Liabilities and Owner's Equity*	
Current Assets			Current Liabilities	
Cash	$35,000		Accounts Payable	$ 2,000
Office Supplies	2,000		Long-Term Liabilities	
Total Current Assets		$ 37,000	Mortgage Payable	55,000
Plant and Equipment			Total Liabilities	$ 57,000
Land	$10,000		Owner's Equity	
Building	60,000		Thomas Cimeron, Capital	50,000
Total Plant and				
Equipment		70,000	Total Liabilities and	
Total Assets		$107,000	Owner's Equity	$107,000

Date and describe each transaction.

E2-14. The following are among the transactions of the Anderson Corporation:

1976
Dec. 1   Capital stock of $50,000 par value was issued for cash.

    4   Purchased land for $10,000 in cash.

    8   Purchased marketable securities (U.S. government bonds) for $5,000 in cash.

  14   Purchased service supplies from Baltimore Company for $800 on account.

  18   Sold the land at cost for $10,000 cash.

  31   Paid $800 to Baltimore Company for balance of account.

Journalize the transactions, post to T accounts, and prepare a trial balance. (Assign appropriate numbers to accounts.)

E2-15. The following trial balance was prepared by the Henry Donnan Company. The trial balance is not in balance and the accounts are not in the proper order, but the account balances are correct.

HENRY DONNAN COMPANY
Trial Balance
December 31, 1976

Account Title	Debits	Credits
Cash	$120,000	
Henry Donnan, Capital		$170,000
Accounts Payable	20,000	
Notes Payable	10,000	
Land		8,000
Building		120,000
Accounts Receivable		14,000
Notes Receivable		12,000
Service Supplies	6,000	
Mortgage Payable		80,000
Totals	$156,000	$404,000

1. Prepare a corrected trial balance showing the accounts in proper order.

2. Prepare a classified report-form statement of financial position.

E2-16. The Ernest Gray Company had the following ledger accounts at June 30, 1976:

	Cash		Acct. No. 101
	110,000		6,000
	800		2,000
			5,000

	Notes Receivable		Acct. No. 112
	3,000		800

	Service Supplies		Acct. No. 131
	8,000		3,000

	Land		Acct. No. 151
	20,000		

	Accounts Payable		Acct. No. 201
	5,000		14,000
			6,000

	Ernest Gray, Capital		Acct. No. 251
			110,000

1. Compute the account balances.
2. Prepare a trial balance.
3. Prepare an account-form statement of financial position.

DP2-1. *(Corporate account-form statement of financial position)* The following alphabetical list of accounts is taken from the records of the Jensen Company at December 31, 1976:

Accounts Payable	$125,000
Accounts Receivable	138,000
Building ·	400,000
Capital Stock	400,000
Cash	250,000
Delivery Equipment	140,000
Land	115,000
Merchandise Inventory	70,000
Mortgage Payable (due July 1, 1993)	280,000
Notes Payable (due April 1, 1977)	110,000
Notes Receivable	18,000
Prepaid Insurance	12,000
Retained Earnings	214,000
Wages Payable	14,000

Required: Prepare an account-form statement of financial position.

DP2-2. *(Liabilities and owner's equity: single-proprietorship statement of financial position)* Refer to DP2-1. Assume that the Jensen Company is a single proprietorship operated by David J. Jensen.

Required: Show how the right side of an account-form statement of financial position would appear.

DP2-3. *(Liabilities and partners' equity: partnership statement of financial position)* Again refer to DP2-1. Assume that the Jensen Company is a partnership owned and operated by David J. Jensen and John T. Jensen and that the two partners have equities as follows:

David J. Jensen	$410,000
John T. Jensen	204,000
Total	$614,000

Required: Show how the right side of the statement of financial position would appear.

DP2-4. *(Development of an accounting system: corporation)* The following transactions occurred at the Westerlin Company during its first month of operations:

1976
May 1 Received a corporate charter and issued all its authorized stock for $100,000 in cash.

       2 Purchased land and building for $60,000. The company paid $20,000 in cash and issued a 20-year mortgage payable for the balance. The land was appraised at $15,000; the building, at $45,000.

       3 Purchased furniture from the Godwin Company for $10,500 on account.

1976

May 15 Paid the Godwin Company $6,500 on account.

20 Sold a portion of the land purchased on May 2 at its approximate cost of $5,000 to the Durham Realty Company on account.

31 Received $4,000 in cash and a 90-day note for $1,000 from the Durham Realty Company.

Required: Using these six transactions, illustrate the five stages discussed in the text:

1. Prepare a statement of financial position after each transaction.
2. Record the transactions in an expanded accounting equation.
3. Record the transactions on separate pages, not divided. (Number the pages.)
4. Record the transactions on separate pages, divided into Debit and Credit columns.
5. Journalize the transactions, post to formal ledger accounts, take a trial balance, and prepare a classified account-form statement of financial position.

DP2-5. *(Transactions peculiar to single proprietorships)* Assume that the Westerlin Company in DP2-4 is a single proprietorship owned and operated by Jay T. Westerlin.

Required: Which transactions would be different under this assumption? Journalize the transactions.

DP2-6. *(Development of an accounting system: single proprietorship)* Thurston Eaton opened a dental office and engaged in the following transactions:

1976

March 1 Opened a bank account, under the business name of Dr. Thurston Eaton, in the amount of $40,000.

2 Purchased land and building for $30,000. Paid $10,000 in cash and issued a 20-year mortgage payable for the balance. The land was appraised at $5,000; the building, at $25,000.

3 Purchased dental equipment and furniture from the Gummo Company for $8,000 on account.

12 Eaton wrote a check on his personal bank account (not his business account) for $3,000 in part payment of the Gummo Company account.

15 Some of the furniture purchased on March 3 was not satisfactory for his office needs, so Eaton sold it on account to an attorney, Thomas Schuester, at its cost of $800.

31 Received $700 from Schuester on account.

Required: Using these six transactions, illustrate the five stages discussed in the text:

1. Prepare a statement of financial position after each transaction.
2. Record the transactions in an expanded accounting equation.
3. Record the transactions on separate pages, not divided. (Number the pages.)
4. Record the transactions on separate pages, divided into Debit and Credit columns.
5. Journalize the six transactions, post to formal ledger accounts, take a trial balance, and prepare a report-form statement of financial position.

P2-1. On December 31, 1976, the assets, liabilities, and stockholders' equity of the Jackson Company are as follows:

Assets (in alphabetical order)	
Accounts Receivable	$ 38,000
Building	100,000
Cash	40,000
Equipment	120,000
Land	20,000
Marketable Securities	90,000
Merchandise Inventory	40,000
Supplies	18,000
Liabilities (in alphabetical order)	
Accounts Payable	40,000
Bonds Payable (due July 1, 1995)	90,000
Dividends Payable	8,000
Interest Payable	12,000
Stockholders' Equity	
Capital Stock	300,000
Retained Earnings	?

Required: Prepare a properly classified account-form statement of financial position.

P2-2. The following is an alphabetical list of the assets, liabilities, and owners' equity of the Michael Company, a single proprietorship, as of December 31, 1976:

Accounts Payable	$ 16,000
Accounts Receivable	17,000
Building	150,000
Cash	60,000
Delivery Equipment	30,000
Land	25,000
Long-Term Notes Payable (due August 1, 2005)	80,000
Marketable Securities	5,000
Merchandise Inventory	32,000
Mortgage Payable (due March 1, 1985)	50,000
Notes Payable	6,000
John Michael, Capital	?
Prepaid Insurance	2,000
Salaries Payable	1,000

Required: Prepare a properly classified report-form statement of financial position.

P2-3. *(Financial policy decision problem)* The following list contains all the current assets and current liabilities of the Lamplighter Company as of December 31, 1976. The list also contains some noncurrent items.

Accounts Payable	$ 5,000
Accounts Receivable	13,000
Cash	6,000
Land	35,000
Marketable Securities	6,000

Merchandise Inventory	60,000
Mortgage Payable (due July 1, 2005)	100,000
Notes Payable (due July 1, 1977)	20,000
Prepaid Insurance	2,500
Salaries Payable	2,000

Required:
1. Compute the current ratio, the acid-test ratio, and the working capital.
2. Assume that you are the loan officer of a bank to which the Lamplighter Company has applied for a 90-day loan of $15,000. Would you grant the loan? Why? Assume that the loan is granted; compute the current ratio, the acid-test ratio, and working capital for the Lamplighter Company immediately following the receipt of the loan.

P2-4. The following lists show selected statement totals for four different firms: Able, Baker, Charles, and Dawson. In each case, the amount for one total is omitted.

	Able	Baker	Charles	Dawson
Current Assets	$200,000	$ 70,000	$?	$ 35,000
Plant and Equipment	400,000	120,000	100,000	180,000
Current Liabilities	100,000	20,000	10,000	15,000
Long-Term Liabilities	150,000	?	26,000	60,000
Capital Stock	350,000	60,000	100,000	?
Retained Earnings	?	10,000	14,000	25,000

Required: Compute the missing figure for each firm.

P2-5. The assets, liabilities, and owner's equity of the Tombstone Company as of December 31, 1976, are as follows:

Cash	$ 8,000
Accounts Receivable	25,000
Notes Receivable	4,000
Merchandise Inventory	8,500
Office Supplies	500
Prepaid Insurance	1,000
Store Equipment	6,000
Building	26,000
Land	7,500
Accounts Payable	15,000
Notes Payable (due May 1, 1977)	8,000
Mortgage Payable (due Feb. 1, 2012)	12,000
Walter K. Tombstone, Capital	51,500

Required:
1. Prepare a report-form statement of financial position.
2. Compute the current ratio, the acid-test ratio, and the working capital.

P2-6. The transactions of the newly organized Finetime Services, Inc., for the week of June 1 to 6, 1976, are given below.

1976
June 1 Received a charter and issued all its authorized capital stock at par for $50,000 in cash.
     2 Purchased land and building at a cost of $60,000. Paid $15,000 in cash and issued a 20-year mortgage payable for the balance. The land is appraised at $15,000; the building, at $45,000.

1976

June 3 Purchased furniture for $3,000 from the Sanford Chair Company on account.

4 Purchased office supplies (stationery, stamps, and envelopes) for $400 in cash.

5 Some of the furniture was found to be defective and was returned to the Sanford Chair Company. The account was reduced by $1,000.

6 Paid the balance due the Sanford Chair Company.

Required: Prepare a classified statement of financial position after each transaction.

P2-7. Successive statements of financial position for the Hand Clinic are given after each of six transactions.

HAND CLINIC
Statement of Financial Position
August 1, 1976

Assets		*Liabilities and Owner's Equity*	
Current Assets		Owner's Equity	
Cash	$130,000	Maurice Hand, Capital	$130,000

HAND CLINIC
Statement of Financial Position
August 2, 1976

Assets			*Liabilities and Owner's Equity*	
Current Assets			Long-Term Liabilities	
Cash		$116,000	Mortgage Payable	$ 86,000
Plant and Equipment			Owner's Equity	
Land	$15,000		Maurice Hand, Capital	130,000
Building	85,000	100,000	Total Liabilities and	
Total Assets		$216,000	Owner's Equity	$216,000

HAND CLINIC
Statement of Financial Position
August 3, 1976

Assets			*Liabilities and Owner's Equity*	
Current Assets			Current Liabilities	
Cash	$116,000		Accounts Payable	$ 6,000
Medical Supplies	6,000	$122,000	Long-Term Liabilities	
Plant and Equipment			Mortgage Payable	86,000
Land	$ 15,000		Total Liabilities	$ 92,000
Building	85,000	100,000	Owner's Equity	
			Maurice Hand, Capital	130,000
			Total Liabilities and	
Total Assets		$222,000	Owner's Equity	$222,000

HAND CLINIC
Statement of Financial Position
August 4, 1976

Assets			*Liabilities and Owner's Equity*	
Current Assets			Current Liabilities	
Cash	$116,000		Accounts Payable	$ 6,000
Notes Receivable	3,000		Long-Term Liabilities	
Medical Supplies	6,000	$125,000	Mortgage Payable	86,000
Plant and Equipment			Total Liabilities	$ 92,000
Land	$ 12,000		Owner's Equity	
Building	85,000	97,000	Maurice Hand, Capital	130,000
			Total Liabilities and	
Total Assets		$222,000	Owner's Equity	$222,000

HAND CLINIC
Statement of Financial Position
August 5, 1976

Assets			*Liabilities and Owner's Equity*	
Current Assets			Current Liabilities	
Cash	$116,000		Accounts Payable	$ 2,000
Notes Receivable	3,000		Long-Term Liabilities	
Medical Supplies	6,000	$125,000	Mortgage Payable	86,000
Plant and Equipment			Total Liabilities	$ 88,000
Land	$ 12,000		Owner's Equity	
Building	85,000	97,000	Maurice Hand, Capital	134,000
			Total Liabilities and	
Total Assets		$222,000	Owner's Equity	$222,000

HAND CLINIC
Statement of Financial Position
August 7, 1976

Assets			*Liabilities and Owner's Equity*	
Current Assets			Current Liabilities	
Cash	$119,000		Accounts Payable	$ 2,000
Medical Supplies	6,000	$125,000	Long-Term Liabilities	
Plant and Equipment			Mortgage Payable	86,000
Land	$ 12,000		Total Liabilities	$ 88,000
Building	85,000	97,000	Owner's Equity	
			Maurice Hand, Capital	134,000
			Total Liabilities and	
Total Assets		$222,000	Owner's Equity	$222,000

Required: Study the successive statements of financial position to determine what transactions have occurred. Prepare a list of these transactions, giving the date and description of each.

BASIC MODEL:
REAL ACCOUNTS

P2-8. The following account numbers and titles were designed for the Herman Car Rental System, a single proprietorship:

101 Cash
111 Accounts Receivable
201 Land
210 Building
215 Automobiles
220 Office Equipment
301 Accounts Payable
310 Notes Payable
400 Henry Herman, Capital

During the first month of operation the following transactions occurred:

1976
Dec. 1   Herman deposited $100,000 in cash in a bank account in the name of the business, Herman Car Rental System, a single proprietorship.

3   Purchased land for $10,000 and a building on the lot for $40,000. A cash payment of $20,000 was made, and a promissory note was issued for the balance.

4   Purchased 15 new automobiles at $3,000 each from the Foreign Motor Company. A down payment of $30,000 in cash was made; the balance was promised to be paid in 30 days.

5   Sold one automobile to Hilton Hertz, one of the company's employees, at cost. The employee paid $2,000 in cash and agreed to pay the balance within 30 days.

6   One automobile proved to be defective and was returned to the Foreign Motor Company. The amount due was reduced by $3,000.

11   Purchased a cash register and office desks for $2,500 for cash.

31   Paid $10,000 in cash to the Foreign Motor Company on account.

Required:
1. Journalize the transactions.
2. Post to T accounts (use account numbers provided).

P2-9. The Nancy Stenographic Service, a newly formed company owned and operated by Nancy Wooten, plans to provide typing, duplicating, and stenographic services to the tenants of the office building it owns and to other clients. The following ledger accounts as of August 31, 1976, are not in the proper sequence.

Cash		Land	
31,470	25,000	5,000	
	1,000		
	200		
	700		
	200		
	100		

Office Supplies		Accounts Payable	
50		100	350
225		80	60

Maintenance Supplies		Mortgage Payable	
250			25,000
220			
515			

Prepaid Insurance		Nancy Wooten, Capital	
1,200			80,000

Duplicating Equipment		Delivery Equipment	
20,000		2,500	

Building		Office Equipment	
70,000		1,000	

Required:
1. Determine the account balances and prepare a trial balance as of August 31, 1976, listing the accounts in proper sequence.
2. Prepare a statement of financial position.

P2-10. The Barringer Garage was incorporated on August 20, 1976. During the first several days of operations, its part-time bookkeeper (a high school student who had had a few months' instruction in bookkeeping) recorded the transactions and rendered the following unbalanced trial balance as of August 31, 1976.

BARRINGER GARAGE
Trial Balance
August 31, 1976

Account Title	Debits	Credits
Accounts Payable	$ 37,100	
Accounts Receivable		$ 20,000
Building	100,000	
Capital Stock	150,000	
Cash	31,000	
Furniture	12,000	
Land		24,000
Marketable Securities		19,200
Mortgage Payable		40,000
Notes Payable	20,700	
Notes Receivable		36,000
Service Supplies	5,600	
Totals	$356,400	$139,200

Required:
1. Assuming that the amounts are correct but that the bookkeeper did not understand the proper debit-credit position of some accounts, prepare a

trial balance showing the accounts in correct statement-of-financial-position order.
2. Prepare a report-form statement of financial position.

P2-11. *(Accounting policy decision problem)* The Barton Corporation has been operating for some years. In November 1976 the accountant of the company disappeared, taking the records with him.

You are hired to reconstruct the accounting records, and with this in mind you make an inventory of all company assets. By checking with banks, counting the materials on hand, investigating the ownership of buildings and equipment, and so on, you develop the following information as of December 31, 1976:

Account Title	Balance	Account Title	Balance
Land	$30,000	Marketable Securities	$ 10,000
Equipment	50,000	Inventories	28,000
Buildings	60,000	Cash on Hand	6,000
Accounts Receivable	20,000	Cash in Banks	106,000

Statements from creditors and unpaid invoices found in the office indicate that $80,000 is owed to trade creditors. A $20,000 long-term mortgage (30 years) is outstanding.

Interviews with the board of directors and a check of the capital stock record book indicate that 2,000 shares of capital stock are outstanding and that the stockholders have contributed $60,000 to the corporation. No record is available regarding past retained earnings.

Required:
1. Prepare a trial balance and a statement of financial position as of December 31, 1976.
2. Write a report to management indicating a simple accounting system that could be used and why you recommend such a system. (*Hint:* Include in the report the kinds of journals, ledgers, and overall system you recommend.)

P2-12. *(Financial policy decision problem)* Accounts included in the trial balance of the Karl Kutz Company as of November 30, 1976, were as follows:

Acct. No	Account Title	Balance
101	Cash	$ 25,200
111	Accounts Receivable	12,000
150	Office Suplies	1,500
200	Land	?
250	Building	?
300	Furniture and Fixtures	9,000
350	Machines	75,000
400	Delivery Equipment	3,500
600	Accounts Payable	4,000
650	Notes Payable	30,000
800	Karl Kutz, Capital	?

Land and building were acquired at a cost of $36,000. It was determined that one-third of the total cost should be applied to the cost of land.
The following transactions were completed during the month of December:

1976

Dec. 2 Paid in full an open-account liability of $200 to the Duncan Company.

3 Collected in full an account receivable of $700 from the Papermoon Corporation.

4 Purchased office supplies from the Boozier Corporation for $500 on account.

8 Kutz made an additional investment of $20,000 in cash in the business.

10 Collected $1,500 from the Parker Company on account.

11 Purchased a machine from the Iber Business Machine Company for $25,000; paid $5,000 in cash, the balance to be paid within 30 days.

15 Paid in full an open-account liability of $600 to the Milton Company.

20 Paid $15,000 in cash to the Iber Business Machine Company in partial settlement of the liability of December 11. Issued a note payable for the balance.

31 Collected in full an account receivable of $400 from the Downy Company.

Required:
1. Journalize these transactions.
2. Enter the balances of November 30, 1976, in ledger accounts, post the December entries, and determine the new balances.
3. Prepare a trial balance as of December 31, 1976.
4. Prepare a statement of financial position.
5. Compute the following:
   a. Working capital
   b. Current ratio
   c. Acid-test ratio
6. Write a brief report to management indicating the ability of the Karl Kutz Company to meet its short-term debt.

P2-13. *(Management policy decision problem)* Once upon a time many, many years ago, there lived a feudal landlord in a small province of Central Europe. The landlord, called the Red-Bearded Baron, lived in a castle high on a hill, and this benevolent fellow was responsible for the well-being of many peasants who occupied the lands surrounding his castle. Each spring, as the snow began to melt and thoughts of other, less influential men turned to matters other than business, the Baron would decide how to provide for all his serf-dependents during the coming year.

One spring, the Baron was thinking about the wheat crop of the coming growing season. "I believe that 30 acres of my land, being worth 5 bushels of wheat per acre, will produce enough wheat for next winter," he mused, "but who should do the farming? I believe I'll give Ivan the Indefatigable and Igor the Immutable the task of growing the wheat." Whereupon Ivan and Igor, two gentry noted for their hard work and not overly active minds, were summoned for an audience with the landlord.

"Ivan, you will farm on the 20-acre plot of ground and Igor will farm the 10-acre plot," the Baron began. "I will give Ivan 20 bushels of wheat for seed and 20 pounds of fertilizer. (Twenty pounds of fertilizer are worth 2 bushels of wheat.) Igor will get 10 bushels of wheat for seed and 10 pounds of fertilizer. I will give each of you an ox to pull a plow but you will have to make arrangements with Feyador, the Plowmaker, for a plow. The oxen, incidentally, are only three years old and have never been used for farming, so they should have a good 10 years of farming ahead of them. Take good care of them, because an ox is worth 40 bushels of wheat. Come back next fall and return the oxen and the plows along with your harvest.''

Ivan and Igor genuflected and withdrew from the Great Hall, taking with them the things provided by the Baron.

The summer came and went, and after the harvest Ivan and Igor returned to the Great Hall to account to their master for the things given them in the spring. Ivan, pouring 223 bushels of wheat onto the floor, said, ''My Lord, I present you with a slightly used ox, a plow broken beyond repair, and 223 bushels of wheat. I, unfortunately, owe Feyador, the Plowmaker, 3 bushels of wheat for the plow I got from him last fall. And, as you might expect, I used all the fertilizer and seed you gave me last spring. You will also remember, my Lord, that you took 20 bushels of my harvest for your own personal use.''

Igor, who had been given 10 acres of land, 10 bushels of wheat, and 10 pounds of fertilizer, spoke next. ''Here, my Lord, is a partially used ox, the plow for which I gave Feyador, the Plowmaker, 3 bushels of wheat from my harvest, and 105 bushels of wheat. I, too, used all my seed and fertilizer last spring. Also, my Lord, you took 30 bushels of wheat several days ago for your own table. I believe the plow is good for two more seasons.''

''Knaves, you did well,'' said the Red-Bearded Baron. Blessed with this benediction and not wishing to press their luck further, the two serfs departed hastily.

After the servants had taken their leave, the Red-Bearded Baron, watching the two hungry oxen slowly eating the wheat piled on the floor, began to contemplate what had happened. ''Yes,'' he thought, ''they did well, but I wonder which one did better?''

Required: Assume that the Red-Bearded Baron was willing to give the peasant who achieved the greater gain a bonus of 1 bushel of wheat. Which peasant would receive the bonus? Support your answer with carefully identified calculations.

(This case was written by Professor W. T. Andrews, Jr., of Guilford College, and was published in *The Accounting Review*, April 1974, under the title of ''Another Improbable Occurrence.'' It is used by permission of the author and of the editor of *The Accounting Review*.)

The Basic Accounting Model: Dynamic Measurements

3

In the previous chapter, changes in the stockholders' equity caused by stockholder investments were discussed. Other changes may be caused by *revenues, expenses,* and *dividends* to stockholders. These changes, and the statements on which they are reflected, are explained in this chapter.

BASIC OPERATING CONCEPTS AND PROCEDURES

REVENUES

The term *revenue* describes the source of inflows of assets received in exchange for services rendered, sales of products or merchandise, gains from sales or exchanges of assets other than stock in trade, and earnings of interest and dividends on investments. It does *not include* increases arising from owners' contributions or from borrowed funds. For revenue to be earned, it does not have to be collected immediately in cash; it is sufficient that claims for cash on customers or clients exist.

Revenue accounts are created to accumulate the amounts earned during a *specified* period; the typical accounting period is one year. Often, however, progressive statements are prepared each month for the information of the management. The title of a revenue account should indicate the nature of the particular revenue; examples are Commissions Earned, Sales, Interest Earned, Dividends Earned, Accounting Fees Earned, and Garage Repair Revenue.

Revenue accounts are *credited when revenue increases;* the particular asset that is received is *debited.* To illustrate the journalizing of revenue transactions, several companies that earned different kinds of revenue are considered.

First, suppose that on August 2, 1976, the Whitside Realty Corporation Limited sells a house and lot and receives a commission of $500 in cash; this can be recorded as follows:

GENERAL JOURNAL					Page 1
1976 Aug.	2	Cash		500	
		Commissions Earned			500
		To record receipt of commission on sale of house and lot.			

Next, assume that on July 30, 1976, I. N. Malvin, CPA,[1] bills the Anderson Company for $1,000 for an annual audit that he had made; his journal entry might look like this:

GENERAL JOURNAL					Page 1
1976 July	30	Accounts Receivable		1,000	
		Accounting Fees Earned			1,000
		To record billing of following client for audit: Anderson Company $1,000			

Suppose that on January 2, 1976, the Georgetown Rental Agency receives $750 in cash for January rent:

GENERAL JOURNAL					Page 1
1976 Jan.	2	Cash		750	
		Rent Earned			750
		To record rental receipts for month of January 1976.			

EXPENSES

Expenses are expired costs of the materials consumed and services received during a specified period and used in the production of revenue during

[1] In Canada and other United Kingdom commonwealths, this practitioner would be designated chartered accountant, or CA.

that same period. Examples of *expense accounts* are Salaries Expense, Rent Expense, and Office Supplies Expense. Expenses are recorded by a debit to the appropriate expense account and a credit to the Cash account, to a liability account, or possibly to some other type of account. The recording process for expenses is illustrated by the following transactions, which took place at the Mason Company.

1976
Jan. 2   Paid $400 in rent for the month of January.
     10   Purchased an advertisement in the local newspaper for $75 in cash.
     15   Paid semimonthly salaries of $600.
     20   Had some office machinery repaired at a cost of $45.

These transactions are recorded in the general journal as follows:

GENERAL JOURNAL			Page 1	
1976 Jan.	2	Rent Expense	400	
		Cash		400
		To record payment of rent for month of January 1976		
	10	Advertising Expense	75	
		Cash		75
		To record payment for advertising.		
	15	Salaries Expense	600	
		Cash		600
		To record payment of semimonthly salaries.		
	20	Repairs Expense — Office Equipment	45	
		Cash		45
		To record payment of repairs to office equipment.		

BASIC OPERATING CONCEPTS

The total expenses for a period are deducted from the total revenues to measure the *net income* (profit) for the period, which in turn reflects the increase in the stockholders' equity resulting from business operations.

Measurement of Net Income

This may be expressed in equation form:

Total revenues − Total expenses = Net income

If the expenses for a period exceed the revenues for that period, a *net loss* results, and the stockholders' equity is decreased. The equation now becomes

$$\text{Total expenses} - \text{Total revenues} = \text{Net loss}$$

Expenses Compared with Costs

It is necessary to distinguish between an *expense* and a *cost*. A *cost* is the amount paid or payable in either cash or the equivalent, for goods, services, or other assets purchased. When a cost no longer has asset status—that is, when its potential to produce future revenue is lost—it is said to be expired and thus to have become an *expense*.

From this statement the following conclusions are warranted:

Expenses = Expired costs (used up in producing this period's revenue)
Assets = Unexpired costs (to be used to produce future revenue)

For example, rent paid in advance for three months is an asset, Prepaid Rent. As time passes, this becomes Rent Expense. The required adjusting process is discussed in detail in the next chapter.

A *disbursement* is a payment in cash or by check. Hence, a machine may be acquired at a cost of $10,000; the transaction is completed by a disbursement in the form of a check for $10,000; and, as the machine is used in operations, it loses part of its service value, or *depreciates.* This is an element of expense, Depreciation Expense.

The basic objective of operating a business is to produce a net income, which results from receiving more from a customer for services rendered than the total expense to the business of producing the services; a loss is incurred when the expense of the services to the enterprise is more than the income received from customers for the services rendered.

Most businesses cannot keep the detailed records necessary to indicate the expense of each service rendered and therefore cannot determine the net income or net loss from each transaction. Even when it is possible, the clerical costs involved in getting the information would not justify the end result. For example, a lawyer bills his client for $1,000 for services performed. How much did it cost the lawyer to perform the service and how much net income did he make on this *one* transaction? The lawyer might total the number of hours he devoted to the case and arrive at an expense in terms of time spent. But how about the rent for his office? the secretary's salary? the telephone bill? the electricity bill?

Since the determination of each expense involved in rendering service for a particular client would require a considerable amount of record keeping, accounting has evolved another and easier method for accomplishing an acceptable result. No attempt is made to determine the cost of each service; instead, records of revenue and expense are kept for a period.

Matching of Expenses against Revenue for a Time Period

At the end of the period, the period's expenses are matched against the period's revenue to determine the net income or net loss for that period. This information is contained in a financial statement called an *income statement,* discussed and illustrated later in this chapter.

Dividends are distributions of net income regardless of whether that income is earned in the current period or in past periods. Although dividends reduce the stockholders' equity, they are *not* expenses; they are not declared and paid for the purpose of producing revenue. A dividend may be recorded by a debit to a special Dividends account and a credit to Cash, or to a liability account if it is to be paid at a date subsequent to the date of declaration. For example, suppose that the Sandra Corporation declared and paid a regular quarterly cash dividend of $1,000 to its stockholders on November 10, 1976; this transaction would be recorded in the general journal of the Sandra Corporation as follows:

GENERAL JOURNAL					Page 1
1976 Nov.	10	Dividends		1,000	
		Cash			1,000
		To record declaration and payment of fourth quarterly dividend.			

EXPANDED RULES FOR DEBITS AND CREDITS

Since new types of accounts have been introduced, the rules for debiting and crediting accounts are expanded and restated:

Debit to record:
1. An increase of an asset
2. An increase of an expense
3. An increase of dividends
4. A decrease of a liability
5. A decrease in the stockholders' equity
6. A decrease in revenue

Credit to record:
1. A decrease of an asset
2. A decrease of an expense
3. A decrease of dividends
4. An increase of a liability
5. An increase in the stockholders' equity
6. An increase in revenue

The relationship of the rules of debits and credits to the accounting equation may be diagramed as follows:

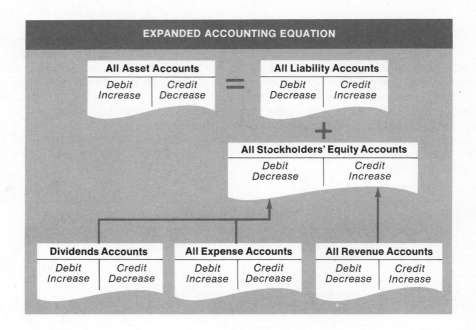

EXPANDED ACCOUNTING EQUATION

All Asset Accounts		
Debit Increase	*Credit Decrease*	=

All Liability Accounts	
Debit Decrease	*Credit Increase*

+

All Stockholders' Equity Accounts	
Debit Decrease	*Credit Increase*

Dividends Accounts	
Debit Increase	*Credit Decrease*

All Expense Accounts	
Debit Increase	*Credit Decrease*

All Revenue Accounts	
Debit Decrease	*Credit Increase*

It is evident from the expanded accounting equation that a *decrease* in the stockholders' equity is debited. Note that when the decrease in the stockholders' equity is recorded in an expense account, the expense account is *increased* (debited); that is, the expense account is designed to *accumulate* a decrease, a reduction, that is later transferred to the stockholders' equity accounts. The specific relationship between the expense accounts and the stockholders' equity accounts is further illustrated as follows:

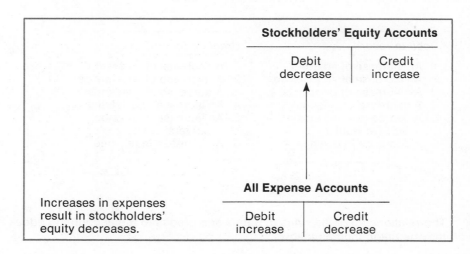

Stockholders' Equity Accounts

Debit decrease	Credit increase

All Expense Accounts

Debit increase	Credit decrease

Increases in expenses result in stockholders' equity decreases.

> Accounts that are incorporated in the statement of financial position and the income statement are kept in a separate book, or collection, called the *general ledger*.

General Ledger

This ledger may actually be a loose-leaf binder, a bound book, cards in open trays, punched cards, or one of the several types of computer data storage devices. Accounts are usually arranged in the sequence in which they will appear in the financial statements—that is, assets, liabilities, stockholders' equity, revenue, and expenses. These accounts are referred to collectively as *general ledger accounts.*

Accounts Receivable Ledger

Many businesses have a large number of customers, and detailed information must be kept of transactions with each one. A separate account thus is required for each customer. If the general ledger were to include each customer's account, it would become too large and unwieldy. Consequently, only one account, Accounts Receivable, is maintained in the general ledger. This account shows the combined increases and decreases in the amounts due from all customers. The individual customer accounts are kept in a separate, or *subsidiary,* ledger called the *accounts receivable ledger.* The Accounts Receivable account, referred to as a controlling account, is a summary account in the general ledger of those individual customers' accounts which are relegated to the subsidiary ledger. After all the transactions for the period have been entered, the balance of the Accounts Receivable account in the general ledger should be equal to the sum of the individual account balances in the subsidiary ledger.

Accounts Payable Ledger

Many businesses have a large number of individual creditors. Consequently, only one account, Accounts Payable, is kept in the general ledger. This account shows total increases and decreases in amounts due to creditors. The individual creditors' accounts are kept in a subsidiary ledger called the *accounts payable ledger.* Accounts Payable, another controlling account, is a summary account in the general ledger of those individual creditors' accounts which are relegated to the subsidiary ledger. After all the transactions for the period have been entered, the balance of the Accounts Payable account in the general ledger should be equal to the sum of the individual account balances in the subsidiary ledger.

Controlling Accounts

As mentioned above, the Accounts Receivable and Accounts Payable accounts appearing in the general ledger are referred to as controlling accounts.

BASIC MODEL:
DYNAMIC
MEASUREMENTS

A *controlling account*, by definition, is any account in the general ledger that controls or is supported by a number of other accounts in a separate ledger.

These accounts contain summary totals of many transactions, the details of which appear in subsidiary ledgers. The accounts receivable ledger is sometimes referred to as the *customers ledger;* the accounts payable ledger, as the *creditors ledger.* Other controlling accounts and their appropriate subsidiary ledgers may be established when enough homogeneous general ledger accounts are created to make it more efficient to relegate these accounts to a separate ledger.

Posting to the General Ledger and the Subsidiary Ledgers

To illustrate the method of posting from the general journal to the general and subsidiary ledgers, the following transaction is considered:

On August 3, 1976, Bookkeeping Services, Inc., billed the following clients for professional services performed:

Jay Johnson	$550
O. M. Omar	120
C. W. Wayne	230

This information is recorded and posted as indicated in Figure 3-1.

Entries to the Accounts Payable controlling account and the accounts payable ledger are handled similarly. An explanation of the encircled figures in Figure 3-1 follows:

❶ Figure 3-1 shows the total posting of the $900 debit to the Accounts Receivable account in the general ledger and detailed posting to the subsidiary ledger accounts. Each customer is debited for the amount shown in the explanation of the general journal entry; the balance is extended to the Balance column; the journal page number is entered in the folio (F) column; and the date is entered. After each posting has been completed, a check mark (√) is entered to the left of each amount in the Explanation column of the general journal to indicate that the amount has been posted to the proper subsidiary ledger account. A check mark is used rather than a page number because subsidiary accounts in the illustration are not numbered but often are kept in alphabetical order.

It will be obvious to the reader that a business such as a department store that makes hundreds of credit sales daily does not list each one in the journal entry explanation; instead, postings to the subsidiary ledger accounts are made from the copies of the sales tickets. The principle, however, is the same, as illustrated in Figure 3-1.

After only a cursory study, it may seem that this dual accounting for accounts receivable would result in double debits that will be incorrectly reflected in the trial balance. Note carefully, however, that only one debit goes into the Accounts Receivable controlling account for later incorporation in the trial balance. The amounts entered in the accounts receivable ledger will not go in the trial balance, but the total of the uncollected balances at the end of a period will be compared with the single balance of the Accounts Receivable controlling account as a check on the accuracy of both the accounts receivable ledger and the Accounts Receivable controlling account in the general ledger.

Figure 3-1 Posting to Control and Subsidiary Accounts

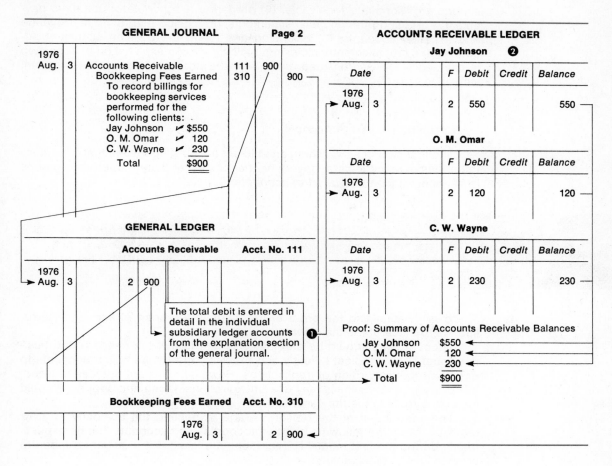

❷   It should be observed that the balance form of ledger account is used for the accounts receivable ledger. This particular form is customarily used in subsidiary ledgers for two reasons: (1) The balances have to be referred to quite often. (2) The form is adaptable to machine accounting, which is frequently employed for subsidiary ledger accounting.

THE ACCOUNTING SEQUENCE ILLUSTRATED

THE ACCOUNTING SEQUENCE

Ten steps in the accounting sequence are illustrated through the example of a newly incorporated business called the Nelson Garage. These steps are: (1) selecting a chart of accounts, (2) journalizing the transactions, (3) posting to

BASIC MODEL: DYNAMIC MEASUREMENTS

the general and subsidiary ledgers, (4) preparing a trial balance, (5) preparing a schedule of accounts receivable, (6) preparing a schedule of accounts payable, (7) preparing the financial statements, (8) closing and ruling the revenue and expense accounts, (9) balancing and ruling the position statement accounts, and (10) taking a postclosing trial balance. An explanation of each step in the sequence is presented along with the accounting procedure for that step.

Selecting a Chart of Accounts

The first step in establishing an efficient accounting system that will satisfy the needs of management, government agencies, and other interested groups is the construction of a *chart of accounts*.

Chart of Accounts

A separate account should be set up for each item that appears in the financial statements to make the statements easier to prepare. The *chart of accounts* is the complete listing of account titles to be used in the entity.

The classification and the order of the items in the chart of accounts corresponds to those of the statements.

Account titles should be carefully selected to suit the needs of the business, and should indicate clearly and precisely the nature of the accounts to ensure proper recording of transactions. However, titles are not standardized; for example, one business may use Unexpired Insurance and another Prepaid Insurance to describe the same asset.

The accountant of the Nelson Garage, expecting the company to grow rapidly, sets up the following chart of accounts—the accounts that he expects to use during the first month of operations are listed with numbers skipped to provide for future expansion.

NELSON GARAGE
Chart of Accounts

Statement of Financial Position Accounts
Asset Accounts (100–299)

Current Assets (100–199)
    101   Cash
    121   Accounts Receivable
    131   Garage Parts and Supplies
    141   Prepaid Insurance

Plant and Equipment (200–299)
    201   Land
    221   Automotive Tools and Equipment

Liability and Stockholders' Equity Accounts (300–499)

Current Liabilities (300–350)
  301   Accounts Payable
  302   Notes Payable

Long-Term Liabilities (351–399)

Stockholders' Equity (400–499)
  401   Capital Stock
  411   Retained Earnings
  421   Dividends

Income Statement Accounts (500–999)

Revenue (500–599)
  501   Garage Repair Revenue

Expenses (600–699)
  601   Rent Expense—Garage Building
  602   Rent Expense—Automotive Tools and Equipment
  604   Salaries Expense
  608   Electricity and Water Expense
  609   Garage Parts and Supplies Used

Clearing and Summary Accounts (900–999)
  901   Income Summary

In this example, a three-digit system is used to number the accounts; a larger business with a number of departments or branches may use four or more digits. Notice that accounts 100–299 represent assets; that accounts 300–499 represent liabilities and stockholders' (owners') equity; and that accounts 500–999 represent income statement accounts. The more detailed breakdown for current assets, plant and equipment, and current liabilities, for example, can be seen in the chart. As stated previously, the gaps between the assigned account numbers allow for additional accounts as they are needed by the business.

Analyzing Transactions and Journalizing

The transactions of the Nelson Garage that occurred during January 1976 are given. Before making entries in the journal, the accountant must analyze each transaction in terms of the basic system of debits and credits that has already been outlined. Following the first five transactions listed, a description of the analytical thinking that must precede the journalizing of these transactions is given as a guide to future action.

1976
Jan. 2 The Corporate charter for the Nelson Garage was received on this date, and the 3,000 shares of authorized capital stock were issued to three stockholders at par for $30,000 in cash. An asset, cash, is received; to record an increase of an asset, it must be debited; therefore, the Cash account is debited for $30,000. The stockholders have a claim against the business; the increase in the stockholders' equity account, Capital Stock, is shown by a credit to that account.

1976
Jan. 3 Rented a temporary garage and paid $300 for the January rent; issued check No. 1. Since all the rent will have expired by the time the financial statements are prepared, it is considered an expense of the month of January. An increase of an expense account is recorded by a debit; therefore, the Rent Expense—Garage Building account is debited. The decrease of the asset cash is recorded by a credit to Cash. A single rent account may be sufficient for all rented buildings and equipment. In this case, the accountant felt that managerial analyses required a separate rent expense account for the garage building.

5 Rented automotive tools and equipment pending purchase of the firm's own. Rent in the amount of $80 was paid for January; issued check No. 2. As in the preceding transaction, all this rent will have expired before the financial statements are prepared; therefore it is considered an expense of January. An increase of an expense account is recorded by a debit—in this case to Rent Expense—Automotive Tools and Equipment. The decrease of the asset cash is recorded by a credit to Cash. Again, a single rent expense account may have been sufficient.

5 Purchased garage parts and supplies described on invoice No. 306 from the Southern Supply Company for $400 on account. The Garage Parts and Supplies account is an asset and is increased by the transaction; the increase in the asset is shown by a debit to Garage Parts and Supplies. Since the purchase was on credit, a liability is created. To record the increase in the liability, the Accounts Payable account is credited. The amount payable to the particular creditor, the Southern Supply Company, must be shown in the books. A note should be made in the Explanation column of the journal to the effect that the creditor is the Southern Supply Company, so that the amount can be posted to the accounts payable ledger.

6 Performed garage repairs for several cash customers; received $1,000 in cash. Cash, an asset, is received; to record the increase of the asset, the Cash account must be debited. The particular source of this asset is a revenue. To record an increase in the revenue, Garage Repairs Revenue is credited.

10 Purchased land as a prospective building site for $10,000. Paid $4,000 in cash (check No. 3) and issued a one-year note for the balance.

12 Made repairs on George Shipman's car for $40. Shipman asked that a charge account be opened in his name; he promises to settle the account within 30 days. This arrangement was authorized by the service manager.

15 Paid $800 in salaries for first half of month (check No. 4 issued to obtain payroll cash).

20 Performed garage repairs for cash customers for $2,000.

26 Made repairs on Jay Munson's truck for $60. A charge account was opened in his name.

28 Made repairs on Robert Batson's car for $120. A charge account was opened in his name.

29 Purchased garage parts and supplies from the Delco Supply House for $250 on account (invoice No. 1004).

30 Paid the Southern Supply Company $300 on account (check No. 5).

31 Paid electricity and water bills for January, $80 (check No. 6).

31 Made garage repairs for cash customers for $1,800.

31 Paid $900 in salaries for last half of month (check No. 7 issued to obtain payroll cash).

31 Paid a $300 cash dividend to the three stockholders (checks No. 8, 9, and 10).

1976

Jan. 31 Purchased automotive tools and equipment for cash, $4,000 (check No. 11). The list price was $5,000.

31 Paid a premium of $600 (check No. 12) on a 12-month comprehensive insurance policy; the policy becomes effective on February 1, 1976.

31 Received a check for $10 from George Shipman as part payment of his account.

31 Took a physical inventory of garage parts and supplies; it showed that parts and supplies costing $375 were on hand, thus indicating that $275 (January 5 purchase $400, plus January 29 purchase $250, minus inventory, $375) worth of garage parts and supplies had been used, becoming an expense. Originally, as parts and supplies were purchased, they were debited to an asset account. Now, as the amount used becomes known, an entry is made debiting an expense account, Garage Parts and Supplies Used, to show that the expense account has been increased, and crediting an asset account, Garage Parts and Supplies, to show that the asset account has been decreased. (This type of transaction is normally recorded in an *adjusting entry,* explained in Chapter 4. It is presented here to broaden the scope of this illustration.)

The results of this analytical reasoning are presented in the following general journal. Note that space is left between entries to ensure that they are separate and distinct.

GENERAL JOURNAL				Page 1	

1976 Jan.	2	Cash
		    Capital Stock
		        To record issuance of capital
		        stock for cash.
			101
			401
				30,000	30,000

	3	Rent Expense—Garage Building
		    Cash
		        To record payment of rent on
		        garage building for month
		        of January, 1976;
		        issued check No. 1.
			601
			101
				300	300

	5	Rent Expense—Automotive Tools
		  and Equipment.
		    Cash
		        To record payment of rent for
		        automotive tools and equip-
		        ment for month of January
		        1976; issued check No. 2.
			602
			101
				80	80

	5	Garage Parts and Supplies
		    Accounts Payable
		        To record purchase of parts
		        and supplies on account on
		        invoice No. 306:
		            Southern Supply Co. ✔ $400
			131
			301
				400	400

GENERAL JOURNAL
Page 1 (cont.)

1976 Jan.	6	Cash	101	1,000	
		Garage Repair Revenue	501		1,000
		To record collections from cash customers for services rendered.			
	10	Land	201	10,000	
		Cash	101		4,000
		Notes Payable	302		6,000
		To record purchase of land; issued check No. 3.			
	12	Accounts Receivable	121	40	
		Garage Repair Revenue	501		40
		To record billing for repairs rendered: George Shipman ✔ $40			
	15	Salaries Expense	604	800	
		Cash	101		800
		To record payment of semimonthly salaries; issued check No. 4 to obtain payroll cash.			

GENERAL JOURNAL
Page 2

1976 Jan.	20	Cash	101	2,000	
		Garage Repair Revenue	501		2,000
		To record collections from cash customers for services rendered.			
	26	Accounts Receivable	121	60	
		Garage Repair Revenue	501		60
		To record billing for repair services rendered: Jay Munson ✔ $60			
	28	Accounts Receivable	121	120	
		Garage Repair Revenue	501		120
		To record billing for repair services rendered: Robert Batson ✔ $120			

1976 Jan.	29	Garage Parts and Supplies 　Accounts Payable 　　To record purchase of parts 　　and supplies on account on 　　invoice No. 1004: 　　　Delco Supply 　　　House　✓ $250	131 301	250	250
	30	Accounts Payable 　Cash 　　To record payment; 　　issued check No. 5: 　　　Southern Supply 　　　Company　✓ $300	301 101	300	300
	31	Electricity and Water Expense 　Cash 　　To record payment of 　　electricity and water bills 　　for month of January; 　　issued check No. 6.	608 101	80	80
	31	Cash 　Garage Repair Revenue 　　To record collections from 　　cash customers for services 　　rendered.	101 501	1,800	1,800
	31	Salaries Expense 　Cash 　　To record payment of salaries 　　for last half of January; 　　issued check No. 7 to obtain 　　payroll cash.	604 101	900	900
	31	Dividends 　Cash 　　To record payment of 　　dividends to stockholders; 　　issued checks No. 8, 9 and 10.	421 101	300	300

GENERAL JOURNAL   **Page 3**

1976 Jan.	31	Automotive Tools and Equipment 　Cash 　　To record purchase of tools 　　and equipment at a cost of 　　$4,000 (list price, $5,000); 　　issued check No. 11.	221 101	4,000	4,000

BASIC MODEL:
DYNAMIC
MEASUREMENTS

GENERAL JOURNAL — Page 3 (cont.)

1976 Jan.	31	Prepaid Insurance	141	600	
		Cash	101		600
		To record payment of insurance premium for 12 months. Insurance is effective February 1, 1976; issued check No. 12.			
	31	Cash	101	10	
		Accounts Receivable	121		10
		To record collection to apply on account: George Shipman ✔ $10			
	31	Garage Parts and Supplies Used	609	275	
		Garage Parts and Supplies	131		275
		To record cost of parts and supplies used during month of January.			

Posting to the Ledgers

As the transactions are posted to the ledger, the account numbers are entered in the general journal folio (F) column. At the same time, the number of the journal page from which the entry is posted is entered in the folio (F) column of the ledger account.

The timing of the posting process is a matter of personal preference and expediency. All postings, however, must be completed before financial statements can be prepared. It is advisable to keep accounts with customers and creditors up to date, so that the account balances are readily available. Because of this, it is probably the best rule to post from the journal to the ledgers on a daily basis.

The three posted ledgers are shown here.

GENERAL LEDGER — Cash — Acct. No. 101

1976 Jan.					1976 Jan.			
2			1	30,000	3		1	300
6			1	1,000	5		1	80
20			2	2,000	10		1	4,000
31			2	1,800	15		1	800
31		23,450	3	10	30		2	300
				34,810	31		2	80
					31		2	900
					31		2	300
					31		3	4,000
					31		3	600
								11,360

Accounts Receivable — Acct. No. 121

1976					1976				
Jan.	12		1	40	Jan.	31		3	10
	26		2	60					
	28	210	2	120					
				220					

Garage Parts and Supplies — Acct. No. 131

1976					1976				
Jan.	5		1	400	Jan.	31		3	275
	29	375	2	250					
				650					

Prepaid Insurance — Acct. No. 141

1976				
Jan.	31		3	600

Land — Acct. No. 201

1976				
Jan.	10		1	10,000

Automotive Tools and Equipment — Acct. No. 221

1976				
Jan.	31		3	4,000

Accounts Payable — Acct. No. 301

1976					1976				
Jan.	30		2	300	Jan.	5		1	400
						29	350	2	250
									650

Notes Payable — Acct. No. 302

					1976				
					Jan.	10		1	6,000

Capital Stock — Acct. No. 401

					1976				
					Jan.	2		1	30,000

GENERAL LEDGER (Continued)

Retained Earnings   Acct. No. 411

Dividends   Acct. No. 421

1976							
Jan.	31		2	300			

Garage Repair Revenue   Acct. No. 501

			1976				
			Jan.	6	1	1,000	
				12	1	40	
				20	2	2,000	
				26	2	60	
				28	2	120	
				31	2	1,800	
						5,020	

Rent Expense—Garage Building   Acct. No. 601

1976							
Jan.	3		1	300			

Rent Expense— Automotive Tools and Equipment   Acct. No. 602

1976							
Jan.	5		1	80			

Salaries Expense   Acct. No. 604

1976							
Jan.	15		1	800			
	31		2	900			
				1,700			

Electricity and Water Expense   Acct. No. 608

1976							
Jan.	31		2	80			

GENERAL LEDGER

Garage Parts and Supplies Used — Acct. No. 609

1976									
Jan.	31			3	275				

Income Summary — Acct. No. 901

ACCOUNTS RECEIVABLE LEDGER

Robert Batson

1976									
Jan.	28					2	120		120

Jay Munson

1976									
Jan.	26					2	60		60

George Shipman

1976									
Jan.	12					1	40		40
	31					3		10	30

ACCOUNTS PAYABLE LEDGER

Delco Supply House

1976									
Jan.	29					2		250	250

Southern Supply Company

1976									
Jan.	5					1		400	400
	30					2	300		100

Preparing a Trial Balance

After the accounts in the general ledger are footed and the balances are obtained, the following trial balance is taken:

(Ch. 3)

NELSON GARAGE
Trial Balance
January 31, 1976

Acct. No.	Account Title	Debits	Credits
101	Cash	$23,450	
121	Accounts Receivable	210	
131	Garage Parts and Supplies	375	
141	Prepaid Insurance	600	
201	Land	10,000	
221	Automotive Tools and Equipment	4,000	
301	Accounts Payable		$ 350
302	Notes Payable		6,000
401	Capital Stock		30,000
421	Dividends	300	
501	Garage Repair Revenue		5,020
601	Rent Expense—Garage Building	300	
602	Rent Expense—Automotive Tools and Equipment	80	
604	Salaries Expense	1,700	
608	Electricity and Water Expense	80	
609	Garage Parts and Supplies Used	275	
	Totals	$41,370	$41,370

Preparing a Schedule of Accounts Receivable

The fact that the trial balance is in balance is presumptive evidence of accuracy of the accounting up to this point; the accountant therefore takes the next step, that of preparing a *schedule of accounts receivable.*

At the end of a designated accounting period (one month in this example), the total of all the balances of customers' accounts should agree with the balance of the Accounts Receivable controlling account in the general ledger. A schedule of accounts receivable usually is prepared to check this agreement. The schedule of accounts receivable taken from the Nelson Garage's accounts receivable ledger shows that the total of all customers' accounts is $210, which agrees with the balance of the Accounts Receivable controlling account.

NELSON GARAGE
Schedule of Accounts Receivable
January 31, 1976

Robert Batson	$120
Jay Munson	60
George Shipman	30
Total Accounts Receivable	$210

Preparing a Schedule of Accounts Payable

The next step is similar to the preceding one; it involves the preparation of a *schedule of accounts payable*.

At the end of the accounting period, the total of the balances of the individual creditors' accounts should equal the balance of the Accounts Payable controlling account. The schedule of accounts payable taken from the Nelson Garage's accounts payable ledger shows that the total of the creditors' accounts is $350, which agrees with the balance of the Accounts Payable controlling account.

NELSON GARAGE
Schedule of Accounts Payable
January 31, 1976

Delco Supply House	$250
Southern Supply Company	100
Total Accounts Payable	$350

Preparing the Financial Statements from the Trial Balance

The income statement, the statement of retained earnings, and the statement of financial position are usually prepared at the end of an accounting period. The first two have not yet been illustrated.

The Income Statement. The income statement shown in Figure 3-2 was prepared from the trial balance of the Nelson Garage.

The heading of the income statement shows the following:

1. Name of the business
2. Name of the statement
3. Period covered by the statement

It is important that the period covered be specified clearly. The date January 31, 1976, is not sufficient; it, alone, does not indicate whether the net income of $2,585 was earned in one day, one month, or one year ended January 31, 1976. The analyst must know how long a period it took for the firm to earn the $2,585.

The determination of net income for the Nelson Garage at this level should not be interpreted as being definitive. For example, a corporation is subject to income taxes; the accounting for income taxes and certain other more complex problems are deferred to later chapters.

There is no standard order for listing accounts in the income statement. Size of each revenue and expense item may be one criterion; or the sequence of the accounts in the general ledger may be used as the basis for establishing the order used in listing the accounts in the income statement.

Figure 3-2
Income Statement

NELSON GARAGE
Income Statement
For the Month Ended January 31, 1976

Revenue		
Garage Repair Revenue		$5,020
Expenses		
Rent Expense—Garage Building	$ 300	
Rent Expense—Automotive Tools		
and Equipment	80	
Salaries Expense	1,700	
Electricity and Water Expense	80	
Garage Parts and Supplies Used	275	
Total Expenses		2,435
Net Income		$2,585
Net Income per Share	$ 0.86	

Net Income per Share

The net income per share, often called earnings per share, of $0.86 is shown at the bottom of the income statement. This figure is determined by dividing the number of shares of capital stock outstanding (the shares in the hands of stockholders), 3,000 shares in the case of Nelson Garage, into the net income of $2,585: ($2,585 ÷ 3,000 ≐ $0.86).

Net income per share is generally considered to be an excellent indicator of future profitability.[2]

The Statement of Retained Earnings. Since the corporation is a creature of the law, there are certain legal restrictions on it, including a requirement that the net income retained in a business be recorded separately from the Capital Stock account. The typical title of the account used to accumulate this information is Retained Earnings. *The statement of retained earnings* shows the changes in that part of the stockholders' equity designated as "retained earnings"; it should cover the same period as the income statement. Since by definition retained earnings are the accumulation of all past net income less any dividends paid out, it follows that net income and dividends for a period must be reflected in the statement. The first end-of-period statement of retained earnings of the Nelson Garage is shown in Figure 3-3.

Figure 3-3
Statement of
Retained Earnings for
New Business

NELSON GARAGE
Statement of Retained Earnings
For the Month Ended January 31, 1976

Net Income for January 1976	$2,585
Deduct Dividends	300
Retained Earnings, January 31, 1976	$2,285

[2] See Chapter 13 for an expanded explanation of earnings per share.

The heading of the statement of retained earnings is similar to that of the income statement.

For a business that has been in existence prior to the current period, there would be an additional item in the statement of retained earnings, the beginning-of-period balance. For example, the statement of the Elizabeth Calloway Company is shown in Figure 3-4.

Figure 3-4
Complete Statement of Retained Earnings

ELIZABETH CALLOWAY COMPANY
Statement of Retained Earnings
For the Month Ended January 31, 1976

Retained Earnings, January 1, 1976	$5,000,000
Add Net Income for January 1976	400,000
Total	$5,400,000
Deduct Dividends	300,000
Retained Earnings, January 31, 1976	$5,100,000

The Statement of Financial Position. Since the retained earnings of the Nelson Garage, as of January 31, 1976, have now been determined (Figure 3-3), it is possible to prepare the formal statement of financial position, as shown in Figure 3-5.

Figure 3-5 Formal Statement of Financial Position

NELSON GARAGE
Statement of Financial Position
January 31, 1976

Assets			*Liabilities and Stockholders' Equity*		
Current Assets			Current Liabilities		
Cash	$23,450		Accounts Payable	$ 350	
Accounts Receivable	210		Notes Payable	6,000	
Garage Parts and Supplies	375		Total Current Liabilities		$ 6,350
Prepaid Insurance	600				
Total Current Assets		$24,635	Stockholders' Equity		
Plant and Equipment			Capital Stock	$30,000	
Land	$10,000		Retained Earnings	2,285	
Automotive Tools and Equipment	4,000				
Total Plant and Equipment		14,000	Total Stockholders' Equity		32,285
Total Assets		$38,635	Total Liabilities and Stockholders' Equity		$38,635

Note that the heading of the statement of financial position contains the single date *January 31, 1976.* This statement reveals the financial position as of the close of business on January 31. It is analogous to a still photograph, whereas the income statement and statement of retained earnings are like moving pictures—they show the changes that have taken place during a specific period.

Closing and Ruling the Revenue and Expense Accounts

Temporary or Nominal Accounts

The revenue, expense, and dividends accounts are used to measure part of the changes that take place in retained earnings during a specified period. For this reason, these accounts are often called *temporary owner's equity accounts,* or *nominal accounts.*

At the end of an accounting period, these accounts must be emptied—or *closed*—so that they may be used to accumulate the changes in retained earnings for the next period. Therefore, *closing entries* are made to transfer the final effects of the temporary stockholders' equity accounts to the Retained Earnings account, which is a *permanent,* or *real,* account.

Permanent or Real Accounts

The term *real* is applied to the accounts that appear in the statement of financial position; these accounts are not closed at the end of a period.

The Closing Procedure. To simplify the transfer of revenue and expense account balances, an intermediate *summary account,* called Income Summary, is used. The balances of all revenue and expense accounts are transferred to this account. The Income Summary account, the balance of which reveals the net income or loss for the period, is then closed by transferring its balance to the Retained Earnings account, a part of the stockholders' equity. This action is justified because net income or net loss accrues to the owners. Since the Dividends account is not an expense account, it is not closed to Income Summary; rather, it is closed directly to Retained Earnings. After the revenue and expense accounts are closed, they are ruled to indicate that they have zero balances and that they are now available to accumulate information for measuring the changes in retained earnings in the next accounting period.

The closing procedure is illustrated in Figure 3-6. An explanation of encircled figures in this figure is as follows:

Entry **1**—The revenue accounts are closed.
Entry **2**—The expense accounts are closed.
Entry **3**—The Income Summary account is closed.
Entry **4**—The Dividends account is closed.

The caption *Closing Entries* is written in the middle of the first unused line in the general journal under the transactions of the period, and the closing entries are begun directly under that.[3] They are posted immediately to the gen-

---

[3] Later a group of entries called *adjusting entries* will be introduced; they will be entered between the transactions and closing entries.

Figure 3-6
The Closing
Procedure

Each Expense Account

| Normal Debit Balance XX | Credit Closing Entry XX |

Each Revenue Account

| Debit Closing Entry XX | Normal Credit Balance XX |

❷   ❶

Income Summary

Expenses XX	Revenue XX
Debit Closing Entry (net income) XX	
XX	XX

❸

Retained Earnings

| Dividends XX | Beginning Normal Credit Balance XX |
| | Net Income XX |

Dividends

| Normal Debit Balance XX | Credit Closing Entry XX |

❹

eral ledger. As indicated in Figure 3-6, the closing entries are made in the following sequence:

Entry 1. All the revenue accounts are debited in a compound entry, and the sum of the revenue items is credited to the Income Summary account.

Entry 2. All the expense accounts are credited in a second compound entry, and the sum of the expense items is debited to the Income Summary account.

Entry 3. After entries 1 and 2 are posted, a credit balance in the Income Summary account represents net income; a debit balance, net loss. The balance of the account is transferred to the Retained Earnings account.

Entry 4. The Dividends account is closed directly to the Retained Earnings account by a debit to Retained Earnings and a credit to Dividends.

Unlike regular transaction entries, which require analysis and judgment, the closing process is purely mechanical and involves only the shifting and summarizing of previously determined amounts. The closing journal entries of the Nelson Garage on January 31, 1976, are shown in Figure 3-7.

The presence of account numbers in the folio column of the journal indicates that the closing journal entries have been posted to the ledger accounts indicated in the journal (see Figures 3-8 and 3-9). Closing may be indicated by the words *Closing entry* in the Explanation columns of the nominal accounts, as shown in Figure 3-8.

Ruling the Closed Nominal Accounts. After the closing entries have been posted, the temporary stockholders' equity accounts consist of equal debit and credit totals; that is, they have zero balances. These accounts (revenue, expense, and dividend) are ruled to separate the amounts entered during one accounting period from the amounts to be entered during the next. Each side is

(Ch. 3)

Figure 3-7
Closing Entries

GENERAL JOURNAL				Page 4	
		Closing Entries			
		❶			
1976 Jan.	31	Garage Repair Revenue	501	5,020	
		Income Summary	901		5,020
		To close revenue to summary account.			
		❷			
	31	Income Summary	901	2,435	
		Rent Expense—Garage Building	601		300
		Rent Expense—Automotive Tools and Equipment	602		80
		Salaries Expense	604		1,700
		Electricity and Water Expense	608		80
		Garage Parts and Supplies Used	609		275
		To close expenses to summary account.			
		❸			
	31	Income Summary	901	2,585	
		Retained Earnings	411		2,585
		To transfer net income to retained earnings.			
		❹			
	31	Retained Earnings	411	300	
		Dividends	421		300
		To close dividends to retained earnings.			

totaled; and the equal debit and credit totals are written on the first available full line. Double lines are then drawn across all the columns, except the Explanation columns, to signify that the accounts have a zero balance. If an account has only one debit and one credit, it is unnecessary to foot the account; double lines are drawn below the individual amounts. Figure 3-8 shows the posted closing entries and the ruling of the nominal accounts.

Balancing and Ruling the Open Real Accounts

To simplify computations in the statement of financial position accounts during the following accounting period and to set apart the amounts from each accounting period, it is customary to bring down the balances of the real accounts, which are still open. The procedure is as follows:

1. The balance of the account is computed. The amount is transferred to the money column on the opposite side, dated as of the last day of the accounting period. The word *Balance* is entered in the Explanation column, and a check mark is placed in the folio (F) column.

GENERAL LEDGER

Dividends   Acct. No. 421

1976					1976				
Jan.	31		2	300	Jan.	31	Closing entry	4	300

Garage Repair Revenue   Acct. No. 501

1976					1976				
Jan.	31	Closing entry	4	5,020	Jan.	6		1	1,000
						12		1	40
						20		2	2,000
						26		2	60
						28		2	120
						31		2	1,800
									5,020
				5,020					5,020

Rent Expense—Garage Building   Acct. No. 601

1976					1976				
Jan.	3		1	300	Jan.	31	Closing entry	4	300

Rent Expense—Automotive Tools and Equipment
                                           Acct. No. 602

1976					1976				
Jan.	5		1	80	Jan.	31	Closing entry	4	80

Salaries Expense   Acct. No. 604

1976					1976				
Jan.	15		1	800	Jan.	31	Closing entry	4	1,700
	31		2	900					
				1,700					
				1,700					1,700

Electricity and Water Expense   Acct. No. 608

1976					1976				
Jan.	31		2	80	Jan.	31	Closing entry	4	80

Garage Parts and Supplies Used   Acct. No. 609

1976					1976				
Jan.	31		3	275	Jan.	31	Closing entry	4	275

Figure 3-8
The Nominal
Accounts Are Closed
and Ruled

BASIC MODEL:
DYNAMIC
MEASUREMENTS

				Income Summary					Acct. No. 901
1976					1976				
Jan.	31	Expenses	4	2,435	Jan.	31	Revenue	4	5,020
	31	Closing entry	4	2,585					
				5,020					
				5,020					5,020

2. The equal debit and credit footings are entered on the next unused full line.
3. Double lines are drawn across all the columns, except the Explanation columns.
4. The balance is written under the double lines on the appropriate side, dated as of the last day of the current accounting period. The word *Balance* is written in the Explanation column, and a check mark is placed in the folio (F) column. It is not necessary to balance and rule an account that contains only one amount. Balancing an account, unlike adjusting and closing, *does not* involve journalizing or posting, because the balance of the account does not change.

The real accounts of the Nelson Garage are shown in Figure 3-9. Note the placement of double lines and balances.

Figure 3-9
The Real Accounts
Are Balanced and
Ruled

					GENERAL LEDGER					
					Cash					Acct. No. 101
1976					1976					
Jan.	2		1	30,000	Jan.	3		1	300	
	6		1	1,000		5		1	80	
	20		2	2,000		10		1	4,000	
	31		2	1,800		15		1	800	
	31	23,450	3	10		30		2	300	
				34,810		31		2	80	
						31		2	900	
						31		2	300	
						31		3	4,000	
						31		3	600	
									11,360	
						31	Balance	✓	23,450	
				34,810					34,810	
1976										
Jan.	31	Balance	✓	23,450						

Accounts Receivable   Acct. No. 121

1976					1976				
Jan.	12		1	40	Jan.	31		3	10
	26		2	60		31	Balance	✓	210
	28	210	2	120					
				220					
				220					220
1976									
Jan.	31	Balance	✓	210					

Garage Parts and Supplies   Acct. No. 131

1976					1976				
Jan.	5		1	400	Jan.	31		3	275
	29	375	2	250		31	Balance	✓	375
				650					
				650					650
1976									
Jan.	31	Balance	✓	375					

Prepaid Insurance   Acct. No. 141

1976			
Jan.	31	3	600

Land   Acct. No. 201

1976			
Jan.	10	1	10,000

Automotive Tools and Equipment   Acct. No. 221

1976			
Jan.	31	3	4,000

Accounts Payable   Acct. No. 301

1976					1976				
Jan.	30		2	300	Jan.	5		1	400
	31	Balance	✓	350		29	350	2	250
									650
				650					650
					1976				
					Jan.	31	Balance	✓	350

Notes Payable   Acct. No. 302

					1976 Jan.	10		1	6,000

Capital Stock   Acct. No. 401

					1976 Jan.	2		1	30,000

Retained Earnings   Acct. No. 411

1976 Jan.	31		4	300	1976 Jan.	31		4	2,585
	31	Balance	✔	2,285			2,285		
				2,585					2,585
					1976 Jan.	31	Balance	✔	2,285

Taking a Postclosing Trial Balance

After the closing entries have been posted and the accounts are ruled and balanced, a *postclosing trial balance* is taken from the general ledger. Since the only accounts with open balances are the real accounts, the accounts and amounts in the postclosing trial balance are the same as those in the statement of financial position. The postclosing trial balance tests the debit and credit equality of the general ledger before the accounts receive postings of the next accounting period. Its use, however, is optional, and a comparison of the general ledger account balances with the statement of financial position will serve the same purpose. In any case, it is absolutely essential to start a new period with the accounts in proper balance; even though the trial balance at the end of the new period would indicate an error; errors made in previous accounting periods are very difficult to trace.

The postclosing trial balance of the Nelson Garage is shown:

NELSON GARAGE
Postclosing Trial Balance
January 31, 1976

Acct. No.	Account Title	Debits	Credits
101	Cash	$23,450	
121	Accounts Receivable	210	
131	Garage Parts and Supplies	375	
141	Prepaid Insurance	600	
201	Land	10,000	
221	Automotive Tools and Equipment	4,000	
301	Accounts Payable		$ 350
302	Notes Payable		6,000
401	Capital Stock		30,000
411	Retained Earnings		2,285
	Totals	$38,635	$38,635

PROCEDURES APPLICABLE TO A SINGLE PROPRIETORSHIP

Since many service businesses are single proprietorships, the procedures discussed in this chapter that affect this form of business organization must be considered. If the Nelson Garage had been started by John Nelson as a single proprietorship, the following accounting differences would apply.

On January 2, 1976, Nelson would make the entire investment of $30,000, instead of three stockholders making an investment in a corporation. This investment by the single proprietor would be recorded in the journal as follows:

		GENERAL JOURNAL		**Page 1**
1976 Jan.	2	Cash	30,000	
		John Nelson, Capital		30,000
		To record investment by proprietor in a business to be called the Nelson Garage.		

The only other regular transaction that would be recorded differently in a single proprietorship is the dividend paid by the corporation on January 31, 1976. A comparable situation in the case of the single proprietor would be his withdrawal of cash (or some other asset) in *anticipation* of the net income that he expects to earn. If Nelson withdraws $300, the transaction would be recorded as follows:

BASIC MODEL:
DYNAMIC
MEASUREMENTS

GENERAL JOURNAL			Page 2	
1976 Jan.	31	John Nelson, Drawing	300	
		Cash		300
		To record withdrawal by proprietor in anticipation of earned income.		

A special account, *John Nelson, Drawing,* would be debited for all withdrawals in anticipation of income, and Cash would be credited; at the end of the period the drawing account would be credited for the net income that is actually earned.

All the other regular transactions of the Nelson Garage would be recorded in exactly the same manner for a single proprietorship as for a corporation.[4]

The only other recording difference between the two forms of business organization is in the closing process. After the revenue and expense accounts are closed, the Income Summary and John Nelson, Drawing accounts will appear as follows:

Income Summary				John Nelson, Drawing	
Expenses	2,435	Revenue	5,020	300	
			2,585		

GENERAL JOURNAL			Page 4	
		Closing Entries for a Single Proprietorship		
		❸		
1976 Jan.	31	Income Summary	2,585	
		John Nelson, Drawing		2,585
		To close net income to drawing account.		
		❹		
	31	John Nelson, Drawing	2,285	
		John Nelson, Capital		2,285
		To close balance of drawing account to capital.		

[4] As indicated on page 142, a corporation must file income tax returns, and these would require accounting entries. No such entries are required in a proprietorship; its net income must be included in the personal tax return of the proprietor.

(Ch. 3)

Entries ③ and ④ are made to complete the closing process in the journal of the single proprietorship (replacing entries ③ and ④ for the corporate form of business, as shown on page 102), in addition to entries ① and ②, also shown on page 102.

The effect of these entries is shown in the following T accounts:

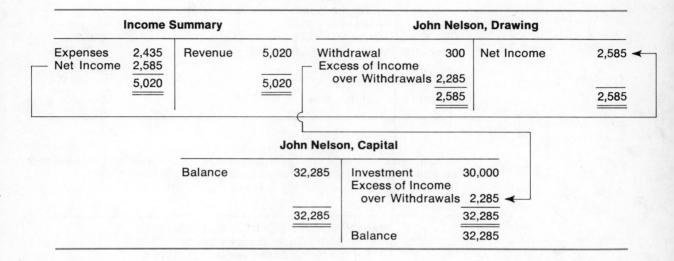

Income Summary			
Expenses	2,435	Revenue	5,020
Net Income	2,585		
	5,020		5,020

John Nelson, Drawing			
Withdrawal	300	Net Income	2,585
Excess of Income over Withdrawals	2,285		
	2,585		2,585

John Nelson, Capital			
Balance	32,285	Investment	30,000
		Excess of Income over Withdrawals	2,285
	32,285		32,285
		Balance	32,285

The net income, or net loss, is transferred to the proprietor's drawing account. This is consistent with the analysis of the withdrawal; since the drawing account is debited for withdrawals in anticipation of income, it should also be credited with the net income actually earned during the period. If the resulting balance of the account is a credit, it indicates that earnings have exceeded withdrawals, so that additional withdrawals can be made. A debit balance indicates an excess of withdrawals over earnings and the possible need for additional investments to cover the deficiency.

Because there are no legal restrictions on the withdrawal of earnings of a single proprietorship, as there are on those of a corporation, the balance of the drawing account is usually closed into the proprietor's capital account at the end of the accounting period.

The statement of financial position of a single proprietorship is the same as that of a corporation, except for the Owner's Equity section. For a single proprietorship, this section appears as shown below.

Owner's Equity
John Nelson, Capital $32,285

Because no Retained Earnings account is required for a single proprietorship, a statement of retained earnings is not prepared; instead, a statement of owner's equity is prepared. The statement of owner's equity for the Nelson Garage as a single proprietorship owned and operated by John Nelson is shown as

---

NELSON GARAGE
Statement of Owner's Equity
For the Month Ended January 31, 1976

John Nelson, Original Investment, January 2, 1976	$30,000
Add Net Income for January, 1976	2,585
Total	$32,585
Deduct Withdrawals	300
John Nelson, Capital, January 31, 1976	$32,285

A statement of owner's equity for a single proprietorship with a beginning balance and an additional investment during January is shown as

---

NANCY WOOTEN SECRETARIAL SERVICES
Statement of Owner's Equity
For the Month Ended January 31, 1976

Nancy Wooten, Capital, January 1, 1976	$500,000
Add Net Income for January, 1976	100,000
Additional Investment	200,000
Total	$800,000
Deduct Withdrawals	50,000
Nancy Wooten, Capital, January 31, 1976	$750,000

INTERRELATIONSHIP OF THE FINANCIAL STATEMENTS

There is a significant interrelationship between the statement of financial position, the statement of retained earnings, and the income statement, as illustrated in Figure 3-10. The income statement shows the net amount remaining after revenues have been matched with expenses for a given period. This amount, the net income, is transferred to the statement of retained earnings, which shows the changes that have taken place in stockholders' equity as a result of the operations of a period. The statement of retained earnings shows additional changes that have taken place in stockholders' equity—in this particular case, dividend payments. The end-of-period balance of retained earnings is transferred to the end-of-period statement of financial position, which presents information as of a moment of time—that is, at the end of the accounting period. The income statement and the statement of retained earnings help to account for the changes in the stockholders' equity during the interval be-

Figure 3-10 Interrelationships of Financial Statements

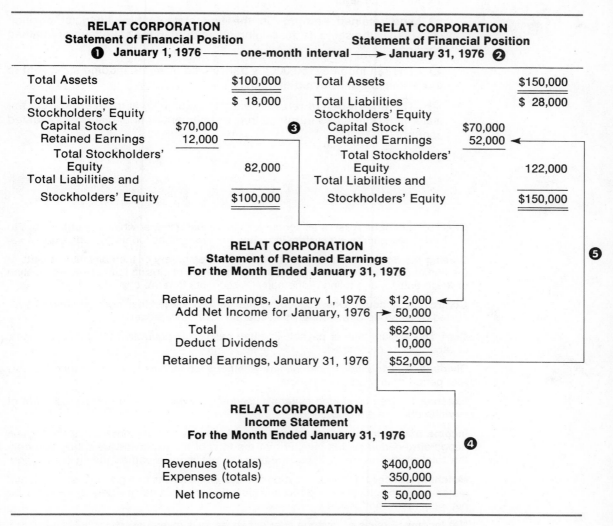

tween statements of financial position. For this reason, it is helpful if the statements are prepared in this sequence: income statement, statement of retained earnings, and statement of financial position.

Summary totals are used so that the statements can be presented on one page. This procedure is not acceptable for solving the end-of-chapter material; details should be given on all statements.

❶ The date of the first statement of financial position is also the beginning date of the statement of retained earnings and the income statement. (*For the Month Ended January 31, 1976,* means the period beginning January 1 and ending January 31.)

(Ch. 3)

❷ The date of the second statement of financial position (January 31, 1976) is also the ending date of the statement of retained earnings and the income statement.

❸ The retained earnings in the first statement of financial position ($12,000) is the same as the beginning amount in the statement of retained earnings.

❹ The net income ($50,000) is transferred from the income statement to the statement of retained earnings.

❺ The end-of-period retained earnings ($52,000) is transferred from the statement of retained earnings to the statement of financial position dated January 31, 1976.

GLOSSARY

Chart of Accounts A list of all accounts in the general ledger which are anticipated to be used. Their numbering system indicates the types of accounts by subgroups.

Closing the Books The process of clearing the temporary or the nominal accounts at the end of a period; this process requires preparation of closing journal entries, posting of these entries, and ruling of the nominal accounts that are closed.

Controlling Account One account in the general ledger that controls, and is supported by, a group of accounts in a separate subsidiary ledger.

Cost The amount paid or payable in either cash or its equivalent for goods, services, or other assets purchased.

Dividend A distribution of net income whether such income is earned during the current period or in a previous period.

Expense Expired costs; the materials used and services utilized in the production of revenue during a specific period.

Income Statement A statement showing all revenue and expense items for a given period arranged in such a manner that the total of the expenses are subtracted from the total of the revenues, thus revealing the net income earned during that period.

Matching Concept The identification of incurred expenses to a given time period, and matching them against earned revenue identified to the same time period, to determine net income for that period.

Net Income Excess of revenue over expenses for a given period.

Net Income per Share Net income divided by average outstanding shares of stock; it is considered to be an excellent indicator of future profitability.

Net Loss Excess of expenses over revenue for a given period.

Nominal Accounts Temporary accounts that are set up to collect and to measure part of the change that takes place in retained earnings or other applicable owners' equity accounts. They are closed out at the end of each accounting period.

Postclosing Trial Balance A trial balance taken of the ledger accounts that have any balances in them—the real accounts—after closing entries have been recorded and posted.

Real Accounts The accounts that are not closed and which are incorporated in the statement of financial position.

Revenue A term describing the source of inflows of assets received in exchange for services rendered, sales of products or merchandise, gains from sales or exchange of assets other than stock in trade, and earnings from interest and dividends on investments.

Schedule of Accounts Payable A listing of the individual creditors with amount owed to each and the total owed to all creditors at a given moment in time.

Schedule of Accounts Receivable A listing of the individual customers (debtors) with the amount owed by each and the total amounts receivable from all customers.

Statement of Retained Earnings A statement showing the changes that occurred in retained earnings during a given period.

Subsidiary Ledger A group of accounts in a separate ledger that provides information in detail about one controlling account in the general ledger.

Q3-1. Define the term *revenue*. Does the receipt of cash by a business indicate that revenue has been earned? Explain. List ten small businesses and professions, and name the major source of revenue for each.

Q3-2. Define the term *expense*. Does the payment of cash by a business indicate that an expense has been incurred? Explain. Distinguish between a dividend and an expense.

Q3-3. The accountant for Ben Potter, owner of a parking lot, listed the parking lot at a cost of $20,000 on the statement of financial position. Potter argues that this amount should be $28,000, because he has recently been offered $28,000 for the lot. Discuss.

Q3-4. What item is common to each of the following pairs of statements: (1) the income statement and the statement of owner's equity, (2) the statement of owner's equity and the statement of financial position as of the beginning of an accounting period, and (3) the statement of owner's equity and the statement of financial position as of the end of an accounting period.

Q3-5. Russell Carter purchased electrical supplies on account from the Dunlap Company for $350 and from Hanlon, Inc., for $100. Carter debited Electrical Supplies, $450, and erroneously credited Accounts Receivable for $450 in the general ledger. The credit postings to the accounts payable ledger were properly made. (a) What effect would the error have on the debit and credit totals of the trial balance taken at the end of the month? (b) What accounts in the trial balance would be incorrectly stated? (c) Would the error be discovered? How?

Q3-6. List the advantages to management of a division of the general and the subsidiary ledgers and the use of controlling accounts. Is it equally advantageous to exclude the schedules of accounts receivable and accounts payable from the general ledger trial balance? Explain.

Q3-7. The following transaction occurred on April 15, 1976: Received bills representing charges for truck maintenance and repairs as follows: Strowd Hill Garage, $150; Thompson Garage, $225.
Showing the proper general journal and general subsidiary ledger accounts, prepare flow diagrams as shown in Figure 3-1 to illustrate posting from the general journal to the general ledger and the accounts payable ledger.

Q3-8. Define *net income per share* and indicate how this statistic is used by investors.

Q3-9. Assume that your firm has 1,000 charge customers. (a) Why would you want to keep your posting up to date? (b) Is it true that posting depends on previous journalizing? (c) Does journalizing, in turn, depend on earlier procedures in the complete accounting system? Explain.

Q3-10. What is the purpose of closing the books? Using T accounts for Revenue, Expenses, Dividends, Income Summary, and Retained Earnings, diagram the closing process.

Q3-11. Distinguish between single proprietorship and corporate accounting for investments and withdrawals, giving journal entry examples.

Q3-12. Draw a diagram showing the interrelationship of the statement of financial position, statement of retained earnings, and income statement.

Q3-13. The balance of retained earnings of the Hudson Company on December 31, 1976, was $2,000 less than on December 31, 1975. Give two possible reasons for the decrease.

EXERCISES

E3-1. A new accountant began work on January 2, 1976. Unfortunately, he made several errors that were discovered by the auditor during the year-end review. For each error described below, indicate the effect of the error by completing the following solution form. Treat each error separately; do not attempt to relate the errors to one another.

Suggested Solution Form

Error	Would the December 31, 1976, Trial Balance Be Out of Balance?		If Yes, by How Much?	Which Would Be Larger?	
	YES	NO		Debit Total	Credit Total
a b etc.					

a. A typewriter was purchased for $450 and cash was paid and credited. The debit was entered twice in the asset account.

b. A debit to the Cash account of $1,192 was posted as $1,129.

c. Cash collections of $925 from customers in settlement of their accounts were not posted to the Accounts Receivable account, but were posted correctly to the Cash account.

d. A purchase of office supplies of $250 was recorded as a credit to Cash and also as a credit to Office Supplies.

E3-2. Some of the possible effects of a transaction are listed:

1. An asset increase accompanied by an asset decrease.
2. An asset increase accompanied by an owner's equity increase.
3. An asset increase accompanied by a liability increase.

4. An asset increase accompanied by a revenue increase.

5. An asset decrease accompanied by a liability decrease.

6. An asset decrease accompanied by owner's equity decrease.

7. An asset decrease accompanied by an expense increase.

8. An expense increase accompanied by a liability increase.

Using the identifying numbers to the left of the listed combinations, indicate the effect of each of the following transactions:

Example: Issued capital stock for cash. *Answer:* (2)

a. Collected a commission on a sale made today.

b. Borrowed money from a bank and issued a note.

c. Collected an account receivable.

d. Paid an account payable.

e. Paid for an ad in a magazine.

E3-3. The following cash receipt transactions occurred at the Amity Realty Corporation during the month of August 1976:

1976
Aug. 1   Issued additional stock for $50,000 in cash.

      7   Received a commission of $2,400 from the sale of a house and lot.

      8   Received $4,500 in cash from the issuance of a note payable to a bank.

     31   Received $250 in interest from U.S. government bonds.

     31   Received $250 in cash for August rent of part of the corporation's building.

Journalize the revenue transactions only.

E3-4. The following were among the cash payment transactions at the Sir Park Garage during the month of May 1976:

1976
May 3   Paid $4,500 for a truck.

      7   Paid $900 in salaries for the month.

      9   Paid $4,000 in settlement of an account.

     12   Paid $300 for a typewriter.

     16   Declared and paid a $1,500 cash dividend to stockholders.

     22   Paid $200 for rent of the office for May.

Journalize the expense transactions only.

E3-5. The August 1976 transactions of the Farrell Travel Service are given below.

1976
Aug. 1   Paid $250 for an advertisement in the Travel section of the *Baltimore Post*.

      2   Arranged a round-the-world trip for Mr. and Mrs. Clyde J. Davis. Collected a commission of $200 in cash from the steamship company.

      3   Arranged fly-now, pay-later European trips for several clients. The Trans-Islandic Airway System agreed to a commission of $700 for services rendered, payment to be made at the end of the month.

      4   Another advertisement was placed in the *Baltimore Post* for $300, payment to be made in 10 days.

BASIC MODEL:
DYNAMIC
MEASUREMENTS

1976
Aug. 16   Robert T. Farrell, owner of the Farrell Travel Service, withdrew $450 from the business for his personal use.

19   Collected $700 from the Trans-Islandic Airway System.

Following the example given for the August 1 transaction, analyze each transaction and prepare the necessary journal entry.

Example:

Aug. 1   **a.** Advertising is an operating expense. Increases in expenses are recorded by debits. Debit Advertising Expense for $250.

b. The asset Cash was decreased. Decreases of assets are recorded by credits. Credit Cash for $250.

c. Journal entry: Advertising Expense   250
                     Cash   250

E3-6.   The Cash account in the general ledger of Houck's Repair Shop is given below.

		Cash		Acct. No. 101
(1)	10,000		(3)	450
(2)	500		(5)	650
(4)	300			

Item 1 is Houck's original investment on June 1. Items 2 and 4 are cash receipts during June, and items 3 and 5 are cash payments made during June.

a. What is the balance of the account to be shown in the trial balance as of the end of June?

b. Will Houck's income statement for the month of June reflect a net loss of $300—the excess of payments ($1,100) over receipts other than the original investment ($800)? Explain.

E3-7.   The following transactions occurred at the Robbins Rug Cleaning Company:

1976
Nov.   1   Billed the following customers for $450 for rug-cleaning work:

Charles Addison	$100
Morton Hamm	150
Barton Rollins	200
Total	$450

31   Received $300 on account from the following customers:

Charles Addison	$ 75
Morton Hamm	100
Barton Rollins	125
Total	$300

a. Prepare general journal entries to record the transactions.

b. Post to general ledger and accounts receivable ledger accounts. (Assign appropriate numbers to general ledger accounts.)

c. Prepare a schedule of accounts receivable.

E3-8. As of December 31, 1976, the ledger of the Baggett Company contained the following accounts and account balances, among others: Cash, $50,000; Accounts Receivable, $30,000; Retained Earnings, $72,500; Commissions Earned, $70,000; Rent Earned, $5,000; Salaries Expense, $40,000; Office Expense, $6,000; Miscellaneous Expense, $15,000; Dividends, $7,000. (All the nominal accounts are included.)
Journalize the closing entries.

E3-9. Financial information for three different corporations follows:

a. Net income for 1976	$ 45,600
Retained earnings at beginning of year	200,000
Dividends declared and paid in 1976	30,000
Retained earnings at end of year	?
b. Net income for 1976	?
Retained earnings at beginning of year	320,000
Dividends declared and paid in 1976	40,000
Retained earnings at end of year	310,000
c. Net loss in 1976	10,000
Retained earnings at beginning of year	?
Dividends declared and paid in 1976	15,200
Retained earnings at end of year	530,000

Supply the missing figures.

E3-10. Financial information for three different single proprietorships follows:

a. Net income for 1976	$100,000
Owner's equity at beginning of year	?
Owner's equity at end of year	190,000
Withdrawals by owner during 1976	17,000
b. Net income for 1976	?
Owner's equity at beginning of year	140,000
Owner's equity at end of year	136,000
Withdrawals by owner during 1976	12,400
c. Net loss in 1976	15,600
Owner's equity at beginning of year	60,000
Owner's equity at end of year	39,600
Withdrawals by owner during 1976	?

Supply the missing figures. (Assume that no additional investments were made during 1976.)

DP3-1. (*Journalizing, posting, trial balance, and schedule of accounts receivable*) The chart of accounts of the Wilson Corporation includes the following accounts and identifying numbers: Cash, 101; Accounts Receivable, 111; Cleaning Supplies, 131; Cleaning and Pressing Equipment, 161; Capital Stock, 251; Cleaning Revenue, 301; Miscellaneous General Expense, 412; Wages Expense, 414.

The company's transactions for December 1976 follow:

1976
Dec. 1 Issued capital stock for $10,000 in cash to start a cleaning business.
    3 Purchased cleaning and pressing equipment for $900 in cash.

DEMON-
STRATION
PROBLEMS

BASIC MODEL:
DYNAMIC
MEASUREMENTS

1976

Dec. 10 Paid $100 in cash for cleaning supplies.

15 Billed the following customers for cleaning work for the first half of the month:

B. Baker	$200
J. James	75
T. Thompson	95

15 Paid $300 in salaries.

21 Paid $120 for miscellaneous general expenses.

26 Received cash from the following customers to apply on account:

B. Baker	$125
J. James	45
T. Thompson	55

31 Paid $300 in salaries.

31 Billed the following customers for cleaning work for the second half of the month:

B. Baker	$185
T. Thompson	105

31 Received $600 from cash customers for the month.

Required:

1. Journalize the transactions.
2. Open accounts and post from the journal to the appropriate ledgers. (Use assigned account numbers for general ledger accounts.)
3. Take a trial balance.
4. Prepare a schedule of accounts receivable.

DP3-2. (*Journalizing, posting, and statements*) Elizabeth Taylor opened an office for the general practice of dentistry. During the month of July 1976, the following transactions occurred:

1976

July 1 Invested $4,000 in the business.

3 Purchased dental supplies on account:

Bettu Dental Supply Company	$400
Safety Supply Company	300

3 Paid $400 for July rent.

7 Paid $300 for miscellaneous general expenses.

9 Received $2,000 in cash for professional services rendered.

10 Purchased dental equipment from Tooth-Fairy Equipment Company for $6,000 on account.

15 Paid on account $250 to the Bettu Dental Supply Company and $200 to the Safety Supply Company.

26 Mailed statements to the following patients for services rendered:

Dorothy Reynolds	$350
Paul Williams	100

31 Paid $2,000 in cash and issued a note payable for $4,000 to the Tooth-Fairy Equipment Company.

31 Received on account in cash $150 from Dorothy Reynolds and $75 from Paul Williams.

31 Determined that $200 of dental supplies had been consumed.

Required:

1. Journalize the transactions.
2. Post to the general ledger, accounts receivable ledger, and accounts payable ledger. (Assign numbers to the general ledger accounts.)
3. Take a trial balance.
4. Prepare schedules of accounts receivable and accounts payable as of July 31, 1976.
5. Prepare an income statement, a statement of owner's equity, and a statement of financial position.
6. Journalize the closing entries and post them.
7. Prepare a postclosing trial balance.

DP3-3. (*Closing entries and postclosing trial balance*) The trial balance of the Fuller Corporation on December 31, 1976, follows:

FULLER CORPORATION
Trial Balance
December 31, 1976

Acct. No.	Account Title	Debits	Credits
101	Cash	$100,000	
111	Accounts Receivable	8,000	
121	Supplies	3,600	
201	Equipment	40,000	
301	Accounts Payable		$ 8,000
401	Capital Stock		100,000
411	Retained Earnings, January 1, 1976		29,700
421	Dividends	4,000	
501	Commissions Earned		30,000
511	Rent Earned		10,000
601	Salaries Expense	13,400	
602	Advertising Expense	2,000	
603	Supplies Used	3,200	
604	Miscellaneous Expense	3,500	
	Totals	$177,700	$177,700

Required:

1. Set up T accounts for Retained Earnings, Dividends, and each revenue and expense account listed in the trial balance. Enter the account balances.
2. Journalize the closing entries and post to the T accounts.
3. Prepare a postclosing trial balance.

P3-1. On August 1, 1976, the Marley Plumbing Company purchased plumbing supplies on account as follows:

Abbott Company	$ 200
Jetters Company	80
Watson, Inc.	520
Total	$ 800

On August 15, 1976, the Marley Plumbing Company paid its creditors on account as follows:

Abbott Company	$ 150
Jetters Company	50
Watson, Inc.	420
Total	$ 620

Required:

1. Prepare general journal entries to record the transactions.
2. Post to general ledger and accounts payable ledger accounts. (Assign appropriate numbers to general ledger accounts.)
3. Prepare a schedule of accounts payable.

P3-2. (*Accounting policy decision problem*) John Stewart decided to start business as a lawyer. Transactions for the month of May 1976 follow:

1976
May 1 Deposited $15,000 in a checking account under the business name, John Stewart, Attorney-at-Law.
   3 Paid $300 for the first month's office rent.
   5 Purchased office equipment for $1,000. Paid $300 in cash and issued a note payable for the balance.
   6 Paid $150 for a one-year insurance policy on the office equipment, effective May 1, 1976.
   7 Paid $200 in cash for office supplies.
   8 Billed the following clients for services rendered:

T. Betterson	$400
J. Deuce	150
F. Fulton	250

   15 Received cash from the following clients:

T. Betterson	$250
J. Deuce	50

   18 Received $900 in cash for services rendered not previously billed.
   20 Withdraw $500 for personal use.
   31 Paid $410 for miscellaneous general expenses for May.

Required:

1. Journalize the transactions.
2. Suggest a chart of accounts for John Stewart and explain why the particular numbers are used in the chart.

P3-3. The Riggsbee Tool Service and Repair Shop was incorporated on June 1, 1976, and capital stock was issued for $20,000 in cash. During the month of June, the corporation completed the following transactions:

1976
June 1 Paid a $250 premium on a one-year comprehensive insurance policy, effective June 1, 1976.
   1 Paid $400 for June rent.

1976

June 2 Purchased shop equipment for $4,000 in cash.

2 Purchased shop supplies on account as follows:

Banning Supply Company $1,500
Dawson Supply House 500
Ridge Tool Company 600

5 Purchased an automobile for $3,500 from Alexander's Motor Company, giving $1,000 in cash and a note payable for the balance.

9 Received $800 in cash for servicing and repairing tools.

10 Paid $100 in cash for advertising space in the *Dawning Sun Paper*.

15 Paid cash for gas, oil, and other automobile expenses for two weeks, $70.

15 Paid $1,500 to the following creditors:

Banning Supply Company $1,000
Dawson Supply House 300
Ridge Tool Company 200

18 Received $600 in cash for repairing tools.

20 Paid $1,000 in cash on the note given for the purchase of the automobile.

21 Declared and paid a $500 dividend.

22 Paid $40 for telephone service.

23 Paid $36 for a new battery for the automobile (debit Automobile Expense).

24 Billed customers $950 for service and repair work:

Easley Carson $375
Milton Lawson 275
Peters Queens 300

25 Paid $25 for cleaning the shop.

25 Received $500 in cash for servicing tools.

26 Purchased additional shop supplies on account:

Banning Supply Company $300
Dawson Supply House 200

27 Paid $60 for electric service.

28 Purchased a typewriter and an adding machine for $650.

29 Received $575 on account from the following customers:

Easley Carson $275
Milton Lawson 100
Peters Queens 200

30 Paid $65 for gas, oil, and other automobile expenses for two weeks.

30 Received $450 from customers for repair work not previously billed.

30 Paid $200 in cash for advertising space in a local magazine.

30 Received a promissory note from Easley Carson for the balance due on his account.

Required:

1. Open the following accounts in the general ledger: Cash, 101; Accounts Receivable, 111; Notes Receivable, 115; Shop Supplies, 136; Prepaid Insurance, 140; Automobile, 201; Shop Equipment, 211; Office Equipment, 221;

Accounts Payable, 301; Notes Payable, 304; Capital Stock, 351; Dividends, 352; Repair Service Revenue, 401; Advertising Expense, 518; Rent Expense, 503; Heat and Light Expense, 505; Telephone and Telegraph Expense, 509; Automobile Expense, 510; Miscellaneous General Expense, 512.

2. Open customers' accounts in the accounts receivable ledger.
3. Open creditors' accounts in the accounts payable ledger.
4. Record all the transactions in the general journal, including the issuance of capital stock.
5. Post to the appropriate ledgers.
6. Prepare a trial balance.
7. Prepare a schedule of accounts receivable.
8. Prepare a schedule of accounts payable.

P3-4. The trial balance of the Capitol Parking Lot shows the following accounts, arranged in alphabetical order:

CAPITOL PARKING LOT
Trial Balance
December 31, 1976

Account Title	Debits	Credits
Accounts Payable		$ 2,000
Accounts Receivable	$13,000	
Cash	43,600	
Capital Stock, 4,000 shares issued and outstanding		40,000
Dividends	1,900	
Equipment Maintenance Expense	2,400	
Heat and Light Expense	1,600	
Interest Earned		1,200
Land	10,000	
Notes Payable		4,000
Notes Receivable	3,000	
Parking Fees Earned		39,300
Salaries Expense	9,000	
Retained Earnings, January 1, 1976		2,500
Supplies on Hand	1,400	
Supplies Used	2,900	
Telephone Expense	200	
Totals	$89,000	$89,000

Required:

1. Prepare a trial balance in proper chart-of-accounts sequence.
2. Prepare an income statement, a statement of retained earnings, and a statement of financial position.
3. Journalize the closing entries.

P3-5. The following statements have been prepared for the Morton Company:

MORTON COMPANY
Statement of Financial Position
March 31, 1976

Assets			*Liabilities and Stockholders' Equity*		
Current Assets			Current Liabilities		
Cash	$2,000		Accounts Payable		$ 600
Repair Parts	1,000		Stockholders' Equity		
Total Current Assets		$ 3,000	Capital Stock	$6,000	
Plant and Equipment			Retained Earnings	3,400	
Land	$2,000		Total Stockholders'		
Building	5,000		Equity		9,400
Total Plant and Equipment		7,000	Total Liabilities and		
Total Assets		$10,000	Stockholders' Equity		$10,000

MORTON COMPANY
Income Statement
For the Month Ended March 31, 1976

Revenue		
Storage Fees		$ 4,970
Expenses		
Office Rent Expense	$ 600	
Salaries Expense	2,000	
Miscellaneous Expenses	670	3,270
Net Income		$ 1,700

During March, the company declared and paid a dividend of $200.

Required: Prepare a statement of retained earnings for the Morton Company for the month of March 1976 and the closing entries as of March 31, 1976.

P3-6. Calvin Atwater, a master plumber, opened his own shop. During the month of January 1976, he completed the following transactions:

1976
Jan. 2 Invested $5,000 in cash in the business.

3 Paid $150 rent for the month of January.

4 Purchased plumbing supplies on account:

Tyrrell Plumbing Company	$600
Union Plumbers, Inc.	200
Waters Plumbing Company	350

6 Purchased from the Porter Motor Company a used truck for $3,500, giving $500 in cash and a note payable for the balance.

9 Paid $800 in cash for shop equipment.

10 Paid $210 in cash for a one-year insurance policy on the shop equipment and truck, effective January 2, 1976.

1976

Jan. 14 Received $450 for a completed plumbing job.

18 Paid creditors on account:

Tyrrell Plumbing Company	$200
Union Plumbers, Inc.	100
Waters Plumbing Company	50

20 Atwater withdrew $300 for his personal use.

Use the following account numbers and titles:

101 Cash
111 Accounts Receivable
121 Plumbing Supplies
131 Prepaid Insurance
241 Truck
245 Shop Equipment
301 Accounts Payable
306 Notes Payable
351 Calvin Atwater, Capital
352 Calvin Atwater, Drawing
401 Rental Revenue
402 Plumbing Revenue
501 Rent Expense
502 Telephone and Telegraph Expense

Required:

1. Journalize the transactions.
2. Post to the appropriate ledger accounts.
3. Take a trial balance.
4. Prepare schedule of accounts payable.

P3-7. The following transactions occurred during March 1976 at the Durham Roof Repair Company:

1976

Mar. 1 Issued 1,500 shares of capital stock for $15,000 in cash.

5 Paid $150 for two days' rental of a derrick and pulley assembly used on a repair job.

6 Purchased U.S. government bonds for $5,000 in cash.

11 Collected $1,400 on completion of roofing repair work.

20 Signed an agreement with Guilford College to repair dormitory roofs for $4,500. The work is to be completed during April and May.

25 Paid a cash dividend of $400 to stockholders.

28 Paid $650 for repair materials used on jobs during the month.

30 Paid $2,500 in salaries and wages.

31 Completed roofing repair work for Thomas Rockness in the amount of $1,850. Rockness promised to pay for the work on April 10, 1976.

Use the following account titles and numbers:

101 Cash
109 Marketable Securities
111 Accounts Receivable
351 Capital Stock
352 Retained Earnings
353 Dividends
401 Repair Service Revenue

501 Salaries and Wages Expense
502 Repair Materials Expense
503 Rental Expense
600 Income Summary

Required:

1. Journalize the transactions.
2. Post to general ledger accounts.
3. Take a trial balance.
4. Prepare an income statement, a statement of retained earnings, and a statement of financial position.
5. Prepare and post the closing entries.
6. Rule the accounts that have no balances.
7. Take a postclosing trial balance.

P3-8. The following information is taken from the books of the Kutz Company:

KUTZ COMPANY
Statement of Retained Earnings
For the Year Ended December 31, 1976

Retained Earnings, January 1, 1976	$100,000
Add Net Income for 1976	200,000
Total	$300,000
Deduct Dividends	70,000
Retained Earnings, December 31, 1976	$230,000

The expenses for 1976 were: salaries expense, $95,000; advertising expense, $19,000; office expense, $16,000; and miscellaneous expense, $28,000. The revenue came from only one source, commissions earned.

Required: Prepare a formal income statement for the Kutz Company. Show your computations of the amounts that are not given.

The Basic Accounting Model: The End-of-Period Process

4

A complete but simple service company illustration, the transactions of the Nelson Garage, was used in Chapter 3. A similar but more complex illustration is used in this chapter to introduce and review the following elements: (1) two accounting methods, (2) *adjustments*—continuous transactions that, for convenience, are not recorded until the end of the period, (3) the *work sheet*—an orderly method of collecting information for the preparation of formal financial statements, (4) the updating of ledger accounts after the work sheet is prepared, (5) a review of the accounting cycle, (6) split entries, and (7) (in the Appendix to the chapter) further managerial analysis.

TWO ACCOUNTING METHODS

Two accounting methods are found in practice: the cash basis and the accrual basis.

CASH BASIS

Under the cash basis of accounting, revenue is recognized when the cash is received, and the revenue is recorded at that time. Expenses are recognized in the period of payment. Recognition of revenue and expenses during an accounting period is based on an inflow and outflow of cash—a matching of cash receipts and cash disbursements to determine operating results during an accounting period. This method of accounting is obviously simple in application; but in most cases *it does not* properly measure net income, because, for example, it does not recognize uncollected revenue items as being earned and unpaid expense items as being incurred until actual payment is made. Hence, it matches only some of the revenues and expenses for a given period. There are instances, however, particularly in small professional and service businesses, in which the cash basis of accounting is used with acceptable results. Hybrid systems, or modifications of the cash-basis system, are often found in practice.

ACCRUAL BASIS

The accrual basis of accounting is founded on the principle that, if the net income of a business for a given period is to be measured properly, all the revenue earned during that period and all the related expenses of earning that income assignable to the period must be considered. Revenues are recognized at the time of sale, and expenses are usually recognized at the time the services are received and used in the production of revenue.

Matching Revenue and Expenses

This process of matching the revenue of a period with the expenses of that period, regardless of when, whether, or how much cash has been received or paid, is the central goal of the accrual basis of accounting and underlies all the discussions in this text.

The difference in net income resulting from the use of each method is best illustrated by an example. The Louise Hale Company, which does landscape gardening, performed work during August for which it charged $1,000. It received $600 on August 15 and $400 on September 10. Wages (the only expense) of $550 were paid on August 31. No work was performed during September.

	Cash Basis		Accrual Basis	
	August	*September*	*August*	*September*
Revenue	$600	$400	$1,000	$-0-
Expense	550	-0-	550	-0-
Net Income	$ 50	$400	$ 450	$-0-

The accrual basis of accounting gives more useful results, because revenue is reflected in the period to which it properly belongs, that is, the period in which it was earned. Net income is the difference between revenue earned and expenses incurred during the accounting period—the difference between the results achieved and the efforts expended. The accrual method, by matching expenses incurred with revenue earned for the period, presents the better measurement of net income. Since the accrual basis of accounting results in more useful financial statements, most businesses keep their books on this basis.

NEED FOR ADJUSTING ENTRIES

During the accounting period, regular business transactions are recorded as they occur. At the end of the period, the accountant may find that the ledger accounts are incomplete: some new accounts must be brought into the books and other accounts must be brought up to date. The journal entries necessary to accomplish this are referred to as *adjusting entries*.

Adjusting Entries

Periodic adjustment of the ledger accounts is indispensable if the financial statements are to reflect the realistic position of the company—its assets and equities—as of the end of the period, and the results of its operations—revenue earned and expenses incurred—during the period.

It is impractical and sometimes impossible to record the day-to-day changes in certain accounts. For example, when the premium payment is made on an insurance policy, the asset Prepaid Insurance is debited. At the end of the accounting period, however, only part of the balance of the Prepaid Insurance account represents an asset. The amount that has expired with the passage of time is an expense, because it represents the cost of insurance protection. At the end of the accounting period, therefore, Prepaid Insurance contains both an asset and an expense element. An adjustment is necessary to record the correct amount of Insurance Expense and to reduce Prepaid Insurance. This type of adjusting entry is referred to as a *short-term cost* apportionment adjustment.

An adjusting entry may be required to record previously unrecorded data. Assume, for example, that a company paid wages on March 28 for the two-week period that ended on that date. However, the employees worked on March 29, 30, and 31. If March 31 is the end of the accounting period, recognition must be given to this unrecorded but incurred expense as well as to the corresponding increase in liabilities, so that the financial statements may show the liability and the proper assignment of the expense to the period. This type of adjustment is referred to as an *accrued expense* adjustment.

A distinction is usually made between adjusting entries and entries that record regular business transactions. Regular business transactions start and complete their cycles within an accounting period. Adjusting entries deal with the transactions that transpire continuously and may be termed *continuous transactions*. It is neither feasible nor necessary to record these continuing changes during the period; rather, they are recorded at the end of each accounting period by means of *summary* adjusting entries. The nature of the adjusting entries varies. The adjusting entry for wages, for example, records a change that has already taken place—the increase in a liability incurred—but is unrecorded. The adjusting entry for Insurance Expense, on the other hand, recognizes the partial consumption of an item that was recorded in an asset account at the time of acquisition.

Adjusting entries may be entered initially in the work sheet with formal recording in the journal deferred until the closing entries are made, or they may be recorded in the journal first and then applied to the work sheet.

PROCESS OF RECORDING ADJUSTMENTS

The various kinds of continuous transactions, or adjustments, may be summarized in the following five groups:

1. *Short-term cost apportionments:* recorded cost that must be apportioned between current and later accounting periods, which could be a month, a quarter, but usually a year. Examples: supplies, prepaid insurance, and prepaid rent.

2. *Short-term revenue apportionments:* recorded revenue that will be apportioned between current and later accounting periods. Examples: rent collected in advance and magazine subscriptions collected in advance.

3. *Long-term cost apportionments:* a type of adjustment similar to short-term cost apportionment except that the recorded cost will usually be apportioned between three or more accounting periods. Example: the cost of a building.

4. *Accrued expenses:* unrecorded expenses incurred in the current period. Example: wages earned by employees after the last pay day in an accounting period.

5. *Accrued revenues:* unrecorded revenues earned in the current period. Example: interest earned on a note receivable held for thirty days in the current period but not due until sometime in the next period.

The Connolly Trucking Company started business on June 1, 1976. As a convenience in illustrating the end-of-period procedures, it is assumed that the books are closed on June 30 (books are customarily closed annually). The trial balance taken from the Connolly Trucking Company's general ledger is shown in Figure 4-1.

The adjusting entries are journalized and posted to the accounts. The separate discussion of each adjusting entry is identified by the letter used to cross-reference the debit and credit adjustments in the Adjustments columns of the *work sheet,* shown in Figure 4-4.

Short-Term Cost Apportionment Adjustments—a, b, and c

There are three steps in adjusting the mixed account involving a short-term cost apportionment.

1. Determining the balance of each account to be adjusted
2. Determining the amount of the asset and expense elements in each account
3. Recording the adjusting entries

Figure 4-1
Trial Balance

CONNOLLY TRUCKING COMPANY
Trial Balance
June 30, 1976

Acct. No.	Account Title	Debits	Credits
101	Cash	$ 5,250	
111	Accounts Receivable	550	
112	Notes Receivable	1,440	
131	Office Supplies	230	
141	Prepaid Insurance	2,160	
142	Prepaid Rent	1,500	
201	Office Equipment	1,400	
211	Trucks	13,000	
301	Accounts Payable		$ 200
302	Notes Payable		8,000
321	Unearned Rent		600
401	Capital Stock		12,000
404	Dividends	500	
501	Trucking Revenue		7,465
601	Heat and Light Expense	40	
602	Maintenance and Repairs Expense	375	
603	Telephone and Telegraph Expense	95	
604	Gas and Oil Expense	525	
605	Wages Expense	1,200	
	Totals	$28,265	$28,265

(a)

On June 1, the Connolly Trucking Company paid $1,500 in cash for three months' rent.

Step 1. The general ledger shows the following balance in the account:

			Prepaid Rent (mixed)			**Acct. No. 142**		
1976 June	1		1	$1,500				

The information in the foregoing ledger account (and other similar illustrations in this chapter) is reproduced from the original ledger and includes folio references for the original data.

Step 2. The amount of expense applicable to June is $500 = ($1,500 ÷ 3 months). On June 30, therefore, Prepaid Rent is a mixed account consisting of an expense element and an asset element.

(Ch. 4)

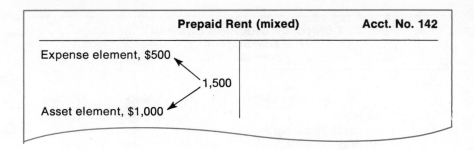

		Prepaid Rent (mixed)			Acct. No. 142
Expense element, $500					
		1,500			
Asset element, $1,000					

Step 3. As stated previously, the timing of the journalizing of the adjustments is optional; it may be delayed until the formal financial statements are prepared and presented to management for its use. Here, however, as a basic teaching device, the adjusting entries for the Connolly Trucking Company are made as each adjustment is explained.

The required adjusting entry is:

		GENERAL JOURNAL		Page 4	
1976 June	30	Rent Expense	606	500	
		Prepaid Rent	142		500
		To record rent expense for June.			

The expense element is thus removed from the mixed account, as shown by the following posting in the ledger accounts.

		Prepaid Rent (asset)				Acct. No. 142	
1976 June	1		1	1,500	1976 June	30	(adjustment)	4	500

		Rent Expense (expense)				Acct. No. 606	
1976 June	30	(adjustment)	4	500				

Prepaid Rent ($1,000) is classified in the statement of financial position as a current asset, and Rent Expense ($500) appears in the income statement as an expense.

(b)

The Connolly Trucking Company paid a premium of $2,160 for a comprehensive three-year insurance policy, effective June 1, 1976.

Step 1. Prepaid Insurance, before adjustment, shows a balance of $2,160. The title Prepaid Insurance classifies it as basically an asset account, but it is in fact a mixed account.

Step 2. An analysis of the account shows that the expense element for the month of June is $60 = ($2,160 ÷ 36 months), and that the unused portion of $2,100 is the asset prepayment benefiting future periods.

Step 3. The following adjusting entry is made:

GENERAL JOURNAL		Page 4	

1976
June 30
	Insurance Expense
	    Prepaid Insurance
	        To record insurance
	        expense for June.
		607
		141
			60
			
			      60

This information is shown in the following ledger accounts:

Prepaid Insurance (asset)					Acct. No. 141		
1976 June	1		1	2,160	1976 June 30 (adjustment)	4	60

Insurance Expense (expense)				Acct. No. 607			
1976 June 30	(adjustment)	4	60				

Prepaid Insurance ($2,100) is classified in the statement of financial position as a current asset, and Insurance Expense ($60) appears in the income statement as an expense.

(c)

Step 1. On the trial balance (Figure 4-1), Office Supplies has a debit balance of $230, representing a purchase made on June 6.

Step 2. The inventory taken on June 30 showed $60 worth of unused supplies; therefore, the expense element is $170 = ($230 − $60).

Step 3. The expense of $170 needs to be removed from the mixed account by the following adjusting entry, and the adjustment information is posted to the accounts shown below the journal entry:

1976								
June	30	Office Supplies Expense				608	170	
		Office Supplies				131		170
		To record supplies used						
		during June.						

Office Supplies (asset)   **Acct. No. 131**

1976					1976				
June	6		1	230	June	30	(adjustment)	4	170

Office Supplies Expense (expense)   **Acct. No. 608**

1976								
June	30	(adjustment)	4	170				

Office Supplies ($60) is classified in the statement of financial position as a current asset and Office Supplies Expense ($170) appears in the income statement as an expense.

Short-Term Revenue Apportionment Adjustment—d

The same three steps are followed in making short-term revenue apportionments of amounts originally recorded in mixed liability accounts.

(d)

On June 1, the Connolly Trucking Company signed a contract for the use of its trucks on a part-time basis and received an advance payment of $600 for six months' rent. At that time, Cash was debited and a liability account, Unearned Rent, was credited for $600. On June 30, only the portion earned in the month of June is transferred from Unearned Rent to Rent Earned; the unearned portion remains in Unearned Rent as a liability, because the Connolly Trucking Company must provide the use of its truck on a part-time basis for another five months.

Step 1. The amount of the unearned rent liability as of June 1, 1976, in the ledger T account is shown below:

Unearned Rent (mixed)   **Acct. No. 321**

					1976				
					June	1		1	600

Step 2. The rent actually earned in June is $100 = ($600 ÷ 6 mos.); on June 30, Unearned Rent is a mixed account and consists of a revenue element and a liability element.

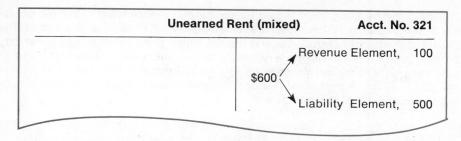

Unearned Rent (mixed)   **Acct. No. 321**

$600 → Revenue Element,   100

$600 → Liability Element, 500

Step 3. The following adjusting entry is made:

		GENERAL JOURNAL		Page 4	
1976 June	30	Unearned Rent	321	100	
		Rent Earned	511		100
		To record revenue earned from rental of trucks during June.			

The revenue element is removed from the mixed account as follows:

Unearned Rent (liability)   **Acct. No. 321**

1976 June	30	(adjustment)	4	100	1976 June	1		1	600

Rent Earned (revenue)   **Acct. No. 511**

					1976 June	30	(adjustment)	4	100

Rent Earned ($100) appears in the income statement as a revenue item, and Unearned Rent ($500) appears in the statement of financial position as a current liability.

Long-Term Cost Apportionment Adjustment—Depreciation—e and f

Two of the remaining adjusting entries involve the recording of long-term asset cost expiration. Three steps similar to the short-term cost apportionments are followed.

(e)

Step 1. The trial balance, Figure 4-1, shows a balance of $1,400 in the Office Equipment account.

Step 2. The equipment, acquired on June 1, is estimated to have a useful life of ten years, or 120 months, and a *salvage value* of $200 at the end of that period. Salvage, or *residual,* value is the estimated price for which an asset may be sold when it is no longer serviceable to the business. In effect, the use of office equipment for ten years has been purchased at a net cost of $1,200 = ($1,400 − $200). A portion of this cost expires in each accounting period during the useful life of the equipment.

Depreciation

This periodic expired cost, called *depreciation expense,* requires no periodic cash outlay, but nevertheless is a continuous expense of operating the business. The portion of the cost of an asset assigned to the accounting period is called *depreciation.* A number of methods may be used in calculating the periodic depreciation charge.

Depreciation expense for the month of June is computed in this case by using the *straight-line method,* in which a uniform portion of the cost is assigned to each period.

$$\frac{\text{Cost} - \text{Salvage value}}{\text{Estimated months of useful life}} = \text{Depreciation for month}$$

The depreciation expense for the office equipment in June is computed as $10.

$$\frac{\$1,400 - \$200}{120} = \$10$$

Step 3. The following adjusting entry is made:

GENERAL JOURNAL				Page 4	
1976 June	30	Depreciation Expense— Office Equipment	609	10	
		Accumulated Depreciation— Office Equipment	201A		10
		To record depreciation for June.			

Both of the foregoing accounts are new accounts.

Contra Account

The second is called an *asset valuation* account or *contra-asset* account, because its balance is deducted from Office Equipment to show the book value, or carrying value, of the asset.

(Ch. 4)

Office Equipment could be credited directly, because the depreciation represents a decrease in the asset; but this procedure is undesirable because it fails to disclose information that is useful to management. Depreciation is an estimate; it is informative to keep asset costs separate from estimated reductions in cost. When separate accounts are used, the original cost and the accumulated depreciation can be determined readily. The June 30 adjusting information is shown in the following ledger accounts:

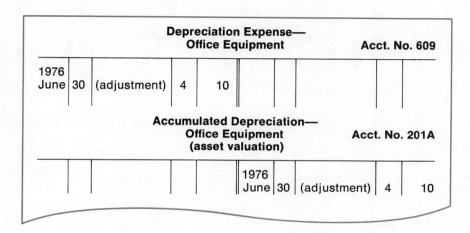

In the statement of financial position (Figure 4-9), the asset valuation account Accumulated Depreciation–Office Equipment is deducted from Office Equipment; the remainder is the *undepreciated cost,* that is, the portion of the cost of the asset that is not yet charged to expense. Depreciation Expense–Office Equipment ($10) is shown in the income statement as an expense.

(f)

Step 1. On June 1, the Connolly Trucking Company purchased two trucks for business use, each costing $6,500. Because the useful life of the trucks is limited, a portion of the cost is allocable to the month of June. It is estimated that their useful life is five years, or 60 months, at the end of which time each truck will have a salvage value of $500.

Step 2. The computation and recording of the depreciation expense for the trucks is similar to that for the office equipment. The depreciation expense for June for the two trucks is calculated by the straight-line method as follows:

$$\frac{\text{Cost of \$6,500} - \text{Salvage value of \$500}}{60 \text{ months}}$$

$$= \$100 \text{ depreciation per month for each truck,}$$
or $200 for two trucks

Step 3. The following adjusting entry is made on June 30 and posted to the accounts shown below the journal entry:

(Ch. 4)

GENERAL JOURNAL   **Page 4**

1976					
June	30	Depreciation Expense—Trucks	610	200	
		Accumulated Depreciation—			
		Trucks	211A		200
		To record depreciation			
		for June.			

Depreciation Expense—Trucks
(expense)   **Acct. No. 610**

1976									
June	30	(adjustment)	4	200					

Accumulated Depreciation—Trucks   **Acct. No. 211A**
(asset valuation)

					1976				
					June	30	(adjustment)	4	200

The classification of these accounts in the financial statements is shown in Figures 4–7 and 4–9.

The Accumulated Depreciation accounts are used to accumulate the periodic charges made to expense and to segregate the deduction for the asset valuation. Depreciation Expense shows the expired cost for the accounting period and is closed along with the other expense accounts in an entry that transfers the total expense to Revenue and Expense Summary. Assume that the same adjusting entry for trucks is made on July 31. After it is posted, the general ledger T accounts for Trucks, Depreciation Expense-Trucks, and Accumulated Depreciation-Trucks appear as follows:

Trucks   **Acct. No. 211**

1976									
June	1		1	13,000					

Accumulated Depreciation—Trucks   **Acct. No. 211A**

					1976				
					June	30		4	200
					July	31		8	200

Depreciation Expense—Trucks									Acct. No. 610
1976 June	30	(adjusting entry)	4	200	1976 June	30	(closing entry)	5	200
1976 July	31	(adjusting entry)	8	200					

The cost of the trucks and the accumulated depreciation are shown on the statement of financial position at July 31 as follows:

Equipment		
Trucks	$13,000	
Deduct Accumulated Depreciation—Trucks	400	$12,600

Accrued Expense Adjustment—g and h

Accrued expenses are expenses that have been incurred in a given period but have not yet been paid. The accountant's job at the end of the accounting period is to record the expense in the proper period of incurrence and also to record the accompanying liability. The accrued expense adjustment described in (g) is that of unrecorded wages expense of $150.

(g)

Step 1. Wages Expense contains two debits of $600 each, representing wages paid biweekly to employees through June 27.

Step 2. The employees earned wages of $150 for work on June 28, 29, and 30, the last three days of the accounting period. Although the company will not pay the employees again until July 11, it has nevertheless incurred $150 of wages expense for these three days, and a $150 liability exists as of June 30.

Step 3. The following adjusting entry is made on June 30 and posted to the accounts shown below the journal entry:

GENERAL JOURNAL					Page 4

1976
June
	30	Wages Expense
		   Accrued Wages Payable
		     To record wages expense
		     accrued during June 28–30,
		     1976.
			605
			311
				150	150

		Wages Expense (expense)			Acct. No. 605		
1976 June	13		2	600			
	27		3	600			
	30	(adjustment)	4	150			

			Accrued Wages Payable (liability)		Acct. No. 311	
			1976 June	30	(adjustment)	4	150

Wages Expense ($1,350) is shown in the income statement as an expense; Accrued Wages Payable ($150) is shown in the statement of financial position as a current liability.

(h)

Step 1. On June 12, the Connolly Trucking Company borrowed $8,000 from the bank and signed a 45-day, 6 percent interest-bearing note payable. This transaction was recorded in the general journal by debiting Cash and crediting Notes Payable for $8,000.

Step 2. The cost of the use of the $8,000—interest expense—continues throughout the 45 days because interest expense accumulates with the passage of time. The total interest expense plus the $8,000 principal amount will be paid to the bank on July 27, the *maturity,* or due, date. However, unpaid interest expense on an interest-bearing note payable for the 18-day period from June 12 through June 30 must be recognized by an adjusting entry debiting Interest Expense and crediting Accrued Interest Payable for $24.

The formula for computing interest is shown in Figure 4-2.

Figure 4-2
Interest Formula

$$\text{Interest} = \text{Principal} \times \text{Interest rate} \times \frac{\text{Elapsed time in days}}{360}$$

The unpaid interest expense accrued on June 30 is computed as follows:

$$\text{Interest} = \$8,000 \times 0.06 \times \frac{18}{360} = \$24$$

The principal multiplied by the interest rate equals the total interest for one year ($8,000 × 0.06 = $480); the interest for a year ($480) multiplied by the elapsed fraction of a year ($18/360$ or $1/20$) is the interest expense for 18 days ($480 × $1/20$), or $24. The use of 360 days in the formula is consistent with commercial practice, the primary reason being simplicity of calculation.

Step 3. The formal adjusting entry is made on June 30 and posted to the accounts indicated below.

BASIC CONCEPTS
AND
METHODOLOGY

(Ch. 4)

GENERAL JOURNAL   Page 5

1976					
June	30	Interest Expense	611	24	
		Accrued Interest Payable	303		24
		To record interest expense			
		accrued during June 12–30,			
		1976.			

Interest Expense (expense)   Acct. No. 611

1976								
June	30	(adjustment)	5	24				

Accrued Interest Payable (liability)   Acct. No. 303

					1976				
					June	30	(adjustment)	5	24

Interest Expense ($24) is reported as an expense in the income statement; Accrued Interest Payable ($24) appears as a current liability in the statement of financial position. This entry gives rise to an *accrued liability.* This term refers to the liability for an expense incurred during one accounting period but payable in a future accounting period. Expenses incurred for which invoices have not yet been received—telephone, heat, light, water, and so on—are also in this category. These may be recorded by debits to appropriate expense accounts and a credit to Accrued Accounts Payable.

Accrued Revenue Adjustment—i

Accrued revenue items are items that have been earned in a given period but for which cash collections have not yet been received. The accountant's job at the end of the accounting period is to record the revenue in the proper period in which it is earned and also to record the accompanying receivable, an asset. The accrued revenue adjustment described in (i) is that of unrecorded earned interest of $4.

(i)

Step 1. The Connolly Trucking Company made a loan of $1,440 to one of its customers, who signed a 30-day, 5 percent interest-bearing note dated June 10. An entry was made debiting Notes Receivable and crediting Cash for $1,440.

Step 2. The company earned interest on the loan for 20 days in June (June 10 through June 30); it will be received on the maturity date, July 10, when the amount due (principal plus total interest) is paid by the customer. Interest earned, like interest expense, accrues with the passage of time. The 20 days' interest earned by June 30 is recorded by an adjusting entry debiting Accrued

Interest Receivable and crediting Interest Earned for $4. Using the formula shown in Figure 4-2, the computation of the interest is

$$\text{Interest} = \$1{,}440 \times 0.05 \times \frac{20}{360} = \$4$$

Step 3. The formal adjusting entry is made on June 30 and posted to the accounts indicated below.

		GENERAL JOURNAL		Page 5	

1976 June	30	Accrued Interest Receivable
		    Interest Earned
		        To record interest revenue
		        accrued during June 10–30,
		        1976.
			113
			521
				4	4

Accrued Interest Receivable (asset)   Acct. No. 113

1976 June	30	(adjustment)	5	4			

Interest Earned (revenue)   Acct. No. 521

			1976 June	30	(adjustment)	5	4

Accrued Interest Receivable ($4) is a current asset in the statement of financial position. Interest Earned is a revenue item in the income statement.

Income Tax Expense Adjustment—j

The income tax expense adjustment is similar to the accrued expense adjustment. A single proprietor or a partner combines his net income from his proprietorship or partnership interest with his income from other sources and computes his tax as an individual taxpayer. A corporation, however, is taxed as a separate entity, and its financial statements must show the tax and the liability for the tax.

(j)

Step 1. It is difficult to determine precisely the tax related to the taxable income for the month of June, because the annual taxable income, on which the tax is based, is not yet known. Nevertheless, the business must make the best possible estimate.

Step 2. The Connolly Trucking Company estimates its income taxes for the month of June to be $1,900.

Step 3. The income tax estimate is journalized on June 30 and posted to the accounts indicated below the general journal.

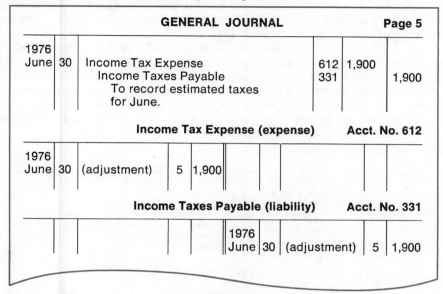

			GENERAL JOURNAL			Page 5
1976						
June	30	Income Tax Expense	612	1,900	
		Income Taxes Payable	331		1,900
		To record estimated taxes for June.			

Income Tax Expense (expense)   **Acct. No. 612**

1976				
June	30	(adjustment)	5	1,900

Income Taxes Payable (liability)   **Acct. No. 331**

			1976				
			June	30	(adjustment)	5	1,900

The income tax expense of $1,900 appears in the income statement; it is deducted from net income before income taxes to determine net income after income taxes (Figure 4-7); Income Taxes Payable appears in the statement of financial position as a current liability.

THE WORK SHEET

The work sheet is a device used by the accountant to facilitate the preparation of the formal financial statements; it is not a substitute for the financial statements. Although the work sheet is not indispensable, it would be difficult in most instances to prepare the statements directly from the journals and ledgers, since that would often require consolidating material from books, cards, and other documents. The work sheet bridges the gap between the accounting records and the formal statements and serves as a convenient device to calculate the effect of the adjustments and to determine the net income, or net loss, before the adjustments are formally entered in the books and posted to the ledger. It furnishes the accountant with a preview of the final statements. Many businesses do not formally close their books at the end of every accounting period; thus, the work sheet substitutes for the formal procedure of recording and posting the usual adjusting and closing entries.

PREPARATION OF THE WORK SHEET

Preparation of the work sheet consists of four steps.
Step 1. The work sheet is headed to show the name of the company, the name of the statement, and the accounting period; the column headings are

entered; the trial balance account titles and amounts are entered either directly from the general ledger or from a prepared listing, if available. The account titles are entered in the space provided and the amounts are entered in the first pair of money columns. The work sheet of the Connolly Trucking Company after completion of step 1 appears in Figure 4-3.

Step 2. The adjustments are entered on the work sheet generally before they are formally journalized. This procedure is followed partly to hasten the preparation of the formal financial statements.

The adjustments are keyed for identification (cross referencing) as they are entered in the Adjustments columns. Any additional accounts required by the adjusting entries are written in below the trial balance. (Alternatively, they may

Figure 4-3 Work Sheet, Step 1: Trial Balance Entered

		CONNOLLY TRUCKING COMPANY Work Sheet For Month Ended June 30, 1976									
Acct. No.	Account Title	Trial Balance		Adjustments		Adjusted Trial Balance		Income Statement		Position Statement	
		Dr.	Cr.	Dr.	Cr.	Dr.	Cr.	Dr.	Cr.	Dr.	Cr.
101	Cash	5,250									
111	Accounts Receivable	550									
112	Notes Receivable	1,440									
131	Office Supplies	230									
141	Prepaid Insurance	2,160									
142	Prepaid Rent	1,500									
201	Office Equipment	1,400									
211	Trucks	13,000									
301	Accounts Payable		200								
302	Notes Payable		8,000								
321	Unearned Rent		600								
401	Capital Stock, 1,000 shares outstanding		12,000								
404	Dividends	500									
501	Trucking Revenue		7,465								
601	Heat and Light Expense	40									
602	Maintenance and Repairs Expense	375									
603	Telephone and Telegraph Expense	95									
604	Gas and Oil Expense	525									
605	Wages Expense	1,200									
	Totals	28,265	28,265								

Trial balance before adjustments.

(Ch. 4)

be listed in sequence with the other accounts without amounts in the Trial Balance columns.) In entry (a), for example, Rent Expense is debited for $500. Since this account does not appear in the trial balance, the title is written on the line immediately below the trial balance totals and the amount is entered directly in the Adjustments Debit column on the same line; the $500 is also entered in the Adjustments Credit column opposite Prepaid Rent. In this adjustment, only one of the accounts involved had to be written in below the trial balance. In entry (e), however, both the debited and the credited accounts had to be written in. After all the adjustments are entered, the Adjustments columns are added as a proof of their equality. Following the completion of step 2 the work sheet appears as shown in Figure 4-4.

Step 3. The amounts extended to the Adjusted Trial Balance columns result from combining the amounts in the Trial Balance columns with the amounts in the Adjustments columns as follows:

a. If there are no adjustments to an account, a debit trial balance amount is extended to the Debit column of the adjusted trial balance, and a credit trial balance amount is extended to the Credit column of the adjusted trial balance.

b. If the account in the trial balance has a debit balance, add its debit adjustments and subtract its credit adjustments. The balance, if a debit, is extended to the Adjusted Trial Balance Debit column; if a credit, it is extended to the Credit column.

c. If the account in the trial balance has a credit balance, add its credit adjustments and subtract its debit adjustments. The adjusted balance is extended to the proper Adjusted Trial Balance column.

d. For the accounts listed below the trial balance totals, the adjustment amount is extended directly to the appropriate Adjusted Trial Balance column.

On completion of step 3, the adjusted trial balance figures will be the same as the balances of the accounts in the general ledger after the adjusting entries have been journalized and posted. Each line on the work sheet represents a general ledger account and functions in the same manner as to the debit and credit position. For example, after adjustment, the Prepaid Rent account appears in the general ledger as follows:

					Prepaid Rent			Acct. No. 142
1976 June	1		1	1,500	1976 June	30	(adjusting entry) 4	500

The new balance is a debit of $1,000, which is the amount shown opposite Prepaid Rent in the Adjusted Trial Balance Debit column of the work sheet.

Following the completion of step 3 the work sheet is shown in Figure 4-5.

Step 4. The amounts in the Adjusted Trial Balance columns are extended either to the Income Statement columns or to the Position Statement columns, depending on their statement classification. Expense and revenue accounts are entered in the Income Statement columns; asset, liability, and stockholders' equity accounts are entered in the Position Statement columns. The four columns are then totaled. The difference between the totals of the Income State-

Figure 4-4 Work Sheet, Step 2: Adjustments Entered

CONNOLLY TRUCKING COMPANY
Work Sheet
For Month Ended June 30, 1976

Acct. No.	Account Title	Trial Balance Dr.	Trial Balance Cr.	Adjustments Dr.	Adjustments Cr.	Adjusted Trial Balance Dr.	Adjusted Trial Balance Cr.	Income Statement Dr.	Income Statement Cr.	Position Statement Dr.	Position Statement Cr.
101	Cash	5,250									
111	Accounts Receivable	550									
112	Notes Receivable	1,440									
131	Office Supplies	230			(c) 170						
141	Prepaid Insurance	2,160			(b) 60						
142	Prepaid Rent	1,500			(a) 500						
201	Office Equipment	1,400									
211	Trucks	13,000									
301	Accounts Payable		200								
302	Notes Payable		8,000								
321	Unearned Rent		600	(d) 100							
401	Capital Stock, 1,000 shares outstanding		12,000								
404	Dividends	500									
501	Trucking Revenue		7,465								
601	Heat and Light Expense	40									
602	Maintenance and Repairs Expense	375									
603	Telephone and Telegraph Expense	95									
604	Gas and Oil Expense	525									
605	Wages Expense	1,200		(g) 150							
	Totals	28,265	28,265								
606	Rent Expense			(a) 500							
607	Insurance Expense			(b) 60							
608	Office Supplies Expense			(c) 170							
511	Rent Earned				(d) 100						
609	Depreciation Expense—Office Equipment			(e) 10							
201A	Accumulated Depreciation—Office Equipment				(e) 10						
610	Depreciation Expense—Trucks			(f) 200							
211A	Accumulated Depreciation—Trucks				(f) 200						
311	Accrued Wages Payable				(g) 150						
611	Interest Expense			(h) 24							
303	Accrued Interest Payable				(h) 24						
113	Accrued Interest Receivable			(i) 4							
521	Interest Earned				(i) 4						
612	Income Tax Expense			(j) 1,900							
331	Income Taxes Payable				(j) 1,900						
	Totals			3,118	3,118						

Letters are used to cross reference the debit and credit adjustments.

Additional accounts for the adjustments.

Adjustments are entered in these columns.

Figure 4-5 Work Sheet, Step 3: Adjusted Trial Balance Entered

Acct. No.	Account Title	Trial Balance Dr.	Trial Balance Cr.	Adjustments Dr.	Adjustments Cr.	Adjusted Trial Balance Dr.	Adjusted Trial Balance Cr.	Income Statement Dr.	Income Statement Cr.	Position Statement Dr.	Position Statement Cr.
	CONNOLLY TRUCKING COMPANY Work Sheet For Month Ended June 30, 1976										
101	Cash	5,250				5,250					
111	Accounts Receivable	550				550					
112	Notes Receivable	1,440				1,440					
131	Office Supplies	230			(c) 170	60					
141	Prepaid Insurance	2,160			(b) 60	2,100					
142	Prepaid Rent	1,500			(a) 500	1,000					
201	Office Equipment	1,400				1,400					
211	Trucks	13,000				13,000					
301	Accounts Payable		200				200				
302	Notes Payable		8,000				8,000				
321	Unearned Rent		600	(d) 100			500				
401	Capital Stock, 1,000 shares outstanding		12,000				12,000				
404	Dividends	500				500					
501	Trucking Revenue		7,465				7,465				
601	Heat and Light Expense	40				40					
602	Maintenance and Repairs Expense	375				375					
603	Telephone and Telegraph Expense	95				95					
604	Gas and Oil Expense	525				525					
605	Wages Expense	1,200		(g) 150		1,350					
	Totals	28,265	28,265								
606	Rent Expense			(a) 500		500					
607	Insurance Expense			(b) 60		60					
608	Office Supplies Expense			(c) 170		170					
511	Rent Earned				(d) 100		100				
609	Depreciation Expense— Office Equipment			(e) 10		10					
201A	Accumulated Depreciation —Office Equipment				(e) 10		10				
610	Depreciation Expense— Trucks			(f) 200		200					
211A	Accumulated Depreciation —Trucks				(f) 200		200				
311	Accrued Wages Payable				(g) 150		150				
611	Interest Expense			(h) 24		24					
303	Accrued Interest Payable				(h) 24		24				
113	Accrued Interest Receivable			(i) 4		4					
521	Interest Earned				(i) 4		4				
612	Income Tax Expense			(j) 1,900		1,900					
331	Income Taxes Payable				(j) 1,900		1,900				
	Totals			3,118	3,118	30,553	30,553				

Balances from the trial balance, adjusted by the amounts in Adjustments columns, are extended here.

Figure 4-6 Work Sheet, Step 4: Remaining Extensions Made

CONNOLLY TRUCKING COMPANY
Work Sheet
For Month Ended June 30, 1976

Acct. No.	Account Title	Trial Balance Dr.	Trial Balance Cr.	Adjustments Dr.	Adjustments Cr.	Adjusted Trial Balance Dr.	Adjusted Trial Balance Cr.	Income Statement Dr.	Income Statement Cr.	Position Statement Dr.	Position Statement Cr.
101	Cash	5,250				5,250				5,250	
111	Accounts Receivable	550				550				550	
112	Notes Receivable	1,440				1,440				1,440	
131	Office Supplies	230			(c) 170	60				60	
141	Prepaid Insurance	2,160			(b) 60	2,100				2,100	
142	Prepaid Rent	1,500			(a) 500	1,000				1,000	
201	Office Equipment	1,400				1,400				1,400	
211	Trucks	13,000				13,000				13,000	
301	Accounts Payable		200				200				200
302	Notes Payable		8,000				8,000				8,000
321	Unearned Rent		600	(d) 100			500				500
401	Capital Stock, 1,000 shares outstanding		12,000				12,000				12,000
404	Dividends	500				500				500	
501	Trucking Revenue		7,465				7,465		7,465		
601	Heat and Light Expense	40				40		40			
602	Maintenance and Repairs Expense	375				375		375			
603	Telephone and Telegraph Expense	95				95		95			
604	Gas and Oil Expense	525				525		525			
605	Wages Expense	1,200		(g) 150		1,350		1,350			
	Totals	28,265	28,265								
606	Rent Expense			(a) 500		500		500			
607	Insurance Expense			(b) 60		60		60			
608	Office Supplies Expense			(c) 170		170		170			
511	Rent Earned				(d) 100		100		100		
609	Depreciation Expense— Office Equipment			(e) 10		10		10			
201A	Accumulated Depreciation —Office Equipment				(e) 10		10				10
610	Depreciation Expense— Trucks			(f) 200		200		200			
211A	Accumulated Depreciation —Trucks				(f) 200		200				200
311	Accrued Wages Payable				(g) 150		150				150
611	Interest Expense			(h) 24		24		24			
303	Accrued Interest Payable				(h) 24		24				24
113	Accrued Interest Receivable			(i) 4		4				4	
521	Interest Earned				(i) 4		4		4		
612	Income Tax Expense			(j) 1,900		1,900		1,900			
331	Income Taxes Payable				(j) 1,900		1,900				1,900
	Totals			3,118	3,118	30,553	30,553	5,249	7,569	25,304	22,984
	Net Income for Month							2,320			2,320
	Totals							7,569	7,569	25,304	25,304

The difference between the Income Statement columns is net income.

Net income is transferred to the Position Statement Credit column.

ment columns is the net income, or net loss, for the period; a net income is indicated if the total of the Credit column exceeds the total of the Debit column. The excess is entered in the Income Statement Debit column and in the Position Statement Credit column just below the column totals. This procedure records on the work sheet the increase in the stockholders' equity resulting from an excess of revenue over expenses during the period. A net loss is indicated if the total of the Income Statement Debit column exceeds that of the Income Statement Credit column. A loss is shown on the work sheet in the Income Statement Credit column and the Position Statement Debit column just below the column totals. The designation Net Income, or Net Loss, for the Month, whichever is pertinent, is entered in the Account Title column on the same line. Following the completion of step 4, the work sheet is illustrated in Figure 4-6.

If the differences between the Income Statement Debit and Credit columns (net income) and the Position Statement Debit and Credit columns are not the same, an error has been made. The totaling and ruling of the last four columns of the work sheet (step 4) is illustrated in Figure 4-6. Note that balancing the last four columns provides only a limited proof of the accuracy of the work sheet—proof that the equality of debits and credits has been maintained throughout its preparation. The extension of the Cash account debit into the Income Statement Debit column, for example, would not destroy the debit-credit relationship of the work sheet, although statements prepared from that work sheet would be inaccurate. Note also that the total of the Position Statement Debit column need not correspond with the total assets reported in the statement. Accumulated Depreciation—Trucks, for example, is extended to the Position Statement Credit column because it represents a position statement account with a credit balance. It is neither an asset nor a liability, but rather a deduction from Trucks, which is extended into the Position Statement Debit column. Since plus and minus symbols are not used on the work sheet, a deduction from an amount in a Debit column is effected by positioning the item to be deducted in the Credit column.

The work sheet may be varied in form—particularly with respect to the number of columns—to meet specific needs of the user. In Figure 5-3, for example, the columns for the adjusted trial balance are omitted.

Preparation of Financial Statements from the Work Sheet

The income statement is prepared from the amounts in the Income Statement columns of the work sheet; the statement of financial position and the statement of retained earnings are prepared from the amounts in the Position Statement columns of the work sheet. In the preparation of financial statements, care should be taken to use each amount just once and in its proper debit and credit relation. The debit-credit relationship is not emphasized by the statements, but it is present. In the statement of financial position, for example, Accumulated Depreciation—Trucks, with a credit balance of $200, is deducted from Trucks, which has a debit balance. Net income (or loss) appears in both the income statement and the statement of retained earnings.

The financial statements of the Connolly Trucking Company for June are shown in Figures 4-7, 4-8, and 4-9. The computation and significance of the items in the Percent columns are discussed later in this chapter. Some form of designation should be used to identify and cross-reference the financial statements; the following is one possibility

Exhibit A for the income statement
Exhibit B for the statement of retained earnings
Exhibit C for the statement of financial position

Figure 4-7
Income Statement

CONNOLLY TRUCKING COMPANY Income Statement For the Month Ended June 30, 1976		Exhibit A
		Percent
Revenue		
Trucking Revenue	$7,465	
Interest Earned	4	
Rent Earned	100	
Total Revenues	$7,569	100.0
Expenses		
Heat and Light Expense	$ 40	0.5
Maintenance and Repairs Expense	375	5.0
Telephone and Telegraph Expense	95	1.3
Gas and Oil Expense	525	6.9
Wages Expense	1,350	17.8
Rent Expense	500	6.6
Insurance Expense	60	0.8
Office Supplies Expense	170	2.3
Depreciation Expense—Office Equipment	10	0.1
Depreciation Expense—Trucks	200	2.6
Interest Expense	24	0.3
Total Expenses	3,349	44.2
Net Income before Income Taxes	$4,220	55.8
Income Tax Expense	1,900	25.1
Net Income after Income Taxes—To Exhibit B	$2,320	30.7
Net Income per Share: $0.23		

Figure 4-8
Statement of
Retained Earnings

CONNOLLY TRUCKING COMPANY Statement of Retained Earnings For the Month Ended June 30, 1976	Exhibit B
Net Income for Month of June, 1976—Exhibit A	$2,320
Deduct Dividends	500
Retained Earnings, June 30, 1976—To Exhibit C	$1,820

Figure 4-9
Statement of
Financial Position

CONNOLLY TRUCKING COMPANY   Exhibit C
Statement of Financial Position
June 30, 1976

Assets

			Percent
Current Assets			
Cash		$ 5,250	21.3
Accounts Receivable		550	2.2
Notes Receivable		1,440	5.9
Accrued Interest Receivable		4	–0–
Office Supplies		60	0.2
Prepaid Insurance		2,100	8.5
Prepaid Rent		1,000	4.1
Total Current Assets		$10,404	42.2
Equipment			
Office Equipment	$ 1,400		
Deduct Accumulated			
Depreciation	10	$ 1,390	5.7
Trucks	$13,000		
Deduct Accumulated			
Depreciation	200	12,800	52.1
Total Equipment		14,190	57.8
Total Assets		$24,594	100.0

Liabilities and Stockholders' Equity

Current Liabilities			
Accounts Payable	$ 200		0.8
Notes Payable	8,000		32.5
Accrued Interest Payable	24		0.1
Accrued Wages Payable	150		0.6
Unearned Rent	500		2.1
Income Taxes Payable	1,900		7.7
Total Current Liabilities		$10,774	43.8
Stockholders' Equity			
Capital Stock	$12,000		48.8
Retained Earnings—Exhibit B	1,820		7.4
Total Stockholders' Equity		13,820	56.2
Total Liabilities and Stockholders' Equity		$24,594	100.0

Since the company was organized on June 1, 1976, it had no beginning balance in the Retained Earnings account; therefore, this item does not appear in the statement.

RECORDING ADJUSTMENTS IN THE GENERAL JOURNAL

If formal adjusting entries are not recorded in the general journal until after the financial statements have been prepared, the adjusting entries may be taken directly from the Adjustments columns of the work sheet and dated as of the last day of the accounting period. The caption "Adjusting Entries" is written

Figure 4-10
Adjusting Entries

GENERAL JOURNAL			Page 4	
1976		*Adjusting Entries*		
June	30	Rent Expense	606	500	
		Prepaid Rent	142		500
		To record rent expense for June.			
	30	Insurance Expense	607	60	
		Prepaid Insurance	141		60
		To record insurance expense for June.			
	30	Office Supplies Expense	608	170	
		Office Supplies	131		170
		To record supplies used during June.			
	30	Unearned Rent	321	100	
		Rent Earned	511		100
		To record revenue earned from rental of trucks during June.			
	30	Depreciation Expense—			
		Office Equipment	609	10	
		Accumulated Depreciation—			
		Office Equipment	201A		10
		To record the depreciation for June.			
	30	Depreciation Expense—Trucks	610	200	
		Accumulated Depreciation—			
		Trucks	211A		200
		To record the depreciation for June.			
	30	Wages Expense	605	150	
		Accrued Wages Payable	311		150
		To record wages expense accrued during June.			

GENERAL JOURNAL					Page 5
1976					
June	30	Interest Expense	611	24	
		Accrued Interest Payable	303		24
		To record interest expense accrued during June.			
	30	Accrued Interest Receivable	113	4	
		Interest Earned	521		4
		To record interest revenue accrued during June.			
	30	Income Tax Expense	612	1,900	
		Income Taxes Payable	331		1,900
		To record estimated taxes for June.			

in the general journal on the line following the last regular general journal entry. After the adjusting entries have been posted, the general ledger account balances will correspond with the amounts in the Adjusted Trial Balance columns of the work sheet. Although the adjusting entries for the Connolly Trucking Company have already been made as they were introduced, to add realism to the accounting job, they are collected and repeated in Figure 4-10. The account numbers in the folio column indicate that they have been posted.

THE RESULT OF ADJUSTING ENTRIES

When all the adjusting entries are recorded in the journal and posted to the general ledger, the mixed elements in the accounts have been eliminated. Accounts consisting of asset and expense elements and accounts containing liability and revenue elements are apportioned so that each element is recorded in a separate account; advance payments for goods and services to be consumed in the future are shown in the appropriate asset accounts; advance receipts for future revenue are shown in liability accounts; and all other supplementary data not previously recorded but necessary for the preparation of financial statements are available in the ledger. The general ledger should contain all the accounts and amounts—expense, revenue, asset, liability, and stockholders' equity—necessary for the presentation of the financial position of the company as of the end of the accounting period and the results of its operations for the period then ended. Failure to adjust a mixed asset or liability account results in incorrect financial statements; failure to disclose all information may result in misleading financial statements.

The need for adjustment, however, and the need for full disclosure do not apply to insignificant, immaterial, or trivial matters.

Materiality

The box of paper clips in the bookkeeper's desk as of the position statement date is an asset of the company, although it has been charged to expense. It is possible, but impractical, to ascertain the asset value of the unused clips and make a corresponding adjusting entry. Because of the insignificance of the unused paper clips, failure to make the adjustment will have no material effect on the financial statements and cannot mislead the user of such statements. A similar situation exists with respect to other minor items of supply or services. The accountant is faced with the problem of determining the line between what is material and what is immaterial—making a value judgment. An item costing $100 may be material in a small business, whereas an item costing $1,000 may be insignificant in a multimillion-dollar business. It is not misleading to combine several insignificant items of expense or revenue into one account;

Figure 4-11
Closing Entries

GENERAL JOURNAL				Page 5
1976		*Closing Entries*		
June	30	Trucking Revenue	501	7,465	
		Rent Earned	511	100	
		Interest Earned	521	4	
		Income Summary	902		7,569
		To close.			
	30	Income Summary	902	5,249	
		Heat and Light Expense	601		40
		Maintenance and Repairs Expense	602		375
		Telephone and Telegraph Expense	603		95
		Gas and Oil Expense	604		525
		Wages Expense	605		1,350
		Rent Expense	606		500
		Insurance Expense	607		60
		Office Supplies Expense	608		170
		Depreciation Expense— Office Equipment	609		10
		Depreciation Expense— Trucks	610		200
		Interest Expense	611		24
		Income Tax Expense	612		1,900
		To close.			
	30	Income Summary	902	2,320	
		Retained Earnings	403		2,320
		To transfer net income to Retained Earnings.			
	30	Retained Earnings	403	500	
		Dividends	404		500
		To close.			

it is misleading, however, to combine a significant loss from a lawsuit with an operating expense account. It may be necessary to disclose an item of an essential nature, regardless of its amount.

CLOSING ENTRIES MAY BE RECORDED DIRECTLY FROM THE WORK SHEET

The caption "Closing Entries" is written in the middle of the first unused line on the journal page under the adjusting entries. The closing entries are recorded (Figure 4-11) and are then posted to the general ledger. They are made directly from the work sheet in the following sequence.

Entry 1. Each account in the Income Statement Credit column is debited, and the sum of the debits is credited to the Income Summary account.

Entry 2. Each account in the Income Statement Debit column is credited, and the sum of the credits is debited to the Income Summary account.

Entry 3. The balance of Income Summary, which, after posting entries 1 and 2, represents the net income or the net loss as shown on the work sheet, is transferred to Retained Earnings.

Entry 4. The balance of the Dividends account is closed into Retained Earnings; the amount of this entry is the amount on the Dividends account line in the Position Statement Debit column of the work sheet.

THE GENERAL LEDGER

The general ledger of the Connolly Trucking Company is reproduced after the adjusting entries and the closing entries have been posted. In reproducing the general ledger, exact dates are used when the information is given in the previous discussion. Otherwise the date of June 30 and the balance of the account as taken from the trial balance in Figure 4-1 are inserted because the detailed transactions were omitted from this example. The notations Balance, A.E. (for adjusting entry), and C.E. (for closing entry) are shown in the Explanation column as an aid in tracing the amounts to their sources. A check mark indicates that the amount was not posted from the journal in this particular illustration.

GENERAL LEDGER

Cash   Acct. No. 101

| 1976 June | 30 | Balance | ✔ | 5,250 | | | |

Accounts Receivable — Acct. No. 111

1976								
June	30	Balance	✓	550				

Notes Receivable — Acct. No. 112

1976								
June	10		2	1,440				

Accrued Interest Receivable — Acct. No. 113

1976								
June	30	A.E.	5	4				

Office Supplies — Acct. No. 131

1976						1976				
June	6		1	230	June	30	A.E.	4	170
						30	Balance	✓	60
				230					230
1976									
June	30	Balance	✓	60					

Prepaid Insurance — Acct. No. 141

1976					1976				
June	1		1	2,160	June	30	A.E.	4	60
						30	Balance	✓	2,100
				2,160					2,160
1976									
June	30	Balance	✓	2,100					

Prepaid Rent — Acct. No. 142

1976					1976				
June	1		1	1,500	June	30	A.E.	4	500
						30	Balance	✓	1,000
				1,500					1,500
1976									
June	30	Balance	✓	1,000					

Office Equipment   Acct. No. 201

Date			Ref	Amount		Date			Ref	Amount
1976 June	1		1	1,400						

Accumulated Depreciation— Office Equipment   Acct. No. 201A

Date			Ref	Amount		Date			Ref	Amount
						1976 June	30	A.E.	4	10

Trucks   Acct. No. 211

Date			Ref	Amount		Date			Ref	Amount
1976 June	1		1	13,000						

Accumulated Depreciation— Trucks   Acct. No. 211A

Date			Ref	Amount		Date			Ref	Amount
						1976 June	30	A.E.	4	200

Accounts Payable   Acct. No. 301

Date			Ref	Amount		Date			Ref	Amount
						1976 June	30	Balance	✔	200

Notes Payable   Acct. No. 302

Date			Ref	Amount		Date			Ref	Amount
						1976 June	12		2	8,000

Accrued Interest Payable   Acct. No. 303

Date			Ref	Amount		Date			Ref	Amount
						1976 June	30	A.E.	5	24

Accrued Wages Payable   Acct. No. 311

Date			Ref	Amount		Date			Ref	Amount
						1976 June	30	A.E.	4	150

Unearned Rent — Acct. No. 321

1976						1976					
June	30	A.E.	4	100		June	1			1	600
	30	Balance	✔	500							
				600							600
						1976					
						June	30	Balance	✔		500

Income Taxes Payable — Acct. No. 331

						1976					
						June	30	A.E.	5	1,900

Capital Stock — Acct. No. 401

						1976					
						June	1			1	12,000

Retained Earnings — Acct. No. 403

1976						1976					
June	30	C.E.	5	500		June	30	C.E.	5	2,320
	30	Balance	✔	1,820							
				2,320							2,320
						1976					
						June	30	Balance	✔		1,820

Dividends — Acct. No. 404

1976						1976					
June	30	Balance	✔	500		June	30	C.E.	5	500

Trucking Revenue — Acct. No. 501

1976						1976					
June	30	C.E.	5	7,465		June	30	Balance	✔		7,465

Rent Earned — Acct. No. 511

1976						1976					
June	30	C.E.	5	100		June	30	A.E.	4	100

Interest Earned   Acct. No. 521

1976					1976				
June	30	C.E.	5	4	June	30	A.E.	5	4

Heat and Light Expense   Acct. No. 601

1976					1976				
June	30	Balance	✔	40	June	30	C.E.	5	40

Maintenance and Repairs Expense   Acct. No. 602

1976					1976				
June	30	Balance	✔	375	June	30	C.E.	5	375

Telephone and Telegraph Expense   Acct. No. 603

1976					1976				
June	30	Balance	✔	95	June	30	C.E.	5	95

Gas and Oil Expense   Acct. No. 604

1976					1976				
June	30	Balance	✔	525	June	30	C.E.	5	525

Wages Expense   Acct. No. 605

1976					1976				
June	13		2	600	June	30	C.E.	5	1.350
	27		3	600					
	30	A.E.	4	150					
				1,350					1,350

Rent Expense   Acct. No. 606

1976					1976				
June	30	A.E.	4	500	June	30	C.E.	5	500

Insurance Expense   Acct. No. 607

1976					1976				
June	30	A.E.	4	60	June	30	C.E.	5	60

BASIC MODEL:
END-OF-PERIOD

Office Supplies Expense   Acct. No. 608

1976 June	30	A.E.	4	170	1976 June	30	C.E.	5	170

Depreciation Expense—Office Equipment   Acct. No. 609

1976 June	30	A.E.	4	10	1976 June	30	C.E.	5	10

Depreciation Expense—Trucks   Acct. No. 610

1976 June	30	A.E.	4	200	1976 June	30	C.E.	5	200

Interest Expense   Acct. No. 611

1976 June	30	A.E.	5	24	1976 June	30	C.E.	5	24

Income Tax Expense   Acct. No. 612

1976 June	30	A.E.	5	1,900	1976 June	30	C.E.	5	1,900

Income Summary   Acct. No. 902

1976 June	30	C.E.	5	5,249	1976 June	30	C.E.	5	7,569
	30	C.E.	5	2,320					
				7,569					7,569

THE POSTCLOSING TRIAL BALANCE

The postclosing trial balance of the Connolly Trucking Company, taken from the general ledger, is shown in Figure 4-12.

Figure 4-12
Postclosing Trial
Balance

CONNOLLY TRUCKING COMPANY
Postclosing Trial Balance
June 30, 1976

Acct. No.	Account Title	Debits	Credits
101	Cash	$ 5,250	
111	Accounts Receivable	550	
112	Notes Receivable	1,440	
113	Accrued Interest Receivable	4	
131	Office Supplies	60	
141	Prepaid Insurance	2,100	
142	Prepaid Rent	1,000	
201	Office Equipment	1,400	
201A	Accumulated Depreciation—Office Equipment		$ 10
211	Trucks	13,000	
211A	Accumulated Depreciation—Trucks		200
301	Accounts Payable		200
302	Notes Payable		8,000
303	Accrued Interest Payable		24
311	Accrued Wages Payable		150
321	Unearned Rent		500
331	Income Taxes Payable		1,900
401	Capital Stock		12,000
403	Retained Earnings		1,820
	Totals	$24,804	$24,804

THE ACCOUNTING CYCLE

In this chapter and the preceding one, the complete *accounting cycle* of a service business concern has been presented. The cycle consists of a series of steps.

1. *Selecting an appropriate chart of accounts,* which consists of selecting the accounts that are likely to be needed for financial statements and designating a numerical index system for these accounts.
2. *Journalizing,* which consists of analyzing and recording transactions in chronological order in the journal.
3. *Posting,* which consists of transferring debits and credits to the appropriate ledgers and to the proper accounts in the ledgers.
4. *Preparing a trial balance,* or summarizing the general ledger accounts to test the equality of debits and credits.
5. *Preparing a schedule of accounts receivable,* which is summarizing the accounts receivable ledger accounts and reconciling the total with the balance of the Accounts Receivable controlling account in the general ledger.
6. *Preparing a schedule of accounts payable,* which is summarizing the accounts payable ledger accounts and reconciling the total with the

balance of the Accounts Payable controlling account in the general ledger.

7. *Preparing the work sheet,* or assembling and classifying information in columnar form to facilitate the preparation of financial statements.
8. *Preparing the financial statements* from the work sheet; these are the income statement, statement of retained earnings, and statement of financial position.
9. *Adjusting the books,* or recording and posting the adjusting entries from the work sheet.
10. *Closing the books,* which consists of recording and posting the closing entries from the Income Statement columns of the work sheet.
11. *Balancing and ruling the real accounts* and bringing the balances forward for the new accounting period.
12. *Taking a postclosing trial balance,* or totaling the open-account balances to prove the equality of the debits and credits in the general ledger.
13. *Analyzing and interpreting the financial statements* by developing percentages, ratios, and other indicators, to make the statements more meaningful.

SPLIT ENTRIES

PURPOSE OF SPLIT ENTRIES

The adjusting entries are recorded in the general journal and posted to the general ledger. Three of the adjusting entries—g, h, and i—involve the accrual of previously unrecorded revenue or expense items assignable to June and require a split form of entry in July, when the transaction cycle culminates in the receipt or payment of cash.

Paying the Accrued Wages Payable

The next regular pay day at the Connolly Trucking Company is on July 11. On July 1, Wages Expense had a zero balance as a result of the closing entries on June 30 but the Accrued Wages Payable account had a credit balance of $150 as a result of the adjusting entries. Assuming that the biweekly wages again amounted to $600, the entry on July 11 to record this payment is

GENERAL JOURNAL				Page 5	
1976 July	11	Accrued Wages Payable		150	
		Wages Expense		450	
		Cash			600
		To record the payment of			
		biweekly wages.			

The result of this entry is to split the biweekly wages of $600 so that $150, which was recognized as a June expense, is debited to Accrued Wages Payable and $450 is recorded as an expense in July. Accrued Wages Payable now has a zero balance.

Paying the Accrued Interest Payable

On the maturity date of the note payable, July 27 (45 days, including 18 days accrued in June), the Connolly Trucking Company pays the bank $8,060, the maturity value. The amount consists of $8,000 principal plus $60, which is 45 days' interest at 6 percent on $8,000, calculated as follows:

$$\text{Interest} = \$8,000 \times 0.06 \times \frac{45}{360} = \$60$$

The entry to record the payment to the bank is

		GENERAL JOURNAL			Page 5
1976 July	27	Notes Payable		8,000	
		Accrued Interest Payable		24	
		Interest Expense		36	
		Cash			8,060
		To record the payment of a			
		note payable.			

The adjusting entry on June 30 allocated 18 days' interest expense ($24) on the note to the month of June. The July entry splits the total interest of $60 so that the $24 liability applicable to June is canceled and the remaining $36 = ($60 − $24) is recorded as interest expense for 27 days in July.

Receiving the Accrued Interest Receivable

On the maturity date of the note receivable, July 10 (30 days, including 20 days accrued in June), the Connolly Trucking Company receives the maturity value, $1,446. The maturity value is determined by adding to the principal, $1,440, 30 days' interest at 5 percent, or $6, computed as follows:

$$\text{Interest} = \$1,440 \times 0.05 \times \frac{30}{360} = \$6$$

The entry to record the receipt from the customer is

GENERAL JOURNAL					Page 5	
1976 July	10	Cash		1,446		
		Notes Receivable				1,440
		Accrued Interest Receivable				4
		Interest Earned				2
		To record the collection of a note receivable.				

On June 30, the adjusting entry accrued 20 days' interest earned on the note, or $4, in June. The total interest earned of $6 is split by the July entry so that the $4 asset, Accrued Interest Receivable, is canceled and the balance of $2 = ($6 − $4) is entered as interest earned in July.

The financial statements are not ends in themselves. Additional information and insight about the business may be obtained by analyzing the relationships within and between the statements to make them more meaningful to management, creditors, and other interested persons. For this purpose percentages are useful.

A percentage analysis of the income statement and statement of financial position of the Connolly Trucking Company is shown in Figures 4-7 and 4-9. In the income statement, the total revenue ($7,569) is 100 percent. Each expense item is expressed as a percentage of the total revenue. The reader can see the distribution of each revenue dollar—that is, the percentage of revenue that has been absorbed by each expense item. Rent Expense, for example, absorbed 6.6 cents of each revenue dollar, and 25.1 cents of each revenue dollar was absorbed by income tax expense.

In the statement of financial position, the total asset amount is used as the base (100 percent), and the percentage of each asset to the total assets is determined by dividing the individual asset by the total assets. Similarly, the percentage of each liability and stockholders' equity item is expressed as a percentage of the total liabilities and stockholders' equity, and is computed by dividing the individual items by the amount of total liabilities and stockholders' equity. Thus,

$$\frac{\text{Cash}}{\text{Total assets}} = \frac{\$5,250}{\$24,594} = 21.3\%$$

$$\frac{\text{Notes payable}}{\text{Total liabilities and stockholders' equity}} = \frac{\$8,000}{\$24,594} = 32.5\%$$

Percentage computations are also made to show the relationship of subtotals to the related totals. The analysis shows that total current assets are 42.2 percent of total assets and that total current liabilities are 43.8 percent of total liabilities and stockholders' equity.

EQUITY RATIOS

A significant measure of the stability of a business is the percentage relationship of the equities of the creditors and the owners in the total assets. These equity ratios for the Connolly Trucking Company are computed as follows:

1. Creditors' interest in assets:

$$\frac{\text{Total liabilities}}{\text{Total assets}} = \frac{\$10,774}{\$24,594} = 43.8\%$$

2. Stockholders' interest in assets:

$$\frac{\text{Total stockholders' equity}}{\text{Total assets}} = \frac{\$13,820}{\$24,594} = 56.2\%$$

BASIC MODEL:
END-OF-PERIOD

The creditors have an equity of 43.8 cents, and the stockholders have an equity of 56.2 cents, of each asset dollar. Many analysts consider the equity ratios equal in importance to the current ratio as indicators of credit strength and sound management. There are no universally accepted percentage relationships to serve as guides for the equity ratios, but it is generally felt that the larger the owner's equity, the stronger the financial condition of the business. A company may, for example, borrow money on a long-term note for working capital purposes. The loan increases the current assets and creates a more favorable current ratio; but it also reduces the stockholders' equity ratio, signaling a possible overdependence on outside sources for financial needs.

GLOSSARY

Accrual Basis The accrual accounting basis assumes that revenue is realized at the time of the sale of goods or services irrespective of when the cash is received; and expenses are recognized at the time the services are received and utilized in the production of revenue irrespective of when payment for these services is made.

Accrued Expenses Expenses that have been incurred—for example, services received and used—in a given period but have not yet been paid or recorded.

Accrued Liability The liability that has accumulated for an expense that has been incurred but not yet paid or recorded.

Accumulated Depreciation The accumulated depreciation account reveals all past depreciation which has been taken on a depreciable plant and equipment item and charged against revenue; it is in essence a postponed credit to the applicable plant and equipment account.

Adjusting Entries Regular continuous entries postponed to the end of an accounting period, for the convenience of the accountant, and made to update revenue, expense, assets, liability, and stockholders' equity accounts as required by the accrual basis of accounting.

Apportionment The dividing of a cost or revenue among two or more periods.

Cash Basis The cash basis of accounting reflects the recognition of revenue at the time that cash is received for the sale of goods and services and the recognition of expenses in the period of the payment for the receipt of a service.

Contra Account A negative element of another account which is shown in a separate account; the contra account should always be shown immediately following the account of which it is a reduction.

Depreciation (Accounting Depreciation) Accounting depreciation is the system of allocation of a part of the cost of a plant and equipment item (that has a limited useful life) over the estimated useful life in a systematic and rational manner.

Long-Term Cost Apportionment Adjustment An adjustment requiring the apportioning of the cost of a long-lived asset between the current period and a future span of time of three or more years.

Materiality An item significant enough in size to influence decisions by statement users that it should receive separate and identified accounting.

Salvage Value The estimated scrap value or resale value that a plant and equipment item has at the end of the estimated life of the asset.

Short-Term Cost Apportionment Adjustment An adjustment which requires that a previously recorded prepaid item be apportioned between the current period and a future short period (usually a year).

Short-Term Revenue Apportionment Adjustment An adjustment which requires that a previously recorded liability involving an advanced collection of a revenue be apportioned between the current period and a future short period (usually one year).

Straight-Line Method of Depreciation A method that allocates the cost of a depreciable asset over the estimated useful life of the asset in equal amounts for each time period.

Work Sheet (Working Papers) A device used by the accountant to collect information rapidly and in an orderly manner for the preparation of the formal end-of-period financial statements.

Q4-1. (a) What are the essential differences between the cash basis of accounting and the accrual basis? (b) Under what conditions is it appropriate to use the cash basis? (c) Under what conditions is it inappropriate to use the cash basis?

Q4-2. (a) What purpose is served by adjusting entries? (b) What events make them necessary? (c) How do they affect the work of the accountant? (d) How does the time period covered by the income statement affect the adjusting entries? (e) How do adjusting entries differ from other entries?

Q4-3. Does the need to make adjusting entries at the end of a period mean that errors were made in the accounts during the period? Discuss.

Q4-4. (a) What is the purpose and function of the work sheet? (b) Can the work of the accountant be completed without the use of the work sheet? (c) Where do the amounts in the first pair of columns on the work sheet come from? (d) What determines the number of columns to be used in the preparation of a work sheet? (e) Why are the parts of each entry in the Adjustments columns cross-referenced with either numbers or letters? (f) How is the amount to be extended into another column determined? (g) What determines the column into which an amount is to be extended? (h) Is the work sheet foolproof? (i) Does the work sheet eliminate the need for formal financial statements?

Q4-5. "Prepaid items are not assets, since these amounts will become expenses in later periods." Comment on this statement.

Q4-6. (a) What is meant by the accounting cycle? (b) What are the steps in the complete cycle? (c) Is it possible for the accountant to vary the sequence in which he performs the steps of the cycle?

Q4-7. Is it possible to prepare the formal financial statements from a four-column work sheet consisting of the trial balance amounts and all the necessary adjustments?

Q4-8. (a) When would the amounts for Depreciation Expense and for Accumulated Depreciation in the adjusted trial balance be the same? (b) When would these amounts be different?

E4-1. Because of an impending paternity suit, the company's accountant quite unexpectedly quit; he took off for parts unknown just before the close of the company's accounting year. In his haste to leave he did not have a chance to discuss what adjusting entries would be necessary at the end of the year, December 31. Fortunately, however, he did jot down a few notes on his memo pad that provide some leads. These are his brief notes:

a. Depreciation on furniture and equipment for the year is $4,000.

b. Charge off $850 of expired insurance from prepaid account for the year.

c. Accrued interest at end of year on notes payable to bank is $1,500; make sure to pick up when adjusting entries are made.

d. No bill received yet from car rental agency for salesmen cars—should be about $1,200 for December.

e. Two days' salaries will be unpaid at year-end; weekly (5 days) total salary is $2,400.

1. On the basis of the available information given above, prepare for each adjustment that should be recorded a general journal entry with brief explanation.

2. What other normal or usual adjustments may have to be recorded in addition to the ones above? Briefly explain each one.

E4-2. Prepare adjusting entries from the following information pertaining to the accounts of Hyper-Video Control Corporation at the end of April 1976:

a. Accrued rent receivable, $280.

b. Accrued interest payable, $75.

c. Accrued taxes payable, $120.

d. Accrued wages payable, $360.

e. A trenching machine was rented during April from the Rent-All Company at the rate of $20 an hour; the machine was used for a total of 80 hours during the month and the corporation had paid $500 to Rent-All Company for the rental of the machine. The $500 payment was debited to Prepaid Equipment Rental Expense.

f. Accrued interest on municipal bonds owned, $150.

g. As of April 30, the unbilled service fees for completed work amounted to $580.

h. The company signed an order form on April 30, 1976, to purchase a trenching machine for $11,500.

E4-3. Thomas Sparrow, an electrician, prepares monthly financial statements. The following transactions occurred during December 1976:

1976
Dec. 15 Billed customers $850 for services rendered this month.

17 Purchased $650 worth of electrical supplies on account.

31 Received $500 in cash from customers billed on December 15.

31 Paid $350 on account for electrical supplies purchased on December 17.

The electrical supplies inventory on December 31 was $150. Journalize the transactions, assuming that Sparrow keeps his books (a) on the cash basis; (b) on the accrual basis. What is the net income (c) on the cash basis? (d) on the accrual basis? Which method should Sparrow use? Why?

E4-4. On January 1, 1976, the Angel Company purchased a new truck for $4,900. It had an estimated useful life of four years and an estimated trade-in value at the end of that time of $500. (a) What is the depreciation expense for 1976? (b) What is the balance in the Accumulated Depreciation—Delivery Equipment account at the end of 1976? of 1977? (c) What will the carrying value of the truck be in the statement of financial position of December 31, 1976? of December 31, 1977? (d) Why is depreciation expense credited to Accumulated Depreciation—Delivery Equipment rather than directly to Delivery Equipment?

E4-5. The trial balance of the Castle Company on December 31, 1976, included the following account balances before adjustments:

Prepaid Insurance	$1,800
Prepaid Advertising Supplies	1,600
Prepaid Rent	2,400
Office Supplies	3,000
Office Equipment	6,600

Data for adjustments on December 31, 1976, were:
a. On November 1, 1976, the company purchased a 2-year comprehensive insurance policy for $1,800.
b. Advertising supplies on hand totaled $450 on December 31, 1976.
c. On September 1, 1976, the company paid one year's rent in advance.
d. The office supplies inventory was $1,400 on December 31, 1976.
e. The office equipment was purchased on July 1, 1976, and has an estimated useful life of 10 years and an estimated salvage value of $600.

Make the adjusting entries.

E4-6. The Black Company employs three sales clerks at a weekly salary of $150 each. They are paid on Friday, the last day of a five-day work week. Make the adjusting entry, assuming that the accounting period ended on Thursday.

E4-7. The statements of financial position of the Dempsey Company as of December 31, 1976 and 1977, showed Office Supplies at $1,600 and $1,800, respectively. During 1977, office supplies totaling $2,600 were purchased. What was the office supplies expense for the year 1977?

E4-8. The balances of the Prepaid Insurance account of the Parris Company were:

December 31, 1976	$1,030
December 31, 1977	620

The income statement for 1977 showed insurance expense of $1,250. What were the expenditures for insurance premiums during 1977?

E4-9. Make the additional closing entries indicated by the following accounts:

John Miller, Capital	John Miller, Drawing
60,000	8,000

Income Summary	
225,000	260,000

E4-10. The Pictorial Magazine Company credited Subscription Revenue for $48,000 received from subscribers to its new monthly magazine. All subscriptions were for twelve issues. The initial issue was mailed during October 1976. Make the adjusting entry on December 31, 1976.

E4-11. The income statement of the Walker Company for the 3-month period ended March 31, 1976, shows net income before income taxes of $140,000. Assuming an income tax rate of 48 percent, make the necessary adjusting entry.

E4-12. From the account balances given below, prepare the adjusting entries.

Account	Account in Trial Balance	Balance After Adjustment
Prepaid Insurance	$ 3,600	$ 1,200
Unearned Rent	1,400	400
Accumulated Depreciation—Building	14,000	20,000
Accrued Salaries and Wages Payable	–0–	900
Accrued Interest Receivable	–0–	220
Accrued Interest Payable	–0–	180

E4-13. Upon examining the books and records of the Gentry Company on December 31, 1976, you find the following: (a) The inventory of office supplies on hand is $250; some partially filled cans of duplicating fluid valued at $3.75 were not inventoried. All purchases of office supplies were debited to Office Supplies Expense. (b) Included in Miscellaneous Expense was a charge of $600 for uninsured losses from a fire.
Indicate the adjustments, if any, that should be made and state why.

E4-14. On September 15 the Sampson Company received a 30-day, 9% note for $600 from a customer. On September 20 the company borrowed $2,400 from the bank on its own 30-day, 9% note. Make entries to adjust the books on September 30, and entries to record the collection and payment of the notes on their respective due dates.

E4-15. The statement of financial position of the Nelson Company at December 31, 1976, shows the following totals:

Current Assets	$26,000
Total Assets	80,000
Current Liabilities	12,000
Total Liabilities	32,000

Prepare analyses that will make these summary totals more meaningful to a reader of the statement.

E4-16. The Nabors Company issued to a supplier of merchandise a 60-day, 9% note for $1,000, dated July 1. On July 16 the company received from a customer a 30-day, 10% note for $800. Make the necessary adjusting entries on July 31.

DP4-1. (*Work sheet*) The general ledger of Center Bowling Lanes, Inc., showed the following balances at December 31, 1976. The books are closed annually on December 31. The company obtains revenue from its bowling alleys and from a refreshment stand that is leased on a concession basis.

Cash	$29,000
Bowling Supplies	8,500
Prepaid Insurance	7,500
Prepaid Rent	6,800
Bowling Equipment	62,000
Accumulated Depreciation	15,000
Mortgage Payable	30,000

Capital Stock	25,000
Retained Earnings	9,280
Dividends	5,000
Bowling Revenue	55,000
Concession Revenue	6,500
Wages Expense	14,500
Repair Expense	3,200
Heat and Light Expense	2,900
Telephone and Telegraph Expense	360
Miscellaneous Expense	1,020

Supplementary data:

a. Bowling supplies on hand based on physical count totaled $650.
b. The balance of the Prepaid Insurance account represents the premium on a 3-year insurance policy, effective January 1, 1976.
c. Rent expense for the year was $4,800.
d. The bowling equipment has an expected useful life of 10 years and an estimated salvage value of $2,000. No equipment was acquired during the year.
e. Salaries earned by employees but unpaid on December 31 were $250.

Required:

1. Record the trial balance on a work sheet.
2. Complete the work sheet.
3. Why is the difference between the totals of the Income Statement columns and the totals of the Position Statement columns the same amount?

DP4-2. (*Adjusting entries*) Certain unadjusted account balances from the trial balance of the Easter Company, a systems consulting firm, for the year ended December 31, 1976, are given below.

Account Title	Debits	Credits
Accounts Receivable	$40,000	
Notes Receivable	18,000	
Prepaid Insurance	2,160	
Office Supplies	1,240	
Automobiles	20,000	
Accumulated Depreciation —Automobiles		$ 4,000
Notes Payable		6,000
Revenue—Consulting Fees		480,000
Interest Earned		600
Rent Earned		2,400
Advertising Expense	1,800	
Rent Expense	40,000	
Salaries Expense	49,000	
Property Taxes Expense	3,350	
Heat and Light Expense	2,400	

Adjustment data on December 31 are as follows:

a. Office supplies on hand totaled $100.
b. Depreciation for the year was $2,000.
c. Estimated heat and light expense not recorded was $250.

d. Of the amount shown for Interest Earned, $200 was unearned as of December 31, 1976.

e. The balance of the Prepaid Insurance account consists of $720 for the premium on a 3-year policy dated July 1, 1976, and $1,440 for the premium on a 3-year policy dated January 1, 1976.

f. Advertising supplies on hand were $140.

g. The balance of the Notes Payable account represents a 9% interest-bearing note dated January 1, 1976, due July 1, 1977.

h. The rent is $4,000 a month.

i. Salaries earned but not paid were $1,300.

j. Property taxes accrued were $190.

k. On January 1, 1976, the Easter Company subleased a section of its rented space. The lease with the tenant specifies a minimum yearly rental of $2,400 payable in twelve installments at the beginning of each month. The maximum annual rental is 5% of sales. The rental adjustment, if any, is due on January 15. The tenant reported sales of $53,000 for 1976.

l. Included in Revenue—Consulting Fees are advance payments of $15,000 by clients for services to be rendered early in 1977.

Required:

1. Record the adjusting entries.

2. Indicate the financial statement classification of each account in each entry.

3. Show the amount reported on the financial statements. Present the data in solution form as shown (Item a is done as an example):

Item	Adjusting Journal Entries December 31, 1976	Dr.	Cr.	Financial Statement Classification	Amount Reported on Financial Statement
a	Office Supplies Expense Office Supplies	1,140	1,140	Expenses Current Assets	$1,140 100

DP4-3. (*Financial statements: closing entries*) Parker Decorators adjusted trial balance, taken from the work sheet for the month ended October 31, 1976, was as follows:

Cash	$ 1,200	
Accounts Receivable	1,800	
Decorating Supplies	4,000	
Prepaid Insurance	2,400	
Land	6,000	
Building	20,000	
Accumulated Depreciation—Building		$11,400
Accounts Payable		4,000
Notes Payable		2,400
Bank Loan Payable (due June 1, 1978)		7,200
Capital Stock, $10 par value		3,000
Retained Earnings		1,380
Dividends	950	
Service Revenue		15,900
Heat and Light Expense	240	

Telephone and Telegraph Expense	80	
Wages Expense	1,600	
Decorating Supplies Expense	6,400	
Insurance Expense	320	
Depreciation Expense—Building	480	
Income Tax Expense	1,500	
Accrued Wages Payable		140
Interest Expense	50	
Accrued Interest Payable		100
Income Taxes Payable		1,500
Totals	$47,020	$47,020

Required:

1. An income statement with a Percent column.
2. A position statement with a Percent column.
3. A statement of retained earnings.
4. Closing entries.
5. The company needs additional cash to increase its volume of business. Suggest alternative means of raising money and the advantages and disadvantages of each alternative.

P4-1. The Lawton Company's adjusted trial balance, taken from the work sheet for the year ended December 31, 1976, was as follows:

Cash	$ 25,700	
Accounts Receivable	21,400	
Machinery and Equipment	42,900	
Accumulated Depreciation		$ 22,000
Accounts Payable		4,040
Notes Payable		8,600
Jason Lawton, Capital		54,360
Jason Lawton, Drawing	4,000	
Service Revenue		60,000
Heat and Light Expense	2,000	
Wages Expense	45,000	
Depreciation Expense	8,000	
Totals	$149,000	$149,000

Required:

1. Enter the adjusted trial balance on a work sheet.
2. Complete the work sheet.
3. Prepare an income statement with a Percent column, a statement of financial position with a Percent column, a statement of owner's equity, and the closing entries.

P4-2. (*Accounting policy decision problem*) Ricca Dixon, a certified public accountant, began practice on March 1, 1976. He kept his accounts on the accrual basis. At the end of the year, the following adjusted trial balance was taken from his work sheet:

Cash	$ 300	
Accounts Receivable	2,300	
Office Supplies	150	
Accrued Salaries Payable		$ 250
Ricca Dixon, Capital		2,000
Ricca Dixon, Drawing	4,400	
Professional Fees		13,040
Rent Expense	2,200	
Insurance Expense	450	
Office Salaries Expense	4,100	
Miscellaneous Expense	1,390	
Totals	$15,290	$15,290

The work sheet shows the following adjustments:

Office Salaries Expense	250	
Accrued Salaries Payable		250
Miscellaneous Expense	60	
Office Supplies		60

Required:

1. Prepare an income statement to determine Dixon's net income on the accrual basis of accounting.
2. Prepare an income statement to determine Dixon's net income on the cash basis of accounting.
3. Which method of accounting should Dixon use? Why?

P4-3. Selected transactions of the Brantley Sales Company for 1976 follow:

1976
Jan. 2 Purchased a 4-year insurance policy for $1,800, effective January 1, 1976.

July 1 Bought two trucks for $12,850. The trucks are expected to last four years, at the end of which time their salvage value will be $850 each.

Dec. 31 Paid $1,200 rent for the three-month period ending March 31, 1977.

    31 Purchased office supplies for $480.

Required:

1. Prepare journal entries to record the transactions.
2. Prepare the adjusting entries as of December 31, 1976. The company closes its books annually on December 31.
3. What adjusting entries would be made if the Brantley Sales Company were on the cash basis?

P4-4. Listed below are the account balances taken from the Trial Balance and Adjusted Trial Balance columns of the work sheet of the Lasley Company for the 12-month period ended June 30, 1976, the first year of operations.

Account Title	Trial Balance	Adjusted Trial Balance
Cash	$ 2,400	$ 2,400
Accounts Receivable	4,000	4,000
Office Supplies	3,500	1,000
Store Supplies	3,000	200
Prepaid Insurance	3,600	1,200
Prepaid Rent	4,800	1,200
Equipment	41,200	41,200
Accounts Payable	14,000	14,000
Capital Stock	39,300	39,300
Dividends	7,000	7,000
Service Revenue	31,000	31,000
Wages Expense	11,000	11,140
Miscellaneous Expense	3,800	3,800
Office Supplies Expense	–0–	2,500
Store Supplies Expense	–0–	2,800
Insurance Expense	–0–	2,400
Rent Expense	–0–	3,600
Depreciation Expense—Equipment	–0–	4,000
Accumulated Depreciation—Equipment	–0–	4,000
Accrued Wages Payable	–0–	140

Required: Reconstruct the Trial Balance, Adjustments, and Adjusted Trial Balance columns of the work sheet.

P4-5. (*Financial policy decision problem*) Following is the trial balance of the Clawson Print Company at October 31, 1976. The company began operations on September 1, 1976. Its fiscal year ends on October 31.

CLAWSON PRINT COMPANY
Trial Balance
October 31, 1976

Account Title	Debits	Credits
Cash	$17,100	
Notes Receivable	12,000	
Accounts Receivable	13,400	
Office Supplies	1,750	
Printing Supplies	2,000	
Prepaid Rent	3,400	
Printing Equipment	22,000	
Accounts Payable		$13,600
Notes Payable		12,200
Jay Clawson, Capital		27,000
Jay Clawson, Drawing	1,500	
Printing Revenue		23,635
Heat and Light Expense	180	
Telephone Expense	145	
Maintenance Expense	360	
Wages Expense	2,600	
Totals	$76,435	$76,435

Other data:

a. A physical count shows that office supplies on hand total $475 and that printing supplies on hand are $700.
b. The monthly rental is $680.
c. Printing equipment acquired on September 1 has an estimated useful life of five years and a salvage value of $2,000.
d. Wages of employees earned but not paid are $400.
e. The note payable is a 1-year note, signed on September 1, and bears interest at 9%.
f. The Notes Receivable account represents a 60-day, 8% interest-bearing note signed by a customer on October 1.

Required:

1. Prepare adjusting entries.
2. Why did Clawson accept the note from the customer?

P4-6. Certain account balances from the trial balance of the Jockey Ridge Company as of June 30, 1976, the end of its fiscal year, are given below.

Account Title	Debits	Credits
Office Supplies	$ 900	
Prepaid Insurance	4,800	
Prepaid Advertising	4,400	
Unearned Rent		$1,200
Rent Expense	4,000	

Examination of the records as of June 30 shows the following:

a. Office supplies on hand totaled $250.
b. A 3-year comprehensive insurance policy was purchased on July 1, 1975, at a premium cost of $4,800.
c. The monthly rent expense is $400.
d. Included in Prepaid Advertising is a payment of $300 for ads to appear during July 1976. The balance is for ads that appeared in prior months.
e. A portion of the floor space was subleased at $100 a month on September 1, 1975. The tenant paid a year's rent in advance on signing the lease.

Required: Record the adjusting entries as of June 30, 1976. The books are closed annually.

P4-7. (*Accounting policy decision problem*) The bookkeeper for the Braxton Company prepared the following condensed income statement for the year ended December 31, 1976, and the condensed statement of financial position as of that date.

Income Statement

Revenue from Services		$40,100
Operating Expenses		
Insurance Expense	$ 1,400	
Miscellaneous Expense	4,600	
Office Supplies Expense	800	
Wages Expense	20,000	26,800
Net Income		$13,300

Statement of Financial Position

Assets

Cash	$ 4,600
Accounts Receivable	8,000
Equipment	40,000
Total Assets	$52,600

Liabilities and Owner's Equity

Accounts Payable	$ 9,800
Ronald Braxton, Capital	42,800
Total Liabilities and Owner's Equity	$52,600

The following items were overlooked entirely by the bookkeeper in the preparation of the statements:

a. The depreciation of equipment (acquired January 1, 1976): estimated life, 10 years; no salvage value.
b. Wages earned but unpaid, $800.
c. Office supplies on hand, $260 (purchases during 1976 were debited to Office Supplies Expense).
d. Unexpired insurance premiums, $400.
e. Heat and light invoices for December, $250.

Required:

1. What adjustments are needed?
2. Prepare revised financial statements.
3. Prepare a schedule reconciling the revised amount of owner's equity with the amount shown in the original statement.
4. In a report to Braxton, state briefly why the accrual basis would be more appropriate for him.

P4-8. After an analysis of the accounts and other records of Pittsborough, Inc., the following information is made available for the year ended December 31, 1976:

a. The Office Supplies account has a debit balance of $720. Office supplies on hand at December 31 total $260.
b. The Prepaid Rent account has a debit balance of $7,200. Included in this amount is $600 paid in December for the succeeding January; $6,600 has expired.
c. The Prepaid Insurance account has a debit balance of $1,920. It consists of the following policies purchased during 1976:

Policy No.	Date of Policy	Life of Policy	Premiums
A63210	January 1	3 years	$1,200
E4522	May 1	2 years	480
X3211	October 1	1 year	240

d. The Prepaid Advertising account has a debit balance of $2,400. Included in this amount is $400 paid to a local monthly magazine for advertising space in its January and February 1977 issues.

BASIC MODEL:
END-OF-PERIOD

e. At the close of the year three notes receivable were on hand:

Date	Face Value	Time of Note	Interest Rate
November 1	$6,000	90 days	9 percent
December 1	7,200	60 days	10 percent
December 16	4,000	30 days	none

f. At the close of the year two notes payable were outstanding:

Date	Face Value	Time of Note	Interest Rate
September 2	$ 6,600	180 days	8 percent
November 1	10,000	90 days	9 percent

g. Salaries and wages accrued totaled $2,000.
h. The Rent Earned account has a credit balance of $9,600. This amount represents receipt of payment on a one-year lease effective May 1, 1976.
i. The Store Equipment account has a debit balance of $13,500. The equipment has an estimated useful life of 10 years and a salvage value of $1,500. All store equipment was acquired prior to January 1, 1976.
j. The Truck account has a debit balance of $6,500. The truck was purchased on June 1, 1975, and has an estimated life of five years and salvage value of approximately $500.
k. Property taxes accrued were $1,400.
l. Estimated income taxes for the year were $4,650.

Required: Prepare the adjusting journal entries required at December 31.

P4-9. (*Accounting policy decision problem*) The closing entries and postclosing trial balance of the Village Realty Company as of December 31, 1976, are given below. A yearly accounting period is used. John Cannon, the proprietor, had a capital balance of $30,000 on January 1, 1976; he made one additional investment during the year.

		GENERAL JOURNAL		Page 12
		Closing Entries		
1976 Dec.	31	Rental Revenue	11,000	
		Commission Revenue	43,200	
		Income Summary		54,200
	31	Income Summary	40,100	
		Rent Expense		3,600
		Insurance Expense		800
		Supplies Expense		300
		Commission Expense		33,000
		Depreciation Expense— Office Equipment		2,000
		Miscellaneous Expense		400
	31	Income Summary	14,100	
		John Cannon, Drawing		14,100
	31	John Cannon, Drawing	4,100	
		John Cannon, Capital		4,100

VILLAGE REALTY COMPANY
Postclosing Trial Balance
December 31, 1976

Account Title	Debits	Credits
Cash	$10,600	
Office Supplies	300	
Prepaid Insurance	3,200	
Office Equipment	32,000	
Accumulated Depreciation—Office Equipment		$ 4,000
Notes Payable to Banks		2,000
John Cannon, Capital		40,100
Totals	$46,100	$46,100

Required:

1. An income statement for 1976.
2. A statement of owner's equity.
3. Cannon believes that the income statement should show a deduction of a reasonable amount for his services to the business. Comment.

P4-10. On October 1, 1976, Jacob Joseph opened a repair shop. During October the following transactions were completed:

1976
Oct. 1 Transferred $3,000 from his personal savings account to a checking account under the name of Joseph's Shop.

2 Paid $185 for office supplies.

3 Purchased secondhand office equipment for $300 in cash.

4 Issued a check for $150 for October rent.

5 Paid a premium of $72 for an insurance policy on the equipment, effective October 1.

6 Purchased repair supplies on account to be used in repair work:

Amber Supply Company	$150
Carson Wire Company	200
Gaddy Supply Company	160
Ronson Repairs, Inc.	140
Total	$650

17 Received $1,250 for repair work completed.

20 Additional repair work was completed, and bills were sent out:

J. K. Blaine	$205
D. J. Dawson	80
H. H. Hooper	70
P. T. Peters	95
Total	$450

22 Paid $45 for the telephone service for the month.

25 Paid the following creditors:

Amber Supply Company	$ 50
Carson Wire Company	100
Gaddy Supply Company	60
Ronson Repairs, Inc.	40
Total	$250

27 Received cash from customers to apply on account:

J. K. Blaine	$105
D. J. Dawson	30
H. H. Hooper	20
P. T. Peters	35
Total	$190

31 Joseph withdrew $400 in cash for his personal use.

Supplementary adjustment data as of October 31, 1976:

a. The insurance premium paid on October 5 is for one year.
b. A physical count shows (1) that office supplies on hand total $65 and (2) that repair supplies on hand are $125.
c. The office equipment has an estimated useful life of five years with no salvage value.

Required:

1. Open the following accounts in the general ledger: Cash, 101; Accounts Receivable, 111; Office Supplies, 136; Repair Supplies, 137; Prepaid Insurance, 140; Office Equipment, 163; Accumulated Depreciation—Office Equipment, 163A; Accounts Payable, 201; Jacob Joseph, Capital, 251; Jacob Joseph, Drawing, 252; Repair Revenue, 301; Insurance Expense, 702; Rent Expense, 703; Office Supplies Expense, 708; Telephone and Telegraph Expense, 709; Repair Supplies Expense, 712; Depreciation Expense–Office Equipment, 717; Income Summary, 800.
2. Open accounts in the accounts receivable ledger for J. K. Blaine, D. J. Dawson, H. H. Hooper, and P. T. Peters.
3. Open accounts in the accounts payable ledger for the Amber Supply Company, Carson Wire Company, Gaddy Supply Company, and Ronson Repairs, Inc.
4. Record all the transactions in the general journal, post to the appropriate ledgers, and enter the general ledger account balances directly in the Trial Balance columns of the work sheet.
5. Enter the adjustment data in the Adjustments columns of the work sheet.
6. Complete the work sheet.
7. Prepare an income statement, a statement of owner's equity, and a statement of financial position (include percentage analyses and equity ratios).
8. Prepare a schedule of accounts receivable.
9. Prepare a schedule of accounts payable.
10. Prepare adjusting entries in the general journal.
11. Post the adjusting entries from the general journal to the general ledger.
12. Prepare closing entries in the general journal, post to the general ledger, and rule the nominal accounts that are closed.
13. Balance and rule the real accounts.
14. Prepare a postclosing trial balance.

Merchandising— Determining and Interpreting the Results of Operations

5

Accounting for businesses that render a service to customers or clients has been discussed up to this point. In this and subsequent chapters, accounting for businesses that buy and sell *merchandise,* or goods, is examined. The principles developed thus far, however, apply to all classes of business enterprise, whether service, merchandising, or manufacturing.

ACCOUNTS FOR A MERCHANDISING BUSINESS

The principal difference in the accounts of a merchandising business from those of a service business is that a merchandising business has to account for the purchase of goods, their handling, and their sale; it has to account not only for operating expenses but also for the *cost of goods* that it has sold. The income statement for a merchandising business, therefore, shows an operating income only if the goods are sold for more than their cost plus all other expenses necessary in operating the business. Since a merchandising business is involved in many activities that are not found in service businesses, additional accounts are needed to report the financial position and operating results of the enterprise. The functions of the merchandising accounts and their classifications in the financial statements are discussed and illustrated in this chapter.

The Sales Account

A sale of merchandise, like a sale of service, is recorded by a credit to a revenue account as shown.

Transaction:
Sold merchandise for $200 on account.
Journal Entry:

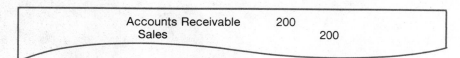

Accounts Receivable	200
Sales	200

The debit to Accounts Receivable (or to Cash if the sale is for cash) records an increase in an asset. The credit to Sales, a revenue account, records an increase in the stockholders' equity. This credit constitutes a recovery of the cost of the merchandise sold as well as a profit. However, each individual sale cannot be divided into a return of cost and a profit. To do so would require such extensive records as to make the accounting impracticable. Therefore, the entire sales price of the goods is recorded as revenue. The entire cost of goods sold becomes a deduction from revenue in the income statement. The result is called *gross margin*.

The Sales Returns and Allowances Account

A customer may return merchandise because it is not exactly what he ordered; or the customer may be entitled to a reduction of the price, or *allowance,* for defective or broken goods that he retains. The effect of the entry to record a return or allowance is the opposite of a sale. However, when Cash or the customer's account is credited, an account entitled Sales Returns and Allowances is debited. This contra account is used, rather than Sales, so that a record may be available of the amount of returns and allowances.

Transaction:
The customer returned $10 worth of the merchandise (see the previous transaction).
Journal Entry:

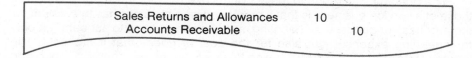

Sales Returns and Allowances	10
Accounts Receivable	10

The Sales Discounts Account

The customer may be allowed a *discount,* or reduction in price, if he pays within a limited period. Since the effect of a discount is to reduce the amount actually received from the sale, Sales Discounts is debited for the amount of the discount. Sales Discounts is a contra account to Sales and is used for the same reason that prompts the use of Sales Returns and Allowances—to supply management with valuable information about the business. When discounts are offered, the customer is in fact being offered the choice of paying (1) the full amount of the invoice or (2) the full amount reduced by the amount of the discount. The seller, however, does not know at the time of the sale whether the customer is going to avail himself of the discount. The customer is charged, therefore, with the full amount of the sale. If the customer pays within the discount period, payment is recorded under the *gross price method* as shown below.

Transaction:
The customer (see the previous transactions) paid his invoice within the discount period, deducting the allowed 2 percent sales discount.
Journal Entry:

Cash	186.20	
Sales Discounts	3.80	
Accounts Receivable		190.00

Computation:

Gross sale price	$200.00
Merchandise returned	10.00
	$190.00
2% discount	3.80
Cash received	$186.20

An alternative procedure, the *sales discounts not taken method,* is discussed later in this chapter.

The following partial income statement of the King Corporation, whose accounts are used for illustrative purposes in this chapter, shows the classification of the Sales and contra Sales accounts.

KING CORPORATION
Income Statement   **Exhibit A**
For the Year Ended December 31, 1976

Sales Revenue		
Sales		$124,200
Deduct: Sales Returns and Allowances	$2,400	
Sales Discounts	1,800	4,200
Net Sales Revenue		$120,000

The Purchases Account

It is customary in a merchandising business to use a separate Purchases account for all merchandise bought for resale. The account is *not* used for the purchase of operating supplies, for example, or for store equipment used in operations. The Purchases account is debited for the cost of the goods bought, shown on the seller's *invoice,* and therefore provides a record of the cost of the goods purchased during the period—not a record of the goods on hand. During the year, Purchases will always have a debit balance; the credits to the account are to close the account or to correct errors requiring offsetting debits to some other account(s).

Transaction:
Purchased merchandise for $800 on account.
Journal Entry:

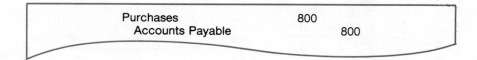

Purchases	800	
Accounts Payable		800

The Transportation In Account

The invoice price of goods may include the cost of transporting the goods from the seller's place of business to that of the buyer. If so, no separation is made, and the entire purchase price is debited to Purchases. If the cost of transportation is not included, the carrier is paid directly by the buyer, who debits the amount to Transportation In. This account is added to Purchases in the income statement to determine the *delivered cost of merchandise.*

The following terms are used in connection with the transportation of merchandise:

1. *F.O.B.* (free on board) *destination* means that the seller bears the freight cost to the buyer's location. (Sometimes the buyer pays the cost and deducts the amount from his payment to the seller.)
2. *F.O.B. shipping point* means that the buyer bears the freight cost from the point of shipment to the destination.

Transaction:
Freight charges of $50 were paid on delivery of merchandise (see the previous transaction); terms of the purchase were F.O.B. shipping point.
Journal Entry:

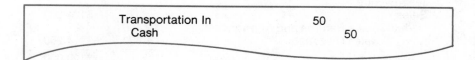

Transportation In	50	
Cash		50

The Purchases Returns and Allowances Account

Goods bought for resale may be defective, broken, or not of the quality or quantity ordered. Either they may be returned for credit, or the seller may make an adjustment by reducing the original price.

Transaction:
Returned to the vendor $100 worth of defective merchandise.
Journal Entry:

Accounts Payable	100	
Purchases Returns and Allowances		100

Purchases Returns and Allowances is a contra account to Purchases. The same result could be accomplished by crediting Purchases, but it is useful to management to have the books show total Purchases as well as total Purchases Returns and Allowances. Analysis of the Purchases Returns and Allowances account may indicate the need for changes in the procedures of ordering and handling merchandise.

The Purchases Discounts Account

The Purchases Discounts account is used to record deductions from the purchase price of goods for payment made within the discount period specified by the seller. At the time of the purchase, the buyer may not know whether he will avail himself of the discount; the account with the seller (Accounts Payable) is therefore credited for the gross purchase price. As in the case of merchandise sales, an alternative procedure, the *discounts lost method* or *net price procedure,* is discussed later in the chapter.

Transaction:
Paid for merchandise (see the previous transactions) within the discount period and deducted the allowed discount of 1 percent.
Journal Entry:

Accounts Payable	700	
Cash		693
Purchases Discounts		7

Computation:

Gross purchase	$800
Merchandise returned	100
	$700
1% discount	7
Cash paid	$693

Merchandise Inventory Account

The system of accounting for merchandise inventory described in this chapter is called the *periodic inventory method.* A different method which yields a continuously updated inventory balance, called the *perpetual inventory system,* is described in Chapter 10.

Merchandise purchased is recorded at cost in Purchases; merchandise sold is recorded at selling price in Sales. Therefore, an account, called Merchandise Inventory, is needed to show the merchandise actually on hand at the end of the accounting period. The amount is determined by making a list of the goods on hand, usually based on an actual count showing physical quantities and their cost. This *ending inventory* is entered in the books and becomes the beginning inventory of the next period. The amount in the ledger account will not be changed until the end of the next accounting period, because the Merchandise Inventory account is not used during the period. Since the account remains open, its balance—the beginning inventory—appears in the trial balance at the end of the period and is transferred to Income Summary when the books are closed. Concurrently, the new ending merchandise inventory is entered as a debit to Merchandise Inventory and a credit to Income Summary. Thus, the amount of the beginning inventory has been eliminated and replaced by the amount of the ending inventory. After the closing entries are posted, the Merchandise Inventory account in the general ledger of the King Corporation appears as shown below.

	Merchandise Inventory		Acct. No. 121
1975 Dec. 31	❶ 15,400	1976 Dec. 31 C.E.	❷ 15,400
1976 Dec. 31	❸ 11,480		

❶ The debit amount of $15,400 is the cost of the merchandise inventory on hand at December 31, 1975 (the beginning inventory).

❷ The credit posting of $15,400 closes the account temporarily and transfers the balance to Income Summary.

❸ The debit posting of $11,480 is the cost of the merchandise inventory on hand at December 31, 1976 (the ending inventory); this amount will remain unchanged in the account until the books are closed again on December 31, 1977.

FUNCTIONS OF THE MERCHANDISE ACCOUNTS

The following T accounts define the functions of the merchandise accounts and their locations in the financial statements. The accounts are presented in their income statement sequence. The description *Balance* in each account refers to the balance before the closing entries have been posted.

After the closing entries are posted, all the merchandise accounts, except Merchandise Inventory, are closed.

Sales

Debited	*Credited*
At the end of the accounting period to close the account.	During the accounting period for the sales price of goods sold.
	Balance
	A credit representing cumulative sales for the period to date.
	Statement Classification
	In the income statement, the first item under sales revenue.

Sales Returns and Allowances

Debited	*Credited*
During the accounting period for unwanted merchandise returned by customers and allowances granted for defective or broken goods.	At the end of the accounting period to close the account.
Balance	
A debit representing cumulative sales returns and allowances for the period to date.	
Statement Classification	
In the income statement, a deduction from sales revenue.	

Sales Discounts

Debited	*Credited*
During the accounting period for the amounts that the customers deduct from the gross sales price when payment is made within the period established by the seller.	At the end of the accounting period to close the account.
Balance	
A debit representing cumulative sales discounts taken by customers for the period to date.	

MERCHANDISING

Sales Discounts (Continued)

Statement Classification In the income statement, a deduction from sales revenue.	

Merchandise Inventory

Debited	*Credited*
At the end of each accounting period for the merchandise actually on hand. *Balance* A debit representing the cost of goods on hand at the beginning of the period. *Statement Classification* 1. In the position statement, under current assets. 2. In the income statement, in the cost of goods sold section, the beginning inventory is added to purchases and the ending inventory is deducted from the cost of merchandise available for sale.	At the end of each accounting period to remove the old inventory from the account (same figure as beginning debit).

Purchases

Debited	*Credited*
During the accounting period for the purchase price of goods bought for resale. *Balance* A debit representing cumulative purchases for the period to date. *Statement Classification* In the income statement, added to the beginning inventory under cost of goods sold.	At the end of the accounting period to close the account.

Transportation In

Debited	Credited
During the accounting period for delivery costs—freight or cartage—on merchandise purchases.	At the end of the accounting period to close the account.

Balance

A debit representing cumulative costs for the period to date incurred by the buyer for the delivery of merchandise.

Statement Classification

In the income statement, in the cost of goods sold section, added to purchases.

Purchases Returns and Allowances

Debited	Credited
At the end of the accounting period to close the account.	During the accounting period for unwanted merchandise returned to the vendor or allowances received for defective or broken merchandise.

Balance

A credit representing cumulative purchases returns and allowances for the period to date.

Statement Classification

In the income statement, in the cost of goods sold section, as a deduction from the gross cost of merchandise purchased.

Purchases Discounts

Debited	Credited
At the end of the accounting period to close the account.	During the accounting period for the amounts of discount from the gross purchase price of merchandise when payment was made within the period established by the seller.

Purchases Discounts (Continued)

Balance

A credit representing cumulative purchases discounts taken for the period to date.

Statement Classification

In the income statement, in the cost of goods sold section, as a deduction from the gross cost of merchandise purchased.

COST OF GOODS SOLD AND GROSS MARGIN ON SALES

Cost of Goods Sold

The *cost of goods sold* is the difference between the cost of the goods available for sale during a period and the cost of the unsold goods on hand at the end of the period.

The term does not identify an active account for the recording of transactions when the periodic inventory method is in use, but rather the result of adding and subtracting the balances of several accounts. The computation is shown as

Cost of goods sold = Beginning inventory + Net cost of purchases − Ending inventory

Net cost of purchases is the total cost of purchases, plus transportation in, less returns, allowances, and discounts.

The income statement of the King Corporation is shown in Figure 5-1. It was prepared from the work sheet in Figure 5-3.

The income statement of the King Corporation shows all the accounts needed to derive the cost of goods sold of $67,200.

Gross Margin

The *gross margin on sales* of $52,800 is what is left after the cost of goods sold of $67,200 is deducted from the net sales revenue of $120,000. The term *gross* indicates that the operating expenses necessary to the conduct of the business must still be deducted to arrive at the *net operating margin*. If the gross margin on sales is less than the operating expenses, the difference is a net operating loss for the period.

Figure 5-1 Income Statement

					Percent

KING CORPORATION   Exhibit A
Income Statement
For the Year Ended December 31, 1976

				Percent
Gross Sales Revenue			$124,200	
Deduct: Sales Returns and Allowances		$ 2,400		
Sales Discounts		1,800	4,200	
Net Sales Revenue			$120,000	100.0
Cost of Goods Sold				
Merchandise Inventory, January 1, 1976			$15,400	
Purchases		$63,580		
Transportation In		4,800		
Gross Delivered Cost of Purchases		$68,380		
Deduct: Purchases Returns and Allowances	$1,500			
Purchases Discounts	3,600	5,100		
Net Cost of Purchases			63,280	
Cost of Merchandise Available for Sale			$78,680	
Deduct Merchandise Inventory				
December 31, 1976			11,480	
Cost of Goods Sold			67,200	56.0
Gross Margin on Sales			$ 52,800	44.0
Deduct Operating Expenses				
Selling Expenses				
Salesmen's Salaries Expense		$12,000		10.0
Transportation Out Expense		2,400		2.0
Advertising Expense		3,000		2.5
Total Selling Expenses			$17,400	14.5
General and Administrative Expenses				
Rent Expense		$ 6,000		5.0
Property Tax Expense		7,800		6.5
Heat and Light Expense		2,160		1.8
Miscellaneous General Expense		480		.4
Insurance Expense		1,920		1.6
Supplies Expense		2,040		1.7
Depreciation Expense—Machinery and Equipment		3,600		3.0
Total General and Administrative Expenses			24,000	20.0
Total Operating Expenses			41,400	34.5
Net Operating Margin			$ 11,400	9.5
Other Revenue				
Interest Earned		$ 125		
Rent Earned		300	$ 425	
Other Expenses				
Interest Expense		$ 75		
Loss on Sale of Equipment		100	175	250
Net Income Before Income Taxes			$ 11,650	
Income Taxes			5,825	
Net Income			$ 5,825	
Net Income per Share		$ 0.5825		

MERCHANDISING

(Ch. 5)   191

THE OPERATING EXPENSE ACCOUNTS

Operating expenses include salaries, postage, telephone and telegraph, heat and light, insurance, advertising, and any other costs incurred for goods or services used in operating the business. The breakdown of operating expenses into a number of detailed accounts facilitates analyses and comparisons that aid in the management of the business. The amount of detail shown depends on the size and type of the business and on the needs and wishes of the management.

The operating expenses are often classified into *selling* and *general and administrative*. The expenses incurred in packaging the product, advertising it, making the sale, and delivering the product are classified as selling expenses. Salesmen's salaries, commissions, and supplies used in the sales department are examples of expenses incurred in making the sale. Expenses of delivering the product include freight paid by the seller (transportation out) and the expense of operating delivery vehicles. Expenses such as rent, taxes, and insurance, to the extent that they are incurred in selling the product, are also classified as selling expenses. All other operating expenses are classified as general and administrative, including office expenses, executive salaries, and the portion of rent, taxes, and insurance applicable to the administrative function of the business. The expenses that are common to both selling and administrative functions may be apportioned on some equitable basis. If an apportionment is not practicable, the account should be classified under the function it serves most. In Figure 5-1, the operating expense accounts that are entirely related to selling are classified as such; all the others are classified as general and administrative. The total operating expenses of $41,400 are deducted from the gross margin on sales of $52,800 to arrive at the net operating margin of $11,400.

If the operating expense accounts in the general ledger are too numerous, it is advisable to remove them to subsidiary selling expense and general and administrative expense ledgers. Two controlling accounts are substituted in the general ledger—Selling Expense Control and General and Administrative Expense Control—in place of the accounts that have been removed. The function of controlling accounts is explained in Chapter 3.

OTHER REVENUE AND OTHER EXPENSES

The Other Revenue and Other Expenses sections of the income statement serve a valuable function; they permit calculation of the net operating margin without it being distorted by extraneous items and link the net operating margin for the period with the net income for that period.

Other Revenue

Some common examples of items classified as other revenue are gains from the sale of securities, dividends on shares of stock owned, and gains from the sale of plant and equipment. In Figure 5-1, the King Corporation shows

$125 in interest earned and $300 in rent earned under Other Revenue. These are additional examples; they are included under Other Revenue because they arose from a source other than the basic business purpose of King Corporation.

Other Expenses

Nonoperating expenses such as interest on money borrowed from the bank or on notes given to creditors for the purchase of merchandise, or losses from the sale of plant and equipment are shown under Other Expenses. In Figure 5-1, the King Corporation shows $75 in interest expense and $100 from a loss on a sale of equipment under this heading.

The King Corporation added $250, the excess of other revenue over other expenses, to the net operating margin. If other expenses exceed other revenue, the expenses are listed first and the excess is deducted from the net operating margin.

In the absence of other revenue or other expenses, net operating margin becomes net income and net operating loss becomes net loss.

Net Income per Share

Assuming that the King Corporation has 10,000 shares of capital stock outstanding, the net income per share is $0.5825 and is shown on the face of the income statement.

COMPLETION OF THE WORK SHEET

The procedure for completing the work sheet of a merchandising business is similar to that of a service business, with the exception of the account for merchandise inventory.

At the end of the period, the balance of the Merchandise Inventory account, the beginning inventory of $15,400, is extended to the Income Statement Debit column of the work sheet because it is part of the cost of merchandise available for sale. The ending inventory, $11,480, is shown in the Income Statement Credit column because it is a deduction from the cost of merchandise available for sale, and in the Position Statement Debit column because it is an asset. This treatment preserves the equality of debits and credits in the work sheet, as shown in Figure 5-2.

The work sheet of the King Corporation is shown in Figure 5-3. There are a number of possible variations in the form; for instance, the Adjusted Trial Balance columns are omitted in this example. The combined Trial Balance and Adjustment column amounts are extended directly to the proper Income Statement or Position Statement columns.

Trial Balance Columns

The account balances in the trial balance are taken from the general ledger of the King Corporation as of December 31, 1976.

Figure 5-2
Partial Work Sheet

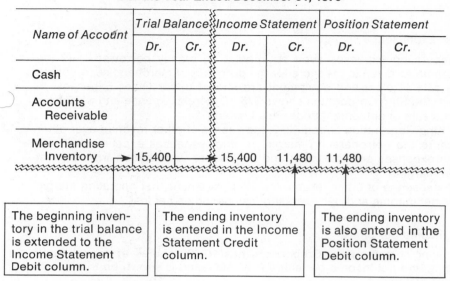

KING CORPORATION
Partial Work Sheet
For the Year Ended December 31, 1976

Name of Account	Trial Balance		Income Statement		Position Statement	
	Dr.	Cr.	Dr.	Cr.	Dr.	Cr.
Cash						
Accounts Receivable						
Merchandise Inventory	15,400		15,400	11,480	11,480	

The beginning inventory in the trial balance is extended to the Income Statement Debit column.

The ending inventory is entered in the Income Statement Credit column.

The ending inventory is also entered in the Position Statement Debit column.

Adjustment Columns

Supplementary records show the following information as of December 31, 1976:

a. Insurance that has expired amounts to $1,920.
b. Office supplies on hand total $1,200.
c. Depreciation on machinery and equipment is computed at $3,600.
d. Income tax expense is estimated to be $5,825.

Figure 5-3 Work Sheet

Acct. No.	Account Title	Trial Balance Dr.	Trial Balance Cr.	Adjustments Dr.	Adjustments Cr.	Income Statement Dr.	Income Statement Cr.	Position Statement Dr.	Position Statement Cr.
	KING CORPORATION **Work Sheet** **For the Year Ended December 31, 1976**								
101	Cash	7,200						7,200	
111	Accounts Receivable	39,800						39,800	
121	Merchandise Inventory	15,400				15,400	11,480	11,480	
131	Office Supplies	3,240			(b) 2,040			1,200	
141	Prepaid Insurance	3,740			(a) 1,920			1,820	
151	Machinery and Equipment	70,100						70,100	
151A	Accumulated Depreciation—Machinery and Equipment		7,200		(c) 3,600				10,800
201	Accounts Payable		17,700						17,700
202	Notes Payable		7,300						7,300
221	Mortgage Payable		20,000						20,000
301	Capital Stock		60,000						60,000
302	Retained Earnings		5,150						5,150
303	Dividends	1,000						1,000	
401	Sales		124,200				124,200		
402	Sales Returns and Allowances	2,400				2,400			
403	Sales Discounts	1,800				1,800			
501	Purchases	63,580				63,580			
502	Transportation In	4,800				4,800			
503	Purchases Returns and Allowances		1,500				1,500		
504	Purchases Discounts		3,600				3,600		
601	Salesmen's Salaries Expense	12,000				12,000			
602	Transportation Out Expense	2,400				2,400			
603	Advertising Expense	3,000				3,000			
701	Rent Expense	6,000				6,000			
702	Property Tax Expense	7,800				7,800			
703	Heat and Light Expense	2,160				2,160			
704	Miscellaneous General Expense	480				480			
801	Interest Earned		125				125		
802	Rent Earned		300				300		
821	Interest Expense	75				75			
822	Loss on Sale of Equipment	100				100			
		247,075	247,075						
705	Insurance Expense			(a) 1,920		1,920			
706	Office Supplies Expense			(b) 2,040		2,040			
707	Depreciation Expense—Machinery and Equipment			(c) 3,600		3,600			
708	Income Tax Expense			(d) 5,825		5,825			
709	Income Taxes Payable				(d) 5,825				5,825
				13,385	13,385	135,380	141,205	132,600	126,775
	Net Income for the Year					5,825			5,825
						141,205	141,205	132,600	132,600

Income Statement Columns

All the account balances that enter into the measurement of net income are extended to the Income Statement columns. The income statement accounts that enter into the determination of gross margin on sales are shown in Figure 5-4.

The difference between the column totals in Figure 5-4 ($140,780 − $87,980 = $52,800) is the same as the gross margin on sales in the formal income statement (Figure 5-1), because all the accounts that enter into the determination of the gross margin are presented. Similar examples could be shown using the other sections of the income and position statements.

Position Statement Columns

All the adjusted amounts used to prepare the statements of financial position and retained earnings are extended to the Position Statement columns.

COMPLETED FINANCIAL STATEMENTS

Figure 5-5 shows the statement of retained earnings and Figure 5-6 shows the classified statement of financial position. These statements and the income statement (Figure 5-1) were prepared after the completion of the work sheet.

Figure 5-4
Abstract from the Work Sheet

Acct. No.	Account Title	Income Statement Dr.	Income Statement Cr.
121	Merchandise Inventory	15,400	11,480
401	Sales		124,200
402	Sales Returns and Allowances	2,400	
403	Sales Discounts	1,800	
501	Purchases	63,580	
502	Transportation In	4,800	
503	Purchases Returns and Allowances		1,500
504	Purchases Discounts		3,600
	Totals of the foregoing items	87,980	140,780

KING CORPORATION Statement of Retained Earnings For the Year Ended December 31, 1976	Exhibit B
Retained Earnings, January 1, 1976	$ 5,150
Add Net Income for the Year—Exhibit A	5,825
Total	$10,975
Deduct Dividends	1,000
Retained Earnings, December 31, 1976	$ 9,975

Figure 5-5
Statement of
Retained Earnings

KING CORPORATION Statement of Financial Position December 31, 1976		Exhibit C

Figure 5-6
Statement of
Financial Position

Assets		*Percent*
Current Assets		
Cash	$ 7,200	6.0
Accounts Receivable	39,800	32.9
Merchandise Inventory	11,480	9.4
Office Supplies	1,200	1.0
Prepaid Insurance	1,820	1.6
Total Current Assets	$ 61,500	50.9
Plant and Equipment		
Machinery and Equipment	$70,100	
Deduct Accumulated Depreciation	10,800	
Total Plant and Equipment	59,300	49.1
Total Assets	$120,800	100.0

Liabilities and Stockholders' Equity		
Current Liabilities		
Accounts Payable	$17,700	14.7
Notes Payable	7,300	6.0
Income Taxes Payable	5,825	4.8
Total Current Liabilities	$ 30,825	25.5
Long-Term Liabilities		
Mortgage Payable	20,000	16.6
Total Liabilities	$ 50,825	42.1
Stockholders' Equity		
Capital Stock	$60,000	49.7
Retained Earnings—Exhibit B	9,975	8.2
Total Stockholders' Equity	69,975	57.9
Total Liabilities and Stockholders' Equity	$120,800	100.0

MERCHANDISING

CLOSING ENTRIES

The procedure for recording the closing entries in a merchandising business is essentially the same as that in a service business (illustrated on pages 101 and 102). The closing entries, including the closing of the beginning merchandise inventory and the recording of the ending inventory, are shown in Figure 5-7. After the closing entries are posted, all the revenue and expense accounts have zero balances. The remaining accounts—the open statement of financial position accounts—are ruled and balanced, and a postclosing trial balance is prepared.

INTERIM FINANCIAL STATEMENTS

Financial statements are prepared at least once a year, at which time the adjusting and closing entries are recorded and posted to the general ledger. The closing of the books at intervals of less than one year is not customary but has been assumed in this text as a convenience in illustrating the periodic summary. Financial statements, however, may be prepared at frequent intervals—monthly or quarterly—without the formal recording and posting of the adjusting and closing entries.

Financial statements may be produced at regular or intermittent intervals during the accounting period for external reasons, such as the establishment of credit for a bank loan, or for the internal use of managers and stockholders. They are referred to as *interim statements* and are prepared with the aid of the work sheet. The general ledger account balances as of the end of the interim period are entered on the work sheet, the adjustments are listed, the adjusted balances are extended to the appropriate Income Statement and Position Statement columns, and formal statements are prepared.

The amounts in the Trial Balance columns of the work sheet represent the cumulative general ledger totals for the year to date and the adjustments are for the same interval; hence, the amounts in the interim income statement are for the year to date. However, if monthly income statements are desired, the amounts on the statements for the previous months are deducted from the amounts on the current statement, thereby providing year-to-date figures as well as results of the current period. The amounts in the Position Statement columns of the work sheet are the correct amounts for the statement of financial position as of the close of the current period.

The preparation of interim statements requires a determination of the cost of the merchandise on hand. Taking a detailed physical inventory, however, is costly and time-consuming and may not be necessary. Alternative methods of determining the ending inventory, such as the gross margin method of inventory valuation and the perpetual inventory system, are discussed in Chapter 10.

Figure 5-7
Closing Entries

GENERAL JOURNAL				Page 12

Closing Entries

1976					
Dec.	31	Merchandise Inventory	121	11,480	
		Sales	401	124,200	
		Purchases Returns and Allowances	503	1,500	
		Purchases Discounts	504	3,600	
		Interest Earned	801	125	
		Rent Earned	802	300	
		Income Summary	901		141,205
		To record the ending inventory and to close the revenue accounts.			
	31	Income Summary	901	135,380	
		Merchandise Inventory	121		15,400
		Sales Returns and Allowances	402		2,400
		Sales Discounts	403		1,800
		Purchases	501		63,580
		Transportation In	502		4,800
		Salesmen's Salaries Expense	601		12,000
		Transportation Out Expense	602		2,400
		Advertising Expense	603		3,000
		Rent Expense	701		6,000
		Property Tax Expense	702		7,800
		Heat and Light Expense	703		2,160
		Miscellaneous General Expense	704		480
		Interest Expense	821		75
		Loss on Sale of Equipment	822		100
		Insurance Expense	705		1,920
		Office Supplies Expense	706		2,040
		Depreciation Expense— Machinery and Equipment	707		3,600
		Income Tax Expense	708		5,825
		To close the beginning inventory and the expense accounts.			
	31	Income Summary	901	5,825	
		Retained Earnings	302		5,825
		To transfer net income to Retained Earnings.			
	31	Retained Earnings	302	1,000	
		Dividends	303		1,000
		To close Dividends to Retained Earnings.			

The financial statements of the King Corporation are analyzed to illustrate some additional ratios commonly used by the management in the analysis of the financial statements. The following amounts used in the illustrations are taken from the December 31, 1975, statement of financial position:

Total liabilities	$58,600
Current assets	71,500
Current liabilities	29,000

Figures are rounded when it is necessary.

Net Operating Margin Ratio and Operating Ratio

The net operating margin ratio shows the relationship of the net operating margin to sales (other revenue and other expenses are excluded).

$$\frac{\text{Net operating margin}}{\text{Net sales revenue}} = \frac{\$11,400}{\$120,000} = 9.5\%$$

The King Corporation earned 9.5 cents for each dollar of net sales. This ratio must be considered together with the rate of return on the stockholders' equity in appraising the earning power of a business. A high net operating margin ratio is not necessarily a favorable indication if it is accompanied by a low rate of return on the stockholders' equity.

The complement of the net operating margin ratio is the operating ratio (90.5 percent) or the amount of each sales dollar absorbed by operations.

Turnover of Merchandise Inventory

The quantity of goods to be kept on hand is a major business decision. It is considered good management to carry as little as possible and to turn it over as rapidly as possible. Good management must guard against excessive inventories, the consequences of which could be an abnormal drain on working capital that could lead to financial difficulties. The greater the inventory, the greater the amount of money tied up, extra space required, and extra handling costs, as well as an increased possibility of loss through shrinkage, style changes, or other factors. Inadequate inventories, on the other hand, may result in higher costs due to buying in smaller quantities and the possible loss of business if the item the customer wants is out of stock. Good management, therefore, requires a careful evaluation of all these factors in establishing inventory levels.

One of the ratios used in inventory analysis is the inventory turnover—the relationship between inventory and cost of goods sold. Since the inventory is shown at cost, the ratio is computed by dividing the cost of goods sold rather than net sales by the average inventory. The figure used may be the average of the beginning and ending inventories of the period or, preferably, the average for the months involved, to minimize the effect of seasonal fluctuations. Although high turnover is usually a sign of good management, this ratio varies widely from one industry to another. A wholesaler of automobile parts and accessories may average five inventory turnovers per year as compared with thirty-five or more for a wholesaler of meat and poultry. Also, a high-volume, low-margin business would have to turn over its inventory more often than a similar business having a low-volume, high-margin policy.

The inventory turnover is computed as shown.

Cost of goods sold	**1**	$67,200
Average merchandise inventory:		
January 1, 1976	**2**	$15,400
December 31, 1976	**3**	11,480
Total	**4**	$26,880
Average (line **4** ÷ 2)	**5**	$13,440
Turnover of inventory (line **1** ÷ line **5**)		5.0

The King Corporation sold and replaced its merchandise inventory five times during the year; that is, the cost of merchandise sold was five times greater than the average cost of merchandise on hand.

Working Capital Turnover

The relationship between working capital and sales tests the efficiency with which the working capital is used. The computation is made as shown below.

	January 1, 1976	*December 31, 1976*
Working capital:		
Current assets	$71,500	$ 61,500
Current liabilities	29,000	30,825
Working capital	$42,500	$ 30,675
Average working capital		
($42,500 + $30,675 = $73,175) ÷ 2		$ 36,588
Net sales		$120,000
Working capital turnover		
($120,000 ÷ $36,588)		3.28

The King Corporation sold $3.28 worth of merchandise for each dollar of working capital. Another viewpoint is that each dollar invested in inventory was recovered, reinvested, and recovered again 3.28 times. The degree of financial strength indicated by this ratio is best determined by comparison with other businesses in the same line.

MERCHANDISING

(Ch. 5)

CASH DISCOUNTS—IMPLICATIONS TO MANAGEMENT

Cash discounts are computed on the net sales price; the conditions of payment are stated on the invoice. Typical cash discount terms are 2/10, n/30 and 1/10, n/60; the term n/30 means that the invoice must be paid without discount within 30 days (or 45 days if the term is n/45). The term of 2/10, n/30 means that if the buyer of merchandise pays within 10 days from the date shown on the invoice, he may deduct 2 percent from the invoice price, or he may take an additional 20 days, or 30 days in all, before paying the gross amount. It is important to recognize the magnitude of the discount offered. This can be done best if the discount is converted into its equivalent annual interest rate. Assuming terms of 2/10, n/30, the cost of the additional 20 days is high, because the loss of the 2 percent discount amounts to one-tenth of 1 percent per day (2% ÷ 20), or 36 percent per 360-day year (0.1% × 360). The prudent businessman should therefore take all cash discounts, even if he has to borrow the money to do so.

MANAGEMENT CONTROL—THE EXCEPTION PRINCIPLE

The control principle of management by exception involves isolating those amounts or accounts which indicate operating inefficiencies, and focusing attention on the areas that might require corrective action. Since only exceptions from the norm require such corrective action, management's task is simplified and expedited by separating from the mass of data the exceptional items for further study.

The alternative method for recording cash discounts, the *discounts not taken method,* illustrates the principle of management by exception. Under the *gross price method* discussed earlier in this chapter, the volume of discounts granted or taken is accumulated in the Sales Discounts and Purchases Discounts accounts. Management is interested primarily, however, not in the amount of discounts taken, since it assumes that all available discounts should be taken, but rather in the exceptions—that is, the discounts not taken.

Sales Discounts Not Taken

Assume that a $1,000 sale is made on April 1, with terms of 2/10, n/30, and that payment is received on April 10. The entries, recorded net of discount, are:

```
1976
Apr.  1   Accounts Receivable        980
              Sales                           980
     10   Cash                       980
              Accounts Receivable             980
```

If the payment were received on April 25, the entry would be:

```
1976
Apr. 25  Cash                              1,000
             Accounts Receivable                      980
             Sales Discounts Not Taken                 20
```

Sales Discounts Not Taken is classified as Other Revenue in the income statement.

Management should make a careful analysis of Sales Discounts Not Taken. A customer who does not take advantage of discount terms of 2/10, n/30, for example, is foregoing savings equivalent to an annual rate of 36 percent. This indicates an unwillingness or an inability to pay debts promptly, significant information in granting credit or evaluating possible losses from uncollectible accounts.

PURCHASES DISCOUNTS LOST METHOD

The rationale for the alternative method of recording purchases discounts under the purchases discounts lost method or net price procedure is the same as for the recording of sales discounts. Purchases are recorded at net of discount, and discounts lost are entered in a special account.

To illustrate the accounting for discounts lost by the purchases discounts lost method, assume that a purchase of $5,000 in merchandise is received on July 1, with terms of 2/10 n/30, and that the invoice is paid on July 10. Purchases and Accounts Payable recorded *net of discount* are:

```
1976
July  1  Purchases                         4,900
             Accounts Payable                        4,900
      10  Accounts Payable                  4,900
             Cash                                     4,900
```

If the invoice were not paid until July 15, the entries would be:

```
1976
July  1  Purchases                         4,900
             Accounts Payable                        4,900
      15  Accounts Payable                  4,900
          Purchases Discounts Lost            100
             Cash                                     5,000
```

Under the discounts lost procedure, the debit to Purchases is $4,900 whether or not the discount is lost, and the loss of $100 appears in a separate general and administrative expense account, isolating the amount for the detection of possible laxities in procedures. The loss of available discounts may indicate a weakness in the organization, such as lack of bank credit or slowness in processing invoices for payment. The cost of goods purchased is not increased when discounts are lost; the amount is classified under other expenses.

There are some disadvantages to recording purchases at the net price: (1) the amount of discounts taken is not reported separately in the income statement; (2) statements from creditors do not agree with the net amounts recorded in the accounts payable ledger; (3) the amounts entered on individual inventory record cards may not agree with the net amounts entered as purchases, since the inventory may be carried at invoice price; (4) the additional information may not justify the increased clerical costs and inconveniences; (5) an adjusting entry is needed at the end of the period to record lapsed discounts by debiting Purchases Discounts Lost and crediting Accounts Payable.

TRADE DISCOUNTS

Another class of discount is the *trade discount,* which, unlike the cash discount, is not recorded in the accounts. A trade discount is a percentage reduction from a list price. The seller prints a catalog in which the prices of the various articles are shown. The actual price charged may differ from the list price because of the class of buyer (wholesalers, retailers, and so on), the quantity ordered, or changes in the catalog. The granting of trade discounts eliminates the need for frequent reprinting of catalogs or printing different lists for different classes of buyers. If more than one discount is given—a so-called *chain discount*—each discount is applied successively to the declining balance to arrive at the invoice price. Thus, the actual price of an item listed at $300 less trade discounts of 20 percent, 10 percent, and 5 percent is $205.20. (Another way to compute the actual price is $300 \times 0.80 \times 0.90 \times 0.95 = $205.20.)

GLOSSARY

Cash Discount A reduction in price offered by terms of sale or purchase to encourage payment within the discount period.

Cost of Goods Sold A computation that appears on the income statement in a separate section. It is calculated by adding net purchases to the beginning inventory to derive the cost of goods available for sale and then deducting from this sum the ending inventory.

Exception Principle A principle of management that involves isolating amounts or accounts that indicate operating inefficiencies to focus attention on the areas that may require corrective action.

F.O.B. Destination The seller of merchandise bears the transportation cost to the buyer's location.

F.O.B. Shipping Point The buyer of merchandise bears the transportation cost from the point of shipment to the destination.

General and Administrative Expenses Amounts paid for goods or services generally reflecting the cost of supporting the marketing of the product other than the direct marketing cost.

Gross Margin The amount obtained by deducting the cost of goods sold from the net sales revenue.

Gross Price Method Accounting for cash discounts by accumulating the amount of the discount in Sales Discounts and in Purchases Discounts accounts.

Interim Statements Financial statements produced at regular or intermittent intervals during the accounting period for internal reasons.

Merchandise Inventory Turnover The ratio that shows the relationship between inventory and cost of goods sold.

Net Cost of Purchases The cost of all merchandise bought for sale including transportation in but reduced by purchases returns and allowances and purchases discounts.

Net Operating Margin Ratio The complement of the operating ratio; an indicator of the earning power of a business.

Net Price Method A procedure illustrative of the principle of management by exception by requiring that purchases and sales be recorded at net of discount prices in anticipation of qualifying for the discount.

Operating Expenses Past or present expenditures for goods or services used or expired in operating the business.

Operating Ratio An indicator of how much it costs to generate a dollar of net revenue; it is found by dividing total revenue deductions—operating expenses plus cost of goods sold—by net sales revenue.

Other Revenue and Other Expenses Extraneous items of ordinary revenue and expense that arise from a source other than the basic business purpose of the company.

Selling Expenses Direct expenses incurred in marketing the product.

Trade Discount A percentage reduction in a list price that, unlike the cash discount, is not recorded in the accounts.

Working Capital Turnover Measures the efficiency with which working capital has been used and is calculated by dividing net sales revenue by the average working capital.

Q5-1. What is the principal difference between the accounts of a merchandising business and those of a service business?

Q5-2. What is the procedure for entering and extending the merchandise inventory accounts on the work sheet of a merchandising business?

Q5-3. (a) What is the function of the Sales account? (b) the Sales Returns and Allowances account? (c) the Sales Discounts account?

Q5-4. (a) What is the function of the Purchases account? (b) the Purchases Returns and Allowances account? (c) the Purchases Discounts account? (d) the Transportation In account?

Q5-5. (a) What is the function of the Merchandise Inventory account? (b) How is its amount determined? In which columns of the work sheet is (c) the beginning inventory shown? (d) the ending inventory?

Q5-6. (a) How is the cost of goods sold determined? (b) Why is the cost of goods sold not recorded at the time of the sale? (c) What is the relationship between the cost of goods sold and the gross margin on sales?

Q5-7. Why is it desirable to show the following items separately on the income statement: (a) operating expenses and other expenses? (b) net operating margin and other revenue?

Q5-8. (a) How does the procedure of closing the books of a merchandising business differ from that of closing the books of a service business? (b) What advantage is gained by including merchandise inventory, beginning and ending, in the closing entries rather than in the adjusting entries? (c) List the various uses an accountant can make of the work sheet.

Q5-9. (a) What is the purpose of interim statements? (b) For whom are they prepared? (c) How are they prepared? (d) What special problems do they create?

Q5-10. Is it true (a) that management need not concern itself with the normal results but only with the exceptions? (b) that only the big exceptions require corrective action? (c) The alternative method for recording cash discounts illustrates the principle of management by exception. Can you think of any other alternative recording methods that further illustrate this principle? (d) What are the disadvantages of recording purchases at the net price?

Q5-11. (a) What is meant by *inventory turnover*? (b) "The greater the turnover of inventory, the greater the gross margin on sales." Is this statement correct? Explain. (c) What is the significance to management of the turnover of merchandise inventory? (d) Is there an advantage in using monthly inventories to compute the turnover?

Q5-12. What ratios or percentages would aid in answering the following questions: (a) Are the operating expenses excessive? (b) Is the company maintaining an efficient relationship between working capital and sales? (c) Are the total selling expenses excessive? (d) Is the merchandise on hand excessive?

Q5-13. Assume that a merchandise transaction was made on September 4. In each case determine the latest possible payment date to allow the discount deduction. (a) 1/10, n/30; (b) 1/10, n/60.

Q5-14. Discuss the significance of each of the following: (a) the operating ratio; (b) the turnover of inventory; and (c) the working capital turnover.

Q5-15. (a) Distinguish between a cash discount and a trade discount. (b) Why are trade discounts used in quoting prices? (c) What are the advantages, if any, of recording purchases of merchandise at the invoice amount less cash discount, or net, over recording the full, or gross, invoice amount? (d) Explain the term *2/10, n/30*. (e) Discuss and illustrate alternative income statement presentations of Purchases Discounts and Sales Discounts.

EXERCISES

E5-1. During the year 1976, the Corvi Sales Company purchased merchandise costing $10,900. In each of the following cases, calculate (a) the total merchandise available for sale, and (b) the cost of goods sold for the year.

Case	Beginning Inventory	Ending Inventory
1	None	None
2	$ 9,000	None
3	12,000	$15,000
4	None	3,000

E5-2. From the following information taken from the books of the Walker Company, prepare a partial income statement through gross margin on sales:

Merchandise Inventory, January 1, 1976	$ 1,800
Merchandise Inventory, January 31, 1976	1,300
Sales	12,900
Transportation In	400
Purchases Discounts	330
Sales Returns and Allowances	210
Purchases	5,600
Sales Discounts	120
Purchases Returns and Allowances	100

E5-3. Prepare general journal entries to record the following transactions on the books of the Baez Company:

1976

July 1 Sold merchandise to the Kane Company for $4,800, terms 2/10, n/30; F.O.B. destination. The Kane Company paid $275 freight on the shipment.

5 The Kane Company returned some unsatisfactory merchandise and received credit for $150.

10 The Kane Company mailed a check to the Baez Company for the net amount due.

E5-4. Prepare general journal entries to record the transactions in E5-3 on the books of the Kane Company.

E5-5. Prepare general journal entries to record the transactions in E5-3 on the books (a) of the Baez Company, and (b) of the Kane Company, assuming that the terms were F.O.B. shipping point.

E5-6. On June 5, Robert Bacon, who uses the net price procedure, purchased merchandise for $5,000; terms 2/10, n/30. The invoice was paid on July 1. (a) Record the purchase and the payment of the invoice. (b) Is the net cost of merchandise the same under both the gross and the net procedures? Show your computations. (c) Assume that Bacon takes advantage of all purchases discounts. Is there any advantage in his using the gross price method of recording the purchase of merchandise?

E5-7. Jean Gaylord, who uses the net price procedure, sold merchandise on May 1 for $6,000; terms 1/10, n/30. The customer paid the invoice on May 20. (a) Record the sale and the collection of the account receivable. (b) Would net sales revenue be the same under both the gross and the net procedures? Show your computations. (c) Compare and contrast the significance to management of the Sales Discounts Not Taken account and the Sales Discounts account.

E5-8. The Cordoza Company grants customer discounts on partial payments made within the discount period. On May 5, the company sold merchandise to Paul DeLobos for $5,000; terms 3/10, n/30. On May 15, the company received $2,500 to apply on account; on June 4, it received a check for the balance of the invoice. (a) Record the transactions for the Cordoza Company using (1) the net price procedure and (2) the gross price procedure. (b) Make the corresponding journal entries for Paul DeLobos.

E5-9. The following information is taken from John Rolando's books as of December 31, 1976:

Trial Balance		Adjustments Data	
1. Prepaid Insurance	$ 1,500	Expired Insurance	$1,000
2. Rent Expense	5,000	Rent paid in advance	1,200
3. Wages Expense	10,000	Accrued wages	500
4. Interest Expense	500	Accrued interest	100
5. Unearned Rent	4,000	Rent earned	2,500
6. Interest Earned	2,000	Unearned interest	600

For each account: (a) prepare the adjusting entry; (b) state the amount to be shown in the income statement; (c) state the amount to be shown in the statement of financial position.

E5-10. The following items are taken from John Inge's trial balance on December 31. The books are closed annually on December 31. All the store equipment was acquired three years ago.

	Debits	Credits
Notes Receivable (90-day, 9% note, dated December 1)	$ 8,000	
Prepaid Insurance (1-year policy, dated Aug. 1)	720	
Prepaid Rent (payable one year in advance on Sept. 1)	1,800	
Store Equipment (10-year life; salvage value $500)	20,500	
Notes Payable (120-day, 10% note, dated November 1)		$4,000
Rent Earned (1-year lease commencing April 1)		4,400

Prepare the adjusting entries.

E5-11. A section of the work sheet of the Ada Nevson Company is presented below. Enter the beginning and the ending inventory amounts in the appropriate columns.

Account Title	Trial Balance		Income Statement		Position Statement	
	Dr.	Cr.	Dr.	Cr.	Dr.	Cr.
Cash	4,000				4,000	
Accounts Receivable	11,000				11,000	
Merchandise Inventory						
Beginning inventory	$ 9,000					
Ending inventory	13,000					

E5-12. (*Financial policy decision problem*) The following information was taken from the financial statements of the Gordon Company.

	December 31, 1975	December 31, 1976
Net income		$ 4,000
Cost of goods sold		48,000
Total operating expenses		36,000
Merchandise inventory	$12,800	11,000
Current assets	29,600	31,000
Sales		92,000
Sales discounts		2,000
Sales returns and allowances		2,000
Current liabilities	15,200	10,000

a. Compute the following:
1. The operating ratio
2. The net operating margin ratio
3. The turnover of merchandise inventory
4. The working capital turnover

b. As a bank officer, would you approve a request by the company for a 2-year loan for $10,000?

E5-13. Footings for the partially completed work sheet of the Cyril Corporation are shown below.

	Income Statement		Position Statement	
	Dr.	Cr.	Dr.	Cr.
	15,650	20,200	43,100	38,550

Complete the work sheet.

E5-14. The Songin Company closes its books annually on December 31. An examination of its insurance policies show the following information:

Policy No.	Unexpired Premium— January 1, 1976	Remaining Life— January 1, 1976
3954	$630	21 months
4872	490	14 months
670	240	6 months

The following policies were purchased during 1976:

Policy No.	Date of Policy	Life of Policy	Prepaid Premium
65412	March 1	2 years	$ 720
8941	August 1	3 years	900
4624	November 1	5 years	2,100

a. What was the balance of the Prepaid Insurance account as of January 1, 1976? The Songin Company debits Prepaid Insurance for all purchases of insurance policies.

b. What was the adjusting entry necessary on December 31, 1976?

c. Reproduce the T accounts for Prepaid Insurance and Insurance Expense as they would appear in the general ledger after the closing entries have been posted on December 31, 1976.

d. Assuming that no additional premiums are paid during 1977, what will be the adjusting entry on December 31, 1977?

E5-15. On January 1, 1974, the Matthew Company entered into a 10-year lease for the rental of a factory from the Seth Investment Corporation. The terms of the lease provided for a rental adjustment whereby the Matthew Company would pay the Seth Investment Corporation for any increase in real estate taxes in excess of a base assessment of $100,000 and a tax rate of $62 per $1,000 of assessed valuation. Make the adjusting entries for the Matthew Company for 1974, 1975, and 1976, assuming the following:

Year	Assessment	Tax Rate per $1,000
1974	$100,000	$65
1975	100,000	68
1976	105,000	70

E5-16. The statement of financial position of the Stein Company at December 31, 1975, showed:

Accrued Interest Receivable	$2,600
Unearned Interest Revenue	300

During 1976, interest collected in cash amounted to $4,800. The statement of financial position at December 31, 1976, showed:

Accrued Interest Receivable	$2,280
Unearned Interest Revenue	195

Compute the amount of interest earned that should appear on the income statement for 1976.

E5-17. The following information was taken from the records of the Mather Company at September 30, 1976, the end of the fiscal year:

a. On April 1, $5,700 was collected as subscription revenue for one year; Unearned Subscription Revenue was credited.

b. On March 1, 1976, a 1-year, 10% note for $5,100 was received from a customer.

c. The company has an 8% mortgage note payable outstanding with a face value of $850,000; the interest on this note is payable semiannually on March 1 and September 1.

d. The store supplies inventory on September 30, 1975, was $10,625; acquisitions of $31,550 for the year were charged to Stores Supplies; a physical count on September 30, 1976, disclosed store supplies costing $14,450 on hand.

Make the adjusting entries.

DEMON-
STRATION
PROBLEMS

DP5-1. (*Cash discounts: gross and net price procedures*) The following transactions were completed by the Hehre Company during June 1976:

1976

June 1   Sold merchandise on account to the Leib Company for $900; terms, 2/10, n/30.

     5   Purchased merchandise from the Jean Company for $1,000; terms, 1½/10, n/30.

     7   Purchased merchandise on account from the Faro Corporation for $850; terms, 1/10, n/30, F.O.B. shipping point.

     7   Sold merchandise to the Mutual Corporation for $1,200; terms, 1/10, n/30.

   10   Paid freight charges of $20 on the merchandise purchased from the Faro Corporation.

   11   Received payment from the Leib Company, less the cash discount.

   12   Received a $100 credit (gross amount) for defective merchandise returned to the Faro Corporation.

   15   Paid the Faro Corporation.

   25   Paid the Jean Company.

   25   Received payment from the Mutual Corporation.

Required:

1a. Journalize the transactions, using the gross price method.

  b. Prepare the cost of goods sold section of the income statement. Assume the following inventories: June 1, $500; June 30, $850.

2a. Journalize the transactions, using the net price procedure.

  b. Prepare the cost of goods sold section of the income statement. Assume inventories as in 1b.

  3. Under the net price procedure, how are Purchases Discounts Lost and Sales Discounts Not Taken classified in the income statement?

DP5-2. (*Work sheet and financial statements*) The trial balance of the Duarte Company for the year 1976 is shown below.

DUARTE COMPANY
Trial Balance
December 31, 1976

Account Title	Debits	Credits
Cash	$ 84,200	
Accounts Receivable	366,300	
Merchandise Inventory	110,000	
Office Supplies	46,200	
Prepaid Insurance	50,900	
Store Equipment	479,100	
Accumulated Depreciation—		
Store Equipment		$ 77,500
Accounts Payable		125,000
Notes Payable		69,300
Capital Stock		570,500
Retained Earnings		132,000
Dividends	44,000	
Sales		1,098,300
Sales Returns and Allowances	22,000	
Sales Discounts	20,300	
Purchases	649,000	
Transportation In	33,000	
Purchases Returns and Allowances		13,200
Purchases Discounts		19,800
Salesmen's Salaries Expense	84,500	
Transportation Out Expense	10,600	
Advertising Expense	31,700	
Rent Expense	42,300	
Heat and Light Expense	15,900	
Miscellaneous Expense	15,600	
Totals	$2,105,600	$2,105,600

Supplementary data on December 31, 1976:
a. Merchandise inventory, $92,400
b. Unexpired insurance, $30,800
c. Office supplies on hand, $17,600
d. Depreciation on store equipment, $10,600
e. Estimated income taxes for the year, $52,800

Required:

1. Complete the work sheet.
2. Prepare an income statement with a percent analysis.
3. Prepare a position statement with a percent analysis.
4. Prepare a statement of retained earnings.
5. Explain the significance of the percent analyses.

DP5-3. (*Financial statement analysis*) The statement of financial position of the Rose Company as of December 31, 1976, follows:

ROSE COMPANY
Statement of Financial Position
December 31, 1976

Assets

Current Assets
Cash	$54,000	
Marketable Securities	27,000	
Accounts Receivable	54,000	
Notes Receivable	16,000	
Merchandise Inventory	108,000	
Prepaid Insurance	11,000	
Total Current Assets		$270,000

Plant and Equipment
Store Equipment	$176,000	
Deduct Accumulated Depreciation	41,000	
Total Plant and Equipment		135,000
Total Assets		**$405,000**

Liabilities and Owner's Equity

Current Liabilities
Accounts Payable	$51,300	
Notes Payable	43,200	
Accrued Wages Payable	13,500	
Total Current Liabilities		$108,000

Long-Term Liabilities
Mortgage Payable (due December 31, 1983)	189,000	
Total Liabilities		$297,000
E. Rose, Capital		108,000
Total Liabilities and Owner's Equity		**$405,000**

Additional data:
a.	E. Rose, Capital, January 1, 1976	$ 81,000
b.	Net sales	324,000
c.	Net income	32,000
d.	Cost of goods sold	162,000
e.	Merchandise inventory, January 1, 1976	135,000
f.	Total operating expenses	130,000

Required:

1. Compute the following (show all your computations): (a) current ratio, (b) working capital, (c) operating ratio, (d) acid-test ratio, (e) turnover of merchandise inventory, (f) net operating margin ratio.
2. Explain the significance of the ratios: (a) to Rose, (b) to the holder of the mortgage, (c) to the holder of the note payable.
3. What additional data are needed for a more comprehensive analysis of Rose's financial statements?

DP5-4. (*Closing entries*) The following account balances were taken from the Income Statement columns of John O'Brien's work sheet for the year ended December 31, 1976:

Account Title	Income Statement	
	Debit	Credit
Merchandise Inventory	23,760	25,650
Sales		62,370
Sales Returns and Allowances	745	
Sales Discounts	1,215	
Purchases	19,210	
Transportation In	1,015	
Purchases Returns and Allowances		610
Purchases Discounts		1,730
Selling Expenses	4,590	
General Expenses	9,720	
Totals	60,255	90,360
Net Income	30,105	
	90,360	90,360

The Position Statement Debit column showed a balance of $3,500 in the John O'Brien, Drawing account.

Required: Prepare closing journal entries.

PROBLEMS

P5-1. The accountant of the Jesson Corporation prepared the following trial balance at December 31, 1976:

JESSON CORPORATION
Trial Balance
December 31, 1976

Account Title	Debits	Credits
Cash	$ 2,850	
Accounts Receivable	92,500	
Prepaid Insurance	4,800	
Merchandise Inventory	104,500	
Store Equipment	57,800	
Accumulated Depreciation—		
Store Equipment		$ 11,400
Accounts Payable		17,000
Notes Payable		38,000
Capital Stock		95,000
Retained Earnings		20,900

Account Title	Debits	Credits
Dividends	19,800	
Sales		345,800
Purchases	161,500	
Advertising Expense	7,000	
Miscellaneous Selling Expense	7,600	
Wages Expense	55,100	
Miscellaneous General Expense	11,200	
Rent Expense	4,600	
Interest Expense	900	
Interest Earned		750
Rent Earned		1,300
Totals	$530,150	$530,150

Additional data:

a. Included in Advertising Expense is a charge of $1,520 for space in the January 1977 issue of a monthly periodical.

b. The Prepaid Insurance account consists of premiums paid on the following policies:

Policy No.	Date of Policy	Life of Policy	Premium
A938	January 1, 1976	6 months	$1,900
J672	September 1, 1976	3 years	2,300
N531	October 1, 1976	1 year	600
Total			$4,800

c. The Store Equipment account consists of the following acquisitions:

Purchase Date	Cost	Useful Life	Salvage Value
Prior to January 1, 1976	$41,800	10 years	$3,800
April 1, 1976	2,700	10 years	400
July 1, 1976	1,900	5 years	200
October 1, 1976	11,400	15 years	1,200
Total	$57,800		

d. A physical count of store supplies shows $475 worth on hand at December 31, 1976. At the time of purchase, Miscellaneous General Expense was debited.

e. On October 1, the Jesson Corporation rented some of its equipment to the Jere Company for eight months under the following terms: $325 a month payable in two payments of $1,300 each on October 1, 1976, and February 1, 1977.

f. Wages earned by employees but unpaid on December 31, 1976, totaled $950.

g. Property taxes of $575 for 1976 are unpaid.

h. An invoice of $575 from the Packing Materials Company, dated December 14, 1976, for shipping cartons is discovered and is to be recorded as a Miscellaneous Selling Expense.

i. Shipping cartons on hand at December 31 were worth $575.

j. The Notes Payable account consists of a 90-day, 9% note dated November 1, 1976, issued to a bank.

k. The merchandise inventory at December 31, 1976, was $85,500. Income taxes for the year were estimated at $21,850.

Required: In schedule form as in the example, show:

a. The adjusting entries.
b. The section of the position statement affected by the adjusting entries.
c. The section of the income statement affected by the adjusting entries.
d. The amount reported on the appropriate financial statement.

Item 1 has been entered as an example.

Item	Explanation	Adjusting Entries		Financial Statement Classification	Amount Reported on Financial Statement
		Dr.	Cr.		
1	Prepaid Advertising	1,520		Current Asset (PS)	1,520
	Advertising Expense		1,520	Selling Expense (IS)	5,480

P5-2. The following balances, arranged in alphabetical order, were taken from the Adjusted Trial Balance columns of the work sheet of the Beaver Corporation for the fiscal year ended June 30, 1976. The inventory on that date was $27,100.

Account Title	Amount
Accounts Payable	$ 9,775
Accounts Receivable	13,650
Accumulated Depreciation—Delivery Equipment	4,550
Advertising Expense	1,425
Capital Stock	53,700
Cash	3,900
Delivery Equipment	13,650
Delivery Expense	2,850
Depreciation Expense—Delivery Equipment	2,150
Dividends	3,900
Gain on Disposal of Marketable Securities	450
Heat and Light Expense	1,160
Income Tax Expense	2,800
Income Taxes Payable	2,800
Insurance Expense	2,240
Interest Earned	325
Interest Expense	210
Loss on Disposal of Land	4,560

Account Title	Amount
Marketable Securities	28,380
Merchandise Inventory, July 1, 1975	29,100
Notes Payable	2,600
Office Supplies	920
Prepaid Advertising	1,170
Prepaid Insurance	1,850
Purchases	77,600
Purchases Discounts	940
Purchases Returns and Allowances	1,600
Rent Earned	2,350
Rent Expense	3,250
Retained Earnings	13,000
Sales	120,250
Sales Discounts	2,100
Sales Returns and Allowances	5,600
Salesmen's Salaries Expense	8,175
Transportation In	1,700

Required:

1. Prepare an income statement for the year ended June 30, 1976.
2. Prepare a statement of retained earnings for the year ended June 30, 1976.
3. Prepare a statement of financial position as of June 30, 1976.

P5-3. The following information was taken from the general ledger of the Helene Corporation on December 31, 1976:

Account Title	Amount
Cash	$ 18,200
Marketable Securities	48,400
Accounts Receivable	106,600
Notes Receivable	18,200
Accrued Interest Receivable	–0–
Merchandise inventory, January 1, 1976	130,000
Store Supplies	–0–
Advertising Supplies	–0–
Prepaid Insurance	6,500
Store Equipment	105,300
Accumulated Depreciation—Store Equipment	26,000
Accounts Payable	57,200
Notes Payable	59,800
Accrued Interest Payable	–0–
Accrued Wages Payable	–0–
Income Taxes Payable	–0–
Accrued Mortgage Interest Payable	–0–
Unearned Rent	–0–
Mortgage Payable (due 1980)	39,000
Capital Stock	130,000
Retained Earnings	39,000
Dividends	14,300
Sales	650,000

Account Title	Amount
Purchases	367,900
Transportation In	6,500
Advertising Expense	12,700
Miscellaneous Selling Expense	19,500
Depreciation Expense—Store Equipment	–0–
Heat, Light, and Power Expense	13,000
Insurance Expense	–0–
Miscellaneous General Expense	22,900
Income Tax Expense	–0–
Rent Expense	12,500
Wages Expense	98,800
Interest Expense	3,900
Interest Earned	1,000
Rent Earned	3,200
Income Summary	–0–

Data for the end-of-period adjustments are as follows:

a. The Prepaid Insurance account consists of the following policies:

Policy Number	Date of Policy	Life of Policy	Premiums
A648	January 1, 1976	3 years	$3,900
P832	July 1, 1976	2 years	2,600

b. The Notes Receivable account consists of a 60-day, 9% note dated December 1, 1976.
c. The Notes Payable consists of a 90-day, 9% note dated December 1, 1976.
d. Purchases of store equipment were as follows:

Purchase Date	Cost	Useful Life	Salvage Value
January 1, 1971	$57,200	10 years	$5,200
April 1, 1976	26,000	20 years	–0–
July 1, 1976	22,100	8 years	1,300

e. Wages earned by employees but unpaid as of December 31, 1976, totaled $1,000.
f. Income taxes for the year were estimated at $9,100.
g. On August 1, 1976, the Helene Corporation rented some store equipment to the O'Leary Company for 12 months and received a check for $3,200 representing the entire year's rental fee.
h. Interest on the mortgage payable is $2,100 a year, paid in semiannual installments on May 1 and November 1, 1976.
i. Inventories on December 31, 1976:

Merchandise	$93,000
Advertising Supplies	3,100
Store Supplies (the original debit was made to Miscellaneous General Expense)	800

Required:

1. Prepare a work sheet for the year ended December 31, 1976.
2. Prepare (a) an income statement, (b) a statement of retained earnings, and (c) a statement of financial position.
3. Prepare the closing entries.

P5-4. The following accounts were taken from the statement of financial position of the Sara Boyajian Company as of June 30, 1976, the end of its first year of operations:

S. Boyajian, Drawing	$10,000
Accounts Payable	22,900
Accounts Receivable	23,600
Cash	15,000
Equipment (net)	7,500
S. Boyajian, Capital	76,300
Merchandise Inventory	39,000
Prepaid Expenses	4,100

The merchandise inventory on July 1, 1975, was $42,000. The net income for the year was $21,300.

Required:

1. Evaluate the company's financial position at June 30, 1976.
2. Compare Boyajian's financial position with what it would have been if she had made a comparable investment in high-quality bonds paying 8% annually and was employed as a manager at an annual salary of $20,000.
3. Assume that when the ending inventory was taken, there was a calculation error which resulted in a $2,500 overstatement of the ending inventory. How would this change your evaluations in requirements 1 and 2?

P5-5. The accounts and balances in the Income Statement columns of Thomas Cohen's work sheet for the year ended December 31, 1976, are given below.

Account Title	Income Statement	
	Dr.	Cr.
Merchandise Inventory	11,400	12,350
Sales		29,070
Sales Returns and Allowances	95	
Sales Discounts	665	
Purchases	13,300	
Transportation In	380	
Purchases Returns and Allowances		190
Purchases Discounts		950
Selling Expenses	3,420	
General Expenses	5,700	
Totals	34,960	42,560
Net Income	7,600	
	42,560	42,560

MERCHANDISING

The Position Statement Debit column of the work sheet showed $1,900 for Thomas Cohen, Drawing.

Required:

1. Prepare an income statement for 1976.
2. Journalize the closing entries.
3. Show the Merchandise Inventory and the Income Summary accounts after the closing entries have been posted.
4. Explain (a) the difference, if any, between the closing entries of a trading business and those of a nontrading business, and (b) whether the Income Summary account may be eliminated.

Accounting Systems: An Introduction

6

The system of recording, classifying, summarizing, and reporting accounting information discussed in the preceding chapters has been satisfactory for teaching the fundamentals of the accounting process, but a business of any size will usually find it necessary to modify the methods of capturing the flow of accounting data to meet the needs of the particular business firm. This chapter describes briefly how a simple system is designed for a business. Since a knowledge of accounting standards is an essential element in the understanding of an accounting system, a discussion of basic accounting standards is included in the Appendix to this chapter.

DESIGN OF A RECORD SYSTEM

The transaction is the basic source of accounting data; it is central to the collection process. Before data processing by any system can begin, some evidence that a transaction has occurred must exist. Source documents, discussed in Chapter 1, such as purchases invoices, sales invoices, and receiver's reports indicate the occurrence of transactions. The data must then be introduced into the system. Data can be captured and processed from these transactions by handwritten procedures, by accounting machines, punched-card equipment, electronic equipment, or by a combination of these methods. The similarity of these concepts of data collection, and that they all lead to the same results, is shown in Figure 6-1. The primary difference is in the methods of collection; however, the greater the volume and variety of information re-

Figure 6-1
Information Flow
Chart

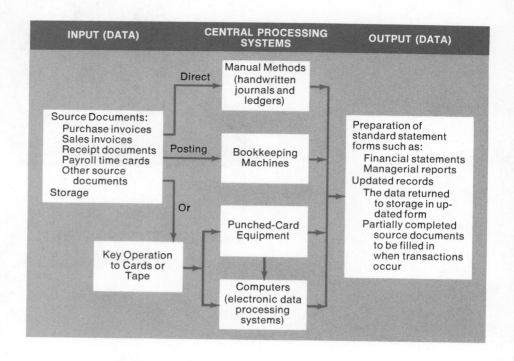

| INPUT (DATA) | CENTRAL PROCESSING SYSTEMS | OUTPUT (DATA) |

quired, the more sophisticated, detailed, and elaborate is the collection process.

The information flow then is from input to output. It is the function of the systems analyst to create a method of collecting these data that will permit management to measure and control its human and physical resources to its best advantage. This design requires a thorough examination of the company's table of organization, its personnel and job descriptions, the current forms in use, the procedures and policies of the organization, and the legal constraints on the business or industry, if the analyst is to gauge the integrity and accuracy of the measurement of the flow of information.

The development of the system will generally be in three stages: (1) *study and design,* (2) *implementation,* and (3) *operation.* The company's operation is studied and a method of collection is proposed for adoption. Once adopted it is put into operation for verification, for review for improvements and redesign, and for testing for effectiveness of the controls. The flow of information from the source of input to the disposition of the output is examined with the following considerations:

1. *Where* will the information be found and stored?
2. *Who* will use the information?
3. *What* will be the application of the information?
4. *When* will the information be needed?

The criteria for selection of the method of collecting the flow of information are listed below.

1. *Speed.* Information should be available when it is needed. The size of the organization is a significant factor in the requirement for timely access to information. The larger the business, the greater will be the amount of data flow.

2. *Accuracy and Reliability of Information.* Error controls should be established in all methods. The more times information is written or manipulated, the greater the opportunity for error.

3. *Volume of Data.* Storage areas or files of data are a major consideration in business data processing because of the mass of data flow. Quick retrieval of this information in usable form is a desirable feature of a good accounting system.

4. *Cost Balanced against Benefits.* The critical criterion is *cost.* The return is not always easily observed or measured; however, the cost is measured per unit or transaction. For instance, the computer is expensive as a system, but its efficiency and volume of usage are making it less expensive per transaction processed. The improvement in the design brought about by the systems examination can bring about economies by eliminating duplication of unneeded services, by increasing productivity, by reducing inventories and capital outlay, and by the improvement of operations. These are important factors in consideration of cost benefit. Clearly, a business should strive for the system that provides the necessary information at the least cost.

5. *Time Cycles.* The frequency of the transactions, the peak periods, and the deadlines are important areas to be determined in the examination.

6. *Priorities and Sequence of Events.* The establishment of the priorities for reports, the need for reports, and the order in which events occur are integral parts of a study of information flow.

7. *Media.* The most efficient type of media for the input, output, and storage must be examined. Can the information be stored on disk or tape, or must it be stored on paper?

Thus, setting up a system for collecting and processing data in a business requires a total examination of the business and its environment. In view of the foregoing, it now becomes necessary to trace the evolution of a simple manual system by expanding the general journal and the ledgers.

EXPANSION OF GENERAL JOURNAL: EVOLUTION OF A SIMPLE MANUAL SYSTEM

As the frequency of similar transactions increases, a more efficient means of processing the resulting data must be devised than the two-column general journal illustrated in the preceding chapters. With the use of this journal each entry must be posted individually to its general ledger accounts, and with the use of subsidiary ledger accounts each entry must be posted a second time. In essence, the data in the journal are repeated in detail in the ledger. In a large business, as thousands of transactions occur each day, some means of streamlining the method and accelerating the processing of these data must be developed.

The accounting records and procedures should be designed to meet the needs of the individual business firm. For example, for a small firm where one accountant records all the transactions, additional columns (each representing an account that receives repetitive entries) may be added to the general journal. As the number of transactions increases, however, and the processing becomes physically impossible for one accountant to perform, it will be necessary to group similar transactions into classes and use a special journal for recording each class of transactions. As a company grows and the volume of transactions further increases, it becomes necessary to use more (and perhaps more complex) accounting machines in the processing of the accounting data.

Special Journals

The manual system illustrated in the following pages saves time in recording the transactions and posting. This system also enables a business to divide the collection process among several employees. Small businesses, or those businesses with limited transactions, find this type of system or adaptations of it useful. Modifying some of the journals and subsidiary ledgers for use with mechanical equipment improves its utility.

The procedures in the preceding chapters can be modified principally by creating several journals for the purpose of recording special classes of transactions. Grouping transactions into classes and using a special journal to record each class offer the opportunity for the rapid and efficient processing of accounting data. The number and kinds of journals used are influenced by the type of business and the information desired. The model used in this text is shown in the following chart:

Journal	Kind of Transaction	Symbol
Sales Journal	Sale of merchandise on account	S
Purchases Journal	Purchase of merchandise on account	P
Cash Receipts Journal	Receipt of cash	CR
Cash Payments Journal	Payment of cash	CP
General Journal	All other transactions that are not grouped in the four classes above—for example, closing and adjusting entries, purchase of merchandise by note, purchase of equipment or supplies on account or by note, sales and purchases returns and allowances.	J

Special journals offer the following advantages:

1. Similar transactions are grouped in chronological order in one place. All credit sales of merchandise, for example, are entered in the sales journal.

2. The repeated writing of each account title—Sales, Purchases, Cash, and so on—is eliminated.
3. Postings are made from column footings in total only—rather than item by item—thereby reducing the volume of work. The general ledger is relieved of unnecessary detail, since fewer postings are made. As a result of the fewer postings, the general ledger is more compact and easier to use, thus reducing the probability of error.
4. Bookkeeping duties may be divided by function. For example, one person may enter information regarding charge sales, taken from *sales* invoices, in the sales journal; a second person may post either from the sales journal or directly from the sales slips to the accounts receivable ledger; a third person may enter cash received from charge customers in the cash receipts journal and post to the accounts receivable ledger; and a fourth person may verify the accuracy of the work by comparing the accounts receivable ledger with the Accounts Receivable controlling account in the general ledger.

This division of responsibilities not only facilitates and accelerates the work flow but also creates some protection against errors and the misappropriation of assets.

An essential feature of *internal control*—the built-in safeguards for the protection of the assets of an enterprise—is the careful planning and supervision of the record keeping of a company and a division of the work so that no one employee has complete control both of an operation of the business and of the recording of that operation.

Internal Control

Sales Journal

All sales of merchandise on account are recorded in the sales journal.[1] To illustrate the use of the sales journal, assume that the following transactions took place at the Hayward Casuals during June, 1976:

1976
June   3   Sold merchandise to Ella Gray, $400; terms 1/15, n/60, invoice No. 1
         4   Sold merchandise to William Ramey, $600; terms 2/10, n/30, invoice No. 2
         5   Sold merchandise to Arthur James, $300; terms 1/5, n/30, invoice No. 3
        30   Sold merchandise to Byron Butts, $800; terms 2/10, n/30, invoice No. 4

When merchandise is sold on account, the transaction is recorded in the sales journal as follows:

1. The date of the transaction is entered in the Date column.

[1] Despite the advantages of management by exception in the alternative methods of recording sales and purchases net of discounts (see Chapter 5), illustrations in Chapter 6 follow the gross procedure to simplify the examples.

(Ch. 6)

Figure 6-2
Simple Sales Journal

			SALES JOURNAL			Page 1
Date		Sales Invoice No.	Account Debited	Terms	F	Amount
1976 June	3	1	Ella Gray	1/15, n/60		400
	4	2	William Ramey	2/10, n/30		600
	5	3	Arthur James	1/5, n/30		300
	30	4	Byron Butts	2/10, n/30		800
	30		Accounts Receivable, Dr.—Sales, Cr.			2,100

2. Sales invoices (or slips) are numbered in sequence; the numbers are entered in chronological order in the Sales Invoice No. column.
3. The name of the customer to whom the sale was made is entered in the Account Debited column.
4. The terms of the sale are listed in the Terms column.
5. If the subsidiary ledger account has a folio, or reference number, it is entered in the folio (F) column when posting is complete; otherwise, a check mark is entered.
6. The amount of the sale is entered in the Amount column.

A simple sales journal is illustrated in Figure 6-2, which shows the entries for the transactions of Hayward Casuals listed above.

Each entry in the sales journal is a debit to the Accounts Receivable account and to the customer's account in the accounts receivable ledger, and a credit to the Sales account. Expressed in the form of a two-column general journal entry, the entry for the sale made on June 1, for example, would be:

Accounts Receivable—Ella Gray	400	
Sales		400

The transaction is *not* actually recorded in both the general journal and the sales journal. It is shown in this manner only to illustrate the difference between the two forms.

Each amount is posted separately as a debit to the accounts receivable ledger, supporting the single debit that is posted at the end of the month to the Accounts Receivable controlling account in the general ledger. Posting to the subsidiary ledger accounts is usually done daily. It is important to have the up-to-date balance of each customer's account readily available so that requests for this information from the customer, the credit department, or others' may be readily fulfilled.[2]

The daily posting is usually done in the following sequence:

1. The amount of the sale is posted to the Debit column of the customer's account and is added to the balance, if any, in the Balance column.
2. The journal symbol and page number (S1) is written in the folio (F) column.
3. The date of the sale is recorded in the Date column.
4. A check mark is placed in the folio (F) column of the sales journal to indicate that the entry has been posted.

At the end of the month, the Amount column of the sales journal is totaled. The total, the date of the transfer, and the sales journal page number are then posted to the debit side of the Accounts Receivable controlling account and to the credit side of the Sales account in the general ledger. The general ledger account numbers are recorded in the sales journal immediately below the footing. To minimize errors, a systematic procedure should be followed in posting. The following sequence is suggested:

Debit posting:
1. The amount is posted to the Debit money column of the Accounts Receivable account in the general ledger.
2. The journal symbol (S1) is written in the folio (F) column of the account.
3. The date is recorded in the Date column.
4. The Accounts Receivable account number is written in parentheses below and to the left of the double rule in the Amount column of the journal.

Credit posting:
5. The same amount as the debit posting is posted to the Credit money column of the Sales account in the general ledger.
6. The journal symbol (S1) is written in the folio (F) column of the account.
7. The date is recorded in the Date column.
8. The Sales account number is written in parentheses below the double rule in the Amount column of the journal, to the right of the debit posting reference number.

Postings from the sales journal of the Hayward Casuals for the month of June 1976 are shown in Figure 6-3.

Purchases Journal

The relationship of the purchases journal and the accounts payable ledger is similar to that of the sales journal and the accounts receivable ledger. All purchases of merchandise on account are recorded in the purchases journal. The transactions of the Hayward Casuals during June 1976 illustrate the use of this journal.

---

[2] A common form of subsidiary ledger account has three money columns—all on the right-hand side—for debits, credits, and balance. This form is introduced on page 45 and is illustrated for machine posting in Figure 6-11.

Figure 6-3
Posting Flow from the
Sales Journal

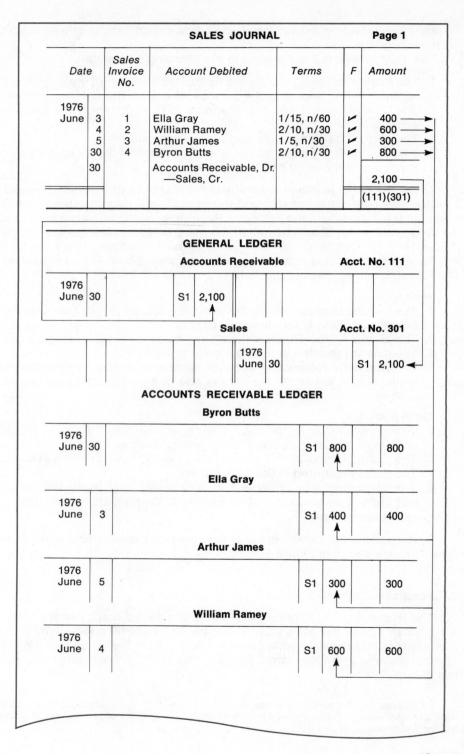

1976

June 3 Purchased merchandise on account from Oakland Clothing Company, $900; terms 2/10, n/20.

     8 Purchased merchandise on account from Southland Apparel, $400; terms 2/10, n/60.

   16 Purchased merchandise on account from San Francisco Clothiers, $500; terms 3/5, n/30.

   28 Purchased merchandise on account from the Dexter Custom Tailors, $700; terms 1/20, n/60.

Figure 6-4 shows how these transactions are recorded in the purchases journal and posted to the general and subsidiary ledger accounts.

Expressed as a two-column general journal entry, the first entry in the purchases journal would be:

Purchases	900	
Accounts Payable—Oakland Clothing Co.		900

The transaction is *not* actually recorded in both the general journal and the purchases journal. It is shown in this manner to illustrate the difference between the two recording forms.

Each transaction is posted separately as a credit to the accounts payable ledger to support the credit posted at the end of the month to the Accounts Payable controlling account in the general ledger. Transactions are usually posted to the subsidiary ledger daily. The date of the entry in the subsidiary ledger account is the invoice date, which is significant in determining if a discount may be taken. At the end of the month, the Amount column of the purchases journal is footed. This total is posted to the Purchases account in the general ledger as a debit. The same total is posted to the Accounts Payable controlling account in the general ledger as a credit.

Cash Receipts Journal

All transactions involving the receipt of cash are entered in the cash receipts journal. A multicolumn form of cash receipts journal is illustrated in Figure 6-5. The column headings typically provide the flexibility necessary to record cash receipts from customers or any other source and to record sales discounts. The form may be varied, particularly in the number and headings of the columns, to meet the needs of the individual business.

Explanation of the various columns in the cash receipts journal follows.

1. The date of the transaction is entered in the Date column.
2. The explanation of the transaction is written in the Explanation column. Every transaction entered in this journal includes a debit to Cash.
3. There are three debit columns. Cash debits are entered in the first Debit column.
4. The Sales Discount Debit column is used for recording discounts granted to customers for paying within the discount period.

Figure 6-4 Posting Flow from the Purchases Journal

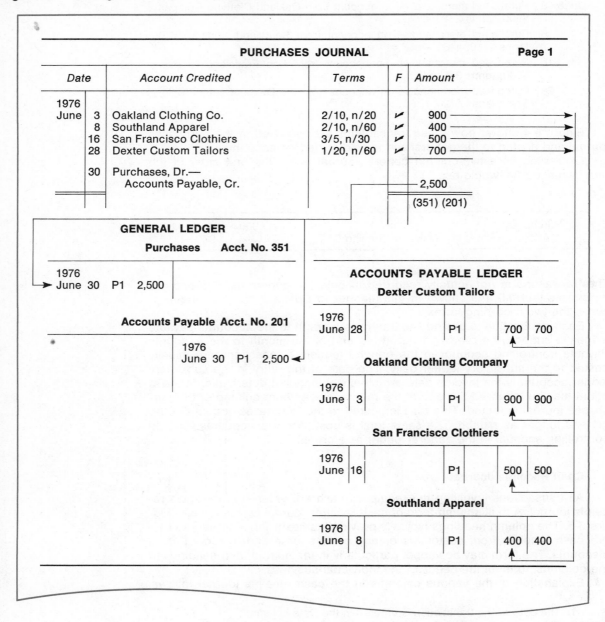

5. The Other Accounts Debit column is for debits to general ledger accounts for which no special columns have been provided.
6. There are three folio columns, two labeled (F), one, ($\checkmark$); a posting symbol indicating that the amount has been posted to the general ledger or to the accounts receivable ledger is placed in the folio column.

Figure 6-5 Column Headings of a Multicolumn Cash Receipts Journal

CASH RECEIPTS JOURNAL										**Page 1**
		Debits					Account Credited	Credits		
Date	Explanation	Cash	Sales Disc.	Other Accounts				Accounts Receivable	Sales	Other Accounts
				Account Title	F	Amount		✓ Amount		F Amount

7. The name of the general ledger or subsidiary ledger account to be credited is written in the Account Credited column.
8. When a charge customer makes a payment on account, an entry is made in the Accounts Receivable Credit column, the first of three credit columns. The amount entered is the actual amount of cash received plus any sales discounts properly taken by the customer.
9. Sales of merchandise for cash are entered in the Sales Credit column.
10. The Other Accounts Credit column is for credits to general ledger accounts for which no special columns have been provided.

The Hayward Casuals cash receipts journal for June 1976 is illustrated in Figure 6-6.

Figure 6-6 Cash Receipts Journal

CASH RECEIPTS JOURNAL										**Page 1**
		Debits					Account Credited	Credits		
Date	Explanation	Cash	Sales Disc.	Other Accounts				Accounts Receivable	Sales	Other Accounts
				Account Title	F	Amount		✓ Amount		F Amount
1976 June 1	Invested in business	2,500					W. Ray, Capital			2,500
10	Payment in full	588	12				William Ramey	600		
15	Cash sales	1,000					Sales		1,000	
18	Payment in full	396	4				Ella Gray	400		
22	Borrowed from bank	600					Notes Payable			600
30	Cash sales	950					Sales		950	
30	Payment on account	100		Notes Receivable		200	Arthur James	300		
30	Totals	6,134	16			200		1,300	1,950	3,100

In previous chapters, transactions involving the receipt of cash were recorded in a simple two-column general journal. Similar transactions are recorded in a cash receipts journal in Figure 6-6. Although each transaction may be entered on a single line, the equality of debits and credits is still maintained through the use of multiple columns. The following is an analysis of the debit-credit relationship of the entries in Figure 6-6 to indicate their effect on the accounts. These transactions, however, are *actually recorded* only in the cash receipts journal, not the general journal.

Transaction:
1976
June   1   William Ray, the owner, invested $2,500 in the Hayward Casuals.

Analysis of Debits and Credits:

Cash	2,500	
W. Ray, Capital		2,500

Cash is debited by entering the amount in the Cash Debit column. Since there is no special column for W. Ray, Capital, the amount is entered in the Other Accounts credit column.

Transaction:
1976
June 10   Received payment in full from William Ramey.

Analysis of Debits and Credits:

Cash	588	
Sales Discounts	12	
Accounts Receivable		600

The sales journal shows that on June 4 merchandise with an invoice price of $600 was sold to William Ramey; terms 2/10, n/30. Since payment was made within 10 days, Ramey deducted $12 from the invoice price and paid $588. Entering the three amounts in the special columns as shown has the same effect on the general ledger as the explanatory debit and credit analysis does. The customer's name is entered in the Account Credited column for posting to the accounts receivable ledger. If cash receipts from charge customers are numerous, a daily total may be entered from an adding machine tape; posting to the subsidiary ledger is done from supporting documents.

Transaction:
1976
June 15   Cash sales for the first half of the month were $1,000.

Analysis of Debits and Credits:

Cash	1,000	
Sales		1,000

(Ch. 6)

The word *Sales* is written in the Account Credited column to fill the space. However, it can be omitted, since both the debit and the credit amounts are entered in the special columns. Although a one-half month summary amount is used to simplify the illustration, cash sales *should be* recorded during each business day.

Transaction:
1976
June 18   Received full payment from Ella Gray.

Analysis of Debits and Credits:

Cash	396	
Sales Discounts	4	
Accounts Receivable		400

The sales journal shows that on June 3 merchandise with an invoice price of $400 was sold to Ella Gray; terms 1/15, n/60. Since payment was made within 15 days, she deducted $4 from the invoice amount and paid $396.

Transaction:
1976
June 22   Borrowed $600 from the bank on a note payable.

Analysis of Debits and Credits:

Cash	600	
Notes Payable		600

Since there is no special column for the Notes Payable account, the amount is entered in the Other Accounts credit column and the name of the account is written in the Account Credited column.

Transaction:
1976
June 30   Cash sales for the last half of the month were $950.

Analysis of Debits and Credits:

Cash	950	
Sales		950

1976
June 30   Received $100 from Arthur James on account and a promissory note payable in 30 days for the balance in his account.

Analysis of Debits and Credits:

Cash	100	
Notes Receivable	200	
Accounts Receivable		300

(Ch. 6)

The sales journal shows that on June 5 merchandise with an invoice price of $300 was sold to Arthur James; terms 1/5, n/30. The Sales Discounts account is not involved in this partial payment because the discount period has expired.

At the end of the month, the columns in the cash receipts journal are footed. Since each line contains equal debits and credits, it follows that the total of the Debit column footings should equal the total of the Credit column footings. This equality should be proved for each special journal before the column totals are posted to the general ledger; otherwise, errors in the special journals may not be detected, the ledger will not have equal total debit and credit balances, and the trial balance will not balance. Moreover, the controlling accounts may not agree with their corresponding subsidiary ledgers. The cash receipts journal of the Hayward Casuals is proved as shown below.

	Debits		Credits
Cash	$6,134	Accounts Receivable	$1,300
Sales Discounts	16	Sales	1,950
Other Accounts	200	Other Accounts	3,100
Total	$6,350	Total	$6,350

Postings from the cash receipts journal of Hayward Casuals are shown in Figure 6-7.

Individual credit postings are made to the accounts receivable ledger to support the $1,300 credit posting to the Accounts Receivable controlling account in the general ledger. A check mark is entered in the folio (✓) column of the cash receipts journal on the line of the entry to indicate that the item has been posted to the customer's account in the subsidiary ledger. The balance of each account is zero; however, any positive balance in an account would normally be a debit. Transactions have already been posted to these accounts from the sales journal.

The totals of the Cash Debit column ($6,134) and the Sales Discounts Debit column ($16) are posted to the respective general ledger accounts. The regular sequence for transferring an amount from a journal to a ledger is followed. The general ledger account number entered in parentheses below the double rule in each column shows that the total has been posted to that account.

The (X) below the Other Accounts Debit column means that the individual amounts contained in the column total have already been posted to the general ledger. The $200 debit to Notes Receivable was posted individually during the month. The account number of Notes Receivable (112) was entered in the folio (F) column of the journal at the time the posting was done.

The Accounts Receivable account is credited for $1,300 and the Sales account is credited for $1,950. These postings are also dated June 30. No posting symbol is used in the folio (F) column on the line of the entry for a cash sale because the item does not require individual posting.

The (X) below the double rule in the Other Accounts credit column indicates that the column total is not to be posted to the general ledger. The total is not posted because the $2,500 credit to W. Ray, Capital, and the $600 credit to Notes Payable were posted separately during the month. The ledger page numbers of these accounts were entered in the folio (F) column of the journal when the posting was done. Note that account numbers 251 and 205 are written in the folio column of the cash receipts journal in Figure 6-7. Postings from the Other Accounts Credit column are dated as of the date of the entry.

The Cash Payments Journal

All transactions involving the payment of cash are entered in the cash payments journal. Most cash payments should be made by check. When payments in currency are required, they may be made from a *petty cash* fund, for which procedures are discussed in Chapter 8.

A typical cash payments journal is illustrated in Figure 6-8 (page 237). The columns provide for recording cash payments, either to creditors or for any other purpose, and for recording purchases discounts.

Explanation of the various columns follows.

1. The date of the disbursement of cash is entered in the Date column.
2. Detailed information is initially recorded on the check stub, which bears the same number as the check. Entries in the cash payments journal are then made from the check stub, and the check number is listed in the Check No. column.
3. An explanation of the transaction is entered in the Explanation column.
4. There are three credit columns; they are located to the left of the debit columns. In a special journal the sequence of columns need not follow the traditional placement. Cash is the first credit and will be used in each transaction entered in this journal.
5. The Purchases Discounts Credit column is used for recording discounts taken on invoices paid within the discount period.
6. Credits to general ledger accounts other than Cash and Purchases Discounts are recorded in the Other Accounts Credit column.
7. There are three folio columns, two labeled (F), one, ($\checkmark$); a posting symbol indicating that the amount has been posted to the general ledger or to the accounts payable ledger is placed in the folio column.
8. The name of the general ledger or subsidiary ledger account to be debited is written in the Account Debited column.
9. When a creditor is paid in full or on account, the amount is entered in the Accounts Payable Debit column. The amount entered is the actual amount of the check plus any purchases discounts taken.
10. The purchase of merchandise for cash is entered in the Purchases Debit column.
11. The Other Accounts Debit column is used for entries to general ledger accounts that have no special column.

The cash payments journal of Hayward Casuals is illustrated in Figure 6-9.

Although each transaction may be entered on a single line, such a practice is not an absolute requirement. Each new transaction entry should begin on a vacant line. The equality of debits and credits is maintained through the use of

Figure 6-7 Posting Flow from the Cash Receipts Journal

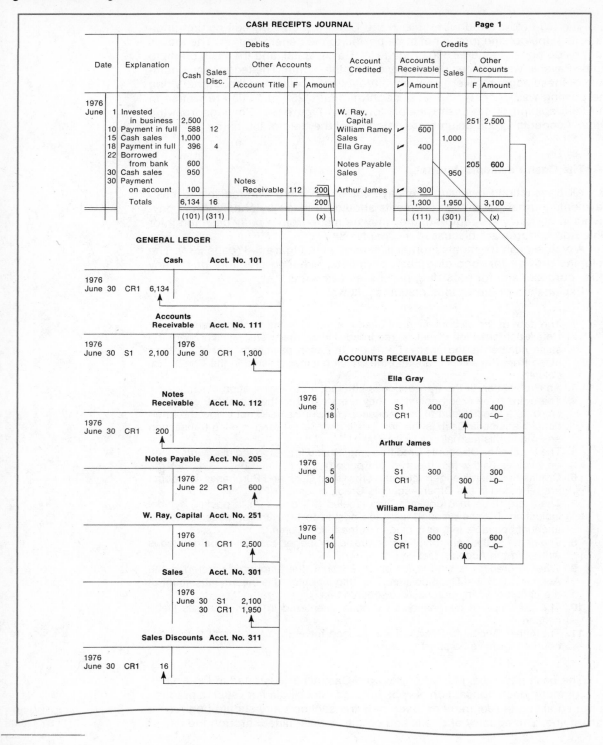

CASH RECEIPTS JOURNAL
Page 1

Date	Explanation	Cash	Sales Disc.	Account Title	F	Amount	Account Credited	✓	Amount	Sales	F	Amount
1976												
June 1	Invested in business	2,500					W. Ray, Capital				251	2,500
10	Payment in full	588	12				William Ramey	✓	600			
15	Cash sales	1,000					Sales			1,000		
18	Payment in full	396	4				Ella Gray	✓	400			
22	Borrowed from bank	600					Notes Payable				205	600
30	Cash sales	950					Sales			950		
30	Payment on account	100		Notes Receivable	112	200	Arthur James	✓	300			
	Totals	6,134	16			200			1,300	1,950		3,100
		(101)	(311)			(x)			(111)	(301)		(x)

GENERAL LEDGER

Cash   Acct. No. 101

1976			
June 30	CR1	6,134	

Accounts Receivable   Acct. No. 111

1976				1976			
June 30	S1	2,100		June 30	CR1	1,300	

Notes Receivable   Acct. No. 112

1976			
June 30	CR1	200	

Notes Payable   Acct. No. 205

				1976			
				June 22	CR1	600	

W. Ray, Capital   Acct. No. 251

				1976			
				June 1	CR1	2,500	

Sales   Acct. No. 301

				1976			
				June 30	S1	2,100	
				30	CR1	1,950	

Sales Discounts   Acct. No. 311

1976			
June 30	CR1	16	

ACCOUNTS RECEIVABLE LEDGER

Ella Gray

1976					
June 3		S1	400		400
18		CR1		400	-0-

Arthur James

1976					
June 5		S1	300		300
30		CR1		300	-0-

William Ramey

1976					
June 4		S1	600		600
10		CR1		600	-0-

(Ch. 6)

multiple columns. The transactions in Figure 6-9 are analyzed in terms of debits and credits to indicate their effect on the accounts. These transactions, however, are *not* actually recorded in both the cash payments journal and the general journal.

Transaction:
1976
June 1   Issued check No. 1 in the amount of $150 for the June rent.

Analysis of Debits and Credits:

Rent Expense	150	
Cash		150

Figure 6-8   Column Headings of a Multicolumn Cash Payments Journal

				CASH PAYMENTS JOURNAL						Page 1		
			Credits					Debits				
Date	Check No.	Explanation	Cash	Purchases Discounts	Other Accounts			Account Debited	Accounts Payable	Purchases	Other Accounts	
					Account Title	F	Amount		✓ Amount		F	Amount

Figure 6-9   Cash Payments Journal

					CASH PAYMENTS JOURNAL						Page 1	
				Credits					Debits			
Date	Check No.	Explanation	Cash	Purchases Discounts	Other Accounts			Account Debited	Accounts Payable	Purchases	Other Accounts	
					Account Title	F	Amount		✓ Amount		F	Amount
1976 June 1	1	June rent	150					Rent Expense				150
11	2	Payment in full	882	18				Oakland Clothing Co.	900			
14	3	Payment in full	392	8				Southland Apparel	400			
15	4	Cash purchases	200					Purchases		200		
30	5	Partial payment	300		NotesPayable		200	San Francisco Clothiers	500			
30	6	Withdrawal of cash	400					W. Ray, Drawing				400
30	7	Various items	100					Misc. General Expense				100
		Totals	2,424	26			200		1,800	200		650

Transaction:
1976
June 11   Paid Oakland Clothing Co. in full; check No. 2.

Analysis of Debits and Credits:

Accounts Payable	900	
Purchases Discounts		18
Cash		882

The purchases journal shows that on June 3 merchandise with an invoice price of $900 was purchased from Oakland Clothing Company; terms 2/10, n/30. Since payment was made within 10 days, a 2 percent discount, or $18, is taken, and a check for $882 is issued. Entering the three amounts in the special columns has the same effect on the general ledger as the explanatory debit and credit analysis does. The creditor's name is entered in the Account Debited column for posting to the accounts payable ledger.

Transaction:
1976
June 14   Paid Southland Apparel in full; check No. 3.

Analysis of Debits and Credits:

Accounts Payable	400	
Purchases Discounts		8
Cash		392

The explanation for this entry is similar to that for the entry of June 11.

Transaction:
1976
June 15   Purchased merchandise and issued a check for the full amount of the invoice; check No. 4.

Analysis of Debits and Credits:

Purchases	200	
Cash		200

Purchases of merchandise on account are entered in the purchases journal. A company may occasionally purchase merchandise for cash, probably from another company with which no credit relationship exists. These cash purchases are recorded directly in the cash payments journal. If cash purchases of merchandise occur frequently, a special Purchases Debit column may be provided in the cash payments journal.

Transaction:
1976
June 30   Paid the San Francisco Clothiers $300 on account (check No. 5) and issued a promissory note for the balance, to be paid in 30 additional days.

Analysis of Debits and Credits:

Accounts Payable	500	
Cash		300
Notes Payable		200

Reference to the purchases journal shows that on June 16 merchandise with an invoice price of $500 was purchased from the San Francisco Clothiers; terms 3/5, n/30. Since the discount period has expired, no discount is taken.

Transaction:
1976
June 30   W. Ray, the owner, withdrew $400 (check No. 6) for his personal use in anticipation of earned income.

Analysis of Debits and Credits:

W. Ray, Drawing	400	
Cash		400

Since there is no special column for personal withdrawals, the cash withdrawal is entered in the Other Accounts Debit column. If such withdrawals are numerous, a special column with the heading W. Ray, Drawing Debit could be provided.

Transaction:
1976
June 30   Issued check No. 7 in the amount of $100 for miscellaneous general expenses.

Analysis of Debits and Credits:

Miscellaneous General Expense	100	
Cash		100

The expense account is debited for various items purchased and consumed during the month.

Before the end-of-the-month postings are made, the columns of the cash payments journal should be footed, and the equality of debits and credits proved as shown below.

	Debits		*Credits*
Accounts Payable	$1,800	Cash	$2,424
Purchases	200	Purchases Discounts	26
Other Accounts	650	Notes Payable	200
Total	$2,650	Total	$2,650

The total debit and total credit postings from this journal to the general ledger are equal.

Posting from the cash payments journal of Hayward Casuals is shown in Figure 6-10.

(Ch. 6)

Figure 6-10 Posting Flow from the Cash Payments Journal

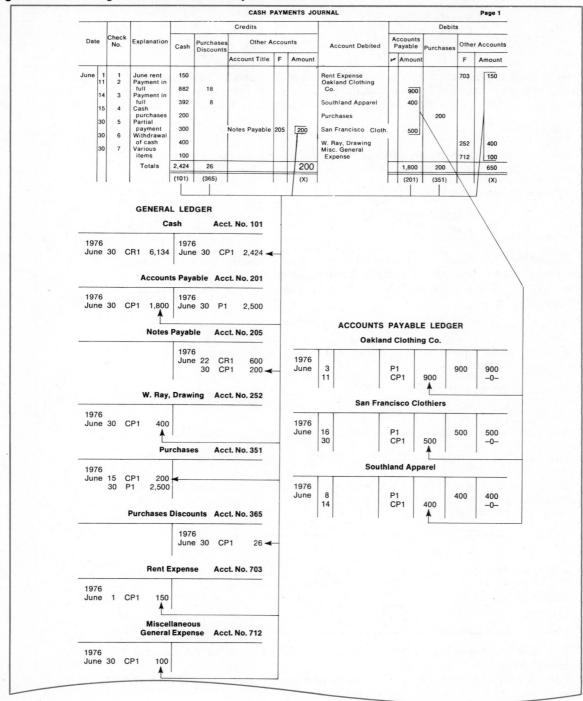

The individual debit postings to the accounts payable ledger support the $1,800 debit posting to the Accounts Payable controlling account in the general ledger. Each check mark in the folio (√) column of the cash payments journal indicates that a posting has been made to the supplier's account in the subsidiary ledger. Note that the balance of each account is either a credit or zero.

The Accounts Payable account is debited for $1,800 as of June 30. The total of the Purchases Debit column, $200, is posted to the Purchases account in the general ledger.

The total of the Other Accounts Debit column is not posted, because it is used to record debits to accounts for which no special columns have been provided; each amount must be posted separately. The numbers of these accounts—703, 252, and 712—are entered in the folio (F) column. The (X) below the double rule in the Other Accounts Debit column indicates that the column total is not posted to the general ledger.

The totals of the Cash Credit column ($2,424) and the Purchases Discounts Credit column ($26) are posted to the general ledger. The basic posting steps are followed. The general ledger account numbers are placed in parentheses below the double rules in the columns to indicate that the postings have been done.

The total of the Other Accounts Credit column is not posted, since each entry in the column has been individually posted at the time the entry is made in the journal. The folio (F) column indicates the account to which the entry was posted.

Combined Cash Receipts and Payments Journal

Many small entities use a combined cash receipts and cash payments journal sometimes called a *cashbook*. This journal is simply a combination of the cash receipts journal and the cash payments journal described earlier. The specialized debit and credit columns (except for cash) would be unique to the needs of the particular entity using it. In addition to small commercial enterprises, such a journal is appropriate to many not-for-profit organizations such as fraternities and sororities and civic clubs and to professional service organizations.

An outline of a simple combined cash receipts and payments journal is presented below.

		Debits			Credits					Other Accounts			
					Cash								
Date	Explanation	Cash	Purchases	Sales Disc.	Check No.	Amount	Accounts Receivable	Sales	Purchases Discounts	Title	F	Debit	Credit

Combined Cash Receipts and Payments Journal

Other Special Journals

Other special journals may be adopted as the need for them becomes apparent. Such a need is indicated if labor may be saved or if the special journal provides an element of flexibility in the accounting system. Examples of other special journals are *sales returns and allowances journal, purchases returns and allowances journal, notes receivable register, notes payable register,* and *voucher register.*

Entries in the General Journal

Although special journals provide for recording frequently recurring transactions, a need for recording (1) unusual current transactions, (2) correcting entries, and (3) adjusting and closing entries remains. For these purposes, a simple two-column general journal is used in conjunction with the special journals.

Unusual Current Transactions. All the transactions that cannot be entered in the special journals are recorded in the general journal. Sales returns and allowances and purchases returns and allowances, for example, are entered in the general journal if special journals for these transactions are not maintained. Other typical current transactions recorded in the general journal include (1) credit purchases of assets other than merchandise inventory, such as plant and equipment or supplies, and the incurrence of liabilities for services; (2) notes received from customers to apply toward accounts receivable; and (3) notes issued to creditors to apply toward accounts payable. The recording of a typical general journal entry is shown below.

			GENERAL JOURNAL		**Page 35**	
1976 July	7		Notes Receivable Accounts Receivable—S. Lee To record receipt of 30-day note in full settlement of account.	112 111/✔	350	350

The amount of this entry, $350, is posted to the general ledger as a debit to Notes Receivable and a credit to Accounts Receivable. The other posting is to the subsidiary ledger to support the corresponding credit to the Accounts Receivable controlling account. A dual credit posting is necessary because the simple two-column general journal—unlike the special journals—does not have classified columns allowing end-of-period posting of column totals.

Note that the detailed explanation of the transaction, which is omitted from special journals (the type of special journal and a reference to an invoice date or number generally suffice to explain a special journal entry), is retained in the general journal because of the unusual nature of the transactions recorded there.

Correcting Entries. If it is discovered that an error has been made in the process of journalizing and posting, it may be corrected by a general journal entry. Erasures should be avoided, because they may create doubt in the minds of persons who examine the records regarding the reason for the erasure. This becomes particularly important when the records are audited, and in cases of litigation when the records may be offered as evidence.

Assume that the following entry, recording the payment of an invoice for repairs to machinery, has been posted (actually journalized in the cash payments journal but for simplicity is shown here in general journal form):

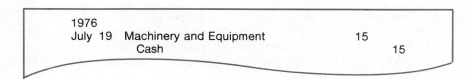

1976		
July 19 Machinery and Equipment	15	
Cash		15

The debit should have been to an expense account; the error may be corrected by the following entry in the general journal:

GENERAL JOURNAL			**Page 40**	
1976 July	26	Maintenance and Repairs Expense	15	
		Machinery and Equipment		15
		To correct entry of July 19 in cash payments journal.		

If an error in a journal entry is discovered before it is posted, it may be corrected by drawing a line through the incorrect account or amount and entering the correction immediately above it.

Adjusting and Closing Entries. Adjusting and closing entries are always recorded in the general journal. These entries were discussed and illustrated in Chapters 3 and 4.

Direct Posting from Business Documents

In many business firms, data can be processed more efficiently and rapidly by posting from the original documents—sales invoices, sales slips, purchase invoices, and so on—directly to the subsidiary ledgers instead of first copying the information in special journals and then posting to the accounts. For example, if sales slips are serially numbered, a binder file of duplicate slips arranged in numerical order could take the place of a more formal sales journal. Amounts from the individual slips could be posted daily to the accounts receivable ledger; at the end of a designated period—a week or a month—the sales slips in the binder file are totaled and the following general journal entry is made:

GENERAL JOURNAL				Page 8

1976 Aug.	31	Accounts Receivable
		    Sales
		        To record charge sales for
		        the month of August, 1976.
			120,000	120,000

A similar procedure may be used to record purchases on account.

If the postings are made from sales slips to the accounts receivable ledger, and if for any reason a special sales journal is still desired, a streamlined journal can be constructed by simply eliminating the Account Debited, Terms, and folio (F) columns, as shown below.

SALES JOURNAL		
Date	Sales Invoice Numbers	Amount

Entries to such a sales journal may be made in batches; for example, a single line may read:

Aug. 12   13,500–13,599   18,329.21

A batch could represent a day's credit sales, or simply a predetermined quantity of invoices or sales slips. The use of *batch totals* is one means of checking the accuracy of posting to subsidiary ledgers.

These changes in procedure and the increasing use of direct posting from original documents are discussed here to add emphasis to a statement made earlier in this chapter: Accounting records and procedures should be designed to meet the needs of the particular business firm.

BOOKKEEPING MACHINE PROCESSING

The simple *posting machine* and similar electromechanical equipment can perform the two basic operations involved in the distribution of business transaction information to appropriate accounts: (1) *listing*—that is, writing such information as cross-reference, date, and amount, and (2) *adding* or *subtracting* amounts. Depending on the complexity of the machine—whether it has one or more *registers,* which allow it to accumulate amounts for further computation, and whether it has a built-in *program* (set of instructions for performing manipulations of data)—it may perform many additional tasks.

In a growing business, as the number of customers and credit transactions increases, the cost of hand posting to the accounts receivable ledger becomes excessive. It may be economical for such a company to buy or rent a simple posting machine that has a *horizontal register* (cross-footer) which can compute the difference between debits and credits on a single line. This type of machine can be used to post debits from sales invoices and credits from receipts to each customer's account in the subsidiary ledger. The operator punches into the machine the beginning balance and both debits and credits, if applicable, to the account, and the machine records this information and prints out a new balance automatically.

The typical ledger account used in machine accounting is the balance-form card shown in Figure 6-11.

A similar procedure is followed to post entries to the accounts payable ledger.

Many firms have accounting systems that permit posting by data-processing equipment to all ledgers, including the general ledger. Economies can be achieved by machine accounting when the volume of similar accounting routines is large enough to enable the bookkeeper to gain speed through repetitive motions that can eventually become habitual. Accuracy and legibility of accounting records are attained by the use of electromechanical and electronic equipment. These machines facilitate proofs of the accuracy of journalizing and posting. The more complex machines perform several stages of accounting—the preparation of specialized reports, journal entries, and ledger posting—in one operation.

OTHER ACCOUNTING SYSTEMS

As a business engages in a larger number of transactions of similar nature, it may be economical to acquire punched-card equipment. This equipment rapidly, accurately, and automatically completes the three basic stages of distributing the details of accounting transactions to the appropriate accounts and reports: (1) recording information on an input medium; (2) classifying the information according to the accounts affected; and (3) summarizing the resulting account balances. Punched-card equipment is also useful for recording, classifying, and summarizing nonfinancial statistical data that help management to make decisions.

Further expansion of the accounting system would lead to the develop-

Date	Explanation	F or Code	Debit	Credit	Balance

Figure 6-11
Typical Machine
Ledger Card

ACCOUNTING
SYSTEMS

ment of electronic data-processing (EDP) systems, which offer the greatest speed, volume, and reliability, and consist of combinations of electronic equipment centered around digital computers. These machines are designed to receive a large mass of input data, perform basic arithmetic operations on the data, make comparison decisions regarding the data, update the previously stored data, almost immediately supply the information or output that results from these operations, and then store the data for later use. These approaches to the processing of data were introduced in Chapter 1; examples of their application are shown in later chapters.

Up to this point, the basic accounting model both for service and for merchandising businesses has been delineated and emphasized. In connection with the study of accounting systems, consideration should be given to the basic principles which form the foundation for accounting entries. Until 1973, the term *generally accepted accounting principles* was used to describe a set of broad rules having substantial authoritative support. The Accounting Principles Board, in its APB statement No. 4, codified and classified these generally accepted accounting principles in October 1970.[1] Then, in 1973, an Accounting Objectives Study Group of the American Institute of Certified Public Accountants (AICPA) issued a report which described certain basic objectives and stated that ". . . the accounting process should consist of an interrelated and compatible system of objectives, standards or principles, and practices or procedures."[2] An *objective* is a basic statement identifying a goal or purpose of accounting, whereas a *standard* is a fundamental guideline that serves as a basis for acceptance or rejection of an accounting method. On the other hand, an *accounting practice* is a specific method for recording of an economic event. The purpose of this Appendix is to provide (1) a historical introduction to authoritative bodies in accounting, (2) a description of the structure and workings of the Financial Accounting Standards Board (FASB), (3) a discussion of accounting objectives, and (4) an explanation of some of the more commonly accepted accounting standards that are in use today.

AUTHORITATIVE BODIES

American Institute of Certified Public Accountants (AICPA)

In 1887, the Association of Public Accountants was formed; in 1916, another group, the Institute of Accountants in the USA, came into being. These two groups merged in 1936 to form the American Institute of Accountants (AIA); in 1957 the name was changed to the American Institute of Certified Public Accountants (AICPA). Since its members are mostly the auditors who perform the attest function, it is easy to understand the power of its influence in developing and prescribing accounting principles. AICPA prepares the examination for the CPA certificate, which, although administered separately in every state in the nation under state law, is uniform throughout the United States. Until 1973, AICPA had an Accounting Principles Board (APB) whose authoritative pronouncements were called *APB Opinions* and *APB Statements*. By the time of the board's replacement, thirty-one APB opinions and four APB statements were in effect to promulgate guidance for accountants.

[1] *APB Accounting Principles,* vol. 2 (Chicago: Commerce Clearing House Inc., 1973), pp. 9057–9119.
[2] Accounting Objectives Study Group, *Objectives of Financial Statements* (New York: American Institute of Certified Public Accountants, 1973), p. 15.

Canadian Institute of Chartered Accountants (CICA)

The Association of Accountants in Montreal (now the Order of Chartered Accountants of Québec) was formed in 1880. In 1883 and 1886, Institutes of Chartered Accountants of Ontario and Manitoba respectively were incorporated; subsequently, other provincial institutes were established. The need to form a definite relationship among the provincial associations resulted in the incorporation of the Dominion Association of Chartered Accountants in 1902; in 1951 the title was changed to the Canadian Institute of Chartered Accountants (CICA). Everyone who holds membership in a provincial institute is automatically a member of the Canadian Institute. The chartered accountant (CA) in Canada fulfills substantially the same role as the CPA in the United States; the CICA serves professional needs similar to those served by the AICPA. In 1970 the Order of Chartered Accountants of Québec pioneered the development of professional practice advisers, who assist CAs with professional problems. Other provinces have subsequently developed similar programs and the Research and Review Committee of the AICPA has expressed interest in this type of service. CICA Research pronouncements and accounting principles are published in the *CICA Handbook,* and these represent standards to be adhered to in most cases by members of the Institute. In addition to the Handbook recommendations, CAs are strongly influenced by American accounting pronouncements and research.

American Accounting Association (AAA)

Beginning in 1916 as an association of accounting instructors, AAA has grown to a large organization today oriented toward accounting research, education research, and matters of academic interest. An example of the work of AAA is the publication, in 1966, of *A Statement of Basic Accounting Theory,* often referred to as "ASOBAT." This book represents two years of work by a committee of nine members—all leaders in the accounting field.

National Association of Accountants (NAA)

The National Association of Cost Accountants was formed in 1919. As its interests broadened to include all aspects of managerial accounting (oriented toward internal users of information), its name was changed to National Association of Accountants (NAA). In addition to its research and publication activities, NAA is the sponsor of the Institute of Management Accounting, which prepares and administers an annual national examination for the Certificate in Management Accounting (CMA).

Financial Accounting Standards Board (FASB)[3]

On June 30, 1972, the Financial Accounting Standards Board was established to replace the Accounting Principles Board. The APB continued the work that it had in process during a transition period, and issued its final APB

---

[3] Most of the material in this section is adapted from "Financial Accounting Standards Board Proposed Rules of Procedure," *Journal of Accountancy,* 134 (November 1972), pp. 75–78.

Figure A6-1 Financial Accounting Standards Organization

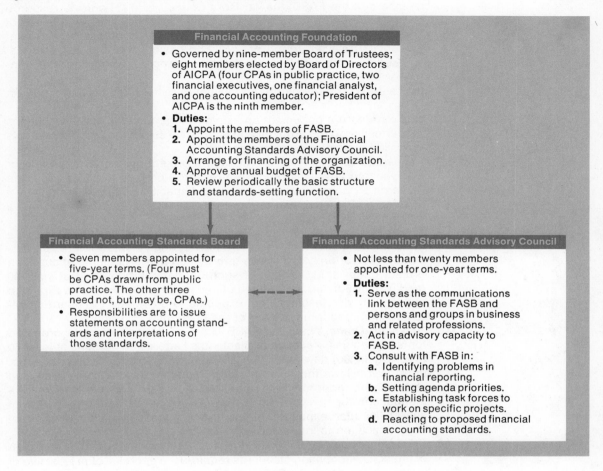

Opinion in June 1973, leaving the FASB as the independent nongovernmental body in the United States to develop and issue standards of financial accounting. The FASB is an element of a three-part structure as shown in Figure A6-1.

The members of the FASB serve full time and are paid for their services. In issuing pronouncements and in conducting other related activities, they act independently of the Board of Trustees of the Foundation. To assist FASB members in their work on a continuing agenda of projects, there are research and administrative personnel. The general procedure followed by FASB consists of the following steps.

1. *Agenda of Projects.* The chairman, with the advice of the board and the members of the Advisory Council, is responsible for maintenance of an agenda of projects. This agenda consists of specific problems to be considered by the board; each has a priority assigned to it.
2. *Task Forces.* Usually, the chairman establishes a task force for each project placed on the agenda of the board. Each task force is normally

(Ch. 6)

headed by an FASB member; other task force members may include members of the FASB, the Advisory Council, and (1) outside resource persons who are particularly aware of the responsibilities and needs of financial statement users or (2) persons with an expertise or viewpoint particularly relevant to the project. The basic job of the task force is:

a. To define the problem and the accounting and reporting issues involved in it.

b. To determine the nature and extent of research to be performed on it.

c. To prepare a document containing the arguments and implications pertaining to the problem and alternative solutions. This document is called a *discussion memorandum.*

3. *Research Projects.* A task force with a project under consideration or the research area may propose a research project. In either case, the research proposal must be directed to a specific issue under study by a task force. The chairman of the FASB has final authority to approve a research project.

4. *Public Hearings.* Using the task force's discussion memorandum as a basis, the FASB normally holds public hearings to allow interested persons an opportunity to provide information and arguments about each project under study. Notice of such hearings is published at least 30 (and usually 60) days in advance of the hearings. Persons who expect to appear and give testimony are expected to provide to the board a written position paper in advance of the hearings.

5. *Exposure Drafts.* When the FASB has a proposed statement prepared for issue, copies are made available to all interested persons at least 30 (and usually 60) days prior to promulgation. This copy, called an *exposure draft,* allows those groups or persons interested in the proposed statement an opportunity to submit to the board comments or recommendations for revision. As in the case of public hearings, notice of availability of an exposure draft is given by press release and by direct communication to interested organizations.

6. *Final Issuances.* For the FASB to issue a statement or an interpretation of financial accounting standards requires the approval of at least five of the seven members. An FASB *statement* generally presents background and discussion of the problem, the opinion of the FASB, and the effective date and method of implementation. As was the case with APB opinions, CPAs are expected to insure that standards contained in FASB statements are followed when they use the words ". . . in accordance with generally accepted accounting principles . . ." in certifying financial statements. An FASB *interpretation* usually relates to a previous FASB statement and contains clarification or additional explanation. Accordingly, an interpretation may be issued without following all the steps outlined in the above procedure.

Other Bodies

While the foregoing probably exert the strongest influence on accounting principles, other bodies in the United States such as the Securities Exchange Commission (SEC), Financial Executives Institute (FEI), New York Stock Ex-

(Ch. 6)

change, Board of Governors of the Federal Reserve System, Internal Revenue Service (IRS), and several regulatory agencies, all play an influential role. An agency of the United States Congress, whose primary goal is to promulgate standards that will achieve consistency in cost accounting practices among companies working on Federal government contracts, is the Cost Accounting Standards Board (CASB). The Comptroller General of the United States is chairman of the CASB; he appoints the other members.

In Canada, each province has a securities commission which exercises a considerable amount of control in the securities markets, particularly in the area of prospectuses. Effective 1972 these provincial commissions formally defined generally accepted accounting principles for financial disclosure as those pronouncements which are set out in the *CICA Handbook*.

ACCOUNTING OBJECTIVES

Three major studies have led to the development of accounting objectives. The 1966 study by the American Accounting Association, referred to as ASOBAT in discussion of AAA, listed four basic criteria for judging the usefulness of accounting information. In 1971, APB Statement No. 4 established seven standards of quality for accounting data, and then, in its 1973 report, *Objectives of Financial Statements,* the AICPA Study Group listed a set of qualitative characteristics of reporting. These are integrated in Figure A6-2.

ASOBAT Criteria (1966)	*APB Statement No. 4 Standards (1971)*	*Objectives Study Group Characteristics (1973)*
1. Relevance	0–1 Relevance	Relevance and materiality
2. Verifiability	0–2 Understandability	Form and substance
3. Freedom from Bias	0–3 Verifiability	Reliability
4. Quantifiability	0–4 Neutrality	Freedom from bias
	0–5 Timeliness	Comparability
	0–6 Comparability	Consistency
	0–7 Completeness	Understandability

Figure A6-2
Comparison of Qualitative Criteria for Accounting Reports

In most of these criteria, there is close agreement in definitions of the terms; all studies give top priority to relevance.

In its 1973 report, *Objectives of Financial Statements,* the AICPA Study Group described twelve objectives of financial statements. They are reproduced below.[4]

1. The basic objective of financial statements is to provide information useful for making economic decisions.
2. An objective of financial statements is to serve primarily those users who have

[4] Copyright © 1973 by the American Institute of Certified Public Accountants, Inc.

ACCOUNTING SYSTEMS

limited authority, ability, or resources to obtain information and who rely on financial statements as their principal source of information about an enterprise's economic activities.

3. An objective of financial statements is to provide information useful to investors and creditors for predicting, comparing, and evaluating potential cash flows to them in terms of amount, timing, and related uncertainty.

4. An objective of financial statements is to provide users with information for predicting, comparing, and evaluating enterprise earning power.

5. An objective of financial statements is to supply information useful in judging management's ability to utilize enterprise resources effectively in achieving the primary enterprise goal.

6. An objective of financial statements is to provide factual and interpretive information about transactions and other events which is useful for predicting, comparing, and evaluating enterprise earning power. Basic underlying assumptions with respect to matters subject to interpretation, evaluation, prediction, or estimation should be disclosed.

7. An objective is to provide a statement of financial position useful for predicting, comparing, and evaluating enterprise earning power. This statement should provide information concerning enterprise transactions and other events that are part of incomplete earnings cycles. Current values should also be reported when they differ significantly from historical cost. Assets and liabilities should be grouped or segregated by the relative uncertainty of the amount and timing of prospective realization or liquidation.

8. An objective is to provide a statement of periodic earnings useful for predicting, comparing, and evaluating enterprise earning power. The net result of completed earnings cycles and enterprise activities resulting in recognizable progress toward completion of incomplete cycles should be reported. Changes in the values reflected in successive statements of financial position should also be reported, but separately, since they differ in terms of their certainty of realization.

9. An objective is to provide a statement of financial activities useful for predicting, comparing, and evaluating enterprise earning power. This statement should report mainly on factual aspects of enterprise transactions having or expected to have significant cash consequences. This statement should report data that require minimal judgment and interpretation by the preparer.

10. An objective of financial statements is to provide information useful for the predictive process. Financial forecasts should be provided when they will enhance the reliability of users' predictions.

11. An objective of financial statements for governmental and not-for-profit organizations is to provide information useful for evaluating the effectiveness of the management of resources in achieving the organization's goals. Performance measures should be quantified in terms of identified goals.

12. An objective of financial statements is to report on those activities of the enterprise affecting society which can be determined and described or measured and which are important to the role of the enterprise in its social environment.

On June 6, 1974, the Financial Accounting Standards Board issued a Discussion Memorandum entitled *Conceptual Framework for Accounting and Reporting: Consideration of the Report of the Study Group on the Objectives of Financial Statements.* In it the FASB presented a hierarchy of objectives, standards, and practices as a tentative framework around which to engender further discussion. FASB's graphical representation is presented in Figure A6-3,

Figure A6-3   Hierarchy of Elements in a Conceptual Framework for Financial Accounting and Reporting

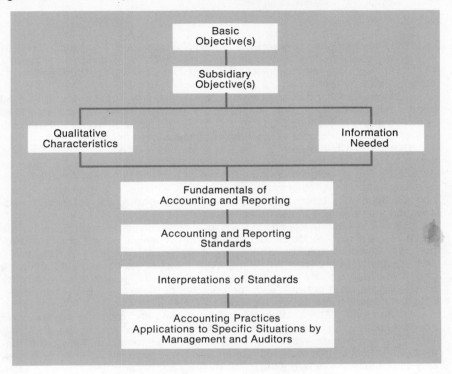

© *Financial Accounting Standards Board*

and is described in the following selected quotations from the Discussion Memorandum.

It should be noted that the hierarchy in Figure 1 [Figure A6-3] provides for more than one *basic objective* should dual or multiple basic objectives be considered appropriate.

The hierarchy also provides for *subsidiary objectives*. Inclusion of a separate box for subsidiary objectives does not necessarily require that certain objectives of accounting be considered less important than others. Rather, that box allows placing in proper perspective any objective(s) that is essentially supportive of the basic objective(s)—that is, any objective(s) that represents a means of attaining the basic objective(s) rather than an ultimate goal in itself.

Information Needed: *APB Statement No. 4* identifies two categories of objectives that serve to further the "basic purpose of financial accounting and financial statements"—general objectives and qualitative objectives.

The *general objectives* relate the content of financial accounting information to the interests and needs of users. The content of financial accounting information can therefore be appraised by determining the extent to which it serves these interests and needs. The *qualitative objectives* indicate the characteristics of useful information and thus provide criteria for appraising the usefulness of financial accounting information. [emphasis supplied]

The two categories of objectives in *APB Statement No. 4* correspond closely to the *information needed* and *qualitative characteristics* boxes in . . .. Hopefully, the more descriptive terminology utilized in the hierarchy will facilitate relating the Objectives Study to it.

Information needed involves identification of the broad categories of financial accounting information needed by users. For example, several of the objectives specified in the Objectives Study deal with specific types of financial statements perceived to be necessary to meet the information needs of users.

Qualitative Characteristics: These are attributes of accounting information which tend to enhance its usefulness. Such qualitative characteristics might be expected to be (1) able to withstand the test of time; (2) pervasive—that is, apply to all accounting entities; and (3) implementable—that is, capable of application and susceptible to objective verification. Certain qualitative characteristics of accounting are described in the Objectives Study.

Below the information needed and qualitative characteristics boxes in the tentative hierarchy are four boxes labeled "fundamentals of accounting and reporting," "accounting and reporting standards," "interpretations of standards," and "accounting practices." While this initial thrust of the conceptual framework project is directed solely toward consideration of the Objectives Study which, for the most part, does not deal with the contents of these lower boxes, some description of their contents may be in order.

Fundamentals: The fundamentals of accounting and reporting are the basic concepts underlying the measurement of transactions and events and disclosing them in a manner meaningful to users of accounting information. They are fundamental in the sense that repeated reference to these concepts will likely be necessary in establishing, interpreting, and applying accounting and reporting standards. Such fundamentals might include the definitions of an accounting entity, assets, liabilities, income, revenue, expense, realization, and others. One or more of such concepts is likely to pervade virtually every Statement of Financial Accounting Standards issued or interpreted by the FASB and virtually every accounting practice.

Accounting and Reporting Standards: These standards represent general solutions to financial accounting problems. The Statements of Financial Accounting Standards emanating from the FASB are expected to contribute to the contents of this box, as well as other boxes as appropriate.

Interpretations of Standards: Interpretations clarify, explain, or elaborate upon the accounting and reporting standards as an aid to their application in accounting practices. As such, they are necessarily derived directly from those standards and generally would be expected to deal with specific aspects of accounting problems.

The FASB is charged with the responsibility of issuing interpretations of Statements of Financial Accounting Standards (including interpretations of Accounting Research Bulletins of the Committee on Accounting Procedure of the AICPA and interpretations of Opinions of the Accounting Principles Board of the AICPA) as it identifies the need for clarification, explanation, or elaboration of existing accounting and reporting standards.

Accounting Practices: Accounting practices are the means to attain the basic objective(s) of financial statements. Accounting practices include the decisions made by managements and auditors in applying the contents of all the other boxes to specific situations. Those applications are reflected in the financial statements with which the entire hierarchy is ultimately concerned.

Although it is not considered necessary to provide here an organized list of generally accepted accounting principles (standards), some of the more important generally accepted concepts are discussed.

Entity Concept. The accountant must maintain separate sets of records for each business enterprise of an owner, and must guard against intermingling of transactions of the enterprise and personal transactions of the owner.

Going Concern. It is assumed that the entity will continue in operation indefinitely unless there is evidence to the contrary. For example, the accountant in a going concern does not record assets at liquidation value; instead the basis chosen for valuation will be one consistent with the idea that the business will continue in existence over the expected useful life of any asset.

Consistency. In some instances there are acceptable alternative methods that can be used in accounting records. Once a choice has been made, the principle of *consistency* holds that the chosen procedure should be followed in all future entries in order to enhance comparability of statements covering different time periods.

Conservatism. Where acceptable alternatives exist, the one normally chosen would be that which produces the least favorable immediate result. The principle of conservatism aims to avoid favorable exaggeration in accounting reports.

Periodicity. Financial statements will be prepared at regular specified time periods before the end of the lifetime of the firm. This principle holds that items of expense and revenue can be allocated to such time periods. Such an assignment to periods is necessary for proper matching of expenses and revenue for income determination.

Objective Evidence Principle. To the greatest extent possible, the amounts used in recording events will be based upon objective evidence as compared to subjective judgment. It will follow that two separate accountants, given the same set of data, would be expected to arrive at the same result. (Without the objective evidence principle, the attest function of CPAs and CAs could not hold the high degree of confidence which it enjoys today.)

Materiality. An item small enough (in dollar amount or in proportion to other items) such that it would not influence a decision based upon the statement in which it is used is immaterial, and the accounting treatment thereof need not follow prescribed accounting principles. (For example, the inventory value of unused stationery in the typing pool or paper clips in the office would not be counted as part of the supplies inventory at the end of a period.)

Full Disclosure. Financial statements should report all significant financial and economic information relating to an entity. If the accounting system does not automatically capture some specific item of significance, it should be included in a footnote to the accounting statements.

Stable-Dollar Concept. This principle assumes that the dollar is sufficiently stable in value to be used as the basic unit of measure in accounting without adjustment for price-level fluctuations. Many accountants challenge the general use of this principle on the grounds that it simply is not true.

Historical Cost Concept. The cost principle holds that actual cost—arrived

ACCOUNTING
SYSTEMS

at through arm's-length bargaining—is the appropriate amount to be used to record the value of a newly acquired asset.

Accrual Basis. Items of expense and revenue should be recognized at the time of occurrence of the economic events that caused them without regard to the timing and amount of cash collections or payments.

Many other concepts and assumptions might be included in the list. As research and study continue, certain standards will be revised and new ones can be expected.

Accounting is a social system designed to meet users' needs. These needs continue to increase in scope and complexity as changes occur in the environment in which users make economic decisions. It is the ongoing task of the FASB to promulgate new and revised accounting standards. Accordingly, the practicing accountant, in order to keep pace with his or her profession, must maintain a constant process of continuing education.

GLOSSARY

Accounting Objective A basic statement identifying a goal or purpose of accounting.

Accounting Practice A specific method for recording of an economic event.

Accounting Principle See *Accounting Standard*.

Accounting Standard A fundamental guideline that serves as a basis for acceptance or rejection of an accounting method. (Formerly called an "accounting principle.")

Accounting System The combination of procedures, forms, and equipment for recording, classifying, summarizing, and reporting of accounting information.

APB Accounting Principles Board of the AICPA.

Attest Function The certification by CPAs as to fairness of the representations made by an entity's financial statements.

Cash Payments Journal A special journal in which all cash payments are recorded.

Cash Receipts Journal A special journal in which all cash receipts are recorded.

CMA An accountant who has passed the national examination and has met the requirements of the Institute of Management Accounting for the Certificate in Management Accounting.

CPA (Certified Public Accountant) An accountant who has passed the national examination and has met the requirements of state law for independent practice in accounting.

Digital Computer A computer that performs arithmetic and logical operations on data under control of an internally stored set of instructions.

Discussion Memorandum A basic document prepared by the FASB with arguments and alternative solutions related to an accounting problem.

EDP System An electronic data-processing system for processing data.

Exposure Draft An advance copy of an FASB issuance made public to provide an opportunity for comment and recommendation by any interested party prior to its formal promulgation.

FASB (Financial Accounting Standards Board) Successor to the APB.

FASB Standard Formally promulgated accounting guidelines from the FASB.

Generally Accepted Accounting Principles The set of accounting standards (see above) that are currently generally accepted as valid.

Internal Control The built-in safeguards for the protection of the assets of an enterprise.

Purchases Journal A special journal in which only purchases of merchandise on account are recorded.

Sales Journal A special journal in which only sales of merchandise on account are recorded.

Q6-1. (a) What is the function of the systems analyst? (b) What are the considerations of the analyst in systems design? (c) In selecting the method or combination of methods of data collection, what criteria are used?

Q6-2. (a) What is the function of special journals? (b) What determines the types of special journals to be used? (c) Do the special journals entirely eliminate the need for a general journal? (d) How do special journals save time and labor? (e) Are there other advantages in using special journals?

Q6-3. What is the rule for entering a transaction (a) in the sales journal? (b) in the purchases journal? (c) in the cash receipts journal? (d) in the cash payments journal? (e) in the general journal?

Q6-4. What is the purpose of an Other Accounts section in a special journal? Describe the posting procedure for items recorded in the Other Accounts section.

Q6-5. The Jetson Company uses sales, purchases, cash receipts, cash payments, and general journals. State the journal in which each of the following transactions and events should be recorded:

1. Sale of merchandise on account
2. Purchase of store supplies on account
3. Return by a customer of a cash sale item for which the customer was given a refund check
4. Purchase of delivery equipment on account
5. Payment to a creditor
6. Sale of merchandise for cash
7. Adjusting entries
8. Purchase of merchandise on account
9. Note receivable issued by a customer in full settlement of his account
10. Return of a credit purchase for which the customer's account was credited
11. Withdrawal of cash by owner for his own use
12. Closing entries
13. Payment of rent
14. Purchase of merchandise for cash
15. Note payable given to a creditor to apply on account
16. Withdrawal of merchandise by the owner for his own use

Q6-6. (a) When are postings made from the purchases journal (1) to the general ledger and (2) to the accounts payable ledger? (b) What is the relationship of the amounts posted? (c) How is it possible to trace postings from the journals to the ledgers? (d) What is the significance of the check mark in the folio (F) column of the purchases journal? (e) Would it be advisable to use code numbers as posting references for creditors' accounts rather than check marks?

Q6-7. The following questions relate to the cash receipts journal illustrated in this chapter: (a) What are the special columns? (b) Why is the journal cross-footed at the end of each month? (c) Explain the postings from this journal (1) to the general ledger and (2) to the accounts receivable ledger.

Q6-8. The column headings listed below might appear in one or more special journals.

1. Other Accounts—Debit
2. Purchases—Debit
3. Accounts Payable—Debit
4. Accounts Receivable—Credit
5. Office Supplies—Debit
6. Other Accounts—Credit
7. Accounts Payable—Credit
8. Cash—Credit
9. Accounts Receivable—Debit
10. Cash—Debit

The company maintains subsidiary ledgers for accounts receivable and accounts payable.
For each of the headings, state the special journal or journals in which it would be found and whether or not the amounts entered in the column would be posted as a total, or separately, or both as a total and separately.

Q6-9. (Appendix). Define (1) an accounting objective, (2) an accounting standard, and (3) an accounting practice.

Q6-10. (Appendix). What is the purpose (1) of a discussion memorandum and (2) of an exposure draft?

Q6-11. (Appendix). In June 1974 the FASB issued a discussion memorandum which contained this question: "For which specific items in the statement of financial position is 'current value' information most likely to be useful to investors and creditors?"
Provide a brief response to the FASB's question.

Q6-12. (Appendix). On September 23, 1974, the FASB held public hearings in New York on the *Conceptual Framework for Accounting and Reporting.* How much advance notice is the FASB expected to give of such hearings? If a person desires to be present at the hearings and to present testimony, what must he or she do first?

EXERCISES

BASIC CONCEPTS AND METHODOLOGY

E6-1. The numbers below indicate the corresponding columns in the cash receipts and cash payments journals of Brevard Company:

Journal	*Column Heading*	*Number*
Cash Receipts	Cash—debit	1
	Accounts Receivable—credit	2
	Sales—credit	3
	Other Accounts—credit	4

Cash Payments	Cash—credit	5
	Accounts Payable—debit	6
	Purchases—debit	7
	Other Accounts—debit	8

Indicate how the following transactions would be entered in the journals by designating the appropriate column numbers for the debits and the credits.

1. Payment to creditor on account
2. Payment of salaries
3. Collection from customer on account
4. Payment of insurance premium for two years
5. Issuance of common stock for cash
6. Cash sale
7. Cash purchase of merchandise

E6-2. The Allison Company made the following merchandise sales on account during May 1976:

1976
May 2 To A. B. Carson, $170.
      3 To D. G. Dawson, $150.
      4 To E. E. Eason, $300.
      7 To J. K. Nelson, $420.
      7 To A. B. Carson, $185.
   12 To D. G. Dawson, $90.
   20 To E. E. Eason, $65.
   31 To J. K. Nelson, $175.

a. Record the transactions in a sales journal similar to the one illustrated in this chapter. The terms on credit sales are 2/10, n/30. Number the sales invoices, starting with 101.
b. Open accounts in the accounts receivable ledger for the customers.
c. Open the following accounts in the general ledger: Accounts Receivable 111 and Sales 301.
d. Post from the sales journal to the accounts receivable ledger and the general ledger.

E6-3. The Clarke Fishing Equipment Shop made the following merchandise purchases during December 1976:

1976
Dec. 1 From the Herman Company on account, $500.
      2 From the Milton Company on account, $200.
      5 From the Queens Company on account, $400.
   13 From the Thompson Supply Company on account, $360.
   17 From the Uriah Company on account, $240.
   19 From the Herman Company on account, $280.
   22 From the Milton Company on account, $210.
   26 From the Herman Company on account, $180.
   30 From the Thompson Supply Company on account, $215.

a. Record the transactions in a purchases journal similar to the one illustrated in this chapter. The terms on all purchases of merchandise on account are 2/10, n/30.

ACCOUNTING
SYSTEMS

b. Open the following accounts in the general ledger: Accounts Payable 201 and Purchases 351.

c. Open accounts in the accounts payable ledger for the creditors.

d. Post from the purchases journal to the accounts payable ledger and the general ledger.

E6-4. The Potter Corporation received its charter on March 1, 1976. During the month of March, it completed the following cash receipt transactions:

1976

Mar. 1 Capital stock of $40,000 was issued at par for cash.

8 Received a check for $196 from Nelson Parker in settlement of a $200 sales invoice.

15 Cash sales for March 1 through 15 were $2,600.

17 Received $120 in cash from Bobo Farrell (no discount).

23 Borrowed $2,000 in cash from the Provincial National Bank and gave a note payable due April 23, 1976.

25 Received a check for $388 from Fred Eckel in settlement of a $400 sales invoice.

31 Cash sales for March 16 through 31 were $3,400.

31 Sold at cost a parcel of land purchased on March 1 for $5,500, receiving $2,500 in cash and a note receivable for the balance.

a. Record the transactions in a cash receipts journal similar to the one illustrated in this chapter.

b. Open the following general ledger accounts:
Cash 101
Accounts Receivable 111
Notes Receivable 115
Land 121
Notes Payable 205
Capital Stock 251
Sales 301
Sales Discounts 311

Post a debit of $890 to Accounts Receivable; date the posting March 31. This amount is from the sales journal.

c. Open the following accounts in the accounts receivable ledger and record the amounts given in the Debit and Balance columns (these are summary totals posted from the sales journal): Fred Eckel, $400; Bobo Farrell, $280; Nelson Parker, $210.

d. Post from the cash receipts journal to the accounts receivable ledger and the general ledger.

e. Prepare a schedule of accounts receivable.

E6-5. The Copper Cliff Company was organized on May 1, 1976. The following cash payments were made during the month:

1976

May 1 Purchased land and building for $50,000. Paid $20,000 in cash and a note for $30,000. Land is appraised at $10,000; building, at $40,000.

10 Paid the Spragge Company $980 in settlement of a purchase made on May 2; the invoice price was $1,000.

15 Cash purchases for May 1 through 15 were $8,000.

1976

May 17 Paid the Kagawong Company $2,000 on account (no discount).

20 Purchased office equipment for $3,000 in cash.

31 Paid the Providence Bay Company $700 on account (no discount).

31 Paid a 9%, 30-day note due this date. Face value of the note was $6,000; interest was $45.

31 Cash purchases for May 16 through 31 were $12,000.

a. Record the transactions in a cash payments journal similar to the one illustrated in this chapter.

b. Open the following general ledger accounts:

Cash 101
Land 201
Building 202
Office Equipment 203
Accounts Payable 301
Notes Payable 302
Purchases 401
Purchases Discounts 402
Interest Expense 501

Enter the following account balances:

1. Cash debit, $150,000—posted from the cash receipts journal.

2. Accounts Payable credit, $5,700—posted from the purchases journal.

3. Notes Payable credit, $6,000—posted from the cash receipts journal.

c. Open the following accounts in the accounts payable ledger and record the amounts given in the Credit and Balance columns (these are summary totals posted from the purchases journal): Kagawong Company, $2,400; Providence Bay Company, $1,800; Spragge Company, $1,500.

d. Post from the cash payments journal to the accounts payable ledger and the general ledger.

e. Prepare a schedule of accounts payable.

E6-6. The Mattehorn Company uses sales, purchases, cash receipts, cash payments, and general journals. On January 31, 1976, it had the following amounts in its general ledger after the books had been closed:

Cash				Accounts Receivable			
1	116,000	2	76,000	3	120,000	4	40,000

Accounts Payable				Sales			
5	16,000	6	39,000	7	156,000	8	120,000
						9	36,000

Purchases				Purchases Returns and Allowances			
10	39,000	12	51,000	13	3,600	14	3,600
11	12,000						

On a sheet of paper, opposite numbers 1 through 14 corresponding to the numbers that appear in the folio columns of the accounts, indicate the most probable journal source for each posting. Use the abbreviations J, S, P, CR, and CP to identify the journals, as shown in the following example:

Number	Journal Source
1	CR

E6-7. A partial cash receipts journal is shown below for the Sanders Company.

CASH RECEIPTS JOURNAL		Page 12	
		Other Accounts Credits	
Account Credited		F	Amount
Capital Stock			10,000
Notes Payable			6,000
Mortgage Payable			50,000
			66,000

(a) Is the total of $66,000 posted to an account? (b) What symbol should be placed under the total to indicate that it has, or has not, been posted? (c) Open general ledger skeleton T accounts and post all the required information for the end of the posting period. Omit dates, but provide account numbers and indicate proper folio references in the T accounts.

E6-8. Partial information relating to the purchases journal and cash payments journal of the Adams Company is given below. (Date and folio (F) information are omitted.)

PURCHASES JOURNAL	Page 8
Account Credited	Amount
Durham Company	5,450
Riggsbee Company	2,350
Tautle Company	1,500
Sang Company	2,500
	11,800

```
        CASH PAYMENTS JOURNAL                    Page 6
                                          ┌─────────────────────────┐
                                          │          Debit          │
        Account Debited                   ├─────────────────────────┤
                                          │    Accounts Payable     │
                                          ├──────────┬──────────────┤
                                          │    ✔     │   Amount     │
────────────────────────────────────────────────────────────────────
   Durham Company                                        5,450
   Riggsbee Company                                      1,000
   Tautle Company                                        1,500
                                                        ───────
                                                         7,950
                                                        ═══════
```

(a) If the purchases from the Durham Company are subject to a 2/10, n/30 discount and the payments are made within eight days of invoice date, would the amount of cash paid be $5,450 or $5,341? (b) Open appropriate general and subsidiary ledger T accounts and post all the foregoing transactions (provide account numbers).

E6-9. (Appendix). You have been asked to correct the following income statement. In addition to a corrected statement, comment on accounting standards that have not been followed.

ELLA'S DRESS SHOPPE
Income Statement
For the Year Ended December 31, 1976

Sales	$250,000
Less amounts uncollected	50,000
Net sales	$200,000
Payments for purchases	110,000
Gross margin on sales	$ 90,000
Operating expense	80,000
Net income from operations	$ 10,000
Gain from adjustment of inventory of dresses to current price level	10,000
Net income	$20,000

Your review of business papers on file reveals the following information:
a. The payments for purchases included a $10,000 carryover from 1975 while $15,000 of the 1976 purchases remain unpaid.
b. Included in operating expenses are these items:
　(1) A 1975 bonus to employees, which was actually paid in January 1976, in the amount of $2,000.
　(2) $150 a month for car payments on Ella's new compact car.
　(3) Depreciation of $500. The 20-year life building cost $40,000, but Ella feels that it deteriorated only about $500 last year.

c. The inventory at December 31, 1975, was $18,000; at December 31, 1976, it was $25,000.

d. You also find in the files a notice from the local tax authorities that the legislature had enacted a 10% tax on all high-fashion clothing effective January 1, 1977. Ella does not know how this tax will affect her sales for 1977, but her attorney has told her that there is a good chance the bill will be found unconstitutional.

E6-10. (Appendix). The Accountants International Study Group is sponsored by the Canadian Institute of Chartered Accountants (CICA), the three institutes of chartered accountants in Great Britain and Ireland, and the American Institute of Certified Public Accountants (AICPA). Suppose this group recommended that specific proposals for rules under the accounting standard of full disclosure be considered by authoritative bodies in all four countries. Show in outline form the steps likely to be taken by groups in the United States.

**DEMON-
STRATION
PROBLEMS**

DP6-1. (*Special journals*) The Quebec Company has been in operation for five years, selling merchandise for cash only. Beginning in January 1976, it plans to start making sales on account. The general ledger of the company shows the following account balances on January 1, 1976.

101	Cash	$40,000
121	Accounts Receivable	–0–
122	Notes Receivable	–0–
131	Merchandise Inventory	60,000
141	Prepaid Insurance	–0–
201	Store Equipment	20,000
201A	Accumulated Depreciation—Store Equipment	8,000
301	Accounts Payable	–0–
302	Notes Payable	–0–
401	Capital Stock	100,000
402	Retained Earnings	12,000
501	Sales	–0–
502	Sales Returns and Allowances	–0–
503	Sales Discounts	–0–
601	Purchases	–0–
602	Purchases Returns and Allowances	–0–
603	Purchases Discounts	–0–
701	Salesmen's Salaries Expense	–0–

Transactions during the month of January:

1976
Jan. 2 Sold merchandise to Thomas Armour on account, $900: terms, 2/10, n/30.

4 Sold merchandise to Billie Burton on account, $300: terms, 2/10, n/30.

6 Sold merchandise to William Canton on account, $600: terms, 2/10, n/30.

7 Sold merchandise to Dunlap Lawson on account, $400: terms, 2/10, n/30.

8 Purchased merchandise from the Milton Company on account, $2,000: terms, 1/10, n/30.

1976
Jan. 9 Purchased merchandise from the Naughton Company on account, $2,600, terms, 1/10, n/30.

10 Purchased merchandise from the Norton Company on account, $750: terms, n/45.

11 Purchased merchandise from the Rumbley Company on account, $1,200: terms, n/60.

12 Received a check from Thomas Armour for the amount due from the sale of January 2.

13 Issued additional capital stock for $10,000 in cash.

15 Cash sales of $9,000 were made.

16 Received a check from Billie Burton for $100 and a 60-day, 10% promissory note for the balance.

17 Received a check for $392 from William Canton in partial settlement of his account—$400 invoice price less $8 discount. Because the check was mailed before the expiration of the discount period, the discount was allowed.

18 Cash sales of $5,000 were made.

18 Purchased store equipment, $4,000, making a down payment of $1,000 and issuing a 120-day, 9% note payable for the balance.

18 Paid $480 for a comprehensive 2-year insurance policy, dating from January 1, 1976.

18 Paid the amount due the Milton Company for the purchases made on January 8.

19 Paid $1,485 in partial settlement of the amount due the Naughton Company: $1,500 invoice price less $15 discount.

20 Paid salesmen's salaries of $1,000.

20 Cash purchases totaled $4,760.

28 Issued a 90-day, 9% note to the Naughton Company in settlement of balance of account.

30 Returned merchandise to the Norton Company and received credit, $160.

31 Credited Dunlap Lawson for $120 for merchandise returned.

Required:

1. Open the necessary general and subsidiary ledgers.
2. Journalize all the charge sales in a sales journal and post them to the accounts receivable ledger. Provide invoice numbers starting with 0001. Summarize the sales journal and make the January 31 postings to the general ledger.
3. Journalize all the charge purchases in a purchases journal and post them to the accounts payable ledger. Summarize the purchases journal and make January 31 postings to the general ledger.
4. Journalize all the cash receipts in a cash receipts journal and post them to the accounts receivable ledger. Summarize and cross-foot the journal and make January 31 postings to the general ledger.
5. Journalize all the cash payments in a cash payments journal and post them to the accounts payable ledger. Provide check numbers starting with 4062. Summarize and cross-foot the journal and make January 31 postings to the general ledger.
6. Journalize any other transactions in a two-column general journal.
7. Prove the balances of the Accounts Receivable and Accounts Payable

accounts by preparing a schedule of accounts receivable and a schedule of accounts payable.

DP6-2. (*Complex examples of cash receipts and cash payments*) The following cash receipts and cash payments requiring multiple debits and/or credits occurred at the Pettegrew Corporation during May 1976:

1976

May 1 Issued an additional 1,000 shares of capital stock to Ronald Paton for the net assets of his single proprietorship.

Assets received:	
Cash	$50,500
Accounts Receivable	9,500
Merchandise Inventory	25,000
Land	20,000
Liability assumed:	
Mortgage Payable	5,000

2 Purchased office equipment for $5,000 and office supplies for $800; paid $4,200 in cash and issued a 90-day, 9% note for the balance.

3 Sold for $9,000 part of the land acquired on May 1 at a cost of $7,000. (Credit Gain on Sale of Land, $2,000.)

4 Paid $3,000 in cash and issued stock with a par value of $9,000 to Nelson, Inc., in settlement of a $12,000 account.

Required: Record the transactions in a cash receipts journal and a cash payments journal as illustrated in this chapter.

PROBLEMS

P6-1. During June 1976 the Builders' Hardware Supply Company completed the transactions listed below.

1976

June 1 Sold merchandise on account to Donald Baty, $2,300.

3 Sold merchandise on account to Robert Ludlow, $920.

7 Issued additional capital stock at par, $3,000.

10 Sold merchandise on account to Richard Mason, $560.

12 Sold merchandise on account to Donald Baty, $710.

13 Received a check from Robert Ludlow for the amount due.

15 Cash sales to date, $4,650.

18 Sold merchandise on account to Joseph Bateman, $380.

20 Borrowed $600 in cash from First State Bank and gave a 30-day, 9% note for that amount.

23 Received a $200 check from Richard Mason to apply on account.

24 Received a check from Joseph Batemen for the amount due.

26 Sold merchandise on account to Robert Briant, $520.

27 Received a check from Donald Baty for the amount due.

28 Sold merchandise on account to Richard Mason, $200.

29 Received a check from Robert Briant for the amount due.

30 Cash sales from June 16 through 30 were $4,060.

30 Received $200 in rent on land for June.

Required:

1. Record the transactions in a sales journal and a cash receipts journal similar to the ones illustrated in this chapter. Terms of 2/10, n/30 apply to all sales on account. (Number the sales invoices, starting with 51.)
2. Open the following accounts in the general ledger: Cash, 101; Accounts Receivable, 111; Notes Payable, 205; Capital Stock, 251; Sales, 301; Sales Discounts, 311; Rent Earned, 351.
3. Open the customers' accounts in the accounts receivable ledger.
4. Post from the two journals to the accounts receivable ledger and general ledger.
5. Prepare a schedule of accounts receivable.

P6-2. The Montreal Company started operations on August 1, 1976. During August, the company used the following accounts:

Cash 101	Sales 401
Accounts Receivable 111	Sales Discounts 402
Notes Receivable 115	Sales Returns and Allowances 403
Prepaid Insurance 117	Purchases 501
Office Supplies 118	Purchases Discounts 502
Land 151	Purchases Returns and Allowances 503
Store Building 154	Transportation In 504
Store Fixtures 156	Salaries Expense 601
Office Equipment 158	Delivery Expense 611
Accounts Payable 201	Office Expense 621
Mortgage Payable 251	Utilities Expense 631
Capital Stock 301	

The following transactions occurred during August:

1976
Aug. 1 Issued for cash capital stock worth $30,000.
1 Purchased a store building and site for $60,000 of which $15,000 is considered land cost. Paid $10,000 in cash and issued a mortgage for the balance.
1 Purchased store fixtures from the Mebane Company for $6,800 on account; terms, n/60.
2 Purchased merchandise from Isaacs, Inc., on account, $4,000; invoice date August 1; terms, 2/10, n/60.
2 Purchased merchandise from Jacob Barstow on account, $8,000; invoice date, August 2; terms, 2/10, n/60.
6 Purchased a 3-year fire insurance policy for $720 in cash.
8 Purchased merchandise for $5,000 in cash.
9 Returned unsatisfactory merchandise to Isaacs, Inc., and received credit for $800.
13 Sold merchandise to Dunn Evanston on account, $8,200; invoice No. 1; terms, 1/10, n/30.
14 Paid Isaacs, Inc., and Jacob Barstow the amounts due.
15 Cash sales from August 1 through 15 were $3,400.
16 Sold merchandise to Hilton Keith on account, $4,700; invoice No. 2; terms 1/10, n/30.
16 Sold merchandise to Lamb Learner on account, $6,300; invoice No. 3; terms, 1/10, n/30.

1976

Aug. 16 Paid salaries for August 1 through 15 totaling $2,650.

19 Sold merchandise to Andrew Melbourne on account, $8,000; invoice No. 4; terms, 1/10, n/30.

21 Purchased merchandise from the Ramsey Company on account, $4,900; invoice date, August 21; terms, 1/10, n/30.

21 Received bill for $130 from the Saffelle Supply Company for items chargeable to Office Expense; terms n/30.

23 Received merchandise returned by Andrew Melbourne; issued credit memo No. 1 for $2,000.

23 Received cash from Dunn Evanston for invoice No. 1, less discount.

26 Received cash from Hilton Keith for invoice No. 2, less discount.

26 Purchased merchandise from Dunkirk, Inc., on account, $9,100; invoice date, August 24; terms, 3/10, n/30. Paid transportation charges of $90. The goods were shipped F.O.B. shipping point.

28 Received $1,300 cash from Lamb Learner and a 9%, 60-day note for the balance.

29 Sold merchandise to Nathan Waters on account, $4,000; invoice No. 5; terms, 1/10, n/30.

29 Paid $215 in cash for electricity.

29 Paid the Ramsey Company on the invoice of August 21, less discount.

29 Received cash from Andrew Melbourne for the balance of invoice No. 4, less discount.

31 Cash sales from August 16 through 31 were $1,950.

31 Paid salaries for August 16 through 31 totaling $2,850.

31 Received a bill for $96 from the Delivu Company for delivery service for the month.

31 Purchased two filing cabinets and a typewriter at a cost of $750 and various office supplies at a cost of $300; paid $350 in cash and issued $700 par value capital stock for the balance.

Required:

1. Record the transactions in a general journal, a cash receipts journal, a cash payments journal, a sales journal, and a purchases journal.
2. Indicate how the postings would be made from the journals by entering the appropriate posting references.

P6-3. Pineland Furniture, Inc., uses a sales journal, a two-column general journal, and a cash receipts journal that includes an Accounts Receivable column. A monthly trial balance is prepared. The accounts receivable ledger is shown below.

SLOAN STORES						
1976 Jan.	1	Balance	✔			900
	10		S6	400		1,300
	19		CR4		900	400
	25		J9		100	300
	28		S6	500		800

SNEPHENS, INC.

1976						
Jan.	1	Balance	✓			350
	5		CR4		350	–
	11		S6	410		410
	20		S6	380		790
	27		CR4		150	640
	30		J10		50	590

SUTTONS, INC.

1976						
Jan.	1	Balance	✓			395
	12		J9		45	350
	15		S6	670		1,020
	31		CR4		250	770

Required:

1. Reconstruct the Accounts Receivable controlling account exactly as it appeared in the general ledger of Pineland Furniture, Inc., after all postings from the journals had been completed, including dates and posting references.
2. Rule and balance the Accounts Receivable account.
3. Verify the ending account balance by preparing a schedule of accounts receivable.

P6-4. The general ledger of Peter Pann Company shows the following account balances on December 1, 1976:

101	Cash	$26,000
111	Accounts Receivable	4,400
115	Notes Receivable	350
125	Merchandise Inventory	40,000
141	Prepaid Insurance	–0–
162	Delivery Equipment	16,000
162A	Accumulated Depreciation-Delivery Equipment	1,600
164	Store Equipment	28,000
164A	Accumulated Depreciation-Store Equipment	4,000
201	Accounts Payable	3,600
205	Notes Payable	–0–
251	Capital Stock	100,000
252	Retained Earnings	5,550
301	Sales	–0–
305	Sales Returns and Allowances	–0–
311	Sales Discounts	–0–
351	Purchases	–0–
361	Purchases Returns and Allowances	–0–
365	Purchases Discounts	–0–
703	Rent Expense	–0–

| 705 | Heat and Light Expense | –0– |
| 714 | Wages Expense | –0– |

The following information was taken from the subsidiary ledgers on November 30, 1976:

ACCOUNTS RECEIVABLE

Customer	Date of Sale	Terms	Amount
Brantley Company	November 24	2/10, n/30	$1,200
Calloway Company			–0–
Fussell Company	November 14	2/10, n/30	1,750
Wharton Company	November 30	2/10, n/30	1,450
			$4,400

ACCOUNTS PAYABLE

Creditor	Date of Purchase	Terms	Amount
Easley Company	November 15	1/25, n/60	$ 930
Hooker Supply Company	November 6	n/30	1,670
Lambert Company	November 20	1/15, n/30	1,000
			$3,600

Transactions for December:

1976

Dec. 1 Purchased merchandise from the Hooker Supply Company on account, $915; terms, n/30.

2 Issued check No. 314 in the amount of $172 for a 1-year insurance policy.

2 Issued a credit memorandum for $50 to the Wharton Company for the return of merchandise on the sale of November 30, 1976.

3 Received a check from the Brantley Company in payment for the sale made on November 24.

3 Paid the Lambert Company for the purchase of November 20; check No. 315.

3 Purchased merchandise from the Easley Company on account, $840; terms, 1/25, n/60.

4 Paid the Hooker Supply Company $670 on account and issued a 60-day, 9% promissory note for the balance due on the purchase of November 6; check No. 316.

4 Paid $240 for the December rent; check No. 317.

10 Paid the Easley Company for the purchase of November 15; check No. 318.

10 Sold merchandise to the Calloway Company on account, $2,100; terms, 2/10, n/30; invoice No. 3072.

11 Issued additional capital stock for $15,000 in cash.

1976

Dec. 12 Received a check for $750 from the Fussell Company for the sale of November 14 and a 10%, 30-day note for the balance due.

12 Sold merchandise to the Brantley Company on account, $1,750; terms, 2/10, n/30; invoice No. 3073.

13 Purchased merchandise from the Lambert Company on account, $1,400; terms, 1/15, n/30.

14 Paid semimonthly salaries totaling $980; checks No. 319–330.

15 Cash sales from December 1 through 15 were $3,750.

17 Sold merchandise to the Fussell Company on account, $1,750; terms, 2/10, n/30; invoice No. 3074.

18 Received a credit memorandum for $100 from the Lambert Company for the return of defective merchandise.

19 Received a check from the Calloway Company for $1,000 on account; no discount was allowed.

20 Purchased merchandise for $4,000 in cash; check No. 331.

21 Received a check for $250 from the Brantley Company and a 9% note for the balance due; no discount was allowed.

27 Received a check from the Fussell Company for the sale of December 17.

28 Paid the Lambert Company for the purchase made on December 13; check No. 332.

30 Paid semimonthly salaries totaling $995; checks No. 333–344.

30 Paid $112 for heat and light for December; check No. 345.

31 Cash sales from December 16 through 31 were $4,550.

31 Purchased merchandise from the Lambert Company on account, $1,450; terms, 1/15, n/30.

Required:

1. Record the transactions in a sales journal, a purchases journal, a general journal, a cash receipts journal, and a cash payments journal.
2. Open in the general ledger the accounts listed above. Using the date December 1, record the account balances.
3. Open the listed accounts in an accounts receivable ledger and an accounts payable ledger. Record the appropriate dates and amounts.
4. Post from the journals to the appropriate ledgers.
5. Prepare a trial balance.
6. Prepare a schedule of accounts receivable and a schedule of accounts payable.

P6-5. Partial journals of the Carbone Company are shown below in skeleton form (Date and folio (F) columns are omitted).

SALES JOURNAL		PURCHASES JOURNAL	
Account	*Amount*	*Account*	*Amount*
N. Ruggles	750	Coleman Co.	260
J. Janes	460	Betro, Inc.	500
K. Goddard	600	Fettig Supply Co.	600
	1,810		1,360

(Ch. 6)

SALES RETURNS AND ALLOWANCES JOURNAL		PURCHASES RETURNS AND ALLOWANCES JOURNAL	
Account	*Amount*	*Account*	*Amount*
J. Janes	60	Betro, Inc.	60
N. Ruggles	70	Coleman Co.	30
	130		90

GENERAL JOURNAL

Notes Receivable	300	
Accounts Receivable—J. Janes		300
Store Equipment	950	
Arnold Carbone, Capital		950

CASH RECEIPTS JOURNAL

Debits			Credits			
Cash	Sales Discounts	Account Credited	Accounts Receivable		Sales	Other Accounts
			✔	Amount		
10,000		Arnold Carbone, Capital				10,000
100		Rent Earned				100
750		Sales			750	
100		J. Janes		100		
294	6	N. Ruggles		300		
198	2	K. Goddard		200		
11,442	8			600	750	10,100

CASH PAYMENTS JOURNAL

Credits			Debits		
Cash	Purchases Discounts	Accounts Debited	Accounts Payable		Other Accounts
			✔	Amount	
2,500		Store Equipment			2,500
98	2	Coleman Company		100	
150		Prepaid Insurance			150
291	9	Fettig Supply Co.		300	
3,039	11			400	2,650

Required:

1. Open general and subsidiary ledger T accounts and post the transactions (provide account numbers).
2. Prepare a trial balance.
3. Prepare a schedule of accounts receivable and a schedule of accounts payable.

P6-6. (*Accounting policy decision problem*) The controller of Mallory College decided to revise the format of the journals used in the accounting department. He started by asking one of his assistants to prepare a summary of the types of transaction experienced by the college. Parts of this summary follow:

1. Students must pay a tuition deposit when their applications for admission are submitted. The deposit is returned only if the college rejects the application.
2. Students must pay additional tuition deposits when they register for specific classes. The deposit is returned only if the college cancels a student's registration during the first ten days of classes; such cancellations are extremely rare.
3. At least one-third of the balance of the tuition must be paid when the semester is one-quarter over; at least two-thirds of the balance must be fully paid when the semester is three-quarters over. Accelerated payments are, of course, permitted.
4. If registration is canceled by a student during the first ten days of classes, the student is not obligated to pay the remainder of the tuition and all payments already made are refunded. If the registration is canceled after the first ten days of classes, the student is obligated to pay the remainder of the tuition, as indicated, for that semester.
5. Students must pay room deposits when their applications for housing are submitted. The deposit is returned only if the college rejects the application of a student or if the student cancels a room application ten days or more before registration begins.
6. Students must pay additional room deposits when they receive their room keys. The deposit is returned only if the college cancels the registration of a student during the first ten days of classes; such cancellations are extremely rare.
7. At least one-third of the balance of the room rent must be paid when the semester is one-quarter over; at least two-thirds of the balance must be paid when the term is one-half over; and the balance must be fully paid when the semester is three-quarters over. Accelerated payments are permitted.
8. If registration is canceled by a student during the first ten days of classes, the student is not obligated to pay the remainder of the room rent. All payments already made are refunded. If the registration is canceled after the first ten days of classes, the student is obligated to pay the remainder of the room rent, as indicated, for that semester.
9. Books and school supplies are sold in the college bookstore for cash only. Discounts are not given. Returns are permitted only on rare occasions—for example, when the wrong books are purchased or when early registration cancellations are made.
10. Books and supplies purchased by the bookstore for resale are subject to payment terms of 1/5, n/30. Transportation charges are paid by the college when the shipments are received. Unused books may be returned for full credit at any time.

ACCOUNTING
SYSTEMS

11. The college regularly (at least monthly) makes payments for the following items:
    a. Salaries of the faculty and clerical staff
    b. Maintenance and repairs for buildings, equipment, and grounds
    c. Supplies to be used by the faculty and staff
    d. Utilities (electricity, gas, heat, telephone, and water)
    e. Retirement of the mortgage and interest thereon
    f. Insurance coverage of several types
12. Depreciation of buildings and equipment is recorded monthly.
13. Interest on individual investments is received twice a year. Since the college has numerous investments, some interest is received every month.

Required:

1. What journals would be most useful to Mallory College?
2. Design the format of the journals that you have indicated as most useful.
3. Justify the inclusion of each column heading in your format.
4. Identify the advantages and disadvantages of these journals.
5. What factors govern the format of the journals to be used?
6. What types of changes will influence changes in format in the future?
7. Explain the connection between these journals and the subsidiary and the general ledgers.
8. Explain the purpose of these journals in the whole accounting process.

Practice Set—Condominium Wholesale Furniture Company

The practice set, containing transactions of the Condominium Wholesale Furniture Company, a single proprietorship, should be assigned after Chapter 6. This is a short set and can be worked in approximately ten hours. The list of transactions and working papers are in a separate package.

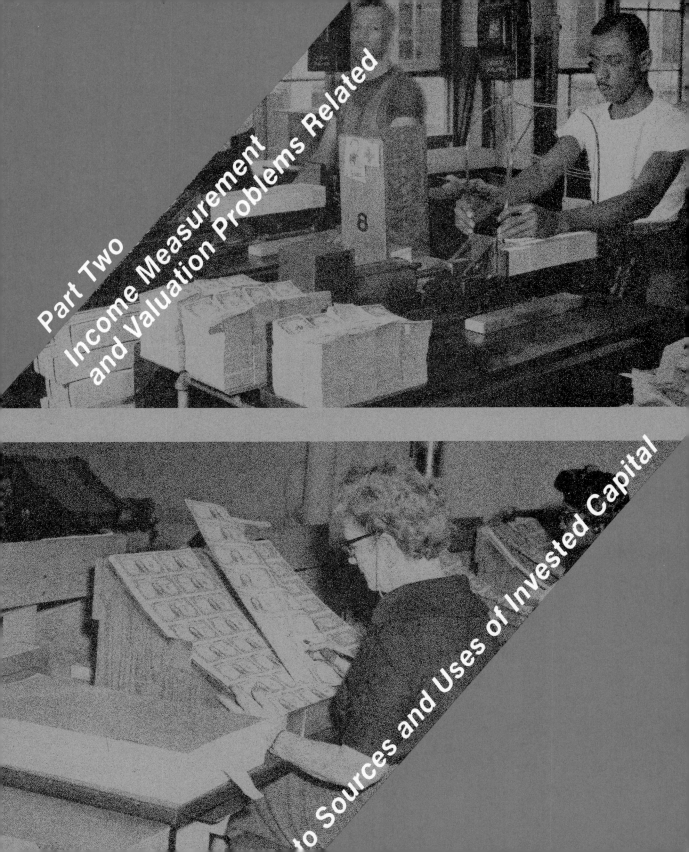

Simple Interest and Compound Interest 7

In periods of high interest rates, it is extremely important for managers to know the rudiments of both simple interest and compound interest. This chapter discusses the basic rudiments of calculating both simple interest and compound interest because they are significant elements in accounting for the borrowing and lending of money. Furthermore, a knowledge of compound interest is essential in the solution of complex problems of calculating insurance probabilities, of determining investment values to yield expected interest rates, and of solving management problems involving the time value of future sums. It is the opinion of the authors that information regarding interest is a necessary introduction to the problem of valuation of assets. Moreover, much of the information contained in this chapter is integrated in Chapters 9, 14, 15, 16, 24, 25, and 26.

DEFINITIONS OF INTEREST

Interest

Interest is the price of credit, a payment made (or collection received) for the use of money or the equivalent of money. Because it is similar to the price of supplies used, interest to the maker—the debtor—is an expense; to the payee—the creditor—interest is a revenue.

Simple Interest versus Compound Interest

Simple interest is interest on the original principal of a note or a time draft, regardless of interest amounts that may have accrued on the principal in past periods, whereas *compound interest* is interest that accrues on unpaid interest of past periods as well as on the principal. In other words, compound interest is interest earned on a principal sum that is increased at the end of each period by the interest for that period.

SIMPLE INTEREST

Assume that Tanya Crayne gives Johnson Evers a 9 percent, 60-day note that has a principal amount of $2,000. The interest specified on a note or a draft, unless otherwise indicated, is an annual fraction or rate on the principal, or face amount, of the instrument. Thus, in Tanya Crayne's note, the price, or charge, for the use of $2,000 for one year, is $180 = ($2,000 × 0.09). Since the term of the note, however, is less than one year, the interest must be computed by multiplying the interest amount for one year by a fraction; the numerator is the term of the note in days and the denominator, the number of days in a year. The formula is

$$\text{Interest} = \text{Principal} \times \text{Rate} \times \text{Time}$$

This is usually stated as I = PRT. In Crayne's note, the interest calculation for the 60-day period is

$$I = \$2{,}000 \times 0.09 \times \frac{60}{360}$$
$$I = \$30$$

It is common commercial practice to assume that the year contains 360 days (or 12 months of 30 days each) in computing interest. This practice is followed here, but it should be understood that the amount of bias in the final interest calculation is 1/73, that is,

$$\frac{365 - 360}{365} = \frac{1}{73}$$

Short-Cut Methods for Calculating Simple Interest

Time can be saved through various short-cut methods of computing simple interest. Two of these are referred to as the *6-percent 60-day method* and the *6-percent 6-day method.* Since the interest at 6 percent for 60 days on any principal is 1 percent = (60/360 × 6%), interest at 6 percent for 60 days on any principal can be figured by moving the decimal point two places to the left in the principal, which is the same as multiplying the principal by 1 percent. Similarly, the interest at 6 percent for 6 days can be figured by moving the decimal point three places to the left in the principal. Either or both of these short methods may be used for note terms other than 6 or 60 days. The term of the note can be stated as a fraction or multiple of 6 or 60 days, and the interest may then be quickly computed.

Short methods can also be applied when the interest rate is other than 6 percent. The interest calculation is first made at 6 percent, then an adjustment is made for the difference between 6 percent and the particular rate.

The following two examples illustrate interest computation by the short methods.

1. Interest at 9 percent on $3,600 for 90 days:

Interest at 6% for 60 days	$36
Interest at 6% for 30 days (½ of $36)	18
Interest at 6% for 90 days	$54
Interest at 3% for 90 days (½ of $54)	27
Interest at 9% for 90 days	$81

2. Interest at 4½ percent on $4,800 for 30 days:

Interest at 6% for 60 days	$48
Interest at 6% for 30 days (½ of $48)	$24
Less interest at 1½% for 30 days (¼ of $24)	6
Interest at 4½% for 30 days	$18

An advantage of the short methods is that they often require relatively simple arithmetical computations, thereby reducing the possibility of error. This is true when interest rates and terms are such that the mathematical manipulations are obvious, but if rates and terms require elaborate adjustments for the use of these methods (for example, 4.25 percent for 27 days), the calculation time will not be reduced, but increased. In such cases it is better to use the basic interest formula, $I = PRT$.

COMPOUND INTEREST

For the purpose of quickly computing the information needed in helping to solve many modern business problems, it is important that the accounting student be familiar with the following four basic types of compound interest computations:

1. Amount of a single invested sum at compound interest
2. Present value of a single given sum due in the future
3. Amount of an ordinary annuity
4. Present value of an ordinary annuity

Amount of a Single Sum at Compound Interest

A simple illustration of the interest compounded annually on a single sum of $100 for four years at 6 percent a year is shown here.

(1)	(2)	(3)	(4)
Year	Amount at Beginning of Year	Annual Amount of Interest (Col. 2 × 0.06)	Accumulated Amount at End of Year (Col. 2 + Col. 3)
1	$100.00	$ 6.00	$106.00
2	106.00	6.36	112.36
3	112.36	6.74	119.10
4	119.10	7.15	126.25
Total		$26.25	

The principal of $100 at the beginning of year 1 has by year 4 grown to $126.25, the *compound amount*.

Each amount in column 4 is 106 percent of the corresponding amount in column 2; that is, $100 × 1.06 × 1.06 × 1.06 × 1.06 = $126.25. This means that 106 percent, or 1.06, has been used as a multiplier four times; thus 1.06 has been raised to the fourth power. The compound amount is, therefore, $100 multiplied by 1.06 to the fourth power, as shown below.

$(1.06)^4$	1.2625
Multiplied by principal	$ 100
Compound amount	$126.25

The compound amount of 1 for n periods is expressed by the following formula:

$$a = (1 + i)^n$$

where a = compound amount of 1 ($1, or any other monetary unit) at interest for n periods
n = number of periods
i = periodic interest rate

The difference between the compound amount and the original principal is the compound interest. The compound interest (I) on 1 for four periods at 6 percent is computed as follows:

$$I = (1 + i)^n - 1$$
$$= (1 + 0.06)^4 - 1$$
$$= 1.2625 - 1$$
$$= 0.2625$$

The calculation of compound interest on $100 for four years at 6 percent compounded annually is

$$\$100 \times 0.2625 = \$26.25$$

Present Value

If $100 is worth $126.25 when it is left at 6 percent compound interest each year for four years, then it follows that $126.25 four years from now is worth $100 now; that is, $100 is the *present value* of $126.25. The present value is the amount that must be invested now to produce the known future value. In compound-amount problems, the future value of a known present value must be determined; in present value problems, the present value of a known future value must be determined. Since the amount of $100 invested at compound interest in the preceding section was in effect determined by multiplying $100 $\times$ 1.06 $\times$ 1.06 $\times$ 1.06 $\times$ 1.06 to arrive at the $126.25 figure, to calculate the present value of $126.25 we must reverse the process. That is, we must take the $126.25 and successively divide by 1.06 as follows:

Year	Amount at End of Year	Divide by		Present Value at Beginning of Year
4	$126.25	$\div$ 1.06	=	$119.10
3	119.10	$\div$ 1.06	=	112.36
2	112.36	$\div$ 1.06	=	106.00
1	106.00	$\div$ 1.06	=	100.00

Observing that the *present value of a single sum* is the reciprocal value of the *amount of a single sum,* the computation can be shortened as shown.

$$\frac{\$126.25}{(1 + 0.06)^4} = \frac{\$126.25}{1.2625} = \$100$$

The general formula for the present value (p) of a single given sum of 1 due in any number of periods is as follows:

$$p = \frac{1}{(1 + i)^n}$$

The present value of 1 at 6 percent interest compounded annually for four years is computed as shown.

$$p = \frac{1}{(1 + i)^n} = \frac{1}{(1 + 0.06)^4} = \frac{1}{1.2625} = 0.79208$$

If the present value of 1 is 0.79208, then the present value of $126.25 is computed as follows:

$$\$126.25 \times 0.79208 = \$100$$

The principal sum that must be deposited at 6 percent interest compounded annually to amount to $126.25 in four years is $100.

(Ch. 7)

Compound Discount

Compound discount (D) is the difference between the future value and the present value; it is expressed by the following formula:

$$D = 1 - \frac{1}{(1 + i)^n}$$

The compound discount on 1 at 6 percent interest, compounded annually, is

$$D = 1 - \frac{1}{(1 + i)^n} = 1 - 0.79208 = 0.20792$$

The calculation of compound discount on $126.25 for four years at 6 percent compounded annually is $126.25 × 0.20792 = $26.25 (rounded).

Ordinary Annuity—Amount

An *ordinary annuity* is a series of equal payments or deposits, also called *rents*, at the end of equal intervals of time with compound interest on these payments. The value of the annuity at the end of the successive time periods is the *amount of the annuity*. The calculation of the amount of an ordinary annuity of four payments of $100 each at 6 percent is shown in Figure 7-1.

Figure 7-1
Amount of an
Ordinary Annuity

(1) Period	(2) Beginning Balance	(3) Interest Earned (6% × Col. 2)	(4) Periodic Payment	(5) Accumulated at End of Period (Col. 2 + Col. 3 + Col. 4)
1	$ –0–	$ –0–	$100	$100.00
2	100.00	6.00	100	206.00
3	206.00	12.36	100	318.36
4	318.36	19.10	100	437.46

The formula for finding the amount (A) of an ordinary annuity of 1 each is as follows:

$$A = \frac{(1 + i)^n - 1}{i}$$

Since the numerator of this equation is the compound interest (*I*), the equation may be restated as

$$A = \frac{I}{i}$$

The amount of an ordinary annuity of four rents of $100 each at 6 percent interest compounded annually may be computed directly as follows:

$$A = \frac{I}{i} = \frac{0.2625}{0.06} \times \$100 = \$437.50$$

Figure 7-1 shows the amount to be $437.46. The $0.04 difference is due to rounding.

Ordinary Annuity—Present Value

The present value of an ordinary annuity is the present value of a series of payments to be made at equal intervals in the future; that is, it is the single sum that, if invested at compound interest now, provides for a stated series of payments or withdrawals at equal time intervals. The formula for the present value of an ordinary annuity of 1 each is as follows:

$$P = \frac{1 - \dfrac{1}{(1 + i)^n}}{i} \quad \text{or} \quad P = \frac{1 - (1 + i)^{-n}}{i}$$

Since the numerator of this equation is the compound discount (D), the equation may be restated as shown.

$$P = \frac{D}{i}$$

The present value of an ordinary annuity of four payments of $100 at 6 percent is calculated as follows:

$$P = \frac{D}{i} = \frac{0.20792}{0.06} \times \$100 = \$346.53$$

The proof that the present value of an ordinary annuity of four payments of $100 at 6 percent is $346.53 is shown below.

Amount invested	$346.53
Interest earned, 1st period (6% × $346.53)	20.79
Amount at end of 1st period	$367.32
Deduct 1st payment	100.00
Balance of investment at beginning of 2d period	$267.32
Interest earned, 2d period (6% × $267.32)	16.04
Amount at end of 2d period	$283.36
Deduct 2d payment	100.00
Balance of investment at beginning of 3d period	$183.36
Interest earned, 3d period (6% × $183.36)	11.00
Amount at end of 3d period	$194.36
Deduct 3d payment	100.00
Balance of investment at beginning of 4th period	$ 94.36
Interest earned, 4th period (6% × $94.36)	5.66
Amount at end of 4th period	$100.02
Deduct 4th payment	100.00
Total (difference is due to rounding)	$000.02

SIMPLE INTEREST
AND COMPOUND
INTEREST

The four basic formulas may be summarized in chart form, using the abbreviated notations, as follows:

$$\text{Present value} \longleftarrow p = \frac{1}{a} \longrightarrow \text{Single payment} \longrightarrow a = (1 + i)^n \longrightarrow \text{Future value}$$

$$\text{Present value} \longleftarrow P = \frac{D}{i} \longrightarrow \text{Series of payments} \longrightarrow A = \frac{I}{i} \longrightarrow \text{Future value}$$

Since $p = 1/a$, $D = 1 - p$, and $I = a - 1$, then the formula for the amount of 1, $a = (1 + i)^n$ is the source for the derivation of the other formulas.

Use of Compound Interest Tables

Compound interest tables are available and are in common use in banking, industry, and elsewhere. Tables of a, p, A, and P of $1 for different periods and at various interest rates are shown in the Appendix tables on pages 1028–1031.

To illustrate how these tables are used, first refer to page 1029, which shows the present value of $1 ($p$). The figure in the 10 percent column for period 10 is 0.385543. This means that $1 due at the end of 10 years, compounded annually at 10 percent interest, if discounted, has a present worth or present value of $0.385543; that is, if $0.385543 is invested today at 10 percent interest compounded annually, it would accumulate to $1 in 10 years. The figures in the table are *discount factors* that produce the present value equivalent of any known future amount when multiplied by that amount. For example, to produce $6,750 10 years from now at 10 percent interest compounded annually, $6,750 × 0.385543, or $2,602.42, must be deposited.

The table on page 1031 shows the present values of series of payments (P) to be made at equal intervals in the future. For example, the figure in the 10 percent column for period 10 is 6.144567. This means that $1 due at the end of each year for 10 years, compounded annually at 10 percent interest, has a present value of $6.144567. The same result can be obtained by using the discount factors from the table on page 1029 to accumulate each present value in the series. The table on page 1031 shortens the process by giving a single discount factor for an entire series. The figures in the present value tables are discount factors that, when multiplied by any series of uniform amounts due at regular intervals in the future, produce the present equivalent of that series of amounts. For example, to produce $1,250 at the end of each year when 10 rents are deposited annually at 10 percent interest compounded annually, $1,250 × 6.144567, or $7,680.71, must be deposited.

The precomputed formula values for a and A as shown on pages 1028 and 1030 are used in a manner similar to that described for p and P above. Several illustrations of these calculations are given below.

Illustration of Computation of Amount of a Single Sum at Compound Interest. Assume that on December 31, 1976, Benjamin Boykin plans to invest in a savings account $10,000 at 6 percent interest compounded annually. He would like to know how much he would have in the savings account on January 1, 1986, when he plans to retire. The problem can be graphically portrayed as follows:

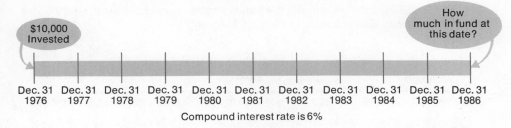

Compound interest rate is 6%

To solve the problem by the use of tables, we must look up the value of *a* for 10 periods at 6 percent on page 1028. This value is 1.790848, which is the value of $(1.06)^{10}$. To obtain the answer, we must multiply the $10,000 by the 1.790848 as shown below.

$$1.790848 \times \$10,000 = \$17,908.48$$

Illustration of Computation of the Present Value of a Given Sum. Assume that Elton Parker desires to have $50,000 in a given fund on December 31, 1986. How much must he invest on December 31, 1976, to produce $50,000 ten years later if the investment earns 6 percent interest compounded annually? Again, the problem can be shown graphically as follows:

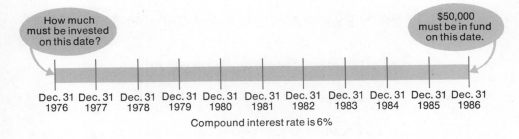

Compound interest rate is 6%

To solve the problem by the use of present value tables, we must look up the value of *p* for 10 periods at 6 percent on page 1029. This value is 0.558395, which is $1/(1.06)^{10}$; then we must multiply the $50,000 by this discount factor, thus:

$$\$50,000 \times 0.558395 = \$27,919.75$$

On December 31, 1976, Parker would have to invest $27,919.75 at 6 percent interest compounded annually to earn $50,000 by December 31, 1986.

Illustration of Computation of the Amount of an Ordinary Annuity at Compound Interest. Assume that John Gainsworthy receives a semiannual bonus of $10,000 on January 2 and July 2. He plans to deposit these bonuses in a savings account which earns interest at 6 percent a year compounded semiannually, or 3 percent each six months. If Gainsworthy starts investing his bonus on

(Ch. 7)

January 2, 1976, how much will he have in the fund on July 2, 1980? The problem can be illustrated graphically as follows:

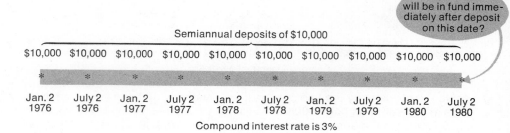

Semiannual deposits of $10,000

How much will be in fund immediately after deposit on this date?

$10,000 $10,000 $10,000 $10,000 $10,000 $10,000 $10,000 $10,000 $10,000 $10,000

Jan. 2 1976   July 2 1976   Jan. 2 1977   July 2 1977   Jan. 2 1978   July 2 1978   Jan. 2 1979   July 2 1979   Jan. 2 1980   July 2 1980

Compound interest rate is 3%

To solve the problem by the use of compound interest tables, we must look up the value of A for 10 rents of 1 each at 3 percent on page 1030. This value is 11.463879, which is a precalculation of

$$\frac{(1.03)^{10} - 1}{0.03}$$

we must then multiply the semiannual deposits of $10,000 each by 11.463879, thus:

$$\$10,000 \times 11.463879 = \$114,638.79$$

Gainsworthy will have $114,638.79 in the fund on July 2, 1980.

Illustration of Computation of the Present Value of an Ordinary Annuity at Compound Interest. Assume that Camilla Peate wishes to make 10 annual withdrawals of $1,000 each from a fund beginning December 31, 1976. How much must she have invested on December 31, 1975, if the balance of the fund will earn interest compounded annually at 6 percent? The problem can be shown graphically as follows:

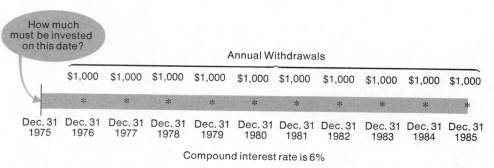

How much must be invested on this date?

Annual Withdrawals

$1,000 $1,000 $1,000 $1,000 $1,000 $1,000 $1,000 $1,000 $1,000 $1,000

Dec. 31 1975   Dec. 31 1976   Dec. 31 1977   Dec. 31 1978   Dec. 31 1979   Dec. 31 1980   Dec. 31 1981   Dec. 31 1982   Dec. 31 1983   Dec. 31 1984   Dec. 31 1985

Compound interest rate is 6%

(Ch. 7)

To solve the problem by the use of compound interest tables, we must look up the value of P for 10 rents of 1 each at 6 percent on page 1031. This value is 7.360087, which is a precalculation of

$$\frac{1 - \dfrac{1}{(1.06)^{10}}}{0.06}$$

The amount to be invested on December 31, 1975, is determined by multiplying $1,000 by 7.360087, thus:

$$\$1,000 \times 7.360087 = \$7,360.09.$$

Use of Tables to Determine Value of Rents in Annuity Problems

In the preceding annuity illustrations, the value of each rent was known, and the problem was to determine either the amount of the annuity or the present value of the annuity. The ordinary compound interest tables may be used to determine the value of each rent or deposit for either type of the foregoing annuity problems. For example, suppose that Thomas Merton had $100,000 to invest on December 31, 1976, and he wanted to start making annual withdrawals on December 31, 1977, and thereafter through December 31, 1986; assume that the fund earns interest at 6 percent compounded annually. This is a present value of an ordinary annuity problem with the present value amount known and the value of each withdrawal or rent unknown. The problem can be graphically presented as follows:

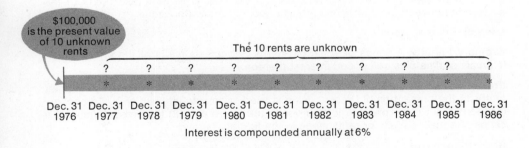

The problem can be solved by dividing $100,000 by P of 10 rents of 1 each at 6 percent. We must look up the value of P of 10 rents of 1 at 6 percent on page 1031, which is 7.360087, and divide the $100,000 by this discount factor, thus:

$$\$100,000 \div 7.360087 = \$13,586.80$$

Merton can then withdraw $13,586.80 on December 31, 1977, and each December 31 thereafter through December 31, 1986.

(Ch. 7)

A similar problem could be solved for the amount of an ordinary annuity where the final amount is known, but the value of each rent is unknown. For example, suppose a firm must have $1,000,000 in 10 years to retire a debt. It wishes to make 10 annual payments in a fund earning 6 percent interest compounded annually; how much must be invested each year? The answer to the problem is $1,000,000 divided by *A* of 10 rents of 1 each at 6 percent, 13.180795, which is $75,867.96.

Uses of Compound Interest Techniques

To reiterate, compound interest must be used to solve complex problems of calculating insurance probabilities, to determine values of investments at given interest yield rates, and to equate the time value of future sums of many management decisions. Elementary problems involving compound interest are illustrated in Chapters 9, 14, 15, 16, 23, 24, and 25. Suggestions are made in several other chapters about how the compound interest techniques could be used.

GLOSSARY

Compound Amount The amount of a single investment plus compound interest for a given number of periods thereon.

Compound Discount The difference between the future value and the present value.

Compound Interest Interest computed not only on the principal but also on any interest that has been earned in the past but not yet paid. This term also refers to the difference between the compound amount and the original principal.

Interest Price of credit.

Ordinary Annuity A series of equal payments or deposits made at the end of equal intervals of time plus compound interest thereon.

Present Value In general, a future sum discounted back by the use of an interest factor to the present time. Present value is used in connection with two approaches: (1) the present value of a single sum due in the future and (2) the present value of a series of equal deposits or rents made in the future.

Rent The amount of each equal annuity payment or deposit made.

Simple Interest Interest on the original principal only.

QUESTIONS

Q7-1. Define the term *interest.* Assume that a man pays $10 for borrowing $100 for a year and 55 cents for a gallon of gasoline. Discuss the nature—similarities and differences—of each of these figures.

Q7-2. Describe two short-cut methods of calculating simple interest. Discuss the reason that the methods will provide correct answers.

Q7-3. Many firms attempt to disguise the effective simple interest rate charged for funds that are loaned. From personal experience or from research, name three ways that are used to disguise the effective simple interest rate.

Q7-4. Distinguish between simple interest and compound interest.

Q7-5. Distinguish between the amount of 1 and the amount of an ordinary annuity of 1.

Q7-6. What is the interest rate per period and the frequency of compounding per year in each of the following:
   a. 6% compounded semiannually?
   b. 5% compounded quarterly?
   c. 9% compounded monthly?

Q7-7. Distinguish between the amount of 1 and the present value of 1.

Q7-8. Distinguish between the present value of 1 and the present value of an ordinary annuity of 1.

Q7-9. Explain how each of the following would be solved without tables:
   a. The present value of $1,000 for 5 years at 6% compounded annually.
   b. The present value of $2,000 for 4 years at 5% compounded semiannually.
   c. The compound discount on $1,000 for 12 years at 4% compounded quarterly.

Q7-10. Donnan wishes to deposit a sum that at 8% interest compounded semiannually will permit two withdrawals: $20,000 at the end of 5 years and $30,000 at the end of 15 years. Analyze the problem to determine the required deposit, stating the procedure to be followed and the tables to be used in developing the solution.

E7-1. Information regarding four notes is given below.

Term of Note	Interest Rate	Principal
60 days	8%	$9,000
90 days	9%	6,000
120 days	10%	4,800
180 days	7%	6,300

Determine the maturity value, principal plus simple interest, of each note.

E7-2. Information regarding four notes held by the Sampson Company is given below.

Date of Note	Term of Note	Interest Rate	Principal
November 1, 1976	90 days	7%	$4,200
November 16, 1976	120 days	10%	6,400
December 1, 1976	60 days	8%	7,200
December 16, 1976	30 days	9%	3,600

Assume that books are closed on December 31, 1976. Compute the amount of simple interest that will be debited to Accrued Interest Receivable.

(Ch. 7)

E7-3. The following information pertains to four notes:

1. $3,465 at 6% for 60 days
2. $4,700 at 9% for 60 days
3. $4,850 at 9% for 120 days
4. $6,210 at 10% for 72 days

Using the short-cut methods discussed in this chapter, compute the amount of simple interest on each note.

E7-4. (*Financial policy decision exercise*) The Dauderis Company Limited needs sources of short-term funds. It has these alternatives:

1. To forego its discounts on purchase of merchandise and pay the invoice price at the latest possible date. These discounts are generally on a 1/10, n/30 basis.
2. To borrow money from the local bank at 10%; but the local bank requires that a minimum balance of 20% of the amount borrowed be maintained.
3. To borrow money from the Hot-Line Finance Company and pay a monthly fee of 2% of the unpaid balance at the beginning of each month.

Assuming that any one of these methods will provide the needed short-term funds, which method should the Dauderis Company Limited use? Indicate why by showing calculations of approximate effective annualized simple interest rates.

E7-5. Using the amount tables on pages 1028 and 1030, solve the following problems:
   a. What is the amount on January 1, 1980, of $20,000 deposited on January 1, 1976, to accumulate interest at 6% compounded annually?
   b. What is the amount on January 1, 1980, of $3,000 deposited on July 1, 1976, to accumulate interest at 6% compounded quarterly?
   c. What is the compound interest on an investment of $3,500 left on deposit for 5 years at 10% compounded annually?

E7-6. Hugh Cameron deposited $8,000 in a special savings account that provides for interest at the annual rate of 18% compounded monthly if the deposit is maintained for 4 years. Using the amount tables on pages 1028 and 1030, calculate the balance of the savings account at the end of the 4-year period.

E7-7. Five equal annual contributions are to be made to a fund, the first deposit to be made on December 31, 1976. Using the amount tables on pages 1028 and 1030, determine the equal contributions that, if invested at 8% compounded annually, will produce a fund of $20,000, assuming that this sum is desired on December 31, 1980.

E7-8. Using the present value tables on pages 1029 and 1031, solve the following problems:
   a. What is the present value on January 1, 1976, of $20,000 due on January 1, 1980, and discounted at 10% compounded annually?
   b. What is the present value on July 1, 1976, of $4,000 due January 1, 1980, and discounted at 12% compounded quarterly?
   c. What is the compound discount on $3,000 for 5 years at 10 percent compounded annually?

E7-9. B. B. Fitch borrows $6,000 that is to be repaid in 24 equal monthly installments with interest at the rate of 1½% a month. Using the tables on pages 1029 and 1031, calculate the equal installments.

E7-10. On January 1, 1976, Charles Sparrow borrows $25,000 from his father to open a business. The son is the beneficiary of a trust created by his favorite uncle from which he will receive $12,000 on January 1, 1985. He signs an agreement to make this amount payable to his father and further to pay his father equal annual amounts from January 1, 1977, to January 1, 1984, inclusive, in retirement of the debt. Interest is to be charged at 10%. What are the annual payments?

DP7-1. (*Computing interest by short-cut methods*) The following information pertains to five notes:

1. $4,200 at 6% for 60 days
2. $5,600 at 9% for 30 days
3. $3,400 at 10% for 72 days
4. $7,600 at 8% for 90 days
5. $10,000 at 7½% for 120 days

Required: Using the short-cut methods discussed in this chapter, compute the amount of interest on each note.

DP7-2. (*Compound interest*) Solve the problem presented in each of the following six cases:

Case A. Jackson Tomes invests $20,000 on January 1, 1976, in a savings account that earns interest at 12% compounded quarterly. What will be the amount in the fund at December 31, 1981?

Case B. Stan Smith receives a bonus of $3,000 each year on December 31. He starts depositing his bonus on December 31, 1976, in a savings account that earns interest at 8% compounded annually. What will be the amount in the fund on December 31, 1981, after he deposits his bonus received on that date?

Case C. John Bates owes $30,000 on a non-interest-bearing note due January 1, 1986. He offers to pay the amount on January 1, 1976, provided that it is discounted at 8% on a compound annual discount basis. What would he have to pay on January 1, 1976, under this assumption?

Case D. Romney Kennedy purchased an annuity on January 1, 1976, which, at a 12% annual rate, would yield $6,000 each June 30 and December 31 for the next 6 years. What must have been the cost of the annuity to Kennedy?

Case E. Five equal annual contributions are to be made to a fund, the first deposit to be made on December 31, 1976. Using the amount tables on pages 1028 and 1030 determine the equal contributions that, if invested at 8% compounded annually, will produce a fund of $25,000 on December 31, 1980.

Case F. Six equal annual withdrawals are to be made beginning December 31, 1977. Using the proper table, determine the equal annual withdrawals if $24,000 is invested at 8% interest compounded annually on December 31, 1976?

P7-1. Information regarding six notes issued by the Delilah Company is given below.

Date of Note	Term of Note	Interest Rate	Principal
August 1, 1976	1 year	8%	$10,000
September 1, 1976	6 months	9%	6,450
November 1, 1976	120 days	10%	5,800
November 16, 1976	90 days	7%	3,000
December 1, 1976	60 days	12%	20,000
December 16, 1976	30 days	8½%	4,000

Required: Assume that the books of the Delilah Company are closed each December 31. Compute the amount of accrued interest payable and make the necessary adjusting entry as of December 31, 1976.

P7-2. Five equal withdrawals are to be made beginning December 31, 1976. Using the proper table, determine the equal annual withdrawals if $20,000 is invested at 10% interest compounded annually on December 31, 1975 (Tables are shown on pages 1028-1031).

P7-3. Using the tables given on pages 1028-1031 solve each of the following problems:
    a. Ten payments of $2,000 are due at annual intervals beginning June 30, 1977. What amount will be accepted in cancellation of this series of payments on June 30, 1976, assuming a discount rate of 8% compounded annually?
    b. Ten payments of $2,000 are due at annual intervals beginning December 31, 1976. What amount will be accepted in cancellation of this series of payments on January 1, 1976, assuming a discount rate of 10% compounded annually?

P7-4. Rogers borrows $50,000 on December 31, 1976, promising to repay this amount on December 31, 1986, together with accrued interest at 8% compounded annually. Rogers plans to make five equal deposits at annual intervals in a special savings fund in order to retire the obligation at its maturity, the first deposit to be made on December 31, 1982. He believes that the fund will earn 10% compounded annually. What amounts are to be deposited?

P7-5. Ray Bowling purchases a new automobile at a cost of $3,800. He pays $800 down and issues an installment note payable by which he promises to pay the balance during the next year in 12 equal monthly installments which include interest at an annual rate of 18% on the remaining unpaid balance at the beginning of each month.

Required:

    1. Compute the equal installment payments.
    2. Compute the interest that will be paid for each of the first two periods.
    3. Indicate the amount of each payment that will be considered to be a reduction of principal.

P7-6. Nicholas needs $30,000 to pay off a mortgage due on December 31, 1982. His plans included the making of 10 annual deposits beginning on December 31, 1973, in accumulating a fund to pay off the mortgage. Without making a precise calculation, Nicholas made three annual deposits of $2,000 each on December 31, 1973, 1974, and 1975, which have been earning interest at 8% compounded annually.

Required: Precisely what will be the equal amount of each of the next seven deposits for the period December 31, 1976, to December 31, 1982, to reach the fund objective, assuming that the fund will continue to earn interest at 8% compounded annually?

P7-7. Rockness is depositing his Christmas bonus in a special savings account. He has been receiving a $2,800 bonus each year. Assume that he will continue to receive this amount and that he deposits these bonuses each December 31 in an account which will earn 10% compounded annually; also assume that the first deposit was made on December 31, 1976.

Required: What amount will be in the account after the deposit on December 31, 1980?

P7-8. The Wolfe Construction Company offers to build a bridge across the canyon for $5,000,000 and agrees to accept in settlement the city's 8% bonds, redeemable in 10 years, interest payable annually. The annual maintenance charges are estimated at $10,000 a year. It is proposed to charge tolls of 25 cents for foot passengers and $1 for vehicles.

Required: On the basis of these charges and assuming a ratio of foot passengers to vehicles of 1 to 20, how many tolls of each class would be necessary *each* year to provide for the sum of annual maintenance, annual interest, and annual deposits to a sinking fund sufficient to retire the bonds at maturity? Assume that the sinking fund will earn 8% compounded annually. (*Hint:* To compute the sinking fund deposit, divide $5,000,000 by the amount of 10 rents of $1 each at 8% compound interest.)

(*AICPA adapted*)

P7-9. On July 1, 1976, Skakle purchases real estate for $80,000 to be paid in ten equal annual installments including interest of 8% on any unpaid balance. The first installment is due on July 1, 1977.

Required: What are the equal payments?

P7-10. Andrews is approaching retirement age. He has inherited a sum of money and desires to purchase an annuity that will yield him $5,000 a year for the next 20 years, first payment to begin one year from the present date.

Required: Assuming that the annuity will yield 8% compounded annually, how much must Andrews deposit today to accomplish his objective?

P7-11. (*Financial policy decision problem*) Because of a severe cash crunch, the Allison Company finds itself needing sources of short-term funds. After investigating all possibilities, the controller lists these alternatives:

1. To forego discounts on the purchase of merchandise and pay the full invoice price at the latest possible date. These discounts are generally on a 1½/10, n/30 basis.
2. To borrow money from the local bank at 12%; but the local bank requires that a minimum balance of 20% of the amount borrowed be maintained throughout the period of the loan.
3. To borrow money from the I. M. Shy Finance Company and pay a monthly fee of 1¾% of the unpaid balance at the beginning of each month.

4. To borrow money from Hard-Line Funds Company on a year's contract basis, agreeing to pay 10% of the original amount borrowed yet agreeing to repay the loan and interest in equal monthly installments.

Required: Assuming that two or more of these sources will be needed to provide adequate short-term funds, indicate the order of the desirability of the sources, starting with the most desirable and extending to the least desirable, by calculating an approximation of the annualized effective simple interest rates for each alternative.

P7-12. (*Financial policy decision problem*) On March 1, 1976, the Border Corporation purchased $100,000 worth of inventory on credit with terms of 1/20, n/60. In the past, Border has always followed the policy of making payment one month (30 days) after the goods are purchased.

A new member of Border's staff has indicated that the company he previously worked for never passed up its cash discounts, and he wonders if this is not a sound policy. It was pointed out, however, that if Border were to pay the bill on March 20 rather than on March 30, the firm would have to borrow the necessary funds for the 10 extra days. Border's borrowing terms with a local bank were estimated to be at 8½% (annual rate) with a 15% compensating balance for the term of the loan. Most members of Border's staff felt that it made little sense to take out an 8½% loan with a compensating balance of 15% in order to save 1% on its $100,000 by paying the account 10 days earlier than they had planned.

Required:

1. In terms of simple effective annual interest cost, would it be to Border's advantage to take the 1% discount by paying the bill 10 days early if to do this it borrowed the necessary amount on the above-mentioned terms?

2. It has also been pointed out to Border that if it does not take advantage of the cash discount, it should wait the entire 60-day period to pay the full bill rather than pay within 30 days. How would your answer to requirement 1 change if Border undertook this policy (that is, just in terms of effective interest cost, would it be to Border's advantage to take the 1% discount by paying the bill 40 days early if to do this they borrowed the necessary amount on the above-mentioned terms?)

3. Your answer to requirement 2 indicates that, in relation to requirement 1, it has become either more desirable or less desirable to borrow in order to take advantage of the 1% cash discount.

    a. If you said more desirable, explain why, given that the only difference is that in requirement 1, if Border does not take the 1% discount, it pays the complete sum at the end of March, while in requirement 2, it would not pay the complete sum until the end of April.

    b. If you said less desirable, make a similar explanation.

(IMA adapted)

Control of Cash Receipts and Cash Disbursements

8

Cash includes any item that a bank customarily accepts for deposit. Coins, *currency* (paper money), bank drafts, cashier's checks, money orders, and bank balances are included in the Cash account. Postdated checks and I.O.U.s are receivables, not cash; postage stamps are prepaid expenses.

Effective management and control of cash is of the greatest importance to a firm, because cash represents instantly available purchasing power and because nearly every transaction ultimately involves the exchange of cash. The problems of good cash management are twofold: (1) a proper cash balance must be maintained at all times, and (2) adequate safeguards must be established to prevent the theft, or misappropriation, of cash. While emphasizing the control of cash, this chapter deals with *petty cash, bank reconciliation, cash forecasting,* the control of cash disbursements through the use of a *voucher system,* and *payroll control.*

CASH ON HAND AND IN BANK

INTERNAL CONTROL

One of the primary functions of management is to protect the assets of a business against avoidable loss. As a business grows in size and complexity, it becomes increasingly important to organize the supervision of the bookkeeping and accounting records to control the receipt of cash, to minimize or prevent the unauthorized disbursement of cash, and to eliminate errors. Employees must be carefully selected and trained, and their duties, responsibilities, and authority clearly defined. Adequate organization also requires the separation of duties, so that no one person is in complete charge of any business transaction. An error—whether intentional or not—is more likely to be discovered if a transaction is handled by two or more persons, so that, as far as possible, the work of each employee who records property is checked automatically by some other employee. It is customary business practice, for example, for one person to make the sale and prepare a sales slip and for another person to receive the cash or record the charge to the customer's account; one person may prepare the payroll and another person make the actual payments to employees; one employee may prepare the check for payment to a creditor, another employee or an officer may sign the check, and a third employee may post the debit to the creditor's account. Adequate organization also provides for a regular follow-up to see how well the accounting work is being done. This system of self-policing is referred to as *internal control*.

Cash Control

Cash is naturally vulnerable to theft or misuse. If cash is handled and controlled properly, both the employer and the employee benefit—the employer safeguards the asset and the employee avoids suspicion of inaccuracy or dishonesty. Embezzlers often begin their criminal careers by temporarily borrowing funds from the company, intending to replace the cash. The intention usually falters. It is to the advantage of both employer and employee to institute such safeguards as will deter employees from misappropriating funds. The safeguards must be designed to prevent the following:

1. Misappropriation of cash on receipt and failure to record the transaction in the cash receipts journal. For example, scrap and waste material may be sold by an employee for cash and not reported.
2. Delay in recording the receipt of cash (the cash being withheld during the interval), or recording false entries. For example, cash may be pocketed on receipt of a payment from a customer but his account may be credited with an offsetting debit to Sales Returns and Allowances.
3. The recording of fictitious charges to expense accounts or other accounts to cover fraudulent cash withdrawals. For example, a branch supervisor may carry a terminated employee's name on the payroll for several additional pay periods, forging the endorsement of the former employee on a fictitious payroll check.

Certain basic controls must be instituted to prevent the misuse of funds. The individual responsibility for each step in the flow of cash must be clearly established. An entry to record the receipt of cash must be made promptly. On receipt all checks should be rubber-stamped *For deposit only* to prevent their misuse. All cash receipts should be deposited intact daily; payments should be made by company check and not out of cash receipts. Mechanical accounting control devices should be used wherever possible.

The protection of cash against losses through fraud, error, and carelessness requires certain fundamental steps, including:

1. A clear segregation of duties and responsibilities.
2. Provision of the necessary facilities, such as cash registers.
3. Furnishing definite written instructions with respect to authorization for and the payment of cash.
4. Organization of the flow and recording of documents so that, whenever possible, the work of one employee is subject to automatic verification by another employee. The handling and recording of cash should be so planned that no one person both receives or disburses cash and records it in the cash journals.
5. Periodic testing to see if internal controls are operating effectively. For example, at unannounced times, recorded cash receipts should be compared with cash on hand and deposits made.

Petty Cash

For adequate internal control, all cash receipts should be deposited intact daily and all disbursements should be made by check. There are occasions, however, when payment by check is impractical, such as for postage, small contributions, express charges, carfare, and minor supplies. A special fund, called the *petty cash fund,* should be set up for these purposes. The fund is placed in charge of one person, and each payment should be supported by a signed receipt, called a *petty cash voucher,* that shows the purpose of the expenditure, the date, and the amount.

To set up the petty cash fund, a check is drawn to the order of the fund custodian and cashed for the amount to be placed in the fund. The journal entry is:

Petty Cash	50	
Cash		50

Safekeeping of the money and the signed vouchers is the responsibility of the custodian, who should be provided with a secure petty cash box or cash register.

When the cash in the fund approaches a stated minimum, or at the end of each month, the fund is replenished; the signed petty cash vouchers serve as evidence of the disbursements. The entry in the cash payments journal to record a check for $43 issued to replenish the petty cash fund for certain expenditures made is:

Postage Expense	12.00	
Telephone and Telegraph Expense	4.00	
Miscellaneous Selling Expense	14.50	
Miscellaneous General Expense	3.75	
Transportation In	8.25	
Cash Over and Short	.50	
Cash		43.00

CONTROL
OF CASH

The Petty Cash account in the general ledger remains at its original balance of $50. It does not change unless the amount of the fund itself is either increased or decreased. It is for this reason that the method described here is called the *imprest* (or fixed) petty cash system. The fund should be replenished at the end of each accounting period to record all the expenses incurred during the period and to bring the amount of cash on hand in the fund up to the balance of the Petty Cash account in the general ledger.

It will be noted that, in the foregoing journal entry, a cash shortage found at the time of replenishment was debited to an expense account, Cash Over and Short. Shortages considered unreasonable should be investigated. Unannounced inspections should be held at intervals to determine that the amount of cash in the fund plus receipted vouchers is equal to the fund amount.

The Bank Statement

It is customary for banks to send depositors a monthly statement together with the canceled checks and notices of bank charges and credits. The statement shows the activities for the month; it should list:

1. Beginning balance
2. Deposits received
3. Checks paid
4. Other charges and credits to the account
5. Ending balance

Frederick Hall's bank statement for September 1976 is shown in Figure 8-1.

The letter combinations listed in the lower section of the bank statement form identify certain entries on the statement.

Certified Check (*CC*). When the depositor requests a check to be certified, the bank immediately deducts the amount of the check from the depositor's balance.

Total of Listed Checks (*LS*). A number of checks issued by the depositor may be presented to the bank for payment on the same day. To conserve space, the bank shows only one entry for the total and attaches a listing of the individual amounts to the checks themselves.

Not Sufficient Funds (*NSF*). Deposits generally include checks received from trade customers. A customer's check that has been deposited may not clear on presentation for payment because the customer's bank balance is less than the amount of the check. If so, the check is deducted from the depositor's balance, the entry is identified by the letters NSF, and the check is returned to the depositor. The legal authority for this deduction is that credit to the depositor's account for checks deposited is conditional on their being honored on presentment.

Service Charge (*SC*). A service charge is a charge by the bank for acting as a depository for funds. The charge is based on the activity of the account in terms of number of items deposited and checks presented for payment. Some banks allow interest on the average daily balance in certain special checking accounts.

Debit Memo (*DM*). A debit memo is a deduction from the depositor's account for additional services rendered (or an adjustment of an error); for example, the charge for collecting a note receivable is reported in a debit memo.

Figure 8-1
Bank Statement

**STATEMENT OF ACCOUNT
WITH
UNITED STATES TRUST COMPANY
BOSTON, MASS.
Acct. No. 037–325079**

Frederick Hall
14 Billings Street
Boston, Mass, 02115

Checks and Other Debits			*Deposits*	*Date*	*Balance*
Balance forward from last statement.				Sept. 1, 1976	7,320.00
			450.00	Sept. 1	7,770.00
49.00	1,237.00			Sept. 2	6,484.00
			48.00	Sept. 3	6,532.00
175.00	1,300.00 CC			Sept. 6	5,057.00
14.00			1,650.00	Sept. 11	6,693.00
			762.00	Sept. 15	7,455.00
28.50	27.25	275.00	1,312.00	Sept. 18	8,436.25
2,000.00	367.00	2.00 DM	500.00 CM	Sept. 29	6,567.25
4.00 SC				Sept. 30	6,563.25

CC—Certified Check
LS—Total of Listed Checks
NSF—Not Sufficient Funds
SC—Service Charge

DM—Debit Memo
CM—Credit Memo
OD—Overdraft

Credit Memo (*CM*). A credit memo is a credit, usually shown in the Deposits column, for items collected (or an adjustment of an error); for example, the collection of a note receivable left at the bank by a depositor is reported in a credit memo.

Overdraft (OD). An overdraft is the amount by which withdrawals exceed the depositor's available balance. The overdraft, if permitted, is usually entered in red in the Balance column. Because of automatic bank loan renewal arrangements or for other reasons, a bank may pay checks even when an overdraft results. The amount of the overdraft is a current liability.

Depositor's Monthly Bank Reconciliation Procedure

The use of a checking account is essential to the control of cash. If all cash receipts are deposited intact and all cash payments are made by check, the records of the bank can be *reconciled* regularly with those of the depositor. The *bank reconciliation* underscores the reciprocal relationship between the bank's records and the depositor's. For each entry in the depositor's books, there should be a counterpart in the bank's books. All debits to Cash in the depositor's books should be matched by credit entries to the depositor's account in the bank's books; all credit entries to Cash in the depositor's books should be matched by debit entries to the depositor's account. For instance, cash received from a customer is recorded in the company's books by debiting Cash and crediting Accounts Receivable; the bank, on receiving the cash, credits the depositor's account. The company records a payment to a creditor by debiting Accounts Payable and crediting Cash; the bank debits the depositor's account.

The records of the depositor and of the bank will not normally agree at the end of the month because of items that appear on one record but not on the other. It is necessary, therefore, to reconcile the two balances and to determine the *adjusted,* or true, cash balance. Discrepancies between the balances may be due to the time lag in recording debits and credits, to special charges and credits of which either the depositor or the bank is unaware, or to errors and irregularities.

The bank reconciliation is prepared as follows:

1. The deposits shown on the bank statement are compared with those entered in the cash receipts journal. Deposits made too late in the month to be credited by the bank on the current statement are referred to as *deposits in transit.* The bank reconciliation for the previous month should be inspected for any deposits in transit at the end of that period; they should appear as the initial deposits of the current period. Any items not on the statement should be investigated.

2. Checks paid and returned by the bank (*canceled checks*) are arranged

Figure 8-2
Format for a Bank Reconciliation

NAME	
Bank Reconciliation	
Date	

Per Books

Cash Balance per Ledger, Date		$xxx
Add: (1) Any proper increases in cash already recorded by the bank that have not been recorded as yet by the firm		
Example: Collection of note by bank	$xx	
(2) Any error in the firm's books that failed to reveal a proper increase in cash or that improperly decreased cash		
Example: Check from customer for $90 entered as $70	xx	xx
Total		$xxx
Deduct: (1) Any proper decreases in cash already recorded by the bank that have not been recorded as yet by the firm		
Example: Bank service charges	$xx	
(2) Any error in the firm's books that failed to reveal a proper decrease in cash or that improperly increased cash		
Example: Check issued in payment to a creditor for $462 entered as $426	xx	xx
Adjusted Cash Balance, Date		$xxx

Figure 8-2

Per Bank

Cash Balance per Bank Statement, Date		$xxx
Add: (1) Any proper increases in cash already recorded by the firm that have not been recorded as yet by the bank		
Example: Deposits in transit	$xx	
(2) Any error by the bank that failed to reveal a proper increase in cash or that improperly decreased cash		
Example: Another depositor's check incorrectly charged to this depositor's account	xx	xx
Total		$xxx
Deduct: (1) Any proper decreases in cash already recorded by the firm that have not been recorded as yet by the bank		
Example: Outstanding checks	$xx	
(2) Any error by the bank that failed to reveal a proper decrease in cash or that improperly increased cash		
Example: Firm's deposit of $679 entered by bank as $697	xx	xx
Adjusted Cash Balance, Date		$xxx

in numerical order and compared with the entries in the cash payments journal. Checks that have not yet been presented to the bank for payment are called *outstanding checks.* The previous bank reconciliation should be inspected for outstanding checks.

FREDERICK HALL
Bank Reconciliation
August 31, 1976

Figure 8-3
Bank Reconciliation

Cash balance per ledger, August 31, 1976		$6,400
Adjusted cash balance, August 31, 1976		$6,400
Cash balance per bank statement August 31, 1976		$7,320
Add: Deposit in transit, August 31, 1976		450
Total		$7,770
Deduct: Outstanding checks		

Check	Amount	
680	$ 49	
694	1,237	
701	84	1,370
Adjusted cash balance, August 31, 1976		$6,400

3. Special debits and credits made by the bank—usually reported in debit or credit memos—are compared with the depositor's books to see if they have already been recorded.

4. Any errors in the bank's or the depositor's records that become apparent during completion of the prior steps are listed.

A format for a bank reconciliation is given in Figure 8-2. Errors and adjustments in the Per Books section require entries in the general journal to correct the books; adjustments in the Per Bank section do not require entries.

Frederick Hall's August bank reconciliation is shown in Figure 8-3. Note that the ending cash balance per the bank is the same as the beginning balance of the September statement (Figure 8-1).

Hall's cash records for September show the following items:

		Cash Deposits	
1976	Sept.	3	$ 48.00
		10	1,650.00
		14	762.00
		18	1,312.00
		30	1,050.00
			$4,822.00

		Checks Issued		
1976	Sept.	2	702	$ 175.00
		5	703	1,300.00
		8	704	14.00
		15	705	82.50
		15	706	312.25
		18	707	27.25
		26	708	2,000.00
		26	709	367.00
		30	710	103.00
				$4,381.00

The statement received from the bank (Figure 8-1) shows a balance of $6,563.25 as of September 30, 1976. The following items were received from the bank together with the bank statement:

Canceled checks:	Check	Amount
	680	$ 49.00
	694	1,237.00
	702	175.00
	703	1,300.00
	704	14.00
	705	28.50
	707	27.25
	708	2,000.00
	709	367.00
	Check of Frederick Hale	275.00

Memos:

Credit memo, $500, for a note receivable collected by the bank on September 29.

Debit memo, $2, dated September 29, for collection fee charged by bank.

Notification of a certified check for $1,300 deducted on September 6. (Even if the certified check, No. 703, had not been canceled by the bank during September, it would not be listed as outstanding, because it has been entered on both Hall's and the bank's records and would therefore not need to be reconciled.)

Service charge notification, $4, dated September 30.

Following receipt of the bank statement, Hall prepares the bank reconciliation statement shown in Figure 8-4 (see Figures 8-1 and 8-3 for support data). The following points should be emphasized:

1. The beginning balance in the Per Books section is taken from the general ledger Cash account; it was determined as shown on page 304.

Figure 8-4
Bank Reconciliation

FREDERICK HALL
Bank Reconciliation
September 30, 1976

Per Books

Cash balance per ledger, September 30, 1976		$6,841.00
Add: Customer's note collected by bank		500.00
Error in entering check No. 705:		
Entered as	$ 82.50	
Correct amount	28.50	54.00
Total		$7,395.00
Deduct: Bank service charge	$ 4.00	
Collection fee	2.00	6.00
Adjusted cash balance, September 30, 1976		$7,389.00

Per Bank

Cash balance per bank statement, September 30, 1976			$6,563.25
Add: Deposit of Sept. 30 in transit to bank			1,050.00
Check of Frederick Hale deducted by bank in error			275.00
Total			$7,888.25
Deduct: Outstanding checks			
	Check	*Amount*	
	701	$ 84.00	
	706	312.25	
	710	103.00	499.25
Adjusted cash balance, September 30, 1976			$7,389.00

Cash balance per ledger, August 31, 1976 (Figure 8-3)	$ 6,400
Add deposits	4,822
Total	$11,222
Deduct checks issued	4,381
Cash balance per ledger, September 30, 1976	$ 6,841

2. Check No. 705 was incorrectly recorded in Hall's books as $82.50 instead of $28.50. The error overstated cash disbursements and therefore understated the ending cash balance by $54 = ($82.50 − $28.50).

3. The beginning balance in the Per Bank section is the last amount in the Balance column of the bank statement for the month of September (Figure 8-1).

4. The deposit of $1,050 made on September 30 was not credited on the bank statement because it was in transit.

5. While determining the outstanding checks, Hall discovered that the bank had deducted in error a check for $275 signed by another depositor, Frederick Hale. This resulted in an understatement of the bank balance on the bank statement. The bank was notified about this error.

6. Check No. 701 was listed as an outstanding check on the bank reconciliation of August 31 (Figure 8-3). Since it has not yet been presented to the bank for payment, it continues to be listed as an outstanding check.

All the items that appear in the Per Bank section of the bank reconciliation for the previous month must be traced to the current month's bank statement. For example, a deposit not credited in the prior month should appear with the initial deposits for the current month; similarly, improper charges or credits of the preceding month should appear as corrections on the current month's statement.

All additions to, and deductions from, the balance per books must be entered on Hall's books to bring the general ledger Cash account balance into agreement with the adjusted cash balance. The Cash account balance of $6,841 should be increased by $548 = ($500 + $54 − $6) to show the actual cash balance of $7,389 as of September 30, 1976.

The required entries are shown below in general journal form:

Cash	498	
Bank Service and Collection Charges Expense	2	
Notes Receivable		500
To record collection of note receivable by bank and related charge.		
Cash	54	
Accounts Payable		54
To record correction of error in entering check No. 705 as $82.50 instead of $28.50.		
Bank Service and Collection Charges Expense	4	
Cash		4
To record bank service charge for September.		

These entries may be made in the cash journals for September if the journals have not been footed and posted, or the following compound entry may be made in the general journal:

Cash	548	
Bank Service and Collection Charges Expense	6	
Notes Receivable		500
Accounts Payable		54
To adjust the Cash account per		
bank reconciliation for September.		

After the entry is posted, Hall's Cash account appears as shown below. Note that the beginning balance for the new period (October) agrees with the adjusted cash balance in the bank reconciliation. Except for the word Balance on September 30 and October 1, the explanations would be omitted in an actual account. They are shown here in parentheses so that the reader may trace the source of each entry.

	Cash			Acct. No. 101	
1976			1976		
Sept. 1	(beginning balance)	6,400	Sept. 30	(checks issued)	4,381
30	(cash deposits)	4,822	30	Balance	7,389
30	(adjustment)	548			
		11,770			11,770
1976					
Oct. 1	Balance	7,389			

Only the items from the reconciliation that either increase or decrease the balance per books need to be entered in the journal. The items that increase or decrease the balance per bank already have been recorded on the depositor's books. Any errors made by the bank should be brought to the bank's attention. If a running cash balance is maintained in the checkbook, the necessary adjustments must also be made there.

The form of bank reconciliation shown in Figure 8-4 is commonly used because the adjusted cash balance is a significant figure; it represents the true cash balance, the amount subject to withdrawal. The form also may be prepared in advance and the items entered directly into the appropriate sections as they are determined.

Cash Over and Short

The daily count of cash in the cash registers may differ from the cash register readings. If the records do not disclose a clerical error, it may be assumed that the overage or the shortage was caused by an error in making change. The discrepancy may be entered temporarily in the books as a debit or a credit to Cash Over and Short. To illustrate, assume that the cash register tape shows cash sales for the day of $100 but the count shows the cash on hand to be $101.50. The journal entry to record the cash sales and the cash overage is:

Cash	101.50	
Sales		100.00
Cash Over and Short		1.50

If the cash count showed $98.50, the entry would be:

Cash	98.50	
Cash Over and Short	1.50	
Sales		100.00

Cash Over and Short is classified on the income statement as general expense if a debit or other revenue if a credit.

MANAGEMENT CONTROLS—CASH FORECASTS

The managers of a business must make certain that adequate cash funds are available at all times. Good management requires that sufficient cash be available for the timely payment of invoices, payrolls, and other costs and operating expenses. An adequate cash balance is also essential to maintain a good credit rating. But excessive cash balances, particularly during inflationary periods when cash suffers a loss of purchasing power, indicate ineffective management of cash resources.

The future cash needs of the business should be anticipated to ensure that payments for purchases and expenses can be met promptly; that bank loans can be paid at maturity; that tax and dividend payments can be met; that funds will be available for additional machinery, equipment, and buildings; and that excess funds, if any, are appropriately invested. All this requires a projected plan, or *cash forecast,* for a number of months in advance. The period covered by the forecast may be one month, three months, six months, or a year, depending on how accurately a company is able to forecast its receipts and disbursements. Some companies make fairly accurate forecasts for the next three-month period and rougher approximations for the remaining nine months. If the cash balance is low and sales are erratic, weekly forecasts may be desirable.

A cash forecast is a projection based on a careful analysis of prior periods, with appropriate adjustments for anticipated changes. The forecast deals exclusively with estimates involving *cash*. Noncash items such as depreciation are excluded. The cash forecast is a summary of projected cash receipts, cash disbursements, and resulting cash balances for the budgeted periods. Cash receipts from customers are projected on the basis of estimated sales and collection patterns experienced in prior periods. Other cash collections are generally lesser in amount and can be readily identified as to period of collectibility. When cash disbursements are forecast, consideration must be given to the various goods and services to be purchased and the timing of the required payments. Detailed operating forecasts are prepared for such items as materials and supplies, utilities, rent, payrolls, and taxes, from which the required cash disbursements are determined. The forms and schedules used should provide for the comparison of actual results with estimates so that any *variances* may be analyzed. If the variances indicate significant errors in the original estimates, corresponding revisions should be made in future forecasts.

The cash forecast of the Sterns Company for the second quarter of 1977 (Figure 8-5) was generated by a computer on the basis of the following input data:

1. Estimated sales (65 percent on credit, 35 percent for cash):

February	$18,000
March	18,000
April	24,000
May	23,000
June	35,000

STERNS COMPANY
Cash Forecast
April, May, June, 1977

Figure 8-5
Cash Forecast

	April	May	June
Estimated Sales	$24,000	$23,000	$35,000
Beginning cash balance	$26,855	$18,199	$ 5,591
Cash receipts			
Cash sales	8,400	8,050	12,250
Credit collections	14,040	14,820	19,695
Total cash available	$49,295	$41,069	$37,536
Disbursement of cash			
Labor	$ 2,420	$ 2,340	$ 3,300
Material purchases	15,750	20,250	18,000
Freight in	840	805	1,225
Administrative	1,750	1,750	1,750
Advertising	5,200	5,200	5,200
Insurance	1,400	1,400	1,400
Interest	129	127	124
Debt payment	307	307	307
Dividend payments	0	0	1,500
Miscellaneous	3,300	3,300	3,300
Total cash disbursement	$31,096	$35,478	$36,106
Ending cash balance	$18,199	$ 5,591	$ 1,430

CONTROL
OF CASH

2. Estimated collections on credit sales: 60 percent during the month of sale, 30 percent during the month following the sale, and 10 percent during the second month following the sale.
3. All purchases of merchandise are typically made and paid for two months in advance of their anticipated sale. Cost of merchandise is 45 percent of the selling price.
4. Other monthly cash expenditures are estimated to be:
   a. Labor, $500 plus 8 percent of sales
   b. Freight in, $3\frac{1}{2}$ percent of sales
   c. Administrative, $1,750
   d. Advertising, $5,200
   e. Insurance, $1,400
   f. Interest, $\frac{3}{4}$ of 1 percent on the unpaid balance of the debt (debt balance as of April 1, $17,200)
   g. Principal repayment, $306.66
   h. Miscellaneous expenses, $3,300
   i. A $1,500 dividend payment is scheduled for June
5. The cash balance on April 1 is estimated to be $26,855.

To compute the cash balance at the end of the month, the beginning balance is added to the estimated cash receipts for that month and the anticipated disbursements for the month are deducted. The ending cash balance of any month is the beginning cash balance of the next month.

The computions and estimated amounts for the month of April are shown below to illustrate the derivation of the numbers in the cash forecast.

Beginning cash balance		$26,855
Cash receipts		
Cash sales (35% of $24,000)		8,400
Credit collections.		
From April sales (.65 × $24,000 × .60)	$ 9,360	
From March sales (.65 × $18,000 × .30)	3,510	
From February sales (.65 × $18,000 × .10)	1,170	14,040
Total cash available		$49,295
Disbursement of cash		
Labor ($500 + [.08 × $24,000])	$ 2,420	
Material purchases (45% of June sales of $35,000)	15,750	
Freight in (.035 × $24,000)	840	
Administrative (given)	1,750	
Advertising (given)	5,200	
Insurance (given)	1,400	
Interest (.0075 × $17,200)	129	
Debt payment (given)	307	
Miscellaneous (given)	3,300	
Total cash disbursement		31,096
Ending cash balance		$18,199

Management uses the cash forecast to determine whether sufficient cash will be available for tax payments, dividends, acquisition of equipment, or purchases of securities as investments. At the end of each month, the actual amount of each item is entered in an extra column headed Actual to provide a month-by-month comparison with the budgeted figures.

CASH DISBURSEMENTS CONTROL

THE VOUCHER SYSTEM

The accounting system must be designed not only to enable the recording of transactions and the preparation of financial statements but also to achieve other managerial objectives: (1) to furnish analyses and reports of past, current, and projected events and (2) to establish internal controls to protect the assets of the business against loss through errors or fraud. The achievement of these objectives goes hand in hand with the achievement of maximum operating efficiency and maximum earnings. A properly functioning voucher system plays a key role in establishing and maintaining effective internal control.

The voucher system is a method of accumulating, verifying, recording, and disbursing all the expenditures of a business. The system covers any transaction, except for payments out of petty cash, that will require the payment of cash, including the purchase of merchandise, services, supplies, and plant and equipment, and the payment of expenses. Expenditures are verified, classified, and recorded when they are incurred. All expenditures must be properly authorized and, except for petty cash transactions, are paid by check.

Reference has been made to the importance of having a built-in system to protect the assets of a business against loss through fraud or error. The voucher system is designed to achieve this internal control by distributing the duties of authorizing expenditures, reporting the receipt of goods or services, and signing checks. This division of duties prevents cash being disbursed from the business without proper approval and then only after verifications made by several members of the organization.

The Voucher

The *voucher* is a serially numbered form that is the written authorization for each expenditure. It is prepared from the seller's invoice or group of invoices or from other documents that serve as evidence of the liability. The voucher form is tailored to meet the needs of the particular business.

The voucher, not the invoice, is the basis for the accounting entry. The invoice, together with acknowledgments or approvals of the receipt of goods or services, and other supporting papers are the underlying documents for the voucher. Supporting papers were described in detail in Chapter 1. The voucher form provides space for:

1. Summary of the invoice data
2. Accounts to be debited

3. Details of payment
4. Initials of persons who have checked accuracy of quantities, unit prices, extensions, and discount terms
5. Signature of the person who authorizes the payment
6. Signature of the person who records the voucher

The Voucher Jacket

The *voucher jacket* is a folded voucher form or envelope that serves both as a voucher and as a cover for the invoice, or group of invoices, from a particular vendor, and related documents. Space is provided on the outside of the jacket form for the details needed for the accounting entry.

Assume that during January 1976 the Ajax Company received ten invoices from a creditor, the Silver Company, with terms of 2/10, n/30. Upon receipt, the invoices are verified for quantities, prices, and extensions and are filed in a voucher jacket. The total price of the invoices, shown on the voucher jacket, is entered in the journal to record the liability and to classify the expenditures. It is then filed with other unpaid vouchers according to their due date so that payment will be made within the discount period. Another advantage of filing unpaid vouchers according to due date is that the amount of cash needed daily to pay vouchers due may be readily determined. Paid vouchers are filed alphabetically in a separate file.

The Voucher Register

The *voucher register* is an elaboration of the purchases journal. It is a journal for recording all liabilities approved for payment. The register is ruled in columns for the frequently used accounts to be charged or credited. The precise form of the register and the number and arrangement of the column headings vary with the needs of the particular business. A suggested outline of a voucher register is presented in Figure 8-6.[1]

The function of the Vouchers Payable account is the same as that of the Accounts Payable account. It is a controlling account—its balance represents the total of the unpaid vouchers recorded in the voucher register. Unpaid vouchers may, therefore, be readily determined to be those without entries on the corresponding line of the Paid column or those in the *unpaid voucher* file. At the end of the period, a list of the unpaid vouchers in the file should be prepared for reconciliation with the balance of the Vouchers Payable account in the general ledger.

The voucher register is used for recording all transactions—of whatever category except petty cash—that are due for payment. Each transaction is entered in the voucher register first, followed by an entry in the check register when payment is made. The vouchers are entered in the voucher register in numerical order. Transactions involving liabilities that are not initially credited to Vouchers Payable—notes payable and accrued expenses, for example—are usually not entered in the voucher register until payment is due. Vouchers are

---

[1] A more detailed discussion of the voucher register is presented in the *Student's Self-Study Guide,* which accompanies this text.

(Ch. 8)

Figure 8-6 Outlines of Voucher Register and Check Register

			Paid		Credit		Debit					Other General Ledger Accounts			
								Selling Expense Control 600		General and Administrative Expense Control 700				Amount	
Date	Voucher No.	Name	Date	Check No.	Vouchers Payable 201	Pur-chases 351	Ac-count No.	F	Amount	Ac-count No.	F	Amount	Account	F	Debit	Credit

VOUCHER REGISTER — Page 8

				Debit	Credits	
Date	Voucher Number	Name	Check Number	Vouchers Payable 201	Purchases Discounts 365	Cash 101

CHECK REGISTER — Page 6

not prepared for accrued expenses; rather, a voucher is prepared for the full amount when the invoice is received or when payment is to be made.

An entry is made in the Credit Vouchers Payable column for the amount due on each voucher. The account or accounts to be debited are indicated on the voucher, and entries are made in one of the special debit columns or in the Other General Ledger Accounts column if no special column is available.

The Check Register

The check register is a book of original entry for all cash disbursements except petty cash; an outline of a check register is presented in Figure 8-6. No payment is made until a specific voucher has been prepared, recorded, and approved. Hence, each entry is a debit to Vouchers Payable, a credit to Cash, and a credit to Purchases Discounts, if any. No other columns are needed, because the transaction already has been classified under an appropriate heading in the voucher register. Checks are entered in the check register in numerical sequence, one line to each check. At the time that the check is entered in the check register, a notation must also be made in the Paid column of the voucher register showing the date of payment and the check number.

Use of the Voucher Register and the Check Register

The voucher register form must be tailored to meet the needs of the particular enterprise. The register provides columns for each general class of expenditure—Selling Expense Control and General and Administrative Expense Control, for example—with space to the left of each general column for the account number of the specific detail account to be debited. This gives the advantage of almost unlimited flexibility combined with economy of space.

(Ch. 8)

The check register will include a Purchases Discounts column if the vouchers are recorded in the voucher register at invoice amounts. This register shows not only the serial number of the check but also the number of the voucher being paid.

Some companies prepare each voucher for the net amount due. This means that if payment is not made within the discount period, an additional voucher will be required, underscoring the expense for lost discounts. The entry in the voucher register for the additional voucher is a debit to Purchases Discounts Lost and a credit to Vouchers Payable. One check is made out for the full amount due as shown by the two vouchers.

Control of Unpaid Vouchers

The unpaid vouchers can be readily determined—they are the ones that have not been marked either "Paid" or "Canceled" in the Paid column. A schedule of unpaid vouchers is prepared at the end of the month; the total should correspond to the balance of the Vouchers Payable account in the general ledger. Thus, the unpaid vouchers file is a subsidiary ledger supporting the Vouchers Payable account.

Elimination of the Accounts Payable Ledger

When the voucher system is used, the subsidiary accounts payable ledger can be eliminated. Each numbered voucher is entered on a separate line in the voucher register and may be considered as a credit to a separate account. When the liability is settled and a notation is made in the Paid column, it is equivalent to a debit to that account. The file of unpaid vouchers replaces the accounts payable ledger. The total of the unpaid vouchers must agree with the total of the Vouchers Payable controlling account.

Advantages of the Voucher System

In a properly functioning voucher system, all invoices must be verified and approved for payment. As a result, responsibility is fixed and the possibility of error or fraud is reduced. The recording of all vouchers in a single journal (the voucher register) provides for prompt recognition and proper distribution of assets, liabilities, costs, and expenses. Economy in recording is effected by the elimination of the accounts payable ledger and by grouping invoices under a single voucher. The maintenance of a chronological unpaid voucher file facilitates the payment of invoices without loss of discounts. This file also enables management to determine its future cash needs for the settlement of liabilities. The systematic filing of paid vouchers provides a ready reference source for data and underlying documents for audit of all disbursements.

On the other hand, the voucher system has certain limitations. The difficulties in handling special transactions and the need for the preparation of separate vouchers or voucher jackets involve extra clerical and accounting work. The elimination of the accounts payable ledger results in a loss of valuable reference data, although this may be overcome by maintaining a file, arranged in alphabetical order by name of vendor, of copies of all vouchers.

MANAGERIAL CONTROL OF PAYROLL

The payroll of a firm is a significant part of total expense, making continuous management control essential. The availability of machines and high-speed electronic equipment has facilitated the processing of payroll data and the establishment of effective controls at a reasonable cost. But the use of an electronic data-processing system for the payroll does not lessen the need for built-in self-policing internal control devices and procedures as part of the payroll system. Computer programs and data-processing systems can be manipulated to defraud the firm.

Effective managerial control of payroll requires that

1. Management has properly authorized the payroll payment.
2. Wages paid be correct and have been received by authorized employees; that is, for example, that no fictitious names or names of persons no longer employed have been listed on the payroll.
3. The numerous reports based on payroll information that are made to governmental agencies, union organizations, and employees be reliable.

Payroll Deductions

It is unusual for an employee to receive the full (*gross*) amount of salary or wages. Some deductions are required by law and must be *withheld* by the employer from the employee's regular pay. These include the following:

1. Federal, state, and local income taxes of the employee
2. Old-Age, Survivors, and Disability Insurance (OASDI) and Hospitalization Insurance Tax (both often referred to as FICA for Federal Insurance Contributions Act, or the social security tax)
3. State unemployment tax (in some states)

Other deductions are optional with the employee, such as for the purchase of U.S. savings bonds or corporate stock; group life, accident, and hospitalization insurance; and savings clubs. Deductions may also be required under union agreements or to settle other claims. The deductions are paid to the Federal and state governments and other designated agencies. Adequate records must be maintained to account for the deductions and their related liabilities and to prepare the required reports to the agencies involved.

Fair Labor Standards Act

The Fair Labor Standards Act—popularly known as the Federal Wage and Hour Law—relates to industries engaged directly in the production of goods for interstate commerce. It currently requires that workers not specifically exempted be paid a minimum hourly rate and an overtime wage of *time and one-half,* or one and one-half times the hourly rate, for time worked over 40 hours a

CONTROL
OF CASH

week. If no more than 40 hours are worked in a week, no overtime compensation need be paid regardless of the number of hours worked in any one day. Employers and employees may, of course, agree to more favorable terms, such as time and one-half for all work over eight hours in any day and double time for Sunday or holiday work. The act does not place a limitation on total working time; it fixes the 40-hour work week as the basis for overtime pay.

Social Security Act and Payroll Deductions

The Social Security Act (approved on August 14, 1935) is a Federal law, operated in part by the states with assistance from the Federal government. The act includes programs to provide benefits to retired workers, their families, and their survivors. It also provides health insurance for the aged (Medicare). These programs are financed by taxes on wages and on self-employment income at rates and maximum base amounts as specified and as changed from time to time by Congress. Funds for the payment of benefits to retired workers are provided by a tax imposed on both employers and employees, at the same rate. Funds for the payment of unemployment benefits are usually provided by a tax on the employer. These financing programs are commonly referred to as the Federal Unemployment Tax Act (FUTA) and the Federal Insurance Contributions Act (FICA). Since all the states have their own state unemployment compensation laws, there is a tie-in between the Federal and the state unemployment compensation systems.

Federal Insurance Contributions Tax. Under the provisions of the Federal Insurance Contributions Act, the employer is required to continue to withhold the employee's share of the tax during each calendar year until the currently prevailing maximum amount has been withheld. An employee who works for more than one employer during the year may, as a result, pay more than the annual maximum. The excess may be treated as income tax withheld by the employee when he files his Federal income tax return (Form 1040). Some groups are exempt from the FICA withholding requirement, and some who are exempted from the Federal income tax withholding requirements are subject to FICA tax withholding. The reader should keep informed of all recent amendments or provisions that may have altered rates, amounts, and eligible groups. Current tables of FICA tax withholding rates are available in Circular E, *Employer's Withholding Tax Guide,* published by the Internal Revenue Service.

Because the FICA tax rate and the applicable maximum earnings base may be changed by Congress at any time,[2] and to simplify the computations, a

[2] Projected tax rates are as follows:

	Old Age Survivor and Disability Insurance	Hospital Insurance	Total
1974–1977	4.95%	0.90%	5.85%
1978–1980	4.95%	1.10%	6.05%
1981–1985	4.95%	1.35%	6.30%
1986–2010	4.95%	1.50%	6.45%
2011 and after	5.95%	1.50%	7.45%

combined rate of 12 percent—6 percent each on employer and on employee—applicable to the first $15,000 paid to an employee during a calendar year is used in all illustrations and problems in this textbook. The accounting principles and recording procedures are the same irrespective of the rates used.

Federal Income Tax Withholding. Employers are required by the Federal Revenue Act to make deductions from each employee's earnings for Federal income taxes. The amount that the employer is required to withhold (certain classes of wage payments are exempt) depends on the total number of exemptions that the employee claims, the employee's earnings, and the frequency of the payroll period. On being hired, the employee fills out an Employee's Withholding Exemption Certificate, Form W-4, indicating the number of exemptions he wishes to claim. He files a new form when he changes the number of his exemptions. The employee may claim exemptions (1) for himself, (2) for his wife (unless she is employed and claims her own exemption), and (3) for each qualified dependent. Additional exemptions may be claimed for old age (65 years or older) and blindness of the claimant or his wife. Since tax rates are subject to change, persons responsible for payrolls should be acquainted with the latest tax rates and regulations, both Federal and state, and in some cases, municipal. The Internal Revenue Service furnishes withholding tables for different payroll periods in its Circular E.

Other Deductions. In some states, employees as well as employers are taxed under the state unemployment insurance programs. A number of states and some cities levy income taxes on the gross earnings of the employee. In some states, employees are taxed to provide funds for the cost of disability benefits. Such additional tax assessments are generally deducted from gross earnings by the employer and remitted to the designated agencies.

Recording and Paying the Payroll

Accurate payroll records are necessary to determine operating expenses and to report earnings information to employees and to Federal, state, and other agencies. The records must show the names, earnings, and payroll deductions of all employees for each pay period. An individual record for each employee showing his earnings and deductions must also be kept. A general journal entry is made to record the payroll for the pay period. Assume that the Burns Company payroll entry for the week ended January 28, 1976, was as follows:

Salesmen's Salaries Expense	1,018.00	
Executive Salaries Expense	750.00	
Office Salaries Expense	320.00	
FICA Taxes Payable (assumed rate of 6%)		125.28
Income Tax Withholdings Payable		218.80
Bond Deductions Payable		47.50
Salaries and Wages Payable		1,696.42
To record the payroll for the week ended January 28.		

The debits are to a selling expense account for $1,018 and to two general and

(Ch. 8)

administrative expense accounts for $1,070, or a total payroll of $2,088, of which the employees' *take-home* pay is $1,696.42.

Employer's Payroll Taxes

In addition to the amounts that he must withhold from employees' pay, the employer must also pay payroll taxes.

Federal Insurance Contributions Act. The FICA tax levies a tax on employers to help finance the social security program. The rates and maximum amounts are the same as those applicable to the employee.

Federal Unemployment Compensation Tax. The Federal Unemployment Compensation Tax Act provides for an additional tax on the employer at a specified rate up to a limited amount of wages paid. To simplify the computations, it will be assumed that the maximum rate is 5 percent on the first $5,000 paid to each covered employee during each calendar year, with 4 percent payable to the state government and 1 percent to the Federal government.

State Unemployment Compensation Tax. All the states have laws requiring the payment of an unemployment compensation tax. Funds are provided by a payroll tax levy on the employer and, in several states, on both the employer and the employees. Unemployed persons who qualify for benefits are paid by a state agency from funds acquired through the tax.

State unemployment tax laws vary in their detail and application. There are maximum rates which may be reduced on a *merit basis* if the employer's annual contributions are sufficiently in excess of withdrawals for unemployment payments made to discharged employees. The *merit-rating plan* provides an incentive to employers to maintain steady employment.

Recording the Employer's Payroll Tax Expense

The employer's payroll tax expense may be recorded at the end of each payroll period or at the end of each month. Assuming that the Burns Company records the payroll tax expense for each payroll and that, because of its merit-rating record, it is subject to a state unemployment tax rate of only 2 percent, the accrued payroll tax liability for the week ended January 28 is computed as follows:

FICA tax ($2,088 $\times$ 0.06)	$125.28
State unemployment compensation tax ($2,088 $\times$ 0.02)	41.76
Federal unemployment compensation tax ($2,088 $\times$ 0.01)	20.88
Total	$187.92

The general journal entry to record the expense is

Payroll Tax Expense	187.92	
FICA Taxes Payable		125.28
State Unemployment Taxes Payable		41.76
Federal Unemployment Taxes Payable		20.88
To record accrued payroll taxes for week ended January 28.		

The debit is to the Payroll Tax Expense account; the three credits are the accrued liabilities to the Federal and state agencies. The liability for FICA taxes ($125.28) matches the amount deducted from the employees' wages. In this entry, payroll taxes were based on $2,088, assuming that all the earnings were subject to payroll taxes. Earnings of any employee in excess of current maximums are not subject to payroll taxes. Assume, for example, that the Burns Company payroll for the week ended October 27 was $3,050, including $1,200 of nontaxable FICA earnings and $2,000 of nontaxable unemployment compensation earnings. The accrued payroll tax liability is computed as follows:

	FICA Tax	Unemployment Taxes
Total payroll	$3,050	$3,050
Payroll (in excess of maximum) not subject to FICA tax	1,200	
Payroll (in excess of maximum) not subject to unemployment taxes		2,000
Payroll subject to taxes	$1,850	$1,050

Payroll taxes	
FICA tax ($1,850 × 0.06)	$111.00
State unemployment compensation tax ($1,050 × 0.02)	21.00
Federal unemployment compensation tax ($1,050 × 0.01)	10.50
Total tax liability	$142.50

The entry to record the payroll taxes and the accrued liability is

Payroll Tax Expense	142.50	
FICA Taxes Payable		111.00
State Unemployment Taxes Payable		21.00
Federal Unemployment Taxes Payable		10.50
To record accrued payroll taxes for week ended October 27.		

Reporting and Payment of Payroll Taxes

The reporting and payment requirements for the employer's payroll taxes and the amounts withheld from employees' earnings are discussed in the following sections.

Income Taxes Withheld and FICA Taxes. The Federal income taxes withheld, FICA taxes withheld from the employees' earnings, and the employer's FICA taxes are reported quarterly. The tax report form is filed during the month following the close of each calendar quarter; for the months of October, November, and December, for example, the form must be filed by January 31. The amounts required to be paid are the amounts accumulated in the Income Tax Withholdings Payable account and in the FICA Taxes Payable account. These amounts are required to be deposited periodically in an approved Federal depositary bank. The deposit must be made by the fifteenth day of the following month. The form (Federal Tax Deposit Form 501) used for this purpose is receipted and returned for submittal with the quarterly tax report (Form 941). Assume that the accounts of the Burns Company show the following tax liabilities on October 31:

Income Tax Withholdings Payable (October)	$910.70
FICA Taxes Payable (October)	295.50

Further assume that the payment of these tax liabilities must be made to a Federal Reserve bank or to an authorized commercial bank before November 15. The entries to record the liability are

Income Tax Withholdings Payable	910.70	
FICA Taxes Payable	295.50	
Vouchers Payable		1,206.20
To record voucher for tax liabilities.		
Vouchers Payable	1,206.20	
Cash		1,206.20
To record payment of tax liabilities.		

By January 31 of each year, the employer is required to give each employee a Withholding Statement, Form W-2, showing his gross earnings and the amounts withheld during the previous calendar year. The employee, in turn, is required to submit a copy of this statement with his Federal income tax return.

State Unemployment Compensation Tax. The employer's state unemployment compensation tax liability is accumulated in the State Unemployment Taxes Payable account. The employer files a tax report form—the form varies with the states—and pays the required tax. Timing of the payments, monthly or quarterly, varies with the states. Assume that for the fourth quarter (October through December) the balance of the State Unemployment Taxes Payable account of the Burns Company was $84.50 on December 31 and that the tax report form must be filed and payment must be made to the proper collecting agency by January 31. The entries to record the vouchering and payment of the accrued liability are

State Unemployment Taxes Payable	84.50	
Vouchers Payable		84.50
To record payment of tax liability.		
Vouchers Payable	84.50	
Cash		84.50
To record payment of tax liability.		

Federal Unemployment Compensation Tax. For deposit purposes, the Federal unemployment tax must be computed on a quarterly basis. If the amount is more than $100, it must be deposited during the month following the quarter. If the tax for the year is $100 or less, it may be paid with Form 940. The tax liability is accumulated during the year in the Federal Unemployment Taxes Payable account. Assume that the Federal Unemployment Taxes Payable account for 1976 (January through December) on the books of the Burns Company shows an accumulated tax liability of $95.50. The form must be filed and payment must be made to the proper Federal agency by January 31, 1977. The entries to record vouchering and payment of the accrued liability are

Federal Unemployment Taxes Payable	95.50	
Vouchers Payable		95.50
To record payment of tax liability.		
Vouchers Payable	95.50	
Cash		95.50
To record payment of tax liability.		

Accrual of Salaries and Wages

If the end of the payroll period does not coincide with the end of the accounting period, an adjusting entry is made for salaries and wages earned but not paid. Assume that the Burns Company closes its books on March 31 and that the last payroll period ended on March 27 (Saturday). The entry to accrue the salaries for the partial pay period is

Salesmen's Salaries Expense	406	
Executive Salaries Expense	300	
Office Salaries Expense	128	
Accrued Salaries and Wages Payable		834
To record salaries and wages accrued		
from March 28 to 31.		

The entire credit for the accrued payroll is made to a single liability account rather than to separate liability accounts for the government and the employees. Amounts to be withheld from employees' earnings for income taxes and for FICA taxes are based on the earnings for an entire payroll period. Insofar as the employer is concerned, the total liability is $834; its breakdown into the several liability accounts does not provide additional useful information and may, therefore, be deferred until the date of payment. The employer's payroll tax expense on the accrued payroll for the partial pay period should be recognized. The entry for the Burns Company is

(Ch. 8)

```
Payroll Taxes Expense                                    75.06
    Accrued Payroll Taxes Payable                                75.06
        To record the employer's payroll tax liability
        on the accrued payroll from March 28 to 31:
            FICA ($834 × 0.06)                    $50.04
            State Unemployment Insurance
            ($834 × 0.02)                          16.68
            Federal Unemployment Tax
            ($834 × 0.01)                           8.34
                Total                             $75.06
```

Suppose that a fictitious company called the Any Company has several hundred employees. A data-processing method that could produce its payroll is a punched card system that uses the three 80-column punched cards for each employee as illustrated in Figure A8-1. Each type of card is identified by the card code in the first column.

The cards illustrated are for employee D. C. Andrews; note that his clock number 8631, the key number that links all cards for D. C. Andrews together, must appear on each of them. The Year-to-Date Balance Card (card number 1) shows the following data:

Card Columns	Information
1	Card code 1 indicates YTD Balance Card
2–4	Andrews is in Department 1
5–8	His employee (clock) number is 8631

Figure A8-1 Punched Card Files

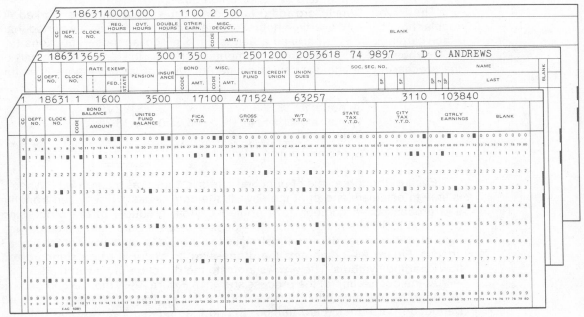

PUNCHED CARD FILES

1. Year-To-Date Balance Card

2. Name, Rate and Fixed Deduction Card

3. Payroll Detail Card

Source: NCR Corporation

CONTROL
OF CASH

(Ch. 8)

9–10	A code showing that an $18.75 savings bond is to be purchased in his name each time his accumulated bond deductions reach $18.75
11–16	The balance accumulated in Andrews' bond deduction account at the beginning of this pay period (that is, to date)
17–24	The total deducted to date this year for a United Fund contribution that Andrews had pledged to pay through payroll deductions. The deductions are $2.50 per pay period.
25–32	Total FICA withheld to date this year
33–40	Total gross pay earned to date this year
41–48	Total Federal income tax withheld to date this year
57–64	Total city wage tax withheld to date this year
65–72	Total earnings for this calendar quarter to date

In a similar manner, fixed information for D. C. Andrews is punched into the Name, Rate, and Fixed Deduction Card (card number 2). The data punched into the card and interpreted at the top edge show that Andrews' rate of pay is $3.655 an hour. The reader will also note that his fixed deductions for each pay period are $3 for insurance, $3.50 for savings bonds, $2.50 for the United Fund, $12 to the credit union, and $2.05 for union dues.

The Payroll Detail Card (card number 3) shows that Andrews worked 40 regular hours and 10 overtime hours (at time and one-half) this pay period, had other earnings of $11 (perhaps a bonus), and miscellaneous deductions (for safety shoes) of $5. Although the computer performs this operation as part of the processing routine, we can calculate Andrews' gross pay manually as follows:

50 hours @ $3.655	$182.75
10 hours overtime @ ($\frac{1}{2} \times$ $3.655)	18.28
Other earnings	11.00
Gross earnings	$212.03

Each of the three sets of punched cards is known as a card *deck*. When it is time to calculate and print the payroll, the card decks are removed from file and processed. In addition to a printed payroll, products of the processing operation include a revised (updated) deck of Year-to-Date Balance cards, listings of deductions, departmental statistical analyses, and the actual payroll checks. Figure A8-2 diagrams the processing procedures using standardized flow-charting symbols. The arrows indicate the direction of flow of work.

At the completion of the process shown in Figure A8-2, the merged deck is re-sorted by machine into the three original decks. The Name, Rate and Fixed Deduction Card deck (card number 2) and the updated Year-to-Date Balance Card deck (card number 1) are returned to file to be used when the payroll is again processed at the end of the next pay period. Commencing with the first day of the next pay period, clock cards and time tickets are used to capture information on hours worked so that a new deck of payroll detail cards can be punched for preparation of the next payroll.

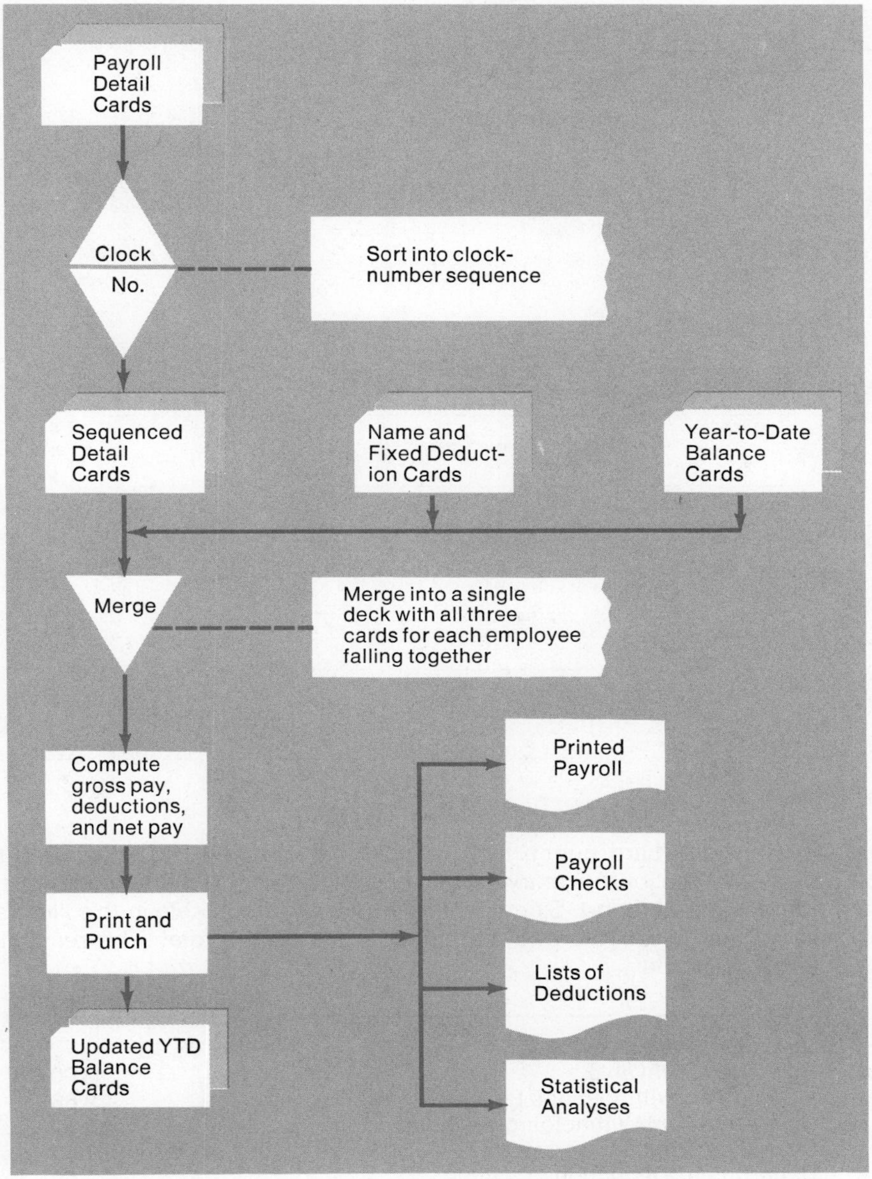

Figure A8-2
Payroll Processing

D. C. Andrews' pay check and the earnings statement detached from the check were printed by the computer and are reproduced in Figure A8-3.

The information in Andrews' earnings statement represents a single line on the printed payroll of the Any Company. The computer which makes the calculations also controls the output devices—the printer that prints the reports and

(Ch. 8)

Figure A8-3 Paycheck and Earnings Statement

Source: NCR Corporation

the checks and the card punch that punches the updated Year-to-Date Balance Card deck. The journal entry for this payroll is made from the total figures on the printed payroll report. Since total figures are not available in this illustration, assume that D. C. Andrews' earnings represent the total. The resulting journal entry would be:

Salaries Expense	212.03	
FICA Taxes Payable		3.00
Income Tax Withholdings Payable		29.68
City Wage Tax Withholding Payable		2.12
Insurance Premiums Payable		3.00
United Fund Deductions Payable		2.50
Savings Bond Deductions Liability		3.50
Union Dues Payable		2.05
Accounts Receivable—Employees		5.00
Credit Union Loans Payable		12.00
Salaries and Wages Payable		149.18

To record the payroll of the week ended September 13.

In this example, note that D. C. Andrews now has accumulated $19.50 = ($16.00 + a new $3.50 deduction) in his savings bond account. Any Company would purchase and deliver to him an $18.75 bond; that transaction would require the following journal entry:

Savings Bond Deductions Liability	18.75	
Cash		18.75
To record purchase and delivery of bond to		
D. C. Andrews, employee.		

GLOSSARY

Bank Reconciliation A statement which shows the specific items that account for the differences between the balance reported by the bank and the amount shown on the depositor's books.

Bank Statement A monthly statement sent by a bank to its depositors together with canceled checks and notices of bank charges and credits.

Cash Forecast Summary of projected cash receipts, cash disbursements, and resulting cash balances for the budgeted periods.

Cash Over and Short An account showing a discrepancy in the daily count of cash between actual cash receipts and cash disbursements and the cash register readings or other supporting documents.

Certified Check A depositor's check, payment of which is guaranteed by a bank by endorsement on the face of the check, the bank having previously deducted the amount of the check from the depositor's balance.

Check Register A book of original entry for all cash disbursements except petty cash.

Deck A set of cards each of which carries the same specified data related to a common subject.

Deposits in Transit Deposits made too late in the month to be credited by the bank on the current statement.

FICA Tax A tax levied on employees and employers to help finance the Federal Insurance Contributions Act provisions of the Social Security program.

Internal Control A built-in system of self-policing for the effective control and safeguarding of cash and other assets.

NSF Check A customer's check that has been deposited but did not clear on presentation for payment because the customer's bank balance was less than the amount of the check.

Outstanding Checks Checks sent to payees but not yet presented to the depositor's bank for payment.

Petty Cash A separate cash fund for the payment of relatively minor items when payment by check is impractical.

(Ch. 8)

Voucher A serially numbered form that is the written authorization for each expenditure prepared from the seller's invoice or group of invoices or from other documents that serve as evidence of the liability.

Voucher Register A columnar journal for recording and summarizing all liabilities approved for payment.

Voucher System A method of accumulating, verifying, recording, and disbursing all the expenditures of a business. It covers all payments except those from the petty cash fund.

QUESTIONS

Q8-1. The Stenn Company employs an office manager, a cashier, an accounts receivable bookkeeper, two clerk-typists, and ten salesmen. The bookkeeper records all charge sales made to customers; she also opens the mail each day and credits the customers' accounts for remittances, turning the money over to the cashier. The monthly bank statement is received directly by the bookkeeper, who prepares the bank reconciliation.

Collections from cash sales are turned over by the salesmen to the cashier, together with a cash sales invoice. The cashier compares these invoices daily with the cash register tapes. Disbursements for petty cash items are made by the cashier out of cash receipts. The cashier fills out a petty cash slip, which is signed by the person receiving the cash. All other disbursements are by check, signed by either the office manager or the owner of the company. Entries in the cash receipts journal and in the cash payments journal are generally made by the office manager. In his absence, the cashier handles the cash receipts journal and the accounts receivable bookkeeper handles the cash payments journal.

(a) What is wrong with this system? (b) What basic internal controls are lacking? (c) Can the system be improved without increasing the present staff?

Q8-2. A company may pay its employees (a) in cash, (b) by checks drawn on the regular checking account, or (c) by checks drawn on a special payroll bank account. Discuss the advantages and disadvantages of each form of payment.

Q8-3. Why is it advantageous to deposit all cash receipts intact and to make all disbursements by check?

Q8-4. (a) What is a petty cash fund? (b) How does it operate? (c) Why should the petty cash fund always be replenished at the end of each accounting period?

Q8-5. Explain the reciprocal relationships between the cash records of the bank and those of the depositor.

Q8-6. Explain the following terms:
  a. Certified check
  b. Total of listed checks
  c. Service charge
  d. Not sufficient funds
  e. Debit memorandum
  f. Credit memorandum
  g. Overdraft

Q8-7. Explain the effect, if any, on the bank statement balance of each of the following bank reconciliation items:
  a. Outstanding checks total $323.
  b. The bank recorded a $650 deposit as $560.

c. The service charge for the month was $7.

d. Deposits in transit total $800.

e. A note payable of $500 made to the bank by the depositor became due.

Q8-8. (a) What is the purpose of a cash forecast? (b) Describe the basic steps in the preparation of a cash forecast. (c) What are some of the problems that may be encountered in the preparation of a cash forecast?

Q8-9. (a) What is the voucher system? (b) What is a voucher? (c) What is a voucher jacket? (d) What is a voucher register? (e) What is a check register? (f) What are the advantages of the voucher system? (g) What are the disadvantages of the voucher system?

Q8-10. (Appendix I) (a) What two types of Federal taxes are most employers required to withhold from their employees' wages? (b) When do taxes withheld become liabilities to the employer? (c) When and in what manner is the employer required to pay to the responsible Federal agency the amounts withheld?

Q8-11. (Appendix I) (a) What are three common payroll taxes levied on an employer? (b) What is the rate of each tax? (c) When and in what manner does the employer pay the tax?

Q8-12. (Appendix I) (a) What are the main purposes of the Federal Wage and Hour Law? (b) Does it limit the number of hours an employee may work? (c) Are all businesses subject to the provisions of this law?

Q8-13. (Appendix I) (a) What classes of employees are subject to the Federal unemployment compensation tax? (b) What is the tax rate? (c) When is a Federal unemployment tax liability incurred? (d) When is the liability paid to the proper government agency?

Q8-14. (Appendix I) (a) What is a state unemployment merit-rating plan? (b) Why are merit ratings assigned by the several states? (c) What are the maximum state unemployment tax rates? (d) How was the maximum rate initially established in the Federal Unemployment Compensation Act? (e) When does the employer become subject to a state unemployment tax liability? (f) When and to whom is the liability paid?

Q8-15. (Appendix II) List some advantages of an automated system of payroll processing to an entity which employs several hundred people.

Q8-16. (Appendix II) In a punched-card system, why is it desirable to have more than one card per employee when it is obvious that many card columns are not being used?

Note: Unless indicated otherwise, the following rates and amounts are to be used in solving the payroll exercises and problems in this chapter:

a. *F.I.C.A. tax:* 6% each on employer and employee, applicable to the first $15,000 paid to an employee during a calendar year.

b. *Federal unemployment compensation tax:* A maximum of 5% on the first $5,000 paid to each covered employee during each calendar year, with 4% payable to the state and 1% to the Federal government.

E8-1. State the underlying reason for each of the following procedures:

a. The ticket taker at the theater tears in half each ticket presented for admission and returns one-half to the theater goer.

b. The clerk in the department store gives the customer his cash register receipt.

c. After the company treasurer signs a batch of checks, he returns the attached supporting documents, but not the checks (which he mails), to the accounting department.

E8-2. (*Management policy decision problem*) The bookkeeper of the Kane Company, in need of money to pay off his debts, "borrows" $500 by pocketing some cash and checks mailed in by customers. He enters appropriate credits to each customer's account for payment made. Can this misappropriation be concealed for a short period? indefinitely? What measures should a company take to prevent the misappropriation of cash or other assets?

E8-3. On May 1, 1976, the Jay Company established a petty cash fund of $675. On May 31, 1976, the fund consisted of cash and other items as follows:

Coins and currency	$142.50
Postage stamps	141.00
Freight and express invoices	192.00
Salvation Army contribution receipt	75.00
Postdated check from an employee	124.50

Make the entries (a) to establish the fund; (b) to replenish the fund; (c) to increase the fund from $675 to $900 on May 31; (d) to reduce the fund from $675 to $450 on May 31.

E8-4. The George Company has an imprest petty cash fund of $1,500. On October 31, 1976, the fund consisted of cash and other items as follows:

Coins and currency		$ 795.00
Vouchers for:		
Transportation In	$337.86	
Telephone	32.25	
Postage Expense	324.48	
Stationery	1.50	696.09
Total		$1,491.09

Assuming that the petty cash fund was not replenished, make the necessary adjusting entry at October 31, 1976.

E8-5. The Old Company's Cash account shows a balance of $20,818.47 as of April 30, 1976. The balance on the bank statement on that date is $23,334.27. Checks for $750, $533.46, and $126.54 are outstanding. The bank statement shows a charge for a check made out by the Olt Company for $75. The statement also shows a credit of $1,200 for a customer's note that had been left with the bank for collection. Service charges for the month were $19.20. What is the true cash balance as of April 30?

E8-6. From the following data prepare a bank reconciliation and entries to adjust the books of the Lans Company as of March 31, 1976:

Balance on bank statement	$6,153.50
Balance on books	5,704.02
Bank service charge	10.86
Credit for a customer's note collected by the bank (includes interest of $7.28)	169.78

Deposit made on March 31, not credited by the bank   330.33
Check No. 786 for $581 was entered in the cash payments jour-
   nal as $518
A customer's check for $16.77 was returned marked NSF on
   March 30.
Outstanding checks:

Check No.	Amount
817	$ 65.00
818	97.57
825	538.09

E8-7. According to the statement that John Fisher received from his bank as of March 31, 1976, his balance was $2,700. He noted the following discrepancies between the bank statement and his records:

   a. A deposit of $500 that was made on March 31 was not shown on the statement.

   b. Outstanding checks as of March 31 were: Nos. 652, $100; 689, $51; 701, $59; and 710, $86.

   c. Check No. 655 for $350, issued on March 10 for advertising expense, was not recorded in the cash payments journal but was paid by the bank on March 16.

   d. A 9%, 90-day note of Thomas Field for $400, maturing on March 31, was discounted by Fisher on March 12, and dishonored at maturity. Dishonor does not show in Fisher's records. The bank charged Fisher's account for the note plus a $2.50 protest fee. Bank service charges for March were $3.

   1. Determine the cash balance on the books before adjustments and prepare a bank reconciliation showing the true cash balances as of March 31, 1976.

   2. Prepare the journal entries necessary to adjust the books.

E8-8. Gross sales of the Gee Company for the year 1976 were $660,000. Accounts receivable were $60,000 at the beginning of the year and $47,200 at the end of the year. Accounts receivable written off during the year were $1,640 and the year's provision for uncollectible accounts was $1,320. Customers returned merchandise for $3,680 in credit and took cash discounts of $7,120. Compute the cash collections made from customers during 1976.

E8-9. The following statement was made by the treasurer of the Donne Corporation: "As nearly as I can determine, 60% of our customers pay within the discount period. Our terms are 3/10, n/30; 80% of the amount due is collected within the 30-day period; 5% of the delinquent receivables remains uncollected at the end of a 60-day period. As a matter of collection policy, at that point I consider such outstanding receivables as doubtful of collection."

   Sales on account for April, May, June, and July were $28,000, $22,000, $26,000, and $34,000, respectively. On the basis of the company's collection experience, compute the monthly forecast of collections on accounts receivable for May, June, and July.

E8-10. The M. Zanger Corporation has been formed to sell appliances on the installment plan. The following estimates are made for the first year of operations:

   a. Selling price per unit $340
   b. Cost to produce per unit   140
   c. Selling and administrative expenses per unit   60

(Ch. 8)

d. Sales (units):

First month	200
Second month	400
Third month	600
Monthly during rest of year	800

e. Terms of sale:

Down payment	80
Monthly for 13 months	20

f. All costs and expenses are paid in the month of sale.

Prepare a statement showing estimated monthly and cumulative cash requirements for the first twelve months.

E8-11. From the following data, prepare a cash forecast for the Martin Company for January, February, and March, 1977. Actual balances as of December 31, 1976, are:

Cash	$44,000
Accounts Receivable	50,000
Accounts Payable	70,000

Estimates for the first quarter of 1977 are:

	January	February	March
Sales on account	$60,000	$40,000	$44,000
Cash sales	24,000	34,000	26,000
Purchases on account	78,000	46,000	54,000
Cash operating expenses	30,000	24,000	18,000
Depreciation expense	4,000	4,000	4,000

Terms of sales and purchases on account are n/30.

E8-12. Actual and projected sales data for the Alfred Company follow:

	Cash Sales	Credit Sales
November, 1975–Actual		$ 42,000
December, 1975–Actual		48,000
January, 1976–Estimated	$24,000	44,000
February, 1976—Estimated	20,000	66,000
March, 1976–Estimated	42,000	108,000

The cash balance on January 1, 1976, was $36,000.
Experience indicates that 50% of the credit sales are collected in the month of the sale, 40% in the month following the sale, and 10% in the second month following the sale. Compute the cash collections by months for the first quarter of 1976.

E8-13. The Rye Company records all vouchers at the net amount. Record the following transactions in general journal form, indicating the proper book of original entry.

1976
Oct. 2 Issued a voucher payable to the White Company for $2,400 worth of merchandise; terms, 2/10, n/30.

   5 Issued a voucher payable to Black, Inc., for $3,000 worth of merchandise; terms, 3/10, n/30.

   12 Issued a check to the White Company in payment of the October 2 voucher.

Nov. 4 Issued a voucher payable to Black, Inc., for the discount not taken on the transaction of October 5.

   4 Issued a check payable to Black, Inc., for the amount due.

E8-14. Grosse, Inc., completed the following transactions, among others, during October 1976:

1976
Oct. 1 Issued voucher No. 45 payable to the Rudy Company for $1,000 worth of merchandise; terms, 2/10, n/30.

   6 Received a credit memorandum for $100 from the Rudy Company for unsatisfactory merchandise returned. Canceled voucher No. 45 and issued voucher No. 61 for the proper amount.

   10 Issued check No. 25 in payment of voucher No. 61, less a 2% discount.

Record the transactions in general journal form, indicating the journal in which each transaction would be properly recorded.

E8-15. The Lemon Company uses a voucher system. During September 1976 the following selected transactions were completed:

1976
Sept. 1 Issued voucher No. 171 payable to the Huff Company for $4,500 worth of merchandise; terms, n/10.

   11 Gave the Huff Company a 20-day, 10% note in payment of voucher No. 171.

   30 Issued voucher No. 189 payable to the Huff Company for the maturity value of the note of September 11.

   30 Issued check No. 97 in payment of voucher No. 189.

Record the transactions in general journal form, indicating the journal in which each transaction would be properly recorded.

E8-16. (Appendix I). J. Handler pays his five employees weekly. The payroll summary for the week ended January 15 follows:

Total earnings		$2,100.00
Deductions		
FICA tax	$126.00	
Federal income tax	460.00	
Union dues	30.00	
Total deductions		616.00
Net amount paid		$1,484.00

Journalize (a) the recording of the payroll and (b) the employers' liability for payroll taxes.

E8-17. (Appendix I). Each of the ten employees of the Lear Company earned over $10,000 during the calendar year 1976. (a) What was the state unemployment tax expense for 1976? (b) Compute the tax expense based on a tax reduced by a merit rating to 0.5%. (c) Compute the Federal unemployment tax expense for 1976.

E8-18. (Appendix I). The following information is obtained from the payroll records of John Hopkins for the week ended July 10:

Total earnings	$3,600
Earnings subject to unemployment compensation tax	1,250
Earnings subject to FICA tax	3,000
Deductions	
FICA tax	180
Federal income tax	540
Accounts receivable	100

Record (a) the payroll and (b) the employer's payroll tax liability.

E8-19. (Appendix I). The payroll records of the Wilson Company for the week ended February 28 showed the following:

Total wages earned		$5,500
Deductions		
FICA tax	$330	
Federal income tax	825	
Accounts receivable	100	1,255
Net amount paid		$4,245

Assuming that a voucher system is used, record in general journal form: (a) total payroll, (b) payment of the payroll, (c) employer's payroll tax expense. Indicate the journal in which each entry would be properly reported.

E8-20. (Appendix I). The following payroll data for the year 1976 were taken from the records of the Kristo Company:

Total wages expense	$45,000
Wages to employees with earnings in excess of $5,000	35,000
Wages to employees with earnings in excess of $15,000	20,000

Calculate the employer's payroll tax expense for the year.

E8-21. (Appendix I). The Loft Company had 15 employees who worked during an entire calendar year. One of them, James Luth, earned $20,000. What was the employer's total expenditure for Luth's services for the year?

E8-22. (Appendix II). Using the punched-card file system shown in Figure A8-1 as a model, assume that an employee receives a raise in pay effective June 28, 1976. Describe the action taken by the data-processing department on receipt of such notification.

E8-23. (Appendix II). Immediately after the payroll-processing run has been completed and card decks sorted for return to separate files, a request is received by telephone from the plant superintendent as follows: "I must know the total hours worked by department 5 last pay period within 20 minutes. Can you do it?"

Sketch a flow chart for a data-processing routine to provide the answer.

DP8-1. (*Recording petty cash fund transactions*) The transactions of the petty cash fund of the Roach Company during the months of July and August 1976 follow:

1976

July 1 Established an imprest petty cash fund in the amount of $350.

      10 Replenished the fund and increased it to $750. The following items were in the petty cash box:

Coins and currency	$12.50
Vouchers for:	
Telephone and telegraph	124.30
. Advances to employees	50.00
Postage stamps	100.00
Miscellaneous office supplies	63.20
Total	$350.00

Aug. 31 Replenished the fund again at the close of the Roach Company's fiscal year. The petty cash box contained the following items:

Coins and currency		$48.64
Vouchers for:		
Telephone and telegraph	$34.47	
Office supplies	23.10	
Postage	141.18	
Traveling expense	201.76	
Entertainment expense	212.32	
Repairs	85.88	
Hardware supplies	2.65	701.36
Total		$750.00

Required: Journalize the transactions.

DP8-2. (*Bank reconciliation*) The Cash account of the Tech Company showed a balance of $2,335.64 on March 31, 1976. The bank statement showed a balance of $2,533.23. Other differences between the information in the firm's Cash account and the bank's records are listed below.

1. A deposit of $130.46 made on March 31 was not recorded by the bank before the bank statement was issued.

2. The following items were returned with the bank statement:

  a. A credit memo for $123.53, the proceeds of a draft for $126.50 drawn on the George Company and accepted by the drawee 60 days ago. The bank deducted $2.97 from the total collected for the cost of collection.

  b. A debit memo for $5.28 for annual rental of a safety deposit box.

  c. A customer's check for $8.25 received on account, which the firm had included in its deposit on March 27, was returned marked NSF.

  d. A canceled check in the amount of $225.50 drawn by the Itek Company and charged by the bank against the account of the Tech Company by mistake. The check is being returned to the bank.

3. Check No. 298 was made out correctly for $19.44 in payment of office supplies, but was entered in the cash payments journal as $19.54.

4. Outstanding checks on March 31 totaled $443.45.

Required:

1. Prepare a bank reconciliation as of March 31, 1976.
2. Prepare the journal entries to adjust the Cash account as of March 31, 1976.

DP8-3. (*Cash forecast*) The Province Company estimates the following sales, purchases, and operating expenses for the first four months of 1976.

	Sales	Purchases	Operating Expenses
January	$400,000	$125,000	$15,000
February	500,000	250,000	17,500
March	450,000	200,000	23,750
April	550,000	550,000	21,250

Balances on January 1, 1976, were:

Accounts Receivable	$75,000
Accounts Payable	50,000

Required:

1. Prepare a schedule of estimated monthly collections for the first four months of 1976. Approximately 25% of sales are for cash; sales on account are on terms of n/30 and are collected in the month following the sale.
2. Prepare a schedule of estimated monthly cash disbursements for the period. Purchases are made on terms of n/15, so that one-half the purchases are paid for in the month of purchase and the remainder in the following month. Operating expenses are paid for in the month in which they are incurred.

DP8-4. (*Voucher register*) A section of a voucher register, showing the unpaid vouchers as of April 30, 1976, is given below:

Date		Vou. No.	Name	Paid		Credit Vou. Pay.	Debit Purch.	Other General Ledger Accounts		
				Date	Ck. No.			Account	Debit	Credit
1976										
April	5	270	Gilbert Spack			2,250				
	10	272	William Murphy			2,000				
	21	291	Baldwin Company			2,250				
	30	305	Norman Geller			1,500				

The following transactions, among others, occurred during May:

1976:
May 1 Issued check No. 651 in payment of voucher No. 270, less 2%.

    1 Issued voucher No. 309 to Herbert Sedlin for $3,750 worth of merchandise; terms, n/15.

    5 Received a credit memorandum from the Baldwin Company for $750

1976
May   for unsatisfactory merchandise returned. Canceled voucher No. 291 and issued voucher No. 310 for the proper amount.

     8   Issued check No. 652 in payment of voucher No. 305, less 1%.

   15   Issued check No. 653 in payment of voucher No. 310, less 1%.

   17   By special agreement with Herbert Sedlin, the purchase of May 1 is to be paid for in installments: $1,250 immediately and the balance by June 16. Canceled voucher No. 309 and issued vouchers No. 311 and 312. Check No. 654 was issued in payment of voucher No. 311.

Required:

1. Enter the unpaid vouchers in a voucher register similar to the one shown (draw double rules under the last entry to exclude the April amounts from the May totals); record the May transactions in the voucher register and a check register.
2. Enter the total of unpaid vouchers as of April 30, $8,250, as a credit in the Vouchers Payable general ledger account; post to Vouchers Payable from the voucher register and check register.
3. Prepare a schedule of unpaid vouchers.

DP8-5. (*Recording transactions in special journals*) The E. Rose Company uses a voucher system. During June 1976, the following selected transactions were completed:

1976
June   1   Purchased $5,000 worth of merchandise from the Ciampa Company; terms, 2/10, n/30.

   10   Made a partial payment on the June 1 purchase. The check is made out for $2,094.75, representing a partial payment on which a discount is allowed.

   15   Paid a 45-day, 12% note for $10,000 due today (the company closed its books on May 31).

   21   Returned merchandise with an invoice price of $500 to the Ciampa Company and received credit.

   25   Paid $1,250 for June rent.

Required: Record the transactions in general journal form and indicate the journal in which each transaction would be properly recorded.

DP8-6. (Appendix I). (*Recording payroll*) The partially completed payroll register of the Hastings Company for the week ended December 11 is given below.

Payroll Register

Name	Earnings		Deductions		Net Amount	Distribution		
	Week Ending December 11	Cumulative Through December 4	FICA Tax	Federal Income Tax		Salesmen's Salaries	Executive Salaries	Office Salaries
Bates, John	170	8,500		25.50		170		
Hanlon, Robert	220	11,000		30.00		220		
Perry, John	400	14,950		75.00			400	
Silver, Clifford	180	4,995		21.60				180
Totals								

Required:

1. Prepare a payroll register similar to the one shown, filling in all the blank columns.
2. Record the Hastings Company's payroll for the week in general journal form.
3. Record the Hastings Company's payroll tax expense in general journal form.

DP8-7. (*Management policy decision problem*)

    a. The manager of a shoe department employing six salesmen has found on a number of occasions that the cash in the register at the end of the day is less than the amounts shown on the record of sales for that day. Each salesman rings up his own sales. What recommendations would you make to the manager?

    b. How do the use of a petty cash system and the regular reconciliation of the bank account protect the company against mistakes and losses?

    c. You note that the independent auditor, when making his examination, reconciles (1) total deposits shown on the bank statements with total receipts shown in the cash receipts journal, and (2) total disbursements shown on the bank statements with total checks drawn as recorded in the cash payments journal. Explain why the auditor makes these reconciliations.

    d. It is essential for a business to establish internal controls to prevent the misappropriation of cash. Does management have other responsibilities relating to cash? Explain.

P8-1. The following data are taken from the records of Hyde, Inc., and from the monthly bank statement furnished them by the National Trust Company:

a. Balance per bank statement, June 30, 1976	$134,655.77
b. Balance per books, June 30, 1976	87,477.74
c. Outstanding checks, June 30, 1976	51,373.47
d. Receipts of June 30, 1976, deposited July 2, 1976	8,507.52
e. Service charge for June, per debit memo	6.16
f. Proceeds of bank loan, June 15, 1976, discounted for 3 months at 10% a year, omitted from the company's books	15,600.00
g. Deposit of June 30, 1976, omitted from bank statement	4,627.86

h. Error on bank statement in entering deposit of June 25, 1976:

Correct amount	$5,091.84	
Entered as	5,090.84	1.00

i. Check of Heid, Inc., charged in error	4,304.00

j. Proceeds of a customer's note collected by bank on June 16, 1976; not entered in the company's books:

Principal	$3,200	
Interest	32	
Total	$3,232	
Less collection fee	8	3,224.00

k. Error on bank statement in entering deposit of June 10, 1976:

Entered as	$5,614	
Correct amount	5,604	10.00

l. Deposit of Hide Corporation credited in error	2,880.00

m. Debit memo for non-interest-bearing note not recorded
by the company $8,000.00

n. A check from Black, Inc., was returned marked NSF;
no entry has been made on the company's records   462.90

Required:

1. Prepare a bank reconciliation as of June 30, 1976.
2. Prepare the journal entries necessary to adjust the books of Hyde, Inc., as of June 30, 1976. The books are closed annually June 30.

P8-2. The Hall Company prepared the following bank reconciliation as of March 31, 1976:

HALL COMPANY
Bank Reconciliation
March 31, 1976

Balance per bank		$24,927.50
Less outstanding checks		
Check	**Amount**	
580	$4,051.00	
599	196.00	
600	6.80	4,253.80
Balance per books		$20,673.70

The bank statement for the month of April was as follows:

SECOND NATIONAL BANK
Statement of account with Hall Company

Checks		Deposits	Date	Balance
			1976	
			April 1	24,927.50
4,051.00			2	20,876.50
196.00	24.00	230.00	1,570.00	6	21,996.50
200.00		390.00	11	22,186.50
124.46	397.00	6.80	16	21,658.24
2,220.00	180.00 NSF		21	19,258.24
1,720.00	30.80	5,000.00	26	22,507.44
5.50 SC		1,521.60	29	24,023.54

Cash receipts for the month:

Date	Amount
April 5	$1,570.00
10	390.00
23	5,000.00
28	1,521.60
30	1,000.00

Cash disbursements for the month:

Check	Amount	Check	Amount
601	$ 24.00	607	$1,364.42
602	1,720.00	608	99.80
603	230.00	609	40.00
604	200.00	610	1,520.00
605	2,220.00	611	124.46
606	287.00	612	397.00

The canceled checks returned by the bank included a check for $30.80 made out by the Hill Company and charged to the Hall Company in error. The NSF check had been received from a customer on account.

Required:

1. Prepare the bank reconciliation as of April 30, 1976.
2. Make the necessary adjusting journal entries.

P8-3. (*Accounting policy decision problem*) The Doone Company has an imprest petty cash fund of $1,000. On June 30, 1976, the end of the company's fiscal year, the composition of the fund was as follows:

Currency and coins		$ 195.88
Vouchers for:		
Postage	$212.16	
Stationery	50.00	
Transportation out	307.24	
Telephone and telegraph	230.60	800.00
Total		$ 995.88
Cash shortage		4.12
Total		$1,000.00

Required:

1. Prepare the entry to replenish the fund on June 30.
2. Assuming that the fund was not replenished, (a) what adjusting entry should be made on June 30? (b) what amount will be reported in the June 30 position statement?
3. Should the custodian of the petty cash fund have the authority to withdraw cash from the bank whenever he needs to replenish the fund?

P8-4. The bookkeeper for the Rock Company prepared the following statement:

ROCK COMPANY
Bank Reconciliation
May 31, 1976

Cash balance per ledger, May 31, 1976	$4,341.10
Deduct bank service charges	4.12
Adjusted cash balance, May 31, 1976	$4,336.98

Cash balance per bank statement, May 31, 1976	$5,590.38
Add deposit in transit	1,314.15
Total	$6,904.53
Deduct outstanding checks	

Check		Amount	
608		$ 476.10	
690		891.44	
695	Certified check for $500		
701		1,200.01	2,567.55

Adjusted Cash Balance, May 31, 1976	$4,336.98

a. How did the bookkeeper determine the amounts to be added or deducted?
b. Why is check No. 695 excluded from the total of outstanding checks?
c. What journal entry is necessary to adjust the books at May 31, 1976?

P8-5. (*Accounting policy decision problem*) You have prepared the financial reports for the Cowan Corporation, which include the following amounts:

Cash balances:	
April 30, 1976	$105,000
April 30, 1975	66,000
Net income:	
For the fiscal year ended	
April 30, 1976	165,000
For the fiscal year ended	
April 30, 1975	180,000

John Cowan, the company's president, says that you must have made a mistake, because you report an increase in the cash balance of $39,000 although earnings for the fiscal year declined by $15,000 from the year before. (a) Is he right? Explain. (b) He asks you what the effect on the cash balance would have been if the company had reported a $15,000 net loss for the period?

P8-6. (*Financial policy decision problem*) Estimates of the Sparrow Manufacturing Company for the first four months of 1976 are as follows:

	January	February	March	April
Sales	$100,000	$120,000	$140,000	$130,000
Purchases	72,000	80,000	80,000	90,000
Payrolls	20,000	24,000	28,000	19,000
Other expenses	10,000	12,000	14,000	13,000

The general ledger includes the following account balances at January 1, 1976:

Cash	$20,000
Accounts Receivable	90,000
Accounts Payable	60,000

All sales are on account on terms of n/30; 90% are collected in the month following the sale; 8% in the second month following the sale; and 2% are ultimately written off as bad debts. All payments on purchases and other expenses are made in the month following the month of purchase. Payrolls are paid during the month. The Accounts Receivable balance of January 1 represents total sales for December of the prior year, and the Accounts Payable balance represents purchases for that month.

Required:

1. Prepare a cash forecast by months for the first four months of 1976.
2. On the basis of the forecast, what financial policy decisions should the company make?
3. (a) Would you recommend daily or weekly cash forecasts? (b) What would be the costs and the benefits of more frequent forecasts?

P8-7. The general ledger of the Camacha Manufacturing Company included the following account balances as of January 1, 1976:

Cash	$ 8,000
Accounts Receivable	84,000
Accounts Payable	43,000

Projected sales, purchases, and cash operating expenses for the first three months of 1976 were:

	January	*February*	*March*
Sales	$72,000	$96,000	$108,000
Purchases	48,000	72,000	60,000
Cash operating expenses	19,000	24,000	18,000

All sales and purchases are on terms of n/30, so that remittances by customers are received in the month following the sale, and all payments for merchandise are made during the month following the purchase. Cash operating expenses are paid for during the month in which they are incurred.

Required: Prepare a schedule showing cash requirements by months for the first quarter of 1976.

P8-8. The Albie Company prepares its vouchers for the net amount due. A section of the voucher register, showing the unpaid vouchers as of June 30, is given below.

Date	Vou. No.	Name	Paid		Credit Vou. Pay.	Debit Purch.	Debit Purch. Disc. Lost	Other General Ledger Account		
			Date	Ck. No.				Account	Debit	Credi
1976 June 1	78	Robert Doyle			98					
3	81	Bennett Co.			1,960					
5	82	Gates & Son			392					

Among the company's July transactions are the following:

1976

July 1 Issued check No. 110 in payment of voucher No. 78.

5 Issued voucher No. 83 payable to Gates & Son for $8 discount lost on the purchase of June 5.

1976

July 6   Issued check No. 111 in payment of vouchers No. 82 and 83.

   10   Issued voucher No. 84 to the Giles Company for $1,000 worth of merchandise; terms, 2/10, n/30.

   14   Issued voucher No. 85 to Warren's, Inc., for $1,500 worth of merchandise; terms 1½/10, n/30.

   16   By special arrangement with the Bennett Company the purchase of June 3 (invoice $2,000; terms, 2/10, n/30) is to be paid for in installments: $800 immediately and the balance on August 16. Issued voucher No. 86 for the purchase discount lost. Canceled vouchers No. 81 and 86 and issued vouchers No. 87 and 88. Issued check No. 112 in payment of voucher No. 87.

   20   Issued check No. 113 in payment of voucher No. 84.

Required:

1. Enter the unpaid vouchers as of July 1 in a voucher register similar to the one shown above; record the July transactions in the voucher register and a single-column check register.
2. Enter the total amount of unpaid vouchers as of July 1 ($2,450) as a credit to the Vouchers Payable general ledger account; post to a Vouchers Payable T account from the voucher register and the check register.
3. Prepare a schedule of unpaid vouchers.

P8-9. (*Financial policy decision problem*) The Zona Company has two notes payable of $150,000 each with due dates of May 31 and June 30, 1976. The company wishes to arrange in advance for any refinancing that may be needed (a) to pay the notes on their due dates and (b) to provide a minimum end-of-month cash balance of $50,000. You are furnished with the following projected data:

Sales		Purchases	
February	$150,000	March	$127,500
March	212,500	April	97,500
April	150,000	May	112,500
May	157,500	June	90,000
June	175,000		

a. The cash balance on April 1 was $40,000.
b. All sales are on terms of 2/10 E.O.M. (a 2% discount is allowed if the invoice is paid by the tenth of the month following the sale). Past experience indicates that 70% of the sales are collected within the first 10 days of the first month following the sale, 20% during the remainder of the first month following the sale, and 8% in the second month following the sale. Bad debts losses are estimated at 2% of sales.
c. Terms of purchases are 2/10, n/30. Since all payments are made within the discount period, two-thirds of the invoices will be paid in the month of the purchase and one-third in the month following the purchase.
d. Operating expenses are $15,000 a month and are paid for when they are incurred. The Zona Company receives $3,750 monthly from property rentals; $6,250 will be realized in June from the sale of obsolete equipment.

Required:

1. Prepare a report, with supporting schedules, advising management of the amount of additional borrowing that will be necessary.
2. Explain to management the usefulness and limitations of the forecast.
3. What specific steps can management take in planning its cash requirements?

4. To what other cash planning and control problems should the management of the Zona Company direct its attention?

5. What suggestions would you offer for improving the cash position of the company?

6. After reviewing your report, one of the officials said: "But these are predictions about the future, and in this business you cannot predict what will happen the next week, or even the next day, so that I personally cannot rely on them." Write a brief answer to this official.

P8-10. (*Financial policy decision problem*) You have been asked to prepare a cash forecast for the Pine Corporation for the first quarter of 1977. In response to your request for past and prospective financial data, you receive the following:

Estimated sales:	
November 1976	$41,000
December 1976	41,000
January 1977	55,000
February 1977	53,000
March 1977	80,000
April 1977	60,000
May 1977	60,000

Seventy percent of the sales are made on account, of which 65% are collected during the month of sale, 30% during the month following the sale, and 5% during the second month following the sale. Thirty percent of the estimated sales are made over the counter for cash. Since the major suppliers require substantial lead time, purchases of merchandise are made three months in advance of sale and are paid for two months in advance of sale. The cost of the merchandise is one-half of the selling price. Other regular monthly cash requirements consist of the following:

Salaries and wages	$1,000
Sales commissions (credit sales only)	10%
General and administrative	$4,000
Insurance	$4,500
Transportation	4% of total sales

A special advertising and promotional campaign is planned that will cost $5,000 payable on March 1. A quarterly dividend payment of $7,500 is scheduled for February 15.

On January 1, 1977, there was an outstanding bank debt of $25,000. The loan must be retired in five months by making principal repayments of $5,000 at the end of each month. Furthermore, interest is payable at the end of each month at 1% a month on the outstanding balance at the beginning of the month. The cash balance on January 1 is estimated to be $30,000.

Required: Prepare the cash forecast for January, February, and March, 1977.

P8-11. (*Financial policy decision problem*) You suggest to James Croyden, owner of the Croyden Manufacturing Company, that it is good business management to plan his cash requirements for at least three months in advance so that he might arrange for bank loans when the cash balance is too low, and might plan to make short-term investments when the cash balance is too high. Croyden's response is: "I don't think that it is worth the effort. It would take me and my financial assistant away from our regular tasks and we wouldn't save enough to make it worthwhile. Furthermore, in my business, I can't plan that far ahead, and my projections would be sheer guesswork."

Required: What is your reaction to Croyden's response?

P8-12. (*Management policy decision problem*) What specific safeguards will be provided by each of the following internal cash control procedures?

1. All cash receipts are deposited intact in a bank account daily.
2. Monthly bank statements are reconciled with the cash records.
3. Periodic unannounced counts are made of the petty cash fund.
4. Checks are issued only if supported by properly authorized vouchers.
5. The person who records cash receipts is not permitted to authorize cash disbursements or to sign checks.
6. The clerks who handle cash are not permitted to make entries in the cash records.
7. The person who approves vouchers for payment is not permitted to sign the checks for those payments.

P8-13. (Appendix I) The TV Sales Company pays its salesmen monthly. On November 30, 1976, the following information was available:

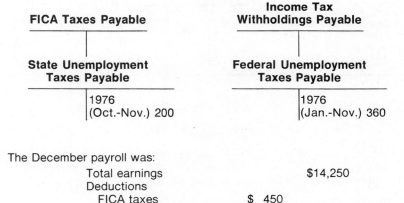

FICA Taxes Payable	Income Tax Withholdings Payable

State Unemployment Taxes Payable	Federal Unemployment Taxes Payable
1976 (Oct.-Nov.) 200	1976 (Jan.-Nov.) 360

The December payroll was:

Total earnings		$14,250
Deductions		
FICA taxes	$ 450	
Federal income taxes	1,650	2,100
Net amount due		$12,150

Required: Copy the T accounts with the November 30 balances and enter the following:

1. The December payroll.
2. The December employer's payroll tax expense. The taxable portion of the December payroll for state and Federal unemployment taxes is $3,000.
3. Checks and appropriate report forms mailed on January 31, 1977, as follows:
   a. To the Internal Revenue Service: a check for December and depositary receipts for October and November.
   b. To the Internal Revenue Service: a check for the Federal unemployment tax liability for 1976.
   c. To the State Division of Employment Security: a check for the state unemployment tax liability for the fourth quarter of 1976.

P8-14. (Appendix I) The following information regarding the payroll of the Brewster Corporation for the week ended July 24, 1976, is given:

Employee	Type of Work	Cumulative Gross Wages to July 17, 1976	Gross Wages for Week Ended July 24
James P. Morris	Salesman	$14,800	$400
Frederick M. Phillips	Salesman	8,500	350
Jane Dolittle	Office Clerk	3,200	150
Thomas O. Waters	Office Clerk	4,900	150

Deductions Other Than FICA

	Federal Income Taxes Withheld	State Income Taxes Withheld	Group Life Insurance Premiums Withheld
James P. Morris	$55	$12	$15
Frederick M. Phillips	33	8	8
Jane Dolittle	15	3	8
Thomas O. Waters	25	7	10

Required:

1. Prepare a journal entry on July 24, 1976, to record and classify the payroll expense.
2. Prepare a journal entry on July 24, 1976, to record the employer's payroll taxes.
3. Prepare a journal entry on July 26, 1976, to record the payment of the payroll.

P8-15. (Appendix I) The general ledger of the Pine Company showed the following data on November 30, 1976:

Name of Account	Period Covered	Amount
Accrued Salaries and Wages Payable		None
FICA Taxes Payable	November	$ 335.00
State Unemployment Taxes Payable	October-November	212.00
Federal Unemployment Taxes Payable	October-November	78.20
Income Tax Withholdings Payable	November	1,210.00
Bond Deductions Payable		320.00
United Fund Payable		125.00
Salaries and Wages Expense	January-November	97,800.00
Payroll Tax Expense	January-November	7,300.00

Following is the payroll summary for December. The last pay period ended December 27.

Total earnings		$8,900.00
Deductions		
FICA taxes	$ 310.00	
Federal income taxes	1,325.00	
U.S. bonds	275.00	
United Fund	150.00	
Total deductions		2,060.00
Net amount paid		$6,840.00

Additional information taken from the records follows:

a. December earnings (through the last pay period) of $2,050.75 were subject to a state unemployment tax rate of 4%.

b. On December 6 a check was issued to Merchants National Bank for the purchase of U.S. savings bonds for $187.50.

c. On December 29, a check was mailed to the United Fund for contributions withheld from employees' earnings through December 27.

d. Wages accrued on December 31 were $1,010.50; the taxable portion for state and Federal unemployment taxes is $350, with rates of 4% and 1%, respectively; the taxable portion for FICA tax is $500.

Required:

1. Record the transactions relating to payroll, payroll deductions, and payroll tax expense for December. Checks are mailed on due date to the proper agencies.

2. List the affected ledger accounts and their balances as of December 31, after all entries have been posted.

P8-16. (Appendix II). (*Management policy decision problem*) As a product of its payroll system, the Xton Company receives a weekly report of year-to-date hours worked and year-to-date total labor cost subdivided by department.

Required: Describe some possible uses of this report (including other reports to be used at the same time):

1. by the plant superintendent
2. by the foremen of production departments
3. by the accounting department

Measurement and Control of Receivables

9

Making sales and purchases on account has become standard business practice. Individuals and businesses alike buy and sell merchandise, invest in stocks and bonds, and even acquire plant and equipment on credit. Consequently, the increasing trend toward the extension of credit terms for transactions involving all types of goods and services has led to a greater need for control and analysis of receivables by management.

SOURCES AND CLASSIFICATION OF RECEIVABLES

There are two classes of trade receivables: accounts receivable, which are claims against customers for sales made on open account, and notes receivable, which are claims against customers supported by written formal promises to pay. From a legal point of view, a note receivable is probably better security than an account receivable because it is a written acknowledgment of the debt; however, in the United States, the unsecured open account form of credit is well established. Nontrade receivables arise from money lent from deposits made, and from other sources.

The various claims should be properly recorded in several separate accounts, one possible classification of which appears below:

1. Accounts Receivable—Trade. This account represents claims against customers for goods sold or for services rendered.
2. Accounts Receivable—Nontrade. This group of accounts represents

claims arising from sources other than normal trade transactions, including:

a. Loans to officers or employees
b. Deposits made on contract bids with public utilities or government agencies
c. Claims against common carriers for loss or damage to goods in shipment, loss claims against insurance companies, and claims against the U.S. Treasury for tax refunds
d. Amounts due from affiliated companies
e. Amounts due or accrued from rentals, interest, and royalties

Notes are similarly classified as trade or nontrade receivables. Nontrade notes receivable should be carried in accounts specifically designated as to source (officers, affiliated companies, rental property) and properly classified on the statement of financial position.

Receivables that are due and collectible within a year should be shown in the Current Assets section of the statement of financial position. The terms *Accounts Receivable* and *Notes Receivable,* if unqualified, should be understood to represent trade receivables collectible within one year or one operating cycle. Nontrade receivables that are not due or are not collectible within a year should be shown under Long-Term Investments.

RECOGNITION OF LOSSES ON UNCOLLECTIBLE ACCOUNTS

Matching Revenue and Expenses

A basic principle in accounting is that the earned revenue of any accounting period and the actual expense incurred in realizing that revenue should be related.

The cost of the goods sold and all other expenses incurred during the period should be related or should be deducted from the revenue of that period. Hence, the cost of a machine is spread over the period during which the machine is used to arrive at a fair measure of the net income for each period. It would be inaccurate to charge the entire cost at the time of purchase or disposal of the machine.

Similarly, since the balance in the Accounts Receivable account represents uncollected amounts included in revenue, losses that may arise through failure to collect any of the receivables should be recognized as an expense of doing business during the period when the sales were made. Thus, accounts receivable originating from sales made for credit in 1976 and determined to be uncollectible in 1977 represent a bad debts expense of the year 1976. It also follows that the Accounts Receivable account in the statement of financial position should be shown at the amount expected to be realized through actual cash collections from customers. If accounts receivable are shown at their gross amount without any accompanying adjustment for the estimated uncollectible portion, then the total assets and the total stockholders' equity would be overstated to the extent of the failure to recognize an expense that arises out of the sale of goods on account.

Recording the Bad Debts Adjustment

To illustrate the recording of a bad debts adjustment, assume that on December 31, 1976, the credit department of the Greene Corporation, having analyzed sales during 1976 and past-due accounts, determines that out of the current year's sales, $550 will be uncollectible. This amount represents a bad debts expense to be shown in the General and Administrative Expenses section of the income statement as a deduction from revenue. The estimated losses pertain to accounts receivable resulting from sales of the current period; therefore, in accordance with the principle of the periodic matching of expenses and revenues, estimated bad debts losses should be charged against revenue.

The adjusting general journal entry recorded on December 31, 1976, and the posting of the entry to the general ledger are shown below.

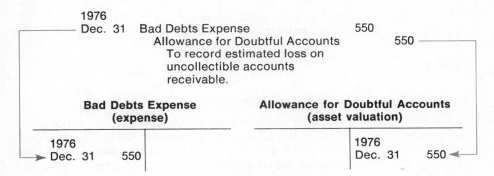

1976			
Dec. 31	Bad Debts Expense	550	
	Allowance for Doubtful Accounts		550
	To record estimated loss on uncollectible accounts receivable.		

Bad Debts Expense (expense)		**Allowance for Doubtful Accounts** (asset valuation)	
1976		1976	
Dec. 31 550		Dec. 31 550	

It is assumed that there was no balance before adjustments in Allowance for Doubtful Accounts and that no account receivable had been written off during the year 1976. These complications are discussed in more detail later in this chapter.

Since the amount of $550 is an estimate and is not related to specific customers' accounts, the credit must be made to a contra (valuation) account. If the credit were to be made directly to Accounts Receivable without corresponding credits to subsidiary accounts, the equality of the controlling account and the subsidiary accounts would no longer exist. The use of the valuation account Allowance for Doubtful Accounts permits a reduction in the asset account without destroying this essential equality. Allowance for Doubtful Accounts is shown in the statement of financial position as a deduction from the related asset account.

Assets		
Current Assets		
Cash		$1,210
Accounts Receivable	$6,945	
Deduct Allowance for Doubtful Accounts	550	6,395
Notes Receivable		1,000

The amount of $6,395 represents the anticipated net realizable value of the accounts receivable.

As actual accounts receivable are determined to be uncollectible during subsequent accounting periods, Allowance for Doubtful Accounts is debited instead of Bad Debts Expense, with offsetting credits to the controlling account and the specific customers' accounts involved. This procedure is required because the expense already has been recognized by the bad debts adjusting entry. A debit to Bad Debts Expense at the time of write-off would cause the loss to be recorded twice.

Assume that on May 1, 1977, the Greene Corporation decides that a claim of $75 against John Landry for a sale made on March 1, 1976, is uncollectible. The entry is:

```
1977
May  1    Allowance for Doubtful Accounts          75
              Accounts Receivable—John Landry              75
              To write off the uncollectible account.
```

Estimating the Amount of Bad Debts Expense

It is necessary for management to make a careful estimate, based on judgment and past experience, of the amount of its uncollectible accounts. Accurate records must be kept and overdue accounts must be carefully analyzed.

There are two alternative approaches commonly used in estimating bad debts. In this text, these methods are referred to (1) as *the income statement approach,* based on the dollar volume of sales, and (2) as *the statement of financial position approach,* based on the amount of receivables.

The Income Statement Approach. The income statement approach associates the bad debts expense directly with dollar volume of sales. Typically the estimate is based on a percentage of sales less sales returns and allowances. The percentage is based on information derived from the company's past experience. It may be desirable to establish the percentage on the basis of charge sales only, excluding cash sales, particularly if the proportion of cash sales to total sales fluctuates from year to year. The method is simple to apply and furnishes an equitable basis for distributing bad debts losses. Since the computation used in this method yields the amount of the bad debts expense for the year, any existing balance in the Allowance for Doubtful Accounts is ignored. A small error in the same direction over the years could accumulate to a large amount in the Allowance for Doubtful Accounts, since its balance is usually ignored in the adjustment process.

To illustrate the adjustment by this approach, assume that an examination of the accounts of a given company for the preceding five years shows that approximately one-half of 1 percent of credit sales have proved to be uncollectible. Assume further that credit sales for a particular year are $100,000 and that there is a credit balance of $85 in Allowance for Doubtful Accounts before adjustments are made. The bad debts expense for the year is $500 = (0.005 × $100,000), and in recording the adjustment, the $85 balance in the Allowance for Doubtful Accounts is ignored. The adjusting entry is

Bad Debts Expense	500	
Allowance for Doubtful Accounts		500

The Statement of Financial Position Approach. The statement of financial position approach requires an adjustment of the existing balance of Allowance for Doubtful Accounts to an amount that, when deducted from Accounts Receivable on the statement of financial position, will show accounts receivable at their net realizable value. In the statement of financial position approach, the amount of accounts receivable rather than sales volume is used as the base for the adjustment. The necessary adjustment for the balance of Allowance for Doubtful Accounts is determined by either of two procedures: (1) the balance necessary to maintain the Allowance for Doubtful Accounts is established by *aging* the accounts receivable (that is, analyzing them by the amount of time they have remained unpaid) and adjusting the existing balance of Allowance for Doubtful Accounts to the proper amount, or (2) the balance of Allowance for Doubtful Accounts is adjusted to an amount equal to an estimated percentage of current accounts receivable. Aging the accounts receivable involves consideration of such factors as the date on which payment was due, the number of days that have elapsed since the due date, and any other available data of a financial nature that give some clue to collectibility of the accounts. A columnar work sheet like the one shown in Figure 9-1 is often used to facilitate the analysis of the Accounts Receivable account. It is sometimes referred to as an *aging schedule.* In an EDP accounting system, the aging schedule is one of the products of data processing.

Figure 9-1
Analysis of Accounts Receivable by Age

WALTER CARTER CORPORATION
Analysis of Accounts Receivable by Age
December 31, 1976

Customer's Name	Total Balance	Not Yet Due	1–30 Days Past Due	31–60 Days Past Due	61–90 Days Past Due	Over 90 Days Past Due
Walter G. Arnold	$ 880	$ 800	$ 80			
Allan Conlon	1,800	1,000	500	$ 300		
Charles Peacock	50				$ 50	
Richard C. Smith	320	100	200	20		
Jerome Werther	960				900	$ 60
[Others]	51,990	27,220	15,460	5,280	730	3,300
Totals	$56,000	$29,120	$16,240	$5,600	$1,680	$3,360
Percent of Total	100	52	29	10	3	6

All the accounts in the subsidiary accounts receivable ledger with their corresponding account balances are listed in the Customer's Name and Total Balance columns. The component charges that make up each balance in the Total Balance column are then extended to the appropriate columns. The aging method yields a more satisfactory Allowance for Doubtful Accounts than does any other method, because the estimate is based on a study of individual customers' accounts rather than on a blanket percentage of a single general ledger account balance. Only a detailed analysis will disclose the accounts that are not past due but which may be uncollectible, and the long overdue accounts that may give indication of eventual collectibility. Yet, if recoveries of accounts receivable previously written off or the write-off in the current year of accounts receivable arising from prior years' sales are run through the Allowance for Doubtful Accounts without any designation of which of these items affect prior years' net income, the bad debts expense of the current year could be greatly distorted.

Management should also compare the current analysis of accounts receivable by age with those of earlier periods, especially the age-group percentages. Currently, 52 percent of the total accounts receivable are not yet due, 29 percent are past due from 1 to 30 days, and so on. When compared with earlier years, percentage increases in the lower age classifications with offsetting decreases in the older classes are favorable.

The analysis in Figure 9-1 may be used to determine the proper balance to be established in Allowance for Doubtful Accounts. To make this determination, companies may apply a sliding scale of percentages based on previous experience to the total amount shown in each column. The computation to determine expected losses for the Walter Carter Corporation is shown below.

	Amount	Estimated Percentage Uncollectible	Allowance for Doubtful Accounts
Not yet due	$29,120	2	$ 582.40
1–30 days past due	16,240	4	649.60
31–60 days past due	5,600	10	560.00
61–90 days past due	1,680	20	336.00
Over 90 days past due	3,360	50	1,680.00
Totals	$56,000		$3,808.00

On the basis of this summary, $3,808 of the outstanding accounts receivable on December 31 may become uncollectible. Consequently, an Allowance for Doubtful Accounts with a balance of $3,808 should be established. Before the adjusting entry is made, the existing balance in the account must be considered. The Walter Carter Corporation has a present credit balance in Allowance for Doubtful Accounts of $200, a provision remaining from earlier periods. The adjusting entry amount will be for $3,608 = ($3,808 − $200); when this amount is transferred to the allowance account, it will bring that account up to $3,808, the estimated probable uncollectible accounts. The adjusting journal entry is

```
1976
Dec. 31   Bad Debts Expense                    3,608
              Allowance for Doubtful Accounts            3,608
              To increase the asset valuation
              account to the estimated loss.
```

Assume, however, that the Allowance for Doubtful Accounts had a debit balance of $300 before adjustment, rather than a credit balance of $200. The adjusting entry would be for $4,108 = ($3,808 + $300); after this entry is posted, the allowance account will contain the desired credit balance of $3,808.

An analysis of accounts receivable by age is time-consuming; if there is a reliable pattern, the Allowance for Doubtful Accounts may be based on a single percentage of accounts receivable computed as follows for the Gnu Corporation:

End of Year	Balance of Accounts Receivable	Total Losses from Uncollectible Accounts
1973	$20,000	$ 800
1974	24,000	480
1975	22,000	700
Totals	$66,000	$1,980

The average loss of the past three years has been 3 percent ($1,980 ÷ $66,000). Assume that at the end of 1976 total accounts receivable are $25,000 and a credit balance of $150 is in the allowance account. Estimated uncollectible accounts at 3 percent of accounts receivable are $750 = ($25,000 × 0.03). The following adjusting entry at the end of 1976 on the books of the Gnu Corporation increases the Allowance for Doubtful Accounts to the desired amount of $750.

```
1976
Dec. 31   Bad Debts Expense                    600
              Allowance for Doubtful Accounts            600
              To increase the asset valuation
              account to the estimated
              uncollectible account.
```

A portion of the information for the following partial statement of financial position is taken from the preceding data.

(Ch. 9)

GNU CORPORATION
Partial Statement of Financial Position
December 31, 1976

Assets

Current Assets		
Cash		$ 3,200
Accounts Receivable	$25,000	
Deduct Allowance for Doubtful Accounts	750	24,250
Notes Receivable		$18,000

Promissory notes receivable arising from the sale of merchandise may also prove to be uncollectible. The amount due from the customer on a dishonored note is removed from Notes Receivable and transferred to Accounts Receivable. The amount will remain in the Accounts Receivable account until it either is collected or is determined to be uncollectible and written off in the usual manner. When notes receivable specifically arise from the sale of merchandise, the current provision for estimated bad debts losses should be adequate to cover outstanding notes receivable and accounts receivable. The following partial statement of financial position presentation shows that the allowance covers Notes Receivable and Accounts Receivable jointly.

GNU CORPORATION
Partial Statement of Financial Position
December 31, 1976

Assets

Current Assets		
Cash		$ 3,200
Accounts Receivable	$25,000	
Notes Receivable	18,000	
Total	$43,000	
Deduct Allowance for Doubtful Accounts and Notes	750	42,250

Writing Off Uncollectible Accounts

When it is decided that a customer's account is definitely uncollectible, the amount due should be written off. Assuming that on February 15, 1977, the Gnu Corporation definitely determined that the account of a customer, Joseph Sacks, is uncollectible, the entry to record the write-off is:

1977			
Feb. 15	Allowance for Doubtful Accounts	50	
	Accounts Receivable—Joseph Sacks		50

This entry has no effect on the net realizable value of the receivables; it only adjusts the balances of the two reciprocal accounts. The entry does not affect expenses, because no expense was incurred on February 15, 1977; the expense was recorded by the adjusting entry of December 31, 1976. Assume that immediately before this entry was made, the books of the Gnu Corporation showed the following balances:

Accounts Receivable	$25,000
Allowance for Doubtful Accounts (credit)	750

When the entry to write of Sacks's account is posted, the result is:

	Balances Before Write-Off	Write-Off	Balances After Write-Off
Accounts Receivable	$25,000	$50	$24,950
Allowance for Doubtful Accounts	750	50	700
Estimated Realizable Value	$24,250		$24,250

This points up the fact that since the loss was recorded in the period when the sale was made, the subsequent write-off does not change assets, liabilities, or stockholders' equity.

Recovery of Bad Debts

An account that is written off as uncollectible may later be recovered in part or in full. In that event, the entry that was made to write off the account is reversed to the extent of the amount recovered or expected to be recovered. Assuming that Joseph Sacks settles with his creditors for 50 cents on the dollar and that a check for $25 is received, the required journal entries are:

1977			
Nov. 15	Accounts Receivable—Joseph Sacks	25	
	Allowance for Doubtful Accounts		25
	To restore the collectible portion of the account previously written off.		
	Cash	25	
	Accounts Receivable—Joseph Sacks		25
	To record payment received.		

The debit and the credit to Accounts Receivable—Joseph Sacks cancel each other, but they are necessary if a complete record of all transactions with the customer is to be maintained. Such a record may be of considerable aid if further extension of credit to Joseph Sacks comes up for consideration at some future date.

CORRECTION OF ERRORS IN ALLOWANCE FOR DOUBTFUL ACCOUNTS

Because of changing economic conditions and the fact that the percentage is based on past losses, errors can and do occur. Assume, for example, that the accountant of the Fountainhead Corporation, after analyzing sales and accounts receivable, determined the following information:

1. Correct bad debts expense for 1976, $4,000.
2. Actual balance in Allowance for Doubtful Accounts before adjustment, $1,000 debit balance.
3. Correct balance which should be in Allowance for Doubtful Accounts before adjustment, $100 credit balance.
4. Cumulative error as a result of past understatement of Allowance for Doubtful Accounts, $1,100.
5. Required balance in Allowance for Doubtful Accounts, $4,100.

The adjusting entry to record the bad debts expense for 1976 and to correct the error in the Allowance for Doubtful Accounts is:

1976			
Dec. 31	Corrections of Prior Years' Income	1,100	
	Bad Debts Expense	4,000	
	Allowance for Doubtful Accounts		5,100
	To correct a material underestimate of uncollectibles and to provide for an adequate allowance balance.		

After the foregoing information is posted to the Allowance for Doubtful Accounts, its balance will yield the estimated correct amount needed for future uncollectibles, $4,100. The correction account is considered to be an ordinary income statement deduction from revenue in arriving at net income.

Allowance for Doubtful Accounts					
1976			1976		
Dec. 31	Balance before Adjustment	1,000	Dec. 31	Adjustment	5,100
				4,100	

Direct Write-Offs in Period of Discovery

A company that uses the direct write-off method postpones recognition of a bad debts expense until the receivable is definitely known to be uncollectible. In this case, an Allowance for Doubtful Accounts is *not* used, and no end-of-period adjusting entry for estimated losses is made. The February 15, 1977, entry on the books of the Gnu Corporation to remove Joseph Sacks's account in full under the direct write-off method is:

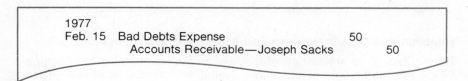

```
1977
Feb. 15   Bad Debts Expense                      50
              Accounts Receivable—Joseph Sacks          50
```

By this method, the loss is recognized in the period of write-off rather than in the period when the sale is made. The direct write-off method, as well as the allowance method previously illustrated, is acceptable for Federal income tax reporting purposes. This method, however, does not charge each accounting period with the losses arising out of sales made in that period and therefore violates the principle of matching expenses and revenue in each accounting period.

An account previously written off in the period of discovery may be subsequently collected in part or in full. Assume again that on November 15, 1977, Sacks makes a settlement of 50 cents on the dollar and issues a check for $25. The required journal entries are:

```
1977
Nov. 15   Accounts Receivable—Joseph Sacks       25
              Bad Debts Recovered                        25
                  To restore the collectible portion of
                  the account previously written off.

      15   Cash                                   25
              Accounts Receivable—Joseph Sacks          25
                  To record payment received.
```

Bad Debts Recovered is a revenue account; its balance may be reported in the Other Revenue section of the income statement.

Comparison of the Two Recording Procedures

The two methods of recording bad debts expense are shown on page 359 in Figure 9-2, assuming the following data:

(Ch. 9)

Allowance for Doubtful Accounts (credit balance, January 1)	$ 4,200
All sales on account	410,000
Cash collections on account	395,000
Sales returns and allowances	4,000
Accounts receivable written off as uncollectible	3,950
Bad debts recovered	250
The basis for estimating bad debt losses is 1 percent of Sales minus Sales Returns and Allowances.	

Valuation Accounts for Returns and Allowances and Cash Discounts

The net realizable amount of receivables on the statement of financial position indicates the amount of collections available to the firm after allowing for bad debts losses. For example, Accounts Receivable of $15,000 and a corresponding Allowance for Doubtful Accounts of $1,000 should result in a company's collecting approximately $14,000. In reality, other deductions may be made that will decrease this amount. Typical deductions are sales returns, sales allowances, cash discounts granted to customers for prompt payments, and collection expenses.

Ideally, all these additional deductions should have corresponding valuation accounts, so that Accounts Receivable in the statement of financial position will be stated at an amount closer to the net amount that will be collected. However, such valuation accounts as Allowance for Sales Returns and Allowances and Allowance for Sales Discounts are rarely used because, as a practical matter, the adjusting entry to debit the expense account will have no significant effect on net income. Moreover, these adjustments are not recognizable for income tax purposes.

Opposite Balances in Accounts Receivable and Accounts Payable

In the accounts receivable ledger, the customers' accounts normally have debit balances. Sometimes an overpayment, a sales return, a sales allowance, or an advance payment may convert the balance into a credit.

Assume that there is a net debit balance of $14,800 in an accounts receivable ledger consisting of 100 accounts, as follows:

98 accounts with a debit balance	$15,000
2 accounts with a credit balance	200
Net debit balance of 100 accounts receivable	$14,800

The debit amount of $15,000 and the credit amount of $200 should appear on the statement of financial position as follows:

Current Assets		Current Liabilities	
Accounts Receivable	$15,000	Credit Balances in Customers' Accounts	$200

Figure 9-2 Two Methods of Accounting for Bad Debts Expense

Transactions (Jan. 1–Dec. 31, 1976)	Estimating Bad Debts Expense	Direct Write-Off

All sales on account.	Accounts
	  Receivable 410,000
	    Sales 410,000
		Accounts
		  Receivable 410,000
		    Sales 410,000

Cash received on account.	Cash 395,000
	  Accounts
	    Receivable 395,000
		Cash 395,000
		  Accounts
		    Receivable 395,000

Sales returns and allowances.	Sales Returns
	  and Allowances 4,000
	  Accounts
	    Receivable 4,000
		Sales Returns
		  and Allowances 4,000
		  Accounts
		    Receivable 4,000

Accounts receivable determined to be uncollectible.	Allowance for
	  Doubtful Accounts 3,950
	  Accounts
	    Receivable 3,950
		Bad Debts Expense 3,950
		  Accounts
		    Receivable 3,950

Bad debts recovered.	Accounts
	  Receivable 250
	    Allowance for
	    Doubtful
	    Accounts 250
	
	Cash 250
	  Accounts
	    Receivable 250
		Accounts
		  Receivable 250
		    Bad Debts
		    Recovered 250
		
		Cash 250
		  Accounts
		    Receivable 250

Adjusting entry, December 31, 1976 ($410,000 − $4,000 =$406,000; $406,000 × 0.01 = $4,060)	Bad Debts Expense 4,060
	  Allowance for
	  Doubtful
	  Accounts 4,060
		(No entry is made)

Closing entry, December 31, 1976	Sales 410,000
	  Sales Returns
	  and
	  Allowances 4,000
	  Bad Debts
	  Expense 4,060
	  Income Summary 401,940
		Sales 410,000
		Bad Debts
		Recovered 250
		  Bad Debts
		  Expense 3,950
		  Sales Returns
		  and
		  Allowances 4,000
		  Income Summary 402,300

The controlling account balance of $14,800 should not be used in the statement of financial position, because it would conceal the current liability of $200. Similarly, if the accounts payable ledger contains creditors' accounts with debit balances, the statement of financial position should show the total credit balances and the total debit balances of accounts payable. For example, if a company has a net balance in the Accounts Payable controlling account of $44,300, with certain subsidiary ledger accounts having debit balances that total $700, it should disclose this information in its statement of financial position as follows:

(Ch. 9)

Current Assets		Current Liabilities	
Debit Balances in Creditors'		Accounts Payable	$45,000
Accounts	$700		

ACCOUNTS RECEIVABLE—MANAGERIAL ANALYSIS

The manager of a business that sells on credit must watch carefully for past-due accounts and guard against possible losses. A detailed analysis of the due date of each customer's account is desirable and should be secured periodically by preparing an aging statement similar to Figure 9-1. Two guides to the overall condition of the accounts receivable are the average collection period and the receivables turnover per year. If goods are sold on terms of 2/10, n/30, the amount of accounts receivable outstanding at any time should be less than the credit sales for the last 30 days, because many of the sales will have been paid within the discount period. If allowance is made for slow-paying accounts, the receivables may represent 30 to 35 days' sales. If the receivables exceed this limitation, a careful analysis of all the accounts should be made.

To illustrate the computation of the average collection period, or number of days' sales uncollected, and the receivables turnover per year, the following data for the Morton Company are assumed:

	1977	1976	1975
Credit sales for year	$183,600	$165,600	$160,000
Trade accounts and notes receivable (net) at end of year	14,420	17,200	$ 15,000

Only receivables (accounts and notes) arising out of sales of merchandise on account are used. The balance of Allowance for Doubtful Accounts is deducted in computing the average trade receivables balance.

Figure 9-3
Managerial Analysis
of Receivables

	1977	1976
1. Net credit sales	$183,600	$165,600
2. Days in year	365	365
3. Net credit sales per day (line 1 ÷ line 2)	$503	$454
4. Average trade receivables [(balance at beginning of year + balance at end of year) ÷ 2]	15,810	16,100
Average collection period (line 4 ÷ line 3)	31 days	35 days
Receivables turnover per year (line 1 ÷ line 4)	11.6 times	10.3 times

If line 1 covered sales for a period of less than one year, then line 2 would be changed accordingly. Thus, if the sales were for a three-month period, line 2 would show 91 days (one-fourth of 365 days).

(Ch. 9)

Average collection periods vary with the line of business. Wholesalers of shoes may average 45 days, compared with grocery wholesalers, whose average is approximately 15 days. In the illustration in Figure 9-3, assuming that sales are on terms of 2/10, n/30, both years show a healthy situation, with 1977 particularly good.

The receivables turnover per year or the ratio of credit sales to receivables is calculated by dividing net credit sales by the average balance of trade receivables. In Figure 9-3, the receivables for the year 1976 have been collected at a rate of approximately 10.3 times a year. For a standard of comparison, the preceding year's rate or the industry rate may be used. An increasing turnover of receivables as exhibited in Figure 9-3 indicates an improvement and reflects a decreasing relative amount of investment of working capital in receivables.

INTERNAL CONTROL—ACCOUNTS RECEIVABLE

As in the case of cash, adequate safeguards must be established for accounts receivable. It is important that persons who maintain the accounts receivable records should not have access to cash. Recording of returns and allowances, discounts, and bad debts write-offs should be authorized by an officer and should be separated from the cash receipt and cash disbursement functions. Statements of account should be checked and mailed to customers by someone other than the accounts receivable bookkeeper. An independent check should be established to see that the statements sent to customers are in agreement with the accounts receivable records. Delinquent accounts should be reviewed periodically by a responsible official. Adequate control over receivables begins with the approved sales order and continues through the remaining stages in the credit sales process: approval of credit terms, recording of shipment, customer billing, recording of the receivable and its collection, and approval of subsequent adjustments.

In addition to the valuation standards and procedures discussed in this chapter, another valuation problem is present in the receivables that are non-interest-bearing or those which vary from the prevailing interest rate. These receivables should be discounted to the statement of financial position date by an appropriate going-market interest rate for the particular grade and quality of applicable security or receivable.[1]

Because of the short period involved, trade accounts receivable are not discounted to the statement of financial position date. In its Opinion No. 21, *Interest on Receivables and Payables,* the Accounting Principles Board, although excluding trade accounts receivable, stated that certain secured and unsecured notes, debentures, bonds, mortgage notes, equipment obligations, and some accounts receivable and accounts payable that are non-interest-bearing or have an unreasonable stated interest rate (but not trade receivables and trade payables) should be discounted to their present value. ("*Present value* is the sum of the future payments discounted to the present date at an appropriate rate of interest."[2])

In its Appendix to Opinion No. 21, the Accounting Principles Board illustrated how the disclosure of the valuation should be achieved:

Example 2—Discount presented separately

	December 31 1970	December 31 1969
Note receivable from sale of property: Non-interest-bearing note due December 31, 1975	$1,000,000	$1,000,000
Less unamortized discount based on imputed interest rate of 8%	320,000	370,000
Note receivable less unamortized discount	$680,000	$630,000

The unamortized discount would be written off over the life of the note as a recognition of periodic interest expense in such a way as to result in a constant rate of interest when applied to the amount outstanding at the beginning of any given period.[3]

---

[1] AICPA, *APB Accounting Principles,* vol. 2 (Chicago: Commerce Clearing House, Inc., 1973), p. 6702.
[2] *Ibid.,* p. 6702.
[3] *Ibid.,* p. 6704.

A type of input/output device that is capable of storing large quantities of data is a magnetic disk. A computer system with such a file would be appropriate for an organization with a large number of customer accounts. Information is recorded on a disk file in a manner similar to magnetic tape recording, although the disk file has a very important advantage—in a disk file every record may be addressed directly by the central processing unit (CPU). When customers' accounts are maintained with a disk system, any single account may be updated or its status ascertained without passing sequentially through the file to locate it.

A typical disk system is illustrated in Figure A9-1.

Figure A9-1   System 3 Disk System

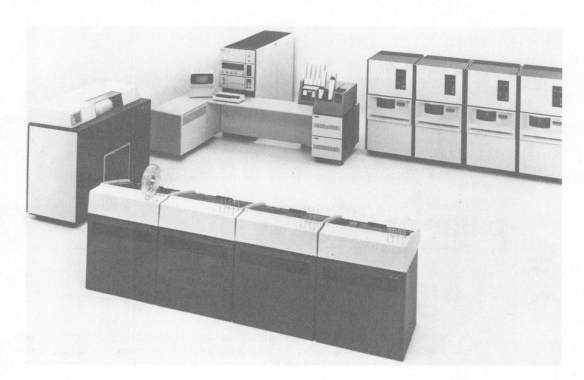

In such a system, debits to the subsidiary ledger are posted simultaneously with the processing run that prepares customer invoices. The procedure for this is flow-charted as follows:

MEASUREMENT
AND CONTROL
OF RECEIVABLES

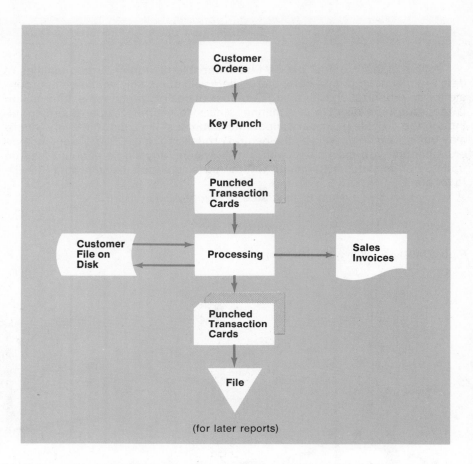

```
                    ┌─────────────┐
                    │  Customer   │
                    │   Orders    │
                    └──────┬──────┘
                           │
                           ▼
                    ┌─────────────┐
                    │  Key Punch  │
                    └──────┬──────┘
                           │
                           ▼
                    ┌─────────────┐
                    │  Punched    │
                    │ Transaction │
                    │   Cards     │
                    └──────┬──────┘
                           │
  ┌──────────┐            ▼              ┌──────────┐
  │ Customer │      ┌──────────┐         │  Sales   │
  │ File on  │◄────►│Processing│────────►│ Invoices │
  │   Disk   │      └────┬─────┘         └──────────┘
  └──────────┘           │
                         ▼
                    ┌─────────────┐
                    │  Punched    │
                    │ Transaction │
                    │   Cards     │
                    └──────┬──────┘
                           │
                           ▼
                        ╲ File ╱
                         ╲────╱
                          ╲  ╱
                           ╲╱

                  (for later reports)
```

Another product of each customer-order-processing run is the dollar total figure to form the journal entry:

Accounts Receivable	xxx	
Sales		xxx

Amounts of collections on account would also be punched into cards daily, and posted to the subsidiary ledger recorded on the disk file with another computer run. A by-product of this processing run is the dollar total for the journal entry:

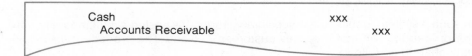

Cash	xxx	
Accounts Receivable		xxx

Figure A9-2 Aged Trial Balance

CUST. NO.	CUSTOMER NAME	TELEPHONE NUMBER	LAST PAY MO	LAST PAY DA	LAST PAY YR	CREDIT LIMIT	TOTAL OUTSTANDING	CURRENT AMOUNT	OVERDUE ACCOUNTS 30 DAYS	OVERDUE ACCOUNTS 60 DAYS	OVERDUE ACCOUNTS 90 & OVER
108	ALLEN & CO.	415-378-1089	2	16	— —	$15,000	$7,296.35	$6,919.77	$ 376.58		
165	ANDERSON AUTO SUPPLY	408-286-6741	1	28	— —	2,500	1,665.49	1,665.49			
178	ANDREWS AND SONS INC	408-262-2074	2	05	— —	750	146.64			$ 146.64	
189	ARGONAUT ENGINEERING	415-867-2506	12	27	— —	2,000	3,125.41	2,111.30	611.54	312.13	$ 90.44
247	BERKLEY PAPER CO	408-251-4189	2	21	— —	6,300	5,289.00	1,185.50	2,652.45	1,400.05	51.00
252	BEST DISTRIBUTION CO	408-296-1667	10	06	— —	1,000	765.44	3.25			762.19
	FINAL TOTALS						$35,241.33*	$21,085.31*	$5,601.57*	$3,831.82*	$998.63*

LAURENTIAN INDUSTRIES INC — AGED TRIAL BALANCE — PAGE 1 — DATE 7/17/— —

Courtesy of International Business Machines Corporation

When the subsidiary ledger is maintained by computer, it is possible to obtain at any time a printout of all accounts with an aging schedule in detail and with the total balance due. Such a report is shown in Figure A9-2.

GLOSSARY

Aging Schedule A columnar work sheet showing the individual receivables by age groups according to time elapsed from due date. The individual age groups are also totaled and a percentage analysis is computed to aid in determining the allowance for doubtful accounts.

Allowance for Doubtful Accounts A valuation account related to accounts receivable showing the amount of estimated uncollectible accounts as of a *given date*.

Average Collection Period The average length of time it takes to collect all trade receivables; it is computed by dividing the average trade receivables by the average credit sales per day.

Bad Debts Expense The account showing the estimated uncollectible credit sales made in a given time period, that is, for one year if the accounting period is a year.

Bad Debts Recovered An account which is credited for the recovery of an account receivable previously written off under the direct write-off method.

Nontrade Receivable Claims against individuals or companies arising from money lent, from deposits made, and from other sources not involving the sale of merchandise or ordinary services.

Notes Receivable Claims against individuals or companies supported by formal written promises to pay. A notes receivable may be either a trade note or a nontrade note.

Trade Receivables Claims against customers arising from sales of merchandise or ordinary services.

Trade Receivables Turnover The number of times each year that the trade receivables are collected; it is computed by dividing net credit sales by the average balance of trade receivables.

(Ch. 9)

Valuation Account A contra asset account; an account which is related to and off-sets, in whole or in part, one or more other accounts. A contra asset account should be deducted from the asset to which it is related to determine a carrying or book value.

Q9-1. List eight different categories of receivables and state the probable financial position statement classification of each. The following format is suggested:

Receivable Item	Probable Financial Position Statement Classification

Q9-2. Discuss the general principle of the valuation of trade receivables.

Q9-3. (a) Explain the function of the Allowance for Doubtful Accounts account. (b) What methods may be used to estimate the allowance for doubtful accounts? (c) How is Allowance for Doubtful Accounts shown on the statement of financial position?

Q9-4. Distinguish between the income statement approach and the statement of financial position approach in estimating the bad debts expense.

Q9-5. A company attempting to state its accounts receivable at their net realizable value may have to establish accounts other than the Allowance for Doubtful Accounts. Name three other valuation accounts for Accounts Receivable.

Q9-6. Briefly contrast the direct write-off method with the allowance method in accounting for bad debts losses.

Q9-7. How would you interpret each entry in the following account?

Allowance for Doubtful Accounts

1976 Mar.	10		J58	2,520	1975 Dec.	31		J50	7,300
1977 Jan.	5		J68	1,500	1976 Dec.	31		J65	6,840
					1977 Apr.	6		J70	1,110

Q9-8. The following entry was made to record the recovery of a bad debt:

| Cash | 450 | |
| Allowance for Doubtful Accounts | | 450 |

Discuss the validity of this method of recording the recovery.

Q9-9. (a) Discuss the reasons for credit balances occurring in Accounts Receivable accounts. (b) How are such balances presented in the statement of financial position?

Q9-10. The Dauderis Company, which had accounts receivable of $59,400 and an allowance for doubtful accounts of $3,400 on January 1, 1976, wrote off in 1976 a past-due account of N. K. Goode for $400. (a) What effect will the write-off have on the total current assets of the company immediately before and after the write-off? (b) on net income for 1976? Explain.

E9-1. The Justa Company maintains a controlling account entitled Receivables, the balance of which at December 31, 1976, was $63,280. The subsidiary ledger and other information reveal the following:

a. 410 trade accounts (debit balances)	$46,000
b. 5 trade accounts (credit balances)	720
c. 6 trade notes	12,000
d. 3 loans to the president and vice presidents	6,000
e. Allowance for Doubtful Accounts	4,000

Show how this information should be reported on the statement of financial position.

E9-2. On December 31, 1976, after adjusting entries had been made, Allowance for Doubtful Accounts had a credit balance of $11,200. During 1976, accounts receivable of $9,800 were written off and accounts receivable totaling $1,200, which were previously written off as uncollectible, were recovered. On January 1, 1976, Allowance for Doubtful Accounts had a credit balance of $10,600. The losses from uncollectible accounts are estimated to be 2% of credit sales. Calculate the credit sales for 1976.

E9-3. The Zeller Company, which uses an Allowance for Doubtful Accounts, had the following transactions involving worthless accounts in 1976 and 1977.

1976
Dec. 31   Recorded bad debts expense of $2,650.

1977
Mar.   6   Wrote off N. K. Garm's account of $610 as uncollectible.
Apr.   12   Wrote off J. J. Jones's account of $680 as uncollectible.
Sept.   6   Recovered $680 from J. J. Jones.

Journalize the transactions.

E9-4. The Watauga Company uses the direct write-off method of accounting for bad debts. It had the following transactions involving worthless accounts in 1976:

1976
Mar.   2   Wrote off Joseph Sack's account of $415 as uncollectible. The merchandise had been sold in 1975.
July   6   Wrote off Herman White's account of $475 as uncollectible.
Dec. 10   Recovered $275 from Joseph Sack.

Journalize the transactions.

E9-5. The Tyrrell Trading Company had charge sales of $610,000 during 1976 and accounts receivable of $60,500 and a credit balance of $250 in Allowance for Doubtful Accounts at the end of the year.

Record the bad debts expense for the year, using each of the following methods for the estimate: (a) Allowance for Doubtful Accounts is to be increased to

4% of Accounts Receivable. (b) Bad debts expense is estimated to be 0.45% of charge sales. (c) Allowance for Doubtful Accounts is to be increased to $3,700, as indicated by an aging schedule. Which method would you choose and why?

E9-6. The trial balance of the Watson Company included the following accounts on August 31, 1976, the end of its fiscal year:

Accounts Receivable	$ 58,000
Allowance for Doubtful Accounts (credit)	250
Sales	390,000

Uncollectible accounts are estimated at 5% of Accounts Receivable. (a) Make the adjusting entry to record the bad debts expense. (b) State the bad debts expense for the year. (c) Show the presentation of Accounts Receivable and Allowance for Doubtful Accounts in the August 31, 1976, position statement. (d) Give the entry to write off the account of an insolvent customer, J. K. Cheshire, for $805.

E9-7. The accounts receivable ledger of the Saffelle Distributing Company shows the following data on December 31, 1976. The general ledger showed a $200 debit balance in Allowance for Doubtful Accounts before adjustments.

Name of Customer	Invoice Date	Amount
Monsanto Sand Company	May 2, 1976	$ 1,200
Naughton Company	August 15, 1976	671
Peters' Plants	December 8, 1976	385
	October 2, 1976	720
Temptation Seedling Company	March 3, 1976	565
Saundrin Company	November 11, 1976	825
Young Fruittrees Company	November 20, 1976	314
	September 4, 1976	484
	July 10, 1976	950
(Others)	December 5, 1976	40,000
Terms of sale are n/30.		

a. Prepare an analysis of accounts receivable by age.
b. Compute the estimated loss based on the following fixed percentages:

		Estimated Percentage Uncollectible
Accounts not due		1.0
Accounts past due:	1–30 days	1.5
	31–60 days	2.5
	61–90 days	8.5
	91–120 days	10.0
	121–365 days	30.0

c. Record the bad debts expense.

(Ch. 9)

E9-8. The Cash account page in the general ledger of the Watsu Corporation has been temporarily misplaced. The following data are available:

	December 31		Year
	1976	1975	1976
Accounts Receivable, Trade	$83,000	$69,000	
Allowance for Doubtful Accounts	6,200	4,800	
Sales			$715,000
Sales Discounts			12,550

During 1976 accounts receivable of $4,700 were written off as uncollectible and one account of $750, written off in 1974, was collected and recorded in the following manner:

Accounts Receivable	750	
Allowance for Doubtful Accounts		750
Cash	750	
Accounts Receivable		750

Compute the cash received from customers during 1976.

E9-9. The following transactions of the First Colony Company occurred during 1976:

1976
Jan. 2 Sold to Borden Combs merchandise with a list price of $8,000 subject to a trade discount of 20%, 10%, and 10%; terms, 2/10, n/30.

10 Received a check from Borden Combs in settlement of his account.

20 Sold merchandise worth $5,000 to Dennis McClees on account; terms, n/10.

Feb. 2 Received a 9%, 3-month note from McClees in settlement of his account.

May 1 McClees dishonored his note. The company charged the note and interest to Accounts Receivable. (*Hint:* Debit Accounts Receivable for face plus total interest.)

a. Journalize the transactions. Use the gross methods of recording receivables and handling cash discounts.
b. What is the equivalent lump-sum trade discount to a 20%, 10%, and 10% chain trade discount? Show computations.

E9-10. The records of the Nabors Company show that amounts due from customers were $400,000 and $460,000 at the beginning and the end of the year 1976, respectively, and that sales for that period were $3,500,000. What conclusions can be drawn regarding the collection of accounts receivable, assuming (a) that terms of sale are 2/10, n/30; (b) that terms of sale are 2/10, n/40; (c) that terms of sale are 2/10, n/40, and 25% of the sales are for cash?

E9-11. The Edenton Company sells on terms of 2/10, 1/20, n/60. Approximately 40% of its sales are for cash. The Accounts Receivable account shows an average balance of $62,768 for 1976. Total sales for the year were $730,400. What is the average collection period?

DP9-1. (*Use of Allowance for Doubtful Accounts*) The following transactions of the Faison Company occurred in 1975, 1976, and 1977. The company uses the estimating procedure in accounting for bad debts.

1975
Dec. 31   Recorded bad debts expense of $5,600 for 1975.

1976
Mar. 12   Wrote off N. O. Goode's account of $720 as uncollectible.

Nov. 8   Wrote off various other accounts of $3,850 as uncollectible.

Dec. 31   Recorded bad debts expense of $5,460 for 1976.

1977
Feb. 9   N. O. Goode remitted $520 of the amount he owed the firm and agreed to pay the remainder in 30 days.

Required: Journalize the transactions.

DP9-2. (*Direct write-off method*) The following transactions of the Goodwin Company occurred in 1976 and 1977. The company uses the direct write-off method of accounting for bad debts.

1976
Jan. 12   Wrote off B. E. Wiry's account of $319 as uncollectible.

Nov. 13   Wrote off I. M. Blokely's account of $219 as uncollectible.
     20   Recovered the $319 from B. E. Wiry.

Dec. 13   Wrote off R. M. Saints' account of $560 as uncollectible.

1977
Mar. 10   Recovered the $219 from I. M. Blokely.

Required: Journalize the transactions.

DP9-3. (*Adjusting entries for bad debts*) The partial trial balance of the Ruth Company at December 31, 1976, before any adjustments are made, is given below:

RUTH COMPANY
Partial Trial Balance
December 31, 1976

	Debits	Credits
Accounts Receivable	$120,000	
Notes Receivable	45,000	
Allowance for Doubtful Accounts and Notes	900	
Sales		$163,750
Sales Returns and Allowances	3,750	

Required: Prepare the adjusting entries for the bad debts expense under the following assumptions: (a) Allowance for Doubtful Accounts and Notes is to be increased to 3% of trade receivables; (b) the bad debts expense is estimated to be 1.5% of net sales.

P9-1. *(Accounting policy decision problem)* The sales revenue section of the annual income statements of four different companies are shown below.

	W Company	X Company	Y Company	Z Company
Sales	$600,000	$20,000,000	$12,000,000	$14,000,000
Deduct: Sales Discounts	$ –0–	$ 300,000	$ 960,000	$ 250,000
Sales Returns and Allowances	–0–	5,000,000	40,000	50,000
Bad Debts	–0–	–0–	–0–	120,000
Transportation Out	–0–	–0–	–0–	100,000
Total Offsets	$ –0–	$ 5,300,000	$ 1,000,000	$ 520,000
Net Sales	$600,000	$14,700,000	$11,000,000	$13,480,000

Required: Identify the unusual situations that you can discover in the four partial income statements. Briefly explain why you think each situation is unusual and whether you think the method of reporting is acceptable by current accounting theory.

P9-2. On January 1, 1976, the balance of Allowance for Doubtful Accounts of the Ricky Company was $3,200. During 1976, uncollectible accounts totaling $3,900 were written off. The company collected $500 on one of these accounts after it had been written off. The balance of Accounts Receivable on December 31, 1976, was $95,000.

Required: Make the journal entries (a) to charge off the worthless accounts during 1976, (b) to record the collection of the $500, and (c) to record the adjusting entry on December 31, 1976, for the bad debts expense. Assume that uncollectible accounts average 5% of the uncollected accounts receivable.

P9-3. *(Accounting policy decision problem)* The Blake Company uses a cash receipts journal, a cash payments journal, a single-column purchases journal, a single-column sales journal, and a two-column general journal. The Accounts Receivable account in the general ledger at June 30, 1976, is given below (posting references have been omitted).

Accounts Receivable

1976			1976		
June 1	Balance	47,000	June 5		3,000
25		3,004	10		250
30		52,400	28		3,004
			30		39,500

During the month, the general journal was used to record transactions with only two customers. The subsidiary ledger accounts of these two customers are shown below.

MEASUREMENT
AND CONTROL
OF RECEIVABLES

Billy Bones						
1976						
June	1	Balance	✔			(600) Cr.
	6		S2	1,400		800
	10		J4		250	550
Tally Rand						
1976						
June	1	Balance	✔			3,000
	5	(20-day note)	J4		3,000	–0–
	25		CP6	3,004		3,004
	28		J4		3,004	–0–

Required:

1. Explain the $600 credit balance on June 1 in Billy Bones's account.
2. What would the posting references for the June 30 entries in the Accounts Receivable controlling account be?
3. What should be the total of the schedule of accounts receivable on June 30?
4. Explain the transaction that resulted in the debit of $3,004 on June 25 in Tally Rand's account.
5. State in narrative form the transactions that resulted in each of the following credits to the Accounts Receivable controlling account: June 5, $3,000; June 10, $250; June 28, $3,004.

P9-4. The Allowance for Doubtful Accounts of the Biltmore Company showed a credit balance of $450 on December 31, 1976, before adjustments were made. The bad debts expense for 1976 is estimated at 3% of the charge sales of $200,000 for the year.

The following transactions occurred during the next two years:

1977
May 1 Wrote off Gordo Durham's $945 account as uncollectible.

Oct. 15 Wrote off Bloke Gordon's account of $1,800 as uncollectible.

Nov. 30 Received a check for $200 in final settlement of Gordo Durham's account written off in May. He had been adjudged bankrupt by the courts.

Dec. 31 An analysis of accounts receivable by age indicated that accounts doubtful of collection totaled $4,650.

1978
Aug. 21 Wrote off J. M. Tonto's $1,950 account as uncollectible.

Dec. 31 Estimated that uncollectible accounts receivable totaled $3,750.

Required:

1. Record in general journal form transactions and events including adjusting entry for December 31, 1976.
2. Post to a T account for Allowance for Doubtful Accounts. Rule and balance the account at the end of each year.

P9-5. The balance of the Accounts Receivable account of the Ramseur Company at December 31, 1976, was $74,460. Two customers' accounts in the subsidiary ledger show credit balances of $3,200 and $1,800.

Required:

1. What amount for Accounts Receivable would be shown under Current Assets on the position statement?
2. How would the credit balances in the customers' accounts be disclosed?

P9-6. The Accounts Receivable controlling account of the Warm Springs Corporation shows a balance of $370,500 on June 30, 1976. A summary of the analysis of accounts receivable by age shows accounts outstanding from the date of the invoice as follows:

Accounts not due		$300,000
Accounts past due:	1–30 days	25,000
	31–60 days	30,000
	61–150 days	12,500
	151 days and over	3,000
	Total	$370,500

On June 30, Allowance for Doubtful Accounts has a debit balance of $310 before adjustments. The adjustment of the Allowance account is to be based on the following schedule of percentages estimated uncollectible:

Accounts not due		½ of 1%
Accounts past due:	1–30 days	4%
	31–60 days	5%
	61–150 days	15%
	151 days and over	40%

Required:

1. Prepare the necessary adjusting entry.
2. Prepare a partial position statement, showing Accounts Receivable and Allowance for Doubtful Accounts.

P9-7. The accounts receivable ledger of the Redoon Company showed the following information on March 31, 1977:

Celeste Jones						
1976						
Aug.	12		S27	4,000		4,000
Sept.	10		S33	800		4,800
	30		CR15		4,000	800
Oct.	12		S45	1,600		2,400
Nov.	4		S52	500		2,900
Dec.	10		CR27		600	2,300
1977						
Jan.	12		S6	700		3,000
	13		CR4		1,600	1,400
	15		S7	850		2,250
	17	Allowance on 1/15 invoice	J2		105	2,145

Diane Lawson

1976							
Nov.	12			S54	2,000		2,000
Dec.	12			CR28		1,000	1,000
1977							
Jan.	29			S9	800		1,800
Mar.	10			S17	500		2,300
	31			CR11		500	1,800

Katherine Melton

1976							
Dec.	12			S56	5,000		5,000
1977							
Jan.	12	Note		J2		4,000	1,000
Feb.	26			S14	2,000		3,000
Mar.	26			S22	3,000		6,000

Ruth Rowdee

1976							
Aug.	1			S24	1,000		1,000
Oct.	12			S45	200		1,200
1977							
Jan.	2	Return		J2		400	800
Feb.	3			S10	700		1,500
	12			S13	300		1,800
Mar.	30			CR11		800	1,000

Required:

1. Prepare an analysis of accounts receivable by age as of March 31, 1977. Assume that the terms of sale are n/30.
2. Make the adjusting entry for the bad debts expense on the basis of the age of the accounts as follows:

Accounts not due		1%
Accounts past due:	1–30 days	2½%
	31–60 days	8%
	61–90 days	15%
	91 days and over	40%

On March 31, 1977, Allowance for Doubtful Accounts has a debit balance of $350 before adjustments.

P9-8. On December 31, 1976, David Jaye's trial balance showed the following:

Accounts Receivable	$82,500
Allowance for Doubtful Accounts (debit)	200

After an analysis of the accounts receivable, it was estimated that the accounts doubtful of collection would amount to $4,200.

During the year 1977, the following transactions occurred:

a. Sales on account were $410,000.

b. Accounts written off as uncollectible totaled $4,010.

c. Collections from customers on account were $350,000. This amount included a receipt of $200 that had been written off during the year as uncollectible.

On December 31, 1977, the accounts doubtful of collection were estimated at $3,650.

Required:

1. Set up T accounts for Accounts Receivable and Allowance for Doubtful Accounts, post the balances as of December 31, 1976, and make the entries for 1976 and 1977 directly into the T accounts.
2. Compute the bad debts expense deduction in the income statement for the year 1977, using: (a) the direct write-off method, (b) the allowance for doubtful accounts method.

P9-9. During November and early December 1976, the Hiller Sales Company had the following sales and receivables transactions. All sales were made on account and carried terms of 2/10, n/30.

1976
Sept. 1   Sold merchandise to T. T. Sousa for $415 on invoice No. 1001.

2   Sold merchandise to R. R. Foley for $2,100 on invoice No. 1002.

7   Credited R. R. Foley for returned merchandise with an invoice price of $300.

9   Received a check from T. T. Sousa for the amount due on invoice No. 1001.

10   Sold merchandise to the First Colony Company for $550 on invoice No. 1003.

13   Received $215.60 in cash from the First Colony Company in partial payment of invoice No. 1003. Discounts are allowed on partial payments.

14   Received a check for the amount due from R. R. Foley.

15   Sold merchandise to the Frying Pan Company for $4,000 on invoice No. 1004.

23   Received a check from the Frying Pan Company for the amount due on invoice No. 1004.

30   Sold merchandise to the Alligator Company for $2,650 on invoice No. 1005.

30   Sold merchandise to the Brickhouse Company for $2,500 on invoice No. 1006.

30   Estimated the bad debts expense for September to be 3.5% of charge sales less sales returns and allowances.

Oct.   8   Received a notice that the First Colony Company had been adjudged bankrupt. The balance of its account was therefore regarded as uncollectible.

Required:

1. Journalize the transactions in general journal form.
2. Post all entries to the Accounts Receivable controlling and subsidiary accounts.
3. Prepare a schedule of accounts receivable at September 30, 1976.

Measurement and Control of Inventory

10

Inventory in a wholesale or retail business—that is, a nonmanufacturing business—is generally understood to mean goods owned by the business for sale to customers. Alternative terms are *merchandise* and *merchandise inventory.* Up to this point in the text, the amount of the merchandise inventory was specified and, therefore, assumed to be correct. The factors involved in arriving at the value of the inventory—classification of items, determination of physical quantities on hand, and techniques of assigning costs—were not stated. These factors, however, are indispensable in valuing the merchandise inventory for the preparation of financial statements.

IMPORTANCE OF INVENTORY VALUATION

The proper valuation, or *costing,* of the merchandise inventory is of considerable importance for income measurement and position statement usefulness. The inventory is often large in proportion to the other items in the financial statements; a misstatement of the inventory will cause a misstatement of the cost of goods sold, gross margin on sales, and net income for the period in which the error occurred, and will also misstate current assets and stockholders' equity as of the end of that period. Furthermore, since the ending inventory of one accounting period is the beginning inventory of the next period, any overstatement or understatement will also misstate the cost of goods sold, gross margin on sales, and net income of the next period.

The following information is taken from the income statements of a retail store for 1975 and 1976:

	1976		1975	
Sales		$300,000		$250,000
Cost of Goods Sold				
Beginning Inventory	$ 90,000		$ 80,000	
Purchases	150,000		120,000	
Total	$240,000		$200,000	
Deduct Ending Inventory	105,000	135,000	90,000	110,000
Gross Margin on Sales		$165,000		$140,000
Expenses		130,000		120,000
Net Income		$ 35,000		$ 20,000

If it is assumed that the ending inventory for 1975 should have been valued at $85,000 rather than $90,000, the effect of the error on the income statements is evident from the corrected statements.

	1976		1975	
Sales		$300,000		$250,000
Cost of Goods Sold				
Beginning Inventory	$ 85,000		$ 80,000	
Purchases	150,000		120,000	
Total	$235,000		$200,000	
Deduct Ending Inventory	105,000	130,000	85,000	115,000
Gross Margin on Sales		$170,000		$135,000
Expenses		130,000		120,000
Net Income		$ 40,000		$ 15,000

The $5,000 overstatement of the ending inventory in 1975 resulted in the following errors of $5,000 in the two income statements:

	1976	1975
Cost of Goods Sold	Overstated	Understated
Gross Margin	Understated	Overstated
Net Income	Understated	Overstated

Since the misstatements cancel each other, the error has no overall effect on the two-year span covered by the statements. That fact, however, does not diminish the seriousness of an inventory valuation error. The interpretation and analysis of the income statement for each period may influence some basic management decisions. Since both income statements are in error, their reciprocal canceling effect does not cancel erroneous interpretations caused by reliance on two incorrect statements.

BASIS OF INVENTORY VALUATION

Inventories are recorded at cost. The term *cost* includes all expenditures "incurred in bringing an article to its existing condition and location."[1] Cost consists of the invoice price of the merchandise (less purchase discounts) plus transportation in, insurance while in transit, and any other expenditures made by the buyer to get the merchandise to his place of business. In the interest of simplifying the clerical task of prorating these other costs to the various items of inventory purchased, they are frequently carried in separate accounts, and the Purchases account shows only the invoice price. If these amounts are significant in relation to the invoice price of the merchandise, a proportionate part should be added to the cost of the goods on hand at the end of the period. The cost of the inventory may be determined in several different ways. The method used to determine cost should be the one that "most clearly reflects periodic income,"[2] with due regard to its usefulness as a measure of financial position and its effect on relevant position statement ratios, its effect on current and subsequent income statements, and possible impact on pricing and purchasing policies.

The term *value* is defined as "the amount at which an item is stated, in accordance with the accounting principles related to that item."[3] "Since accounting is predominantly based on cost, the proper uses of the word *value* in accounting are largely restricted to the statement of items at cost, or at modifications of cost."[4]

The accountant, therefore, usually expresses *value* in terms of *cost*.

Valuation of Assets at Cost

There are, of course, other concepts of value; the accountant's valuation is *historical,* or prior, cost, which is objective, being subject to measurement. It is this objectivity which accounts for the predominance of historical cost as a valuation basis. The economist, on the other hand, relates value to current and anticipated prices for better comparability and matching of expired costs with revenue. The distinction between these two concepts is especially important during periods of rapidly rising prices with their concomitant effect on financial statement valuations. Many persons in and out of the profession question the usefulness of cost as a valuation concept when prices are unstable. The *Report of the Study Group on the Objectives of Financial Statements* (AICPA, October 1973) states that "financial statements might contain data based on a combina-

[1] AICPA, *APB Accounting Principles,* vol. 2 (Chicago: Commerce Clearing House, Inc.), 1973, p. 6014.
[2] *Ibid.,* p. 6015.
[3] *Ibid.,* p. 9509.
[4] *Loc. cit.*

tion of valuation bases," that "management is accountable for the values of assets as well as for their costs," and that "current values should also be reported when they differ significantly from historical cost." (See Chapter 27, pages 1007 and 1008, for a discussion of valuation techniques.)

INVENTORY SYSTEMS

Two systems for determining inventory quantities on hand are in use: periodic (physical count) and perpetual (continuous record).

Periodic Inventory. With the periodic inventory system, the value of the inventory for statement of financial position presentation and for the determination of the cost of goods sold is determined at the end of each annual accounting period by a complete physical count and pricing of all inventory items. (Estimated gross margin rates described later in this chapter may be used to determine the cost of goods sold during interim periods.) Acquired goods not on hand are assumed to have been sold. Merchandise losses through misappropriation, breakage, or other causes are included in the cost of goods sold as a deduction from revenue, although these goods do not actually create revenue. Small retail businesses often use the periodic system as a matter of expediency, since it does not require a continuous record of inventory balances.

Perpetual Inventory. The perpetual inventory system provides for a continuous book inventory of items on hand; it is a method of record keeping. An inventory record card, often called a *stock record card,* or a record in a computer storage device is kept for each inventory item acquired; when units are purchased or sold, the inventory record for the item must be adjusted accordingly to show the quantity on hand at any time. The maintenance of continuous inventory records does not preclude the need for a complete annual physical inventory. Some companies that use the perpetual inventory system take physical counts of portions of the inventory during the course of the year to test whether the records are in agreement with quantities actually on hand. This practice may be followed, instead of taking a complete annual physical inventory.

A perpetual inventory may be costly to maintain, especially when the inventory includes numerous items of small value. A company may, therefore, maintain continuous records for only certain classifications of its inventory. A hardware supply company, for example, may find it feasible to use the perpetual inventory system only for items with a high unit selling price and the periodic inventory system for all other items.

PERPETUAL AND PERIODIC INVENTORY SYSTEMS COMPARED

With the periodic inventory system assumed in the preceding chapters, the beginning inventory is shown in a Merchandise Inventory account, and all purchases are entered in a Purchases account. The cost of goods sold does not appear as an account balance in the general ledger but is determined only after the physical inventory is taken at the end of the period. With the perpetual inventory system, however, the beginning inventory and all purchases are shown as debits in a Merchandise Inventory (asset) account. The cost of all goods sold is debited to a Cost of Goods Sold Account and credited to the Merchandise Inventory account. The balance of the Merchandise Inventory account is the cost of the goods remaining in the inventory, provided there have been no shrinkages or other losses. The Merchandise Inventory account is a controlling account supported by a subsidiary inventory ledger made up of inventory record cards for all items.

The entries in summary journal form for both systems are shown below.

Periodic Inventory

(1)

Purchases	254.00	
Accounts Payable		254.00
To record April purchases.		

(2)

Accounts Receivable	467.50	
Sales		467.50
To record April sales of 85 units at $5.50 each.		

Perpetual Inventory

(1)

Merchandise Inventory	254.00	
Accounts Payable		254.00
To record April purchases.		

(2)

Accounts Receivable	467.50	
Sales		467.50
To record April sales of 85 units at $5.50 each.		

(3)

Cost of Goods Sold	214.00	
Merchandise Inventory		214.00
To record the cost of 85 units sold (amounts from Issued column, Figure 10–1).		

After entries 1 and 3 under the perpetual inventory system are posted, the affected accounts in the general ledger appear as shown below.

Cost of Goods Sold

| April 30 | 214 | |

Merchandise Inventory

| April 1 Balance | 44 | April 30 Cost of Goods sold 214 |
| 30 Purchases | 254 | |

The Merchandise Inventory account shows a balance of $84, which is the cost of goods on hand to be reported in the statement of financial position for April 30.

The perpetual inventory cards (Figures 10-1, 10-2, and 10-3) combine a system of control of inventory quantities with a method of assigning costs. Some companies employ the perpetual inventory card form only for controlling quantities; receipts, issues, and running balances are recorded, but the procedure for determining the cost of the inventory is the same as with the periodic system. One advantage of using perpetual inventory cards is that financial statements may be prepared without taking a physical inventory; this is an important advantage to businesses that require frequent, usually monthly, statements.

Information on quantities on hand is useful for determining when and how much to order and for comparison with periodic physical counts for detecting discrepancies and errors.

ASSIGNING THE COST OF INVENTORY

The total cost of goods available for sale must be allocated between the cost of goods sold and the cost of goods on hand. With the periodic inventory system, this allocation is made at the end of each accounting period; with the perpetual inventory system, it is made after each sale and each acquisition.

The process of assigning costs would be relatively simple if each item acquired could be marked and identified with a specific invoice cost. Such a procedure is possible in certain businesses in which the items are large or otherwise readily traceable. In most instances, however, specific identification of each inventory item is neither feasible nor practical, particularly when successive acquisitions are commingled in common storage facilities. The problem is complicated further because acquisitions of like items are usually made at fluctuating prices. Consequently, a method of assigning costs to merchandise items—with either a perpetual or a periodic inventory system—based on an *assumed* flow of goods and expired costs must be adopted and followed consistently for inventory valuation purposes and for matching costs with revenues. (The principle of consistency is discussed later in this chapter.) The most commonly used methods of assigning costs to inventory items are:

1. First-in, first-out (FIFO)
2. Last-in, first-out (LIFO)
3. Moving average
4. Weighted average
5. Specific identification

When costs are determined by either the FIFO or the LIFO cost procedure, the inventory used—periodic or perpetual—must be clearly stated. This is especially significant with LIFO costing, because the resulting cost assignments may be different.

To illustrate the various methods of assigning costs to inventories, the following information pertaining to a single inventory item, a steel lock, stock item number 7004 is given. Prior to April 1, 1976, the specific identification method of inventory valuation was in use.

1976

April 1   Inventory on hand consisted of 20 units, purchased at $2.20 each.

       5   Purchased 60 units at $2.60 each.

    12   Sold 55 units.

    15   Purchased 35 units at $2.80.

    30   Sold 30 units.

For convenience, the data are rearranged as follows:

	Units	Unit Cost	Total Cost
Inventory, April 1	20	$2.20	$ 44
Purchases			
April 5	60	2.60	156
15	35	2.80	98
Goods available for sale	115		$298
Sales			
April 12	55		
30	30		
Total	85		
On hand, April 30	30	(115 − 85)	

First-In, First-Out (FIFO) Costing. The FIFO method of determining the cost of goods on hand and the cost of goods sold is based on the assumption that the units are sold in the order in which they were acquired; that is, the oldest units on hand are sold first, the units acquired next are the next to be sold, and so on. This assumption relates only to the method of accounting and not to the actual physical movement of the goods although it may approximate the actual physical flow. What is significant, however, is the monetary value. The unsold units on hand at the date of the inventory are assumed to be the units acquired most recently. Consequently, for income measurement, earlier costs are matched with revenue and the most current costs are used for position statement valuation. A detailed perpetual inventory card illustrating the FIFO procedure for assigning costs is shown in Figure 10-1.

As each shipment of goods is received, the quantity, unit cost, and total cost are recorded in the appropriate columns. When goods are issued, the unit cost of the oldest goods on hand is recorded in the Unit Cost column; this cost is then multiplied by the number of units, and the total is written in the Total Cost column. The balance on hand, unit cost, and total cost for each shipment from which units are assumed to remain are recorded in the Balance column.

The cost of the 55 units sold on April 12 is assumed to consist of the 20 units on hand on April 1 and 35 units from the April 5 purchase. The cost of the 30 units sold on April 30 is assumed to consist of the remaining 25 units from the April 5 purchase and 5 units from the April 15 purchase. Therefore, the 30 units on hand on April 30 are assumed to be from those purchased on April 15. The cost of the units sold may be summarized as follows:

Cost of goods available for sale (beginning inventory plus purchases)	$298
Cost of April 30 ending inventory (30 units at $2.80)	84
Cost of goods sold	$214

Figure 10-1 Perpetual Inventory Card (FIFO)

ITEM: LOCK, STEEL, NO. 7004   LOCATION S-5

Date		Ref.	Received (or Purchased)			Issued (or Sold)			Balance		
			Quantity	Unit Cost	Total Cost	Quantity	Unit Cost	Total Cost	Quantity	Unit Cost	Total Cost
1976 April	1	Balance							20	2.20	44.00
	5	P.O.* 673	60	2.60	156.00				20	2.20 }	
									60	2.60 }	200.00
	12	S.T.† 401				20	2.20 }				
						35	2.60 }	135.00	25	2.60	65.00
	15	P.O. 690	35	2.80	98.00				25	2.60 }	
									35	2.80 }	163.00
	30	S.T. 407				25	2.60 }				
						5	2.80 }	79.00	30	2.80	84.00

* Purchase Order
† Shipping Ticket

When FIFO costing is used, the amount of the ending inventory as well as the amount of the cost of goods sold is identical with either the periodic or the perpetual inventory system, because in each instance the goods on hand are assumed to consist of the most recently acquired units.

Last-In, First-Out (LIFO) Costing. LIFO costing is based on the assumption that the cost of goods sold should be based on prices paid for the most recently acquired units and that the inventory consists of the oldest units on hand. The major advantage claimed for this procedure is that during periods of continuously rising prices, the higher prices of the most recent purchases are included in the cost of goods sold, thereby reducing the gross margin on sales and the taxable income. It is further claimed that the cost of goods sold is more realistic, because LIFO costs most nearly approximate current replacement costs, thereby achieving a closer matching of costs with revenue. The application of LIFO costing is illustrated in Figure 10-2.

Sold goods are listed at the unit cost of the latest acquisition, up to the amount assumed to be still on hand. For instance, the 55 units sold on April 12 are assumed to have come from the units received on April 5. The balance on hand, unit cost, and total cost for each receipt from which units are assumed to be on hand are recorded in the Balance column.

(Ch. 10)

Figure 10-2 Perpetual Inventory Card (LIFO)

		Received (or Purchased)			Issued (or Sold)			Balance		
ITEM: LOCK, STEEL, NO. 7004 LOCATION S-5										
Date	Ref.	Quantity	Unit Cost	Total Cost	Quantity	Unit Cost	Total Cost	Quantity	Unit Cost	Total Cost
1976 April 1	Balance							20	2.20	44.00
5	P.O. 673	60	2.60	156.00				20	2.20 ⎱	
								60	2.60 ⎰	200.00
12	S.T. 401				55	2.60	143.00	20	2.20 ⎱	
								5	2.60 ⎰	57.00
15	P.O. 690	35	2.80	98.00				20	2.20 ⎱	
								5	2.60 ⎬	
								35	2.80 ⎰	155.00
30	S.T. 409				30	2.80	84.00	20	2.20 ⎱	
								5	2.60 ⎬	
								5	2.80 ⎰	71.00

The inventory on April 30 is assumed to consist of:

$$
\begin{array}{lll}
20 \text{ units at} & \$2.20 = & \$44 \\
5 \text{ units at} & 2.60 = & 13 \\
5 \text{ units at} & 2.80 = & \underline{14} \\
\overline{30 \text{ units}} & & \underline{\$71}
\end{array}
$$

The cost of goods sold is $227 (goods available for sale, $298, less ending inventory, $71). This figure is obtainable by adding the Total Cost column of the Issued (or Sold) section of the inventory card.

If the *periodic inventory system* were used, the 30 units in inventory on April 30 would be assumed to consist of the beginning inventory of 20 units and 10 units from the purchase of April 5 for a total cost of $70. The cost of the units sold would be $228:

Cost of goods available for sale (beginning inventory plus purchases)	$298
Cost of April 30 inventory	70
Cost of goods sold	$228

Note that, unlike FIFO costing, the valuations of the cost of goods sold and ending inventory under LIFO costing may be different, depending on whether the perpetual or the periodic inventory system is used. When LIFO costing is

(Ch. 10)

used with the perpetual inventory system, prices at the beginning of the period that would be reflected in the ending valuation with the periodic inventory system may be dropped from the running balance as goods are issued. When the inventory is taken only at the end of the period, the various dates of sales are ignored. The LIFO procedure may be used appropriately with either periodic inventories or perpetual inventories even though the results may be different; the system selected, however, should be followed consistently. The following tabulation illustrates the different results of LIFO costing with the perpetual and the periodic inventory systems:

	Perpetual Inventory	Periodic Inventory
Inventory, April 1	$ 44	$ 44
Purchases	254	254
Total goods available for sale	$298	$298
Inventory, April 30	71	70
Cost of goods sold	$227	$228

Figure 10-3 Perpetual Inventory Card (Moving Average Costing)

		Received (or Purchased)			Issued (or Sold)			Balance		
Date	**Ref.**	Quantity	Unit Cost	Total Cost	Quantity	Unit Cost	Total Cost	Quantity	Unit Cost	Total Cost
1976 April 1	Balance							20	2.20	44.00
5	P.O. 673	60	2.60	156.00				80	2.50	200.00 (a)
12	S.T. 401				55	2.50	137.50	25	2.50	62.50
15	P.O. 690	35	2.80	98.00				60	2.675	160.50 (b)
30	S.T. 409				30	2.675	80.25	30	2.675	80.25

ITEM: LOCK, STEEL, NO. 7004   LOCATION S-5

Computations

(a)	(b)
20 at $2.20 = $ 44.00	25 at $2.50 = $ 62.50
60 at 2.60 = 156.00	35 at 2.80 = 98.00
80 $200.00	60 $160.50
Average $2.50	Average $2.675

(Ch. 10)

Moving Average Costing. Under moving average costing, the cost of each purchase is added to the cost of units on hand, and the total cost is divided by the total quantity on hand to find the average price. Units issued are priced at the average price until additional units are purchased; then a new average price is computed. This method tends to level off price fluctuations. The application of moving average costing is shown in Figure 10-3.

Weighted Average Costing. Under weighted average costing—not to be confused with moving average costing—the ending inventory is priced at the end of each accounting period at a unit cost computed by dividing the total cost of goods available for sale by the physical units available for sale. Similarly, all quantities sold are stated at a uniform price—the computed average price for the period (typically one month). The assignment of costs to goods sold during the month must be delayed until the end of the month so that the weighted average cost computation can be made.

The average cost for the period, the inventory valuation, and the cost of goods sold are computed as follows:

Date			Units	Unit Cost	Total
1976					
April	1	Beginning inventory	20	$2.20	$ 44.00
	5	Purchase	60	2.60	156.00
	15	Purchase	35	2.80	98.00
			115		$298.00

$$\text{Average unit cost} = \frac{\text{Cost of goods available for sale}}{\text{Units available for sale}} = \frac{\$298}{115} = \$2.5913$$

Units on hand, April 30	30
Inventory valuation (30 × $2.5913)	$77.74
Units sold	85
Cost of goods sold (85 × $2.5913)	$220.26

Specific Identification Costing. The specific identification method of inventory valuation may be used if each item (automobiles, diamond rings, or other items) purchased can be identified specifically with the related underlying documents. Some businesses mark the specific cost in code on every unit so that each item of inventory as well as each unit sold may be valued. Valuation by specific identification can be used with either the perpetual or the periodic inventory system. In either case, the cost of units sold as well as the cost of units remaining on hand is determined by reference to the related specific invoices.

In many instances, whether because of the volume of items involved or because the items are of a kind that make individual coding impossible, the method of specific identification is impracticable. Similar items acquired on different dates and at different prices may be commingled, or *fungible* (interchangeable) items—wheat in bins, coal in piles—might be matched with unrelated invoices, thereby misstating net income. Furthermore, some costs are common to groups of items—shipping, insurance, handling—and may not be readily identifiable with specific items.

(Ch. 10)

The most common cost methods of inventory valuation have been discussed in this chapter; others may be used in special circumstances. In a particular business, the method selected should be the one that will best measure net income.

If there are no significant price changes in the merchandise handled during a given period and the quantity held does not change, FIFO, LIFO, and moving average costing will produce approximately the same results. If, however, the prices of the goods acquired fluctuate significantly during the period and the inventory turnover is rapid, the method of inventory valuation used will have a direct effect on the financial statements. In Figure 10-1, the price of the item fluctuated from $2.20 to $2.80 during the month. To illustrate the comparative effect of rising prices on the financial statements under perpetual FIFO, moving average, and LIFO costing, the basic data (page 383) for the preceding discussions are used again. Two additional assumptions are made: (1) The selling price of each unit is $5.50, and (2) the operating expenses for the month are $100. These computations of income are for a single inventory item. The effect of the different methods on net income would be proportionately increased with increasing volume and number of items. The effect of the three methods of allocating inventory cost and cost of goods sold under the stated assumptions is further highlighted in Figure 10-4, which is abstracted from the preceding income computations.

During a period of rising prices, FIFO costing results in the highest ending inventory valuation, gross margin on sales, and net income and the lowest cost of goods sold. Given the same rising market conditions, the LIFO inventory

Figure 10-4
Summary Tabulation

	FIFO	Moving Average	LIFO
Sales (85 units × $5.50)	$467.50	$467.50	$467.50
Cost of goods sold (see Figures 10–1, 10–2, and 10–3 for computations)	214.00	217.75	227.00
Gross margin on sales	$253.50	$249.75	$240.50
Deduct operating expenses	100.00	100.00	100.00
Net income	$153.50	$149.75	$140.50

	FIFO	Moving Average	LIFO
Ending inventory	$ 84.00	$ 80.25	$ 71.00
Cost of goods sold	214.00	217.75	227.00
Gross margin on sales	253.50	249.75	240.50
Net income	153.50	149.75	140.50

INCOME
MEASUREMENT
AND VALUATION

(Ch. 10)

method gives the opposite results: lowest ending inventory valuation, gross margin on sales, and net income and highest cost of goods sold. During a period of falling prices, FIFO results in the lowest ending inventory valuation, gross margin on sales, and net income and the highest cost of goods sold; LIFO gives the opposite results.

The major advantage of LIFO costing is that during a prolonged period of generally rising prices, lower year-to-year earnings are reported with a concomitant income tax advantage. A major disadvantage is that during inflationary periods LIFO costing results in a significant understatement of current assets, which limits the significance and usefulness of the position statement. LIFO's purpose is to match revenue with current cost, rather than with earliest cost, as is done under FIFO costing.

Figure 10-4 shows that the amounts for the income statement items listed under moving average costing fall between the corresponding amounts for FIFO and LIFO costing. The same position would be maintained in a falling market. Moving average costing reduces the effect of widely fluctuating prices and results in a valuation closer to FIFO than to LIFO.

The position statement classifies the ending inventory as a current asset; consequently, this statement as well as the income statement is affected by the method of inventory valuation used. The ending inventory is often the largest single item in the Current Assets section and has, therefore, a decided effect on the current ratio, the reported amount of working capital, the merchandise inventory turnover, the total stockholders' equity, and related ratios.

Historical cost is the primary basis used for inventory valuation. Some accountants recommend the use of replacement cost for inventory valuation. This may be defined as the current cost of replacing the inventory items at the inventory date, in the ordinary course of business, assuming access to the usual sources of supply and at volumes in which the goods are usually purchased. The accountants who criticize the use of historical cost argue that FIFO does not segregate gains from changing price levels and that LIFO eliminates the effects of changing price levels from income. Others recommend reporting parallel figures showing both historical cost and current costs, thereby providing the user with a better basis for evaluating past performance and for predicting future performance. The use of current costs would eliminate the need for a cost-flow assumption—LIFO, FIFO, average—and would result in a better matching of expired cost and revenue. The position statement valuation would also be more significant. "Where current value varies obviously and significantly from historical cost, the accountant should feel compelled to modify the recorded amount. Replacement cost may prove to be the most meaningful basis for modification of inventory and plant and equipment under some circumstances."[5]

LOWER OF COST OR MARKET (LCM)

The various methods of inventory valuation discussed thus far in this chapter are methods of arriving at the cost of the inventory.

[5] Arthur Andersen & Co., *Accounting and Reporting Problems of the Profession*, 4th ed., 1973, p. 54.

However, a long-standing convention in accounting holds that inventories may be valued at the *lower of cost or market*.

"A departure from the cost basis of pricing the inventory is required when the utility of the goods is no longer as great as its cost. Where there is evidence that the utility of goods, in their disposal in the ordinary course of business, will be less than cost, whether due to physical deterioration, obsolescence, changes in price levels, or other causes, the difference should be recognized as a loss of the current period. This is generally accomplished by stating such goods at a lower level commonly designated as *market*."[6] The term *market* generally means the cost of replacing the goods as of the position statement date.

Application of Lower of Cost or Market

The process of valuing the inventory at LCM occurs at the end of the accounting period when financial statements are prepared. It may be applied (1) to each item individually, (2) to each major inventory category, or (3) to the entire inventory. On the basis of the inventory tabulations in Figure 10-5 (FIFO costing is assumed), the valuation under each procedure is as follows (Items A and B are assumed to constitute category X and the remaining items constitute category Y):

1. If each item is valued individually, the inventory is reported as $5,725 (column 6).
2. If the inventory is valued by major categories, it is reported as $5,925 (column 7).
3. If the inventory is valued in total, it is reported as $6,225 (column 8).

When applying LCM, "market" shall not be more than "net realizable value," that is, the estimated resale price of the item less expected costs to complete and sell. However, "market" shall be not less than "net realizable value" reduced by a normal profit margin.

Evaluation of LCM

The reason for LCM inventory valuation is to avoid the anticipation of profits and to provide for all foreseeable losses. This practice was developed when the influence of the grantor of credit was paramount and when primary emphasis was on the statement of financial position and on conservative asset valuations. It is based on the assumption that a drop in the purchase price of goods will be followed by a corresponding drop in the selling price of those goods, thereby reducing or eliminating the normal profit margin.

LCM lacks theoretical support: (1) It is a departure from the cost concept. (2) It is inconsistent, because presumed losses are anticipated but potential gains from an increase in the purchase price of goods are ignored, and some

[6] AICPA, *op. cit.*, p. 6015.

Figure 10-5 Application of LCM

Column Nos.	1	2	3	4	5	6	7	8
						Lower of Cost or Market		
						Basis		
Item	Quantity	Unit Cost	Unit Market Price	Total Cost	Total Market	Unit	Major Category	Total Inventory
Category X:								
Item A	100	$10	$9.00	$1,000	$ 900	$ 900		
Item B	200	4	6.00	800	1,200	800		
Subtotal				$1,800	$2,100		$1,800	
Category Y:								
Item C	400	1	1.25	$ 400	$ 500	$ 400		
Item D	600	6	5.00	3,600	3,000	3,000		
Item E	250	3	2.50	750	625	625		
Subtotal				$4,750	$4,125		4,125	
Totals				$6,550	$6,225			$6,225
Ending Inventory-LCM						$5,725	$5,925	$6,225

goods may be priced at cost and others at market when LCM is applied to individual items or categories. (3) The expectation of lower selling prices may not materialize, thereby distorting the income of several periods. The rule of lower of cost or market is generally applied to individual items—the required procedure for Federal income tax reporting—rather than to the whole inventory.

> For income tax reporting, a consistent procedure must be followed from year to year.

Consistency of Reporting for Tax Determination

Either cost or the lower of cost or market is acceptable for tax purposes, except for goods valued under LIFO costing. The Federal income tax regulations state that on adoption of LIFO costing, no other method of inventory valuation may be used in annual statements, including reports to stockholders or creditors. The use of LCM is not permitted in conjunction with LIFO costing, although this does not preclude the disclosure, by footnote or parenthesis, of the excess of the FIFO valuation of the inventory over the LIFO valuation.

MEASUREMENT
AND CONTROL
OF INVENTORY

STATEMENT OF FINANCIAL POSITION DISCLOSURE— INVENTORY

Studies of financial reports prepared by leading corporations show that LCM is the most commonly used basis of valuation for inventories, the only other common basis being cost. Cost, of course, includes LIFO, FIFO, and weighted average valuations, by either the perpetual or the periodic inventory system. LIFO costing is the method most frequently used.

Some typical examples of how inventories are reported in statements of financial position from the published annual reports of business corporations are shown below.

(1)
Current Assets
    Merchandise Inventories—at lower of cost
        or market $2,500,000

Note: Inventories are reported at the lower of FIFO cost or estimated market on the basis of specific items and classes of merchandise. Obsolete stock is carried at estimated salvage value.

(2)
Current Assets
    Merchandise Inventories $3,250,549

Note: Inventories are stated at cost, certain inventories at average cost, and others at FIFO cost. These costs are not in excess of market value.

(3)
Current Assets
    Merchandise Inventories $552,100

Note: Inventories are stated at the lower of cost or market. During 1976, the company adopted LIFO costing for a portion of its inventories. The effect of this change was to reduce net income by $27,000, and Federal income taxes by $12,000. FIFO costing is used for the rest of the inventories.

GROSS MARGIN METHOD OF ESTIMATING INVENTORIES

Taking a physical inventory or maintaining perpetual inventory records is often costly and time-consuming. For some purposes—preparing monthly financial statements, checking the accuracy of a physical inventory, or estimating inventory value when an accurate valuation cannot be made, as in the case of a fire loss—the *gross margin* method of estimating the inventory is used.

Assume that during the previous three years the Needham Company has averaged a gross margin rate on sales of 30 percent, as shown below.

	Prior Years			
	1	2	3	Totals
Sales	$124,000	$142,000	$154,000	$420,000
Cost of Goods Sold	87,420	97,980	108,600	294,000
Gross Margin	$ 36,580	$ 44,020	$ 45,400	$126,000
Gross Margin Rate	29.5%	31%	29.5%	30%

For the current year, the following data are available from the records of the company:

Inventory—January 1, 1976	$ 20,000
Purchases during 1976	110,000
Sales during 1976	160,000

Under the gross margin method, the estimated inventory on December 31, 1976, would be computed as follows:

a. Sales − Gross margin = Cost of goods sold

$160,000 − (0.30 × $160,000) = $112,000

b. Beginning inventory + Net cost of purchases − Cost of goods sold = Ending inventory

$20,000 + $110,000 − $112,000 = $18,000

On the basis of the foregoing computations, the complete income statement is as follows:

NEEDHAM COMPANY
Income Statement
For the Year Ended December 31, 1976

Sales (given)		$160,000
Cost of Goods Sold		
Inventory, January 1, 1976 (given)	$ 20,000	
Purchases (given)	110,000	
Total	$130,000	
Estimated Inventory, December 31, 1976 (item b)	18,000	
Cost of Goods Sold (item a)		112,000
Gross Margin (Sales − Cost of Goods Sold)		$ 48,000

This method is based on the assumption that the rate of gross margin on sales is substantially the same in every period. It is accurate, therefore, only to the extent that the assumed gross margin rate reflects the experience of the current period. It is essential that a careful study be made of possible differences between the past data from which the assumed rate is derived and the corresponding current data. Appropriate adjustments should be made for significant differences. The inventory on hand at the end of the current period computed by this method is the amount that would result at a gross margin rate equal to the assumed rate.

RETAIL METHOD OF ESTIMATING INVENTORIES

Another method of estimating the ending inventory, commonly used by chain and department stores, is the *retail inventory* method. Its value is twofold: It serves as a means of computing the ending inventory without a physical count; it provides a method of centrally controlling inventories that consist of a variety of items dispersed over several departments or several branch stores. Goods are charged to the departments or branches at their selling price, records of both cost and selling price of goods purchased are kept centrally, and records of sales are kept in the usual manner. From these records, the inventory valuation may be prepared at any time. The estimated inventory at retail is derived by deducting the sales during the period from the total goods available for sale priced at retail. This amount is then converted to cost by applying the cost percentage (the ratio of the cost of goods available for sale to the retail price of those goods). This is illustrated in Figure 10-6.

Changes in previously established retail prices by increases (called *markups*) or decreases (called *markdowns*) are often necessary. Depending on how these changes are applied in computing the cost-to-retail ratio, the ending inventory may approximate lower of cost or market, LIFO, FIFO, or replacement cost.

Both the gross margin method and the retail inventory method are based on a calculation of the gross margin rate. The gross margin method uses past experience as a basis; the retail inventory method uses current experience. The gross margin method is, therefore, less reliable, because past experience may be different from the current experience.

Figure 10-6
Retail Inventory Method

	Cost	Retail
Inventory at beginning of period	$ 20,000	$ 30,000
Purchases during period	180,000	270,000
Total goods available	$200,000	$300,000
Cost percentage (ratio of cost to retail) $\dfrac{\$200,000}{\$300,000} = 66\frac{2}{3}\%$		
Sales during period		258,000
Inventory at retail		$ 42,000
Estimated inventory at cost (66⅔% of $42,000)	$28,000	

A physical inventory should be taken periodically. This inventory is first computed at the retail selling prices marked on the goods, reduced to cost by using the cost percentage, and then compared with the inventory value computed in the manner shown in Figure 10-6. If there have been losses due to thefts or shrinkage, the valuation based on the physical inventory will be less than that shown by the records, and an adjustment is made for the decrease.

The retail inventory method offers a means of determining a company's inventory at frequent intervals without taking a physical count—a valuable tool for purposes of preparing financial statements or other reports that require an inventory valuation. Its reliability rests on the assumption that the percentage of cost to retail is fairly uniform within the several departments of the company and for all the various items sold, and that the percentage is equally applicable to the goods sold and the goods unsold. If that is not the case, separate records should be maintained for the different departments and for the different items handled. Use of the retail inventory method is permissible for Federal income tax purposes.

CONSISTENCY IN APPLICATION OF PROCEDURES

Different procedures may be used in different areas of accounting.

It is of paramount importance, therefore, that the selected method should be followed consistently from year to year.

Consistency

Inconsistency in inventory pricing, cost allocations, and financial statement presentation would make year-to-year comparisons of operating results and financial position meaningless. Since such comparisons often serve as the basis for managerial decisions and decisions of external users of accounting information, the importance of consistency becomes evident.

The concept of consistency may be applied at several levels. Consistency is important not only in the matter of valuation procedures followed but also with respect to the classification of items in financial statements. Consistency in classification applies to the grouping of items within each statement as well as to year-to-year consistency. The principle of consistency does not preclude required changes properly made and fully disclosed. A change from FIFO to LIFO inventory costing, for example, requires an explanation accompanying the financial statements of the year of change, giving the nature of the change and its effect.

INVENTORY CONTROL

The principle of the separation of duties discussed on page 296 is equally applicable to merchandise. Internal controls must be established to protect against loss, theft, and misappropriation of inventory. The system for receiving, storing, issuing, and paying for the merchandise must provide for such records and supporting documents and for the assignment of individual responsibility and accountability as will safeguard the assets. Absence of control over inventories can be a serious detriment to the successful management of a business. An excessive inventory is expensive to carry. Studies made indicate that the costs of carrying an inventory—taxes, insurance, warehousing, handling, and inventory taking—may be as high as 25 percent of the original purchase price. This is exclusive of lost potential earnings (interest) on the funds tied up in inventories. On the other hand, sufficient items and quantities must be stocked to provide customers with good service.

Maintaining a proper balance, to avoid both shortages and excesses of inventory, requires organization and planning. Control plans must provide for day-to-day comparisons of projected inventory acquisitions with current sales volume. A reduction in sales volume will result in excess inventories unless adjustments are made.

Inventory Turnover

The cost of goods sold divided by the average inventory gives the *inventory turnover,* a useful guide in inventory control (see page 200). The turnover rate may be computed for individual items or for major categories in order to establish item-by-item control.

Ratio of Inventory to Working Capital

The ratio of inventory to working capital is an indication of the amount of working capital invested in inventory and the amount of currently maturing obligations that will have to be met with proceeds from the sale of the inventory. If, for example, a firm's ending inventory is $330,000 and its working capital is $300,000, the ratio is:

$$\frac{\text{Ending inventory}}{\text{Working capital}} = \frac{\$330,000}{\$300,000} = 110\%$$

This ratio, being greater than 100 percent, indicates that the current debt cannot be paid in full from cash on hand and proceeds from receivables, but will require, in addition, part of the proceeds from the sale of inventory.

Maximum and Minimum Levels

It is customary to establish maximum and minimum stock levels for inventory items, so that the purchasing agent is automatically notified when the balance on hand is at the minimum quantity and the item must be replenished. Minimum levels should be set to allow for anticipated sales requirements during the time required for placing the replenishment order and receiving the goods, with a margin for unforeseen delay. Maximum balances should be set, based on sales requirements, minimum stock point, and the most economical buying quantities.

Economical Buying Quantities

Deciding the quantity to purchase involves considering the cost of acquisition and the cost of carrying the items. Ordering large quantities often results in a lower unit purchase price and lower transportation costs per unit, but the saving is offset by the increased cost of carrying the inventory. Carrying cost includes taxes, insurance, storage, losses due to obsolescence and deterioration, interest on the investment, and other factors. The point at which the aggregate of all the cost elements—cost to order, carrying cost, and purchase cost—is lowest indicates the most economical quantity to order or the number of orders to place each year.

PERIODIC PHYSICAL INVENTORIES

A periodic physical count of the entire inventory is an essential element of inventory control. A physical count (that is, a count by weight or measure) and valuation serve to confirm perpetual inventory records. If perpetual records are not maintained, an annual physical inventory is an absolute necessity for the preparation of financial statements. A physical count also aids in reviewing the condition of the goods on hand and detecting errors or laxity in the system of accounting for storing and handling merchandise.

The taking of a physical inventory requires careful planning—setting the date, selecting and instructing the inventory takers, and establishing controls and procedures. It is advantageous to select a business year that ends when quantities are low and when the inventory taking will interfere least with the regular operations of the business. When necessary, technically trained personnel must be available to assist in identifying items; others must be available to move bulky items or to reach items not easily accessible.

It is common practice to attach consecutively numbered tags to all inventory items for recording the counts as they are made. On completion of the count, the filled-in tags are removed and checked to ensure that they have all been returned. The inventory items and quantities are then accumulated on inventory sheets showing descriptions, quantities, unit costs, and total costs. If tags are not used, the inventory count is entered directly on the inventory sheets. The unit costs to be shown on the inventory sheets depend on the costing method employed—LIFO, FIFO, and so on. If there is a discrepancy between the records and the count, the inventory records are brought into agreement with the physical count. The cause of the discrepancy should be traced so that steps may be taken to prevent a recurrence.

Item descriptions on the inventory tags must be complete and accurate. To eliminate confusion resulting from incorrect or inadequate item descriptions, the tags may be prepared in advance from the stock records.

Some inventory items cannot be counted, measured, or weighed conveniently, such as piles of coal, large quantities of nails dumped in bins, and partially used tanks or containers of materials. Other appropriate means must be devised to estimate the quantities of such items on hand. Obsolete or damaged merchandise must be identified clearly and excluded from the inventory if it is unsalable. If such goods are salable at a reduced price, they should be valued at the reduced price less any selling costs.

Since the inventory is taken as of a specific date, a careful record must be kept of acquisitions, withdrawals, and goods in transit during the inventory period. Goods on hand for which the liability has been recorded are included in the inventory; goods held for shipment and charged to the customer must be excluded. Goods owned but located elsewhere—at a branch warehouse or under *consignment*—must be included in the inventory.

Business organizations who carry large numbers of items in inventory often need a perpetual system, but find both clerical costs and error rates are high when they maintain the stock record cards in Figures 10-1, 10-2, and 10-3 by hand-posting methods. Accordingly, they adopt an electronic data-processing system to maintain these stock records. The concept of an individual stock record for each item still applies, but the record itself may be recorded on punched card, magnetic tape, or magnetic disk or drum.

One such computer system, IBM System 3, can use a 96-column punched card. Like the more commonly used 80-column card illustrated in Figure A8-1 (page 321), the 96-column card carries data represented by holes punched in the columns. The 96-column card differs from the 80-column card not only in shape and size, but also in the code used to represent data. In both cases, however, the data are *machine-sensible*—that is, they can be read by machine and transmitted into the central processing unit of a computer, where calculations are made and the results transmitted back from the computer both in printed reports and in updated stock record cards.

As in the hand-posted perpetual system, a separate master stock record card is used for each item carried in the inventory. Figure A10-1 illustrates such a card. The card pictured is blank; no data have been punched in it. It will be noted that, with changed format, spaces are available for the basic data such as item stock number, description, receipts, issues, and balance on hand. Also, like most perpetual inventory cards, it shows the quantity on order. (What may appear to the reader to be duplication in the 96-column card actually is not.) The upper portion contains printed information; the lower portion carries the coded punched data. The card is therefore both *human-sensible* and *machine-sensible*.

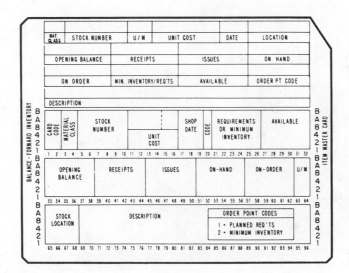

Figure A10-1
An Item Master Card

Source: IBM Corporation

MEASUREMENT
AND CONTROL
OF INVENTORY

(Ch. 10)

Figure A10-2
A Transaction Card

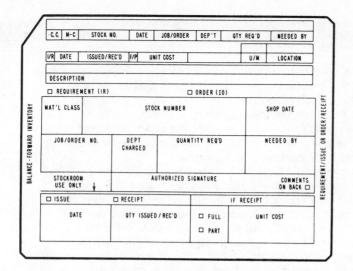

Courtesy of International Business Machines Corporation

Figure A10-3 IBM 5424 Multifunction Card Unit

Courtesy of International Business Machines Corporation

(Ch. 10)

With what is known as a *balance forward* system, a second type of 96-column card generally known as a *transaction card* is used. In the balance forward system, a separate transaction card is key punched for each transaction for each inventory item. A single stock item—for example, the steel lock, stock No. 7004, used in the examples throughout this chapter—may have one or more receipts, several sales, an order placed, and a correction or an adjustment all occurring on the same day. Each of these events is recorded on a source document. For those cited there would have been prepared one or more receiver's reports, several sales tickets, a purchase order, and a journal voucher. From these source documents, information would be punched into a separate transaction card for each event. Figure A10-2 is an illustration of such a transaction card.

Again, the illustrated card is a blank one; it has no data punched in it. At the end of each day, the cards are brought together, the file of item master cards is

Figure A10-4   A Simplified Balance Forward Procedure

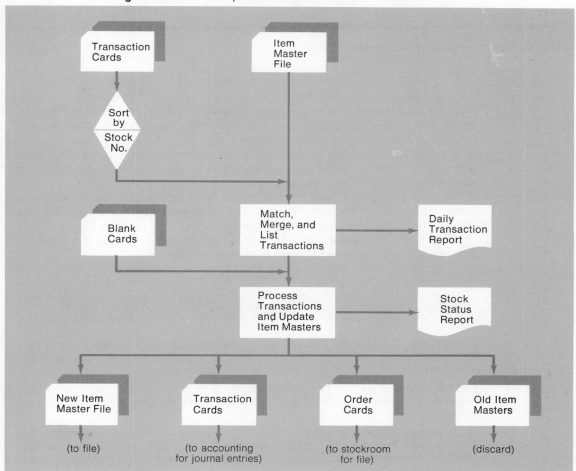

Figure A10-5 Stock Status Report

DATE 2/14/--				STOCK STATUS REPORT				PAGE 17					
ITEM NO.	DESCRIPTION	QUANTITY ON HAND	QUANTITY ON ORDER	TRANSACTION QUANTITY	QUANTITY B/O	AVERAGE UNIT COST	EXTENDED COST	LAST RECEIPT	LAST ISSUE	MIN. BAL.	MAX. BAL.		
411116	B500 TWINLITE SOCKET BLUE	458	500			.35	160.30			800	1600		
	ADJUSTMENT			42		.35	14.70						
	RECEIPT			500		.37	185.00						
	ISSUE			50-		.36	18.00-						
		950*				.36	342.00	2/11/--	2/14/--				
411122	B506 SOCKET ADAPTER BROWN	325				.19	61.75			300	800		
	ISSUE			20-		.19	3.80-						
	ISSUE			38-		.19	7.22-						
	ISSUE			10-		.19	1.90-						
		257*				.19	48.83	12/19/--	2/11/--	UNDER			
411173	C151C SILENT SWITCH IVORY	50	150			1.16	58.00			100	200		
	RECEIPT			150		1.20	180.00						
		200*				1.19	238.00	2/10/--	2/03/--				
411254	A210 PULL CORD GOLD	62	75			2.25	139.50			80	165		
	ISSUE			16		2.25	36.00						
	ISSUE			30		2.25	67.50						
		16*	75			2.25	36.00	11/17/--	2/09/--				
	FINAL TOTALS			BEG. INV.	48295.26								
				CHANGE	700.08								
				NEW VALUE	48995.34								

updated, and the desired printed reports are produced. The file of item master cards is maintained in stock number sequence, but the deck of transaction cards, which were generated as events occurred, are in no specified order at the end of the day's punching. A single piece of equipment, shown in Figure A10-3, has the capability of sorting the transaction cards and merging them with the item master cards into a single deck in which all cards bearing on a single stock number fall together.

The cards are then read into the computer, which adds receipts, subtracts sales, makes other adjustments, and computes new quantity and dollar balances. The steps in the system are shown in the flow chart in Figure A10-4.

The types of reports prepared in this process depend upon the needs of the individual firm. A typical report is shown in Figure A10-5.

GLOSSARY

Consistency The concept that uniformity—with full disclosure for any departures—from year to year, especially in inventory pricing, cost allocation, and financial statement presentation, is essential to make comparisons meaningful.

FIFO A method of determining the cost of goods on hand and the cost of goods sold based on the assumption that the units are sold in the order in which they were acquired.

Gross Margin Method A method of estimating inventory value by deducting the cost of goods sold from the total cost of goods available for sale, the cost of goods sold being the product of the average gross margin percentage for prior periods applied to sales for the current period.

INCOME
MEASUREMENT
AND VALUATION

(Ch. 10)

Inventory Turnover The cost of goods sold divided by the average inventory.

LIFO A costing method based on the assumption that the cost of goods sold should be calculated on prices paid for the most recently acquired units and that the units on hand consist of the oldest units acquired.

Lower of Cost or Market (LCM) An inventory valuation method by which units are valued at the lower of either original acquisition cost or at replacement cost (market) for those units in inventory whose replacement cost has fallen below original acquisition cost.

Moving Average An inventory costing method by which the cost of each purchase is added to the cost of units on hand, and the total cost is divided by the total quantity on hand to find the average unit price.

Periodic Inventory An inventory system of record keeping by which the value of the inventory for statement of financial position presentation and for the determination of the cost of goods sold is determined at the end of each annual period by a complete physical count and pricing of all inventory items.

Perpetual Inventory An inventory system of record keeping that provides for a continuous book inventory of items on hand.

Retail Method A method of estimating inventory value by applying the current gross margin ratio (the ratio of the cost of goods to the selling price) to net sales to derive the cost of goods sold which, when deducted from sales, equals the selling price of the inventory. The inventory valued at retail is then converted to cost by the application of the gross margin ratio.

Specific Identification An inventory costing method by which the unit cost is identified specifically with the related supporting acquisition document.

Weighted Average A costing method by which the ending inventory and the cost of goods sold are priced at the end of each accounting period at a unit cost computed by dividing the total cost of goods available for sale by the physical units available for sale.

Q10-1. Distinguish between the terms *cost* and *value* when used in connection with inventory valuations. Is this distinction imperative during periods of price stability? during periods of rising prices? during periods of falling prices?

Q10-2. Why are accountants reluctant to abandon the assumption that the dollar is a stable unit of valuation?

Q10-3. Why is it important that the selected system of inventory valuation be applied consistently from year to year? Does strict compliance with the principle of consistency preclude a change from FIFO to LIFO?

Q10-4. Distinguish between the perpetual and the periodic inventory systems. Does the perpetual inventory system eliminate the need for a physical inventory count?

Q10-5. How do overstatements or understatements of inventory affect net income in the period when the error is made? in the following period?

Q10-6. What effect do the different methods of inventory valuation have on the financial statements?

Q10-7. Compare the gross margin method with the retail inventory method.

Q10-8. An audit of the records of the Shelley Corporation showed that the ending

MEASUREMENT
AND CONTROL
OF INVENTORY

inventory on December 31, 1975, was overstated by $7,600 and that on December 31, 1976, the inventory was understated by $9,300. What was the effect of the errors on the income statement for each year? What was the overall effect for the two-year period?

Q10-9. The Cole Company maintains perpetual inventory cards for all merchandise items. An inventory is taken annually. Serially numbered perforated tags are placed on or alongside the various items. The inventory is taken by teams of two employees: One employee fills in the description and quantity of the item on each section of the tag; the other checks both the description and the count and removes the second half of the tag. The removed portions of the tags are then sent to the office, where the information is entered on inventory sheets and priced on the basis of lower of cost or market.
Explain the purpose of each step of this procedure. Criticize the procedure followed. State what precautionary steps must be taken prior to the actual inventory count, during the count, and immediately following the completion of the count.

Q10-10. Explain the effect on the statement of financial position valuation and on the income determination of the use of LIFO as compared with FIFO (a) if prices have risen during the year; (b) if prices have fallen during the year.

Q10-11. (a) Define the term *market* as used in lower of cost or market inventory valuation. (b) What is the rationale for LCM? (c) Does LCM always produce conservative financial statements?

Q10-12. Explain the means by which a company can protect itself against errors, theft, or the improper use of inventory items.

Q10-13. (a) What is the relationship between the actual physical flow of goods in and out of inventory and the method used for inventory valuation? (b) What inventory valuation method should a company use if, as new shipments of inventory items are received, they are commingled with identical items on hand in storage bins?

Q10-14. As a stockholder, how would you evaluate the adoption of LIFO by your company?

Q10-15. (Appendix). When perpetual inventory records are maintained on punched cards, tape, or direct access media, is a separate card or record kept for each item? Are there major differences in the information available about each item between manual stock record cards and automated stock record systems?

Q10-16. (Appendix). What is the purpose of an item master card? a transaction card?

EXERCISES

E10-1. The records of the Stark Company show the following data as of December 31, 1976:

a. Cost of merchandise on hand, based on a physical count $50,000

b. Merchandise sold to a customer, but held for him pending receipt of shipping instructions (included in item a) 1,800

c. Merchandise shipped out on December 30, F.O.B. destination; expected delivery time is 8 days 2,200

d. Merchandise purchased on December 28, F.O.B. shipping point, delivered to a carrier on December 29; expected delivery date is January 5 750

INCOME
MEASUREMENT
AND VALUATION

e. Cost of spoiled merchandise (to be given away);
not included in item a   200

What is the value of the inventory on December 31, 1976, for financial statement reporting purposes?

E10-2. The following items were included in the income statements of the Egypt Company for the years ended December 31, 1976 and 1975:

	December 31	
	1976	1975
Cost of goods sold	$ 69,000	$ 76,000
Gross margin	142,000	135,000
Net income	35,000	20,000

An audit of the records revealed that the merchandise inventory at December 31, 1975, was understated by $4,000. What was the effect of the error on the amounts given?

E10-3. The year-end inventory of the Kidder Company consisted of the following groups of items, priced at cost and at market:

Item	Cost	Market
A	$60,000	$63,000
B	40,000	40,000
C	80,000	78,000
D	50,000	42,000

What inventory amount should be used in the financial statements? Why?

E10-4. The inventory of the Lear Company on January 1 and December 31, 1976, consisted of 21,250 and 31,250 units, respectively, of Commodity X-1. The beginning inventory was priced at $1,700. The following purchases were made during the year:

Date	Quantity	Cost
January 10	12,500	$1,125
April 15	21,250	1,800
July 5	30,000	2,850
October 2	7,500	750
December 15	20,000	1,600

Determine the cost of the December 31, 1976, inventory by each of the following methods: (a) LIFO; (b) FIFO; (c) weighted average. Assume that the periodic inventory system is used.

E10-5. The beginning inventory, purchases, and sales of an item by the Golemme Company for the month of July 1976 were as follows:

1976
July 1   Inventory on hand consisted of 100 units at $3.15 each.
    12   Sold 50 units.
    15   Purchased 40 units at $3.00 each.
    17   Purchased 60 units at $2.70 each.
    19   Sold 30 units.
    26   Purchased 50 units at $3.45 each.
    29   Sold 40 units.

What was the value of the units on hand on July 31 (a) under the perpetual inventory moving average method and (b) under the periodic inventory weighted average method?

E10-6. The following information pertains to a stock item of the Dailey Corporation:

1976
January 1	On hand	10,000 units at $9.00
February 14	Purchase	12,000 units at 9.75
June 12	Purchase	14,000 units at 9.00
November 12	Purchase	10,000 units at 9.50
December 31	On hand	12,000 units

The periodic inventory system is used. Compute the value of the inventory on December 31, 1976, (a) under FIFO and (b) under LIFO.

E10-7. The DeVey Company calculates its inventory by the gross margin method for interim statement purposes. The inventory on January 1 was $53,200, net purchases during January were $139,650, and net sales for the month were $199,500. The gross margin rate is estimated at 35% of net sales. What was the estimated inventory on January 31?

E10-8. The entire stock of the Knit Company was destroyed by fire on June 22, 1976. The books of the company (kept in a fireproof vault) showed the value of goods on hand on June 1 to be $40,000. Transactions for the period June 1 through June 22 resulted in the following amounts:

Sales	$98,780
Sales Returns	2,105
Purchases	79,800
Purchases Returns	1,815
Transportation In	1,475

The rate of gross margin on sales for the previous three years averaged 35%. Determine the cost of the inventory destroyed by the fire.

E10-9. The books of Hopper Department Store show the following data for the leather goods department for the year 1976, its first year of operations:

Purchases (at cost)	$4,900
Purchases (at original selling price)	8,650
Markups	560
Markdowns	280
Sales	8,175

Compute the inventory on December 31, 1976, by the retail method. (*Hint:* Include the markups but exclude the markdowns in the computation of the cost percentage.)

E10-10. (a) From the following data, compute the cost of the ending inventory:

Sales	$30,000
Beginning inventory (cost)	12,500
Beginning inventory (retail)	17,500
Purchases (cost)	17,500
Purchases (retail)	22,500

(b) Recompute the ending inventory, assuming the following additional items:

(*Hint:* Include the markups but exclude the markdowns in the computation of the cost percentage.)

Transportation In	$750
Purchases Returns (cost)	500
Purchases Returns (retail)	750
Sales Returns	1,000
Markups	875
Markdowns	625

E10-11. Goldstein Co., a specialty clothing store, uses the retail inventory method. The following information relates to 1976 operations:

Inventory January 1, 1976, at cost	$14,200
Inventory January 1, 1976, at sales price	20,100
Purchases in 1976 at cost	32,600
Purchases in 1976 at sales price	50,000
Additional markups on normal sales price	1,900
Sales (including $4,200 of items which were marked down from $6,400)	60,000

The cost of the December 31, 1976, inventory determined by the retail inventory method, is: (a) $9,800, (b) $6,370, (c) $6,743, (d) $6,543. (*Hint:* Include the markups but exclude the markdowns in the computation of the cost percentage.)

AICPA adapted

E10-12. (Appendix). At the end of a sales day, about 500 sales tickets have been sent to the data-processing department, where the following steps will be taken:

1. Updating the item master file.
2. Sorting into stock number sequence.
3. Merging with item master file.
4. Punching a transaction card for each item on each sales ticket.
5. Separating the decks and return to storage.

Place these steps in the proper sequence.

DP10-1. (*Accounting policy decision problem: Inventory valuation*) On January 1, 1976, the Fisher Company had an inventory of 500 units of a product that cost $27 each. January receipts and issues were as follows:

Received		Issued	
January 3	200 units at $28	January 2	100 units
January 10	300 units at 32	January 8	200 units
January 23	100 units at 29	January 17	300 units
		January 26	200 units

Required:

1. Compute the January 31 inventory using (a) FIFO based on a periodic inventory, (b) LIFO based on a perpetual inventory, and (c) weighted average.
2. Prepare summary journal entries for the transactions, assuming the use of LIFO and the perpetual inventory system, and post to the following T accounts: Merchandise Inventory, Accounts Receivable, Accounts Payable, Cost of Goods Sold, and Sales. The unit selling price was $42.
3. What is the purpose of a perpetual inventory system?

4. Would you recommend recording quantities only on the perpetual records and eliminating unit costs and total costs?

5. (a) Does the use of a perpetual inventory system eliminate the need for taking periodic physical inventories? (b) How will differences between the physical count and the amounts shown on the perpetual records be accounted for? What are some causes for such differences?

6. Which method of inventory valuation would you recommend to Fisher Company management (a) giving reasons for your choice, and (b) stating the effect of your recommendation on the financial statements?

DP10-2. (*Management policy decision problem: Inventory valuation—retail inventory method*) The records of the Tarrasch Company show the following information on January 31, 1976:

	Cost	Sales Price
Merchandise Inventory—		
January 1, 1976	$ 12,700	$18,100
Purchases during January	118,000	176,000
Transportion In	1,600	
Purchases Returns and		
Allowances	4,460	6,650
Markups		17,400
Markdowns		1,800
Sales		180,000

Required:

1. Find the lower of cost or market value of the January 31 inventory, using the retail inventory method.

2. Why are markdowns excluded in arriving at the cost-to-retail ratio? How would you describe the valuation if markdowns are not excluded? if both markups and markdowns are excluded?

3. The Tarrasch Company has had frequent inventory shortages in certain of its departments. What steps should management take to eliminate these shortages?

DP10-3. (*Accounting policy decision problem: Inventory valuation—gross margin method*) A fire destroyed the entire inventory of the Mannes Corporation on December 23, 1976. The following information is available for the years 1975 and 1976 (to the date of the fire):

	1976	1975
Merchandise Inventory, January 1	$ 36,200	$ 34,450
Sales	142,800	136,600
Sales Returns and Allowances	2,750	3,100
Purchases	120,000	103,300
Purchases Returns and Allowances	6,350	7,300
Transportation In	4,800	5,460

Required:

1. Estimate the amount of the inventory destroyed by the fire.
2. How reliable is the estimate?
3. Should this method be used for financial reporting purposes to eliminate the need for physical inventory taking?

P10-1. (*Accounting policy decision problem*) Purchases and sales data for the first three years of operation of the Andover Company for a single item were as follows (purchases are listed in order of acquisition):

	1974	*1975*	*1976*
Sales	19,200 units at $52	24,000 units at $62	29,000 units at $68
Purchases	6,500 units at $25	9,000 units at $35	11,000 units at $43
	10,000 units at $27	10,000 units at $37	7,500 units at $46
	8,000 units at $33	6,500 units at $40	8,000 units at $48

Required:

1. Prepare a schedule showing the number of units on hand at the end of each year.
2. Compute the year-end inventories under the periodic inventory system for each of the three years, using (a) FIFO and (b) LIFO.
3. Prepare income statements for each of the three years through gross margin on sales on the basis (a) of FIFO, (b) of LIFO, and (c) of weighted average.
4. Which method of inventory valuation do you think is the most logical? Why?
5. (a) As a manager, which method would you prefer, assuming that you are paid a bonus based on earnings? (b) which method would you prefer if you were (1) a present shareholder; (2) a prospective shareholder.

P10-2. The following data are from the inventory records of a single item of the Lawn Company:

Purchases	*Sales*	*Balance*
		100 units at $1.10
200 units at $1.30		
100 units at 1.40		
	120 units at ?	
40 units at 1.50		
	60 units at ?	
	40 units at ?	
100 units at 1.60		

Required: Determine the ending inventory and the cost of goods sold using:

1. FIFO and (a) the periodic inventory system, (b) the perpetual inventory system.
2. LIFO and (a) the periodic inventory system, (b) the perpetual inventory system.
3. Weighted average and the periodic inventory system.

P10-3. The Weir Machine Company buys and sells planers. Purchases and sales during March 1976 are shown below.

	Purchases	*Sales*
March 2	88 units at $300	
3		160 units
9	84 units at $375	
15	92 units at $340	
20		60 units
25	88 units at $360	
30		172 units

The inventory on March 1 consisted of 100 units at $450 each.

Required:

1. Compute the cost of goods sold during March, using LIFO and the periodic inventory system.
2. Compute the cost of goods sold during March, using FIFO and the perpetual·inventory system.

P10-4. (*Accounting policy decision problem*) In October 1976, the Hodge Company began buying and selling a recently patented stamping machine. Transactions for the month follow:

1976
Oct. 2   Purchased a machine at $9,900.
  7   Purchased a machine at $10,500.
  15 Sold a machine at $21,000.
  20 Purchased a machine at $12,000.
  28 Sold a machine at $21,000.
  Operating expenses for October were $12,000.

Required:

1. Record the information on perpetual inventory records, using each of the following methods: (a) FIFO, (b) moving average, and (c) LIFO.
2. Prepare an income statement based on each of the three methods of inventory valuation.
3. Give reasons for the variations in the cost of goods sold and the net income in the three statements.
4. What factors should be considered when choosing a method of inventory valuation?
5. Assume that Hodge is about to purchase another machine before the end of the month but asks you first (a) how the purchase will affect the net income for the month, and (b) whether he should defer the purchase until early in November. The price will not change. What would you recommend?

P10-5. (*Accounting policy decision problem*) The inventory of the Kaufman Upholstering Company on December 31, 1976, consisted of the following items:

		Unit	
	Quantity	Cost	Market
Frames			
Type F-1	110	$14.25	$15.50
Type F-12	75	26.00	22.50
Type F-15	60	21.50	21.00
Springs (sets)			
Type S-1	760	7.28	8.50
Type S-12	625	10.50	11.50
Type S-15	340	8.60	6.00

Required:

1. Compute the ending inventory at the lower of cost or market, applied (a) to each item, (b) to each category, and (c) to the entire inventory.
2. What is the effect of each application of LCM on the gross margin in the current year? in the following year?

3. It is maintained by some that LCM pricing is inherently inconsistent and that its application may result in income distortions. Discuss.

P10-6. (*Accounting policy decision problem*) The following data relate to an inventory item of the Morris Company:

	Units	Unit Cost
Beginning balance	180	$3.00
First purchase	300	3.00
Second purchase	600	3.30
First sale	525	
Third purchase	750	3.60
Second sale	825	
Fourth purchase	300	3.75
Third sale	150	

Required:

1. Compute the cost value of the ending inventory under each of the following methods: (a) Weighted average—periodic, (b) FIFO—perpetual, (c) LIFO—perpetual, (d) FIFO—periodic, and (e) LIFO—periodic.
2. Assume that the current replacement costs of all the items in the inventory have increased significantly since they were acquired. How would this change your answer? What would be the effect of using the current replacement costs?

P10-7. The records of the Fair Boutique show the following information for the month of June 1976:

Sales	$200,000
Markups	15,000
Markdowns	26,250
Transportation In	3,000
Purchases at cost	142,500
Purchases at retail	210,000
Inventory—June 1, at cost	52,500
Inventory—June 1, at retail	75,000

Required: Compute the June 30 inventory at the lower of cost or market, using the retail inventory method. (*Hint:* Include the markups but exclude the markdowns in the computation of the cost percentage.)

P10-8. (*Accounting policy decision problem*) The Rook Company estimates its merchandise inventory when preparing monthly financial statements. The following information is available on April 30:

	Cost	Retail
Merchandise Inventory, April 1	$120,000	$ 195,000
Purchases during April (net)	975,000	1,650,000
Transportation In during April	6,000	
Sales during April (net)		960,000

Required:

1. Compute the estimated inventory on April 30, using the gross margin method. On the basis of past experience, Rook estimates a rate of gross margin of 40% for the current year.
2. Compute the estimated inventory on April 30, using the retail inventory method.

MEASUREMENT
AND CONTROL
OF INVENTORY

(Ch. 10)

411

3. (a) Give the reason for the difference in the ending inventory under the two methods. (b) Which method is more reliable? Why?

P10-9. The Singer Company closes its books annually on December 31, at which time the merchandise inventory is determined by a physical count. For its monthly interim statements, however, inventory estimates based on the gross margin method are used. Condensed partial income statements for the years 1973, 1974, and 1975 follow:

	1973	*1974*	*1975*
Sales	$437,500	$500,000	$550,000
Cost of Goods Sold	262,500	295,000	319,000
Gross Margin	$175,000	$205,000	$231,000

The merchandise inventory on December 31, 1975, was $87,500. During January 1976, sales were $55,000 and purchases were $50,000.

Required:

1. Compute the inventory on January 31, 1976, based (a) on the gross margin rate for the prior three years and (b) on the average of the past three annual gross margin rates.
2. Which gross margin rate should be used? Why?

P10-10. James Pitkin, the owner of a retail store, has always carried fire insurance on his inventory. Under the terms of the policy, he is to collect from the insurance company 80% of any loss of merchandise inventory from fire.

On the morning of August 2, 1976, Pitkin's store was destroyed by fire. The fixtures and the inventory were a total loss. The records, which were kept in a fireproof safe, were not destroyed.

Operations for the period January 1 through August 1 resulted in the following balances:

Sales	$34,320
Heat, Light, and Water Expense	102
Inventory—January 1, 1976	4,800
Transportation In	600
Salaries and Wages	7,280
Purchases	23,800
Sales Returns and Allowances	112
Salesmen's Commissions	2,080
Purchases Returns and Allowances	460
Sales Discounts	608
Purchases Discounts	140

Pitkin's records also include an income statement for the year ended December 31, 1975, which is condensed as follows:

Sales		$68,800
Cost of Goods Sold		48,160
Gross Margin		$20,640
Expenses		
Selling	$6,000	
General	7,760	13,760
Net Income		$ 6,880

Required: Compute the amount of merchandise inventory lost in the fire and the amount that Pitkin may expect to collect from the insurance company.

P10-11. (*Accounting policy decision problem*) On July 1, 1976, Seth Matthew established the Matthew Company with an investment of $20,000 in cash. Purchases and sales of an item during the month are shown below.

1976
July 1 Purchased $2,880 units at $19.20.

  10 Sold 1,680 units at $32.

  13 Purchased 2,400 units at $20.40.

  17 Sold 2,640 units at $32.

  22 Purchased 3,600 units at $21.20.

  30 Sold 2,160 units at $32.

Operating expenses were $22,400. Cash settlements on all transactions were completed by the end of the month.

Required:

1. Prepare perpetual inventory schedules, using (a) FIFO, (b) LIFO, and (c) moving average.
2. Prepare income statements and statements of financial position based on each method of inventory valuation.
3. Explain why the different methods yield different results. Which method is correct?
4. What other factors should Matthew consider in his choice of a method of inventory valuation?
5. Which method would you recommend? Explain.
6. FIFO reflects price increases on goods on hand in net income but these are not real profits because, as the inventory is depleted, replacement costs will be higher. Do you agree? Explain.

P10-12. (*Accounting policy decision problem*) The following notes accompanied the annual reports of companies A, B, and C:

Company A

Inventories are stated at the lower of cost or market. The inventories at December 31, 1976, include $67,427 of precious metals of the A Industries Division, of which amount approximately 78% is valued at cost prices under the last-in, first-out method of valuation. At December 31, 1976, the market value of such precious metal inventories exceeded the carrying value by $26,234. Taxes on income would become payable on any realization of this excess by reason of reduction of precious metals inventories.

Required:

1. Discuss the purpose of this note?
2. (a) Would you recommend that the precious metal inventories be stated at their market values? (b) If so, what entry would you make? (c) What would be the effect on the statement of financial position and the income statement? (d) What accounting principles are involved?
3. What inventory management policies would be needed to avoid the additional taxes on income referred to in the last sentence?

Company B

Inventories consist of the following:

	December 31	
	1976	1975
At the lower of cost (principally first-in, first-out, and average) or market:		
Finished goods	$ 65,980	$ 57,537
Work in process	21,083	21,593
Raw materials and supplies	55,443	31,025
At cost (whiskey, other spirits, and wine):		
Tax paid	28,721	
In bond	293,599	
	$464,826	$110,155

A substantial portion of in-bond inventories of whiskey, other spirits, and wine in storage for aging over a period of several years are classified as current assets in accordance with general practice prevailing in the distilling industry. Inventories of whiskey, other spirits, and wine, under existing Federal and other applicable laws, are subject to payment of excise taxes and other levies on removal from bonded or other government-controlled premises.

Required:

1. What principle supports the classification of inventories "in storage for aging" as a current asset?
2. What caused the quadrupling of the company's inventory during the year?
3. Are the inventory valuation procedures used by the company "conservative?" Explain.

Company C

The amounts of inventories were determined using the following methods:

Lower of cost or market	$348,165
Cost, less amortization (primarily theatrical and television films)	124,664
Estimated net sales price (commodities, primarily sold but not shipped)	15,403
	$488,232

Required: Discuss the inventory valuation procedures of this company. Indicate the existing conditions justifying the use of amortized cost and estimated selling price for parts of the inventory.

P10-13. (*Accounting policy decision problem*) The following information was extracted from the financial records of the Oaklite Corporation:

	1976	1975	1974
Sales	$500,000	$450,000	$300,000
Purchases	275,000	230,000	200,000
End-of-year inventory	80,000	60,000	55,000

The Oaklite Corporation began operations at the beginning of 1974 and has used the FIFO method of inventory valuation. John Jordan, who was appointed president of the corporation early in 1977, seeks your advice regarding inventory accounting policy and inventory management, and raises the following questions (assume that increases in end-of-year inventories are due entirely to price increases):

1. What would have been the difference in net income if the company had used the LIFO method of inventory valuation?
2. What would have been the effect (a) on total assets and on stockholders' equity if LIFO had been used? (b) on the inventory turnover rates?
3. What are the implications of a changeover to LIFO in terms (a) of financial reporting and disclosure requirements and (b) of the actual physical flow of the goods?
4. What should be the central objective of the firm's inventory policies and procedures?

Jordan believes that both counting and pricing errors were made when physical inventories were taken, and he wants to know (a) the effect of inventory errors on the financial statements, (b) what steps he should take to prevent such errors, and (c) whether there is any way of avoiding the disrupting and time-consuming effects of the annual physical inventory taking.

Required: Write a report answering Jordan's specific questions, and add any other comments that may be useful to him.

P10-14. The following financial statements were prepared by the Joslin Corporation and given to its independent CPA for use in his annual audit of the firm's accounts and records:

JOSLIN CORPORATION
Income Statement
For the Year Ended December 31, 1976

Net Sales Revenue		$240,000
Cost of Goods Sold		
Merchandise Inventory, January 1, 1976	$ 30,000	
Purchases (net)	125,000	
Cost of Merchandise Available for Sale	$155,000	
Deduct Merchandise Inventory,		
December 31, 1976	23,000	
Cost of Goods Sold		132,000
Gross Margin on Sales		$108,000
Operating Expenses		81,500
Net Income		$ 26,500

JOSLIN CORPORATION
Statement of Financial Position
December 31, 1976

Assets

Current Assets	
Cash	$ 15,000
Accounts Receivable	80,000
Merchandise Inventory	23,000
Other Current Assets	5,000
Total Current Assets	$123,000
Plant and Equipment (net)	120,000
Total Assets	$243,000

MEASUREMENT
AND CONTROL
OF INVENTORY

Liabilities and Stockholders' Equity

Current Liabilities		
Accounts Payable		$ 35,000
Other Current Liabilities		26,000
Total Current Liabilities		$ 61,000
Long-Term Liabilities		40,000
Total Liabilities		$101,000
Stockholders' Equity		
Capital Stock	$120,000	
Retained Earnings	22,000	
Total Stockholders' Equity		142,000
Total Liabilities and Stockholders' Equity		$243,000

As a result of his audit, the CPA found the following errors or omissions:

1. The ending inventory was overstated by $1,250 as a result of a number of counting and pricing errors of goods on hand.
2. Several purchases on account totaling $750 made late in December were not recorded although the goods were received and included in the ending inventory.
3. A sale of merchandise on December 30 for $800 which cost $500 was not recorded until January 5, 1977. The goods were not included in the ending inventory.
4. A sale of merchandise on account for $500 late in December was not recorded, but the goods sold, which cost $300, were included in the ending inventory.
5. A purchase on account for $800 was not recorded. The goods were received on December 31 but were not included in the ending inventory.
6. A purchase made late in December was recorded when payment was made on January 10, 1977. The goods, costing $850, were received on December 24, 1976, and were included in the ending inventory.

Required: Prepare revised financial statements.

P10-15. (*Management policy decision problem*) The Raiso Construction Company maintains a central warehouse for storage of hardware items, wiring and electrical supplies, and plumbing supplies. The inventory has gradually increased until about 2,000 different items are stored in the warehouse. Robert Raiso feels that there is no need for an inventory control system, because his warehouse operator has been with the company for years and, as he says, "Henry knows where everything is."

Required: On the basis of ability to produce a daily stock status report, list for Raiso some advantages of a computer application.

Plant and Equipment— Acquisition, Depreciation, and Disposal

11

Industrial expansion often requires large expenditures for land, buildings, machinery, and equipment. When such expenditures must be made in an economic environment marked by sweeping technological changes, inflation, and high levels of taxation, the accounting problems become both more complicated and more controversial. This chapter deals with the determination of and accounting for the cost of plant assets, the allocation of these asset costs to the appropriate accounting periods, the disposal or retirement of plant assets, and related problems of management planning and control.

The term *plant and equipment* denotes all assets of a tangible and relatively permanent nature, acquired for use in the regular operations of the business, not for resale, and whose use or consumption will cover more than one accounting period. This classification includes land, buildings, machinery, trucks, fixtures, tools, office machines, furniture and furnishings, patterns, and dies. The terms *plant assets, capital assets, fixed assets, tangible assets,* and *noncurrent assets* are often used as synonyms for plant and equipment. The term *intangible assets* denotes nonphysical rights and expected benefits that come from the ownership of these intangible assets.

COST OF PLANT AND EQUIPMENT

The cost of plant and equipment includes the purchase price (less any discount) plus all other expenditures required to secure title and to get the asset ready for operating use. The cost of buildings includes permit fees, engineering fees, and remodeling costs. The cost of machinery includes transportation, installation, and all other costs incurred in preparing the machinery for operations.

Assume that a company purchases a machine for $5,000 at terms of 2/10, n/60, with freight to be paid by the buyer. Installation of the machine requires specialized electrical wiring and the construction of a cement foundation. All these expenditures are charged to the asset account. The total asset cost includes the following:

Purchase price	$5,000
Deduct 2% cash discount	100
Net purchase price	$4,900
Transportation	125
Cost of wiring	75
Construction of a special foundation	110
Total asset cost	$5,210

The entry for the purchase of the machine is the net cash paid on purchase.

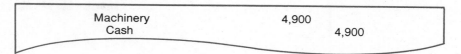

Machinery	4,900	
Cash		4,900

The entry for the freight payment is:

Machinery	125	
Cash		125

The entry to record the payment for installation of the machine is:

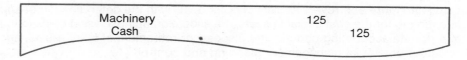

Machinery	185	
Cash		185

When these entries are posted, the Machinery account shows a total cost for the machine of $5,210. If the discount of $100 is not taken, it should still be deducted from the purchase price of $5,000 and charged to Discounts Lost—Nonmerchandise Items. An asset acquired in some manner other than by cash payment—for example, by gift or issuance of securities—is valued on the basis of the amount of cash that would be required for its acquisition (*fair market value*). When a used plant asset is acquired, all expenditures incurred in getting the asset ready for use—paint, replacement parts, and so on—are charged to the asset account.

The cost of land includes brokers' fees, legal fees, transfer taxes, as well as costs incurred in preparing the land for use, such as grading, clearing, and the removal of unwanted existing structures. Land is shown separately on the position statement, because it is not subject to depreciation. However, improvements to land—landscaping, lighting, parking areas, fencing—which deteriorate through usage, are subject to depreciation and should be classified in a separate account, such as Land Improvements.

DEPRECIATION OF PLANT AND EQUIPMENT

Depreciation is not necessarily a measure of the decline in the value of an asset, but rather a recognition that depreciable assets used in the business have a predictable and limited service life over which asset costs should be allocated for income measurement. The emphasis is on the periodic charge to expense rather than the resulting position statement valuation.

> Since most plant and equipment assets have a limited useful life, their cost is properly allocable as an expense to the accounting periods in which the assets are used.

Allocation of Plant and Equipment Costs

Although the serviceable life of the asset cannot be definitely known at the time of its acquisition, the cost of the asset cannot be considered as an expense chargeable entirely either to the period of acquisition or to the period of disposal. It is better to make an estimation of the useful life of the asset for purposes of making the periodic charge to expense than to omit the charge on the grounds that there is no strictly scientific way of making such an estimation.

Depreciation should be distinguished from *depletion.* Depletion (discussed later in this chapter) refers to the process of estimating and recording the periodic charges to operations due to the exhaustion of a natural resource, such as coal, oil, or standing timber. Although *amortization* is often used as a general term to cover write-downs of assets, it is most commonly used to describe periodic allocation of costs of intangible assets.

Several factors limit the serviceability of plant assets, chiefly wear and tear through ordinary use, accidental damage, inadequacy, level of repairs or maintenance, and obsolescence. Inadequacy may be due to changes in the nature of the business—method of manufacture, location, or type or design of product—that necessitate the disposition or replacement of plant assets. Obsolescence is due to technological advances that necessitate replacement of an existing asset with a new model.

Estimated Useful Life (EUL)

It is often difficult to predict the useful service life of an asset. The estimate is important, because the amount of cost assigned to each period (depreciation

PLANT AND EQUIPMENT

for a period) is deducted from current revenue, thereby affecting net income for the period. Past experience, standard operating policies, and equipment replacement policies may be used in estimating the period during which the asset can or will be used by the business. A machine may be able to withstand wear and tear for perhaps twenty years, but it may be used for only ten years because it has become too slow or too small for current requirements; or it may have to be replaced because the particular model has become obsolete. In any case, the cost is allocated over the *estimated useful life* (EUL) of the asset.

The 1971 Revenue Act established the Class Life Asset Depreciation Range (ADR) system permitting taxpayers to take as a reasonable allowance for depreciation on all types of tangible property an amount based on any period of years within a range specified for designated classes of assets. This system is designed to minimize disputes between the taxpayer and the Internal Revenue Service regarding useful lives, salvage value, and repair allowances. For example, the printing, publishing, and allied industries have a guideline life of eleven years, with a range from nine to thirteen years.

Estimated Salvage Value

The amount of the asset to be depreciated is its acquisition cost minus the amount that is expected to be recovered when the asset is ultimately scrapped, sold, or traded in (salvage or residual value). If an expenditure will be required in dismantling or removing the asset, the estimated gross salvage value is reduced by the anticipated removal cost. It is frequently assumed that the salvage value will be offset by the removal cost; in this case, depreciation is computed on the total cost of the asset. Also, total cost may be depreciated when the salvage value is known to be negligible. A company may trade in any assets that have a market value. For example, some businesses trade in cars, trucks, and office equipment for new models after a period of use. In such instances, the estimated cash market value at the date of trade-in should be deducted in arriving at the depreciable amount. Experience will enable the company to arrive at a salvage value factor.

Under the Class Life ADR system, for tax accounting the taxpayer can disregard salvage value completely when computing periodic charges, but the account cannot be depreciated below a reasonable salvage value.

Methods of Computing Depreciation

A number of methods are used to calculate periodic depreciation charges; each may give a significantly different result. The method selected in any specific instance should be based on a careful evaluation of all the factors involved, including estimated useful life, intensity of use, rapidity of changes in the technology of the industry and of the equipment, and revenue-generating potential. The objective is to charge each period in proportion to the benefits received during that period from the total pool of expected benefits over the asset's useful life. Procedures for allocating the cost of the asset to each accounting period within its service life are based on either uniform or varying charges. By the use of certain methods, the amounts charged to each period may be irregular, or they may follow a regularly increasing or decreasing pattern.

The method selected for computing depreciation is crucial, because the amount of the charge affects the income measurement for current and future periods and the carrying value of the asset in the position statement. This in turn affects some of the ratios and analyses used to measure the effectiveness of management in the use of plant and equipment assets.

Straight-Line Method. Under the straight-line method, depreciation is considered a function of time, and a uniform portion of the cost is allocated to each accounting period. Degrees of use, age, or efficiency factors are not considered in determining the amount of depreciation to be assigned to each period. The straight-line method may be expressed as follows:

$$\frac{\text{Cost less salvage value}}{\substack{\text{Number of accounting periods in} \\ \text{estimated useful life of asset}}} = \substack{\text{Depreciation for each} \\ \text{accounting period}}$$

Assume that a machine costing $5,210, with an estimated service life of five years and an estimated net salvage value of $210, is purchased on January 2, 1976. The annual depreciation charge is:

$$\frac{\$5,210 - \$210}{5} = \$1,000$$

The straight-line method is popular primarily because it is simple to use. It assumes, however, level operating efficiency, repair and maintenance, and revenue contributions.

Production Methods. Production methods relate depreciation to usage or to results rather than time, recognizing either working hours or units of output with each unit being charged with an equal amount regardless of decline in service effectiveness, decline in revenue generated, or level of repair and maintenance requirements.

The *working-hours method* requires an estimate of useful life in service hours instead of years. The charge to depreciation for an accounting period is determined as follows:

$$\frac{\text{Cost less salvage value}}{\text{Total estimated working hours}} = \substack{\text{Depreciation expense} \\ \text{per hour}}$$

$$\substack{\text{Depreciation} \\ \text{expense} \\ \text{per hour}} \times \substack{\text{Working hours} \\ \text{for the} \\ \text{period}} = \substack{\text{Depreciation} \\ \text{expense for} \\ \text{the period}}$$

An alternative computation procedure is:

$$\text{Cost less salvage value} \times \frac{\substack{\text{Working hours} \\ \text{for the period}}}{\substack{\text{Total estimated} \\ \text{working hours}}} = \substack{\text{Depreciation} \\ \text{expense for} \\ \text{the period}}$$

Assume, for example, that a machine costing $21,000 with a salvage value of $1,000 is expected to render 40,000 hours of service. If it is used for 5,000 hours during an accounting period, the computation for that period would be:

$$\frac{\$21,000 - \$1,000}{40,000 \text{ hrs.}} = \$0.50 \text{ per service hour}$$

$0.50 × 5,000 hrs. = $2,500 depreciation expense for the period

Under the *production-unit method,* depreciation is computed on units of output, and therefore an estimate of total units of output is required. If the machine in the previous example had an estimated productive life of 10,000 units and if 1,500 units were processed during the current period, the charge to depreciation for the period would be:

$$\frac{\$21,000 - \$1,000}{10,000 \text{ units}} = \$2 \text{ per unit produced}$$

$2 × 1,500 units = $3,000 depreciation expense for the period

The production methods allocate cost in proportion to the use that is made of the asset, the assumption being that there is a correlation between units of use and revenue generated. The straight-line method ignores use, emphasizing the fact that the asset is available; depreciation expense is regarded as a measure of such availability, irrespective of the extent of use.

Declining-Amount Methods. The use of a declining-amount method results in larger depreciation charges during the early years of asset life with gradually decreasing charges in later years. Some commonly used forms are the *declining-balance method* and the *sum-of-the-years'-digits method.*

Under the *declining-balance method,* a uniform depreciation rate is applied in each period to the remaining *carrying value* (cost less accumulated depreciation). For Federal income tax purposes, the rate may not exceed twice the straight-line rate (*double-rate* declining balance) for most new assets. Another commonly used rate is *150 percent declining balance,* which is one and one-half times the straight-line rate. The computation is made without an adjustment for salvage, even though the asset cannot be depreciated below a reasonable salvage value, presumably because the arithmetic of this formula is such that it will never reduce the asset balance to zero. At the end of the EUL, therefore, the remaining balance (less salvage) may be depreciated under the straight-line method over a period determined at that time or by an adjustment in the amount of the depreciation for the final period, or it may continue to be reduced at the fixed percentage of the carrying value until it is retired from use.

Assume that a $10,000 machine is purchased on January 2, 1976, with an estimated life of ten years and an estimated net salvage value of $500. A 20 percent depreciation rate—twice the straight-line rate of 10 percent—applied to the remaining carrying value gives the following results for the first three years:

Year	Computation	Annual Depreciation	Accumulated Depreciation	Carrying Value
1976	20% × $10,000	$2,000	$2,000	$8,000
1977	20% × 8,000	1,600	3,600	6,400
1978	20% × 6,400	1,280	4,880	5,120

The entry to record the depreciation charge for 1978 and the position statement presentation of the machine at the end of that year are as follows:

Depreciation Expense—Machinery and Equipment	1,280	
Accumulated Depreciation—		
Machinery and Equipment		1,280

Plant and Equipment
Machinery and Equipment $10,000
Deduct Accumulated Depreciation   4,880 $5,120

Under the *sum-of-the-years'-digits method,* depreciation for any year is determined by multiplying the cost less salvage of the asset by a fraction, the denominator of which is the sum of the numbers of the years of estimated useful life of the asset and the numerator of which is the number of the specific period applied in reverse order, or the number of years remaining, including the current year.

Assume that a machine costing $15,300 is purchased on January 2, 1976; the EUL is five years and the estimated salvage value is $300. The denominator of the fraction used is $1 + 2 + 3 + 4 + 5 = 15$. The annual depreciation is computed as follows:

Year	Years Digits	Fraction	Annual Depreciation
1976	5	$5/15 \times \$15,000$	$ 5,000
1977	4	$4/15 \times 15,000$	4,000
1978	3	$3/15 \times 15,000$	3,000
1979	2	$2/15 \times 15,000$	2,000
1980	1	$1/15 \times 15,000$	1,000
Total	15		
Total depreciation for 5 years			$15,000

For long-lived assets, the sum-of-the-years'-digits can be found by using

PLANT AND
EQUIPMENT

the formula for a simple arithmetic progression, $s = n/2\,(a + l)$, where $n =$ EUL, $a = 1$, and $l =$ the last year. In the previous example, the computation would be:

$$\text{number of years in series} = n/2\,(a + l) = 5/2\,(1 + 5) = 15$$

On the basis of the same facts, the results under the double-rate declining-balance method (20% $\times$ 2) are as follows (amounts are rounded to nearest dollar):

Year	Computation	Annual Depreciation	Accumulated Depreciation	Carrying Value
1976	40% of $15,300	$6,120	$ 6,120	$9,180
1977	40% of 9,180	3,672	9,792	5,508
1978	40% of 5,508	2,203	11,995	3,305
1979	40% of 3,305	1,322	13,317	1,983
1980	40% of 1,983	793	14,110	1,190

A comparison of the three methods shows the following depreciation under each:

Year	Straight Line	Double-Rate Declining Balance (40%)	Sum of the Years' Digits
1976	$ 3,000	$ 6,120	$ 5,000
1977	3,000	3,672	4,000
1978	3,000	2,203	3,000
1979	3,000	1,322	2,000
1980	3,000	793	1,000
Totals	$15,000	$14,110	$15,000

The double-rate declining-balance method results in the highest depreciation in the first year because of the higher rate and the higher base ($15,300 as compared with $15,000). However, an undepreciated amount of $1,190 = ($15,300 − $14,110) remains at the end of the fifth year. If the machine is to be kept in service, $890 = ($1,190 − $300) may be written off on a straight-line basis over the remaining period of use.

Group Rates and Composite Rates

Some companies simplify the computation of depreciation and charge depreciation uniformly to all service years including the final one by use of a *group* or *composite* rate, applied either to all the assets owned or to each major asset category. The term *group* refers to a number of homogeneous assets.

When a group rate is applied to a number of nonhomogeneous assets, it is called a *composite* rate; it is a special application of the group rate. The group rate is especially useful if there are a large number of individual units with similar service lives and relatively low costs (for example, railroad tracks and ties, telephone poles and cables, and restaurant and hotel furniture). The use of a group rate eliminates the clerical work necessary to compute individual periodic depreciation and the need for detailed records of accumulated amounts. Its use is satisfactory if the assets are kept for relatively long periods and if variations in individual rates, either over or under the group rate, tend to cancel out.

Several methods may be used to develop a composite rate; one is illustrated below.

Asset	Cost	Estimated Salvage Value	Depreciable Cost	EUL (Years)	Annual Depreciation (Straight Line)
A	$20,000	$2,000	$18,000	6	$3,000
B	15,000	–0–	15,000	10	1,500
C	10,200	600	9,600	12	800
	$45,200	$2,600	$42,600		$5,300

The *composite life* for this group of assets is 8.04 years, computed as follows:

$$\frac{\text{Depreciable cost}}{\text{Annual depreciation}} = \frac{\$42,600}{\$5,300} = 8.04 \text{ years of average life}$$

A group rate may be used with either straight-line depreciation or a declining-amount method. Assuming that the straight-line method is used, the annual rate to be applied is:

$$\frac{\text{Annual depreciation}}{\text{Total cost}} = \frac{\$5,300}{\$45,200} = 0.1172, \text{ or } 11.72\%$$

Total depreciation at a mean rate of 11.72 percent, applied each year for 8.04 years to the total cost of $45,200, will be $42,600 = ($45,200 × 0.1172 × 8.04, adjusted for rounding), the amount to be depreciated. The annual depreciation charge is $5,297.44 = ($45,200 × 11.72%).

When any unit in the group is disposed of, it is assumed that it has been fully depreciated and no gain or loss on disposal is recognized. Underdepreciation on items in the group used for less than their estimated useful lives is assumed to be offset by overdepreciation on items used longer than their EULs. Although accumulated depreciation records on the individual units in the group are not kept, a record of original costs is kept.

Assume that asset A is retired at zero salvage value after four years of service. The entry to record the retirement is:

(Ch. 11)

```
Accumulated Depreciation              20,000
    Asset Account                                20,000
        To record retirement of Asset A; salvage
        value is zero.
```

If $4,000 in salvage value were realized, the entry would be:

```
Accumulated Depreciation              16,000
Cash                                   4,000
    Asset Account                                20,000
        To record sale of asset A
        for $4,000.
```

The debit to Accumulated Depreciation is the cost of the asset less proceeds from the sale.

Given accurate estimates of EUL and salvage values, the carrying value of the group is zero when the last item in the group is retired and there is indeed no gain or loss on disposal. But because errors in forecasting are likely and because an error made on one item affects the rate used on all other items in that group, it is essential that the rate be revised whenever acquisitions or disposals change the composition of the group with respect to types of assets, estimated useful lives, and so on. The Internal Revenue Service permits the application of a single rate to groups of accounts, composite accounts, and accounts classified as to use.

Depreciation for Partial Accounting Periods

A consistent method should be followed for recording depreciation on assets acquired or retired during the accounting period. A variety of procedures are used. One that is popular because of its simplicity is to consider that a plant asset is purchased as of the beginning of the month of acquisition if it is purchased on or before the fifteenth of the month, and to consider that a plant asset is purchased on the first day of the following month if it is purchased on or after the sixteenth of the month, the minimum measurable unit of time for the depreciation expense charge being one month.

Assume that a machine costing $6,500 with an estimated life of ten years and salvage value of $500 was purchased on November 10, 1976. Depreciation on the machine for the calendar year 1976, using straight line, is:

$$\frac{\$6,500 - \$500}{10} \times \frac{2}{12} = \$100$$

The year-end entry to record depreciation on the machine for two months is:

(Ch. 11)

```
Depreciation Expense—Machinery and Equipment          100
    Accumulated Depreciation—Machinery and Equipment          100
```

If the machine had been acquired on or after November 16, the amount in the entry would be $50. Depreciation may have to be recorded for a partial accounting period when an asset is sold, discarded, or exchanged for another asset. In these situations, depreciation must be recorded to the date of the event, assuming that the asset has not already been fully depreciated. The amount of depreciation to be charged for the month of disposal is based on the method followed for acquisitions. The rules must be applied consistently.

DEPRECIATION METHODS COMPARED—MANAGEMENT CONSIDERATIONS

The process of recording depreciation gives recognition to the expiration of asset cost through use. Its primary purpose is cost allocation, not to report the plant asset at the amount for which it could be sold currently. Plant assets are not acquired for resale.

Purpose of Depreciation

The method that is most practical and meaningful for the user should be selected. Since the amount of the depreciation deduction has a direct effect on net income and since the alternative methods of calculating depreciation result in different amounts, the method chosen may significantly affect the income tax liability. The declining-amount methods, in contrast to the straight-line method, reduce the tax liability and conserve working capital during the early life of the asset by deferring or postponing tax payments for some period. These funds become available for investment in new plant and equipment or for any other use management chooses. A company may use one method for income tax reporting and a different method for financial reporting.

The straight-line method is simple to apply and is satisfactory under conditions of fairly uniform usage. Two objections to the method are:

1. The straight-line depreciation charge results in a uniform deduction from revenue without adjustment for variation in sales volume or rate of output during the period.
2. If expenditures for repairs increase gradually with continued use of the asset, the deduction from revenue for the combined expenses of repairs and depreciation will increase annually, thus distorting the reported income.

The production methods allocate depreciation in proportion to usage or output. This is important if usage is the dominant cause of loss in usefulness of the asset. It should be emphasized that the estimate of useful life is based on anticipated total usage before disposal of the asset regardless of the reason—wear and tear, obsolescence, or inadequacy.

The declining-amount methods are based on the hypothesis that the service rendered by a plant asset is greatest in the early years of use; hence, that

PLANT AND
EQUIPMENT

depreciation charged under these methods results in a more accurate matching of expense and revenue. The rapidity of the decline in service value varies with the demand for the product and the rate of technological progress. If revenues drop significantly during the early years of use and if rapid changes in technology shorten the economic life of the asset, then the deduction of larger amounts of depreciation in early years is matched by the relatively larger revenues, and the concomitant diminishing depreciation deductions in later years are matched against the diminishing revenues of those years.

Another reason for using the declining-amount methods is that as an asset gets older, it requires more maintenance. The increasing maintenance expenses in later years are offset by the diminishing depreciation expense, thus equalizing, to some extent, the total expenses of the asset and thereby achieving a better matching of expense with revenue. The declining-amount methods more closely reflect the economic fact that an investment in an asset is made for the purpose of realizing a desired annual rate of return on the unrecovered portion of the investment. "Entrepreneurs . . . buy the asset to make a profit; hence, conceptually, they discount the bundles of future net services which they purchase. Therefore, by inference, an *ideal depreciation* method is one which allocates cost in such a way as to produce a uniform return on remaining unamortized investment in all periods at the rate of return implicit in the original transaction by which the asset was acquired."[1] The difficulty here is to measure the revenue contribution of a particular asset from a group of assets that collectively generate the revenue for the period.

When a plant and equipment item is depreciated, the depreciable cost of the asset is written off over its useful life. Depreciation expense is included in the income statement as a deduction from revenue. The process of recording depreciation does not provide or segregate funds for the replacement of the property at the end of its EUL; an asset should be depreciated even if there is no intention of replacing it. The acquisition of a new asset creates a new series of depreciation charges. Of course, depreciation deductions reduce income taxes, but the amount by which the tax liability is reduced does not necessarily remain in the business as cash available for the replacement of equipment. It may be employed for a multitude of other purposes—inventory expansion, dividends, and so on. It is possible for a business to segregate an amount of cash equal to the periodic depreciation charges, but such funds, if available, probably would result in a greater return when used in the regular operations of the business.

CAPITAL AND REVENUE EXPENDITURES

Capital versus Revenue Expenditures

The term *expenditure* refers to a payment or a promise to make a future payment for benefits received—that is, for assets or services. Expenditures made on plant and equipment assets during the period of ownership may be classified as *capital expenditures* or *revenue* expenditures. A capital expenditure results in an addition to an asset account; a revenue expenditure results in an addition to an expense account.

[1] Isaac N. Reynolds, "Selecting the Proper Depreciation Method," *Accounting Review* (April 1961), pp. 243–44.

(Ch. 11)

Capital expenditures are payments for asset alterations, additions, and replacements that are significant in amount and which will benefit two or more accounting periods; therefore, through the depreciation process, these expenditures are expenses of such future accounting periods. They prolong the useful life of the asset, make it more valuable, or make it more adaptable. Most commonly they are recorded as increases in plant and equipment; the expenditure is said to have been *capitalized*. Original purchases of land, buildings, machinery, and office equipment are also capital expenditures.

Expenditures for extraordinary repairs made to equipment during its life are also classified as capital expenditures if they extend the useful life or capacity of the asset or otherwise make the asset more serviceable (for example, replacing a manually operated elevator with a fully automated one). Some accountants view an extraordinary repair as a restorative process; they record the increase in the asset by debiting Accumulated Depreciation, thereby canceling past depreciation charges.

Revenue expenditures benefit a current period and are made for the purpose of maintaining the asset in satisfactory operating condition. A routine repair or the replacement of a minor part that has worn out is an expense of the current accounting period, to be deducted from the revenue for the period. These expenditures do not increase the serviceability of the asset beyond the original estimate, but rather represent normal maintenance costs.

Careful distinction between capital and revenue expenditures is one of the fundamental problems of accounting; it is essential for the matching of expenses and revenue and, therefore, for the proper measurement of net income. A capital expenditure recorded as a revenue expenditure—as, for example, a purchase of office equipment charged to Office Expense—causes an understatement of net income in that year. If the error is not corrected, net income for the following years will be overstated by the amount of depreciation expense that would otherwise have been recognized. Conversely, a revenue expenditure recorded as a capital expenditure—as, for example, an office expense charged to Office Equipment—overstates net income for that year. If the error is not corrected, net income for the following years will be understated by the depreciation charge on the overstated portion of the Office Equipment account.

DISPOSAL OF PLANT AND EQUIPMENT

An asset may be disposed of by sale, by being *traded in* as part of the purchase price of a replacement, or by simply being discarded. The accounting treatment of sales and of discards is similar; the treatment of *trade-ins* is somewhat different.

An asset may still be in use after it is fully depreciated—that is, when the balance of the Accumulated Depreciation account, assuming that the salvage value is zero, is equal to the cost of the asset. In this case, no further depreciation is taken and no further entries are required until the asset is disposed of. In the statement of financial position, the Plant and Equipment amount may be followed by a notation of the portion that represents fully depreciated assets still in use.

Sale or Discard of Plant and Equipment

When an asset is sold or discarded, the entry for the transaction must remove the appropriate amounts from the asset and the accumulated depreciation accounts. Assume, for example, that a company acquires a truck on January 2, 1976, at a cost of $5,000. Depreciation is recorded on a straight-line basis at the rate of $1,000 annually (salvage value is assumed to be zero). Five possible situations, together with the methods of accounting for the disposal of the truck, are illustrated.

Example 1—*Discard of fully depreciated asset.* The truck is discarded on March 1, 1981 (in the sixth year).

```
1981
March 1   Accumulated Depreciation–Trucks          5,000
             Trucks                                          5,000
```

The purpose of this entry is to eliminate the accumulated charges from the Accumulated Depreciation account and to reduce the asset account by the original cost of the truck. No depreciation expense would be recorded for the truck for the time it was in use during 1981 because the truck has been completely depreciated by December 31, 1980, the end of its fifth year of use.

Example 2—*Sale of fully depreciated asset.* The truck is sold on March 1, 1981, for $50.

```
1981
March 1   Cash                                         50
          Accumulated Depreciation–Trucks          5,000
             Trucks                                          5,000
             Gain on Disposal of Equipment                     50
```

Gains and losses on disposal of plant assets are measured by the difference between the carrying value of an asset and the proceeds from its disposal: a gain results when the proceeds are greater than the carrying value; a loss results when the proceeds are less than the carrying value. If the asset is fully depreciated, as in the example, the carrying value is zero and the gain is the full amount realized from the sale. A gain or a loss may be indicative of errors in estimating the asset's useful life, salvage value, or both, in which case the gain or loss is, in fact, a correction of prior years' earnings. Also, the carrying value of the asset and, therefore, the gain or loss on disposal are affected by the depreciation procedure used. Gain on Disposal of Equipment is shown in the income statement under Other Revenue. A loss would be shown under Other Expenses.

Example 3—*Sale of asset at a price equal to carrying value.* The truck is sold on July 1, 1980, for $500. The first entry is to record the depreciation for the current year, up to the date of the sale.

```
1980
July 1   Depreciation Expense–Trucks              500
             Accumulated Depreciation–Trucks              500
             To record depreciation on trucks for the
             six-month period 1/1/80 to 7/1/80.
```

The Accumulated Depreciation account now has a credit balance of $4,500, as shown below.

```
                Accumulated Depreciation—Trucks
                        12/31/76      1,000
                        12/31/77      1,000
                        12/31/78      1,000
                        12/31/79      1,000
                         7/1/80         500
```

The entry to record the sale is:

```
1980
July 1   Cash                                      500
         Accumulated Depreciation–Trucks         4,500
             Trucks                                        5,000
```

Example 4—*Sale of asset at a price above carrying value.* The truck is sold on July 1, 1980, for $600. The entry to record the depreciation for the current year, up to the date of the sale, is the same as in Example 3 and is assumed to have been made. The following entry is made to record the sale:

```
1980
July 1   Cash                                      600
         Accumulated Depreciation—Trucks         4,500
             Trucks                                        5,000
             Gain on Disposal of Equipment                  100
```

The gain of $100 is computed as follows:

```
        Cost of truck                       $5,000
        Deduct accumulated depreciation      4,500
        Carrying value of truck             $  500
        Amount received                        600
           Gain on disposal                 $  100
```

PLANT AND
EQUIPMENT

Example 5—*Sale of asset at a price below carrying value.* The truck is sold on July 1, 1980, for $400 in cash. Again, the entry to record the depreciation applicable to the year of sale is the same as in Example 3 and is assumed to have been made. The entry to record the disposal is:

1980		
July 1	Cash	400
	Accumulated Depreciation—Trucks	4,500
	Loss on Disposal of Equipment	100
	Trucks	5,000

The loss of $100 is computed as follows:

Cost of truck	$5,000
Deduct accumulated depreciation	4,500
Carrying value of truck	$ 500
Amount received	400
Loss on disposal	$ 100

Loss on Disposal of Equipment is shown in the income statement under Other Expenses.

Trade-in of Plant and Equipment—Recognition of Gain or Loss

It is common practice to exchange, or trade in, used property when new property is acquired. If the trade-in allowance is not arbitrarily excessive (as a partial offset to an unrealistic list price of the new asset), it may be considered the proper selling price of the old asset, and the new asset is recorded at its list price. After the accumulated depreciation up to the date of the trade-in is recorded, the carrying value of the old asset is compared with its trade-in allowance. A gain is recognized if the trade-in allowance is greater than the carrying value, and a loss is recognized when the trade-in allowance is less than the carrying value. When the carrying value and the trade-in allowance are equal, however, there is no recognized gain or loss. If the list price or trade-in allowance is not realistic, the new asset should be recorded at its *cash market price,* or the cash payment plus the *fair market value* of the asset traded in. The gain or loss can then be measured by the difference between the cash market price of the new equipment and the total of the cash outlay and the carrying value of the old equipment.

Example 1—*Trade-in allowance greater than fair market value.* A truck with a cost of $5,000 and accumulated depreciation up to the date of the trade-in of $4,500 is exchanged for a new truck listed at $6,000. A trade-in allowance of $1,000 is granted on the old truck. The fair market value of the old truck, however, is only $600. The entry to record the trade-in is:

Truck (new)	5,600	
Accumulated Depreciation—Trucks	4,500	
Truck (old)		5,000
Cash		5,000
Gain on Disposal of Equipment		100

The new truck is recorded at its cash market price—the cash payment ($5,000) plus the fair market value ($600) of the old truck. The inflated list price is reduced by the excess ($400) of the trade-in allowance ($1,000) over the fair market value ($600) of the old truck, as shown below.

List price	$6,000
Deduct trade-in allowance	1,000
Cash payment	$5,000
Fair market value of old truck	600
Fair market price of new truck	$5,600

The gain on the trade-in is computed in either of the two following ways:

1. Cost of old truck		$5,000
Accumulated depreciation to date of trade-in		4,500
Carrying value		$ 500
Fair market value		600
Gain on trade-in		$ 100
2. Cash market price of new truck		$5,600
Cash outlay for new truck	$5,000	
Carrying value of old truck	500	5,500
Gain on trade-in		$ 100

The following three examples illustrate the possibilities involved in trade-ins when the trade-in allowance is *equal* to the fair market value of the truck traded in.

Example 2—*Trade-in allowance greater than carrying value.* A truck that cost $5,000 with accumulated depreciation of $4,500 up to the date of the trade-in is exchanged for a new one listed at $4,000; the trade-in allowance is $800. The fair market value of the old truck is $800. Again, the new truck is recorded at its cash market price—the cash payment plus the fair market value of the old truck. The transaction is recorded as follows:

PLANT AND
EQUIPMENT

Truck (new)	4,000	
Accumulated Depreciation—Trucks	4,500	
Cash		3,200
Truck (old)		5,000
Gain on Disposal of Equipment		300

The gain on disposal of the truck is computed as follows:

Cost of old truck	$5,000
Accumulated depreciation to date of trade-in	4,500
Carrying value—unrecovered cost	$ 500
Trade-in allowance	800
Gain on trade-in	$ 300

Example 3—*Trade-in allowance less than carrying value.* The old truck in Example 2 is traded in for an allowance of $400.

Truck (new)	4,000	
Accumulated Depreciation—Trucks	4,500	
Loss on Disposal of Equipment	100	
Cash		3,600
Truck (old)		5,000

The loss on disposal of the truck is computed as follows:

Cost of old truck	$5,000
Accumulated depreciation to date of trade-in	4,500
Carrying value—unrecovered cost	$ 500
Trade-in allowance	400
Loss on trade-in	$ 100

Example 4—*Trade-in allowance the same as carrying value.* The old truck in Example 2 is traded in for an allowance of $500.

Truck (new)	4,000	
Accumulated Depreciation—Trucks	4,500	
Cash		3,500
Truck (old)		5,000

There is no gain or loss in this case because the trade-in allowance is the same as the carrying value.

Trade-in of Plant and Equipment—Nonrecognition of Gain or Loss

An alternative procedure for recording exchanges of assets is required by the Internal Revenue Service. The cost of the new asset for income tax purposes must consist of the carrying value of the old asset plus the required additional expenditure (cash paid or its equivalent), or:

$$\text{Cost of new asset} = \text{Carrying value of old asset} + \text{Expenditure}$$

The excess of trade-in allowance over carrying value is viewed not as a gain but as a reduction from an inflated list price, whereas the excess of carrying value over trade-in value is viewed not as a loss but as an addition to the cost of the new asset. List prices and trade-in values are not recognized in the accounts. They enter only into the computation of the required cash outlay. Under this rule, the unrecognized gain or loss on the exchange is absorbed in the cost valuation of the new asset. An objective of the Internal Revenue Service's rule of nonrecognition of gain or loss on the trade-in of assets of like kind is to prevent the shifting of income for income tax purposes from one year to the next. A company with a large gain on a trade-in could defer trading the asset until the following tax year, thereby shifting the gain to that year.

> The income tax method of recording asset exchanges violates the accounting principle that plant and equipment, like inventories, should be recorded at actual cash (or equivalent) cost. Future periodic charges for depreciation should be based on cost rather than on a conglomerate figure that may reflect a sale price adjustment of the new asset as well as the unrecovered cost of the old asset. A gain or a loss on an asset exchange is an integral part of the complete transaction cycle and should, therefore, be recognized.

Recording of Assets at Cost

The income tax method is frequently used to account for exchanges so that further analysis and adjustment may be avoided when income tax returns are prepared, but this tendency to adjust accounting principles to conform with tax rules for the sake of expediency should not be condoned.

CHANGING DEPRECIATION CHARGES

The periodic depreciation charge may require revision as the result (1) of a capital expenditure that does not prolong the useful life of the original asset and (2) of errors in the original EUL. In either case, the new depreciable cost is typically allocated over the remaining life of the property on which the expenditure was made. Assume, for example, that an additional wing costing $8,000 is added to a five-year-old factory building. The original cost of the building was

$33,000, the estimated salvage value was $3,000, and the estimated useful life was twenty-five years. The straight-line method of depreciation has been used. The calculation of the revised annual depreciation charge is:

Original cost	$33,000
Deduct five years' accumulated depreciation ($30,000 $\times$ 0.04 = $1,200 per year $\times$ 5 years)	6,000
Carrying value	$27,000
Additional cost	8,000
New carrying value	$35,000
Deduct estimated salvage value	3,000
New depreciable cost	$32,000
New annual depreciation charge, based on a remaining useful life of 20 years ($32,000 $\times$ 0.05)	$ 1,600

If the improvement prolongs the life of the asset or increases its salvage value, the calculations must be altered to give effect to such changes. For example, if after the addition of the wing the remaining useful life was estimated to be twenty-four years and the estimated salvage value was $3,800, the revised annual depreciation charge would be determined as follows:

New carrying value	$35,000
Deduct estimated salvage value	3,800
New depreciable cost	$31,200
New annual depreciation charge, based on a remaining useful life of 24 years ($31,200 $\times$ 0.04167)	$ 1,300

DISCLOSURE REQUIREMENTS

Disclosure requirements for property, plant, and equipment are stated in APB Opinion No. 12:

4. Disclosure of the total amount of depreciation expense entering into the determination of results of operations has become a general practice. The balances of major classes of depreciable assets are also generally disclosed. Practice varies, however, with respect to disclosure of the depreciation method or methods used.
5. Because of the significant effects on financial position and results of operations of the depreciation method or methods used, the following disclosures should be made in the financial statements or in notes thereto:

a. Depreciation expense for the period,
b. Balances of major classes of depreciable assets, by nature or function, at the balance-sheet date,
c. Accumulated depreciation, either by major classes of depreciable assets or in total, at the balance-sheet date, and
d. A general description of the method or methods used in computing depreciation with respect to major classes of depreciable assets.[2]

The following is an extract from an annual report of the Weldotron Corporation:

PROPERTY AND EQUIPMENT—at cost (Note 1C)

Land	**70,942**
Fixtures, equipment, tools and dies	**981,179**
Leasehold improvements	**325,233**
Automotive equipment	**40,658**
	1,418,012
Less accumulated depreciation and amortization	**580,472**
	837,540

C. Depreciation and Amortization

For financial reporting purposes, the Company and its consolidated subsidiaries follow the policy of providing depreciation and amortization on the straight-line method over the estimated useful lives of the assets which are as follows:

Fixtures and Equipment	3 to 10 Years
Automobile Equipment	2 to 4 Years
Leasehold Improvements	5 to 25 Years

For income tax purposes, depreciation is computed using various accelerated methods with the same useful lives as for financial reporting purposes. Costs of additions and betterments are capitalized, and maintenance and repairs are charged to expense when incurred. Upon retirement or sale, the cost of the asset and the related depreciation are removed from the accounts and any gain or loss on disposal is charged or credited to income.

Some companies report only totals in the body of the position statement with details in an accompanying note.

XYZ COMPANY

	(000 omitted)
Property, Plant, and Equipment (Note 4)	$31,500
Deduct accumulated depreciation	17,700
Net property, plant, and equipment	$13,800

---

[2] AICPA, *APB Accounting Principles,* vol. 2 (Chicago: Commerce Clearing House, Inc., 1973), p. 6595.

Note 4 (Continued) (000 omitted):

	Cost	Accumulated Depreciation	Book Value
Land	$ 258		$ 258
Buildings and improvements	6,000	$ 2,850	3,150
Machinery	23,200	13,733	9,467
Office equipment	552	429	123
Automotive equipment	1,490	688	802
Totals	$31,500	$17,700	$13,800

DEPLETION OF NATURAL RESOURCES

Natural resources, or wasting assets, such as oil wells, mines, or timber tracts, should be recorded in the asset account at cost. As the resource is extracted, its asset value is reduced. This reduction in value, or expiration of the cost, of the asset resulting from production is called *depletion* and may be recorded on the books by a debit to the Depletion Cost account and a credit to the Accumulated Depletion account. Or, theoretically, since the depletion cost item becomes part of the cost of the merchandise inventory, it may be debited directly to the inventory account. Thus, the depletion amount would become an expense chargeable against revenue on the income statement only when the goods are sold. In the statement of financial position, accumulated depletion is deducted from the cost of the resource.

The periodic depletion charge is usually calculated on an output basis similar to the production-unit method of recording depreciation. The cost of the wasting asset is divided by the estimated available units of output, to arrive at a per unit depletion charge. The number of units removed during the accounting period multiplied by the per unit depletion charge represents depletion for that period. For example, if the asset is a mineral measured in tons:

$$\frac{\text{Cost} - \text{Salvage}}{\text{Estimated tons to be mined}} = \text{Depletion}$$

Assume that a mine costs $180,000 and contains an estimated 400,000 tons of ore. It is estimated that the net salvage value will be $20,000. The per unit depletion charge is:

$$\frac{\$180,000 - \$20,000}{400,000} = \$0.40 \text{ per ton}$$

If 10,000 tons are mined during an accounting period, the depletion charge is 10,000 $\times$ $0.40, or $4,000, and the entry to record the depletion for that period is:

Ore Inventory	4,000	
Accumulated Depletion—Mine		4,000

The Ore Inventory account should also be debited with the additional costs of the extraction process such as labor and overhead.

At the end of the accounting period, the amount of the recorded depletion cost remaining in the Ore Inventory account is the number of units on hand multiplied by the per unit depletion charge. Assume that 2,000 tons remain unsold at the end of the period. The entry required is a debit to Cost of Goods Sold for $3,200 (expired depletion) plus four-fifths of applicable labor and over-head, and a credit to the Ore Inventory account for this total amount.

The cost of goods sold is deducted in the income statement from the revenue realized from the sale of 8,000 tons of ore. The balance of the Ore Inventory account includes not only the allocated portion of mine depletion cost but also the proportionate amount of labor and other costs of extracting the ore (*overhead*). This is illustrated in the following T account flow chart:

Ore Inventory				Cost of Goods Sold	
Depletion	4,000	3,200			
Other:			($3,200 plus		
Salaries	xxx	xxx	proportionate		
Wages	xxx	xxx	amounts)		
Over-			→ xxx		
head	xxx	xxx			

In the above example, a balance of $800 of the depletion cost and one-fifth of the labor and other costs remain in the Ore Inventory account. The other four-fifths (8,000 tons) is transferred to Cost of Goods Sold. For income tax purposes the depletion deduction for a tax year may also be figured as a percentage of the gross income subject to maximum and minimum limits. These limits do not, however, preclude deductions over the life of the asset greater than the cost of the asset. The intended purpose of the percentage depletion allowance is to encourage further exploration and development of natural resources.

PLANT AND EQUIPMENT—MANAGEMENT ANALYSIS

The investment by a company in plant and equipment assets may vary considerably, depending on the nature of the business. Manufacturing concerns require a greater investment in machinery and equipment than do retail or wholesale firms. The relationship of the plant and equipment to total assets and to sales should be in proper proportion for the industry. If the amount invested in plant and equipment is too high, fewer funds are available for working capital purposes. Depreciation charges will also be high, resulting in either higher sales prices or lower profits. Finally, the long-term liabilities will be greater, resulting in greater interest costs and the need for funds to pay off debts as they mature.

The following ratios are used to determine whether there has been an overinvestment in plant and equipment:

1. Plant and equipment to long-term liabilities
2. Plant and equipment to stockholders' equity
3. Net sales to plant and equipment

The ratio of plant and equipment to long-term liabilities is obtained by dividing the total carrying value of the plant and equipment by the long-term liabilities. This comparison is of particular significance to the long-term creditors if any of the plant and equipment has been mortgaged as security for loans. A reduced ratio reflects an increased dependence on long-term borrowing to finance plant and equipment acquisitions.

The ratio of plant and equipment to stockholders' equity is obtained by dividing the total carrying value of the plant and equipment by the stockholders' equity. An investment in plant and equipment that exceeds the stockholders' equity in the corporation indicates a possible overinvestment in plant and equipment, thus resulting in higher interest, taxes, maintenance expenses, and depreciation charges, and lower working capital. A heavy investment in land, buildings, and machinery greatly restricts the mobility of a company if a change in plant location or type of product manufactured is desirable.

The ratio of net sales to plant and equipment, or plant and equipment turnover, is found by dividing net sales by the total carrying value of the plant and equipment. A decreasing ratio underscores a possible overinvestment in plant and equipment.

These analyses, when based on historical cost, do not reflect the effect of changing economic and technological conditions and market price fluctuations. The Accounting Objectives Study Group of the AICPA concluded that different valuation bases are preferable for different assets and liabilities and that "financial statements might contain data based on a combination of valuation bases."[3] In addition to historical cost, the report describes other valuation bases that have been advocated.

Exit Values: A valuation basis quantifying assets and liabilities by the amounts that would be received or paid currently as a result of non-distress liquidation.

Current Replacement Cost: A valuation basis quantifying assets in terms of present prices for items equivalent in capacity or service. Earnings computed by this method also include, in a separate category, changes in the replacement costs of assets.

Discounted Cash Flows: A valuation basis quantifying specific assets and liabilities, or the enterprise as a whole, by discounting all expected cash flows at a rate reflecting both time values and risks.[4]

PLANT AND EQUIPMENT REPLACEMENT—MANAGEMENT CONSIDERATIONS

The decision to replace plant and equipment items and the timing of the replacement is often a complex matter requiring careful analysis by management. The decision is particularly difficult when it involves not merely the re-

[3] *Objectives of Financial Statements* (New York: AICPA, 1973), p. 41.
[4] *Ibid.*, p. 41.

placement of a worn-out or obsolete unit, but the acquisition of a machine with a different purchase price, capacity, or operating cost. The problem of asset replacement involves a careful study of the expense of doing the given task with the present unit as compared with the expense of using the new unit. Generally, a replacement is advisable if the larger profits resulting from the use of the new equipment will justify the additional investment required. This consideration is discussed in detail in Chapter 25.

APPENDIX I Intangible Assets

Intangible assets are nonphysical rights that are of future value to the business because they shelter the firm from competition or provide other similar advantage to the owner. Some intangibles, whether purchased or self-developed, such as patents, copyrights, franchises, and leaseholds, can be readily identified and their cost measured. Others, such as goodwill, are not specifically identifiable or measurable.

The procedure for the amortization, or periodic write-off of a portion of the cost, of an intangible asset is the same as for computing and recording depreciation on a plant and equipment item by the straight-line method. The amount to be amortized annually is computed by dividing the asset cost by the legal life or the estimated useful life, whichever is shorter. The entry is a debit to an amortization account and a credit directly to the asset account. The straight-line method is generally used in view of the difficulties and uncertainties in estimating useful economic life and future benefits.

Difficulties and uncertainties arise from the uniqueness of intangibles. The estimated useful life may be limited by law (copyright), by contract, by legislation (franchise), or by the economic factors of demand and competition (patents). Other intangibles (goodwill, trademarks) have an unlimited or indefinite life. Furthermore, some can be separately identified (franchise), whereas others cannot be, because they relate to the total entity (goodwill); finally, some intangibles are purchased, while others are developed within the firm.

In its Opinion Number 17, the AICPA Accounting Principles Board concluded "that a company should record as assets the costs of intangible assets acquired from others, including goodwill acquired in a business combination. A company should record as expenses the costs to develop intangible assets which are not specifically identifiable. The Board also concludes that the cost of each type of intangible asset should be amortized by systematic charges to income over the period estimated to be benefited. The period of amortization should not, however, exceed forty years."[1]

PATENTS

The United States Patent Office grants *patents,* or exclusive rights to the owners to produce and sell their inventions or discoveries for a period of seventeen years. All the costs involved in developing and acquiring a patent are included in the intangible asset Patents account. The cost of a patent may be large and should be capitalized and amortized over the economic useful life of the asset or seventeen years, whichever is shorter. The Patents account may be credited directly for the amortized portion; the account debited is called Amortization of Patent Cost or Patent Amortization Expense.

[1] *Op. cit.,* p. 6662.

COPYRIGHTS

A *copyright* is an exclusive right to publish a literary or an artistic work, granted by the government. The copyright is recorded at cost and is subject to amortization either over its legal life—twenty-eight years—or its useful economic life. If the copyright is obtained directly, the cost is small and is usually written off entirely in the first year. If it is purchased, the cost may be large enough to warrant periodic amortization. In practice, however, since revenues from copyrighted material are uncertain and are often limited to a relatively brief period, the cost of a copyright is added to the other costs of the first printing and enters into the inventory cost of the books or other printed materials.

FRANCHISES

A *franchise* is a monopolistic right granted by a government or an entity in the private sector to render a service or to produce a good. A right to operate a bus line or a railroad or the exclusive use of a television transmitting channel is a valuable asset to the owner. The cost of obtaining the franchise is amortized over its life. Franchises are also used in industry whereby a manufacturer grants a dealer the exclusive privilege to sell the manufacturer's product within a defined geographical area.

LEASEHOLDS AND LEASEHOLD IMPROVEMENTS

Leaseholds are rights to the use of land, buildings, or other property. They are frequently paid for in advance and should be classified as capital expenditures. Leasehold improvements, such as buildings, are sometimes constructed on leased property. Leaseholds and leasehold improvements should be amortized over the life of the lease or over the estimated useful life of the asset, whichever is shorter. With respect to lease commitments that have not been classified as capital expenditures, the APB states that "financial statements of lessees should disclose sufficient information regarding noncapitalized lease commitments to enable users of the statements to assess the present and prospective effect of those commitments upon the financial position, results of operations, and changes in financial position of the lessees."[2]

GOODWILL

Goodwill is a general term embodying a variety of intangible factors relating to the reputation of a firm and its ability to realize above-normal net income

---

[2] *Op. cit.*, p. 6818.

returns on an investment. Such factors as favorable customer relations; loyal and competent employees; possession of valuable patents, franchises, or copyrights; a high-quality product; and efficient management all aid in the development of goodwill. Self-developed goodwill is not recorded on the books. However, if the assets and goodwill of one company are purchased by another, the purchased goodwill should be recorded as an asset at cost.

The amount to be paid for goodwill is usually a product of a bargaining process between the buyer and the seller. The debit to Goodwill is the excess of the cost (purchase price) over the amounts allocable to assets other than Goodwill.

"Cost is measured by the amount of cash disbursed, the fair value of other assets distributed, the present value of amounts to be paid for liabilities incurred, or the fair value of consideration received for stock issued. . . ."[3]

RESEARCH AND DEVELOPMENT

In theory, current expenditures for research and development should be capitalized to the extent that they will benefit future periods whether in the form of new or better products, reduced costs, or other benefits; when future benefits are uncertain, research and development costs should be expensed. Prior to FASB Standard No. 2, in practice, a number of alternatives were used, varying from charging all expenditures to income when incurred to deferring all expenditures and amortizing them over the years of benefit.

Since future benefits from research are difficult to estimate—especially pure research, although less so for new or better product development—current practice favors expensing research and development costs when incurred. The recently issued FASB Standard No. 2 requires that most research and development costs be treated as expenses when incurred and that all costs capitalized at the effective date of the Standard be written off as a prior period adjustment. An exception to the foregoing general conclusion occurs when research and development is done on a contract basis for another company. These costs should be accounted for in accordance with accounting standards for contracts in general.

ORGANIZATION COSTS

This is an intangible asset resulting from expenditures made incidental to incorporation and is discussed further in Chapter 12.

[3] *Op. cit.*, p. 6665.

To support depreciation charges for tax purposes, to maintain strong internal control, and to enhance the quality of planning, it is important to maintain accurate and detailed records of plant and equipment. The type of fixed asset record system suitable for an entity depends upon a number of factors, such as the quantity of fixed assets, the amount invested in them, the reports needed to operate the type of enterprise, and the type of data-processing equipment available.

One very flexible system utilizes a disk storage system to maintain the master file of fixed assets. A disk system was illustrated in Figure A9-1; records are stored by coded characters made up of magnetic spots on a disk with each *record* (all the information pertaining to one asset) directly accessible to the central processing unit. Asset acquisitions and deletions are read onto the master disk file from punched cards. Figure A11-1 is a simplified flow chart of the system.

Indicated in the flow chart are three typical reports. Any (or all) could be the product of a processing run. The fixed asset register, one of these reports, is shown in detail in Figure A11-2; comments on specific portions of it are keyed to the circled numbers in the figure.

❶ If this is a business in which all depreciation is charged as an operating expense of the current year, the adjusting entry to be recorded at December 31 can be taken from the register:

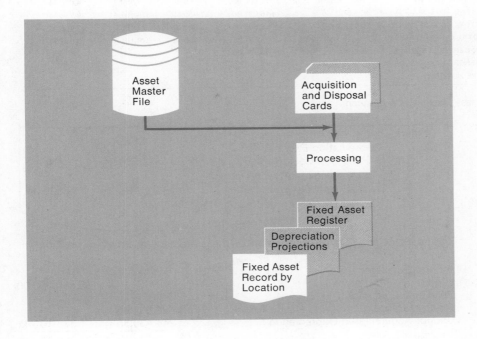

Figure A11-1
Fixed Asset Record Processing.

PLANT AND
EQUIPMENT

(Ch. 11)

445

Figure A11-2 Fixed Asset Register

```
FXRSNO                                    YOUR COMPANY NAME
                                         FIXED ASSET REGISTER                        12/30/76        PAGE  1
DEPRCN.METHOD.0-ST.LN.1-SUM.YRS.DIG.2-DOUBL DECL.BAL.3-DOUBL.DECL.BAL.TO ST.LN.4-SUM YRS.DG.6MOS. 5-SUM YRS.DG.12 MOS.
```

SERIAL NO	A C	ACCT NO	LOC DEP	DEPR METH	DESCRIPTION	CAPTL DATE	LIFE	MOS DEP	TOT. CAPTLZ VALUE	ACCUMULATED DEPRECIATN	REMAINING VALUE	CUR. YEAR DEPRECIATION
00100	1	0100	01	0	MILLING MACHINERY-1	1/01/72	5	48	10,000.00	8,000.00	2,000.00	2,000.00
00110	1	0100	01	1	MILLING MACHINERY-2	1/01/72	5	48	10,000.00	9,333.20	666.80	1,333.20
00120	1	0100	01	2	MILLING MACHINERY-2	1/01/72	5	48	10,000.00	8,704.00	1,296.00	864.00
00130	1	0100	01	3 *	MILLING MACHINERY-4	1/01/72	5	48	10,000.00	8,920.00	1,080.00	1,080.00
00140	1	0100	01	3	MILLING MACHINERY-5	1/01/72	5	48	10,000.00	8,704.00	1,296.00	864.00
00150	2	0200	01	2	MILLING MACHINERY-6	1/01/72	5	48	12,000.00	10,704.00	1,296.00	864.00
00160	2	0200	01	3 *	MILLING MACHINERY-7	1/01/72	5	48	12,000.00	10,920.00	1,080.00	1,080.00
00170	2	0200	02	1	MACHINERY & EQUIPM.	7/01/72	12	42	116,031.96	56,822.09	59,209.87	13,887.48
00180	3	0200	20	0	LATHE	2/01/70	5	60	6,000.00	6,000.00		100.00
00190	1	0200	02	2	MILLING MACHINERY-3	7/01/72	5	42	10,000.00	8,272.00	1,728.00	1,152.00
00200	1	0200	02	3 *	MILLING MACH-3	7/01/71	5	54	10,000.00	9,424.00	576.00	1,152.00
01000	5	0300	01		BOOK SHELF	1/01/72			100.00			
02000	5	0300	01		LAMP	1/01/71			50.00			
03000	3	0300	01	0	EXECUTIVE DESK	1/01/69	5	60	500.00	500.00		
04000	4	0400	08		LAND-PLANT	7/01/54	99		5,850,900.00			
05000	1	0400	08	0	BUILDING-OFFICE	1/01/72	25	48	250,000.00	40,000.00	210,000.00	10,000.00
06000	1	0400	09	1	EQUIPMENT-GROUP	7/01/72	5	42	11,000.00	8,000.00	3,000.00	1,666.50
06010	1	0400	09	1	SURFACE GRINDER	7/01/72	5	42	11,000.00	8,000.00	3,000.00	1,666.50
10010	1	0100	01	0	DRILL PRESS-1	1/16/75	4	12	10,000.00	2,500.00	7,500.00	2,500.00
10020	1	0100	01	0	DRILL PRESS-2-SALVG	5/01/75	4	8	11,000.00	1,666.98	9,333.02	1,666.98
10030	1	0100	01	3	DRILL PRESS-3-SALVG	6/01/75	4	7	12,000.00	3,500.00	8,500.00	3,500.00
11010	1	0200	02	1	DRILL PRESS-4-N SALV	4/01/75	4	9	10,000.00	3,000.28	6,999.72	3,000.28
11015	1	0200	02	4	DRILL PRESS-4-N SALV	4/01/75	4	6	10,000.00	2,000.32	7,999.68	2,000.32
11016	1	0200	02	5	DRILL PRESS-4-N SALV	4/01/75	4	12	10,000.00	4,000.24	5,999.76	4,000.24
11020	1	0200	02	1	DRILL PRESS-5-SALVG	4/01/75	4	9	12,000.00	3,000.28	8,999.72	3,000.28
11030	2	0200	02	1	DRILL PRESS-6-BONUS	4/01/75	4	9	11,000.00	4,000.28	6,999.72	4,000.28
12010	1	0300	03	2	FORK LIFT-DBL-NOSAL	2/01/75	4	11	8,000.00	3,666.66	4,333.34	3,666.66
12020	1	0300	03	3	FORK LIFT-DBL-SL SAL	2/01/75	4	11	9,000.00	4,125.00	4,875.00	4,125.00
12030	2	0300	03	3	FORK LIFT-DBL-SL-BON	2/01/75	4	11	9,000.00	4,666.66	4,333.34	4,666.66
21010	1	0500	20	1	DRILL PRESS-4B	4/01/75	4	6	10,000.00	2,000.32	7,999.68	2,000.32
21020	1	0500	20	5	DRILL PRESS-5A	4/01/75	4	12	12,000.00	4,000.24	7,999.76	4,000.24

	TOT. CAPTLZ VALUE	ACCUMULATED DEPRECIATN	REMAINING VALUE	CUR. YEAR DEPRECIATION
TOTAL CAPITAL ASSETS-ACTIVE-CODE 1 & 2	616,031.96	237,930.55	378,101.41	79,736.94
TOTAL CAPITAL ASSETS-FULLY DEPRECD-CODE-3	6,500.00	6,500.00		100.00
TOTAL CAPITAL ASSETS- 1, 2 & 3	622,531.96	244,430.55	378,101.41	79,836.94
TOTAL NON DEPRECIABLE ASSETS-CODE-4	5,850,900.00			
TOTAL EXPENSED ITEMS-CODE-5	150.00			
TOTAL CODE-9 RECORDS TO BE DELETED-				

Courtesy of International Business Machines Corporation.

```
1976
Dec. 31    Depreciation Expense—
              Plant and Equipment                    79,836.94
              Accumulated Depreciation—
                Plant and Equipment                               79,836.94
              To record depreciation for the year.
```

❷ The Plant and Equipment section of the statement of financial position will show:

Plant and Equipment:		
Land		$5,850,900.00
Buildings, Equipment, and Machinery	$622,531.96	
Deduct Accumulated Depreciation	244,430.55	378,101.41
Total		$6,229,001.41

Figure A11-3 Fixed Asset Report by Location

FXRLOC					FIXED ASSET REPORT BY LOCATION				12/30/76		PAGE	6
LOC. DEPT	SERIAL NO	A C	D M		CAPTLZ DATE	LIFE YRS	MONS DEPR	CAPITALIZED VALUE	DEPRECIATION ACCUMULATED CUR. YEAR CUR. PERIOD			SALVAGE
20	00180	3	0	LATHE	2/01/70	5	060	6,000.00	6,000.00	100.00		
	21010	1	4	DRILL PRESS—4B	4/01/75	4	006	10,000.00	2,000.32	2,000.32		
	21020	1	5	DRILL PRESS—5A	4/01/75	4	012	12,000.00	4,000.24	4,000.24		2,000.00
20	DEPARTMENT TOTAL CODES—1, 2 & 3							28,000.00	12,000.56	6,100.56		2,000.00
	GRAND TOTAL-DEPRECIABLE ASSETS-CODES-1, 2 & 3							622,531.96	245,888.89	78,295.28	3,000.00	20,000.00

Courtesy: IBM Corporation

❸ A footnote would show that $6,500 of the above plant assets were fully depreciated, but were still in service.

❹ Another footnote would show that the straight-line method is being used to depreciate the building, but that most plant equipment is being depreciated by accelerated methods.

Figure A11-3 shows the last page of a six-page departmental breakdown. Although the concept of factory overhead will be covered in a later chapter, it is noted that this report provides the departmental allocation of depreciation charges. On page 6 of the report, for example, the current year figure of $6,100.56 for Department 20 is part of the manufacturing cost in that department, and will be charged to factory overhead.

This company has three divisions some of which have more than one department. From Figure A11-4 we can learn that Department 8 has $250,000 of depreciable equipment (the building), and that Department 9 has $22,000 of depreciable assets. Projections of depreciation charges for next year using

Figure A11-4 Depreciation Projection Report.

								DEPRECIATION PROJECTION REPORT		1/01/76		PAGE 2	
DIVN	ACCT CLAS	DEPT LOC.	SERIAL NO	DEPR METH	DATE CAPITLZD	LIFE YRS	TOT. CAPITLZD VALUE	PROJEC. FOR TAX PURPOSE CURRENT YEAR NEXT YEAR		PROJEC. ST. LINE-INTERNAL CURRENT YEAR NEXT YEAR			
2	400	8	05000	0	1/01/72	25	250,000.00	10,000.00	10,000.00	10,000.00	10,000.00		
2	400	8	DEPT TOTAL				250,000.00	10,000.00	10,000.00	10,000.00	10,000.00		
2	400	9	06000	1	7/01/72	5	11,000.00	1,333.30	666.70	2,000.00	1,000.00		
2	400	9	06010	1	7/01/72	5	11,000.00	1,333.30	666.70	2,000.00	1,000.00		
2	400	9	DEPT TOTAL				22,000.00	2,666.60	1,333.40	4,000.00	2,000.00		
2	400	ACCOUNT TOTAL					272,000.00	12,666.60	11,333.40	14,000.00	12,000.00		
2	DIVISION TOTAL						278,500.00	12,666.60	11,333.40	14,000.00	12,000.00		
3	500	20	21010	4	4/01/75	4	10,000.00	3,499.86	2,499.90	2,500.00	2,500.00		
3	500	20	21020	5	4/01/75	4	12,000.00	2,999.88	1,999.92	2,500.00	2,500.00		
3	500	20	DEPT TOTAL				22,000.00	6,499.74	4,499.82	5,000.00	5,000.00		
3	500	ACCOUNT TOTAL					22,000.00	6,499.74	4,499.82	5,000.00	5,000.00		
3	DIVISION TOTAL						22,000.00	6,499.74	4,499.82	5,000.00	5,000.00		
	GRAND TOTAL—PROJECTION						622,531.96	71,511.51	48,764.30	72,570.19	54,169.48		

Courtesy: IBM Corporation

various accelerated methods for tax purposes and straight-line for internal reporting are shown with subtotals by department and in total.

These are only three of many possible reports that could be obtained from this fixed asset information system. Other reports would serve for capital budgeting, internal control, or production planning in addition to those which provide data for accounting entries.

GLOSSARY

Amortization Often used as a general term to cover write-down of assets; it is most commonly used to describe periodic allocation of costs of intangible assets.

Capital Expenditure A payment or a promise to make a future payment for asset acquisitions.

Depletion The process of estimating and recording the periodic charges to operations because of the exhaustion of a natural resource.

Depreciation—Composite Rate A charge for depreciation using a blanket rate applied to a number of nonhomogeneous assets.

Depreciation—Declining-Amount Method A depreciation method that results in larger depreciation charges during the early years of the asset life with gradually decreasing charges in later years.

Depreciation—Group Rate A charge for depreciation using a blanket rate applied to a group of homogeneous assets.

Depreciation—Production Methods Charges for depreciation based on usage or results rather than time (mileage, units of output).

Depreciation—Straight Line A depreciation method that allocates a uniform portion of the depreciable asset cost to each accounting period.

Depreciation—Sum of the Years' Digits A declining-amount method of depreciation.

Goodwill A general term embodying a variety of intangible factors relating to the reputation of a firm and its ability to generate above-normal earnings.

Intangible Assets Nonphysical rights and expected benefits that come from the ownership of such assets.

Revenue Expenditure Expenditure that benefits a current period and is made for the purpose of maintaining assets in satisfactory operating condition.

Salvage Value The amount of asset cost that is expected to be recovered when the asset is ultimately scrapped, sold, or traded in.

Tangible Assets Land, structures, and equipment of a tangible and relatively permanent nature, acquired for use in the regular operations of the business.

QUESTIONS

Q11-1. What does the term *plant and equipment* encompass?

Q11-2. (a) List some expenditures other than the purchase price that make up the cost of plant and equipment. (b) Why are cash discounts excluded from the cost of plant and equipment? (c) What problems in cost determination arise when used plant assets are acquired?

(Ch. 11)

Q11-3. (a) What distinguishes a capital expenditure from a revenue expenditure? (b) What is the effect on the financial statements if this distinction is not properly drawn?

Q11-4. Student A maintains that if a plant asset has a fair market value greater than its cost after one year of use, no depreciation need be recorded for the year. Student B insists that the fair market value is irrelevant in this context. Indicate which position you support and give your reasons.

Q11-5. What are some of the factors that must be considered (a) when the depreciation method to be used is chosen? (b) when depreciation is recorded?

Q11-6. The basis for depreciation is generally original (historical) cost. Is there any other basis that could logically be used?

Q11-7. Since the total amount to be depreciated cannot exceed the cost of the asset, does it make any difference which method is used in calculating the periodic depreciation charges?

Q11-8. Describe the conditions that might require the use of each of the following methods of depreciation: (a) straight line, (b) production, (c) declining amount.

Q11-9. (a) Distinguish between the composite rate and the group rate of depreciation. (b) Give reasons to support the use of these procedures and state their underlying assumptions.

Q11-10. What procedures may be followed in recording depreciation on assets acquired during the accounting period?

Q11-11. What is the relationship, if any, between the amount of the annual depreciation charges on plant assets and the amount of money available for the new plant assets?

Q11-12. What accounting problems result (a) from the trade-in of one like plant asset for another? (b) from the sale of a plant asset?

Q11-13. (a) Distinguish between the terms *depreciation, depletion,* and *amortization.* (b) How is the periodic depletion charge determined?

Q11-14. (a) What are intangible assets? What factors must be considered (b) when the acquisition of intangibles is recorded? (c) when intangibles are amortized?

Q11-15. What ratios are useful in evaluating the level of investment in plant assets?

Q11-16. It has been argued that with proper maintenance certain equipment will last almost indefinitely, in which case depreciation is not necessary. Do you agree? Explain.

Q11-17. The legislative enactment of the assets depreciation range (ADR) regulations under the new title "class life system" in the Revenue Act of 1971 allows a company (select the best answer):
  a. To write off machinery and equipment items for tax purposes using lives up to 20% shorter or 20% longer than the established guideline lives at the election of management.
  b. To use typically short lives for machinery and equipment items for tax purposes without having to substantiate these lives by relating them to actual useful lives.
  c. To deduct for tax purposes an asset repair which extends the useful life of an asset, to the extent repairs do not exceed the repair allowance range.
  d. To eliminate the use of the "reserve ratio test" on assets acquired after December 31, 1970.

PLANT AND
EQUIPMENT

(Ch. 11)

e. To do all of the above.

Q11-18. (Appendix II). How are data stored on a disk? Can the record of any single asset item be read from the disk file by the CPU?

Q11-19. (Appendix II). If fixed assets are maintained on a disk system, what accounting entry (entries) can be made with much less effort than under a manual system?

E11-1. For each of the following items, indicate the account to be debited:
 a. Expenditure for installing machinery
 b. Expenditure for trial run of new machinery
 c. Expenditure for conveyor system for machinery
 d. Payment of delinquent taxes on land (taxes were delinquent at the date of purchase of the land)
 e. Expenditure for extensive plumbing repairs on a building just purchased
 f. Sales tax paid on new machinery just purchased
 g. Payment of incorporation fees to the state
 h. Expenditure for a major overhaul that restores a piece of machinery to its original condition and extends its useful life
 i. Expenditure for an addition to a building leased for 20 years
 j. Amount paid for a purchased business in excess of the appraised value of the net assets

E11-2. The Bhaby Company made the following expenditures on the acquisition of a new machine:

Invoice cost ($19,000) less 2% cash discount	$18,620
Transportation charges	570
Installation charges	950
Property insurance—premiums for three years	570
Materials and labor used during test runs	285

What is the cost of the machine?

E11-3. The Wildey Manufacturing Company acquired an old building for $48,000 and spent $15,000 to put it into usable condition. One year later, an additional expenditure of $1,200 was made for painting, plumbing, and electrical repair work. Record all the expenditures.

E11-4. The Fay Corporation purchased a machine for $10,000; terms, 1/10, n/60. Record (a) the acquisition of the machine and (b) payment of the invoice within the discount period.

E11-5. The Nitze Corporation solicited bids for a new wing for its factory building. The lowest bid received was $25,000. The corporation decided to do the work with its own staff, and the wing was completed for a total cost of $22,000. Record the expenditure.

E11-6. On April 1, 1976, a calculating machine used in the office of the Andrea Company was sold for $400. The sale was recorded by a debit to Cash and a credit to Office Equipment for $400. The machine had been purchased on October 1, 1973, for $1,200 and had been depreciated at the rate of 10% annually (no salvage value) through December 31, 1975. The Andrea Com-

INCOME
MEASUREMENT
AND VALUATION

450

pany closes its books annually on June 30. Make an entry to correct the accounts as a result of the transaction.

E11-7. On February 1, 1973, the Tyre Corporation acquired a truck costing $15,000 with an estimated useful life of five years and a salvage value of $1,000. On August 1, 1976, the truck was traded in for a new one with a cash market price of $20,000. The dealer allowed $4,200 on the old truck, and the balance was paid in cash. Record the trade-in on the books of the Tyre Corporation, on the basis (a) of recognition of gain or loss and (b) of nonrecognition of gain or loss. (c) Contrast the entries in (a) and (b) and state how the nonrecognition of the gain or loss in (b) is compensated for.

E11-8. The Boston Corporation purchased a truck on January 2, 1976, for $12,500. It had an estimated useful life of six years and a trade-in value of $500. Compute the depreciation charge for the year 1976 under the following methods: (a) straight line, (b) sum of the years' digits, (c) double-rate declining balance, and (d) production, assuming an operating life of 100,000 miles and 18,000 miles of actual use the first year.

E11-9. On January 2, 1976, the Fleet Company purchased land and an old building for $200,000. The land is appraised at $20,000; the building is estimated to have a useful life of 20 years and a salvage value of $10,000. After three years' use, the building was remodeled at a cost of $75,000. At this time, it was estimated that the remaining useful life of the building would be 25 years with a salvage value of $20,000. Using the straight-line method of depreciation, give the entries (a) for the purchase of the land and building, (b) for depreciation for 1976, (c) for remodeling costs, and (d) for depreciation for 1979.

E11-10. The Eybe Corporation acquired a building for $150,000 with an estimated useful life of 20 years and an estimated salvage value of $12,000. Five years later, an addition to the building was constructed at a cost of $30,000. Using straight-line depreciation, compute the annual depreciation charges before and after the construction of the addition to the building.

E11-11. The Phillips Company acquired three machines as follows:

| | Machine | | |
	A	B	C
Cost	$95,000	$75,000	$89,000
Estimated salvage value	7,000	5,000	9,000
Estimated life (years)	11	10	8

Assuming that the straight-line method is used, compute (a) the composite life for the three machines and (b) the annual depreciation rate.

E11-12. The unadjusted trial balance of the Beatrice Company at December 31, 1976, includes the following accounts:

Patents (granted January 2, 1976)	$30,000
Copyrights (acquired July 1, 1976)	7,800
Goodwill	6,750
Research and Development (new products)	12,500
Organization Costs	3,750

(a) What is the basis of valuation of each of these accounts? (b) What adjustments should be made on December 31, 1976? (c) What additional information is needed to complete requirement (b)?

E11-13. The Pauline Corporation reported a net income of $150,000 for the year 1976. The president of the corporation noted that the beginning and ending inventories were $600,000 and $750,000, respectively, although the physical quantities on hand were relatively stable. She also noted that deductions for depreciation averaged 10% on plant and equipment costing $1,350,000, although the current dollar value of the assets is estimated at $1,800,000. The president suggests that the reported net income is erroneous. Comment.

E11-14. The Dune Company purchased a mine for $336,000. It was estimated that the land contained 1,120,000 tons of a recoverable mineral deposit, and that after recovery of the deposits the land would have a salvage value of $16,000. During the first year, 96,000 tons were recovered and 80,000 tons were sold. Labor and overhead costs were $160,000. Determine (a) the cost of goods sold and (b) the ending inventory valuation.

E11-15. The comparative financial statements of the Marjorie Corporation show the following information:

	Plant and Equipment	Long-Term Liabilities	Stockholders' Equity
December 31, 1976	$154,000	$70,000	$210,000
1975	140,000	67,000	161,000
1974	119,000	60,000	147,000
1973	126,000	63,000	140,000

Sales:	1976	$420,000
	1975	308,000
	1974	280,000
	1973	252,000

(a) Compute the appropriate ratios and (b) evaluate the significance of the ratios.

E11-16. The condensed income statement of the Gail Company for the year ended March 31, 1976, was as follows:

Sales		$500,000
Cost of Goods Sold		300,000
Gross Margin		$200,000
Operating Expenses		
(includes depreciation expense of $20,000)		125,000
Net income		$ 75,000

(a) Assuming that beginning and ending Accounts Receivable, Accounts Payable, and Merchandise Inventory balances were approximately the same, how much cash was generated by operations? (b) Did the depreciation expense deduction result in a direct cash increase of $20,000? Explain.

E11-17. (*Accounting policy decision problem*) (a) "The government gave away $2.7 billion in tax revenue." (b) "An unwarranted windfall." (c) "A bonanza." These are some of the statements made by some public officials and economists following an announcement by the U.S. Treasury Department reducing the depreciation provision period by about 20%.

1. Do you agree with the above quotations? Explain.
2. What is the Treasury Department's motive in permitting faster write-offs?
3. What is the effect of the Treasury Department's action on net income after taxes?

E11-18. (Appendix II). A new asset is acquired by a company using the disk system described in Figure A11-1. What procedures would be followed to record the new asset on the disk file?

DEMON-
STRATION
PROBLEMS

DP11-1. (*Computing depreciation expense*) The St. Johns Company began business on July 1, 1976, with three new machines. Data for the machines are as follows:

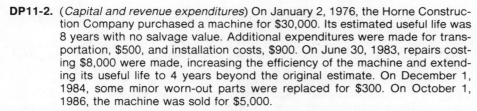

Machine	Cost	Estimated Salvage Value	EUL (years)
A	$ 93,000	$ 9,000	12
B	126,000	14,000	10
C	34,000	6,000	7

Required: Compute the depreciation expense for the first two years by each of the following methods: (a) straight line, (b) sum of the years' digits, (c) double-rate declining balance, and (d) composite rate based on straight-line depreciation.

DP11-2. (*Capital and revenue expenditures*) On January 2, 1976, the Horne Construction Company purchased a machine for $30,000. Its estimated useful life was 8 years with no salvage value. Additional expenditures were made for transportation, $500, and installation costs, $900. On June 30, 1983, repairs costing $8,000 were made, increasing the efficiency of the machine and extending its useful life to 4 years beyond the original estimate. On December 1, 1984, some minor worn-out parts were replaced for $300. On October 1, 1986, the machine was sold for $5,000.

Required: Give the journal entries to record (a) the purchase, (b) annual depreciation for 1976, (c) the extraordinary repair on June 30, 1983, (d) annual depreciation for 1983, (e) the ordinary repair on December 1, 1984, and (f) the disposal on October 1, 1986.

DP11-3. (*Asset sale; trade-in*) On January 2, 1976, the Lorne Corporation purchased a machine costing $20,000 with a useful life of 10 years and salvage value of $2,000. Assume that the sum-of-the-years'-digits method is used to record depreciation.

Required: Give the journal entries to record the sale or trade-in of the machine, on the basis of each of the following assumptions:

1. Sale of the machine for $3,000 at the end of the sixth year.
2. Sale of the machine for $4,000 at the end of the fourth year.
3. Trade-in of the machine at the end of the sixth year for a new machine listed at $25,000. The corporation paid $15,000 in cash to acquire the new machine. (Recognize the gain or loss on the exchange.)
4. Assuming the same facts as in (3), record the trade-in under the income tax method.

DP11-4. (*Management policy decision problem*) The board of directors of the Mainline

Corporation, after reviewing the following data taken from the firm's records, is concerned about a possible overinvestment in plant and equipment.

	1974	1975	1976
Current Assets	$104,000	$118,000	$120,000
Plant and Equipment	40,000	64,000	88,000
Current Liabilities	52,000	58,000	68,000
Long-Term Liabilities	22,000	36,000	39,000
Capital Stock	32,000	32,000	54,000
Retained Earnings	38,000	56,000	48,000
Net Sales	130,000	160,000	168,000

Required:

1. You have been asked to prepare a report on this matter to the board of directors. Include appropriate analyses and computations to support your conclusions.
2. Assume you are a prospective shareholder. How would this report influence your evaluation of the company?

DP11-5. (*Accounting policy decision problem*) The Hopper Corporation has acquired depreciable plant and equipment items totaling $100,000. Using a 10-year life and no salvage value, calculate the effect on net income for the first three years for each of the following methods of depreciation:
a. Straight line
b. Sum of the years' digits
c. Double-rate declining balance

The company is subject to a combined state and federal income tax rate of 50%.

DP11-6. (*Computing depreciation expense*) The Stang Corporation acquired a compressor on July 1, 1976, at a cost of $25,000. The compressor had an estimated useful life of eight years and a salvage value of $2,500. Two years later the compressor was completely overhauled and rebuilt at a cost of $5,000. These improvements were expected to increase the estimated useful life of the compressor by four years from July 1, 1978.

Required: Prepare all entries through December 31, 1978. The company reports on a calendar-year basis and uses straight-line depreciation.

PROBLEMS

P11-1. The Scollay Corporation purchased land and buildings for $450,000; the buildings were demolished at a cost of $17,000, salvaged materials were sold for $4,000, and a new building was constructed on the site for $4,000,000. The following additional expenditures were incurred during construction:

Fees for permits and licenses	$1,500
Interest on money borrowed for payment of construction costs	2,000
Architectural fees	25,000
Insurance	1,500
Real estate taxes	2,000
Land grading and leveling	10,000
Promotional literature describing the new facility	1,000
Trees, shrubs, and other landscaping costs	7,500

Required: Open T accounts for (a) Land, (b) Buildings, and (c) Operating Expenses. Post the transactions to the accounts.

INCOME
MEASUREMENT
AND VALUATION

P11-2. On January 2, 1976, a piece of machinery was acquired by Norbert, Inc., for $9,000. It was estimated to have an eight-year life and a salvage value at the end of that time of $750.

Required: Prepare tables showing periodic depreciation over the eight-year period, for each assumption listed:

1. Depreciation is to be calculated by the straight-line method.
2. Depreciation is to be calculated by the sum-of-the-years'-digits method.
3. Depreciation is to be calculated by the double-rate declining-balance method.
4. Repair charges are estimated at $400 for the first year and are estimated to increase by $200 in each succeeding year; depreciation charges are to be made on a diminishing scale so that the sum of depreciation and estimated repairs is the same over the life of the asset.

P11-3. The Vida Corporation purchased a machine on January 3, 1976, at a cost of $30,000. In addition, the corporation paid $500 to have the machine delivered and $2,500 to have it installed. The estimated useful life of the machine is six years with a trade-in value of $5,000 at the end of that time.

Required: Prepare four separate schedules, showing the annual depreciation charge for the six-year period under each of the following methods: (a) straight line; (b) production, assuming a total operating life of 40,000 hours with actual annual hours of use as follows: 5,000; 7,000; 9,000; 6,000; 6,000; 7,000; (c) double-rate declining balance; and (d) sum of the years' digits.

P11-4. On January 2, 1976, the Dolan Company purchased a new machine for $75,000 with an estimated salvage value of $5,000 and an estimated useful life of six years, or 9,000 machine-hours. The plant manager expects to use the machine for 2,200 hours during 1976, and 1,500 hours during 1977.

Required:

1. Compute the depreciation expense for each of the first two years by the following methods: (a) straight line, (b) production, (c) sum of the years' digits, and (d) double-rate declining balance.
2. Assume that the Dolan Company is in an industry in which rapid changes in technology have, in the past, made existing equipment obsolete. How does this affect the estimate of the asset's useful life?

P11-5. The following information was taken from the books of the Marjorie Corporation.

	Machine A	Machine B	Machine C
Date acquired	January 2, 1976	January 2, 1977	January 2, 1978
Cash payment	$30,800	$8,800	$39,600
Estimated salvage value	2,000	2,400	4,400
Estimated useful life in years	5	6	7
Method of depreciation	Sum of the years' digits	Straight line	Double-rate declining balance

On January 2, 1977, machine A, with a value of $18,800, was traded for machine B, which listed for $28,000.

Required:

1. Give all the necessary entries to record the transactions through December 31, 1978. The books are closed annually on December 31.

2. What is the entry for the trade-in of machine A for machine B when the income tax method is used?

P11-6. The Gull Corporation acquired two factory buildings. Subsequently, major improvements were made to roofs and foundations, extending the useful life of each building. The following information was taken from the records:

	Building A	Building B
Date acquired	1/2/76	7/1/76
Original cost	$46,000	$68,000
Estimated salvage value	$ 2,000	$ 5,000
Estimated useful life	10 years	20 years
Date improvements completed	7/1/77	7/1/77
Improvement costs	$5,000	$13,000
Revised estimated salvage value	$1,500	$ 3,500
Remaining estimated useful life	12 years	20 years
Method of depreciation	Straight line	Straight line

Required:

1. Give the journal entries to record the transactions, including year-end adjustments through December 31, 1978. The books are closed annually on December 31.
2. What factors influence the estimate of the useful life of the buildings?
3. (a) What other methods of depreciation can be used? (b) What additional information would be needed?

P11-7. The general ledger of the Norma Company includes the following accounts:

Machinery and Equipment			
1972			
Jan. 2	A 15,000		
1973			
Apr. 1	B 16,500		
1975			
June 1	C 22,500		

Accumulated Depreciation—Machinery and Equipment		
	1972	
	Dec. 31	2,500.00
	1973	
	Dec. 31	3,737.49
	1974	
	Dec. 31	4,150.00
	1975	
	Dec. 31	5,462.49

The straight-line method is used, the machines have no salvage value, and gains and losses on trade-ins are recognized. Details regarding the computation of accumulated depreciation are summarized as follows:

Machine	Date Acquired	Cost	EUL (Years)	Accumulated Depreciation (12/31/75)
A	1/2/1972	$15,000	6	$10,000.00
B	4/1/1973	16,500	10	4,537.50
C	6/1/1975	22,500	10	1,312.50

On January 2, 1976, machine A was traded in for machine D, with a cash outlay of $13,500. The cash value of the new machine is $19,500. Its estimated useful life is 10 years.

On August 2, 1976, machine B was traded in for machine E. The new machine lists for $24,000 and its estimated useful life is six years. A trade-in allowance of $12,000 is received on the old machine; the fair market value of the old machine is $10,500.

Required:

1. Record all the necessary entries for the year 1976 through December 31.
2. Record the trade-in of machine B, assuming that it had been depreciated under the sum-of-the-years'-digits method instead of the straight-line method.

   Note: Computations for depreciation for machine B for the years 1973 and 1974, using the sum-of-the-years'-digits method, would be as follows:

	1973	*1974*
April 1, 1973, through March 31, 1974:		
$^{10}\!/_{55} \times \$16,500 = \$3,000$ allocable to:		
1973: ¾ × $3,000	$2,250	
1974: ¼ × $3,000		$ 750
April 1, 1974, through March 31, 1975:		
$^{9}\!/_{55} \times \$16,500 = \$2,700$, allocable to:		
1974: ¾ × $2,700		2,025
Totals	$2,250	$2,775

P11-8. The Machinery and Equipment account of the Beatrice Corporation shows the following at the beginning of 1976:

Asset	Cost	Estimated Salvage Value	EUL (Years)
A	$ 400	–0–	5
B	1,000	–0–	8
C	2,000	200	10

During 1976, the company acquired 50 pieces of small machinery to perform a repetitive machining operation. The machines cost $400 each, had no sal-

PLANT AND EQUIPMENT

vage value, and had an estimated weighted average useful life of five years. The company uses a blanket rate for all machinery and equipment.

Required:

1. Record the retirement during the year of asset C, which had been acquired five years ago.
2. Record the sale of one of the small machines for $200.
3. Record depreciation expense for the year.

P11-9. (*Management policy decision problem*) The 1976 annual report of the Fiske Engine Company, Inc., includes the following data:

	December 31	
	1976	*1975*
Net sales	$410,633	$366,489
Net earnings	18,350	13,153
Total shareholders' equity	130,205	115,762
Long-term liabilities	87,208	72,153
Property, plant and equipment at net book value	104,445	103,955
Total assets	278,065	251,342
Shares of common stock outstanding at end of year	6,045	5,475

Required:

1. Prepare such ratios as you consider useful by a present or prospective shareholder in evaluating the company.
2. On the basis of these ratios, (a) what is your assessment of the company? (b) why might these ratios be misleading? (c) why do you consider them useful?

P11-10. (*Accounting policy decision problem*)
   a. Cutler-Hammer, Inc., explains in its report to its shareholders that depreciation provisions were generally computed by the sum-of-the-years'-digits method "which distributes the greatest cost of the assets to the early years of their estimated lives." Do you agree with the apparent rationale for using this method of depreciation? Explain fully.
   b. Assume that Cutler-Hammer had been using the straight-line method. Would its adoption of the sum-of-the-years'-digits method be more likely to insure the availability of funds that will be needed to replace assets when they are no longer useful?
   c. What is the relationship between the balance in the Accumulated Depreciation—Machinery account and the availability of funds for replacing machinery? What is the relationship between the quantity and quality of a company's repair and maintenance programs and the amount and rate of the provisions for depreciation?
   d. International, Inc., reported to its shareholders that effective January 1, 1976, two subsidiary companies, for financial reporting purposes, changed from an accelerated method to the straight-line method of computing depreciation. Indicate (a) the probable reason for the changeover, (b) which accounts are affected, and (c) the effect on the financial statements.

P11-11. (*Accounting policy decision problem*) The following statements were extracted from notes accompanying annual reports:

a. Trade names and goodwill acquired through purchases prior to 1968 are being amortized over a 25-year period; subsequent purchases aggregating $1,530,000 will be amortized when it becomes evident that the value of the asset has diminished.

b. Television and feature film costs are amortized in the proportion of rentals earned to date to management's estimate of ultimate rentals. If management's estimate indicates a loss, the full amount of the loss is charged against income.

c. Franchises consist of contracts to import whiskeys, liquors, and other distilled spirits which, in the opinion of the management, have continuing value and accordingly are not amortized. Other intangibles of $3,670,363 are being amortized over periods not exceeding 20 years.

d. The company follows the practice of accumulating costs applicable to immature fruit crops including care-taking expenses and depreciation. Costs during the year are capitalized and charged to earnings when the fruit crop is sold.

Required:

1. Comment critically on each of the foregoing notes and state your suggestions.
2. Do any of the methods used violate the proper matching of revenue and expense?
3. What alternative methods might have been used in each instance?
4. Do the methods used indicate an explicit attempt to influence reported net income? If so, in what way?
5. What are some specific circumstances underlying the choice of accounting method in each case?

P11-12. (*Accounting policy decision problem*) Buzzards Bay, Inc., recently began operations as a manufacturer and wholesaler of glassware. Management has been holding regular meetings at which decisions are made regarding various company policies. One of the items on the agenda for the next scheduled meeting is the depreciation policy of the company. Brian Mills, the company treasurer and controller, is responsible for developing relevant supporting data. As a staff assistant to Mills, you are responsible for gathering the information that he requests.

You select the following data from the Plant and Equipment section of the general ledger:

Land	$ 20,000
Buildings	200,000
Furniture, fixtures, machinery, and equipment	300,000
Transportation equipment	16,000
Kilns	28,000

On the basis of information that has been obtained from reliable sources, you suggest to Mills the following useful lives and salvage values for the assets:

Buildings	30 years and $30,000
Furniture, fixtures, machinery, and equipment	10 years and $20,000
Transportation equipment	8 years and $2,400
Kilns	8 years and no salvage value

On the basis of comprehensive forecasts of sales and expenses, management estimates net income before depreciation and income taxes as follows:

First year of operations	$ 90,000
Second year of operations	100,000
Third year of operations	150,000

The company is subject to a Federal corporate income tax rate of 22% on the first $25,000 of taxable income and 48% on all taxable income in excess of $25,000. Also, management plans to use the same depreciation amounts on both the corporate financial statements and the corporate tax returns.

Required: As preparation for Mills's presentation at the forthcoming meeting, you are instructed to do the following:

1. Using the straight-line, sum-of-the-years'-digits, and double-rate declining-balance methods, prepare depreciation schedules for the first three years of operations.
2. Calculate the net income under each method.
3. Describe the effect of each method on the company's cash balance during the first three years of operations.

P11-13. (*Accounting policy decision problem*) The Brittany Corporation purchased a new machine at a cost of $55,000. The machine is expected to produce 20,000 units over its estimated useful life of five years as follows:

Year	Number of Units
1976	3,000
1977	4,000
1978	6,000
1979	5,000
1980	2,000

Required:

1. Compute the annual depreciation charges under each of the following methods (assume $5,000 salvage value):
   a. Straight line
   b. Sum of the years' digits
   c. Double-rate declining balance
   d. Units of production
2. What factors should be considered in selecting a depreciation method?
3. Which method do you recommend? Why?

P11-14. The Prence Hotel Corporation buys certain small appliances in batches of 50 units. Past experience indicates that the useful life of the units in a batch is as follows:

Years of Life	Number
1	3
2	11
3	22
4	11
5	3
	50

On January 1, 1976, the corporation acquired 50 units at a cost of $100 each. The actual years-of-service life of these units was:

Year of Retirement	Number
1976	2
1977	12
1978	24
1979	11
1980	1
	50

The 24 units that were discontinued from use at the end of 1978 were sold to a scrap dealer for $120. All the other units had no salvage value.

Required:

1. Record depreciation for each year using the group rate method of depreciation.
2. Record the retirement of the units at the end of 1978.

P11-15. The Globe Company purchased a tract of land at a cost of $200,000. It was estimated that the land contained 1,000,000 tons of a recoverable ore deposit and that after recovery of the deposits, the land would have a resale value of $25,000. Costs of clearing the area and drilling mine shafts was $300,000. During 1976, the first year of operations, 90,000 tons were recovered and 70,000 tons were sold for $8 a ton. Labor and overhead costs were $200,000, and general and administrative expenses were $50,000.

Required:

1. Prepare the income statement for the year.
2. Prepare a partial statement of financial position showing how the foregoing would be reported as at December 31, 1976.

P11-16. (Appendix I). Following are certain selected transactions and events of the Bailey Corporation relating to its plant and equipment accounts.
   a. Purchased a machine on January 1, 1976, at a cost of $8,000 with an estimated life of 10 years and no salvage value. On July 1, 1978, the machine was traded in for a new model with a cash market price of $10,000. The trade-in allowance was $5,000. The fair market price of the old machine was $4,000.
   b. On April 1, 1976, acquired patent rights to a new product at a cost of $25,000. The patent was approved by the U. S. Patent Office one year ago. The Bailey Corporation expects to earn well above normal profits on the patented product for about five years, at which time competing products will reduce earnings to normal levels.
   c. On July 1, 1976, the company purchased equipment for $40,000 plus a 3% sales tax, terms, 2/10, n/60. The invoice was paid within the discount period. The estimated useful life of the equipment was 15 years with no salvage value. Additional expenditures were made for freight, $750; installation costs, $1,500; and costs of a trial run, $250. On April 1, 1977, the company built an adapter to the equipment in its own plant at a cost of $2,000. The adapter increased the speed and output of the equipment by 10%. The bid price for the work by an outside contractor was $2,500.

d. The president suggests to his controller that depreciation on some of the equipment should be accelerated to increase funds that will be needed for their early replacement, because he expects some of the specialized machines to become technically obsolete within a few years. He also wants to capitalize the cost of an extensive advertising campaign on several new products that was conducted during 1976 at a cost of $25,000 and which, he expects, will help to generate sales of the products for at least three years.

Required:

1. (Item a) Make all necessary entries through December 31, 1978. The company uses straight-line depreciation and reports on a calendar-year basis.
2. (Item b) Make all necessary entries through December 31, 1977.
3. (Item c) Make all necessary entries through December 31, 1977.
4. (Item d) How should the controller respond to the president's suggestions?

P11-17. (Appendix II). (*Management policy decision problem*) Clouse Company already has a 96-column card reading capability and disk files in its computer system. Both payroll accounting and inventory control functions are now performed by the computer. The number of plant and equipment assets has grown to the point that two people spend full time maintaining the records and computing depreciation charges for monthly work sheets for management, and quarterly and annual reports to stockholders. Since the computer system has both idle time and unused disk storage capacity, Douglas Clouse wonders why fixed asset records cannot be handled as an additional data-processing application.

Required: List for Clouse some costs and some savings that would arise from his idea.

Paid-In Capital—Single Proprietorships, Partnerships, and Corporations

12

The owner's, partners', or stockholders' equity of a business results from assets contributed by the proprietor, partners, or stockholders and from earnings reinvested in the business. The characteristics of a single proprietorship, a partnership, and a corporation and the accounting for single proprietorship, partnership, and corporate capital contributions are presented in this chapter. The entries for the regular operating transactions are the same for all forms of business organization; only the entries for the formation of the business, the withdrawal of funds, and the closing process are different. The accounts used for recording the paid-in capital in a single proprietorship, a partnership, and a corporation are shown in Figure 12-1 on page 465.

SINGLE PROPRIETORSHIPS AND PARTNERSHIPS

SINGLE PROPRIETORSHIPS

The accounting procedures applicable to the capital accounts of single proprietorships were discussed and illustrated in the introductory chapters of this text. A brief review follows.

To illustrate the accounts used for recording the paid-in capital and other owner's equity items of a single proprietorship, assume that on January 2, 1976, James Leary formed the Leary Appliance Company with a cash investment of $20,000. On June 15, he withdrew $6,000 in anticipation of earnings; a summary of the accounts on December 31 showed the net income for the year to be $10,000. The entries to record these events are:

1976				
Jan. 2	Cash		20,000	
	James Leary, Capital			20,000
	To record investment by proprietor to form a retail appliance business to be called the Leary Appliance Company.			
June 15	James Leary, Drawing		6,000	
	Cash			6,000
	To record withdrawal by proprietor in anticipation of earned income.			
Dec. 31	Income Summary		10,000	
	James Leary, Drawing			10,000
	To close net income to the Drawing account.			
31	James Leary, Drawing		4,000	
	James Leary, Capital			4,000
	To close the balance of the Drawing account.			

The James Leary, Drawing, account is debited for all withdrawals in anticipation of earned income and is credited at the end of the period with the actual net income. It is then closed by transferring its balance to the Capital account.

The Owner's Equity section of the statement of financial position as of December 31, 1976, would appear as follows:

Owner's Equity	
James Leary, Capital	$24,000

The statement of owner's equity for 1976 would appear as shown below.

LEARY APPLIANCE COMPANY
Statement of Owner's Equity
For the Year Ended December 31, 1976

James Leary, Capital (investment, January 2, 1976)	$20,000
Add Net Income for the Year	10,000
Total	$30,000
Deduct Withdrawals	6,000
James Leary, Capital, December 31, 1976	$24,000

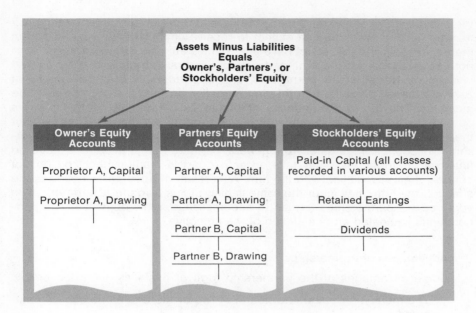

Figure 12-1
Accounts for
Recording Capital

**Assets Minus Liabilities
Equals
Owner's, Partners', or
Stockholders' Equity**

Owner's Equity Accounts	Partners' Equity Accounts	Stockholders' Equity Accounts
Proprietor A, Capital	Partner A, Capital	Paid-in Capital (all classes recorded in various accounts)
Proprietor A, Drawing	Partner A, Drawing	Retained Earnings
	Partner B, Capital	Dividends
	Partner B, Drawing	

PARTNERSHIPS

A partnership, according to the Uniform Partnership Act, is "an association of two or more persons to carry on, as co-owners, a business for profit." It is a contractual association whereby the partners pool their financial resources, services, skills, and knowledge and as a result hope to accomplish together what any one of them could not achieve individually. This association of two or more persons should be effected by a written contract called the *articles of copartnership*. The law, however, does not require any written agreement and, in the absence of any evidence to the contrary, considers that the partners intend to share equally in profits or losses. Any other method of distributing profits or losses must be clearly agreed upon by all the partners.

The partnership form of business organization is the least common of the three principal forms. It is most often found in the professional fields, primarily medicine, accounting, and law, in which a personal responsibility exists. Professional practice in corporate form is recognized by most states and by the Internal Revenue Service for Federal income tax purposes.

Types of Partnerships

Most trading partnerships are *general partnerships*. In this type of association, the members are called *general partners*. They take an active part in the business, and each partner is subject to unlimited liability. If the partnership is unable to meet its obligations, the creditors may look to the personal assets of any of the partners for the full payment of the partnership debts.

The Uniform Partnership Act allows some partners, but not all, a limited personal liability equal to the amounts that they have agreed to contribute to the business. Once they have made the agreed contributions, neither the partnership nor the creditors can expect to receive any further financial aid from them. *Limited partners* cannot have their names appear in the firm name, cannot act as agents for the firm, and cannot withdraw any part of their agreed investment. Not all states permit this form of partnership organization. *Silent partners* do not participate in the firm management and are not known to be members. They do have a financial interest in the partnership. *Secret partners* do participate in the management of the firm and have a financial interest, but their association with the firm is not revealed to persons outside the partnership. *Nominal partners* differ from general partners in that they have made no financial contributions. They take an active part in management and do not conceal their association with the firm. As a result of open participation in the affairs of the firm, they incur the same liability status as general partners. *Joint ventures* are partnerships formed to accomplish a single objective. The partnership is liquidated on completion of the objective.

Advantages of Partnerships

Some advantages of the partnership form of business are listed below.

1. The money, skill, and knowledge of two or more persons can be combined.
2. Partnerships can be formed easily and quickly.
3. Government regulations do not limit the sphere of activity of a partnership. Partnerships may change from one type of business to another at will or may expand without limitation, whereas a corporation is limited to the sphere of activity stated in its charter, although if stated broadly enough, it too may engage in multiple activities.
4. A partnership can act promptly as a business enterprise in all matters (withdrawal of funds, for example). A corporation may be restricted in its actions on certain matters by its charter, bylaws, or by state laws.
5. Many of the formal government reports required of the corporation are not required of the partnership.
6. Income taxes are not levied against partnerships, although they are required to file information returns. The partners, however, report on their individual tax returns their distributive shares of partnership income as shown on the partnership information return. The partnership itself is not an income taxable entity.

Disadvantages of Partnerships

Some disadvantages of the partnership form are given below.

1. The liability of general partners is unlimited. They are jointly and individually liable for all the debts of the partnership.
2. The life of the partnership is limited. Death, withdrawal, or admission of a partner; agreement to terminate; bankruptcy; and incapacity are all causes for the termination of a partnership relationship. By amending the existing partnership agreement, a new partnership can be brought into existence without cessation of the actual business carried on by the enterprise.

3. The general partnership is a mutual agency; that is, each partner may act in business matters as the agent of the partnership, and the remaining partners will be bound by his actions. If a partner purchases, in the name of the firm, merchandise used in the course of business, the other partners are also liable, although they may not have consented to or even been aware of the purchase.
4. The partners may find it difficult to cooperate, thus leading to dissolution of the partnership.
5. Partial or entire partnership interests may be difficult to transfer to another individual.
6. The ability of a partnership to raise funds is limited.

Nature of Partnership Accounting

The partnership form of business organization presents no new problems in accounting for assets, liabilities, expense, and revenue. The primary difference between a single proprietorship and a partnership is that the accounts of the partnership must show the equities of each of the individual partners of the partnership.

Each partner's share of ownership is recorded in an equity account, and its balance is in turn reported on the statement of financial position. On formation of a partnership, the contribution of each partner is also recorded in that equity account. To illustrate, assume that Robert Walsh and John Snow form a partnership, each investing $8,000 in cash. The opening entry is shown below.

Cash	16,000	
Robert Walsh, Capital		8,000
John Snow, Capital		8,000
To record the investments of the partners		
in the Walsh and Snow Company.		

It is not necessary that each partner invest the same amount of cash. Assuming Walsh contributed $5,000 and Snow $10,000, the following entry is required:

Cash	15,000	
Robert Walsh, Capital		5,000
John Snow, Capital		10,000

Neither is it necessary that the original contributions be limited to cash. Assume that Walsh contributed land worth $3,000, a building worth $20,000, and merchandise costing $6,200, and that the partnership assumed his mortgage payable of $10,000 and $200 in interest accrued on the mortgage. Snow invested $15,000 in cash. The opening entry is shown below:

Cash	15,000	
Merchandise Inventory (or Purchases)	6,200	
Land	3,000	
Building	20,000	
Mortgage Payable		10,000
Accrued Mortgage Interest Payable		200
Robert Walsh, Capital		19,000
John Snow, Capital		15,000

Function of Partnership Equity Accounts. It is possible to record all equity changes in the partnership Capital accounts. However, since several individuals are involved, it is generally desirable to detail the reasons for equity changes in *capital subdivision* accounts, referred to as *personal, current,* or *drawing* accounts. The functions of partnership equity accounts are explained in the following paragraphs.

The following T account shows the recording of transactions in the Capital accounts:

Name of Partner, Capital
(separate account for each partner)

1. Withdrawals of permanent capital are recorded as debits.	1. The original investment is recorded as a credit.
2. A Drawing account debit balance is closed into this account at end of the period.	2. Additional permanent investments are also credited to this account.
	3. A Drawing account credit balance is closed into this account at end of the period.

After the closing entries have been posted, each Capital account normally has a credit balance showing the partner's equity in the net assets of the firm. A debit balance indicates a deficiency. An additional investment must be made by the partner to provide for the cumulative excess of his withdrawals and losses over his investments and profits.

The following types of transactions are recorded in the Drawing account:

Name of Partner, Drawing
(separate account for each partner)

1. Withdrawals in anticipation of profits earned during the period are debited to this account.	1. Each partner's share of net income for the period is recorded as a credit.
2. Each partner's share of any net loss for the period is recorded as a debit to his Drawing account.	

The balance of the Drawing account is transferred periodically to the partner's Capital account. A partner's Drawing account is similar to the Drawing account of a single proprietor.

Sharing of Profits and Losses. The allocation of profits and losses to the partners is based on mutual agreement. If no articles or other evidence of agreement exists, the law assumes that profits and losses are to be divided equally even when the factors of investment, ability, or time are unequal. Since allocation is based on mutual agreement, there are many ways to distribute profits and losses. The more common are:

1. Earnings are divided in an agreed ratio.
2. Interest is allowed on the capital investments and the balance is distributed in an agreed ratio.
3. Salaries are allowed to the partners, interest is allowed on capital investments, and the balance is distributed in an agreed ratio.

To illustrate these methods of sharing profits and losses, assume the following figures:

Robert Walsh, Capital		John Snow, Capital	
	1976		1976
	Jan. 2 19,000		Jan. 2 15,000
	July 1 6,000		July 1 5,000

Income Summary	
	1976
	Dec. 31 12,000

1. *Agreed ratio.* The partners may agree to divide the net income in any ratio. If, for example, Walsh contributes twice as much time to the business as Snow, and if earnings are distributed accordingly, the entry to distribute the net income is:

Income Summary	12,000	
Robert Walsh, Drawing		8,000
John Snow, Drawing		4,000
To distribute the net income for the year in 2 to 1 ratio.		

2. *Interest and agreed ratio.* The partners may agree to allow for differences in capital investments as well as for differences in services rendered by allowing interest on capital balances and distributing the remainder in an agreed ratio. *Interest, as it is used here, is not an expense but rather a mecha-*

nism for dividing a portion of the earnings in the ratio of contributed capitals, with the remainder divided in some other ratio. If 6 percent interest is allowed on opening capital balances, the division is as follows:

	Walsh	*Snow*	*Total*
Interest on opening capital			
6% of $19,000	$1,140		
6% of $15,000		$ 900	
Total interest			$2,040
Remainder: ⅔ and ⅓	6,640	3,320	9,960
Totals	$7,780	$4,220	$12,000

The entry to record this distribution of net income is:

Income Summary	12,000	
Robert Walsh, Drawing		7,780
John Snow, Drawing		4,220
To distribute the net income for the year divided 2:1 after allowing for 6% interest on opening capital balances.		

3. *Salaries, interest, and agreed ratio.* A part of the net income may be divided to recognize differences in capital balances, another part to recognize differences in the value of services rendered, and the remainder in an agreed ratio. Such a computation follows:

	Walsh	Snow	Total
Salary allowances	$4,000	$2,000	$ 6,000
Interest on opening capital			
6% on $19,000	1,140		
6% on $15,000		900	
Total			2,040
Remainder divided equally	1,980	1,980	3,960
Totals	$7,120	$4,880	$12,000

The entry to record the distribution is:

Income Summary	12,000	
Robert Walsh, Drawing		7,120
John Snow, Drawing		4,880
To distribute the net income for the year equally after allowing for salaries and interest on capital balances.		

In the absence of an agreement to the contrary, the salary and interest distributions must be made even though the net income is less than the total of such distributions. The excess is divided in the same ratio used for dividing an excess of net income over total salaries and interest. To illustrate, assume the same facts as in the previous example except that the net income for the year is $7,000. The computation is:

	Walsh	Snow	Total
Salary allowances	$4,000	$2,000	$6,000
Interest on opening capital			
6% on $19,000	1,140		
6% on $15,000		900	2,040
Totals	$5,140	$2,900	$8,040
Deduct excess of salary and interest allowances over net income			
Net income $7,000			
Deduct allowances 8,040			
Excess divided equally	(520)	(520)	(1,040)
Distribution of net income	$4,620	$2,380	$7,000

The entry to record the distribution is:

Income Summary	7,000	
Robert Walsh, Drawing		4,620
John Snow, Drawing		2,380
To distribute the net income for the year.		

Partnership Financial Statements. The changes in partners' equity accounts during the year are shown in a statement of partners' equities. Its form is similar to the statement of owner's equity for a single proprietorship and the statement of retained earnings for a corporation. It is a supporting statement for the total partners' equities reported in the statement of financial position. Assume that Walsh and Snow each withdrew $3,000 during the year. The statement of partners' equities for the Walsh and Snow Company is shown as:

WALSH AND SNOW COMPANY
Statement of Partners' Equities
For the Year Ended December 31, 1976

	Walsh	Snow	Total
Balances, January 2, 1976	$19,000	$15,000	$34,000
Add additional investments	6,000	5,000	11,000
Net income	4,620	2,380	7,000
Totals	$29,620	$22,380	$52,000

PAID-IN
CAPITAL

	Walsh	Snow	Total
Deduct withdrawals	3,000	3,000	6,000
Balances, December 31, 1976	$26,620	$19,380	$46,000

The entries to close the partners' Drawing accounts are as follows:

Robert Walsh, Drawing	1,620	
Robert Walsh, Capital		1,620
To close partner's drawing account (net income credit, $4,620, minus withdrawals debit, $3,000).		
John Snow, Capital	620	
John Snow, Drawing		620
To close partner's drawing account (withdrawal debit, $3,000, minus net income credit, $2,380).		

The financial statements of a partnership are similar to those of a single proprietorship. The allocations of net income to the partners may be shown below the Net Income line of the income statement or, if they are too numerous, in a supplementary statement. The statement of financial position shows the individual capital account balances as of the end of the period and their total; or, if they are too numerous, the individual balances are shown in the supplementary statement of partners' equities.

Admission of a New Partner

The admission of a new partner technically dissolves the old partnership although, in the absence of complete dissolution or winding up, the business continues as before. A new partner either (1) may purchase his interest from one or more of the other partners or (2) may be admitted as a partner by making an investment in the partnership.

If the new partner buys his interest from one of the original partners, partnership assets are unchanged, because the transfer of assets is directly between the persons involved. The only entry on the partnership books is a transfer of the agreed share from the old partner's capital account to a capital account opened for the new partner. Assume that A and B are partners, each with capital balances of $50,000 and that A, with B's consent, sells one-half of his interest to C for $30,000. The entry required to record C's admission is:

A, Capital	25,000	
C, Capital		25,000

The amount paid by C to A has no effect on this entry, since there is no change in partnership assets or total capital. The $5,000 gain is a personal profit to A, which occurs outside the entity.

C may be admitted by making a contribution of cash or other assets directly to the firm, thereby increasing partnership assets and total capital. The amount credited to the incoming partner's capital account may be measured by the value of his investment. The admission of a new partner is often the occasion for recognizing goodwill—attributable to either the new partner or the old partnership—or a bonus may be allowed the old partners or the incoming partner. If the old partnership has been successful, the new partner may agree, as a condition, that part of his investment be considered a bonus from him to the old partners, or he may agree to the recognition of goodwill being credited to the old partners. On the other hand, if the old partners need additional resources—the funds, the skills, or both—that the new partner will contribute, they may agree to credit the new partner with an amount greater than his investment in the form of either a bonus or goodwill.

Assume that A and B are partners, sharing gains and losses equally, with capital account balances of $15,000 and $21,000. Some conditions under which C, a new partner, may be admitted, and the resulting journal entries, are illustrated below.

1. C is admitted to a one-third interest by investing $20,000, total capital to be $60,000.

Cash	20,000	
Goodwill	4,000	
A, Capital		2,000
B, Capital		2,000
C, Capital		20,000

Goodwill is recognized and is credited to the old partners in their profit-and-loss-sharing ratios.

2. C is admitted to a one-third interest by investing $24,000, total capital to be $60,000.

Cash	24,000	
A, Capital		2,000
B, Capital		2,000
C, Capital		20,000

C pays $24,000 but is credited with $20,000, the excess being credited to the old partners as a bonus.

3. C invests $15,000 for a one-third interest, total capital to be $51,000.

PAID-IN
CAPITAL

Cash	15,000	
A, Capital	1,000	
B, Capital	1,000	
C, Capital		17,000

In this illustration, the old partners provide a special inducement to C by crediting him with $2,000 more than his actual investment as a bonus.

Liquidation of a Partnership

A partnership may be terminated by selling the assets, paying the creditors, and distributing the remaining cash to the partners. This process is called *liquidation* of a partnership; conversion of assets to cash is called *realization.* Gains and losses resulting from the sale of assets must first be distributed to the capital accounts in profit-and-loss-sharing ratios before making any distribution of cash to the partners. If, after all gains and losses are distributed, a partner's capital account shows a debit balance, that partner must pay in the deficiency from his personal resources.

To illustrate, assume that A, B, and C, whose statement of financial position is shown below, decide to sell their noncash assets, pay their creditors, and distribute the remaining cash to themselves.

A, B, AND C
Statement of Financial Position
August 31, 1976

Assets

Cash	$ 25,000
Other Assets	125,000
	$150,000

Liabilities and Partners' Equities

Liabilities	$ 50,000
A, Capital	50,000
B, Capital	30,000
C, Capital	20,000
	$150,000

The noncash assets are sold for $140,000; profits and losses are shared equally. The summary below shows the liquidation sequence.

	Cash	Other Assets	Liabilities	Capital A	Capital B	Capital C
Balances before realization	$ 25,000	$ 125,000	$ 50,000	$ 50,000	$ 30,000	$ 20,000
❶ Sale of assets at a gain	140,000	(125,000)		5,000	5,000	5,000
Balances	$ 165,000		$ 50,000	$ 55,000	$ 35,000	$ 25,000
❷ Payment of creditors	(50,000)		(50,000)			
Balances	$ 115,000			$ 55,000	$ 35,000	$ 25,000
❸ Cash distribution to partners	(115,000)			(55,000)	(35,000)	(25,000)

Amounts to be distributed to the partners ③ are the balances in their capital accounts after each partner is credited with his share of the gain on the sale of the assets ①.

Sale of assets at a loss in the process of liquidation may result in a capital deficiency in a partner's capital account. If the partner cannot cover the deficiency from his personal assets, it is allocated to the other partners as an additional loss in the profit-and-loss-sharing ratio that exists between themselves. If, for example, the assets in the foregoing illustration are sold for $50,000, C's one-third share of the resulting loss of $75,000 = ($125,000 − $50,000) is $25,000, or $5,000 more than the balance in his capital account. The payments to A and B must be such as to leave credit balances in their accounts that will exactly absorb each partner's share of C's $5,000 deficiency if C is unable to cover it. This is accomplished by treating C's deficiency as an additional loss and distributing it to A and B in their profit-and-loss-sharing ratio (which is now 1 to 1), or $2,500 to each partner.

A summary statement follows:

	Cash	Other Assets	Liabilities	Capital A	Capital B	Capital C
Balances before realization	$ 25,000	$ 125,000	$ 50,000	$ 50,000	$ 30,000	$ 20,000
Sale of assets at a loss	50,000	(125,000)		(25,000)	(25,000)	(25,000)
Balances	$ 75,000		$ 50,000	$ 25,000	$ 5,000	$(5,000)
Payment to creditors	(50,000)		(50,000)			
Balances	$ 25,000			$ 25,000	$ 5,000	$(5,000)
Cash distribution to partners	(25,000)			(22,500)	(2,500)	
Balances				$ 2,500	$ 2,500	$(5,000)

If C subsequently pays the $5,000 to the partnership, the amount will be distributed equally to A and B and all the accounts will be reduced to zero balances. Failing that, the $5,000 debit balance in C's account will be distributed to A and B and all accounts reduced to zero balances.

(Ch. 12)

CHARACTERISTICS OF A CORPORATION

In a famous 1819 decision, John Marshall, Chief Justice of the United States, gave this classic definition of a corporation: "A corporation is an artificial being, invisible, intangible, and existing only in contemplation of law."

Legal Entity

The corporation is, from both the legal and the accounting points of view, a special and separate being, or separate *legal entity,* created by law.

That is the characteristic which makes it almost ideally suited to doing business. The weaknesses inherent in single proprietorships and partnerships do not generally exist with the corporate form. The death or retirement of a single proprietor or of a partner may terminate the business, whereas the corporate form continues indefinitely irrespective of changes in stockholders.

A stockholder may sell his stock whenever he chooses without the prior consent of other stockholders, with the corporation simply recording the change in ownership; a partner wishing to sell his interest must first get the consent of all the other partners. The purchase and sale of stock is a relatively simple matter because of the existence of stock exchanges (the New York Stock Exchange, for example). The sale and transfer of a block of stock from one holder to another is a private matter between the buyer and the seller. Except for a change of names and addresses in the stockholders ledger, the transfer does not affect the issuing corporation.

Single proprietors and general partners are fully liable to the firm's creditors. Their personal fortunes—in addition to their investments in the business—may have to be used. A stockholder, on the contrary, having paid for his stock in full, is not further liable either to the corporation or to satisfy the creditors' claims. For example, the possible losses of an investor who pays $500 to a corporation for ten shares of $50 par value stock is limited to $500. This is a distinct advantage to the investor in a corporation. It may also be a disadvantage, especially to the smaller corporation seeking credit. Since satisfaction of creditor claims is limited to the assets of the corporation, the extent of credit tends to be limited to the level of corporate assets.

Because the corporation is treated as a legal entity, separate and distinct from the stockholders who own it, it enjoys the same legal rights and privileges as do a single proprietor and a partner, and may therefore engage in any type of business activity authorized by the charter. The corporate form of business organization is of great advantage for a large business because it may sell its stock to anyone willing to invest and is, therefore, able to raise large sums of capital. Most large-scale businesses are incorporated and do a much larger volume of business than all other forms of business organization. Many small businesses are also incorporated—frequently with only a few stockholders—because of the advantages that the corporate form offers.

The corporate form also has its disadvantages. Because it is an artificial legal being created by the state, it must file reports with the state in which it was organized; it may engage in only that type of business for which it was chartered; it cannot distribute profits arbitrarily, as do partnerships, but must treat all shares of stock of the same class alike; and it is subject to special taxes and fees. Corporate laws vary from state to state and are often complex. The rights and obligations of corporations, directors, and stockholders are therefore often difficult to determine. The business corporation is taxed as a legal entity, and its pro rata distributions of earnings to stockholders (in the form of dividends) are also taxed as personal income of the recipient. The earnings of single proprietorships and partnerships, on the other hand, are taxed only once, as the personal income of the owners.

Ownership of Corporations

Ownership in a corporation is represented by shares of stock, which may be owned by individuals, or by other corporations, or by estates and trusts. Each share of stock represents a fractional part of the ownership. Ownership of a corporation may be vested in a single individual who owns all the stock, in a family whose members own all the stock, or by hundreds of thousands of stockholders. The holders of stock in a corporation are entitled to certain rights, including the right to participate in the distribution of earnings and the right to vote at elections of members of the board of directors, thereby participating, albeit indirectly, in the management of the corporation.

Organizing a Corporation

A corporation may be organized for a number of reasons. The purpose may be to start a new business or to buy a previously existing single proprietorship or partnership. It should be emphasized that the work of organizing a corporation must be done by competent attorneys, since it often involves complex legal matters.

To form a corporation it is first necessary for at least three incorporators to file a form known as the "Articles of Incorporation" with the secretary of state or the corporation commissioner (or other designated official of the state in which the company is incorporating), setting forth the name and address of the proprosed corporation with the nature of the business it is to operate, a description of the classes of stock and the number of shares of each class to be authorized, and any other information required by the state in which incorporation takes place. On approval of the application, a charter is issued by the state.

The incorporators then hold the initial stockholders' meeting. Capital stock certificates are issued, the stockholders elect a board of directors, and a set of rules and regulations (known as *bylaws*) governing the internal activities of the corporation is approved. The directors in turn elect the officers of the corporation, who execute the policies approved by the board of directors for the operation of the business.

Organization Costs. The formation of a corporation makes certain expenditures necessary, including legal fees, fees and commissions paid to promoters, and statutory fees and taxes. Since these expenditures are made to bring the

PAID-IN
CAPITAL

corporation into existence, they may be regarded as of benefit during the entire life of the corporation and may therefore be charged to an asset entitled Organization Costs, which is classified as an intangible asset in the position statement. Since the life of a corporation is indefinite, there is theoretical justification for retaining the account on the books indefinitely. In practice, however, organization costs are amortized over the early years of the corporation, because they are considered as having limited potential for generating future earning power. Under the Internal Revenue Code, organization costs may be written off over a period of not less than five years. The entry to record the periodic amortization of organization costs is:

| Amortization of Organization Costs | xxx | |
| Organization Costs | | xxx |

The Amortization of Organization Costs account is classified in the income statement as a general and administrative expense.

Stockholders. The stockholders occupy the top position in the corporate organization chart. The stockholders may attend annual and special meetings and participate in the management of the company by voting on matters presented for their consideration. If a stockholder is unable to attend the meeting, he may designate someone else—often the secretary of the corporation—to cast his vote by *proxy.* A stockholder is normally entitled to one vote for each share of voting stock he holds. The meeting of stockholders need not be a routine event, particularly if conflicting groups are attempting to gain control. On such occasions, each group seeks to obtain the largest number of proxy votes to assist it in acquiring control.

Board of Directors and Officers. The stockholders elect the board of directors, who are then primarily responsible for the affairs of the corporation. All decisions reached by the board as a unit are recorded in a *minute book;* the recorded decisions are referred to as *minutes of meetings of the board of directors.* The accountant makes frequent reference to these minutes as the underlying authority for transactions affecting the accounts, particularly the capital stock accounts.

The board of directors selects the officers—president, vice-presidents, treasurer, controller, and so on—who carry on the daily activities of the corporation. But the responsibility of the board of directors does not end with the selection of officers. Directors are in effect trustees with responsibility to stockholders and creditors alike; they are legally liable for any acts they may perform that are not authorized by the corporate charter or bylaws. Only the board of directors may declare dividends.

Capital Stock

Ownership in a corporation is represented by its stock, which is divided into shares representing fractional ownership. There may be more than one class of stock, each in turn divided into shares. Each share in a class of stock must be treated like every other share in that class with respect to whatever rights and privileges attach to it.

Whenever there is more than one class of stock, one of the classes may enjoy the right to receive dividends, for example, before the other classes of stock. By the same token, certain restrictions, such as not having the right to vote, may be placed on a particular class of stock. If only one class of stock is issued, it is refered to as *common stock;* if two classes of stock are issued, they are usually referred to as common stock and *preferred stock.* There may be subclasses of stock within each major class, also with specific rights, privileges, and restrictive provisions.

The rights and privileges attached to common stock are:

1. The stockholder's right to sell or otherwise to dispose of all shares owned.
2. The stockholder's so-called *preemptive right* to purchase any additional new issues of stock in proportion to his current holdings in that class of stock.
3. The right to vote.
4. The right to participate in dividend distributions when a dividend is declared.

Stock Certificate. A *stock certificate* is a printed or an engraved serially numbered document issued to the stock purchaser as evidence of ownership of the stated number of shares of capital stock of the issuing corporation. Transfer of the shares from one person to another is accomplished by filling in the assignment section on the reverse of the stock certificate. The buyer sends the assigned stock certificate to the corporation or to its transfer agent, who records the transfer on the corporation's capital stock records, cancels the old certificate, and issues a new one to the new owner. Stock certificates are often bound with attached stubs in the same manner as checkbooks. The perforated stock certificate is removed, and the stub is filled in and retained by the corporation as a permanent record.

Stockholders Ledger. The *stockholders ledger* furnishes the detail for the Capital Stock controlling accounts in the general ledger. An account is opened for each stockholder to show the certificates issued or canceled and the number of shares held. This record is used for purposes of establishing the voting and dividend rights of each stockholder. Only those persons whose names appear in the stockholders ledger are recognized as share owners.

Stock Transfer Journal. The purpose of the *stock transfer journal* is to record transfers or exchanges of stock from one person to another. The date, certificate numbers (old and new), and number of shares exchanged are recorded in it. The work is often done by independent *transfer agents*—banks or trust companies—who handle the recording of the sale and transfer of stock. The stock transfer journal may be used for posting to the subsidiary stockholders ledger. The function of recording all certificates issued and canceled is often done by a *registrar,* also usually a bank or a trust company.

With millions of shares being bought and sold on the stock exchanges daily, it has become necessary that most large corporations (or their independent transfer agents and registrars) use computers to maintain the stockholders ledger and stock transfer journal. The basic record for each stockholder is stored on magnetic tape or a direct access storage device, such as the disk file illustrated in Figure A9-1.

Sources of Capital

Operating transactions of corporations are recorded in the same manner as those of single proprietorships and partnerships. The chart of accounts must be designed, however, to distinguish between the primary sources of corporate capital. These sources are (1) investments by stockholders and (2) retained earnings from operations. This distinction is essential because state laws provide that earnings may be distributed to the stockholders but that, both for the protection of corporate creditors and for the continued operation of the business, investments must not be distributed. Hence, separate accounts should be kept for the following:

1. The par or stated value of each class of stock
2. Each type of paid-in capital other than the par or stated value of stock, including premiums (by class) on issuance of stock, proceeds from sale of treasury stock in excess of cost, and donated capital
3. Equity arising from revaluation of assets
4. The discount (by class) on stock issued below par value
5. Retained earnings (explained in Chapter 13)

Data from these separate accounts must be clearly set forth in the Stockholders' Equity section of the corporate statement of financial position.

Authorized and Unissued Capital Stock

The charter granted by the state of incorporation authorizes the newly formed corporation to issue a designated number of shares of capital stock. The corporation usually secures authorization to issue more shares than it anticipates issuing at the outset. This allows for additional sales in the future without seeking further authorization by the state. The total number of shares issued cannot exceed the number of shares authorized.

General ledger accounts for authorized but unissued stock need not be opened. Detail with respect to the number of shares authorized is customarily included as part of the description in the Stockholders' Equity section of the position statement. The position statement presentation may be as shown below.

Stockholders' Equity
  Paid-in Capital
    Common Stock, $100 per value, authorized 1,000 shares,
    issued 500 shares $50,000

Classes of Stock

As previously stated, stock is usually issued in two classes, *common* and *preferred*.

Preferred Stock. One of the reasons for issuing two or more classes of stock is to endow one class with certain features that will make it more salable. The attractive feature of preferred stock is that, when a dividend declaration is made by the board of directors, the preferred stockholders must be paid at the stated rate and amount for the class of stock before payments are made to other stockholders. The same preference applies when a corporation is dissolved: assets remaining after satisfaction of creditor claims are used first to redeem the claims of preferred stockholders; the remainder of the assets, if any, are paid to the other stockholders. Preferred stockholders, on the other hand, are often restricted to a specific dividend rate and do not, therefore, benefit from extra earnings. A preferred stockholder is usually denied the right to vote.

Common Stock. If a corporation issues only one class of stock, then all shares are treated alike, and, there being no preferences, that class of stock is called common stock. If there is more than one class, the class that does not have preferences and that shares only in the remainder of earnings or assets distribution is known as common stock. This class of stock does have voting privileges.

Par Value Stock

The term *par value* refers to a specific dollar amount per share, which is printed on the stock certificate, representing the minimum amount that must be paid to the issuing corporation by the original purchaser of the stock; otherwise the purchaser may be held liable for the *discount,* or difference, in case of future claims by the corporate creditors. This contingent liability for the discount passes from the original buyer to successive buyers, provided each buyer in the chain is made aware of the fact that the particular stock had been acquired in the first instance at a discount.

> The par value may be any amount set forth in the corporation's charter and is rarely an indication of what the stock is actually worth. Par value is used as the basis for recording the stock on the corporate books. Many state laws designate par value as *legal capital,* the amount that cannot be returned to stockholders unless all creditor claims have been satisfied. Beyond that, it may have little or no significance. It is often established at a nominal value (referred to as low par value) to preclude contingent stockholder liability.

Par Value

The use of par value stock used to be considered advantageous to the stockholder and the creditor, since it requires payment in full or the assumption of a liability for the discount. The market value of stock, however, is determined not by its par value but rather by the value of the corporation's net assets and by its earnings. Furthermore, in some cases, evasive schemes were evolved to by-pass the par value rule, and creditors also found it difficult to recover the stock discount from stockholders in a bankrupt company. The evasive schemes usually involved the issuance of *watered* stock—that is, the transfer of property or the rendering of services to the corporation for its capital stock at highly inflated values, thereby overstating the stockholders' equity in the position statement. Sometimes this stock would then be given back to the corporation for sale at whatever price it would bring without any liability for the discount because the stock had already been fully paid for. The Securities and Exchange Commission of the Federal government may and does interfere when obviously inflated values are assigned to assets being turned over in payment for capital stock, so that the flagrant abuses of past periods have been checked. The investor and the creditor, therefore, enjoy a high degree of protection against unprincipled promoters.

No-Par Value Stock

Since par value was often misleading, *no-par value* stock began to be used widely in order to overcome some of the disadvantages of the par value stock. The use of no-par value stock made it unnecessary to resort to evasive schemes for by-passing the contingent liability arising from a sale of par value stock at a discount. The attempted evasion of the par value rule through overvaluation of assets or services would no longer be necessary. Differences of opinion can and do exist, however, with regard to the proper value to be placed on an asset in exchange for stock, and resort to the use of no-par value stock has not eliminated this problem.

Stated Value ◄ When no-par value stock is issued, the directors often assign a *stated*, or uniform, value to each share. This value becomes the basis for recording the stock on the corporate books, and the accounting is the same as for par value stock.

Since in most cases the directors may change the stated value—unlike the par value—at will, there is usually no occasion for recording a discount on the sale of no-par value stock.

To compare the entries for the issuance of stock, assume that the King Corporation issues 1,000 shares of common stock for $110,000.

1. Assuming that the par value of the stock is $100,

Cash	110,000	
Common Stock		100,000
Premium on Common Stock		10,000

2. Assuming that the stock is no-par value with a $75 stated value.

Cash	110,000	
Common Stock		75,000
Paid-in Capital—Excess over Stated Value of Common Stock		35,000

3. Assuming that the stock is no-par value and has no stated value.

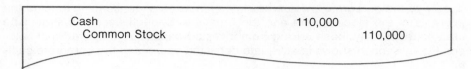

Cash	110,000	
Common Stock		110,000

Several other items denoting the concept of value give a more direct indication of the worth of the stock. The term *book value* is used to indicate the value per share based on net assets (assets minus liabilities), or stockholders' equity. The book value of a share of stock of any class is derived by dividing the total stockholders' equity applicable to that class by the number of shares of stock of that class issued and outstanding. If the market value of the assets is either above or below their recorded cost values, then the book value per share computed in the above manner is not a fair indication of its true worth. The term *market value* is used to indicate the amount that a share will bring the seller if the stock is offered for sale. Market prices change daily and can be determined readily for many stocks by reference to the stock market quotations carried in daily newspapers or to a financial magazine or financial service publication.

Legal, or Stated, Capital

The term *legal capital,* or *stated capital,* is incorporated in the laws of a number of states for the purpose of placing a restriction on the return of capital to the stockholders. The purpose of this restriction is to protect the creditors, because it prevents the stockholders from withdrawing their investment, either as dividends or by the reacquisition of capital stock, to the point where there may be insufficient funds left to satisfy creditors' claims. The creditors of a corporation do not have access to the personal resources of the stockholders; their only protection is in the corporate assets. *Legal capital* is the minimum amount of capital that must be left in the corporation and that cannot be withdrawn by the stockholders. Since there is a legal limit on stockholder withdrawals, creditors are assured that in the event of corporate losses the investors as a group will absorb the losses up to the amount of the stated capital.

There is considerable variation in the several state laws as to the method of determining and applying such provisions; the accountant may require the assistance of an attorney on questions involving legal capital. In some states, for example, legal capital is considered to be the total proceeds from the sale of stock. In other states, the directors of a corporation that has issued no-par value stock may, by resolution, designate a portion of the paid-in capital as the stated capital, or the state may designate a minimum amount. On par value stock, the stated capital is the par value of all the shares issued. When, as is often the case, the par value is low in relation to the issue price, the stated capital will be much less than the total paid in by shareholders. In such a situation legal capital is not a significant constraint on amounts to be distributed to stockholders, and the security of the creditors depends rather on the firm's operating and financial policies and resources.

(Ch. 12)

Recording Stock Transactions

Great care needs to be taken to record stock transactions in strict compliance with the corporate laws of the state of incorporation, keeping in mind the interests of the stockholders and the creditors. Enough accounts should be created, especially those arising from invested capital, so that the Stockholders' Equity section shows in adequate detail the sources of the corporate capital.

Authorization and Issuance of Stock. The initial entry on a corporate set of books may be a simple narrative statement setting forth certain basic data taken from the corporate charter, including the name of the corporation, the date of incorporation, the nature of the business, and the number and classes of shares authorized to be issued. Assume that the following three transactions took place at the Crown Corporation, which is organized as a wholesale hardware supply business authorized to issue 2,000 shares carrying $100 par value.

1. One-half the stock is issued at par value for cash.

Cash	100,000	
Common Stock		100,000

2. A total of 900 shares is issued for $40,000 in cash plus land and buildings having a fair cash value of $10,000 and $40,000, respectively.

Cash	40,000	
Land	10,000	
Buildings	40,000	
Common Stock		90,000

3. A total of 100 shares is issued to the organizers of the corporation in payment for their services.

Organization Costs	10,000	
Common Stock		10,000

The Stockholders' Equity section of the Crown Corporation statement of financial position after the foregoing transactions shows the following:

Stockholders' Equity	
Paid-in Capital	
Common Stock, $100 par value; authorized and issued 2,000 shares	$200,000

Issuance of Stock at a Premium. Assume that a corporation is organized with an authorized capital of $100,000, consisting of 1,000 shares of $100 par value stock, which are issued for $108,000. The entry is:

Cash	108,000	
Common Stock		100,000
Premium on Common Stock		8,000

When capital stock is offered for sale, the price it will bring depends not only on the condition and reputation of the corporation, but also on the availability of funds for investment and other external factors. When stock is issued above its par value, the difference is credited to Premium on Common Stock or to Paid-in Capital—Excess over Par Value of Common Stock. The account represents the excess of the issue price per share over the par value per share. Although the premium appears in a separate account, it is part of the total capital paid in by investors. By use of a separate account for the excess over par value paid in on the stock, the par value may be shown readily in the statement of financial position. If more than one class of stock has been issued at a premium, separate premium accounts should be kept. Issuance of stock in excess of par or stated value does not constitute earnings, and premiums therefrom should never be recorded in accounts showing corporate earnings.

Immediately following the issuance of the 1,000 shares for $108,000, the Stockholders' Equity section appears as shown below.

Stockholders' Equity		
Paid-in Capital		
Common Stock, $100 par value;		
authorized and issued 1,000 shares	$100,000	
Premium on Common Stock	8,000	
Total Paid-in Capital		$108,000

Issuance of Stock at a Discount. Assume that a corporation is organized with an authorized capital of $100,000, consisting of 1,000 shares of $100 par value stock, which are issued for $90,000. The entry is:

Cash	90,000	
Discount on Common Stock	10,000	
Common Stock		100,000

When the issue is for less than par value—that is, when the stock has been issued at a discount—the difference between the par value and the issue price of the stock is charged to Discount on Common Stock. Purchasers of stock at

PAID-IN
CAPITAL

a discount are contingently liable to the corporation's creditors for the amount of the discount. When such stock is transferred, the discount liability is noted on the stock certificate as foreknowledge that the liability passes to the new owner. In most states, par value stock may *not* be issued at a discount. The account appears as a deduction in the Stockholders' Equity section of the position statement and designates the existence and amount of the contingency as shown below.

Stockholders' Equity		
Paid-in Capital		
Common Stock, $100 par value;		
authorized and issued 1,000 shares	$100,000	
Discount on Common Stock	10,000*	
Total Paid-in Capital		$ 90,000
* Deduction.		

The use of premium and discount accounts makes it possible to show in the position statement the par value, or stated value, as well as the amount actually contributed. Premiums and discounts should not be offset. If, for example, a corporation that is authorized to issue 1,000 shares of $100 par value common stock issues 500 shares at $105 a share and later issues 250 shares at $98 a share, separate premium and discount accounts should be set up. The position statement presentation would be as shown below.

Stockholders' Equity		
Paid-in Capital		
Common Stock, $100 par value;		
authorized 1,000 shares; issued 750 shares	$75,000	
Premium on Common Stock	2,500	
Discount on Common Stock	500*	
Total Paid-in Capital		$77,000
* Deduction.		

If only the net excess of $2,000 ($2,500 premium less $500 discount) is reported, the existence of the discount liability is concealed from readers of the statement.

The descriptions of stock issuance transactions in the previous sections were based on the assumption that full payment for the stock was received and the stock certificates were issued at once. This condition normally exists for small or closely held corporations. In the following transactions, *subscriptions,* or pledges to buy the stock, are taken first, and payment is made later in single lump sums or in installments. The purchaser signs a formal, legally enforceable *subscription contract* in which he agrees to buy a certain number of shares of stock and to make certain specified payments. The stock certificates are not issued until completion of the payment.

The Subscriptions Receivable account is similar in nature and function to the Accounts Receivable account. It is a current asset and shows the amount due on stock that has been subscribed but has not been fully paid for. It is debited for the issue price, not necessarily the par or stated value, of the stock and is credited for collections as they are received. Like the Accounts Receivable account, it is a controlling account with supporting detail kept in a subsidiary *subscribers ledger,* which contains the accounts of the individual subscribers. When more than one class of stock is issued, separate Subscriptions Receivable accounts should be kept for each class.

The Capital Stock Subscribed account is a temporary capital stock account. It shows the amount of stock that has been subscribed, but the stock certificates for the amount in the account have not been issued pending receipt of the payments still due on the stock as shown in the Subscriptions Receivable account. The account is credited for the par or stated value of the subscribed stock and is debited for the par or stated value when the stock is issued, with the permanent Capital Stock account being credited. If no-par value shares without a stated value are issued, the Capital Stock Subscribed account is debited or credited for the full subscription price.

The subscriber to stock normally acquires the full status of a stockholder with all rights and privileges even though he is not in possession of the stock certificate. The stock subscription agreement, however, may restrict such rights until full payment is received.

Issuance by Subscription at a Premium. The Reed Corporation is authorized to issue 6,000 shares of $100 par value common stock. On July 1, 5,000 shares are issued at a price of $105 a share for cash and subscriptions are received for 1,000 shares. A 60 percent down payment is received; the remaining 40 percent is payable in two installments of $21,000 each on August 2 and September 1. The journal entries are:

1976					
July	1	Cash		525,000	
		Common Stock			500,000
		Premium on Common Stock			25,000
		To record the issuance of			
		5,000 shares of $100 par			
		value stock for cash at $105			
		a share.			

PAID-IN
CAPITAL

1976
July
	1	Subscriptions Receivable—
		Common Stock
		    Common Stock Subscribed
		    Premium on Common Stock
		        To record the receipt of
		        subscriptions for 1,000
		        shares of $100 par value
		        stock at $105 a share.
			105,000	100,000
				5,000

	1	Cash
		    Subscriptions Receivable—
		    Common Stock
		        To record the receipt of a
		        60% down payment on the
		        stock subscription of July 1.
			63,000	63,000

Aug.	2	Cash
		    Subscriptions Receivable—
		    Common Stock
		        To record the receipt of
		        the first 20% installment
		        on the stock subscription
		        of July 1.
			21,000	21,000

Sept.	1	Cash
		    Subscriptions Receivable—
		    Common Stock
		        To record the receipt of
		        the second and final
		        installment on the
		        stock subscription
		        of July 1.
			21,000	21,000

	1	Common Stock Subscribed
		    Common Stock
		        To record the issuance of
		        stock certificates for
		        1,000 shares of stock.
			100,000	100,000

When stock is subscribed at a premium, the entire excess over par or stated value is credited to the Premium on Stock account at the time the stock is subscribed (see the first entry of July 1). The premium is recognized at the time of subscription—not proportionately as installments are collected. The amount of the entry for the issuance of the stock certificates is the par or stated value of the stock; the existence of a premium or discount does not affect the amount recorded.

Partial statements of financial position as of July 1 and September 1 are shown below.

July 1, 1976

Assets

Current Assets
  Subscriptions Receivable–Common Stock $ 42,000

Stockholders' Equity

Paid-in Capital
  Common Stock, $100 par value; authorized 6,000
    shares, issued 5,000 shares $500,000
  Common Stock, subscribed but not issued, 1,000 shares   100,000
  Premium on Common Stock   30,000

September 1, 1976

Stockholders' Equity

Paid-in Capital
  Common Stock, $100 par value; authorized and
    issued 6,000 shares $600,000
  Premium on Common Stock   30,000

If the Reed Corporation issued the stock at $95 a share, the entries on July 1 to record the issue and subscription would include debits of $25,000 and $5,000 to Discount on Common Stock. All other entries would be the same except that the amounts for the entries in Cash and Subscriptions Receivable—Common Stock would be reduced. The Discount on Common Stock account, like the Premium on Common Stock account, is recorded in full when the subscription is received and is not involved when the installment payments are received. The Discount on Common Stock account is reported in the position statement as a negative Paid-In Capital item in the Stockholders' Equity section.

If preferred stock is issued in addition to common stock, special accounts would be opened as required for Subscriptions Receivable—Preferred Stock, Preferred Stock Subscribed, Discount on Preferred Stock, and Premium on Preferred Stock.

Depending on the statutes of the state of incorporation, a defaulting subscriber may (1) forfeit the amounts he paid in, (2) forfeit only the loss resulting from the resale of the shares, or (3) receive the number of shares he could have purchased for the amounts paid in.

GLOSSARY

Capital Stock Shares representing fractional ownership in a corporation; may consist of several classes with varying rights and privileges.

Common Stock If only one class of capital stock is issued, it is called common stock.

(Ch. 12)

Corporation From both the legal and the accounting points of view, the corporation is a special and separate being, or separate legal entity, created by law.

Organization Costs Expenditures necessary to bring the corporation into existence.

Paid-In Capital Amounts invested by stockholders that are credited to accounts other than capital stock.

Par Value The nominal or face value printed on a stock certificate representing the minimum amount to be paid to the issuing corporation by the original purchaser.

Partnership An association of two or more persons to carry on, as co-owners, a business for profit.

Preferred Stock A class of capital stock having preferences as to dividends and as to assets upon liquidation.

Stated Capital The minimum amount of capital that must be left in the corporation for the protection of creditors, and which cannot be withdrawn by the stockholders.

Stock Certificate A printed or engraved serially numbered document issued to the stock purchaser as evidence of ownership of the stated number of shares of capital stock of the issuing corporation.

Stock Subscription A pledge to buy capital stock with payment to be made later in a single lump sum or in installments.

Stock Transfer Journal The journal in which are recorded the transfers or exchanges of stock from one person to another.

Stockholders Ledger A subsidiary ledger showing the account of each stockholder, the certificates issued or canceled, and the number of shares held.

Q12-1. (a) What are some of the distinct features of the partnership form of business organization? (b) What are its advantages? (c) What are its disadvantages?

Q12-2. Describe each of the following: (a) general partner, (b) limited partner, (c) secret partner, (d) nominal partner.

Q12-3. Compare the partnership form of business organization with the single proprietorship and corporate forms.

Q12-4. Why should agreements reached in forming a partnership be in writing? What are some of the matters that should be specifically covered in a partnership agreement?

Q12-5. Can a partnership business continue after the death or retirement of one of the partners? Explain.

Q12-6. James Brown and Cedric Lee formed a partnership. Brown invested $10,000 in cash; Lee invested land and a building with a cash market value of $25,000. Five years later they agree to terminate the partnership, and Lee demands the return to him of the land and building. Is he justified in his demand?

Q12-7. D. Myers and S. Sacks agreed orally to form a partnership as of January 10, 1976. They postponed formalization of their agreement pending the return of their attorney, who was out of town. D. Myers invested $40,000 in cash; S. Sacks invested land and buildings worth $20,000 and $80,000, respectively. On January 11, the building was completely destroyed by an accidental explosion, and they terminated their partnership. Sacks claims that both the land and the $40,000 belong to him. Is he right? Explain.

INCOME
MEASUREMENT
AND VALUATION

(Ch. 12)

Q12-8. Frank Fish and Homer Little are partners with capital account balances of $40,000 each. They share profits one third and two thirds, respectively. (a) Is this an equitable arrangement? (b) Assume that 10% interest on capital balances is agreed on. How will profits of $12,000 be distributed? (c) What account should be charged for the interest on the capital balances?

Q12-9. Douglas Evans and Stanley Byrd form a partnership by oral agreement. The matter of profit distribution is not discussed. Evans invests $15,000 and Byrd, $10,000. At the end of the first year, Evans contends that he should be credited with 60% of the profits of $10,000. Byrd disagrees. (a) Is Evans right? (b) How could this disagreement have been avoided?

Q12-10. (a) What books and records do corporations have that are not necessary for single proprietorships or partnerships? (b) What is meant by the following terms: authorized capital stock, stock certificate, share of stock, par value stock, no-par value stock?

Q12-11. What is meant (a) by preferred stock? (b) by common stock? (c) by stockholders' equity? (d) by retained earnings?

Q12-12. What is the purpose and function of the following corporate records: subscription ledger, stockholders' ledger, stock transfer journal, minute book?

Q12-13. Distinguish between authorized and unissued stock and issued and outstanding stock.

Q12-14. Student A says that if he were buying stock, he would purchase only stock having a par value. Student B takes the opposite viewpoint. Discuss.

Q12-15. What is legal capital? How is it determined? How does it differ from contributed capital? retained earnings? stockholders' equity? Why should the state of incorporation regulate the amount that may be distributed to stockholders in the form of dividends?

Q12-16. Student A says that Subscriptions Receivable is a current asset; student B argues that the account belongs in the Stockholders' Equity section. Discuss.

Q12-17. Define and give the significance of each of the following terms: (a) par value of stock; (b) preemptive right; (c) market value of stock; (d) preferred stock; (e) corporation.

E12-1. Enter the following transactions in appropriate T accounts:
  a. Thomas Wojeck and James Lord form a partnership with cash investments of $25,200 and $19,800, respectively.
  b. Wojeck and Lord withdrew $5,400 and $9,000, respectively, in anticipation of earnings.
  c. Wojeck made an additional cash investment of $3,600, and Lord turned over to the partnership the title to a parcel of land with a fair market value of $10,800.
  d. The net income for the period was $23,400 (profits and losses are shared equally).

E12-2. In their partnership agreement, Tom Jones and Ernest Raymond agreed to divide profits and losses as follows: (a) 10% interest on average capital balances, (b) salaries of $10,800 each, and (c) the remainder shared equally. Prepare a schedule showing the distribution of net income of $35,100, assum-

PAID-IN
CAPITAL

ing average capital balances of $18,000 and $36,000 for Jones and Raymond, respectively.

E12-3. The following information relates to the partnership of A and B:

Average capital balances for 1976	
A	$72,000
B	84,000
Net income for 1976	9,600

The partnership agreement states that profits shall be divided as follows:

Salary allowances:
A $9,600
B   7,200
Interest allowance: 9% on average capital balances
Remainder:
A ¼
B ¾

Prepare the closing journal entries to distribute the net income in accordance with the partnership agreement.

E12-4. James Queene, owner of the Quality Store, asks you to determine his equity in the business at December 31, 1976. You determine his net income for the year from the store to be $39,000. In addition, the following transactions occurred during the year:

Original investment	$45,000
Additional investment	6,000
Personal withdrawals	24,000

(a) Post the transactions to appropriate T accounts, and (b) prepare a statement of owners' equity.

E12-5. Paul Haley and John Galvin formed a partnership on June 8, 1976. Haley contributed $10,000 in cash, land worth $6,000, a building appraised at $40,000 (the land and the building are encumbered by a mortgage of $8,000, which is assumed by the partnership), and a truck valued at $2,000. Galvin contributed $10,000 in cash.
(a) Make the entries to record the formation of the partnership. (b) Why may Haley be willing to enter into a partnership in which he contributes five times as much as his partner?

E12-6. The LePaz Corporation, organized on September 30, 1976, was authorized to issue 15,000 shares of $20 par value common stock.

1976
Oct.   1   Issued 200 shares to an attorney for services, valued at $4,000, in organizing the corporation.
     25   Issued for cash 3,000 shares at $22 a share.
Nov. 10   Issued for cash 2,000 shares at $23 a share.

Record the transactions.

E12-7. (Appendix) The Tilley Corporation was authorized to issue 30,000 shares of no-par value common stock with a $20 stated value and 10,000 shares of 10% preferred stock, $100 par value. At the end of one year of operations, the

Tilley Corporation's trial balance included the following account balances:

Preferred Stock	$660,000
Common Stock	440,000
Subscriptions Receivable—Common	106,000
Subscriptions Receivable—Preferred	275,000
Preferred Stock Subscribed	330,000
Common Stock Subscribed	165,000
Premium on Common Stock	77,000
Discount on Preferred Stock	44,000

How much cash has been collected from the stock transactions?

E12-8. The Richard Powers Corporation acquired the plant and equipment of the K. Raffol Company in exchange for 20,000 shares of its $25 par value common stock. Record the acquisition, assuming that if the assets had been acquired for cash, the purchase price would have been (a) $525,000; (b) $450,000.

E12-9. The Spiller Corporation is authorized to issue 15,000 shares of $50 par value common stock. The following transactions occurred:

1. Issued for cash 3,000 shares at par value.
2. Issued 100 shares to the promotors for services valued at $5,000.
3. Issued 100 shares to attorneys for services, valued at $5,000, in organizing the corporation and securing the corporate charter.
4. Issued 1,800 shares in exchange for a factory building and land valued at $85,000 and $12,000, respectively.
5. Issued for cash 1,500 shares at $45 a share.
6. Issued for cash 3,000 shares at $60 a share.

Record the transactions.

E12-10. The India Corporation was authorized to issue 5,000 shares of common stock. Record the issue of 4,000 shares at $7\frac{1}{4}$, assuming (a) that the shares have a $5 par value; (b) that the shares have no-par and no stated value; (c) that the shares have a stated value of $3.

E12-11. (Appendix). The Zona Corporation was authorized to issue 20,000 shares of no-par value common stock and 20,000 shares of $20 par value preferred stock. Organizers of the corporation received 3,000 shares of the no-par value common stock for services valued at $8,500. A total of 3,000 shares of the preferred stock was issued for cash at $18 a share, and 3,000 shares of common stock were issued for cash at $5 a share. A total of 4,000 shares of preferred stock was subscribed at $12 a share. One-half the subscribers paid in full. (a) Record the transactions in T accounts. (b) Prepare a statement of financial position.

E12-12. (Appendix). The Stockholders' Equity section of the Tout Corporation's position statement as of December 31, 1976, shows the following:

Common Stock, $100 par value; authorized 1,000 shares:	
subscribed but not issued 900 shares	$90,000
Discount on Common Stock	3,000*
Premium on Common Stock	10,000

The Current Assets section shows:

Subscriptions Receivable	$50,000

How much cash has been collected from the stock subscribers?

E12-13. (*Financial policy decision problem*) The 1976 annual report of M. H. Fish Company includes the following note to its financial statements:

During the year the stockholders approved a change in the authorized capital stock of the company from 15,000 shares, $100 par value preferred stock to 500,000 shares, no-par value, and from 2,000,000 shares, $1 par value common stock to 3,000,000 shares, $1 par value common stock. (a) What was the effect of these changes on the company's financial statements? (b) What was the purpose of the changes?

DEMON-
STRATION
PROBLEMS

DP12-1. (*Recording partnership transactions*) The following selected transactions occurred in the partnership of Collins and Condin:

1976

Jan. 2   Clark Collins and Daniel Condin formed a partnership on this date, making the following investments:

Collins invested $55,000 in cash. Condin contributed his equity in a building and lot. The partners agreed that the building was worth $90,000 and the land, $15,000. There was a mortgage on the land and building with a face value of $27,000; the mortgage carried an interest rate of 9%, and the interest was last paid on October 1, 1975. The partnership assumed all liabilities relating to the investment.

Mar. 1   Collins withdrew $800 cash in anticipation of income to be earned.

Apr. 1   Condin withdrew merchandise from the business. The merchandise cost $600 and had a selling price of $800. The firm uses the periodic inventory system.

Oct. 1   Collins was allowed to withdraw $12,000 in cash to pay a personal debt. This amount exceeds any anticipated income to be earned.

Required: Record the transactions.

DP12-2. (*Distribution of partnership profits and losses*) Edward Hand and Maurice Strong formed a partnership on January 1, 1976, with investments of $25,000 and $40,000, respectively.

On July 1, 1976, Strong invested an additional $10,000. On October 1, 1976, Hand and Strong withdrew $6,000 and $5,000 respectively, in anticipation of earnings.

Required: Make the appropriate journal entries to record the distribution of profits and losses on the basis of each of the following assumptions:

1. Net income is $12,000, profits and losses are shared equally.
2. Net loss is $5,000; the partnership agreement provides that profits are to be distributed 55% to Hand and 45% to Strong; the method of distributing losses was not specified.
3. Net income is $10,000, to be distributed in the ratio of capital balances as of December 31, 1976.
4. Net income is $20,000, to be distributed as follows: salaries of $10,000 to Hand and $12,000 to Strong; interest of 8% on ending capital balances; remainder to be distributed equally.

DP12-3. (Appendix). (*Recording capital stock issuance; stockholders' equity*) The Bechet Company was organized on July 1, 1976, with authority to issue 50,000 shares of $50 par value preferred stock and 30,000 shares of no-par value, $15 stated-value common stock. The following transactions occurred during the year:

1976

July 1 Issued for cash 24,000 shares of preferred stock at $51 a share.

10 Issued for cash 16,000 shares of common stock at $20 a share.

15 Issued for cash 4,000 shares of preferred stock at $49 a share.

20 Received subscriptions for 8,000 shares of common stock at $17 a share with a down payment of 50% and the balance due on September 30.

31 Received subscriptions for 12,000 shares of preferred stock at $51 a share; one-half the price was received on subscription, with the remainder due on September 30.

Aug. 2 Issued 100 shares of preferred stock to an attorney in payment for services, valued at $5,000, rendered in organizing the corporation.

Sept.15 Issued 2,000 shares of common stock in exchange for land and a building appraised at $12,000 and $35,000, respectively.

30 Collected the installment due on the subscriptions of July 20 and July 31.

30 Net income from operations, after income taxes, for the period July 1 to September 30 was $50,000 (debit Other Assets).

Required:

1. Record the transactions in appropriate T accounts.
2. Prepare the Stockholders' Equity section of the statement of financial position as of September 30, 1976.

P12-1. C. Bunnell and R. Byrne form a partnership.

Required: Journalize their investments, based on each of the following assumptions:

1. Each partner invests $6,000 in cash.
2. Bunnell invests $7,000 in cash, and Byrne invests $9,000 in cash.
3. Bunnell invests $2,000 in cash, land worth $8,000, a building worth $20,000, and merchandise worth $3,000. Byrne invests $25,000 in cash.
4. Bunnell invests $3,000 in cash, land worth $5,000, and a building worth $20,000. The partnership agrees to assume a mortgage payable of $10,000 on the land and building. Byrne invests $3,000 in cash, store equipment worth $6,000, and merchandise worth $2,000.
5. Before the formation of the partnership, Bunnell and Byrne were competitors. They decide to form the partnership for their mutual advantage; the partnership assumes their existing assets and liabilities at book values as follows:

PAID-IN
CAPITAL

	Bunnell	Byrne
Cash	$ 6,000	$ 7,000
Accounts Receivable	13,000	16,000
Merchandise Inventory	30,400	22,200
Delivery Equipment (net)	7,000	10,400
Store Equipment (net)	12,000	20,000
Totals	$68,400	$75,600
Accounts Payable	$26,800	$24,400
Notes Payable	10,000	12,000
Bunnell, Capital	31,600	
Byrne, Capital		39,200
Totals	$68,400	$75,600

6. Assume the same facts as in assumption 5, except that the merchandise and equipment are to be recorded at their fair market valuations as follows:

	Bunnell	Byrne
Merchandise Inventory	$28,000	$22,000
Delivery Equipment (net)	8,000	10,000
Store Equipment (net)	10,000	14,000

P12-2. Arthur Dublin and Lowell Dworin form a partnership to operate a food brokerage business.

Required: Record their initial investments, on the basis of each of the following assumptions:

1. Dublin and Dworin each invest $10,000 in cash.
2. Dublin and Dworin invest $4,000 and $2,500 in cash, respectively.
3. Dublin invests $4,000 in cash, merchandise worth $7,500, a building worth $30,000, and land worth $9,000; Dworin invests $10,000 in cash, office equipment worth $6,000, and store equipment worth $10,000.
4. Dublin and Dworin transfer the following assets and liabilities to the partnership as their initial investments:

	Dublin	Dworin
Cash	$ 6,000	$ 4,500
Accounts Receivable	10,000	12,000
Merchandise Inventory	20,000	17,000
Delivery Equipment (net)	12,000	–0–
Store Equipment (net)	–0–	11,000
Accounts Payable	15,000	16,000
Notes Payable to Bank	13,000	15,000

P12-3. Barry Fuchs, John Galvin, and Tom Gee formed a partnership on May 1, 1975, with investments of $15,000, $11,000, and $13,000, respectively. Profits and losses were to be shared equally. During the next twelve months, Fuchs and Galvin made additional investments of $5,000 each; Gee invested an additional $6,000 and withdrew $2,500. Net income for the period was $30,000.

Required: Prepare (a) a statement of partners' equities for the year ended April 30, 1976, and (b) entries to close the partners' Drawing accounts.

P12-4. Peter Warg and Rae Burn formed a partnership on January 2, 1976. Certain relevant accounts are given as of December 31, 1976:

Peter Warg, Capital		Rae Burn, Capital	
1976	1976		1976
Aug. 1 10,000	Jan. 1 80,000		Jan. 1 100,000
	July 1 20,000		Dec. 1 12,000

Peter Warg, Drawing		Rae Burn, Drawing	
1976		1976	
Dec. 31 6,000		Dec. 31 8,000	

The net income for 1976 was $10,000. The following provisions appeared in the articles of copartnership:

Net income shall be divided as follows:
Salary allowances: Warg, $6,000; Burn, $8,000
Interest allowances: 9% on beginning-of-year capital balances
Remainder: divided 55% to Warg and 45% to Burn

Required: Prepare the journal entries to distribute the net income to the partners' accounts and to complete the closing process.

P12-5. Assume that A and B are equal partners, each with a capital balance of $39,000. Record the admission of C under each of the following assumptions:

a. A sells his interest to C for $42,000.
b. C invests $39,000 for a one-fourth interest.
c. C invests $39,000 for a one-fourth interest, total capital to be $130,000.
d. C invests $39,000 for a one-third interest, total capital to be $117,000.
e. C invests $45,500 for a one-third interest, total capital to be $136,500.
f. C invests $26,000 for a one-third interest, total capital to be $117,000.
g. C invests $46,800 for a one-fourth interest, total capital to be $124,800.
h. C invests $46,800 for a one-half interest, total capital to be $124,800.

P12-6. A, B, and C, whose financial position information is shown below, have decided to liquidate their partnership. Their general ledger shows the following balances on March 31, 1976:

Cash	$10,000
Accounts Receivable	12,500
Inventories	50,000
Machinery	62,500
Accounts Payable	10,000
A, Capital	25,000

B, Capital	37,500
C, Capital	62,500

Proceeds from the sale of noncash assets were as follows:

Accounts Receivable	$ 7,500
Inventories	22,500
Machinery	12,500

Required: Prepare a schedule in good form showing the final distribution of the remaining cash following the sale of the assets and the payment of creditors.

P12-7. (Appendix) On December 31, 1976, the ledger of the Knowles Company included the following accounts:

Notes Receivable	$ 15,000
Merchandise Inventory	75,000
Marketable Securities—U.S. Government Bonds	8,000
Common Stock ($100 par value)	300,000
Retained Earnings	100,000
Subscriptions Receivable—Common Stock	40,000
Preferred Stock ($10 par value)	150,000
Goodwill	30,000
Common Stock Subscribed	150,000
Organization Costs	20,000
Premium on Preferred Stock	12,000
Building	225,000
Premium on Common Stock	30,000
Notes Receivable Discounted (*Hint:* A contra to Notes Receivable)	7,000
Cash	90,000
Research and Development Costs	110,000

Required: Prepare the Stockholders' Equity section of the statement of financial position as of December 31, 1976.

P12-8. (Appendix). John Dill, an investor, and Richard Paris, an inventor, decided to form Hewlett, Inc., to manufacture and sell a product developed by Paris. The corporation is chartered by the state, with 10,000 shares of $100 par value common stock authorized.

   a. Dill invests $200,000 and Paris invests $140,000 in cash for stock at par value. Paris is issued an additional $75,000 in stock at par value in payment for his patent on the product to be manufactured.
   b. The corporation issues 200 shares of common stock at par value to each promoter as payment for promotion and incorporation fees.
   c. Hewlett, Inc., sells stock on a subscription basis to five investors. Each investor subscribes to 200 shares of the common stock at $105 per share, making a down payment of 40% of the subscription price. The remainder is to be paid at a later date.
   d. Four of the five subscribers pay the remaining installment.

Required: Journalize the transactions.

P12-9. (Appendix). The Burns Corporation was organized on January 2, 1976, with authority to issue 10,000 shares of $100 par value common stock. The following transactions occurred during the year:

1976

Jan.	10	Issued for cash 150 shares at $102 per share.
Feb.	18	Issued for cash 150 shares at $98 per share.
Mar.	1	Issued 2,000 shares for land and a building with a fair market value of $200,000. One-eighth the total valuation was allocable to the land.
June	1	Received subscriptions for 1,000 shares at $104 per share, payable 40% down and the balance in two equal installments due on August 2 and October 1.
	10	Paid $5,000 for legal fees incurred in organizing the corporation.
July	5	Purchased equipment for $60,000 in cash.
Aug.	2	Received the installment due on the subscription of June 1.
Oct.	1	Received the installment due on the subscription of June 1.
Dec.	15	Received subscriptions for 1,000 shares at $97 a share payable 40% down and the balance in two equal installments due on February 15, 1977, and April 15, 1977.
	31	Recorded the following entry, summarizing the net effects of the results of operations before income taxes for the year:

Cash	35,000	
Accumulated Depreciation—Building		6,000
Accumulated Depreciation—Equipment		3,000
Income Summary		26,000

	31	Recorded the income tax liability of $4,500.
	31	Closed the Income Summary account.

Required:

1. Record the transactions in appropriate T accounts.
2. Prepare a statement of financial position as of December 31, 1976.

P12-10. (Appendix). The following selected transactions occurred at the newly formed Love Corporation:

1976

July	1	Received a charter authorizing the issuance of 5,000 shares of $50 par value preferred stock and 50,000 shares of no-par value common stock with a stated value of $5 per share.
	2	Issued 25,000 shares of common stock at $10 per share for cash.
	2	Issued 500 shares of common stock to an incorporator for a patent that he had perfected.
	3	Received subscriptions from four investors for 250 shares each of preferred stock at $52.50.
	5	Received 60% down payments on the subscriptions from all four subscribers.
	20	Received payment in full from three of the preferred subscribers, and issued the stock.
	31	Received payment in full from the fourth preferred subscriber, and issued the stock.
Aug.	10	Received a subscription from Yok Lie for 500 shares of the preferred stock at $49 a share.
	12	Collected 60% of Lie's subscription total. The balance is due on September 1, 1976.

PAID-IN
CAPITAL

(Ch. 12)

499

Required: Record the transactions.

P12-11. The accountant for Bruce and Thomas, interior decorators, prepared the following trial balance at December 31, 1976:

Cash	$ 4,850	
Accounts Receivable	12,600	
Supplies	3,800	
Prepaid Insurance	2,750	
Office Equipment	12,000	
Accumulated Depreciation—Office Equipment		$ 3,500
Building	80,000	
Accumulated Depreciation—Building		10,000
Accounts Payable		4,500
Accrued Salaries Payable		500
Mortgage Payable		20,000
Edward Bruce, Capital		25,000
Edward Bruce, Drawing	15,000	
Ray Thomas, Capital		20,000
Ray Thomas, Drawing	12,000	
Professional Fees		85,000
Supplies Used	3,000	
Depreciation Expense—Office Equipment	1,200	
Depreciation Expense—Building	4,000	
Utilities Expense	1,200	
General Expense	1,500	
Property Tax Expense	1,000	
Interest Expense	1,600	
Salaries Expense	12,000	
	$168,500	$168,500

Required:

1. Prepare an income statement for the year showing the distribution of net income to each partner. The partners have agreed to divide profits and losses as follows: (a) 10% interest on capital balances at the beginning of the year, (b) salaries of $15,000 each, and (c) the remainder equally. Each partner made an additional investment of $3,000 on July 1, 1976.
2. Prepare a statement of partners' equities for the year.
3. Prepare a statement of financial position as of December 31, 1976.

P12-12. John Healy and Frank Ford, equal partners in a plastics manufacturing company, wish to expand their production facilities. They plan to dissolve the partnership and to transfer all partnership assets and liabilities to a newly formed corporation authorized to issue 100,000 shares of $5 par value voting common stock and 1,000 shares of $100 par value, 8% nonvoting preferred stock.

The accounts of the partnership at the time of the transfer to the corporation, to be called the Healford Corp., Inc., are listed on page 501.

Cash	$ 5,500	
Accounts Receivable	12,400	
Allowance for Doubtful Accounts		$ 860
Merchandise Inventory	20,000	
Prepaid Expenses	1,000	
Land	10,000	
Building (net)	58,000	
Equipment (net)	30,000	
Accounts Payable		20,000
Accrued Liabilities		1,040
John Healy, Capital		57,500
Frank Ford, Capital		57,500
	$136,900	$136,900

The following transactions occurred immediately following incorporation:

1. Each partner was issued common stock at par in amounts equal to his partnership interest.
2. Issued 40 shares of preferred stock at $103 a share for cash.
3. Issued 15,000 shares of common at $5.50 a share for cash.
4. Cash payments were made for incorporation fees, $500, legal services in forming the corporation, $750, and printing costs for the stock certificates, $250.

Required:

1. Record the transactions on the books of the corporation (the partnership books are used).
2. Prepare a statement of financial position.
3. What did Healy and Ford gain by incorporating their partnership? What did they sacrifice?

Dividends, Retained Earnings, and Treasury Stock

13

The stockholders' equity in a corporation arises from a number of sources. It is of the utmost importance that these sources be clearly distinguished and stated. It is equally important that the terminology used to designate them be precise and meaningful.

The various sources of the stockholders' equity discussed in this chapter and in Chapter 12 are outlined in Figure 13-1.

PAID-IN CAPITAL

As implied in the previous chapter, *paid-in capital* may include items other than the par or stated value of stock. Among these, in addition to premiums on common or preferred stock, may be donations and amounts arising from asset revaluations.

Excess over Par or Stated Value

The premium on stock, or excess over par or stated value, is that part of the capital paid in by stockholders that is not credited to the capital stock accounts. Some accountants refer to it as *capital surplus,* but this term may be confusing, as other accountants use it to designate retained earnings. Separate paid-in capital accounts are kept so that the position statement shows the specific sources of capital. Such precise source accounts are also desirable to establish the availability of source of funds for dividends or other distributions to stockholders, in states that permit such distributions.

Donations

A gift or donation to a corporation increases the assets and the stockholders' equity and is credited to Paid-In Capital—Donations. Gifts of land, buildings, or other facilities are sometimes made by a local organization to encourage a corporation to do business in the area. Sometimes donations of assets or stock are made by the stockholders to a company in financial difficulties to enable it to raise funds.

A contribution of land and buildings by a town to a newly established firm is recorded by the receiving corporation at the fair market value of the assets contributed as shown below (the fair market values are assumed).

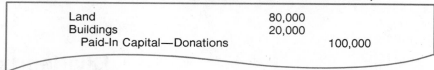

Land	80,000	
Buildings	20,000	
Paid-In Capital—Donations		100,000

Figure 13-1
Sources of
Stockholders' Equity

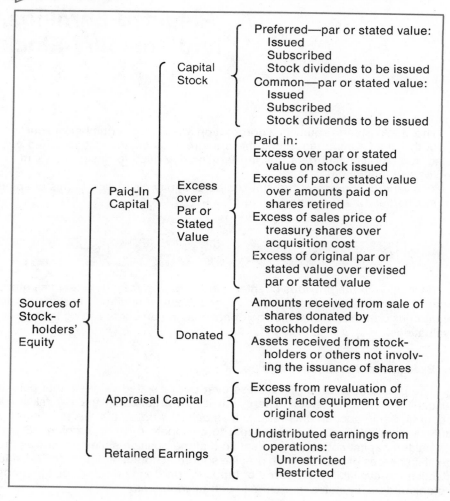

To help a corporation in raising needed working capital, its stockholders, instead of investing additional funds, may donate a portion of their fully paid stock to the corporation. Such stock is known as *treasury stock,* explained later in this chapter. Sales of the donated stock for cash are recorded by a debit to Cash and a credit to Paid-In Capital—Donations.

REVALUATIONS

The upward revaluation of corporate assets, generally following a continuing increase in price levels, results in an increase in stockholders' equity. The practice of revaluing assets to reflect current market values is contrary to current practice, but the usefulness of historical cost amounts is limited when there is a wide disparity between original cost and market or replacement values.

The Study Group of the AICPA on the Objectives of Financial Statements concluded that "different valuation bases are preferable for different assets and liabilities. That means that financial statements might contain data based on a combination of valuation bases."[1] The group also stated that "current values should also be reported when they differ significantly from historical cost,"[2] and that earnings computed by a valuation basis quantifying assets in terms of present prices should "include, in a separate category, changes in the replacement cost of assets."[3] In some cases, current value estimates would be reported in footnotes; in others, specific assets would be revalued and their new carrying costs entered in the accounts. If the revision is upward, there is a corresponding increase in stockholders' equity that came neither from additional investment nor from earnings. Accordingly, it would be improper to report it as paid-in capital or as part of retained earnings. Instead, it should be credited to an appraisal capital account that carries a title descriptive of the event. (The debit is usually not made directly to the asset, but to an adjunct account such as Land—Appreciation in Value.)

RETAINED EARNINGS

Undistributed earnings from regular operating transactions are classified as *retained earnings.* These are sources of stockholders' equity other than transactions involving the company's own stock and revaluations. Such terms as *earned surplus, retained income, accumulated earnings,* and *earnings retained for use in the business* are also used to designate the earnings that have not been distributed to the stockholders as dividends.

[1] Report of the Study Group on the Objectives of Financial Statements (New York: AICPA, 1973), p. 41.
[2] *Ibid.,* p. 64.
[3] *Ibid.,* p. 41.

The creation of special Restricted Retained Earnings accounts indicates that a portion of the earnings of the corporation is not available for dividends. This does not mean that a special cash fund has been set up, nor does the restriction provide cash funds. The restrictions do not in any way alter the total retained earnings or the total stockholders' equity. The segregation of retained earnings is an accounting device by which a corporation, following a resolution of the board of directors, intentionally reduces the amount of earnings available for dividend distributions, thus indicating its intention to conserve corporate assets for other purposes. The restriction of retained earnings does not reduce the overall retained earnings but merely *earmarks,* or sets aside, a portion of the earnings in an account specifically designated to indicate its purpose. The same information can be communicated by a footnote or by a parenthetical notation.

Each restricted account, although separated from the parent Retained Earnings account, is nevertheless a part of retained earnings and is so classified in the Stockholders' Equity section of the position statement. When the special account has served its purpose and the requirement for which it was set up no longer exists, the amount in the restricted account is returned to the Retained Earnings account.

Restrictions may be either voluntary or involuntary. A restriction for plant expansion, for example, may be set up by voluntary action of the board of directors. The purpose of this restriction is to show management's intention to retain cash or other assets for use in connection with a projected plant expansion program rather than to distribute them in the form of dividends. When cash dividends are paid, the assets of the corporation are depleted. To the degree, then, that dividend declarations are restricted, assets are retained for other business purposes such as plant expansion. Involuntary restrictions may be required either by state statute, covered later in this chapter, or by contract. When a corporation enters into an agreement for a long-term loan, the terms of the contract may require periodic restrictions of retained earnings, accumulating over the term of the loan to an amount equal to the loan. The purpose of the restriction is to reduce the amount of cash earnings that might otherwise be distributed to the stockholders as dividends, and to improve the corporation's ability to make periodic interest payments and any other payments required under the terms of the loan. The restriction does not ensure the availability of working capital; it does, however, limit the use of working capital for dividend distributions. The journal entry to record this type of restriction is a debit to Retained Earnings and a credit to Retained Earnings—Restricted for Long-Term Loan Retirement. This entry is reversed whenever its intended purpose has been accomplished and continuance of the restriction is no longer necessary.

The term *dividend* refers to the distribution of cash, stock, or other corporate property by a corporation to the stockholders. A dividend must be declared formally by the board of directors, a record of which should be entered in the minute book; the entry should indicate the date the dividend was declared, the *record date* to determine the eligibility of *stockholders of record* on that date, and the date of the payment. For a cash dividend distribution to be made, there must be accumulated unrestricted retained earnings and there must be assets available for distribution. If there are no accumulated earnings, the dividend becomes a reduction in paid-in capital, which is normally illegal. There may be adequate earnings but insufficient cash or other readily distributable type of assets. A corporation may have a good earnings record but no cash available for dividends because the cash may have been used to acquire other assets (land, buildings, machinery, or inventory), or funds are being accumulated for an anticipated expansion program or other corporate needs. Only the board of directors has the authority to determine whether a dividend is to be paid, to which classes of stock it is to be paid, and the time, manner, and form of payment. This applies to all classes of stockholders, preferred and common.

The board of directors is the ultimate authority in regard to dividend declaration. There have been court cases in which stockholders have attempted to force a dividend declaration that they felt was being deliberately withheld by the board of directors. Except in rare instances, courts have been reluctant to interpose and order dividend payments. Once formal action has been taken by the board, however, the declaration immediately becomes a current liability of the corporation. The state corporation laws contain dividend provisions that must be observed by the board of directors. It is customary, for example, particularly for larger corporations with numerous stockholders, to make a public announcement of the dividend declaration in newspapers or magazines.

The term *dividend* is most often used to designate a cash distribution. A dividend may be paid in property other than cash; a company may, for example, distribute marketable securities or merchandise. A well-known distillery once declared a dividend and made a pro rata distribution of whiskey late in December. The term *stock dividend* is used to designate the distribution of additional shares of stock to existing stockholders. The term *liquidating dividend* refers to a distribution of assets by a company being liquidated, or a distribution whose effect is to reduce the stockholders' equity from paid-in or revaluation capital. Thus, a liquidating dividend is a distribution of paid-in capital when there are no accumulated retained earnings or when a deficit exists. The term *ex-dividend* indicates that the quoted price of the shares is exclusive of a dividend declared and payable on a specified future date to shareholders of record as of a specified date prior to the payment date.

Declaration of a Dividend

The dividend may be stated as a percent of par or as a specified amount per share. Following is a typical dividend notice:

DIVIDENDS,
RETAINED EARNINGS,
TREASURY STOCK

The holder of 100 shares of common stock of the National Gas Company will be mailed a check for $47.50 on January 15, 1977. An investor who buys the stock in time to be recorded as its owner by December 31, 1976, the record date, will receive the dividend. An investor who buys stock of this company after December 31, 1976, is said to buy the stock *ex-dividend*—that is, without the right to receive the latest declared dividend. Stock traded on the stock exchanges is quoted ex-dividend typically three days prior to the record date to allow time for the recording and delivery of the securities. During the interval between December 31, 1976, and January 15, 1977, the company prepares the list of eligible stockholders and performs all other tasks incident to the mailing of the dividend checks.

With the stockholders ledger stored on disk or tape, the complete job of writing dividend checks can be performed by a computer. The amount of the dividend per share is read into the computer along with each stockholder's record. Since each record shows the number of shares owned by that shareholder, the computer calculates the amount due and prints the dividend checks.

Recording Cash Dividends

To illustrate the recording of a cash dividend, assume that on August 2, 1976, the board of directors of Magnetics, Inc., declared a quarterly dividend of $3,000 on 2,000 shares of $100 par value 6 percent preferred stock, and a $2,000 dividend on 10,000 shares of $10 par value common stock. The dividends are payable on September 1, 1976, to stockholders of record at the close of business on August 14, 1976. The entries to record the dividend declaration and the payment are as follows:

```
1976
Aug.   2   Dividends—Common Stock              2,000
           Dividends—Preferred Stock           3,000
              Dividends Payable—Common
                 Stock                                          2,000
              Dividends Payable—Preferred
                 Stock                                          3,000
                    To record the declaration
                    of a dividend on the
                    outstanding preferred and
                    common stock, payable
                    September 1, 1976, to
                    stockholders of record on
                    August 14, 1976: 1.5
                    percent on $200,000
                    preferred, and 2 percent
                    on $100,000 common.

Sept.  1   Dividends Payable—Common
              Stock                             2,000
           Dividends Payable—Preferred
              Stock                             3,000
                 Cash                                           5,000
                    To record payment of
                    dividends to stockholders
                    of record on August 14,
                    1976.
```

Each Dividends account is closed out at the end of the accounting year to Retained Earnings. The use of a Dividends account has the advantage of segregating dividends declared during the year; it also keeps Retained Earnings clear of charges that would require analysis at the end of the year when the statement of retained earnings is prepared. The Dividends account is a temporary stockholders' equity account; it has a debit balance and represents a reduction in the stockholders' equity. It is shown on the statement of retained earnings as a deduction from the total of the beginning balance of Retained Earnings plus net income and other credits to Retained Earnings. Dividends Payable, on either common or preferred stock, is a current liability.

Dividends on Preferred Stock

As mentioned in Chapter 12, preferred stock enjoys certain dividend preferences. The right to a dividend of a preferred stockholder must await a formal declaration by the board of directors. On declaration, the preferred stockholders are entitled to a stated amount per share before any dividend distribution is made to holders of common stock.

If the preferred stock is *cumulative,* undeclared dividends are accumulated and must be paid together with the current dividend before any dividend payment is made on common stock. If the preferred stock is *noncumulative,* a

(Ch. 13)

dividend passed (not formally declared by the board of directors) in any one year is lost forever. Preferred stock may be either *participating* or *nonparticipating*. If the preferred stock is participating, it receives its specified dividend rate and a share of any additional dividends declared. The manner of determining the amount of the additional dividend depends on the terms of the stock contract. If the preferred stock is fully participating, it participates on a pro rata basis at the same rate based on par value with the common stock in dividend distributions after the common stock has received an amount equal to the stipulated preference rate on the preferred stock. The participation may be limited in the stock contract to a specified rate or amount per share. If the preferred stock is nonparticipating, it receives the stipulated rate only, and the balance of the dividend distribution, irrespective of amount, is paid to the common stockholders. Most preferred stock issues are cumulative and nonparticipating.

The extent to which preferred stockholders participate in distributions above the regular rates depends on the specific provisions of the corporate charter. The following examples illustrate the application of the dividend preference of preferred stock.

1. *Cumulative and Nonparticipating.* A corporation has outstanding 1,000 shares of 5 percent cumulative preferred stock and 2,000 shares of common stock, each with a par value of $100. Undistributed earnings are $75,000, there are no dividends in arrears, and a $27,000 dividend is declared. Assuming that the preferred stock is nonparticipating, the required journal entry for the dividend declaration is shown below.

Dividends—Preferred Stock	5,000	
Dividends—Common Stock	22,000	
Dividends Payable—Preferred Stock		5,000
Dividends Payable—Common Stock		22,000

2. *Cumulative and Fully Participating.* Assume the same facts as in example 1, except that the preferred stock is cumulative and fully participating—that is, the preferred stock shares at an equal rate with the common stock in the amount distributed in excess of the 5 percent preferred dividend and a comparable dividend on the common stock. The required journal entry is shown here.

Dividends—Preferred Stock	9,000	
Dividends—Common Stock	18,000	
Dividends Payable—Preferred Stock		9,000
Dividends Payable—Common Stock		18,000

The allocation is computed as follows:

	To Preferred	To Common
Current rate at 5%, or $5 per share:		
To preferred stock: 1,000 shares × $5	$5,000	
To common stock: 2,000 shares × $5		$10,000
Participation at 4%, or $4 per share:		
To preferred stock: 1,000 shares × $4	4,000	
To common stock. 2,000 shares × $4		8,000
Total distribution	$9,000	$18,000

Note that each stockholder receives $9 a share because the preferred stock is fully participating, and the common stock receives a current rate equal to the preference rate on preferred stock.

3. *Cumulative and Partly Participating.* Assume the same facts as in example 2, except that the preferred stock participates to a maximum of 2 percent, or $2 a share, above its preference rate; the allocation of the $27,000 is computed as follows:

	To Preferred	To Common
Current rate	$5,000	$10,000
Participation:		
Preferred stock: 1,000 shares × $2	2,000	
Common stock: remainder		10,000
Total distribution	$7,000	$20,000

Preferred stock participates at the stated maximum only if the proportionate distribution to the common stock—at a rate on the par value, or in an amount per share on no-par value stock—equals or exceeds the distribution to the preferred stock. In this example, the preferred rate per share is $7 and the common rate is $10. The amount actually received on participation may be less than $2 a share, as shown in the following example.

4. *Dividend Arrearage.* This example is based on the same facts as in example 3, except that there is a dividend *arrearage* (amounts owed from previous periods) on the preferred stock of $9,000. The dividend distribution is computed as follows:

To preferred stock:	
Arrearage	$ 9,000
Current year's preference dividend	5,000
Participation	1,000
Total to preferred	$15,000
To common stock:	
Remainder	12,000
Total distribution	$27,000

The distribution to the preferred stock due to the participation provision is computed as follows:

Total dividend		$27,000
Deduct: Arrearage payment	$ 9,000	
Current year's preference—preferred stock	5,000	
Current year's rate—common stock	10,000	24,000
Available for participation		$ 3,000
Number of shares outstanding		3,000
Rate per share on participation		$ 1
To preferred stock: 1,000 × $1		$ 1,000

Preferred stock may also be preferred in distributing assets; this means that if the corporation is liquidated, the preferred stockholders must be paid before any liquidating payments are made to the common stockholders. The manner of the preference application depends on the wording in the stock contract. The preference may be for the par value of the preferred stock, the par value and accumulated dividends, or some other stipulated amount. If the preferred stock is not preferred as to assets, then the assets are usually distributed to all classes of stockholders on an equal basis proportionate to the respective par values.

Stock Dividends

The term *stock dividend* refers to the issuance by a corporation of additional shares of its authorized stock without additional payment of any kind by the stockholders. There are various occasions for the declaration of a stock dividend, such as:

1. A large unappropriated retained earnings balance
2. A desire by the directors to reduce the market price of the stock
3. A desire to increase the permanent capitalization of the company by converting a portion of the retained earnings into capital stock
4. A need to conserve available cash

A stock dividend does not change the total stockholders' equity in the corporation; it simply effects a transfer of retained earnings to paid-in capital. A cash dividend, on the other hand, decreases both the assets and the stockholders' equity. A stock dividend has no effect on either total assets or total stockholders' equity; the change is entirely within the Stockholders' Equity section (Retained Earnings decreases and Paid-In Capital increases). To illustrate, assume that the Truro Corporation, with $500,000 common stock, $100 par value, outstanding, and retained earnings of $80,000 declares a $50,000 stock dividend. The effect of the declaration on the stockholders' equity is shown on page 513.

Stockholders' Equity

	Immediately before Declaration	Immediately after Declaration	Immediately after Stock Issuance
Stockholders' equity:			
Common stock, $100 par value	$500,000	$500,000	$550,000
Stock dividends to be issued		50,000	
Retained earnings	80,000	30,000	30,000
Total stockholders' equity	$580,000	$580,000	$580,000

The Stock Dividends To Be Issued account is part of the stockholders' equity. It is not a liability, because its reduction will result not in a reduction of a current asset but rather in an increase in capital stock. The account should therefore be shown under Capital Stock in the Stockholders' Equity section of the position statement.

It is evident that a stock dividend has no effect on the total stockholders' equity; the relative interest of each stockholder is, therefore, unchanged. For example, John Green, a stockholder with 100 shares before the stock dividend, will have 110 shares after the stock dividend. His proportionate holdings remain unchanged at 2 percent of the total stock outstanding. Hence, all his rights and privileges are unaltered, as shown below.

	Line	Before Declaration	After Declaration
Total stockholders' equity	1	$580,000	$580,000.00
Number of shares outstanding	2	5,000	5,500
Stockholders' equity per share (line 1 ÷ line 2)	3	$ 116	$ 105.45
Shares owned by John Green	4	100	110
Green's equity (line 4 × line 3)	5	$ 11,600	$ 11,600.00

A stock dividend, nevertheless, is significant to the stockholder. The dividend does not alter the recipient's equity in the company and is not, therefore, considered income. There is no income tax on a stock dividend. If the stock dividend does not cause a significant decline in the price of stock, the stockholder's gain is equal to the market value of the new shares received. If, in addition, the corporation does not reduce the amount of its cash dividends per share, the stockholder gains the dividends on the additional shares. It is this aspect— the expectation of greater dividends as well as the availability of more shares

DIVIDENDS, RETAINED EARNINGS, TREASURY STOCK

(Ch. 13)

for possible ultimate profitable resale—that creates a favorable reception for a stock dividend.

A stock dividend provides certain advantages to the corporation. Its earnings are capitalized (that is, earnings are transferred to capital stock accounts); there is no reduction in working capital; and the corporation may plow back its earnings for expansion or other purposes. The corporation also may wish to reduce the market price of its shares in order to attract more buyers; by issuance of more shares, the price per share will decrease. At the same time, a stock dividend makes possible larger total dividend distributions without a change in the regular dividend rate.

When there are two classes of stockholders, the stock dividend normally applies only to the common stockholders. Payment, however, may be in either preferred or common stock. The various court rulings are not consistent with respect to the rights of preferred stockholders to participate in a stock dividend, although generally no such rights inhere in preferred stock.

Small Stock Dividends. The AICPA has recommended that for small dividends—those involving the issuance of less than 20 or 25 percent of the number of shares previously outstanding—the corporation should transfer from retained earnings to capital stock and paid-in surplus accounts an amount equal to the fair value of the additional shares issued.[4] To illustrate, assume that the market value of the shares issued by the Truro Corporation was $60,000 (500 shares at $120 a share) and that the board of directors, in authorizing the stock dividend, directed that the dividend be recorded at market value. The entries to record the declaration and stock issuance are:

Stock Dividends (or Retained Earnings)	60,000	
Stock Dividends To Be Issued		50,000
Paid-in Capital—Excess Over		
Par or Stated Value on Stock Dividends		10,000
Stock Dividends To Be Issued	50,000	
Common Stock		50,000

If the account Stock Dividends is used, it would be closed to Retained Earnings at the end of the year.

The AICPA's rationale with respect to small stock dividends is that since the market value of the shares previously held remains substantially unchanged and since "many recipients of stock dividends look upon them as distributions of corporate earnings and usually in an amount equivalent to the fair value of the additional shares issued"—that is, as a cash dividend—the accounting should be such as to show the amount of retained earnings available for future dividend distribution.

Large Stock Dividends. For large stock dividends—those involving the is-

[4] AICPA, *Accounting Principles,* vol. 2 (Chicago: Commerce Clearing House, Inc., 1973), p. 6024.

suance of more than 25 percent of the number of shares previously outstanding—the AICPA recommends that there is no need to capitalize retained earnings other than to the extent occasioned by legal requirements.[5] This means that for large stock dividends, the amount of retained earnings capitalized is represented by the par or stated value of the shares issued. To illustrate, assume that the Truro Corporation declares a stock dividend of 2,500 shares, or 50 percent of the 5,000 shares previously outstanding. The entry to record the stock issuance is shown below.

Stock Dividends (or Retained Earnings)	250,000	
Common Stock		250,000
To record the issuance of 2,500 shares of additional common stock as a stock dividend.		

The rationale with respect to large stock dividends is that the effect is to reduce materially the share market value, and the transaction is "a split-up effected in the form of a dividend." There is, therefore, no need to capitalize retained earnings beyond the legal requirements.

Stock Split-Ups

A corporation may wish to reduce the par value of its stock, or it may desire to reduce the price at which the stock is being issued to make it more salable. This is accomplished by a stock split-up whereby the shares outstanding are increased and the par or stated value per share is reduced; there is no change, however, in the total par or stated value of the outstanding shares. No journal entries are required, and *there is no change in retained earnings.* The capital stock ledger account headings are changed to show the new par or stated value per share and the subsidiary stockholders ledger is revised to show the new distribution of shares.

Assume, for example, that a corporation has outstanding 100,000 shares of $50 par value common stock. The current market price of the stock is $175 a share. The corporation, wishing to reduce this high market price to create a broader market for a forthcoming additional stock issue, reduces the par value from $50 to $25 and increases the number of shares from 100,000 to 200,000. This is called a "2-for-1 split-up," because the number of shares owned by each shareholder is doubled. The split in shares may be accomplished by calling in all the old shares and issuing certificates for new shares on a 2-for-1 basis or by issuing an additional share for each old share previously owned. This action is recorded either by a memorandum notation in the capital stock account or by the following journal entry:

[5] *Ibid.,* p. 6025.

Common Stock, $50 par value	5,000,000	
Common Stock, $25 par value		5,000,000
To record a 2-for-1 split-up,		
increasing the number of		
outstanding shares from 100,000		
to 200,000 and reducing par value		
from $50 to $25.		

It may be assumed that the market price of the shares will now be reduced sufficiently to enhance the marketability of the new issue.

Both stock dividends and stock splits change the number of shares outstanding without changing the pro rata share of ownership of each stockholder or total stockholder equity. A stock dividend, unlike a stock split, requires a transfer from Retained Earnings to Paid-In Capital, and increases the capital stock account by the par or stated value of the dividend shares. A stock split, unlike a stock dividend, changes the par or stated value of the capital stock without changing the balances of any accounts.

TREASURY STOCK

A corporation may reacquire some of its own stock, preferred or common, either by purchase or gift or in settlement of a debt. Such stock is known as *treasury stock.* Treasury stock, if it has been fully paid for originally, may be issued at a price below par or stated value without the assumption of the usual contingent discount liability by the purchaser of discount stock to the corporation's creditors for the amount of the discount. Another feature of treasury stock is that it need not first be offered to present stockholders in compliance with their preemptive rights to participate in any additional issues. Treasury stock does not fall into the category of new issues; it is the corporation's own stock that has been issued and later reacquired. It is issued, but not outstanding, stock and therefore does not have voting or dividend rights.

A corporation may purchase some of its own stock, at or below the market price, to bolster a sagging market or to meet the needs under a plan whereby the company's own stock is distributed to its employees in lieu of other compensation. Sometimes the stock is purchased because it is available at a favorable price. Acquisition of treasury stock has the effect of reducing the assets and the stockholders' equity. The Treasury Stock account, therefore, should appear in the Stockholders' Equity section as a deduction from the total paid-in capital. Since the acquisition of treasury stock results in a distribution of corporate assets to stockholders, some states have enacted restrictive provisions pertaining to this kind of stock to protect the corporate creditors. If a corporation faces financial difficulties, certain influential stockholders could have the corporation buy back their shares, thereby reducing the amount available for the creditors and other stockholders. The restrictive provisions vary widely among the states. Some states require a restriction of retained earnings to the extent of the disbursement for the treasury stock.

Recording the Purchase of Treasury Stock

When a corporation reacquires shares of its own stock, the Treasury Stock account is debited for the cost of the shares acquired. To illustrate, assume that the Lee Corporation reacquires ten shares of its own stock at $55 a share. The entry is as shown below.

Treasury Stock—Common	550	
Cash		550

The purchase of the ten shares of stock reduces cash by $550 and the stockholders' equity by $550. It also reduces the number of shares outstanding. It does not reduce the amount of issued stock, because the purchase of the shares is recorded not by a debit to Common Stock but by a debit to a special Treasury Stock account, which is shown in the Stockholders' Equity section as a deduction from Total Paid-In Capital and Retained Earnings.

Issuance of Treasury Stock—Above Cost

The reissuance of treasury stock is recorded by a credit to Treasury Stock for the cost of the shares. The difference between the cost and the issue price of treasury stock when it is issued above cost is credited to Paid-In Capital from Treasury Stock Transactions. To illustrate, assume that the Lee Corporation reissues five shares for $65 a share. The entry is shown here.

Cash	325	
Treasury Stock—Common		275
Paid-In Capital from Treasury Stock		
Transactions—Common		50

The Stockholders' Equity section of the Lee Corporation's position statement after the reissuance of the five shares is shown below (other amounts are assumed).

Stockholders' Equity
Paid-In Capital
Common Stock, $50 par value; authorized and issued
1,000 shares of which five shares are held
in treasury $50,000

Stockholder's Equity (Continued)	
Premium on Common Stock	2,500
From Treasury Stock Transactions	50
Total Paid-In Capital	$52,550
Retained Earnings	20,000
Total Paid-In Capital and Retained Earnings	$72,550
Deduct Cost of Treasury Stock—Common	275
Total Stockholders' Equity	$72,275

Issuance of Treasury Stock—Below Cost

The entry to record the issuance of treasury stock below cost depends on the existence of capital accounts that are not considered to be part of the stated capital. To illustrate, assume that the Lee Corporation issues the five remaining shares of treasury stock (which cost $275) for $225. The difference of $50 is charged to Paid-In Capital from Treasury Stock Transactions, as follows:

Cash	225	
Paid-In Capital from Treasury Stock Transactions	50	
Treasury Stock—Common		275

If the negative difference on the issue of the shares exceeds the amount in Paid-In Capital from Treasury Stock Transactions—Common, the excess is charged to any other Paid-In Capital account arising from the original issuance of the same class of stock (Excess over Par or Stated Value, for example) and not a part of the stated capital. In the absence of such accounts, the difference between the cost and the selling price of the treasury stock is charged to Retained Earnings.

Treasury Stock Donated

One or more shareholders may donate a portion of their shares to the corporation for reissuance to raise needed cash. Shares acquired by donation do not affect the position statement, as there is no change in the assets, liabilities, or stockholders' equity. On acquisition, a memorandum is made in the Treasury Stock account indicating the date and the number of shares donated. When the shares are reissued, the proceeds are credited to Paid-In Capital—Donations. Assume that on May 1, 100 shares are donated to the Lee Corporation by its principal stockholder. The shares are reissued on June 15 at $45 a share. Upon receipt of the shares, the following memorandum is made in the Treasury Stock account:

Treasury Stock

May 1	100 shares donated

The journal entry to record the reissuance is shown below.

Cash	4,500	
Paid-In Capital—Donations		4,500
To record the reissuance		
for cash of 100 shares of		
donated treasury stock.		

A memo entry should also be made in the Treasury Stock account to record the reissuance of the shares.

Book Value of Capital Stock

The value of a share of stock may be expressed in terms of par, market, or book value. The book value of a share of stock, or the stockholders' equity per share, assuming that there is only one class of stock outstanding, is computed as follows:

	Line	Amount
Total stockholders' equity	1	$750,000
Number of shares outstanding	2	6,000
Book value per share (line 1 ÷ line 2)	3	$ 125

When more than one class of stock is outstanding, it becomes necessary to determine the liquidation claims of each class against the net assets of the corporation (assets minus liabilities). If, for example, the preferred stock is cumulative and nonparticipating and there are dividends in arrears, the stockholders' equity is divided between the two classes on the basis of the preferences accorded to the preferred stock. Assume that a corporation has the following capital structure:

(Ch. 13)

Common stock, $100 par value; issued 1,000 shares	$100,000
Preferred stock (6%), $100 par value; cumulative, nonparticipating; issued 1,000 shares	100,000
Excess over stated value of no-par common stock	5,000
Retained earnings	45,000
Retained earnings—restricted for plant addition	10,000
Total stockholders' equity	$260,000

Dividends are in arrears for the preceding year and the current year. The book value of a share of preferred stock at the end of the year is computed as follows:

Preferred stock, $100 par value; issued 1,000 shares	$100,000
Dividends in arrears (2 years × $6,000)	12,000
Total equity of preferred stockholders	$112,000
Number of shares outstanding	1,000
Book value per share	$ 112

The book value of a share of common stock is computed as shown:

Total stockholders' equity	$260,000
Deduct equity of preferred stockholders	112,000
Total equity of common stockholders	$148,000
Number of shares outstanding	1,000
Book value per share	$ 148

If the preferred stock is participating, an additional portion of the retained earnings is allocated to the preferred stockholders' equity based on the participation provisions. Hence, in computing the book value of preferred stock, its preference rights—dividends in arrears, dividend participation rights, and preference in dividing the assets on dissolution—must be known.

The book value and the market value of a share of stock may be and usually are different in amount.

Market Value

The market value of a share of stock—the price that a share of stock commands on the stock exchange—reflects price level changes; available investment funds; economic, political, and psychological factors; and so on.

(Ch. 13)

Since these factors are not reflected in the accounts, there is often a disparity between book and market values. The book value per share is what each stockholder would receive for each share held in the theoretical event of liquidation after the assets are sold without gain or loss. Since the valuations on the books—especially for inventories and plant and equipment—do not necessarily reflect market conditions, the book value of a share of stock may be of little significance as an indicator of the resale value of the stock.

Of greater usefulness to the investor are the ratios of earnings and dividends to the market value of the shares, because it is the cash represented by the market value of the shares that can be put to other uses. Three such ratios are

$$\text{Earnings yield rate} = \frac{\text{Earnings per share}}{\text{Market value per share}}$$

$$\text{Dividend yield rate} = \frac{\text{Dividends per share}}{\text{Market value per share}}$$

$$\text{Price-earnings ratio} = \frac{\text{Market price per share}}{\text{Earnings per share}}$$

A careful analysis of the relationship and trend of these ratios indicates the profitability of the firm as related to the market value of its shares, its ability to pay dividends, and its growth prospects.

ACCOUNTING FOR CORPORATE INCOME TAXES

Because the corporation is treated as a legal entity, separate and distinct from its stockholders, it is taxed as a business entity. The tax is based on corporate net income before taxes and is recorded by an entry such as:

Income Tax Expense	xxx	
Income Taxes Payable		xxx

The Income Tax Expense account is deducted in the income statement from income before taxes to arrive at net income after taxes. Income Taxes Payable is classified as a current liability in the position statement.

PAID-IN CAPITAL IN STATEMENT OF FINANCIAL POSITION

The Stockholders' Equity section of the Dwight Corporation's statement of financial position as of December 31, 1976, and the statement of retained earnings for 1976 are shown in Figure 13-2. Each item in the statement is numbered and is discussed in the following paragraphs. Duplicate numbers are used for related items. Brief technical account titles may be used, for convenience, in journals and ledgers, because these records are for internal use only and the

DWIGHT CORPORATION
Partial Statement of Financial Position
December 31, 1976

Stockholders' Equity
Paid-In Capital

❶   Preferred Stock, 5 percent cumulative, nonparticipating, $100 par value, authorized 2,500 shares; issued 2,000 shares $200,000

❶   Premium on Preferred Stock   10,000

       Total Paid In by Preferred Stockholders $210,000

❷   Common Stock, no par value, $40 stated value; authorized 7,000 shares, issued 5,000 shares of which 500 shares are held in treasury $200,000

❷   Excess over Stated Value on Common Stock   50,000

       Excess from Reduction of Stated Value of 5,000 shares of Common Stock from $50 to $40 per share   50,000

❸   From Treasury Stock Transactions— Common   2,500

❺   Common Stock Subscribed but not Issued   12,000

       Total Paid In by common Stockholders   314,500

       Other Paid-In Capital

❼   Donation of Land by Town of Needham   50,000

       Total Paid-In Capital $574,500

❽   Appraisal Capital—Excess of Appraised Value of Land over Cost   10,000

❻   Retained Earnings (of which $27,500 is restricted for treasury stock acquisitions and $45,000 for anticipated plant expansion)   200,000

       Total $784,500

❹   Deduct Cost of Treasury Stock— Common   27,500

       Total Stockholders' Equity $757,000

functions of the accounts are understood by the users. However, for external reporting, these account titles should either be replaced or be supplemented by descriptive language to minimize possible misunderstanding by nontechnical readers of the statement. The nature and significance of the items should

Figure 13-2
(Continued)

DWIGHT CORPORATION
Statement of Retained Earnings
For the Year Ended December 31, 1976

❻ Retained Earnings, January 1, 1976	$130,000
❻ Net Income for 1976	120,000
Total	$250,000
❻ Dividends	50,000
Retained Earnings, December 31, 1976	$200,000

not be obscured by the use of jargon or the absence of supporting detail.

❶ On the date of its organization, the Dwight Corporation issued 2,000 shares of preferred stock at $105 per share. The total par value of these shares (2,000 × $100 = $200,000) is labeled Preferred Stock. This amount represents part of the legal, or stated, capital. The excess ($5 × 2,000) over the par value of the preferred stock is reported separately as Premium on Preferred Stock.

❷ The Dwight Corporation also issued 5,000 shares of no-par value common stock at $60 per share. The stated value of the shares—originally $50 per share but reduced to $40 per share on December 31—multiplied by the number of shares issued ($40 × 5,000) is shown as Common Stock. The excess of the issue price ($60) over the original stated value ($50) multiplied by the number of shares issued ($10 × 5,000), not being part of the stated capital, is shown separately as Paid-In Capital—Excess over Stated Value on Common Stock. The excess of the original stated value ($50) over the revised stated value ($40), multiplied by the number of shares issued ($10 × 5,000), is also entered separately, for the same reason; it is labeled Paid-In Capital—Excess from Reduction of Stated Value of 5,000 Shares of Common Stock from $50 to $40 per Share.

❸ On July 10, the Dwight Corporation acquired 1,000 shares of its own common stock for $55 per share. On August 2, it sold 500 shares for $60 per share. The excess of the issue price over the cost is shown as Paid-In Capital from Treasury Stock Transactions.

❹ On July 10, the Dwight Corporation reacquired 1,000 shares of its own common stock for $55,000. The laws of the state in which it is incorporated limit the payment of dividends to the extent of the amount in the unrestricted Retained Earnings account. Since the effect of a purchase of treasury stock is similar to a cash dividend—a reduction in corporate assets and in the stockholders' equity—the limitation applies equally to dividend payments and to treasury stock acquisitions. A company with free retained earnings of $25,000, for example, may either reacquire treasury stock or declare cash dividends, or do both, provided the total disbursement is not over $25,000. Such a restriction prevents a corporation from bypassing restrictions on dividend distributions and improves the protection of the corporate creditors. The amount of $27,500 ($55,000 from the transaction of July 10 less $27,500 from the transaction of August 2) appears twice in the Stockholders' Equity section: (1) as a parenthetical note following retained earnings and (2) as a reduction in the stockholders' equity resulting from a distribution of $27,500 in cash to the stockholders from whom the stock was acquired.

⑤ Subscriptions have been received from key employees under a stock option plan for 300 shares of common stock. Stock certificates will be issued on receipt of the uncollected portion of the subscription price as shown in the asset account Common Stock Subscriptions Receivable.

⑥ The beginning Retained Earnings balance represents undistributed earnings from prior years. The corporation earned $120,000 from operations for the year; $50,000 was to be distributed to the stockholders on January 15, 1977; $72,500 was restricted for specific purposes; and the remainder, $127,500, is unrestricted.

⑦ A building site with an estimated cash market value of $50,000 was donated by the town of Needham as an inducement to the Dwight Corporation to establish itself there. This gift increased the assets and the paid-in capital.

⑧ The $10,000 increase in the Land account following an appraisal of the current market value of the land increased the assets and the stockholders' equity.

Reported earnings, earnings per share, and the selling price of shares expressed as a multiple of earnings per share are of primary interest to most investors. These figures are not a satisfactory substitute for a thorough financial analysis, but investors consider them key tools in their investment decisions.

The introduction and popularity in the past decade of a variety of unique securities that were, in substance, the equivalent of common stock resulted in the issuance of APB Opinions Number 9 and 15 by the Accounting Principles Board of the American Institute of Certified Public Accountants (AICPA). These opinions require that earnings per share (EPS) be presented on the face of the income statement and provide specific guidelines for earnings per share calculations.

Prior to the issuance of Opinions 9 and 15, earnings per share were calculated by dividing net income applicable to common stock by the number of common shares outstanding. Opinion Number 15 calls for a dual reporting of EPS:

1. Primary EPS $= \dfrac{\text{Applicable net income}}{\substack{\text{Common stock outstanding} \\ \text{plus} \\ \text{Common stock equivalents} \\ \text{that will decrease EPS}}}$

2. Fully Diluted EPS $= \dfrac{\text{Applicable net income}}{\substack{\text{Common stock outstanding} \\ \text{plus} \\ \text{Common stock equivalents} \\ \text{plus} \\ \text{Other securities with} \\ \text{conversion privileges that} \\ \text{will decrease EPS}}}$

The APB Opinions have converted EPS from a historically oriented figure to a *pro forma* and predictive figure. "Primary *EPS* is the amount of earnings attributable to each share of common stock outstanding and common stock assumed to be outstanding to reflect the dilutive effect of common stock equivalents."[6] Dilution is a reduction of the amount which would otherwise be reported as EPS. "A common stock equivalent is not common stock in form but rather derives a large portion of its nature from its common stock characteristics or conversion privileges. Such a security typically contains provisions enabling its holder to become a common stockholder."[7]

"Examples of common stock equivalents are: options and warrants, preferred stock or debt convertible into common stock if the stock or debt yields less than 66⅔% of the bank prime interest rate at time of issuance, and agree-

[6] AICPA, *APB Accounting Principles,* vol. 2 (Chicago: Commerce Clearing House, Inc., 1973), p. 9573.
[7] *Ibid.,* p. 9572.

DIVIDENDS,
RETAINED EARNINGS,
TREASURY STOCK

ments to issue common stock with the passage of time as the only condition to issuance."[8]

"*Fully diluted EPS* is the amount of earnings attributable to each share of common stock outstanding and common stock assumed outstanding to reflect the dilutive effect of common stock equivalents and other potentially dilutive securities."[9] Thus, primary EPS is based on the outstanding common stock plus common stock equivalents, and fully diluted EPS is based on primary EPS plus the number of common shares represented by convertible securities not included in primary EPS.

To illustrate, assume a company with the following earnings and equities:

Net income	$100,000
6 percent convertible bonds, convertible three common shares for each $100 bond	$ 60,000
6 percent convertible preferred stock, $100 par, convertible one common share for each share of preferred.	1,000 shares
Common stock	10,000 shares
Calculation of primary EPS:	
Actual net income (A)	$100,000
Adjusted shares outstanding:	
Actual shares outstanding	10,000
Additional shares issuable to preferred stockholders	1,000
Adjusted shares outstanding (B)	11,000
Primary EPS (A ÷ B)	$ 9.09

Calculation of fully diluted EPS:	
Adjusted net income:	
Actual net income	$100,000
Interest reduction if bonds converted; 6 percent net of 50 percent tax effect (0.06 × $60,000) 0.5	1,800
Adjusted net income (A)	$101,800
Adjusted shares outstanding:	
Actual shares outstanding	10,000
Additional shares issuable:	
To preferred shareholders	1,000
To bondholders (600 × 3)	1,800
Adjusted shares outstanding (B)	12,800
Fully diluted EPS (A ÷ B)	$ 7.95

[8] *Ibid.*, p. 9572.
[9] *Ibid.*, p. 9574.

(Ch. 13)

In its Opinion No. 15, the APB concluded that for primary EPS calculations, a convertible security is considered to be a common stock equivalent if its cash yield based on its market price is less than two-thirds of the bank prime interest rate at the time of its issuance. In the foregoing example it is assumed that the 6 percent convertible bonds are *not* common stock equivalents. When bonds are treated "as if" converted, the actual net income is adjusted accordingly by adding back the net after-tax effect on net income of the bond interest expense deduction.

Many other complex problems may be involved in calculating EPS. They are beyond the scope of this text. Volume 2 of APB *Accounting Principles* includes Opinion No. 15 and a detailed interpretation of the opinion.

GLOSSARY

Appraisal Capital The title of the account credited for the increase in stockholders' equity resulting from the upward revaluation of assets.

Book Value The net amount at which an account or an account group appears on the books. For capital stock, it represents the portion of the stockholders' equity assigned to a class of stock divided by the number of shares of that class of stock issued and outstanding.

Deficit The caption used in the position statement to designate a Retained Earnings account which has a debit balance.

Dividend A distribution of cash, stock, or other corporate property by a corporation to stockholders.

Dividend Yield Rate Dividends per share divided by the market value per share.

Earnings per Share Net income divided by the average number of common shares outstanding during the year.

Earnings Yield Rate Earnings per share divided by the market value per share.

Fully Diluted Earnings per Share Applicable net income divided by common stock outstanding plus common stock equivalents plus other securities with conversion privileges that will decrease EPS.

Price-Earnings Ratio Market price per share divided by earnings per share.

Primary Earnings per Share Applicable net income divided by common stock outstanding plus common stock equivalents that will decrease EPS.

Retained Earnings Undistributed earnings from regular operations and gains from sale of assets.

Retained Earnings—Restricted The portion of retained earnings not available for dividends.

Revaluation Capital See *Appraisal Capital.*

Stock Dividend The issuance by a corporation of additional shares of its authorized stock without additional payment by the stockholders.

Stock Split-up An increase in the number of shares of stock outstanding without a change in the total par or stated value of the outstanding shares.

Treasury Stock A company's own stock previously issued and outstanding but reacquired either by purchase or gift or in settlement of a debt.

QUESTIONS

Q13-1. (a) What are the major subdivisions of the Stockholders' Equity section of the statement of financial position? (b) Why must particular care be taken in subdividing the Stockholders' Equity section?

Q13-2. (a) What is the purpose of restricting retained earnings? (b) Is the restriction of retained earnings tantamount to the establishment of a special cash fund?

Q13-3. The following quotation is adapted from the notes to the financial statements of a large company, "Retained earnings of $28,500,000 are restricted from payment of cash dividends on common stock because of a promissory note agreement. Further restrictions of $1,700,000 are made to cover the cost of the company's own common stock reacquired."
What is the significance of this note (a) to a short-term creditor, (b) to a long-term creditor, (c) to a stockholder?

Q13-4. What is meant by the term *book value?* How is book value computed? Has it any real significance as a financial measure of the worth of stock?

Q13-5. Preferred stock enjoys certain preferences. (a) What are these preferences? (b) How do they affect dividend distributions?

Q13-6. (a) What is a stock dividend? (b) What conditions prompt the declaration of a stock dividend? (c) How does a stock dividend affect (1) the total stockholders' equity, (2) the total assets, (3) the book value per share, (4) the taxable income of the recipient, (5) the market price per share?

Q13-7. (a) What is accomplished by a stock split-up? (b) How is it recorded? (c) How does it affect (1) the total stockholders' equity, (2) the book value per share, (3) the market price per share?

Q13-8. (a) What is treasury stock? (b) Why do corporations buy back their own shares? (c) How does the reacquisition of a company's own shares affect its financial position? (d) Why do some states place certain restrictions on treasury stock acquisitions? (e) How is the purchase of treasury stock recorded? (f) How is the issuance of treasury stock recorded? (g) How does the issuance of treasury stock affect the financial statements?

Q13-9. *Limited liability* is one of the distinguishing characteristics of the corporate form of organization. In state corporation law, limited liability is recognized in a number of the provisions relating to financial aspects of the corporation. Indicate three such provisions that are relevant to the financial and accounting aspects of the stockholders' equity.

Q13-10. (Appendix). What are the uses and the limitations of earnings-per-share data? What is a common stock equivalent? Compare and contrast primary earnings per share with fully diluted earnings per share.

EXERCISES

E13-1. The outstanding capital stock of the Hague Corporation consisted of the following:

9% preferred stock, par value $50 (6,000 shares)	$300,000
Common stock, par value $25 (18,000 shares)	450,000

Earnings from operations for the year 1976 were $110,000. Compute the earnings per share on the preferred and common stocks.

E13-2. The Stockholders' Equity section of the Guild Company's statement of financial position shows the following:

Common Stock, no-par value, issued 15,000 shares	$270,000
Retained Earnings	90,000
Total	$360,000

What is the cumulative effect on stockholders' equity of each of the following events, occurring in sequence: (a) the declaration of a 5% stock dividend; (b) the distribution of the dividend; (c) the acquisition of 200 shares of the company's own stock for $18 a share; (d) the issuance of these shares for $20 a share; (e) the declaration of a $1-per-share cash dividend; (f) the payment of the dividend.

E13-3. The Depot Corporation, having 50,000 shares of $10 par value common stock authorized and issued, finds itself in need of working capital. The stockholders agree to donate 10% of their holdings to the corporation. The shares are then reissued at $12 a share. Record the transactions.

E13-4. The Pamet Company restricted retained earnings of $30,000 to cover a lawsuit by a customer. The lawsuit was ultimately settled for $15,000. Make all the necessary journal entries.

E13-5. The Lind Corporation has issued and outstanding 4,000 shares of $25 par value common stock and 2,000 shares of $50 par value 9% cumulative and nonparticipating preferred stock. Glenda Linnell owns 10 shares of the common stock, which she purchased at $50 a share; John Little owns 20 shares of preferred stock, which he acquired for $105 a share.
(a) What basic rights and privileges does Linnell have? (b) Little? (c) How are these shares reported on the Lind Corporation's statement of financial position? (d) How much will Linnell and Little each receive if over a three-year period the corporation distributes earnings of $8,000, $16,000, and $38,000? (e) How much would Little receive if the preferred stock were cumulative and fully participating?

E13-6. The Murphy Corporation entered into an agreement with the town of Tipton to build a plant there. The town donated land and buildings valued at $40,000 and $100,000, respectively. Record the transaction.

E13-7. The Petow Corporation was authorized to issue 50,000 shares of $1 par value common stock, all of which was issued to the principal incorporator in payment for machinery and equipment he sold to the corporation. Shortly thereafter, the incorporator donated 25,000 shares to the corporation. The shares were then reissued for cash at an average price of $1.50 a share.

a. Make all the necessary journal entries.
b. Prepare statements of financial position immediately before and immediately after the reissuance of the donated shares.

E13-8. The capital stock of the Pierce Corporation consists of no-par value common stock with a $5 stated value. Record: (a) the issuance of 750 shares at $10 a share, (b) the reacquisition of 200 shares at $9 a share (restriction of retained earnings is not required), (c) the reissuance of the treasury stock at $12 a share, (d) a reduction in the stated value to $3 a share, (e) a 2-for-1 stock split-up.

E13-9. The Pina Corporation has issued and outstanding 3,000 shares of common stock and 1,500 shares of 8% preferred stock, each with a par value of $50. Retained earnings are $75,000, and the directors declare a $50,000 cash dividend. Record the dividend declaration, assuming (a) that the preferred stock is cumulative and nonparticipating and there are no dividends in arrears; (b) that the preferred stock is cumulative and participates up to $4 a share above the regular 8% rate; (c) that the preferred stock is cumulative and fully participating, and there was no dividend declaration during the previous year.

E13-10. The Pike Mining Company's statement of financial position shows the following:

Common stock, par value $50; 10,000 shares	$500,000
Retained Earnings	250,000

Give the effect on these accounts of each of the following situations: (a) All the stock is called in and 20,000 shares of no-par value stock are issued, the entire proceeds constituting legal capital. (b) The old shares are replaced by 20,000 shares of no-par value, $40 stated-value common stock. (c) Each stockholder receives a stock dividend of one additional share for every three shares he now holds.

E13-11. Indicate the effect, if any, of each of the following transactions on total retained earnings of the Pilgrim Company.

1. The board of directors declared a stock dividend to be issued one month from the current date.
2. Issued the stock dividend declared in transaction 1.
3. Wrote off Accounts Receivable against the Allowance for Doubtful Accounts.
4. Paid accounts payable.
5. Collected accounts receivable.
6. Issued $50 par value common stock at $45 a share.
7. Restricted retained earnings for contingencies.
8. Issued $50 par value preferred stock at $55 a share.
9. Purchased machinery on open account.
10. Issued long-term notes and received cash in return.

E13-12. On July 31, 1976, the directors of the Sisk Corporation, after a successful year with its new products, declared $80,000 in dividends on all classes of stock. There are outstanding 5,000 shares of $40 par value, 8% cumulative preferred stock participating to 10%, and 25,000 shares of no-par common stock. Dividends on the preferred stock are in arrears for the preceding two years. Common stock also has not received any dividends for the preceding two years. The same number of shares of preferred stock was outstanding on July 31, 1975; however, on July 31, 1974, only 4,000 shares of preferred stock were outstanding. The Common Stock account has remained unchanged for more than three years. Compute the amount of dividends each class will receive as a result of the dividend declaration.

E13-13. The following is part of note 8 accompanying the August 31, 1976 statement of financial position of the Gordon Corporation:

> Capital Stock
> Each holder of Class A Stock or Class B Stock has one vote per share. Each and all shares vote as one class except that they are entitled to vote separately by classes in cases of certain amendments to the certificate of incorporation affecting the rights of the capital stock, and except as may be required by law. The holders of the Class A Stock and the Class B Stock are entitled to receive dividends when and as declared by the Board of Directors. Cash dividends must be declared and paid on each class at the same time but dividends on Class B Stock shall be 5 percent (or $\frac{1}{20}$th) per share of the dividends per share on Class A Stock. The holders of Class A Stock and Class B Stock participate equally share for share in any stock or liquidating dividends to stockholders. The shares of Class B Stock are convertible into Class A Stock at any time at the option of the holder on a share-for-share basis. On June 1, 1980, should any share of Class B Stock be outstanding, they shall each, without further action of the company or the holder thereof, become one share of Class A Stock.

Give some reasons why a company might issue more than one class of capital stock. What are the advantages to the stockholders? to the corporation?

E13-14. The unclassified statement of financial position of the Quality Corporation is shown below.

QUALITY CORPORATION
Statement of Financial Position
December 31, 1976

Assets

Cash	$ 15,000
Accounts Receivable	35,000
Merchandise Inventory	40,000
Other Assets	10,000
Total Assets	$100,000

Liabilities and Stockholders' Equity

Liabilities		
Accounts Payable		$ 15,000
Notes Payable		5,000
Total Liabilities		$ 20,000
Stockholders' Equity		
Common Stock, $100 par value	$50,000	
Retained Earnings	30,000	80,000
Total Liabilities and Stockholders' Equity		$100,000

The members of the board of directors are considering several dividend distribution plans. They seek your advice with respect to these alternatives: (a) a cash dividend of 20%, (b) a stock dividend of 50%, (c) no dividend distribution. Discuss.

E13-15. The following information relates to three companies in the same industry:

Company	Dividends per Share	Earnings per Share	Latest Market Price
A	None	$11	$35
B	$4	5	40
C	6	10	80

On the basis of only the foregoing, which company represents the most attractive investment opportunity? Explain.

E13-16. (Appendix). The 1976 net income of Mack Co. was $100,000, and 100,000 shares of its common stock were outstanding during the entire year. In addition, there were outstanding options to purchase 10,000 shares of common stock at $10 a share. These options were granted in 1974 and none had been exercised by December 31, 1976. Market prices of Mack's common stock during 1976 were:

January 1	$20 a share
December 31	40 a share
Average price	25 a share

The amount which should be shown as Mack's fully diluted earnings per share for 1976 is (rounded to the nearest cent):

a. $\dfrac{\$100{,}000}{110{,}000 \text{ shares}} = \$0.91.$

b. $\dfrac{\$100{,}000}{105{,}000 \text{ shares}} = \$0.95.$

c. $\dfrac{\$100{,}000}{106{,}000 \text{ shares}} = \$0.94.$

d. $\dfrac{\$100{,}000}{107{,}500 \text{ shares}} = \$0.93.$

(*IMA adapted*)

E13-17. (Appendix). On January 2, 1976, Lang Co. issued at par $10,000 of 4% bonds convertible in total into 1,000 shares of Lang's common stock. These bonds are common stock equivalents for purposes of computing earnings per share. No bonds were converted during 1976.

Throughout 1976 Lang had 1,000 shares of common stock outstanding. Lang's 1976 net income was $1,000. Lang's income tax rate is 50%.

No potentially dilutive securities other than the convertible bonds were outstanding during 1976. Lang's primary earnings per share for 1976 would be: (a) $1.00, (b) $0.50, (c) $0.70, (d) $0.60.

(*AICPA adapted*)

DP13-1. (*Recording corporate transactions; stockholders' equity*) Following is the Stockholders' Equity section of the statement of financial position of the Skelly Corporation as of December 31, 1975.

Common Stock, no-par value; issued and outstanding 50,000 shares		$600,000
Retained Earnings		
Restricted		
For Lawsuit Damages	$ 50,000	
For Plant Expansion	250,000	
Unrestricted	150,000	450,000
Total Stockholders' Equity		$1,050,000

The following transactions occurred during the year 1976 (restriction of retained earnings is required):

1. Acquired 7,500 shares of its own common stock at $12 a share.
2. Paid $6,000 in settlement of the lawsuit for injuries.
3. Issued 4,000 shares of treasury stock at $17 a share.
4. One of the stockholders donated land and a building worth $25,000 and $75,000, respectively.
5. Paid a cash dividend of $1.50 a share.
6. Reduced the retained earnings restriction for plant expansion by $50,000.
7. Wrote off organization costs of $12,000.
8. Net income for the year after income taxes was $60,000 (make the closing entry).

Required:

1. Enter the December 31, 1975, balances in T accounts.
2. Journalize the transactions and post to the appropriate accounts.
3. Prepare the Stockholders' Equity section of the statement of financial position as of December 31, 1976.
4. What is the effect of the retained earnings restrictions (a) on the financial statements and (b) on the individual shareholders?
5. Why did the company write off its organization costs?

DP13-2. (*Effect of cash and stock dividends*) The Stockholders' Equity section of the Shute Corporation's statement of financial position consists of the following accounts:

Common Stock, $100 par value; issued 500 shares	$50,000
Retained Earnings	35,000
Total Stockholders' Equity	$85,000

Required:

1. (a) Prepare the journal entries to record the declaration and the payment of an $8-per-share cash dividend. (b) Compute the book value per share of the common stock immediately before the declaration of the dividend and immediately after the payment of the dividend.
2. Assume that the corporation declares a stock dividend instead of a cash dividend, each stockholder to receive one dividend share for each 5 shares he now holds. Complete requirements 1a and 1b on the basis of this assumption.
3. John Vanden owns 50 shares of Shute Corporation stock. What was his equity (a) before the stock dividend and (b) after the stock dividend?

4. Discuss the purpose, advantages, and disadvantages of a stock dividend from the viewpoint (a) of the stockholder and (b) of the issuing corporation.

5. Suppose the board of directors declared a 2-for-1 stock split, which the stockholders approved. How would this affect John Vanden? the company's position statement? the earnings per share?

DP13-3. (*Computing dividend distributions*) The Usher Corporation has outstanding 4,000 shares of $100 par value common stock and 4,000 shares of $100 par value 10% preferred stock.

Required: Journalize the declaration of the cash dividend based on each of the following assumptions:

1. The preferred stock is cumulative and nonparticipating; dividends declared, $75,000.

2. The preferred stock is cumulative and fully participating; dividends declared, $75,000.

3. The preferred stock is cumulative and nonparticipating, and dividends have not been declared for the current year or for the two years preceding the current year; dividends declared, $150,000.

4. The preferred stock is cumulative and fully participating, and dividends have not been declared for the current year or the preceding year; dividends declared, $150,000.

5. Assume the same facts as in requirement 4 except that dividends declared were $40,000.

DP13-4. (*Financial policy decision problem*) The 1976 annual report of Williams Corporation states in a note to its financial statements that "The terms of certain note agreements restrict the payment of cash dividends on common stock. The amount of retained earnings not so restricted on December 31, 1976, was approximately $122,000."

Required:

1. Of what usefulness is the statement regarding the amount of restricted retained earnings? the amount not restricted?

2. The cash dividend distributions during 1976 were $14,908; net income for the year was $84,010. Do the stockholders have the right to dividends up to $14,908? up to $122,000?

3. Total shareholders' equity at December 31, 1976, was $860,703. Does this indicate what the shareholders would receive in the event of liquidation? of sale? Explain.

P13-1. On March 1, 1976, the Mack Corporation was authorized to issue 25,000 shares of $25 par value common stock and 2,000 shares of 9% preferred stock, $100 par value. The following transactions occurred between March 1 and December 31, 1976:

1. Issued 6,000 shares of common stock at $25 a share and 1,500 shares of preferred stock at $102 a share.

2. Purchased the assets of the Willow Run Company at their fair cash value: the assets consisted of land worth $20,000, buildings worth $150,000, and plant and equipment worth $200,000. Issued 14,000 shares of common stock in payment.

3. Purchased 1,000 shares of its own common stock at $22.50 a share. (The laws of the state of incorporation require a restriction of retained earnings equal to the cost of treasury stock.)
4. Established a restriction on retained earnings for contingencies of $20,000.
5. Issued 400 shares of treasury stock for $23 a share.
6. Earnings through December 31 after Federal income taxes were $90,000 (make the closing entry).
7. Declared a 75 cents-per-share dividend on the common stock and a $4.50 dividend on the preferred stock.

Required:

1. Record the transactions in appropriate T accounts.
2. Prepare the Stockholders' Equity section of the statement of financial position as of December 31, 1976.

P13-2. The Stockholders' Equity section of the Wiggin Corporation's statement of financial position as of June 30, 1975, is shown below.

Stockholders' Equity
Common Stock, $50 par value; issued 2,000 shares	$100,000
Retained Earnings	65,000
Total Stockholders' Equity	$165,000

The following transactions occurred during the next twelve months:

1. Established a retained earnings restriction of $10,000 for a pending lawsuit.
2. Received, as a donation from the town of Lenox, land and a building worth $20,000 and $115,000, respectively.
3. Declared a 2% stock dividend. The shares to be issued are currently quoted at $55 a share.
4. Purchased 100 shares of its own stock for $54 a share.
5. Issued the stock certificates for the stock dividend.
6. Received 200 shares of stock as a gift from one of the stockholders of the corporation.
7. Issued 100 of the donated shares for $5,600.
8. Issued 50 shares of treasury stock for $3,000.
9. Net income for the year after income taxes was $35,000 (make the closing entry).

Required:

1. Enter the balances as of June 30, 1975, in T accounts.
2. Record the transactions directly into the T accounts.
3. Prepare the Stockholders' Equity section of the statement of financial position as of June 30, 1976.

P13-3. The condensed statement of financial position of the Glass Corporation as of December 31, 1976, was as follows:

Total Assets	$1,450,000
Liabilities	$ 400,000
Preferred Stock, 9%, $50 par value; cumulative	200,000
Common Stock, no-par value; stated value $5	600,000
Premium on Preferred Stock	20,000

DIVIDENDS,
RETAINED EARNINGS,
TREASURY STOCK

Excess over Stated Value of Common Stock	30,000
Retained Earnings—Restricted for Plant Expansion	100,000
Retained Earnings	100,000
Total Liabilities and Stockholders' Equity	$1,450,000

Required:

1. Find the book value per share of common stock, assuming that there are no dividend arrearages. The liquidating value of the preferred stock is equal to the par value.
2. Find the book value per share of common stock, assuming that dividends on the preferred stock are in arrears for the years 1975 and 1976.
3. What is the significance of the book value per share?
4. What is the interrelationship between book value per share and market value per share?

P13-4. (*Accounting policy decision problem*) The following information is taken from the Stockholders' Equity section of the Wiesel Corporation's statement of financial position as of December 31, 1976:

Preferred Stock, 10%, cumulative and nonparticipating, $100 par value; authorized and issued 3,000 shares	$300,000
Common Stock, no-par value; stated value $20; authorized 40,000 shares; issued 20,000 shares	400,000
Excess over Stated Value of Common Stock	840,000
Retained Earnings—Restricted for Plant Expansion	80,000
Retained Earnings—Restricted for Bond Redemption	40,000
Retained Earnings—Unrestricted	300,000
Total Stockholders' Equity	$1,960,000

Dividends on the preferred stock are in arrears for 1975 and 1976.

Required:

1. Compute the book value per share of the common stock.
2. Assume that the market value of the Wiesel Corporation common stock was one-half the book value per share. Does this indicate that faulty accounting principles or procedures were used? Give some reasons for the difference in book and market values per share.

P13-5. The following account balances were taken from the ledger of the Whitney Company as of December 31, 1976:

Excess from Revaluation of Building	$ 72,000
Premium on Preferred Stock	60,000
Paid-In Capital—Donated	144,000
Paid-In Capital from Treasury Stock Transactions—Common	12,000
Preferred Stock, 9%, $100 par value; issued 9,600 shares	960,000
Retained Earnings—Restricted for Plant Additions	192,000
Retained Earnings—Restricted for Contingencies	24,000
Paid-In Capital—Excess of Original Stated Value over Revised Stated Value of Common Stock	180,000

Common Stock, no-par value; stated value $20; issued	
24,000 shares	480,000
Retained Earnings	396,000
Treasury Stock—Common (600 shares)	120,000
Paid-In Capital—Excess over Stated	
Value of Common Stock	48,000
Estimated Income Taxes Payable	115,000
Organization Costs	24,000

Required:

1. Prepare the Stockholders' Equity section of the statement of financial position as of December 31, 1976.
2. Give a brief statement of the origin and function of each account.

P13-6. A listing of the balances of all the Stockholders' Equity accounts, taken from the statement of financial position of Tesson, Inc., at December 31, 1976, is given below.

Preferred stock, $100 par value; 10% cumulative; entitled to $105 per share plus cumulative dividends in arrears in liquidation; authorized 5,000 shares, issued 4,000 shares of which 250 are held in treasury	$400,000
Paid-In Capital in excess of par value of preferred stock	12,000
Paid-In Capital from treasury stock transactions—preferred	1,000
Common stock, no-par value; stated value $40; authorized 10,000 shares, issued 8,000 shares	320,000
Stock dividend, to be issued at stated value 2,000 common shares	80,000
Paid-In Capital in excess of stated value of common stock	28,000
Paid-In Capital from stock dividend—common stock	8,000
Discount on Common Stock	500
Land donated by Lee County	20,000
Retained earnings	
Restricted in the amount of treasury stock purchased at cost	20,750
Unrestricted	50,150
Treasury stock, preferred—at cost	20,750

Required:

1. Prepare a properly classified Stockholders' Equity section.
2. Compute (a) the amount contributed by the preferred stockholders, (b) the amount contributed by the common stockholders, (c) the book value per share of common stock, (d) the book value per share of preferred stock, assuming that one year's preferred dividends are in arrears.
3. How does the reacquisition by a company of its own shares affect (a) the financial statements? (b) the individual shareholders?

P13-7. The Stockholders' Equity section of the Fitz Corporation's statement of financial position as of December 31, 1975, was as follows:

Stockholders' Equity	
Capital Stock	
Preferred Stock, 10%, $50 par value; authorized and issued 5,000 shares	$ 250,000
Common Stock, $40 par value; authorized and issued 15,000 shares	600,000
Premium on Common Stock	75,000

| Retained Earnings | 300,000 |
| Total Stockholders' Equity | $1,225,000 |

Transactions for the year 1976:

1. Declared a $70,000 cash dividend for 1976. (The preferred stock is cumulative and nonparticipating; there are no dividends in arrears.)
2. Paid the dividend declared in transaction 1.
3. Purchased 1,000 shares of its own preferred stock for $75 a share (a restriction of retained earnings is not required).
4. Established a restriction on retained earnings of $15,000 for contingencies.
5. Issued 400 shares of treasury stock for $80 a share.
6. Earnings from operations for the year after income taxes were $225,000 (make the closing entry).
7. Issued 300 shares of treasury stock for $95 a share.
8. The principal stockholder donated to the corporation a warehouse valued at $40,000.

Required:

1. Prepare journal entries to record the transactions.
2. Post to T accounts.
3. Prepare the Stockholders' Equity section of the statement of financial position as of December 31, 1976.
4. Why do you think the principal stockholder donated his warehouse to the corporation?

P13-8. (*Accounting policy decision problem*) The following information was taken from the ledger of Guay, Inc., as of September 30, 1976:

Cash	$ 60,000
Accounts Receivable	190,000
Cash Dividends Payable	55,000
Organization Costs	2,000
Common Stock Subscribed	150,000
Preferred Stock Subscribed	250,000
Common Stock, $5 par value	325,000
Preferred Stock, $10 par value	400,000
Subscriptions Receivable—Common Stock	30,000
Subscriptions Receivable—Preferred Stock	40,000
Premium on Preferred Stock	50,000
Premium on Common Stock	30,000
Retained Earnings	150,000
Retained Earnings—Restricted for Contingencies	20,000
Paid-In Capital—Donated	25,000
Paid-In Capital from Treasury Stock Transactions—Common	10,000
Retained Earnings—Restricted for Retirement of Preferred Stock	40,000
Discount on Common Stock	20,000
Allowance for Doubtful Accounts	12,000
Retained Earnings—Restricted for Plant Addition	50,000
Estimated Income Taxes Payable	30,000
Accumulated Depreciation—Building	20,000

Required:

1. Prepare the Stockholders' Equity section of the statement of financial position as of September 30, 1976.
2. Give several possible alternatives for the manner of grouping and sequencing the accounts when preparing the Stockholders' Equity section of the statement of financial position.
3. Which of the subtotals in the Stockholders' Equity section are most significant to the reader? Why?

P13-9. The Guest Corporation was organized on April 1, 1976, with authority to issue 15,000 shares of no-par value common stock and 7,500 shares of 9% preferred stock, $50 par value. During 1976, the following transactions occurred:

1. Issued 750 shares of preferred stock at $56 a share.
2. Issued 6,000 shares of common stock for cash at $15 a share. A stated value of $12 a share is set by the board of directors for the common stock.
3. Issued 150 shares of common stock, in lieu of a $2,000 fee, to the corporation's attorneys for their services in drafting the articles of incorporation and a set of bylaws.
4. Acquired 300 shares of common stock for $3,500 from the estate of a deceased stockholder.
5. Reissued the 300 shares of the treasury stock at $15 a share.
6. Declared a 9% dividend on preferred stock and a 30 cents-per-share dividend on common stock. The dividends are payable on January 10, 1977, to stockholders of record on December 31, 1976. The board also authorized the restriction of retained earnings of $15,000 for plant expansion.

Required: Prepare the journal entries to record the transactions.

P13-10. (*Financial policy decision problem*) An analysis of the Treasury Stock account of Grosch, Inc., shows the following debit entries during 1976:

Date	Lot No.	Description	No. of Shares	Class of Stock	Amount
1976					
Jan. 10	1	Purchase	192	Common	$7,680
Feb. 16	2	Purchase	128	Preferred	2,560
Apr. 20	3	Purchase	80	Common	3,360
May 3	4	Gift	40	Preferred	1,000
3	5	Gift	40	Common	1,280

The following credit entries were made:

Date	Lot No.	Description	No. of Shares	Class of Stock	Amount
1976					
Feb. 5	1	Sale	80	Common	$3,520
11	1	Sale	32	Common	1,380
16	1	Sale	32	Common	1,250
Mar. 1	2	Sale	112	Preferred	2,800
Apr. 20	3	Sale	64	Common	2,950
22	1	Sale	32	Common	1,100
July 20	4	Sale	40	Preferred	800
26	5	Sale	32	Common	650

DIVIDENDS, RETAINED EARNINGS, TREASURY STOCK

The bookkeeper has followed the policy of debiting the account at cost for purchases and at the prevailing market price for gifts; all credits to the account are for the net proceeds from sales. The common stock was originally issued at a substantial premium; the preferred stock was originally issued at par value.

Required:

1. Give the journal entries to correct the Treasury Stock account (compute costs by specific identification).
2. Give the journal entry to restrict an amount of retained earnings equal to the cost of the shares on hand.
3. Is it appropriate for a company to trade in its own stock?
4. Give some reasons why a company may want to reacquire its own shares.

P13-11. (*Financial policy decision problem*) The 1976 annual report of the AMJ Corporation included an explanatory note, a portion of which is shown below:

Shareholders' Equity

The Board of Directors on June 5, 1975, declared a 100 percent common stock distribution on common shares, payable July 17, 1975. The per share amounts in the consolidated statement of income have been adjusted retroactively to reflect this July 1975 stock distribution.

Series preference stock, no par value, amounting to 1,000,000 shares have been authorized. The initial series of such series preference stock is the $3.20 preference stock of which 215,000 shares are authorized and 76,654 are outstanding. This preference stock ranks junior as to dividends and in liquidation to the $3 preferred stock of which 112,254 shares are authorized and 47,088 are outstanding.

The $3 preferred and the $3.20 preference shares are each convertible into 3.6 common shares, have liquidating preferences of $65 and $100 per share, respectively, redeemable beginning in 1980 at $68 and $103 per share, respectively, and are entitled to one vote per share. The company has been advised by counsel that there are no restrictions on income retained in the business as a result of the excess of liquidating preference over stated value of the preferred stocks.

In January 1976, the company increased the number of authorized shares of common stock from 7,000,000 to 45,000,000 shares. Of the common shares authorized but unissued at December 31, 1976, a total of 15,949,307 was reserved for conversion of preferred stocks and convertible subordinated debentures and for exercise of stock options and warrants.

Required:

1. What was achieved by the 100% common stock distribution (a) from the corporation's viewpoint? (b) from the stockholders' viewpoint?
2. How did the stock distribution affect the statement of financial position?
3. What is the purpose of the conversion privilege attaching to the preferred shares?
4. What is the significance of the advice by counsel regarding retained earnings restrictions?
5. Give some reasons for the large increase in the number of authorized shares of common stock.

P13-12. (*Accounting and financial policy decision problem*) The Martin Development Corporation was formed ten years ago to acquire real estate for the development of suburban housing and shopping areas. It was originally organized as a closed corporation, financed by the investments of five businessmen. During the first year of operations, the board of directors, which consisted of the five original stockholders, voted to restrict the payment of dividends and to reinvest all earnings, if any, in the expanding projects of the corporation. This policy was favored by all the members of the board of directors, although one of them, Peter Holt, was reluctant. To placate him, the other members did agree on different occasions to issue two stock dividends and a stock split-up.

After another year of operations, the board of directors agreed, except for Holt, to issue some preferred stock to a number of persons who had indicated an interest in the organization. Holt, being suspicious of the motivations of the new investors, offered his stock to the corporation. The other members of the board of directors voted to buy all his shares at 10% more than their book value. Holt accepted the offer. Shortly thereafter, preferred stock was issued to the new investors.

A review of the sequence of events affecting the Stockholders' Equity section of the corporation's statement of financial position follows:

1. The corporate charter was received, authorizing the issuance of 20,000 shares of $100 par value voting common stock and 40,000 shares of $50 par value cumulative, 10%, participating to 12% (for the latest year only), nonvoting preferred stock. The preferred stock can become fully voting on a per share basis when preferred dividends are in arrears, beginning with the third year of arrearage.
2. Each of the five original stockholders purchased 500 shares of common stock at par value.
3. The corporation reported a net loss of $8,500 for the first year of operations.
4. The corporation reported a net income of $17,500 for the second year of operations.
5. The directors voted to restrict all retained earnings for the expansion of operations.
6. The corporation reported a net income of $40,000 for the third year of operations.
7. The directors voted to restrict all retained earnings for the expansion of operations.
8. The directors voted to issue a 10% stock dividend and to release the appropriate amount of restricted retained earnings.
9. The corporation reported a net income of $55,000 for the fourth year of operations.
10. The directors voted to issue a 20% stock dividend.
11. The corporation reported a net income of $65,000 for the fifth year of operations.
12. The corporate charter was changed, authorizing the issuance of 50,000 shares of $50 par value voting common stock (the preferred stock authorization was not changed).
13. The directors voted a 2-for-1 common stock split-up.
14. The corporation reported a net income of $75,000 for the sixth year of operations.
15. Holt sold all his shares of common stock to the corporation for 110 percent of book value. The directors voted to restrict an equal amount of retained earnings.
16. New investors purchased 5,000 shares of preferred stock at par value.
17. The corporation reported a net income of $90,000 for the seventh year of operations.

18. At the end of the first two full years since the preferred stock was issued, the directors declared a $130,000 cash dividend.

19. The directors voted to sell one-fourth of the treasury stock to another local investor for 5% more than its cost. An equal amount of retained earnings was released. The other three-fourths of the treasury stock was canceled.

20. The corporation reported a net income of $80,000 for the eighth year of operations.

Required:

1. Record the foregoing events.
2. Why did the directors decide to pay a cash dividend? What was the amount of the cash dividend per share?
3. Prepare a partial statement of financial position showing the Stockholders' Equity section on completion of the twenty events.

P13-13. (Appendix). (*Financial policy decision problem*) The income statement of the Hambley Corporation for the year ended December 31, 1976, was as follows:

Revenue		$200,000
Costs and expenses (exclusive of interest on bonds)	$150,000	
Interest on bonds	10,000	160,000
Net income before taxes		$ 40,000
Income taxes (50%)		20,000
Net income		$ 20,000

The following securities were outstanding:

	Units
No-par common stock (shares)	2,000
9% bonds, $1,000 maturity value, each convertible into 20 shares of common stock	200

Required:

1. Compute the primary and fully diluted earnings per share (assume the bonds do not qualify as common stock equivalents).
2. Assume that, in addition to the above, there are outstanding 1,000 shares of 9% preferred stock, $100 par, each convertible into one share of common stock. Compute primary and fully diluted earnings per share.
3. Calculate primary and fully diluted earnings per share, assuming the bonds qualify as common stock equivalents.

P13-14. (Appendix). The following facts are used to answer questions 1 and 2. Roxby Company has a net income of $152,000 after applicable Federal and state income taxes. It has a capital structure as follows:

Shares	*Class*	*Annual Dividend*
10,000	A Preferred	$3
20,000	B Preferred	$1
40,000	Common	Discretionary

Each share of Class B preferred is convertible into 3 shares of common and at date of issuance it did not satisfy the tests for a common stock equivalent.

1. Primary earnings per share for Roxby Company would be shown in financial reports as: (a) $4.10, (b) $3.80, (c) $3.05, (d) $2.55, (e) $1.02.
2. Fully diluted earnings per share for Roxby Company would be shown in financial reports as: (a) $3.05, (b) $2.10, (c) $1.52, (d) $1.22, (e) $1.02.
   (*IMA adapted*)

P13-15. (Appendix). On September 1, 1975, the Top Lofty Corporation issued $250,000 of 7%, 10-year convertible debenture bonds at 102. Each $100 bond was convertible into three shares of common stock. The bank prime rate at the time of issuance was $11\frac{1}{4}$%. On January 1, 1977, the corporation issued 10,000 shares of 6% convertible preferred, $100 par, for $105 a share, with each share convertible into two shares of common stock. The bank prime interest rate was then $11\frac{3}{4}$%. At the beginning of the year, 100,000 shares of common stock were outstanding. Earnings for the year after taxes of 50% were $200,000.

Required:

1. Compute the primary and the fully diluted earnings per share for 1977, assuming that no additional shares of common stock were issued during the year.
2. Compute the primary and the fully diluted earnings per share for 1977, assuming that on January 2, 1977, 10,000 shares were issued to holders of 5,000 shares of convertible preferred.

P13-16. (Appendix). (*Financial policy decision problem*) Comment on each of the following statements adapted from published annual reports:

a. Company A:

Earnings per Share
Per share computations are based on the average number of shares outstanding during the year, adjusted to include shares issued in poolings of interests. Conversion of convertible debt, exercise of stock options and warrants, and issuance of contingent shares would not result in a material dilution of earnings per share.

b. Company B:

Per Share Income Data
Per share income amounts have been calculated in accordance with Opinion Number 15 of the Accounting Principles Board of the American Institute of Certified Public Accountants. In compliance with this opinion the company has elected to classify as common stock equivalents (common shares assumed to be outstanding for the calculation of primary earnings per share) only those securities issued prior to June 1, 1969, which were classified as residual securities under Accounting Principles Board Opinion Number 9. As a result, the company's preferred stocks are considered common stock equivalents and the computation of primary earnings per share gives effect to the full conversion of the preferred stocks into common shares. Fully diluted earnings per share assume, in addition to full conversion of preferred stocks, exercise of the outstanding warrants and the outstanding stock options with the proceeds applied in the following steps:
a. Purchase 20 percent of the company's common stock outstanding at average market price during the period.

b. Payment of all long- and short-term obligations including convertible subordinated debentures and,

c. The balance invested in government securities.

The weighted average number of shares for the primary computation was 8,352,000 and 4,959,000 for 1976 and 1975, and for the fully diluted computation was 16,675,000 and 5,421,000 shares, respectively.

c. Company C:

Earnings per Common and
Common Equivalent Share

Earnings per common and common equivalent share is based on the weighted average number of common and common equivalent shares outstanding during the periods. The number of shares used in the calculation of earnings per common and common equivalent share in 1976 and 1975 (adjusted for the 1976 2-for-1 split) is 4,498,398 and 4,583,686, respectively. Earnings per common share—assuming full dilution is based upon the common and common equivalent shares outstanding plus the common shares that would have been issued had the 5½-percent subordinated bonds been converted when issued in 1976 and, in 1975, had the 4¾-percent convertible subordinated debentures been converted when issued. Conversion of the preferred stock and issuance of contingent shares have not been assumed as their effect on earnings per share is antidilutive.

In computing the per share effect of assumed exercise of dilutive stock options, proceeds from the exercise of stock options are assumed to have been used to purchase shares of the company's common stock and the net increase in the number of shares outstanding has been added to the weighted average of shares outstanding. Interest charges (less applicable income tax) on the bonds and debentures have been added to income in computing the per share effect of the assumed conversions.

Short-Term Debt Financing

14

Business firms often find it more economical to use some means of short-term financing than to pay cash for various purchases. A popular form of short-term financing is the purchase of merchandise, supplies, and equipment on 30-, 60-, or 90-day open charge accounts. Cash terms—no carrying charges are assigned—are often extended for a period of ninety days or more. During this period, cash may be obtained from new sales and used to pay for merchandise obtained on the open charge accounts. This form of financing has already been discussed in Chapter 5. Several other short-term financing devices are considered in this chapter; they are:

1. Issuance of notes to trade creditors
2. Borrowing from banks on a company's own notes
3. Discounting notes receivable from customers

Managers faced with the decision about which method to choose must consider for each method both its current and expected future availability and its effective cost. In general, a financial manager should choose the method or methods that will produce and continue to produce the desired short-term funds at the lowest long-run cost. In applying this general rule to specific financial decisions, management must consider such related variables as the availability of collateral, financial institutional connections, and the attendant effect on long-term debt financing.

A *negotiable promissory note* may be defined as an unconditional written promise to pay a specified sum of money to the order of a designated person, or to bearer, at a fixed or determinable future time or on demand.

A typical note is illustrated in Figure 14-1. Richard Baldwin, the *maker,* gives Edward Fenn, the designated *payee,* a 9 percent, 60-day note for $2,000, dated April 19, 1976, in payment for a purchase of merchandise.
The outstanding characteristics of a note are the following:

1. The instrument must be in writing, signed by the maker.
2. The instrument must contain an unconditional promise to pay a sum certain in money.
3. The instrument may be payable to the order of a designated person, the payee, or it may be payable to bearer (that is, anyone who holds the note).
4. The instrument must be payable either on demand or at a determinable time in the future.
5. The instrument may or may not be interest bearing.

The ownership of a negotiable promissory note is transferred simply by delivery if it is payable to the bearer; otherwise, it is transferred by endorsement and delivery.

A *blank endorsement* consists of a signature of the owner, or the payee, on the back of the instrument. A *full endorsement* consists of a notation on the back of the document, "Pay to the order of [name of person or company]," accompanied by the signature of the owner. If the endorser—the owner who is transferring the document—wishes to pass title to the instrument and at the same time to relieve himself of any further liability, he places his signature on the back of the note and adds the phrase "without recourse" (this is a *qualified endorsement*).

From the viewpoint of the maker, Richard Baldwin, the note illustrated in Figure 14-1 is a liability and is recorded by crediting Notes Payable. From the viewpoint of the payee, Edward Fenn, the same note is an asset and is recorded by debiting Notes Receivable. At the maturity date, Edward Fenn, or his *agent,* the First National Bank, will expect to receive $2,030 in cash for the note and interest, and Richard Baldwin will expect to pay $2,030 in cash.[1]

Maturity Dates of Notes and Their Determination

The *term* of a note may be expressed in years, months, or days. To determine the maturity of a note expressed in months or years, count the number of months or years from the issuance date. For example, a two-year note dated April 3, 1976, is due on April 3, 1978, and a two-month note dated April 3, 1976, is due on June 3, 1976. Occasionally, when time is expressed in months, there may be no corresponding date in the maturity month, in which case the last day of the month of maturity is used; a three-month note dated March 31 is due on

---

[1] See Chapter 7 for a discussion of approaches to the calculation of simple interest.

Figure 14-1 A Promissory Note

$ _2,000.00_	_Boston, Mass._	_April 19, 1976_

Sixty days _____ after date ___ _I_ ___ promise to pay

to the order of _____ _Edward Fenn_ _____

~~~~~ _Two Thousand and no/100_ ~~~~~ Dollars

Payable at _____ _First National Bank_ _____

Value received ___ _with interest at 9%_ ___

No. ___ _40_ ___ Due ___ _June 18,_ ___ 1976   _Richard Baldwin_

June 30, and a one-month note dated January 29, 30, or 31 is due on the last day of February. If the term of the note is expressed in days, the maturity is found by counting forward the specified number of days after the date of the note, excluding the date of the note but including the maturity date. The note of Richard Baldwin in Figure 14-1 has an issuance date of April 19; the due date of June 18 is determined as follows:

Total days in April	30
Date of note in April	19
Number of days note runs in April (excluding April 19)	11
Total days in May	31
Total number of days note has run through May 31	42
Due date in June (60 days minus 42 days)	18
Term of the note	60

If the term of a note that is expressed in days includes an entire month, count the actual number of days in that month. The determination of the number of calendar days in a term expressed in months is the same as the calculation for a term expressed in days. Thus, a two-month note dated April 19 is due 61 days later on June 19. Interest may be computed for either 60 or 61 days. Though banks generally compute interest by using the exact number of days— 61 days in the example—on their direct loans, the usual commercial practice is to calculate interest (as in the example) for two months of 30 days each, or 60 days rather than 61 days. The typical commercial practice is followed in this text; that is, the interest computation on a one-month note is based on 30 days; on a two-month note, 60 days; and so on.

SHORT-TERM
DEBT
FINANCING

(Ch. 14)

Recording Procedure Involving Notes Payable

All notes payable may be recorded in a single Notes Payable account in the general ledger, disclosing supplementary details including name of payee, the interest rate, and the terms of the note, as shown below.

GENERAL LEDGER

Notes Payable   Acct. No. 205

1976				1976			
Dec.	24	F. T. Anson (paid)	450	Nov.	15	B. B. Baker, 7%, 60 days	2,000
					24	F. T. Anson, 8%, 30 days	450
				Dec.	3	C. L. Jones, 8%, 90 days	800
					10	F. E. Merrick, 8%, 60 days	1,000
					18	P. O. Paulson, 8%, 90 days	950

Issuance of Notes for Plant and Equipment. The following examples illustrate the use of notes payable in the acquisition of plant and equipment.

Assume that on July 10, 1976, the Able Company buys from the Bourrim Machine Company a bookkeeping machine at a cost of $2,000; the creditor agrees to take a 90-day, non-interest-bearing note for the purchase price. This transaction is recorded as follows:

1976				
July	10	Office Equipment	2,000	
		Notes Payable		2,000
		To record the purchase of a bookkeeping machine and the issuance of a 90-day, non-interest-bearing note to the Bourrim Machine Company.		

On the maturity date, 90 days later, the payment of the note is recorded as follows:

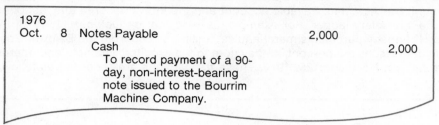

```
1976
Oct.   8   Notes Payable                  2,000
              Cash                                    2,000
              To record payment of a 90-
              day, non-interest-bearing
              note issued to the Bourrim
              Machine Company.
```

Although the transaction of October 8, 1976, should be entered in the Able Company's cash payments journal, for teaching purposes a general journal entry is shown to illustrate the *effect* of the transaction.

Few creditors accept non-interest-bearing notes. Therefore, in the second example, assume that the Able Company purchases the same bookkeeping machine, but gives the Bourrim Machine Company a 9 percent, 90-day note. The journal entry is similar to the previous one.

```
1976
July   10   Office Equipment              2,000
              Notes Payable                         2,000
              To record the purchase of a
              bookkeeping machine and
              the issuance of a 9%, 90-
              day note to the Bourrim
              Machine Company.
```

On October 8, 1976, the payment of the note and interest to the Bourrim Machine Company is recorded as follows:

```
1976
Oct.   8   Notes Payable                  2,000
              Interest Expense                45
                 Cash                                 2,045
                 To record payment of a 9%,
                 90-day note and interest to
                 the Bourrim Machine
                 Company.
```

Issuance of Notes for Merchandise. A business may use notes as a means of postponing payment for merchandise purchased for resale. These transactions could be recorded as were those in the preceding section; but since the volume of business done with a particular supplier or customer must be known for managerial purposes, such as applying for quantity discounts, it is helpful to have a subsidiary ledger account showing the total history of all transactions with a particular firm. To supply management with this information, the accountant may wish to record all merchandise transactions involving notes through the Accounts Payable account and the individual creditors' accounts in the subsidiary ledger. For example, assume that on October 11, 1976, the Able Company purchases merchandise costing $1,800 from the Baldwin Company and issues a 9 percent, 45-day note to the creditor. The note and interest are paid on November 25, 1976. These transactions are recorded as follows:

1976				
Oct.	11	Purchases	1,800.00	
		Accounts Payable—Baldwin Company		1,800.00
		To record merchandise purchased.		
	11	Accounts Payable—Baldwin Company	1,800.00	
		Notes Payable		1,800.00
		To record the issuance of a 9%, 45-day note to the Baldwin Company.		
Nov.	25	Notes Payable	1,800.00	
		Interest Expense	20.25	
		Cash		1,820.25
		To record payment of a note and interest to the Baldwin Company.		

Issuance of Notes in Settlement of Open Accounts. A firm may issue a note to an open-account creditor as a means of postponing payment further, or a creditor may require a debtor to give a note if the account is past due. The entry for the issuance of a note in settlement of an open account payable is similar to the second entry dated October 11 in the previous section.

Issuance of Notes to Borrow from Banks. A business faced with the possibility of losing cash discounts may find it advantageous to borrow money from a bank to pay the open accounts within the discount periods. A 2/10, n/30 cash discount, for example, represents an annual cost saving of 36 percent, as was illustrated in Chapter 5. It is a sound financial decision to borrow money at 9 percent, for example, to prevent the loss of a 36 percent cost saving.

There are two ways in which banks and other grantors of credit handle notes: (1) money may be borrowed on an interest-bearing note signed by the borrower, or (2) money may be advanced on a non-interest-bearing note *discounted* by the borrower. In the first case, the borrower receives the face value of the note and pays the face value plus the accumulated interest on the maturity date. In the second case, the note is non-interest bearing, because the interest, or *discount,* is deducted in advance, and the borrower receives only the discounted value. At the maturity date, the borrower pays the face value of the note. The element of interest is present in either case: the difference is primarily one of form. There may also be notes that are non-interest bearing as far as both the maker and the payee are concerned.

Assume that on March 1, 1976, the Able Company borrows $5,000 from the First National Bank, giving a 9 percent, 60-day note, and that on April 30 it pays the bank for the note and interest. The issuance and payment of the note are recorded in the Able Company's books as follows:

1976			
Mar. 1	Cash	5,000	
	Notes Payable		5,000
	To record a 9%, 60-day note issued to the First National Bank.		
Apr. 30	Notes Payable	5,000	
	Interest Expense	75	
	Cash		5,075
	To record payment of a 9%, 60-day note to the First National Bank.		

Assume that on May 1, 1976, the Able Company borrows money from the City National Bank, discounting its own $5,000, 60-day, non-interest-bearing note at the *discount rate* of 9 percent. The amount of cash received in this case is $4,925, or $5,000 less a discount of $75, computed by applying the discount rate to the face value for the discount period of 60 days. If the maturity date falls within the current accounting period—the calendar year is assumed—the following entries are made in the Able Company's books:

1976			
May 1	Cash	4,925	
	Interest Expense	75	
	Notes Payable		5,000
	To record a non-interest-bearing note issued to the City National Bank discounted at 9% for 60 days.		
June 30	Notes Payable	5,000	
	Cash		5,000
	To record payment of a non-interest-bearing note to the City National Bank.		

Assume that the Able Company had issued the note on December 16,

1976. Since the maturity date falls in the accounting year 1977, the following entry would be made:

```
1976
Dec.  16   Cash                                 4,925
           Discount on Notes Payable               75
               Notes Payable                             5,000
               To record a non-interest-
               bearing note discounted at
               9% for 60 days.
```

The $75 discount is not prepaid and should not be debited to Prepaid Interest, as is sometimes done. The interest is not paid until the note matures. At that time, the net amount borrowed of $4,925 plus total interest of $75 is paid; therefore, the balance of Discount on Notes Payable represents a potential interest expense. Accordingly, adjusting entries are required at December 31, 1976 and 1977, to transfer the applicable expense portions of the balance of Discount on Notes Payable to the Interest Expense account of the respective years; the entries are illustrated later in this chapter.

Discount on Notes Payable should be shown in the statement of financial position as a contra account to Notes Payable under Current Liabilities to indicate clearly the source of the net amount of funds received from creditors. Later, as adjustments are made to the Discount on Notes Payable account, the difference between the Notes Payable account and the balance of the Discount on Notes Payable account shows the net amount borrowed plus accrued interest on that amount.

In reference to the March 1 and May 1 bank loans, the amount paid at maturity was $75 more than the amount received from the bank by the borrower. However, the borrower had the use of $5,000, or the full face value of the interest-bearing note (March 1 bank loan), whereas only $4,925 was available from the non-interest-bearing discounted note. The *effective interest rate* (i) on a discounted note may be computed by the following formula:

$$i = \frac{D}{P} \times \frac{12}{T}$$

where D = the amount of the discount
$\quad\quad P$ = the net proceeds
$\quad\quad 12$ = months in the year, and
$\quad\quad T$ = the term of the note in months

The effective interest in the example is not 9 percent; rather, it is:

$$i = \frac{\$75}{\$4,925} \times \frac{12}{2} = 1.522843\% \times 6 = 9.137\%$$

The accountant should carefully determine the effective interest rate of a loan, since this is relevant to making any short-term financial decision.

A *discount* may be defined as a deduction made from a gross future sum.

The amount of the discount on a note is the difference between its value on the date of discount and its future value at maturity. Since discount and interest are similar in that each represents the charge for the use of money, the Interest Expense account is used in this text to record the incurred portion of expense for each of these items. The use of the Interest Expense account is further extended when a firm discounts customers' notes receivable, another short-term financing device discussed in this chapter.

End-of-Period Adjustments

Since interest is incurred continuously throughout the life of a note payable, it is necessary to make adjusting entries for the interest expense on those notes payable that mature in a later accounting period. Two kinds of adjustment are considered: the accrual of interest on an interest-bearing note payable and the expense apportionment on a discounted note payable.

Assume that the Boston Company has the following accounts in its general ledger as of December 31, 1976:

					Notes Payable	Acct. No. 205
				1976 Dec.	1 Hamilton Co., 9%, 90 days	4,650
					16 Bank of Orange 120 days, discounted at 9%	3,600

		Discount on Notes Payable		Acct. No. 205A	
Dec. 1976	16		108		

At December 31, 1976, the following two adjusting entries are made:

```
1976
Dec.  31   Interest Expense                      34.88
               Accrued Interest Payable                     34.88
                  To record accrued interest
                  on the note issued to the
                  Hamilton Co.; Interest for 30
                  days at 9% on $4,650 is
                  $34.88.
      31   Interest Expense                      13.50
               Discount on Notes Payable                    13.50
                  To record the transfer of
                  $13.50 interest from the
                  Discount on Notes Payable
                  account to the Interest
                  Expense account on the
                  note discounted at the Bank
                  of Orange.
```

Comments on these two entries follow.

1. The amount of the accrued interest on a note issued to the Hamilton Company is figured at 9 percent for 30 days, the number of days after December 1, including December 31. Of course, no interest for the time period after December 31, 1976, should be recorded as an expense of 1976.

2. The second adjusting entry transfers interest from the Discount on Notes Payable account to the Interest Expense account. There are two methods by which the interest expense of $13.50 for 1976 can be determined. (1) The amount of the discount may be multiplied by a fraction consisting of the age of the note as of the adjustment date divided by the term—in the example, $15/120 \times \$108 = \$13.50$. (2) An ordinary interest computation may be made—interest at 9 percent on $3,600 for 15 days is $13.50.

On March 1, 1977, when the Boston Company pays the Hamilton Company for the note and interest, the following journal entry is made:

```
1977
Mar.  1   Notes Payable                       4,650.00
          Accrued Interest Payable               34.88
          Interest Expense                        69.75
              Cash                                         4,754.63
                 To record payment of a 9%,
                 90-day note and interest to
                 the Hamilton Co.
```

The credit to Cash of $4,754.63 represents the payment of two liabilities already on the books, Notes Payable and Accrued Interest Payable, and a payment of interest expense of $69.75 = (9\% \times 60/360 \times \$4,650)$ entirely applicable to 1977.

The payment of the $3,600 on April 15, 1977, to the Bank of Orange is recorded in the following journal entry:

```
1977
Apr.  15  Notes Payable                        3,600
              Cash                                        3,600
              To record payment of a
              note to the Bank of Orange.
```

Since the note is non-interest bearing, no interest is recorded at the time of payment. However, there is a $94.50 balance in the Discount on Notes Payable account, which represents an expense of the year 1977. The following adjusting entry is made as of December 31, 1977, to transfer this amount to the Interest Expense account:

```
1977
Dec.  31  Interest Expense                     94.50
              Discount on Notes Payable                   94.50
              To apportion the amount of
              interest expense applicable
              to the year 1977.
```

NOTES RECEIVABLE FINANCING PROBLEM

Another financial device often employed to obtain short-term funds is discounting customers' notes receivable. Before this is discussed, however, it would be helpful to understand the accounting for notes received from customers.

In general, the accounting for notes receivable is similar to that for notes payable; however, some procedures warrant additional discussion.

Recording Procedures

Many businesses make use of promissory notes to create a negotiable instrument that may be easily discounted at a bank should the need for funds arise. These businesses include firms selling high-priced durable goods such as furniture, farm machinery, and automobiles. Notes receivable are also received by a financial institution when it lends money.

It is perhaps even more important to keep good accounting records for notes receivable than it is for notes payable. After all, the payee of a note payable will send a statement to the maker that a note is due, so there is little danger that the maker will overlook the due date. The holder of notes receivable must have his records arranged so that he can notify the debtor that the note is due. This requires that notes receivable be filed chronologically by maturity date in a tickler file that is properly safeguarded.

All notes receivable are usually recorded in a single general ledger account. The tickler file of notes receivable plus the general ledger account containing such information as the maker, the term, the interest rate, and any collateral pledged make it unnecessary for a firm to maintain a subsidiary notes receivable ledger. The Notes Receivable account of the Carson Company is shown here.

		Notes Receivable					Acct. No. 111	
1976 Nov.	1	C. Adams, 45 days, 8%		775	1976 Dec.	16	C. Adams	775
Dec.	20	B. Baker, 90 days, 9%		425				
	20	L. Wilson, 60 days, 8%		500				

Each debit posting indicates that an asset, Notes Receivable, has been acquired from a customer; each credit entry indicates that a particular note has been settled by payment or renewal or has been dishonored. In addition to the dollar amounts in the money columns, the Explanation columns give the maker's name, the term of the note, the interest rate, and any other relevant information.

If the volume of transactions warrants it, a special notes receivable register, like a notes payable register, could be created. Special Debit and Credit money columns could be inserted, along with memorandum columns for supplementary information. This register could serve as both a journal and a subsidiary record of notes receivable.

Receipt of a Note for a Sale

Assume that on March 5, 1976, the Dawson Company sells merchandise to John Roch and receives a 9 percent, 90-day note for $650. The following entries are made:

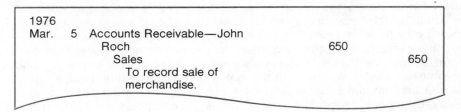

1976				
Mar.	5	Accounts Receivable—John Roch	650	
		Sales		650
		To record sale of merchandise.		

(Ch. 14)

```
1976
Mar.   5   Notes Receivable                        650
               Accounts Receivable—John
                  Roch                                              650
                  To record the receipt of a
                  9%, 90-day note from
                  John Roch.
```

The first entry is made so that the customer's account in the subsidiary ledger will contain a complete record of all credit sales transactions. This information is useful to management in making decisions about collection efforts and further extension of credit.

On June 3, 1976, when the Dawson Company receives payment from John Roch, the following entry is made:

```
1976
June   3   Cash                                   664.63
               Notes Receivable                               650.00
               Interest Earned                                 14.63
                  To record receipt of
                  payment from John Roch
                  for note and interest due
                  today.
```

The Interest Earned account is a revenue account. The balance of this account is closed at the end of the accounting period to the Income Summary account.

Receipt of a Note in Settlement of an Open Account. Assume that Ralph Towne owes the Dawson Company $1,850, due on July 10, 1976. On August 1, the Dawson Company agrees to accept a 60-day, non-interest-bearing note with a face value of $1,877.75 (the amount receivable, $1,850, plus interest at 9 percent for 60 days) in settlement of the open account. This procedure is common among retailers who plan to discount their notes at banks. Banks prefer that most, if not all, of their notes be noninterest bearing. Since the maturity date of this note falls within the current accounting period—the calendar year is assumed—the following entry is made:

```
1976
Aug.   1   Notes Receivable                     1,877.75
               Accounts Receivable—Ralph
                  Towne                                        1,850.00
               Interest Earned                                 27.75
                  To record receipt of a 60-
                  day, non-interest-bearing
                  note, with interest of
                  $27.75 included in the
                  face value, from Ralph
                  Towne.
```

(Ch. 14)

The credit of the entire $27.75 to the revenue account, Interest Earned, is permissible, since that amount will become revenue by the time the books are closed on December 31.

On September 30, when payment is received, the following entry is made:

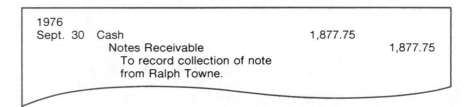

```
1976
Sept. 30   Cash                                1,877.75
               Notes Receivable                            1,877.75
               To record collection of note
               from Ralph Towne.
```

If the note of August 1, 1976, had been received on December 1, 1976, all the interest would not be earned by December 31, 1976. The following entry is required:

```
1976
Dec.   1   Notes Receivable                    1,877.75
               Accounts Receivable—Ralph
               Towne                                        1,850.00
               Unearned Interest (included in
               face of notes receivable)                       27.75
               To record receipt of a 60-
               day, non-interest-bearing
               note, with interest of
               $27.75 included in the
               face value, from Ralph
               Towne.
```

The Unearned Interest account, credited for $27.75, represents the interest that will be partly earned in 1976 and partly earned in 1977. The unearned interest should *not* be classified as a current liability, as is sometimes done. Rather, it should be shown as a contra account to Notes Receivable, to reduce that account to an estimate of its present value; this figure, the carrying value, increases as the note approaches maturity date, and represents the approximate amount that could be received by discounting the note at a bank. The Unearned Interest account will require adjusting entries at December 1976 and 1977, to apportion the amount of applicable revenue earned in the respective years to the operations of those years. This procedure is described later in this chapter.

Dishonor of a Note Receivable by the Maker. If a note cannot be collected at maturity, it is said to be *dishonored* by the maker. Another term that is often used is *defaulting* on a note. Once the maturity date of a note passes without the note being collected, an entry should be made transferring the face value of the note plus any uncollected accrued interest to the Accounts Receivable account.

Assume that on June 1, 1976, Ronald Ronson issued a 9 percent, 90-day note for $2,000 to the Dawson Company. At the maturity date, August 30, 1976, Ronson fails to pay the amount of the note and interest, at which time the following entry is made on the books of the Dawson Company:

1976			
Aug. 30	Accounts Receivable—Ronald Ronson	2,045	
	Notes Receivable		2,000
	Interest Earned		45
	To record the dishonor by Ronald Ronson of a 9%, 90-day note.		

Two questions arise in connection with this entry: (1) Why should $45 be recognized as revenue and credited to the Interest Earned account? (2) Why should the amount of the note and interest not be written off to Allowance for Doubtful Accounts?

Under the accrual concept, the interest has been earned. It represents a valid claim against the maker of the note; if the face of the note is collectible, then so is the interest. This leads to the answer to the second question: The fact that a note is uncollectible at its maturity is not a definite indication that it will never be collected. Unless there is some evidence to the contrary, most business firms assume that notes will ultimately be collected. Certainly, if the amounts involved are material, all possible steps including legal action will be taken to collect both accounts and notes receivable, and only after such steps have failed will an account be written off to Allowance for Doubtful Accounts.

The transfer of dishonored notes and interest to Accounts Receivable accomplishes two things: (1) the Notes Receivable account is relieved of past-due notes, reflects only the current notes, and therefore represents a highly liquid asset; and (2) use of the Accounts Receivable account emphasizes the legal fact of dishonor (legally, a past-due note is the same as an open account claim against a customer) and presents a complete picture of all transactions with the customer.

End-of-Period Adjusting Entries

The adjusting entries for interest on notes receivable parallel the adjusting entries for interest on notes payable. The major problem is accurate measurement of the revenue Interest Earned and the asset Accrued Interest Receivable, or the contra account Unearned Interest. To illustrate the adjusting entries and the effect they have on the accounting for notes and interest in the next accounting period, assume that the Eason Company has the following accounts in its general ledger as of December 31, 1976:

Notes Receivable			Acct. No. 111

1976 Nov.	1	Linda Phillips, 9%, 150 days	1,720
Dec.	1	George Archer, 90-day, non-interest-bearing note, but interest of $54 is in the face	2,454

			Unearned Interest	Acct. No. 111A
		1976 Dec.	1	Interest in face of George Archer note	54

At December 31, 1976, the accountant for the Eason Company makes the following adjusting entries:

1976				
Dec.	31	Accrued Interest Receivable	25.80	
		Interest Earned		25.80
		To record the accrued interest on the Linda Phillips note at 9% for 60 days.		
	31	Unearned Interest	18.00	
		Interest Earned		18.00
		To record the transfer of 1/3 of $54 interest on the note from George Archer from the Unearned Interest account to the revenue account.		

Comments on these adjustments follow:

1. The accrued interest receivable on the note from Linda Phillips is figured at 9 percent for 60 days, the number of days after November 1 including December 31. No interest for the period after December 31, 1976, should be recorded as revenue in the year 1976.

2. The second adjustment involves the apportionment of interest revenue earned in a given period, 1976, to that period.

On March 1, 1977, when the Eason Company collects the George Archer note, the following entry is made:

```
1977
Mar.  1  Cash                              2,454
            Notes Receivable                        2,454
               To record collection of a
               note from George Archer.
```

Since the note is non-interest bearing on the face, no interest is recorded at the time of collection. However, a balance of $36 remains in the Unearned Interest account, representing revenue earned in the year 1977. Thus, an adjusting entry is necessary as of December 31, 1977, to transfer this amount to the Interest Earned account:

```
1977
Dec.  31  Unearned Interest                 36
             Interest Earned                          36
                To apportion the amount of
                interest revenue applicable
                to the year 1977.
```

A slightly different problem is associated with the collection of the note from Linda Phillips. The following entry is made on March 31, 1977, when the note is collected:

```
1977
Mar.  31  Cash                           1,784.50
             Notes Receivable                      1,720.00
             Accrued Interest Receivable               25.80
             Interest Earned                           38.70
                To record collection of a
                9%, 150-day note and
                interest from Linda Phillips.
```

The debit of $1,784.50 to Cash represents the collection of two receivables already on the books, Notes Receivable and Accrued Interest Receivable, and of a revenue, Interest Earned of $38.70, which was earned in, and is entirely applicable to, the year 1977.

(Ch. 14)

For a business that receives a large number of notes from customers, it may be economically advantageous to obtain cash by discounting these notes at a bank rather than hold them to maturity. If the credit rating of the firm is good, most banks will usually discount customers' notes receivable because, if the maker fails to pay the maturity value when it is due, the firm that has discounted the note—having previously endorsed it—must make payment to the bank.

Contingent Liability

This obligation is referred to as a *contingent liability*.

Determining the Cash Proceeds

As far as the bank is concerned, it is making a loan to the borrower based on the maturity value of the note, including any interest, because that is the amount the bank will collect from the maker at the maturity date. The discount that the bank deducts is based on a stipulated rate of the maturity value for the period the note has to run.

The sequence for computing the proceeds of a discounted note is:

1. The maturity value, or the principal plus the total interest to maturity, is determined.
2. The discount period, or the number of days the note still has to run after the date of the discount, is found.
3. The discount is computed at the stipulated bank rate for the discount period.
4. The discount is deducted from the maturity value to find the cash proceeds.

This sequence may be stated as:

$$P = MV - (MV \times d \times RL)$$

where P = the cash proceeds
MV = the maturity value
d = the rate of discount
RL = the remaining life of the note

Assume that on April 19, 1976, the Faison Company receives from Edward Goodson a 9 percent, 60-day note for $2,000 in settlement of a past-due open account. This transaction is recorded as follows:

```
1976
Apr.  19   Notes Receivable                    2,000
              Accounts Receivable—
              Edward Goodson                            2,000
                 To record receipt of a
                 9%, 60-day note from
                 Goodson in settlement of
                 a past-due open account.
```

On May 1, 1976, the Faison Company, needing short-term funds, decides to discount Goodson's note at the bank's rate of 8 percent. Calculation of the proceeds follows:

```
1. Maturity value of note (principal of $2,000
   plus total interest of $30)                           $2,030.00
2. Due date                               June 18
3. Period of discount:
      May 1–May 31 (not counting May 1)   30 days
      June 1–June 18 (including June 1)   18 days
                                          48 days

4. Discount at 8% for 48 days on the
   maturity value:
      Interest on $2,030 at 6% for 60 days   $20.30
      Less interest on $2,030 at 6% for
      12 days (⅕ × $20.30)                      4.06
      Interest on $2,030 at 6% for 48 days   $16.24
      Add interest on $2,030 at 2% for
         48 days (⅓ × $16.24)                   5.41
      Discount (or interest) on $2,030 at
         8% for 48 days                                     21.65
             Total cash proceeds                        $2,008.35
```

Recording the Proceeds

The entry on the Faison Company's books is:

```
1976
May   1   Cash                              2,008.35
             Notes Receivable Discounted                 2,000.00
             Interest Earned                                 8.35
                To record the discounting of
                Edward Goodson's 9%, 60-
                day note at the bank at 8%.
```

The Notes Receivable Discounted account is used to indicate that the Faison Company, having, endorsed the note before turning it over to the bank, is now obligated to pay the bank if Goodson fails to do so; that is, the Faison Company would have to pay the $2,000 contingent liability plus the $30 interest at 9 percent for 60 days, plus any *protest fee* charged by the bank. The obligation assumed by the Faison Company is contingent on Goodson's payment, and the account is therefore referred to as a *contingent liability account.* This account brings the existence of the contingent liability to the attention of the reader of the statement of financial position.

| Full Disclosure | In preparing financial statements, full disclosure of all essential facts is of paramount importance. |

Goodson does not need to be informed that the note has been discounted, and no entry is required on his books; his obligation to pay the maturity value of the note on its presentation by the legal holder in due course remains unchanged.

Presentation on the Statement of Financial Position

Assume that on May 31 the Notes Receivable account shows a balance of $3,500 (including the $2,000 note discounted on May 1). The statement of financial position prepared on that date may disclose the existence of the contingent liability by a footnote or supplementary note to the statement of financial position as follows:

Assets

Current Assets
    Notes Receivable (see Note 1) $1,500

    Note 1: The company is contingently liable for notes receivable discounted in the amount of $2,000.

Disclosure of the contingent liability can also be made by offsetting Notes Receivable Discounted against Notes Receivable in the statement of financial position in the following manner:

Assets

Current Assets		
Notes Receivable	$3,500	
Deduct Notes Receivable Discounted	2,000	
Net Notes Receivable		$1,500

Payment of a Discounted Note

If notification of dishonor is not received from the bank (the bank normally does not notify the borrower of payment by the maker), it is assumed that the maker has paid the note at the maturity date, and the borrower is released from his contingent liability. The entry on the Faison Company's books to eliminate the contingent liability is:

1976			
June 18	Notes Receivable Discounted	2,000	
	Notes Receivable		2,000
	To eliminate the contingent liability on Goodson's note, which was discounted on May 1, 1976.		

The entry on Edward Goodson's books on the date of payment is:

1976			
June 18	Notes Payable	2,000	
	Interest Expense	30	
	Cash		2,030
	To record payment to the bank for a 9%, 60-day note issued to the Faison Company on April 19, 1976.		

The debit to Interest Expense is for the full 60-day period. It is assumed that no adjusting entry has been made for any interest expense.

Nonpayment of a Discounted Note

If Edward Goodson dishonors the note at the maturity date, the bank must follow a certain formal procedure involving the preparation of notarized protest documents to establish the legal basis for the collection of the full amount from the Faison Company. Assuming that the bank charges a protest fee of $5, the following entries are made on the Faison Company's books when the company pays the bank the face value of the note, the interest, and the protest fee.

(Ch. 14)

```
1976
June 18    Accounts Receivable—Edward Goodson        2,035
              Cash                                                2,035
                 To record payment of Edward
                 Goodson's note, which was discounted
                 and is now dishonored by Goodson:

                       Protest Fee          5
                       Interest            30
                       Face value     $2,000

                       Total          $2,035

        18    Notes Receivable Discounted            2,000
                 Notes Receivable                            2,000
                    To record the elimination of the
                    contingent liability and Goodson's
                    discounted and dishonored note.
```

Note that Accounts Receivable, instead of Notes Receivable Discounted, is debited in the entry recording the cash payment. This procedure avoids the error of treating discounted notes as though they were actual liabilities; since payment is made as soon as the contingency is realized, no book liability need be recorded. The second journal entry is necessary to remove the contingent liability after the cash payment for the dishonored note is made.

The fact that a note is dishonored does not mean that it will be definitely uncollectible or that it should be written off to Allowance for Doubtful Accounts. Goodson, in this case, may pay at a later date, either voluntarily or on a court order. The account remains open in the accounts receivable ledger until it is settled or definitely determined to be uncollectible and written off.

Use of Compound Interest in Installment Payments

A popular form of short-term debt is the obligation that requires installment payments. Often this kind of obligation provides that it be liquidated by a series of equal payments that are to include both principal and accrued interest. The future principal obligation represents the present value of an annuity, the equal payments being calculated by dividing the principal sum owed by the present value of an annuity of $1. To illustrate, assume a debt of $1,000 incurred as of August 1, 1976, is to be paid off by twelve equal *monthly* installments including both principal and interest. Interest at the nominal annual rate of 18 percent, or monthly rate of 1½ percent, accrues on the unpaid balance, and the first payment is to be made on August 31, 1976. The monthly payments are determined by dividing $1,000 by 10.9075052, the present value of an annuity of twelve rents of $1 each at 1½ percent. The equal payments, then, are $91.68.

Under the assumption that the obligation is represented by the issuance of an installment notes payable, entries that would be made on August 31 and September 30, 1976, appear below. Similar entries would be made in subsequent periods.

Transaction	Books of Party Issuing Note		Books of Party Receiving Note	

August 1, 1976. Note for $1,000 is issued.	Purchases (or Cash) 1,000.00
	    Notes Payable*
		1,000.00	Notes Receivable* 1,000.00
			    Sales (or Cash)
				1,000.00

August 31, 1976. Monthly payment is made.	Notes Payable 76.68
	Interest Expense 15.00
	    Cash
		91.68	Cash 91.68
			    Notes Receivable
			    Interest Earned
				76.68
				15.00

September 30, 1976. Monthly payment is made.	Notes Payable 77.83
	Interest Expense 13.85
	    Cash
		91.68	Cash 91.68
			    Notes Receivable
			    Interest Earned
				77.83
				13.85

* If the item arises out of a transaction involving the sale of merchandise, it should first be recorded in open Accounts Payable and Accounts Receivable accounts.

A ROUGH APPROXIMATION OF THE COST OF BORROWING MONEY

An essential factor in all short-term financial decisions is the effective cost of the particular means of financing. Even though legislation requires the disclosure of the effective annual interest cost of borrowed funds, debtors should be familiar with the computations involved in the determination of these rates, or at least in approximating these rates. This knowledge is particularly important when individuals are faced with the decision for selecting a single method from among several alternative short-term financing methods.

With installment purchase plans where the effective interest rate is not stated, it is particularly helpful to know a method of quickly approximating this rate. Such an approximation involves making the simplifying assumption that each payment constitutes equal reductions in the principal amount owed; thus the average debt for the interest period is the original principal divided by two. Then the interest for the period can readily be compared with the average outstanding principal. One must be very careful to "annualize"[2] any interest rate that is determined. To illustrate this approximation, assume that merchandise costing $1,000 is purchased; this amount is to be paid in twenty-four equal monthly installments of $50 each (which includes interest). The calculation is as follows:

1. Average outstanding principal = $1,000/2 = $500.
2. Annual absolute interest cost:
Total interest for two years = ($50 × 24) − $1,000 = $200.
Interest for *one* year = $200 ÷ 2 = $100.
3. Rough approximation of effective annual interest rate
= $100/$500 = 20 percent per year, or 1.67 percent each month.

[2] The term *to annualize* is used to mean to translate whatever periodic interest that is stated to an equivalent interest rate for a one-year period.

A *draft* is a written order to pay, such as a bank check, with the same negotiability as a note, for which it is often used as a substitute. Commercial drafts, excluding checks, are used to enforce the collection of open accounts, to obtain the advantages of both a written acknowledgment and a negotiable instrument, and for C.O.D. (collect on delivery) shipments.

The person who issues the order and draws the draft is the *drawer;* the person to whom it is addressed and who is to make payment is the *drawee;* and the person to whom payment is to be made is the *payee.* If the drawer names himself as the payee—a common occurrence with commercial drafts—the draft becomes a two-party document similar to a note. The types of drafts used in business are (1) *ordinary checks,* (2) *certified checks,* (3) *cashier's* or *treasurer's checks,* (4) *sight drafts,* (5) *time drafts,* and (6) *trade acceptances.*

An *ordinary check* is one form of a three-party sight draft; it is accounted for as cash received from a customer or as cash paid when a check is written. A *certified check* is a check that has been stamped *certified* by a bank and for which the bank reduces the drawer's account immediately at the time of certification. A *casher's,* or *treasurer's, check* is purchased from a bank; such a check is written by officials of a bank and is guaranteed by the bank; cashiers' checks are treated as cash items.

A *commercial sight draft,* a demand for payment by the person to whom money is owed, may be used to attempt to collect money from a customer who has a past-due account, or may be used to make a C.O.D. sale. The sight draft, attached to the *order bill of lading* (the document authorizing the passage of title to the goods and a receipt given by the common carrier), is mailed to the customer's bank. Since the customer cannot get the merchandise without the bill of lading, the payment of the draft must precede receipt of the bill of lading and delivery of the goods by the warehouse or the transportation firm. To help account for the shipment of merchandise, a journal entry may be made at the time the sight draft is drawn, debiting Accounts Receivable and crediting Sales. No entry would be made for the draft itself at this time, because the drawing of a draft is simply an intent until the draft is accepted. When the draft is honored by payment and the drawer is notified of the fact, Cash and an expense account for any collection fee charged by the bank are debited and Accounts Receivable is credited.

A *time draft* is due after the passage of a specified period. The drawer presents the instrument to the drawee, who indicates his agreement to pay the draft at maturity by writing "Accepted" across the face of the draft and signing it properly. The accounting entry usually made on the drawee's book when the drawee accepts a time draft drawn by a creditor for an amount of a past-due open account is a debit to Accounts Payable and a credit to Notes Payable. When he receives the accepted draft from the debtor, the drawer debits Notes Receivable and credits Accounts Receivable. The accounting for any interest that the draft bears is similar to that for notes. The interest may accrue from the date of the draft—*60 days from date*—or from the date the draft was accepted by drawee—*60 days from sight.* A *trade acceptance* is a special form of time draft used in connection with a specific sales transaction. The document is

(Ch. 14)

drawn by the seller of merchandise. Its acceptance by the buyer serves as an acknowledgment of the purchase, and it then assumes the same status as a note. Trade acceptances may be used to ensure prompt payment and to borrow money.

GLOSSARY

Blank Endorsement The signature of the owner, the payee, on the back of a negotiable instrument; the endorsement guarantees the validity of the instrument and warrants the payment of the instrument in case of dishonor by the maker at maturity.

Cashier's Check A check drawn by the cashier of a bank on itself; cashier's checks are sold to individuals or businesses for a small fee.

Certified Check An ordinary bank check, personal or business, stamped "Certified" and signed by an official of the bank; thus the bank reduces the drawer's account when the check is certified and guarantees the check.

Contingent Liability An amount that may become a liability in the future *if* certain events occur.

Discount An amount subtracted from a future sum to determine the present value or cash proceeds.

Discount on Notes Payable An account which discloses the amounts (or unexpired portion thereof) subtracted from the maturity value of notes payable to arrive at proceeds. As such, it represents future interest expense; it should be disclosed on the statement of financial position as a contra item to the applicable Notes Payable account.

Dishonored Note A note that has not been paid by the maker at the maturity date.

Draft A written order signed by the drawer directing the drawee to pay a specified sum of money to the order of a designated person or to bearer (the payee), at a fixed or determinable future time or on demand.

Effective Interest The correct interest computed on only the remaining balance of an unpaid debt for the specific time period, usually stated as an annual fraction of the unpaid debt.

Full Endorsement An endorsement consisting of a notation on the back of a negotiable instrument of "Pay to the order of [name of person or company]" accompanied by the signature of the owner; the full endorsement requires the subsequent endorsement of the named endorsee before the instrument can be transferred further.

Maturity Date The date on which a negotiable instrument is due and payable.

Maturity Value The amount payable (or receivable) on a negotiable instrument at its maturity date; it includes face value plus any stated interest.

Non-Interest-Bearing Note A note which does not bear any interest on the face; the principal sum named in the note is the maturity value of the note.

Notes Payable A promissory note issued by an individual or a firm; it is a liability account of the issuing firm.

Notes Receivable A promissory note received from a customer or client; it represents an asset to the owner of the note.

SHORT-TERM
DEBT
FINANCING

Notes Receivable Discounted An account that discloses the contingent liability for customers' notes which have been discounted with others and endorsed either in blank or in full.

Promissory Note An unconditional written promise to pay a specified sum of money to the order of a designated person, or to bearer, at a fixed or determinable future time or on demand.

Protest Fee A fee charged by a bank or financial institution for a note which is dishonored (not paid) at maturity.

Qualified Endorsement An endorsement accompanied by the phrase "without recourse," which tends to relieve the endorser of any further liability.

Sight Draft A demand for immediate payment to oneself (the drawer) or to another person (that is, when draft is presented for payment); an ordinary check is a sight draft.

Time Draft A draft that is due after the passage of a specified period; the time may be measured from the date that the draft is drawn or from the date that the draft is accepted by the drawee.

Trade Acceptance A special form of time draft arising out of a specific sales transaction.

Unearned Interest An amount included in the face value of a note receivable; it represents future interest revenue, and should be disclosed on the statement of financial position as a contra item to Notes Receivable.

Q14-1. Explain the following terms or procedures: (a) negotiable instrument, (b) the 6%, 60-day method, (c) interest-bearing note, (d) maker of a note, and (e) payee of a note.

Q14-2. Explain the following terms or procedures: (a) discounting a note, (b) bank discount rate, (c) contingent liability, (d) proceeds, (e) maturity value, and (f) dishonored note.

Q14-3. The accountant for the Virgin Islands Company recorded the receipt of a note on a sale to Joseph Sales as follows:

Notes Receivable	875	
Sales		875

State how you think the transaction should have been recorded and give your reason.

Q14-4. The Saxon Company negotiated with the Providence Bank a 90-day loan (reference l), which was paid on its due date (reference m). It arranged with the Queens Bank for another 90-day loan (reference x), which was also paid when due (reference y).

Cash		Notes Payable to Bank		Interest Expense	
(l) 3,000	(m) 3,045	(m) 3,000	(l) 3,000	(m) 45	
(x) 2,955	(y) 3,000	(y) 3,000	(x) 3,000	(x) 45	

Describe the type of negotiable instrument used (a) by the Providence Bank; (b) by the Queens Bank. (c) Which loan is more favorable to the Saxon Company? Why?

Q14-5. On July 1, 1976, Able gives Baker a 9%, one-year $20,000 note and is given credit for the face of the note. Baker transfers the note by a blank endorsement to Carter on September 1, at which date the note is applied on account at its face value plus accrued interest. Describe all entries for the year 1976 relevant to the note, including receipt and transfer of the note, adjusting and closing entries for any interest transactions on the books (a) of Able, who closes his books annually on December 31, (b) of Baker, who closes his books quarterly at the end of each calendar quarter, and (c) of Carter, who closes his books monthly.

Q14-6. The following account balances appear in the general ledger of the Hobson Company:

Notes Receivable		Notes Payable		Notes Receivable Discounted	
70,000			40,000		30,000

(a) What is the amount of customer notes outstanding? (b) What is the amount of customer notes in the Hobson Company's possession? (c) What is the amount of discounted customer notes? (d) What is the Hobson Company's contingent liability on discounted notes? (e) Do the accounts furnish enough data to compute the company's working capital position? (f) How would these accounts be shown in the position statement?

Q14-7. Six transactions related to a sale to a customer are recorded in the T accounts below. Describe each transaction.

Cash		Accounts Receivable		Notes Receivable	
(c) 1,808	(d) 1,822	(a) 1,800	(b) 1,800	(b) 1,800	(e) 1,800
(e) 1,832		(d) 1,822	(f) 1,822		

Notes Receivable Discounted		Sales		Interest Earned	
(e) 1,800	(c) 1,800		(a) 1,800		(c) 8
					(f) 10

(Ch. 14)

Q14-8. (a) What is a contingent liability? (b) May there be more than one person contingently liable on a particular note? Explain. (c) What items must a person who is contingently liable on an interest-bearing note pay if the maker dishonors the note on its due date?

Q14-9. Discuss the managerial factors that a company must consider in determining what method of short-term financing it should choose.

Q14-10. Describe briefly how a person may approximate the effective interest rate on installment purchase plans where the interest rate is not explicitly stated.

E14-1. Information regarding five notes is given below.

Date of Note	Term of Note	Interest Rate	Principal
(1) March 1, 1976	60 days	8%	$2,000
(2) April 5, 1976	90 days	9%	3,000
(3) August 24, 1976	15 days	10%	4,000
(4) September 13, 1976	3 months	7%	1,500
(5) November 3, 1976	2 months	11%	4,800

Determine the maturity date and maturity value of each note.

E14-2. The following were among the transactions of the Trollingwood Company for 1976 and 1977:

1976
Jan. 2 Purchased $5,000 worth of merchandise from the Biltmore Company, and issued a 9%, 45-day note.

Feb. 16 Paid note and interest due the Biltmore Company.

Mar. 15 Issued a 10%, 90-day note to the Melton Company in settlement of an open account of $4,000.

June 13 Paid the Melton Company $3,000 on principal and all the interest for the preceding 90 days; issued a new 9%, 60-day note for the balance of the principal.

Aug. 12 Paid the remaining amount due the Melton Company.

Dec. 1 Issued a 9%, 90-day note to the Donnan Company in settlement of an open account of $8,000.

1977
Mar. 1 Paid the amount due the Donnan Company.

Journalize the transactions, including any necessary adjusting entries on December 31, 1976.

E14-3. The following were among the transactions of the Dawson Company for 1976 and 1977.

1976
Aug. 3 Discounted its own 90-day, non-interest-bearing note, made out to the Bank of Plymouth in the principal amount of $9,000, at a discount rate of 9%.

1976

Nov. 1 Paid the Bank of Plymouth the amount due.

Dec. 1 Discounted its own 90-day, non-interest-bearing note, made out to the Bank of York in the principal amount of $6,000, at a discount rate of 9%. (Assume that the books are closed on December 31).

1977

Mar. 1 Paid the amount due the Bank of York.

Journalize the transactions, including any necessary adjusting entries on December 31, 1976, and 1977.

E14-4. The following were among the transactions of the Easley Corporation for 1976 and 1977:

1976

Apr. 19 Sold merchandise worth $900 to H. H. Nixon and received a 9%, 60-day note.

June 18 Collected the amount due from H. H. Nixon.

June 21 Received a 9%, 120-day note from A. C. Deece in settlement of an open account for $3,000.

Oct. 19 A. C. Deece dishonored his note.

Nov. 15 Received a 9%, 90-day note from I. M. Gooding in settlement of an open account of $4,000.

1977

Feb. 13 Collected the note and interest from I. M. Gooding.

Journalize the transactions, including any necessary adjusting entries as of December 31, 1976.

E14-5. The following were among the transactions of the Hobson Company for 1976 and 1977:

1976

Mar. 1 Received a 90-day, non-interest-bearing note from Larry Alvins, the principal amount of which included a past-due open account of $4,600 plus interest at 9% for 90 days. (The books are closed annually on December 31.)

May 30 Collected the amount due from Alvins.

Dec. 1 Received a 120-day, non-interest-bearing note from Melvin Rollins, the principal amount of which included a past-due open account of $5,000 plus interest at 8% for 120 days.

1977

Mar. 31 Collected the amount due from Rollins.

Journalize the transactions, including any necessary adjusting entries on December 31, 1976, and 1977.

E14-6. Nikolai Company completed the following transactions in 1976 and 1977:

1976

Aug. 1 Sold $800 worth of merchandise to the Hoffman Company on account.

Oct. 8 Received a 90-day, 9% note in full settlement of the Hoffman account.

Dec. 5 Discounted the above note at 8% at the Bank of Columbia.

1977

Jan. 6 The December 6 note was paid at maturity.

Journalize the transactions on the books of Nikolai Company and the Hoffman Company, including any necessary adjusting entries on December 31, 1976.

E14-7. On September 5, 1976 the Best Company sold $3,600 worth of merchandise to Bazley Company on account and received a 9%, 60-day note. This note was discounted at 9% on October 20, 1976, at the Foxboro Bank. At maturity date the note was dishonored by the Bazley Company, and the Best Company paid the maturity value plus a $3 protest fee. Journalize the transactions on the books of the Best Company.

E14-8. Evans Johnson received from Lawrence Key a 9%, 120-day note for $6,000 dated March 3, 1976. Thirty days later Johnson discounted with Phillip Holding Key's note at 10%. Key paid the note at maturity.

Journalize the transactions on the books of Johnson and of Holding.

E14-9. (Appendix). Lynne Powell owed the Fritig Company $600 for merchandise that she had purchased. Since the debt was past due, Fritig drew a sight draft and sent it to Powell's bank for collection. Powell paid the sight draft. The bank charged $2 for its services.

Journalize the transactions on the books of Lynne Powell and the Fritig Company.

E14-10. The Kinder Company accepts trade notes from its customers. As of December 31, 1976, it had accepted only one: an 8%, 90-day note on December 1, 1976. At the end of the year, the following adjusting entry was made:

1976
Dec. 31 Accrued Interest Receivable   32
        Interest Earned   32
           To record interest at 8% for 30 days on the note
           received from Robert Glass December 1 in settle-
           ment of an open account receivable.

Reconstruct the entry made on December 1 to record the receipt of the note from Robert Glass. Show all your calculations.

E14-11. Betsy Camerson is considering purchasing merchandise with an invoice price of $6,000, which she will be required to pay in twelve monthly installments of $560 each. Before she makes her decision, she would like to know the approximate annual effective interest rate involved in the installment contract. Calculate the approximate annual effective interest rate of this installment purchase.

E14-12. B. B. Fitch borrows $1,000, to be repaid in 24 equal monthly installments with interest at the rate of $1\frac{1}{2}$% a month. Using the tables on pages 1029 and 1031 calculate the equal installments.

DP14-1. (*Computing maturity dates*) The following notes were received by Aldersgate, Inc.:

Date of Note	Term of Note
March 10, 1976	90 days
April 5, 1976	60 days
March 10, 1976	4 months
April 5, 1976	2 months
January 31, 1976	1 month

Required: Determine the maturity date of each note.

DP14-2. (*Computing interest by short-cut methods*) The following information pertains to five notes:

1. $4,200 at 6% for 60 days
2. $5,600 at 9% for 90 days
3. $3,400 at 8% for 120 days
4. $7,600 at 10% for 90 days
5. $8,000 at 12% for 72 days

Required: Using the short-cut methods, compute the amount of interest on each note.

DP14-3. (*Journalizing notes payable transactions*) The Watson Company completed the following transactions during 1976 and 1977:

1976
Jan. 2 Purchased $4,800 worth of merchandise from the Nunn Company; issued a 9%, 60-day note.

Mar. 3 Paid the Nunn Company the amount due for the note and interest.

      3 Issued a 9%, 45-day note for $3,600 to Cohoon, Inc., in settlement of an open account.

Apr. 17 Paid Cohoon, Inc., $2,600 on the March 3 note plus all the interest; issued a new 10%, 30-day note for the balance of the principal.

May 17 Paid Cohoon, Inc., for the April 17 note.

June 1 Discounted at a discount rate of 9% its own $6,000, 30-day, non-interest-bearing note, made out to the First Anytown Bank.

July 1 Paid the First Anytown Bank the amount due.

Dec. 1 Issued to the Queens Company a 9%, 90-day note for $6,000 in settlement of an open account.

Dec. 16 Discounted at a discount rate of 9% its own $20,000, 60-day, non-interest-bearing note, made out to the First National Bank.

1977
Feb. 14 Paid the First National Bank the amount due.

Mar. 1 Paid the amount due to Queens Company for the note issued on December 1, 1976.

Required: Journalize the transactions, including any necessary adjusting entries on December 31, 1976 and 1977.

DP14-4. (*Journalizing notes receivable transactions*) The following were among the transactions of the Ransom Company for 1976 and 1977:

1976
Jan. 6 Sold merchandise worth $2,400 to Harry Geer and received a 9%, 45-day note.

1976

Feb. 20 Collected the amount due from Harry Geer.

Mar. 1 Received a 9%, 75-day note for $3,600 from N. O. Ricardo in settlement of an open account.

May 15 N. O. Ricardo dishonored his note.

June 1 Sold merchandise worth $3,000 to Gene Bettie and received a 90-day, non-interest-bearing note for the amount of the sale plus interest at 9%.

Aug. 30 Collected the amount due from Gene Bettie.

Nov. 16 Received a 9%, 120-day note for $4,800 from J. T. Tomkins in settlement of an open account.

Dec. 1 Received a 90-day, non-interest-bearing note from Janie Council in settlement of an open account of $4,000. Interest of $90 was included in the face value.

1977

Mar. 1 Received the amount due from Janie Council.

16 Received the amount due from J. T. Tomkins.

Required: Journalize the transactions, including any necessary adjusting entries on December 31, 1976 and 1977.

DP14-5. (*Journalizing notes discounted transactions*) Record in general journal form the following note transactions on the books of Ben Johnson, the maker, and Walter Hinton, the payee:

1. On July 1, Ben Johnson purchased $4,400 worth of merchandise on account from Walter Hinton.
2. Ben Johnson gave to Walter Hinton a 9%, 90-day note, dated August 21, in settlement of his account.
3. On August 31, Walter Hinton discounted Ben Johnson's note at the Bank of Vancouver at a discount rate of 9%.
4. On maturity date, Ben Johnson paid the bank the maturity value of the note.

DP14-6. (*Effective interest computation*) The following transactions occurred at the McCauley Company:

1. Discounted at a bank at 9% its own 90-day, non-interest-bearing note for $10,000.
2. Borrowed $7,200 in cash from a bank; interest at 9% on $7,200 is added to the note, making the principal amount of the note $7,848. The note is to be paid off in monthly installments over 12 months ($654 each month).

Required: Compute the effective interest cost in each case.

DP14-7. (*Application of compound interest techniques*) B. E. Delayee purchases a new refrigerator at a cost of $1,200. He pays $200 down and issues an installment note payable on which he promises to pay the balance during the next year in 12 equal monthly installments including interest at 18% on the remaining unpaid balance at the beginning of each month.

Required:

1. Compute the equal installment payments.
2. Prepare the journal entries to record the first two installment payments.

P14-1. The Los Alto Company completed the following transactions with Hoot Holton:

1976

Jan. 10 Sold $2,000 worth of merchandise to Holton on account.

Mar. 1 Received a 9%, 60-day note in full settlement of the account.

17 Discounted the note at 8% at the Branch Bank.

May 5 Received a notice from the bank that Holton failed to honor the note due on April 30, 1976.

5 Paid the bank the maturity value of the note plus a protest fee of $3.50.

19 Received a check from Holton for the full amount due, plus interest at 9% on the maturity value of the old note from the due date to the present.

Required: Record the transactions in general journal form on the books of the Los Alto Company.

P14-2. (*Financial policy decision problem*) Carlene Martin borrowed $4,000 from the Hill Trust Company, giving her 9%, 60-day note. On the same day, Martin borrowed from the United Bank Company by discounting her $4,000 note for 60 days at 9%.

Required:

1. Give the entries in general journal form to record (a) both bank loans and (b) the payments of the loans on the maturity date.
2. Explain which loan was more favorable to Martin.

P14-3. During 1976, the Good-All Manufacturing Company completed the following transactions, among others:

1976

Jan. 3 Purchased merchandise worth $3,000 from the Gardner Company, giving a 9%, 30-day note, payable at the First State Bank.

4 Sold $4,000 worth of merchandise to Sam King on account.

6 Sold $2,000 worth of merchandise to Cotten Moss on account.

8 Purchased merchandise worth $1,000 from Marlow Company on account.

10 Gave Marlow Company a 9%, 30-day note, in settlement of open account (Jan. 8 purchase), payable at the Brambley Bank.

12 Cotten Moss gave a 9%, 20-day note, payable at the First State Bank.

15 Sam King gave an 8%, 30-day note, payable at the Chawta Bank.

16 Sold $5,000 worth of merchandise to Elton Primrose on account.

24 Received from Elton Primrose a 10%, 20-day note, payable at the Worcester Bank.

24 Sold $7,000 worth of merchandise to Banton Company and received a 9%, 30-day note, payable at the Quebec Bank.

Feb. 1 Cotten Moss's note of January 12 was dishonored.

2 Paid the Gardner Company for the note due today.

9 Paid the Marlow Company for the note due today.

13 Received a check from Elton Primrose for $2,000 plus interest, and

accepted a new 9%, 90-day note, payable at the Worcester Bank, for the balance of the note of January 24.

Feb. 14   Received payment from Sam King in settlement of his note due to-day.

     23   Received a check from Banton Company for $3,000 plus interest, and accepted a new 9%, 30-day note, payable at the Quebec Bank, for the balance of the note of January 24.

     28   Discounted at the Leamon Bank at 9% Banton Company's note of February 23.

Mar. 25   Received notice that Banton Company had dishonored its note of February 23. Paid the bank the maturity value of the note plus a $4 protest fee.

Required: Record the transactions in general journal form.

P14-4. On November 1, 1976, the Columbia Company adopted a policy of requesting customers whose accounts have become past due to substitute interest-bearing notes for the open account. In many cases, the company discounts the notes receivable obtained from customers. The bank charges 9% discount on such transactions.

The following ledger accounts reflect the note transactions, interest expense, and interest earned during November and December. The company closes its books at the end of the calendar year, December 31.

		Notes Receivable						Acct. No. 104	
1976					1976				
Nov.	6	B. C. Dawson, 30-day	J3	1,400	Dec.	6	B. C. Dawson	J5	1,400
	24	C. D. Dermott, 60-day	CP2	3,000					
Dec.	12	D. E. East, 90-day	J7	8,000					
	18	A. M. Ball, 8%, 30-day	J8	2,400					

		Notes Receivable Discounted						Acct. No. 104A	
					1976				
					Dec.	9	C. D. Dermott	CR2	3,000
						20	A. M. Ball	CR2	2,400

		Notes Payable						Acct. No. 202	
					1976				
					Nov.	18	Rawl Company, 8% 90-day (settle open account)	J4	4,200

				Interest Earned					**Acct. No. 311**
				1976					
				Dec.	6	B. C. Dawson	J5	10.50	
					9	C. D. Dermott	CR2	10.74	
					31	Adjustment	J10	38.00	

				Interest Expense					**Acct. No. 413**
1976									
Dec.	20	A. M. Ball	CR2	0.91					
	31	Adjustment	J11	40.13					

Required:

1. Prepare in general journal form all the entries made by the Columbia Company to record the information in the ledger accounts. Assume that all the notes bear interest at the rate of 9% unless otherwise indicated. Also assume that the accounts include the necessary adjustments for interest at December 31. For the two notes receivable discounted, determine whether the bank in fact charged interest at an annual rate of 9% (show your computation).
2. Show how the facts regarding all the notes should be disclosed in the statement of financial position.

P14-5. On June 30, the Noontide Company's trial balance included the following accounts:

Notes Receivable	$14,500
Notes Receivable Discounted (credit)	6,000

The notes receivable register showed the following supporting details:

Note No.	Face Value	Date of Note	Term of Note	Interest Rate	Remark
1	$3,500	May 29, 1976	60 days	8%	Discounted at bank on June 30, 1976; bank discount rate 9%
2	2,500	May 1, 1976	120 days	10%	Discounted at bank on June 16, 1976; bank discount rate 9%
3	4,500	June 16, 1976	30 days	7%	
4	4,000	June 21, 1976	90 days	9%	

The disposition of the four notes was:

Note 1: Paid at the bank by the maker on the maturity date.
Note 2: Dishonored by the maker. The Noontide Company paid the bank the maturity value of the note plus $4 protest fee.
Note 3: Paid by the maker on the maturity date.
Note 4: On July 10, 1976, the Noontide Company's own $3,200 non-interest-bearing note was due at the bank. Noontide Company paid its $3,200 note by discounting note 4 (the bank discount rate was 9%) and received the balance due in cash. The maker of note 4 paid the bank on the maturity date.

Required: Prepare in chronological order dated general journal entries to record the disposition of each note.

P14-6. (*Financial policy decision problem*) The Faison Appliance Company sells a standard stove for $120 in cash or on terms of $12.50 down and $20 a month for six months. In order to meet competition, the company is considering changing its credit terms to a $12.50 down payment and $10 a month for 12 months.

Required: Compute the effective annual interest rate (a) under the present plan and (b) under the proposed plan. Use the approximating method discussed in the text. (c) Which financing method should be chosen?

P14-7. At December 31, 1976, the Slavino Appliance Company's ledger contained the following information in the Notes Receivable and Notes Payable accounts:

Analysis of notes receivable:

Maker	Date of Note	Principal	Term of Note	Interest Rate	Remarks
A. Addison	Nov. 2, 1976	$ 3,600	90 days	9%	
W. Butler	Dec. 8, 1976	4,800	60 days	8%	
M. Goodwin	Dec. 16, 1976	4,090	90 days		Interest of $90 included in face value
· Total		$12,490			

Analysis of notes payable:

Payee	Date of Note	Principal	Term of Note	Interest Rate	Remarks
Leuter Company	Nov. 10, 1976	$ 5,000	120 days	8%	
Nelson Company	Nov. 20, 1976	6,000	90 days	9%	
Hill Bank	Dec. 1, 1976	8,000	120 days		Discounted at 9%
Total		$19,000			

Required: Prepare the adjusting journal entries. Show your calculations, properly labeled.

Long-Term Debt Financing

15

The financial managers of modern corporations are constantly faced with the problem of how and where to get corporate capital for both short-term and long-term needs. The various alternative sources are outlined as follows:

1. Investments of the owners (discussed in Chapter 12)
2. Retention of earnings (discussed in Chapter 13)
3. Financing by creditors, which may create current or long-term liabilities (discussed in Chapter 14 and in this chapter)

Only a summary review of current liabilities is given in this chapter, since they have been discussed in various other parts of this text, particularly Chapter 14. In this chapter more detailed attention is paid to long-term debt financing instruments such as bonds payable, mortgages payable, and liabilities under pension contracts.

REVIEW OF CURRENT LIABILITIES

As previously defined, current liabilities represent obligations, the liquidation of which requires the use of current assets or the creation of other current liabilities within a year or an operating cycle, whichever is the longer period. Various kinds of current liabilities have been discussed elsewhere in this text, such as:

Bank overdrafts
Accounts payable, trade; or vouchers payable
Notes payable, trade
Notes payable, bank
Maturing bonds payable
Current installments of serial bonds payable
Credit balances in customers' accounts
Accrued interest payable

Sales taxes payable
FICA taxes payable
State unemployment compensation taxes payable
Federal unemployment compensation taxes payable
Federal income taxes payable
Employees' income tax withholdings payable
Unearned subscriptions

Bonds payable, though they may have been originally issued with lives as long as fifty years or more, are classified as a current liability on the statement of financial position prepared at the end of the fiscal year immediately preceding the year they mature. Unearned subscriptions are not liquidated by the use of current assets but are earned within the next year or the operating cycle; current assets are consumed in the earning process. Current liabilities are generally presented on the statement of financial position at their full maturity value.

All these current liabilities provide cash or some other asset, such as merchandise. They are significant to a financial manager, since payment or refunding must be accomplished; but the management of current liabilities may also influence decisions made in regard to long-term debt financing. For example, if the dollar amount of unsecured accounts payable outstanding is considerable, these short-term creditors may bring pressure to bear to prevent the issuance of long-term secured bonds payable, an act that would give prior claims on assets to the long-term debt instrument holders.

BONDS PAYABLE

One of the means used by businesses and governments to acquire funds that will not be repaid for many years is the issuance of bonds. A *bond,* or *bond certificate,* is a written promise under the corporate seal to pay a specific sum of money on a specified or determinable future date to the order of a person named in the certificate or to the order of the bearer. An example of a corporate bond is the 9% sinking fund debentures, due 1995, issued by the Burlington Industries, Inc.

Bonds are usually issued in denominations of $100, $500, $1,000 or $5,000 each; this variation enables the issuing company to obtain funds from many different classes of investors. Denominations smaller than $100 are used by the United States government in its Series E Savings Bond issues. On the other hand, municipal bond issues in $5,000 denominations are also common.

Bonds may be issued directly by the borrowing corporation or they may be transferred to banks, brokers, or other underwriting syndicates who, in turn, market the bonds through their own channels. *Bondholders* are creditors of the corporation; with the exception noted above, the Bonds Payable account is a long-term liability. Bonds contain provisions for interest to be paid at regularly stated intervals. Interest is usually paid semiannually on industrial bonds.

A bond, like a promissory note, represents a corporate debt to the lender, which must be satisfied from the assets of the corporation in preference to stockholders' equity claims. The main functional difference between bonds and promissory notes is that bonds are used in long-term financing, whereas promissory notes are used in short-term financing. The contract or covenant between the corporation and its bondholders is called a *bond indenture*.

BONDS COMPARED WITH CAPITAL STOCK

A better knowledge of bonds may be obtained if they and related concepts are compared with capital stock. The following parallel listing should help the reader understand more fully the nature of bonds.

Bonds	Capital Stock
Bondholders are creditors.	Stockholders are owners.
Bonds Payable is a long-term liability account.	Capital Stock is a stockholders' equity account.
Bondholders, along with other creditors, have primary claims on assets in liquidation.	Stockholders have residual claims on assets in liquidation.
Interest is typically a fixed charge; it must be paid or the creditors can institute bankruptcy proceedings against the debtor corporation.	Dividends are not fixed charges; even preferred dividends are at best only *contingent charges*.
Interest is a valid expense.	Dividends are not expenses; they are distributions of net income.
Interest is deductible in arriving at both taxable and business income.	Dividends are not deductible in arriving at taxable and business income.
Bonds do not carry voting rights.	All stock carries voting rights unless they are expressly denied by contract, as is usually the case with preferred stock.

CLASSIFICATIONS OF BONDS

There are many types of bonds, each tailored to meet the particular financial needs of the issuing corporation. Some common classifications of bonds are described in the following paragraphs.

Registered Bonds. Registered bonds are issued in the name of the bondholder. They require proper endorsement on the bond certificate to effect a transfer from one owner to another. The debtor corporation or its transfer agent, usually a bank or trust company appointed by the corporation, maintains complete ownership records. Large corporations (or their transfer agents) maintain computer records of bondholders. The file of records of registered bonds is updated in the same manner as the stockholders ledger; thus the computation of interest due on registered bonds and the actual writing of checks in payment simply require the execution of a computer program on each interest date. Bonds may be registered as to both principal and interest, in which case interest checks are issued only to bondholders of record. It is possible, however, to register the principal only (*coupon bonds*); the owner detaches *interest coupons* from the bond certificate and deposits them at the stated interest dates at his bank or at a designated bank.

Bearer Bonds. Bonds may be issued without being registered in the name of the buyer; title to them is vested in the *bearer*. The procedure for making interest payments is the same as with coupon bonds. This method is least burdensome to the issuing corporation, but the owner must take particular care against loss or theft of the certificates, or unauthorized removal of the coupons attached to the bonds.

Secured Bonds. A *secured* bond is one for which the issuing corporation pledges some part of the corporate property as security for the bond. The property pledged may consist of land and buildings (*real estate mortgage* bonds), machinery (*chattel mortgage* bonds), negotiable securities (*collateral trust* bonds), or other corporate property. Several loans may use the same property for collateral; this gives rise to *first mortgage* bonds and *second mortgage* bonds. The numbers indicate the order to be followed in satisfying the mortgage-holders' claims if the corporation does not meet its obligations under the *bond indenture*—the contract between the corporation and the bondholder. In the event of default, *foreclosure* and sale of the property follow. Second and third mortgage bonds necessarily carry a higher interest rate than first mortgage bonds because of the order of priority of payment in the event of a default; thus, they are not as marketable as first mortgage bonds and are more costly to the borrowing company. It is, therefore, desirable for the borrower to raise the required funds through a single, large first mortgage bond issue.

Unsecured Bonds. Unsecured bondholders rank as general, or ordinary, creditors of the corporation and rely on the corporation's general credit. Such bonds are commonly referred to as *debenture* bonds, or often simply as *debentures.* Sometimes debenture bonds are issued with a provision that interest payments will depend on earnings; such bonds are called *income* bonds.

Bonds may have other special features; for instance, the bonds may mature in serial installments (*serial* bonds), which means that specified portions of the outstanding bonds will mature in installments and will be paid at stated intervals. Sometimes the issuing corporation retains an option to call in the bonds before maturity (*callable* bonds); or, in other cases, the bondholder may be given an option to exchange his bonds for capital stock (*convertible* bonds). The bond indenture may require the issuing corporation to deposit funds, often to a trustee for the bondholders, at regular intervals to insure the availability of adequate funds for the redemption of the bonds at maturity (*sinking fund* bonds).

MANAGEMENT REASONS FOR ISSUING BONDS INSTEAD OF CAPITAL STOCK

Among the many factors influencing management in regard to the issuance of bonds instead of capital stock is that management may be enabled to tap another market source of creditor funds that it would not be able to tap by the issuance of stock. For example, many banks and other financial institutions are not permitted by law or regulation to buy stocks, but they are allowed to buy bonds.

A second factor is *leverage,* or *trading on the bondholders' equity.* This practice can be described simply: If funds can be borrowed at an interest rate of 6 percent and utilized in the business to earn 14 percent after taxes, then the additional earnings of 8 percent (14% − 6%) accrue to the common stockholders. However, there is always the possibility of the opposite result: in other words, the borrowed funds may earn less than the cost of borrowing—an instance of unfavorable leverage.

A third reason why corporations decide to issue bonds instead of capital stock is that there is a high income tax rate on corporate net income. If a corporation pays at least half its net income in Federal and state income taxes, it naturally considers the issuance of bonds as a means of effecting a considerable tax saving.

To illustrate the way that leverage and heavy income taxes affect financial decision making involving the choice of alternative methods of fund raising, assume that the Hunt Corporation, which has $100 par value common stock outstanding in the amount of $1,000,000, needs $500,000 to purchase additional plant and equipment. Three plans are under consideration: Plan 1 is to issue additional common stock at $100 par value; Plan 2 is to issue 8% preferred stock at $100 par value, cumulative and nonparticipating; Plan 3 is to issue 7% bonds.

	Plan 1	Plan 2	Plan 3
Common stock	$1,000,000	$1,000,000	$1,000,000
Additional funds	500,000	500,000	500,000
Total	$1,500,000	$1,500,000	$1,500,000
Net income before bond interest and income taxes	$ 350,000	$ 350,000	$ 350,000
Deduct bond interest expense	–0–	–0–	35,000
Net income after bond interest expense	$ 350,000	$ 350,000	$ 315,000
Deduct income taxes (assumed rate of 50%)	175,000	175,000	157,500
Net income after income taxes	$ 175,000	$ 175,000	$ 157,500
Deduct dividends on preferred stock	–0–	40,000	–0–

	Plan 1	Plan 2	Plan 3
Available for common stock dividends	$ 175,000	$ 135,000	$ 157,500
Pro forma earnings per share on common stock (15,000 shares outstanding under Plan 1; 10,000 shares under Plans 2 and 3)	$11.67	$13.50	$15.75

All the plans assume that the securities will be issued at par value, that earnings of $350,000 annually before the bond interest expense is deducted will be maintained, and that an income tax rate of 50 percent will prevail.

Assuming that earnings per share on common stock is an accepted decision-making criterion, Plan 3 appears to be the most promising for the common stockholders, particularly if the annual earnings exceed $350,000, because the bond interest rate is fixed. If the annual earnings fall below $350,000, one of the other plans may become more advantageous. Since the securities market and corporate net earnings remain uncertain, there is no exact mathematical formula to solve this financial problem. The decision requires sound judgment based on past experience and projected future needs.

A fourth reason for the issuance of bonds instead of common stock is that bonds, and to a lesser extent preferred stock, aid in offsetting losses due to shrinkage in the purchasing power of the funds invested in assets. Bonds, for example, carry fixed contract maturity values in terms of the monetary unit at the maturity date. If the value of the dollar decreases before the bonds are paid, a gain resulting from the use of the more valuable money received at the time of borrowing accrues to the owners of the business.

A fifth factor is control. The issuance of additional common stock may result in a loss of management control, because the ownership of the corporation is distributed over a larger number of stockholders. Bondholders, on the other hand, are creditors and do not participate in managerial decisions, except in the rare instances when this is a specific provision of the bond indenture.

Other reasons may influence the decision of management to issue bonds; but these five factors indicate the scope of the problem.

AUTHORIZING THE BOND ISSUE

Even after management decides that bonds should be issued, it is faced with months of preliminary work before the bonds can actually be *floated*, or sold. For example, the exact amount to be borrowed, the *contract* or *nominal interest rate* (the rate on the bond certificate that applies to the face value), the maturity date, and the assets, if any, to be pledged must be determined. The

INCOME
MEASUREMENT
AND VALUATION

586

(Ch. 15)

provisions of the bond indenture must be chosen with extreme care. For instance, should the bonds be callable, and should they be convertible into some other form of security? Careful long-range financial planning helps to reduce the cost of securing the long-term funds. For example, if there is any chance that the company will need additional funds in the near future, management should not close the door on the possibility of marketing additional bonds by pledging the company's total mortgageable assets. In this case, management probably should seek authority for a bond issue large enough to meet all foreseeable needs.

The financial vice-president, working with other corporate officers, is responsible for finding answers to these and other questions. He prepares a written report for the board of directors, summarizing the proposed features of the bond financing and stating why the funds are needed, how they are to be used, and the means of ultimately retiring the bond issue. Various alternative methods of raising funds, such as those shown in the example of the Hunt Corporation, are presented to point up the financial advantage of issuing the bonds.

The board of directors studies this written report, along with the laws of the state in which the company is incorporated, the corporate charter, and the corporate bylaws, before passing a resolution recommending to the stockholders that bonds be issued; a record of the resolution is entered in the minute book of the corporation. Next, the proposal is presented to the stockholders for their approval. Once this approval has been gained, the board of directors prepares a resolution instructing the proper corporate officers to issue the bonds and sign the necessary documents. The final step is the issuance of a formal certified statement that the approval of the board of directors and the stockholders has been obtained. Approval by the stockholders is required because the bondholders have a preferred position; as creditors, they have a prior claim to the assets of the corporation in the event of liquidation.

ACCOUNTING FOR ISSUANCE OF BONDS

No formal journal entry is required to record the authorization of the bond issue by the stockholders, but a memorandum should be made in the Bonds Payable account indicating the total amount authorized. This information is needed when the statement of financial position is prepared, since it should disclose the total authorization as well as the amount issued.

The issue price, usually stated as a percentage of the face value, is affected primarily by the prevailing market interest rate on bonds of the same grade. Bonds are graded by various financial institutions; the grade depends on the financial condition of the issuing corporation. The highest grade is AAA; the next, AA; and in descending order: A, BBB, BB, B. If, on the issue date, the stated interest rate applicable to the face value of the bonds—also called *contract,* or *nominal,* rate—is established at the prevailing market interest rate for the particular grade of bonds, the authorized bonds will sell at face value.

On the other hand, if there is a disparity between the contract bond interest rate and the prevailing market rate for that grade of bonds, the bonds will sell at a price above or below face value, that is, at a *premium* or a *discount*.

Bonds Issued at Face Value. The first example relates to the simple situation in which a corporation issues bonds at face value (sometimes called issuance *at par*) on an interest date. The same sequence is followed in each of the first three examples. First, an entry is made to record the issuance of the bonds; next, any peculiarity of financial statement presentation is discussed; after this, the accounting procedure for interest payments is described; finally, the recording of the *retirement* of the bonds at the maturity date is shown.

Assume that on July 1, 1976, the Grogan Corporation is authorized to issue 8% debenture bonds with a face value of $200,000 and a maturity date of June 30, 1996. Interest is paid semiannually on June 30 and December 31. All the bonds are issued on July 1, 1976, at 100, or face value, and the following entry is made:

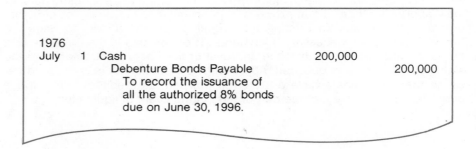

```
1976
July  1  Cash                              200,000
            Debenture Bonds Payable                    200,000
            To record the issuance of
            all the authorized 8% bonds
            due on June 30, 1996.
```

The similarity between this entry and that for the issuance of notes, discussed in Chapter 14, is clear.

A statement of financial position prepared after this transaction would report the bond issue as follows:

Long-Term Liabilities	
8% Debenture Bonds Payable, due June 30, 1996	$200,000

The following entry records the payment of interest on December 31, 1976, (the bond issue and interest payment entries are normally made in the cash receipts and cash payments journals):

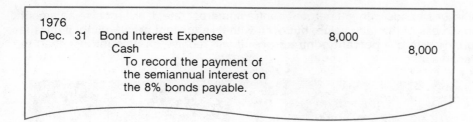

```
1976
Dec.  31    Bond Interest Expense              8,000
               Cash                                            8,000
               To record the payment of
               the semiannual interest on
               the 8% bonds payable.
```

A similar entry is made each June 30 and December 31 until the bonds are retired. It is possible for all the interest paid by the corporation to be recorded in a single Interest Expense account; however, in the present case, the interest on bonds payable is considered to be material enough to warrant a separate general ledger account.

On June 30, 1996, the bonds are retired by the payment of cash to the bondholders. The following compound entry is made on that date to record the last interest payment and the retirement of the bonds:

```
1996
June  30    Debenture Bonds Payable         200,000
            Bond Interest Expense             8,000
               Cash                                          208,000
               To record the final interest
               payment and retirement of
               the 8% bonds payable due
               today.
```

Bonds Issued at a Discount or a Premium. If the average effective market interest rate on bonds of any particular grade exceeds the contract interest rate of bonds of the same grade being issued, investors will offer less than the face value of the bonds in order to make up the difference between the rates. The difference between the issue price and the maturity value, plus receipts of the semiannual interest, will give the investors a return on their investments approximating the yield of similar amounts invested at the prevailing market interest rate. By the same token, if the stated interest rate is more favorable than the current market rate, investors will tend to offer more than the face value, because they know that the premium paid will, in effect, be returned to them to the extent that the periodic interest payments exceed the amount that they would otherwise receive on investments made at the current market rate.

Two examples are presented to emphasize the reasons for bonds selling at a premium or a discount. First, assume that the Strong Company has an AAA financial rating and is planning to issue debenture bonds. Assume also that all the AAA debenture bonds on the market have an effective average market interest rate of 8 percent. If the Strong Company issues debenture bonds with an 8 percent contract interest rate, it will receive the face value of the bonds; if

(Ch. 15)

it issues bonds with a 9 percent contract interest rate, it will receive an amount in excess of the face value; but even with its excellent credit rating, if it issues bonds with a 7 percent contract rate, it will receive an amount less than the face value.

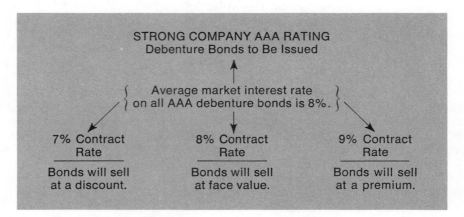

STRONG COMPANY AAA RATING
Debenture Bonds to Be Issued

Average market interest rate on all AAA debenture bonds is 8%.

| 7% Contract Rate | 8% Contract Rate | 9% Contract Rate |
| Bonds will sell at a discount. | Bonds will sell at face value. | Bonds will sell at a premium. |

The second example will help to show that the financial condition of a company is not the basic determinant of the issue price of the company's bonds. Assume that the Weak Company, with a BB financial rating, intends to issue first mortgage bonds. Further assume that the average effective market interest rate on BB first mortgage bonds is 9 percent. If the Weak Company issues its bonds with a 9 percent contract interest rate, it will receive the face value of the bonds. Even with its relatively poor credit rating, if it issues bonds with a 10 percent contract interest rate, is will receive an amount in excess of the face value; but if it issues bonds with an 8 percent contract interest rate, it will receive an amount less than the face value.

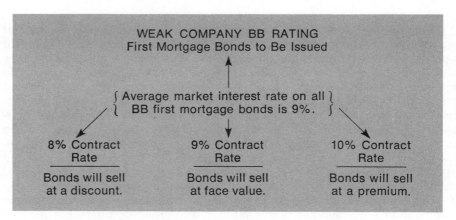

WEAK COMPANY BB RATING
First Mortgage Bonds to Be Issued

Average market interest rate on all BB first mortgage bonds is 9%.

| 8% Contract Rate | 9% Contract Rate | 10% Contract Rate |
| Bonds will sell at a discount. | Bonds will sell at face value. | Bonds will sell at a premium. |

Calculation of the Exact Price of Bonds to Yield a Given Rate

The exact price that an investor must pay for the bonds to yield a given effective rate can be determined by a compound interest computation or by reference to a *bond yield table*. To illustrate the compound interest computation, assume that a 10-year (20 semiannual periods), 8%, $1,000 bond with interest paid semiannually is to yield 6 percent (or 3 percent every six months). The issue price is calculated as shown below.

Present value of $1,000 for 20 periods at 3%:	
$1,000 × 0.553676	$ 553.68
Add present value of 20 interest payments of $40 each at 3%:	
$40 × 14.877475	595.10
Total price to yield 6% annually	$1,148.78

Accounting for Bonds Issued at a Premium—Straight-Line Amortization Method

Assume that on July 1, 1976, the Hunt Corporation is authorized to issue 8% first mortgage bonds with a face value of $300,000 and a maturity date of June 30, 1991. Interest is paid semiannually on June 30 and December 31. All the bonds are issued on July 1, 1976, at 103; that is, at 103 percent of their face value; and the following entry is made:

1976				
July	1	Cash	309,000	
		First Mortgage Bonds Payable		300,000
		Premium on Bonds Payable		9,000
		To record the issuance of		
		8% first mortgage bonds		
		due June 30, 1991.		

A statement of financial position prepared on July 1, 1976, would show Bonds Payable and Premium on Bonds Payable as follows:

Long-Term Liabilities		
8% First Mortgage Bonds Payable, due		
June 30, 1991	$300,000	
Premium on Bonds Payable	9,000	
Total Long-Term Liabilities		$309,000

The assets pledged as security for the bonds payable would be disclosed in the following footnote:

Land and buildings costing $600,000 (market value $650,000) are pledged as security for the bonds payable.

(Ch. 15)

This method of disclosure is consistent with the concept that the right side of the statement of financial position describes the sources of business funds. Of course, the Premium account will be reduced by periodic amortization and thus will be smaller on each subsequent statement; but, again, this procedure is consistent with the concept that when bonds are issued at a premium, each interest payment contains, in effect, a payment of the interest earned on the investment and also a partial return of the amount borrowed from the investor. If part of the $309,000 borrowed is repaid, a statement of financial position prepared at a later date would naturally show a smaller amount. The footnote describing the assets pledged as security for the long-term debt is a disclosure of important information that may influence the decision of an investor to buy or not to buy the company's bonds.

The amount received from the issuance of the bonds is $9,000 greater than the amount that must be repaid at maturity. This amount is not a gain, for it is illogical to assume that revenue can result directly from the borrowing process. The premium arose because the contract rate of interest on the bonds issued was higher than the prevailing market rate on similar grade bonds; therefore, it is sound accounting practice to allocate part of the premium on bonds payable to each period as a reduction of the periodic bond interest expense. The straight-line method of allocation is most commonly used, and will be emphasized in this text; however, the compound interest method of premium and discount amortization is illustrated in the Appendix to this chapter. In summary, the total bond interest expense over the life of a bond issue is equal to the total amount of cash paid in interest reduced by the amount of the premium.

The bond interest expense of the Hunt Corporation is recorded on December 31, 1976, as follows:

1976			
Dec. 31	Bond Interest Expense	11,700	
	Premium on Bonds Payable	300	
	Cash		12,000
	To record the semiannual bond interest payment and amortization; the amount of the amortization is $\frac{1}{2} \times \frac{1}{15} \times \$9,000 = \$300$		

If the $9,000 premium on the bonds payable represents a reduction in interest over the entire 15-year life of the bonds, it is evident that by the straight-line amortization method the reduction in interest for the six months ended December 31, 1976, is $9,000 divided by 30 semiannual periods (calculated as $\frac{1}{2} \times \frac{1}{15} \times \$9,000$ in the journal entry), or $300.

This compound entry emphasizes that the $12,000 constitutes the payment of effective bond interest expense of $11,700 and a partial return of the amount borrowed, the $300 amortized. (It is suggested that, for the problems in this text, premiums or discounts on bonds payable be amortized each time the bond interest expense is recorded to emphasize that this amortization is an adjustment of the bond interest expense.) Even though the compound entry is acceptable, two separate entries may be made: (1) one entry to record the payment of the semiannual bond interest, and (2) a separate entry to record the semiannual amortization of the premium.

Assuming the use of straight-line amortization of the premium on bonds payable, the validity of the $11,700 semiannual bond interest figure can be established as follows:

Cash payments		
Face value of bonds at maturity		$300,000
Total interest—8% × 15 years × $300,000		360,000
Total cash payments		$660,000
Cash receipts		
Bonds with face value of $300,000 issued at 103		309,000
Net interest expense for 15 years		$351,000
Net semiannual interest expense		
$351,000		
30 semiannual periods		$ 11,700

A formula for the approximation of effective interest rate (i) on bonds issued at a premium can be stated as follows:

$$i = I \div \left(F + \frac{P}{2} \right)$$

where I = annual absolute interest, adjusted for amortization of premium
F = face value of bonds

P = total premium (so that $\dfrac{P}{2}$ = average premium)

The effective interest rate on the Hunt Corporation bonds is approximately 7.68 percent [$23,400 ÷ ($300,000 + $9,000/2)]—that is, the absolute effective amount of annual interest divided by the average carrying value (face value plus unamortized premium) of the bonds issued. Exact effective rates may be determined readily from bond yield tables or by using compound interest techniques. The effective interest rate computation emphasizes the face that the premium on the bonds results in a downward adjustment of the 8 percent contract rate to the effective rate.

Assume that the 8% first mortgage bonds payable are retired on June 30, 1991. After the June 30, 1991, semiannual interest payment entry is made, the Premium on Bonds Payable account has a zero balance. The second entry, recording the retirement of the bonds at maturity, is similar to the one that records the retirement of the Grogan Company bonds in the first bond example.

(Ch. 15)

```
1991
June  30   Bond Interest Expense              11,700
           Premium on Bonds Payable              300
              Cash                                       12,000
                 To record the last
                 semiannual interest payment
                 on the 8% bonds payable
                 and the last semiannual
                 amortization of bond
                 premium.

      30   First Mortgage Bonds Payable     300,000
              Cash                                      300,000
                 To record the retirement of
                 the 8% bonds payable at
                 maturity.
```

Accounting for Bonds Issued at a Discount—Straight-Line Amortization Method

Assume that on July 1, 1976, the Ironson Company is authorized to issue 7% debenture bonds with a face value of $400,000 and a maturity date of June 30, 1986. Again, assume that interest is paid semiannually on June 30 and December 31. All the bonds are issued on July 1, 1976, at 97. The discount is caused by the difference in the prevailing market interest rate on similar grades of debenture bonds and the contract rate of interest on the bonds issued. In the case of the Ironson Company's debenture bonds, their contract interest rate is lower than the prevailing market rate on a similar grade of securities. The issuance of these bonds may be recorded as follows:

```
1976
July   1   Cash                             388,000
           Discount on Bonds Payable          12,000
              Debenture Bonds Payable                  400,000
                 To record the issuance of
                 7% debenture bonds due
                 June 30, 1980.
```

A statement of financial position prepared on July 1, 1976, would disclose Bonds Payable and Discount on Bonds Payable as follows:

Long-Term Liabilities		
7% Debenture Bonds Payable, due June 30, 1986	$400,000	
Deduct Discount on Bonds Payable	12,000	
Total Long-Term Liabilities		$388,000

Note the similarity of this method to the disclosure of a premium on bonds payable.

The following compound entry records the first semiannual interest payment by the Ironson Company and semiannual amortization of the Discount on Bonds Payable account.

1976			
Dec. 31	Bond Interest Expense	14,600	
	Cash		14,000
	Discount on Bonds Payable		600
	To record semiannual bond interest payment and amortization; the amount of amortization is		
	$\frac{1}{2} \times \frac{1}{10} \times \$12,000 = \$600$		

This entry indicates that the effective semiannual interest expense is $14,600, not $14,000. Assuming that the straight-line method of amortization is used, the effective interest is equal to the cash interest payment plus a pro rata share of the discount, which is, in effect, a part of the total interest cost over the entire life of the bonds. This accounting procedure, therefore, recognizes the reason for the discount on the bonds—that the contract rate of interest was lower than the prevailing market interest rate on similar grades of securities.

Assuming the use of straight-line amortization of the discount on bonds payable, the proof of this semiannual bond interest expense can be established as follows:

Cash payments	
Face value of bonds at maturity	$400,000
Total interest—7% × 10 years × $400,000	280,000
Total cash payments	$680,000
Cash receipts	
Bonds with face value of $400,000 issued at 97	388,000
Net interest expense for 10 years	$292,000
Net semiannual interest expense	
$\dfrac{\$292,000}{20 \text{ semiannual periods}}$	$ 14,600

A formula for the approximation of effective interest rate (i) on bonds issued at a discount can be stated as follows:

$$i = I \div \left(F - \frac{D}{2} \right)$$

where I = annual absolute interest, adjusted for amortization of discount
F = face value of bonds
D = total discount (so that $\dfrac{D}{2}$ = average discount)

The effective interest rate is approximately 7.41 percent [$29,200 ÷ ($400,000 − $12,000/2)]. Again, an exact effective interest rate may be determined readily from bond yield tables or by using compound interest techniques. The bond discount results in an upward adjustment of the 7 percent contract rate to its effective yield rate of 7.41 percent.

On June 30, 1986, the 7% debenture bonds payable are retired. After the June 30, 1976, semiannual interest payment entry is made, the Discount on Bonds Payable account has a zero balance. The second entry records the retirement of the bonds at maturity.

1986			
June 30	Bond Interest Expense	14,600	
	Cash		14,000
	Discount on Bonds Payable		600
	To record the last semiannual interest payment and final amortization of bond discount on the 7% bonds payable.		
30	Debenture Bonds Payable	400,000	
	Cash		400,000
	To record the retirement of the 7% bonds payable at maturity.		

Amortization and End-of-Period Adjustments

The preceding examples emphasized the basic accounting procedures and the reasons for amortizing bond premiums and discounts. A more complex problem involving the issuance of bonds between interest dates is presented below.

Bonds may be authorized by the stockholders but not issued for several months or even years because market conditions are not favorable. Some of the bonds may be issued and the rest held until a specific need for the additional funds arises. Often, the time needed for clerical work delays issuance past an interest date. The interest on bonds issued between interest dates will have accrued from the last interest date to the date of issuance. Since the bonds carry an inherent promise to pay not only the face value at maturity but six months' interest at each interest date, it is customary in these cases for the investor to pay the issue price of the bonds plus an amount equal to the accrued interest. In turn, the first interest payment will be for one full interest period—six months' interest—thereby returning to the purchaser the accrued interest that he paid plus the interest earned from the date of purchase to the current interest date.

Assume that on October 1, 1974, the Johnson Company is authorized to issue 9% debenture bonds with a face value of $1,000,000 and a maturity date of October 1, 1984. The semiannual interest dates are April 1 and October 1.

(Ch. 15)

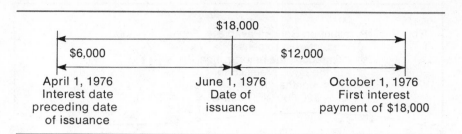

Figure 15-1
Accumulation of
Interest

The bonds are held until June 1, 1976, when bonds with a face value of $400,000 are floated at 105 plus accrued interest. The amount of cash that the Johnson Company receives is $426,000: $420,000 for the bonds plus $6,000 for accrued interest. Note that the promise to pay six months' interest is not retroactive beyond April 1, 1976, the interest date preceding the date of issuance. On October 1, 1976, the purchaser of the bonds receives an interest payment of $18,000, although the interest on $400,000 at 9 percent from June 1 to October 1 is only $12,000. The payment includes a return of the $6,000 that the investor paid for accrued interest on June 1, as illustrated in Figure 15-1.

The Johnson Company records the bond issuance as shown below.

1976		
June 1 Cash	426,000	
Debenture Bonds Payable		400,000
Premium on Bonds Payable		20,000
Accrued Bond Interest		
Payable		6,000
To record the issuance of		
bonds at 105 plus		
accrued interest.		

The accrued interest is credited to a current liability account, since it must be repaid on the next interest date.

The entries to record the payment of semiannual interest and the amortization of bond premium are shown below.

1976		
Oct. 1 Bond Interest Expense	12,000	
Accrued Bond Interest Payable	6,000	
Cash		18,000
To record the payment of		
semiannual interest on 9%		
bonds payable.		

```
1976
Oct.   1   Premium on Bonds Payable              800
               Bond Interest Expense                          800
                   To record the amortization
                   of the bond premium for
                   four months:
                       $20,000 ÷ 100 mos. × 4 = $800
```

The entry for the interest payment reflects the amounts shown in Figure 15-1; that is, the semiannual cash payment includes a return of $6,000 for the accrued interest that was sold to the investor plus $12,000 for interest actually earned by the investor for the four months' use of his money.

Amortization Period   The amortization covers only the period from the date of issuance to the maturity date.

The date of authorization and even the preceding interest date are not relevant to the start of the amortization period. For the bonds of the Johnson Company, the amortization period begins on June 1, 1976, and ends on October 1, 1984, a total of 100 months. The amount of bond premium to be amortized each month is $200 = ($20,000 ÷ 100 mos.); the amount for four months is $800 = ($200 × 4).

Assuming that the Johnson Company closes its books on a calendar-year basis, the following adjusting entries are made on December 31, 1976:

```
1976
Dec.   31   Bond Interest Expense               9,000
                Accrued Bond Interest
                    Payable                                  9,000
                    To record the accrual of
                    bond interest for three
                    months.
        31   Premium on Bonds Payable             600
                Bond Interest Expense                         600
                    To record the
                    amortization of bond
                    premium for three months:
                        3 × $200 = $600
```

The effect of the end-of-year adjustments is that the Bond Interest Expense account reflects the correct interest expense ($19,600) incurred for the seven months during which the bonds were outstanding (June 1 to December 31).

The Bond Interest Expense account is closed to Income Summary. The Accrued Bond Interest Payable account is shown as a current liability on the statement of financial position and remains on the books until the next regular interest date.

On April 1, 1977, the next regular interest date, the following entries are made to record the payment of interest and the amortization of the bond premium:

1977				
Apr.	1	Bond Interest Expense	9,000	
		Accrued Bond Interest Payable	9,000	
		Cash		18,000
		To record the payment of semiannual bond interest.		
	1	Premium on Bonds Payable	600	
		Bond Interest Expense		600
		To record the amortization of bond premium for three months.		

Note that only three months' amortization of the bond premium is recorded. This coincides with the three months' bond interest expense incurred and recorded to April 1, 1977.

RETIREMENT AND REFUNDING OF BONDS PAYABLE

The borrowing company may retire its outstanding bonds at the maturity date by paying the contract face value in cash. Even if the bonds were originally issued at a premium or a discount, the entry to record the retirement is a debit to Bonds Payable and a credit to Cash for the face value. Serial bonds are retired in serial installments. Assume, for example, a $500,000, 10-year serial bond issue, $50,000 to be retired at face value at the end of each year. The annual retirement entry is again a debit to Bonds Payable and a credit to Cash for $50,000. The retirement schedule is established by the issuing corporation and may provide for several retirement dates beginning a fixed number of years after the date of issue.

Other methods of retiring bonds include (1) the retirement of all or part of a bond issue by call, or purchase on the open market before the bonds are actually due, (2) the retirement of bonds by *refunding,* or refinancing by issuing new bonds on new terms, (3) the conversion of bonds payable into capital stock, and (4) the retirement of bonds with sinking fund assets and the attendant problem of accumulating the sinking fund.

Retirement of Bonds before Maturity. A corporation that has issued bonds may find itself with more cash than it expects to need for operations, thus permitting it to retire all or part of its outstanding bonded indebtedness prior to

(Ch. 15)

maturity date. Management may decide to retire the bonds immediately if the cash is available, if there appears to be no better alternative use now or in the future for the excess cash, and if it wishes to decrease the fixed charges for the bond interest. For bonds to be retired by a corporation before maturity, the indenture must contain a *call provision,* permitting the issuing corporation to redeem the bonds by paying a specified price, usually slightly above face value; or if the bonds are not callable, the issuing company may redeem them before the maturity date by purchasing them on the open market. Retirement of bonds below the carrying value adjusted to the date of retirement results in a gain; a loss is incurred if the purchase price exceeds the adjusted carrying value. Gains and losses on the retirement of bonds payable are classified in the income statement under Other Revenue or Other Expense.

Refunding. Bonds also may be retired by refunding, or refinancing by issuing new bonds on new terms. The proceeds from the new issue are specifically designated for the retirement of the old bond issue. The old bondholders may be given the option of exchanging their bonds for the new bonds at the call price. This procedure helps reduce the refinancing costs of the issuing corporation. A refunding decision may be warranted if it is possible to redeem bonds with a relatively high interest rate and to substitute bonds with a lower interest rate. Other reasons for refunding are to replace an issue about to mature with a new issue, thus extending the maturity date, or to retire outstanding bonds containing such stringent restrictive provisions as a closed mortgage lien or a requirement that funds be accumulated to retire the bonds.

In the accounting procedure for refunding, the retirement should be recorded in entries similar to those described in the preceding section. Accounting for the new issue is the same as described earlier in this chapter.

Conversion of Bonds into Common Stock. To make certain bonds more attractive to investors, and thus to increase their marketability, the bond agreement may give investors the option of exchanging bonds on a given interest date, or dates, for a certain number of shares of stock, usually common, of the issuing company. These securities, referred to as convertible bonds, have the advantage of offering the investor an initial fixed return on his investment combined with an opportunity to share in profitable operations of the issuing company by later conversion of the bonds to stock. The terms and conditions for conversion are designated in the bond indenture. Conversion is at the option of the bondholder, so that if earnings are unfavorable he does not need to exercise the conversion privilege and may retain the fixed return and greater security of the bonds. The conversion of bonds into stock changes the legal and accounting status of the security holder from creditor to owner. When conversion occurs, the generally accepted accounting procedure is to transfer the carrying value of the convertible bonds payable to paid-in capital accounts, which probably will include both Common Stock and Premium on Common Stock.

Bond Sinking Fund. The borrowing corporation may agree in the bond indenture to accumulate funds to retire the bonds at maturity. Periodic cash payments are made to a sinking fund trustee, usually a bank or a trust company. These payments are ordinarily invested in revenue-producing securities. When the bonds mature, the sinking fund trustee sells the securities, and the proceeds are used to pay the bondholders. In some instances the corporation itself may act as trustee, thereby retaining control over the activities of the sinking fund.

To illustrate the operation of a simple nonactuarial sinking fund managed by a trustee, assume that on the authorization date, January 1, 1976, Wells, Inc., issues 10-year sinking fund bonds with a face value of $500,000. The bond indenture provides that at the end of each year a deposit of $50,000—reduced by any net earnings of the funds from its investments—be made to the trustee. The entry to record the initial deposit with the trustee is shown below.

```
1976
Dec.  31   Bond Sinking Fund                    50,000
               Cash                                          50,000
                   To record the initial sinking
                   fund deposit with the
                   trustee.
```

The Bond Sinking Fund account is a controlling account. The trustee must invest all the available cash in the fund in revenue-producing securities. As a practical matter, it would not always be possible for the trustee to invest odd amounts of cash or to purchase securities immediately on the receipt of cash. Hence, the bond sinking fund is composed of a number of individual items, such as cash, securities, and accrued interest receivable. It is unnecessary for Wells, Inc., to maintain a separate general ledger account for each asset contained in the bond sinking fund.

If, at the end of the second year, the trustee reports net earnings of $1,500 from investments in bonds, the following entries record the second deposit:

```
1977
Dec.  31   Bond Sinking Fund                     1,500
               Interest Earned                                1,500
                   To record net earnings of
                   the bond sinking fund per
                   report of the trustee.

      31   Bond Sinking Fund                    48,500
               Cash                                          48,500
                   To record the second
                   sinking fund deposit with the
                   trustee; the amount is
                   $50,000 less earnings of
                   $1,500, or $48,500.
```

The following entry is made to record the retirement of the bonds at maturity by the payment of assets in the bond sinking fund:

(Ch. 15)

```
1986
Jan.    1   Sinking Fund Bonds Payable        500,000
            Bond Sinking Fund                              500,000
              To record the retirement of
              bonds by the trustee.
```

The Bond Sinking Fund account is classified in the Assets section as a long-term investment on each statement of financial position except the one prepared at the end of the year preceding the date of the retirement of the bonds. On this statement, Bond Sinking Fund should be shown as a current asset and Sinking Fund Bonds Payable should be disclosed as a current liability.

The actuarial method of accumulating a sinking fund provides for an equal sum to be deposited periodically with the trustee. It is assumed that these deposits, accumulating at compound interest, will equal the principal sum needed to retire the debt at maturity. This equal sum (in the Wells, Inc., case) is determined by dividing the required maturity amount of $500,000 by the amount of an ordinary annuity of 10 rents of $1 each at the estimated annual earning rate of the fund. If, at the retirement date, the accumulated funds exceed the required amount, the excess is returned by the trustee to the corporation; a shortage, on the other hand, requires an additional deficiency payment from the corporation.

Restriction on Retained Earnings for Bond Redemption. In addition to the requirement for sinking fund deposits, the bond indenture may require a restriction on retained earnings up to the amount in the sinking fund. The bondholders thus are provided with twofold protection: the sinking fund ensures the availability of adequate cash for the redemption of the bonds, and the restriction on retained earnings for bond redemption reduces the amount available for distribution as dividends to the stockholders. This restriction enhances the company's working capital position and its ability to meet its regular needs as well as its requirements for bond interest and bond sinking fund payments. An improved working capital position also is advantageous in enabling the company to meet its regular operational cash requirements and to maintain a favorable credit standing.

To illustrate, assume that the bond indenture of Wells, Inc., provides for a restriction of retained earnings. The entry at the end of each year is:

```
Dec.  31   Retained Earnings                  50,000
             Retained Earnings—
             Restricted for Bond
             Redemption                                    50,000
               To record the restriction
               of retained earnings equal
               to the annual increase in
               the bond sinking fund.
```

Retained Earnings—Restricted for Bond Redemption is shown in the Stockholders' Equity section of the statement of financial position under Retained Earnings. It should be noted that the provisions of the bond indenture may require (1) the creation of the bond sinking fund only, (2) a restriction on retained earnings until the bonds are redeemed only, or (3) both a bond sinking fund and a restriction on retained earnings. When the bonds are redeemed at maturity, the contractual restriction on retained earnings is removed. The journal entry to record the removal of the restriction is:

```
1986
Jan.   1   Retained Earnings—Restricted
               for Bond
               Redemption                    500,000
               Retained Earnings                        500,000
                   To remove the restriction
                   on retained earnings on
                   retirement of the bonds.
```

The unrestricted Retained Earnings account now has been increased by an amount equal to the maturity value of the bonds. The equivalent amount in funds may not be available for distribution to the stockholders, because it has been permanently committed to the operations of the business in the form of plant expansion or debt retirement. In essence, the stockholders have been contributing capital to the corporation through earnings retained in the business that might otherwise have been distributed as dividends. Formal recognition of this fact is often made in the form of a declaration of a stock dividend.

OTHER LONG-TERM LIABILITIES

Among long-term liabilities found on the statement of financial position are those arising from the use of long-term financing devices such as secured or unsecured long-term notes and continuing obligations incurred under employee profit-sharing and pension plans and similar forms. Brief comments are made about each of these.

Instead of issuing bonds, a corporation may borrow from financial institutions, such as banks or insurance companies. A group of banks or insurance companies may jointly finance the transaction. By this arrangement, the corporation eliminates the need for dealing with many bondholders. The corporation issues long-term notes to the lending institutions. Such notes may also provide for a sinking fund and for a restriction on retained earnings. Notes are usually issued at face value; hence the accounting for these items is similar to that for short-term notes. They may be for a short period with optional renewal provi-

(Ch. 15)

sions. Renewable notes are often used when the bond interest rate is unfavorable.

Long-term financing may involve the pledging of specific assets. A corporation may, for example, acquire funds for plant expansion or other purposes by placing a mortgage on its plant and equipment. This creates a long-term liability—Mortgage Payable. Sometimes the lending institution advances funds for the construction of the plant and upon completion takes a mortgage on the newly constructed plant. This is known as a *construction mortgage payable*. The title of the liability account should clearly indicate the nature and type of instrument used.

Accounting for liabilities under pension contracts and similar forms is rather complex and specialized; therefore, only very brief comments are made in this text. The accounting for employees' pension costs and the related liability depends on whether the employees' rights in such plans are forfeitable or nonforfeitable. Under the forfeitable plans, a separate trust must be established; hence the company's long-term liability is usually limited to the cumulative amount of each year's contribution to the pension or profit-sharing trust. Under the nonforfeitable plan, the company simply accrues the liability on the books and records the offsetting expense. The amounts involved are usually determined by the use of compound actuarial tables.

The computation by use of present value techniques of the exact price of an 8% 10-year $1,000 bond sold to yield 6 percent was determined to be $1,148.78 calculated on page 591. If this bond were authorized and issued by the Edwards Corporation on January 1, 1976, with a maturity data of December 31, 1985, and with interest dates of June 30 and December 31, it would be recorded as follows:

```
1976
Jan.   1   Cash                              1,148.78
              Bonds Payable                              1,000.00
              Premium on Bonds Payable                     148.78
                 To record issuance of 8%
                 bonds to yield 6%.
```

An alternative to the straight-line method of amortization is the compound-interest method, sometimes called the *effective-yield* method of amortization. In other words, the interest expense is reported at the effective or yield rate multiplied by the carrying value of the bonds with the amount of amortization being the difference between the effective interest so computed and the nominal interest, calculated by multiplying the nominal interest rate by the face value of the bonds.

The effective-interest calculation and attendant compound-interest amortization for June 30 and December 31 appear below.

```
1976
June  30   Bond Interest Expense (3% ×
              $1,148.78)                      34.46
           Premium on Bonds Payable
              ($40.00 − $34.46)                5.54
              Cash                                          40.00
                 To record payment of
                 interest and amortization
                 of premium on a 6%
                 annual yield basis.

Dec.  31   Bond Interest Expense [(3% ×
              ($1,148.78 − $5.54)]            34.30
           Premium on Bonds Payable
              ($40.00 − $34.30)                5.70
              Cash                                          40.00
                 To record payment of
                 interest and amortization
                 of premium on a 6%
                 annual yield basis.
```

LONG-TERM
DEBT
FINANCING

(Ch. 15)

A similar procedure is used when the compound-interest method of amortization is applied to bonds issued at a discount.

It should be noted that the foregoing procedure will produce a constant yield on the carrying value of the bonds payable, face plus unamortized premium or face minus unamortized discount. Compare this with the results achieved with the straight-line method of amortization: a constant absolute interest amount related to bond carrying value that will be reduced over time will produce an "effective" interest rate that increases in subsequent years. The compound-interest method of amortization is superior to the straight-line method because of this peculiarity; but because of the complexity of the compound-interest calculation, the attendant effective-yield method of amortization is seldom used in practice.

GLOSSARY

Amortization of Premium or Discount on Bonds Payable The periodic writing off of the premium or discount on bonds payable as a decrease or an increase to interest expense; amortization can be accomplished by the straight-line method or by the compound-interest method.

Bearer Bond A bond issued without the owner's name being registered; the title to this kind of bond is deemed to be vested in the holder of the bond.

Bond A written promise under the corporate seal to pay a specified sum of money on a specified or determinable future date to the order of a person named in the bond certificate or to the order of bearer.

Bond Certificate Evidence that a loan has been made to a corporation; it contains the written promise under the corporate seal to pay a specific sum of money on a specified or determinable future date to the order of a person named in the certificate or to the order of bearer.

Bondholder A creditor who has lent money to a corporation or government and has received a bond certificate as evidence of the loan.

Bond Indenture A contract between the corporation issuing bonds and the bondholder; it will contain all privileges, restrictions, covenants, and other provisions, contained in this form of contract.

Bond Sinking Fund Segregation of assets for the purpose of retiring bonds usually at maturity.

Callable Bond A bond for which the issuing corporation retains an option to retire the bonds before maturity at a specified price on specific dates.

Carrying Value of Bonds Payable The face or principal amount of the bonds payable plus the unamortized premium, or face minus the unamortized discount on bonds payable.

Compound-Interest Method of Amortization Sometimes referred to as the effective-yield method of amortization; the periodic amortization is the difference between the nominal rate of interest computed on the face value of the bonds and the effective-yield rate of interest computed on the book value of the investment at the beginning of the current interest period.

Contract or Nominal Interest Rate The rate of interest that is written in a bond indenture; it is the rate based on face or principal amount that will be paid on the stated periodic interest dates.

Convertible Bond A bond that contains a provision entitling the bondholder to exchange the bond for capital stock at the bondholder's option.

Coupon Bond A bond that has the periodic interest coupon attached to the bond certificate.

Current Liabilities Obligations the liquidation of which requires the use of current assets or the creation of other current liabilities within a year or an operating cycle whichever is the longer period.

Debenture Bond Often referred to as a debenture; it is an unsecured bond—one that carries no specific pledge of collateral.

Discount on Bonds Payable The amount by which the face value of bonds exceeds the price received for the bonds on issuance; it arises because the nominal (contract) rate of interest is lower than the going market rate of interest on similar grade bonds.

Effective-Yield Rate The constant rate of interest that, when applied to all future cash flows from an investment on a discount basis, will reduce those flows to the present market price or value of the investment.

Income Bond A bond with a provision that interest payments will depend upon earnings.

Leverage Usually refers to the practice of trading on the bondholders' equity; that is, the practice of borrowing money at a given rate of interest and utilizing the borrowed funds in the business to earn a higher rate of return than the borrowing rate.

Premium on Bonds Payable The excess of the price received for bonds payable above face value; it arises because the nominal (contract) rate of interest is higher than the going market rate of interest on similar grade bonds.

Registered Bond A bond whose owner's name is recorded by the issuing corporation; for this bond to be transferred to another individual, it must be endorsed and a request must be filed to have the owner's name changed on the records of the issuing corporation.

Secured Bond A bond for which the issuing corporation pledges some part of the firm's property as security in case of financial difficulty.

Serial Bonds Bonds that mature in periodic installments and will be paid at stated intervals of time.

Trading on the Bondholders' Equity A practice of borrowing money at a given rate of interest and utilizing the borrowed funds in the business to earn a higher rate of return than the borrowing rate.

Unsecured Bond A bond for which there is no specific pledge of assets for security; these are also called debenture bonds.

Q15-1. Distinguish between *nominal* and *effective* interest rates on bonds.

Q15-2. On January 1, 1976, the Durham Sales Company issued 20-year, 8% bonds having a face value of $2,000,000. Interest is payable semiannually on June 30 and December 31. The proceeds to the company were $1,900,000; that is, on January 1, 1976, the bonds had a market price of 95% of face value.

Explain the nature of the $100,000 difference between the face value and the market value of the bonds on January 1, 1976.

Q15-3. What is the difference (a) between a stock certificate and a bond? (b) between a bond and a promissory note?

Q15-4. Identify the following terms: (a) registered bonds, (b) bearer bonds, (c) secured bonds, (d) unsecured bonds, (e) serial bonds, (f) convertible bonds, (g) coupon bonds, (h) income bonds.

Q15-5. A corporation needs cash for the acquisition of plant and equipment. It is considering three alternative sources: additional common stock, 9% preferred stock, and 8% bonds. (a) What are some of the factors involved in this decision? (b) Will the decision affect the present common stockholders? Discuss.

Q15-6. (a) What are the general requirements for the approval of a bond issue? (b) Should the stockholders always approve a bond issue? Why?

Q15-7. (a) Why does the buyer of a bond purchased between interest dates pay the seller for accrued interest on the bond? (b) Is the accrued interest included in the stated purchase price of the bond?

Q15-8. Why are bonds not always issued at the prevailing interest rate, thereby eliminating bond discount or bond premium?

Q15-9. (a) What is the difference to the issuing corporation between common stock issued at a premium and bonds issued at a premium? (b) Does revenue result from either?

Q15-10. On December 31, 1976, a corporation has serial bonds outstanding with a face value of $1,000,000. These bonds mature annually in $200,000 amounts, beginning June 30, 1977. How will this be shown on the position statement as of (a) December 31, 1976, (b) December 31, 1977, and (c) December 31, 1978?

EXERCISES

E15-1. On the date of authorization, January 1, 1976, the Kaboodle Corporation issued 20-year, 8% bonds with a face value of $800,000 at 100. Interest is payable each January 1 and July 1.

1. Record the issuance of the bonds.
2. Record the first interest payment.
3. Record the accrued interest expense on December 31, 1976.
4. Record the retirement of the bonds on January 1, 1996, by the payment of cash.

E15-2. On the date of authorization, January 1, 1976, the Columbia Corporation issued 10-year, 9% bonds with a face value of $500,000 at 102. Interest is payable each January 1 and July 1.

1. Record the issuance of the bonds.
2. Record the first interest payment and amortization of the premium by the straight-line amortization method.
3. Record the accrued interest expense and amortization of the premium on December 31, 1976.
4. Open a Bond Interest Expense account and post the transactions.

INCOME
MEASUREMENT
AND VALUATION

(Ch. 15)

5. Prepare a schedule proving the interest cost for 1976 by the straight-line amortization method.

6. Compute the approximate effective interest rate.

E15-3. (Appendix). On the date of authorization, July 1, 1976, the Baker Investment Company issued 10-year, 8% bonds with a face value of $1,000,000 at a price to yield 10%. Interest is payable June 30 and December 31.

1. Compute the value of the bonds to yield 10% (that is, 5% each six months).

2. Record the issuance of the bonds on July 1, 1976.

3. Record the December 31, 1976, and June 30, 1977, interest payments with accompanying amortization, using the effective-yield, or compound interest, method of amortization.

4. Briefly compare the reasons for using the effective-yield method of amortization as compared to the straight-line method of amortization.

E15-4. On the date of authorization, July 1, 1976, the Carter Corporation issued 20-year, 8% bonds with a face value of $600,000 at 98. Interest is payable each January 1 and July 1.

1. Record the issuance of the bonds.

2. Record the accrued interest expense and amortization of the discount on December 31, 1976.

3. Record the interest payment on July 1, 1977, and amortization of the discount by the straight-line amortization method.

E15-5. On October 1, 1976, the Myrtle Corporation issued 8% bonds with a face value of $500,000 at 103 plus accrued interest. The bonds mature on June 1, 1984, and interest is paid each June 1 and December 1. The straight-line amortization of premium is recorded each time bond interest expense is recorded. Prepare all the entries relating to the bond issue during 1976.

E15-6. On the authorization date, January 1, 1976, the Richey Corporation issued 10-year bonds with a face value of $2,000,000. Under the terms of the bond indenture, a sinking fund is to be maintained to provide for the retirement of the bonds at maturity. Deposits are to be made with a trustee at the end of each year in amounts that, when added to the sinking fund earnings, will total $200,000. Record (a) the deposit with the trustee on December 31, 1976, (b) earnings of $17,500 during the second year, (c) the deposit with the trustee on December 31, 1977, and (d) the retirement of the bonds at maturity by the trustee.

E15-7. Assume that the bond indenture (see E15-6) requires a restriction on retained earnings equal to the amount of the sinking fund. Record (a) the restriction at the end of 1976 and 1977 and (b) the removal of the restriction at the maturity date.

E15-8. (*Financial policy decision exercise*) In addition to 8% bonds with a face value of $1,600,000 outstanding, the total capitalization of the Plymouth Corporation at December 31, 1976, is:

8% Preferred Stock, Nonparticipating	$2,400,000
Common Stock	3,200,000
Retained Earnings	800,000

1. Prepare a schedule showing the distribution of earnings of $560,000 before

bond interest expense but after income taxes, and compute the rate of
return on the investment of each of the equity groups—bondholders, preferred stockholders, and common stockholders.
2. Prepare a similar schedule, assuming a distribution of $320,000.
3. Which rate of return reflects a favorable leverage position?

E15-9. On the date of authorization, January 1, 1976, the Wellon Company issued 10-
year, 8% bonds. Interest is paid semiannually on January 1 and July 1. On July
1, 1976, the accountant for the Wellon Company prepared the following journal
entry to record the payment of bond interest and the straight-line amortization
of the discount:

```
1976
July 1   Bond Interest Expense                        14,350
           Cash                                                    14,000
           Discount on Bonds Payable                                  350
             To record the bond interest expense
             for the preceding six months.
```

From this information, reconstruct the journal entry that was made to record
the issuance of the bonds. Show all your calculations.

E15-10. On July 1, 1976, the Safetee Company issued 10-year bonds with a face of
$1,000,000. Under the terms of the bond indenture, a sinking fund is to be
maintained to provide for the retirement of the bonds at maturity. The sinking
fund will earn an annual return of 8%. Beginning June 30, 1977, ten annual,
equal deposits are to be made to the sinking fund. Using the actuarial
method—that is, appropriate compound interest techniques—compute the
amount of the equal deposits to the sinking fund.

**DEMON-
STRATION
PROBLEMS**

DP15-1. (*Accounting for the issuance of bonds*) In each of the following cases, assume (a) 8% bonds with a face value of $1,000,000, (b) date of authorization,
January 1, 1976, (c) interest payable each January 1 and July 1, (d) maturity
date of bonds, January 1, 1986, and (e) year ends December 31.

	Case A	Case B	Case C	Case D	Case E
Date of issuance	Jan. 1, 1976	Jan. 1, 1976	Jan. 1, 1976	Mar. 1, 1976	Jan. 1, 1976
Issue price	100	102	97	101 plus accrued interest	at a price to yield 10%

Required:

1. For cases A, B, C, and D, prepare all journal entries for 1976, assuming
the use of the straight-line amortization method.
2. For case E, prepare all journal entries for 1976, assuming the use of the
compound interest method of amortization. (Appendix)
3. For cases B and C, prepare a schedule proving the interest cost for 1976
by the straight-line amortization method.
4. For cases B and C, calculate the approximate effective interest rate.

DP15-2. (*Retirement of bonds before maturity*) On April 1, 1976, the Sanford Company issued 8% bonds with a face value of $600,000 at 106 plus accrued interest. The bonds have a maturity date of August 1, 1984, and interest is paid each February 1 and August 1. On December 1, 1977, the Sanford Company purchased its own bonds with a face value of $200,000 on the open market at 102 plus accrued interest.

Required: Assuming that the books of the Sanford Company are closed each December 31, prepare all the entries relevant to the bonds for the years 1976 and 1977.

DP15-3. (*Accounting for bond sinking fund*) On the date of authorization, January 1, 1976, the Pittsboro Corporation issued four-year sinking fund bonds with a face value of $800,000 at 100. The sinking fund indenture requires an annual contribution at the end of each of the four years to provide for the retirement of the bonds at maturity. As an added protection, the terms of the bond indenture require that retained earnings be restricted in an annual amount equal to the total addition to the sinking fund. The Pittsboro Corporation is to make a deposit to the Anytown Bank, which has been named trustee of the sinking fund, of amounts that when added to the sinking fund earnings will total $200,000 each year. The Anytown Bank guaranteed the Pittsboro Corporation a return of 8% annually. The bank will credit the Sinking Fund account with this return each December 31.

Required:

1. Record the issuance of the sinking fund bonds.
2. Give all the entries for the four years to record the deposits to the sinking fund and the related restrictions on retained earnings.
3. Record the retirement of the sinking fund bonds by the trustee on the maturity date and the removal of the retained earnings restriction.
4. Assuming that *equal* amounts are to be deposited to the sinking fund under an actuarial method, calculate what the equal amounts would be.

P15-1. On the date of authorization, March 1, 1976, the Greensboro Corporation issued 10-year, 8% bonds with a face value of $600,000 at 103. Interest is payable each March 1 and September 1.

Required:

1. Record the following transactions during 1976: (a) issuance of the bonds, (b) first interest payment and straight-line amortization of the premium, (c) accrual of interest on December 31, 1976, and amortization of the premium.
2. Calculate the approximate effective interest rate paid.
3. State how Bonds Payable and Premium on Bonds Payable should be shown on the statement of financial position prepared as of December 31, 1976, assuming that the bonds are unsecured debenture bonds.

P15-2. On the date of authorization, April 1, 1976, the Boone Company issued 20-year, 7% bonds with a face value of $500,000 at 97. Interest is payable each April 1 and October 1.

LONG-TERM
DEBT
FINANCING

Required:

1. Record the following transactions during 1976: (a) issuance of the bonds, (b) first interest payment and straight-line amortization of the discount, (c) accrual of interest on December 31, 1976, and amortization of the discount.
2. Calculate the approximate effective interest rate paid.
3. State how Bonds Payable and Discount on Bonds Payable should be shown on the statement of financial position as of December 31, 1976, assuming that the bonds are first mortgage bonds with land and buildings pledged as security.

P15-3. On April 1, 1976, the stockholders of the Samuel Corporation authorized the issuance of 20-year, 8% first mortgage bonds with a face value of $1,000,000. The bonds mature on April 1, 1996, and interest is payable each April 1 and October 1.

Required: Make journal entries to record the following transactions:

1976
June 1 Issued bonds at 102 plus accrued interest.
Oct. 1 Paid the semiannual interest. (Assume that premium on bonds payable is amortized by the straight-line method each time bond interest expense is recorded.)
Dec. 31 Accrued the bond interest.
31 Closed the Bond Interest Expense account.
1977
Apr. 1 Paid the semiannual interest.
Oct. 1 Paid the semiannual interest.
Dec. 31 Accrued the bond interest.

P15-4. Selected accounts from three trial balances of the Cameron Corporation are presented.

	Adjusted		Unadjusted
	12/31/74	12/31/75	12/31/76
Debits			
Bond Interest Expense	$ 7,100	$ 42,600	$ 31,950
Credits			
Accrued Bond Interest Payable	11,250	11,250	–0–
9% Bonds Payable—			
issued 11/1/74	500,000	500,000	500,000
Premium on Bonds Payable	23,400	21,000	19,200

The data from the adjusted trial balances are correct. The bonds were issued between interest payment dates.

Required:

1. Compute the following: (a) original issue price as of November 1, 1974, (b) maturity date, (c) semiannual interest payment dates.
2. Reconstruct the journal entry to record the issuance of the bonds on November 1, 1974.
3. Prepare any required adjusting entries as of December 31, 1976.

P15-5. (Appendix). On July 1, 1976, the Isaiah Corporation issued 10-year, 9% bonds with a face value of $1,000,000 at a price to yield 8%. Interest is payable June 30 and December 31.

Required:

1. Prepare journal entries to record the following transactions, assuming that the compound interest amortization method (effective-yield method) is used:

1976
July 1 Issued all the bonds for cash.
Dec. 31 Paid the semiannual interest and recorded the proper amortization.
1977
June 30 Paid the semiannual interest and recorded the proper amortization.
Dec. 31 Paid the semiannual interest and recorded the proper amortization.

P15-6. On March 1, 1976, the authorization date, the Abraham Company issued 10-year, 10% debenture bonds with a face value of $400,000 at 106. Interest is payable each March 1 and September 1. The company closes its books on December 31. The following selected transactions and adjustments were made:

1976
Mar. 1 Issued all the bonds for cash.
Sept. 1 Paid the semiannual interest.
Dec. 31 Accrued the bond interest.
1977
Mar. 1 Paid the semiannual interest.
Sept. 1 Paid the semiannual interest.
Dec. 31 Accrued the bond interest.
1981
Mar. 1 Paid the semiannual interest.
Sept. 1 Paid the semiannual interest.
Dec. 31 Accrued the bond interest.
1986
Mar. 1 Paid the semiannual interest.
1 Paid the bonds outstanding at maturity.

Required: Record the foregoing transactions. (Assume that the premium is amortized by the straight-line method each time the bond interest expense is recorded.)

P15-7. On January 1, 1976, the Jacob Corporation authorized and issued 10-year, 8% sinking fund bonds with a face value of $1,000,000. The bond indenture provided (a) for an annual deposit with a trustee at the end of each year of $100,000 less sinking fund earnings since the previous deposit and (b) for an annual restriction on retained earnings.

Required: Record the following selected transactions relating to the bond issue:

1976
Dec. 31 Made the initial deposit with the sinking fund trustee.
31 Made the restriction on retained earnings.

(Ch. 15)

1977
Dec. 31   Received a report of sinking fund earnings of $7,600.
     31   Made the deposit with the sinking fund trustee.
     31   Made the restriction on retained earnings.
1985
Dec. 31   Paid the bonds at maturity.
     31   Removed the contractual restriction on retained earnings.

P15-8.   (*Financial policy decision problem*) The Drew Furniture Company is considering the introduction of a new product line. Plant and inventory expansion equal to 50% of present asset levels will be necessary to handle the anticipated volume of the new product line. New capital will have to be obtained to finance the asset expansion. Two proposals have been developed to provide the added capital.

Proposal 1.   Raise the $100,000 by issuing 10-year, 12% bonds. This will change the capital structure from one with about 20% debt to one with almost 50% debt. The investment banking house estimates that the price-earnings ratio, now 12 to 1, will be reduced to 10 to 1 if this method of financing is chosen.

Proposal 2.   Raise the $100,000 by issuing new common stock. The investment banker believes that the stock can be issued to yield $33⅓. The price-earnings ratio would remain at 12 to 1 if the stock is issued. The present market price is $36.

The company's most recent financial statements are presented below.

DREW FURNITURE COMPANY
Statement of Financial Condition
As of December 31, 1976

Assets		*Equities*	
Current	$ 65,000	Debt 5%	$ 40,000
Plant and Equipment	135,000	Common Stock	100,000
		Retained Earnings	60,000
	$200,000		$200,000

DREW FURNITURE COMPANY
Income Statement
For the Year Ended December 31, 1976

Sales	$600,000
Operating Costs	538,000
Operating Income	$ 62,000
Interest Charges	2,000
Net Income Before Taxes	$ 60,000
Federal Income Taxes	30,000
Net Income	$ 30,000

Required:

1. The vice-president of finance asks you to calculate the earnings per share and the market value of the stock (assuming the price-earnings ratio given is a valid estimate) for the two proposals assuming total sales (including the new product line) of (a) $400,000, (b) $600,000, (c) $800,000. Costs exclusive of interests and taxes are about 90% of sales.
2. Which proposal would you recommend? Your answer should indicate: (a) the criteria used to judge the alternatives, (b) a brief defense of the criteria used, (c) the proposal chosen in accordance with the criteria.
3. Would your answer to (2) change if a sales level of $1,200,000 or more could be achieved? Explain.
4. What reason(s) would the investment broker give to support the estimate of a lower price-earnings ratio if debt is issued?

(IMA adapted)

P15-9. On January 1, 1976, the Do-rite Corporation issued 10-year bonds with a face value of $2,000,000. Under the terms of the bond indenture, a sinking fund is to be maintained to provide for the retirement of the bonds on January 1, 1986. Assume that the sinking fund will earn an annual return of 10% and that ten equal deposits are to be made to the sinking fund beginning December 31, 1976.

Required:

1. Using the actuarial method, compute the amount of the equal deposits to the sinking fund.
2. Prepare journal entries to record the deposits on December 31, 1976, and December 31, 1977, and the earning of 10% on debt instruments held by the sinking fund trustee.

P15-10. The David Company issued 8% bonds on September 1, 1976, at a certain price plus accrued interest. The bonds mature on June 1, 1986. Interest is paid each June 1 and December 1. The accountant for the company recorded the first semiannual bond interest payment as follows:

1976
Dec. 1	Bond Interest Expense	6,274	
	Accrued Bond Interest Payable	5,314	
	Discount on Bonds Payable		960
	Cash		10,628
	To record the payment of semiannual bond interest and the straight-line amortization of the discount for three months.		

Required:

1. Compute the following: (a) face value of bonds issued, (b) original issue price and discount.
2. Reconstruct the journal entry to record the issuance of the bonds on September 1, 1976.

P15-11. (*Financial policy decision problem*) The board of directors of the Nathan Corporation has approved the recommendation of the management to expand the production facilities. The firm currently manufactures only heavy machinery, but plans are being developed for diversifying the corporation's activities through the production of smaller and more versatile equipment.

The directors have concluded that whereas a number of factors should influence their choice of the method of financing to be used in obtaining approximately $3,000,000 needed, prime attention should be devoted to observing the expected income effect on the corporate equity of the common stockholders. They are considering the following methods of providing funds:

1. They can issue 50,000 shares of $50 par value common stock at a net price of $60 a share.
2. They can issue 30,000 shares of $100 par value, 8½%, cumulative, nonparticipating preferred stock at a net price of $100 a share.
3. They can issue $3,000,000 face value of 20-year, 8% bonds at a net price of 101.
4. They can issue $3,000,000 face value of 20-year, 7% bonds at a net price of 98.

The corporation's current liability and stockholders' equity structure is:

Current liabilities	$ 240,000
8% bonds payable due in 10 years	360,000
7% preferred stock, cumulative and nonparticipating, $100 par value; authorized 100,000 shares; issued 16,000 shares	1,600,000
Common stock, $50 par value; authorized 200,000 shares; issued 40,000 shares	2,000,000
Excess over par value received—common stock	200,000
Retained earnings	800,000

Management expects that the investment of $3,000,000 will yield a return of 18% before income taxes, which will be computed at a 48% rate. The corporation is currently realizing a return of 16% on all long-term capital before income taxes.

Required:

1. Using a form like the following, compare the expected effect of each proposed financing method on the corporate equity of the common stockholders.

	Currently (before expansion)	After Issuing Common Stock	After Issuing Preferred Stock	After Issuing 8% Bonds	After Issuing 7% Bonds
Cash proceeds available for investment					
Net income before bond interest and income taxes					
Less: Bond interest expense					
Net income before income taxes					
Less: Income tax expense					

	Currently (before expansion)	After Issuing Common Stock	After Issuing Preferred Stock	After Issuing 8% Bonds	After Issuing 7% Bonds
Net income					
Less: Full dividend to preferred stockholders					
Portion of net income applicable to common stockholders					
Net income applicable to each share of outstanding common stock					
Portion of net income applicable to common stockholders as a percentage of common stockholders' equity					

2. Applying the single expressed criterion established by the directors, what method of financing should be employed? Why?
3. Discuss other factors that must influence a decision of this type.
4. Without prejudice to your answer in requirement 3, assume that the directors decide to issue the 8% bonds, prepare the general journal entries: (a) to record the issuance of the bonds; (b) to record the periodic interest payment six months after the issuance of the bonds; (c) to record the adjusting entry immediately prior to closing the books four months after entry b; (d) to record the periodic interest payment two months after entry c; (e) to record the periodic interest payment and the retirement of the bonds at maturity.
5. A decrease in the tax rate will tend to favor which method of financing? An increase will tend to favor which method? Explain why.

Short-Term and Long-Term Investments

16

Management may wish to invest excess funds not needed for current operations because of temporary reductions in inventory and accounts receivable. Available temporary excess cash is often invested in the securities of other companies for a favorable return in the form of interest or dividends; the investments should be made in securities for which a ready market exists so that they can be sold when cash is required. Such investments are classified as current assets because they can be and will be converted into cash in a relatively short period of time when there is a seasonal shortage of cash. If the securities are to be held until they mature, or if they are not readily salable, the investments are classified as long-term investments on the statement of financial position. Investments are often also made for the purpose of obtaining control of another company, whose productive or other facilities are needed by the investing company. Such investments should be shown on the statement of financial position as long-term investments.

SHORT-TERM INVESTMENTS OR MARKETABLE SECURITIES

A firm should give serious consideration to the investment of any seasonal excess of cash as it becomes available. In this way, it maximizes its income by putting idle, non-revenue-producing funds to work when they are not needed in the operations of the business. If it is expected that the funds will be needed in the near future, they can be invested in readily marketable securities. These securities should be high-grade bonds or other debt instruments or even *blue-chip* stocks that are not likely to fluctuate widely in price and, when sold, will return as much as or more than the amount that was originally invested. Of course, this kind of security yields a relatively low rate of return, a common characteristic of readily marketable, high-grade securities. Only a few securities qualify as marketable; these are United States government bonds, AAA industrial bonds, and certain blue-chip stocks that are listed on the various stock exchanges. The accounting examples that follow illustrate the recording of the purchase of bonds accompanied by the receipt of interest and the purchase of stock accompanied by the receipt of dividends.

TEMPORARY INVESTMENT IN BONDS

Assume that on March 1, 1976, Owens Company purchases as temporary investments 6% bonds of the Peters Company with a face value of $30,000 at 102 plus accrued interest. Interest is paid on January 1 and July 1. The brokerage fee and other costs incident to the purchase are $60. This information is recorded as follows:

1976			
Mar.	1 Marketable Securities—Bonds		
	of Peters Company	30,660	
	Accrued Bond Interest		
	Receivable	300	
	Cash		30,960
	To record the purchase of bonds of Peters Company as temporary investments.		

Recording Assets at Cost

1. In accordance with the generally accepted principle of recording all assets at cost, Marketable Securities are recorded at full cost, including the brokerage fee and other incidental costs.

2. The account title, Marketable Securities—Bonds of Peters Company, includes the general ledger control account Marketable Securities and the name of the individual bond for posting to a subsidiary record, typically in the form of an *investment register*.
3. The transaction involves the purchase of two different assets: the bonds and the accrued bond interest. The amount of the accrued interest

should be set up in a separate account (and not merged with Marketable Securities), since it is a different asset.

The receipt of semiannual interest on July 1, 1976, is recorded as follows:

1976				
July	1	Cash	900	
		Accrued Bond Interest		
		Receivable		300
		Bond Interest Earned		600
		To record the receipt of		
		semiannual bond interest on		
		bonds of the Peters		
		Company.		

1. The six months' interest represents a collection of the receivable that was purchased on March 1 and the amount of interest that was earned for the four-month period from March 1 to July 1.
2. Note that the premium element of the cost of the bonds is not amortized. Neither the premium element nor the discount element of the cost of bonds purchased as *temporary investments* is amortized, because the purchasing firm is uncertain about how long it will hold the temporary investments. On the other hand, the premium or the discount on bonds purchased as long-term investments *is amortized*.

To complete the cycle, assume that on August 1, 1976, Owens Company found that it needed cash and decided to sell the bonds of the Peters Company. They were sold at $101\frac{3}{4}$ (net of brokerage fees and other costs) plus accrued interest; the transaction is recorded as follows:

1976				
Aug.	1	Cash	30,675	
		Loss on Disposal of Marketable		
		Securities	135	
		Marketable Securities—		
		Bonds of Peters Company		30,660
		Bond Interest Earned		150
		To record the sale of		
		marketable securities.		

1. The computation of the loss on disposal of marketable securities is:

Original full cost of bonds	$30,660
Selling price of bonds ($30,000 × 101.75%)	30,525
Loss on disposal of marketable securities	$ 135

2. The cash received comes from two sources: the sale of the bonds, $30,525, and the sale of the accrued interest, $150.

3. The Marketable Securities account must be credited with the same amount, the cost, for which it was originally debited.

Loss on Disposal of Marketable Securities is shown in the income statement under Other Expenses. Management must consider this loss, along with the Bond Interest Earned, in evaluating the success of its decision to invest in the bonds of Peters Company.

TEMPORARY INVESTMENT IN STOCKS

To illustrate the recording of a purchase of stock as a temporary investment, assume that on April 1, 1976, Arlex Company purchases 200 shares of Hurley Corporation $100 par value preferred stock at $105 per share. Brokerage fees are $108. The entry to record the purchase is:

1976				
Apr.	1	Marketable Securities— Preferred Stock of Hurley Corporation	21,108	
		Cash		21,108
		To record the purchase of 200 shares of Hurley Corporation $100 par value preferred stock at $105 per share.		

1. The amount of the debit to the asset is the full cost. The par value is of no significance to the investor except as a possible base to measure the amount of dividends to be received when the dividend rate is stated as a percentage of par value.

2. Dividends do not legally accrue; therefore, no recognition is given to this feature even for preferred stock until the dividend is actually declared. If Hurley Corporation had declared a dividend on its preferred stock, and Arlex Company had purchased the 200 shares between the declaration date and the dividend record date, then Arlex Company should divide the purchase price between Marketable Securities and Dividends Receivable. One important facet of stock market behavior should be mentioned. The market price of both common and preferred stock reflects investors' anticipation of the ultimate declaration of dividends. In other words, if all other variables were constant, the market price of stock on which dividends are regularly declared would go up gradually from one dividend date to the next in approximately the same manner that interest accrues on bonds. On the dividend record date,

(Ch. 16)

the market price per share would drop by the amount of the dividend per share.

Assume that on July 1, 1976, a quarterly dividend of $1.50 per share is received on the 200 shares of the Hurley Corporation stock. The entry to record the dividend is:

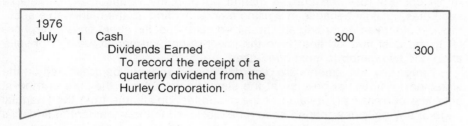

```
1976
July   1   Cash                              300
               Dividends Earned                        300
                   To record the receipt of a
                   quarterly dividend from the
                   Hurley Corporation.
```

Dividends Earned is classified under Other Revenue on the income statement.

Again, to meet a seasonal cash shortage, on September 15, 1976, the preferred stock of Hurley Corporation is sold for $106.50 per share (net of brokerage fees and other costs). The sale is recorded as follows:

```
1976
Sept. 15   Cash                              21,300
               Marketable Securities—
               Preferred Stock of Hurley
               Corporation                            21,108
               Gain on Disposal of
               Marketable Securities                     192
                   To record the sale of
                   preferred stock of
                   Hurley Corporation at
                   $106.50 per share.
```

Gain on disposal of marketable securities is determined as follows:

Selling price of preferred stock (200 × $106.50)	$21,300
Original full cost	21,108
Gain on disposal of marketable securities	$ 192

Gain on Disposal of Marketable Securities is shown on the income statement under Other Revenue. Management must consider this amount, along with Dividends Earned, in evaluating the success of its decision to buy the preferred stock as a temporary investment.

(Ch. 16)

VALUATION OF MARKETABLE SECURITIES

Ideally, all current assets should be shown at current market price on the statement of financial position. However, this represents a departure from another generally accepted accounting standard, the use of historical cost. Only rarely do firms use the current market price in the valuation of marketable securities,[1] mainly because in a rising market, writing up the marketable securities would mean recording an unrealized gain. Specific attention is given here (1) to the cost method and (2) to the lower-of-cost-or-market method of valuation, the two methods most often used.

Temporary investments are recorded at cost and may be presented on the statement of financial position at the same figure. Even if they are carried at cost, the current market value of the securities, obtainable from the financial page of any daily newspaper, should be disclosed in the statement of financial position by a parenthetical notation as shown below to enable the reader to evaluate the item for purposes of financial position analysis.

Assets

Current Assets		
Cash		$ 562,000
Marketable Securities (shown at cost; current market price, $175,000)		158,000
Accounts Receivable	$200,000	
Deduct Allowance for Doubtful Accounts	8,000	192,000
Merchandise Inventory		300,000
Prepaid Insurance		2,000
Total Current Assets		$1,214,000

Note that even though the current market value is disclosed parenthetically, the securities are valued at cost; that is, only the original cost is added into the figures that are totaled. The cost method is consistent with the fundamental principle of matching expired costs (or expenses) and revenues as well as with income tax requirements.

Many firms value their marketable securities at the lower of cost or market. In effect, these firms value their securities at cost or *realizable cost,* whichever is the lower. The objective of this valuation method is to recognize the effect of market price declines without recognizing market price increases.

Conservatism

Thus, it adheres to the concept of conservatism, the recognition of all anticipated losses but not the recognition of unrealized gains.

Although there are two possible approaches to applying the lower of cost or

[1] An exception are increases in market prices of marketable securities held by investment companies (see AICPA *APB Accounting Principles,* vol. II (Chicago: Commerce Clearing House, Inc., 1973), p. 9095.

market method to marketable securities (the *unit* method and the *total securities* method), the unit method—taking the lower of cost or market for each security owned—is the most conservative and the only method discussed in this text. To illustrate, assume that the lower of cost or market unit method is applied to the securities owned by Duncan Company as of December 31, 1976, as shown.

Marketable Securities	Cost (at time securities were acquired)	Market (December 31, 1976)	Lower of Cost or Market
Preferred Stock of Anison Company	$12,550	$12,000	$12,000
Preferred Stock of Bassom Company	16,470	16,200	16,200
Bonds of Connors Company	20,000	20,500	20,000
Totals	$49,020	$48,700	$48,200

If the lower of cost or market unit method is applied to these three securities, the amount to appear in the statement of financial position for Marketable Securities is $48,200, which represents the December 31, 1976, market price of the stocks of Anison and Bassom Company plus the cost of the bonds of Connors Company. The adjusting entry necessary to give recognition to the valuation may take one of two forms: (1) direct asset reduction or (2) creation of a valuation account. Since cost must be retained for income tax requirements and other managerial evaluations, it is suggested that the second method is desirable and that the following valuation adjusting entry is proper:

1976		
Dec. 31 Recognized Decline in Value of Marketable Securities	820	
Allowance for Decline in Value of Marketable Securities		820
To give recognition to the lower of cost or market unit method of valuation.		

The statement of financial position then shows the following:

Assets

Current Assets		
Marketable Securities (at cost)	$49,020	
Deduct Allowance for Decline in Value of Marketable Securities	820	
Marketable Securities at Lower Cost or Market		$48,200

The account Recognized Decline in the Value of Marketable Securities is closed to the Income Summary, and the $820 loss is reported on the income statement under Other Expenses.

To complete the cycle, suppose that on January 15, 1977, Duncan Company sells the preferred stock of Anison Company for $12,060. This transaction is recorded as follows:

1977		
Jan. 15 Cash	12,060	
Allowance for Decline in Value of Marketable Securities	550	
Marketable Securities— Preferred Stock of Anison Company		12,550
Gain on Sale of Marketable Securities		60
To record the sale of preferred stock of Anison Company.		

Observe that the gain or loss on the sale must be determined by comparing the selling price with the lower of cost or market figure used for the statement of financial position valuation. For the Anison Company stock, the gain is computed by comparing the $12,060 received with the $12,000 carrying value. It should be understood that the $60 gain is not recognized for tax purposes; instead a $490 loss is reported on the tax return for 1977 since securities that had cost $12,550 were sold for $12,060.

LONG-TERM INVESTMENTS

In addition to its primary operational activities, a firm may make investments in stocks, bonds, and other securities that are expected to contribute to the success of the business largely by making independent contributions to business revenue. These investments may be temporary or long term. As suggested in the preceding section, investments are called *marketable securities* and are classified as current assets only when they are readily marketable and it is the *intention of management* to convert them into cash when there is a seasonal need for such action. Investments that do not qualify as marketable securities are classified as long-term investments on the statement of financial position.

INVESTMENT IN STOCKS

A company may buy stock in another company specifically for the dividend revenue, or it may acquire control of another company—a *subsidiary*—thereby expanding and diversifying its operations and gaining a more prominent competitive position, possibly accompanied by a steady supply of merchandise or the creation of sales outlets. The acquisition of a controlling interest in one or more subsidiary corporations frequently leads to the combining of the financial statements of the affiliated companies into single consolidated statements.

Stock may be acquired directly from the issuing company, but it is more likely to be purchased through a broker on the New York Stock Exchange, the American Stock Exchange, or other exchange in this or other countries. If shares of stocks are not listed on an exchange—that is, sold through securities dealers—they are said to be sold *over the counter*.

The Cost Method of Recording and Valuation of Long-Term Investment in Stock

Long-term investment in stocks as well as temporary investments are initially recorded at full cost including brokerage fees and postage. APB Opinion No. 18 recommends that an investing company that buys less than 20 percent of the common stock of a company should account for this investment by the so-called cost method which is described below. If cash is paid for the purchase of stock, there is no problem in establishing cost. In other cases, problems of valuation may arise. A sound accounting rule is to record the investment in stocks at the most objective measurement of the cash equivalent cost of the securities. Since dividends do not legally accrue, no recognition is given to the purchase of Dividends Receivable unless the issuing corporation has officially declared a dividend and the investing corporation purchases the stock between the dividend declaration date and the record date. To illustrate both cases, assume, first, that on July 1, 1976, the Satterfield Company purchases 1,000 shares of $100 par value common stock of James Corporation at 105 with a broker's fee of $440. The investor's total cost is $105,440, and the following entry is made:

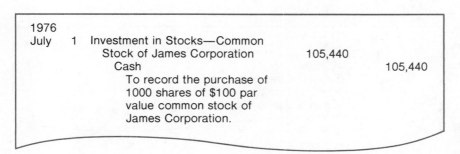

1976				
July	1	Investment in Stocks—Common Stock of James Corporation	105,440	
		Cash		105,440
		To record the purchase of 1000 shares of $100 par value common stock of James Corporation.		

Observe that the asset Investment in Stocks is debited for the cost, not the par value, of the stock. The account title shows the general ledger controlling account, Investment in Stocks, and the subsidiary account title, Common Stock of James Corporation. The information about the specific stock is transferred to an investment register, which serves in place of a more formal subsidiary ledger.

To illustrate the handling of declared dividends, consider the purchase on

July 20, 1976, by Satterfield Company of 100 shares of common stock of Iser Company at 102½ plus a brokerage fee of $42. On July 10, 1976, the board of directors of Iser Company had declared a $1 per share dividend, payable on August 10, 1976, to stockholders of record on July 25, 1976. The purchase price of $102.50 per share includes the cost of all rights. An analysis of this price, therefore, reveals that $101.50 is the cost of each share of stock, excluding the brokerage fees, and $1 per share is the cost of the Dividends Receivable purchased. This transaction is recorded in the journal as follows:

1976				
July	20	Investment in Stocks—Common		
		Stock of Iser Company	10,192	
		Dividends Receivable	100	
		Cash		10,292
		To record the purchase of 100 shares of common stock of Iser Company with a $1 per share dividend receivable.		

When the dividend is received on August 10, an entry is made debiting Cash and crediting Dividends Receivable for the $100. Similarly, if a firm sells its stock in a company in the interval between a cash dividend declaration and the dividend record date, it should give recognition to a dividend revenue.

Normally, for convenience, a cash dividend is not recorded until the cash is actually received. For example, if Satterfield Company receives a $0.60 per share quarterly dividend on the stock of James Corporation on November 10, 1976, it records this information as follows:

1976				
Nov.	10	Cash	600	
		Dividends Earned		600
		To record the receipt of a $0.60 per share dividend from the James Corporation.		

A necessary exception to the foregoing rule is the case of a dividend declared in one year and payable in another year.

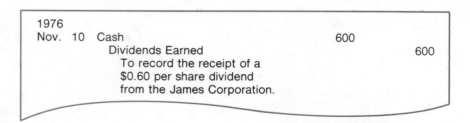

Recognizing Declared Dividends

Sound accrual accounting theory dictates that the dividend revenue be recognized in the year in which the dividend is declared, not in the year in which it is paid.

(Ch. 16)

In this case, an entry is made on or before the last day of the fiscal year in which the dividend is declared, debiting Dividends Receivable and crediting Dividends Earned. Then, when the dividend is actually received in the subsequent accounting period, an entry is made debiting Cash and crediting Dividends Receivable.

Today, frequent use is made of stock dividends and stock split-ups to reduce the market price per share and thus to put the stock in a more favorable price range. The additional shares received by an investing company are not revenue to the stockholder. Only a memorandum entry is necessary to record the increase in the number of shares owned. The unit cost is decreased, however, because of the larger number of shares held after the stock dividend is issued. For example, assume that James Corporation declares a 100 percent stock dividend (a 2-for-1 split-up would be treated in the same way). The receipt of the additional 1,000 shares on December 12, 1976, by Satterfield Company is noted in the journal as follows (the original 1,000 shares had cost $105,440):

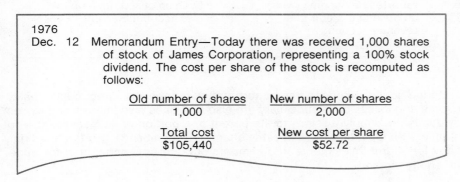

1976
Dec. 12 Memorandum Entry—Today there was received 1,000 shares of stock of James Corporation, representing a 100% stock dividend. The cost per share of the stock is recomputed as follows:

Old number of shares	New number of shares
1,000	2,000
Total cost	New cost per share
$105,440	$52.72

The gain or loss per share on any subsequent sale of James Corporation stock is determined by comparing the selling price with the adjusted cost of $52.72 per share.

The Dividends Earned balance is disclosed in the income statement under Other Revenue, whereas the Investment in Stocks account is reported in the statement of financial position under Long-Term Investments, a noncurrent caption appearing between Current Assets and Plant and Equipment. The most commonly used method of valuation for long-term investments (where ownership is less than 20 percent) is *cost*. When, however, there is a material and presumably permanent decline in the market value of the investment, an adjustment may be made crediting the investment account and debiting the Loss from Decline in Market Value of Investment in Stocks account.

The Equity Method of Accounting for Investment in Subsidiary

In the illustrations thus far, investments in other corporations have been carried at cost and revenue from these investments has been recognized only as dividends were declared. In its Opinion No. 18, the APB concluded that ownership of 20 percent or more of the voting stock of another company was evidence of ability to exercise control. Accordingly, the APB ruled that, when a

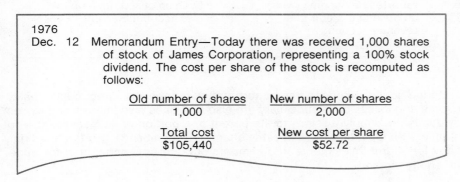

(Ch. 16)

corporation's investment in a subsidiary, domestic or foreign, is large enough to presume ability to control it, the *equity method* should be used to account for the investment.[2]

Under the equity method, the initial purchase is recorded at cost. However, after the initial acquisition, the investment account of the parent company fluctuates in value to recognize income or losses and dividends declarations of the subsidiary. A simplified illustration of the effect of the equity method is as follows:

Investment in Common Stocks—Subsidiary S

Increased by initial purchase of stock at cost	Decreased by parent's share of dividend declarations.
Increased by proportionate share of subsidiary's reported net income (with an offsetting credit to a revenue account, Subsidiary Income)	Decreased by proportionate share of subsidiary's net loss (with an offsetting debit to a loss account, Subsidiary Loss)

Using the equity method, a parent corporation recognizes an economic reality: income and losses of its subsidiary are also part of its own income and losses; dividends are simply a return to the parent of a portion of its investment—not income. APB Opinion No. 18 became effective December 31, 1971; accordingly many long-term investments in common stock are now accounted for under the equity method.

INVESTMENT IN BONDS—STRAIGHT-LINE AMORTIZATION

A number of institutional investors are prohibited by law from buying common stock; others are restricted in the amount of common stock they may buy. Organizations such as banks, insurance companies, some trusts, and pension funds acquire bonds as sound investments. Industrial companies also frequently buy bonds, either for the interest revenue to be received or for reasons of business connection.

Accounting for the purchase of long-term bonds is practically the mirror image of accounting for the issuance of bonds, with one exception: *no premium or discount accounts are used when the bonds are purchased above or below face value.* To measure the bond interest revenue properly, the amount of the discount or premium is amortized, but the offsetting debits or credits are to the Bond Interest Earned account. Two examples are presented to illustrate the accounting for investment in bonds; the second example involves more complex issues than the first.

[2] AICPA, *APB Accounting Principles,* vol. 2, (Chicago: Commerce Clearing House, Inc., 1973), p. 6673.

Figure 16-1 Entries for Bonds on Books of Issuer and Investor, Assuming the Use of the Straight-Line Amortization Method

Transaction	Books of Aman Company (Issuer)	Books of Boston Finance Company (Investor)

1976
May 1 Aman Company issued the Bonds to Boston Finance Company at 98.
	1976
	May 1 Cash 294,000
	Discount on
	  Bonds Payable 6,000
	    Bonds Payable 300,000
	      To record the issuance of bonds at 98.
		1976
		May 1 Investment in
		  Bonds—
		  Aman Company
		  Bonds 294,000
		    Cash 294,000
		      To record the purchase of bonds at 98.

Nov. 1 Aman Company paid semiannual interest to Boston Finance Company.	Nov. 1 Bond Interest
	  Expense 10,500
	    Cash 10,500
	      To record payment of semiannual interest.
		Nov. 1 Cash 10,500
		    Bond Interest
		    Earned 10,500
		      To record the receipt of semiannual interest.

1 Amortized discount for six months.	1 Bond Interest
	  Expense 300
	    Discount on
	    Bonds Payable 300
	      To record the amortization of bond discount for six months:
	$6/120 \times \$6000 = \$300$
		1 Investment in
		  Bonds—
		  Aman Company
		  Bonds 300
		    Bond Interest
		    Earned 300
		      To record the discount accumulated for six months.

Dec. 31 Accrued interest for two months.	Dec. 31 Bond Interest
	  Expense 3,500
	    Accrued Bond
	    Interest Payable 3,500
	      To record the accrual of interest for two months.
		Dec. 31 Accrued Bond
		  Interest
		  Receivable 3,500
		    Bond Interest
		    Earned 3,500
		      To record the accrual of interest earned for two months.

31 Amortized discount for two months.	31 Bond Interest
	  Expense 100
	    Discount on
	    Bonds Payable 100
	      To record the amortization of bond discount for two months:
	$2/120 \times \$6000 = \$100$
		31 Investment in
		  Bonds—
		  Aman Company
		  Bonds 100
		    Bond interest
		    Earned 100
		      To record the discount accumulated for two months.

Example 1. *Boston Finance Company Purchases Bonds from Aman Company.* Assume that on May 1, 1976, Aman Company places a 7%, $300,000 bond issue with Boston Finance Company at 98. The interest is payable on May 1 and November 1 and the bonds mature on May 1, 1986. The entries on both the issuing company's and the investing company's books for the year 1976 are shown in Figure 16-1.

The discount accumulation (comparable to the discount amortization for the issuer) results in a debit to the asset account and a credit to the Bond Interest Earned account. For better measurement of periodic revenue from the securities, the discount on long-term investments on the investor's books is accumulated over the outstanding life of the bonds, starting with the date of purchase and ending with the maturity date. Otherwise, the amount of the discount would have to be recognized as a gain in the accounting period during which the bonds mature. Such a gain would reflect only the failure to adjust the Bond Interest Earned account in prior accounting periods.

The income statement of Boston Finance Company for the year ended December 31, 1976, includes Bond Interest Earned of $14,400 = ($14,000 + $400). Accrued Bond Interest Receivable of $3,500 is shown in the December 31, 1976, statement of financial position under Current Assets. The Investment in Bonds is shown under Long-Term Investments on the statement of financial position at $294,400 = ($294,000 + $400). At maturity, the investment account will have a balance of $300,000. It will have been increased by periodic discount accumulation entries to the $300,000 figure.

Example 2. *Western Company Purchases Bonds of Malcolm Company.* Only the investor's entries are shown in the more complex example. Assume that on March 1, 1976, Western Company purchases 9% bonds of Malcolm Company with a face value of $200,000 at 104 plus accrued interest. Interest is paid on May 1 and November 1. The bonds mature on November 1, 1992. The Western Company holds the bonds until August 1, 1980, at which time it sells them at 103½ plus accrued interest. The 1976 entries for the purchase of the bonds, receipt of interest, straight line amortization of premium element of cost and accrual of bond interest, and the 1980 entries to record the sale are presented as follows:

1976				
Mar.	1	Investment in Bonds—Malcolm Company Bonds	208,000	
		Accrued Bond Interest Receivable	6,000	
		Cash		214,000
		To record the purchase of 9% bonds at 104 plus accrued interest.		
May	1	Cash	9,000	
		Bond Interest Earned		3,000
		Accrued Bond Interest Receivable		6,000
		To record the receipt of semiannual interest from the Malcolm Company.		

1976					
May	1	Bond Interest Earned Investment in Bonds— Malcolm Company Bonds To record the premium amortization for two months: 2/200 × $8000 = $80		80	80
Nov.	1	Cash Bond Interest Earned To record the receipt of semiannual interest from the Malcolm Company.		9,000	9,000
	1	Bond Interest Earned Investment in Bonds— Malcolm Company Bonds To record the premium amortization for six months: 6/200 × $8000 = $240		240	240
Dec.	31	Accrued Bond Interest Receivable Bond Interest Earned To record the accrual of interest for two months on the Malcolm Company Bonds.		3,000	3,000
	31	Bond Interest Earned Investment in Bonds— Malcolm Company Bonds To record the premium amortization for two months: 2/200 × $8000 = $80		80	80
1980					
Aug.	1	Accrued Bond Interest Receivable Bond Interest Earned To accrue the interest for three months on the bonds to be sold.		4,500	4,500
	1	Bond Interest Earned Investment in Bonds— Malcolm Company Bonds To record the premium amortization for three months: 3/200 × $8000 = $120		120	120

```
1980
Aug.  1   Cash                                      211,500
            Investment in Bonds—
              Malcolm Company Bonds                               205,880
            Accrued Bond Interest
              Receivable                                            4,500
            Gain on Sale of Bonds                                   1,120
                 To record the sale of
                 bonds of Malcolm
                 Company at 103½ plus
                 accrued interest.
```

1. On March 1, 1976, two assets are purchased; separate accounts are maintained for each asset, particularly since Accrued Bond Interest Receivable is a current asset and Investments in Bonds is a noncurrent asset.
2. For better measurement of periodic bond interest revenue, the premium element of the cost of the bonds is amortized over the outstanding life of the bonds. The amortization credit is made to the Investment in Bonds account.
3. The gain on the sale of bonds is determined as follows:

Selling price of bonds ($200,000 at 103.50%)		$207,000
Deduct: Book value at date of sale		
Original cost	$208,000	
Total amortization to August 1, 1980		
(53 months × $40 per month)	2,120	
Book value at date of sale		205,880
Gain on sale of bonds		$ 1,120

LONG-TERM INVESTMENT IN SECURED AND UNSECURED NOTES

Other types of long-term investments may be made, particularly by financial institutions. Notes secured by mortgages or deeds of trust and unsecured notes are typical. The accounting principles and procedures applicable to these investments are similar to those for investment in bonds. For example, mortgage notes are often acquired at a discount, in which case accounting theory dictates that the mortgage note be recorded at cost and the amount of the discount be accumulated (amortized) over the remaining outstanding life of the note. After the entry is made to record the periodic cash interest, the discount accumulation entry is made, debiting Investment in Mortgages and crediting Interest Earned.

In addition to the effective interest yield computations discussed in Chapter 15, another important ratio is used by investors in bonds—the *number of times bond interest expense is earned.* This ratio is of special interest to bond investors as a measure of the safety of their investment; it is an indication of a firm's ability to meet its annual bond interest requirement. To illustrate, assume that Analee Corporation has bonds outstanding with a face value of $500,000 and that in 1976 it reports bond interest expense of $40,000, income taxes of $50,000, and net income (after income taxes) of $80,000. Since bond interest expense is deductible in determining taxable income, the following formula seems appropriate:

Number of times bond interest expense is earned =

$$\frac{\text{Net income} + \text{Income tax expense} + \text{Annual bond interest expense}}{\text{Annual bond interest expense}}$$

Substituting the amounts given for Analee Corporation,

Number of times bond interest expense is earned

$$= \frac{\$80,000 + \$60,000 + \$40,000}{\$40,000}$$

$$= 4.5 \text{ times}$$

A ratio of 4.5 times appears to be relatively safe for the investors holding bonds of Analee Corporation, although there are no established universal standards of safety. The safety margin depends in part on the type of collateral used, the type of business in which the firm is engaged, and the liquidity of the firm. Investors in a private utility with mortgageable plant assets, for example, may feel secure with a ratio of 2.5 times; whereas investors in other businesses without mortgageable assets may feel insecure with a ratio smaller than 5 times.

Another investor-oriented ratio similar to the foregoing one is the *number of times preferred dividends is earned.* This ratio is of particular interest to investors in preferred stock as a safety measure for their investment. To illustrate, assume that Analee Corporation has 7% preferred stock outstanding with a par value of $1,000,000. Since preferred dividends are *not* deductible in determining taxable income, the following formula is appropriate:

Number of times preferred dividends is earned =

$$\frac{\text{Net income (after taxes)}}{\text{Annual preferred dividends}}$$

Substituting the amounts given for Analee Corporation,

Number of times preferred dividends is earned $= \dfrac{\$80,000}{\$70,000}$

$$= 1.14 \text{ times}$$

The adequacy of this ratio must be interpreted in the same manner as that described for the number of times bond interest expense is earned; that is, the safety margin that is acceptable will depend in part on the type of business in which the firm is engaged, the liquidity of the firm, and other factors.

The method of accounting for the amortization of the premium or discount elements involved in the investment in bonds described earlier in this chapter is referred to as the straight-line method. If an investor buys bonds to yield a given effective interest rate, he may want to reflect in his records this constant rate of return on the book value of the investment. In this case, he would use the compound interest or effective yield method of amortizing the premium or discount elements of the investment in bonds.

To illustrate this particular method of accounting, assume that on January 1, 1976, Harold Baskin purchased the one 8%, 10-year, $1,000 bond issued by Edwards Corporation described in Chapter 15 (see pages 590 and 605) to yield 6 percent. Baskin would pay $1,148.78 for the bond as calculated on page 591. The purchase of the bond on January 1, 1976, and the compound interest or effective interest calculation and attendant compound-interest amortization for June 30 and December 31, 1976, appear below:

1976				
Jan. 1	Investment in Bonds—Edwards Corporation Bond		1,148.78	
	Cash			1,148.78
	To record the purchase of the Edwards Corporation bond to yield an annual rate of 6 percent.			
June. 30	Cash		40.00	
	Bond Interest Earned (3% × $1,148.78)			34.46
	Investment in Bonds— Edwards Corporation Bond ($40.00 − $34.46)			5.54
	To record the receipt of semiannual interest and the amortization of the premium element on a 6 percent annual yield basis.			
Dec. 31	Cash		40.00	
	Bond Interest Earned [3% × ($1,148.78 − $5.54)]			34.30
	Investment in Bonds— Edwards Corporation Bond ($40.00 − $34.30)			5.70
	To record the receipt of semiannual interest and the amortization of the premium element on a 6 percent annual yield basis.			

SHORT- AND LONG-TERM INVESTMENTS

(Ch. 16)

A similar procedure is used when the compound-interest method of amortization is applied to the investment in bonds purchased at a discount.

Two comments should be made about the foregoing procedure.

1. The procedure will produce a constant rate of return on the book value of the investment in bonds.
2. The accounting is essentially the mirror image of the accounting for the issuance of bonds described in Chapter 15 except that separate premium and discount accounts are not maintained; therefore, the amount of the premium amortization is credited to the Investment in the Bonds account and the amount of the discount accumulation is debited to the Investment in Bonds account.

GLOSSARY

Blue-Chip Stocks or Bonds High-grade stocks and AAA-rated bonds that are listed on one of the stock exchanges.

Conservatism The concept that adheres to the idea of recognizing all possible losses for a period without recognizing gains until fully realized through sales.

Investment in Secured Notes Purchased notes for which a pledge of specific assets has been made by the company issuing the secured notes.

Investment in Unsecured Notes Purchased notes of a given firm for which no pledge of specific assets has been made.

Long-Term Investments Investment in stocks, bonds, other securities, and certain other kinds of property that management intends to hold for a long period.

Lower-of-Cost-or-Market-Unit Method The lower value of the cost or the market for each security is determined; then the lower unit values are summed to determine the lower of cost or market value for marketable securities.

Marketable Securities High-grade, readily marketable securities purchased by a firm usually to be held for a short period; they are classified as current assets on the statement of financial position.

Number of Times Bond Interest Is Earned A ratio which measures a degree of safety margin of an investment in bonds; it is computed by dividing the sum of net income plus income tax expense plus annual bond interest expense by the annual bond interest expense.

Number of Times Preferred Dividends Is Earned A ratio which indicates a certain degree of margin of safety of investment in preferred stock; it is computed by dividing net income for a period by the periodic preferred dividend requirement.

Realizable Cost The amount which could be obtained by the sale of investment securities is a measure of possible realizable cost when securities are not to be sold.

Subsidiary A company, the majority of whose voting capital stock is held by another company, referred to as the parent company.

Temporary Investments Investment in high-grade, blue-chip securities that management intends to hold for a relatively short period; *marketable securities* is a synonymn of *temporary investments*.

INCOME
MEASUREMENT
AND VALUATION

638

(Ch. 16)

Q16-1. Generally speaking, the accounting for investment in bonds is the mirror image of the accounting for the issuance of bonds. Discuss: state the differences and similarities in the accounting for each. Be specific in regard to the account titles used and the accounting for temporary investments and long-term investments.

Q16-2. What are marketable securities? How are they classified on the statement of financial position?

Q16-3. List four types of investments that may qualify as marketable securities.

A16-4. Name and discuss the methods of valuation of marketable securities.

Q16-5. Discuss the accounting involved in the lower-of-cost-or-market method of valuation of marketable securities. Give journal entries to illustrate your discussion.

Q16-6. Why do firms acquire stock as a long-term investment?

Q16-7. Do dividends legally accrue? Can a firm buy dividends receivable? Explain.

Q16-8. What is a stock split-up? Discuss the accounting for a stock split-up from the point of view of the investor. Would there be any difference in the accounting for a stock dividend as compared to the accounting for a stock split-up from the point of view of the investor?

Q16-9. Name the various groups of investors who typically buy bonds as a long-term investment.

Q16-10. State the financial position statement classifications of (a) Bond Sinking Fund, (b) Accrued Bond Interest Receivable, (c) Accrued Bond Interest Payable.

E16-1. On July 1, 1976, the Decidor Company purchased 8% AAA first mortgage bonds of the Goode Company with a face value of $100,000 at 102½ plus $68 brokerage fees. Interest is payable on July 1 and January 1.

1. If these bonds were purchased as a *temporary investment,* what account title(s) would be debited and for what amount(s).
2. If these bonds were purchased as a *long-term investment,* what account title(s) would be debited and for what amount(s).
3. Explain briefly the difference in accounting for the purchase of the bonds and the subsequent treatment of the investment as a temporary investment as compared to a long-term investment.

E16-2. The Marko Company had the following transactions in *temporary* investments during 1976:

1976
Mar. 1 Purchased 8% AAA bonds of Alpha Company with a face value of $100,000 at 102 plus accrued interest. Interest is paid on January 1 and July 1. Brokerage fees and other costs incident to the purchase were $65. The bonds have a maturity date of July 1, 1996.

Apr. 10 Purchased 400 shares of $100 par value 8% preferred stock of Omega Company at $105 a share. Dividends are paid semiannually on January 1 and July 1. Brokerage fees and other costs incident to the purchase were $125.

1976

July 1   Received the semiannual interest from the Alpha Company.

5   Received the semiannual dividends from the Omega Company.

Aug. 1   Sold the bonds of Alpha Company at 102½ plus accrued interest.

Journalize the transactions.

E16-3. The Grey Company had the following *temporary* investments as of December 31, 1976:

	Cost	Market Price at December 31, 1976
Bonds of Charleton Company	$40,000	$38,400
Preferred Stock of Deece Company	20,000	20,200

On February 1, 1977, immediately after receiving and recording the semiannual interest, the Grey Company sold the bonds of Charleton Company for $38,000. Assuming the use of a valuation offset account, record the necessary adjusting entry under the lower-of-cost-or-market method as of December 31, 1976, and the sale on February 1, 1977.

E16-4. The Neal Company had the following transactions in *long-term* investment in stocks during 1976:

1976

Jan. 5   Purchased 3,000 shares of $100 par value common stock of Burlingraine Company at 106. The Burlingraine Company had declared a $1 per share dividend on January 2, 1976, payable on January 20, 1976, to stockholders of record January 10, 1976.

20   Received the cash dividend from the Burlingraine Company.

Mar. 10   Purchased 2,000 shares of $100 par value common stock of Burlingraine Company at 110.

July 1   Received a $1.20 per share cash dividend from the Burlingraine Company.

Dec. 1   The Burlingraine Company split up its stock two for one. The Neal Company exchanged 5,000 shares of $100 par value stock for 10,000 shares of no-par value stock.

31   The Burlingraine Company declared an $0.80 a share cash dividend payable January 18, 1977, to stockholders of record on December 31, 1976.

Journalize the transactions using the cost method.

E16-5. On January 1, 1976, the Barton Corporation purchased as a *long-term* investment 9% bonds of Carson Corporation with a face value of $400,000 at 102. The bonds have a maturity date of January 1, 1986. Interest is payable each January 1 and July 1. Record (a) the purchase of the bonds by the Barton Corporation and (b) all the necessary remaining entries for 1976. Use the straight-line method of amortization.

E16-6. Assume that the Barton Corporation (see E16-5) purchased the Carson Corporation bonds at 99 instead of 102. Prepare all the required entries for 1976. Use the straight-line method of amortization.

E16-7. On May 1, 1976, the Hobson Company purchased as a *long-term* investment 8% bonds of Potter Company. Interest is paid semiannually on May 1 and

November 1. The bonds mature on May 1, 1988. On November 1, 1976, the accountant for the Hobson Company prepared the following entry to record the receipt of bond interest and the amortization of the premium:

1976			
Nov. 1	Cash	6,000	
	Investment in Bonds—Potter Company Bonds		375
	Bond Interest Earned		5,625
	To record the receipt of bond interest from the Potter Company and to amortize the premium for six months by the straight-line method.		

From this information, reconstruct the journal entry that was made to record the purchase of the bonds. Show all your calculations.

E16-8. (*Appendix*). On July 1, 1976, the Taylor Company purchased as a *long-term* investment 10%, 10-year bonds of Roughton Company with a face value of $200,000 at a price to yield 8% (4% each six months). Interest is paid June 30 and December 31. Maturity date of the bonds is June 30, 1986.

1. Compute the price paid for the bonds, using compound interest techniques.
2. Record the purchase of the bonds on the books of the Taylor Company and record the receipt of interest on December 31, 1976, and June 30, 1977, and the amortization of the premium element, using the compound interest method.

DP16-1. (*Accounting for marketable securities*) The Amy Stephenson Company had the following transactions in temporary investments during 1976:

1976

Feb. 1 Purchased 8% bonds of Kaboodle Company with a face value of $300,000 at 109 plus accrued interest. Interest is paid each May 1 and November 1. Brokerage fees and other costs incident to the purchase were $180. The bonds have a maturity date of November 1, 1996.

Mar. 15 Purchased 500 shares of $100 par value, 8% preferred stock of Brown Corporation at $104 a share. Dividends are paid semiannually on March 15 and September 15. The Brown Corporation had declared the regular semiannual cash dividend on its preferred stock on March 10, 1976, payable on March 25, 1976, to stockholders of record on March 20, 1976. Brokerage fees and other costs incident to the purchase were $102.

25 Received the semiannual dividend from the Brown Corporation.

May 1 Received the semiannual interest on the bonds of Kaboodle Company.

Sept. 20 Received the semiannual dividends on the preferred stock of Brown Corporation.

Oct. 1 Sold bonds of Kaboodle Company with a face value of $150,000 at 112 plus accrued interest.

Nov. 1 Received semiannual interest on the remaining bonds of Kaboodle Company.

Dec. 31 Accrued the interest on the bonds of Kaboodle Company.

Required: Journalize the transactions.

DP16-2. (*Valuation of marketable securities*) The Elton Parker Company had the following *temporary* investments as of December 31, 1976:

	Cost	Market Price at December 31, 1976
Bonds of Godwin Company	$31,480	$32,050
Preferred stock of Hobson Company	15,000	14,700
Preferred stock of Isaacs Company	32,100	30,500

On February 1, 1977, the Elton Parker Company sold the preferred stock of Hobson Company for $14,300. On March 1, 1977, the company sold the preferred stock of Isaacs Company for $31,000.

Required:

1. Assuming that a valuation offset account is used, record the necessary adjusting entry under the lower-of-cost-or-market method.
2. Show how the investments should be shown on the end-of-period financial statement.
3. Record the sales of marketable securities in 1977.

DP16-3. (*Accounting for long-term investment in stocks*) The Investment Company had the following transactions involving long-term investment in stocks in 1976:

1976
Jan. 6 Purchased 4,000 shares of $100 par value common stock of Summer Company at 108.

May 1 Received a $2.50 a share cash dividend from the Summer Company.

June 1 Purchased 2,000 shares of $100 par value common stock of Summer Company at 116.

Sept. 1 The Summer Company split up its stock four for one. The Investment Company exchanged 6,000 shares of $100 par value stock for 24,000 shares of no-par value stock.

Oct. 10 The Investment Company sold 2,500 shares of the stock of Summer Company for $41 a share. On October 5, the Summer Company declared a $1.20 a share cash dividend payable on October 25 to stockholders of record on October 20.

25 Received the cash dividend on the remaining shares of stock of Summer Company.

Required:

1. Journalize the transactions using the cost method.
2. Show how the long-term investment in stocks should be shown on the statement of financial position at December 31, 1976.

DP16-4. (*Accounting for the purchase of bonds as a long-term investment*) Assume that Boston, Inc., purchased 9% bonds of Montreal Corporation under each of the following conditions (the authorization date is January 1, 1976).

(Ch. 16)

	Case A	Case B	Case C	Case D
Face value of each bond	$1,000	$500	$10,000	$1,000
Term of bond issued (years)	10	20	20	10
Interest payable	Jan. 1 and July 1	Jan. 1 and July 1	Jan. 1 and July 1	Jan. 1 and July 1
Date of purchase	Jan. 1, 1976	Jan. 1, 1976	Mar. 1, 1976	Jan. 1, 1976
Number of bonds purchased	10	20	5	50
Purchase price	100	98½	102 (plus accrued interest)	at a price to yield 8%

Required: For each case, record (a) purchase of the bonds, (b) receipt of the first interest payment, accompanied by the entry to record proper amortization, and (c) the adjusting entry for interest accrual on December 31, 1976, accompanied by the entry to record proper amortization. (In cases B and C use the straight-line amortization method, and in case D use the compound interest method.)

P16-1. The Valley Company had the following temporary investments as of December 31, 1976:

	Cost	Market Price at December 31, 1976
Bonds of Milton Company	$21,000	$21,200
Preferred stock of Owen Company	18,500	18,100
Preferred stock of Ransom Company	27,000	26,500

The following transactions involving the investments occurred in 1977:

1977
Jan. 15 Sold the preferred stock of Owen Company for $18,200.
Feb. 15 Sold the preferred stock of Ransom Company for $26,450.

Required:

1. Assuming the use of a valuation offset account, record the necessary adjusting entry under the lower-of-cost-or-market method.
2. Show how the temporary investments should be shown on the end-of-period financial statement.
3. Record the sales of the temporary investments in 1977.

P16-2. The Sparks Company had the following transactions involving *temporary* investments during 1976:

1976
Jan. 1 Purchased 7% AAA bonds of Good-deal Company with a face value of $150,000 at 101 plus accrued interest. Interest is paid each March 1 and September 1. Brokerage fees and other costs incident to the purchase were $140. The bonds have a maturity date of September 1, 1985.

1976

Mar. 1 Received semiannual interest on bonds of Good-deal Company.

15 Purchased 500 shares of $50 par value, 8% preferred stock of Riggsbee Company at $60 a share. Dividends are paid semiannually on February 15 and August 15. Brokerage fees and other costs incident to the purchase were $104.

Aug. 15 Sold 100 shares of preferred stock of Riggsbee Company at $65 a share. On August 10, the board of directors of the Riggsbee Company declared the regular semiannual dividend on this stock payable on August 25 to stockholders of record on August 20.

25 Received the dividend on the remaining preferred stock of Riggsbee Company.

Sept. 1 Received semiannual interest on the bonds of Good-deal Company.

Oct. 1 Sold the bonds of Good-deal Company at 102 plus accrued interest.

Required: Journalize the transactions.

P16-3. On May 1, 1976, the Slavino Company purchased as a *long-term* investment 8% bonds of Albermarle Company with a face value of $200,000 at 102. The bonds mature on May 1, 1986, and interest is paid each May 1 and November 1. The books are closed each December 31.

Required: Journalize all necessary entries on the books of the Slavino Company for 1976 and 1977, assuming that proper straight-line amortization is recorded each time bond interest is recorded.

P16-4. The Parento Company had the following transactions involving *long-term* investment in stocks in 1976:

1976

Jan. 4 Purchased 4,000 shares of $50 par value common stock of Sunny Company at 58.

Feb. 10 Purchased 6,000 shares of $50 par value common stock of Sunny Company at 62. On February 2, the Sunny Company declared a $1.20 a share cash dividend payable February 26 to stockholders of record on February 21.

26 Received the cash dividend on the stock of Sunny Company.

Mar. 2 Purchased 4,000 shares of $50 par value common stock of Sunny Company at 64.

Sept. 10 The Sunny Company declared a 100% stock dividend. The Parento Company received 14,000 additional shares of $50 par value common stock from the Sunny Company.

Nov. 1 Sold 5,000 shares of the common stock of Sunny Company at 36.

Dec. 31 The Sunny Company declared a $0.65 a share cash dividend payable January 16, 1977, to stockholders of record on December 31, 1976.

Required:

1. Journalize the transactions using the cost method.
2. Show how the long-term investment in stock should be shown on the statement of financial position of the Parento Company as of December 31, 1976.

P16-5. On April 1, 1976, the Brickhouse Company purchased as a *long-term* investment 9% bonds of Rock Company with a face value of $500,000 at 98 plus accrued interest. The bonds mature on August 1, 1984, and interest is paid each February 1 and August 1. On July 1, 1980, the Brickhouse Company sold bonds with a face value of $200,000 at 100 plus accrued interest. The books are closed each December 31.

Required:

1. Journalize all necessary entries on the books of the Brickhouse Company for 1976, assuming that proper straight-line amortization is recorded each time bond interest is recorded.
2. Assuming that the proper accounting is carried out in the years 1977 through 1979, prepare all the entries for the year 1980, including the receipt of interest on February 1 and August 1, the proper discount accumulation, the sale of the bonds on July 1, and the accrual of interest and other necessary adjusting and closing entries at December 31.

P16-6. On June 1, 1976, the Keller Company purchased as a *long-term* investment 9% bonds of Hinton Company at a certain price plus accrued interest. Interest is payable semiannually on April 1 and October 1. The bonds mature on October 1, 1995. On October 1, 1976, the accountant for the Keller Company prepared the following entry to record the receipt of bond interest and the amortization of the premium:

```
1976
Oct.  1   Cash                                            9,900
              *Investment in Bonds—Hinton Company Bonds              200
               Accrued Bond Interest Receivable                    3,300
               Bond Interest Earned                                6,400
               To record the receipt of semiannual bond in-
               terest from the Hinton Company and to amor-
               tize the premium for four months by the
               straight-line method.
```

Required:

1. Compute and state separately (a) the face value of bonds, (b) the original purchase price of bonds.
2. From the information given, reconstruct the journal entry to record the purchase of the bonds by the Keller Company.

P16-7. (Appendix). On March 1, 1976, the Investure Company purchases as a *long-term* investment 7%, 20-year bonds of Whello Company with a face value of $500,000 at a price to yield 8% (4% each six months). Interest dates are March 1 and September 1. The maturity date of the Whello bonds is March 1, 1996.

Required:

1. Compute the price Investure Company would pay for the bonds, using compound interest techniques.
2. Record the purchase of the bonds; the receipt of interest on September 1, 1976, with the accompanying amortization, using the compound interest method; and the accrual of interest receivable on December 31, 1976, with the accompanying amortization using the compound interest method. (*Hint:* Figure the amortization of discount for a full six months and calculate two-thirds of this amount for a four-month period.)

P16-8. (*Financial policy decision problem*) John Gardner received an inheritance of $300,000. He plans to invest this amount in bonds which he contemplates holding for several years. After consulting with his broker and other advisers, he has narrowed his decision to the following four bonds:

1. 10%, 10-year, grade A debenture bonds of Alpha Company, which are selling at 104.
2. 8%, 10-year, grade AAA first mortgage bonds of Beta, which are selling at 99.
3. 6%, 10-year, grade A debenture bonds of Kappa Company, which are selling at 80.
4. 9%, 10-year, grade AAA debenture bonds of Delta Company, which are selling at 100.

Required:

1. Compute the approximate effective interest yield on each $1,000 bond, and prepare a list indicating the order of yield from the highest to the lowest.
2. Which bond would be the safest? What criteria should you use? What additional information would be helpful in determining safety of principal and safety of interest? Discuss the method of rating bonds.
3. Which bond would you recommend that John Gardner buy? Give reasons for your answer.

Part Three

Financial Reporting:

Analysis and Interpretive Problems

Disclosure in Financial Reporting: Interpretation and Analysis Issues

17

The accounting department of a business organization is responsible for preparing a number of different kinds of reports, the purposes of which are listed below.

1. Primarily external users; (a) for annual (or periodic) financial reports, (b) for prospectuses, and (c) for special reports to grantors of credit.
2. Primarily for internal users; various managerial reports and analyses.

These reports are discussed in this chapter in terms of their history and functions.

The importance of financial reporting to outside groups has paralleled the growth of the corporate form of enterprise. Early American corporations revealed very little financial information to anyone outside the internal management. Annual financial reports to stockholders were meager and consisted usually of condensed and unaudited financial statements.

With the growth of corporations, the New York Stock Exchange became interested in such information that was being furnished to stockholders. In 1898, for example, the exchange, in reviewing the application of a particular company for a listing of its stock, requested that the applicant present detailed statements to the stockholders prior to each annual meeting. This was the genesis of the detailed annual corporate reports made available today to the stockholders. These reports, in addition to a summary letter from the president or the chairman of the board of directors, contain detailed audited comparative statements of financial position and income and other descriptive and analytical information about the present and future outlook for the corporation. A detailed discussion of authoritative bodies whose rulings influence accounting reports was included in the Appendix to Chapter 6. Certain regulatory functions are also discussed in Chapter 27.

Corporate financial reports may take a slightly different form when a corporation requests a loan from a bank or establishes a line of credit. The grantor of credit under these circumstances will dictate the kind and form of reports. Often, only a statement of financial position will be required. In other cases, in addition to the statement of financial position, an income statement, a statement of changes in financial position (discussed in Chapter 18), and other statistical and financial reports may be required in narrative form.

MANAGEMENT NEEDS FOR FINANCIAL DATA

If users of financial statements are to make intelligent decisions based on accounting data, they must understand these data. A major function of the accounting department of a corporation, therefore, is to supply the necessary financial reports to management in meaningful form. The accounting department records the data, prepares the financial statements, and also may prepare ratio, trend, and percentage analyses. The financial data are used by the corporate executives, who are responsible for the stewardship of the business, to measure past performance in terms of costs and revenue, to determine the efficiency and effectiveness of the various departments, to determine future business policies, and to report to the stockholders.

The format of managerial reports often cannot be predetermined. The particular form depends on the decision that is to be made. If these reports are to be most beneficial, however, they should (1) be current, (2) contain sufficient details regarding the particular problem to be solved, and (3) present acceptable alternatives.

There is a constantly increasing reliance by business executives on information systems. Large-scale production, wide geographical distribution, the increasing trend toward corporate business expansion with a concomitant delegation of authority, complex income tax legislation, and increasing government regulation of business are some of the factors requiring greater management reliance on corporate financial reports.

PURPOSE OF FINANCIAL STATEMENTS

Financial statements, whether in an annual report to stockholders, a prospectus for investors, or a report to grantors of credit or to management, should be prepared carefully. They should furnish the least-informed reader with enough information to enable him to make an intelligent decision concerning some aspect of the entity.

Forty years ago the purpose of financial statements appearing in annual corporate reports was stated rather well by a group of very forward-thinking accountants as follows:

> Financial statements are prepared for the purpose of presenting a periodical review or report on progress by the management and deal with the status of the investment in the business and the results achieved during the period under review. They reflect a combination of recorded facts, accounting conventions, and personal judgments; and the judgments and conventions applied affect them materially. The soundness of the judgments necessarily depends on the competence and integrity of those who make them and on their adherence to generally accepted accounting principles and conventions.[1]

Recorded facts refers to the data in financial statements as taken from the accounting records. The amounts of cash, accounts receivable, and plant and equipment, for example, represent recorded facts. *Accounting standards* are basic assumptions or conditions accepted by common consent. These standards are concerned with the problems of asset valuation, allocation of expenditures between asset and expense classifications in the accounting period, and the proper measurement of income.

Accounting statements are prepared on the assumption that each enterprise is a separate entity, that all business transactions can be expressed in dollars, that the enterprise will continue in business indefinitely, and that reports will be prepared at regular intervals.

Basic Financial Reporting Concepts

Accounting is ultimately an art and not an exact science, and financial statements must therefore reflect the opinion and judgment of the accountant and of management.

Importance of Personal Judgment

For example, the estimated life and the method of depreciation to be used in the valuation of plant and equipment, the method of inventory valuation, the valuation of intangibles (patents, goodwill, and so on) are some areas that require opinion and judgment. Equally competent accountants, given the same set of facts, may arrive at different results. Thus, the element of personal judgment and preference affects the financial statements.

In short, the basic purpose of financial statements is to transmit to interested groups, both external and internal, information that is useful in making economic decisions.

Basic Purpose of Financial Statements

[1] "Examination of Financial Statements by Independent Public Accountants," *Bulletin of American Institute of Certified Public Accountants,* (January, 1936), p. 1.

If the purpose of financial statements, as stated in the previous section, is to be achieved, these statements must be constructed in a manner that will make them as understandable and as useful as possible to the reader. In preparing financial statements, the accountant should do his best to obtain an interpretive presentation of the information included in the statements. The following four basic devices are commonly utilized to achieve the desired interpretive statement presentation:

1. *Classification.* Items are presented together in classes to emphasize the similarity of the items within each class and to arrive at meaningful class totals.
2. *Arrangement.* Individual items, classes, totals, and other information are arranged within a statement to indicate important relationships in the data. The disclosure of total current assets and total current liabilities in juxtaposition helps in evaluating the ability of a business to meet its current obligations.
3. *Order.* The order in which figures are shown directs attention to the most important data and reinforces the arrangement. For instance, the final figure on a typical income statement is the net income—the most important amount.
4. *Description.* Modern financial reports do not necessarily carry titles taken verbatim from the general ledger. Rather, serious consideration is given to the selection of words to ensure that descriptions of dollar amounts are both accurate and understandable.

Statement of Financial Position

The statement of financial position, or balance sheet, shows the financial position—the cost (or cost less accumulated amortization) of the assets, the liabilities, and the equity of the owner or owners—as of a specific point in time. As previously explained, the statement may be prepared in one of two forms—account or report. A skeleton of the account form of position statement is shown below. (See pages 1012–1015 for examples of actual statements published in annual reports.)

Heading	
Assets	*Liabilities and Stockholders' Equity*
Current Assets	Current Liabilities
Long-Term Investments	Long-Term Liabilities
Plant and Equipment	Deferred Credits
Intangible Assets	Total Liabilities
Deferred Charges	Stockholders' Equity
Total Assets	Total Liabilities and Stockholders' Equity

The chief advantage of this form of statement of financial position is that the juxtaposition of subgroups helps to show the relationship of certain data and therefore facilitates statement analysis and interpretation.

An outline of a typical report form of position statement follows:

Heading

Assets

Current Assets
Long-Term Investments
Plant and Equipment
Intangible Assets
Deferred Charges
Total Assets

Liabilities and Stockholders' Equity

Current Liabilities
Long-Term Liabilities
Deferred Credits
  Total Liabilities
Stockholders' Equity
Total Liabilities and Stockholders' Equity

The advantages of this form include (1) ease of preparation and (2) expansibility. Since the totals do not have to be placed on the same line, this form of the statement is easier to prepare. In addition, a large number of items may be presented in an orderly manner.

The lists of class headings include several new terms. These are defined and illustrated on the following pages. The traditional class headings also are reexamined in light of the large number of items that have been introduced since classified statements were first discussed in Chapter 2.

Current Assets. "The term *current assets* is used to designate cash and other assets or resources commonly identified as those which are reasonably expected to be realized in cash or sold or consumed during the normal operating cycle of the business,"[2] or one year, whichever is the longer period. A normal operating cycle is the length of time it takes a business to purchase an entire stock of goods, convert them to accounts receivable, and collect the accounts receivable. One business may complete a single operating cycle in two years, whereas another business may have four cycles within a single year. In the latter case, the year is normally chosen as the length of time for determining the currency of assets; in the former case it would be two years.

Included under Current Assets are Cash, Marketable Securities, Accounts Receivable, Accrued Interest Receivable, Notes Receivable, Merchandise Inventory, Prepaid Insurance, and other prepaid expenses that will be consumed within an operating cycle. Even though short-term prepaid expenses are not

---

[2] AICPA, *APB Accounting Principes,* vol. 2 (Chicago: Commerce Clearing House, Inc., 1973), p. 6010.

converted into cash as such, it is logical to include them among the current assets because in a break-even or profit-making operation their total cost will be recovered through revenue within the year or operating cycle.

Current assets are often subdivided into *quick current assets* and *trading current assets.* The quick current assets include cash and the items that can be converted into cash rather rapidly, such as marketable securities and the receivables. The trading current assets include the inventories and prepaid expenses. This method of subdividing current assets is useful in financial statement analysis; for example, the acid-test ratio (Chapter 2) is determined by dividing quick current assets by total current liabilities.

Long-Term Investments. The second asset caption is generally Long-Term Investments; it includes stocks and bonds purchased from other companies, long-term funds, long-term receivables, the cash-surrender value of life insurance policies owned by the company, and land held for future use. To restrict the name "long-term investments" to this particular group of assets is somewhat misleading, because all assets represent investments. Nevertheless, it is a commonly accepted practice to include only the nonoperating, long-term assets under this caption. Since these assets are usually reported at cost, the analyst should be aware of their possible undervaluation or overvaluation in relation to market values, especially during periods of fluctuating prices. Good financial reporting will disclose current market values when they can be determined.

Plant and Equipment. This group of assets includes those tangible, long-lived assets used in the operations of the business rather than being held for resale. Among these assets are land, buildings, machinery and equipment, and delivery equipment. Often called *fixed assets* or *fixed tangible assets,* these assets usually are disclosed on the statement of financial position in order of decreasing permanence, beginning with land and buildings.

A word of caution should be injected at this point. A generally accepted principle is that plant and equipment should be carried at original cost in the case of land and original cost less accumulated depreciation in the case of depreciable assets. Since this brief description is preparatory to the discussion of financial statement analysis, it should be kept in mind that most plant and equipment accounts contain a commingling of dollars with different purchasing powers. Sound financial statement analysis must take this fact into account, or perhaps even require that necessary price-level adjustments be made to the data being used in analysis relationships.

Intangible Assets. This group includes the long-term assets that have no physical form or substance. They represent rights to future benefits and make a significant contribution to the production of revenue, typically by legally sheltering the company from competition. Many intangible assets are owned by entities. Some of them are current, such as Accounts Receivable; others are noncurrent, such as investments in bonds and stocks. The items generally listed under Intangible Assets are goodwill, trademarks, copyrights, organization costs, patents, licenses, franchises, secret formulas, processes and designs, leases, leaseholds, and leasehold improvements. Since only long-term assets appear under the caption Intangible Assets, it seems that the more descriptive caption *Intangible Long-Term Assets* should be used.

Some of the items in this group—goodwill, for example—are suspect in the view of some analysts. Yet they may represent highly valuable present and future benefits. The analyst must judge whether they are valued realistically in terms of their future usefulness to the firm.

Deferred Charges. Under the matching concept, costs incurred in one period that will increase revenue or reduce expenses in a future period should be deferred when incurred and then allocated to the period or periods benefited. Long-term unallocated debits against future operations commonly are referred to as deferred charges. This title to some extent describes all assets. Buildings depreciate and are allocated to future operations; merchandise is sold and its cost is allocated against future revenue; and even cash is held to acquire the assets that, in turn, become expenses, thus being allocated against future operations. Despite this fact, only certain items are generally shown under Deferred Charges; for instance, Long-Term Prepaid Expenses and Discount on Bonds Payable. Each of these items would be better disclosed under some other statement of financial position caption. The first is an intangible fixed asset; the next should be offset against Bonds Payable under Long-Term Liabilities.

Other items that may be found under this classification include costs of plant relocation, start-up costs, advertising, intangible drilling and development, and future income tax benefits. There is little in accounting theory to justify the use of the classification Deferred Charges. The analyst should question whether these are truly assets having future benefits or whether they are so classified for the sole purpose of transferring current operating expenses to future periods.

Current Liabilities. Current liabilities represent obligations the liquidation of which requires the use of current assets or the creation of other current liabilities within a year or operating cycle, whichever is longer. Accounts Payable, Notes Payable, Accrued Expenses Payable, Sales Taxes Payable, and Unearned Revenue are typically carried under this caption, as well as currently maturing installments of long-term debts, such as the installment of serial bonds due within the coming year or operating cycle.

In much financial statement analysis, current liabilities are related either to current assets or to some subdivision of current assets. Thus it is important that any obligation which does not require the use of a current asset to liquidate it should not be classified as a current liability or else the resulting analyses will be misleading.

Long-Term Liabilities. Obligations that will not be liquidated until after the current year or operating cycle are referred to as Long-Term Liabilities, or Long-Term Debt. Shown under this caption are Bonds Payable, Mortgage Payable, Long-Term Contracts Payable, Liability under Pension Contracts, and Long-Term Leases Payable. Proper disclosure dictates that maturity dates and other relevant information concerning these liabilities be clearly shown on the statement of financial position.

The analyst must examine and evaluate all footnotes and other disclosures that describe the terms and conditions of the liabilities. Contingent liabilities—obligations under leases, long-term contract commitments, and pending litigations—whether quantified and included in total liabilities or whether only mentioned in the notes and comments, require careful analysis and evaluation.

Deferred Credits. Appearing on many statements of financial position is the caption Deferred Credits or Deferred Revenue, which represents long-term unallocated credits to future operations. As with the term *deferred charges, Deferred Credits* does not properly describe the items generally appearing under it, which are long-term unearned revenues such as unrealized gross margin on installment sales, premium on bonds payable, and similar items. In some instances deferred credits represent a transfer of current revenue to a future period (for example, deferred gross margin on installment sales) rather than a liability. Others (for example, deferred federal income taxes) arise from a tax-postponement policy that may be of long and indefinite duration. Typically, this kind of caption becomes a catchall classification for amounts that do not precisely fit under another caption. In attempting to analyze financial statements, it is extremely important to recognize this fact. Often a statement may have to be recast before it can be analyzed properly. As with deferred charges, there is little in financial reporting theory to justify this statement of financial position category.

Stockholders' Equity. The Stockholders' Equity section of a statement of financial position for a corporation should not only disclose the major sources of capital, but should also show certain legal, financial, or other restrictions that are imposed on withdrawals either from invested capital or from earnings. The rights and preferences of the different classes of stockholders and their ranking in the event of liquidation should also be disclosed.

ACCOUNTING POLICIES AND FOOTNOTES TO STATEMENTS

The proper purpose of footnotes is to furnish descriptive detail and explanatory support data for items quantified in the body of the statement. Their purpose is to help the analyst to understand and to appraise the quantitative amounts in the statement proper. They should not be used as a substitute for a quantifiable amount or as a means of evading or avoiding a difficult or troublesome measurement decision. Footnotes are customarily used to disclose methods of inventory pricing, depreciation methods, terms and conditions of long-term debt, contingent liabilities, long-term lease provisions, and other items.

In recognition of the fact that "the usefulness of financial statements for purposes of making economic decisions about the reporting entity depends significantly upon the user's understanding of the accounting policies followed by the entity,"[3] the APB concluded in its Opinion No. 22 that "a description of all significant accounting policies of the reporting entity should be included as an integral part of the financial statements."[4] Disclosures should identify and describe the accounting standards selected from existing acceptable alternatives and any unusual or innovative applications of generally accepted accounting principles.

[3] AICPA, *APB Accounting Principles,* vol. 2 (Chicago: Commerce Clearing House, Inc., 1973) p. 6710.
[4] *Loc. cit.*

THE AUDITOR'S OPINION

The primary purpose of an audit of his client's financial statements by the CPA is to enable the auditor, in his role as an independent and objective examiner of the accounting records and other evidence, to express an opinion on the fairness of the presentation of financial position and results of operations. Although management is primarily responsible for the integrity of the statements, the auditor assumes personal responsibility to those who rely on his opinion—investors, credit grantors, and others—about the fairness of management's representations. The auditor bases his opinion on his examination "made in accordance with generally accepted auditing standards" and including "such tests of the accounting records and other auditing procedures considered necessary in the circumstances." The analyst must, therefore, be assured not only of the CPA's technical competence but also of his integrity and judgment.

If the auditor is limited by his client or others in the scope of his examination, if the client's statements do not fairly present financial position and results of operations, or if they are not in accordance with generally accepted accounting principles, then the auditor will either qualify his opinion, disclaim rendering an opinion, or render an adverse opinion. Since statements filed with the SEC—and typically with banks, stock exchanges, and others—must be accompanied by a "clean" certification, the omission of an opinion or even the qualification of an opinion, presents very serious problems to the client. This, in turn, places a serious public responsibility on the CPA.

EXTRAORDINARY ITEMS, AND PRIOR-PERIOD ADJUSTMENTS

Prior to the issuance of APB Opinion No. 9, there was quite a controversy about whether the income statement or the statement of retained earnings should be used to report such items (referred to at that time as extraordinary items) as losses from fires or natural hazards, nonrecurring gains or losses on the retirement of bonds payable or the disposal of assets, and corrections of errors in the net income of prior periods. One group argued that if amounts of these items are substantial and if they are included in the income statements, they would distort net income; thus this group of advocates stated that these items should be disclosed in the statement of retained earnings. This view was referred to as the *current operating performance concept.* Opponents argued that all items affecting the calculation of net income should appear in the income statement. The foregoing items do affect the long-run income of a firm; thus many accountants argue that they should be disclosed in the income statement. This view was labeled the *all-inclusive income statement concept.*

To illustrate the variation that could occur in net income under the two historical concepts, assume, for example, that the Baxter Company earns an ordinary income of $50,000 for each of the three years 1976 through 1978; in addition, in the first year, it sells for a gain of $100,000 a patent that it developed but did not use; in the second year, it sells other plant assets for a gain of $70,000; and in the third year, it experiences an uninsured fire loss of $50,000 in the plant. Under the current operating performance concept, the Baxter Company's net income would be reported as $50,000 each year. However, under the all-inclusive concept, the net income would be reported as shown below.

	1976	1977	1978
Ordinary Income	$ 50,000	$ 50,000	$50,000
Extraordinary Gain (loss)	100,000	70,000	(50,000)
Net Income before Income Taxes	$150,000	$120,000	$ –0–

Advocates of the current operating performance concept argued that under this theory, net income reflects what took place under normal business conditions and that the income statement comparability is thereby enhanced. On the other hand, adherents of the all-inclusive concept maintain that the periodic income statement should record the total income history of the company; that allowing the omission of extraordinary items from the income statement furnishes an opportunity to conceal pertinent information; and that the omission or inclusion of certain items in borderline cases may make possible the manipulation of reported net income.

APB Opinion No. 9 states that all items of gain or loss recognized during the period with the single exception of "prior period adjustments" (carefully defined) should be disclosed in the income statement. The extraordinary items, described carefully in terms of nature and amount, should be segregated from the results of recurring, normal operations and disclosed separately in the income statement. Those few items which qualify as "prior period adjustments" should be shown as adjustments of the opening balance of retained earnings in the statement of retained earnings. Prior-period adjustments are

... those material adjustments which (a) can be specifically identified with and directly related to the business activities of particular prior periods, and (b) are not attributable to economic events occurring subsequent to the date of the financial statements for the prior period, and (c) depend primarily on determination by persons other than management, and (d) were not susceptible of reasonable estimation prior to such determination.[5]

The APB goes on to say, "Such adjustments are rare in modern financial accounting." Then it lists examples of prior-period adjustments as

... material, nonrecurring adjustments or settlements of income taxes, or renegotiation proceedings, or of utility revenues under rate processes. Settlements of significant amounts resulting from litigation or similar claims may also constitute prior period adjustments.[6]

[5] AICPA, *APB Accounting Principles,* vol. 2 (Chicago: Commerce Clearing House, Inc., 1973), p. 6561.
[6] *Loc. cit.*

The intent of the APB in Opinion No. 9 was to move virtually all the way toward the all-inclusive income statement concept. In actual practice, however, the classification of items as "extraordinary" or "ordinary" was unreliable and tilted in whatever direction best served the client's perceived needs to "manage the amounts reported as net income before extraordinary items and net income after extraordinary items." As a consequence, Opinion No. 30 was issued to further define and restrict the classification of items as extraordinary. The board stated that an extraordinary item "should possess a high degree of abnormality"[7] and "the underlying event or transaction should be of a type that would not reasonably be expected to recur in the forseeable future, taking into account the environment in which the entity operates." The following were cited as examples of gains and losses that should not be reported as extraordinary.[8]

(a) Write-down or write-off of receivables, inventories, equipment leased to others, deferred research and development costs, or other intangible assets.
(b) Gains or losses from exchange or translation of foreign currencies, including those relating to major devaluations and revaluations.
(c) Gains or losses on disposal of a segment of a business.
(d) Other gains or losses from sale or abandonment of property, plant, or equipment used in the business.
(e) Effects of a strike, including those against competitors and major suppliers.
(f) Adjustment of accruals on long-term contracts.

STATEMENTS ILLUSTRATED

Multiple-Step Income Statement. The multiple-step income statement is illustrated in Figure 17-1. The groupings in this statement furnish the following essential data: gross margin on sales, operating income, net income before income taxes, and extraordinary items. These figures are valuable in making statistical analyses, in comparing current data with prior periods of the company and with data of the industry, and in financial planning. The usefulness of this form of statement to management justifies its popularity. Note that the deduction for income taxes is proportionate to net income before income taxes and that the extraordinary loss is on a net after tax credit basis (loss of $12,000 reduced by a tax credit of $6,000). See Chapter 26 for a detailed discussion of intraperiod income tax allocation.

Figure 17-2 illustrates the reporting of a prior-period adjustment. Figure 17-3 is a combined statement of income and retained earnings. This form is favored by those who wish to report within one statement all changes in retained earnings during the year. A disadvantage of this form is that it does not end with the amount of net income.

Single-Step Income Statement. The single-step income statement shows all the revenue items and the amount of total revenues, followed by a listing of all costs and expenses the total of which is deducted from total revenue to

---

[7] *Ibid.*, p. 6813.
[8] *Ibid.*, p. 6814.

DISCLOSURE IN
FINANCIAL
REPORTING

Figure 17-1
Multiple Step Income
Statement

EVANS COMPANY
Condensed Income Statement
For the Year Ended December 31, 1976

Net Sales Revenue	$390,000
Cost of Goods Sold	200,000
Gross Margin on Sales	$190,000
Deduct Selling and General Expenses	60,000
Net Income Before Income Taxes	$130,000
Income Taxes (50% of $130,000)	65,000
Net Income Before Extraordinary Items	$ 65,000
Deduct Extraordinary Item (net of applicable income tax reduction of $6,000)	
Loss from Riot Damages	6,000
Net Income	$ 59,000

Figure 17-2
Statement of
Retained Earnings

EVANS COMPANY
Statement of Retained Earnings
For the Year Ended December 31, 1976

Retained Earnings, December 31, 1975	$220,000
Adjustment of Prior-Years Income:	
Settlement of 1974 damage suit	(7,500)
Adjusted Retained Earnings, December 31, 1975	$212,500
Net Income per Income Statement	59,000
Total	$271,500
Dividends Declared	25,000
Retained Earnings, December 31, 1976	$246,500

Figure 17-3
Combined Statement
of Income and
Retained Earnings

EVANS COMPANY
Combined Statement of Income and Retained Earnings
For the Year Ended December 31, 1976

Net Sales Revenue		$390,000
⌇⌇⌇		
Net Income After Extraordinary Items		
(Figure 17–1)		$ 59,000
Retained Earnings, December 31, 1975	$220,000	
Adjustment of Prior Years' Income:		
Settlement of 1974 damage suit	(7,500)	
Adjusted Retained Earnings, December 31, 1975		212,500
Total		$271,500
Dividends Declared		25,000
Retained Earnings, December 31, 1976		$246,500

determine net income. This form of statement has the advantage of easy readability. There are no intermediate additions and deductions, with accompanying labeled subtotals, that may confuse the untrained reader. It is primarily for this reason that this form has become increasingly popular in recent years. The single-step statement is best adapted for annual reports to stockholders, since they are not vitally interested in operating details.

Certain intermediate figures that are important for management purposes, such as the cost of goods sold, the gross margin on sales, and the net income before income taxes, are not shown. Furthermore, only a skilled reader is able to determine operating income, because extraordinary items are intermingled with ordinary items. The income statement of the Evans Company is illustrated in single-step form in Figure 17-4 but is modified so as to report the extraordinary loss in accordance with the disclosure requirements of APB Opinion No. 9. Some items are omitted to avoid duplication of material in Figure 17-1.

Figure 17-4
Single-Step Income
Statement

EVANS COMPANY
Income Statement
For the Year Ended December 31, 1976

Revenue		
Net Sales Revenue		$390,000
Revenue Deductions		
Cost of Goods Sold	$200,000	
Selling and General Expenses	60,000	
Income Taxes	65,000	325,000
Net Income Before Extraordinary Item		$ 65,000
Extraordinary Loss (net of applicable		
income tax reduction of $6,000)		
Loss from Riot Damages		6,000
Net Income		$ 59,000

ACCOUNTING CHANGES

In another effort to improve reporting practices, the APB in Opinion No. 20 stated that an accounting principle, once adopted, should be changed "only if the enterprise justifies the use of an alternative acceptable accounting principle on the basis that it is preferable."[9] It stated further that the reason why the newly adopted accounting principle is preferable should be clearly explained, that the cumulative effect of the change should be shown in net income of the period of the change between "extraordinary items" and "net income." The intent of the opinion was to restrict the opportunities for changing net income by switching back and forth, as expediency dictates, between alternative ac-

[9] AICPA, *APB Accounting Principles,* vol. 2 (Chicago: Commerce Clearing House, Inc., 1973), p. 6689.

counting methods. The arbitrary "management" of operating results, whether it be to smooth out peaks and valleys in periodic net income, or for any other management purpose, is detrimental to the integrity of the reports. If income fluctuates, so be it and "let the chips fall where they may." The effort should be to achieve the truth in reporting as closely as it can be perceived.

INTERPRETATION AND ANALYSIS OF FINANCIAL DATA

Before an individual can adequately understand and evaluate financial statement data, he must (1) understand the nature and limitations of accounting, (2) understand the terminology of accounting and business, (3) have some knowledge of business, and (4) be acquainted with the nature and tools of financial statement analysis. The major problem for current consideration is a further look at the tools of financial statement analysis.

Tools of Financial Statement Analysis

The figures in financial statements may be said to have significance in at least three different respects. First, in themselves they are measures of absolute quantity. When an analyst sees that a company has $50,000 in cash, he understands that figure in terms of current purchasing power. However, the absolute amount does not tell him whether it is adequate for the current needs of the particular company. Some other means of determining its significance is required. Second, a degree of significance is indicated when figures are compared with similar amounts for other years and other companies. If $50,000 in cash was shown on the statement of financial position at the end of the previous year, if that amount was sufficient at that time, and if no changes in needs are foreseen, then it may be assumed that a cash balance of $50,000 is adequate now. A third determinant of significance is the consideration of financial data in conjunction with related figures. When current assets are compared with current liabilities, the dollars of current assets behind each dollar of current liabilities can be determined.

The various tools of financial statement analysis are related to the ways in which financial data have significance. These tools are (1) comparative statements, (2) percentage analyses, (3) ratio analyses, and (4) a combination of the three. A brief review of the various standards of comparisons will indicate methods of using these tools of financial statement analysis. The central theme of any analysis is the evaluation of financial data through comparisons and measurement by some consistent standard to determine performance. Three types of standard have been proposed: (1) a company's past performance, (2) performance of companies in the same field, and (3) industry comparisons. In using each of these standards, the analyst should be aware of certain basic limitations. For example, if a company earned only $100 last year and earns $200 during the current year, it has improved 100 percent; yet it is still not a growth company. In a like manner, the performance of other companies and the industry standards have similar pitfalls. Even with these difficulties, these standards of comparison can be extremely beneficial as a means of revealing improvements and regressions, and thus can be helpful in the interpretation of statement data.

Percentage and ratio analyses have been illustrated throughout this text, but little has been said about comparative statements as such. In the following discussion, emphasis is placed on comparative statements; then a summary chart of the major ratios that have been discussed is presented.

Comparative Financial Statements

A study of the financial position of a company and the results of its operations for a period is more meaningful if the analyst has available the statements of financial position and the income statements for several periods. Trends can be better ascertained when three or more financial statements are compared. It is not uncommon to find comparative statements for ten years in annual reports. One large corporation in its recent annual report showed comparative financial statements covering a period of fifteen years.

> For effective analysis, the statements being compared must be based on the consistent application of generally accepted accounting principles over the period covered by the comparison. If there is an absence of comparability, it should be made known in the accountant's report.
>
> **Comparability of Data on Statements**

The effect on net income, for example, of a changeover from FIFO to LIFO in valuing inventories must be clearly disclosed in the report.

The AICPA makes the following recommendations regarding comparative financial statements:

> The presentation of comparative financial statements in annual and other reports enhances the usefulness of such reports and brings out more clearly the nature and trends of current changes affecting the enterprise. Such presentation emphasizes the fact that statements for a series of periods are far more significant than those for a single period and that the accounts for one period are but an installment of what is essentially a continuous history.
>
> In any one year it is ordinarily desirable that the balance sheet (statement of financial position), the income statement, and the surplus statement (statement of retained earnings) be given for one or more preceding years as well as for the current year. Footnotes, explanations, and accountant's qualifications which appeared on the statements for the preceding years should be repeated, or at least referred to, in the comparative statements to the extent that they continue to be of significance. . . . This procedure is in conformity with the well-recognized principle that any change in practice which affects comparability should be disclosed.[10]

The use of comparative information in annual corporate reports to stockholders is nearly universal. Other devices are also used to present the entire financial story as clearly and attractively as possible. Although there is no uni-

[10] AICPA, *APB Accounting Principles,* vol. 2 (Chicago: Commerce Clearing House, Inc. 1973), pp. 6008–6009.

(Ch. 17)

formity in the kind of visual and statistical aids used, some of the more common are comparative statements with accompanying *trend percentages; common-size* statements, which present individual figures as percentages of a base total or some other established norm; pictorial statements using bar or line graphs to emphasize particular trends, ratios, or relationships; and pie charts showing the allocation of each company sales dollar. Any of these methods of presentation can make an interesting and informative report, aimed at perhaps the largest audience in the history of corporate reporting. Some of these devices are illustrated in this chapter.

Comparative Statement of Financial Position. Successive statements of financial position of a company may be given side by side, showing only the dollar amounts. These statements can be made more meaningful if the dollar amount of increase or decrease and the percentage of increase or decrease are also shown. This form of statement is illustrated in Figure 17-5, the comparative position statement of the Melvin Company. In this illustration, the year 1975 is the base year and represents 100 percent. Accounts Receivable increased by 30.8 percent ($8,000 ÷ $26,000) during 1976; Notes Payable decreased by 5 percent ($1,000 ÷ $20,000); and Cash increased by $16,000, or 100 percent. The December 31, 1976, cash balance is twice the December 31, 1975, balance; Retained Earnings as of December 31, 1976, are almost twice the amount shown on December 31, 1975. No additional plant and equipment assets were acquired; the decreases reflect the annual depreciation deductions.

The change that occurred during 1976 for the Melvin Company is apparently favorable. Current assets increased by 42.3 percent, whereas current liabilities increased by only 18.5 percent. The total stockholders' equity increased by 20 percent; this is reflected by an increase in all the current assets. The favorable position of Retained Earnings, accompanied by an increase in working capital, was accomplished without resort to long-term borrowing, because Mortgage Payable and Notes Payable have decreased during the period. Additional working capital was acquired by the sale of stock.

Comparative Income Statement. A single income statement is just one link in a continuous chain reporting the operating results of the business. Comparative income statements are required for an analysis of trends and for making decisions regarding possible future developments. An income statement showing the results of operations for a single year is inadequate for purposes of analyzing the significance of the changes that have occurred.

The comparative statement of income and retained earnings of the Melvin Company is shown in Figure 17-6. The year 1975 is again used as the base year. Gross Margin on Sales increased by 25.4 percent, Net Income before Income Taxes increased by 67.2 percent; and Total Operating Expenses decreased by 0.6 percent. These favorable changes resulted primarily from an increase in sales. The provision for income taxes increased by 106.4 percent, because of the sharp change in the Federal corporate tax rate on earnings in excess of $25,000. In 1975, it was assumed that the entire net taxable income of $23,000 was subject to only the normal corporate tax rate; whereas, in 1976, $13,450 = ($38,450 − $25,000) was assumed to be subject to both the normal and the surtax rates.

There is a close relationship between the cost of goods sold, the volume of

Figure 17-5 Comparative Statement of Financial Position

MELVIN COMPANY
Comparative Statement of Financial Position
December 31, 1976 and 1975

	December 31 1976	December 31 1975	Amount of Increase or (Decrease) during 1976	Percent of Increase or (Decrease) during 1976
Assets				
Current Assets				
Cash	$ 32,000	$ 16,000	$16,000	100.0
Accounts Receivable (net)	34,000	26,000	8,000	30.8
Inventories	45,000	36,000	9,000	25.0
Total Current Assets	$111,000	$ 78,000	$33,000	42.3
Plant and Equipment				
Land	$ 7,000	$ 7,000	$ –0–	–0–
Building (net)	116,000	119,000	(3,000)	(2.5)
Store Equipment (net)	23,000	25,000	(2,000)	(8.0)
Total Plant and Equipment	$146,000	$151,000	$ (5,000)	(3.3)
Total Assets	$257,000	$229,000	$28,000	12.2
Liabilities and Stockholders' Equity				
Current Liabilities				
Accounts Payable	$ 34,000	$ 26,000	$ 8,000	30.8
Notes Payable	19,000	20,000	(1,000)	(5.0)
Accrued Payables	11,000	8,000	3,000	37.5
Total Current Liabilities	$ 64,000	$ 54,000	$10,000	18.5
Long-Term Liabilities				
Mortgage Payable	55,000	60,000	(5,000)	(8.3)
Total Liabilities	$119,000	$114,000	$ 5,000	4.4
Stockholders' Equity				
Capital Stock	$109,000	$100,000	$ 9,000	9.0
Retained Earnings	29,000	15,000	14,000	93.3
Total Stockholders' Equity	$138,000	$115,000	$23,000	20.0
Total Liabilities and Stockholders' Equity	$257,000	$229,000	$28,000	12.2

---

sales, and net income before income taxes. In periods of exceptionally high sales volume, net income before income taxes tends to rise (percentage of increase, 67.2) at a faster rate than do sales (percentage of increase, 30.5). In periods of declining sales volume, earnings fall more sharply than sales. This is because a significant part of the operating expenses are constant (or fixed)— they are not affected by the current sales volume. Such fluctuations in net

Figure 17-6 Comparative Statement of Income and Retained Earnings

MELVIN COMPANY
Comparative Statement of Income and Retained Earnings
For the Years Ended December 31, 1976 and 1975

	Years Ended December 31 1976	Years Ended December 31 1975	Amount of Increase or (Decrease) during 1976	Percent of Increase or (Decrease) during 1976
Sales (net)	$197,000	$151,000	$46,000	30.5
Cost of Goods Sold	123,000	92,000	31,000	33.7
Gross Margin on Sales	$ 74,000	$ 59,000	$15,000	25.4
Operating Expenses				
Selling Expenses				
Advertising Expense	$ 1,200	$ 1,100	$ 100	9.1
Sales Salaries Expense	18,300	17,900	400	2.2
Depreciation Expense—				
Store Equipment	2,000	2,000	–0–	–0–
Total Selling Expenses	$ 21,500	$ 21,000	$ 500	2.4
General Expenses				
Depreciation Expense—Building	$ 3,000	$ 3,000	$ –0–	–0–
Insurance Expense	675	650	25	3.8
Miscellaneous General Expense	425	350	75	21.4
General Salaries Expense	7,200	8,000	(800)	(10.0)
Total General Expenses	$ 11,300	$ 12,000	$ (700)	(5.8)
Total Operating Expenses	$ 32,800	$ 33,000	$ (200)	(0.6)
Operating Income	$ 41,200	$ 26,000	$15,200	58.5
Other Expenses				
Interest Expense	2,750	3,000	(250)	(8.3)
Net Income Before Income Taxes	$ 38,450	$ 23,000	$15,450	67.2
Income Taxes	14,450	7,000	7,450	106.4
Net Income After Income Taxes	$ 24,000	$ 16,000	$ 8,000	50.0
Retained Earnings, January 1	15,000	9,000	6,000	66.7
Total	$ 39,000	$ 25,000	$14,000	56.0
Dividends Declared	10,000	10,000	–0–	–0–
Retained Earnings, December 31	$ 29,000	$ 15,000	$14,000	93.3

income can be eliminated if unit sales prices are increased in periods of low sales volume and reduced in periods of high sales volume. Such a pricing policy, however, would be undesirable from the customers' viewpoint and im- practicable from the company's viewpoint. It becomes important, therefore, that management know the volume at which profits begin. This figure, the *break-even point,* is that volume of sales at which the business will neither make a profit nor incur a loss. Break-even analysis is discussed and illustrated in Chapter 23.

Percentage increases or decreases are calculated only when the base figure is positive. When there is no figure for the base year or when base year amounts are negative, there is no extension into the Percent of Increase or (Decrease) column. When there is a positive amount in the base year and none in the following year, the percent of decrease is 100, as shown below.

	1976	1975 (Base Year)	Amount of Increase or (Decrease) During 1976	Percent of Increase or (Decrease) During 1976
Notes Receivable	$3,000	–0–	$3,000	
Notes Payable	–0–	$2,000	(2,000)	(100)
Net Income or (Loss)	4,000	(1,000)	5,000	

Trend Percentages

Comparative financial statements for several years may be expressed in terms of trend percentages.

Management can more readily study changes in financial statements between periods by establishing a base year and expressing the other years in terms of the base year. The base year, may be any typical year in the comparison—the first, the last, or any of the other years.

Trend Percentages

To illustrate, a partial comparative income statement is presented in Figure 17-7. The amounts in Figure 17-7 are converted into trend percentages with 1975 as the base year, as shown in Figure 17-8.

Each item in the 1975 column of Figure 17-7 is assigned a weight of 100 percent. All the amounts in other years are expressed as trend percentages, or percentages of the figures for the base year. Each base year amount is divided into the same item for the other years. Trend percentages for sales, for example, are calculated as follows: 1976: $95,000 ÷ $100,000 = 95; 1977: $120,000 ÷ $100,000 = 120; and 1978: $130,000 ÷ $100,000 = 130. When the base year amount is larger than the corresponding amount in another year, the trend percentage is less than 100 percent; conversely, when the base year amount is the lesser of the two, the trend percentage is over 100 percent.

The trend percentage statement is an analytical device for condensing the absolute dollar data of comparative statements. The device is especially valuable to management because readability and brevity are achieved by substituting percentages for large dollar amounts, which in themselves are difficult to compare. Trend percentages are generally computed for the major items in the statements; minor amounts are omitted, the objective being to highlight the significant changes.

An evaluation of the trend percentages requires a careful analysis of the

DISCLOSURE IN
FINANCIAL
REPORTING

Figure 17-7
Partial Comparative
Income Statements
for Four Years*

	1975	1976	1977	1978
Sales (net)	$100,000	$95,000	$120,000	$130,000
Cost of Goods Sold	60,000	58,900	69,600	72,800
Gross Margin on Sales	$ 40,000	$36,100	$ 50,400	$ 57,200
Total Selling Expenses	$ 10,000	$ 9,700	$ 11,000	$ 12,000
Net Income before Income Taxes	$ 5,000	$ 3,800	$ 8,400	$ 10,400

* The years are listed in ascending order to facilitate analysis when data for three or more years are given. The reverse (descending order) is usually found in corporate annual reports.

interrelated items. Sales, for example, may show increases over a four-year period leading up to a trend percentage of 150 percent for the fourth year. This is unfavorable if it is accompanied by trend percentages of 200 percent for cost of goods sold, 175 percent for selling expenses, and 95 percent for net income before income taxes. Other unfavorable trends include an upward trend in receivables and inventories accompanied by a downward trend in sales, and a downward trend in sales accompanied by an upward trend in plant and equipment. Favorable trends would be an increase in sales accompanied by a decrease in cost of goods sold and selling expenses or an increase in current assets accompanied by a decrease in current liabilities.

Figure 17-8
Comparative Trend
Percentages for Four
Years*

	1975	1976	1977	1978
Sales (net)	100%	95%	120%	130%
Cost of Goods Sold	100	98	116	121
Gross Margin on Sales	100	90	126	143
Total Selling Expenses	100	97	110	120
Net Income before Income Taxes	100	76	168	208

* The years are listed in ascending order to facilitate analysis when data for three or more years are given. The reverse (descending order) is usually found in corporate annual reports.

Trend percentages show the degree of increase and decrease; they do not indicate the causes of the changes. They do, however, single out unfavorable developments for further analysis and investigation by management. A marked change may have been caused by inconsistency in the application of accounting principles, by fluctuating price levels, or by controllable internal factors (for example, an unnecessary increase in merchandise inventory or a decrease in operating efficiency).

Common-Size Statements

Trend percentages provide for *horizontal statement analysis;* common-size statements provide for *vertical analysis* (see Figure 17-9). It is important for the analyst to compare changes on the financial statements that occur from period to period with certain base totals within those periods.

Thus total assets, total liabilities and stockholders' equity, and total sales are each converted to a base of 100 percent. Each item within each classification is expressed as a percentage of the base; each asset, for example, is expressed as a percentage of total assets. Since these bases represent 100 percent in all the statements in the comparison, there is a common basis for analysis; therefore, the statements are referred to as "common-size statements."

Common-size Statements

Comparisons can be made within the company, with other companies in the same industry, or with entire industry figures. Thus, important relationships can be discerned even when comparisons are made with companies of unlike size; and any significant differences may indicate that a decision should be made. The common-size statement supplemented by additional analytical financial data are effective tools for a historical financial study of a business or industry.

If comparisons are to be made of one company with one or more other companies or with an entire industry, it must first be carefully established that the data in the comparison are based on reasonably uniform and consistent accounting methods and principles.

Consistency Standard

The comparative common-size statement of financial position and the comparative common-size income statement are shown in Figures 17-9 and 17-10.

Common-Size Statement of Financial Position. In the common-size position statement of the Melvin Company (Figure 17-9), the method of converting dollar amounts into common-size percentages, using data from Figure 17-9, is shown below.

$$\frac{\text{Accounts receivable (1976)}}{\text{Total assets (1976)}} = \frac{\$34,000}{\$257,000} = 13.2\%$$

Accounts Receivable in 1976 represent 13.2 percent of the total assets. For each dollar of total assets there were 13.2 cents of accounts receivable.

$$\frac{\text{Accounts payable (1975)}}{\text{Total liabilities and stockholders' equity (1975)}} = \frac{\$26,000}{\$229,000} = 11.4\%$$

Accounts Payable for 1975 represents 11.4 percent of total liabilities and stockholders' equity. For each dollar of total liabilities and stockholders' equity there were 11.4 cents of accounts payable.

Each current asset item has increased both in dollar amount and as a percentage of the total assets. Total current assets for 1976 have increased by 9.1 percent (43.2% − 34.1%) over 1975; total current liabilities for 1976 have

Figure 17-9
Comparative
Common-Size
Statement

MELVIN COMPANY
Comparative Common-Size Statement of Financial Position
December 31, 1976 and 1975

	December 31		Common-Size Percentages December 31	
	1976	1975	1976	1975
Assets				
Current Assets				
Cash	$ 32,000	$ 16,000	12.5	7.0
Accounts Receivable (net)	34,000	26,000	13.2	11.4
Inventories	45,000	36,000	17.5	15.7
Total Current Assets	$111,000	$ 78,000	43.2	34.1
Plant and Equipment				
Land	$ 7,000	$ 7,000	2.8	3.0
Building (net)	116,000	119,000	45.1	52.0
Store Equipment (net)	23,000	25,000	8.9	10.9
Total Plant and Equipment	$146,000	$151,000	56.8	65.9
Total Assets	$257,000	$229,000	100.0	100.0
Liabilities and Stockholders' Equity				
Current Liabilities				
Accounts Payable	$ 34,000	$ 26,000	13.2	11.4
Notes Payable	19,000	20,000	7.4	8.7
Accrued Payables	11,000	8,000	4.3	3.5
Total Current Liabilities	$ 64,000	$ 54,000	24.9	23.6
Long-Term Liabilities				
Mortgage Payable	55,000	60,000	21.4	26.2
Total Liabilities	$119,000	$114,000	46.3	49.8
Stockholders' Equity				
Capital Stock	$109,000	$100,000	42.4	43.7
Retained Earnings	29,000	15,000	11.3	6.5
Total Stockholders' Equity	$138,000	$115,000	53.7	50.2
Total Liabilities and Stockholders' Equity	$257,000	$229,000	100.0	100.0

increased by only 1.3 percent. Thus, the working capital position has been strengthened. Increases in net income and proceeds from the sale of stock are reflected by increases in each current asset item. The company did not invest in plant and equipment; the decreases in Store Equipment and Building are due to deductions for annual depreciation charges.

The ratio of stockholders' equity to total assets has increased, with corresponding decreases in the ratio of total liabilities to total assets. On December 31, 1975, the ratio of total liabilities to total assets was 49.8 percent; a year later

Figure 7-10
Comparative
Common-Size Income
Statement

MELVIN COMPANY
Comparative Common-Size Income Statement
For the Years Ended December 31, 1976 and 1975

	Year Ended December 31		Common-Size Percentages Year Ended December 31	
	1976	1975	1976	1975
Sales (net)	$197,000	$151,000	100.0	100.0
Cost of Goods Sold	123,000	92,000	62.4	60.9
Gross Margin on Sales	$ 74,000	$ 59,000	37.6	39.1
Operating Expenses				
Selling Expenses				
Advertising Expense	$ 1,200	$ 1,100	0.6	0.7
Sales Salaries Expense	18,300	17,900	9.3	11.9
Depreciation Expense—				
Store Equipment	2,000	2,000	1.0	1.3
Total Selling Expenses	$ 21,500	$ 21,000	10.9	13.9
General Expenses				
Depreciation Expense—				
Building	$ 3,000	$ 3,000	1.5	1.9
Insurance Expense	675	650	0.4	0.4
Miscellaneous				
General Expenses	425	350	0.2	0.2
General Salaries Expense	7,200	8,000	3.7	5.4
Total General Expenses	$ 11,300	$ 12,000	5.8	7.9
Total Operating Expenses	$ 32,800	$ 33,000	16.7	21.8
Net Operating Margin	$ 41,200	$ 26,000	20.9	17.3
Other Expenses				
Interest Expense	2,750	3,000	1.4	2.0
Net Income before				
Income Taxes	$ 38,450	$ 23,000	19.5	15.3
Income Taxes	14,450	7,000	7.3	4.7
Net Income	$ 24,000	$ 16,000	12.2	10.6

this decreased to 46.3 percent. The overall financial position of the Melvin Company has improved.

Common-Size Income Statement. The common-size income statement of the Melvin Company is shown in Figure 17-10. Examples of the conversion of income statement dollar amounts into common-size percentages are shown below.

$$\frac{\text{Gross margin on sales (1976)}}{\text{Net sales (1976)}} = \frac{\$74,000}{\$197,000} = 37.6\%$$

(Ch. 17)

Gross margin on sales for 1976 represents 37.6 percent of net sales; for each dollar of net sales there was a margin of 37.6 cents.

$$\frac{\text{Total operating expenses (1975)}}{\text{Net sales (1975)}} = \frac{\$33,000}{\$151,000} = 21.9\%$$

Total operating expenses for 1975 represent 21.9 percent of net sales; for each dollar of net sales there were 21.9 cents of total operating expenses.

A comparison of the cost of goods sold for the two years shows an increase of 1.5 percent (62.4% − 60.9%) and a corresponding decrease in the gross margin. This relatively modest change may indicate an increase in markdowns from original sales prices. Increases in amounts and percentages of inventories accompanied by a decrease in gross margin may indicate an overinvestment in inventories.

The change in total operating expenses is favorable. Sales increased by $46,000 = ($197,000 − $151,000), whereas total operating expenses remained approximately the same. The Melvin Company has increased the efficiency of its operations by increasing dollar sales without increasing its operating costs—a favorable development. The amount of increase in income taxes is at best a partially uncontrollable factor.

In addition to the analyses already illustrated, other ratios such as sales returns and allowances to sales revenue, sales discounts to sales revenue, purchase returns and allowances to purchases, and purchases discounts to purchases furnish information useful to management for controlling various activities, especially when they are compared from period to period.

Rate of Return on Total Investment

The relationship of the earnings of a corporation to its total resources is an important indicator of the effectiveness of management in generating a return to suppliers of capital, as well as a method of predicting future earnings. The rate of return on total investment may be computed as shown below.

Net income for the year 1976 plus interest expense		Ⓐ	$ 26,750
Average total liabilities:			
Balance, December 31, 1975	$114,000		
Balance, December 31, 1976	119,000		
Total	$233,000		
Average ($233,000 ÷ 2)		Ⓑ	$116,500
Average stockholders' equity:			
Balance, December 31, 1975	$115,000		
Balance, December 31, 1976	138,000		
Total	$253,000		
Average ($253,000 ÷ 2)		Ⓒ	$126,500
Total average equities		Ⓓ	$243,000
Rate of return on total investment (line A ÷ line D)			11.0%

The Melvin Company earned 11.0 cents for each dollar invested in the company—whether by outside creditors or by stockholders. Since total equities are equal to total assets, it may also be said that the Melvin Company earned 11.0 cents on each dollar of assets used in the business.

Rate of Return on Stockholders' Equity

The relationship between earnings and the stockholders' investment is a significant measure of the profitability of a business and is of particular interest to the corporate shareholders. This rate is computed as shown here.

Net income for the year 1976	Ⓐ	$24,000
Average stockholders' equity (above)	Ⓑ	$126,500
Rate of return on stockholders' equity (Line A ÷ Line B)		19%

The rate of return on the stockholders equity is twice the rate of return on total investments. This means that the return to stockholders is well above the fixed rates on the mortgage payable and the notes payable, and the rate—if any—on the accounts payable. The difference of 8.0% = (19.0% − 11.0%) between the two rates is called the capital leverage factor. The Melvin Company is favorably "trading on the equity" of its stockholders by using that portion of total equities as a cushion or base from which to borrow from external sources at rates below those generated on stockholders' equity.

Use of the Company's Revenue Dollar

Annual reports often include graphic presentations of the disposition of each revenue dollar. These may take the form of a pie chart, bar graph, or simple statement. Such a presentation is often more meaningful to the reader than a detailed income statement and is popular for its simplicity and effectiveness.

A revenue-dollar statement for Melvin Company is shown below.

	1976	1975
Each sales dollar was allocated as follows:		
Cost of Goods Sold	$0.624	$0.609
Selling Expenses	0.109	0.139
General Expenses	0.058	0.079
Interest Expense	0.014	0.020
Income Taxes	0.073	0.047
Net Income	0.122	0.106
Total Sales Dollar	$1.000	$1.000

Ratios

A tabulation of twenty significant ratios arranged in an outline of their primary measurements is shown in Figure 17-11, indicating the range of possibili-

Figure 17-11 Major Ratios

SIGNIFICANT RATIOS

Chapter Reference	Page Number	Ratio	Computation of Ratio	Indicates
A. Short-Run Solvency Measurements				
2	54	Current Ratio ✶	$$\dfrac{\text{Current Assets}}{\text{Current Liabilities}}$$	The ability of a business to meet its current obligations
2	55	Acid-Test Ratio ✶ (quick ratio)	$$\dfrac{\text{Quick Current Assets } (\text{cash } \& \text{ A/R})}{\text{Current Liabilities}}$$	The ability of a business to meet quickly unexpected demands for working capital from assets readily convertible into cash
9	360	Average Number of Days' Sales Uncollected (Collection Period)	$$\dfrac{\text{Average accounts receivable}}{\text{Net sales}} \times 365$$ OR (1) Net Sales $\div$ 365 = Net Sales Per Day (2) $$\dfrac{\text{Average Trade Receivables}}{\text{Net Sales Per Day}}$$	The rapidity with which the accounts receivable are collected; the average number of days elapsing from the time of sale to the time of payment
5	201	Merchandise Inventory ✶ Turnover	$$\dfrac{\text{Cost of Goods Sold}}{\text{Average Inventory}}$$	The number of times the merchandise inventory was replenished during the period, or the number of dollars in the cost of goods sold for each dollar of inventory
20	793	Materials Turnover	$$\dfrac{\text{Materials Used}}{\text{Average Materials Inventory}}$$	The number of times the materials inventory was replaced during the period, or the number of dollars of materials used in manufacturing for each dollar of inventory on hand.
20	794	Finished Goods Turnover	$$\dfrac{\text{Cost of Goods Sold}}{\text{Average Finished Goods Inventory}}$$	The number of times the finished goods inventory was sold and replaced during the period, or the number of dollars of cost of finished goods sold for each dollar of finished goods on hand
B. Long-Run Solvency Measurements				
4	165	Creditors' Equity Ratio ✶	$$\dfrac{\text{Total Liabilities}}{\text{Total Assets}}$$	The amount of creditor sources of total assets
4	165	Stockholders' Equity ✶ Ratio	$$\dfrac{\text{Stockholders' Equity}}{\text{Total Assets}}$$	The amount of owner sources of total assets
11	440	Plant and Equipment to Long-Term Liabilities	$$\dfrac{\text{Plant and Equipment (net)}}{\text{Long-Term Debt}}$$	The adequacy of protection to long-term debtors

Figure 17-11 (Continued)

SIGNIFICANT RATIOS (cont.)

Chapter Reference	Page Number	Ratio	Computation of Ratio	Indicates
11	440	Plant and Equipment to Stockholders' Equity	$$\frac{\text{Plant and Equipment (net)}}{\text{Stockholders' Equity}}$$	The extent to which owner sources are being used to finance plant and equipment acquisitions
16	635	Number of Times Preferred Dividends Is Earned ✱	$$\frac{\text{Net Income}}{\text{Annual Preferred Dividend}}$$	The primary measure of the safety of an individual's investment in preferred stock —the ability of a firm to meet its preferred dividend requirement
16	635	Number of Times Bond Interest Is Earned	$$\frac{\text{Net Income} + \text{Income Taxes} + \text{Annual Bond Interest Expense}}{\text{Annual Bond Interest Expense}}$$	The primary measure of the safety of an individual's investment in bonds—the ability of a firm to meet its bond interest requirement

C. Earning Power and Growth Potential Measurements

Chapter Reference	Page Number	Ratio	Computation of Ratio	Indicates
17	673	Net Income to Stockholders' Equity ✱	$$\frac{\text{Net Income}}{\text{Average Stockholders' Equity}}$$	The profitableness of the business expressed as a rate of return on the stockholders' equity
5	200	Operating Ratio ✱	$$\frac{\text{Cost of Goods Sold} + \text{Operating Expenses}}{\text{Net Sales Revenue}}$$	The number of cents needed to generate one dollar of sales
11	440	Sales to Plant and Equipment (Plant Turnover)	$$\frac{\text{Net Sales}}{\text{Average Plant and Equipment (net)}}$$	Dollar of sales per dollar of investment in plant and equipment assets
13	525	Earnings Per Share of Common Stock ✱	$$\frac{\text{Net Income minus Annual Preferred Dividend}}{\text{Outstanding Common Shares}}$$	The company's earning power as related to common stockholders' equity
17	672	Return on Total Investment ✱	$$\frac{\text{Net Income} + \text{Interest Expense}}{\text{Average Total Assets}}$$	The profitableness of the business expressed as a rate of return on total investments by both owners and creditors.
13	521	Earnings Yield Rate ✱	$$\frac{\text{Earnings per Share}}{\text{Market Value per Share}}$$	Earnings as related to market value of the shares
13	521	Dividends Yield Rate ✱	$$\frac{\text{Dividends per Share}}{\text{Market Value per Share}}$$	Dividend payout as related to market value of the shares
13	521	Price-Earnings Ratio ✱	$$\frac{\text{Market Price per Share}}{\text{Earnings per Share}}$$	Profitability of the firm as related to market value of each share

D. Financial Structure Measurements: These measurements can be determined from common-size statements of financial position, which shows the composition of items on each side of the position statement.

E. Asset Utilization Ratios: These are measures of asset turnover or the dollars of sales generated by each dollar of investment in total assets or in each individual asset.

F. Operating Performance Ratios: These are measures which show the relationship of each income statement item or groups of items to sales.

ties in the analysis of financial statements. With the aid of these ratios, the skilled analyst is better able to evaluate the managerial efficiency and financial stability of a company.

FINANCIAL STATEMENT ANALYSIS—INFLUENCES

The techniques and procedures for the analysis of financial statements discussed thus far are useful tools for gaining an insight into the financial affairs of a business. The analyst must, however, evaluate many other influences that, although not specifically reflected in the statements, may nevertheless influence the future of the company. Careful evaluation must be made of the possible effect on the company of sudden changes in key management personnel, shifts in employee or customer loyalty, development of new competing products, as well as broad shifts in the social, political, or economic environment. Another factor that must be evaluated with care is the impact of changing price levels on the statements. (This problem is covered in Chapter 19.) Differences in financial statements may also be due to the wide variations that exist within the framework of generally accepted accounting principles and procedures—in the valuation of inventories, the selection of depreciation bases, the treatment of intangibles, and the method of disclosing extraordinary and nonrecurring items, for example.

GLOSSARY

Accounting Standards Basic assumptions or conditions accepted by common consent.

All-Inclusive Concept The concept that extraordinary items should be disclosed in the income statement.

Auditor's Opinion The statement made by the auditor regarding his audit work and his opinion on the fairness of the presentation of financial position and results of operations.

Comparative Statements Successive financial statements of a company given side by side.

Current Assets Cash and other assets that are reasonably expected to be realized in cash or sold or consumed during the normal operating cycle of the business or one year, whichever is longer.

Current Liabilities Obligations whose liquidation will require the use of current assets, or the creation of other current liabilities, within a year or operating cycle, whichever is longer.

Current Operating Performance Concept The concept that extraordinary items should be disclosed in the statement of retained earnings rather than in the income statement.

Deferred Charges Long-term unallocated charges against future operations.

Deferred Credits Long-term unallocated credits to future operations.

Extraordinary Items Events and transactions that are of an unusual nature and that recur infrequently.

Intangible Assets Long-term assets, without physical form or substance, representing rights to future benefits which are without physical form or substance.

Long-Term Investments Nonoperating long-term assets.

Long-Term Liabilities Obligations that will not be liquidated until after the current year or the operating cycle.

Multiple-Step Income Statement A form of income statement that groups revenue and deductions so as to arrive at a series of intermediate subtotals culminating in net income after extraordinary items.

Rate of Return on Stockholders' Equity Net income divided by average stockholders' equity.

Rate of Return on Total Investment Net income plus interest expense divided by the average total equities (liabilities plus stockholders' equity).

Single-Step Income Statement A form of income statement in which all revenues appear in one section, and all deductions from revenue in another section, without any intermediate subtotals.

Stockholders' Equity The excess of assets over liabilities; the section of the statement of financial position that shows the amounts and sources of assets from investors and from earnings.

Trend Percentages An analytical device for condensing the absolute dollar data of comparative statements.

Q17-1. (a) What are some limitations of financial statements? (b) List and discuss some factors contributing to the development of financial reporting to outside groups.

Q17-2. (a) Discuss the characteristics of a good managerial report. (b) Discuss the purposes of financial statements.

Q17-3. Discuss the four basic devices that are commonly used to achieve interpretative statement presentation.

Q17-4. What major classifications may be applied (a) to assets, (b) to liabilities, and (c) to stockholders' equity items? Indicate the nature of the data that are reported within each classification.

Q17-5. (a) Give an example (1) of an asset offset, (2) of a liability offset, and (3) of a stockholders' equity offset. (b) When is an offset improperly applied?

Q17-6. (a) Define the term *contingent liability*. (b) State three ways in which Notes Receivable Discounted may be disclosed on the financial statements.

Q17-7. How has the AICPA's *APB Opinions No. 9* and *No. 30* altered the accountant's view (a) of the current operating performance concept of income reporting and (b) of the all-inclusive income statement concept?

Q17-8. "The financial statement analyst should have available comparative statements, showing changes in absolute amounts and percentage changes." Explain.

Q17-9. Comment on the significance of each of the following factors to the financial statement analyst:

1. A steadily increasing price level
2. An increase in inventory
3. An increase in plant and equipment
4. An increase in sales
5. An increase in sales and a decrease in accounts receivable
6. An increase in liabilities

Q17-10. Trend percentages are of limited usefulness (a) because they do not indicate whether the change is favorable or unfavorable, (b) because the change may be in relation to a year that is not typical or normal, and (c) because they do not measure the effectiveness of management. Discuss.

Q17-11. What are the advantages and limitations to the analyst of the following: (a) comparative statements, (b) trend percentages, and (c) common-size percentages?

Q17-12. Explain how each of the following would be determined:

1. A company's earning power
2. The extent to which owner sources have been used to finance plant and equipment acquisitions
3. The adequacy of protection to long-term debtors
4. The rapidity with which the accounts receivable are collected
5. The ability of a business to meet quickly the unexpected demands for working capital

Q17-13. What ratios or other analytical devices will help to answer the following questions?

1. Is there an overinvestment in plant and equipment?
2. Are the assets distributed satisfactorily?
3. Is there adequate protection for creditors?
4. How is the business being financed?
5. Are earnings adequate?
6. Is there a satisfactory relationship between creditor and owner financing?
7. Are costs and expenses too high? Are sales adequate?

Q17-14. (a) What knowledge must an analyst possess to enable him to evaluate financial statement data successfully? (b) What are some of the influences that are not specifically reflected in financial statements but which an analyst must evaluate to draw correct inferences from his analysis of financial statements?

EXERCISES

E17-1. The following items are among those which would appear on the statement of financial position as of December 31, 1976, for the Hanna Company:

1. Marketable Securities
2. Subscriptions Receivable—Common Stock
3. Notes Receivable
4. Notes Receivable Discounted
5. Discount on Notes Payable
6. Discount on Bonds Payable
7. Discount on Common Stock
8. Unearned Interest Included in Face Value of Notes Receivable
9. Treasury Stock—Common

10. Stock Dividend to Be Issued—Common

Indicate the statement of financial position classification of each item.

E17-2. The following information is available for the Hamblin Company as of December 31, 1976:

Gain from sale of equipment	$ 30,000
Net sales revenue	900,000
Income taxes—1976	110,000
Selling and administrative expenses	225,000
Cost of goods sold	440,000
Loss on write-off of abandoned equipment	4,000
Uninsured loss through fire	5,000
Adjustment for cost of maintenance and repairs charged to plant and equipment	3,500
Retained earnings, Dec. 31, 1975 (credit)	60,000
Dividends declared	50,000
Income tax refund for prior years	15,000

Prepare (a) a multiple-step income statement and (b) a statement of retained earnings for the Hamblin Company for the year ended December 31, 1976.

E17-3. Refer to E17-2. (a) Prepare a combined statement of income and retained earnings. (b) Prepare a single-step income statement.

E17-4. Assume that you have been hired as chief accountant for the Jones Company on December 31, 1976, before the books were closed. In looking back over the accounting records you discover the following errors:

1. The December 31, 1975, merchandise inventory was overstated by $3,500 because some merchandise items had been included twice.

2. On December 31, 1975, accrued interest payable of $350 had not been recorded; this amount was recorded as an expense in 1976 when it was paid.

3. The liability for invoices from merchandise suppliers is not recorded until the goods are inspected and marked, although merchandise in the receiving and marking department is correctly included in the physical inventory taken at the end of the year. The cost of the uninspected and unmarked merchandise in the receiving and marking department at end of 1975 and 1976 was:

December 31, 1975	$2,575
December 31, 1976	4,750

Prepare correcting journal entries as of December 31, 1976.

E17-5. The following groups of items are presented for various companies as of December 31, 1976 and 1977, or for the years then ended:

	1977	1976
1. Sales	$248,000	$192,000
Cost of Goods Sold	160,000	128,000
Operating Expenses	40,000	32,000
Net Income	36,000	24,000
2. Current Liabilities	120,000	80,000
Mortgage Bonds Payable	180,000	200,000
3. Common Stock	480,000	400,000

	1977	1976
Preferred Stock	120,000	160,000
Retained Earnings (deficit)	(4,000)	40,000
4. Cash	57,000	85,000
Accounts Receivable	52,000	56,000
Inventories	24,000	32,000
Other Current Assets	1,500	1,000
Land	8,000	8,000
Buildings	200,000	168,000
Accumulated Depreciation—Buildings	30,000	24,000

Compute the percentage increase or decrease for each item, and indicate possible reasons for the changes.

E17-6. Assume the following transactions:

1. Borrowed cash from the bank; issued a $5,000, 60-day, 9% note.
2. Purchased machinery for $60,000; paid $25,000 in cash and issued a 120-day note for the balance.
3. Sold for $25,000 some plant and equipment items that had a book value of $30,000.
4. Wrote off $1,500 of uncollectible accounts to Allowance for Doubtful Accounts.
5. Declared a stock dividend of $35,000.
6. Paid $4,800 to trade creditors.

Indicate the effect of the foregoing transactions on the working capital.

E17-7. The following information is given:

	1977	1976
Net Sales	$1,397,000	$1,122,000
Cost of Goods Sold	935,000	814,000
Selling Expenses	154,000	121,000
General Expenses	88,000	77,000
Other Revenue	4,000	7,000
Other Expenses	2,000	9,000
Income Taxes	134,000	66,000

(a) Prepare a comparative income statement with common-size percentages.
(b) Indicate the favorable and unfavorable changes.

E17-8. The following condensed information is taken from the statement of the Muldoon Company:

	December 31	
	1977	1976
Current Assets	$456,000	$340,000
Plant and Equipment (net)	580,000	600,000
Current Liabilities	260,000	244,000
Long-Term Liabilities	200,000	240,000
Capital Stock	450,000	400,000
Retained Earnings	126,000	56,000

Prepare a condensed comparative statement of financial position, showing the dollar amounts and the percentages of increase or decrease during 1977.

E17-9. The following balances were taken from the books of the Murphy Corporation as of May 31, 1977 and 1976:

	May 31	
	1977	1976
Current Assets	$115,000	$ 85,000
Plant and Equipment	145,000	152,500
Current Liabilities	65,000	55,000
Long-Term Liabilities	57,500	65,000
Common Stock	112,500	100,000
Retained Earnings	25,000	17,500

Prepare a comparative statement of financial position showing common-size percentages.

E17-10. The following revenue and expense data of the Moor Company for the year 1976 are given:

Sales	$315,000
Cost of Goods Sold	195,000
Selling Expenses	27,000
General Expenses	18,000
Interest Expense	3,750
Income Taxes	35,625
Net Income	35,625

Prepare a revenue-dollar statement.

E17-11. In the left-hand column a series of transactions is listed; in the right-hand column, a series of ratios:

Transaction	Ratio
1. Declaration of a cash dividend	Current ratio
2. Write-off of an uncollectible account receivable	Receivables turnover
3. Purchase of inventory on open account	Acid-test ratio
4. Issuance of 10-year mortgage bonds	Rate of return on total assets
5. Issuance of additional shares of stock for cash	Creditor equity ratio
6. Issue of stock dividend on common stock	Earnings per share
7. Appropriation of retained earnings	Rate of return on stockholders' equity
8. Purchase of supplies on open account	Current ratio
9. Payment to short-term creditor in full	Acid-test ratio
10. Payment of accounts payable, taking the cash discount	Inventory turnover

State whether each transaction will cause the indicated ratio to increase, decrease, or remain unchanged. For the current ratio, receivables turnover, acid-test ratio, and inventory turnover, assume that the ratio is greater than 1:1 before each transaction occurred.

E17-12. On December 31, 1975, the stockholders' equity section of the balance sheet of Mason Co. was as follows:

Common stock (Par value $1; 1,000 shares authorized; 300 shares issued and outstanding)	$ 300
Additional paid-in capital	1,800
Retained earnings	2,000
	$4,100

On January 2, 1976, the board of directors declared a stock dividend of one share for each three shares owned. Accordingly, 100 additional shares of stock were issued. On January 2 the fair market value of Mason's stock was $10 a share.

Required: Answer the following questions: The most appropriate presentation of Mason's stockholders' equity on January 2, 1976, following the issuance of the 100 additional shares is:

a.

Common stock (Par value $1; 1,000 authorized shares; 400 shares issued and outstanding)	$ 400
Additional paid-in capital	1,700
Retained earnings	2,000
	$4,100

b.

Common stock (Par value $1; 1,000 shares authorized, 400; shares issued and outstanding)	$ 400
Additional paid-in capital	1,800
Retained earnings	1,900
	$4,100

c.

Common stock (Par value $1; 1,000 shares authorized; 400 shares issued and outstanding)	$ 400
Additional paid-in capital	2,700
Retained earnings	1,000
	$4,100

d.

Common stock (Par value $1; 1,000 shares authorized; 400 shares issued and outstanding)	$ 400
Additional paid-in capital	2,400
Retained earnings	1,300
	$4,100

(*AICPA adapted*)

**DEMON-
STRATION
PROBLEMS**

DP17-1. (*Statement of financial position*) The following terms appear on various statements of financial position:

Current Assets	Deferred Charges
Long-Term Investments	Current Liabilities
Plant and Equipment	Long-Term Liabilities
Intangible Assets	Stockholders' Equity

Required:

1. Define and give several examples of each term.
2. Indicate three ways of grouping the items in formal statements of financial position.

DP17-2. (*Correcting errors*) Assume that you are hired as chief accountant of the Palmer Company as of December 31, 1976, before the books are closed. To familiarize yourself with the accounting procedures, you review the records for the two preceding years and discover the following errors:

a. The depreciation on the building was recorded as $2,000 in 1975; it should have been $4,000.

b. The December 31, 1975, inventory was understated by $2,500.

c. The company purchased a typewriter on July 1, 1975, at a cost of $500. This amount was debited to Office Expense. Normally, the Palmer Company depreciates office equipment by the straight-line method, using a five-year life.

d. The liability for a $3,000 purchase was not recorded as of December 28, 1976, when the purchase was made, although the amount was correctly included in the December 31, 1976, periodic inventory.

Required: Prepare correcting and adjusting entries as of December 31, 1976.

DP17-3. (*Single-step income statement and multiple-step income statement*) The following information is taken from the books of the Paradise Company on December 31, 1976:

Retained Earnings, December 31, 1975 (credit)	$ 26,000
Loss from Sale of Land	2,400
Sales	224,000
Loss from Flood	3,200
Cost of Goods Sold	112,000
Adjustment for Cost of Machinery Charged to Equipment Repairs	2,800
Income Taxes	34,000
Understatement of Depreciation in Prior Years	4,800
Selling and General and Administrative Expenses	36,000
Dividends Declared	20,000

Required:

1. Prepare a multiple-step income statement and a statement of retained earnings.

2. Prepare a combined statement of income and retained earnings.

3. Prepare a single-step income statement.

DP17-4. (*Comparative statements: amount and percentage of increase or decrease*) The condensed comparative statements of Page, Inc., follow:

PAGE, INC.
Comparative Statement of Financial Position
December 31, 1977 and 1976

	December 31	
	1977	1976
Current Assets	$270,000	$232,500
Plant and Equipment	285,000	307,500

	December 31	
	1977	1976
Total Assets	$555,000	$540,000
Current Liabilities	$103,500	$ 81,750
Long-Term Liabilities	105,000	112,500
Total Liabilities	$208,500	$194,250
Capital Stock	$300,000	$300,000
Retained Earnings	46,500	45,750
Total Stockholders' Equity	$346,500	$345,750
Total Liabilities and Stockholders' Equity	$555,000	$540,000

PAGE, INC.
Comparative Statement of Income and Retained Earnings
For the Years Ended December 31, 1977 and 1976

	Years Ended December 31	
	1977	1976
Sales (net)	$742,500	$825,000
Cost of Goods Sold	564,000	615,000
Gross Margin on Sales	$178,500	$210,000
Operating Expenses	123,000	142,500
Net Income Before Income Taxes	$ 55,500	$ 67,500
Income Taxes	27,750	33,750
Net Income	$ 27,750	$ 33,750
Retained Earnings, January 1	45,750	45,000
Total Net Income and Retained Earnings	$ 73,500	$ 78,750
Dividends Declared	27,000	33,000
Retained Earnings, December 31	$ 46,500	$ 45,750

Required:

1. Prepare a comparative statement of income and retained earnings, showing the amount and percentage of increase or decrease during 1977.
2. Prepare a comparative position statement, showing the amount and percentage of increase or decrease during 1977.
3. Write a report indicating whether the financial condition and operating results are favorable or unfavorable and stating your reasons.

DP17-5. (*Comparative statements—trend percentages*) The following information is taken from the books of the Rockwood Company:

	1976	1977	1978	1979
Sales	$337,500	$368,750	$390,625	$421,875
Cost of Goods Sold	195,000	217,100	229,000	246,000
Accounts Receivable	50,000	57,500	61,000	67,000
Merchandise Inventory	87,500	101,500	107,625	114,625
Net Income	30,000	30,600	31,500	32,400

Required:

1. Calculate the trend percentages (1976 is the base year).
2. Point out the favorable and unfavorable tendencies.

DP17-6. (*Common-size statements: revenue-dollar statements*) The comparative condensed financial statements of the Becker Company are as follows:

BECKER COMPANY
Comparative Statement of Financial Position
December 31, 1977 and 1976

	December 31	
	1977	1976
Current Assets	$152,000	$185,250
Plant and Equipment	399,000	308,750
Total Assets	$551,000	$494,000
Current Liabilities	$ 98,800	$218,500
Long-Term Liabilities	239,400	114,000
Total Liabilities	$338,200	$332,500
Capital Stock	$186,200	$142,500
Retained Earnings	26,600	19,000
Total Stockholders' Equity	$212,800	$161,500
Total Liabilities and Stockholders' Equity	$551,000	$494,000

BECKER COMPANY
Comparative Income Statement
For the Years Ended December 31, 1977 and 1976

	Years Ended December 31	
	1977	1976
Sales (net)	$960,000	$855,000
Cost of Goods Sold	550,800	483,750
Gross Margin on Sales	$409,200	$371,250

| | Years Ended December 31 | |
	1977	1976
Operating Expenses		
Selling Expenses	$204,600	$165,000
General Expenses	120,900	82,500
Total Operating Expenses	$325,500	$247,500
Net Income	$ 83,700	$123,750

Required:

1. Prepare (a) a comparative common-size statement of financial position, (b) a comparative common-size income statement, and (c) a comparative revenue-dollar statement.

2. Discuss the financial condition and operating results of the company, emphasizing favorable and unfavorable trends.

PROBLEMS

P17-1. The postclosing trial balance of the Nickerson Corporation is given below.

NICKERSON CORPORATION
Postclosing Trial Balance
December 31, 1976

Cash	$ 90,000	
Marketable Securities (at cost; market value is $28,000)	25,000	
Accounts Receivable	72,000	
Allowance for Doubtful Accounts		$ 3,000
Merchandise Inventory	225,000	
Accrued Bond Interest Receivable	6,000	
Prepaid Insurance	3,000	
Bond Sinking Fund	10,000	
Investment in Bonds— Excel Company Bonds	100,000	
Delivery Equipment	8,000	
Accumulated Depreciation— Delivery Equipment		2,000
Machinery and Equipment	450,000	
Accumulated Depreciation— Machinery and Equipment		50,000
Accounts Payable		122,000
Estimated Income Taxes Payable		50,000
Accrued Bond Interest Payable		6,000
First Mortgage 8% Bonds Payable		100,000
Discount on First Mortgage Bonds Payable	1,200	
Second Mortgage 10% Bonds Payable		50,000
Premium on Second Mortgage Bonds Payable		1,000

Preferred Stock, 10%, $100 par value		200,000
Common Stock, $50 par value		300,000
Retained Earnings		58,200
Prepaid Rent	2,000	
Retained Earnings—		
Restricted for Plant Addition		40,000
Retained Earnings—Restricted for First		
Mortgage Bond Redemption		10,000
Totals	$992,200	$992,200

Required: Prepare the statement of financial position for the Nickerson Corporation as of December 31, 1976, showing working capital and net assets on the left-hand side balanced by stockholders' equity on the right-hand side.

P17-2. Assume that you are hired as chief accountant of the Nichols Company as of December 31, 1976, before the books are closed. To familiarize yourself with the accounting procedures of the firm, you review the records for the two preceding years and discover the following errors:

a. The depreciation of the building was recorded as $1,000 in 1975; it should have been recorded as $10,000.

b. The December 31, 1975, inventory was overstated by $3,500.

c. An unrecorded bill in the amount of $1,850 for a 1975 purchase was paid in 1976; Purchases was debited.

d. The freight cost of $700 incurred for the purchase of machinery was debited to Transportation In on September 15, 1975, when the amount was paid. No part of this cost was assigned to the December 31, 1975, inventory. Machinery is depreciated by the straight-line method, assuming a 20-year life.

e. Merchandise costing $1,500 was sold on credit for $2,000 on December 21, 1975; it was returned on December 29, 1975. No entry was made in 1975 to record the return; the entry debiting Sales Returns and Allowances was made on January 5, 1976. The merchandise was included in the December 31, 1975, inventory at the selling price.

Required: Prepare correcting journal entries.

P17-3. The following information is taken from the books of the Flagship Company on December 31, 1976:

Retained Earnings, December 31, 1975 (credit)	$ 127,500
Sales	1,125,000
Dividends Declared	97,500
Selling and General and Administrative Expenses	420,000
Loss on Sale of Securities	7,500
Income Taxes	49,500
Cost of Goods Sold	585,000
Loss on Disposal of Equipment	10,500
Overstatement of Depreciation in Prior Years	12,000
Gain from Disposal of Building	22,500

Required:

1. Prepare a multiple-step income statement and a statement of retained earnings.
2. Prepare a combined statement of income and retained earnings.
3. Prepare single-step income statement.

P17-4. (*Financial policy decision problem*) The Yee Company presents the following comparative information as of December 31, 1976 and 1977:

	1977	1976
Cash	$ 15,200	$ 14,000
Accounts Receivable	16,800	10,000
Notes Receivable	15,200	4,000
Inventories	26,000	28,000
Machinery and Equipment (net)	36,000	40,000
Land	16,000	16,000
Building (net)	40,000	48,000
Accounts Payable	22,000	18,800
Notes Payable (current)	6,000	11,600
Mortgage Payable (long-term)	28,000	40,000
Capital Stock ($100 par value)	100,000	80,000
Retained Earnings, January 1 (credit)	?	8,000
Sales (net)	154,000	120,000
Cost of Goods Sold	100,000	74,000
Operating Expenses	28,800	28,000
Income Taxes	13,600	9,200
Dividends Declared	12,000	7,200

Required:

1. Prepare comparative financial statements, including the amounts and the percentages of change during 1977.
2. Write a report to management indicating the favorable and unfavorable financial and operating trends.

P17-5. Condensed comparative financial statements for the Wagner Manufacturing Company appear below.

WAGNER MANUFACTURING COMPANY
Comparative Statements of Financial Position
October 31, 1978, 1977, and 1976
(in thousands of dollars)

Assets	1978	1977	1976
Current Assets	$ 13,600	$15,000	$20,000
Plant and Equipment (net of accumulated depreciation)	84,000	72,000	60,000
Intangible Assets	6,000	8,000	10,000
Total Assets	$103,600	$95,000	$90,000

Liabilities and Stockholders' Equity	1978	1977	1976
Liabilities			
Current Liabilities	$ 10,400	$10,000	$ 8,000
Long-Term Liabilities			
(net of discount)	19,600	19,200	18,800
Stockholders' Equity			
Capital Stock ($50 par)	48,000	40,000	40,000
Capital in Excess of Par Value	3,600	2,000	2,000
Retained Earnings	22,000	23,800	21,200
Total Liabilities and			
Stockholders' Equity	$103,600	$95,000	$90,000

WAGNER MANUFACTURING COMPANY
Comparative Income Statements
For the Years Ended October 31, 1978, 1977, and 1976
(in thousands of dollars)

	1978	1977	1976
Net Sales	$280,000	$240,000	$200,000
Cost of Goods Sold	210,000	174,000	140,000
Gross Margin on Sales	$ 70,000	$ 66,000	$ 60,000
Selling Expenses	$ 27,600	$ 24,800	$ 20,000
Administrative Expenses	29,400	28,800	28,000
Interest Expense	980	960	940
Total Expenses	$ 57,980	$ 54,560	$ 48,940
Net Income Before Income Taxes	$ 12,020	$ 11,440	$ 11,060
Provision for Income Taxes	6,140	5,920	5,660
Net Income After Income Taxes	$ 5,880	$ 5,520	$ 5,400

Required:

1. Compute the trend percentages for all statement of financial position items, using 1976 as the base year.
2. Prepare common-size comparative income statements for the three-year period, expressing all items as percentage components of net sales.
3. Comment on the significant trends and relationships revealed by the analytical computations in requirements 1 and 2.

P17-6. In the following schedule, certain items taken from the income statements of the Monroe Company have been expressed as percentages of net sales:

	Percentage of Net Sales	
	1977	1976
Net Sales	100	100
Beginning Inventory	16	10
Net Purchases	60	68
Ending Inventory	12	8
Selling Expenses	15	13
Administrative Expenses	9	8
Provision for Income Taxes	3.6	2.7

Net sales were $300,000 in 1976; they increased by 25% in 1977. Average accounts receivable were $30,000 in 1977 and $32,000 in 1976. Credit sales were 75% of total sales in both years.

Required:

1. Did the net income increase or decrease in 1977 as compared with 1976, and by how much? Prepare a comparative income statement to support your answer.
2. Compute the average length in days of the company's receivables turnover days for both years, showing the basis of your computation.

P17-7. Statements for the Wahtola Company as of December 31, 1976, follow:

WAHTOLA COMPANY
Income Statement
For the Year Ended December 31, 1976

Gross Sales	$887,400
Sales Returns and Allowances	13,500
Net Sales	$873,900
Cost of Goods Sold	624,000
Gross Margin on Sales	$249,900
Operating Expenses	195,900
Net Income from Operations	$ 54,000
Interest on Mortgage Payable	2,400
Net Income before Income Taxes	$ 51,600
Federal Income Taxes	18,600
Net Income after Income Taxes	$ 33,000

WAHTOLA COMPANY
Statement of Financial Position
December 31, 1976

Assets

Current Assets			
Cash		$ 36,000	
Accounts Receivable	$285,000		
Deduct Allowance for Doubtful Accounts	18,000	267,000	
Inventory		240,000	
Total Current Assets			$543,000
Plant and Equipment			
Land		$ 60,000	
Building	$180,000		
Deduct Accumulated Depreciation	36,000	144,000	
Store Equipment	$ 45,000		
Deduct Accumulated Depreciation	21,000	24,000	
Total Plant and Equipment			228,000
Total Assets			$771,000

Liabilities and Stockholders' Equity

Current Liabilities		
Accounts Payable	$259,800	
Accrued Expenses Payable	87,000	
Total Current Liabilities		$346,800
Long-Term Liabilities		
Mortgage Payable		60,000
Total Liabilities		$406,800
Stockholders' Equity		
Preferred Stock, 6%, $100 Par Value	$ 60,000	
Common Stock, $100 Par Value	240,000	
Retained Earnings	64,200	
Total Stockholders' Equity		364,200
Total Liabilities and Stockholders' Equity		$771,000

On December 31, 1975, the inventory was $300,000 and the total stockholders' equity was $345,000.

Required: Compute the following (carry to two decimal places):
Current ratio
Acid-test ratio
Inventory turnover
Percent of year's net sales uncollected
Ratio of stockholders' equity to total assets
Ratio of net sales to stockholders' equity
Ratio of plant and equipment assets to long-term debt
Earnings per share of common stock
Percent of net income to average stockholders' equity
Number of times preferred dividends is earned
Number of times mortgage interest is earned

P17-8. (*Financial policy decision problem*) Certain financial information for the Glazer Company and the Quaid Company as of the end of 1976, are shown below.

	Glazer Company	Quaid Company
Current Assets	$ 720,000	$ 660,000
Plant and Equipment	3,048,000	2,310,000
Accumulated Depreciation	(480,000)	(360,000)
Patents	12,000	–0–
Goodwill	–0–	30,000
Total Assets	$3,300,000	$2,640,000
Current Liabilities	$ 390,000	$ 204,000
Bonds Payable, 9%, due in 10 years	600,000	720,000
Preferred Stock, 10%, $100 par value	720,000	480,000
Common Stock, $25 par value	1,200,000	900,000
Retained Earnings	270,000	180,000

	Glazer Company	Quaid Company
Retained Earnings Restricted for Contingencies	120,000	–0–
Premium on Common Stock	–0–	156,000
Total Liabilities and Stockholders' Equity	$3,300,000	$2,640,000
Analysis of Retained Earnings.		
Balance, beginning of year	$ 273,600	$ 148,800
Net Income for year	224,400	118,800
Dividends: Preferred	(50,400)	(33,600)
Dividends: Common	(57,600)	(54,000)
Additions to Retained Earnings— Restricted for Contingencies	(120,000)	–0–
Balance, end of year	$ 270,000	$ 180,000
Market price of common stock per share	$ 40	$ 40
Market price of preferred stock per share	110	107

Required: Under the assumption that the two companies are generally comparable, write a brief answer to each of the following questions. Use only the ratios that will most reasonably substantiate your answer and indicate why. Compute the amount of each ratio and percentage indicated (carry your computations to one place beyond the decimal point).

1. Since the market prices of the bonds are not given, what ratios would aid potential investors to determine which bonds would probably sell at the higher price and which bonds would probably yield the higher return?
2. What ratio(s) would aid potential investors in preferred stock to determine which company's preferred stock is the safer investment?
3. To what extent is each company benefiting from the leverage factor inherent in the existence of the bonds? of preferred stock?
4. What are the dividend yield rates and earnings per share for the common stock of each company?

P17-9. (*Financial policy decision problem*) The Walters Corporation has issued convertible bonds under an agreement to maintain net assets, defined in the agreement as assets minus all liabilities except the convertible bonds, at an amount not less than 230% of the convertible bonds outstanding; to maintain current assets at not less than 200% of the current liabilities; and to maintain working capital at not less than 100% of the convertible bonds outstanding.

On December 31, 1976, the corporation's adjusted trial balance was as follows:

WALTERS CORPORATION
Adjusted Trial Balance
December 31, 1976

	Debits	Credits
Cash	$ 30,000	
Marketable Securities	225,000	

	Debits	Credits
Accounts Receivable	222,000	
Allowance for Doubtful Accounts		$ 9,000
Inventory	339,000	
Prepaid Expenses	18,000	
Land	54,000	
Building	468,000	
Accumulated Depreciation—Building		63,000
Equipment	672,000	
Accumulated Depreciation—Equipment		126,000
Accounts Payable		207,000
Notes Payable, 4-Year (due 12/20/79)		225,000
Accrued Expenses Payable		18,000
Convertible Bonds Payable		600,000
Common Stock		450,000
Retained Earnings		330,000
Totals	$2,028,000	$2,028,000

In January 1977, it was discovered that title had passed as of December 31, 1976, on incoming merchandise costing $100,000. Since the merchandise was not on hand, it was not included in the inventory. The corporation had recorded $50,000 of collections from customers received on January 2, 1977, under the date of December 31, 1976, on the theory that such collections in all probability were in the mail before midnight, December 31, 1976. In the afternoon of January 2, 1977, the corporation wrote and mailed checks to creditors, dating and recording the checks as of December 31, 1976; the checks amounted to $50,000, equal to the collections in transit.

Required:

1. Contrast, by means of comparative ratios, the reported conditions with those you believe more fairly indicate the status of the corporation. Limit your comparison to the ratios mentioned in the agreement with the bond-holders.
2. Comment briefly on your findings.

P17-10. (*Financial policy decision problem*) Following is the Stockholders' Equity section of the statement of financial position of Castley, Inc., as of December 31, 1976:

CASTLEY, INC.
Partial Statement of Financial Position
December 31, 1976

Stockholders' Equity

Paid-In Capital
  Capital Stock
    Preferred Stock—9% cumulative,
      entitled to $105 a share plus
      cumulative dividends in arrears in
      liquidations; $100 par value;

---

authorized 20,000 shares, issued and outstanding, 16,000 shares of which 1,000 are held in treasury	$1,600,000	
Common Stock—no par value, $40 stated value; authorized 40,000 shares; issued and outstanding, 32,000 shares	1,280,000	
Stock Dividend to be Issued, 8,000 shares	320,000	$3,200,000
Paid-In Capital in Excess of Par or Stated Value		
Premium on Preferred Stock	$ 48,000	
From Treasury Stock Transactions—Preferred	4,000	
Excess Over Stated Value on No-Par Common Stock	112,000	
From Stock Dividend—Common	32,000	
Discount on Common Stock	(2,000)	194,000
Donated Capital (land donated by Suffolk County)		30,000
Total Paid-In Capital		$3,424,000
Retained Earnings		
Restricted, not available for dividends— equal to cost of treasury stock	$ 83,000	
Unrestricted	200,600	283,600
Total		$3,707,600
Deduct cost of Treasury Stock—Preferred		83,000
Total Stockholders' Equity		$3,624,600

Required:

1. Why did Castley, Inc., restrict a part of its retained earnings?
2. (a) What is the book value per share of common stock? (b) What is its significance to a potential investor in common stock of the corporation? (c) What is the book value of the preferred stock? (d) What is its significance?
3. Why did Castley, Inc., reacquire some of its own shares?
4. What is the significance of the two major subdivisions of the Stockholders' Equity section?
5. Total retained earnings as at December 31, 1976, amount to $283,600. What future transactions or events will increase this amount? reduce it?
6. What would be the effect on the foregoing stockholder equity accounts, if, early in 1977, the corporation (a) declared a 50% stock dividend, (b) declared a 2-for-1 stock split, (c) issued 500 shares of common stock to holders of $25,000 of its convertible debenture bonds, and (d) issued additional common stock at a premium for cash.

P17-11. The L. Konrath Company is considering extending credit to the D. Hawk Company. It is estimated that sales to the D. Hawk Company would amount to $2,000,000 each year. The L. Konrath Company is a wholesaler that sells throughout the Midwest. The D. Hawk Company is a retail chain operation that has a number of stores in the Midwest. The L. Konrath Company has had a gross margin of approximately 60% in recent years and expects to have a similar gross margin on the D. Hawk Company order. The D. Hawk Company order is approximately 15% of the L. Konrath Company's present sales. Recent statements of the D. Hawk Company are as follows:

D. HAWK COMPANY
Statement of Financial Position
As of December 31
(000,000 omitted)

Assets	1974	1975	1976
Current Assets			
Cash	$ 2.6	$ 1.8	$ 1.6
Government Securities (Cost)	.4	.2	—
Accounts and Notes Receivable (Net)	8.0	8.5	8.5
Inventories	2.8	3.2	2.8
Prepaid Assets	.7	.6	.6
Total Current Assets	$14.5	$14.3	$13.5
Property, Plant, and Equipment (Net)	4.3	5.4	5.9
Total Assets	$18.8	$19.7	$19.4

Equities	1974	1975	1976
Current Liabilities			
Notes Payable	$ 3.2	$ 3.7	$ 4.2
Accounts Payable	2.8	3.7	4.1
Accrued Expenses & Taxes	.9	1.1	1.0
Total Current Liabilities	$ 6.9	$ 8.5	$ 9.3
Long-Term Debt; 6%	3.0	2.0	1.0
Total Liabilities	$ 9.9	$10.5	$10.3
Shareholders' Equity	8.9	9.2	9.1
Total Equities	$18.8	$19.7	$19.4

D. HAWK COMPANY
Income Statement
For the Year Ended December 31
(000,000 omitted)

	1974	1975	1976
Net Sales	$24.2	$24.5	$24.9
Cost of Goods Sold	16.9	17.2	18.0
Gross Margin	$ 7.3	$ 7.3	$ 6.9
Selling Expenses	$ 4.3	$ 4.4	$ 4.6
Administrative Expenses	2.3	2.4	2.7
Total Expenses	$ 6.6	$ 6.8	$ 7.3
Earning (loss) Before Taxes	$ .7	$ .5	$(.4)
Income Taxes	.3	.2	(.2)
Net Income (Loss)	$ .4	$ .3	$(.2)

DISCLOSURE IN
FINANCIAL
REPORTING

Required:

1. Calculate for the year 1976 the following ratios:
   a. rate of return on total assets
   b. acid-test ratio
   c. return to sales
   d. current ratio
   e. inventory turnover
2. As part of the analysis to determine whether or not Konrath should extend credit to Hawk, assume the ratios below were calculated from Hawk Company statements. For each ratio indicate whether it is a favorable, unfavorable, or neutral statistic in the decision to grant Hawk credit. Briefly explain your choice in each case.

	1974	1975	1976
1. Rate of return on total assets	1.96%	1.12%	(.87)%
2. Return to sales	1.69%	.99%	(.69)%
3. Acid-test ratio	1.73/1	1.36/1	1.19/1
4. Current ratio	2.39/1	1.92/1	1.67/1
5. Inventory turnover (times)	4.41	4.32	4.52
6. Equity relationships			
Current liabilities	36.0%	43.0%	48.0%
Long-term liabilities	16.0	10.5	5.0
Shareholders	48.0	46.5	47.0
	100.0%	100.0%	100.0%
7. Asset relationships			
Current assets	77.0%	72.5%	69.5%
Property, plant & equipment	23.0%	27.5%	30.5%
	100.0%	100.0%	100.0%

3. Would you grant credit to D. Hawk Co.? Support your answer with facts given in the problem.
4. What additional information, if any, would you require before making a final decision?

(IMA adapted)

Statement of Changes in Financial Position

18

The income statement and the statement of retained earnings disclose the causes of part of, but not all, the changes that take place in the items appearing in the statements of financial position at the beginning and the end of a given period. Businesses engage in a variety of financial transactions, the details of which are not disclosed in either the income statement or the statement of retained earnings. Information regarding the changes in working capital, cash, and/or other financial items are summarized in a fourth major statement entitled *statement of changes in financial position*.

EVOLUTION OF CONTENT OF STATEMENT OF CHANGES IN FINANCIAL POSITION

Prior to 1971, various statements of sources and uses of funds (the typical name given at that time to the present statement of changes in financial position) were presented in some but not all annual reports. These older statements defined funds in several different ways; concepts used included working capital, cash only, cash and securities, current assets, quick assets, or all financial resources. The concept of funds most often employed was that of *working capital;* and, thus, a statement of sources and uses of working capital was frequently included in many annual reports.

In 1971, the Accounting Principles Board in *APB Opinion No. 19* recommended that the broader concept of "all financial resources" be used, that the title of the statement be statement of changes in financial position, and that this statement be a basic financial statement for each period for which an income statement is presented.[1] This latter requirement means that the statement of changes in financial position is mandatory in financial reports and is equal in status to the other three end-of-period financial statements.

APB Opinion No. 19 requires a business to disclose in the statement of changes in financial position "all important aspects of its financing and investing activities regardless of whether cash or other elements of working capital are directly affected."[2] Although the *Opinion* specifically permits flexibility in form, content, and terminology in the statement, it strongly suggests that information about *sources and uses of working capital or cash* be appropriately described, in addition to the inclusion of other financial information such as the issuance of bonds payable in exchange for land, the issuance of common stock to acquire plant and equipment items, the conversion of bonds into common stock, and other financial transactions that *do not affect* working capital.

The statement of changes in financial position has two broad purposes:

1. To strengthen financial planning by providing historical information on sources and uses of financial resources.
2. To help explain to financial statement users the causes of changes in financial position from one statement of financial position prepared as of a given date to the one prepared as of the end of the next period.

Typically, in the preparation of a statement of changes in financial position, attention is *usually* focused first on working capital and then on those financing and investing activities not affecting working capital. It is therefore appropriate that we turn first to a careful consideration of working capital—specifically the preparation of a statement of changes in financial position on a working capital basis. After this narrower concept is carefully identified, the broader concept of "all financial resources" will be illustrated.

STATEMENT OF CHANGES IN FINANCIAL POSITION—WORKING CAPITAL BASIS

The chief sources of working capital are operations, additional investments by owners, long-term borrowing, and the sale of assets. The chief uses of working capital are to increase noncurrent assets, retire long-term debt, reduce the owner's or the stockholders' equity, and provide for the declaration of dividends. The statement of changes in financial position on a working capital basis emphasizes the interrelationship of the sources (inflows) and uses (outflows) of working capital. A chart of working capital inflows and outflows based on an analogy between the flow of working capital through a business and the flow of water into and out of a container is shown in Figure 18-1.

[1] AICPA, *APB Accounting Principles,* vol. 2 (Chicago: Commerce Clearing House, Inc., 1973), p. 6680.
[2] *Ibid.,* p. 6680.

Figure 18-1
Working Capital
Inflows and Outflows

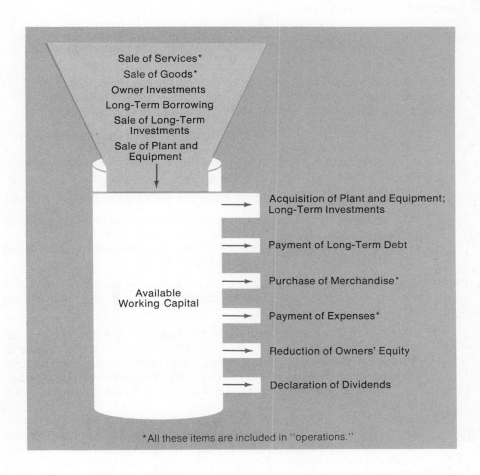

Sale of Services*
Sale of Goods*
Owner Investments
Long-Term Borrowing
Sale of Long-Term Investments
Sale of Plant and Equipment

Available Working Capital

Acquisition of Plant and Equipment; Long-Term Investments

Payment of Long-Term Debt

Purchase of Merchandise*

Payment of Expenses*

Reduction of Owners' Equity

Declaration of Dividends

*All these items are included in "operations."

Purpose of the Statement of Changes in Financial Position on a Working Capital Basis

It is often difficult for management and others to understand how the net income for a period was disposed of and the effect of the flow of working capital through the business. Readers of the conventional financial statements often ask such questions as: Where did the working capital come from? What was done with it? What happened to the various asset items during the period? Why did working capital decrease although earnings were favorable? Why were dividends not larger? Is the company solvent? Where did the working capital for replacement or expansion come from? What kind of financial decisions were made during the period? The statement of changes in financial position helps to answer these questions.

The smooth flow of working capital into and out of a business is the result of a continuing series of managerial decisions, often requiring a high level of skill and judgment. The statement helps the reader to understand not only the

(Ch. 18)

financial well-being of the company but also the effectiveness of the financial policies of its management.

Approaches to the Problem of Determining the Sources and Uses of Working Capital

In determining the information to be included in the statement of changes in financial position prepared under a working capital basis, a source of working capital—a cause of increase in working capital—must result:

1. In an increase in current assets without a corresponding increase in current liabilities, or
2. In a decrease in current liabilities without a corresponding decrease in current assets.

A use of working capital—a cause of decrease in working capital—must result:

1. In a decrease in current assets without a corresponding decrease in current liabilities, or
2. In an increase in current liabilities without a corresponding increase in current assets.

Since these sources and uses are compiled for a specific period, a month or a year, there are two possible alternative approaches to the solution of the problem.

1. An analysis of every transaction occurring during the period which affects a current asset or a current liability to determine the causes of changes in the working capital figure. This method would require much work, because many changes in both current assets and current liabilities *do not* change working capital—for example, the collection of accounts receivable.
2. An analysis of every transaction occurring during the period which affects a noncurrent account—long-term investments, plant and equipment, intangible assets, long-term liabilities, and stockholders' equity—to determine the causes of change in working capital. This approach is a shorter one; it can be used because every change in working capital must result in a change in one or more of the noncurrent accounts.[3] This is the approach that is used in the following pages to determine the sources and uses of working capital that will be incorporated in the statement of changes in financial position—working capital basis.

Classification of Transactions

Since there is great variety in the transactions that enter into the inflow and outflow of working capital, it is helpful to classify them in distinctive categories, on the basis of their effect on working capital.

1. *Transactions that change a current and a noncurrent account.* For example, the acquisition of a tract of land for cash changes working capital and

---

[3] For a mathematical proof of this statement, see Ching-Wen Kwang and Albert Slavin, "The Mathematical Unity of Funds-Flow Analyses," *NAA Bulletin,* Section 1, January 1965, pp. 49–56.

is, therefore, reported in the statement of changes in financial position—working capital basis.

2. *Transactions that change current asset or current liability accounts but have no effect on working capital.* For example, the purchase of merchandise on account and the settlement of an account receivable change the current accounts but do not change the amount of working capital; hence, they are not reported in the statement of changes in financial position—working capital basis. On the other hand, it should be noted that the purchases of merchandise and sales of merchandise are reported in the statement by being included in the overall category of "changes caused by operations" as illustrated in the following pages.

3. *Transactions that change noncurrent accounts only.* For example, the acquisition of a tract of land by a company in exchange for its own stock does not change working capital and is, therefore, not reported in the statement prepared on a working capital basis. Other transactions in this category include the conversion of bonds payable into common stock, and plant and equipment revaluations. It is apparent, however, that information about the acquisition of assets of a material amount by the use of nonworking capital items, should be shown on the statement of changes in financial position. The omission of this information is a definite weakness of the statement prepared on a rigid working capital basis.

Working Capital Provided by Operations

A primary source of working capital is the regular operating activities of the business. The determination of working capital from this source is complicated by the fact that the change in working capital may be greater than, or less than, the net income shown in the income statement. To illustrate, assume that the Cowan Company's income statement for the year ended December 31, 1976, is as follows:

COWAN COMPANY
Income Statement
For the Year Ended December 31, 1976

Sales		$10,000
Cost of Goods Sold		7,000
Gross Margin on Sales		$ 3,000
Operating Expenses		
Depreciation—Plant and Equipment	$ 400	
Other	2,100	2,500
Net Income		$ 500

An analysis of this statement in terms of the change in working capital resulting from operations shows the following:

COWAN COMPANY
Income Statement
(converted from accrual basis to a working capital basis)
For the Year Ended December 31, 1976

	Income Statement	Working Capital Increase or (Decrease)	Explanation
Sales	$10,000	$10,000	Increase in cash or accounts receivable
Cost of Goods Sold	7,000	(7,000)	Decrease in inventories
Gross Margin on Sales	$ 3,000	$ 3,000	
Operating Expenses			
Depreciation— Plant and Equipment	$ 400	–0–	Decrease in net income and the carrying value of plant and equipment
Other	2,100	(2,100)	Decrease in cash or increase in accounts payable
Total Operating Expenses	$ 2,500		
Total Outflow of Working Capital		$ (2,100)	
Net Income	$ 500		
Working Capital Provided by Operations		$ 900	

For brevity, the required adjustment to net income to compute working capital from operations may be determined by working backward as follows:

Working Capital Provided by Operations	
Net Income (before extraordinary items)	$500
Add Nonworking Capital Charges to Income Summary:	
Depreciation Expense—Plant and Equipment	400
Working Capital Provided by Operations Exclusive of Extraordinary Items	$900

APB Opinion No. 19 requires that in disclosing the working capital provided by operations "net income before extraordinary items" be the starting figure. Since there are no extraordinary items in the Cowan Company illustration, the net income figure is also net income before extraordinary items. It must not be inferred from the mechanics of this procedure that the $400 depreciation expense increased working capital and is thereby a source of working capital. The deduction of depreciation expense merely decreased net income without effecting a corresponding decrease in working capital. Accordingly, the net income figure usually must be adjusted to determine working capital provided by operations. An income statement is likely to include several items of this kind—for example, depreciation, amortization of intangible assets, and loss on disposal of plant assets—representing costs and expenses that enter into income determination but do not affect working capital in the current period. The relevant expenditures either were made in a prior period or will be made in a future period. The recognition of depreciation is essential to income measurement, but it does not change the amount of working capital.

To illustrate the preparation of a simple form of the statement of changes in financial position on the working capital basis, the position statement of the Fairfield Company, Inc., is given.

FAIRFIELD COMPANY, INC.
Comparative Statement of Financial Position
December 31, 1976 and 1975

	December 31 1976	December 31 1975	Increase or (Decrease)
Assets			
Current Assets			
Cash	$ 30,000	$ 32,000	$ (2,000)
Accounts Receivable (net)	65,000	52,000	13,000
Merchandise Inventory	112,000	92,000	20,000
Unexpired Insurance	3,000	4,000	(1,000)
Total Current Assets	$210,000	$180,000	$ 30,000
Plant and Equipment	$470,000	$438,000	$ 32,000
Deduct Accumulated Depreciation	105,000	98,000	7,000
	$365,000	$340,000	$ 25,000
Total Assets	$575,000	$520,000	$ 55,000
Liabilities and Stockholders' Equity			
Current Liabilities			
Accounts Payable	$ 60,000	$ 81,000	$ (21,000)
Bank Loans Payable (short term)	31,500	26,500	5,000
Accrued Payables	3,500	2,500	1,000
Total Current Liabilities	$ 95,000	$110,000	$ (15,000)

FAIRFIELD COMPANY, INC.
Comparative Statement of Financial Position
December 31, 1976 and 1975

Stockholders' Equity			
Capital Stock	$410,000	$350,000	$ 60,000
Retained Earnings	70,000	60,000	10,000
Total Stockholders' Equity	$480,000	$410,000	$ 70,000
Total Liabilities and			
Stockholders' Equity	$575,000	$520,000	$ 55,000

Step 1 in preparing the statement of changes in financial position on a working capital basis is to determine the changes in working capital. Such an analysis is easily made in Schedule D-1 shown below.

FAIRFIELD COMPANY, INC.   **Schedule D-1**
Schedule of Changes in Working Capital
For the Year Ended December 31, 1976

	December 31		Changes in Working Capital	
	1976	*1975*	*Increase*	*Decrease*
Current Assets				
Cash	$ 30,000	$ 32,000		$ 2,000
Accounts Receivable (net)	65,000	52,000	$13,000	
Merchandise Inventory	112,000	92,000	20,000	
Unexpired Insurance	3,000	4,000		1,000
Total Current Assets	$210,000	$180,000		
Current Liabilities				
Accounts Payable	$ 60,000	$ 81,000	21,000	
Bank Loans Payable				
(short-term)	31,500	26,500		5,000
Accrued Payables	3,500	2,500		1,000
Total Current Liabilities	$ 95,000	$110,000		
Working Capital	$115,000	$ 70,000		
Net Increase				
in Working Capital				45,000
			$54,000	$54,000

Step 2 is to analyze the changes in all the noncurrent accounts.

(Ch. 18)

FAIRFIELD COMPANY, INC.
Analysis of Changes in Noncurrent Accounts
For the Year Ended December 31, 1976

	(Debit) or Credit	Effect on Working Capital	
		Increase	Decrease
Plant and Equipment			
Balance, 12/31/75	$(438,000)		
Acquisitions during 1976	(32,000)		$ 32,000
Balance, 12/31/76	$(470,000)		
Accumulated Depreciation—Plant and Equipment			
Balance, 12/31/75	$ 98,000		
Depreciation for 1976	7,000	$ 7,000*	
Balance, 12/31/76	$ 105,000		
Capital Stock			
Balance, 12/31/75	$ 350,000		
Stock Issued	60,000	60,000	
Balance, 12/31/76	$ 410,000		
Retained Earnings			
Balance, 12/31/75	$ 60,000		
Net Income for 1976	35,000	35,000	
Dividends declared	(25,000)		25,000
Balance, 12/31/76	$ 70,000		
		$102,000	$ 57,000
Net Increase in Working Capital			45,000
		$102,000	$102,000

*Nonworking capital charge to Income Summary.

Step 3 is to prepare a statement of changes of financial position—working capital basis for 1976, as shown on page 706.

The T-Account Method

Although a statement of changes in financial position on a working capital basis can be prepared directly from a comparative position statement as in the preceding example, it becomes more difficult to prepare as the number of

FAIRFIELD COMPANY, INC. **Exhibit D**
Statement of Changes in Financial Position—Working Capital Basis
For the Year Ended December 31, 1976

Working Capital Was Provided by:		
Operations		
Net Income (before extraordinary items)		$ 35,000
Add Nonworking Capital Charges against Operations		
Depreciation of Plant and Equipment		7,000
Working Capital Provided by Operations Exclusive		
of Extraordinary Items		$ 42,000
Issuance of Capital Stock		60,000
Total Working Capital Provided		$102,000
Working Capital Was Used for:		
Purchase of Equipment	$32,000	
Declaration of Dividends	25,000	
Total Working Capital Used		57,000
Net Increase in Working Capital		
(See Schedule D-1)		$ 45,000

transactions and accounts to be analyzed increases. Some systematic method is needed to facilitate the analysis of the transactions required for the preparation of the formal statement. Several techniques may be used for this purpose, all of which lead to the same result. The technique known as the *direct*, or *T-account*, method[4] is often used because of its relative simplicity and clarity. The basic steps are as follows:

Step 1. A schedule of changes in working capital is prepared.

Step 2. A T account is opened for each *noncurrent* position statement item and the amount of the net increase or decrease, obtained from the comparative position statement, is entered in each account. Increases in assets and decreases in liabilities and stockholders' equity accounts are debit changes and are entered on the debit side; decreases in assets and increases in liabilities and stockholders' equity accounts are credit changes and are entered on the credit side. A single horizontal line is then drawn under each amount, across the account.

Step 3. Two additional T accounts, Working Capital Summary and Operating Summary, are opened. The Working Capital Summary account represents all the current asset and current liability accounts; the amount entered in this account is, therefore, the net change in working capital as determined in step 1: it is a debit if there is a net increase; a credit if there is a net decrease. The Operating Summary account is used to determine the amount of working capital provided by operations. No entry is made in this account at this point. The amounts entered in the T accounts are added to make sure that total debits equal total credits.

Step 4. The net changes entered in the T accounts in steps 2 and 3 repre-

[4] Based on William J. Vatter, "A Direct Method for the Preparation of Fund Statements," *The Journal of Accountancy,* June, 1946, pp. 479–489.

(Ch. 18)

sent, in summary form, all the transactions that occurred during the period. These transactions are now reconstructed by separate entries below the horizontal lines in the appropriate T accounts. An offsetting debit or credit to a noncurrent account may be to:

1. *Another noncurrent account.* Although such a transaction does not affect working capital, the entry is made so that all changes may be explained.
2. *Working Capital Summary.* This account is debited or credited for transactions other than revenue and expense that affect working capital and noncurrent accounts.
3. *Operating Summary.* This account is debited or credited for transactions affecting revenue, expense, and noncurrent accounts. It adjusts the net income figure to a figure representing working capital provided by operations.

Step 4 is completed only when the balance of the amounts below the horizontal line in each account is equal to the net change entered above the horizontal line in steps 2 and 3. This ensures that all the transactions that affect working capital have been accounted for. Each entry should be identified by a letter or number, together with a brief notation giving the source of the entry to facilitate the preparation of the formal statement.

Step 5. The balance of Operating Summary is closed into Working Capital Summary.

Step 6. The formal statement of changes in financial position on a working capital basis is prepared. Operating Summary shows the details of working capital provided by operations. Working Capital Summary contains details of sources and uses of working capital; the debit entries represent sources, the credit entries are uses.

The comparative position statement of the Plymouth Corporation and related supplementary data are used to illustrate the step-by-step T-account method for the preparation of a statement of changes in financial position—working capital basis.

PLYMOUTH CORPORATION
Comparative Position Statement
December 31, 1976 and 1975

	December 31		Increase or (Decrease)
	1976	1975	
Assets			
Current Assets			
Cash	$ 16,000	$ 21,000	$(5,000)
Accounts Receivable (net)	19,600	16,600	3,000
Merchandise Inventory	31,000	21,000	10,000
Total Current Assets	$ 66,600	$ 58,600	$ 8,000
Long-Term Investments (at cost)	$ 22,000	$ 19,000	$ 3,000

(Ch. 18)

PLYMOUTH CORPORATION
Comparative Position Statement
December 31, 1976 and 1975

	December 31		Increase or (Decrease)
	1976	1975	
Plant and Equipment			
Land	$ 18,000	$ 18,000	$ −0−
Buildings	126,000	110,000	16,000
Accumulated Depreciation— Buildings	(38,000)	(35,000)	(3,000)*
Machinery	152,000	125,000	27,000
Accumulated Depreciation— Machinery	(37,000)	(25,000)	(12,000)*
Total Plant and Equipment	$221,000	$193,000	$28,000
Intangible Assets	$ 9,000	$ 10,000	$ (1,000)
Total Assets	$318,600	$280,600	$38,000

Liabilities and Stockholders' Equity

Current Liabilities			
Accounts Payable	$ 23,000	$ 19,000	$ 4,000
Notes Payable	3,500	4,000	(500)
Total Current Liabilities	$ 26,500	$ 23,000	$ 3,500
Long-Term Liabilities			
Mortgage Payable	32,000	35,000	(3,000)
Total Liabilities	$ 58,500	$ 58,000	$ 500
Stockholders' Equity			
5% Preferred Stock, $100 par value	$ 55,000	$ 50,000	$ 5,000
Common Stock, no-par value, $10 stated value	125,000	110,000	15,000
Premium on Common Stock	13,000	10,000	3,000
Retained Earnings	67,100	52,600	14,500
Total Stockholders' Equity	$260,100	$222,600	$37,500
Total Liabilities and Stockholders' Equity	$318,600	$280,600	$38,000

*These items represent increases to contra asset accounts, which in turn represent decreases in assets.

PLYMOUTH CORPORATION
Income Statement
For the Year Ended December 31, 1976

Sales		$125,000
Cost of Goods Sold		70,000
Gross Margin on Sales		$ 55,000
Operating Expenses		
Depreciation—Machinery	$12,000	
Depreciation—Building	3,000	
Amortization of Intangibles	1,000	
Other	20,675	36,675
Operating Margin		$ 18,325
Gain on Sale of Investments		1,000
Net Income		$ 19,325

An analysis of the income statement, the statement of retained earnings, and the changes in the noncurrent items discloses the following supplementary information:

1. Net income per statement. $19,325
2. Depreciation
   a. Machinery   12,000
   b. Building   3,000
3. Amortization of intangible assets   1,000
4. Dividends declared and paid   4,825
5. Payment on mortgage payable   3,000
6. Investments costing $4,000 were sold for $5,000 (the gain of $1,000 was included in net income). Since investments increased by $3,000, additional investments costing $7,000 = ($4,000 + $3,000) must have been acquired.
7. Plant and Equipment
   a. No machinery was sold during the period. Acquisitions, therefore, must have cost $27,000.
   b. No buildings were disposed of during the period. Acquisitions, therefore, must have cost $16,000.
8. Issuance of Stock
   a. Preferred—50 shares at par value
   b. Common—1,500 shares at $12 per share

STATEMENT OF
CHANGES IN
FINANCIAL
POSITION

(Ch. 18)

709

Step 1. A schedule of changes in working capital is prepared.

PLYMOUTH CORPORATION Schedule D–1
Schedule of Changes in Working Capital
For the Year Ended December 31, 1976

	December 31 1976	December 31 1975	Changes in Working Capital Increase	Changes in Working Capital Decrease
Current Assets				
Cash	$16,000	$21,000		$ 5,000
Accounts Receivable (net)	19,600	16,600	$ 3,000	
Merchandise Inventory	31,000	21,000	10,000	
Total Current Assets	$66,600	$58,600		
Current Liabilities				
Accounts Receivable	$23,000	$19,000		4,000
Notes Payable	3,500	4,000	500	
Total Current Liabilities	$26,500	$23,000		
Working Capital	$40,100	$35,600		
Net Increase in Working Capital				4,500
			$13,500	$13,500

Step 2. A T account is opened for each noncurrent position statement item and the amount of change during the year is entered. A single horizontal rule is drawn under each amount, as shown below.

Long-Term Investments		**Mortgage Payable**	
3,000		3,000	

Buildings		**5% Preferred Stock**	
16,000			5,000

Accumulated Depreciation —Buildings		**Common Stock**	
	3,000		15,000

Machinery		Premium on Common Stock	
27,000			3,000

Accumulated Depreciation —Machinery		Retained Earnings	
	12,000		14,500

Intangible Assets	
	1,000

Step 3. Two additional T accounts are opened—Working Capital Summary and Operating Summary. The net change in working capital is entered in the Working Capital Summary account, and a rule is drawn. It is suggested that before proceeding to step 4 the accountant test the accuracy of the debit and credit changes in the T accounts including the net change in working capital: the sum of the debit changes should equal the sum of the credit changes.

Operating Summary		Working Capital Summary	
		4,500	
		Increases in working capital	Decreases in working capital

Step 4. All the transactions for the year are reconstructed in separate summary entries and reflected below the horizontal rules of each account. The entries indicated by the changes in the comparative position statements and the supplementary data are made directly to the T accounts. They are shown in general journal form only to facilitate the explanation. They are posted to the T accounts only—*not to the regular general ledger accounts.*

(a)		
Operating Summary—Net Income	19,325	
Retained Earnings		19,325

The amount of $19,325, the net income for the period, was originally re-corded as a closing entry by a debit to Income Summary and a credit to Re-tained Earnings. In this entry, Operating Summary is debited in place of Income Summary. Since the balance of the Operating Summary account will show the amount of working capital provided by operations, this entry assumes a net increase in funds of $19,325 resulting from the revenue and expense transac-tions for the period.

(b)

Operating Summary—Depreciation of Machinery	12,000	
Accumulated Depreciation—Machinery		12,000

This entry represents the annual depreciation charge, the original debit being to Depreciation Expense—Machinery, an expense account. It is evident that the assumption made in entry (a), that all expenses decrease working capi-tal, is not valid. Working capital is used to acquire machinery, but the periodic allocation of this cost as a deduction from revenue does not affect working capital. The debit in this entry will, therefore, be added to the debit from entry (a) in determining the amount of working capital provided by operations.

(c)

Operating Summary—Depreciation of Buildings	3,000	
Accumulated Depreciation—Buildings		3,000

The reason for this entry is the same as for entry (b). It is another of the required adjustments to net income to compute working capital provided by operations.

(d)

Operating Summary—Amortization of Intangibles	1,000	
Intangible Assets		1,000

This entry represents the amortization of a cost incurred in a prior period. The reason for the entry is the same as for entry (b); another adjustment to net income.

(e)

Retained Earnings	4,825	
Working Capital Summary—Declaration of Dividends		4,825

Dividends were declared and paid, resulting in a decrease in working capi-tal. If the dividends were declared but not paid, the credit to Dividends Payable would increase current liabilities and decrease working capital. Entry (e) would, therefore, be the same.

(f)			
Working Capital Summary—Sale of Investments		5,000	
Long-Term Investments			4,000
Operating Summary—Gain on Sale of Investments			1,000

Securities that cost $4,000 were sold for $5,000. The gain on the sale is an ordinary item and is included in the reported net income of $19,325, and in Operating Summary through entry (a). But the effect of the sale was to increase working capital by a total of $5,000; hence, the debit to Working Capital Summary for $5,000 in entry (f). Furthermore, the increase in working capital resulting from the gain ($1,000) should be reported as an integral part of the total increase in working capital from sale of investments ($5,000) and not as a part of working capital provided by operations. The credit of $1,000 to Operating Summary, therefore, cancels a like amount included in Operating Summary through entry (a).

The T account for Long-Term Investments now appears as shown.

Long-Term Investments		
3,000		
	(f)	4,000

Since the balance below the horizontal line must be the same as the balance above the line, a debit entry of $7,000 must be made. It may be assumed that securities costing $7,000 were acquired. In practice, reference would be made to the records to confirm this assumption.

(g)			
Long-Term Investments		7,000	
Working Capital Summary—Purchase of Investments			7,000
(h)			
Machinery		27,000	
Working Capital Summary—Purchase of Machinery			27,000

The explanation for entry (h) is the same as for entry (g). Since no machinery was sold during the period, it may be assumed that the net change represents acquisitions.

(i)			
Buildings		16,000	
Working Capital Summary—Acquisition of Building			16,000
(j)			
Working Capital Summary—Issuance of Preferred Stock		5,000	
5% Preferred Stock			5,000

STATEMENT OF
CHANGES IN
FINANCIAL
POSITION

Fifty shares of preferred stock were issued at par value.

	(k)		
Working Capital Summary—Issuance of Common Stock	18,000		
Common Stock			15,000
Premium on Common Stock			3,000

Fifteen hundred shares of common stock were issued at $12 a share.

	(l)		
Mortgage Payable	3,000		
Working Capital Summary—Payment of			
Mortgage Payable			3,000

The decrease in Mortgage Payable is assumed to be due to a cash payment.

At this point, the balance below the horizontal line in each noncurrent account is equal to the net change above the line, all the transactions affecting funds having been reproduced.

Step 5. The balance in the Operating Summary account is now $34,325, representing the working capital provided by operations. This balance is transferred to Working Capital Summary.

	(m)		
Working Capital Summary—Working Capital			
Provided by Operations	34,325		
Operating Summary			34,325

The completeness and accuracy of the work is verified by the equality of the balances above and below the rule of the Working Capital Summary account.

Long-Term Investments				Mortgage Payable		
	3,000				3,000	
(g)	7,000	(f)	4,000	(l)	3,000	
bal.						
3,000						

Buildings			5% Preferred Stock		
	16,000				5,000
(i)	16,000			(j)	5,000

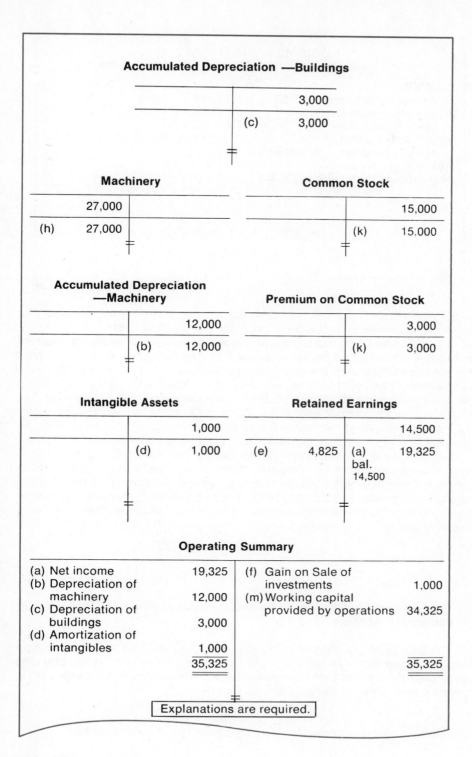

Accumulated Depreciation —Buildings

			3,000
		(c)	3,000

Machinery

	27,000		
(h)	27,000		

Common Stock

			15,000
		(k)	15.000

Accumulated Depreciation —Machinery

			12,000
		(b)	12,000

Premium on Common Stock

			3,000
		(k)	3,000

Intangible Assets

			1,000
		(d)	1,000

Retained Earnings

			14,500
(e)	4,825	(a)	19,325
		bal.	
		14,500	

Operating Summary

(a)	Net income	19,325	(f) Gain on Sale of investments	1,000
(b)	Depreciation of machinery	12,000	(m) Working capital provided by operations	34,325
(c)	Depreciation of buildings	3,000		
(d)	Amortization of intangibles	1,000		
		35,325		35,325

Explanations are required.

(Ch. 18)

Working Capital Summary

	4,500		
(f) Sale of investments	5,000	(e) Cash dividends	
(j) Issuance of preferred		declared	4,825
stock at par value	5,000	(g) Purchase of	
(k) Issuance of common		investments	7,000
stock at premium	18,000	(h) Purchase of	
(m) Working capital		machinery	27,000
provided by operations	34,325	(i) Purchase of buildings	16,000
bal. 4,500		(l) Payment on mortgage	3,000

Explanations are required.

Note that explanations are required for the last two summary accounts so that the formal statements can be prepared from these two accounts.

It is suggested that the accountant place some symbol in the noncurrent accounts to indicate that he has explained all the changes that have occurred in these accounts during the year. An equals sign (=) written across the vertical line of the T account is an excellent symbol to describe that the accountant has completed his task. When all the T accounts have an equals sign (=) written across the vertical line of the T, the accountant can quickly ascertain that he has completed the total work requirement on the T accounts. He can then proceed to step 6, the preparation of the formal statement.

Step 6. The formal statement of changes in financial position on the working capital basis can now be prepared directly from the Working Capital Summary and Operating Summary accounts: the debits represent sources of working capital; the credits represent uses of working capital. Supporting figures for working capital received from operations must be taken from the Operating Summary account. The statement is shown on page 717.

The Statement of Changes in Financial Position—Working Capital Basis: Managerial Analysis

The statement of changes in financial position of the Plymouth Corporation arranged in common-size form, is shown in Figure 18-2. An analysis in question and answer form to indicate how this statement may be used by management, investors, and other interested persons follows.

1. What was the net change in working capital? An increase of $4,500.

PLYMOUTH CORPORATION   **Exhibit D**
Statement of Changes in Financial Position—Working Capital Basis
For the Year Ended December 31, 1976

Working Capital Was Provided by:		
Operations		
Net Income (before extraordinary items)		$19,325
Add Nonworking Capital Charges against Operations		
Depreciation of Machinery		12,000
Depreciation of Building		3,000
Amortization of Intangibles		1,000
Total		$35,325
Deduct Nonworking Credits to Operations		
Gain on Sale of Investments		1,000
Working Capital Provided by Operations		
Exclusive of Extraordinary Items		$34,325
Sale of Investments		5,000
Issuance of Preferred Stock		5,000
Issuance of Common Stock		18,000
Total Working Capital Provided		$62,325
Working Capital Was Used for		
Purchase of Investments	$ 7,000	
Purchase of Machinery	27,000	
Purchase of Buildings	16,000	
Declaration of Dividends	4,825	
Payment of Mortgage Payable	3,000	
Total Working Capital Used		57,825
Net Increase in Working Capital		
(see Schedule D–1)		$ 4,500

2. What was the effect of plant and equipment acquisitions on working capital? The purchase of additional machinery and buildings decreased available working capital by $43,000, or 69 percent of available working capital ($43,000 ÷ $62,325). Note, however, that net income as shown in the income statement was $19,325, whereas the working capital provided by operations was $34,325; the difference is represented by the deductions from revenue for depreciation on machinery ($12,000) and buildings ($3,000).

3. What working capital was made available from investment by owners? from operations? These two sources thus provided approximately 92 percent of the available working capital ($57,325 ÷ $62,325). The remaining 8 percent came from the sale of investments for $5,000.

4. What working capital came from outside borrowing? None.

5. What working capital came from the sale of noncurrent assets? The sale of investments increased working capital by $5,000.

6. What was the effect of the dividend declaration on working capital? Dividends declared totaled $4,825, which decreased working capital. The declaration of dividends represents approximately 25 percent of net income ($4,825 ÷ $19,325) and 8 percent of available working capital ($4,825 ÷ $62,325).

PLYMOUTH CORPORATION   **Exhibit D**
Statement of Changes in Financial Position—Working Capital Basis
For the Year Ended December 31, 1976

		Amount	Percent
Working Capital Was Provided by:			
Operations			
Net Income (before extraordinary items)		$19,325	
Add Nonworking Capital Charges against Operations			
Depreciation of Machinery		12,000	
Depreciation of Building		3,000	
Amortization of Intangibles		1,000	
Total		$35,325	
Deduct Nonworking Credits to Operations			
Gain on Sale of Investments		1,000	
Working Capital Provided by Operations			
Exclusive of Extraordinary Items		$34,325	55.1
Sale of Investments		5,000	8.0
Issuance of Stock			
Preferred	$ 5,000		
Common	18,000	23,000	36.9
Totals		$62,325	100.0
Working Capital Was Used for			
Purchase of Investments		$ 7,000	11.2
Purchase of Machinery		27,000	43.3
Purchase of Buildings		16,000	25.7
Declaration of Dividends		4,825	7.8
Payment on Mortgage		3,000	4.8
Net Increase in Working Capital		4,500	7.2
Totals		$62,325	100.0

ALL-FINANCIAL RESOURCES CONCEPT OF FUNDS

As early as 1963, *APB Opinion No. 3* encouraged *but did not require* firms to present a statement of financial position statement broadened to include "all financial resources" as supplementary information in financial reports.[5] When *APB Opinion No. 19* was issued in 1971, it made this statement a basic statement and also made mandatory the use of the all financial resources concept rather than a concept limited to working capital or cash.

A summary of additional pertinent provisions of *APB Opinion No. 19* follows:

1. The statement should begin with the income or loss before extraordinary items, if any, and add back (or deduct) items recognized in determining income (or

[5] *Ibid.,* p. 6512.

(Ch. 18)

loss) which did not use (or provide) working capital (or cash in some cases) during the period in order to determine working capital provided by operations.

2. The items to be added back (or deducted) in 1 above should be clearly presented to avoid the interpretation that they provided resources (e.g., "Add— Expenses not requiring outlay of working capital in the current period" or non-working capital charges or credits to operations.)

3. The effects of extraordinary items (see *APB Opinions 9 and 30*) should be reported separately from the effects of normal operating items.

4. The effects of all financing and investing activities, as well as working capital (or cash in some cases) should be *individually* disclosed.

5. If the format shows the flow of working capital and two-year comparative statements of financial position are presented, the detailed changes in working capital accounts nevertheless must be presented, i.e., a schedule of working capital changes should be prepared or the same information be included in the formal statement of changes in financial position.

6. Working capital (or cash) provided from (or used in operations) should be appropriately described [e.g., Working capital provided from (used in) operations for the period, exclusive of extraordinary items].

7. There should be flexibility in form, content, and terminology in the statement: flexibility should be used to develop the presentation that is most informative in the circumstances.

8. It is strongly recommended that isolated statistics of working capital and cash, especially per-share amounts, not be presented.

APB Opinion No. 30, issued in June, 1973, requires that for an item to be extraordinary it must be of an *unusual nature,*

> . . . the underlying event or transaction should possess a high degree of abnormality and be of a type clearly unrelated to, or only incidentally related to, the ordinary and typical activities of the entity, taking into account the environment in which the entity operates[6]

and it must have an *infrequency of occurrence,*

> . . . the underlying event or transaction should be of a type that would not reasonably be expected to recur in the foreseeable future, taking into account the environment in which the entity operates.[7]

These two criteria will make most gains and losses *ordinary* items. Perhaps earthquake loss or a flood loss would qualify as an extraordinary item. Generally speaking, however, the net income before extraordinary items will be the net income figure, that is, the bottom figure reported on the income statement.

Differences between Working Capital Concept and All-Financial Resources Concept

An interpretation of the information contained in *APB Opinion No. 19* indicates that the all-financial resources concept would include the following:

[6] *Opinions of the Accounting Principles Board, No. 30,* "Reporting the Results of Operations," (New York: 1973) p. 564.
[7] *Ibid.,* p. 565.

1. Sources and uses of working capital (or cash in some cases), plus
2. Sources and uses of other financial resources not affecting working capital, such as:
   a. Issuance of bonds payable or other long-term debt instrument in exchange for plant and equipment items.
   b. Issuance of capital stock in exchange for plant and equipment items.
   c. Conversion of bonds payable into common stock.
   d. Conversion of preferred stock into common stock.
   e. The exchange of one plant and equipment item for another plant and equipment item.

Each item listed in 2 above would be shown both as a source of financial resources and as a use of financial resources. Consider, for example, the issuance of bonds payable for land:

1. The issuance of bonds payable would be listed as a source of financial resources, and
2. The acquisition of land would be listed as a use of financial resources.

Not all changes in statement of financial position items are to be listed as sources and uses of financial resources. Specifically excluded by *APB Opinion No. 19* are the following:

1. Stock dividends
2. Restrictions on retained earnings.

These items are considered primarily to be accounting changes that do not alter the basic nature of financial resources.

Illustration of the All-Financial Resources Concept. The following information is given for the Fundo Company:

THE FUNDO COMPANY
Comparative Statements of Financial Position
December 31, 1976 and 1975

	December 31 1976	December 31 1975	Change Increase (Decrease)
Cash	$ 525,000	$ 415,000	$110,000
Accounts Receivable (net)	90,000	80,000	10,000
Merchandise Inventory	593,000	400,000	193,000
Prepaid Insurance	6,000	5,000	1,000
Land	100,000	–0–	100,000
Machinery	450,000	400,000	50,000
Accumulated Depreciation —Machinery	(30,000)	(20,000)	10,000
	$1,734,000	$1,280,000	

THE FUNDO COMPANY
Comparative Statements of Financial Position
December 31, 1976 and 1975

Accounts Payable	$ 25,000	$ 20,000	5,000
Dividends Payable	50,000	10,000	40,000
9% Bonds Payable	300,000	–0–	300,000
Premium on 9%			
Bonds Payable	9,000	–0–	9,000
Convertible Preferred Stock	–0–	150,000	(150,000)
Common Stock, $10 par	900,000	800,000	100,000
Premium on			
Common Stock	50,000	–0–	50,000
Retained Earnings	400,000	300,000	100,000
	$1,734,000	$1,280,000	

Additional information

a. Net income for 1976 was $150,000.
b. A dividend of $50,000 was declared on December 15, 1976, payable on January 12, 1977.
c. On December 28, 1976, the company traded in a machine, which had cost $100,000 and had an accumulated depreciation of $10,000, for new machinery costing $150,000; the trade-in allowance which was equal to fair market value of the old machine was $80,000; the balance was paid in cash. The loss of $10,000 is an ordinary loss.
d. The annual depreciation expense on machinery was $20,000.
e. On January 1, 1976, the company issued at 105 for cash 9 percent bonds with a face value of $200,000. The maturity date of the bonds is January 1, 1986.
f. On December 31, 1976, the company issued directly to Hall Realty Company 9 percent bonds with a face value of $100,000 at 100 for land valued at $100,000.
g. The convertible preferred stock was converted during 1976 into 10,000 shares of $10 par value common stock.
h. The annual amortization of premium on 9 percent bonds payable was $1,000.

Solution to the problem follows:

STATEMENT OF
CHANGES IN
FINANCIAL
POSITION

(Ch. 18)

721

THE FUNDO COMPANY　　　**Schedule D-1**
Schedule of Changes in Working Capital
For the Year Ended December 31, 1976

	December 31		Changes in Working Capital	
	1976	1975	Increase	Decrease
Current Assets				
Cash	$ 525,000	$415,000	$110,000	
Accounts Receivable (net)	90,000	80,000	10,000	
Merchandise Inventory	593,000	400,000	193,000	
Prepaid Insurance	6,000	5,000	1,000	
Total Current Assets	$1,214,000	$900,000		
Current Liabilities				
Accounts Payable	$ 25,000	$ 20,000		$ 5,000
Dividends Payable	50,000	10,000		40,000
Total Current Liabilities	$ 75,000	$ 30,000		
Working Capital	$1,139,000	$870,000		
Net Increase in Working Capital				269,000
			$314,000	$314,000

Even when the all-financial resources basis is used, *APB Opinion No. 19* requires the details of the changes in individual working capital items to be presented. One method is to prepare a schedule of changes in working capital as indicated in the foregoing illustrations.

For the purpose of clarity the entries to the T accounts are presented in general journal form. The entries will be lettered to correspond to the letters preceding the additional information. Since the all-financial resources concept is being followed, the account equivalent to working capital summary has been renamed *Financial Resources Summary*. This change of name seems to be indicated because the new summary account will be used not only to record sources and uses of working capital, but also to record those sources and uses of financial resources that do not affect working capital.

(a)

Operating Summary—Net Income	150,000	
Retained Earnings		150,000

(b)

Retained Earnings	50,000	
Financial Resources Summary—Declaration of Dividends		50,000

The foregoing transaction represents a use of financial resources, since it decreases working capital even though it will not be paid until 1977.

(c)

Financial Resources Summary—Disposal of Machinery	80,000	
Machinery	150,000	
Operating Summary—		
Loss on Disposal of Machinery	10,000	
Accumulated Depreciation—Machinery	10,000	
Machinery		100,000
Financial Resources Summary—Purchase of Machinery		150,000

(d)

Operating Summary—		
Depreciation of Machinery	20,000	
Accumulated Depreciation—Machinery		20,000

(e)

Financial Resources Summary—Issuance of 9% Bonds Payable at 105	210,000	
9% Bonds Payable		200,000
Premium on 9% Bonds Payable		10,000

(f)

Financial Resources Summary—Issuance of 9% Bonds Payable at 100	100,000	
9% Bonds Payable		100,000
Land	100,000	
Financial Resources Summary—Purchase of Land		100,000

Even though the bonds in this transaction are issued directly to the realtor for the land, the transaction must be disclosed both as a source of financial resources and as a use of financial resources. The two entries are suggested as a means of more carefully delineating this problem.

(g)

Financial Resources Summary—Issuance of Common Stock	150,000	
Common Stock, $10 par Value		100,000
Premium on Common Stock		50,000
Convertible Preferred Stock	150,000	
Financial Resources Summary—Retirement of Convertible Preferred Stock		150,000

This transaction is similar to entry (f)—it must be shown as both a source and a use of financial resources. The paid-in capital in excess of the $10 par value was credited to Premium on Common Stock.

(Ch. 18)

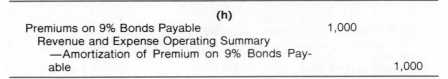

(h)

Premiums on 9% Bonds Payable	1,000	
Revenue and Expense Operating Summary		
—Amortization of Premium on 9% Bonds Payable		1,000

The amount of the amortization of premium on 9 percent bonds payable is a nonworking credit against operations; that is, it resulted in an increase in net income, by way of decreasing bond interest expense, without increasing working capital.

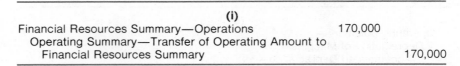

(i)

Financial Resources Summary—Operations	170,000	
Operating Summary—Transfer of Operating Amount to		
Financial Resources Summary		170,000

The T accounts with the foregoing entries posted to them appear below:

Land		Machinery	
100,000		50,000	
(f) 100,000		(c) 150,000	(c) 100,000
		bal. 50,000	

Accumulated Depreciation—Machinery		9% Bonds Payable	
	10,000		300,000
(c) 10,000	(d) 20,000		(e) 200,000
			(f) 100,000
	bal. 10,000		bal. 300,000

Premium on 9% Bonds Payable		Convertible Preferred Stock	
	9,000	150,000	
(h) 1,000	(e) 10,000	(g) 150,000	
	bal. 9,000		

Common Stock, $10 Par

		100,000
	(g)	100,000

Premium on Common Stock

		50,000
	(g)	50,000

Retained Earnings

				100,000
(b)	50,000	(a)	150,000	
		bal. 100,000		

Operating Summary

(Working Capital Provided by Operations)

(a) Net Income	150,000	(h)	Amortization of Premium of 9% bonds Payable	1,000
(c) Loss on Disposal of Machinery	10,000	(l)	To Financial Res. Summary	179,000
(d) Depr. of Machinery	20,000			

Financial Resources Summary

Net Increase in Working Capital	269,000			
(c) Disposal of Machinery	80,000	(b)	Declaration of Dividends	50,000
(e) Issuance of 9% Bonds Payable at 105	210,000	(c)	Purchase of Machinery	150,000
(f) Issuance of 9% Bonds Payable at 100	100,000	(f)	Purchase of Land	100,000
(g) Issuance of Common Stock	150,000	(g)	Retirement of Convertible Preferred Stock	150,000
(i) Operations	179,000			450,000
bal. 269,000	719,000			

STATEMENT OF
CHANGES IN
FINANCIAL
POSITION

(Ch. 18)

725

The formal statement of changes in financial position is shown in Exhibit D.

THE FUNDO COMPANY **Statement of Changes in Financial Position** **For the Year Ended December 31, 1976**		**Exhibit D**
Financial Resources Were Provided by Operations		
Net Income (before extraordinary items)		$150,000
Add Nonworking Capital Charges to Operations		
Loss on Disposal of Machinery		10,000
Depreciation of Machinery		20,000
Total		$180,000
Deduct Nonworking Capital Credits to Operations		
Amortization of Premium on 9% Bonds Payable		1,000
Working Capital Provided by Operations		
Exclusive of Extraordinary Items		$179,000
Disposal of Machinery		80,000
Issuance of 9% Bonds Payable at 105		210,000
Issuance of 9% Bonds Payable at 100		100,000
Issuance of Common Stock		150,000
Total Financial Resources Provided		$719,000
Financial Resources Were Used for		
Declaration of Dividends	$ 50,000	
Purchase of Machinery	150,000	
Purchase of Land	100,000	
Retirement of Convertible Preferred Stock	150,000	
Total Financial Resources Used		450,000
Net Increase in Working Capital (See Schedule D–1)		$269,000

STATEMENT OF CHANGES IN FINANCIAL POSITION—CASH BASIS

The specific content of the statement of changes in financial position, whether sources and uses of working capital, cash, all-financial resources, or some other concept of funds, will depend upon the purposes and objectives that users of this statement have in mind. For many short-run purposes, a statement based on cash is definitely of more importance than perhaps any other fund concept; such a statement is quite useful to management and analysts in budgeting and forecasting cash requirements. With the extremely high interest rates in effect today, the administration of cash is of paramount importance.

The basic logic of the analysis for a cash-basis statement of changes in financial position is the same as for a working-capital basis statement: an analysis of the relationships of the items in the financial statements. The causes of the changes in cash—the sources and uses of cash—are determined by analyzing the changes in all accounts other than Cash. Figures from the income statement are used to determine the changes in cash as a result of operations, and figures from the position statement together with supplementary data reveal the remaining causes for the changes in cash.

As with working capital provided by operations, a major problem is the determination of the cash generated by operations; this problem is complicated by the fact that the revenue and expense figures used for income measurement are different from cash receipts and cash disbursements. The time lag in the settlement of accounts with customers and creditors and the prepayment of certain expenses, for example, necessitate the conversion of accrual-basis revenue and expense amounts to the cash equivalent.

Thus in applying the T-account procedure for purposes of preparing a statement of changes in financial position on a cash basis, it is necessary to open a T account for every position statement account for which a periodic change is recorded, including an Operating Summary account and the Cash Summary account. The transactions causing changes in cash are reconstructed in summary form through a process of analyzing the changes in all accounts other than Cash and by reference to supplementary information. Since the procedural approach is similar to the two preceding illustrations, an expanded example is not shown here.

STATEMENT OF FINANCIAL ACTIVITIES

The AICPA Objectives of Financial Statements Study Group concluded that

An objective is to provide a statement of financial activities useful for predicting, comparing, and evaluating enterprise earning power. This statement should report mainly on factual aspects of enterprise transactions having or expected to have significant cash consequences. This statement should report data that require minimal judgment and interpretation.[8]

This suggested statement of financial activities would be a variation of the statement of changes in financial position prepared on a cash basis. The recommended statement purports to measure changes in terms of a highly probable effect on cash. The Objectives Study Group went on to say:

Accordingly, transactions that establish highly probable receipts and disbursements of cash should be emphasized in the financial activities statement. For example, in most cases, the statement should report sales of product rather than collection of the related receivable. Similarly, it should report purchases of product rather than payments of resulting obligations. Sales, purchases, other acquisitions, and similar activities should be grouped to show their overall effect on the changes in net liquid assets (cash, plus highly probable cash receipts, less highly probable cash disbursements.)
The statement should also disclose acquisitions of long-term assets, incurrence of long-term debt, capital contribution and distributions and related transactions, as

[8] AICPA, *Objectives of Financial Statements,* (New York: American Institute of Certified Public Accountants), pp. 38–39.

well as purchase commitments, lines of credit, sales backlog, leases, and other activities with likely cash consequences.[9]

The Objectives Study Group emphasized that the "purpose of the statement is to present an ordered array of financial activities to emphasize factual information about transactions, so that the user can make his own interpretation of their significance."[10]

Whether the suggested name of the statement or its content will be adopted by the accounting profession is still a matter of conjecture. For the recommendations of this Study Group to be adopted, the Financial Accounting Standards Board would have to issue a standards statement incorporating the objectives of the AICPA Objectives Study Group.

GLOSSARY

All-Financial Resources A concept of funds which includes the disclosure of not only the sources and uses of working capital or cash, but also other financial and investment information that does not affect working capital.

Changes in Working Capital Working capital can be increased by transactions which increase current assets without increasing current liabilities or by transactions which decrease current liabilities without decreasing current assets; working capital can be decreased by transactions which decrease current assets without decreasing current liabilities or by transactions which increase current liabilities without increasing current assets.

Current Account Any current asset or current liability account.

Direct T-Account Method A method of determining the sources and uses of funds; T accounts for all noncurrent accounts are set up which show only the net change that has occurred during a year; then those transactions which cause these changes are reconstructed; and in this analytical process the sources and uses of funds are determined.

Financial Resources Summary A T account in the direct T-account method used to record on the debit side the sources of all financial resources and on the credit side the uses of all financial resources.

Funds In the context of the statement of changes in financial positions, funds may mean cash, working capital, net quick assets, cash and marketable securities, current assets, or all-financial resources, depending upon the needs of the user.

Noncurrent Account Any account on the statement of financial position *other than* current assets and current liabilities; specifically, a noncurrent account is any one of the long-term investments: plant and equipment, intangibles, long-term liabilities, or stockholders' equity accounts.

Operating Summary A T account in the direct T-account method used to record the working capital provided by or used in operations.

Statement of Changes in Financial Position A statement showing sources and uses

[9] *Ibid.,* p. 38.
[10] *Ibid.,* pp. 37–38.

of funds prepared either (1) on all-financial resources basis (recommended by *APB Opinion No. 19*), (2) on working capital basis, (3) on cash basis, or (4) on some other concept of funds.

Statement of Financial Activities A statement similar to the statement of changes in financial position that reports mainly on factual aspects of enterprise transactions having or expected to have significant cash consequences.

Working Capital Current assets less current liabilities, or that part of current assets not required to liquidate current liabilities.

Working Capital Summary A T account in the direct T-account method used to record on the debit side all sources of working capital and on the credit side all uses of working capital.

Q18-1. What is meant by the term *funds*? Discuss three popular concepts of funds.

Q18-2. In its *Opinion No. 19,* the APB recommended what concept of funds for typical presentation in annual reports?

Q18-3. The statement of changes in financial position is now a fourth major financial statement subject to the independent auditor's opinion. Secure an annual report (from your library) dated prior to 1971 and one dated after 1971 and compare the difference in location of the statement in the annual report and the difference in the title and content of the statement. Check to see whether the statement of changes in financial position prepared after 1971 conforms to the criteria stated in *APB Opinion 19.*

Q18-4. What is the purpose of the statement of changes in financial position?

Q18-5. How may working capital provided by operations be determined?

Q18-6. What are the chief sources of working capital from operations? the chief uses of working capital for operations?

Q18-7. Certain transactions are eliminated from the statement of changes in financial position—working capital basis. Why? Give some examples.

Q18-8. How may the statement of changes in financial position—working capital basis be used to advantage by management? by investors? by others?

Q18-9. How may the statement of changes in financial position—cash basis be used to advantage by management? by investors? by others?

Q18-10. What are some of the sources of information for the preparation of the statement of changes in financial position—working capital basis?

Q18-11. What is the effect of a dividend declaration on working capital? of the payment of a dividend?

Q18-12. What is the effect of depreciation of plant and equipment (a) on working capital? (b) on cash?

Q18-13. The net income as shown on the income statement and the working capital provided by operations are different amounts. Why?

Q18-14. Which items are included in a statement of changes in financial position prepared under total financial resources concept that are not included on a statement prepared under the working capital concept?

Q18-15. Does the statement of changes in financial position eliminate the need for the statement of financial position? for the income statement? Discuss.

Q18-16. What is the effect on working capital of a change to an accelerated method of depreciation?

Q18-17. In arriving at working capital provided by operations, certain items are added to net income and other items are deducted. Illustrate and explain.

Q18-18. The AICPA Objectives of Financial Statements Study Group recommended that a statement of financial activities be prepared. How does this statement differ from the statement of changes in financial position? Compare the recommended statement of financial activities with the statement of changes in financial position prepared under total financial resources concept.

Q18-19. The accounts receivable of a business totaled $30,000 at the beginning of the year and $24,000 at the end of the year. Accounts receivable written off as uncollectible during the year amounted to $2,600 and cash discounts allowed to customers amounted to $1,200. The sales for the year were $70,000. What were the cash receipts during the year from sales of the current and prior periods?

Q18-20. The purchases of merchandise of a business amounted to $100,000 during 1976. Accounts payable at the beginning and end of the year were $33,000 and $29,600, respectively; notes payable given to trade creditors in settlement of open accounts were $8,000 at the beginning of the year and $8,800 at the end of the year. Returns and allowances on purchases were $870. What were the cash payments during 1976 for purchases of 1976 and prior periods?

EXERCISES

E18-1. For each of the following transactions, state whether (a) it was a source of working capital, (b) it was a use of working capital, or (c) it had no effect on working capital:

1. Purchased U. S. Treasury notes maturing in six months.
2. Issued a stock dividend to common stockholders.
3. Restricted retained earnings for anticipated plant expansion.
4. Issued common stock in exchange for a building.
5. Acquired machinery for $50,000; paid $20,000 in cash and issued a long-term note for the balance.
6. Reacquired some outstanding preferred stock for retirement.
7. Issued additional common stock at a premium for cash.
8. Issued bonds directly to preferred shareholders to retire preferred stock.

E18-2. Refer to E18-1 and state which of the transactions are a source or use of total financial resources yet are *not* a source or use of *working capital.*

E18-3. Comparative financial statements of the Casless Corporation showed the following balances:

	December 31	
	1976	*1975*
Cash	$100,000	$104,000
Other Current Assets	220,000	230,000
Plant and Equipment (net)	280,000	220,000
Current Liabilities	220,000	230,000
Stockholders' Equity	380,000	324,000

There were no disposals of plant and equipment during the year. Dividend payments totaled $20,000.

Prepare a schedule explaining the cause of the decrease in working capital in spite of reported net income of $76,000.

E18-4. The Plant and Equipment section of the Seero Company's comparative statement of financial position shows the following amounts:

	December 31	
	1976	1975
Plant and Equipment		
Machinery	$275,000	$250,000
Deduct Accumulated Depreciation	125,000	120,000
Total Plant and Equipment	$150,000	$130,000

Acquisitions of new machinery during the year totaled $70,000. The income statement shows depreciation charges of $35,000 for the year and a loss from machinery disposals of $12,000.

Determine the original cost and accumulated depreciation of machinery sold during the year and the proceeds of the sale; prepare a partial statement of changes in financial position—working capital basis.

E18-5. For each of the following cases, compute the working capital generated by operations.

	a	b	c	d	e
Net income (loss) per income statement	$30,000	$(30,000)	$110,000	$90,000	$(40,000)
Depreciation of plant and equipment	4,000	4,000	9,000	6,000	2,000
Gain (loss) on sale of long-term investments			(2,000)	4,000	(1,000)
Periodic amortization of discount on bonds payable			2,000	1,000	500
Periodic amortization of patents				1,000	600

E18-6. During the year 1976, the changes in the accounts of the Miller Company were as follows:

	Increases	Decreases
Cash		$20,000
Accounts Receivable	$ 12,000	
Merchandise Inventory	40,000	
Long-Term Investments	12,000	

	Increases	Decreases
Plant and Equipment	116,000	
Accumulated Depreciation	8,000	
Accounts Payable	15,000	
Taxes Payable		1,000
Mortgage Payable		12,000
Common Stock	92,000	
Retained Earnings	58,000	

Additional information:

a. Net income per income statement, $77,300

b. Dividends declared, $19,300

c. There were no disposals of plant or equipment during the year.

Prepare a statement of changes in financial position—working capital basis for the year 1976

E18-7. The following information regarding the changes in financial position is indicated for the year 1976 for the All-Resourco Company.

THE ALL-RESOURCO COMPANY
Comparative Statements of Financial Position
December 31, 1976 and 1975

	December 31		Change Increase (Decrease)
	1976	1975	
Cash	$262,500	$207,500	$ 55,000
Accounts Receivable (net)	45,000	40,000	5,000
Merchandise Inventory	296,500	200,000	96,500
Prepaid Insurance	3,000	2,500	500
Land	50,000	–0–	50,000
Machinery	225,000	200,000	25,000
Accumulated Depreciation Machinery	(15,000)	(10,000)	5,000
	$867,000	$640,000	
Accounts Payable	$ 12,500	$ 10,000	2,500
Dividends Payable	25,000	5,000	20,000
9% Bonds Payable	150,000	–0–	150,000
Premium on 9% Bonds Payable	4,500	–0–	4,500
Convertible Preferred Stock	–0–	75,000	(75,000)
Common Stock, $10 par	450,000	400,000	50,000
Premium on Common Stock	25,000	–0–	25,000
Retained Earnings	200,000	150,000	50,000
	$867,000	$640,000	

Additional information:

a. Net income for 1976, $75,000.

b. A dividend of $25,000 was declared on December 16, 1976, payable on January 14, 1977.

c. On December 27, 1976, the company traded in a machine which cost $50,000 and had an accumulated depreciation of $5,000 for new machinery costing $75,000; the trade-in allowance, which was equal to fair market value of the old machine, was $40,000; the balance was paid in cash. The loss of $5,000 is an ordinary loss.

d. The annual depreciation expense on machinery was $10,000.

e. On January 1, 1976, the company issued 9% bonds with a face value of $100,000 at 105 for cash. The maturity date of the bonds is January 1, 1986.

f. On December 31, 1976, the company issued directly to Biltmore Realty Company 9% bonds with a face value of $50,000 at 100 for land valued at $50,000.

g. The convertible preferred stock was converted during 1976 into 5,000 shares of $10 par value common stock.

h. The annual amortization of premium on 9% bonds payable was $500.

1. Prepare a schedule of changes in working capital.

2. Prepare a statement of changes in financial position using the total financial resources concept for 1976. Use the direct T-account approach.

E18-8. The financial statements of Easley Company are given below.

EASLEY COMPANY
Income Statement
For the Year Ended December 31, 1976

Net Sales		$130,000
Cost of Goods Sold		94,600
Gross Margin on Sales		$ 35,400
Expenses		
Salaries Expense	$18,400	
Depreciation Expense	3,000	
Rent Expense	4,800	
Supplies Expense	2,000	28,200
Net Income		$ 7,200

EASLEY COMPANY
Statement of Financial Position Accounts
December 31, 1976 and 1975

	December 31	
	1976	1975
Debits		
Cash	$32,340	$22,720
Accounts Receivable	12,220	14,440
Inventory	16,200	16,200
Supplies on Hand	600	1,400
Equipment	30,000	24,000
	$91,360	$78,760

(Ch. 18)

EASLEY COMPANY
Statement of Financial Position Accounts
December 31, 1976 and 1975

Credits		
Accounts Payable—Inventory	$ 7,800	$ 6,200
Accrued Rent Payable	800	400
Accrued Salaries Payable	600	200
Accumulated Depreciation	12,600	9,600
Capital Stock	50,000	50,000
Retained Earnings	19,560	12,360
	$91,360	$78,760

Without the use of T accounts, prepare a schedule of net cash generated by operations for 1976.

DP18-1. (*Statement of changes in financial position—working capital basis*) The December 31, 1975 and 1976, statements of financial position of the Burley Company carried the following debit and credit amounts:

	December 31	
	1976	1975
Debits		
Cash	$ 20,400	$ 25,200
Accounts Receivable (net)	70,200	65,800
Merchandise Inventory	170,400	172,800
Prepaid Expenses	3,000	3,600
Office Equipment	10,000	11,200
Store Equipment	59,600	56,600
Totals	$333,600	$335,200
Credits		
Accumulated Depreciation—		
Office Equipment	$ 5,000	$ 4,800
Accumulated Depreciation—		
Store Equipment	15,000	13,000
Accounts Payable	44,800	47,000
Notes Payable	20,000	10,000
Common Stock, $10 par value	220,000	200,000
Premium on Common Stock	13,000	11,000
Retained Earnings	15,800	49,400
Totals	$333,600	$335,200

Additional information:
a. The net loss for 1976 was $3,800.

DEMON-STRATION PROBLEMS

FINANCIAL
REPORTING

b. Depreciation expense on office equipment was $1,000; on store equipment, $3,400.

c. Office equipment that was carried at its cost of $1,200 with accumulated depreciation of $800 was sold for $600. The gain was credited directly to Retained Earnings.

d. Store equipment costing $4,400 was purchased.

e. Fully depreciated store equipment that cost $1,400 was discarded and its cost and accumulated depreciation were removed from the accounts.

f. Cash dividends of $8,000 were declared during the year.

g. A 2,000-share stock dividend was declared and issued. On the date of declaration, the common stock of the company had a fair market value of $11 a share.

Required: Prepare a statement of changes in financial position for 1976 using the *working capital basis*. Use the direct T-account approach.

DP18-2. (*Statement of changes in financial position—total financial resources*) The Kwick-Chango Corporation reported the following information in regard to changes in financial position during 1976.

THE KWICK-CHANGO CORPORATION
Comparative Statements of Financial Position
December 31, 1976 and 1975

	December 31 1976	December 31 1975	Change Increase (Decrease)
Cash	$ 787,500	$ 622,500	$165,000
Accounts Receivable (net)	135,000	120,000	15,000
Merchandise Inventory	889,500	600,000	289,500
Prepaid Insurance	9,000	7,500	1,500
Land	150,000	–0–	150,000
Machinery	675,000	600,000	75,000
Accumulated Depreciation on Machinery	(45,000)	(30,000)	15,000
	$2,601,000	$1,920,000	
Accounts Payable	$ 37,500	$ 30,000	7,500
Dividends Payable	75,000	15,000	60,000
9% Bonds Payable	450,000	–0–	450,000
Premium on 9% Bonds Payable	13,500	–0–	13,500
Convertible Preferred Stock	–0–	225,000	(225,000)
Common Stock, $10 Par	1,350,000	1,200,000	150,000
Premium on Common Stock	75,000	–0–	75,000
Retained Earnings	600,000	450,000	150,000
	$2,601,000	$1,920,000	

Additional information:

a. Net income for 1976, $225,000.

b. A dividend of $75,000 was declared on December 12, 1976, payable on January 16, 1977.

c. On December 29, 1976, the company traded in a machine which had cost $150,000 and had an accumulated depreciation of $15,000 for new machinery costing $225,000; the trade-in allowance, which was equal to fair market value of the old machine, was $120,000; the balance was paid in cash. The loss of $15,000 is an ordinary loss.

d. The annual depreciation expense on machinery was $30,000.

e. On January 1, 1976, the company issued 9% bonds with a face value of $300,000 at 105 for cash. The maturity date of the bonds is January 1, 1986.

f. On December 31, 1976, the company issued directly to Orange Realty Company 9% bonds with a face value of $150,000 at 100 for land valued at $150,000.

g. The convertible preferred stock was converted during 1976 into 15,000 shares of $10 par value common stock.

h. The annual amortization of premium on 9% bonds payable was $1,500.

Required:

1. Prepare a separate schedule of changes in working capital.

2. Prepare a statement of changes in financial position for 1976 using the *total financial resources basis.* Use the direct T-account approach.

DP18-3. (*Statement of changes in financial position—working capital and cash basis*) The following data are taken from the books of the Walker Corporation (amounts are in thousands of dollars):

	December 31	
	1976	1975
Debits		
Cash	$ 630	$ 570
Marketable Securities	212	100
Receivables (net)	290	250
Inventories	190	140
Long-Term Investments	140	220
Machinery	1,000	700
Buildings	1,200	400
Land	70	70
Totals	$3,732	$2,450
Credits		
Accumulated Depreciation	$ 550	$ 300
Accounts Payable	200	150
Notes Payable	100	50
Mortgage Bonds Payable	1,000	500
Common Stock	1,100	800
Premium on Common Stock	110	–0–
Retained Earnings	672	650
Totals	$3,732	$2,450

WALKER CORPORATION
Income Statement
For the Year Ended December 31, 1976

Sales		$1,200
Cost of Goods Sold		674
Gross Margin on Sales		$ 526
Operating Expenses		
Depreciation—Machinery	$100	
Depreciation—Buildings	160	
Other Expenses	200	460
Net Income from Operations		$ 66
Gain on Sale of Long-Term Investments—		
Ordinary		24
Total		$ 90
Loss on Sale of Machinery—Ordinary		
(proceeds were $30)		10
Net Income		$ 80

Required:

1. Prepare a statement of changes in financial position—working capital basis for 1976.
2. Prepare a statement of changes in financial position—cash basis for 1976.

DP18-4. (*Working capital generated by operations*) You are given the following single-step combined statement of income and retained earnings:

CALIFORNIA COMPANY
Statement of Income and Retained Earnings
For the Year Ended December 31, 1976

Revenue and Other Credits		
Sales		$300,000
Interest Earned		5,250
Correction of Prior Year's Income—		
Overstatement of 1974 Depreciation of		
Machinery		2,500
Total		$307,750
Expenses, Losses and Other Charges		
Cost of Goods Sold	$235,000	
Salaries and Wages Expense	20,000	
Bad Debts Expense	2,000	
Advertising Expense	5,000	
Depreciation Expense	30,000	
Office Expense	10,000	
Loss on Reduction of Marketable		
Securities to Market	2,500	
Loss on Sale of Machinery	4,000	
Interest Expense	2,000	
Total		$310,500
Net Loss for the Year		$ (2,750)

CALIFORNIA COMPANY
Statement of Income and Retained Earnings
For the Year Ended December 31, 1976

Retained Earnings, December 31, 1975		505,250
Total		$502,500
Deduct: Dividends declared June 2, 1976, and paid July 2, 1976	$ 50,000	
Dividends declared December 2, 1976, to be paid January 2, 1977	75,000	
Stock dividends declared and issued in 1976	100,000	
Total		225,000
Retained Earnings, December 31, 1976		$277,500

Interest Earned represents a receipt of $5,025 in cash and the amortization of discount on bonds purchased for investments (long term) of $225. The Interest Expense figure was increased by $175 for amortization of discount on bonds payable and was decreased by $100 for amortization of a premium on bonds payable.

Required:

1. Starting with the net loss for the year, compute, in schedule or T-account form, the working capital provided (or used) by operations during 1976.
2. Compute the amount of working capital provided or used in connection with the dividend policy of the company.

P18-1. The comparative statements of financial position of the Tyrrell Company, as of December 31, 1976 and 1975, disclosed the following:

	December 31	
	1976	**1975**
Debits		
Cash	$ 96,000	$ 126,000
Accounts Receivable (net)	117,600	99,600
Merchandise Inventory	170,000	130,000
Long-Term Investments	136,000	120,000
Machinery	700,000	600,000
Buildings	540,000	450,000
Land	100,000	100,000
Patents	36,000	40,000
Totals	$1,895,600	$1,665,600

	December 31	
	1976	1975
Credits		
Accumulated Depreciation—Machinery	$ 80,000	$ 60,000
Accumulated Depreciation—Buildings	70,000	40,000
Accounts Payable—Trade	110,000	100,000
Notes Payable—Trade	16,000	20,000
Mortgage Payable	100,000	120,000
Common Stock	1,100,000	1,000,000
Retained Earnings	419,600	325,600
Totals	$1,895,600	$1,665,600

Additional information:
a. Net income for the year was $94,000.
b. There were no sales or disposals of plant or equipment during the year.

Required: Prepare a statement of changes in financial position using the *working capital basis for 1976.*

P18-2. The following data of the Morrison Company are given in three parts (amounts are in thousands of dollars):

Part I		
	December 31	
	1976	1975
Debits		
Current Assets	$210	$120
Plant and Equipment (net)	300	250
Totals	$510	$370
Credits		
Current Liabilities	$ 80	$ 40
Common Stock	300	300
Retained Earnings	130	30
Totals	$510	$370

Depreciation for period is $10.

Assume the same facts, except that Plant and Equipment cost and Accumulated Depreciation are itemized as follows:

	December 31	
	1976	1975
Debits		
Current Assets	$210	$120
Plant and Equipment	340	280
Totals	$550	$400
Credits		
Accumulated Depreciation	$ 40	$ 30
Current Liabilities	80	40
Common Stock	300	300
Retained Earnings	130	30
Totals	$550	$400

Part III

Assume the same debit and credit amounts as in Part II. Assume further that during the year a machine having an original cost of $20,000 and accumulated depreciation of $10,000 was sold for $14,000.

Required: For each part, prepare a statement of changes in financial position for 1976 using the *working capital basis.*

P18-3. Following is the comparative postclosing trial balance of the Grand-Prix Company:

GRAND-PRIX COMPANY
Comparative Postclosing Trial Balance
December 31, 1976 and 1975

	December 31	
	1976	1975
Debits		
Cash	$ 17,500	$ 25,000
Accounts Receivable (net)	47,500	40,000
Merchandise Inventory	130,000	97,500
Marketable Securities	–0–	55,000
Prepaid Expenses	2,000	1,250
Plant and Equipment	250,000	150,000
Patents	32,000	34,000
Totals	$479,000	$402,750

GRAND-PRIX COMPANY
Comparative Postclosing Trial Balance
December 31, 1976 and 1975

Credits

Accumulated Depreciation—		
Plant and Equipment	$ 67,500	$ 50,000
Accounts Payable	50,000	30,000
Common Stock	250,000	250,000
Retained Earnings	111,500	72,750
Totals	$479,000	$402,750

Additional data:
a. Net income for the period was $62,500.
b. Dividends declared were $23,750.
c. The marketable securities were sold at a gain (included in a) of $7,500.
d. Equipment with an original cost of $10,000 and accumulated depreciation of $5,000 was sold at an ordinary loss (included in a) of $1,000.
e. Patents are being amortized over their legal life of 17 years.

Required: Prepare a statement of changes in financial position for 1976 using the *working capital basis*.

P18-4. Data of Suskin, Inc., are given below.

	December 31	
	1976	1975
Debits		
Cash	$ 30,000	$ 22,500
Accounts Receivable	45,000	40,000
Merchandise Inventory	20,000	16,000
Investments (Long Term)	15,000	25,000
Machinery	20,000	12,500
Buildings	45,000	37,500
Land	5,000	5,000
Totals	$180,000	$158,500
Credits		
Allowance for Doubtful Accounts	$ 1,500	$ 1,000
Accumulated Depreciation—Machinery	3,750	1,500
Accumulated Depreciation—Buildings	9,000	6,000
Accounts Payable	20,000	16,500
Accrued Payables	2,250	1,750
Mortgage Payable	17,500	20,000
Common Stock	100,000	100,000
Retained Earnings	26,000	11,750
Totals	$180,000	$158,500

STATEMENT OF
CHANGES IN
FINANCIAL
POSITION

Additional data:
a. Net income for the year was $30,000.
b. Dividends declared during the year were $15,750.
c. Investments that cost $10,000 were sold during the year for $12,500. The gain is an ordinary one and is included in a.
d. Machinery that cost $2,500, on which $500 in depreciation had accumulated, was sold for $3,000. The gain is ordinary and is included in a.

Required: Prepare a statement of changes in financial position for 1976 using the *working capital basis.*

P18-5. You are given the following information from the books of the Alberta Corporation:

ALBERTA CORPORATION
Statement of Financial Position Accounts
December 31, 1976 and 1975

| | December 31 | | Change |
| | | | Increase |
	1976	1975	(Decrease)
Debits			
Cash	$ 26,400	$ 31,200	$ (4,800)
Accounts Receivable	95,200	64,800	30,400
Merchandise Inventory	44,000	56,000	(12,000)
Machinery	164,800	174,800	(10,000)
Sinking Fund Cash	20,000	–0–	20,000
Totals	$350,400	$326,800	$ 23,600
Credits			
Allowance for Doubtful Accounts	$ 5,600	$ 5,000	$ 600
Accumulated Depreciation— Machinery	32,400	36,400	(4,000)
Accounts Payable	42,000	48,400	(6,400)
Dividends Payable	4,000	–0–	4,000
Bonds Payable	40,000	–0–	40,000
Premium on Bonds Payable	1,900	–0–	1,900
Capital Stock	200,000	200,000	–0–
Retained Earnings	4,500	37,000	(32,500)
Retained Earnings— Restricted for Sinking Fund	20,000	–0–	20,000
Totals	$350,400	$326,800	$ 23,600

ALBERTA CORPORATION
Statement of Retained Earnings
For the Year Ended December 31, 1976

Balance, December 31, 1975		$37,000
Add: Net Income for year ended December 31, 1976		1,500
Total		$38,500
Deduct: Dividends Declared and Paid in Cash	$10,000	
Dividend Declared Payable January 15, 1977	4,000	
Appropriation for Sinking Fund	20,000	34,000
Balance, December 31, 1976		$ 4,500

ALBERTA CORPORATION
Income Statement
For the Year Ended December 31, 1976

Sales		$170,900
Cost of Goods Sold		130,000
Gross Margin on Sales		$ 40,900
Operating Expenses		
Salaries Expense	$29,400	
Bad Debts Expense	600	
Depreciation of Machinery	7,000	
Taxes Expense	800	
Insurance Expense	600	38,400
Net Income from Operations		$ 2,500
Other Ordinary Expenses		
Bond Interest Expense	$2,100	
Deduct Amortization of Bond Premium	100	
Net Bond Interest Expense	$ 2,000	
Other Ordinary Revenue		
Gain on Sale of Machinery	1,000	1,000
Net Income to Retained Earnings		$ 1,500

Additional data:
a. Bonds payable in the amount of $40,000 were issued on April 30, 1976, at 105.
b. Machinery that cost $14,000 and had accumulated depreciation of $11,000, was sold for $4,000 in cash.

Required: Prepare a schedule of working capital changes and a statement of changes in financial position—working capital basis for 1976 by the T-account approach. Submit all supporting computations, including the T accounts.

P18-6. The comparative statements of financial position of the Rhodes Company as of December 31, 1976 and 1975, and related supplementary data are as follows:

RHODES COMPANY
Comparative Position Statements
December 31, 1976 and 1975

	December 31	
	1976	1975
Assets		
Current Assets		
Cash	$ 50,000	$ 46,000
Marketable Securities	80,000	70,000
Accounts Receivable (net)	130,000	124,000
Merchandise Inventory	120,000	100,000
Total Current Assets	$ 380,000	$ 340,000
Investments (at cost)	$ 160,000	$ 20,000
Plant and Equipment		
Land	$ 100,000	$ 100,000
Buildings (net)	450,000	350,000
Machinery (net)	400,000	280,000
Total Plant and Equipment	$ 950,000	$ 730,000
Total Assets	$1,490,000	$1,090,000
Liabilities and Stockholders' Equity		
Current Liabilities		
Accounts Payable—Trade	$ 190,000	$ 180,000
Notes Payable—Trade	20,000	50,000
Total Current Liabilities	$ 210,000	$ 230,000
Long-Term Liabilities		
Mortgage Bonds Payable	150,000	50,000
Total Liabilities	$ 360,000	$ 280,000
Stockholders' Equity		
5% Preferred Stock, $100 par value	$ 200,000	$ –0–
Common Stock, $10 par value	700,000	700,000
Retained Earnings	230,000	110,000
Total Stockholders' Equity	$1,130,000	$ 810,000
Total Liabilities and Stockholders' Equity	$1,490,000	$1,090,000

Additional data:
a. Net income for the year 1976 was $140,000.
b. Dividends declared during year were $20,000.

c. Depreciation was: Machinery, $40,000; Buildings, $20,000.

d. There were no plant and equipment disposals during the year.

e. The Company issued 2,000 shares of 8% preferred stock at par value.

f. Investments costing $20,000 were sold for $28,000. The gain is an ordinary one and is included in Item a.

Required:

1. Prepare a separate schedule of changes in working capital.
2. Prepare a separate schedule of working capital provided by operations.
3. Prepare a statement of changes in financial position for 1976 using the working capital basis. Use the direct T-account approach.

P18-7. You are given the following partial statement data and other information for the Meade Company:

Position Statement Data

	December 31	
	1976	1975
Debits		
Plant and Equipment	$550,000	$400,000
Credits		
Accumulated Depreciation	235,000	200,000
Bonds Payable	50,000	–0–
Premium on Bonds Payable	2,500	–0–

Income Statement Data

	1976
Depreciation Expense	$ 60,000
Gain on Disposal of Plant and Equipment	4,000

Additional data:

a. Plant and equipment acquisitions during the year were $175,000.

b. Bonds payable were issued on December 31, 1976 at 105 for a total of $52,500.

Required:

1. Set up T accounts for Plant and Equipment, Accumulated Depreciation, Bonds Payable, Premium on Bonds Payable, Operating Summary, and Working Capital Summary. Place the net changes that occurred during 1976 in the first four accounts.
2. Make all the necessary entries in the accounts to accumulate information for the statement of changes in financial position, using the working capital basis.

P18-8. The Opry Company revealed the following information regarding its changes in financial position during 1976:

THE OPRY COMPANY
Comparative Statements of Financial Position
December 31, 1976 and 1975

	December 31 1976	December 31 1975	Change Increase (Decrease)
Cash	$ 918,750	$ 726,250	$192,500
Accounts Receivable (net)	157,500	140,000	17,500
Merchandise Inventory	1,037,750	700,000	337,750
Prepaid Insurance	10,500	8,750	1,750
Land	175,000	–0–	175,000
Machinery	787,500	700,000	87,500
Accumulated Depreciation— Machinery	(52,500)	(35,000)	17,500
	$3,034,500	$2,240,000	
Accounts Payable	$ 43,750	$ 35,000	8,750
Dividends Payable	87,500	17,500	70,000
9% Bonds Payable	525,000	–0–	525,000
Premium on 9% Bonds Payable	15,750	–0–	15,750
Convertible Preferred Stock	–0–	262,500	(262,500)
Common Stock, $10 par	1,575,000	1,400,000	175,000
Premium on Common Stock	87,500	–0–	87,500
Retained Earnings	700,000	525,000	175,000
	$3,034,500	$2,240,000	

Additional information:
a. Net income for 1976, $262,500.
b. A dividend of $87,500 was declared on December 19, 1976, payable on January 14, 1977.
c. On December 30, 1976, the company traded in a machine which cost $175,000 and had an accumulated depreciation of $17,500 for new machinery costing $262,500; the trade-in allowance which was equal to fair market value of the old machine was $140,000; the balance was paid in cash. The loss of $17,500 is an ordinary loss.
d. The annual depreciation expense on machinery was $35,000.
e. On January 1, 1976, the company issued 9% bonds with a face value of $350,000 at 105 for cash. The maturity date of the bonds is January 1, 1986.
f. On December 31, 1976, the company issued directly to Lynch Realty Company 9% bonds with a face value of $175,000 at 100 for land valued at $175,000.
g. The convertible preferred stock was converted during 1976 into 17,500 shares of $10 par value common stock.
h. The annual amortization of premium on 9% bonds payable is recorded by the straight-line method.

Required:
1. Prepare a separate schedule of changes in working capital.

2. Prepare a statement of changes in financial position for 1976 using the *total financial resources concept.* Use the direct T-account approach.

P18-9. You have completed the field work in connection with your audit of the Ames Corporation for the year ended December 31, 1976, and are ready to prepare a statement of changes in financial position for inclusion in your audit report. The following schedule shows the statement of financial position accounts at the beginning and end of the year.

	December 31 1976	December 31 1975	Change Increase (Decrease)
Debits			
Cash	$ 282,400	$ 320,000	$ (37,600)
Accounts Receivable	490,000	410,000	80,000
Inventory	695,000	660,000	35,000
Prepaid Expenses	10,000	8,000	2,000
Investment in Sunno Co.	106,000	–0–	106,000
Cash Surrender Value of Life Insurance	2,100	1,800	300
Land	52,500	52,500	–0–
Buildings	566,500	507,500	59,000
Machinery	186,600	190,000	(3,400)
Patents	71,000	60,000	11,000
Goodwill	40,000	50,000	(10,000)
Discount on Bonds Payable	4,680	–0–	4,680
	$2,506,780	$2,259,800	$ 246,980
Credits			
Accrued Taxes Payable	$ 92,000	$ 80,000	$ 12,000
Accounts Payable	301,280	280,000	21,280
Dividends Payable	60,000	–0–	60,000
Bonds Payable—4%	125,000	–0–	125,000
Bonds Payable—6 %	–0–	100,000	(100,000)
Allowance for Doubtful Accounts	45,300	40,000	5,300
Accumulated Depreciation— Buildings	407,000	400,000	7,000
Accumulated Depreciation— Machinery	141,000	130,000	11,000
Premium on Bonds Payable	–0–	1,600	(1,600)
Capital Stock—no par	1,301,200	1,453,200	(152,000)
Additional Paid-In Capital	14,000	–0–	14,000
Retained Earnings— Restricted for Plant Expansion	10,000	–0–	10,000
Retained Earnings	10,000	(225,000)	235,000
	$2,506,780	$2,259,800	$ 246,980

Statement of Retained Earnings Data

December 31, 1975	Balance (deficit)	$ (225,000)
March 31, 1976	Income for first quarter of 1976	25,000
April 1, 1976	Transfer from additional paid-in capital	200,000
	Balance	$ –0–
December 31, 1976	Income for last three quarters of 1976	80,000
	Dividend declared—	
	payable January 21, 1977	(60,000)
	Restricted for plant expansion	(10,000)
	Balance	$ 10,000

Your working papers contain the following information:

a. *Income statement data for year ended December 31, 1976:*

Income before other ordinary operating revenues and expenses	$106,450	
Add gain on retirement of 6% bonds	550	$107,000
Deduct loss on sale of machinery		2,000
Net income		$105,000

b. On April 1, 1976, with the official sanction of the state of incorporation, the Ames Corporation wrote off the existing deficit against additional paid-in capital created by reducing the stated value of the no-par stock.

c. On November 1, 1976, 8,000 shares of no-par stock were sold for $62,000. The board of directors voted to regard $6 a share as stated capital.

d. A patent was purchased for $16,000.

e. Machinery was purchased for $4,600 and installed in December 1976. A check for this amount was sent to the vendor in January 1977.

f. During the year, machinery which had a cost basis of $8,000 and on which there was accumulated depreciation of $5,000 was sold for $1,000. No other fixed assets were sold during the year. The resulting loss is considered to be an ordinary loss.

g. The 6%, 20-year bonds were dated and issued on January 2, 1964. Interest was payable on June 30 and December 31. The bonds were sold originally at 104. They were retired at 101 and accrued interest on March 31, 1976.

h. The 4%, 40-year bonds were dated January 1, 1976, and were sold on March 31 at 97 and accrued interest. Interest is payable semiannually on June 30 and December 31. Expense of issuance was $1,020.

i. The Ames Corporation acquired 80% control in Sunno Co. on January 2, 1976, for $100,000. The income statement of Sunno Co. for 1976 shows a net income of $7,500. The equity method of accounting for investments is used.

j. Extraordinary repairs to buildings of $7,000 were charged to Accumulated Depreciation—Building.

Required: From the above information prepare a statement of changes in financial position for 1976 using the *total financial resources concept* and a schedule of working capital changes. T accounts are required.

(*AICPA adapted*)

P18-10. You are given the following information about certain items for two companies during a year:

Accounts Receivable—beginning of year	$ 54,000	$ 80,000
Accounts Receivable—end of year	70,000	76,000
Sales	210,000	300,000
Uncollectible Accounts Written Off	1,000	1,500
Cash Discounts on Sales	2,000	5,000

Required: For each company determine the amount of cash received from customers.

P18-11. You are given the following information about certain items for two companies during a year:

	1	2
Beginning Inventory	$ 24,000	$ 30,000
Ending Inventory	20,000	36,000
Purchases	150,000	170,000
Beginning Accounts Payable	20,000	28,000
Ending Accounts Payable	24,000	20,000
Discounts on Purchases	2,000	3,000

Required: For each company determine the amount of cash disbursements for merchandise.

P18-12. The data of Cashew Company follows:

CASHEW COMPANY
Comparative Position Statements
December 31, 1976 and 1975

	December 31	
	1976	1965
Debits		
Cash	$ 52,000	$ 74,000
Accounts Receivable (net)	180,000	192,000
Merchandise Inventory	200,000	160,000
Investments (Long Term)	24,000	20,000
Land	40,000	30,000
Buildings (net)	320,000	200,000
Machinery (net)	400,000	300,000
Totals	$1,216,000	$976,000
Credits		
Accounts Payable	$ 150,000	$130,000
Accrued Payables	6,000	8,000
Mortgage Payable	140,000	116,000
Common Stock	600,000	500,000
Retained Earnings	320,000	222,000
Totals	$1,216,000	$976,000

CASHEW COMPANY
Income Statement
For the Year Ended December 31, 1976

Sales		$1,620,000
Cost of Goods Sold		960,000
Gross Margin on Sales		$ 660,000
Operating Expenses		
Depreciation—Machinery	$ 40,000	
Depreciation—Buildings	20,000	
Other Operating Expenses	442,000	502,000
Net Income		$ 158,000

Additional data:

a. Dividends paid during year were $60,000.

b. The increase in long-term investments, machinery, buildings, and land were from purchases for cash.

c. Common stock worth $100,000 was issued at par value.

Required: Prepare a statement of changes in financial position for 1976 using the cash basis.

P18-13. (*Financial policy decision problem*) You have been assigned by the acquisitions committee of Control Group, Inc., to examine a potential acquisition, Retailers, Inc. This company is a merchandising firm that appears to be available because of the death of its founder and principal shareholder. Recent statements of Retailers, Inc., are shown below.

RETAILERS, INC.
Comparative Statements of Financial Position
As of January 31

	1976	1975	1974
Cash	$ 130,000	$ 120,000	$ 100,000
Accounts Receivable	430,000	370,000	300,000
Inventory	400,000	400,000	200,000
Fixed Assets	900,000	800,000	700,000
Less Accumulated			
Depreciation	(325,000)	(250,000)	(200,000)
Total Assets	$1,535,000	$1,440,000	$1,100,000
Accounts Payable	$ 300,000	$ 260,000	$ 220,000
8% Notes Payable			
Due 1/31/84	280,000	280,000	–0–
Common Stock Outstanding	690,000	690,000	690,000
Retained Earnings	265,000	210,000	190,000
Total Equity	$1,535,000	$1,440,000	$1,100,000

RETAILERS, INC.
Income Statements
For the Years Ended January 31

	1976	1975
Sales	$2,943,000	$2,629,000
Cost of Goods Sold	$2,200,000	$2,000,000
Wages	350,000	300,000
Supplies	42,600	36,600
Depreciation	100,000	75,000
Interest Charges	22,400	22,400
Loss on Sale of Fixed Assets	75,000	105,000
Total Deductions	$2,790,000	$2,539,000
Net Income Before Taxes	$ 153,000	$ 90,000
Income Taxes	68,000	40,000
Net Income	$ 85,000	$ 50,000

RETAILERS, INC.
Changes in Financial Position
For the Years Ended January 31

	1976	1975
Sources		
Net Income	$ 85,000	$ 50,000
Add back: Depreciation	100,000	75,000
Loss	75,000	105,000
Notes Payable	–0–	280,000
Total	$260,000	$510,000
Uses		
Net Fixed Assets Purchased	$200,000	$230,000
Dividends Paid	30,000	30,000
Total	$230,000	$260,000
Increase (Decrease) in Net Working Capital	$ 30,000	$250,000

Required:

1. Calculate the inventory turnover (a) for 1975; (b) for 1976. (c) Is the turn-over better or worse in 1976 than in 1975?
2. Calculate the current ratio for 1976.
3. Calculate a rate of return on the stockholders' equity for 1976.
4. Describe the cash flow for 1976 by redrawing the statement of changes in financial position to explain the changes in cash position instead of net working capital.
5. Does the amount shown for net fixed assets purchased equal the funds spent for newly acquired assets? Explain your answer.
6. The statement of changes in financial position (formerly the funds statement) is now required in published financial reports. What reasons are given to support the requirement that this statement be included in published financial reports?

(IMA adapted)

Price Level Reporting Problems

19

Since the basis for entry of amounts into the accounting records is historical cost, the financial reports of entities after a few years reflect summary dollar figures made of individual acquisitions in different years. For example, the building may have been purchased in 1965, a piece of machinery may have been acquired in 1970, and the inventory may represent a mixture of carryover from 1975 and purchases in 1976.

In the statement of financial position, the historical costs of these and other assets are added to obtain total assets, the *stable-dollar assumption* incorporating the concept that a 1965 dollar, a 1970 dollar, a 1975 dollar, and a 1976 dollar all represent equal amounts of purchasing power.	**Stable-dollar Assumption**

This is simply an unrealistic assumption.

The purchasing power of the dollar varies significantly from period to period.

As the general level of prices of all goods and services rises, the purchasing power of the dollar declines—a change known as *inflation*. Conversely, as the general level of prices of all goods and services falls, the purchasing power of the dollar increases—a change known as *deflation*. Such changes in the value of the dollar are known as *general purchasing power* changes.	**General Purchasing Power**

Changes in general purchasing power should be differentiated from changes in price levels of specific commodities or services such as farm products or medical services. These are changes in specific purchasing power of the dollar; they are influenced by specific factors not common to all goods and services.

In 1974, the Financial Accounting Standards Board (FASB) noted that inflation, after holding at average rates of 2.3 percent and 2 percent a year for the periods 1950–1958 and 1960–1968 respectively, had moved to an average rate of 5.1 percent a year from 1969 to 1973. Accordingly, the FASB added to its original agenda the question of requiring reporting of the effects of general price-level changes as supplemental information to the conventional historical dollar financial statements. The cost standard on which historical dollar statements are based is not abandoned in the preparation of general price-level statements. Many variables can affect the current value of financial statement items; no variable except the change in general price level is considered in restating data for changes in general purchasing power. After an amount is restated, it still represents cost, that is, cost repriced in terms of general purchasing power and *not a current replacement value.*

The Accounting Principles Board, in APB Statement No. 3, discussed various types of indexes which might be used to make adjustments to reflect purchasing power changes.[1]

Price Index	A *price index* is a statistical average of prices expressed as a percentage of a base period.

The U. S. Department of Labor compiles a consumer price index (CPI), which has several major subdivisions such as food, housing, apparel, and upkeep or medical care, and a wholesale price index (WPI), which also has several subdivisions. Among the wholesale price index subdivisions are farm products, processed foods and feeds, textiles and apparel, fuels and related products and power, machinery and equipment, and several others. A number of specific indexes are compiled privately. There is general agreement, however, that the best available index of general price levels in the United States since 1929 is the gross national product implicit price deflator (GNP deflator) published annually by the U. S. Department of Commerce, Bureau of Economic Analysis.

COMPARABILITY OF STATEMENTS

The overall effect of price level adjustments is illustrated by the stockholders' equity per share of a major corporation in its 1973 annual report:

Year	1973	1972	1971	1970	1969
Stockholders' equity per share as reported	$30.25	$28.76	$28.31	$28.09	$26.61
Stockholders' equity per share converted to 1973 dollars	30.25	29.76	30.77	31.95	31.93

[1] AICPA, *APB Accounting Principles,* vol. 2 (Chicago: Commerce Clearing House, Inc., 1973), pp. 9008–9055.

As reported in historical cost dollars, there appears to be a substantial increase from 1969 to 1970, a steady increase in the 1970–1972 period, and again a substantial increase in 1973. When all figures are converted to dollars of 1973 purchasing power, however, the 1969–1970 increase almost disappears, the steady increase for the 1970–1972 period appears as a steady decline, and the substantial increase in 1973 is a rather modest one.

To convert the foregoing figures to a set of comparable data—in this case, dollars of 1973 purchasing power—the GNP deflator index was used. It could be argued that some other index may be more appropriate, but the implications of this example are clear. Historical dollar figures used to portray comparative data in financial reports can be quite misleading when inflation or deflation is present over the time period of comparison. Furthermore, if the nature of the resulting reported earnings and dividend distributions is not a reliable indicator of the firm's potential, then the usefulness of the statements is limited. Certainly, the usefulness of the comparative statements of prior periods is severely limited if material price changes occurred during the time span covered by such statements.

To overcome these shortcomings, and to avoid this commingling of "shoes and ships and sealing wax"—that is, of dollars of different sizes with different purchasing power dimensions—a conversion to a uniform or "common dollar" basis is necessary. An expenditure of $10,000 for a tract of land, for example, represents a commitment of $10,000 of current purchasing power. The subsequent reporting of that item in financial statements should be in terms of dollars of purchasing power as of statement date. If, a year later, prices in general have increased by 10 percent, the land should then be reported at $11,000 or $10,000 × 110/100. Thus, the land will be stated in dollars of uniform size or in "common dollars"—that is, in dollars with a purchasing power size prevailing at statement date. The cost remains at $10,000, but it has been restated in more units of lesser purchasing power. The $1,000 increase is a recognition of the change in the value of the measuring unit, a recognition of the fact that there has been a 10 percent increase in the *general* level of prices, so that $11,000 is now required to buy all kinds of goods and services that could have been bought for $10,000 a year before. The $1,000 increase is not a gain, but its recognition means that assets and paid-in capital will have been increased by an amount sufficient to maintain the general purchasing power of the paid-in capital at its original level. The purchasing power needed to replace the specific tract of land may be greater than, or less than, $11,000, depending upon the currently prevailing market conditions for that specific asset. The discussion in this chapter is related only to general, not specific, price-level changes. If the tract of land has a current market value of $15,000, it will still be restated at $11,000. The additional $4,000 = ($15,000 − $11,000) is due to a specific price change and is not recognized in statements adjusted for general price-level changes.

If the essence of the financial reporting process is to measure and report purchasing power, then the items being compared must be expressed in terms

(Ch. 19)

of a common, stabilized, or comparable purchasing power yardstick. Clearly, a $100 investment that matures when the price level has doubled cancels the investment, but the two $100 amounts cannot be compared to measure the result of the investment. The investor's original $100 is worth $200 now (200/ 100 × $100), and he has lost $100 in terms of dollars at maturity. Similarly, the $100 he receives at maturity is worth only $50 in terms of dollars at the time the investment was made (100/200 × $100).

It is necessary to distinguish between the amount or number of dollars (money value) and the kind and amount of goods and services those dollars command (real value). Such distinction is necessary because changing price levels cause changes in purchasing power, which in turn create the gap between money values and real values. To illustrate, assume a person earns $100 a year over a three-year period as follows:

	1974	1975	1976
a. Money value (current dollars)	$100	$100	$100
b. Price index (base year: 1974)	100	125	150
c. Real value (divide a by b and multiply by 100)	$100	$ 80	$ 66.67
d. Adjusted value (divide b by a)	$100	$125	$150

A dollar in 1975 buys only as much as 80 cents bought in 1974; $100 in 1976 buys only as much as $66.67 bought in 1974. To maintain his purchasing power over the period, this person would need to receive $125 in 1975 and $150 in 1976. He needs $1.50 in 1976 to buy what $1 would have bought in 1974. The dollar will buy more goods and services when prices fall; the dollar will buy fewer goods and services when prices rise. This fluctuation in the purchasing power of the dollar results from fluctuating price levels. Changes in price levels may be measured by index numbers.

Use of Index Numbers to Adjust Costs

The following steps are required to convert historical cost dollars into dollars of a uniform purchasing power:

1. Convert to base-year dollars by dividing by the price index of the date on which the amount was incurred.
2. Convert the amount in step 1 to year-end dollars by multiplying by the current year-end index.

These steps may be expressed by the formula

Cost measured in current year-end dollars =

$$\text{Historical cost} \times \frac{\text{Current index}}{\text{Index at date of origin}}$$

The problems of price-level changes as related to the basic matching concept have been discussed thus far. A somewhat different problem arises in connection with monetary assets or money items—cash, notes receivable, accounts receivable, accrued receivables, notes payable, accounts payable, accrued payables, and bonds payable. These items are fixed in terms of the total number of dollars that will be collrected on the assets and the number of dollars that must be paid to creditors on the liabilities regardless of changes in prices. The purchasing power, however, of the cash to be collected or to be paid fluctuates. Cash or claims to cash are worth less or will buy less during periods of rising prices and, conversely, in periods of falling prices, they are worth more and will buy more. By the same token, the reduction of indebtedness during periods of rising prices is eased by payment in current or cheaper dollars. The opposite is true if prices are falling. The relative effect of changing price levels on monetary assets and liabilities will result in a purchasing power monetary gain or loss depending upon the relative balance in existence and the movement of the price level, whether rising or falling. These gains and losses "should be recognized as part of the net income of the period in which the general price level changes."[2]

To illustrate monetary or purchasing power gain or loss, assume the following information (Figure 19-1) taken from the statements of financial position of Andover Corporation.

Figure 19-1 Andover Corporation Net Monetary Assets

	December 31		
	1975	1976	Increase
Cash	$412,000	$570,000	$158,000
Accounts Receivable	300,000	368,000	68,000
Totals	$712,000	$938,000	$226,000
Accounts Payable	$209,000	$260,000	$ 51,000
Bonds Payable	300,000	300,000	–0–
Totals	$509,000	$560,000	$ 51,000
Net Monetary Assets	$203,000	$378,000	$175,000
Assumed Price Index:	1975–average	100	
	1975–end of year	120	
	1976–average	150	
	1976–end of year	165	

To simplify the illustration, it is assumed that the average price levels during 1975 and 1976, respectively, were 100 and 150 and that end-of-year levels were 120 and 165. The relevant multipliers and related conversion factors to restate to dollars of general purchasing power as at December 31, 1976, are

---

[2] AICPA, *APB Accounting Principles,* vol. 2 (Chicago: Commerce Clearing House, Inc., 1973), p. 9015.

PRICE LEVEL
REPORTING
PROBLEMS

computed by dividing the index number at December 31, 1976, by each of the other index numbers. Thus, for items originating during 1975, the index number for the current position statement date, December 31, 1976, is divided by the average index for 1975 (165 ÷ 100, or 1.65). An item acquired during 1975 at a cost of $100 is restated in current dollars as at December 31, 1976, as $100 × 1.65, or $165. The $100 cost in 1975 is equal to a cost of $165 at December 31, 1976. Conversion factors are computed as follows:

1. For items originating during 1975:

$$\frac{\text{December 31, 1976}}{\text{Average for 1975}} = \frac{165}{100} = 1.65$$

2. For 1975 year-end:

$$\frac{\text{December 31, 1976}}{\text{December 31, 1975}} = \frac{165}{120} = 1.375$$

3. For items originating during 1976:

$$\frac{\text{December 31, 1976}}{\text{Average for 1976}} = \frac{165}{150} = 1.10$$

4. For 1976 year-end:

$$\frac{\text{December 31, 1976}}{\text{December 31, 1976}} = \frac{165}{165} = 1.00$$

All monetary items appearing in Figure 19-1 are converted in terms of December 31, 1976, dollars in Figure 19-2 as follows:

1. All amounts as at the end of 1975 are multiplied by 165/120, or by the conversion factor, 1.375.
2. All amounts originating during 1976—the changes during the year—are multiplied by 165/150 or 1.10.
3. The amounts in (1) and (2) are compared with the appropriate December 31, 1976, balances to measure the purchasing power gain or loss.
4. The net loss or net gain is computed by deducting gains from losses or losses from gains.

The $289,600 purchasing power loss resulting from the conversion of money assets reflects the extent to which money asset growth has failed to keep pace with the increase in the price level during 1976. The required increase in money assets to maintain purchasing power parity in the face of price-level increase during 1976 is as follows:

On 1975 year-end balances (37.5% of $712,000)	$267,000
On increases during 1976 (10% of $226,000)	22,600
Total	$289,600

The $195,975 purchasing power gain resulting from the conversion of money liabilities reflects a reduction in the debt burden due to the decline in the purchasing power of the dollar. The $509,000 indebtedness as of Decem-

Figure 19-2 Purchasing Power Gains and Losses

ANDOVER CORPORATION
Purchasing Power Gains and Losses
For Year Ended December 31, 1976

	Amount (From Figure 19–1)	Conversion Factor	Converted to 12/31/76 Dollars	
Conversion of monetary assets:				
Balance, December 31, 1975	$712,000	1.375	$ 979,000	
Increase during 1976	226,000	1.100	248,600	
Total	$938,000		$1,227,600	
Deduct December 31, 1976 unconverted balance			938,000	
Purchasing power loss				$289,600
Conversion of monetary liabilities:				
Balance, December 31, 1975	$509,000	1.375	$ 699,875	
Increase during 1976	51,000	1.100	56,100	
Total	$560,000		$ 755,975	
Deduct December 31, 1976 unconverted balance			560,000	
Purchasing power gain				195,975
Net purchasing power loss				$ 93,625

ber 31, 1975, is fixed by contractual agreement. But repayment will be in dollars that have lost 37.5 percent of their purchasing power. It may be reasonably assumed that the Andover Corporation has used creditor funds in the manufacture and sale of a product whose selling price has been increased to correspond with the increasing price level. Repayment of debt, however, is fixed at the amounts owed prior to the price-level increase. The excess, therefore, represents a purchasing power gain. If the $509,000 indebtedness as of December 31, 1975, were to be repaid in terms of December 31, 1976, dollars, the required payment would be $699,875, computed as follows:

Liabilities (unadjusted)	$509,000
Adjustment for price level increase ($509,000 × 37.5%)	190,875
Total (adjusted)	$699,875

The adjusted total of $699,875 has the same purchasing power as $509,000 had one year earlier. If all 1975 year-end debts were paid on December 31, 1976, the creditors will have incurred a purchasing power loss of $190,875 and Andover Corporation will have realized a corresponding purchasing power gain. The price level adjustment for the increase in liabilities during 1976 is $51,000 × 0.10, or $5,100. The total of the two adjustments ($190,875 + $5,100) represents a pur-

(Ch. 19)

chasing power gain of $195,975 from the conversion of money liabilities. Combining loss and gain results in a net purchasing power loss of $93,625.

NONMONEY ITEMS AND CHANGING PRICE LEVELS

The money items, being fixed by the customary legal relationship between banks, customers, and creditors, *are not* restated in the current statements. They are already stated in current dollars (when comparative statements are presented, money items for prior periods *are* restated). Regardless of changing price levels, there is no quantitative change in the dollars on deposit in the bank or in the numerical amount of the settlement between debtors and creditors. Only the purchasing power of these items changes and this is what gives rise to gains and losses. The opposite is true of the other position statement items—merchandise inventory, land, plant and equipment, common stockholders' equity, and so on. It is necessary to convert or restate the nonmoney items. The purchasing power represented by the dollar amount of these items is not fixed contractually, and they are not stated in terms of current dollars; rather, the purchasing power of the dollar amount of these items fluctuates with changes in price levels and must, therefore, be converted to the current dollar basis. Such conversion does not give rise to purchasing power gains and losses, however; the change is due only to a change in the measuring yardstick; it is not an economic event such that gives rise to a real gain or loss. Contrariwise, the money items are not converted because they are already stated in current dollars, but the qualitative change in their purchasing power while they are being held does give rise to gains and losses.

Illustrative Problem

The financial statements of the Andover Corporation illustrate, in summary form, the procedure for the price-level conversion of such statements (Figures 19-3 and 19-4). The multipliers used are based on the same price index assumptions as those in Figure 19-1. The explanation of the conversions follows the presentation of the unconverted and converted statements.

The derivation of the purchasing power loss of $93,625 is shown in Figure 19-2. Amounts for the changes in the monetary items during 1976 were taken from the statements of financial position. A similar schedule is shown in Figure 19-5 except that the changes in the monetary items during 1976 are taken from the income statement for that year.

Conversion of Combined Statement of Income and Retained Earnings
Sales. Sales were made uniformly throughout the year. The conversion is, therefore, at the average price index for 1976, or

$$\$750,000 \times 1.100 = \$825,000.$$

Cost of Goods Sold. The computation and conversion for the cost of goods sold is shown in Figure 19-6.

ANDOVER CORPORATION
Comparative Statements of Financial Position
As of December 31, 1976 and 1975

Figure 19-3
Comparative
Statements of
Financial Position

	Unconverted December 31		Converted December 31	
Assets	1976	1975	1976	1975
Cash	$ 570,000	$ 412,000	$ 570,000	$ 566,500
Accounts Receivable	368,000	300,000	368,000	412,500
Merchandise Inventory	50,000	30,000	55,000	49,500
Land	40,000	40,000	66,000	66,000
Plant and Equipment	1,150,000	1,150,000	1,897,500	1,897,500
Accumulated Depreciation	(465,000)	(350,000)	(767,250)	(577,500)
	$1,713,000	$1,582,000	$2,189,250	$2,414,500

Liabilities and Stockholders' Equity

Accounts Payable	$ 260,000	$ 209,000	$ 260,000	$ 287,375
Bonds Payable	300,000	300,000	300,000	412,500
Capital Stock	975,000	975,000	1,608,750	1,608,750
Retained Earnings	178,000	98,000	20,500	105,875
	$1,713,000	$1,582,000	$2,189,250	$2,414,500

(deduction)

ANDOVER CORPORATION
Combined Statement of Income and Retained Earnings
For the Year Ended December 31, 1976

Figure 19-4
Combined Statement
of Income and
Retained Earnings

	Unconverted	Converted
Sales	$750,000	$825,000
Costs and Expenses:		
Cost of Goods Sold	$430,000	$489,500
Depreciation	115,000	189,750
Other Expenses	125,000	137,500
Total	$670,000	$816,750
Operating Income	$ 80,000	$ 8,250
Purchasing Power Loss		(93,625)
Net Income (Loss)	$ 80,000	$ (85,375)
Retained Earnings, January 1, 1976	98,000	105,875
Retained Earnings, December 31, 1976	$178,000	$ 20,500

Figure 19-5
Purchasing Power
Gains and Losses

ANDOVER CORPORATION
Schedule of Purchasing Power Gains and Losses
For the Year Ended December 31, 1976

	Unconverted	Conversion Factor	Converted
Net Monetary Assets, December 31, 1975 (Figure 19-1)	$203,000	1.375	$ 279,125
Add: Sales (Figure 19-4)	750,000	1.100	825,000
	$953,000		$1,104,125
Deduct:			
Purchases (Figure 19-6)	$450,000	1.100	$ 495,000
Other Expenses (Figure 19-4)	125,000	1.100	137,500
	$575,000		$ 632,500
Net Monetary Assets, December 31, 1976 (converted)			$ 471,625
Deduct December 31, 1976 (unconverted)	$378,000		378,000
Purchasing Power Loss			$ 93,625

Figure 19-6
Conversion of Cost of
Goods Sold

Inventory, January 1	$ 30,000 × 1.65 =	$ 49,500
Purchases	450,000 × 1.100 =	495,000
Total	$480,000	$544,500
Inventory, December 31	50,000 × 1.100 =	55,000
Cost of Goods Sold	$430,000	$489,500

The beginning inventory was acquired during 1975 and the purchases were made uniformly during 1976. the Andover Corporation uses the first-in, first-out method of inventory valuation.

Depreciation. The converted cost of plant and equipment is $1,897,500. Assuming a straight-line rate of 10 percent, the converted depreciation expense is 10 percent of $1,897,500, or $189,750. An alternative method is to multiply the unconverted depreciation expense by the same factor used in converting the related asset, or

$$115,000 \times 1.65 = \$189,750$$

Other Expenses. Other expenses were incurred during the year. The conversion computation is:

$$125,000 \times 1.100 = \$137,500$$

Conversion of Position Statement as of December 31, 1975

The monetary items—Cash, Accounts Receivable, Accounts Payable, and Bonds Payable are converted from year-end 1975 to their December 31, 1976, equivalents by the factor 1.375. All other items except retained earnings are assumed to have originated when the price index was 100; the applicable conversion factor is, therefore, 1.65. Retained earnings is a balancing figure arrived at by subtracting total liabilities and capital stock from total assets.

> Retained earnings in the restated balance sheet [statement of financial position] at the beginning of the first year for which general price-level restatements are prepared can be computed as the balancing amount. This avoids the impractical alternative of restating all prior financial statements since the inception of the company. Retained earnings in subsequent restated balance sheets is determined from the restated statements of income and retained earnings.[3]

Conversion of Position Statement as of December 31, 1976.
The monetary assets and liabilities are, by definition, payable in current dollars and need not, therefore, be converted. All other items except the December 31, 1976, inventory and retained earnings are assumed to have originated when the price index was 100; the applicable conversion factor is, therefore, 1.65. The retained earnings amount of $20,500 is detailed in Figure 19-4.

Analysis of Unconverted and Converted Statements

A comparison of some ratios in the converted and unconverted statements underscores the striking effect of the conversion of the statements into current dollar terms. The ratio of operating income to sales, for example, is:

$$\text{Unconverted:} \frac{\$80,000}{\$750,000} = 10.67\%$$

$$\text{Converted:} \frac{\$8,250}{\$825,000} = 1\%$$

Position statement ratios for the nonmoney items also change drastically. For example, ratio of operating income to stockholders' equity is:

$$\text{Unconverted:} \frac{\$80,000}{\$1,153,000} = 6.94\%$$

$$\text{Converted:} \frac{\$8,250}{\$1,629,250} = 0.51\%$$

Book value per share (assume 9,000 shares outstanding) is:

$$\text{Unconverted:} \frac{\$1,153,000}{9,000} = \$128.11$$

$$\text{Converted:} \frac{\$1,629,250}{9,000} = \$181.03$$

[3] AICPA, *APB Accounting Principles,* vol. 2 (Chicago: Commerce Clearing House, Inc., 1973), p. 9023.

(Ch. 19)

In a time when corporate annual reports are making extensive use of such devices as bar charts to show comparative data for a number of years, it is important that the readers of such reports understand the implications of price-level changes that have occurred over the period of comparison. Whether such charts have been prepared from converted or unconverted figures and whether ratios and book value per share figures are from adjusted or unadjusted data are questions that must be raised. The importance of these questions, of course, becomes greater in direct proportion to the degree of inflation or deflation that is occurring.

GLOSSARY

Conversion Factor The decimal equivalent of the ratio of a stated year (usually the current one) to a base year.

Deflation A downward change in the general price level resulting in an increase in the purchasing power of the dollar.

Historical Cost The original cost of an asset, including net purchase price and all other costs required to place it into service.

Inflation An upward change in the general price level resulting in a decrease in the purchasing power of the dollar.

Modified Historical Cost Historical cost offset by a figure that recognizes the amount of original benefits already extracted from an asset.

Monetary Items Assets and liabilities that are fixed in terms of dollars regardless of changes in price level.

Nonmoney Items Assets with a dollar value that would be expected to change with changes in price levels.

Price Index A statistical average of prices expressed as a percentage of a base period.

Purchasing Power Gains and Losses Actual gains and losses arising out of holding monetary items during periods of inflation and deflation.

QUESTIONS

Q19-1. Why should accountants concern themselves with price-level fluctuations?

Q19-2. Give three illustrations of distortions or inaccuracies in conventional financial statements resulting from changes in dollar purchasing power.

Q19-3. Why is the historical-cost dollar not always reliable as a basis for management decision?

Q19-4. What are the probable effects of rising costs on earnings? Illustrate.

Q19-5. A member of the board of directors of Allyn Corporation refused to vote for a proposed $250,000 dividend declaration. He contended that the reported net earnings of $300,000, after adjustments for price-level changes, were inadequate to justify the proposed declaration. Comment on his position.

Q19-6. Zal Corporation constructed plant A in 1976 at a cost of $2,000,000. Ten years later, it built plant B, a similar plant, in another city at a cost of $4,000,-000. What are the competitive advantages of plant A over plant B?

Q19-7. How may changes in price levels be measured?

Q19-8. What is a price index? How is it constructed? How may it be used?

Q19-9. Does the use of LIFO resolve the problem of inventory price fluctuation? What is the effect of LIFO (a) on net income, (b) on working capital?

Q19-10. What is the relationship between rising prices and accumulated depreciation?

Q19-11. It has been said that the central problem of accounting is the proper matching of expense and revenue. How do rising prices affect this problem?

Q19-12. What is the relative effect of changing price levels on monetary assets and liabilities?

Q19-13. What gives rise to a monetary purchasing power gain or loss? Illustrate.

Q19-14. In what specific areas of decision making may accounting data adjusted for price-level changes be used to advantage? In what areas is the use of such data of no advantage?

Q19-15. What is the effect of adjusting accounting data for rising prices on the financial statement ratios?

Q19-16. Summarize the arguments for and against the conversion of historical-dollar amounts into "real" dollars by the use of price index numbers. Should the converted amounts supplement or replace the historical amounts in financial statements?

Q19-17. On July 1, 1951, a corporation issued $5,000,000 in bonds to mature on June 30, 1976. What is the relative gain or loss position on June 30, 1976, (a) of the issuing corporation, (b) of the bondholders? How do the financial statements reflect such gains and losses?

E19-1. Students A and B each received cash birthday gifts of $750. Student A purchased a bond with a maturity value of $1,000 in 8 years. Student B purchased a tract of land. Prepare adjusted statements of financial position for A and B 8 years later, assuming the price index has doubled during the interval.

EXERCISES

E19-2. Rock Corporation acquired the following plant and equipment assets:

Year	Cost	Index
1956	$400,000	100
1966	300,000	150
1976	700,000	200

Convert these amounts to 1976 equivalent dollars. Discuss the significance of the converted amounts.

E19-3. Rowe Corporation constructed a plant at a cost of $600,000 in 1957 when the price level stood at 100. A similar plant was built in 1976 when the price level was 175. What was the approximate cost of the second plant? What is the effect of the increased cost of the new plant on this company's competitive position? Should the depreciation base on the original plant be changed? Comment on the effect of such a change.

PRICE LEVEL
REPORTING
PROBLEMS

E19-4. Leo Corporation sales for the years 1975 and 1976 were $500,000 and $650,000, respectively. Price indexes were:

	1975	1976
January 1	150	200
December 31	200	250

Assuming no seasonal fluctuations in sales and uniform price-level changes, what significant conclusions may be drawn from the sales data for the two years?

E19-5. Land Corporation began business on July 1, 1976, by acquiring merchandise costing $200,000. On July 31, 1976, 65% of the merchandise was sold. The price index rose from 120 to 125 during the month. Compute the adjusted cost of goods sold and cost of goods on hand as of July 31.

E19-6. Gill Corporation was formed to operate an office building that cost $400,000. Operating data for the first year were:

Income from rentals	$80,000
Operating costs (exclusive of depreciation)	40,000
Depreciation	16,000

Assume all transactions are for cash and are incurred or received uniformly throughout the year. The price level doubled during the year. Prepare a general price level statement of financial position as of December 31, 1976, and an adjusted operating statement for the year.

E19-7. Wilde Corporation had on hand on January 1, 1976, 6,000 units of merchandise costing $60,000 that were acquired when the price level was 120. During 1976, 8,500 units were acquired at a cost of $120,000, when the price level was 125. Sales for the period totaled 12,000 units. The index at the end of the period was 130.

Compute, in terms of year-end dollars, (a) cost of goods sold and cost of goods on hand using FIFO, and (b) cost of goods sold and cost of goods on hand using the conventional LIFO procedure.

E19-8. The machinery and equipment account of Mann Corporation consisted of two separate acquisitions: (1) ten machines costing a total of $160,000 with an estimated service life of 20 years, no salvage value, acquired when the price level was 90; and (2) five machines costing $125,000, with an estimated service life of 10 years, no salvage value, acquired when the price level was 120. The first group of machines has been in use six years; the second group, four years. Straight-line depreciation is used. The index now stands at 150.

Compute (a) the adjusted and unadjusted carrying value of the machines, and (b) the adjusted and unadjusted depreciation expense for the current year.

E19-9. The sales manager and the financial vice-president of the Polaride Company disagree on the significance of the company's sales increases during the last three years. Gross sales were as follows:

1974	$4,000,000
1975	5,500,000
1976	7,000,000

Relevant price indices were, respectively, 100, 140, and 190. The sales manager is satisfied with the level of "growth" in sales during the three-year period.

The financial vice-president argues to the contrary that there has been a steady decline in sales. Who is correct? Why?

DP19-1. (*Preparation of converted income statement*) The following trial balance was taken from the books of Rollo Company as of December 31, 1976.

ROLLO COMPANY
Trial Balance
December 31, 1976

	Debits	Credits	Price Level
Cash	$ 96,000		115
Notes and Accounts Receivable	144,000		115
Merchandise Inventory,			
Jan. 1, 1976	88,000		100
Plant and Equipment	640,000		100
Notes and Accounts Payable		$ 120,000	115
9% Mortgage Bonds Payable		200,000	100
Common Stock ($100 par)		560,000	100
Retained Earnings, Jan. 1, 1976		64,000	100
Sales		1,280,000	115
Purchases	960,000		115
Operating Expenses			
(excluding dep'n.)	240,000		115
Depreciation Expense	46,000		100
Interest Expense	10,000		115
	$2,224,000	$2,224,000	

Merchandise Inventory, December 31, 1976, $144,000, (price level, 115). Indicated price levels at acquisition dates are based on the following assumptions:

January 1	100
December 31	130
Year's Average	115

Required:

1. Prepare a conventional income statement for the year and a statement of financial position as of December 31, 1976.
2. Prepare converted statements.
3. Compute the following ratios for each set of statements: (a) net income to net sales; (b) book value per share of common stock; (c) current ratio; (d) net income to stockholders' equity.

DP19-2. (*Computing monetary purchasing power gain or loss*) The position statements of Wills Company as of December 31, 1975 and 1976, included the following:

	December 31	
	1975	1976
Cash	$275,000	$300,000
Notes and Accounts Receivable	200,000	225,000
Notes and Accounts Payable	112,500	150,000
9% Mortgage Bonds Payable	125,000	125,000

Price levels were:

	1975	1976
Beginning of year	100	120
Average for year	110	135
End of year	120	150

Required: Prepare a schedule showing the monetary purchasing power gain or loss during 1976.

P19-1. During the period 1940–1976, the Mills Corporation acquired six parcels of land in the area surrounding its home plant (all parcels were approximately equal in size) as follows:

Lot No.	Year	Cost	Price Index
1	1940	$10,000	43.9
2	1950	12,000	80.2
3	1958	20,000	100.0
4	1965	30,000	110.9
5	1968	40,000	117.6
6	1976	75,000	140.0

Required:

1. How should these parcels be shown in the company's statement of financial position as at the end of 1976?
2. Indicate some alternative methods of presentation.
3. State the method you consider as being the most useful, explaining your choice fully.
4. What additional information is needed?

P19-2. Refer to P19-1. Assume that the Mills Corporation sold lot number 5 for $75,000 when the price index was 150. What was the gain or loss on the sale? Explain fully.

P19-3. The Keyes Corporation acquired machinery costing $150,000 three years ago, when the price index was 110. The current price index is 150. The estimated useful life of the equipment is 10 years.

Required:

1. How should the equipment be shown in the Keyes Corporation's statement of financial position?
2. What is the effect on the company's results of operations for the current year if price-level change is ignored? on total assets?

P19-4. The Roy Corporation's merchandise inventory, on January 1, 1976, was $100,000. Merchandise purchases during the year were as follows:

June 20	$500,000
September 1	400,000

Goods on hand as of December 31 cost $175,000. Prevailing price indexes were as follows:

January 1	120
June 20	130
September 1	135
December 31	140

Required: Calculate the cost of goods sold for the year. (Use FIFO.)

P19-5. The net monetary assets of the Glynn Corporation were $300,000 on January 1, 1976, and $600,000 on December 31, 1976. Price indexes were:

January 1	125
Average during year	140
December 31	150

Required:

1. Calculate the purchasing power gain or loss for the year.
2. Calculate the purchasing power gain or loss, assuming no change in net monetary assets.

P19-6. Refer to P19-5. Assume that net monetary assets increased $500,000 during the year and that nonmonetary assets increased $300,000.

Required: Calculate the company's purchasing power gain or loss for the year.

P19-7. The Machinery account of the Zanger Corporation shows the following:

Year	Acquisitions	Disposals	Average Price Index
1973	$200,000	20,000	110
1974	150,000	50,000	120
1975	250,000	60,000	125
1976	100,000	40,000	130
12/31/76 (year end)			140

Required:

1. Restate the Machinery account in terms of the December 31, 1976, price index.
2. What is the balance in the accumulated depreciation account, assuming (a) 10-year life, straight-line depreciation, no end-of-life value; (b) full year's depreciation in year of acquisition and none in year of disposal.

P19-8. Following is the condensed income statement of the David Company for the year 1976:

Sales		$400,000
Cost of Goods Sold		
Inventory, January 1	$ 40,000	
Purchases (net)	260,000	
Total	$300,000	
Inventory, December 31	60,000	240,000
Gross Margin on Sales		$160,000

Operating Expenses		
Depreciation	$ 20,000	
General and Administrative	100,000	120,000
Net Income		$ 40,000

Price index assumptions:

January 1	110
December 31	150
All plant and equipment	100
Inventory, January 1	105
All other items (average index for year)	125

Required: Prepare a corrected income statement based on the end-of-year price index.

Cost Accumulation and Control— General Manufacturing Operations

20

Up to this point, the accounting for only service and trading businesses has been considered. A trading business buys merchandise in finished form and sells it in the same form. A manufacturing company, on the other hand, buys materials that it converts into finished products by the application of labor and other factory costs. The accounting standards and procedures, however, are the same for both manufacturing and nonmanufacturing businesses. Additional accounts are opened to record the activities involved in the manufacturing process—the conversion of materials into finished goods. From these accounts the schedule of cost of goods manufactured may be prepared; this shows the cost of materials consumed, direct labor costs, and the other factory costs incurred in the manufacture of the finished product over a stated period.

MATERIALS USED

All materials that are economically traceable to the finished product are referred to as *materials, raw materials,* or *direct materials.* Because many of these materials are fabricated by other manufacturers, the titles "materials" and "direct materials" are used here rather than "raw materials." The cloth used in the manufacture of a suit, for example, is classified as a "direct material." Some materials, although an integral part of the finished product, are not classified as direct materials because the cost or the quantity used is small or because it would be uneconomical to trace and determine the cost and amount of certain materials that are incorporated in the finished product. The thread used in manufacturing a garment, for example, may not be regarded as a direct material, although it can otherwise be clearly identified with the end product. The cost of the thread would be accounted for, as are certain other indirect factory costs, which are discussed later in this chapter.

The cost of materials used during an accounting period in the manufacture of a product may be determined by the periodic inventory method in the same manner as is the cost of goods sold in a trading business. The procedure necessary to account for *materials, direct labor,* and *manufacturing overhead* in a manufacturing company may be illustrated by the following sequence of transactions.

The Acme Manufacturing Company had materials on hand on January 1, 1976, costing $8,200. During the month of January, entries and postings were made as follows (only the general ledger accounts necessary for the illustration are shown):

(1)

Materials Purchases	79,500	
Accounts Payable		79,500
To record purchases of materials on account.		

(2)

Transportation In on Materials Purchases	2,250	
Accounts Payable		2,250
To record freight charges on materials purchased.		

(3)

Accounts Payable	3,250	
Materials—Purchases Returns and Allowances		3,250
To record credit received for materials returned.		

(4)

Accounts Payable	80,000	
Materials—Purchases Discounts		1,600
Cash		78,400
To record payment of invoice of materials purchased.		

GENERAL LEDGER

Materials Inventory

1976		
Jan. 1 Balance	8,200	

COST
ACCUMULATION,
AND CONTROL;
FINANCIAL
PLANNING

774

(Ch. 20)

Materials Purchases

1976 Jan. 31 (1)	79,500		

Transportation In on Materials Purchases

1976 Jan. 31 (2)	2,250		

Materials—Purchases Returns and Allowances

		1976 Jan. 31 (3)	3,250

Materials—Purchases Discounts

		1976 Jan. 31 (4)	1,600

Materials on hand on January 31 were $9,700. The Materials Used section of the schedule of cost of goods manufactured for the month of January is shown in Figure 20-1.

ACME MANUFACTURING COMPANY   Schedule A-1
Partial Schedule of Cost of Goods Manufactured
For the Month Ended January 31, 1976

Materials Used			
Materials Inventory, January 1, 1976			$ 8,200
Materials Purchases		$79,500	
Transportation In on Materials Purchases		2,250	
Gross Cost of Materials Purchases		$81,750	
Deduct Purchases Returns and Allowances	$3,250		
Deduct Purchases Discounts	1,600	4,850	
Net Cost of Materials Purchases			76,900
Cost of Materials Available for Use			$85,100
Deduct Materials Inventory, January 31, 1976			9,700
Cost of Materials Used			$75,400

Figure 20-1
Computation of Materials Used

DIRECT LABOR

The wages paid to employees performing operations directly on the product being manufactured are referred to as *direct labor*. Direct labor is the cost of wages paid for work involving the construction, composition, or fabrication of the end product.

The following journal entries demonstrate the recording of direct labor:

(5)		
Direct Labor	58,300	
Salaries and Wages Payable (and		
payroll tax withholding liabilities)		58,300
To record the direct labor costs incurred		
during January (payroll deduction		
details have been omitted).		

(6)		
Direct Labor	2,700	
Accrued Wages and Salaries Payable		2,700
To record direct labor costs accrued.		

The debit total of $61,000 = ($58,300 + $2,700) is the direct labor cost for the month. This amount is entered in the schedule of cost of goods manufactured on one line immediately following the amount for materials used.

MANUFACTURING OVERHEAD

All factory costs incurred in the manufacturing process other than the cost of materials used and direct labor are classified as *manufacturing overhead*. Other terms used for this group of costs are *indirect manufacturing costs* and *manufacturing burden*.

Inventoriable or Product Costs

For a manufacturing company, manufacturing overhead, along with direct materials and direct labor, are product costs and not period expenses; that is, these costs are incorporated in the inventory of manufactured goods.

COST ACCUMULATION, AND CONTROL; FINANCIAL PLANNING

Selling expenses and general and administrative expenses are not considered manufacturing overhead, because they reflect the administrative and distributive functions of the business and are not part of the manufacturing function. Most of the accounts listed in the schedule of cost of goods manufactured (see

(Ch. 20)

Figure 20-2) are self-explanatory. Others are explained in the following paragraphs.

Indirect labor is the labor cost for the workers whose efforts are not directly identified with the conversion of specific materials into specific finished products. Wages paid to employees who schedule and supervise the work of others, for example, would be classified as indirect labor. The term also includes the wages of repair and maintenance crews, guards, janitors, and cost accounting clerks assigned to the manufacturing function.

Amortization of patents represents that part of the cost of patents allocable to the current accounting period. It is assumed that these patents are for manufacturing processes. The cost of the patents should be amortized over the economically useful life or the remaining legal life of the asset, whichever is shorter. The Patents account may be credited directly for the amortized portion. The amortized portion is debited to Amortization of Patents, listed under Manufacturing Overhead. The unamortized balance of Patents is reported on the statement of financial position as an intangible asset.

Small tools used represents the cost of special small tools used up by workmen during the accounting period. It is possible to depreciate small tools by methods similar to those used for machinery and equipment. This procedure is difficult, however, because of the great variety of tools used and their relatively small value. In addition, small hand tools are easily lost or broken, and their useful life is difficult to predict. To overcome this practical difficulty, small tools may be accounted for as follows: The acquisition cost is debited to the asset account Small Tools; at the end of each accounting period an inventory of tools on hand is taken and priced; the discrepancy between the balance in the asset account and the inventory count represents the cost of tools broken, discarded, or lost. The entry to adjust the Small Tools account to the inventory amount is a debit to Small Tools Used, a manufacturing overhead item, and a credit to Small Tools, a plant and equipment asset.

A separate account may be opened in the general ledger for each manufacturing overhead item; however, if these accounts are numerous, a subsidiary *manufacturing overhead ledger* may be set up. Its controlling account in the general ledger is Manufacturing Overhead.

The journals of the Acme Manufacturing Company showed the following additional entries (entry 7 was made during the month; the others represent end-of-period adjustments):

(7)			
Factory Rent	2,000		
Heat, Light, and Power	12,000		
Indirect Labor	9,100		
Equipment Maintenance and Repairs	2,900		
Miscellaneous Factory Costs	2,950		
Accounts Payable (and payroll tax withholding liabilities)		28,950	
To record overhead costs incurred during the month. (There was no accrued indirect labor, and payroll deduction details have been omitted.)			

(8)

Depreciation—Machinery and Equipment	3,500	
Accumulated Depreciation—		
Machinery and Equipment		3,500
To record one month's depreciation		
of machinery and equipment.		

(9)

Factory Insurance	1,100	
Prepaid Insurance		1,100
To record the expiration of one month's		
insurance.		

(10)

Factory Property Tax	1,600	
Accrued Property Taxes Payable		1,600
To record property taxes accrued		
on the factory building.		

(11)

Amortization of Patents	950	
Patents		950
To amortize the patent cost for January.		

(12)

Small Tools Used	250	
Small Tools		250
To adjust the asset account to the		
inventory valuation.		

GENERAL LEDGER

Depreciation—Machinery and Equipment

1976		
Jan. 31 (8)	3,500	

Factory Rent

1976		
Jan. 31 (7)	2,000	

Heat, Light, and Power

1976		
Jan. 31 (7)	12,000	

COST
ACCUMULATION,
AND CONTROL;
FINANCIAL
PLANNING

778

(Ch. 20)

Amortization of Patents

1976			
Jan. 31	(11)	950	

Small Tools Used

1976			
Jan. 31	(12)	250	

Factory Insurance

1976			
Jan. 31	(9)	1,100	

Factory Property Tax

1976			
Jan. 31	(10)	1,600	

Indirect Labor

1976			
Jan. 31	(7)	9,100	

Equipment Maintenance and Repairs

1976			
Jan. 31	(7)	2,900	

Miscellaneous Factory Costs

1976			
Jan. 31	(7)	2,950	

TOTAL PERIOD MANUFACTURING COSTS

Total period manufacturing costs are made up of the costs of materials used, direct labor, and manufacturing overhead, as shown below.

(Ch. 20)

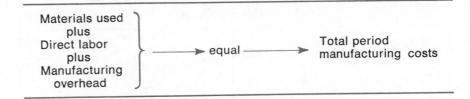

| Materials used plus Direct labor plus Manufacturing overhead | equal | Total period manufacturing costs |

WORK-IN-PROCESS INVENTORY

The fabrication of a product is a continuing and repetitive process. At any time, therefore, partly finished products will be on hand in various stages of completion; they are known as *work in process* or *goods in process*. At the end of the accounting period, the work in process is inventoried and its value determined. Since the cost of these partly finished units is included in the total period manufacturing costs, the end-of-period work-in-process inventory is deducted from the total costs to arrive at the cost of goods manufactured. Work-in-Process Inventory is classified as a current asset in the statement of financial position. The ending inventory of one period is the beginning inventory of the next period and enters into the cost of goods manufactured for that next period.

The Acme Manufacturing Company had a beginning work-in-process inventory on January 1 of $2,900. On January 31, the ending work-in-process inventory was $3,600. Note that the inventories include the cost of materials, labor, and overhead assignable to the unfinished product.

The completed schedule of cost of goods manufactured is shown in Figure 20-2.

FINISHED GOODS AND COST OF GOODS SOLD

The Cost of Goods Sold sections of the income statements of a merchandising business and of a manufacturing business are compared in Figure 20-3. The amounts are from the statements of the King Corporation (Figure 5-1) and the Acme Manufacturing Company. The cost of goods manufactured in the Acme Manufacturing Company statement is equivalent to the net cost of purchases in the King Corporation statement. The significant difference, however, is that the cost of goods manufactured is supported by a detailed schedule that presents three distinct cost elements, a variety of accounts, and two inventories. The calculation of net cost of purchases, on the other hand, involves only four accounts.

It is assumed in Figure 20-3 that the Acme Manufacturing Company had a beginning finished goods inventory of $12,100 and an ending inventory of $10,150. The term *finished goods* means the completed goods ready for sale and corresponds to the merchandise inventory of a trading business.

COST
ACCUMULATION,
AND CONTROL;
FINANCIAL
PLANNING

(Ch. 20)

Figure 20-2
Completed Schedule
of Cost of Goods
Manufactured

ACME MANUFACTURING COMPANY   Schedule A-1
Schedule of Cost of Goods Manufactured
For the Month Ended January 31, 1976

Materials Used			
Materials Inventory, January 1, 1976			$ 8,200
Materials Purchases		$79,500	
Transportation In on			
Materials Purchases		2,250	
Gross Cost of Materials Purchases		$81,750	
Deduct Purchases Returns			
and Allowances	$3,250		
Purchases Discounts	1,600	4,850	
Net Cost of Materials Purchases			76,900
Cost of Materials Available for Use			$ 85,100
Deduct Materials Inventory,			
January 31, 1976			9,700
Cost of Materials Used			$ 75,400
Direct Labor			61,000
Manufacturing Overhead			
Depreciation—			
Machinery and Equipment		$ 3,500	
Factory Insurance		1,100	
Factory Rent		2,000	
Factory Property Tax		1,600	
Heat, Light, and Power		12,000	
Indirect Labor		9,100	
Amortization of Patents		950	
Equipment Maintenance and Repairs		2,900	
Small Tools Used		250	
Miscellaneous Factory Costs		2,950	
Total Manufacturing Overhead			36,350
Total Period Manufacturing Costs			$172,750
Add Work-in-Process Inventory,			
January 1, 1976			2,900
Total			$176,650
Deduct Work-in-Process Inventory,			
January 31, 1976			3,600
Cost of Goods Manufactured			$172,050

MANUFACTURING SUMMARY

It is possible to close all the manufacturing accounts directly into the Income Summary account. However, since the determination of the cost of goods manufactured is in part a process of adjusting, it is helpful to indicate

(Ch. 20)

Figure 20-3
Comparison of Cost of
Goods Sold Sections

Merchandising Business		Manufacturing Business	
Cost of Goods Sold		Cost of Goods Sold	
Merchandise Inventory, 1/1/1976	$15,400	Finished Goods Inventory, 1/1/1976	$ 12,100
Purchases (net)	63,280	Cost of Goods Manufactured (Schedule A-1)	172,050
Cost of Merchandise Available for Sale	$78,680	Cost of Finished Goods Available for Sale	$184,150
Deduct Merchandise Inventory, 12/31/1976	11,480	Deduct Finished Goods Inventory, 1/31/1976	10,150
Total Cost of Goods Sold	$67,200	Total Cost of Goods Sold	$174,000

this fact by showing the cost of goods manufactured in a temporary general ledger account called *Manufacturing Summary.* All account balances that enter into the calculation of the cost of goods manufactured are transferred to this account. In turn, the final balance of this account, which is the cost of goods manufactured, is closed into the Income Summary account. The closing entries are entered in the general journal, and the procedure followed is the same as for a trading concern. The closing entries may be made directly from the work sheet.

The closing entries for the Acme Manufacturing Company are given below.

Closing Entries
(13)

Manufacturing Summary	190,200	
Materials Inventory (beginning)		8,200
Work-in-Process Inventory (beginning)		2,900
Materials Purchases		79,500
Transportation In on Materials Purchases		2,250
Direct Labor		61,000
Depreciation—Machinery and Equipment		3,500
Factory Insurance		1,100
Factory Rent		2,000
Factory Property Tax		1,600
Heat, Light, and Power		12,000
Indirect Labor		9,100
Amortization of Patents		950
Equipment Maintenance and Repairs		2,900
Small Tools Used		250
Miscellaneous Factory Costs		2,950
To close all the manufacturing accounts with debit balances.		

(Ch. 20)

(14)

Materials Inventory (ending)	9,700	
Work-in-Process Inventory (ending)	3,600	
Materials—Purchases Returns and		
Allowances	3,250	
Materials—Purchases Discounts	1,600	
Manufacturing Summary		18,150
To record the ending inventories and		
to close all the manufacturing accounts		
with credit balances.		

(15)

Income Summary	172,050	
Manufacturing Summary		172,050
To close the Manufacturing Summary		
account and to transfer the cost of		
goods manufactured to Income Summary.		

(16)

Income Summary	12,100	
Finished Goods Inventory (beginning)		12,100
To close the beginning finished goods		
inventory into Income Summary.		

(17)

Finished Goods Inventory (ending)	10,150	
Income Summary		10,150
To record the ending finished goods		
inventory.		

Entries 16 and 17 may be recorded as part of the compound entries closing out the remaining income statement accounts. If they are made separately, the balance of Income Summary after entries 16 and 17 are posted shows the cost of goods sold.

GENERAL LEDGER

Manufacturing Summary

1976				1976				
Jan. 31	(13)		190,200	Jan. 31	(14)			18,150
				31	(15)			172,050
			190,200					190,200

Finished Goods Inventory

1976				1976		
Jan.	1	Bal.	12,100	Jan. 31	(16)	12,100
	31	(17)	10,150			

Income Summary

1976				1976		
Jan.	31	(15)	172,050	Jan. 31	(17)	10,150
	31	(16)	12,100			

At this point, the $174,000 balance of the Income Summary account is the cost of goods sold, as shown in Figure 20-3. The remaining closing entries for the Acme Manufacturing Company are the same as for a merchandising business.

WORK SHEET FOR A MANUFACTURING COMPANY

There is only one essential difference between a work sheet for a manufacturing company and one for a merchandising company. In the work sheet for a manufacturing company, a pair of columns is added, headed Manufacturing, into which are extended the debit and credit account balances representing the elements of the cost of manufacturing—that is, all the accounts that enter into the preparation of the schedule of cost of goods manufactured. The difference between the totals of these columns is the cost of goods manufactured, which is then transferred to the Income Statement Debit column.

The function of the other work sheet columns is the same as in a merchandising company. The remaining illustrations and discussion in this chapter are based on the work sheet of the Carol Manufacturing Company, shown in Figure 20-4. It should be observed that a different illustration is used here in order to add complexities that were not appropriate to the elementary illustration of the Acme Manufacturing Company.

ENDING INVENTORIES ON THE MANUFACTURING WORK SHEET

The materials inventory on December 31, 1976, was $51,500. This amount is entered on the Materials Inventory line as a debit in the Position Statement columns and as a credit in the Manufacturing columns. The ending inventory is

(Ch. 20)

Figure 20-4 Work Sheet for a Manufacturing Company

CAROL MANUFACTURING COMPANY
Work Sheet
For the Year Ended December 31, 1976

Account Title	Trial Balance Dr.	Cr.	Adjustments Dr.	Cr.	Manufacturing Dr.	Cr.	Income Statement Dr.	Cr.	Position Statement Dr.	Cr.
Cash	12,000								12,000	
Accounts Receivable	78,350								78,350	
Allowance for Doubtful Accounts		650		(a) 1,037						1,687
Materials Inventory	58,300				58,300	51,500			51,500	
Work-in-Process Inventory	31,725				31,725	47,000			47,000	
Finished Goods Inventory	23,200						23,200	19,600	19,600	
Prepaid Insurance	2,100			(b) 1,500					600	
Office Equipment	6,050								6,050	
Accumulated Depreciation—Office Equipment		2,000		(d) 605						2,605
Store Equipment	10,000								10,000	
Accumulated Depreciation—Store Equipment		4,000		(d) 1,000						5,000
Machinery and Equipment	51,000								51,000	
Accumulated Depreciation—Machinery and Equipment		10,000		(c) 10,200						20,200
Accounts Payable		29,200								29,200
Capital Stock		180,000								180,000
Retained Earnings		12,855								12,855
Dividends	10,000								10,000	
Sales		420,000						420,000		
Sales Returns and Allowances	5,200						5,200			
Sales Discounts	2,400						2,400			
Materials Purchases	91,000				91,000					
Materials—Purchases Returns and Allowances		2,800				2,800				
Materials—Purchases Discounts		2,650				2,650				
Direct Labor	98,530		(e) 3,500		102,030					
Indirect Labor	21,200		(e) 1,400		22,600					
Rent	12,000				9,600		{1,800 S / 600 G}			
Heat, Light, and Power	8,100				7,290		{405 S / 405 G}			
Advertising Expense	6,500						6,500			
Salesmen's Salaries Expense	50,000		(e) 5,100				55,100			
Executive Salaries Expense	60,500						60,500			
Office Salaries Expense	26,000						26,000			
	664,155	664,155								
Bad Debts Expense			(a) 1,037				1,037			
Insurance			(b) 1,500		1,050		{300 S / 150 G}			
Depreciation—Machinery and Equipment			(c) 10,200		10,200					
Depreciation Expense—Office Equipment			(d) 605				605			
Depreciation Expense—Store Equipment			(d) 1,000				1,000			
Accrued Wages and Salaries Payable				(e) 10,000						10,000
Income Tax Expense			(f) 7,368				7,368			
Income Taxes Payable				(f) 7,368						7,368
			31,710	31,710	333,795	103,950				
Cost of Goods Manufactured						229,845	229,845			
					333,795	333,795	422,415	439,600	286,100	268,915
Net Income							17,185			17,185
							439,600	439,600	286,100	286,100

S = Selling Expenses
G = General and administrative expenses

a current asset; furthermore, it must be deducted from the cost of materials available to determine the cost of materials used. This deduction is effected on the work sheet by entering the amount in the Manufacturing Credit column.

The work-in-process inventory at the end of the year was $47,000; it is entered on the Work-in-Process Inventory line. The debit in the Position Statement columns sets up the new inventory (a current asset), and the credit in the Manufacturing columns is used in computing the cost of goods manufactured.

The finished goods inventory on December 31, 1976, was $19,600; it is entered on the Finished Goods Inventory line. Again, the debit in the Position Statement columns establishes the new inventory (a current asset); the credit in the Income Statement columns is deducted from the cost of goods available to derive the cost of goods sold.

Adjusting Entries on the Manufacturing Work Sheet

The entries in the Adjustments columns of the work sheet are based on the information that follows. The letters correspond to those used on the work sheet.

(a)

The Bad Debts Expense was estimated at ¼ of 1 percent of gross sales less sales returns and allowances. The amount of the adjustment was computed as indicated below.

Gross Sales	$420,000
Deduct Sales Returns and Allowances	5,200
	$414,800
Bad Debts Expense Percentage	× 0.0025
Bad Debts Expense	$ 1,037

The entry is as shown below.

1976			
Dec. 31	Bad Debts Expense	1,037	
	Allowance for Doubtful Accounts		1,037

The debit records the estimated bad debts charge; the credit increases Allowance for Doubtful Accounts to $1,687 = ($650 + $1,037). This adjustment debits an expense, not a manufacturing, account.

(b)

Insurance of $1,500 has expired; this is recorded by the following entry:

COST
ACCUMULATION,
AND CONTROL;
FINANCIAL
PLANNING

786

(Ch. 20)

```
1976
Dec. 31   Insurance                    1,500
               Prepaid Insurance                    1,500
```

The debit records the cost of the expired insurance; the credit decreases the asset account. Note that Insurance is a factory overhead account and not a period expense.

(c)

The annual depreciation rate for factory machinery and equipment is 20 percent. Since all the equipment was acquired prior to 1976, a full year's depreciation is taken, based on the amount shown in the trial balance. The computation is as follows:

Cost of machinery and equipment	$51,000
Annual depreciation rate	× 0.20
Depreciation for 1976	$10,200

The entry is as shown below.

```
1976
Dec. 31   Depreciation—Machinery and Equipment 10,200
               Accumulated Depreciation—
                  Machinery and Equipment                    10,200
```

The debit records the depreciation of the machinery and equipment; the credit increases the Accumulated Depreciation—Machinery and Equipment account.

(d)

The annual depreciation rate for both office equipment and store equipment is 10 percent. All the office and store equipment was acquired prior to 1976; consequently a full year's depreciation is taken, based on the amount of each account shown in the trial balance. The computations are as follows:

	Office Equipment	Store Equipment
Cost	$6,050	$10,000
Annual depreciation rate	× 0.10	× 0.10
Depreciation for 1976	$ 605	$ 1,000

(Ch. 20)

The entry is given below.

1976			
Dec. 31	Depreciation Expense—Office Equipment	605	
	Depreciation Expense—Store Equipment	1,000	
	Accumulated Depreciation—Office Equipment		605
	Accumulated Depreciation—Store Equipment		1,000

The debits record the depreciation expense for the office and store equipment; the credits increase the corresponding Accumulated Depreciation accounts.

(e)

The accrued wages and salaries payable as of December 31, 1976, were:

Direct labor	$ 3,500
Indirect labor	1,400
Salesmen's salaries	5,100
Total	$10,000

The entry is:

1976			
Dec. 31	Direct Labor	3,500	
	Indirect Labor	1,400	
	Salesmen's Salaries Expense	5,100	
	Accrued Wages and Salaries Payable		10,000

The debits record all the wages and salaries incurred but not paid; the credit records the accrued liability. Here is an example of debits both to manufacturing accounts and to a period expense.

(f)

The estimated income tax liability is $7,368. The entry is shown below.

1976			
Dec. 31	Income Tax Expense	7,368	
	Income Taxes Payable		7,368

The debit records the estimated income tax; the credit records the estimated income tax liability.

COST
ACCUMULATION,
AND CONTROL;
FINANCIAL
PLANNING

788

(Ch. 20)

Allocation of Costs and Expenses on the Work Sheet

In the Trial Balance and Adjustments columns, there are certain accounts representing cost incurred partly in the manufacturing processes and partly in the selling and general and administrative functions. Assume that a study was made late in 1975 to find an equitable method for allocating these items. As a result of this study, the following bases for allocation were decided on:

Item	Basis for Allocation
Rent	Square footage of building space used
Heat, light, and power	Actual readings from meters in the factory, in the sales rooms, and in the general and administrative areas
Insurance	Cost of comprehensive policies covering the buildings allocated on the basis of square footage; other insurance costs charged directly to manufacturing, selling, or general and administrative expense

From these bases, converted to percentages, the following allocations were made:

			ALLOCATION				
		Manufacturing		Selling		General	
Item	Total	%	Amount	%	Amount	%	Amount
Rent	$12,000	80	$9,600	15	$1,800	5	$600
Heat, light, and power	8,100	90	7,290	5	405	5	405
Insurance	1,500	70	1,050	20	300	10	150

On the line of the work sheet for each of these items, the total of the Trial Balance and Adjustments columns is extended to the appropriate column. The Rent debit balance of $12,000, for example, is distributed as follows: $9,600 = ($12,000 × 0.80) is extended to the Manufacturing Debit column; $1,800 = ($12,000 × 0.15) and $600 = ($12,000 × 0.05) are extended to the Income Statement Debit column. Note that the $9,600 is classified as manufacturing overhead under Factory Rent (Figures 20-4 and 20-8); the $1,800 is classified as a selling expense, Rent Expense (Figures 20-4 and 20-5). The $9,600 portion is carried as a product cost and not as an expense, because it is part of the cost of the finished product; it becomes an expense only when the product is sold. Until such time, overhead costs are assets; that is, they are part of either work in process (asset) or finished goods (asset). The $1,800 portion of the rent is classified as Rent Expense, because it does not enter into the cost of goods manufactured (finished goods) but is rather an expense of the period in which it is incurred. This distinction also applies to heat, light, and power and to

(Ch. 20)

insurance. All the overhead accounts and all portions of accounts allocated to manufacturing are product cost accounts.

The letters S and G after the amounts identify the specific income statement classifications of selling or general and administrative expenses. These letters may be further used for amounts extended as a lump sum in a single column to facilitate the precise classification of the accounts if the formal income statement is prepared directly from the work sheet.

FINANCIAL STATEMENTS

The Manufacturing columns of the work sheet contain all the amounts required for the preparation of the schedule of cost of goods manufactured in their proper debit or credit relationship; each amount is used once. Similarly, the Income Statement and Position Statement columns contain all the figures needed for the preparation of the income statement, statement of retained earnings, and statement of financial position. The financial statements are illustrated in Figures 20-5, 20-6, 20-7, and 20-8.

As indicated in Chapter 18, a *statement of changes in financial position* must also be prepared. Because the format of this statement for a manufacturing firm is essentially the same as that indicated in Chapter 18, the statement is not repeated here.

MANUFACTURING ACCOUNTING—MANAGERIAL ANALYSIS

A company must control its inventories and its cost of operations. Excessive inventories must be avoided because they may result in losses due to changes in style, obsolescence, and price fluctuations. Several ratios and comparisons are indicators of such potential losses. Ratios and trends vary from industry to industry, but within any given industry, or especially within a single company, valuable trends and ratios can be established. Amounts for the year 1975 for the Carol Manufacturing Company have been assumed. Amounts for 1976 are from the statements in Figures 20-5, 20-6, 20-7, and 20-8.

Turnover of Materials

An overinvestment or underinvestment in materials may be brought to management's attention by comparing the materials turnover with that of prior periods or of other similar companies. An overinvestment in materials inventory should be avoided, because it ties up working capital and storage space and creates the possibility of loss through shrinkage, style and price changes, and so on. Conversely, an underinvestment in inventory must be avoided to ensure a steady flow of materials into production and to prevent the possible incurrence of higher costs through a shoestring buying policy. The turnover of materials inventories is shown in Figure 20-9.

COST
ACCUMULATION,
AND CONTROL;
FINANCIAL
PLANNING

790

(Ch. 20)

Figure 20-5
Income Statement

CAROL MANUFACTURING COMPANY
Income Statement
For the Year Ended December 31, 1976

Exhibit A

Sales Revenue			
Sales			$420,000
Deduct: Sales Returns and			
Allowances		$ 5,200	
Sales Discounts		2,400	7,600
Net Sales Revenue			$412,400
Cost of Goods Sold			
Finished Goods Inventory,			
January 1, 1976		$ 23,200	
Add Cost of Goods Manufactured			
(Schedule A-1)		229,845	
Cost of Finished Goods Available			
for Sale		$253,045	
Deduct Finished Goods Inventory,			
December 31, 1976		19,600	
Cost of Goods Sold			233,445
Gross Margin on Sales			$178,955
Operating Expenses			
Selling			
Rent Expense	$ 1,800		
Heat, Light, and Power Expense	405		
Advertising Expense	6,500		
Salesmen's Salaries Expense	55,100		
Insurance Expense	300		
Depreciation Expense—			
Store Equipment	1,000		
Total Selling Expenses		$ 65,105	
General and Administrative			
Rent Expense	$ 600		
Heat, Light, and Power Expense	405		
Executive Salaries Expense	60,500		
Office Salaries Expense	26,000		
Bad Debts Expense	1,037		
Insurance Expense	150		
Depreciation Expense—			
Office Equipment	605		
Total General and			
Administrative Expenses		89,297	
Total Operating Expenses			154,402
Net income Before Income Taxes			$ 24,553
Income Tax Expense			7,368
Net Income After Income Taxes			$ 17,185

Net Income per Share: $0.95

Figure 20-6
Statement of
Financial Position

CAROL MANUFACTURING COMPANY **Exhibit B**
Statement of Financial Position
December 31, 1976

Assets

Current Assets			
Cash		$ 12,000	
Accounts Receivable	$78,350		
Deduct Allowance for			
Doubtful Accounts	1,687	76,663	
Materials Inventory		51,500	
Work-in-Process Inventory		47,000	
Finished Goods Inventory		19,600	
Prepaid Insurance		600	
Total Current Assets			$207,363
Plant and Equipment			
Office Equipment	$ 6,050		
Deduct Accumulated Depreciation	2,605	$ 3,445	
Store Equipment	$10,000		
Deduct Accumulated Depreciation	5,000	5,000	
Machinery and Equipment	$51,000		
Deduct Accumulated Depreciation	20,200	30,800	
Total Plant and Equipment			39,245
Total Assets			$246,608

Liabilities and Stockholders' Equity

Current Liabilities			
Accounts Payable		$ 29,200	
Accrued Wages and Salaries Payable		10,000	
Income Taxes Payable		7,368	
Total Current Liabilities			$ 46,568
Sotckholders' Equity			
Capital Stock, $10 Par Value		$180,000	
Retained Earnings (Exhibit C)		20,040	
Total Stockholders' Equity			200,040
Total Liabilities and Stockholders' Equity			$246,608

Figure 20-7
Statement of
Retained Earnings

CAROL MANUFACTURING COMPANY **Exhibit C**
Statement of Retained Earnings
For the Year Ended December 31, 1976

Retained Earnings, January 1, 1976	$12,855
Net Income for the Year (Exhibit A)	17,185
Total	$30,040
Deduct Dividends	10,000
Retained Earnings, December 31, 1976	$20,040

COST
ACCUMULATION,
AND CONTROL;
FINANCIAL
PLANNING

792

(Ch. 20)

Figure 20-8
Schedule of Cost of
Goods Manufactured

CAROL MANUFACTURING COMPANY Schedule A-1
Schedule of Cost of Goods Manufactured
For the Year Ended December 31, 1976

Materials Used			
Materials Inventory, January 1, 1976			$ 58,300
Materials Purchases		$91,000	
Deduct: Purchases Returns			
and Allowances	$2,800		
Purchases Discounts	2,650	5,450	
Net Cost of Materials Purchases			85,550
Cost of Materials Available for Use			$143,850
Deduct Materials Inventory,			
December 31, 1976			51,500
Cost of Materials Used			$ 92,350
Direct Labor			102,030
Manufacturing Overhead			
Indirect Labor		$22,600	
Factory Rent		9,600	
Heat, Light, and Power		7,290	
Factory Insurance		1,050	
Depreciation—Machinery and			
Equipment		10,200	
Total Manufacturing Overhead			50,740
Total Period Manufacturing Costs			$245,120
Add Work-in-Process Inventory,			
January 1, 1976			31,725
Total			$276,845
Deduct Work-in-Process Inventory,			
December 31, 1976			47,000
Cost of Goods Manufactured (to Exhibit A)			$229,845

In 1976, for every $1 in the average materials inventory there was $1.68 worth of materials used in the manufacture of the finished products. The numbers 1.68 and 1.44 represent the number of times the materials were replaced during the year. These turnover rates may be converted to days by dividing the number of days in a year by the turnover.

Figure 20-9
Materials Turnover

		1976	1975
Materials used	**(a)**	$92,350	$86,670
Materials inventories			
Beginning of year		$58,300	$61,900
End of year		51,500	58,300
Average	**(b)**	$54,900	$60,100
Materials turnover (a ÷ b)		1.68	1.44

Figure 20-9
Materials Turnover
(continued)

		1976	1975
Number of days in year	**(a)**	365*	365
Turnover (from Figure 20–9)	**(b)**	1.68	1.44
Number of days' inventory (a ÷ b)		217	253

* For purposes of comparability, it is assumed that each year has 365 days, even though there are 366 days in the leap year 1976.

The number 217 for 1976 means that during that year the company had, on the average, materials on hand sufficient for 217 days' use. This information, together with such factors as available sources of supply and the length of time required to obtain the material, makes it possible to recognize and to initiate action to control overstocking or understocking of inventories.

Turnover of Finished Goods

The computation of the finished goods turnovers for the Carol Manufacturing Company for the years 1976 and 1975 is shown in Figure 20-10.

Figure 20-10
Turnover of Finished
Goods

		1976	1975
Cost of goods sold	**(a)**	$233,445	$197,142
Finished goods inventories			
Beginning of year		$ 23,200	$ 24,650
End of year		19,600	23,200
Average	**(b)**	$ 21,400	$ 23,925
Finished goods turnover (a ÷ b)		10.91	8.24

In 1976, for every $1 in the average finished goods inventory there was $10.91 worth of finished goods sold. The computation for converting these turnover rates to days is:

		1976	1975
Number of days in year	**(a)**	365*	365
Turnover (from Figure 20–10)	**(b)**	10.91	8.24
Number of days' inventory (a ÷ b)		33	44

* For purposes of comparability, it is assumed that each year has 365 days, even though there are 366 days in the leap year 1976.

The Carol Manufacturing Company had improved the finished goods inventory turnover in 1976 as compared to 1975. In terms of the number of days' sales requirements, the inventory has been decreased from 44 days to 33 days.

There are a variety of factors that influence the finished goods inventory turnover trend and which must be considered before any conclusions are

COST
ACCUMULATION,
AND CONTROL;
FINANCIAL
PLANNING

794

(Ch. 20)

drawn. The ratio is influenced by actual or anticipated changes in prices, volume, basis of inventory valuation, the presence of obsolete or unsalable goods in the inventory, and so on. If, for example, a higher turnover is the result of an increased volume of sales due to lowered prices, gross margin may not increase. If, however, the amount of the inventory and the rate of gross margin are relatively stable, an increased turnover will result in an increase in gross margin. Again, such increases in gross margin may not result in increased earnings if the more rapid turnover is accompanied by increases in advertising and other costs of distributing the product.

Manufacturing Costs

The percentage relationships of materials used, direct labor, and manufacturing overhead to total period manufacturing costs also provide significant information about the business. If these percentages are disproportionate to those of prior periods or similar companies, they may indicate to management the need for investigation. The computations of the relationships for the Carol Manufacturing Company for 1976 are:

		Percentage
$\dfrac{\text{Materials used}}{\text{Total period manufacturing costs}} = \dfrac{\$92,350}{\$245,120} =$		38
$\dfrac{\text{Direct labor}}{\text{Total period manufacturing costs}} = \dfrac{\$102,030}{\$245,120} =$		41
$\dfrac{\text{Manufacturing overhead}}{\text{Total period manufacturing costs}} = \dfrac{\$50,740}{\$245,120} =$		21
Total		100

Each dollar of the total period cost of manufacturing consisted of materials, 38 cents; direct labor, 41 cents; and manufacturing overhead, 21 cents.

Unit Cost Analysis

An important measure of management efficiency is the cost of manufacturing each unit. It is in the interest of management to keep the unit cost of the product as low as possible. Any increase in unit cost results in either a decrease in gross margin or an increase in the selling price. Assume that the Carol Manufacturing Company manufactures a single product and that it manufactured 20,000 units in 1976. The unit cost is computed as shown in Figure 20-11.

$$\frac{\text{Cost of goods manufactured}}{\text{Number of units manufactured}} = \frac{\$229,845}{20,000} = \$11.49 \text{ (cost per unit)}$$

Figure 20-11
Unit Cost
Computation

To determine operating results in manufacturing accounting, it is necessary to take physical inventories of materials, work in process, and finished goods. The valuation of the work-in-process and finished goods inventories is difficult to determine because the cost of the components incorporated in these inventories cannot be easily associated with the physical articles. The next two chapters deal with the more elaborate methods used in cost accounting, which enable management to trace the flow of unexpired costs directly to the products.

If the Carol Manufacturing Company produced only a single product and manufactured 20,000 units (see Figure 20-11), management could cost each inventory unit at $11.49. However, if the company produced several different products, it would have to install a device for costing the ending work-in-process and finished goods inventories. The cost of materials per unit of the product can usually be measured accurately by reference to materials requisitions. Direct labor cost per unit can also be determined satisfactorily by observation coupled with the keeping of time and cost records. The unit cost of factory overhead is difficult to determine directly. It is necessary to determine a high correlative relationship between factory overhead cost and some common measure to the commodities produced. Direct labor cost is usually a fair indicator, because the passage of time is an element in both direct labor and factory overhead costs. More direct labor time implies more use of factory facilities, which results in more factory overhead cost for that product. This relationship of factory overhead and direct labor cost—called the *overhead rate*—for the Carol Manufacturing Company (see Figure 20-8) is as shown here.

$$\frac{\text{Total manufacturing overhead}}{\text{Direct labor}} = \frac{\$50,740}{\$102,030} = 49.7\%$$

For each dollar of direct labor cost incurred on a given product, 49.7 cents worth of manufacturing overhead will be allocated to it. For example, the per unit cost of the ending inventories of finished goods and work in process of products A and B were computed as shown below.

Finished Goods Inventory		
	Product A	*Product B*
Materials (from requisitions)	$ 5.00	$ 4.00
Direct labor (from payroll records)	4.00	6.00
Manufacturing overhead ($4 × 0.497)	1.99	
($6 × 0.497)		2.98
Total inventory cost per unit	$10.99	$12.98

COST
ACCUMULATION,
AND CONTROL;
FINANCIAL
PLANNING

796

(Ch. 20)

Work-in-Process Inventory

	Product A	Product B
Materials (from requisitions)	$ 3.00	$ 2.00
Direct labor (from payroll records)	2.30	1.20
Manufacturing overhead ($2.30 × 0.497)	1.14	
($1.20 × 0.497)		.60
Total inventory cost per unit	$ 6.44	$ 3.80

In some manufacturing operations it is necessary to forecast production requirements for long periods in advance so that necessary materials, personnel, and equipment will be available for each production run. In the Burlington Plant of the J. I. Case Company, forecasts for the ensuing fifteen months are updated monthly. Each forecast is key-punched into cards and processed against various files, as shown in Figure A20-1.

The files against which the forecast requirements are matched are maintained on random access storage devices (such as disk or drum) and contain the necessary data to do the following:

1. Explode each forecast production item into its component parts and assemblies.
2. Further expand the parts and assembly requirements into material requirements for those that are to be made locally.

Figure A20-1   Monthly Requirements Generation Procedure

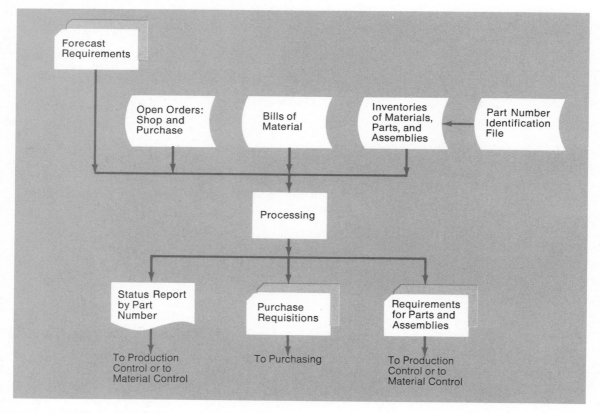

Source: J. I. Case Company, Racine, Wisconsin.

3. Match the parts, assembly, and material requirements against inventories to generate purchase requisition cards for items that need to be purchased and requirements cards for items that are to be made.

Figure A20-1 portrays only a broad overview of the many subsystems that make up the overall production and control system. It should be obvious, however, from this and the data-processing examples shown in other chapters that the work of an accountant has progressed far beyond the simple mechanics of bookkeeping operations.

GLOSSARY

Amortization of Patents The amount of patent cost applicable to a given time period; it is an element of manufacturing overhead for a manufacturing firm.

Cost of Goods Manufactured The cost of the units of finished products completed during a given period; it is calculated by adding the beginning work-in-process inventory to the three period manufacturing cost groups and deducting the ending work-in-process inventory.

Cost of Goods Sold for Manufacturing Firm Often referred to as cost of sales; it is computed by adding the beginning finished goods inventory to the cost of goods manufactured for the period and subtracting the ending finished goods inventory.

Direct Labor The cost of the wages paid to employees performing operations directly on the product being manufactured.

Finished Goods The inventory of finished products of a manufacturing firm.

Indirect Labor The labor cost of those workers whose efforts are *not* directly identified with the conversion of specific material into specific finished products; for example, the factory janitor's salary is an indirect labor cost.

Manufacturing Firm A firm which fabricates finished products out of basic materials by applying direct labor costs and other manufacturing costs to convert the basic materials into finished goods.

Manufacturing Overhead All factory costs incurred in the manufacturing process *other* than the cost of direct materials used and direct labor; examples are indirect labor, small tools used, factory insurance, and so forth.

Manufacturing Overhead Allocation Basis Certain costs are joint costs incurred in several company functions including the manufacturing function. These costs must be allocated to the respective functions by some equitable method; hence an allocation base is selected that will achieve the foregoing stated objective; for example, rent may be allocated on the basis of square footage of building space used by each function.

Manufacturing Summary A summary account used in the closing process for a manufacturing firm to which all items used in the calculation of cost of goods manufactured are closed.

Materials The inventory, at cost, of material held for consumption in fabricating the finished product of a manufacturing firm; synonomous terms are *raw materials* or *direct materials*.

Materials Used The cost of the materials used in manufacturing during a given period;

under the periodic inventory method the amount is the sum of beginning materials inventory plus cost of materials purchases less ending materials inventory.

Period Manufacturing Costs Those product manufacturing costs which are accumulated for a given period; these comprise direct materials used, direct labor, and manufacturing overhead items.

Turnover of Finished Goods Inventory The number of times on the average the entire inventory of finished goods is sold during a given time period.

Turnover of Materials Inventory The number of times on the average that an entire materials inventory is used during a given time period.

Work in Process The inventory of partly finished products in various stages of completion at any given time.

Q20-1. "The accounting standards and procedures are the same for both the manufacturing and the nonmanufacturing types of business." Justify this statement by showing that accounting in the two types of business is the same in regard to inventory items.

Q20-2. A manufacturing firm has three inventory controlling accounts and a fourth inventory account that is closely related to the other three. Name each of these accounts and describe briefly what the balance in each at the end of any accounting period represents.

Q20-3. Explain each of the following terms: (a) materials used, (b) direct labor, and (c) manufacturing overhead.

Q20-4. What are the criteria for distinguishing between direct labor and indirect labor?

Q20-5. Distinguish between total *period manufacturing costs* and *cost of goods manufactured.*

Q20-6. Describe the purpose and function of the Manufacturing columns in the work sheet. Where in the work sheet would the amounts normally contained in the Manufacturing columns be entered if the Manufacturing columns were eliminated?

Q20-7. During a given period the cost of materials used by a manufacturing firm was $50,000. The materials inventory increased by $5,000 during the period, and materials purchases returns amounted to $2,000. What was the delivered cost of materials purchased?

Q20-8. The books of the Brooks Corporation showed the following information:

Inventories	12/31/1976	12/31/1975
Finished goods	$24,000	$18,000
Work in process	17,250	10,500
Materials	15,900	19,050

Explain how each amount will be shown (a) in the work sheet, (b) in the schedule of cost of goods manufactured, (c) in the income statement, and (d) in the statement of financial position.

Q20-9. When a given cost is applicable partly to manufacturing and partly to the administrative or selling function, how is the amount allocated in the work sheet? Discuss a possible alternative method.

Q20-10. State the formula and purpose of the turnover (a) of materials and (b) of finished goods.

Q20-11. Identify some of the problems involved in the measurement of the periodic inventories of work in process and finished goods.

EXERCISES

E20-1. The following data are taken from the books of the Sink Company for the year 1976:

Materials purchases	$150,000
Direct labor	300,000
Manufacturing overhead	300,000
Materials inventory change (amount of increase of ending inventory over beginning inventory)	45,000
Work-in-process inventory (net change—decrease)	30,000
Finished goods inventory (net change—increase)	15,000

Determine (a) the cost of goods manufactured and (b) the cost of goods sold.

E20-2. Manufacturing overhead is 20% of cost of goods manufactured. Direct labor is 30% of sales and 60% of cost of goods manufactured. Ending materials inventory is $8,000 more than beginning materials inventory. Sales totaled $200,000 for the year. Compute the net cost of materials purchased during the year. This company never has any work-in-process inventory at the end of each period.

E20-3. Compute the missing amounts in the following tabulation:

	Beginning Inventory of Materials	Materials Purchases	Transportation In on Materials	Materials Purchases Returns And Allowances	
1.	$2,250	$12,900	$?	$450	
2.	?	3,750	450	300	
3.	5,250	?	1,050	·300	(*continued below*)

	Materials Purchases Discounts	Net Cost of Materials Purchases	Cost of Materials Available for Use	Ending Inventory of Materials	Cost of Materials Used
1.	$225	$14,250	$?	$?	$12,750
2.	?	3,750	8,250	?	5,400
3.	600	?	29,850	7,500	?

E20-4. Compute the missing amounts in the following tabulation:

	Net Sales	Beginning Inventory of Finished Goods	Cost of Goods Manufactured	Cost of Finished Goods Available for Sale	
1.	$61,500	$?	$45,000	$60,000	
2.	?	37,500	?	?	
3.	90,000	?	60,000	90,000	(*continued below*)

	Ending Inventory of Finished Goods	Cost of Goods Sold	Gross Margin on Sales
1.	$?	$ 38,250	$?
2.	15,000	121,500	30,000
3.	?	?	15,750

E20-5. Compute the missing amounts in the following tabulation:

	Cost of Materials Used	Direct Labor	Manufacturing Overhead	Total Period Cost of Manufacturing	
1.	$ 15,750	$?	$ 18,000	$ 55,500	
2.	?	75,000	90,000	203,250	
3.	375,750	600,000	450,000	?	(*continued below*)

	Beginning Work-in-Process Inventory	Ending Work-in-Process Inventory	Cost of Goods Manufactured
1.	$ 7,500	$?	$52,500
2.	150,000	187,500	65,750
3.	150,000	225,000	?

E20-6. The Bumpus Corporation acquired certain patent rights for $180,000 and spent an additional $92,000 in further developing them.

  1. Record the acquisition and development of the patents.
  2. Record the patent amortization for one year on the basis of a full legal life.
  3. Record the patent amortization on the basis of an assumed useful economic life of eight years.

E20-7. The following Small Tools account is from the books of the Huyett Corporation:

Small Tools	
1976	
Jan. 1 Balance 20,800	
Aug. 3 Purchase 5,200	

The inventory of small tools on hand on December 31, 1976, was priced at $13,500, based on a physical count.

  1. How is the cost of small tools used determined? What part of the Small Tools account is allocated to the current accounting period?
  2. Prepare the entry to adjust the Small Tools account.

E20-8. The adjusted trial balance of the Kincaid Corporation included the following items:

Rent	$7,000
Heat, light, and power	4,200

Insurance	2,400
Taxes	2,000
Depreciation	4,000

The accountant for the Kincaid Corporation determined the following allocation percentages:

	Manufacturing	Selling	General
Rent	80%	15%	5%
Heat, light, and power	90	3	7
Insurance (plant and equipment)	60	20	20
Taxes	70	20	10
Depreciation	75	10	15

Enter the account balances in the Adjusted Trial Balance columns of a manufacturing work sheet and, using the allocation percentages given, extend the items to the appropriate columns of the work sheet.

E20-9. The following data are taken from the books of the Kearney Manufacturing Company:

	1976	1975
Materials used	$ 70,500	$ 67,500
Materials inventories		
Beginning of year	43,500	48,000
End of year	39,000	43,500
Cost of goods sold	175,500	168,000
Finished goods inventories		
Beginning of year	20,625	21,750
End of year	17,250	20,625

1. Compute the turnover of materials and finished goods.
2. What were the average inventories in terms of days, on the basis of a 365-day year?

E20-10. The following data are revealed by the financial statements of the Lowder Corporation:

Materials Inventory, December 31, 1975	$353,000
Materials Purchases, 1976	546,000
Materials Inventory, December 31, 1976	306,000
Direct Labor, 1976	600,000
Manufacturing Overhead, 1976	300,000
Work-in-Process Inventory, December 31, 1975	198,000
Work-in-Process Inventory, December 31, 1976	255,000
Finished Goods Inventory, December 31, 1975	138,000
Finished Goods Inventory, December 31, 1976	120,000

What significant relationships may be determined from these figures?

DP20-1. (*Computation of materials used*) The following information is available from the records of the Hayes Manufacturing Company:

Materials inventory, December 31, 1975	$ 19,125
Materials inventory, December 31, 1976	15,000
Materials purchases, 1976	300,000
Transportation in on materials purchases, 1976	6,000

| Materials purchases returns and allowances, 1976 | 7,500 |
| Materials purchases discounts, 1976 | 5,250 |

Required: In schedule form, compute the cost of materials used in 1976.

DP20-2. (*Computation of cost of goods sold*) The following information is available from the records of the Briley Company:

Finished goods inventory, December 31, 1975	$ 37,500
Cost of goods manufactured in 1976	450,000
Finished goods inventory, December 31, 1976	45,000
Work-in-process inventory, December 31, 1975	15,750
Work-in-process inventory, December 31, 1976	18,975

Required: In schedule form, compute the cost of goods sold in 1976.

DP20-3. (*Journal entries; schedule of cost of goods manufactured; analysis*) The Nanney Manufacturing Company uses a regular accounts payable system of recording liabilities for materials purchases. During 1976, the firm completed certain transactions as follows:

1. Purchased materials on account for $125,500.
2. Paid transportation charges amounting to $4,100 on materials.
3. Received $5,500 credit for materials returned.
4. Issued checks for $100,500 in payment of liability for materials purchased for $102,500 (discounts taken were $2,000).
5. Paid direct labor wages of $75,000 (ignore payroll taxes).
6. Paid the following items: factory rent, $5,500; heat, light, and power, $6,800; indirect labor, $5,200; and miscellaneous factory costs, $1,200.
7. Made year-end adjusting entries to record expired factory insurance of $2,500; small tools costs of $1,500, and depreciation on machinery and equipment of $7,500.

Required:

1. Journalize the transactions and post to T accounts.
2. Prepare a schedule of cost of goods manufactured. Inventories were as follows:

	Beginning	*Ending*
Materials	$10,500	$8,500
Work in process	4,000	4,600

3. Journalize the entries to close the nominal manufacturing accounts.
4. Compute the materials turnover in terms (a) of rate and (b) of days.
5. Determine the percentage relationship of materials used, direct labor, and manufacturing overhead to total period manufacturing costs.

DP20-4. (*Work sheet, statements, and closing entries*) The condensed adjusted trial balance of the Wentz Corporation on December 31, 1976, after adjustment, consisted of the following:

Cash	$ 30,000
Accounts Receivable	21,000
Finished Goods, December 31, 1975	18,000
Work in Process, December 31, 1975	12,000
Materials, December 31, 1975	15,000
Plant and Equipment	75,000

COST
ACCUMULATION,
AND CONTROL;
FINANCIAL
PLANNING

804

(Ch. 20)

Accumulated Depreciation—Plant and Equipment	15,000
Accounts Payable	36,000
Common Stock ($100 par value)	75,000
Retained Earnings	27,000
Sales	126,000
Materials Purchases	45,000
Direct Labor	30,000
Manufacturing Overhead	24,000
Selling Expenses	6,000
General Expenses	3,000

Inventories on December 31, 1976:

Finished goods	$15,000
Work in process	18,000
Materials	21,000

Required: Prepare (a) a manufacturing work sheet, (b) a schedule of cost of goods manufactured, (c) an income statement, (d) a statement of financial position, and (e) the closing entries.

P20-1. The following information is from the books of the Wilson Company:

PROBLEMS

Inventories

	June 30, 1975	June 30, 1976	Year Ended June 30, 1976
Materials	$ 30,000	$ 34,500	
Work in Process	44,700	43,050	
Finished Goods	110,250	106,350	
Materials Purchases			$413,250
Transportation In—Materials			20,550
Direct Labor			465,000
Manufacturing Overhead			394,500

Required:

1. Compute the total period cost of manufacturing.
2. Compute the cost of goods manufactured.
3. Compute the cost of goods sold.

P20-2. The following information is available for the Rosenberg Corporation:

	12/31/1975	1976	12/31/1976
Inventories			
Materials	$18,000		$16,500
Work in Process	21,000		27,000
Finished Goods	33,000		32,250
Materials purchased during year		$55,000	
Direct Labor		33,000	
Manufacturing Overhead		25,500	

Required: Prepare a schedule of cost of goods manufactured for 1976.

P20-3. The Soyars Manufacturing Company's partial statement of financial position as of December 31, 1975, is given on page 806.

Materials Inventory		$ 9,450
Work-in-Process Inventory		12,300
Finished Goods Inventory		14,250
Prepaid Insurance		1,425
Patents		3,000
Machinery and Equipment	$37,500	
Deduct Accumulated Depreciation	4,500	33,000
Office Equipment	$15,000	
Deduct Accumulated Depreciation	1,500	13,500

Condensed transactions for 1976:

1. Sales on account for the year were $375,000.
2. Collections from customers were:

Accounts receivable	$315,000
Deduct discounts taken	3,600
Total	$311,400

3. Materials purchases on account were $117,450.
4. Freight and other transportation charges on materials purchases were $3,450.
5. Credit received for materials returned was $5,625 (credit Accounts Payable).
6. Accounts payable were paid as follows:

Accounts Payable	$90,000
Deduct discounts taken	2,250
Checks issued	$87,750

7. Direct labor paid for the year was $93,000 (ignore payroll taxes).
8. Insurance paid for the year was $6,750.
9. The following additional items were paid:

Rent	$ 7,800
Property taxes	1,650
Indirect labor (ignore payroll taxes)	13,950
Building maintenance and repairs	4,500
Miscellaneous factory overhead costs	2,250
Office salaries (ignore payroll taxes)	15,600
Heat, light, and power	9,750
Salesmen's salaries (ignore payroll taxes)	20,700

Inventory and adjustment data:
a. Depreciation rates: machinery and equipment, 5%; office equipment, 4%.
b. Amortization of patents, $750.
c. Prepaid insurance, $1,200.
d. Wages and sslaries payable (not yet recognized):

Direct labor	$1,275
Indirect labor	225
Salesmen's salaries	1,800
Office salaries	1,500

e. Ending Inventories: materials, $9,900; work in process, $11,250; and finished goods, $13,200.

COST
ACCUMULATION,
AND CONTROL;
FINANCIAL
PLANNING

806

(Ch. 20)

f. Allocation data:

	Manufacturing	Selling	General
Rent	80%	15%	5%
Property Taxes	85	10	5
Maintenance and Repairs	90	5	5
Heat, Light, and Power	75	10	15
Insurance	80	10	10

Required:

1. Enter the December 31, 1975, balances in T accounts.
2. Record the transactions for 1976, including the adjusting entries, in general journal form and post to the T accounts.
3. Prepare a schedule of cost of goods manufactured.
4. Prepare the closing entries to accumulate the cost of goods manufactured and to transfer the balance to the appropriate account.

P20-4. The King Manufacturing Company was created on January 1, 1976. Selected transactions that occurred during the year are given below.

1. Received a charter authorizing the issuance of 50,000 shares of $50 par value common stock.
2. Issued for cash 30,000 shares of common stock at $55 a share.
3. Paid the following factory payrolls:

	Gross Wages	FICA Taxes Withheld	Employees' Federal Income Taxes Withheld	Employees' State Income Taxes Withheld
Direct labor	$50,000	$3,000	$7,575	$1,550
Indirect labor	5,000	300	600	150

4. Record the employer's payroll taxes (use assumed rates: 6% for FICA taxes, 2.1% for state unemployment, and 0.5% for Federal unemployment taxes).
   The gross wages were subject to all payroll taxes. Debit Payroll Taxes—Factory for the total; treat this as a manufacturing overhead item.
5. The December 31, 1976, inventories were as follows: materials, $15,000; work in process, $6,000; and finished goods, $16,250.

Required:

1. Journalize the transactions, assuming general manufacturing operations and the use of periodic inventories.
2. Prepare the journal entries to record the three ending inventories.

P20-5. Following are the Manufacturing columns of the work sheet of the Redfern Corporation for the year ended December 31, 1976:

	Manufacturing Debits	Manufacturing Credits
Materials Inventory	$ 45,000	$ 43,500
Work-in-Process Inventory	30,000	37,500
Materials Purchases	105,000	
Direct Labor	52,500	

	Manufacturing	
	Debits	Credits
Indirect Labor	11,250	
Rent	4,800	
Heat, Light, and Power	3,600	
Depreciation—Plant and Equipment	4,500	
Miscellaneous Factory Costs	3,750	
	$260,400	$ 81,000
Cost of Goods Manufactured (40,000 units)		179,400
	$260,400	$260,400

Required:

1. Prepare a schedule of cost of goods manufactured for 1976.
2. Compute the significant ratios and percentages.
3. Journalize the closing entries pertaining to the manufacturing functions.

P20-6. The following accounts and amounts, arranged in alphabetical order, were taken from the completed work sheet of the Margeson Manufacturing Corporation:

Accounts Receivable	$ 42,750
Accumulated Depreciation—Machinery and Equipment	14,700
Advertising Expense	2,175
Allowance for Doubtful Accounts	900
Bad Debts Expense	825
Cash	3,825
Depreciation—Machinery and Equipment	1,650
Direct Labor	23,250
Factory Insurance	2,250
Factory Rent	4,500
Finished Goods Inventory, December 31, 1975	35,250
Finished Goods Inventory, December 31, 1976	31,800
Heat, Light, and Power—Factory	2,175
Indirect Labor	6,450
Machinery and Equipment	34,500
Materials Inventory, December 31, 1975	27,750
Materials Inventory, December 31, 1976	28,125
Miscellaneous Factory Costs	2,955
Prepaid Insurance	1,650
Purchases—Materials	69,225
Purchases Discounts—Materials	2,250
Purchases Returns and Allowances—Materials	1,800
Sales	222,750
Sales Discounts	3,150
Sales Returns and Allowances	2,100
Salesmen's Salaries Expense	20,250
Small Tools	9,300
Small Tools Used	975
Transportation In—Materials	1,125
Work-in-Process Inventory, December 31, 1975	22,500
Work-in-Process Inventory, December 31, 1976	18,000

COST
ACCUMULATION,
AND CONTROL;
FINANCIAL
PLANNING

808

(Ch. 20)

Required:

1. Prepare the schedule of cost of goods manufactured for 1976.

2. Prepare a partial income statement through Gross Margin on Sales for 1976.

3. Prepare the Current Assets section of the statement of financial position.

P20-7. The adjusted trial balance of the Markham Company for the year ended December 31, 1976, is shown below.

MARKHAM COMPANY
Adjusted Trial Balance
December 31, 1976

	Debits	Credits
Cash	$ 24,450	
Accounts Receivable	59,835	
Allowance for Doubtful Accounts		$ 1,800
Materials Inventory	44,400	
Work-in-Process Inventory	2,385	
Finished Goods Inventory	18,150	
Prepaid Insurance	640	
Machinery and Equipment	67,950	
Accumulated Depreciation— Machinery and Equipment		30,480
Office Equipment	12,015	
Accumulated Depreciation— Office Equipment		5,700
Accounts Payable		21,900
Income Taxes Payable		5,250
Accrued Wages and Salaries Payable		8,250
Capital Stock, $100 Par Value		90,000
Retained Earnings		52,650
Sales		330,000
Sales Returns and Allowances	4,050	
Sales Discounts	1,875	
Purchases—Materials	68,700	
Purchases Returns and Allowances— Materials		2,065
Purchases Discounts—Materials		2,250
Direct Labor	76,605	
Depreciation—Machinery and Equipment	7,800	
Indirect Labor	16,350	
Rent	10,800	
Heat, Light, and Power	6,900	
Insurance	2,625	
Advertising Expense	5,700	
Salesmen's Salaries Expense	76,950	
Executive Salaries Expense	34,050	
Bad Debts Expense	1,650	
Depreciation Expense—Office Equipment	1,215	
Income Taxes Expense	5,250	
Totals	$550,345	$550,345

Additional data:

December 31, 1976, inventories:

Materials	$18,790
Work in Process	1,690
Finished Goods	42,900

Allocation percentages:

Item	Manufacturing	Selling	General
Rent	70	20	10
Heat, light, and power	80	10	10
Insurance	70	15	15

Required: Prepare:

1. A schedule of cost of goods manufactured for 1976.
2. An income statement.
3. A statement of financial position.

P20-8. The postclosing trial balance of the Press Manufacturing Company on December 31, 1975, is shown below.

PRESS MANUFACTURING COMPANY
Postclosing Trial Balance
December 31, 1975

	Debits	Credits
Cash	$ 37,875	
Accounts Receivable	19,500	
Allowance for Doubtful Accounts		$ 975
Materials Inventory	27,000	
Work-in-Process Inventory	36,000	
Finished Goods Inventory	33,000	
Prepaid Insurance	1,800	
Supplies Inventory	640	
Patents	1,500	
Small Tools	1,010	
Machinery and Equipment	37,500	
Accumulated Depreciation		12,000
Accounts Payable		42,000
Accrued Wages and Salaries Payable		9,000
Dividends Payable		30,000
Income Taxes Payable		20,250
Common Stock, $100 par value; issued 600 shares		60,000
Retained Earnings		21,600
Totals	$195,825	$195,825

Condensed transactions for 1976:
  1. The accrued wages and salaries payable as of December 31, 1975, consisted of the items listed below (no entry is required; this detailed information is needed for a later entry).

Direct Labor	$3,000
Indirect Labor	2,250
Salesmen's Salaries	1,800
Executive Salaries	1,950

2. Sales on account for the year were $225,000.

3. Collections from customers were:

Accounts receivable	$195,000
Deduct discounts allowed	1,950
Amount collected	$193,050

4. Purchased materials on account for $54,000.

5. Dividends due stockholders were paid in the amount of $30,000.

6. Freight and other transportation charges on materials were paid in the amount of $900.

7. Credit received for materials returned totaled $1,650.

8. Accounts payable for materials were paid as follows:

Accounts payable	$59,250
Deduct discounts taken	1,185
Amount paid	$58,065

9. Payrolls *paid* during year were (ignore the payroll taxes):

Direct labor	$24,000
Indirect labor	10,950
Salesmen's salaries	14,250
Executive salaries	15,450

10. The following items were also paid:

Small Tools	$ 450
Insurance (debit Prepaid Insurance)	1,800
Supplies	1,080
Rent	9,000
Repairs and Maintenance	3,750
Miscellaneous General Expenses	1,800
Miscellaneous Selling Expenses	630
Heat, Light, and Power	2,700

11. Dividends declared by the board of directors were $12,000.

12. Accounts receivable written off during year amounted to $1,350.

13. Merchandise returned by customers and credit granted totaled $3,450.

14. Paid income taxes of $20,250.

Inventory and adjustment data:

a. Depreciation of machinery and equipment is 10% of original cost.

b. All patents had an economic life of 10 years as of the beginning of the year.

c. Prepaid Insurance as of December 31, 1976, was $1,425.

d. Provision for doubtful accounts is estimated at ½ of 1 percent of net sales.

e. The small tools inventory as of December 31, 1976, was $1,215.

f. Supplies on hand as of December 31, 1976, amounted to $525.

g. Estimated income taxes were $39,750.

h. December 31, 1976, inventories were:

Materials	$28,500
Work in Process	31,500
Finished Goods	30,000

GENERAL
MANUFACTURING
OPERATIONS

i. Allocation percentages are as follows:

Item	Manufacturing	Selling	General
Insurance	80	10	10
Supplies	70	20	10
Rent	80	15	5
Repairs and Maintenance	90	5	5
Heat, Light, and Power	80	15	5

Required:

1. Enter the December 31, 1975, postclosing trial balance amounts in appropriate ledger T accounts.
2. Record the condensed transactions for 1976 and post to T accounts (omit dates and posting references).
3. Prepare (a) a work sheet, (b) a schedule of cost of goods manufactured, (c) an income statement, (d) a statement of retained earnings, and (e) a statement of financial position.
4. Compute the turnover of materials.
5. Compute the turnover of finished goods.
6. Determine the percentage relationship of materials used, direct labor, and factory overhead to the total period costs of manufacturing.
7. Assume that the Press Manufacturing Company produced a single product. Determine the unit cost based on 75,000 units manufactured during the year.

P20-9. (*Accounting policy decision problem*) The Laffiteau Manufacturing Company produces a single commodity. A summary of its activities for 1976 follows:

	Units	Amount
Sales	90,000	$900,000
Materials inventory, 12/31/1975		48,000
Work-in-process inventory, 12/31/1975		60,000
Finished goods inventory, 12/31/1975	18,000	72,000
Materials inventory, 12/31/1976		36,000
Work-in-process inventory, 12/31/1976		75,000
Finished goods inventory, 12/31/1976	24,000	?
Materials purchases		192,000
Direct labor		135,000
Manufacturing overhead costs		108,000

Required:

1. Prepare a schedule of cost of goods manufactured for 1976. Indicate on the schedule the number of units completed for the year and the cost per unit of finished goods.
2. Determine the gross margin on sales for the year, assuming that the transfer of the cost of finished goods to cost of goods sold is on the last-in, first-out basis. Show all your computations.
3. Discuss the accounting concepts underlying the selection of the LIFO basis versus the FIFO basis. Which of these two methods should be chosen if sound accounting concepts are followed? Why?

P20-10. The accountant for the Mayo Manufacturing Company made several errors during 1976 and previous years, as indicated below.
   a. Purchases of materials are not recorded until payment is made, although the company purports to be on the accrual basis. In January 1976, $6,900

COST
ACCUMULATION,
AND CONTROL;
FINANCIAL
PLANNING

812

(Ch. 20)

was paid for materials received in 1975. As of December 31, 1976, $4,125 worth of materials for which payment had not been made were on hand.

b. The December 31, 1975, inventory of materials was understated by $4,500.

c. Machinery used in manufacturing was purchased on January 1, 1975, at a cost of $8,250. This machinery was debited to Repairs and Maintenance and was reported as part of the operating expenses for 1975. No depreciation has been taken on this machinery. Normally, the company depreciates factory machinery under the sum-of-the-years'-digits method, using a 10-year life.

Required: Assuming that provisions of APB Opinion No. 30 are followed and that the books have not been closed for 1976, prepare correcting and adjusting entries as of December 31, 1976.

Cost Accumulation and Control—Job Order and Process Cost Systems

21

Cost accounting, a tool of management, is concerned with three basic objectives: (1) unit cost determination, (2) cost control, and (3) cost analysis. The calculation of relevant unit product costs enables management to obtain better inventory valuation; and this, in turn, enables management to determine more exactly the net income figure. In addition, this information helps management in making many decisions, particularly those involved in the determination of profitable selling prices and the development of means of reducing costs. The control of costs is achieved by the establishment and use of a system of perpetual inventory accounts, budgets, and other predetermined cost information. For example, when subsidiary perpetual inventory records related to the general ledger accounts are maintained, control is more constant and systematic, and inventory valuations are more accurate. Cost information is available at any time for managerial analysis, thereby permitting the observation and control of cost trends and cost movements.

COST ACCOUNTING SYSTEMS

The flow of the product and its related costs through the factory can be determined by a historical *job order cost system* or a *process cost system*. The job order cost system is used when each unit maintains its identity and unit costs can be specifically associated with the physical units in the job order, as in job printing. A process cost system is used for manufacturing processes in which costs of any one unit cannot be distinguished from another unit and production is largely continuous, as in the petroleum industry. Accordingly, costs for the total output of a productive operation are determined over a time period, and the unit cost is determined by dividing the total cost by the number of units produced.

A cost system under both the job order and process approaches may be either *historical* or *standard.* In a historical cost system, the actual costs of materials requisitioned and labor expended are recorded when they are used on the job. Manufacturing overhead is usually allocated on the basis of a predetermined overhead rate.

On the other hand, when a standard cost system is employed, predetermined costs are incorporated in the inventory accounts. Each product has an established standard cost for materials, labor, and overhead. The flow of costs through the production process is measured at both standard cost and actual cost, and all variations are recorded in *variance accounts.* By constantly analyzing the variance accounts, management can quickly determine the reasons for variances and initiate proper remedial action. Standard costs are discussed in more detail in Chapter 22. The remainder of this chapter is concerned with the examination of historical cost systems.

GENERAL ACCOUNTING COST ACCUMULATION COMPARED WITH A COST ACCOUNTING SYSTEM FOR A MANUFACTURING COMPANY

A manufacturing company may accumulate costs under a general accounting system sometimes referred to as a noncost system, as described in the preceding chapter, or it may accumulate costs under a cost accounting system. The difference between the two systems is the method of cost determination and control. In a general accounting system for a manufacturing firm, the cost of goods manufactured in any particular period is determined by assembling appropriate account balances in a schedule of cost of goods manufactured. The shortcoming of this procedure is that the cost of each product, process, job, unit, or department—each *cost center*—is not known. Furthermore, the use of a periodic inventory does not provide as satisfactory a means of controlling the cost of materials used in manufacturing as does the perpetual inventory approach.

A sound cost accounting system, therefore, involves the use of the perpetual inventory plan, which provides (1) for a system of inventory control through controlling accounts and (2) for a flow of costs through ledger accounts for Materials Inventory, Factory Payroll, and Manufacturing Overhead, culminating in cost accumulations for work in process, finished goods, and cost of goods sold. In this flow and accumulation, it is necessary to reiterate the distinction between *product costs* and expenses. Product costs are initially assets; they have been reclassified in form but continue to be classified as assets in the form of inventories. These asset costs become expenses when they expire and are utilized in producing revenue for the company, thus becoming deductions from revenue. In a trading business, sales salaries and all selling and general and administrative expenses are expired costs and are expenses of the period in which they are incurred. Factory wages and all other costs of manufacturing,

(Ch. 21)

on the other hand, are initially unexpired product costs (assets, not expenses) in the form of the finished product. When the finished product is sold, it becomes an expired cost, or an expense—cost of goods sold.

There are three stages in the flow of costs: (1) *recognition* (asset); (2) *transference,* or internal reclassification (asset)—transference of materials, direct labor, and manufacturing overhead through work in process into finished goods; and (3) *expiration,* or conversion of asset into expense—finished goods are sold and thus become expired costs or expenses, that is, the cost of goods sold.

JOB ORDER COST SYSTEM

Figure 21-1 shows the flow of job order costs through the general ledger accounts. The debits and credits represent current transactions; balances represent ending inventories.

The debits to Materials Inventory, Factory Payroll, and Manufacturing Overhead in the figure reflect the recognition of assets. Transference, or the inter-

Figure 21-1 Flow Chart for Job Order Cost System

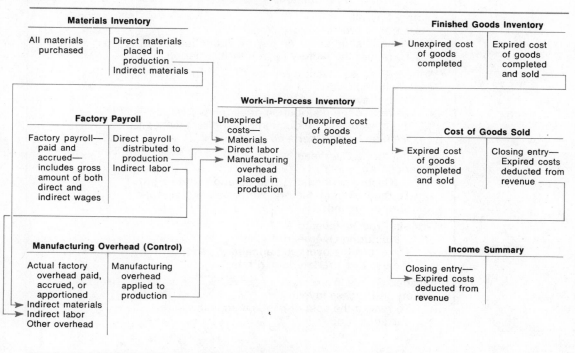

nal regrouping of assets, is reflected by the three debits to Work-in-Process Inventory with offsetting credits to Materials Inventory, Factory Payroll, and Manufacturing Overhead; the debit to Finished Goods Inventory and the credit to Work-in-Process Inventory are for the cost of work completed. Expiration is reflected by the debit to a *Cost of Goods Sold* account, set up to accumulate expired manufacturing costs, and the credit to Finished Goods Inventory for the cost of work completed and sold. The debit to Income Summary and the credit to Cost of Goods Sold for the expired cost of finished goods sold during the period is a closing entry and reflects the deduction of expired costs—expenses—from realized revenues for the period.

The flow of costs illustrated in Figure 21-1 can be summarized in journal form, as follows:

Materials Inventory	xx	
Accounts Payable		xx
To record purchase of materials and supplies		
to be used in the manufacturing process.		
Work-in-Process Inventory	xx	
Manufacturing Overhead	xx	
Materials Inventory		xx
To record the issuance of direct and indirect		
materials to production.		
Factory Payroll	xx	
Cash or Accrued Factory Wages Payable		xx
(and liabilities for all payroll deductions)		
To record the factory payroll for the period.		
Work-in-Process Inventory	xx	
Manufacturing Overhead	xx	
Factory Payroll		xx
To record the distribution of all factory wages—		
direct wages to production and indirect wages to		
Manufacturing Overhead.		
Manufacturing Overhead	xx	
Various Accounts		xx
(Cash, Accumulated Depreciation, and so on)		
To record actual factory overhead paid, accrued,		
or apportioned.		
Work-in-Process Inventory	xx	
Manufacturing Overhead		xx
To record the overhead applied to production by		
the use of a predetermined rate.		
Finished Goods Inventory	xx	
Work-in-Process Inventory		xx
To record the cost of goods completed in the		
current period.		

COST
ACCUMULATION,
AND CONTROL;
FINANCIAL
PLANNING

818

(Ch. 21)

```
Cost of Goods Sold                                    xx
    Finished Goods Inventory                             xx
        To record the expired cost of goods sold during
        the period.
Income Summary                                        xx
    Cost of Goods Sold                                   xx
        To close the Cost of Goods Sold account at the
        end of the period.
```

Cost Control Accounts

Cost control accounts are controlling accounts used with a cost system. The function of the cost control accounts is the same as that of the controlling accounts in a general accounting system—Accounts Receivable and Accounts Payable, for example. Some commonly used cost control accounts and the related subsidiary ledgers or records are:

Cost Control Accounts	Subsidiary Ledgers or Records
Work-in-Process Inventory	Job order cost sheets
Finished Goods Inventory	Finished goods perpetual inventory cards
Materials Inventory	Material perpetual inventory cards
Factory Payroll	Individual employee payroll records
Manufacturing Overhead	Manufacturing overhead ledger cost accounts

Many forms and documents are used in conjunction with the flow and accumulation of costs. These are omitted here, except for the basic *job order cost sheet* (Figure 21-2), because they are usually tailored to meet specific needs and, therefore, vary widely in scope and content.

Work in Process

The Work-in-Process Inventory account and its subsidiary job order cost sheets accumulate production cost data for single items or a group of items. A job order cost sheet is kept for each job in process. During the accounting period, the costs of material, labor, and manufacturing overhead are entered on a cost sheet. Work-in-Process Inventory is a summary controlling account, the details of which are shown on the job order cost sheets. A job order cost sheet for the Wilson Company is shown in Figure 21-2 (the amounts are assumed). The amount of manufacturing overhead costs applied is explained later in this chapter.

The summary entry to record the data that are entered on the cost sheet in Figure 21-2 is:

Work-in-Process Inventory	753.00	
Materials Inventory		425.50
Factory Payroll		227.50
Manufacturing Overhead		100.00

The balance of the Work-in-Process Inventory account should correspond to the total charges for materials, labor, and overhead entered on the job order cost sheets for all jobs started but not yet completed.

The job order cost sheet provides management with each element of the cost per unit. Once the variances between actual and budgeted costs and their causes are known, required remedial action may be initiated. In addition, the job order cost sheet may serve as a guide for future budgeting and pricing policies.

Finished Goods

The entry to record the transfer of work completed to the Finished Goods Inventory account is shown below (the items are two Type B motors at $376.50 each).

Finished Goods Inventory	753	
Work-in-Process Inventory		753

A corresponding debit entry for $753 for two motors is made on the subsidiary *finished goods perpetual inventory card* for Type B motors. When finished goods are sold, entries are made to record (1) the selling price and (2) the cost of goods sold. The entries to record the sale by the Wilson Company of one Type B motor for $750 are as shown below.

Accounts Receivable	750.00	
Sales		750.00
Cost of Goods Sold	376.50	
Finished Goods Inventory		376.50

Corresponding entries would be made in the subsidiary finished goods ledger and the accounts receivable ledger.

The perpetual inventory records for finished goods are of value to management in furnishing current inventory data and in inventory control. The avail-

COST
ACCUMULATION,
AND CONTROL;
FINANCIAL
PLANNING

820

(Ch. 21)

Figure 21-2 Job Order Cost Sheet

Quantity and Description	2 Type B Motors		Job. No.	53	
Date Started	1/2/1976		Date Completed	1/19/1976	
For	Stock				

	Direct Materials			Direct Labor		
Date	Requisition Number	Amount	Date	Time Ticket Number	Hours	Amount
1976			1976			
1/2	475	125.00	1/2	892	8	40.00
1/5	481	75.50	1/4	901	8	34.00
1/19	490	225.00	1/10	909	6	25.50
			1/11	915	8	40.00
			1/12	917	6	24.00
			1/15	920	8	34.00
			1/19	925	6	30.00
	Total	425.50		Totals	50	227.50

Summary

	Amount	Per Unit
Materials	$425.50	$212.75
Labor	227.50	113.75
Overhead 50 hours at $2.00	100.00	50.00
Totals	$753.00	$376.50

ability of goods to fill telephone or across-the-counter orders, for example, may be determined without delay by reference to the perpetual inventory cards. The taking of a complete physical inventory at one time with its attendant interruption of normal operational activities is not necessary; the count of inventory items on hand may be compared with the finished goods ledger cards on a continuing basis.

Materials

Control of materials involves the recording, reconciling, efficient use, and verification of quantitative data; it is essential to effective management. The receipt of material is recorded from the approved vendor's invoice by a debit to Materials Inventory and a credit to Accounts Payable or Vouchers Payable;

(Ch. 21)

each different type of item purchased is entered on an individual *materials perpetual inventory card,* sometimes referred to as a *stores ledger card.* Transfer of materials from the storeroom is effected on receipt of an authorized materials requisition form, which shows quantity, stock and job numbers, unit price, and total price; a requisition for indirect materials refers to an identifying account in the manufacturing overhead ledger. Work-in-Process Inventory or Manufacturing Overhead is debited and Materials Inventory is credited for the transfers. On the subsidiary records, appropriate charges are made either to the job order cost sheet or to the manufacturing overhead ledger, with corresponding credits to the materials ledger cards. The pricing procedure used may be FIFO, moving average, or any other acceptable method.

Consistency	The selected pricing method must be used consistently.

The reconciliation of material control is effected when the dollar balances of the individual materials ledger cards agree in total with the dollar balance of the Materials Inventory controlling account.

Under the perpetual inventory system for the control of materials, quantities of stock on hand may be determined readily from the records at any time; this eliminates the need for a complete physical inventory at the end of each accounting period. Verification by physical count of goods on hand and comparison with materials ledger cards can be a continuing process resulting in a minimum of interruption to plant operation.

Factory Payroll

Time cards, and *time tickets,* showing daily hours worked by employees are sorted by type of labor—direct and indirect. If an employee changes jobs during the day, a new time ticket is prepared. Time tickets serve as the basis for the distribution of employee wages either to job order cost sheets (direct labor) or to manufacturing overhead accounts (indirect labor, such as supervision, factory clerical, idle time, or overtime). At the end of each pay period, a summary entry of the total labor costs incurred is made, usually from the factory payroll register, debiting Factory Payroll and crediting Accrued Factory Wages Payable and other liabilities. Payroll details are entered regularly on individual employees' earnings record cards from the factory payroll register. The total debits to the Factory Payroll controlling account should agree with the total gross earnings on the individual employees' earnings record cards. A summary entry is also made at the end of the accounting period, debiting Work-in-Process Inventory for direct labor and Manufacturing Overhead for indirect labor and crediting Factory Payroll, to distribute the total factory payroll costs. The Factory Payroll account thus serves as a clearing account—all the charges to it are redistributed to other accounts.

Manufacturing Overhead

Manufacturing overhead includes all costs incurred in the manufacturing process other than the costs of materials and labor charged directly to job

COST
ACCUMULATION,
AND CONTROL;
FINANCIAL
PLANNING

822

(Ch. 21)

order cost sheets. All actual manufacturing overhead costs incurred are debited to the Manufacturing Overhead controlling account. At the same time individual overhead items—factory supplies used, indirect labor, depreciation of factory machinery, and others—are also debited to the various accounts in the subsidiary manufacturing overhead ledger.

The specific identification of the direct material and labor costs incurred on a given job order can be determined readily. Manufacturing overhead, however, cannot be economically identified with a specific job order. Some manufacturing overhead items—depreciation, insurance, rent, and property taxes, for example—are related to the passage of time and are not affected by production volume, whereas other manufacturing overhead costs—power, cutting oil, and small tools, for example—vary with the volume of production. If completed product costs are to be currently available to management, it becomes necessary to apply manufacturing overhead to job order cost sheets on a predetermined, or estimated, basis.

> The calculation of a predetermined overhead rate is based (1) on expected manufacturing overhead based on budgeted production and (2) on an estimated cost factor related to expected future production.

Overhead Rate

A cause and effect, or high correlative, relationship should exist between the cost factor selected and the manufacturing overhead cost. To illustrate, assume that the Wilson Company estimates manufacturing overhead costs at $800,000 and expects a production level of 400,000 direct labor hours during 1976. In this plant, there is a close relationship between direct labor hours and manufacturing overhead. The predetermined overhead rate for 1976 is calculated as follows:

$$\frac{\text{Estimated manufacturing overhead}}{\text{Estimated direct labor hours}} = \frac{\$800,000}{400,000} = \$2 \text{ per direct labor hour}$$

If a given job requires 50 labor hours (see Figure 21-2), a charge of $100 (50 hours × $2) would be recorded on that job order cost sheet for overhead. The entry in the controlling accounts would be:

Work-in-Process Inventory	100	
Manufacturing Overhead		100

If actual direct labor hours during 1976 are 400,000, as estimated, the Wilson Company will have charged $800,000 = (400,000 hours × $2) in manufacturing overhead costs to the various job order cost sheets. If, as is likely, a variance exists between the actual and the estimated amounts, there will be a balance in the Manufacturing Overhead account; a debit balance indicates overhead underapplied (overhead applied is less than actual overhead) and a credit balance indicates overhead overapplied (overhead applied is more than actual overhead). Although the under- or overapplied manufacturing overhead affects work in process, finished goods, and cost of goods sold, it generally, in practice, is treated as an adjustment to the largest of these items, the cost of goods sold and is closed into that account. The amount of over- or underapplied overhead should be relatively small at all times. Variances arise through variations in actual volume of production from budgeted volume, variations in actual price levels from budgeted, and errors or waste. Persistent variations may necessitate a revision of the predetermined rate. This, in turn, may involve adjustments of the sales price of the product, revisions of purchase commitments (for overhead services and supplies), and so on. Careful investigation should be made to trace specific causes so that proper remedial steps may be taken.

Other bases for applying manufacturing overhead are (1) direct labor dollars, (2) machine hours, (3) units of production, and (4) material cost. The computation of a predetermined overhead rate using any of these bases is the same as for direct labor hours. Assume that the Wilson Company selects the material cost basis and estimates the direct material cost to be $3,200,000 for budgeted production in 1976. The computation of the predetermined overhead rate based on material cost is as follows:

$$\frac{\text{Estimated manufacturing overhead}}{\text{Estimated material cost}} = \frac{\$800,000}{\$3,200,000} = 25\% \text{ of material cost}$$

The overhead to be applied to Job Order 53 (Figure 21-2) would be $106.38 (direct material cost of $425.50 × 0.25 predetermined overhead rate).

Selecting the Basis of Allocation. An important management decision is the selection of the proper basis for allocating overhead. The basis that should be selected is one that charges the job with an amount of manufacturing overhead most nearly corresponding to the actual manufacturing overhead costs incurred on the job. Each available basis—with due consideration for economy and practicability in application—has particular merits under particular circumstances. A detailed analysis should be made of all cost and production factors involved prior to the selection of a base, and should be continuously reconsidered. The direct labor hours method, for example, is used widely because it recognizes the causal relationship of time and overhead cost; an increase in direct labor hours on a job will result in a corresponding increase in the factory overhead charged to that job. Some may object to its use because of certain added clerical costs in recording and reconciling hours of direct labor by jobs.

The direct labor dollars method is economical to administer. Direct labor costs are readily available from the payroll records. Reference to direct labor hours may, therefore, be omitted from the job order cost sheets for clerical simplicity. The method may, however, result in an inequitable overhead charge when there are differentials in wage rates for employees performing the same type of operation with the same degree of skill. Assume, for example, that a factory with a predetermined overhead rate of 50 percent of labor costs has the following identical jobs in process concurrently:

Job No.	Materials	Labor	Overhead	Total
110	$50	$30 = (10 hours × $3)	$15 = ($30 × 0.50)	$ 95
111	$50	$40 = (10 hours × $4)	$20 = ($40 × 0.50)	$110

COST
ACCUMULATION,
AND CONTROL;
FINANCIAL
PLANNING

824

(Ch. 21)

Assume that the production process primarily uses automatic machines, with the cost of depreciation on machinery and equipment representing approximately 80 percent of the total overhead cost. Overhead is most equitably charged to production in this instance by using a machine-hours basis. Additional clerical costs are incurred, however, in recording machine hours and allocating them to jobs.

A satisfactory predetermined rate should accomplish two objectives in distributing overhead to job order cost sheets: (1) accuracy, resulting in a minimization of over- or underapplied manufacturing overhead; (2) equitability, resulting in a charge to each job of a logically defensible share of overhead. If these objectives are met, the overhead applied to each job will correspond closely to the actual overhead costs incurred on those jobs.

Departmentalization of Manufacturing Overhead. Up to this point, a single predetermined overhead rate, or *blanket rate,* has been used to distribute factory overhead costs to jobs. If the operations are organized by departments, predetermined departmental overhead rates are desirable to achieve closer control of overhead costs and more accurate product and unit cost figures. Costs are accumulated for each department—both *service* and *producing.* Producing departments are the departments that are in actual contact with the job or product—milling, cutting, assembling, and others. A service, or *indirect,* department services the producing departments—power, maintenance, and storage, for example.

To establish predetermined overhead rates, each department head submits a budget of his anticipated direct overhead costs (costs incurred within the department) for the budget period. Estimated indirect overhead costs (costs incurred in more than one department) are then allocated to the producing and service departments. The allocation of indirect costs to all the departments and the reallocation of service department costs to the producing departments require the selection of appropriate bases for such allocations. The resulting estimated total is the budgeted departmental overhead. Total budgeted departmental overhead is then divided by the appropriate allocation base—the anticipated total direct labor dollars, probable total machine hours, and so on, to arrive at the predetermined rate to be used.

PROCESS COST SYSTEM

The process cost system is used by companies in which the manufacturing process is continuous and uniform—that is, where there is a continuous flow of units of a product through successive departments. Process costing is used by firms engaged in such diverse industries as pharmaceuticals, chemicals, petroleum, gas, electricity, plastics, and mining. Basic differences between job order costing and process costing are these: In job order costing, all costs are identified with specific jobs, and unit costs are computed when the job is completed; in process costing, there is a continuous flow of units of a product unrelated to specific jobs, and emphasis is placed on homogeneous output for a given period. Unit costs are computed for time intervals rather than for specific jobs. Material, labor, and manufacturing overhead costs are charged to the manufacturing department in which they are used, and at the end of a period—usually a month—the unit cost of the product in that department is determined by dividing the total departmental manufacturing cost by the total number of units of the product processed through that department.

Flow of Costs in a Process Cost System

The distinction between direct and indirect materials and labor in a process cost system may be different from that in a job order cost system. In many cases, what was an indirect cost in a job order cost system may now be a direct cost because it can be specifically identified with a particular department; if it cannot, the cost remains an element of manufacturing overhead.

In some cases, actual manufacturing overhead may be charged directly to the departments, thus eliminating the application of overhead by a predetermined rate; however, if certain manufacturing overhead costs, particularly those of a company that operates a seasonal business, cannot be assigned directly to departments, a predetermined rate should be used.

The flow of the three elements of cost through a hypothetical two-process pharmaceutical company that manufactures a single homogeneous product called Allegrow is illustrated in Figure 21-3. Certain basic materials used in the manufacture of this product are started first in the Cooking Department. After the drug is cooked for several hours, it is transferred to the Finishing Department, where additional materials are added and the product is finished and bottled in pint jars for sale.

The flow of costs illustrated in Figure 21-3 can be summarized in the following journal entries:

Work-in-Process—Cooking Department	xx	
Work-in-Process—Finishing Department	xx	
Manufacturing Overhead	xx	
Materials Inventory		xx
To record materials issued.		
Work-in-Process—Cooking Department	xx	
Work-in-Process—Finishing Department	xx	
Manufacturing Overhead	xx	
Factory Payroll		xx
To record the distribution of factory wages incurred during the period.		
Work-in-Process—Cooking Department	xx	
Work-in-Process—Finishing Department	xx	
Manufacturing Overhead		xx
To record the allocation of actual overhead to the producing departments.		
Work-in-Process—Finishing Department	xx	
Work-in-Process—Cooking Department		xx
To record the cost of Allegrow transferred to the Finishing Department from the Cooking Department.		

Figure 21-3 Flow Chart for Process Cost System

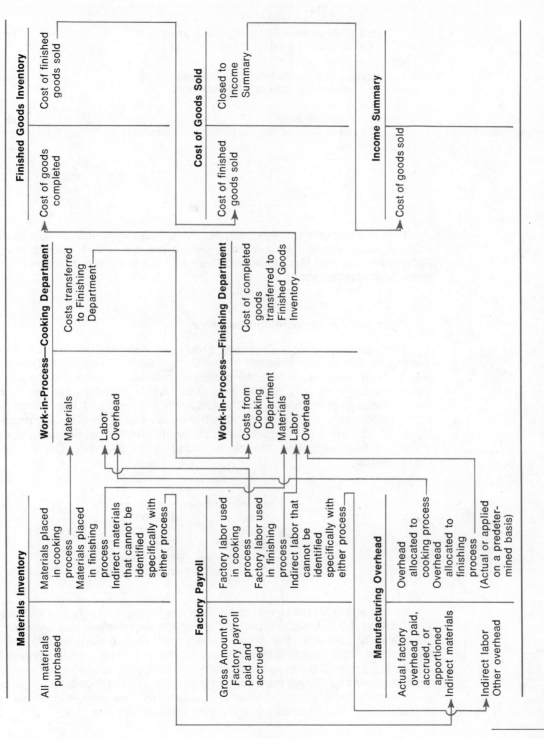

(Ch. 21)

Finished Goods Inventory		xx	
Work-in-Process—Finishing Department			xx
To record the cost of Allegrow finished.			
Cost of Goods Sold		xx	
Finished Goods Inventory			xx
To record the cost of Allegrow sold.			
Income Summary		xx	
Cost of Goods Sold			xx
To close Cost of Goods Sold at the end of the period.			

Only the flow of costs involving the three major cost accounts is illustrated in the journal entries. The entries to record the debits to Materials Inventory, Factory Payroll, and Manufacturing Overhead are the same as those in the job order cost illustrations.

Process Cost Accounting Illustration

The Atkins Chemical Company produces a single hypothetical product, Bettergum, which is processed in two departments, Blending and Aging. On July 1, 1976, there is no beginning work-in-process inventory in the Blending Department. During July, 50,000 units of Bettergum are started in the Blending Department; of this amount, 40,000 units are finished and transferred to the Aging Department. As of July 31, 10,000 units are still in the blending process—these are 100 percent complete as to materials and 50 percent complete as to labor and overhead. The July costs added in the Blending Department are shown below.

Materials	$10,000
Labor	13,500
Overhead	11,250

In the Aging Department, there is a beginning (July 1) work-in-process inventory of 4,000 units, 75 percent complete as to labor and overhead; no materials are added in the Aging Department. During July, 40,000 units are received from the Blending Department. Of the 44,000 units of Bettergum to be accounted for in the Aging Department, 38,000 units are finished and transferred to Finished Goods Inventory, and on July 31, 6,000 units are in process, $33\frac{1}{3}$ percent complete as to labor and overhead. The work-in-process inventory and costs added in July in the Aging Department are:

COST
ACCUMULATION,
AND CONTROL;
FINANCIAL
PLANNING

828

(Ch. 21)

July 1 work-in-process inventory	$ 5,300
July costs	
Materials	–0–
Labor	14,800
Overhead	13,320

Generally, the detailed information regarding a process cost system is summarized on a *cost of production report;* but for this basic presentation, only the individual items and sections of this report will be discussed.

Quantity Schedule—Blending. A *quantity schedule* is prepared for each department, showing the number of units of the product processed during a given period. Such a schedule for the Blending Department is illustrated in Figure 21-4. The stage of completion for the July 31 work-in-process inventory is an average estimate; in other words, the Bettergum that has just entered the Blending Department has material added but no labor or overhead; the Bettergum that is almost ready to leave the department has almost all the labor and overhead absorbed; thus, the average work in process *in this case* has all the material cost and one-half the labor and overhead costs.

	Units
Quantity to be accounted for	
Units in process at beginning of period	–0–
Units started in process	50,000
Total	50,000
Quantity accounted for	
Transferred to Aging Department	40,000
Units still in process at end of period	10,000 (all material—
	½ L and O)
Total	50,000

Figure 21-4
Quantity Schedule, Blending Department

Schedule of Equivalent Production—Blending. Equivalent production is the finished unit equivalent of the units completely and partially processed in a given period; in other words, it is the finished number of whole units that could have been completed if all the effort and costs for the period had been applied only to wholly finished units. The conversion of work-in-process units to equivalent whole units is necessary when computing unit costs, because there may be a different number of units—called *equivalent production units*—for material, for labor, and for overhead. The schedule of equivalent production for the Blending Department is illustrated in Figure 21-5 shown on page 830.

In the Blending Department, there is no beginning work-in-process inventory to complete; hence zeros are entered in the Materials column and in the L and O column (Figure 21-5). Units started and finished in this period (July) totaled 40,000 and are shown in both the Materials column and the L and O column. The ending work-in-process inventory consists of 10,000 units; its

(Ch. 21)

Figure 21-5 Schedule of Equivalent Production, Blending Department

	Materials	L and O ·
Beginning work-in-process inventory (to complete)	–0–	–0–
Units started and finished (this period)	40,000	40,000
Equivalent whole units contained in ending work-in-process inventory (stage of completion)	10,000 (10,000 × 100%)	5,000 (10,000 units × ½)
Equivalent production units	50,000	45,000

stage of completion is such that all the materials have been received (10,000 is entered in the Materials column), and one-half labor and overhead has been absorbed (5,000 is entered in the L and O column). This is based on the assumption that the costs expended in completing one-half the work on 10,000 units are the same as the costs of completing 5,000 units.

Unit Cost Computation—Blending. Unit costs are computed for each element—materials, labor, and overhead. Each cost element in the Total Cost column is divided by the corresponding equivalent units produced, to derive the unit costs indicated in Figure 21-6.

Figure 21-6
Unit Cost
Computation,
Blending Department

	Total Cost		
Element	Amount	Equivalent Units	Unit Cost
Materials	$10,000	50,000	$0.20
Labor	13,500	45,000	0.30
Overhead	11,250	45,000	0.25
Totals	$34,750		$0.75

Accumulated Cost Distribution—Blending. The total accumulated cost distribution of the Blending Department ($34,750) is accounted for by the $30,000 = (40,000 units × $0.75) transferred to the Aging Department and the $4,750 that appears in the ending work-in-process inventory; this is computed as follows:

Materials	10,000 units × $0.20	$2,000
Labor	10,000 units × ½ × $0.30	1,500
Overhead	10,000 units × ½ × $0.25	1,250
Work-in-Process Inventory—Blending Department (July 31, 1976)		$4,750

The same schedules and computations are now made for the second pro-

Figure 21-7
Quantity Schedule,
Aging Department

	Units*
Quantity to be accounted for	
Units in process at beginning of period	4,000 (¾ L and O)
Units received from Blending Department	40,000
Total	44,000
Quantity accounted for	
Transferred to Finished Goods Inventory	38,000
Units still in process at end of period	6,000 (⅓ L and O)
Total	44,000

* No materials are added in the Aging Department.

cess in the Aging Department. Note that there is an added complication in this process, a beginning work-in-process inventory of 4,000 units.

Quantity Schedule—Aging. The quantity schedule for the Aging Department is shown in Figure 21-7.

Schedule of Equivalent Production—Aging. The 4,000 units in the beginning work-in-process inventory were three-fourths complete as to the elements of labor and overhead on July 1. Therefore, these 4,000 units receive one-fourth of their labor and overhead during this cost period (July); each should be equated with one-fourth of a unit of labor and of overhead. Consequently, 1,000 units (4,000 units × ¼) are entered in the L and O column, as shown in Figure 21-8. The number of units started and finished during this period is determined as follows:

$$\begin{bmatrix} \text{Units transferred to} \\ \text{finished goods} \\ \text{inventory} \\ 38,000 \end{bmatrix} - \begin{bmatrix} \text{Units in beginning} \\ \text{work-in-process} \\ \text{inventory} \\ 4,000 \end{bmatrix} = \begin{bmatrix} \text{Units started and} \\ \text{finished} \\ \\ 34,000 \end{bmatrix}$$

These 34,000 units are recorded in the L and O column. Each unit in the ending work-in-process inventory of 6,000 units received one-third of its labor and overhead this month. The stage of completion of the ending work-in-process inventory, expressed in terms of whole units, is 2,000 (6,000 units × ⅓); this figure is recorded in the L and O column. The total of the L and O column (37,000 units) represents equivalent production units for the month of July.

	Materials	L and O
Beginning work-in-process inventory (to complete)	–0–	1,000 (4,000 units × ¼)
Units started and finished	–0–	34,000
Equivalent whole units contained in ending work-in-process inventory (stage of completion)	–0–	2,000 (6,000 units × ⅓)
Equivalent production units	–0–	37,000

Figure 21-8
Schedule of
Equivalent
Production, Aging
Department

JOB ORDER
AND PROCESS
COST SYSTEMS

(Ch. 21)

Unit Cost Computation—Aging. Since no materials are added in the Aging Department, the departmental unit cost is computed by dividing the cost of labor and overhead added in July by the equivalent production for July. This computation is shown in Figure 21-9.

Figure 21-9
Unit Cost
Computation, Aging
Department

Total Cost			
Element	*Amount*	*Equivalent Production*	*Unit Cost*
Labor	$14,800	37,000	$0.40
Overhead	13,320	37,000	0.36
Totals	$28,120		$0.76

It should be noted, however, that the total unit cost of goods started, completed, and transferred to the finished goods inventory during July is $1.51 (the unit cost of $0.75 from the Blending Department plus the unit cost of $0.76 from the Aging Department).

Accumulated Cost Distribution—Aging. The total cost to be accounted for in the Aging Department is shown below.

Work-in-Process Inventory, July 1 (beginning)	$ 5,300
Cost from the preceding department, the Blending Department, transferred to the Aging Department during July.	
40,000 units × unit cost of $0.75	30,000
Cost added to the foregoing units by the Aging Department during July (labor and overhead only)	28,120
Total cost for which an accounting must be made	$63,420

This cost is accounted for by the amount assigned to the 38,000 units finished and transferred to the storeroom and the amount assigned to the July 31 work-in-process inventory. The beginning work-in-process inventory and the new July production (started and finished) are typically recorded separately and are costed on the first-in, first-out basis; that is, the beginning work-in-process inventory is assumed to be completed before the new production is completed and costed. The cost of the completed 4,000 units which were in the July 1 (beginning) work-in-process inventory, the cost of the new production of 34,000 units which were started and finished during July, and the cost of the 6,000 units in the July 31 (ending) work-in-process inventory are shown below.

(Ch. 21)

Accumulated Cost Distribution
 The completed cost of the 4,000 units in the
  beginning work-in-process inventory:
   Cost of the July 1 Work-in-Process
    Inventory, from June $5,300
   Added July cost to complete these
    4,000 units:
   Labor added 4,000 × ¼ × $0.40 $400
   Overhead added 4,000 × ¼ × $0.36 360   760
    Total cost of the 4,000
     completed (unit cost, $1.515) $ 6,060
 The completed cost of the new production,
  the units started and finished
  during July:
   34,000 × $1.51   51,340
    Total cost of the 38,000 units
     completed $57,400
 The cost of the Work-in-Process Inventory,
  July 31:
   Cost from the Blending Department
    6,000 × $0.75 $4,500
   Labor added during July
    6,000 × ⅓ × $0.40   800
   Overhead added during July
    6,000 × ⅓ × $0.36   720
    The cost of the Work-in-Process
     Inventory, July 31   6,020
Total Accumulated Cost Distribution $63,420

It should be observed that the total cost of the first 4,000 units finished and transferred to finished goods is $6,060, or $1.515 per unit, and that these units have a different cumulative unit cost from the cumulative unit cost of $1.51 for the new production which was started and finished during July. Thus there is a variation in the unit cost of the two groups of items. Also note that the total cost of the ending work-in-process inventory of $6,020 added to the total cost of the 38,000 units finished of $57,400 equals $63,420, which is the accumulated cost to be distributed and for which an accounting must be made.

Cost of Production Report

 The schedule of equivalent production, the quantity schedule, the accumulated costs, and the distribution of these for each department or process are combined into what is normally referred to as a *cost of production report*. The cost of production report is a valuable aid in controlling costs; it may be used for comparisons with prior company costs, current industry costs, and predetermined estimates. The report can be expanded to include the description and total cost of each item of material, each labor operation, and each item of overhead, together with corresponding unit costs. A careful study and analysis of day-to-day variations in unit costs as shown on daily cost reports may reveal losses or inefficiencies that might otherwise continue for an indefinite period. Because of its complexity, however, this report is not presented in this basic accounting text.

(Ch. 21)

Flow of Process Costs—Summary Journal Entries

Summary entries to record the flow of costs for the Atkins Chemical Company are shown below (assuming that the same units manufactured were sold).

(a)

Work-in-Process Inventory—Blending Department	10,000	
Materials Inventory		10,000

(b)

Work-in-Process Inventory—Blending Department	13,500	
Work-in-Process Inventory—Aging Department	14,800	
Factory Payroll		28,300

(c)

Work-in-Process Inventory—Blending Department	11,250	
Work-in-Process Inventory—Aging Department	13,320	
Manufacturing Overhead		24,570

(d)

Work-in-Process Inventory—Aging Department	30,000	
Work-in-Process Inventory—Blending Department		30,000

(e)

Finished Goods Inventory	57,400	
Work-in-Process Inventory—Aging Department		57,400

(f)

Cost of Goods Sold	57,400	
Finished Goods Inventory		57,400

Work-in-Process Inventory—Aging Department has a debit balance on July 1 of $5,300, which is the value of the beginning work-in-process inventory. Entry (d) transfers costs from the Blending Department to the Aging Department. When the finished goods are sold, the costs are transferred to Cost of Goods Sold, entry (f), and the customers are billed for the sales.

It should be noted that the accountant of the Atkins Chemical Company was able to assign all materials and labor costs to the applicable department; hence, none of these costs had to be considered as manufacturing overhead.

SUGGESTIONS FOR APPLICATIONS OF ELECTRONIC DATA-PROCESSING PROCEDURES

The cost accounting area affords an excellent opportunity to utilize the electronic data-processing procedures discussed throughout this text. For example:

1. In inventory control, punched cards could be used in the maintenance of the perpetual inventory of materials and finished goods.
2. Direct and indirect labor time cards could be prepunched with employee name, badge number, and job or department code and used to

COST
ACCUMULATION,
AND CONTROL;
FINANCIAL
PLANNING

834

(Ch. 21)

facilitate automatic data-processing of the payroll and accumulating and distributing the costs to various functions.

3. In a similar manner, materials requisition cards could be prepunched with job or department code to facilitate the automatic data-processing of materials costs.

GLOSSARY

Cost Center A subentity or segment within a firm for which costs are accumulated; examples are job, process, unit of product, department, or subdepartment.

Cost Control Accounts Controlling accounts used with a cost system such as Work-in-Process Inventory, Factory Payroll, Manufacturing Overhead, and others.

Cost of Production Report A report combining the schedule of equivalent production, the quantity schedule, the accumulated costs, the distribution, and the calculation of unit cost for each department.

Cost of Goods Sold Account An account used to accumulate the cost of products sold when a perpetual inventory system is employed.

Equivalent Production Units The number of equivalent whole units produced in a time period. It is the units started and finished during a period plus partial completions converted into equivalent whole units.

Expense A period expired cost that is utilized in the production of revenue.

Factory Payroll Account An account used in a cost accounting system to show on the debit side the gross direct and indirect labor cost for a period; the entire amount is cleared out or shifted out of the account to either a work-in-process inventory account or to the manufacturing overhead control account.

Historical Cost System A cost system established to record only actual or historical costs; the job order and process systems can be designed to record only historical costs.

Job Order Cost Sheet A subsidiary record used with a job order cost accounting system to record the direct materials used, the direct labor incurred, and the manufacturing overhead applied to the specific job.

Job Order Cost System A cost accounting system that is used when costs can be specifically associated with the physical units in the specific production or job order; most job order systems accumulate historical cost only but could be designed to accumulate some form of predetermined-type cost.

Perpetual Inventory Card A subsidiary record for each of the materials that will be used in production and for each item of finished goods.

Predetermined Overhead Rate A rate used to allocate manufacturing overhead to work in process to accomplish two basic objectives: accuracy and equitability; it should be calculated by relating the budgeted overhead cost to budget amount of some high correlative factors.

Process Cost System A cost system which is used for manufacturing processes in which costs cannot be traced to specific units and in which production is largely continuous, as in the petroleum industry; a process system can accumulate either historical costs or standard costs.

Producing Department A department engaged directly in the production of the product being manufactured.

Product Cost A cost incorporated in the inventories of work in process and finished goods; it is an asset.

Quantity Schedule A schedule showing the units of product processed during a given time period for a particular process.

Service Department A department that provides a service for other service departments as well as producing departments—for example, the heating plant of a factory.

Standard Cost System A cost system devised to accumulate both standard costs (predetermined cost based on a given philosophy of cost) and historical cost; any differences between the two costs are measured and recorded in variance accounts.

Time Ticket A record of the daily number of hours, hourly rate, and total wages maintained for a factory laborer for each job or process for different amounts of time spent on these respective jobs and processes.

Unit Cost The amount of cost of direct labor, direct materials used, and factory overhead that is incorporated in one unit of product.

QUESTIONS

Q21-1. Name two approaches to the various types of cost systems. Which produces more meaningful information for management? Explain.

Q21-2. The three stages in the flow of costs are recognition, transference, and expiration. Explain these stages.

Q21-3. What factors should be taken into account in deciding whether to use a job order cost system or a process cost system in any given manufacturing situation?

Q21-4. What is the difference between *product cost* and *expense*?

Q21-5. What subsidiary ledgers or records are controlled by each of the following general ledger accounts: (a) Work-in-Process Inventory; (b) Materials Inventory; (c) Factory Payroll; (d) Manufacturing Overhead; and (e) Finished Goods Inventory?

Q21-6. (a) What is the function of a job order cost sheet? (b) What documents may furnish direct material and direct labor costs for the job order cost sheet? (c) How is manufacturing overhead applied? (d) What controlling account in the general ledger controls the data on the job order cost sheets?

Q21-7. (a) Define the term *manufacturing overhead*. (b) What are the debit and credit functions of the Manufacturing Overhead controlling account? (c) Why is a predetermined overhead rate used in applying overhead to job order cost sheets? (d) Explain the causes and the significance of over- and underapplied overhead.

Q21-8. (a) How is a predetermined overhead rate computed? (b) What bases may be used in applying manufacturing overhead to job order cost sheets? (c) What are the objectives in distributing overhead to job order cost sheets?

Q21-9. (a) What types of industry are likely to use a process cost system? (b) What are the differences between a job order cost system and a process cost system? (c) Describe the accumulation of costs when a process cost system is used.

Q21-10. A given manufacturing cost may be indirect if a job order cost system is used, but may be direct if a process cost system is used. Explain and give two examples.

E21-1. The information shown below was taken from the job order cost sheets used by the Tillery Manufacturing Company for the manufacture of its only product, Glub. Assume that all units of Glub manufactured prior to August 20 had been sold.

Job Order Number	Balance, September 1	Production Cost in September	Remarks
1062	$2,000		Completed 8/20
1063	2,500		Completed 8/30
1064	700	$1,950	Completed 9/8
1065	450	2,050	Completed 9/12
1066	350	2,100	Completed 9/18
1067		1,740	
1068		910	

Jobs 1062, 1063, and 1064 were sold and were delivered to customers in September. From the foregoing information, compute the following:

1. Work-in-process inventory at September 1
2. Finished goods inventory at September 1
3. Cost of goods sold during September
4. Work-in-process inventory at September 30
5. Finished goods inventory at September 30

E21-2. The following are among the transactions of the Jolly Manufacturing Company:

1. Issued $120,000 worth of materials for use on jobs and $6,000 for general factory use.
2. Distributed factory payroll, consisting of $150,000 of direct labor and $12,000 of indirect labor.
3. Applied manufacturing overhead at 60% of direct material cost.
4. Completed jobs that cost $144,000.

Prepare journal entries to record the transactions.

E21-3. The Work-in-Process Inventory as of the end of a period is as follows:

Work-in-Process Inventory			
Direct materials	60,000	Finished goods	174,000
Direct labor	84,000		
Manufacturing overhead	42,000		

There is one job in process at the end of the month. The direct materials charged to this job total $3,000.

Determine the amount charged to this job for direct labor and manufacturing overhead. Assume that manufacturing overhead is applied to production on the basis of direct labor cost.

JOB ORDER
AND PROCESS
COST SYSTEMS

E21-4. The following account is from the ledger of the Williams Manufacturing Company:

Manufacturing Overhead (Control)			
1976 Actual	307,005	1976 Applied	304,875

(a) Before this account is closed, three accounts are understated because of underapplied overhead. Name these three accounts. (b) Give the entry to close the Manufacturing Overhead account.

E21-5. Various cost data for the Bailey Company are given as follows:

Direct labor for 1976	$82,500
Direct material for 1976	30,000
Manufacturing overhead for 1976	83,325
Materials inventory, 12/31/76	18,000
Work-in-process inventory, 12/31/76	12,000
Finished goods inventory, 12/31/76	22,500

(a) On the basis of direct labor cost, what was the manufacturing overhead rate? (b) If the direct labor cost in the finished goods inventory was $9,000, what did the direct materials cost?

E21-6. The following information is taken from the records of a firm that produces one standardized product in a single process:

a. Beginning work-in-process inventory: 1,500 units, 75% complete as to materials and 40% complete as to direct labor and manufacturing overhead.
b. Finished and transferred to finished goods inventory: 45,000 units during the period.
c. Ending work-in-process inventory: 750 units, 60% complete as to materials and 20% complete as to direct labor and manufacturing overhead.

Compute the equivalent production for each element of cost for the period.

E21-7. The following information is taken from the books of the Cornick Company in August 1976:

Schedule of Equivalent Production

	Materials	L and O
Equivalent production of Zonker	15,000	12,000

The beginning work-in-process inventory consisted of 1,500 units, 70% complete as to materials and 40% complete as to direct labor and overhead. The August 1976 cost to manufacture was:

Materials	$ 45,000
Direct Labor	36,000
Manufacturing Overhead	30,000
Total	$111,000

Cost of the beginning work-in-process inventory was $8,400. There were 7,500 units of Zonker started and finished during August.

COST
ACCUMULATION,
AND CONTROL;
FINANCIAL
PLANNING

838

(Ch. 21)

Compute the total cost of only the 7,500 units that were started and finished during August 1976.

E21-8. The Andrews Chemical Company manufactures its product in a single processing department. The costs of production for 1976 were:

Materials	$300,000
Direct labor	211,500
Manufacturing overhead	176,250

During the year, 150,000 units were started in process, of which 138,000 units were transferred to the finished goods inventory. On December 31, 1976, 12,000 units were still in process, having received all materials and one-quarter of labor and overhead. The finished goods inventory on December 31, 1975, consisted of 30,000 units costing $4.95 each. On December 31, 1976, there were 18,000 finished units on hand. There was no work-in-process inventory as of December 31, 1975. The finished goods inventory is costed on the first-in, first-out basis.

Calculate the cost of the December 31, 1976, inventories of finished goods and work in process.

E21-9. The Apple Manufacturing Company produces a single product requiring a single process. Following are data for the month of May 1976:

a. Beginning work-in-process inventory: 18,000 units, 100% complete as to materials and 50% complete as to direct labor and manufacturing overhead; cost $27,000.
b. Started in process: 72,000 units.
c. Added within department during the period: materials, $216,000; direct labor, $72,000; overhead, $36,000.
d. Completed: 81,000 units.
e. Units in process on May 31, 9,000; all material, and one-third completed as to labor and overhead.

Compute (a) the unit cost of material, direct labor, and overhead for May 1976; (b) the total cost to be accounted for; (c) the cost of completed units; and (d) the cost of the ending work-in-process inventory.

DP21-1. (*Job order cost system*) The Barry Manufacturing Company completed the following transactions during the month of April 1976:

1. Purchased materials for $75,000.
2. Requisitioned materials for production as follows:

Job 101	$18,000
Job 102	12,000
Job 103	7,500
Job 104	4,500
Total	$42,000

3. Requisitioned materials for general factory use, $6,000 (charge Manufacturing Overhead).
4. Paid the factory payroll totaling $72,000 (ignore payroll taxes). The direct factory labor cost was distributed as follows:

DEMON-
STRATION
PROBLEMS

JOB ORDER
AND PROCESS
COST SYSTEMS

	Hours	Amount
Job 101	7,500	$15,000
Job 102	4,500	9,000
Job 103	10,500	23,625
Job 104	9,000	20,250
Total		$67,875

Indirect labor used cost $4,125.
5. Incurred additional overhead costs of $64,125 (credit Accounts Payable).
6. Applied manufacturing overhead to job order cost sheets at the rate of $1.75 per direct labor hour.
7. Completed Jobs 101, 102, and 103 and transferred them to finished goods.
8. Sold Jobs 101 and 102 on account for $135,000.
9. Transferred the balance of Manufacturing Overhead to Cost of Goods Sold.

Required:

1. Prepare journal entries to record the transactions.
2. Post to a Work-in-Process Inventory T account.
3. Post to a T account for each of the four jobs.
4. Verify the ending work-in-process inventory.

DP21-2. (*Process cost system with a single process*) The Boone Manufacturing Company began operations on January 1, 1976. It plans to manufacture a single standardized product called Uno, which requires a single process.

During January it started and finished 12,000 units of Uno. There was no January 31 work-in-process inventory. The company's costs for January were:

Materials	$ 78,000
Direct labor	102,000
Manufacturing overhead	122,400
Total	$302,400

During February, the company started and finished 13,500 units of Uno; it had 600 units in process as of February 28, 1976, in the following stage of completion:

Materials	75%
Direct labor and manufacturing overhead	50%

Costs for February were:

Materials	$ 86,490
Direct labor	113,160
Manufacturing overhead	135,792
Total	$335,442

During March, the company completed 15,000 units, including the beginning work-in-process inventory. It had 750 units in process as of March 31 in the following stage of completion:

Materials	100%
Direct labor and manufacturing overhead	60%

COST
ACCUMULATION,
AND CONTROL;
FINANCIAL
PLANNING

840

(Ch. 21)

Costs for March were:

Materials	$ 91,800
Direct labor	121,200
Manufacturing overhead	145,440
Total	$358,440

Required: For each month, where applicable, (a) prepare a schedule of equivalent production; (b) compute the unit cost of materials, direct labor, and manufacturing overhead; (c) compute the total cost to be accounted for; (d) compute the cost of completed units; and (e) compute the cost of the ending work-in-process inventory.

DP21-3. (*Process cost system with two processes*) The Braswell Company manufactures a product in two processes. In Process 1, all the material is added when the units of the product are started in process; in Process 2, materials are added as the last step in the processing. During July 1976, the company started 12,000 units in Process 1; 9,000 units were completed and sent to Process 2. The remaining 3,000 were one-half complete in Process 1. There were 1,500 units three-quarters complete in Process 2 at the beginning of the month; at the end of the month 2,700 were on hand, two-thirds complete. The following costs were incurred:

	Process 1	Process 2
Beginning work-in-process inventory	$ –0–	$13,005
Materials	36,000	3,900
Labor	16,800	8,475
Manufacturing overhead	23,100	6,780

Required:

1. Calculate the equivalent units produced.
2. Calculate the unit cost of material, direct labor, and overhead for July.
3. Calculate the cost of the units completed and transferred.
4. Calculate the cost of the ending work-in-process inventory in each process.

P21-1. The following ledger accounts show certain cost flows for a period:

Materials Inventory

Inventory	54,000	Returned to vendors	2,700
Purchases	66,000	Direct	105,000
Returned from jobs	6,000	Indirect	3,000

Factory Payroll			**Manufacturing Overhead**	
90,000	Direct 81,000	Materials	3,000
	Indirect 9,000	Labor	9,000
		Other	43,650

Finished Goods Inventory

Beginning Inventory	0		
	218,430		

Manufacturing overhead is applied to production on the basis of 70% of direct labor cost.

Required: Reconstruct the journal entries affecting the Work-in-Process Inventory account and post to a Work-in-Process Inventory T account.

P21-2. The following were among the transactions completed by the Chapman Manufacturing Company during the month of December (assume that there was no work-in-process inventory on December 1, 1976):

1. Purchased materials for $108,000.
2. Requisitioned materials for production as follows:

Job 90	$24,000
Job 91	21,000
Job 92	27,000
Job 93	15,000
Total	$87,000

3. Requisitioned materials for general factory use, $9,000 (charge Manufacturing Overhead).
4. Paid the factory payroll for December of $126,000 (ignore payroll taxes). Direct labor was distributed as follows:

Job 90	$ 30,000
Job 91	27,000
Job 92	34,500
Job 93	22,500
Total	$114,000

Indirect labor cost $12,000.
5. Recorded additional actual overhead costs for December of $108,000 (credit Accounts Payable).
6. Applied manufacturing overhead to job order cost sheets at the rate of 150% of direct material cost.
7. Completed Jobs 90, 91, and 93 and transferred them to finished goods inventory.
8. Sold Jobs 90 and 93 on account for $210,000.
9. Closed the balance of Manufacturing Overhead into Cost of Goods Sold.

Required:

1. Journalize the transactions.
2. Post to a Work-in-Process Inventory T account.

COST
ACCUMULATION,
AND CONTROL;
FINANCIAL
PLANNING

842

(Ch. 21)

3. Post to T accounts for each of the jobs.
4. Verify the ending work-in-process inventory.

P21-3. The Cherry Manufacturing Company completed the following transactions during August:

1. Purchased materials on account for $156,000.
2. Requisitioned direct materials totaling $90,000 for job orders.
3. Used indirect materials worth $9,000.
4. Returned to the vendor during August materials worth $3,000.
5. Returned materials to the storeroom: from job orders, $3,600; from indirect materials issued, $1,500.
6. Paid a total factory payroll of $195,000 for August (ignore payroll taxes).
7. Distributed the factory payroll as follows: direct labor, $192,600; indirect labor, $2,400.
8. Recorded additional actual overhead costs of $87,000 for August.
9. Applied manufacturing overhead to production at 50% of direct labor cost.
10. Completed jobs during the month costing $345,000.
11. Sold finished goods on account as follows: selling price, $555,000; cost of finished goods sold, $333,000.
12. Allowed credit for finished goods returned by customers, $4,500. These finished goods cost $2,700.
13. Closed out the over- or underapplied manufacturing overhead to Cost of Goods Sold.

Required: Journalize the transactions.

P21-4. (*Management policy decision problem*) The Crane Company uses a job order cost system for assigning manufacturing costs to its products. Management has decided to change from a system of allocating actual manufacturing overhead to jobs at the end of each month to a system of allocating overhead at a predetermined rate.

At the beginning of 1976, the following estimates of production costs for the year were made:

Direct materials	$375,000
Direct labor	450,000
Manufacturing overhead	675,000

There was no work in process on January 1, 1976. During the first three months of 1976, actual production costs were:

	January	February	March
Direct materials	$15,000	$22,125	$22,275
Direct labor	20,250	24,375	30,375
Manufacturing overhead	30,000	37,500	45,000

Required:

1. The company uses the direct labor dollar method to allocate manufacturing overhead to the various jobs. On the basis of the estimated production cost for 1976, what should the predetermined rate for allocating manufacturing overhead be? In light of the actual costs for the three months given, is this rate realistic? Support your answer by computations.
2. In summary form, record the materials requisitioned for the various jobs; the distribution of the direct labor payroll; and, using the rate derived in require-

ment 1, the assignment of manufacturing overhead to the various jobs for the month of January.

3. All goods worked on during the three-month period were completed except for Job 1062, which had accumulated direct materials costing $600 and direct labor costing $450. All goods completed during the period were sold except Job 1091, which had a total assigned cost of $1,500. Record, in general journal entry form, the completion of work during the period and the cost of goods sold during the period.

P21-5. (*Accounting policy decision problem*) The Eastwood Manufacturing Company prepared the following budgeted data for the year 1976:

Manufacturing overhead	$450,000
Direct material cost	$225,000
Machine hours	900,000
Direct labor hours	150,000
Direct labor cost	$450,000
Units of production	1,350,000

Required:

1. Calculate the predetermined overhead rate for the company for 1976 on each of the following bases: (a) direct material cost, (b) machine hours, (c) direct labor hours, (d) direct labor cost, and (e) units of production.
2. Data on Job 45, which was completed during 1976, are as follows: direct materials cost, $480; direct labor hours, 1,020; direct labor cost, $3,330; machine hours, 1,995; units, 3,000. (a) Compute the cost of Job 45, using each of the bases from requirement 1. (b) Which method of applying overhead do you recommend? (c) Why?

P21-6. The Frazelle Oil Company produces a product in a single process. Following are data for the month of May:

a. In process as of April 30: 3,000 units, 60% complete as to materials and 10% complete as to direct labor and manufacturing overhead
b. Started in process during May: 39,000 units
c. In process on May 31: 4,500 units, 75% complete as to materials and 20% complete as to direct labor and manufacturing overhead

Required: Prepare a schedule in good form showing the equivalent units produced in May.

P21-7. Cost information for Department 3 of the Gardner Company for June is shown below (there was no beginning work-in-process inventory).

	Total Cost	Unit Cost
Production costs		
Costs from preceding department	$270,000	$ 1.80
Costs added during June within department		
Materials	$ 60,000	
Direct labor	82,800	
Manufacturing overhead	27,600	
Total costs added	$170,400	
Total costs	$440,400	

COST
ACCUMULATION,
AND CONTROL;
FINANCIAL
PLANNING

844

(Ch. 21)

	Units
Quantity to be accounted for	
Units transferred from Department 2	150,000
Quantity accounted for	
Units completed and transferred to storeroom	132,000
Units unfinished at end of month	18,000
Total	150,000

The work in process in Department 3 at the end of June is complete as to materials and one-third complete as to direct labor and manufacturing overhead.

Required:

1. Compute the equivalent units produced in June.
2. Compute the unit cost of production in Department 3 for materials, labor, and manufacturing overhead added in Department 3.
3. Compute the total cost and unit cost of goods transferred to finished goods inventory.
4. Compute the cost of the work-in-process inventory in Department 3 at the end of June.

Show computations in good form.

P21-8. The Holland Company started manufacturing a new product on November 1; it required processing in two departments, Cooking and Drying. Total cost and unit data for the month were:

	Department	
	Cooking	*Drying*
Costs		
Materials	$138,240	$ –0–
Labor	75,048	168,370
Overhead	49,608	153,470
Totals	$262,896	$321,840
	Units	*Units*
Quantity to be accounted for		
Started in process	48,000	
Received from preceding department		41,000
Totals	48,000	41,000
Quantity accounted for		
Transferred to next department	41,000	36,000
Units in process (all materials added)		
$\frac{1}{5}$ complete as to labor and overhead	7,000	
¼ complete as to labor and overhead		5,000
Totals	48,000	41,000

Required:

1. Prepare a schedule of equivalent production for each department.
2. Compute the unit cost of production for each department for materials, labor, and manufacturing overhead.
3. Compute the total cost and unit cost of goods transferred out of each department.
4. Compute the cost of the November 30 work-in-process inventory for each department.

Show computations in good form.

P21-9. The Kerr Chemical Company manufactures a product in two processes: grinding and blending. Materials are complete when a unit is started in the Grinding Department, but are added continuously in the Blending Department. During September, the company started 36,000 units in the Grinding Department; at the end of the month 6,000 of them were in the work-in-process inventory, one-quarter complete. The others went to the Blending Department, where there were 9,000 units, one-third complete, at the start of the month, and 12,000 units, three-quarters complete, at the end. Costs were as follows:

	Department	
	Grinding	*Blending*
Work in process, August 31	$ –0–	$27,360
Direct materials	39,600	16,500
Direct labor	22,050	26,400
Manufacturing overhead	15,750	21,450

Required:

1. Prepare a schedule of equivalent production for each department.
2. Prepare a quantity schedule for each department.
3. Compute the unit cost of production for each department for materials, labor, and manufacturing overhead.
4. Compute the total cost and unit cost of goods transferred out of each department.
5. Compute the September 30 work-in-process inventory for each department.

Show computations in good form.

COST
ACCUMULATION,
AND CONTROL;
FINANCIAL
PLANNING

846

(Ch. 21)

Cost Accumulation and Control—Standard Costs, Direct Costing, Responsibility Accounting

22

A historical cost system furnishes information that often becomes available too late for many decisions. If data are to be received in time for most decisions, a system must be designed to yield predetermined or precomputed costs, the output of a *standard cost system.* This chapter deals with the rudiments of standard costs, the question of direct costing, and an introduction to responsibility accounting.

STANDARD COSTS

Standard costs are precomputed costs based on a given philosophy of what standards should be for the purpose of measuring cost. For example, the *engineering* or *ideal standards* are predetermined costs of manufacturing a unit of product based on the use of the most efficient laborers working under the most ideal conditions possible. Another widely used standard concept is referred to as the *average attainable standards.* These standards are predicated on the concept that the cost of a unit of product should be that resulting from the manufacture of a unit of product by an average laborer working under average normal factory conditions. Ideal standards can seldom be attained and thus may discourage the productivity of laborers and create a morale factor in the plant. The average attainable standards may serve to spur the capabilities of laborers and thus appear to be reasonable criteria for measuring the adequacy of a company's performance.

Standard costs are similar to budgets in that both are predetermined. Both standard costs and budgets aim at the same objective—managerial control. Standard costs are the anticipated costs of a product; to be useful to management they must be computed with great care.

Each product has a *standard cost card* that shows what costs should be incurred under normal operating conditions. Actual costs of the product may also be recorded on the card. The basic objective is to compare each element of standard cost with each element of actual cost so that differences may be identified for study and remedial action.

PRINCIPLE OF MANAGEMENT BY EXCEPTION

Job order and process costing procedures, as described in the previous chapter, deal with actual historical costs except for the use of predetermined overhead rates. In many industries, the use of predetermined costs has been extended to all costs of manufacturing through the use of standard costs. The comparison of actual costs with standard costs or the analysis of actual cost variances from standard costs makes possible *management by exception*. It is the exceptions and their causes that must be determined and remedied. Costs can be controlled better when variances and their causes are known promptly. Standard costs may be used with either job order costing or process costing. They also may be used effectively for the control of selling and administrative costs of a company to measure the efficiency of those functions.

The use of overhead standards is related to the grouping of costs in the overhead budget. Budgetary control results when budgets and standards are harmonized effectively. One cannot function properly without the other, for the budget is, in effect, a summary of standard costs. The materials purchases budget, for example, can be prepared readily when production requirements are known and the standard quantity of material required for the end product and standard unit cost have been determined.

FIXED MANUFACTURING OVERHEAD BUDGET

Budgeted overhead is sometimes based on the assumption of a *fixed* or static budget; that is, it is based on a predetermined level of production. The individual items in such a budget are often not even classified into fixed or variable elements. A fixed overhead budget based on an anticipated production level of 10,000 units of finished product of the Stetson Manufacturing Company is shown in Figure 22-1.

Such a budget is of limited use to management in its control-exercising function, because variations of actual costs from budgeted costs arise whenever the total number of units produced is different from that on which the budget was based.

COST
ACCUMULATION,
AND CONTROL;
FINANCIAL
PLANNING

848

(Ch. 22)

Figure 22-1
Fixed Manufacturing
Overhead Budget

STETSON MANUFACTURING COMPANY
Manufacturing Overhead Budget for 10,000 Units
For the Month Ending July 31, 1976

Item	Amount
Depreciation—Factory Building	$ 3,000
Factory Property Taxes	200
Insurance—Factory Building	300
Other Fixed Costs	16,500
Factory Supplies	500
Light and Power	800
Indirect Labor	600
Other Variable Costs	8,100
Total	$30,000

FLEXIBLE MANUFACTURING OVERHEAD BUDGET

A budget that gives recognition to varying levels of production and to the costs that change with these levels, often called the *flexible budget,* overcomes the shortcomings of the fixed budget by providing management with a basis for analyzing—and, therefore, controlling—the variances between budgeted and actual costs. This is accomplished by comparing actual expenditures with previously established budgeted amounts, adjusted for varying levels of production. A series of budgets is prepared, showing estimated or standard costs at various levels of production. Since it is not practicable to set up budgets for every possible level of operation, interpolation may be necessary if, for example, the flexible budgets are at 5,000 unit intervals and actual production falls at a point between the intervals. The preparation of a flexible budget involves an analysis of the degree and extent to which each item of overhead cost is affected by changes in volume of production. The flexible budget, therefore, is essentially a series of fixed budgets. The preparation of any one budget in the series is the same as for a single fixed budget.

Cost Behavior Patterns. A prerequisite to this type of budget planning is a knowledge of the patterns of cost (cost behavior) within the various cost functions. Up to this point the assumption has been made that all costs are strictly fixed or strictly variable. This assumption does not hold true in a number of situations. In Figure 22-2, cost curves are given to illustrate diagrammatically four types of cost patterns. Some costs, for a given period, may be relatively fixed *in total,* regardless of changes in production. Depreciation, property taxes on factory buildings, and fire insurance are examples of these costs. As indicated previously, these are referred to as *fixed costs;* they produce a curve similar to that indicated in Figure 22-2a.

Other costs, such as supplies, may be relatively variable; that is, they vary *in total* in proportion to changes in output. These costs are referred to as *variable costs* and produce a curve similar to that indicated in Figure 22-2b.

(Ch. 22)

Figure 22-2
Patterns of Cost
Behavior

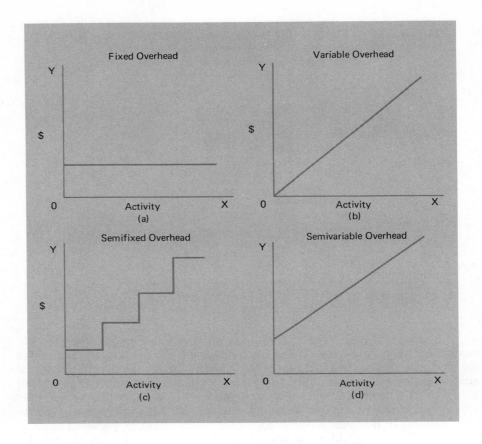

Certain other costs may change in total in the direction of changes in production, but these changes are not proportionate. Two examples of these kinds of costs are referred to as *semifixed costs* and *semivariable costs*. The semifixed costs vary in steps. For example, one inspector of finished goods may be needed for outputs of 0 to 10,000 units; two inspectors may be needed for outputs of 10,001 to 20,000 units, and so on. The salaries of the inspectors would be a *semifixed cost* (see the cost curve in Figure 22-2c). On the other hand, assume that a foreman receives a base salary of $10,000 plus a bonus of 2 percent of the revenue produced by sales of products made by his department. His salary would contain both a fixed component—the base salary—and a variable component—the bonus based on sales generated by his department. This kind of cost is referred to as a *semivariable cost* and produces a cost curve as indicated in Figure 22-2d.

Illustration of Flexible Budget. When the flexible budget is prepared, the fixed and variable components of each semivariable cost must be resolved.

COST
ACCUMULATION,
AND CONTROL;
FINANCIAL
PLANNING

850

(Ch. 22)

	90%	95%	100%	105%
Direct Labor Hours	27,000	28,500	30,000	31,500
Fixed costs				
Depreciation—factory building	$ 3,000	$ 3,000	$ 3,000	$ 3,000
Factory property taxes	200	200	200	200
Insurance—factory building	300	300	300	300
Other costs	16,500	16,500	16,500	16,500
Total fixed costs	$20,000	$20,000	$20,000	$20,000
Variable costs				
Factory supplies	$ 450	$ 475	$ 500	$ 525
Light and power	720	760	800	840
Indirect labor	540	570	600	630
Other costs	7,290	7,695	8,100	8,505
Total variable costs	$ 9,000	$ 9,500	$10,000	$10,500
Total costs	$29,000	$29,500	$30,000	$30,500

Figure 22-3
Flexible
Manufacturing
Budget

Moreover, the production range of the semifixed costs must be known so that the amounts may be indicated as being fixed for only that particular range. For example, indirect labor may remain constant for the 85 and 90 percent production capacity, but it may be indicated at a higher fixed amount for the 95 and 100 percent production capacity. The range over which cost behavior is predictable is known as the *relevant volume range*.

Relevant Volume Range

To illustrate the flexible budget, assume that the Stetson Manufacturing Company produces a single, uniform product, and that its costs can be resolved into fixed and variable components. The flexible manufacturing overhead budget for the month of July is shown in Figure 22-3.

The 100 percent of capacity level used in Figure 22-3 is not intended to indicate the maximum plant capacity. Rather, it is the level at which it is considered theoretically sound to charge all fixed overhead costs to the finished products as being properly utilized; that is, no part of the fixed overhead costs should be considered as *idle time cost,* a lost cost. Hence, the Stetson Manufacturing Company may select 90 percent, 95 percent, or some other actual level as the standard level of output on which to base its predetermined overhead rate and the point from which to measure overapplied or underapplied overhead. It may be assumed that the level of 30,000 direct labor hours or 10,000 units of output represents the company's practical operating capacity over a relatively long period.

Figure 22-3 indicates (1) that fixed costs are constant at all four levels of capacity, (2) that overhead is to be applied with direct labor hours as a basis, and (3) that variable costs are in direct proportion to capacity levels. This is evident from the following computations relating to the 100 percent and 95 percent columns:

STANDARD COSTS;
DIRECT COSTING;
RESPONSIBILITY
ACCOUNTING

$$30,000 \text{ direct labor hours} \times 95\% = 28,500 \text{ hours}$$
$$\$500 \text{ in factory supplies} \times 95\% = \$475$$
$$\$10,000 \text{ in total variable costs} \times 95\% = \$9,500$$

The Stetson Manufacturing Company produces 10,000 units at its 100 percent of capacity level. Each unit requires three hours of direct labor.

Illustration of Standard Cost Accounting

A standard cost accounting system is illustrated by the continuation of the activities of the Stetson Manufacturing Company for the month of July 1976.

Standard Cost Card. The accountant working with engineers develops standards usually based on a given concept of standard cost, which may be the cost of the average performance of laborers working under normal operating conditions or average attainable standards. The standard cost card of the Stetson Manufacturing Company reveals the following standard cost per unit:

Materials: 2 pieces of Material K-12 at $5	$10
Labor: 3 hours at $3	9
Overhead: 3 hours at $1 (See Figure 22-3)	3
	$22

The predetermined overhead rate for the month of July, based on the 100 percent column (from Figure 22-3), is shown in Figure 22-4.

Figure 22-4
Predetermined
Overhead Rate

$$\text{Variable cost per hour} = \frac{\text{Variable costs}}{\text{Total hours}} = \frac{\$10,000}{30,000} = \$0.33\tfrac{1}{3}$$

$$\text{Fixed cost per hour} = \frac{\text{Fixed costs}}{\text{Total hours}} = \frac{\$20,000}{30,000} = \$0.66\tfrac{2}{3}$$

$$\text{Predetermined overhead rate (per hour)} \qquad \$1.00$$

The hourly rate also may be computed as follows:

$$\frac{\text{Total budget manufacturing overhead}}{\text{Total budgeted direct labor hours}} = \frac{\$30,000}{30,000} = \$1 \text{ per hour}$$

Flow Chart of a Standard Cost System. Figure 22-5 shows the flow of standard costs through the Stetson Manufacturing Company. Each of these indicated steps is illustrated and discussed in conjunction with the accounting for the activities and transactions described below.

July Cost Information for the Stetson Manufacturing Company. During July, 10,000 units were started and 9,880 units were completed; the beginning work-in-process inventory consisted of 80 units, which had received all the material and one-fourth of the labor and overhead; there were 200 units in the ending work-in-process inventory, which had received all materials and one-fifth of the

COST
ACCUMULATION,
AND CONTROL;
FINANCIAL
PLANNING

852

Figure 22-5 Flow Chart of a Standard Cost System

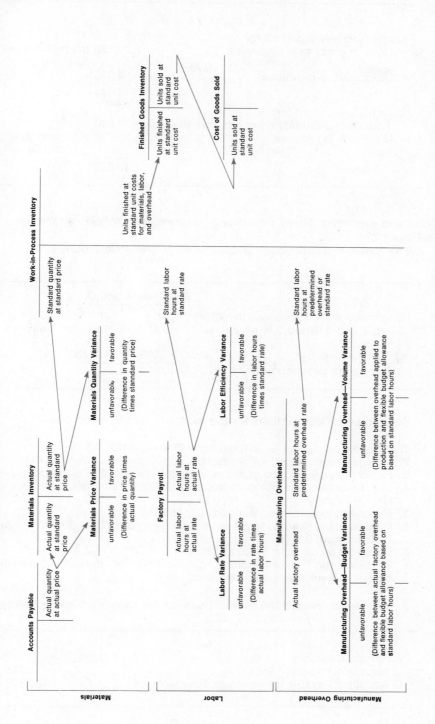

STANDARD COSTS;
DIRECT COSTING;
RESPONSIBILITY
ACCOUNTING

(Ch. 22)

853

Figure 22-6
Quantity Schedule for
July

	Units
Quantity to be accounted for	
Units in process at beginning	80 (all material—
	¼ L and O)
Units started in process	10,000
Total	10,080
Quantity accounted for	
Transferred to finished goods inventory	9,880
Units still in process	200 (all material—
	⅕ L and O)
Total	10,080

labor and overhead. These data may be expressed in schedule form, as shown in Figure 22-6.

The equivalent production is computed as shown in Figure 22-7.

Figure 22-7
Schedule of
Equivalent Production
for July

	Materials	L and O
Beginning work-in-process inventory	–0–	60 (80 units × ¾)
Started and finished this period	9,800	9,800 (9,880 units—
		80 units)
Unit still in process	200	40 (200 × ⅕)
Equivalent production units	10,000	9,900

A summary of transactions for the month of July is given below.

1. Materials purchased: 20,200 pieces of Material K-12 at $4.98 each
2. Materials requisitioned for production: 20,100 pieces of Material K-12
3. Factory payroll incurred during July: 29,600 hours at $3.05 an hour
4. Direct labor applied: standard hours for 9,900 units of finished product times standard rate
5. Manufacturing overhead incurred: $29,850
6. Manufacturing overhead applied to production: $29,700 = (9,900 × $3)
7. Units finished: 9,880
8. Units sold on account: 9,500 at $30
9. Manufacturing Overhead controlling account closed and variances entered in budget and volume variance accounts

The entries to record the transactions for the month are given below.

(a)

Materials Inventory	101,000	
Materials Price Variance		404
Accounts Payable (or Vouchers Payable)		100,596

COST
ACCUMULATION,
AND CONTROL;
FINANCIAL
PLANNING

854

(Ch. 22)

	Quantity	Price		Amount
	Actual: 20,200 ×	Standard: $5.00		$101,000
	Actual: 20,200 ×	Actual: $4.98		100,596
	Materials price variance (favorable)			$ 404

(b)

Work-in-Process Inventory	100,000	
Materials Quantity Variance	500	
Materials Inventory		100,500

	Quantity	Price		Amount
	Actual: 20,100 ×	Standard: $5.00		$100,500
	Standard: 20,000 ×	Standard: $5.00		100,000
	Materials quantity variance (unfavorable)			$ 500

10,000 equivalent production units (see Figure 22–7)
<u>× 2</u> standard pieces per unit
<u>20,000</u> standard units of material

(c)

Factory Payroll	90,280	
Salaries and Wages Payable		
(and other payroll deduction liabilities)		90,280
29,600 actual hours × $3.05 = $90,280		

(d)

Work-in-Process Inventory	89,100	
Labor Rate Variance	1,480	
Labor Efficiency Variance		300
Factory Payroll		90,280

Rate Variance

	Hours	Rate		Amount
	Actual: 29,600 ×	Actual: $3.05		$90,280
	Actual: 29,600 ×	Standard: $3.00		88,800
	Labor rate variance (unfavorable)			$ 1,480

Efficiency Variance

	Standard: 29,700 ×	Standard: $3.00		$89,100
	Actual: 29,600 ×	Standard: $3.00		88,800
	Labor efficiency variance (favorable)			$ 300

9,900 equivalent production units (see Figure 22–7)
<u>× 3</u> standard hours per unit
<u>29,700</u> total standard labor hours

(e)

Manufacturing Overhead	29,850	
Prepaid Insurance (and other accounts)		29,850

(f)

Work-in-Process Inventory	29,700	
Manufacturing Overhead		29,700

29,700 standard labor hours × $1 per hour
predetermined overhead rate = $29,700

(g)

Finished Goods Inventory	217,360	
Work-in-Process Inventory		217,360

9,880 completed units × $22 standard
unit cost = $217,360

(h)

Cost of Goods Sold	209,000	
Accounts Receivable	285,000	
Finished Goods Inventory		209,000
Sales		285,000

9,500 units × $22 standard unit cost = $209,000
9,500 units × $30 unit selling price = $285,000

(i)

Manufacturing Overhead—Volume Variance	200	
Manufacturing Overhead—Budget Variance		50
Manufacturing Overhead		150

The Manufacturing Overhead controlling account after entry (i) is posted appears as follows:

Manufacturing Overhead		
Entry (e) 29,850	Entry (f) 29,700	
	Entry (i) 150	
29,850	29,850	

The actual manufacturing overhead incurred ($29,850) exceeded the overhead applied ($29,700); therefore, the debit balance of $150 represents underapplied overhead. Further analysis indicates that the $150 is made up of a credit budget variance of $50 and a debit volume variance of $200. In deriving these two amounts, reference must be made to the flexible budget to determine the budget allowance based on standard labor hours for the actual work completed (29,700 units). Since a breakdown of the fixed and variable elements in the predetermined overhead rate is available, computations for the flexible

(Ch. 22)

budget allowances for 29,700 labor hours on work completed may be made as follows (see Figure 22-4):

Fixed costs	$20,000
Variable costs 29,700 hours × $0.33⅓	9,900
Flexible budget allowance	$29,900

If a breakdown of the fixed and variable elements is not available, the $29,900 may be derived directly from the flexible budget schedule (Figure 22-3):

$$\frac{\text{Standard labor hours for work done}}{\text{Budgeted direct labor hours}} = \frac{29,700}{30,000} = 99\%$$

The flexible budget allowance at this 99 percent level may now be interpolated as follows:

95% (28,500 hours)	$29,500
100% (30,000 hours)	30,000
5% difference	$ 500
1% difference	100
4%	$ 400

The flexible budget allowance at 99 percent level is:

95%	$29,500
4%	400
99%	$29,900

The underapplied overhead of $150 may be analyzed as follows:

1. Budget variance:

Flexible budget allowance for 99% capacity attained	$29,900
Actual overhead incurred	29,850
Budget variance (favorable)	$ 50

2. Volume variance:

Flexible budget allowance for 99% capacity attained	$29,900
Overhead applied during July (29,700 hours × $1)	29,700
Volume variance (unfavorable)	$ 200

The budget variance is favorable, because the actual overhead costs incurred are less than the flexible budget allowance at the 99 percent of actual

(Ch. 22)

capacity level. The volume variance is unfavorable, because a portion (1 percent) of the available plant facilities were not used, resulting in a loss of $200, computed alternatively as follows:

Budgeted hours	30,000
Standard hours for capacity attained	29,700
Idle capacity hours	300
Fixed overhead rate per hour	$ 0.66⅔
Cost of idle capacity	$ 200

The idle capacity, or unfavorable volume variance, represents the portion of the fixed costs that was not absorbed because full production (30,000 hours) was not achieved. Had the volume of activity exceeded 100 percent (30,000 standard labor hours), an excess capacity, or favorable volume variance, would have resulted.

Practice varies with respect to the disposition of the variance accounts. Many accountants view standard costs as being realistic costs; therefore, they view the variances as losses, or, if they are favorable, as gains. They would close the variances to the Income Summary account. Another method is to treat the variances as costs of the period in which they are incurred—that is, to close all the variance accounts into Cost of Goods Sold. This may either be done monthly or be deferred until the end of the annual accounting period. Deferral may be practical if the variances tend to offset each other owing to seasonal volume fluctuations.

The standard cost of the 80 units (all material and one-quarter labor and overhead) in the beginning work-in-process inventory of the Stetson Manufacturing Company is comprised of the following cost elements:

Materials: 80 units × $10 standard cost	=	$ 800
Labor: 80 units × ¼ × $9 standard cost	=	180
Overhead: 80 units × ¼ × $3 standard cost	=	60
Total		$1,040

The Work-in-Process Inventory ledger account appears as shown below.

Work-in-Process Inventory

Beginning balance	1,040	Entry (g)	
Entry (b) materials	100,000	finished goods	217,360
Entry (d) labor	89,100		
Entry (f) overhead (2,480)	29,700		

COST
ACCUMULATION,
AND CONTROL;
FINANCIAL
PLANNING

858

(Ch. 22)

The $2,480 debit balance in the account represents the standard cost of 200 units in the ending work-in-process inventory, which is verified as follows:

Cost Element	Units in Process	Stage of Completion	Standard Unit Cost	Total Standard Cost
Materials	200	100%	$10	$2,000 = (200 × $10)
Labor	200	20%	9	360 = (200 × ⅕ × $9)
Overhead	200	20%	3	120 = (200 × ⅕ × $3)
Total work in process				$2,480

MANAGERIAL INTERPRETATION OF VARIANCES

As a first step in the managerial interpretation of variances, it is necessary to identify who has primary responsibility for each of the variances. For example, the purchasing department is responsible, in part at least, for the materials price variance. Supervisory factory personnel, however, may have some influence on materials prices when these individuals specify certain brand-named materials or materials of certain grade and quality. Factory supervisory personnel have primary responsibility for the materials quantity and labor efficiency variances. The personnel department is partly responsible for the labor rate variance (although others in the factory may have some influence here—for example, hiring policies). Top factory heads are responsible for the overhead volume variance; those who acquire and use overhead items are responsible for the overhead budget variance.

When any variance is large enough, an investigation should be made to see if corrective action should be taken. For example, if the actual price of materials is substantially above the standard, a study should be made—possibly by the accountant working with the individual (or individuals) who has primary responsibility for the materials price variance—to see if this cost could be reduced by buying in larger quantities, by the substitution of other materials, or by taking other measures. The other variances are analyzed in a similar manner. It is important, moreover, to know what variances *are not* large enough to justify an investigation, as these studies may be extremely costly and hence, for small differences, unprofitable for management.

DIRECT COSTING

A primary purpose of cost accounting is to furnish management with meaningful accounting data for use in decision making. With this in view, a number of companies have adopted a cost method referred to as *direct cost-*

ing. Direct costing is contrasted with absorption, or conventional, costing. Under direct costing, all manufacturing costs are segregated into product costs and period expenses on the basis of the variability of costs with volume. For direct costing purposes, costs that vary with changes in volume are considered product costs; those which do not vary are treated as period expenses. The cost of goods sold and the cost of goods in inventory are valued on the basis of variable product costs alone—direct labor, direct material, and variable manufacturing overhead. Fixed manufacturing overhead costs are reported as expenses for the period and are deducted from the gross margin. Thus, the reported excess of revenue over variable costs and expenses, or *marginal income,* under direct costing reflects directly the effect of sales volume. Costs that are incurred to make a given level of plant productive facilities available—that is, costs that do not vary with the amount of work done but expire with the passage of time—are excluded in valuing both the cost of goods sold and the cost of goods on hand. Absorption costing, which treats *all* manufacturing costs as product costs, on the other hand, reflects the factors of both sales and production volume.

The ledger accounts under direct costing provide for the segregation of costs into their fixed and variable elements; the income statement is usually prepared to show *marginal income*—sales minus variable costs—from which fixed costs are deducted to arrive at net income. This is in contrast to absorption costing, under which the fixed and variable elements are mingled within the individual accounts. The separation of costs into their fixed and variable elements enables management to analyze the effect of volume changes on these cost elements and on net income. Under direct costing, fixed costs are deducted in the period when they are incurred, whereas under absorption costing, a portion of the fixed costs remains in inventory; hence the reported net income will differ under the two systems. When production exceeds sales, a portion of the fixed costs will remain in inventory under the absorption costing method, cost of goods sold will be less, and net income will be higher than under the direct costing method. The results are reversed when sales exceed production. Reported earnings under absorption costing may, therefore, rise with falling sales volume if production volume is increased, and fall with rising sales volume if production falls.

The difference between direct costing and absorption costing is illustrated by the operational data for the Directo Manufacturing Company. During 1976, the company produced 40,000 units of a new product and sold 32,000 units at $25 each. Cost of production and operating expenses are as follows:

Direct materials	$120,000
Direct labor	80,000
Manufacturing overhead—fixed	200,000
Manufacturing overhead—variable	240,000
Selling and administrative expenses—fixed	60,000
Selling and administrative expenses—variable	40,000

Thus the product unit cost figures under each cost concept is:

Absorption costing:	$\dfrac{\$640{,}000 \text{ Total manufacturing costs}}{40{,}000 \text{ Units produced}} = \$16$
Direct costing:	$\dfrac{\$440{,}000 \text{ Total variable manufacturing costs}}{40{,}000 \text{ Units produced}} = \$11$

The company did not have a beginning finished goods or work-in-process inventory, because the product is new; also assume that it did not have a work-in-process inventory at December 31, 1976. Two abbreviated income statements, distinguishing between the two costing concepts, are shown below.

DIRECTO MANUFACTURING COMPANY
Income Statement—Absorption Costing
For the Year Ended December 31, 1976

Sales	$800,000
Cost of Goods Sold	512,000*
Gross Margin on Sales	$288,000
Selling and Administrative Expenses	100,000
Net Income	$188,000

* *Calculation:* $16 per unit × 32,000 units sold = $512,000.

DIRECTO MANUFACTURING COMPANY
Income Statement—Direct Costing
For the Year Ended December 31, 1976

Sales		$800,000
Cost of Goods Sold		352,000*
Gross Margin on Sales		$448,000
Variable Operating Expenses		
Selling and Administrative Expenses		40,000
Marginal Income		$408,000
Fixed Operating Expenses and Costs		
Manufacturing Overhead	$200,000	
Selling and Administrative Expenses	60,000	
Total Fixed Operating Expenses and Costs		260,000
Net Income		$148,000

* *Calculation:* $11 per unit × 32,000 units sold = $352,000.

Since there was no beginning finished goods inventory, the $40,000 variation in net income results solely from the amount of fixed costs contained in the ending finished goods inventory ($5 × 8,000 units = $40,000).

(Ch. 22)

Certain comparative operational results under direct costing and absorption costing are summarized below.

1. In any given year when units produced are greater than units sold, reported net income under direct costing is less than under absorption costing.

2. When units produced are less than units sold, reported income under direct costing is greater than under absorption costing.

3. When units sold and units produced are the same, reported income is the same under both methods.

4. Under direct costing, increases and decreases in units sold result in proportionate increases and decreases in marginal income because only variable costs are assigned to the cost of units produced.

5. Under direct costing, the emphasis is on the number of units sold, and the net income or net loss will, therefore, move in the same direction as the sales volume. Net income or net loss cannot increase or decrease, however, in direct proportion to sales volume because unit fixed costs do not stay constant. Under absorption costing, emphasis is on both production and sales, and the net income and net loss do not, therefore, show the expected relationship to sales.

6. Under direct costing, inventory valuations are determined with fixed costs excluded and are always smaller than inventory valuations computed under absorption costing, which includes fixed manufacturing overhead costs. Therefore, working capital (current assets less current liabilities) reported on the statement of financial position under the direct costing method will always be smaller.

In conclusion, note that the difference between the results under direct costing and absorption costing stems from the amount of fixed manufacturing costs allocated to finished goods and work-in-process inventories. The advocates of direct costing argue that these fixed costs are not a part of the cost of goods manufactured during a given period. Rather, these are the costs of having the capacity to produce; hence, they are expenses and should be charged against revenue irrespective of physical production. Proponents of absorption costing argue that fixed manufacturing costs are as essential to the production of goods as are variable costs and certainly add an element of economic utility to the finished product. Moreover, net income from the sale of any unit of a product does not emerge until after the total cost of bringing that product to the point of sale has been recovered.

Unquestionably, the delineation of costs into their fixed and variable components is useful to management in studying cost-volume-income relationships. To include only variable costs in finished goods and work-in-process inventories however, leaves some doubt about the validity of the valuation of those items for such purposes as securing loans and issuing capital stock. Moreover, the undervaluation of inventories leaves some doubt about the validity of subsequent income measurement. For these reasons, direct costing has not attained the status of a generally accepted accounting procedure. Some firms, however, have set up their records on a direct costing basis; then for financial reporting and tax purposes they convert their statements to an absorption costing basis.

COST
ACCUMULATION,
AND CONTROL;
FINANCIAL
PLANNING

862

(Ch. 22)

In Chapter 1, planning and controlling functions of management were described briefly to illustrate an important managerial use of accounting information. Another approach is to examine the various cost accumulation techniques from the viewpoint of a responsibility accounting of the planning and control functions.

Responsibility accounting traces cost, expense, and revenue measurements to specific segments of the organization (usually a department, division, or section thereof). Periodic comparisons of actual figures with budgeted, planned figures can then provide a basis for the evaluation of performance of each such organizational element and for corrective action where needed (controlling).

Responsibility Accounting

At the very outset, it should be pointed out that responsibility accounting does not require a separate set of accounting records. The accounts for developing product costs described in Chapters 20, 21, and this chapter must be classified or subdivided by areas of organizational responsibility. For each area of organizational responsibility, it is necessary that cost control accounts be further broken down into controllable and noncontrollable costs and that they be classified and coded in the same manner as are the budget categories. Although the design of such an information system is complex, its operation is relatively simple after the systems application work is completed. The system can be designed so that the actual data processing can be done by a computer.

Fundamental to responsibility accounting is the budget for the operating period. In actual practice, a company's budget consists of a hierarchy of budgets and supporting schedules which culminates in projected financial statements. A simplified budget structure is graphically presented on page 864.

The starting point in preparing a budget for a business is usually planned or projected sales. Once the sales summary (see budget structure above) is determined, other forecasts and budgeted schedules will be determined on the basis of the projection of sales. Thus it is extremely important that the best possible estimate of future sales be made. The several techniques of preparing the sales budget and other accompanying summaries and schedules are covered in cost accounting and managerial accounting textbooks; thus they are not discussed here.

It should be observed, however, that the work of behavioral scientists in recent years has made clear that the reduction of the budget formulation process to a mechanical routine—especially if imposed upon the organization without participation of those whose work is directly effected—often leads to results that are contrary to overall organizational goals.

Before illustrating briefly a generalized approach to a responsibility accounting system, let us restate Figure 22-3 on a responsibility basis for 30,000 direct labor hours as shown on page 864.

STANDARD COSTS;
DIRECT COSTING;
RESPONSIBILITY
ACCOUNTING

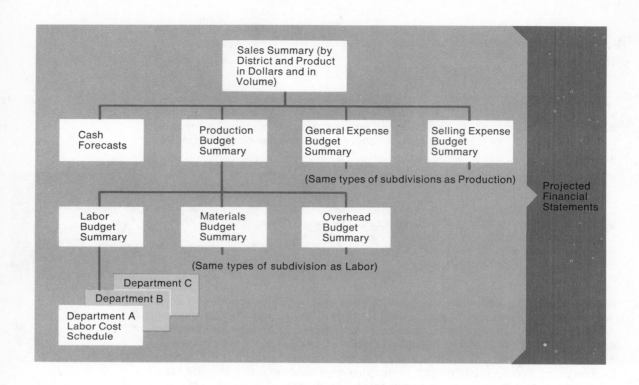

STETSON MANUFACTURING COMPANY
Manufacturing Overhead Budget—30,000 Direct Labor Hours
Month of July 1976

	Producing Departments		Service Departments		Total All Depts.
	Dept. A	Dept. B	Dept. X	Dept. Y	
Fixed costs (not controllable)	$ –0–	$ –0–	$ –0–	$ –0–	$20,000*
Variable costs.					
Factory supplies	300	200	–0–	–0–	500
Light and power	400	220	80	100	800
Indirect labor	350	200	25	25	600
Other costs	4,000	3,000	600	500	8,100
Total costs	$5,050	$3,620	$ 705	$ 625	$30,000

* These costs are not controllable; for responsibility performance measurement, they are not budgeted to the various departments.

COST
ACCUMULATION,
AND CONTROL;
FINANCIAL
PLANNING

864

Assuming that the Stetson Company attained this level in July, a performance report could be produced from the accounting records and the budget shown on page 865.

(Ch. 22)

STETSON MANUFACTURING CORPORATION
Department A—Manufacturing Overhead
Planned versus Actual Performance—July, 1976

| Budget Item | Expenditures | | Variance* |
	Budget	Actual	
Factory supplies	$ 300	$ 295	$ 5F
Light and power	400	410	10U
Indirect labor	350	500	150U
Other costs	4,000	3,975	25F
Totals	$5,050	$5,180	$ 130U

* F indicates a favorable variance;
  U indicates an unfavorable variance.

Similar reports are issued for other departments for the overhead budget and for each other schedule in the budget structure. Managers at all levels are responsible for explaining the variances from planned results and for initiating corrective action where indicated. Note, for example, that indirect labor in Department A has exceeded budget by more than 40 percent.

Responsibility accounting is not limited to commercial enterprises; the concept can also apply to government or not-for-profit organizations. The major difference is that, for these latter groups, there is greater focus on cost control, since the generation of revenue does not involve continuous effort, as it does in a business firm.

GLOSSARY

Absorption Costing A cost system whereby direct materials, direct labor, and all factory overhead including both fixed and variable components are assigned to the units of products manufactured.

Average Attainable Standards Standards or predetermined costs of manufacturing a unit of product, based on the use of average laborers working under average normal factory conditions.

Budget A financial plan for a future period developed in organizational detail.

Controlling The management function which consists of monitoring actual versus planned activity and taking corrective action where appropriate.

Direct Costing A cost system whereby only direct materials, direct labor, and *variable* overhead are assigned to the units of products manufactured; the fixed elements of overhead are treated as period expenses.

Engineering or Ideal Standards Standards or predetermined costs of manufacturing a unit of product based on the use of the most efficient laborers working under the most ideal conditions possible.

Fixed Budget A budget based on one specific predetermined level of production.

Fixed Costs Costs that, without change in present productive capacity, are not affected by change in volume of output.

STANDARD COSTS;
DIRECT COSTING;
RESPONSIBILITY
ACCOUNTING

(Ch. 22)

Flexible Budget A budget that gives recognition to varying levels of production and to the costs that change with these levels; a series of fixed budgets at different levels of production.

Flexible Budget Allowance for Overhead The amount of budgeted overhead for the capacity that is actually attained.

Idle Capacity The cost of *not* fully utilizing the machinery, plant, and other fixed factors of production; an unfavorable manufacturing overhead volume variance is one measure of cost of idle capacity.

Labor Efficiency Variance The difference in actual and standard labor hours multiplied by the standard rate.

Labor Rate Variance The difference in actual and standard rate of direct labor multiplied by the actual hours of direct labor.

Management by Exception Management's concentration on material differences between two sets of data—for example, the difference between standard costs and actual costs.

Manufacturing Overhead Budget Variance The difference between the actual factory overhead and the flexible budget allowance based on production attained.

Manufacturing Overhead Volume Variance The difference between overhead applied to production and the flexible budget allowance based on production attained.

Marginal Income Excess of revenue above variable cost of goods sold and other variable operating expenses.

Materials Price Variance The difference between the actual and the standard price of materials multiplied by the actual quantity purchased.

Materials Quantity Variance The difference between the actual and the standard quantity of materials used multiplied by the standard price.

Planning The function that defines the goals and objectives of the organization.

Relevant Volume Range The range of production capacity over which cost behavior is predictable.

Responsibility Accounting Tracing of cost, expense, and revenue to specific segments of the organization, with periodic comparisons of actual versus planned performance.

Semifixed Costs Costs that vary in steps; they are not affected by changes in volume of output within a short range of output.

Semivariable Costs Costs that include both a fixed and a variable component.

Standards A philosophy or concept adapted for creating predetermined costs of materials, labor, and overhead incorporated in the unit of product manufactured.

Standard Cost Card The document which describes the standard quantity and standard price of materials, labor, and overhead that should be incorporated in each unit of product manufactured.

Standard Costs Predetermined costs of a unit of product based on a given standards concept.

Variable Costs Costs that are affected in total by changes in the volume of output; costs that vary proportionately with the changes in some base such as production.

Q22-1. How does a standard cost system make possible the application of the principle of management by exception?

Q22-2. (a) What is the difference between a fixed budget and a flexible budget? (b) Why is it desirable to establish the variable and fixed factors of the predetermined overhead rate?

Q22-3. (a) What is meant by the average attainable standard cost of a unit? (b) Why is a standard cost system an effective means of cost control? (c) Identify and explain six variance accounts used in a standard cost system.

Q22-4. (a) What is meant by "budget allowance based on standard costs"? (b) How may the budget and volume variances be analyzed? (c) When should the standard costs be changed?

Q22-5. Standard cost as discussed in this text applies to a manufactured product; is it possible to extend the general principle of standard cost to the cost of services? Explain and give examples.

Q22-6. What is the basic difference between an income statement based on direct costing procedures and one based on the absorption costing method?

Q22-7. Give the advantages and the disadvantages of direct costing to management.

Q22-8. On January 1, 1976, the Duda Company had on hand 2,000 units of a given product; it manufactured 20,000 units and sold 12,000 units. Which costing method—direct or absorption—will produce the smaller net income for 1976? Explain the reason for the difference.

Q22-9. "All costs are controllable at one time or another in the life of a firm." In the basic format of responsibility accounting, discuss this statement.

Q22-10. If responsibility accounting does not require a separate set of accounting records, how is it implemented?

E22-1. Select the correct answer:

  1. Which of the following statements is true for a firm that uses "direct" (variable) costing?
     a. The cost of a unit of product changes because of changes in number of units manufactured.
     b. Profits fluctuate with sales.
     c. An idle facility variation is calculated by a direct cost system.
     d. Product costs include "direct" (variable) administrative costs.
     e. None of the above.

  2. When a firm prepares financial reports by using absorption costing, it may find that:
     a. profits will always increase with increases in sales.
     b. profits will always decrease with decreases in sales.
     c. profits may decrease with increased sales even if there is no change in selling prices and costs.
     d. decreased output and constant sales result in increased profits.
     e. none of the above.

(IMA adapted)

E22-2. Ten pounds of a given material at $1.30 a pound are standard for the production of a given product manufactured by the Larson Company. During August, 28,000 pounds of the particular materials were purchased at $1.32 a pound;

24,000 pounds were put into process; 2,470 equivalent units of the finished product were produced.

Determine the materials price and quantity variances.

E22-3. Six gallons of a given material at $2.20 a gallon are standard for the production of a given product manufactured by the Elliott Company. During March 1976, the following transactions (in summary form) took place:

1. Materials purchased were 34,000 gallons at $2.16 a gallon.
2. Materials requisitioned for production totaled 31,530 gallons.
3. Equivalent production for March was 5,250 equivalent units of the finished product.

Journalize the transactions involving materials, including the materials price and quantity variances.

E22-4. The Taylor Company's standard cost card for one of its products showed the following direct labor charge:

4 hours at $5.50 an hour

Standard direct labor hours for production for the month of April were 4,800; actual direct labor hours were 4,720 at a total cost of $26,432.

Determine (a) the labor rate variance and (b) the labor efficiency variance.

E22-5. The Hoffman Company's standard cost card for its product, Chemtide, showed the following direct labor charge:

7 hours at $4 an hour

The following were among the transactions that occurred during June 1976:

1. Factory payroll incurred during June was 60,920 direct labor hours, at a total cost of $242,460.
2. The standard direct labor cost was assigned to 8,680 equivalent finished units.

Journalize the transactions involving direct labor, including the labor rate · variance and the labor efficiency variance.

E22-6. The Wooten Company maintains a standard cost system and a flexible overhead budget, as shown below.

	70%	80%	90%	100%
Standard direct labor hours	140,000	160,000	180,000	200,000
Variable costs	$28,000	$32,000	$36,000	$40,000
Fixed costs	50,000	50,000	50,000	50,000
Total costs	$78,000	$82,000	$86,000	$90,000

Normal capacity is budgeted at the 100% level of 200,000 direct labor hours; the standard overhead rate is 45 cents an hour. During the period, the company worked 196,000 actual direct labor hours. Overhead was applied to production on the basis of 197,000 standard hours. Actual overhead incurred was $88,000.

Determine the manufacturing overhead (a) volume variance and (b) budget variance. (c) Prove the volume variance, using alternative computations.

E22-7. The Holmes Company produced 10,000 units of a new product during 1976; 8,000 units were sold at $25 each. Cost of production and operating expenses were as follows:

(Ch. 22)

Direct materials	$30,000
Direct labor	20,000
Manufacturing overhead—fixed	50,000
Manufacturing overhead—variable	60,000
(there was no ending work-in-process inventory)	
Selling and administrative expenses—fixed	15,000
Selling and administrative expenses—variable	10,000

Prepare an income statement, using the direct costing method.

E22-8. The Sparrow Company had a finished goods inventory of 6,000 units of a given product as of January 1, 1976, with a cost of $48,600 under the absorption costing method, or a cost of $30,000 under the direct costing method. There was no beginning work-in-process inventory.

During 1976, the Sparrow Company manufactured 113,000 units of the particular product. The fixed manufacturing overhead cost totaled $339,000 during 1976, and the variable unit cost was the same as in 1975. The company sold 100,000 units of the product at $18 each and used the FIFO method of assigning costs to the cost of goods sold. There was no ending work-in-process inventory.

Operating expenses for the year were:

| Selling and administrative expenses—fixed | $32,800 |
| Selling and administrative expenses—variable | 44,000 |

Prepare an income statement for 1976 using (a) the direct costing method and (b) the absorption costing method.

E22-9. An important concept in management accounting is that of "responsibility accounting."

Required:

1. Define the term "responsibility accounting."
2. What conditions are necessary for effective responsibility accounting?
3. What benefits are said to result from responsibility accounting?
4. Listed below are three charges found on the monthly report of a division which manufactures and sells products primarily to outside companies. Division performance is evaluated by the use of return on investment. You are to state which, if any, of the following charges are consistent with the responsibility accounting concept. Support each answer with a brief explanation.
   a. A charge for general corporation administration at 10% of division sales.
   b. A charge for the use of the corporate computer facility. The charge is determined by taking actual annual computer department costs and allocating an amount to each user on the ratio of its use to total corporation use.
   c. A charge for goods purchased from another division. The charge is based on the competitive market price for the goods.

(IMA adapted)

DP22-1. (*Standard cost accounting with a flexible budget*) The Berta Objects Company used a standard cost system and a fixed manufacturing overhead budget in 1975, as follows:

DEMON-
STRATION
PROBLEMS

Direct labor hours	80,000

Fixed costs	
Depreciation—factory building	$ 32,000
Factory taxes	2,400
Depreciation—machinery and equipment	64,000
Other costs (item data omitted)	141,600
Total fixed costs	$240,000

Variable costs	
Light and power	$ 8,000
Factory supplies	4,000
Other costs (item data omitted)	68,000
Total Variable Costs	$ 80,000
Total manufacturing overhead	$320,000

In 1976, the management decided to prepare a flexible overhead budget at 80, 90, 100, and 110 percent of capacity levels of production. The 1975 budget represents a normal capacity of 100 percent. The standard unit cost of the product is

Materials: 1 piece of Material Y-37		$ 6
Direct labor: 2 hours at $5		10
Manufacturing overhead: 2 hours at $4		8
Total		$24

Production data for 1976:

1. There was no beginning work-in-process inventory.
2. 39,600 units started in production.
3. 38,000 units completed.
4. 800 units in process (all materials added and one-quarter labor and overhead).

Condensed transactions for 1976:
1. Materials purchased totaled 40,000 pieces at $6.04.
2. Materials requisitioned for production were 39,620 pieces.
3. Direct labor was 77,000 hours at $4.96 an hour.
4. Manufacturing overhead totaled $308,800.
5. Manufacturing overhead was applied to production on the basis stated.
6. Units finished were 38,000.
7. Units sold were 37,600 at $44 each.
8. Manufacturing Overhead control account was closed and variances were entered in budget and volume variance accounts.

Required:

1. Construct the flexible budget.
2. Record the transactions for 1976.
3. Post to a Work-in-Process Inventory T account and prove the ending balance.
4. Prepare a schedule analyzing the manufacturing overhead volume variance.

DP22-2. (*Absorption and direct costing*) The Directorium Manufacturing Company produced 80,000 units of a new product during 1976 and sold 60,000 units at $50 each. Costs for 1976 were as follows:

(Ch. 22)

	Fixed Costs	Variable Costs
Direct materials		$200,000
Direct Labor		160,000
Manufacturing overhead	$440,000	320,000
Selling and administrative expenses	280,000	80,000

There was no ending work-in-process inventory.

Required:

1. Prepare comparative income statements for the year 1976, using (a) the absorption cost method and (b) the direct cost method.
2. Give the reasons for the difference in reported net income or net loss in requirements 1(a) and 1(b).

DP22-3. (*Responsibility accounting*) Prince Edward Company, a distributor of art objects, offers a cash discount of 2% to customers paying their accounts within 10 days of sale, but charges 18% a year or 1½% a month on all accounts not paid within 30 days of sale. Each department decides which of its customers will be allowed to buy on credit. The net sales of each department are computed by subtracting the cash discount actually taken on department sales. Interest revenue from finance charges is allocated to the departments on the basis of credit sales made during the current month. A summary of these monthly transactions follows:

	Total	Dept. A	Dept. B	Dept. C
Cash sales (net of cash discount)	$300,000	$ 40,000	$120,000	$140,000
Cash discounts on credit sales collected within 10 days	4,700	1,800	2,600	300
Total sales	670,000	140,000	280,000	250,000
Interest revenue on credit sales not collected in 30 days	15,600	4,216	6,746	4,638

Required:

1. Discuss the method of allocating cash discounts and the revenue from interest charges for responsibility accounting purposes.
2. Compute the net revenue due to credit sales, assigning the discounts and interest revenue in a manner which you believe would produce more useful results for management use.

P22-1. The budgeted data for the Hillsborough Company at 100 percent of capacity follow:

Direct labor hours	240,000
Variable overhead costs	$120,000
Fixed overhead costs	$180,000

Required:

1. Prepare a flexible overhead budget at 85%, 90%, 95%, 100%, and 105% of capacity.
2. Compute the overhead rate at each capacity.

(Ch. 22)

P22-2. Following are the budgeted data for the Pittsborough Company for the first three months of 1976, based on a normal capacity level of 100%.

Units	120,000
Direct materials	$360,000
Direct labor cost	$240,000
Direct labor hours	120,000
Fixed overhead costs	
Depreciation—machinery and equipment	$ 20,000
Factory taxes	8,000
Factory insurance	12,000
Miscellaneous	20,000
Variable overhead costs	
Light and power	10,000
Factory supplies	4,000
Miscellaneous	16,000

Required:

1. Construct a flexible manufacturing overhead budget at levels of 85%, 90%, 95%, 100%, and 105%.
2. Prepare standard cost cards for the product at each level of activity; compute separate variable and fixed cost rates per direct labor hour.

P22-3. The standard cost card for the Tarborough Company showed the following information on its commodity, Slinko.

Materials: 4 gallons of Slough at $4 each	$16
Direct labor: 6 hours at $6	36
Total materials and direct labor cost	$52

Production data for 1976:
1. Beginning work-in-process inventory: 200 units, 60% complete as to materials and 40% complete as to direct labor and manufacturing overhead.
2. Completed during 1976, 40,000 units.
3. Ending work-in-process inventory: 4,000 units, 80% complete as to materials and 50% complete as to direct labor and manufacturing overhead.

Transactions involving materials and labor during 1976:

1. Purchased 192,000 gallons of Slough at $4.04 a gallon.
2. Requisitioned 172,480 gallons of Slough for production.
3. Factory payroll incurred during the period was 247,680 hours at a total cost of $1,491,033.60 (ignore payroll taxes).
4. A standard direct labor cost was assigned to production on the basis of information contained on the standard cost card.

Required: Record the foregoing information in journal form, clearly establishing all material and labor variances in appropriate accounts.

P22-4. The Carrborough Company manufactures a single product in several styles, all of which are uniform as to material quantity and production time requirements. The standard cost sheet for all products is as follows:

Materials: 32 pieces at $4		$128
Direct labor: 40 hours at $6		240
Manufacturing overhead: 40 hours at $2		80
Total		$448

The standard cost was the same for July and August. Overhead distribution is based on direct labor hours. The condensed flexible overhead budget for August 1976 is:

	50%	75%	100%	125%
Direct labor hours	4,800	7,200	9,600	12,000
Variable costs	$4,800	$7,200	$9,600	$12,000
Fixed costs	9,600	9,600	9,600	9,600
Total costs	$14,400	$16,800	$19,200	$21,600

Production data for August:
1. Beginning work-in-process inventory: 20 units, 80% complete as to materials and 50% complete as to direct labor and manufacturing overhead.
2. Completed during the period, 244 units.
3. Ending work-in-process inventory: 12 units, 100% complete as to materials and 50% complete as to direct labor and manufacturing overhead.

Transactions for the month included the following:
1. Materials purchased totaled 8,200 pieces at $3.96.
2. Materials issued for production totaled 8,160 pieces.
3. Labor costs incurred were 10,040 direct labor hours at $5.90; standard labor cost was transferred to the work-in-process inventory.
4. Manufacturing overhead incurred was $20,800.
5. Manufacturing overhead was applied to production.
6. Recorded units completed.
7. Sold 260 units for $750 each.
8. Closed the Manufacturing Overhead controlling account and entered the variances in budget and volume variances accounts.

Required:

1. Give the journal entries for the month.
2. Post to a Work-in-Process Inventory T account and verify the ending balance.
3. Prepare a schedule to account for the manufacturing overhead volume variance.

P22-5. The Vanceborough Company manufactures a single product in several styles, all of which are uniform as to quantity of materials and production time requirements. The standard cost card for all products reveals the following quantities and costs:

Materials	12 pieces × $2	$ 24
Direct labor	16 hours × $8	128
Manufacturing overhead	16 hours × $8	128
Total		$280

The normal (100%) standard budgeted overhead costs consist of:

Direct labor hours	8,000
Variable costs	$16,000
Fixed costs	48,000
Total costs	$64,000

Production data for July 1976 (there was no June 30, 1976, work-in-process inventory):
1. Completed: 500 units.
2. In process as of July 31: 20 units, 40% complete as to materials and 30% complete as to labor and overhead.

Selected transactions for the month of July 1976 included the following:
1. Materials purchased were 6,400 pieces at $1.96.
2. Materials issued for production totaled 6,120 pieces.
3. Manufacturing overhead incurred was $65,600.
4. Manufacturing overhead was applied to production.
5. Closed the Manufacturing Overhead controlling account and entered the variances in budget and volume variance accounts.

Required:

1. Prepare the journal entries to record the transactions.
2. Prepare the end-of-period entries to close the four established variances.

P22-6. The standard cost card for the Greensborough Company shows the following information on its commodity, Dunker:

Materials: 8 pounds of Dinklo at $3.00	$24
Direct labor: 4 hours at $4	16
Total material and direct labor cost	$40

The schedule of equivalent production reveals the following figures:

Materials	*Direct Labor*
104,000 units	103,200 units

Selected transactions for the month of November 1976 included the following:
1. Purchased 862,400 pounds of Dinklo at $2.98 a pound.
2. Requisitioned for production 831,800 pounds of Dinklo.
3. Factory payroll incurred during the period was 412,400 hours at a total cost of $1,640,800 (ignore payroll taxes).
4. Standard direct labor costs were assigned to production at the standard rate.

Required:

1. Prepare the journal entries to record the transactions.
2. Prepare the end-of-period entries to close the four established variances.

P22-7. (*Accounting policy decision problem*) On January 1, 1975, the Townville Manufacturing Company began the manufacture of a new product. Management is disturbed because, in spite of a substantial increase in sales, profits decreased during 1976. The cost accountant explains that reported marginal income does not necessarily fluctuate in proportion to sales unless the statements are prepared on the direct costing basis. Operating data for 1976 and 1975 follow:

	1976	1975
Units sold	160,000	120,000
Units produced	100,000	200,000
Sales price per unit	$ 36.00	$ 36.00
Variable manufacturing cost per unit	12.00	12.00
Fixed manufacturing overhead	1,600,000	1,600,000
(There was no ending work-in-process inventory)		
Variable selling and administrative expenses per unit sold	0.40	0.40
Fixed selling and administrative expenses	64,000.00	64,000.00

Required:

1. Prepare income statements for 1976 and 1975, using the absorption costing method. In a parallel column, prepare an income statement for 1976 only, assuming sales of 180,000 units. Assume the use of FIFO.
2. Prepare income statements for 1976 and 1975, using the direct costing method. In a parallel column, prepare an income statement for 1976 only, assuming sales of 180,000 units.
3. Under what conditions will the net income be the same under either method?

P22-8. On January 1, 1976, the Greenville Company had a finished goods inventory of 11,200 units of its commodity, Sweetgum, which had a cost of $123,200 under the absorption costing method and a cost of $84,000 under the direct costing method.

During 1976, the Greenville Company manufactured 351,300 units of Sweetgum. The fixed manufacturing overhead costs totaled $1,405,200 during 1976 and the variable unit cost was the same as in 1975. The company sold 200,000 units of Sweetgum at $20 each and used the LIFO method of assigning costs to the cost of goods sold.

Operating expenses for the year were:

Selling and administrative expenses—fixed	$40,000
Selling and administrative expenses—variable	36,000

Required:

1. Prepare income statements for 1976, using (a) the absorption costing method and (b) the direct costing method.
2. Prepare a schedule to account for the difference in net income or net loss.

P22-9. You are the head office accountant for the Eccles Corporation, which is decentralized. The chairman of the board has heard that divisional managers avoid making investments which would lower their present rate of return on investment. The chairman is concerned, because he believes that in certain cases this practice could be detrimental to overall company profitability.

Required:

1. *Briefly,* under what conditions would this action on the part of divisional managers be detrimental to overall company profitability? (If you wish, you may use your calculation in requirement 2 to illustrate your answer.)

STANDARD COSTS;
DIRECT COSTING;
RESPONSIBILITY
ACCOUNTING

2. Using the following information, calculate an alternative "measure" of divisional managers performance which would overcome the problem referred to by the chairman.

	Division A	Division B
Sales	$5,000,000	$7,000,000
Controllable Costs	4,500,000	6,400,000
Controllable Investment	2,000,000	3,000,000

The company can raise substantial amounts of capital at an annual rate of interest of 10%.

3. Briefly explain how your "measure" of performance overcomes the problem referred to by the chairman.

P22-10. The Rockness Company produces farm equipment at several plants. The business is seasonal and cyclical. The company has attempted to use budgeting for planning and controlling activities, but the variable nature of the business has caused some company officials to be skeptical about the usefulness of budgeting to the company. The accountant for the Gibsonville plant has been using a system he calls "flexible budgeting" to help his plant management control operations.

The company president asks him to explain what the term means, how he applies the system at the Gibsonville plant, and how it can be applied to the company as a whole. The accountant presents the following data as part of his explanation.

Budget data for 1976
Normal monthly capacity of the
plant in direct labor hours   10,000 hours
Material costs   6 lb. @ $1.50 $9.00 unit
Labor costs   2 hr. @ $3.00 $6.00 unit

Overhead estimate at normal monthly capacity
Variable (controllable)

Indirect labor	$ 6,650
Indirect materials	600
Repairs	750
Total variable	$ 8,000

Fixed (noncontrollable)

Depreciation	$ 3,250
Supervision	3,000
Total Fixed	$ 6,250
Total Fixed and Variable	$14,250

Planned units for January 1976, 4,000
Planned units for February 1976, 6,000

Actual data for January 1976:

Hours worked	8,400
Units produced	3,800
Costs incurred:	
Material (24,000 lbs.)	$36,000
Direct Labor	25,200
Indirect Labor	6,000
Indirect Materials	600

COST
ACCUMULATION,
AND CONTROL;
FINANCIAL
PLANNING

876

(Ch. 22)

Repairs	1,800
Depreciation	3,250
Supervision	3,000
Total	$75,850

Required:

1. Prepare a budget for January.
2. Prepare a report for January comparing actual and budgeted costs for the actual activity for the month.
3. Can flexible budgeting be applied to the nonmanufacturing activities of the company? Explain your answer.

(IMA adapted)

P22-11. The Roby Corporation manufactures and sells a single product. The cost system used by the company is a standard cost system. The standard cost *per unit* of product is shown below:

Material—1 lb. of plastic @ $2		$ 2.00
Direct labor 1.6 hr. @ $4		6.40
Variable overhead cost		3.00
Fixed overhead cost		1.45
		$12.85

The overhead cost per unit was calculated from the following annual overhead cost budget for a 60,000 unit volume.

Variable Overhead Cost	
Indirect labor 30,000 hr. @ $4	$120,000
Supplies—Oil 60,000 gal. @ $0.50	30,000
Allocated variable service department costs	30,000
Total Variable Overhead Cost	$180,000
Fixed Overhead Cost	
Supervision	$ 27,000
Depreciation	45,000
Other fixed costs	15,000
Total Fixed Overhead Cost	$ 87,000
Total Budgeted Annual Overhead Cost at 60,000 Units	$267,000

The charges to the manufacturing department for November, when 5,000 units were produced, are given below:

Material 5,300 lb. @ $2	$10,600
Direct labor 8,200 hr. @ $4.10	33,620
Indirect labor 2,400 hr. @ $4.10	9,840
Supplies—Oil 6,000 gal. @ $0.55	3,300
Allocated variable service department costs	3,200
Supervision	2,475
Depreciation	3,750
Other	1,250
Total	$68,035

STANDARD COSTS;
DIRECT COSTING;
RESPONSIBILITY
ACCOUNTING

The purchasing department normally buys about the same quantity as that used in production during a month. In November 5,200 pounds were purchased at a price of $2.10 a pound.

Required:

1. Calculate the following variances from standard costs for the data given:
   a. materials purchase price
   b. materials quantity
   c. direct labor wage rate
   d. direct labor efficiency
   e. overhead budget
2. The company has divided its responsibilities such that the purchasing department is responsible for the price at which materials and supplies are purchased. The manufacturing department is responsible for the quantities of materials used. Does this division of responsibilities solve the conflict between price and quantity variances? Explain your answer.
3. Prepare a report that details the overhead budget variance. The report, which will be given to the manufacturing department manager, should display only that part of the variance which is the responsibility of the manager, and should highlight the information in ways that would be useful to that manager in evaluating departmental performance and when considering corrective action.
4. Assume that the department manager performs the timekeeping function for this manufacturing department. From time to time, analysis of overhead and direct labor variances have shown that the department manager has deliberately misclassified labor hours (for example, he has listed direct labor hours as indirect labor hours and vice versa) so that only one of the two labor variances is unfavorable. It is not feasible economically to hire a separate timekeeper. What should the company do, if anything, to resolve this problem?

(IMA adapted)

P22-12. The Brummet Company manufactures a fuel additive which has a stable selling price of $40 a drum. Since losing a government contract, the company has been producing and selling 80,000 drums a month, 50% of normal capacity. Management expects to increase production to 140,000 drums in the coming fiscal year.

In connection with your examination of the financial statements of the Brummet Company for the year ended September 30, 1976, you have been asked to review some computations made by Brummet's cost accountant. Your working papers disclose the following about the company's operations:

1. Standard costs per drum of product manufactured:
   Materials:

8 gal. of miracle mix	$16
1 empty drum	1
	$17
Direct labor—1 hr.	$ 5
Factory overhead	6

2. Costs and expenses during September 1976:
   Miracle mix:
   500,000 gal. purchased at cost of $950,000; 650,000 gal. used

COST
ACCUMULATION,
AND CONTROL;
FINANCIAL
PLANNING

878

(Ch. 22)

Empty drums:
  94,000 purchased at cost of $94,000; 80,000 used
Direct labor:
  82,000 hr. worked at cost of $414,100
Factory overhead:

Depreciation of building and machinery (fixed)	$210,000
Supervision and indirect labor (semivariable)	460,000
Other factory overhead (variable)	98,000
	$768,000

3. Other factory overhead was the only actual overhead cost that varied from the overhead budget for the September level of production; actual other factory overhead was $98,000, and the budgeted amount was $90,000.

4. At normal capacity of 160,000 drums a month, supervision and indirect labor costs are expected to be $570,000. All cost functions are *linear*.

5. None of the September 1976 cost variances is expected to occur proportionally in future months. For the next fiscal year, the cost standards department expects the same standard usage of materials and direct labor hours. The average prices expected are: $2.10 per gallon of miracle mix, $1 per empty drum, and $5.70 per direct labor hour. The current flexible budget of factory overhead costs is considered applicable to future periods without revision.

6. The company uses the two-variance method of accounting for overhead.

Required:

1. Prepare a schedule computing the following variances for September 1976: (a) materials price, (b) materials quantity variance, (c) labor rate variance, (d) labor efficiency variance, (e) controllable (budget or spending) overhead variance, and (f) volume (capacity) overhead variance. Indicate whether variances were favorable or unfavorable.
2. Prepare a schedule of the actual manufacturing cost per drum of product expected at production of 140,000 drums a month, using the following cost categories: materials, direct labor, fixed factory overhead, and variable factory overhead.

(AICPA adapted)

Cost, Volume, and Income Analyses in Management Decisions

23

Before costs can be analyzed and interpreted for managerial use, a specific conception of the nature and content of various costs must be known. Therefore, certain basic cost concepts are reviewed or discussed here.

Fixed costs are the costs that, without change in present productive capacity, are not affected by changes in volume of output. For instance, rent on a factory building is a fixed cost because it does not change when productive volume increases or decreases.

Variable costs are costs that are affected in total by changes in the volume of output. The cost of materials, for example, is a variable cost because it increases in direct proportion to the increase in the number of units produced.

Semifixed costs are costs that vary in steps; they are not affected by changes in volume of output within a given range of output. For example, one inspector may be required for an output of 0 to 10,000 units; two may be required for outputs of 10,001 to 20,000 units; and so on. Semivariable costs are costs that include both a fixed and a variable component. An example is a foreman who receives a base salary plus a bonus determined by a percent of production.

Marginal costs (or *differential costs*) are the differences in cost between two levels of output, or the additional cost necessary to produce an additional unit.

Opportunity cost is the cost of foregoing one thing to get an alternative; for example, a company may make a large investment in plant and equipment, thereby giving up an opportunity to invest in bonds.

Out-of-pocket costs are costs that give rise to cash expenditures, such as wages, in contrast to depreciation, which requires no cash disbursement in the current period.

As a general rule, no single cost concept is relevant for all the decisions that must be made. Different kinds of decisions require different kinds of cost calculations. The problems of determining periodic net income are different from the problems met by management in day-to-day operations. Cost calculations that serve one purpose will not always serve another.

Business decisions are made after alternative courses of action are considered; the identification of the alternatives to be considered is itself a very important aspect of decision making. A rational decision depends upon a determination of the expected consequences of each of the various alternatives. It is only the prospective differences in consequences that influence the choice. Only the factors that are affected by the choice should be viewed as relevant to the decision.

If a cost is the same for each alternative under consideration, that cost should have no bearing on the outcome of the decision. As a general rule, fixed costs are common to all alternatives and hence have little meaning to many managerial problems. The relevant costs for the majority of business decisions are variable costs; however, it must be realized that in the long run all costs are variable; hence, for long-run decisions, all costs are relevant. Moreover, in those short- and intermediate-run decisions involving the addition of an element of fixed cost, the cost that is added becomes, in effect, a variable cost for the particular decision to be made. In other words, marginal cost as defined is simply that cost which is variable for the specific decision under consideration—that is, the variable cost as such plus any additional fixed cost per unit, because of new facilities, that will be incurred in implementing the decision.

The average total absorption cost described in Chapters 21 and 22 is acceptable for measuring the amount of inventories for statement presentation, for the calculation of net income, and for long-run decisions; for example, a firm would not build a new plant unless it was sure of earning a return after the recovery of total expired costs. As a general rule, however, these average unit cost figures are unacceptable as a guide to short-run decisions.

In decision making, all relevant differences are necessarily future differences, starting from the moment of decision. Past events cannot be changed by a decision made today. Past costs in dollars of any size are not relevant costs except for possible recovery values. Present and estimated future costs are the only relevant costs. It should be emphasized, however, that sometimes the only guides to present and future costs are past book figures.

Some of the specific managerial decisions for which special cost analyses must be prepared are discussed in this chapter. As will be shown in the following discussion, these analyses may require the use of data not readily available from regular accounting records. The more complex decisions involving the acquisition of plant assets and those decisions requiring the use of quantitative techniques are discussed in Chapters 24 and 25.

BREAK-EVEN ANALYSIS

The *break-even point* is the volume of sales at which the business will neither earn income nor incur a loss; it is the point at which expired costs, or

COST
ACCUMULATION,
AND CONTROL;
FINANCIAL
PLANNING

882

(Ch. 23)

expenses, and revenue are exactly equal. The break-even point indicates to management the volume of sales needed to cover total costs and expenses, which must be broken down into only two basic components—fixed and variable. Sales in excess of the break-even point result in a net income, because fixed costs have been recovered at the break-even sales volume.

Break-even analysis is an aid to management in policy making because it highlights the effect on income of changes in selling prices, volume of sales, *product mix* (changes in the type of products sold), variable costs, and fixed costs. An understanding of the interaction of these factors assists management in budgeting and income planning and in evaluating the effects of alternative courses of action.

Computation of the Break-Even Point

Since the break-even point is the volume of sales at which the business will neither earn net income nor incur a loss, the following basic formula is indicated:

$$S_{BEP} - (FC + VC_{BEP}) = 0,$$

where S_{BEP} = sales at break-even point.
FC = total fixed costs
VC_{BEP} = variable costs at break-even point

Further, since S_{BEP} is the unknown element in the equation and since VC_{BEP} depends on a knowledge of the sales at break-even point, VC_{BEP} has to be stated as a percentage of sales. With this in mind, the equation can be restated as follows:

$$S_{BEP} = FC + VC_{BEP}$$

$$VC_{BEP} = \frac{TVC}{TS} S_{BEP}.$$

And because,

where TVC = total variable cost for whatever volume of actual or budgeted sales is used in the computation
TS = total sales volume that corresponds to the total variable cost, the equation may be restated thus:

$$S_{BEP} = FC + \frac{TVC}{TS} (S_{BEP}).$$

Rearranging the terms yields,

$$S_{BEP} - \frac{TVC}{TS} (S_{BEP}) = FC,$$

and, factoring out S_{BEP}, we have

$$S_{BEP} \left(1 - \frac{TVC}{TS}\right) = FC.$$

(Ch. 23)

Now, by dividing both sides by $1 - \dfrac{TVC}{TS}$, we obtain the basic break-even dollars formula,

$$S_{BEP} = \frac{FC}{1 - \dfrac{TVC}{TS}}$$

Sometimes unit variable cost and unit selling price—say VC and SP—are known. If so, $\dfrac{VC}{SP}$ can be substituted in the formula for $\dfrac{TVC}{TS}$. In either case, the expression is the ratio of variable cost to sales. To illustrate, assume that the budgeted data of Jackson Corporation are as shown in Figure 23-1.

The break-even point is $175,000, computed as follows:

$$\frac{\$105,000}{1 - (\$120,000/\$300,000)} = \frac{\$105,000}{1 - 0.40} = \frac{\$105,000}{0.60} = \$175,000$$

The mechanics of the break-even computation are further illustrated by the following equation:

$$\text{Variable cost percentage} = \frac{\text{Total variable costs}}{\text{Total sales}} = \frac{\$120,000}{\$300,000} = 0.40$$

Thus, 40 percent of sales is required to cover the variable costs.

	Percent
Break-even sales	100
Variable costs	40
Fixed costs at break-even point	60

Figure 23-1
Data for Break-Even
Computation

	Fixed	Variable	Budgeted Net Income Calculation
Budgeted sales:			
20,000 units $15 each			$300,000
Budgeted costs			
Direct materials		$ 25,000	
Direct labor		35,000	
Factory overhead	$ 50,000	40,000	
Selling expenses	30,000	15,000	
Administrative expenses	25,000	5,000	
Totals	$105,000	$120,000	225,000
Budgeted Net Income			$ 75,000

COST
ACCUMULATION,
AND CONTROL;
FINANCIAL
PLANNING

884

(Ch. 23)

Then 60 percent of each sales dollar (the *contribution margin percentage*) is available to cover the fixed costs.

$$S_{BEP} = \frac{\text{Fixed costs}}{\text{Contribution margin percentage}} = \frac{\$105,000}{0.60} = \$175,000 =$$

Volume of sales at break-even point

Proof of this solution follows:

Break-even sales		$175,000
Costs		
Variable (40%)	$ 70,000	
Fixed (60%)	105,000	175,000
Net income		$ –0–

The Break-Even Chart

One effective means of presenting the relationship of fixed and variable costs to sales at different volume levels is the *break-even chart.* The two charts shown (Figures 23-2 and 23-3) are based on data in Figure 23-1. It is assumed that the total quantity produced can be sold at $15. Total sales are measured on the 45 degree line rising from the origin in both charts. In Figure 23-2, the vertical line (*Y* axis) represents dollars from which both total sales and various costs can be read; the horizontal line (*X* axis) represents sales unit volume and percent of plant capacity.

The fixed costs, assumed to be unaffected by volume changes, are, therefore, represented by a horizontal line running parallel to the *X* axis. Total costs, which are affected by volume changes, are represented by a straight line starting at the fixed cost intersection on the *Y* axis and rising to the right of the chart. The point at which the total sales and total cost lines meet is the break-even point; at this point costs equal sales so that there is neither income nor loss. The spread between the lines above the intersection measures the amount of income; the spread between the lines below the intersection measures the amount of loss.

In Figure 23-2, the fixed costs line is below the variable costs line. In Figure 23-3, an inverted break-even chart, the fixed costs line is above the variable costs line to show clearly the portion of the fixed costs remaining to be recovered (loss area) before income is realized. The break-even point in the two forms is, of course, the same.

Both charts show the *relevant volume range,* which is the operating range span over which all costs are likely to be predictable as fixed or variable. This range excludes extremely high and low levels of volume where the probability of the cost behavior patterns would most likely be different from those indicated for the output of the relevant volume range; for example, semifixed costs are lower at the lower volume range and are higher at the higher volume range. The information contained in the relevant volume range of the chart is, thus, more reliable for decision making than is the information contained in the non-relevant range area of the chart.

(Ch. 23)

Figure 23-2
Typical Break-Even
Chart

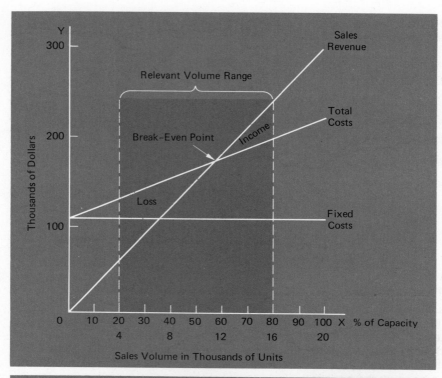

Figure 23-3
Inverted Break-Even
Chart

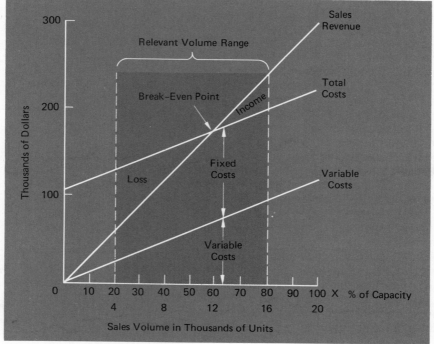

COST
ACCUMULATION
AND CONTROL;
FINANCIAL
PLANNING

886

(Ch. 23)

The charts are based on certain assumptions regarding the relationship between prices and costs and the relative proportions of the various products sold. Further assumptions are that costs are either fixed or variable, that variable costs are affected proportionately by volume changes, and that beginning and ending inventories, price levels, product mix, and technical plant and labor efficiency will remain essentially unchanged. The degree and the effect of these factors on actual and assumed conditions must be carefully balanced and evaluated in break-even analysis. Break-even charts may be prepared from budgeting data as a forecast of costs and income, or they may be based on data taken from the books as a historical presentation of cost-volume-income relationships.

The break-even point in terms of units or in terms of percentage of plant capacity used may be determined from the X-axis scale. The amounts at the break-even point are as shown (see Figure 23-2):

Break-even percent of plant capacity	58.3
Break-even units (assuming a single product or a constant mix)	11,667

The break-even percentage of operating capacity may also be verified mathematically as follows:

$$\frac{\text{Break-even sales volume}}{\text{Budgeted sales volume}} = \frac{\$175,000}{\$300,000} = 58.3\%$$

The break-even point in units is proved in the following equation:

$$
\begin{aligned}
x &= \text{number of units sold at break-even point at \$15 each} \\
\$15x &= \$15(0.4x) + \$105,000 \\
\$\ 9x &= \$105,000 \\
x &= 11,667
\end{aligned}
$$

The same computation may be made in the following terms:

$$\text{Unit}_{BEP} = \frac{\text{Fixed costs}}{\text{Unit dollars contribution margin}} = \frac{\$105,000}{\$9} = 11,667 \text{ or,}$$

Line		
1	Unit sales price (see Figure 23–1)	$ 15
2	Unit variable cost (0.40 × \$15)	6
3	Unit contribution (amount available for the recovery of fixed costs and profit)	$ 9
4	Fixed costs	$105,000
5	Unit break-even sales (line 4 ÷ line 3)	11,667

This is simply dividing the unit cost contribution into fixed cost to determine how many times it must be earned (units sold) to pay the fixed costs. The proof of this calculation is shown below.

Sales (11,667 × $15)		$175,000*
Costs		
Variable (11,667 × $6)	$ 70,000*	
Fixed	105,000	175,000
Net Income		$ –0–

* Adjusted for rounding.

As indicated, cost variability in break-even analysis has been based on the assumption that costs can be segregated into two groups—those which vary directly with volume and those which are unaffected by volume changes. This assumption is an oversimplification, and care must be taken against reaching possible erroneous conclusions, particularly for conclusions based on information outside the relevant volume range area. As shown in Chapter 22, the course of many costs is quite erratic in relation to volume. This is particularly true of second-shift costs, fringe benefits, and so on. Few if any costs are uniform in terms of units of output or time except within relatively limited volume ranges, referred to here as the *relevant volume range*.

Other limitations, in summary, are (1) if the break-even chart is based on data of only one or just a few periods, the results obtained may not be typical of the company's experience; and (2) the chart is not well designed for firms that sell a great variety of products, the proportions of which may change.

MARGINAL INCOME STATEMENTS

Marginal income, or contribution to fixed cost, is the excess of revenue over related variable costs and variable expenses. The marginal income statement, therefore, separates costs and expenses into their fixed and variable elements. It is a convenient means of presenting data to management when charts or other forms might not be as serviceable. The break-even sales volume can be calculated readily from such a statement. A marginal income statement and break-even computation for the Jackson Corporation is shown in Figure 23-4 (see Figure 23-1 for supporting data).

From information shown in Figure 23-4, the following basic equations may be derived:

Sales − Variable costs = Marginal income
Marginal income − Fixed costs = Net income
Marginal income ÷ Sales = Marginal income percentage or contribution margin percentage
Unit selling price − Unit variable cost = Contribution per unit

COST
ACCUMULATION,
AND CONTROL;
FINANCIAL
PLANNING

888

(Ch. 23)

Figure 23-4
Marginal Income
Statement

Sales (net): 20,000 units × $15 each	$300,000
Variable costs and expenses	120,000
Marginal income	$180,000
Fixed costs and expenses	105,000
Net income	$ 75,000
Marginal income (or contribution) percentage	60%
Break-even dollar volume: $105,000 ÷ 0.60	$175,000
Break-even point in units: $\dfrac{\$105,000}{\$15 - 0.4\,(\$15)}$	11,667

$$\text{Fixed costs} \div \text{Contribution margin percentage} = \text{Break-even point in sales dollars}$$
$$\text{Fixed costs} \div \text{Contribution per unit} = \text{Break-even point in units}$$

A marginal income statement is prepared to emphasize the contribution of each sales dollar toward the recovery of fixed costs and toward net income. Marginal income must equal fixed costs if the firm is to break even; marginal income must exceed fixed costs if a net income is to be realized. Thus, in Figure 23-4, 60 cents out of each sales dollar contributes toward the recovery of fixed costs up to sales of $175,000; out of each dollar of sales thereafter, 60 cents contributes to net income. Note that a marginal income statement used for decision making in a manufacturing firm requires the application of direct-costing techniques (see Chapter 22).

MARGIN OF SAFETY

The *margin of safety* is the dollar volume of sales above the break-even point, or the amount by which sales may decrease before losses are incurred. The margin of safety for the Jackson Corporation is

Sales	$300,000
Deduct break-even sales	175,000
Margin of safety	$125,000

A loss will not be incurred unless sales decrease by more than $125,000. The *percentage of safety* is computed as follows:

$$\frac{\text{Margin of safety}}{\text{Net sales}} = \frac{\$125,000}{\$300,000} = 0.4167$$

(Ch. 23)

Any decreases in sales up to 41.67 percent can be absorbed before a loss is incurred.

There is a relationship between the contribution percentage and the percentage of safety. It is:

$$\text{Contribution percentage} \times \text{Percentage of safety} = \text{Profit as a percent of sales}$$

For the Jackson Corporation at a sales level of $300,000:

$$0.60 \times 0.4167 = 0.25, \text{ or } 25\%$$

Note that 25 percent of $300,000 = $75,000, which is the net income shown in Figure 23-4.

MARGINAL INCOME PLANNING

The effect of any prospective changes in operations can be determined rapidly when data on costs are divided between the fixed and variable elements. This kind of evaluation and analysis is demonstrated in the following two cases.

Case 1. The Excel Manufacturing Company is considering the possibility of expanding its present plant facilities at a time when the plant is operating at full capacity. Two important factors that must be known before the decision is made are the sales volume required with the planned expansion to earn the current income and an appraisal from the marketing department of whether this figure can be reached and exceeded.

Assume the following data for the Excel Manufacturing Company:

	Under Present Plant Facilities		Under Proposed Plant Facilities	
Sales		$600,000		$800,000
Variable costs	$180,000		$240,000	
Fixed costs	350,000	530,000	462,000	702,000
Net income		$ 70,000		$ 98,000

The following basic formula (expanded from the break-even formula) is appropriate to determine the sales volume required with the planned expansion to earn a specified amount of income:

$$S = VC_S + FC + I,$$

where S = dollar volume of sales to attain I
VC_S = variable costs at the specifically required sales volume
I = specified income

COST
ACCUMULATION,
AND CONTROL;
FINANCIAL
PLANNING

890

(Ch. 23)

Thus, the formula can be stated:

$$S = \frac{FC + I}{1 - \dfrac{TVC}{TS}}$$

The data for the company may be substituted in the foregoing formula to determine the volume of sales needed to maintain current net income:

$$S = \frac{\$462,000 + \$70,000}{1 - (\$240,000/\$800,000)} = \$760,000$$

This is verified in conventional income statement form as follows:

Sales (S)		$760,000
Variable costs (0.30S)	$228,000	
Fixed costs	462,000	690,000
Net income (currently being earned)		$ 70,000

It is assumed in this illustration that the variable cost rate will continue to be 30 percent of sales. It is possible that the additional facilities may permit an increase in the productivity of labor or purchasing economies, thus causing a decrease in the variable cost rate. Other factors must be considered in determining whether the proposed expansion is warranted. The acquisition of additional plant and equipment involves long-term investments, possible long-term financing, and increased taxes, insurance, maintenance, and other costs. Management should be reasonably assured that it will be able to make sustained use of the added facilities.

Case 2. A corporation is considering the purchase of some special machines. Management will buy the machines if their cost can be recovered in three years—that is, if the marginal income (less out-of-pocket related fixed costs other than depreciation) generated by these machines over a three-year period is equal to their cost. Assume the following facts:

1. The machines cost $180,000.
2. The annual revenue generated by the machines will total $200,000.
3. The variable cost is 60 percent of sales.

The marginal income is $80,000 a year, computed as follows:

$$[(1.00 - 0.60) \times \$200,000] = \$80,000$$

If the annual fixed cost on these machines other than depreciation—property taxes, insurance, and so on—amounts to $6,000 a year, then the remainder, or $74,000 = ($80,000 − $6,000) a year, is recovery of the cost of the machines. At this rate, the cost of the machines will be recouped in approximately 2.4 years, determined as follows:

$$\frac{\$180,000}{\$74,000} = 2.4 \text{ years}$$

If this is the only variable on which the decision rests, then the special machines should be purchased. A more complete discussion of this and other problems involving investments in plant assets may be found in Chapter 25.

PRICING OF SPECIAL ORDERS

A decision with which management is often confronted is whether or not to accept a special order involving the production of additional units beyond outstanding commitments. An analysis of preexisting cost patterns will not necessarily furnish the required data for such a decision. Each new situation requires a new cost analysis. The probable effect of the additional order on fixed manufacturing costs, selling and administrative expenses, selling price, and possible reduction in direct material costs resulting from increased volume buying must be analyzed carefully.

If the price of the special order exceeds its marginal costs—which will equal variable costs if unused capacity is available and if there are no alternative uses for this available capacity—the offer should be accepted. To illustrate, assume the following total unit cost data for the Jason Company, based on a budgeted annual production of 60,000 units:

Manufacturing costs	
Direct materials	$ 2.00
Direct labor	2.50
Variable overhead costs	1.50
Total variable costs	$ 6.00
Fixed overhead costs ($180,000 ÷ 60,000 units)	3.00
Total unit cost	$ 9.00
Fixed selling and administrative expenses	$100,000.00

The Jason Company has been offered a long-term contract for 20,000 additional units annually at a unit price of $8.50. Since the purchaser is to attach his own label to the product, the Jason Company's established price of $15 each will not be affected. Because fixed costs are not affected by the volume of production, fixed manufacturing overhead, fixed selling expenses, and fixed administrative expenses, $280,000 in this case, will not be increased by the new order. Therefore, since the special offer price of $8.50 exceeds the unit variable cost of $6, which is also the unit marginal cost, the regular sales are not affected, and a gain of $50,000 is realized on the additional order, the offer should be accepted. The comparative budget data shown on page 893 verify this conclusion.

COST
ACCUMULATION,
AND CONTROL;
FINANCIAL
PLANNING

892

(Ch. 23)

JASON COMPANY
Budgeted Comparative Income Statement
For the Year Ending December 31, 1976

	Budgeted Production	Additional Order	Totals
Sales			
60,000 units at $15.00	$900,000		
20,000 units at 8.50		$170,000	$1,070,000
Variable Manufacturing Costs			
60,000 units at $ 6.00	360,000		
20,000 units at 6.00		120,000	480,000
Marginal Income	$540,000	$ 50,000	$ 590,000
Fixed Costs*	280,000		280,000
Net Income	$260,000	$ 50,000	$ 310,000

* Includes fixed manufacturing overhead cost of $180,000 and selling and administrative expenses of $100,000, which are assumed to be fixed costs.

The data also indicate the possibility of developing a new market through price reductions made possible by the absorption of fixed costs in the regular volume of business. This may be particularly effective when a product is sold in a foreign market or in any decisions involving levels of output or the cost of additional volume.

PRODUCT PRICING

An intricate relationship exists between the factors of price, cost, and volume. An understanding of this relationship is imperative, because it underlies virtually every decision confronting management. It is essential, therefore, that management make continuing analyses of its selling prices, particularly for competitive products.

One of the knottiest problems is calculating the effect of price on the volume of sales in terms of both short-run and long-run effects. The cost analyst plays a significant role in pricing-policy decisions by projecting the effect on costs and income of the sales volumes that may be expected at different prices.

The method of accumulating costs to arrive at total costs has been discussed in previous chapters. Total costs consist of direct costs (direct materials and labor), variable manufacturing overhead (power, supplies, maintenance), and fixed manufacturing overhead (insurance, taxes, depreciation). The process of establishing a predetermined overhead rate involves an allocation of the fixed manufacturing overhead on some arbitrary basis as well as an estimated volume factor that becomes the denominator in the overhead rate formula. The pricing of the product on this total cost basis is often considered unsatisfactory (1) because the allocation of overhead items is inherently impre-

(Ch. 23)

Figure 23-5
Marginal Income at
Various Prices

Sales Price per Unit	Quantity	Projected Sales Volume	Variable Costs ($40 per unit)	Marginal Income
$80.00	40,000	$3,200,000	$1,600,000	$1,600,000
78.00	45,000	3,510,000	1,800,000	1,710,000
75.00	55,000	4,125,000	2,200,000	1,925,000
72.50	57,000	4,132,500	2,280,000	1,852,500
67.00	65,000	4,355,000	2,600,000	1,755,000

cise, (2) because the projected volume on which the overhead rate is based is also imprecise, and (3) because total cost is not relevant to short-run decisions.

In general, however, the unit price that yields the greatest marginal income is the price that should be used for a particular product. Following this approach, therefore, a schedule should be prepared based on variable costs only, such as the one in Figure 23-5 showing the probable volume of sales and the marginal income that will result at each of the several price levels under consideration. It may be assumed that the volume-price relationships are estimated from the results of a market survey based on test sales in selected areas and from questionnaires.

A sales price of $75 a unit will provide the greatest marginal income—that is, $1,925,000. The $75 selling price does not provide the greatest margin on each unit sold; the unit marginal income is $35 compared with $40 at the $80 selling price. The increased sales volume at the lower price, however, results in a greater total marginal income..

When more than one product is priced, it is necessary to find a combination of price and volume that results in the greatest marginal income. Assume, for example, that the Baker Company manufactures two different products, X and Y, that require nearly identical production processes. Variable unit costs are $10 for product X and $10 for product Y. Facilities are available to produce a combined total of 11,000 units. The following schedule was prepared to aid management in its pricing policy:

Sales Price per Unit	Quantity	Projected Sales Volume	Variable Cost	Marginal Income
Product X				
$22	4,000	$ 88,000	$40,000	$48,000
20	5,000	100,000	50,000	50,000
16	7,000	112,000	70,000	42,000
Product Y				
$26	3,000	$ 78,000	$36,000	$42,000
23	5,000	115,000	60,000	55,000
22	7,000	154,000	84,000	70,000

COST
ACCUMULATION,
AND CONTROL;
FINANCIAL
PLANNING

894

(Ch. 23)

A combination of 5,000 units of X and 7,000 units of Y results in the largest possible marginal income ($50,000 + $70,000 = $120,000). If, however, plant capacity cannot be efficiently expanded beyond the previously assumed level of 11,000 units, the most profitable combination is 4,000 units of X and 7,000 units of Y, for a total marginal income of $118,000 = ($48,000 + $70,000).

The establishment of prices based on marginal income is the customary practice in retailing. Prices are set on the basis of a percentage markup on cost. The markup must be delicately adjusted to gauge the responsiveness of consumer demand. Studies may be made to determine the percentage of change in revenue that results from each percentage price change (elasticity of demand) for products whose sales potential fluctuates inversely with changes in price.

In these examples, it is assumed that fixed costs remain the same at all the indicated sales levels and that net income is, therefore, maximized at prices that provide the greatest marginal income. Total unit costs (fixed and variable) depend, however, on total volume, and total volume in turn depends upon the price charged. It is for this reason that cost studies also should be made showing estimates of total cost and net income at the various sales levels. Such studies might indicate maximum net income at levels different from the marginal income studies. In the last analysis, a firm must recover total costs, not just variable costs. Long-term pricing based on marginal income might result in prices set too close to the marginal income point, possibly resulting in needless cutthroat competition within the industry.

Another factor is that the firm may not be motivated exclusively by the maximum income objective. In the long run, or even in the short run, a just price resulting in a reasonable income may prove ultimately to be the best price. A short-run price based on maximized income may operate adversely in the long run by depressing future demand. There is also the possibility that competing costs and prices are such as to permit setting a price above the level indicated by the marginal income analysis if the firm should so decide.

DECIDING TO MAKE OR TO BUY

Management must often decide whether to make or to buy a particular part, product, or plant asset. If the plant facilities have already been acquired, the capacity is available, quality can be assured, and there are no negative factors, the decision depends upon a comparison of marginal costs, which in this case are equal to variable costs, with the outside purchase price of the item. (If other fixed costs have to be added, then marginal cost would be larger than variable cost.) If the variable production cost of the item—the marginal cost—is less than the quoted purchase price, then the item should be manufactured; if the quoted purchase price is less than the variable cost of the item, it should be purchased.

Assume that the Ames Company manufactures a particular part at a unit cost of $6.80 and that this cost consists of the following:

Direct materials	$1.50
Direct labor	2.50
Variable overhead costs	1.20
Total variable costs	$5.20
Fixed overhead costs	1.60
Total unit cost	$6.80

The Ames Company can purchase this part from a reliable manufacturer for $6.05. If the available plant facilities represent sunk costs that cannot be recovered by some other use of the facilities (the fixed overhead unit cost of $1.60), then the firm should continue to make the part. The variable costs of $5.20 are less than the quoted purchase price of $6.05, and the difference might be used to defray part of fixed overhead costs. If, on the other hand, the Ames Company can make an alternative and profitable use of those facilities for other purposes, it should buy the part. Under this assumption, fixed overhead costs must be included in the total cost of the part, because the company is foregoing the opportunity of making an alternate use of the facilities. With fixed overhead costs included, the unit cost to make is greater than the cost to buy—that is, $6.80 compared with $6.05.

This involves a decision whether to continue making a product or to buy it. The parallel problem—to manufacture a part or a product that is currently being purchased—involves essentially the same factors for consideration, together with such other relevant factors as the effect of the change on inventories and on working capital, on net income before and after taxes, on the rate of return on capital employed, and on the rate of return on sales. Finally, intangible factors at the top management level would also enter into the decision to make or to buy.

DEPARTMENT, TERRITORY, OR PRODUCT ABANDONMENT

The decision whether or not to abandon a supposedly unprofitable department, territory, or product involves a careful analysis of the effect of the abandonment on the fixed and variable costs and the marginal income. If a department, territory, or product produces any marginal income, it should not be abandoned unless the newly created capacity—that is, a substituted new department, territory, or product—could be committed to a more profitable use.

The departmental income statement of the Stevens Clothing Company is shown in Figure 23-6. The accountant for the company has been asked by the management to study the probable effect on total costs if the Children's Department is eliminated. Management is aware that although closing the department will entirely eliminate sales, cost of goods sold, and gross margin, certain other costs currently chargeable to the department will continue. A careful analysis reveals the cost tabulation shown in Figure 23-7.

COST
ACCUMULATION,
AND CONTROL;
FINANCIAL
PLANNING

896

(Ch. 23)

Figure 23-6 Departmental Income Statement

STEVENS CLOTHING COMPANY
Income Statement
For the Year Ended December 31, 1976

	Men's Department	Women's Department	Children's Department	Combined
Sales (net)	$78,910	$128,000	$34,400	$241,310
Cost of Goods Sold	53,656	90,444	26,630	170,730
Gross Margin on Sales	$25,254	$ 37,556	$ 7,770	$ 70,580
Deduct Operating Expenses				
Advertising Expense	$ 981	$ 1,590	$ 429	$ 3,000
Salesmen's Salaries	9,050	12,030	3,515	24,595
Commissions Expense	750	1,100	240	2,090
Rent Expense	2,160	3,600	1,440	7,200
Depreciation Expense—				
Store Equipment	400	500	100	1,000
Supervisor's Salary	2,603	5,196	1,301	9,100
Office Salary	1,158	2,313	579	4,050
Insurance Expense	480	600	120	1,200
Bad Debts Expense	75	175	50	300
Miscellaneous General Expenses	400	500	100	1,000
Heat and Light Expense	450	750	300	1,500
Total Operating Expenses	$18,507	$ 28,354	$ 8,174	$ 55,035
Net Operating Income or (Loss)	$ 6,747	$ 9,202	$ (404)	$ 15,545

As a result of this study, the effect of discontinuing the Children's Department can be reasonably forecast as follows:

Net operating income of all departments (Figure 23–6)		$15,545
Reduction in gross margin on sales (Figure 23–6)	$7,770	
Reduction in variable costs (Figure 23–7)	4,454	
Reduction in net operating income		3,316
Combined net operating income with Children's Department eliminated		$12,229

On the basis of this calculation, the Children's Department should not be eliminated even though it shows a net loss. The department contributed to the earnings of the company by absorbing a part of the fixed expenses. Elimination of the department will reduce net operating income by $3,316.

COST, VOLUME, AND INCOME ANALYSES

(Ch. 23)

Figure 23-7
Effect on Costs of
Elimination of
Children's
Department

	Operating Costs Charged to Children's Department	Effect of Elimination of Children's Department	
		Eliminated	Not Eliminated
Variable Costs			
Advertising	$ 429	$ 429	
Salesmen's Salaries	3,515	3,515	
Commissions	240	240	
Insurance	120	120	
Bad Debts	50	50	
General	100	100	
Fixed Costs			
Rent	1,440		$1,440
Depreciation—			
Store Equipment	100		100
Supervisor's Salary	1,301		1,301
Office Salaries	579		579
Heat and Light	300		300
Totals	$8,174	$4,454	$3,720

Children's Department fixed costs (Figure 23–7)	$3,720
Deduct net loss (Figure 23–6)	404
Reduction in net operating income	$3,316

If this department is discontinued, the other departments will have to absorb that part of the fixed cost which is now absorbed by the Children's Department, $3,316, which is the contribution to fixed costs or marginal income. This would result in a comparable decrease in the combined net income.

Another way of verifying this information is to compute the marginal income earned by the Children's Department: revenue of $34,400, less variable costs of $31,084 (cost of goods sold of $26,630 plus variable operating expenses of $4,454), equals $3,316, the advantage to the total firm of continuing the Children's Department.

In this example, the information used is net operating income (or income before income taxes and other expenses and revenue). Since a loss reduces income taxes, the value of the Children's Department to the total firm would really be larger than the $3,316 indicated. To simplify the problem, the effect of income taxes on the decision has been ignored. Of course, income taxes are pertinent to the problem, but their inclusion in this instance will not change the final decision.

There are, in addition, certain intangible factors that would result from the elimination of the Children's Department and which cannot be measured by an analysis of the income statement. This department brings in customers; busi-

COST
ACCUMULATION,
AND CONTROL;
FINANCIAL
PLANNING

898

(Ch. 23)

ness may be lost, because some customers will not be able to buy clothing for the entire family in one location. Furthermore, customers who intend to purchase children's clothing only are exposed to the displays of the other two departments, which may result in additional purchases from these other departments. Finally, the reduction in the volume of purchases may have a negative effect on the ability of the company to get quantity discounts.

GLOSSARY

Break-Even Point The volume of sales at which the business will neither earn income nor incur a loss.

Contribution Margin Percentage Marginal income divided by sales.

Fixed Costs Costs that, without a change in present productive capacity, are not affected by changes in volume of output.

Make-Buy Decision The decision whether to make a product or to buy it outside.

Margin of Safety The dollar volume of sales above the break-even point.

Marginal Costs The change in total cost that occurs with a small change in output.

Marginal Income The excess of revenue over related variable costs and variable expenses.

Opportunity Costs The cost of foregoing one thing—investment, operation, material, process, and so on—to get an alternative.

Out-of-Pocket Costs Costs that give rise to cash expenditures.

Percentage of Safety The margin of safety divided by net sales.

Relevant Volume Range The operating-range span over which all costs are likely to be predictable as fixed or variable.

Semifixed Costs Costs that are not affected by changes in volume of output within a given range.

Semivariable costs Costs that include both a fixed and a variable component.

Variable Costs Costs that are affected in total by changes in the volume of output.

Q23-1. Define the following terms: (a) sunk costs, (b) variable costs, and (c) out-of-pocket costs.

Q23-2. What is meant by the statement "Different costs for different purposes"? Illustrate, by explaining, how an element of depreciation, as a cost, might be treated differently for different purposes.

Q23-3. (a) Costs relevant to a decision must be present or estimated future costs. Explain. (b) Can past costs ever be relevant to a given decision?

Q23-4. (a) What is meant by the term *break-even point?* (b) How is it computed? (c) What are its practical applications? (d) What are its limitations?

Q23-5. Define the following terms: (a) operating capacity, (b) product mix, (c) margin of safety, and (d) marginal income statement.

Q23-6. Under what circumstances would it be advantageous for a manufacturer in the United States to accept a long-term contract for his product from a foreign buyer?

Q23-7. The sales price of a product should be the amount that will result in the largest marginal income. Comment.

Q23-8. Is maximum income the sole objective in determining the sales price of a new product?

Q23-9. (a) What use does management make of cost data in deciding to make or buy a certain part? (b) Should fixed costs enter into the decision?

Q23-10. (a) Is it possible for one of three departments in a retail store to show a net loss even though its elimination would decrease the total net income of the entire store? (b) What other intangible factors must be considered when deciding whether or not a certain department should be eliminated?

Q23-11. Cost-volume-earnings analysis (break-even analysis) is used to determine and express the interrelationships of different volumes of activity (sales), costs, sales prices, and sales mix to earnings. More specifically, the analysis is concerned with what will be the effect on earnings of changes in sales volume, sales prices, sales mix, and costs.
1. Certain terms are fundamental to cost-volume-earnings analysis. Explain the meaning of each of the following terms:
   a. Fixed costs
   b. Variable costs
   c. Relevant volume range
   d. Break-even point
   e. Margin of safety
   f. Sales mix
2. Several assumptions are implicit in cost-volume-earnings analysis. What are these assumptions?

(AICPA adapted)

EXERCISES

E23-1. For the year 1976, the Till Company estimates fixed costs at $312,000 and variable costs at $2.10 a unit.

1. How many units must be sold to break even, assuming a unit sales price of $5.20?
2. Prepare an income statement to prove your answer.

E23-2. The Run Company has fixed costs of $704,000 a year. Its variable costs are $10.60 a unit and its sales price is $17.60 a unit. It is considering the purchase of machinery that will increase the fixed costs to $819,000 a year, but will enable the company to reduce variable costs to $7.75 a unit.

1. Compute the break-even point before and after the acquisition of the new machinery, giving it in both sales dollars and units of product.
2. If net income before the acquisition is $140,000, how many units will have to be sold after the machinery is acquired to maintain the net income?

E23-3. The fixed costs in the Eastern Company are now $1,175,000 a year. They are

COST
ACCUMULATION,
AND CONTROL;
FINANCIAL
PLANNING

900

(Ch. 23)

expected to increase to $1,225,000 next year. Variable costs will also go up from $7.05 to $7.70 a unit. Its product sells for $15.50 a unit.

How much sales revenue must be obtained to have a net income (before taxes) of $115,000 next year?

E23-4. A new machine costing $510,000 is under consideration. The product it makes sells for $16 a unit and requires materials costing $3.50, direct labor of $5.10, and other variable costs of $0.50 a unit. Sales of 65,000 units a year are assumed. Applicable annual fixed costs other than depreciation amount to $19,000.

Over what period would this investment be recovered?

E23-5. The Jackson Company manufactures and sells 2,500,000 units of its product in the United States annually. The selling price per unit is $32; variable costs are $13 a unit; and fixed costs are $16 a unit.

Should the company accept an additional order to sell 800,000 units abroad (a) at $12 a unit? (b) at $12.65 a unit; (c) at $14.40 a unit; (d) at $16.80 a unit? Explain your answer to each question.

E23-6. The Rowely Company was organized early in 1976. During 1976, it produced 9,600 units and sold 8,960 units; costs for the year were:

Variable costs	
Direct materials	$34,560
Direct labor	46,080
Manufacturing overhead	55,200
Selling and administrative expenses	14,400
Fixed costs	
Manufacturing overhead	21,600
Selling and administrative expenses	9,600

The selling price per unit is $35.

1. Calculate the break-even point.
2. Prepare a marginal income statement for 1976.
3. Compute the margin of safety, expressed as a dollar amount.

E23-7. Roxby, Inc., can sell 35,000 units of its product at $13 a unit. The variable costs of this product are $5 a unit. However, a reduction in sales price to $10 a unit would increase units sold to 56,000. The greater volume of production would reduce variable costs to $4 a unit; fixed costs are expected to increase by $24,000.

Should Roxby reduce its selling price? Explain and support with computations.

E23-8. The Plymouth Company manufactures Exoze; unit costs are as follows:

Direct materials	$ 9.60
Direct labor	6.40
Variable overhead costs	3.20
Subtotal	$19.20
Fixed overhead costs	4.80
Total	$24.00

The company can purchase this part for $21.50.

Should Exoze be purchased: (a) if fixed overhead unit cost of $4.80 is a sunk cost? (b) if an alternative and profitable use can be made of the plant facilities now devoted to making Exoze?

E23-9. The following operational information is available for Lou's Department Store for 1976:

	Department			
	1	2	3	Total
Net operating income or (loss)	$20,000	$40,000	$(10,000)	$ 50,000
Marginal income	44,000	75,000	4,000	123,000

1. Should department 3 be eliminated?
2. If department 3 is eliminated and the 1977 operating results for departments 1 and 2 are the same as in 1976, how much higher (or lower) will the 1977 net operating income be?

E23-10. In a recent period Zero Company had the following experience:

Sales (10,000 units @ $200) $2,000,000

	Fixed	Variable	
Costs:			
Direct material	$ -0-	$ 200,000	
Direct labor	-0-	400,000	
Factory overhead	160,000	600,000	
Administrative expenses	180,000	80,000	
Other expenses	200,000	120,000	
Total costs	$540,000	$1,400,000	1,940,000
Net income			$ 60,000

Each item below is independent.

1. Calculate the break-even point for Zero in terms of units and sales dollars. Show your calculations.
2. What sales volume would be required to generate a net income of $96,000? Show your calculations.
3. What is the break-even point if management makes a decision that increases fixed costs by $18,000? Show your calculations.

(AICPA adapted)

DP23-1. (*Break-even sales; income planning in conjunction with expansion of plant facilities*) The Heald Manufacturing Company is operating at full capacity. It has under consideration a plan for the expansion of its plant facilities. Current and projected income statement data are shown below.

	Under Present Plant Facilities		Under Proposed Plant Facilities	
Sales		$500,000		$750,000
Variable costs	$200,000		$300,000	
Fixed costs	240,000	440,000	360,000	660,000
Net income		$ 60,000		$ 90,000

Required:

1. What is the present break-even point?
2. What is the break-even point under the proposed plan?
3. What will be the amount of sales necessary to realize the current net income of $60,000 under the proposed plan?
4. Prepare an income statement to prove your answer to requirement 3.

DP23-2. (*Acceptance or rejection of an offer*) The Boot Shop is operating at 65% capacity, producing 225,000 pairs of men's fancy boots annually. Actual unit cost and selling price data for the year 1976 are as follows:

Direct materials	$10
Direct labor	6
Variable overhead costs	3
Total variable costs	$19
Fixed overhead costs ($1,800,000 ÷ 225,000)	8
Total unit cost	$27
Selling price	$51

The company has been offered a long-term contract to sell 80,000 pairs of men's boots annually to a Mexican importing firm at $23 a pair. This will not affect domestic sales. Fixed overhead costs of $1,800,000, as well as fixed selling and administrative costs of $1,600,000, will not be affected by the new order.

Required: Prepare comparative statements for management indicating whether or not this long-term contract should be accepted.

DP23-3. (*Product pricing*) After conducting a market survey of its new product, the Coolidge Company prepared the following estimates:

Sales Price per Unit	Estimated Sales (units)
$40	58,000
$38	74,000
$35	86,000
$34	93,000
$26	102,000

Variable costs are estimated at $8 a unit.

Required: Determine the price that will result in the maximum marginal income and the maximum net income.

DP23-4. (*Make or buy decision*) The Britten Manufacturing Company can produce a part at the following costs:

Direct materials	$7.20
Direct labor	9.60
Variable overhead costs	4.00
Subtotal	$20.80
Fixed overhead costs	6.40
Total unit costs	$27.20

COST, VOLUME,
AND INCOME
ANALYSES

The company can purchase the part for $22.40.

Required: Should the part be purchased: (a) if fixed overhead unit cost of $6.40 is a sunk cost? (b) if an alternative and profitable use can be made of those plant facilities now devoted to making the part?

DP23-5. (*Department abandonment*) The following condensed marginal income statement is available for the Reynolds Department Store for 1976.

	Department			
	A	B	C	Total
Sales (net)	$560,000	$480,000	$400,000	$1,440,000
Variable costs	288,000	432,000	192,000	912,000
Marginal income	$272,000	$ 48,000	$208,000	$ 528,000
Fixed costs	160,000	128,000	109,000	397,000
Net operating income (or loss)	$112,000	$(80,000)	$ 99,000	$ 131,000

Required:

1. Should Department B be eliminated? Explain.
2. Assume that none of the fixed costs can be eliminated if Department B is abandoned, and that the 1977 operational results for Departments A and C are the same as in 1976. Prepare a condensed marginal income statement for 1977, assuming that Department B is eliminated.

P23-1. The Fall Company estimates its costs at full capacity as follows:

Fixed	$336,000
Variable	192,000

Fixed costs are constant at all levels of operation; variable costs vary in direct proportion to sales. Sales at full capacity are estimated at $640,000.

Required:

1. Calculate the break-even point.
2. Determine the break-even percentage of operating capacity.
3. Prepare a marginal income statement, assuming full capacity sales.
4. Compute the margin of safety, expressed as a dollar amount.
5. Compute the margin percentage safety.

P23-2. The management of the Murrow Corporation prepared the following budgeted income statement for the year 1976:

	Fixed	Variable	
Estimated sales (112,000 units at $25)			$2,800,000
Estimated costs			
Direct materials		$425,600	
Direct labor		224,000	
Factory overhead	$656,000	512,000	
Selling	128,000	65,600	
Administrative	96,000	32,800	
	$880,000	$1,260,000	2,140,000
Estimated net income			$ 660,000

COST
ACCUMULATION,
AND CONTROL;
FINANCIAL
PLANNING

904

(Ch. 23)

Required:

1. (a) Compute the break-even point. (b) Prove the break-even point. (c) Compute the break-even point expressed as a percentage of operating capacity. (d) Compute the break-even point in units, assuming a constant product mix. (e) Compute the margin of safety, expressed both as a percentage and as a dollar amount.
2. Prepare a marginal income statement.
3. Prepare a break-even chart.

P23-3. The estimate of the Crown Manufacturing Company is that fixed costs will total $1,150,000 during 1976 and that variable costs will be $11 a unit.

Required:

1. At a selling price of $24 a unit, at what level of revenue will the company break even?
2. At a selling price of $26 a unit, at what level of revenue will the company break even?
3. In order to earn $800,000 before taxes, how many units will have to be sold at a price of $25?

P23-4. (*Management policy decision problem*) The East Company can sell 70,000 units of its product at $26 a unit. The variable costs of this product are $10 a unit. However, a reduction in sales price to $22 a unit would increase units sold to 80,000. The greater volume of production would reduce variable costs to $8 a unit; fixed costs are expected to increase by $96,000.

Required: Should the East Company reduce its selling price? Explain, showing supporting computations.

P23-5. The condensed income statement for Cyril, Inc., is given below.

CYRIL, INC.
Condensed Income Statement
For the Year Ended December 31, 1976

Net Sales		$800,000
Deduct Costs and Expenses		
Variable	$400,000	
Fixed	240,000	640,000
Net Income		$160,000

The directors of Cyril are considering a plant expansion program from the present 100% sales capacity of $800,000 to $1,200,000. The expansion would increase annual fixed costs by $120,000. Variable costs would remain directly proportional to sales, and the expansion would not change the current relationship of variable costs to sales.

Required:

1. What is the current break-even point?
2. What will the break-even point be under the proposed plan?
3. What dollar amount of sales is required under the proposed plan to equal the current net income of $160,000?

(Ch. 23)

4. Prepare an income statement to prove your answer to requirement 3.

P23-6. (*Management policy decision problem*) The Beane Corporation is considering whether to purchase some special machines. Management does not wish to buy the machines unless their cost can be recovered in three years. The following information is available:

1. Cost of the machines is $575,000.
2. Sales revenue generated by new machines is estimated to be $640,000.
3. Variable cost is 65% of sales.
4. Annual fixed costs other than depreciation total $20,000.

Required:

1. On the basis of the criterion of the three-year recovery period, should the special machines be purchased? Support your answer with a computation of the period required for the investment of $575,000 to be recovered.
2. Discuss briefly any other factors that should be considered by management in deciding whether to acquire the special machines.

P23-7. (*Management policy decision problem*) The Lane Company is currently operating at its full capacity of 200,000 units annually. Costs are as follows:

Direct materials	$640,000
Direct labor	320,000
Variable overhead	160,000
Fixed overhead	96,000
Variable selling and administrative expenses	64,000
Fixed selling and administrative expenses	48,000

The product is sold under Lane Company brand for $10. Humphrey Distributors, Inc., offers to purchase 80,000 units annually for the next five years at $6.60 a unit. This offer, if accepted, will not affect the current selling price, because Humphrey Distributors will sell under its own brand name. Acceptance of the offer will have the following results:

1. Labor costs on the additional 80,000 units will be 1½ times the regular rate.
2. Variable selling and administrative expenses will increase by 8 cents a unit on the additional units only.
3. The required additional materials can be purchased at a 5% volume discount.
4. All other cost factors will remain the same.

Required: Should Lane Company accept the offer? Show all your computations in support of your conclusion.

P23-8. The Flora Company has the facilities to produce two additional products, Horex and Borex, which require approximately the same production processes. The following data were made available to management to aid in establishing sales prices and product mix:

(Ch. 23)

Horex		Borex	
Estimated Sales Units	*Sales Price per Unit*	*Estimated Sales Units*	*Sales Price per Unit*
9,600	$104	7,200	$122
11,600	98	12,000	112
16,400	75	16,800	104
Variable costs per unit are $40.		Variable costs per unit are $56.	

Required: What product mix of Horex and Borex will result in the largest marginal income?

P23-9. (*Management policy decision problem*) The Rail Company is presently purchasing a package of five parts used in the manufacture of its finished product. Comparative costs to manufacture the parts and to buy them outside are as shown:

Part No.	*Estimated Materials Labor, and Variable Overhead to Make*	*Cost to Buy*
1	$28.80	$32.00
2	13.60	12.00
3	10.40	8.80
4	8.00	11.20
5	14.40	16.00
Totals	$75.20	$80.00

The Rail Company has the capacity to produce these parts, and at the present time it has no alternative profitable use for the facilities. Making the parts will not increase fixed costs of $100,000.

Required:

1. What is the proper decision? The finished product sells for $140.
2. Assume that the Rail Company is presently purchasing 32,000 units of each part annually, that it can use the available plant facilities to make and sell annually 16,000 units of a new product without increasing fixed costs, and that this will result in an estimated marginal income of $10.40 a unit. What is the proper decision under these circumstances?

P23-10. (*Management policy decision problem*) The management of the Welch Company is considering the elimination of Department B. The departmentalized income statement follows:

(Ch. 23)

WELCH COMPANY
Income Statement
For the Year Ended December 31, 1976

	Dept. A	Dept. B	Combined
Sales (net)	$214,400	$72,000	$286,400
Cost of Goods Sold	108,800	48,000	156,800
Gross Margin on Sales	$105,600	$24,000	$129,600
Operating Expenses			
Advertising Expense	$ 6,720	$ 1,920	$ 8,640
Salesmen's Salaries Expense	16,000	9,600	25,600
Office Salaries Expense	5,600	2,720	8,320
Insurance Expense	1,440	960	2,400
Bad Debts Expense	1,600	800	2,400
Miscellaneous General Expense	2,880	1,440	4,320
Rent Expense	17,600	8,000	25,600
Depreciation Expense—Store Equipment	3,200	1,920	5,120
Total Operating Expenses	$ 55,040	$27,360	$ 82,400
Net Operating Income (Loss)	$ 50,560	$ (3,360)	$ 47,200

The following additional data have been submitted to management on the proposed elimination of Department B:

1. There will be a 15% decline in the sales of Department A. The cost of goods sold varies directly with the sales volume.

2. The operating expenses of Department A will decrease as follows:
   a. Insurance Expense by 4%
   b. Bad Debts Expense by 9%
   c. Miscellaneous General Expense by 12%

3. The elimination of Department B will have the following effect on the operating expenses of Department B:
   a. Advertising expense, salesmen's salaries, insurance expense, and bad debts expense will be eliminated.
   b. Of the apportioned miscellaneous general expense, 80% will not be incurred.
   c. Office salaries will be reduced by $1,500 through the dismissal of some part-time employees.
   d. There will be no reduction in rent expense or in depreciation expense—store equipment.

Required:

1. Prepare a statement showing the probable effect on operating costs if Department B is eliminated.
2. Prepare a statement showing the effect on net income if Department B is eliminated.

P23-11. (*Management policy decision problem*) The Tall Company has three sales territories, X, Y, and Z. Management is considering the elimination of Territory

(Ch. 23)

X. The following condensed information has been prepared to aid in making this decision:

TALL COMPANY
Marginal Income Statement
For the Year Ended December 31, 1976

| | Territory | | | |
	X	Y	Z	Total
Sales (net)	$350,000	$400,000	$600,000	$1,350,000
Variable Costs	210,000	160,000	240,000	610,000
Marginal Income	$140,000	$240,000	$360,000	$ 740,000
Fixed Costs	200,000	100,000	150,000	450,000
Income (Loss)	$ (60,000)	$140,000	$210,000	$ 290,000

None of the fixed costs of Territory X can be eliminated.

Required: Prepare a report to aid management in deciding whether to discontinue Territory X.

P23-12. (*Management policy decision problem*) The Parham Oil Company operates a chain of service stations throughout the local area. Each station sells the usual service station products: gasoline, oil, tires, batteries, automobile accessories. All the products are purchased in bulk by the home office and delivered on a scheduled basis to each station. If a station manager foresees that the quantities he will need will vary by more than 5% from the scheduled quantities, he calls the home office at least twenty-four hours in advance of the anticipated delivery time and changes the standing order.

Being an astute businessman, Otis Lester, the president and major stockholder of the company, has the accountant prepare a separate income statement for each station. Also, he often asks for income statements by product line within each station. His main concern at this time, however, is the poor overall operating results of the station located in Johnson City. This station was once considered profitable, but since a nearby military base was closed, business has declined. The most recent income statement is typical of each of the past three years.

Sales		$177,000
Cost of Goods Sold		138,000
Gross Margin on Sales		$ 39,000
Operating Expenses (listed alphabetically)		
Advertising (Company-oriented and allocated equally to each station)	$ 1,520	
Attendants' Salaries (the number of attendants is adequate for the current volume)	16,800	
Depreciation—Building and Equipment	8,000	

Home Office Expenses (allocated to each station based on station sales)	7,200	
Insurance (fire and public liability)	1,120	
Interest on average book Investment (a book charge only; all long-term funds are provided by the stockholders)	7,680	
Local Property Taxes and Privilege Licenses	6,100	
Manager's Bonus	640	
Manager's Salary	7,700	
Payroll Taxes (attendants' salaries and manager's salary and bonus)	1,675	
Repairs and Maintenance (on building and equipment)	440	
Station Supplies	5,600	
Utilities (electricity, heat, telephone, and water)	500	
Total Operating Expenses		64,975
Net Loss		$ (25,975)

Required:

1. As a management consultant with the local certified public accounting firm, what would you recommend to Lester as the course of action regarding the station in Johnson City? Some possibilities are (a) to continue to operate as is, (b) to discontinue operation, (c) to initiate local advertising, and (d) to sell the station. If your recommendation is to sell the station, what is the minimum amount that Lester should accept?
2. Give the reason(s) for your recommendation.
3. What overall business objective will your recommendation help to achieve? Justify this objective.
4. Support your recommendation with appropriate computations.
5. Identify some nonaccounting factors that could influence a decision of this type.
6. Which accounting techniques, if any, do you think should be changed? How should they be changed? Why should they be changed?
7. If the division into variable and fixed costs remains as it is and current accounting procedures are continued, by how much must sales increase in order for this station to break even?
8. How much must sales be in order for this station to report a net income of $10,000?

P23-13. (*Management policy decision problem*) The Vernom Corporation, which produces and sells to wholesalers a highly successful line of summer lotions and insect repellents, has decided to diversify in order to stabilize sales throughout the year. A natural area for the company to consider is the production of winter lotions and creams to prevent dry and chapped skin.

After considerable research, a winter products line has been developed. However, because of the conservative nature of the company management, Vernom's president has decided to introduce only one of the new products for this coming winter. If the product is a success, further expansion in future years will be initiated.

The product selected (called Chap-off) is a lip balm that will be sold in a

COST
ACCUMULATION,
AND CONTROL;
FINANCIAL
PLANNING

910

lipstick-type tube. The product will be sold to wholesalers in boxes of 24 tubes for $8 a box. Because of available capacity, no additional fixed charges will be incurred to produce the product. However, a $100,000 fixed charge will be absorbed by the product to allocate a fair share of the company's present fixed costs to the new product.

Using the estimated sales and production of 100,000 boxes of Chap-off as the standard volume, the accounting department has developed the following costs:

Direct Labor	$2.00/box
Direct Materials	3.00/box
Total Overhead	1.50/box

Vernom has approached a cosmetics manufacturer to discuss the possibility of purchasing the tubes for Chap-off. The purchase price of the empty tubes from the cosmetics manufacturer would be $.90 per 24 tubes. If the Vernom Corporation accepts the purchase proposal, it is estimated that direct labor and variable overhead costs would be reduced by 10% and direct material costs would be reduced by 20%.

Required:

1. Should the Vernom Corporation make or buy the tubes? Show calculations to support your answer.
2. What would be the minimum purchase price acceptable to the Vernom Corporation for the tubes? Support your answer with an appropriate explanation.
3. Instead of sales of 100,000 boxes, revised estimates show sales volume at 125,000 boxes. At this new volume, additional equipment, at an annual rental of $10,000, must be acquired to manufacture the tubes. However, this incremental cost would be the only additional fixed cost required, even if sales increased to 300,000 boxes. (The 300,000 level is the goal for the third year of production.) Under these circumstances, should the Vernom Corporation make or buy the tubes? Show calculations to support your answer.
4. The company has the option of making and buying at the same time. What would be your answer to requirement 3 if this alternative was considered? Show calculations to support your answer.
5. What nonquantifiable factors should the Vernom Corporation consider in determining whether they should make or buy the lipstick tubes?

(IMA adapted)

P23-14. (*Management policy decision problem*) Victor Calderone started a pizza restaurant in 1972. He rented a building for $400 a month. Two women were hired to work full time at the restaurant and six college boys were hired to work 30 hours a week delivering pizza. An outside accountant was hired (at $300 a month) for tax and bookkeeping purposes. The necessary restaurant equipment and delivery cars were purchased with cash. Calderone has noticed that expenses for utilities and supplies have been rather constant.

Calderone increased his business between 1972 and 1976. Profits have more than doubled since 1972. Calderone does not understand why his profits have increased faster than his volume.

The following projected income statement for 1976 has been prepared by the accountant:

CALDERONE COMPANY
Projected Income Statement
For the Year Ended December 31, 1976

Sales		$95,000
Cost of Food Sold	$28,500	
Wages & Fringe Benefits of Restaurant Help	8,150	
Wages & Fringe Benefits of Delivery Boys	17,300	
Rent	4,800	
Accounting Services	3,600	
Depreciation of Delivery Equipment	5,000	
Depreciation of Restaurant Equipment	3,000	
Utilities	2,325	
Supplies (Soap, Floor Wax, etc.)	1,200	73,875
Net Income Before Taxes		$21,125
Income Taxes		6,338
Net Income		$14,787

Note: The average pizza sells for $2.50. Assume that Calderone pays 30% of his income in income taxes.

Required:

1. What is the break-even point in number of pizzas that must be sold?
2. What is the cash flow break-even point in number of pizzas that must be sold?
3. If Calderone withdraws $4,800 for personal use, how much cash will be left from the 1976 income producing activities?
4. Calderone would like an after-tax net income of $20,000. What volume must be reached in number of pizzas sold in order to obtain the desired income?
5. Briefly explain to Calderone why his profits have increased at a faster rate than his sales.
6. Briefly explain to Calderone why his cash flow for 1976 will exceed his profits.

(IMA adapted)

P23-15. (*Management policy decision problem*) E. Berg and Sons build custom-made pleasure boats which range in price from $10,000 to $250,000. For the past 30 years, Edward Berg, Sr., has determined the selling price of each boat by estimating the costs of material, labor, and a prorated portion of overhead, and adding 20% to these estimated costs.

For example, a recent price quotation was determined as follows:

Direct Materials	$ 5,000
Direct Labor	8,000
Overhead	2,000
	$15,000
Plus 20%	3,000
Selling price	$18,000

The overhead figure was determined by estimating total overhead costs for the year and allocating them at 25% of direct labor.

COST
ACCUMULATION,
AND CONTROL;
FINANCIAL
PLANNING

912

(Ch. 23)

If a customer rejected the price and business was slack, Berg, Sr., would often be willing to reduce his markup to as little as 5% over estimated costs. Thus, average markup for the year is estimated at 15%.

Ed Berg, Jr., has just completed a course on pricing and believes the firm could use some of the techniques discussed in the course. The course emphasized the contribution margin approach to pricing and Berg, Jr., feels such an approach would be helpful in determining the selling prices of the custom-made pleasure boats.

Total overhead, which includes selling and administrative expenses for the year, has been estimated at $150,000, of which $90,000 is fixed and the remainder is variable in direct proportion to direct labor.

Required:

1. Assume that the customer in the example rejected the $18,000 quotation and also a $15,750 quotation (5% markup) during a slack period. The customer countered with a $15,000 offer.
   a. What is the difference in net income for the year between accepting or rejecting the customer's offer?
   b. What is the minimum selling price Berg, Jr., could have quoted without reducing or increasing net income?
2. What advantages does the contribution margin approach to pricing have over the approach used by Berg, Sr.?
3. What are the pitfalls, if any, to contribution margin pricing?

(IMA adapted)

P23-16. (*Management policy decision problem*) The Justa Corporation produces and sells three products, A, B, and C; these are sold in a local market and in a regional market. At the end of the first quarter of the current year, the following income statement has been prepared:

	Total	Local	Regional
Sales	$1,300,000	$1,000,000	$300,000
Cost of Goods Sold	1,010,000	775,000	235,000
Gross Margin	$ 290,000	$ 225,000	$ 65,000
Selling Expenses	$ 105,000	$ 60,000	$ 45,000
Administrative Expenses	52,000	40,000	12,000
	$ 157,000	$ 100,000	$ 57,000
Net Income	$ 133,000	$ 125,000	$ 8,000

Management has expressed special concern with the regional market because of the extremely poor return on sales. This market was entered a year ago because of excess capacity. It was originally believed that the return on sales would improve with time, but after one year no noticable improvement can be seen from the results as reported in the above quarterly statement.

In attempting to decide whether to eliminate the regional market, management has studied the following data:

	Products		
	A	B	C
Sales	$500,000	$400,000	$400,000
Variable Manufacturing Costs as a Percentage of Sales	60%	70%	60%
Variable Selling Expenses as a Percentage of Sales	3%	2%	2%

COST, VOLUME, AND INCOME ANALYSES

Sales by Markets

Product	Local	Regional
A	$400,000	$100,000
B	300,000	100,000
C	300,000	100,000

The administrative expenses and fixed manufacturing costs are common to the three products and to the two markets and are fixed for the period. Remaining selling expenses are fixed for the period and separable by market. All fixed expenses are based on a prorated yearly amount.

Required:

1. Prepare the quarterly income statement, showing contribution margins by markets.
2. Assuming there are no alternative uses for the Justa Corporation's present capacity, would you recommend dropping the regional market? Why or why not?
3. Prepare the quarterly income statement, showing contribution margins by products.
4. It is believed that a new product can be ready for sale next year if the Justa Corporation decides to go ahead with continued research. The new product can be produced by simply converting equipment presently used in producing Product C. This conversion will increase fixed costs by $10,000 a quarter. What must be the minimum contribution margin per quarter for the new product to make the changeover financially feasible?

(*IMA adapted*)

P23-17. (*Management policy decision problem*) R. A. Ro and Company, maker of quality handmade pipes, has experienced a steady growth in sales for the past five years. Increased competition, however, has led John Ro, the president, to believe that an aggressive advertising campaign will be necessary next year to maintain the company's present growth.

To prepare for next year's advertising campaign, the company's accountant has prepared and presented Ro with the following data for the current year, 1975:

Cost Schedule

Variable Costs:	
Direct Labor	$8.00/pipe
Direct Materials	3.25/pipe
Variable Overhead	2.50/pipe
Total Variable Costs	$13.75/pipe
Fixed Costs	
Manufacturing	$ 25,000
Selling	40,000
Administrative	70,000
Total Fixed Costs	$135,000
Selling Price, per pipe:	$25.00
Expected Sales, 1975 (20,000 units)	$500,000
Tax Rate: 40%	

Ro has set the sales target for 1976 at a level of $550,000 (or 22,000 pipes).

COST
ACCUMULATION,
AND CONTROL;
FINANCIAL
PLANNING

914

(Ch. 23)

Required:

1. What is the projected after-tax net income for 1975?
2. What is the break-even point in units for 1975?
3. Ro believes an additional selling expense of $11,250 for advertising in 1976, with all other costs remaining constant, will be necessary to attain the sales target. What will be the after-tax net income for 1976 if the additional $11,250 is spent?
4. What will be the break-even point in dollar sales for 1976 if the additional $11,250 is spent for advertising?
5. If the additional $11,250 is spent for advertising in 1976, what is the required sales level in dollar sales to equal 1975 after-tax net income?
6. At a sales level of 22,000 units, what is the maximum amount which can be spent on advertising if an after-tax net income of $60,000 is desired?

(IMA adapted)

Quantitative Techniques for Decision Making

24

The executive of a business—as well as all individuals—is involved in the continuous process of decision making. Some of the decisions that he makes will have a long-range effect and may be crucial to the very survival of the firm. When the executive makes the right decisions and executes them properly, he will have succeeded in his most important function. The purpose of this chapter is to examine the decision-making process and to discuss several of the quantitative techniques or models useful in executive decision making. A model is a representation or an approximation of a real-life situation or process. The model makes it possible to project the possible consequences of a decision and to pretest that decision prior to making the actual commitment involved. Models may represent the ideal or the pragmatic, they may be concrete or abstract, they may be operating or nonoperating. Hence they describe and inform.

The executive makes his decisions and choices with the foreknowledge that he has control over only some of the factors involved, such as the amount of money required, the manpower requirements, and the amount of materials needed, but he cannot control such outside forces as the reaction of competitors, the state of the economy, the weather, and many others.

Decision making requires all kinds of information at each state of the decision-making process. The decision maker must be clear as to his objectives, must ask the right questions, and must gather data. He must examine past decisions and measure past performances as guides to the future, and he must make a careful evaluation of the risks involved and the probable gains and losses. He must know what the alternatives are as well as the constraints in men, money, materials, and technical and managerial expertise, and must compare these alternatives with the resources that will be required. He must make the best use of his resources. He does this by choosing the best of the available alternatives. If there are no alternatives, there is no choice and no decision to make. To choose, the decision maker must know what his (the firm's) goals and objectives are. If the decision maker knows his objectives, if he can measure the possible outcomes of each available alternative, he will then choose that alternative which comes closest to achieving his objective.

ROLE OF ACCOUNTING IN DECISION MAKING

The use of mathematical models may appear to be a departure from what is commonly recognized as the domain of accounting. But conventional accounting, with its reliance on historical cost, often does not furnish the kind of information needed by the business executive for making decisions. Accounting provides information that may lead to prediction. It does not seek optimal solutions and does not indicate what would have occurred if an alternative decision had been made; that is, accounting does not measure the optimum allocation of resources—the opportunity cost of the decision. If fundamental concepts and models from mathematics, economics, and the natural and behavioral sciences provide tools for improving the decision-making process, then the accountant must integrate these into his work. Otherwise, he forfeits his role in the vital planning and control functions of the firm.

Since the decision maker must choose, he must formulate guidelines and criteria—cost minimization, optimum return on investment, maximum sales—by which to judge and measure each of the available alternatives from which he will make his choice. Scientific models and the computer provide the decision maker with the means for systematizing the choice process. This is the purpose of the models and techniques discussed below.

DECISIONS UNDER RISK

Probability

Since the decision maker must choose from several alternatives, prior to the choice decision he must measure the probable outcome of each alternative for comparison. But the outcome of an alternative cannot always be predicted with certainty, and most decisions affecting the future involve some lack of certainty. The theories of probability provide the means for measuring the risk and uncertainty in the decision. Technically, a decision problem under risk is when the probability of each outcome is known; a decision problem under uncertainty is when the probability of each outcome is, by definition, unknown and a decision under conditions of certainty is a situation in which all possible outcomes are known. The tossing of a coin provides a simple illustration. Numbers are assigned to all possible outcomes of an event. The scale used is 1 and the range is from 0 to 1, with 0 as the measure of an event that can never occur—two heads on the toss of a single coin—and 1 as the measure of an

(Ch. 24)

event that is certain to occur—either a head or a tail on the toss of a coin. If the event is the showing of a head on the toss of a fair coin, the only possible outcome is either a head or a tail, and the number 1/2 is assigned to each outcome. Numbers are assigned on the basis of logic or subjective judgment or by experimentation and testing. Logic dictates assigning 1/2 to the probability of a head on the toss of a coin, 1/6 that the roll of a die will produce a 5, and 1/52 to the probability of a draw of the jack of clubs from a complete and well-shuffled deck of cards. Similarly, if two defective flashlight batteries are commingled with six good batteries in a container, the likelihood of selecting a good battery is 6/8 and the probability of selecting a defective battery is (8/8 − 6/8) = 2/8. Subjective judgment or intuition dictates the probability to be assigned to the event that it will rain tomorrow or to the event of a rise in the Dow-Jones stock market averages. On the other hand, if the owner of a store wants to know the probability of there being more than ten customers in his store during a particular hour of a particular day, he can make actual counts over a period of days and calculate the probability based on the number of times the event occurred over the number of tests he conducted. However evaluated, the same rules can be used for calculating all these probabilities.

From this it can be generalized that the probability of an equally likely event is 1 divided by the number of possible events ($1/n$), the events being mutually exclusive—a single toss of a coin will not show *both* a head and a tail—and collectively exhaustive—on any single toss of the coin, it is certain that either a head or a tail will show.

Numbers can also be assigned to the event head on the first toss of a coin followed by a head on the second toss of the coin, or to the probability of three heads on three consecutive tosses of a coin. These probabilities are diagramed in Figure 24-1.

The sum of the probabilities on each toss is still the sum of the separate probabilities, but the probabilities of each of the possible outcomes of the two tosses combined is the product of their individual probabilities or $0.5 \times 0.5 = 0.25$. These can be read by tracing each of the four equally likely paths (HH, HT, TH, TT), the probability of any of the four paths being 1/4. The first set of branches traces the two possible outcomes on the first toss of the coin and the second set traces the possible outcomes of the second toss. The possible outcomes on the second toss are not affected by the results of the first toss. To avoid having to show each item separately—a laborious task when the number of tosses is large and to avoid a possibly confusing array of numbers—a *frequency* distribution such as that shown in Figure 24-2 may be prepared.

The concepts discussed above can be applied to business decision making, although frequency distributions such as those shown in Figure 24-2 are not as easily determinable, and equally likely outcomes cannot be assumed. But if a decision is to be made—whether or not to market a new product, to bid on a contract, or to predict the weather or some other state of nature—it is better to gather the available information and establish the probabilities than to proceed purely from hunch. Systematization of the analytical process will, in itself, improve the decision-making process. If, further, the probability of each outcome is associated with a dollar value, an *expected value* can be derived. Expected value is the arithmetic average of all possible values and is calculated by multiplying the numerical value of each possible outcome by its related probability and summing the products.

(Ch. 24)

Figure 24-1 Tree Diagram: 2 and 3 Coin Tosses

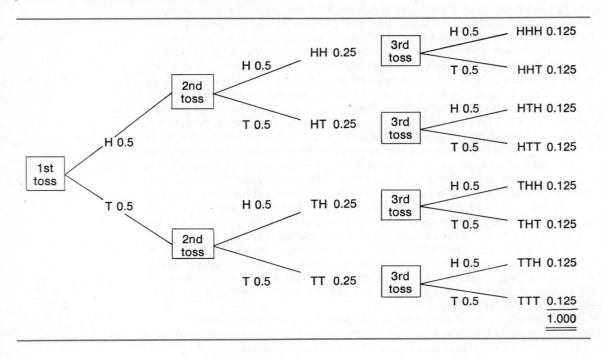

To illustrate, assume that a salesman, in planning his calls for the next day, is undecided whether to call on customer A in city X or customer B in city Y. His decision is based on the maximum expected dollar value of the order. He cannot call on both A and B. The size of the order is directly affected by whether or not it is raining on the day of the call. The weather bureau predicts a 20 percent

Figure 24-2
Frequency
Distribution: 2 and 3
Coin Tosses

Outcomes 2 Tosses	Frequency	Probability
2 heads	1	0.25
1 head and 1 tail	2	0.50
2 tails	1	0.25
	4	1.00
Outcomes 3 Tosses		
3 heads	1	0.125
2 heads and 1 tail	3	0.375
1 head and 2 tails	3	0.375
3 tails	1	0.125
	8	1.000

COST
ACCUMULATION,
AND CONTROL;
FINANCIAL
PLANNING

920

(Ch. 24)

chance of rain the next day for both cities. A convenient means of structuring this information, together with the expected order sizes in dollars, is in the form of a *payoff matrix* with the rows representing the alternatives or strategies and the columns representing the risks and uncertainties or states of nature as shown in Figure 24-3. Since the salesman's goal is to maximize his expected value and since strategy S₁ has the higher expected value, he should visit customer A.

Figure 24-3
Payoff Matrix

State of Nature	N_1	N_2
Probability	20%	80%
Weather	Rain	Sunny
S1: Customer A	$100	$300
S2: Customer B	200	250

S1: EV = 0.2($100) + 0.8($300) = $260
S2: EV = 0.2($200) + 0.8($250) = $240

Probabilities may be applied to both positive and negative values, thereby making it possible to bring differing viewpoints to bear on a decision. Assume, for example, that there is a 70 percent chance that a certain decision will result in a $10,000 gain and a 30 percent chance that it will result in a $5,000 loss. The expected value of the decision is calculated as follows:

0.7 ($10,000)	=	$7,000
0.3 (−5,000)	=	−1,500
Expected value		$5,500

DECISIONS UNDER CERTAINTY

Inventory Models

How much of each size, style, or color, to carry in stock, how much and how frequently to order or how much to produce in a given production run are crucial policy decisions for the businessman. The extreme positions are (1) to stock enough so as to be able to fill all orders and never be out of stock or (2) to produce only on receipt of an order from a customer. But either of these extremes would be too costly or impractical for most businesses. What is needed is a policy that will balance supply and demand at an economical level consistent with the firm's goals, whether they be to maintain stable employment, maximum customer satisfaction, stable production runs, maximum earnings, or maximum sales.

The expenses involved in inventory decisions fall into two categories: (1) those which increase with increases in lot size ordered (handling and storing, spoilage and obsolescence, insurance, taxes, rent, heat, light, cost of capital) and (2) those expenses which decrease with increases in lot size (clerical,

QUANTITATIVE
TECHNIQUES
FOR DECISION
MAKING

setup, back ordering, loss of orders and customer goodwill, shipping). Thus, as one cost increases, the other decreases. The objective is to minimize total cost involved. This is achieved when the quantity ordered is that amount at which the cost of ordering is exactly equal to the cost of carrying the goods on hand. To illustrate, assume a company uses 12,000 units annually of a steel part that costs $10 each. It costs $150 to place an order, and the annual carrying costs are 4 percent of the cost of the part or 40 cents ($10 × 0.04) per unit on hand. The schedule in Figure 24-4 shows that the optimum ordering frequency is 4 orders a year and the optimum order quantity is 3,000 parts.

Figure 24-4   Optimal Lot Size

(1) Orders per Year	(2) Quantity per Order (12,000 ÷ col. 1)	(3) Order Cost (col. 1 × $150)	(4) Carrying Cost (½ of col. 2 × $0.40)	(5) Total Annual Cost (cols. 3 + 4)
12	1,000	$1,800	$ 200	$2,000
6	2,000	900	400	1,300
4	3,000	600	600	1,200
3	4,000	450	800	1,250
2	6,000	300	1,200	1,500
1	12,000	150	2.400	2,550

In Figure 24-4, six different order sizes were tested to arrive at the optimum lot size. A much simpler way to solve this kind of a problem is to use a formula based on the general model shown in Figure 24-5. This model can be best explained by relating it to the specific data in Figure 24-4. The curves in Figure 24-5 are not intended to represent the specific facts on which Figure 24-4 is based but rather as a picture of the general model.

Curve C_1, annual ordering cost, represents those costs which decrease with increases in lot size and is represented in part by column 3 of Figure 24-4. The amount represented by a point on this curve is a function (a) of the cost of placing one order, (b) of the total demand for the year, and (c) of the quantity per order. The number of orders per year is the annual demand divided by the quantity per order.

Curve C_2, annual carrying cost, shows those costs which increase with increases in lot size and is represented in part by column 4 of Figure 24-4. The amount represented by a point on this curve is a function (a) of the annual carrying cost per unit and (b) of one-half the ordering quantity (one-half of column 2 or average inventory).

Curve TC is the total annual cost, or the sum of curves C_1 and C_2, and is represented by column 5 in Figure 24-4.

The actual shapes of the three curves will vary with the facts in any specific situation.

Since the objective is to minimize the total C_1 and C_2 costs and since curve TC represents that total, it follows that the optimum ordering quantity is represented by the lowest point on the curve TC, the point at which the slope is zero. It is directly above the crossover point of curves C_1 and C_2; that is, the sum of

COST
ACCUMULATION
AND CONTROL;
FINANCIAL
PLANNING

922

(Ch. 24)

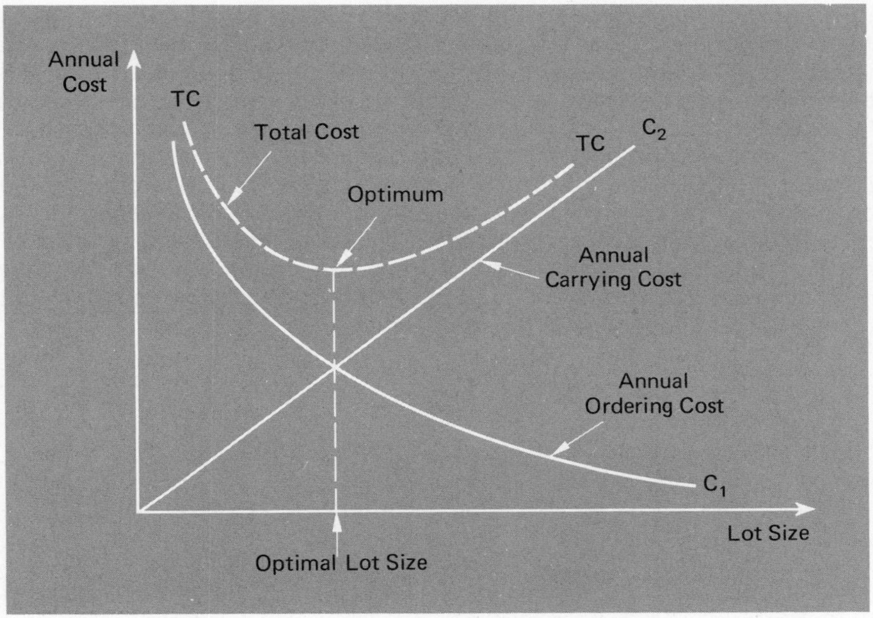

Figure 24-5
Optimal Lot Size

Figure content labels: Annual Cost, TC, Total Cost, Optimum, C₂, TC, Annual Carrying Cost, Annual Ordering Cost, C₁, Lot Size, Optimal Lot Size

C_1 and C_2 must correspond to the lowest point on the TC curve. This point is represented by four orders per year and 3,000 units per order at which point columns 3 and 4 are equal (C_1 and C_2 costs) and is the lowest amount in column 5 (curve TC).

The purpose of the formula is to find that point on the TC curve whose cost is equal to the sum of the C_1 and C_2 curves at the point at which they cross over. The model assumes certainty as to ordering and carrying costs, demand, order lead time, receipt of order, and all orders being received when the inventory is zero.

The mathematical formula is as follows:

$$EOQ = \sqrt{\frac{2C_{0.1}D}{C_{0.2}i}}$$

where EOQ = economic ordering quantity
$C_{0.1}$ = cost of placing one order
D = annual demand, in units, for the inventory item under consideration
$C_{0.2}$ = annual cost of carrying inventory as a percent of its cost price
i = unit cost of the inventory item under consideration

The Inventory Cycle

Inventory decisions involve commitment of resources to meet future and uncertain demands. The amount committed must be justified by the return on

(Ch. 24)

the resources committed. This is accomplished by minimizing the costs involved in ordering and carrying the inventory. Figures 24-4 and 24-5 show that the economic order quantity or optimum lot size is the point at which ordering costs and carrying costs are equal. A diagram of the inventory cycle is shown in Figure 24-6. The solid vertical lines show the increase in inventory when an order is received, the height of the line being determined by the amount received or the EOQ. The downward sloping lines represent the gradual depletion of the inventory from time to time as goods are sold. A second order, represented by a broken vertical line, is placed at time T_1 and is received at time T_2, the interval between T_2 and T_1 representing the lead time needed for an order to be placed and delivered. When the second order is received, the units on hand will again be at the target level.

Figure 24-6
Inventory Cycle

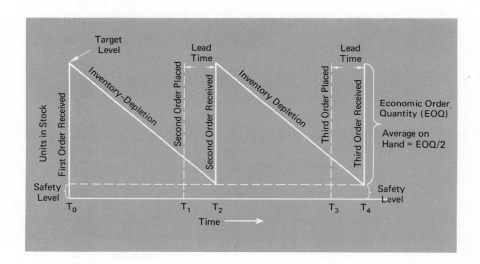

MARGINAL INCOME ANALYSIS

A basic management decision-making problem is how best to allocate scarce resources—whether human, financial, or material—when various opportunities are available. If, for example, the consequences of a decision choice on revenue, expenses, and contribution margin or marginal income can be projected, the tool of marginal analysis will indicate the best choice.

To illustrate marginal income analysis, assume that the following data were developed from the cost records of an automobile dealership showing the monthly profit margins if the sales force is assigned to the departments in the numbers indicated below.

COST
ACCUMULATION,
AND CONTROL;
FINANCIAL
PLANNING

924

(Ch. 24)

Number of Salesmen	Margin If Assigned to		
	New Cars	Used Cars	Parts
1	$1,000	$ 500	$ 600
2	1,400	1,000	700
3	1,700	1,300	800
4	2,000	1,600	850
5	2,400	1,800	900

When these data are rearranged to show the incremental margin that is generated by the addition of one more sales person, the results are shown below.

Number of Sales Persons	Margin If Assigned to					
	New Cars		Used Cars		Parts	
1		$1,000		$500		$600
2	($1,400-$1,000)	400	($1,000-$ 500)	500	($700-$600)	100
3	(1,700- 1,400)	300	(1,300- 1,000)	300	(800- 700)	100
4	(2,000- 1,700)	300	(1,600- 1,300)	300	(850- 800)	50
5	(2,400- 2,000)	400	(1,800- 1,600)	200	(900- 850)	50

If the decision criterion is to maximize profits, then the assignment of additional sales persons should be made in the order indicated:

		Department	Total Margin
(a)	If 1 sales person	New Cars	$1,000
(b)	If 2 sales persons:		
	1	New Cars	$1,000
	1	Parts	600
	2		$1,600
(c)	If 3 sales persons:		
	2	As in (b)	$1,600
	1	Used Cars	500
	3		$2,100
(d)	If 4 sales persons:		
	3	As in (c)	$2,100
	1	Used Cars	500
	4		$2,600
(e)	If 5 sales persons:		
	4	As in (d)	$2,600
	1	New Cars	400
	5		$3,000

Linear programming is a technique used for analyzing a problem so as to arrive at the optimum choice from related alternatives involving the allocation of scarce resources subject to certain constraints. The nature of the optimum solution depends on the objectives. Assuming that available resources in men, machines, and money are restricted, the decision to produce one product may limit the resources available for the production of another product, because different products require a different mix of scarce resources as well as a different market demand and profit margins. The optimum solution is that which allocates the available resources so as to maximize profits or minimize expense.

The starting point is to state the *objective function*, which is a statement of the mathematical model for the solution to the problem of allocating scarce resources. It is a measurement of the expected outcome from a proposed strategy. When the number of alternatives is large, the computer and advanced linear programming models are used. When the problem involves two alternatives, it can be solved graphically by lines drawn on a quadrant representing equations expressing the constraints. The optimum solution can then be read visually from the graph. The graph of the equations are straight lines connecting two identified points, the assumption being that each production unit requires a fixed amount of a scarce resource. Thus, if one unit of product A requires two hours of machine time, then two units are assumed to require four hours; if one unit of product A contributes $5, then two units are assumed to contribute $10.

When all the lines have been drawn, the boundaries of the *technically feasible* or acceptable solution area will have been defined. Within this area there is an infinite number of possible solutions. The optimum solution will be at one of the corner points. The coordinates of that point representing the optimum mix of products are determined and the contribution is then calculated.

Illustration 1. Assume the Jordan Company makes products A and B. Product A requires two hours of cutting machine time and two hours of polishing machine time. Product B requires an hour of cutting machine time and three hours of polishing machine time. Daily available machine time capacity is restricted to 10 hours for the cutting department and 18 hours for the polishing department. Each item is sold separately; contribution margins (selling price less variable expenses) are $3 for product A and $2 for product B. The objective function is:

$$\text{Maximize } Z = \$3A + \$2B$$

where A = number of units of product A to be produced daily
B = number of units of product B to be produced daily
Z = profit to be maximized

The purpose is to find those numbers (coordinate points) which, when substituted for A and B in the objective function, will maximize profits. The next step is to introduce into the statement of the problem the constraints represented by the limited available machine hour capacity.

Constraint I—Cutting: $2A + 1B \leq 10$

One unit of A requires two hours of cutting capacity and one unit of B requires one hour of cutting capacity. The combined requirements cannot exceed 10 hours. Thus, if total cutting machine capacity were devoted to producing either A's or B's, the department could cut either five units of A ($5 \times 2 = 10$), or 10 units of B ($10 \times 1 = 10$).

Constraint II—Polishing: $2A + 3B \leq 18$

One unit of A requires two hours of polishing machine capacity and one unit of B requires three hours of polishing machine capacity. The combined capacity requirements for the production of A's and B's can be less than, or equal to, but cannot be greater than, 18 hours. Thus, the firm could process either nine units of A or six units of B in this department ($9 \times 2 = 18$ or $6 \times 3 = 18$). Figure 24-7 summarizes these facts in the problem; Figure 24-8 shows the solution.

Several combinations can be produced within the constraints—that is, within the area of technical feasibility. What is needed is that combination which provides the maximum contribution margin. The graph shows the feasibility area, the area within which all the possible combinations can be produced without violating the cutting and polishing department constraints. The boundaries for each constraint are drawn by identifying and connecting two points, one on each axis. The two points for the cutting department constraint are 10 on the vertical axis and 5 on the horizontal axis identified as follows:

Constraint: $2A + 1B = 10$
when $A = 0$, then $B = 10$ and
when $B = 0$, then $A = 5$

Similarly, the two points for the polishing department are 9 and 6, identified as follows:

Constraint: $2A + 3B = 18$
when $A = 0$, then $B = 6$ and
when $B = 0$, then $A = 9$

Any combination of A's and B's on the line will equal 18. This means that all such combinations will utilize the maximum available polishing department capacity of 18 hours daily.

The technically feasible area is bounded by the corner points identified by

(Ch. 24)

Figure 24-7 Summary Schedule for Linear Program

THE JORDAN COMPANY
Summary Schedule

| | Department | | Contribution Margin |
	Cutting	Polishing	
1. Machine hours per unit:			
Product A	2	2	$ 3
Product B	1	3	2
2. Total hours available	10	18	
3. Maximum output and contribution margin			
if produce either all A's or all B's:			
Product A	10 ÷ 2 = 5 ①	18 ÷ 2 = 9	5 × $3 = $15 ①
Product B	10 ÷ 1 = 10	18 ÷ 3 = 6 ②	6 × $2 = 12 ②
4. Contribution margin if optimum mix			
is produced.			
Product A (3 units at $3 each)			$ 9
Product B (4 units at $2 each)			8
			$17

Notes

❶ Since only five A's can be cut, the available polishing capacity for four additional units cannot be used. Cutting is the bottleneck.

❷ Since only six B's can be polished, the available cutting capacity for four additional units cannot be used. Polishing is the bottleneck.

Figure 24-8
Graph of Optimum
Product Mix

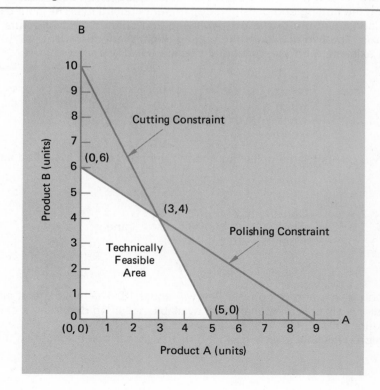

COST
ACCUMULATION,
AND CONTROL;
FINANCIAL
PLANNING

928

(Ch. 24)

the coordinates (0, 0), (0, 6), (3, 4), and (5, 0). The optimum product combination is at the corner (3, 4). Marginal contribution (Z) for each of the corner points are shown below.

Coordinates	Product A	Product B	Objective Function $Z = \$3A + \$2B$
(0, 0)	0	0	$\$3(0) + \$2(0) = \$\ 0$
(0, 6)	0	6	$3(0) +\ \ 2(6) =\ \ 12$
(3, 4)	3	4	$3(3) +\ \ 2(4) =\ \ 17$
(5, 0)	5	0	$3(5) +\ \ 2(0) =\ \ 15$

Illustration 2. The following problem was programmed for solution by a computer.[1]

1. *Description of problem*

Product	Time Required in Hours per Unit				Contribution Margin
	Machine Shop	Pre-Assembly	Assembly	Finishing	
Table—style No. 1 (T_1)	1	½	4	2	$\$\ 8$
Table—style No. 2 (T_2)	1	1	8	2½	15
Chair—style No. 1 (C_1)	2	1	2	4	6
Chair—style No. 2 (C_2)	2	2	4	5	11
Total hours available	40	40	120	80	

2. *Objective function*

$$\text{Maximize } Z = \$8T_1 + \$15T_2 + \$6C_1 + \$11C_2$$

where T_1 = the number of style #1 tables to be produced daily
T_2 = the number of style #2 tables to be produced daily
C_1 = the number of style #1 chairs to be produced daily
C_2 = the number of style #2 chairs to be produced daily
Z = profit to be maximized

3. *Constraints*
  a. Machine Shop: $1T_1 + 1T_2 + 2C_1 + 2C_2 \leq 40$
  b. Pre-Assembly: $\tfrac{1}{2}T_1 + 1T_2 + 1C_1 + 2C_2 \leq 40$
  c. Assembly: $4T_1 + 8T_2 + 2C_1 + 4C_2 \leq 120$
  d. Finishing: $2T_1 + 2\tfrac{1}{2}T_2 + 4C_1 + 5C_2 \leq 80$

[1] Courtesy of John C. Southern, Glen Raven Mills, Inc.

e. $T_1 \geq 0$, $T_2 \geq 0$, $C_1 \geq 0$, $C_2 \geq$ (cannot produce a negative number of units)

4. Copy of printout of optimum solution follows:

```
ACE FURNITURE CO.                                                          2
                                                     PAGE NO.   3
                                                     RUN  NO.   1

  VARIABLE   ENTRIES  SOLUTION     UPPER        LOWER       CURRENT     REDUCED
             TYPE     ACTIVITY     BOUND        BOUND        COST        COST

   TABLE1   LL   5      0.0     ************      0.0        8.000      -0.200
   PROFIT   B*   0    264.667   ************  ************  -1.000      -1.000
   TABLE2   B*   5      9.334   ************      0.0       15.000       0.0

   CHAIR1   LL   5      0.0     ************      0.0        6.000      -0.900
   CHAIR2   B*   5     11.334   ************      0.0       11.000       0.0
   MACHSHOP B*   0     32.000      40.000         0.0        0.0         0.0

   PRE-ASSB B*   0     32.000      40.000         0.0        0.0         0.0
   ASSEMBLY UL   0    120.000     120.000         0.0        0.0        -1.584
   FINISH   UL   0     80.000      80.000         0.0        0.0        -0.934
```

The optimum mix consists of daily production runs of 9⅓ style No. 2 tables and 11⅓ style No. 2 chairs. Note that all available assembly and finishing hours will be used, but only 32 of the available 40 hours will be used in the other two shops.

DECISIONS UNDER UNCERTAINTY

If neither the outcome resulting from an action nor the probability of such outcome is known, there are still decision criteria that can be used in models. An example is *minimax* (the strategy that minimizes the maximum loss). Assume the following payoff matrix for a sports concessionaire who can sell only one type of beverage:

	Gain or (Loss)		
Decision \ **Weather**	**Hot**	**Cold**	**Medium**
Sell Hot Coffee	($ 50)	$300	$75
Sell Cold Drinks	$200	($ 30)	$75

COST
ACCUMULATION,
AND CONTROL;
FINANCIAL
PLANNING

930   (Ch. 24)

If the decision maker uses the *minimax* criterion, the decision will be to sell cold drinks, because that strategy is the one in which the worst that can happen is a $30 loss, whereas the other could cause a $50 loss. In contrast, the decision maker could use the *maximax* criterion (the strategy that maximizes the possible gain). If maximax is used, he will sell coffee, because there is a chance to gain $300 compared with a gain of $200 if he sells cold drinks.

GLOSSARY

Expected Value The arithmetic average of all possible values.

Linear Programming A technique used for analyzing a problem so as to arrive at the optimum choice from related alternatives involving the allocation of scarce resources subject to certain constraints.

Marginal Income Analysis A method of structuring decisions involving the allocation of scarce resources when various opportunities are available.

Maximax A decision-making strategy that maximizes the possible gain under conditions of uncertainty.

Minimax A decision-making strategy that minimizes the maximum possible loss under conditions of uncertainty.

Optimum Lot Size The number of units to be ordered or the number of units to be produced on a production run so that minimum costs are incurred or maximum benefits are generated.

Payoff Matrix A rectangular array for structuring information such as, for example, probabilities of expected values.

Probability A theory that provides the means for measuring the likelihood of the occurrence of a chance event in a decision when the outcome cannot be predicted with certainty.

QUESTIONS

Q24-1. (a) What is a model? (b) Identify some accounting models you are familiar with. (c) What purposes do accounting models serve? (d) What are their limitations?

Q24-2. (a) What is the role of accounting in decision making? (b) Of what concern is the work of behavioral scientists to the accountant?

Q24-3. (a) How may an executive apply probability theory to his decision making? (b) Does this preclude the use of intuition, hunch, or common sense?

Q24-4. (a) What is meant by "expected value"? (b) What is a "payoff matrix"? (c) How are these terms related?

Q24-5. (a) What is the central objective in inventory decisions? (b) What information is needed for inventory decisions? (c) Describe the optimal lot size inventory model.

Q24-6. (a) Describe the linear programming model. (b) What is meant by the terms "objective function," and "feasible solution"? (c) What is the criterion for determining the optimum product mix?

(Ch. 24)

Q24-7. In problems that can be solved graphically when two products are involved, is there a limit to the number of constraining equations involved?

Q24-8. Which of these alternatives would decrease contribution per unit margin the most?
a. a 15 percent decrease in selling price
b. a 15 percent increase in variable expense
c. a 15 percent increase in selling price
d. a 15 percent decrease in variable expense
e. a 15 percent decrease in fixed expenses

(IMA adapted)

EXERCISES

E24-1. Some companies have long-run objectives other than profit maximization, such as service to the public or enhancing the power of the central management group. How does this affect the work of the accountant?

E24-2. Should the accountant include in his measurements of a company's performance the cost to society of the air or water pollutants being discharged by the company's production processes? Explain.

E24-3. A manufacturer produces products X and Y, which are processed in two departments. Department I can process either 1,000 X's or 2,000 Y's and Department II can process either 2,000 X's or 1,000 Y's.
(a) Assuming contribution margins of $12 for each product, what is the optimum product mix? (b) Under what conditions will profits be maximized (1) if only X's are produced, or (2) if only Y's are produced?

E24-4. The Josephson Company uses 240,000 units of product Y, which costs $1 each. The cost of placing an order is $400 and the average cost of carrying a unit is $0.10. What is the optimum ordering frequency, assuming usage is spread evenly throughout the year?

E24-5. In break-even analysis, a number of assumptions typically are made. Which of the following assumptions typically is not made? Explain.
a. Volume is the only relevant factor affecting cost.
b. No change between beginning and ending inventory.
c. The sales mix will be maintained as volume changes.
d. Prices of cost factors fluctuate proportionally with volume.
e. None of the above.

(IMA adapted)

E24-6. An accountant would typically have which of the following in mind when referring to the "margin of safety"?
a. excess of budgeted or actual sales over the variable costs and the fixed costs at break even
b. excess of budgeted or actual sales revenue over fixed costs
c. excess of actual sales over budgeted sales
d. excess of sales revenue over variable costs
e. none of the above

(IMA adapted)

E24-7. If fixed costs decrease while variable cost per unit remains constant, the new

COST
ACCUMULATION,
AND CONTROL;
FINANCIAL
PLANNING

932

(Ch. 24)

variable contribution margin in relation to the old will be which of the following? (a) unchanged, (b) higher, (c) lower, (d) indeterminate, (e) none of the above.

(IMA adapted)

E24-8. Expected annual usage of a particular raw material is 2,000,000 units, and the standard order size is 10,000 units. The invoice cost of each unit is $500, and the cost to place one purchase order is $80. Select the best answer for each of the following:

1. The average inventory is: (a) 1,000,000 units, (b) 5,000 units, (c) 10,000 units, (d) 7,500 units.
2. The estimated annual order cost is: (a) $16,000, (b) $100,000, (c) $32,000, (d) $50,000.

(AICPA adapted)

E24-9. The graph below applies to items 1 and 2. Select the best answer.

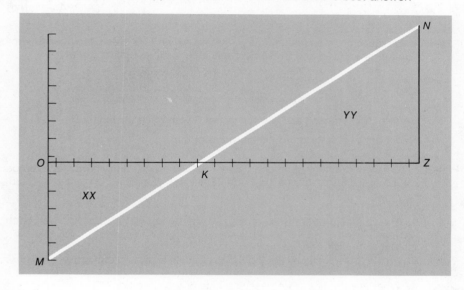

1. On the profit/volume chart above:
   a. Areas *XX* and *YY* and point *K* represent profit, loss, and volume of sales at break-even point, respectively.
   b. Line *O-Z* represents volumes of sales.
   c. Two lines *O-M* and *N-Z* represent fixed costs.
   d. Line *M-N* represents total costs.
   e. None of the above is true.

2. The vertical scale represents:
   a. volume of sales.
   b. units produced.
   c. profit above O and loss below O.
   d. contribution margin.
   e. none of the above.

(IMA adapted)

E24-10. Gyro Gear Company produces a special gear used in automatic transmissions. Each gear sells for $28, and the company sells approximately 500,000 gears each year. Unit cost data for 1976 are presented below:

Direct material $6.00
Direct labor   5.00

	Variable	Fixed
Other costs:		
Manufacturing	$2.00	$7.00
Distribution	4.00	3.00

Gyro has received an offer from a foreign manufacturer to purchase 25,000 gears. Domestic sales would be unaffected by this transaction. If the offer is accepted, variable distribution costs will increase $1.50 a gear for insurance, shipping, and import duties. The relevant unit cost to a pricing decision on this offer is which of the following? (a) $17.00, (b) $14.50, (c) $28.50, (d) $18.50.

(AICPA adapted)

DP24-1. Thermiquetron, Inc., manufactures models AX and BY steam facial units. Production processes and available capacities for the coming month are:

Cutting   100 AX or 150 BY
Wiring   200 AX or 100 BY
Assembly   150 AX or 100 BY

Contribution margins are $60 for model AX and $80 for model BY.

Required: Calculate the optimum product mix.

DP24-2. A company orders 12,000 units a year at $30 a unit. Carrying costs average 6% of the cost of goods on hand. The cost of placing an order is $125.

Required:

1. The optimum quantity to order and the number of orders to place each year.
2. The total inventory cost.
3. Prove your results by setting up a schedule similar to that shown in Figure 24-4.
4. What are the underlying assumptions of your solution?
5. What is the effect on total costs if it later turns out that the actual ordering costs were $150 an order?

DP24-3. The York Corporation is considering introducing a new product. Cost and marketing studies indicate that the item can be sold for $15 each. Production costs are uncertain, because the company has no experience with this product, but the production manager provides the following estimates:

	Probability	Unit Cost
Most optimistic	0.10	$4
Most probable	0.75	6
Most pessimistic	0.15	8

The sales manager predicts that he can easily sell the entire projected output of 100,000 units for the first year.

Required: What is the expected profit the first year?

DP24-4. The Robney Company is a restaurant supplier which sells a number of products to various restaurants in the area. One of the products is a special meat cutter with a disposable blade.

The blades are sold in packages of 12 blades for $20 a package. After a number of years, it has been determined that the demand for the replacement blades is at a constant rate of 2,000 packages a month. The packages cost the Robney Company $10 each from the manufacturer and require a three-day lead time from date of order to date of delivery. The ordering cost is $1.20 an order and the carrying cost is 10% a year.

Robney is going to use the economic order quantity formula below.

$$EOQ = \sqrt{\frac{2\ (\text{Annual requirements})\ (\text{Cost per order})}{(\text{Price per unit})\ (\text{Carrying cost})}}$$

Required:

1. Calculate:
   a. Economic order quantity.
   b. Number of orders needed per year.
   c. Total cost of buying and carrying blades for the year.
2. Assuming there is no reserve (for example, safety stock) and that the present inventory level is 200 packages, when should the next order be placed? (Use 360 days in a year.)
3. Discuss the problems that most firms would have in attempting to apply this formula to their inventory problems.

(IMA adapted)

P24-1. The Harlile Electric Company manufactures and distributes two models of epilators, AG and BG. The major production processes are wiring and cutting. Available resources and required time in hours are as follows:

	Model		Available Capacity
Process	AG	BG	(hours)
Wiring	1	2	30
Cutting	4	3	100

Required:

1. Graph the technically feasible area for model AG and model BG, identify all corner points, and determine the optimum mix, assuming contribution margins of $175 for model AG and $225 for model BG.
2. Calculate the contribution of each model for each corner point.

P24-2. The Richard Company has been using manually operated equipment to service its customers. Automatic equipment is now available and the company has conducted a cost-benefit study to determine whether to replace its conventional equipment.

The study indicates that annual revenue will continue at its present level of $50,000.

Comparative costs of using the conventional equipment and automatic equipment are estimated as follows:

QUANTITATIVE
TECHNIQUES
FOR DECISION
MAKING

	Manual	Automatic
Equipment	$12,000	$15,000
Salvage	1,000	2,000
Supplies, annual	1,000	1,500
Maintenance, annual	100	150
Overhaul:		
End of year 2	500	
End of year 3		1,000

Assume that the estimated useful life for either type of equipment is five years and that the company's cost of capital is 16%.

Required:

1. Should the company invest in automatic equipment?
2. What are the underlying assumptions and the advantages and disadvantages of your analysis for this decision?

P24-3. The Rainex Company is considering introducing a new product. Cost and marketing studies indicate that the item can be sold for $12 each. Production costs are uncertain, because the company has no experience with this product, but the production manager provides the following estimates:

	Probability	Unit Cost
Most optimistic	0.10	$4
Most probable	0.75	6
Most pessimistic	0.15	8

The sales manager predicts that he can easily sell the entire projected output of 150,000 units for the first year.

Required: What is the expected profit for the first year?

P24-4. Harry Kane, developer and designer of a steam hair-waving machine, is prepared to distribute his product nationally. He asks you for a forecast of the number of units he might expect to distribute the first year. After surveying a number of large cities, you arrive at the following estimates:

Units	Probability
1,500	0.1
2,000	0.3
2,500	0.4
3,000	0.2
	1.0

The selling price of the machine is $350. A manufacturer has agreed to produce the machine for $175 each. Shipping expenses will average $12 a unit. Distribution will be through contractors' representatives, who will receive a $125 commission on each unit. Kane's other expenses are $35,000 annually.

Required: What are Kane's expected earnings the first year?

P24-5. Girth, Inc., makes two kinds of men's suede leather belts. Belt A is a high-quality belt. Belt B is of somewhat lower quality. The company earns $7 for each unit of belt A sold, and $2 for each unit sold of belt B. Each unit (belt) of A requires twice as much manufacturing time as is required for a unit B. Further, if only belt type B is made, Girth has the capacity to manufacture 1,000 units a day. Suede leather is purchased by Girth under a long-term contract

COST
ACCUMULATION,
AND CONTROL;
FINANCIAL
PLANNING

936

which makes available to Girth enough leather to make 800 belts a day (A and B combined). Belt A requires a fancy buckle, of which only 400 a day are available. Belt B requires a different (plain) buckle, of which 700 a day are available. The demand for the suede leather belts (A or B) is such that Girth can sell all that it produces.

The accompanying graph displays the constraint functions based upon the facts presented above.

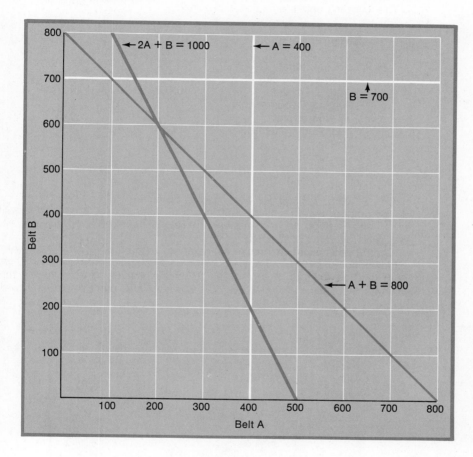

Required:

1. Using the graph, determine how many units of belt A and belt B should be produced to maximize daily profits.
2. Assume the same facts above except that the sole supplier of buckles for belt A informs Girth, Inc., that it will be unable to supply more than 100 fancy buckles per day. How many units of each of the two belts should be produced each day to maximize profits?
3. Assume the same facts as in **2** except that Texas Buckles, Inc., could supply Girth, Inc., with the additional fancy buckles it needs. The price would be $3.50 more than Girth is paying for such buckles. How many, if any, fancy

(Ch. 24)

buckles should Girth buy from Texas Buckles? Explain how you determined your answer.

(IMA adapted)

P24-6. Part A. The Witchell Corporation manufactures and sells three grades, A, B, and C, of a single wood product. Each grade must be processed through three phases—cutting, fitting, and finishing—before it is sold.

The following unit information is provided:

	A	B	C
Selling Price	$10.00	$15.00	$20.00
Direct Labor	$ 5.00	$ 6.00	$ 9.00
Direct Materials	$ 0.70	$ 0.70	$ 1.00
Variable Overhead	$ 1.00	$ 1.20	$ 1.80
Fixed Overhead	$ 0.60	$ 0.72	$ 1.08
Materials Requirements in Board Feet	7	7	10
Labor Requirements in Hours:			
Cutting	3/6	3/6	4/6
Fitting	1/6	1/6	2/6
Finishing	1/6	2/6	3/6

Only 5,000 board feet per week can be obtained.

The cutting department has 180 hours of labor available each week. The fitting and finishing departments each have 120 hours of labor available each week. No overtime is allowed.

Contract commitments require the company to make 50 units of A a week. In addition, company policy is to produce at least 50 additional units of A, 50 units of B, and 50 units of C each week to remain actively in each of the three markets. Because of competition, only 130 units of C can be sold each week.

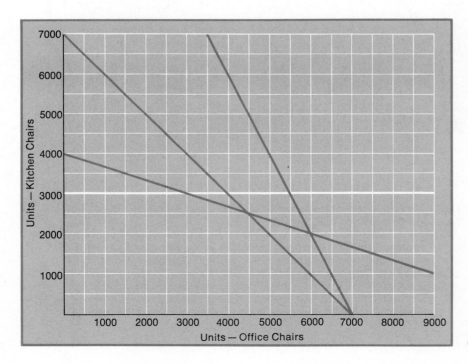

COST
ACCUMULATION,
AND CONTROL;
FINANCIAL
PLANNING

938

(Ch. 24)

Required: Formulate and label the linear objective function and the constraint functions necessary to maximize the contribution margin.

Part B. The graph shown on page 938 presents the constraint functions for a chair manufacturing company whose production problem can be solved by linear programing. The company earns $8 for each kitchen chair sold and $5 for each office chair sold.

Required:

1. What is the profit maximizing production schedule?
2. How did you select this production schedule?

P24-7. The customary letter to the stockholders from the company president included in the firm's annual report typically includes a statement that its greatest asset is its employees. The annual report of one company, for example, includes the following statement:

The Future. The progress of your company last year and all through the sixties primarily is the result of the superior performance and dedication of our management-employee team. It is their creativity, their production and marketing skills, and their abilities to capitalize on the potentials and facilities of the company that encourage confidence of even greater growth of your company in this new decade.

It has been suggested that the company should quantify its human resources for inclusion in the financial statements.

The following bases have been proposed:

1. Cost of recruitment, training, and retraining
2. Replacement cost
3. Capitalized value of excess earnings attributed to human resources
4. Present value of future employee earnings

Required:

1. Do you agree that a firm's human resources should be quantified? If you do, which method would you use?
2. How would quantification aid in the evaluation of the firm's performance and financial position?
3. Will readers or employees resent the idea of quantifying human beings in the manner of plant assets?
4. How will the amounts be amortized? What factors would have to be considered in establishing amortization policies?
5. What variables would have to be considered in constructing the measurement model?

QUANTITATIVE
TECHNIQUES
FOR DECISION
MAKING

(Ch. 24)

939

Capital Budgeting Decisions 25

Capital budgeting refers to the allocation and commitment of funds to long-term capital investment projects. The amount of such investments or expenditures is usually large, and they are made in expectation of benefits to be received over a number of years. Capital budgeting concerns itself with the development, selection, and evaluation of proposals for plant expansion and modernization, equipment replacement, product development, and so on. The nature of these investments and their effect on the long-range welfare of a company make it imperative that they be analyzed and evaluated with the utmost care.

BUDGETING CAPITAL EXPENDITURES

Types of Capital Expenditure

The types of capital expenditure can perhaps best be illustrated by questions involving capital investment decisions, such as the following:

1. *Expansion.* Shall we buy additional equipment to supply the actual or anticipated increase in demand for our product? Shall we expand our facilities to produce new products? Shall we acquire the necessary facilities to make parts we are now buying from outside sources?
2. *Replacement.* Shall we replace present equipment with new and more efficient equipment? Shall we automate our production lines? Shall we buy machine A or machine B? Shall we lease the new equipment or shall we buy it?

3. *Other.* Some investments are made on noneconomic grounds. Expenditures for recreational facilities for use by employees, for example, are not made to reduce costs or increase revenue, but rather to improve employer-employee relations. An investment to eliminate sound nuisances or smoke hazards may be made in compliance with local ordinances; but even if it is not mandatory, a company may choose to make such an investment in acknowledgment of corporate social responsibility.

Rate of Return

Business people make investments to get a satisfactory return. What constitutes a satisfactory rate of return depends on a number of factors, including available funds, available investment opportunities, cost of obtaining funds, and degree of uncertainty and risk. In the long run, the rate of return must be adequate to attract new capital.

The choice of an appropriate rate of return is central to the capital budgeting decision, since it has a direct influence on the decision. The choice may be based on the *investment opportunity* concept, which is a subjective evaluation of the available investment opportunities and their respective earnings rates. The selected rate of return is the rate that the funds could earn if they were invested in the best available alternative project. Since funds used on project A, for example, are not available for use on project B, the amount that could have been earned on project B is sacrificed. The amount or rate so sacrificed constitutes an opportunity cost, or the minimum rate that must be earned on project A, the project chosen.

The choice of a cutoff rate may be based on a different concept, the *cost of capital.* The premise for the use of the cost of capital as the minimum rate of return is that the project should earn at least as much as the cost of the funds invested in the project, whether using available capital or new capital. A rate of return (or cost) on new capital investment that is less than the rate of return on old capital investment would have a dilutive effect and decrease the return to owner' equity. This, in turn, may decrease the market value of the firm's stock.

The minimum rate of return or the cost of capital is difficult to measure and varies with each company. Stated in its simplest terms, it represents a weighted average of the cost to the company of common stock equity capital as measured by the ratio of the market value of the stock to the dividend rate, and the cost of long-term debt as measured by the rate of interest on the debt. But other variables such as reinvested earnings, future dividend rates, and changes in the market value of the shares complicate the calculations. Furthermore, some argue that the cost of capital is independent of the firm's capital structure and depends only upon the riskiness represented by the investment and the stream of earnings that it generates.

Budgeting Decisions

The capital budgeting decision involves making a choice among alternatives. Available proposals usually exceed available funds, so that a system must be established for ranking the proposals and selecting the most desirable ones.

COST
ACCUMULATION,
AND CONTROL;
FINANCIAL
PLANNING

942

(Ch. 25)

Since the capital budgeting decision is an investment decision, it may be subjected to the same criterion that any prudent investor uses—that is, the gain or the rate of return to be realized on the investment. This, in turn, furnishes the rationale for the selection, once the desired minimum rate of return has been fixed.

Present Value Concept

The present value concept refers to the conversion of cash inflows and outflows over a period to a common point in time for purposes of comparing capital expenditures. The concepts of compound amounts and present values are used in this conversion process: Since dollar amounts can be moved forward in time by compounding or backward in time by discounting, direct comparisons can be made of cash flows occurring in different periods. If, for example, an investment in a piece of equipment will reduce operating costs by $100 a year for four years, and the company has opportunities to invest its funds in other projects yielding a return of 10 percent a year, it can afford to pay $316.99 for this piece of equipment and still realize a 10 percent rate of return on the investment. The factor comes from the 10 percent column for Period 4 (Appendix Table 4, Compound Interest Tables). The computation is as follows:

$$\$100 \times 3.169865 = \$317 \text{ (rounded)}$$

The company could pay $317 for the equipment even if it had to borrow the $317 at 10 percent interest. The fact that the company could repay the loan and interest with the funds derived from the annual $100 costs savings and still be as well off as it would be before the equipment was purchased is demonstrated by the following calculation:

Amount borrowed	$317.00
Interest for 1st year	31.70
Total	$348.70
First payment	100.00
Amount due at beginning of 2d period	$248.70
Interest for 2d year	24.87
Total	$273.57
Second payment	100.00
Amount due at beginning of 3d period	$173.57
Interest for 3d year	17.36
Total	$190.93
Third payment	100.00
Amount due at beginning of 4th period	$ 90.93
Interest 4th year	9.09
Total	$100.02
Fourth payment	100.02

(Ch. 25)

The discrepancy of 2 cents is due to rounding. Payments are assumed to have been made at the end of each year. The assumed saving of $100 each year in operating costs enables the company to recover the loan or the investment of $317 plus annual interest of 10 percent on the unrecovered balance. Note that any residual salvage value of the equipment has been ignored.

Capital expenditures are subject to the same test as any other kind of investment, the earning of a satisfactory profit. Investments in government securities are, of course, qualitatively different from investments in machinery, because the element of certainty of return on the investment is greater. But the essential objectives of the two types of investment are the same, a satisfactory rate of return. Since sums moved forward or backward in time can be converted to a comparable basis by the application of present value factors, such application to the solution of capital budgeting problems follows logically. The formulas that apply to the analysis of financial investments apply equally to the analysis of capital expenditures.

COMPARING CAPITAL EXPENDITURES

Determining the Relevant Cash Flows. A capital investment generates a flow of cash into and out of the business over a period. A comparison of several investment projects from which the best choice is to be made involves a comparison of the expected cash flows under the several alternatives. The concern is with future, not past, costs and with relevant costs—that is, the costs that will be different. Clearly, a cost or a revenue amount that will be the same under all the alternatives from which a choice is to be made is not relevant, since it will not change the decision. The appropriateness for the emphasis on cash flow to the exclusion of valuations based on generally accepted accounting principles must be considered within the context of the capital budgeting problem. The measurement of revenue and expense—the measurement of net income—*is not* relevant to the timing of the related cash flows. The measurement of a rate of return on a specific investment proposal *is* affected by the timing of the cash flows due to the time value of money. There is no conflict between conventional income measurements and rate of return measurements; the goals and end-uses of each are different.

Present Value Method

Under the present value method, the cash flows are discounted to the present, using the firm's cost of capital as the discounting rate. If the present value of the inflows exceeds the present value of the outflows, the investment is desirable. If the present value of the outflows exceeds the present value of the inflows, the investment is undesirable. The measurement of a proposed capital expenditure by the present value method requires a determination of the following:

1. Net cash investment
2. Net cash inflows
3. Estimated useful life of the investment

COST
ACCUMULATION,
AND CONTROL;
FINANCIAL
PLANNING

944

(Ch. 25)

4. Excess present value

For example, assume that the West Company is planning to buy a new press for $25,000, with an estimated useful life of 10 years. Freight and installation costs will be $1,500. The press being replaced originally cost $20,000, has a carrying value of $8,000 and a remaining life of 10 years, and can be sold for $4,000. The new press is not expected to change revenue but is expected to reduce labor costs, including fringe benefits, by $5,500, and to increase power costs by $1,000. Maintenance, taxes, and insurance will be unchanged. The advisability of the replacement is being questioned. The company's cost of capital is 14 percent.

Step 1: Net cash investment. The initial step in the measurement of the rate of return is to determine the net amount of the initial cash investment required by the specific capital expenditure proposed. This usually consists of the purchase price of the asset, transportation, installation, and any other costs incurred to prepare the asset for operation. If the project involves the replacement of an old asset, the proceeds from the sale of the old asset are deducted in arriving at the amount of the net investment.

The net cash investment for the West Company is computed as follows:

Purchase price of new press	$25,000
Freight and installation	1,500
Total	$26,500
Deduct proceeds from sale of old press	4,000
Net investment	$22,500

The carrying value of the old press is irrelevant, because it represents a past, or sunk, cost, not a future cost. Whatever the carrying value, the net investment is $22,500. What is relevant is the selling price of the old machine, because it represents a reduction of the cash investment.

Step 2: Net cash inflows. The West Company proposal falls into the cost reduction category. The relevant cash outflows are the costs that will be different—the *differential costs*—if the proposal is adopted. The expected change in annual operating cash flows will be as follows:

Cost decreases—labor	$5,500
Deduct cost increases—power	1,000
Net annual saving	$4,500

This step involves a careful analysis of all operating costs to determine which costs will be increased and which decreased. Only those cost changes which will change cash flows are relevant. Changes in costs due, for example, to changes in cost allocations without corresponding changes in cash flow are irrelevant for this purpose, even though they are essential to the accounting process.

(Ch. 25)

Step 3: Estimated useful life. The rate of return on an investment project is directly affected by the estimated useful life of the project. The serviceable life of an asset cannot be definitely known at the time of its acquisition, and it may be difficult to estimate, but an approximation or judgment must be made. The estimate is based not on physical life but on economic life. The question to be answered is: How long will the project contribute earnings to the firm? A machine with an estimated physical life of 10 years may have to be replaced after only one year due to changes in the nature of the business—method of manufacture; location, type, or design of product; and so on. Advances in technology may necessitate replacement of an existing machine even if it is in perfect condition. The relevant factor is earning power, not necessarily physical life, the life used for financial reporting, or the life used for Federal income tax reporting.

Step 4: Excess present value. The relative desirability of an investment is indicated by the difference, at a common point of time, between the cost of the investment and the expected earnings from that investment discounted at the desired minimum rate. The greater the excess of the present value of the earnings over the net cash investment, the more desirable the investment. Using the West Company figures, the excess present value is calculated as follows:

Present value of earnings at 14% rate for 10 years:	
$4,500 × 5.216115	$23,472.52
Net cash investment	22,500.00
Excess present value	$ 972.52

Since the present value of the earnings exceeds the investment, the project is desirable. If, however, the desired minimum is increased to 16 percent, the present value of the earnings is less than the investment; at 16 percent, therefore, the investment is undesirable. The computation is as follows:

Net cash investment	$22,500.00
Present value of earnings at 16% rate for 10 years:	
$4,500 × 4.833227	21,749.52
Excess over present value	$ 750.48

Excess Present Value Index. The excess present value index is the ratio of the present value of the earnings to the required investment. This ratio, or *profitability index,* is useful as a ranking device for investments varying in size and economic life. An index of 1.00 or more indicates that the earnings equal or exceed the desired minimum rate. The higher the index, the more desirable the project. The indexes for the West Company at 14 percent and 16 percent are shown below.

$$\frac{\text{Present value of earnings at 14\%}}{\text{Investment}} = \frac{\$23,472.52}{\$22,500.00} = 1.04$$

COST
ACCUMULATION,
AND CONTROL;
FINANCIAL
PLANNING

946

(Ch. 25)

$$\frac{\text{Present value of earnings at 16\%}}{\text{Investment}} = \frac{\$21,749.52}{\$22,500.00} = 0.967$$

The index at 16 percent, being less than 1.00, indicates that the earnings are not high enough to earn a 16 percent return on the $22,500 investment.

Rate of Return Method

The net cash investment of the West Company ($22,500), the annual net cash earnings ($4,500), and the economic life (10 years) having been determined, these relationships can now be combined to compute a rate of return on the investment and, concurrently, the return of the investment. In the language of compound interest, the rate of return will be that rate—the *internal rate of return* or the *time-adjusted rate of return*—at which the present values of the cash inflows and outflows offset each other. This means that if the company were to borrow funds to finance the investment at that internal rate of return, it would recover its investment as well as the interest on the borrowed funds. The computation on page 943 shows, for example, that an investment of $317 now is exactly equal to a future inflow of $100 at the end of each year for four years at 10 percent interest; that is, the present value of the inflows exactly offsets the present outflow. This means that the rate of return on the $317 investment is exactly 10 percent.

The rate of return computation for the West Company involves finding a discount rate that, applied to the net cash inflows of $4,500 over the 10-year period, equals $22,500, the net cash investment. This can be found by the process of trial and error. When positive and negative present values are found, the exact rate can be derived by interpolation. This procedure is illustrated on page 948. However, when the cash flows are *uniform,* as in the West Company problem, the time-consuming trial-and-error method can be avoided. The predicted annual earnings of $4,500 must, in each of the 10 years, contribute to the recovery of a portion of the net cash investment of $22,500 and a return on the yet unrecovered portion of the investment. What is needed is a present value of an annuity of 1 factor, that, when applied to the annual cash inflows of $4,500, equals $22,500. This factor must be the net cash investment divided by the net cash inflow, or $22,500 ÷ $4,500 = 5.000000.

The quotient 5 is the ratio of the investment to the annual earnings. The factors in Appendix Table 4 are likewise ratios of investments to earnings: of an investment of $1 to various rates and lives of earnings. Since the problem is to find a discount factor that, when applied to the earnings, exactly equals the investment, that factor must be the investment (numerator) divided by the earnings (denominator).

Appendix Table 4 lists combinations of three elements: (1) economic life, (2) interest rate, and (3) discount factor. Given any two of these elements, the third element can be read off directly. Given the factor 5.000000 and the economic life, 10 years, the third element, the rate, can be read directly from the table.

The rate of return can now be found by referring to Appendix Table 4, in the row corresponding to the economic life, and for the factor closest to 5, the quotient of the investment divided by the earnings. The column heading under which this figure is found is the approximate rate. The factors in the 14 percent and 16 percent columns are 5.216115 and 4.833227. The rate may therefore be estimated at roughly 15 percent.

The trial-and-error method yields the same result. Assuming that the first rate tried was 14 percent and the next was 16 percent, the results would be as shown below.

Net cash investment	$22,500.00
Present value of earnings at 14% rate for 10 years:	
$4,500 × 5.216115	23,472.52
Difference	972.52
Net cash investment	$22,500.00
Present value of earnings at 16% rate for 10 years:	
$4,500 × 4.833227	21,749.52
Difference	$ (750.48)

The positive difference at 14 percent indicates a rate above 14 percent; the negative difference at 16 percent indicates a rate below 16 percent; the true rate is therefore between 14 percent and 16 percent. If an investment of $22,500 is made today with an estimated life of 10 years, and if the required minimum rate of return is 15 percent, then the project will have to produce annual cash earnings of $4,500 to repay the investment.

Depreciation, Income Taxes, and Capital Budgeting

For financial and income tax reporting, the costs of plant and equipment assets are amortized over the useful lives of the assets; a portion of the cost of the assets is deducted from revenue in measuring net income. Such revenue deductions, although essential to the income measurement process, are irrelevant to the capital budgeting decision, because they do not represent actual cash outflows. The inclusion of the entire net cash investment as a cash outflow makes it unnecessary to allocate portions of the cost over the asset's useful life as revenue deductions. Only the actual acquisition of the asset, not its allocation to income, involves cash. But the periodic depreciation deduction does reduce net income and therefore the amount of the income tax, which does represent a cash outflow. Furthermore, the use of accelerated depreciation methods has a direct effect on the pattern of the income tax cash outflows and thereby influences the rate of return.

Assuming that the West Company is subject to an income tax rate of 50 percent, the loss on the sale of the old press will result in a $2,000 tax benefit as shown below.

Carrying value	$8,000
Selling price	4,000
Deductible loss	$4,000
Tax rate	0.50
Tax deduction	$2,000

COST
ACCUMULATION,
AND CONTROL;
FINANCIAL
PLANNING

948

(Ch. 25)

Although the book loss is $4,000, the net after-tax effect of the sale is a loss of only $2,000, since, if the sale did not take place, the West Company's cash outflow for income taxes would be $2,000 greater. In this case, the net cash investment would be as shown here.

Cost of new press		$26,500
Proceeds from sale of old press	$4,000	
Tax deduction from loss on sale of old press	2,000	6,000
Net cash investment		$20,500

If the old press were sold at a gain, the tax on the gain would be deducted from the proceeds in computing the net cash investment.

The depreciation deduction and income taxes affect not only the net investment but also the net cash inflow. The change in the annual depreciation deduction changes taxable net income, which, in turn, changes the net cash earnings after taxes. The net cash earnings after taxes for the West Company, assuming the use of the straight-line depreciation method, is as follows:

Annual cash savings before taxes			$4,500
Deduct income taxes on applicable earnings			
Annual cash savings before taxes		$4,500	
Increase in annual depreciation deduction			
on new press: 10% of $26,500	$2,650		
on old press: 10% of $20,000	2,000	650	
Increase in taxable net income		$3,850	
Income taxes: 50% × $3,850			1,925
Net cash earnings after taxes			$2,575

Irregular Cash Flow Patterns

The capital budgeting proposals discussed thus far involved a single present net cash investment and uniform savings over the entire life span. Some projects, however, produce irregular cash flow patterns. The present value of a stream of earnings is influenced directly by both the amount and the timing of the inflow. The rate of discount increases with time, so that cash inflows of early years have a higher present value than corresponding inflows of later years. The analysis must, therefore, identify both the amount and the time pattern by years. To illustrate, assume that a company makes an immediate investment of $100,000 in a plant for the manufacture of a new product. Earnings rise in the second year, as the market for the product is developed, then fall in the third year under the impact of competition. An additional investment is made in the third year for an intensive advertising campaign. Because of the uneven cash flow, each amount must be multiplied by the appropriate present value of 1 factor, as shown (assumed cost of capital is 20 percent).

Year	Cash Inflow (Outflow)	Present Value of $1 Discounted at 20% (Appendix Table 2)	Present Value
1	$40,000	0.833333	$ 33,333
2	50,000	0.694444	34,722
3	25,000	0.578704	14,468
	(10,000)	0.578704	(5,787)
4	45,000	0.482253	21,701
5	30,000	0.401878	12,056
Total			$110,493

The excess present value and index are computed as follows:

Present value of cash flows	$110,493
Present value of original investment	100,000
Excess present value	$ 10,493
Excess present value index: $110,493 ÷ 100,000	1.10493

The exact rate of return may be found by trial and error. The cash flows are discounted, using different trial rates, until a rate is found at which the net present value is zero. At this rate, the net inflows equal the amount of the investment. The trial-and-error computation, using trial rates of 20 and 24 percent, follows:

Year	Cash Inflow (Outflow)	Present Value Factors		Present Values of Cash Flows	
		20%	24%	20%	24%
1	$40,000	.833333	.80645	$ 33,333	$ 32,258
2	50,000	.694444	.65036	34,722	32,518
3	25,000	.578704	.52449	14,468	13,112
	(10,000)	.578704	.52449	(5,787)	(5,245)
4	45,000	.482253	.42297	21,701	19,034
5	30,000	.401878	.34111	12,056	10,233
				$110,493	$101,910

The second trial rate of 24 percent shows present value inflows of $101,910, which, when compared with the net investment of $100,000, gives a rate of return larger than 24 percent; the actual rate would be approximately 25 percent.

(Ch. 25)

Annual Cost of an Investment

Businessmen customarily think in terms of annual costs. Statements of financial position and earnings reports are in annual terms. Capital budgeting problems may also be expressed in terms of annual costs. This is useful not only because it is a customary way of thinking but also because it provides a common basis for the comparison of two projects with different economic lives. The decision is based on whether the annual earnings expected from the investment exceed the annual cost of the investment over the estimated life.

The annual cost of an investment may be found by dividing the net investment by the present value factor corresponding to the desired rate of return and estimated life. Returning to the West Company proposal, if the company used a cutoff rate of 16 percent, the annual cost, given the net investment of $22,500 and a useful life of 10 years, is:

$$\frac{\text{Investment}}{\text{Present value factor for } i = 16\%, n = 10} = \frac{\$22,500}{4.833227} = \$4,655 \text{ (rounded)}$$

Since the estimated savings are $4,500, the project will not earn the 16 percent rate. If, however, the desired minimum is 14 percent, the annual cost becomes

$$\frac{\text{Investment}}{\text{Present value factor for } i = 14\%, n = 10} = \frac{\$22,500}{5.216115} = \$4,314 \text{ (rounded)}$$

The annual cost at 14 percent is $4,314, which is less than the estimated annual earnings of $4,500. The project therefore meets the 14 percent minimum rate test.

Annual cost computations are useful for a variety of capital expenditure problems. To illustrate, assume that a company is considering the advisability of investing in data-processing equipment that will reduce annual clerical costs from $30,000 to $18,000. The equipment costs $60,000 and has an estimated useful life of 10 years. Assuming that the desired rate of return is 10 percent, the annual cost comparison is as shown below.

Present costs		$30,000
Proposed costs		
Clerical	$18,000	
Equipment	9,765	27,765
Annual saving		$ 2,235

The computation of the annual cost of the equipment is as follows:

$$\frac{\text{Investment}}{\text{Present value factor for } i = 10\%, n = 10} = \frac{\$60,000}{6.144567} = \$9,765 \text{ (rounded)}$$

The annual saving indicates (1) that the rate of return is greater than 10 percent, (2) that the 10 percent rate of return can be realized even if proposed costs increase by $2,235 or (3) that the company could pay up to $73,735 = [($30,000 − $18,000) × 6.144567] for the equipment and still realize a 10 percent rate of return, as shown.

Present costs		$30,000
Proposed costs		
Clerical	$18,000	
Equipment	12,000	30,000
Annual saving		$ −0−

In this situation, the computation of the annual cost of the equipment is as follows:

$$\frac{\text{Investment}}{\text{Present value factor for } i = 10\%, n = 10} = \frac{\$73,735}{6.144567} = \$12,000$$

Payback

Payback, or *payout,* is a method of measuring the desirability of a project in terms of a single criterion: How soon will the cash invested in the project be returned? It is a measure of the time required for the accumulated cash earnings from a project to equal the cash investment, or

$$\frac{\text{Investment}}{\text{Annual net cash flow}} = \text{Payback}$$

In theory, the shorter the payback time, the less the risk. The popularity of payback is due to its simplicity and to its effectiveness as an initial screening measure, especially for high-risk investments in which the useful life is difficult to project. It is also useful in evaluating projects of such obvious merit that refined analysis is not needed, and projects showing no financial merit. Its limitations are that it ignores (1) the useful life, (2) the amount and pattern of cash flows beyond the payback point, (3) disposal values, (4) the time value of money, and (5) the profitability of the investment. To illustrate, assume the following figures:

Project	Net Investment	Annual Net Cash Savings
A	$10,000	$ 5,000
B	20,000	10,000

The payback on both projects is two years; on this basis they are equally desirable. However, if it is further assumed that Project A has a two-year life and

Project B a five-year life, it becomes obvious that these proposals are not equally desirable.

Although the rate-of-return method and the present value method will often point to the same choice, in some situations the two methods yield conflicting results. Given two or more investments with only one to be undertaken, the rate-of-return method ignores the sizes of the investments. The rate of return on the incremental cash flows generated by the incremental investment may be below the acceptable rate. In such cases, the present value method yields the more accurate rate and should be used.

The primary objective is to present an approach to the quantification of capital expenditures. The concept of present values has theoretical validity and practicability in the capital budgeting process. It provides the basis for a systematic analysis of available alternative investment proposals. But sophistication and refinement of procedure cannot insure a best choice if the data are wrong. The data used are projections of expectations—often long range—involving revenue, costs, equipment life, human and material performance, and so on. Under such conditions of uncertainty, skillful managerial judgment is imperative. Finally, there are irreducible factors that cannot be quantified. An investment may have a direct or indirect effect on employee morale or on relations with the community, which, if not carefully judged, could cause irreparable harm. There is usually no single right answer. Sophisticated analytical procedures will not mitigate the effects of poor judgment as to market potential, available resources, and environmental factors—economic, political, and social.

GLOSSARY

Annual Cost of an Investment Net investment divided by the present value factor corresponding to the desired rate of return and estimated life.

Capital Budgeting The allocation and commitment of funds to long-term capital investment projects.

Cost of Capital A bench mark used in capital budgeting decisions; the minimum rate of return should be not less than the cost of the funds invested in the project.

Excess Present Value A bench mark used in capital budgeting decisions with the desirability of an investment indicated by the difference, at a common point of time, between the cost of the investment and the expected earnings from that investment discounted at the desired minimum rate.

Internal Rate of Return The rate at which the present value of cash inflows and outflows offset each other.

Investment Opportunity Concept The concept that, in a capital budgeting decision, the appropriate rate of return is based on the subjective evaluation of the available investment opportunities and their respective earnings rates.

Payback A method of measuring the desirability of a project in terms of how soon the cash invested in a project will be returned.

Present Value Method The conversion of cash inflows and outflows over time to the present, using the firm's cost of capital as the discounting rate, for purposes of comparing capital expenditures.

Time-Adjusted Rate of Return See *Internal Rate of Return*.

QUESTIONS

Q25-1. What is capital budgeting? Why are the principles of compound interest relevant to capital budgeting?

Q25-2. What is meant (a) by simple interest? (b) by compound interest? (c) by present value? (d) by compound discount? (e) by ordinary annuity amount? (f) by present value of an ordinary annuity?

Q25-3. What kind of investment problems lend themselves to rate-of-return measurement techniques?

Q25-4. What constitutes a satisfactory rate of return? How is a rate selected? How is it determined?

Q25-5. What is meant by the term *discounted cash flow?*

Q25-6. Why is it appropriate in making capital budgeting decisions to emphasize the relevant cash flows rather than revenue and expense valuations based on generally accepted accounting principles?

Q25-7. What are the steps to be taken in measuring the rate of return on a proposed capital expenditure?

Q25-8. How is the annual cost of an investment measured? Of what use is such a measurement?

Q25-9. What is meant (a) by excess present value? (b) by excess present value index?

Q25-10. What is the relevance of depreciation and income taxes to capital budgeting problems?

Q25-11. (a) Define *payback.* What are (b) its advantages? (c) its disadvantages?

Q25-12. What limitations are inherent in the application of present value to capital budgeting problems?

Q25-13. "The excess present value method is wrong because it ignores depreciation." Comment on this statement.

Q25-14. "The method of depreciation does not affect the capital budgeting decision." Comment on this statement.

EXERCISES

Note: For all exercises and problems, use an interest rate of 20% unless otherwise instructed.

E25-1. Students A and B have expressed contrary views to you regarding each of the following matters and ask your help in settling their differences:

1. The amount of $75 today is more valuable than $100 five years from today.
2. It is worthwhile to invest $4,500 now in a canteen operation that will earn about $1,200 a year for the next five years.
3. It is better to invest $6,000 in food vending machines that will earn about $2,500 a year for five years than to invest $9,200 in a similar business that will earn about $3,300 a year for five years.
4. An investment of $35,000 in a business that will earn $5,600 a year for ten years will not earn a 10% return.
5. To justify a $75,000 investment in a ten-year concession operation, earnings would have to be at least $18,000 a year.
6. Projects A and B each involve a $3,000 investment but the net cash proceeds for the first year are $2,900 and $2,500, respectively. Project A should therefore be selected.

E25-2. What is the approximate rate of return on an investment with an initial cash outlay of $20,000 and net cash inflows of $6,000 a year for five years?

E25-3. A machine that costs $20,000 will reduce present operating costs by $4,000 a year (net). What is the approximate rate of return if the life of the machine is (a) 10 years? (b) 20 years? (c) What must the minimum useful life of the machine be if the required rate of return is 16%?

E25-4. A company has an opportunity to make one of three possible investments, as follows:

	1	2	3
Investment	$48,000	$60,000	$70,000
Estimated net cash inflow			
Year 1	15,000	20,000	25,000
Year 2	23,000	30,000	35,000
Year 3	25,000	34,000	45,000

For each investment determine (a) the payback period, (b) the excess present value, (c) the excess present value index, and (d) the time-adjusted rate of return.

E25-5. The engineer for the Waibel Corporation has proposed the installation of certain equipment that he estimates will produce the following net after-tax savings over a five-year period:

Year	Savings
1	$1,800
2	2,200
3	2,500
4	2,800
5	2,800

What is the maximum amount that should be paid for the equipment? (Assume a minimum rate of return of 16%.)

E25-6. The Ventura Machine Company is considering replacing a machine presently in use and carried on the books at $12,000 with a new machine costing $25,000. The new machine will make possible cost reductions of $4,000 annually for 10 years. The old machine, which could otherwise be continued in use for another 10 years, can be sold for $5,200.

Assuming the use of straight-line depreciation, a desired rate of return of 20%, and an income tax rate of 50%, should the replacement be made?

E25-7. What is the maximum amount that should be paid for a business that will earn $15,000 a year for five years, at the end of which time it can be sold for about $40,000?

E25-8. Net cash earnings from the introduction of a new product are expected to be $90,000 for 10 years. An initial investment of $450,000 will have to be made. (a) What is the internal rate of return? (b) Should the investment be made if the cost of capital is 16%?

E25-9. A new design computer is being considered for the design engineering group of the automotive division of the Kelsey Manufacturing Company, Inc. The investment will have no effect on revenue but will reduce operating expenses by $1,000,000 a year for the next seven years.

The equipment will cost $3,000,000, has an estimated useful life of 6 years, and a salvage value of $600,000 at the end of the sixth year. Annual fixed costs are $100,000. These will not change. Should the investment be made, assuming a desired rate of return of 16%?

DEMON-
STRATION
PROBLEMS

DP25-1. (*Payback; excess present value; internal rate of return*) Correy, Inc., plans to invest $200,000 in certain improved metal fabrication equipment that is expected to save $70,000 (net after taxes) annually for ten years. Additional working capital of $20,000 will be required. Assume a 50% income tax rate and straight-line depreciation with no salvage value.

Required:

1. Compute the payback period.
2. Compute the excess present value.
3. Compute the internal rate of return.

DP25-2. (*Payback; excess present value; rates of return*) The National Machine Company plans to spend $100,000 on land for the construction of a factory and an adjoining warehouse. Preparation of the site for construction (deductible as an expense) will be $50,000; construction of buildings will cost $1,650,000, and additional working capital of $100,000 will be needed. The new facilities are expected to bring savings of $400,000 (before taxes and depreciation) annually for ten years. The sum-of-the-years'-digits method of depreciation is used. Assume a 50% income tax rate.

Required: Determine whether the plan should be undertaken.

DP25-3. (*Payback, excess present value; rates of return*) The Cork Company is considering a proposal to add an electrozinc-plating unit for finishing work now being done by outside contractors at an average cost of $0.027 a pound. Annual requirements are 2,500,000 pounds. Two types are available.

	Semiautomatic	*Fully Automatic*
Purchase price	$25,000	$ 50,000
Operating costs per unit	$ 0.024	$0.01955
Economic life	8 years	8 years

Required: Determine which type of unit is preferable.

COST
ACCUMULATION,
AND CONTROL;
FINANCIAL
PLANNING

956

(Ch. 25)

P25-1. The Renay Chemical Company is considering the advisability of buying a new reactor that can handle products at high temperatures. The reactor will make possible annual savings in labor and maintenance costs of about $12,000. Data regarding the new reactor are as follows:

Purchase price	$50,000
Salvage value	5,000
Estimated life	15 years

Required: Determine whether the reactor should be purchased.

P25-2. The Kahn Corporation owns 60 concrete block buildings that house certain metering and control equipment. To maintain good public relations with the residents and officials of the towns in which the buildings are located, it is necessary to paint the buildings regularly at an annual cost of $23,000. It has been proposed that the buildings be covered with aluminum siding at a cost of $70,000; this will eliminate all further maintenance. The guarantee period is 15 years.

Required: Determine whether the proposal should be approved.

P25-3. The B. G. Baker Company is planning to buy a continuous gelatin dryer to replace the hand nets currently used to perform the drying operation. The useful life of the dryer is ten years and its installed cost is $400,000. The old equipment has a carrying value of $75,000 and can be sold for $30,000.

The new dryer will reduce labor costs and fringe benefits by $100,000 annually and will eliminate the need for nets at a saving of $30,000 each year. Maintenance costs will increase by $20,000 annually. The new dryer is expected to improve the quality of the product and eliminate some presently existing sanitation problems.

The company uses the straight-line method of depreciation and is subject to a combined Federal and state income tax of 50%. The present equipment can be used for another ten years.

Required: Determine whether the dryer should be purchased to replace the old equipment.

P25-4. John Ford, the plant engineer for the Jones Company, has been asked to procure equipment that will improve the present method used by the company for shearing bar stock. He finds three different systems, each of which will improve present methods and reduce space requirements. The costs of the systems are as follows:

A	$ 60,000
B	90,000
C	100,000

The work to be done by the new equipment currently requires 3,300 hours annually at an hourly variable cost of $24.02. The new systems will do the same work in 1,100 hours at the following rates:

A	$29
B	26
C	21

The company plans to depreciate the new equipment over eight years, using the straight-line method, and is subject to a 50% combined state and Federal income tax rate. No salvage value is expected.

The old equipment is fully depreciated and has no salvage value. The new system will not require increased working capital.

Required:

1. Compute the payback period.
2. Compute the internal rate of return.

P25-5. The Rosen Company is considering the replacement of conventional drilling equipment with a numerically controlled drilling machine. The purchase price of the machine, including controls, is $60,000. Freight and installation costs are $1,800. Other first-year expenses include a programmer at $15,000 and training fees of $2,000. The useful life of the machine is ten years. Projected annual savings are as follows:

Reduction in tooling costs	$13,857
Reduction in tool wear and tear	600
Reduced scrap and rework costs	494
Reduced floor space: 200 square feet × $3.00 per square foot	600
Reduced maintenance	600
Reduction in labor and fringe benefits	8,000

After the first year, the part-time services of a programmer will be needed at an annual cost of $3,500.

Required: Compute the internal rate of return, assuming no salvage value, a 50% income tax rate, and straight-line depreciation.

P25-6. The Crowell Company needs equipment to produce about 1,500 microcircuits a week for the next five years. Rapidly evolving microcircuit technology makes projections for any period longer than five years hazardous. Two methods are being considered, as follows:

	A	B
Investment for equipment	$30,000	$36,000
Variable costs per 1-inch microcircuit		
(exclusive of transistors and diodes)	0.83	0.80

The choice of method will not affect sales volume, because the microcircuits are incorporated into a larger piece of equipment. No salvage value is expected.

Required: Determine which investment should be made.

P25-7. A new design computer is being considered for the design engineering group of the automotive division of the Svensen Manufacturing Company, Inc. The investment will have no effect on revenue but will reduce operating expenses by $750,000 a year for the next eight years.

The equipment will cost $3,000,000, has an estimated useful life of eight years, and a salvage value of $400,000 at the end of the eighth year. Annual fixed costs are $90,000. These will not change.

Required: Should the investment be made, assuming a desired rate of return of 16%?

P25-8. The Lynd Company has the following two investment proposals under consideration:

(Ch. 25)

| | **Proposal** | |
	Product A	*Product B*
Investment	$250,000	$250,000
Salvage	$5,000	$15,000
Estimated life (years)	5	5
Unit selling price	$1.25	$1.00
Variable cost per unit	$0.75	$0.60
Fixed costs—annual	$180,000	$150,000

Projected unit sales and their probabilities are as follows:

| *Product A* | | *Product B* | |
Units	Probability	Units	Probability
1,000,000	0.1	900,000	0.2
800,000	0.2	700,000	0.6
600,000	0.4	400,000	0.2
400,000	0.2		
200,000	0.1		
	1.0		1.0

Required: Which investment proposal should the company choose? Explain fully. Assume 14% cost of capital.

P25-9. The Gaynor Corporation performs accurate light machining operations on numerous small parts for certain scientific instruments. Orders are for small lots, each requiring special jigs and fixtures. The company has been investigating the possible use of numerically controlled machining techniques, which would make possible multiple machining operations in one setup and eliminate the need for the special jigs and fixtures. This, in turn, would lessen the problems of quality control and reduce inventory requirements. Companies now using numerically controlled equipment report reductions in machining time of from 50% to 80% and can produce parts of a quality higher than that produced with conventional machinery. Subsequent studies by the Gaynor Corporation indicate possible savings in the following areas:

1. Labor hours
2. Variable overhead
3. Inventory carrying costs
4. Scrap and rework
5. Inspection
6. Tooling costs

The company has made a study of the savings that would result on 195 parts suitable for numerically controlled machining to be phased into the new program in two stages: 98 parts at the beginning of the first year and the remainder at the beginning of the second year.

Labor hours. The 195 parts currently require 11,000 machining hours annually at an average hourly rate of $2.80 (including fringe benefits). The same parts can be machined on numerically controlled equipment in 6,000 hours.

Variable overhead. The present overhead rate is $7 a direct labor hour. This amount includes 20 cents for fringe benefits and 41 cents for depreciation and other nonvariable costs.

Inventory carrying costs. The average inventory cost of the 195 parts is $50,000, with an annual turnover ratio of 4:1. Use of numerically controlled equipment would require an average inventory cost of $16,250. Inventory carrying charges are presently 20%, but since present storage space and stores personnel would remain unchanged, annual savings of about $5,000 are anticipated.

Scrap and rework. A review of the quality control records and monthly rework reports showed rework costs due to shop errors for the 195 parts of about $3,000. The built-in self-monitoring devices of the numerically controlled equipment should eliminate at least 90% of rework costs.

Inspection. Since the numerically controlled equipment is highly accurate within the guaranteed limits, it will be necessary to inspect only the first piece of each lot and one or two other pieces, instead of every piece. This will reduce inspection costs by $3,000 annually.

Tooling costs. Anticipated savings relating to tooling result (1) from design and fabrication of tools for new parts and (2) from maintenance of existing tools. Design and fabrication of new parts suitable for the numerically controlled equipment is expected to number 43, 85, and 85, respectively, for the first three years of use, after which the two-shift capacity of the machine will have been reached. Numerically controlled tooling is $75 a part, compared with the current $300 a part. Savings from general tool maintenance would continue on an annual basis at $5,000 yearly.

The cost of the numerically controlled equipment is $140,000, consisting of the following:

Basic machine price	$112,000
Tool holders and accessories	20,000
Installation	8,000
Total	$140,000

In addition, one-time costs of $11,000 would be incurred for the basic program for producing tapes and for training programmers and operators.

It is estimated that the equipment will be worth $14,000 at the end of its expected six-year life. The company uses the sum-of-the-years'-digits method of depreciation and is subject to a 50% income tax rate. Its cost of capital is 16%.

Required: Write a report to management, giving your recommendations and reasons for the action you recommend, together with supporting schedules and exhibits.

P25-10. The Beta Corporation manufactures office equipment and distributes its products through wholesale distributors.

Beta recently learned of a patent on the production of a semiautomatic paper collator that can be obtained at a cost of $60,000 cash. The semiautomatic model is vastly superior to the manual model that the corporation now produces. At a cost of $40,000, present equipment could be modified to accommodate the production of the new semiautomatic model. Such modifications would not affect the remaining useful life of four years or the salvage value of $10,000 that the equipment now has. Variable costs, however, would increase by $1 a unit. Fixed costs, other than relevant amortization charges, would not be affected. If the equipment is modified, the manual model cannot be produced.

(Ch. 25)

The current income statement relating to the manual collator appears as follows:

Sales (100,000 units @ $4)		$400,000
Variable costs	$180,000	
Fixed costs*	120,000	
Total costs		$300,000
Net Income before income taxes		$100,000
Income taxes (40%)		40,000
Net income after income taxes		$ 60,000

* All fixed costs are directly allocable to the production of the manual collator and include depreciation on equipment of $20,000, calculated on the straight-line basis with a useful life of 10 years.

Market research has disclosed three important findings on the new semiautomatic model. First, a particular competitor will certainly purchase the patent if Beta Corporation does not. In this case, Beta Corporation's sales of the manual collator would fall to 70,000 units a year. Second, if no increase in the selling price is made, Beta Corporation could sell approximately 190,000 units a year of the semiautomatic model. Third, because of the advances being made in this area, the patent will be completely worthless at the end of four years.

Because of the uncertainty of the current situation, the raw materials inventory has been almost completely exhausted. Regardless of the decision reached, substantial and immediate inventory replenishment will be required. The engineering department estimates that if the new model is to be produced, the average monthly raw materials inventory will be $20,000. If the old model is continued, the inventory balance will average $12,000 a month.

Required:

1. Prepare a schedule which shows the incremental after-tax cash flows for the comparison of the two alternatives. Assume that the corporation will use the sum-of-the-years'-digits method for depreciating the costs of modifying the equipment.
2. Assuming that the incremental after-tax cash flows calculated in requirement 1 and the annual incomes for the two alternatives are as given in the following schedule, will Beta Corporation, if it has a cost of capital of 18%, decide to manufacture the semiautomatic collator? Use the net present value decision rule and assume that all operating revenues and expenses occur at the end of the year.

Year	Incremental Cash Flow (000 omitted)	Annual Income (000 omitted)	
		Manual	SemiAutomatic
1 Beginning	$−110	—	—
1 End	+ 40	$24	$39
2 End	+ 40	24	39
3 End	+ 40	24	39
4 End	+ 50	24	39

Interest factors for 18%:

Period	Present Value of $1.00	Present Value of $1 a period Received at End of Period	Accumulated Value of $1.00	Accumulated Value of $1 a Period Received at End of Period
1	.85	.85	1.18	1.00
2	.72	1.57	1.39	2.18
3	.61	2.18	1.64	3.57
4	.52	2.70	1.94	5.21

3. Calculate the accounting rate of return for each project. Using this method, would you recommend that Beta manufacture the semiautomatic collator? Explain.
4. What additional analytical techniques, if any, would you consider before presenting a recommendation to management? Why?
5. What concerns would you have about using the information as given in the problem to reach a decision in this case?

(*IMA adapted*)

P25-11. The Baxter Company manufactures toys and other short-lived fad items.

The research and development department came up with an item that would make a good promotional gift for office equipment dealers. Aggressive and effective effort by Baxter's sales personnel has resulted in almost firm commitments for this product for the next three years. It is expected that the product's value will be exhausted by that time.

In order to produce the quantity demanded, Baxter will need to buy additional machinery and to rent some additional space. It appears that about 25,000 square feet will be needed. 12,500 square feet of presently unused, but leased, space is available now. (Baxter's present lease, with 10 years to run, costs $3 a foot.) There is another 12,500 square feet adjoining the Baxter facility which Baxter will rent for three years at $4 a square foot a year if it decides to make this product.

The equipment will be purchased for about $900,000. It will require $30,000 in modifications, $60,000 for installation, and $90,000 for testing; all these activities will be done by a firm of engineers hired by Baxter. All the expenditures will be paid for on January 1, 1976.

The equipment should have a salvage value of about $180,000 at the end of the third year. No additional general overhead costs are expected to be incurred.

The following estimates of revenues and expenses for this product for the three years have been developed.

	1976	1977	1978
Sales	$1,000,000	$1,600,000	$800,000
Material, Labor, and Incurred Overhead	$ 400,000	$ 750,000	$350,000

	1976	1977	1978
Assigned General Overhead	40,000	75,000	35,000
Rent	87,500	87,500	87,500
Depreciation	450,000	300,000	150,000
	$ 977,500	$1,212,500	$622,500
Income Before Tax	$ 22,500	$ 387,500	$177,500
Income Tax (40%)	9,000	155,000	71,000
	$ 13,500	$ 232,500	$106,500

Required:

1. Prepare a schedule which shows the incremental, after-tax cash flows for this project.
2. If the company requires a two-year payback period for its investment, will it undertake this project? Show your supporting calculations clearly.
3. Calculate the after-tax accounting rate of return for the project.
4. A newly hired business school graduate recommends that the company consider the use of the net present value analysis to study this project. If the company sets a required rate of return of 20% after taxes, will this project be accepted? Show your supporting calculations clearly. (Assume all operating revenues and expenses occur at the end of the year.)

Discount Factors for 20% (rounded off)

Period	Present Value of $1	Present Value of $1 a Period Received at End of Period	Accumulated Value of $1	Accumulated Value of $1 a Period Received at End of Period
1	.83	.83	1.20	1.00
2	.69	1.52	1.44	2.20
3	.58	2.10	1.73	3.64
4	.48	2.58	2.07	5.37

U.S. TREASURY DEPARTMENT
INTERNAL REVENUE SERVICE

AUDIT DIVISION

Federal Income Taxes 26

The major justification for the inclusion of an introduction to Federal income taxes in an elementary text is the need to emphasize the primary differences between traditional business income and taxable income. Accordingly, in this chapter, consideration is given (1) to highlights of Federal income taxation, (2) to income tax planning problems as a foundation for observing some examples of differences between book net income and taxable income, (3) to the impact of income taxes on business decisions, and (4) to some elementary financial reporting problems.

FEDERAL INCOME TAX

To acquaint the student with a few of the intricacies of the Federal income tax structure, this section includes discussions (1) of classes of taxpayers, (2) of tax accounting methods, (3) of individual income taxes, (4) of the partnership informational return, and (5) of corporate income taxes.

Classes of Taxpayers

Four kinds of separate entities are subject to the income tax: individuals, corporations, estates, and trusts; each must file a return and, if applicable, each must pay a tax on its taxable income.[1] Single proprietorships and partnerships

[1] Some trusts, all of whose income goes to beneficiaries, file tax returns for information purposes only. The income received from these trusts by the individual beneficiaries should be reported on their individual tax returns. Under these circumstances, the trust would not pay any income taxes.

are not taxed as separate entities. Rather, the single proprietor reports his business income along with all his personal income on Form 1040, the U. S. Individual Income Tax Return. The partnership files a separate informational return, Form 1065, but each partner reports his share of net income, together with his personal nonpartnership income on his Form 1040.

Tax Accounting Methods

The Internal Revenue Code sets forth rules, and the Internal Revenue Service establishes regulations, regarding the inclusion and exclusion of certain revenue and expense items and the use of certain methods and procedures in computing taxable income.

The Internal Revenue Code, however, permits taxpayers to select certain options, among them the alternative of choosing the cash or the accrual basis of computing net income under certain circumstances. To reiterate, on the cash basis, income is recognized when cash is received and expenses are considered to be incurred when the cash expenditure is made. Although the cash basis usually is not a satisfactory method of measuring net business income, for tax purposes it is well suited for individuals not engaged in business and also, to a lesser extent, for businesses in which inventories, payables, and receivables are not a major factor. An individual whose only income is salary is required to use the cash basis.

The cash basis allowed for income tax purposes is modified in two ways: (1) The cost of a long-lived asset cannot be deducted in the year of its purchase; the taxpayer must treat the item as an asset and apportion its cost over its useful service life. (2) Revenue is recognized when it is constructively received, that is, when the revenue is in the control of the taxpayer. For example, interest credited to a savings and loan account is deemed to be constructively received even though the cash is not yet in the hands of the taxpayer.

The taxpayer should choose the method permissible under the law that will postpone and avoid taxes, thereby conserving working capital and achieving the lowest long-run tax cost.

The accrual basis of measuring income has been discussed in preceding chapters of this text. Under this method, revenue is recognized in the period when a sale is made or a service is rendered, irrespective of when cash is received; and expenses are recognized in the period when services are received and utilized in the production of revenue. The accrual basis is required of those businesses in which production, purchases, and sales of merchandise are significant factors. Any taxpayer other than a salaried person who maintains a set of accounting records may elect to use the accrual basis.

INDIVIDUAL INCOME TAX

The individual taxpayer computes his tax by following the outline provided on the U. S. Individual Income Tax Return, Form 1040. Figure 26-1 presents the basic content of Form 1040 and shows the tax formula for individuals.

Gross Income. All income not specifically excluded by law is includable in

FEDERAL
INCOME TAXES:
CONTEMPORARY
TOPICS

968

(Ch. 26)

Figure 26-1 Individual Income Tax Chart

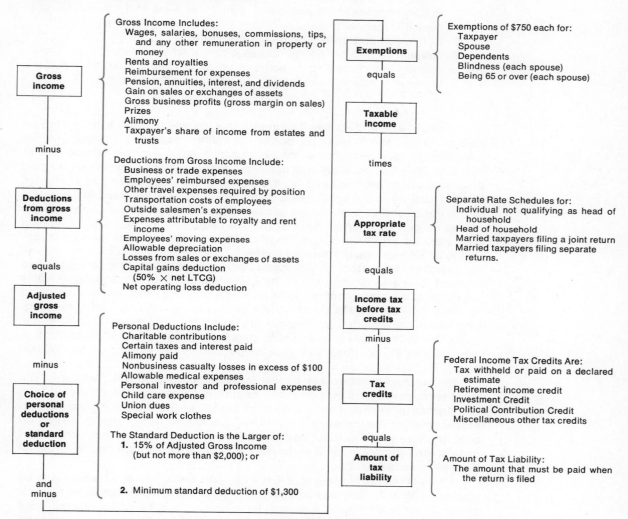

Gross Income Includes:
  Wages, salaries, bonuses, commissions, tips, and any other remuneration in property or money
  Rents and royalties
  Reimbursement for expenses
  Pension, annuities, interest, and dividends
  Gain on sales or exchanges of assets
  Gross business profits (gross margin on sales)
  Prizes
  Alimony
  Taxpayer's share of income from estates and trusts

Deductions from Gross Income Include:
  Business or trade expenses
  Employees' reimbursed expenses
  Other travel expenses required by position
  Transportation costs of employees
  Outside salesmen's expenses
  Expenses attributable to royalty and rent income
  Employees' moving expenses
  Allowable depreciation
  Losses from sales or exchanges of assets
  Capital gains deduction
    (50% × net LTCG)
  Net operating loss deduction

Personal Deductions Include:
  Charitable contributions
  Certain taxes and interest paid
  Alimony paid
  Nonbusiness casualty losses in excess of $100
  Allowable medical expenses
  Personal investor and professional expenses
  Child care expense
  Union dues
  Special work clothes

The Standard Deduction is the Larger of:
  1. 15% of Adjusted Gross Income
     (but not more than $2,000); or

  2. Minimum standard deduction of $1,300

Exemptions of $750 each for:
  Taxpayer
  Spouse
  Dependents
  Blindness (each spouse)
  Being 65 or over (each spouse)

Separate Rate Schedules for:
  Individual not qualifying as head of household
  Head of household
  Married taxpayers filing a joint return
  Married taxpayers filing separate returns.

Federal Income Tax Credits Are:
  Tax withheld or paid on a declared estimate
  Retirement income credit
  Investment Credit
  Political Contribution Credit
  Miscellaneous other tax credits

Amount of Tax Liability:
  The amount that must be paid when the return is filed

gross income. In addition to the items mentioned in Figure 26-1, gambling winnings and income from illegal activities must be included in gross income.

The following are specifically excluded by law, Treasury regulations, or court decisions:

1. Interest on state and municipal bonds and notes
2. Qualified dividends received by each spouse who actually owns stock, not to exceed $100 for each owner
3. Gifts, inheritances, and bequests received
4. Life insurance proceeds received on the death of the insured
5. Amounts received from workmen's compensation, unemployment compensation, and other kinds of insurance, with a limit of usually $100 a week, under certain conditions

FEDERAL
INCOME
TAXES

6. Social security receipts
7. Return of investment portion of annuity receipts and other returns of capital investments
8. GI benefits and certain veteran's payments
9. Income earned by United States citizens while residing in a foreign country and from foreign sources up to $20,000 a year, provided the taxpayer remains in the foreign country at least 18 months.

Capital Gains and Losses. The income tax treatment of gains and losses on sale of capital assets—stocks, bonds, and other qualifying property—is extremely important, because net long-term capital gains are taxed at one-half, or less than one-half, the rates applicable to ordinary income. The amount of gain or loss is the difference between the selling price and the tax basis. The tax basis is cost when the asset was acquired by purchase, the basis in the hands of the donor and in some cases fair market value when the property was acquired by gift, fair market value at date of death (or the alternative valuation date used for estate tax purposes) when the property was acquired by inheritance, and other legally specified bases.

Gains or losses from capital assets held for six months or less are classified as short term and 100 percent of the gain must be reported. Short-term gains are taxed as ordinary income. Gains and losses arising from capital assets held for more than six months are classified as long term; only one-half of net long-term gains are included in adjusted gross income. The maximum rate of tax applicable to the gross (before the 50 percent reduction) gain is 25 percent on the first $50,000 of gross gain plus 35 percent of the excess above $50,000 gain.

In computing deductible capital losses, the sum of 100 percent of the short-term losses plus 50 percent of long-term losses may be deducted from other gross income up to a maximum of $1,000, or the taxable income, whichever is smaller. The unused portion of the capital loss, however, may be carried over to future years, without any limitation on the number of years, and offset against the ordinary income of those years, not to exceed the maximum limitations per year as stated.

The income tax law requires that long-term and short-term transactions be combined in a certain way in computing adjusted gross income. In the first place, all long-term gains and long-term losses must be offset against each other in order to determine the net long-term gain or loss. In a similar manner, short-term gains and losses must be combined. The combination and netting of long-term and short-term items produce a number of situations that require further explanation. For example, a taxpayer may have both a net long-term gain and a net short-term gain. In this case, he would treat the two items separately: the entire short-term gain would be included in gross income and treated as ordinary income. Similarly, if a taxpayer has net short-term losses and net long-term losses, he would combine 100 percent of the short-term capital loss plus 50 percent of the long-term capital loss into one figure, and would deduct up to $1,000 in the computation of adjusted gross income. Still further, it is possible for a taxpayer to have either short-term or long–term gains greater than opposite type losses of a long-term or short-term nature. These must be combined to arrive at either a net long-term gain or a net short-term

Figure 26-2
Capital Gain and
Loss Rules

Case A		Case B	
Net LTCG	$5,000	Net LTCL	$1,000
Net STCG	1,000	Net STCL	500
		Total Capital Loss	$1,500
		Less: 50 percent of net LTCL	500
		Deductible Capital Loss	$1,000

Includable in AGI:

All the STCG is included, but only one-half LTCG; the total included in AGI is $3,500.
Note that the entire gain of $6,000 is included in gross and that a deduction of $2,500 from gross income is allowed to calculate the amount to be included in AGI of $3,500.

Deductible from Gross Income:

Only $1,000 is deductible in the current year to arrive at AGI.

Case C		Case D	
Net LTCG	$4,000	Net LTCL	$4,200
Net STCL	2,500	Net STCG	5,600
Net capital gain (long-term)	$1,500	Net capital gain (short term)	$1,400

Includable in AGI:

50 percent of the $1,500, or $750, is included.

Includable in AGI:

The entire $1,400 would be included and taxed as ordinary income.

Abbreviations used in this illustration are:
Net LTCG—Net long-term capital gain
Net STCG—Net short-term capital gain
Net LTCL—Net long-term capital loss
Net STCL—Net short-term capital loss
AGI—Adjusted gross income

gain, depending on the characteristic of the dominant gain. These rules are illustrated in Figure 26-2.

Deductions from Gross Income. The various classes of deductions from gross income are indicated in Figure 26-1. In general, they are self-explanatory. A brief word about a few should suffice.

Business expenses are the ordinary and necessary expenses of carrying on a trade, business, or profession. In actual practice, business expenses are

(Ch. 26)

deducted from business revenue on a separate Schedule C to Form 1040, and only the net income from business is included in adjusted gross income.

Allowable employee expenses are necessary and must actually be incurred in connection with the employment.

Losses from sales or exchanges may qualify as capital losses and hence would follow the rules summarized in Figure 26-2.

The *capital gains deduction* is 50 percent of the net long-term capital gains (as determined in Figure 26-2). Legally, 100 percent of long-term capital gains qualifies as gross income. As indicated previously, however, in deriving the long-term capital gains to be included in adjusted gross income, it is necessary to deduct the capital gains deduction from the legal gross income item, the 100 percent amount of net long-term capital gain.

Personal Deductions or Percentage Standard Deduction and Minimum Standard Deduction. A taxpayer has the option of itemizing personal deductions, some of which are listed in Figure 26-1, or taking the standard deduction, whichever will benefit him most. Some of the personal deductions have limits. For example, contributions to recognized charitable, religious, educational, and other eleemosynary organizations are limited to a percentage that may vary from 20 to 50 percent of adjusted gross income. The limitation depends upon whether the eleemosynary organization is publicly supported or is a certain type of private foundation. Publicly supported organizations include religious, educational, community chest, and other charitable organizations that derive the majority of their funds from the general public. The nonpublicly supported charities that have a limitation of 20 percent include private foundations that do not distribute all their revenue within two and one-half months following the close of the year to qualifying charities. If the contributions to the publicly supported organizations are at least 30 percent of adjusted gross income, the limit is 50 percent of adjusted gross income; but if these contributions to the publicly supported organizations are not 30 percent of adjusted gross income, the limit is 20 percent of adjusted gross income plus the amount of the special contribution to the qualifying publicly supported organizations.

Gross medical expenses include doctor, hospital, dental fees, the cost of medicines and drugs in excess of 1 percent of adjusted gross income, travel to receive medical treatment, and medical and hospital insurance.

Deductible medical expenses consist of one-half the medical and hospital insurance, not to exceed $150, plus the amount of medical and dental expenses and remaining medical and hospital insurance in excess of 3 percent of adjusted gross income, with no maximum limit. To illustrate the computation of the deductible medical expenses, assume that a taxpayer has an adjusted gross income of $20,000; medical and hospital insurance of $360; drugs of $310; and other medical, dental, and hospital expenses of $1,800. (See computation on page 973).

The optional standard deduction is the larger of the allowable *percentage standard deduction* or the *minimum standard deduction*. The percentage standard deduction is 15 percent of adjusted gross income with a maximum amount of $2,000. A married taxpayer filing a separate return is allowed the same percentage, but only up to one-half the indicated maximum amount.

The minimum standard deduction is designed primarily to remove poverty level taxpayers from the tax rolls. For those taxpayers who are required to file a

FEDERAL
INCOME TAXES:
CONTEMPORARY
TOPICS

972

(Ch. 26)

Deductible Medical Expenses:
  One-half of medical and hospital insurance,
    ½ × $360 = $180; this exceeds $150,
    thus the deductible portion is $ 150.00
Gross Medical:
  Remaining medical and hospital insurance $ 210.00
  Allowable drugs:
    Gross drugs $310
    Less: 1% of $20,000 (AGI)   200   110.00
  Other medical, dental, and
    hospital expenses   1,800.00
Gross Medical $2,120.00
Less: 3% × $20,000 (AGI)   600.00   1,520.00
Deductible Medical Expense $1,670.00

return and who elect to use the minimum standard deduction rather than the percentage standard deduction, the amount of the deduction is $1,300. For a married taxpayer filing a separate return, it is $650.

Exemptions. A personal exemption of $750 is allowed for the taxpayer, for his spouse if a joint return is filed, and for each person who qualifies as a *dependent* of the taxpayer. The taxpayer and spouse may claim special exemptions if he or she is blind, or if either is 65 years or over.

Under the law, a dependent is a person (1) who receives over one-half his support from the taxpayer, (2) who is closely related to the taxpayer or lives in his home, (3) who has received less than $750 in gross income during the year, unless the dependent is a child of the taxpayer under 19 years old or a full-time student, and (4) who has not filed a joint return.

Individual Income Tax Rates. Once the taxable income is properly determined, the income tax before credits is computed by multiplying the appropriate tax rates by the net taxable income. The tax rates that are applied depend upon the rate qualification of the taxpayer. There is a separate tax schedule for a single person who does not qualify as head of household, a schedule for an individual who does qualify as head of household, a schedule for a married couple filing a joint return, and still another schedule for married taxpayers filing separate returns. All these rates are progressive; that is, those with the lowest taxable income are taxed at the lowest rate and those with larger taxable incomes are taxed at progressively higher rates. The progressive character of the individual tax rate can be observed from Figure 26-3, which shows the individual income tax rates, starting at 14 percent and rising gradually to 70 percent. (The taxpayer must consult the latest rates, which are furnished by the Internal Revenue Service, before he prepares his Federal income tax return.)

The separate tax schedule for married taxpayers is designed to eliminate tax inequity for married couples in states having community property laws that permit them to divide gross income and for couples in states that do not have such laws. Married couples filing a joint return determine their income tax before credits by applying the rates indicated in Rate Schedule No. 2 of Figure 26-

Figure 26-3
Individual Income Tax
Rate Schedule

	Individual Income Tax Rates for Filing in 1974							
	Rate Schedule No. 1		Rate Schedule No. 2		Rate Schedule No. 3		Rate Schedule No. 4	
	Separate Returns (Unmarried taxpayers)		Joint Returns (Married taxpayers and surviving spouses)		Head of Household Returns		Separate Returns (Married taxpayers)	
Taxable Income	Tax	Rate on Excess	Tax	Rate on Excess	Tax	Rate on Excess	Tax	Rate on Excess
Up to $500		14%		14%		14%		14%
500	$ 70	15	$ 70	14	$ 70	14	$ 70	15
1,000	145	16	140	15	140	16	145	16
1,500	225	17	215	15	220	16	225	17
2,000	310	19	290	16	300	18	310	19
3,000	500	19	450	17	480	18	500	19
4,000	690	21	620	19	660	19	690	22
6,000	1,110	24	1,000	19	1,040	22	1,130	25
8,000	1,590	25	1,380	22	1,480	23	1,630	28
10,000	2,090	27	1,820	22	1,940	25	2,190	32
12,000	2,630	29	2,260	25	2,440	27	2,830	36
14,000	3,210	31	2,760	25	2,980	28	3,550	39
16,000	3,830	34	3,260	28	3,540	31	4,330	42
18,000	4,510	36	3,820	28	4,160	32	5,170	45
20,000	5,230	38	4,380	32	4,800	35	6,070	48
22,000	5,990	40	5,020	32	5,500	36	7,030	50
24,000	6,790	40	5,660	36	6,220	38	8,030	50
26,000	7,590	45	6,380	36	6,980	41	9,030	53
28,000	8,490	45	7,100	39	7,800	42	10,090	53
32,000	10,290	50	8,660	42	9,480	45	12,210	55
36,000	12,290	50	10,340	45	11,280	48	14,410	55
38,000	13,290	55	11,240	45	12,240	51	15,510	58
40,000	14,390	55	12,140	48	13,260	52	16,670	58
44,000	16,590	60	14,060	50	15,340	55	18,990	60
50,000	20,190	62	17,060	50	18,640	56	22,590	62
52,000	21,430	62	18,060	53	19,760	58	23,830	62
60,000	26,390	64	22,300	53	24,400	58	28,790	64
64,000	28,950	64	24,420	55	26,720	59	31,350	64
70,000	32,790	66	27,720	55	30,260	61	35,190	66
76,000	36,750	66	31,020	58	33,920	62	39,150	66
80,000	39,390	68	33,340	58	36,400	63	41,790	68
88,000	44,830	68	37,980	60	41,440	64	47,230	68
90,000	46,190	69	39,180	60	42,720	64	48,590	69
100,000	53,090	70	45,180	62	49,120	66	55,490	70
120,000	67,090	70	57,580	64	62,320	67	69,490	70
140,000	81,090	70	70,380	66	75,720	68	83,490	70
160,000	95,090	70	83,580	68	89,320	69	97,490	70
180,000	109,090	70	97,180	69	103,120	70	111,490	70
200,000	123,090	70	110,980	70	117,120	70	125,490	70

Examples of Use of Tax Tables

1. Unmarried taxpayer with taxable income of $23,000:

Tax on first $22,000	$5,990
Tax on excess: 40% × $1,000	400
Total tax	$6,390

2. Married taxpayer filing joint return with taxable income of $84,000:

Tax on first $80,000	$33,340
Tax on excess: 58% × $4,000	2,320
Total tax	$35,660

FEDERAL
INCOME TAXES:
CONTEMPORARY
TOPICS

974

(Ch. 26)

3, the tax rates that are specifically applicable to married taxpayers filing joint returns.

It should be noted that marital status is determined as of December 31 of a given taxable year. For example, if a couple were married on December 31, 1974, they would qualify to file a joint return for the entire taxable year of 1974.

The special tax schedule for head of household (Rate Schedule No. 3 of Figure 26-3) provides an element of relief for widows or widowers and others who qualify as head of household to compensate them partially for the additional family burden that they must carry. Only the following persons may qualify as head of household: (1) one who is unmarried (or separated) at the end of the taxable year, and (2) one who is married at the end of the year to an individual who was a nonresident alien at any time during the taxable year. Moreover, the individual must have furnished over one-half the cost of maintaining as the taxpayer's home a household that during the entire year, except for temporary absences, was occupied as the principal place of abode and as a member of such household (1) by any related person, other than the taxpayer's unmarried child, grandchild, or stepchild for whom the taxpayer is entitled to a deduction for an exemption, unless the deduction arises from a multiple support agreement, or (2) by the taxpayer's unmarried child, grandchild, or stepchild, even though such child is not a dependent. The rates, as shown in Rate Schedule No. 3 of Figure 26-3, are lower than for nonhead-of-household unmarried individuals but are higher than those for married couples filing joint returns.

Use of the Tax Tables. The Internal Revenue Service provides tax tables for taxpayers who have adjusted gross income of less than $10,000. The use of these tax tables is simply a short-cut method of figuring the income tax. The tables are based on the taxpayer's personal exemptions and the relevant standard deduction in place of itemized personal deductions and certain credits. It should be noted that a taxpayer desiring to make use of the minimum standard deduction must use the tax tables provided by the Internal Revenue Service. The special tax tables are prepared by the Internal Revenue Service and are mailed to the taxpayer at the same time Form 1040 is mailed.

Although there are four different classes of income taxpayers, there are only two different basic rate structures, the individual and corporate structures. An estate or a trust is subject to the income tax rates applicable to a single individual who does not qualify as head of household—that is, at the rates shown in Rate Schedule No. 1 of Figure 26-3. The corporate rate structure is considered in connection with the discussion of the corporate income tax.

Exceptions to the Schedule Tax Rates. There are two exceptions to the rates as published in Figure 26-3. First, the Revenue Act of 1969 imposed a new minimum tax on large taxpayers who have certain "tax preference items" such as accelerated depreciation, stock options, long-term capital gains, and other tax preference items. Form 4625, Computation of Minimum Tax, must be filed if a taxpayer has tax preference items in excess of $15,000, even though there may be no minimum tax due.

The other exception to the tax rate schedule is for large taxpayers who have large amounts of net long-term capital gains. To illustrate, assume that in 1974, Mr. and Mrs. Sam Samuelson had the following taxable income indicated on a joint return:

$75,000 Net Taxable Income Excluding
Net Long-Term Capital Gains
25,000 Net Long-Term Capital Gains
before 50 percent reduction

By including $12,500 of net long-term capital gains in taxable income, there would be $87,500 of taxable income and an indicated tax of $37,690, computed as follows:

Tax on first $80,000	$33,340
Add Tax on Remaining $7,500: 58% × $7,500	4,350
Indicated Tax	$37,690

Yet since long-term capital gains were subject in 1974 to a maximum tax of 25 percent on the first $50,000 and 35 percent on the excess of the amount above $50,000, without giving consideration to the 50 percent reduction, the actual tax would be $36,720, computed as follows:

Tax on ordinary taxable income of $75,000	
Tax on first $70,000	$27,720
Tax on remaining $5,000: 55% × $5,000	2,750
Tax on ordinary taxable income	$30,470
Tax on capital gains of $25,000	6,250
Total income tax for 1974	$36,720

Tax Credits. After the income tax has been computed, certain special credits may be deducted from this amount in computing the amount of the tax liability currently outstanding. Tax credits are typically allowed for the following:

1. Income Tax Withheld or Paid on Declared Estimate. A taxpayer takes credit for all salary withholding income taxes and for advance payments made on the basis of his Declaration of Estimated Income Tax, Form 1040-ES.

2. Retirement Income Credit. Persons who have worked for at least 10 years, in which at least $600 was earned in each year, who are now receiving qualifying retirement pay, and individuals over 65 who meet the same earnings test and who receive primarily rents, interest, and dividends are entitled to a tax credit of 15 percent of qualifying retirement income—rents, interest, dividends, and other—up to $1,524, or a maximum credit of $228.60; however, if a husband and wife, both 65 or over, file a joint return and if either one meets the 10-year work test, then the tax credit of 15 percent may be applied to qualifying retirement income up to $2,286, or a maximum credit of $342.90. The maximum allowable credit on a joint return where *both husband and wife* show retirement income of $1,524 is $457.20.

FEDERAL
INCOME TAXES:
CONTEMPORARY
TOPICS

976

(Ch. 26)

3. Investment Credit. A 7 percent investment tax credit applied to qualifying business equipment acquired is allowed.

4. Political Contribution Credit or Deduction. The 1971 Revenue Act provides a credit amounting to one-half a taxpayer's actual political contribution, made after December 31, 1971, with a maximum credit of $12.50, or $25 for a couple filing a joint return; alternatively the taxpayer could elect to take an itemized personal deduction for such actual contribution, made after December 31, 1971, up to a maximum $50, or $100 for a couple filing a joint return.

5. Miscellaneous Tax Credits. A few other rather infrequent tax credits are allowed. For example, a credit is allowed for taxes paid to foreign countries on income that is also taxed by the United States.

Income Averaging

Those taxpayers who have unusual fluctuations in income can use the allowable averaging device to ease the tax bite in peak income years. For income averaging to apply, the taxpayer must have at least $3,000 of "averagable income" which can be made up of almost any kind of ordinary or capital gains income. Schedule G of Form 1040 provides the instructions and formula required for income averaging. The basic logic back of the taxing of fluctuating peak income is to tax the excess amount above an average base period income at a lower bracket rate that it would be taxed if the gross amount were included in taxable income.

Illustrative Problem—Individual Income Tax

The following hypothetical case illustrates the major features of the individual Federal income tax computation:

John Thompson, who is 44 years old, is married to Faye Thompson, who is 40 years old. They have two children: a son, John, Jr., 10 years old; and Mary Kay, 20 years old, who is attending college. The Thompsons furnish over one-half the support of both their children, although Mary Kay works as a summer camp counselor and earned $900 in 1974.[2] Thompson owns and operates a grocery store under the name of Thompson Groceries. Mrs. Thompson did not earn any income in 1974. Relevant business and personal information for the family is shown in Figure 26-4.

The computation of the tax liability on a joint return filed by the Thompsons appears in summary form in Figure 26-5. Supporting information is shown in Schedules 1 through 5.

Partnerships are not taxed as separate entities. Rather, the relevant revenues and expenses of the partnership are reported on an informational return,

---

[2] The year 1974 rather than 1976 is used in the discussion in this chapter because statements made are based on the law in effect during 1974. The Federal tax rates are subject to change at any time.

FEDERAL
INCOME
TAXES

Figure 26-4
Tax Information—
John and Faye
Thompson

Income
  Net income from Thompson Groceries (gross margin on
    sales of $50,000 less operating expenses of $40,000) $10,000
  Interest on U.S. Bonds   1,000
  Interest on State of Massachusetts Bonds   1,800
  Dividends on stock jointly owned   3,200
  Net long-term capital gain from sale of 100 shares of
    National Carbon Company stock:

Date Acquired	Date Sold	Tax Basis (Cost)	Selling Price	
2/10/68	3/6/74	$4,000	$5,000	1,000

  Net short-term capital gain from sale of 200 shares of
    United Widgets Company stock:

Date Acquired	Date Sold	Tax Basis (Cost)	Selling Price	
1/10/74	4/1/74	$2,000	$2,500	500

Expenditures
  Contribution to church and university   800
  Contribution to Community Chest   200
  Interest paid on personal loans   300
  Property taxes paid to town and county   692
  State taxes paid
    Sales tax   158
    Automobile license tags   24
    Gasoline tax   100
  Family medical expenses
    Doctor and hospital fees   200
    Drugs and medicine   100
  Amount paid in 1974 as a result of filing Form 1040-ES,
    Declaration of Estimated Income Tax   1,700

Figure 26-5
Computation of the
Tax Liability

JOHN AND FAYE THOMPSON
Computation of Income Tax Liability
Taxable Year 1974

Gross Income (Schedule 1)		$55,500
Deductions from Gross Income		
Operating Expenses of the Grocery Store (from Figure 26-4)	$40,000	
Capital Gains Deduction 50% × Net LTCG of $1,000	500	
Total Deductions from Gross Income		40,500
Adusted Gross Income		$15,000
Personal Deductions (Schedule 2)	$2,250	
Personal Exemptions (Schedule 3)	3,000	5,250
Taxable Income		$ 9,750
Federal Income Tax for 1974 (Schedule 4)		$ 1,765
Tax Credits (Schedule 5)		1,700
Net Tax Liability		$ 65

FEDERAL
INCOME TAXES:
CONTEMPORARY
TOPICS

978

(Ch. 26)

Schedule 1—Gross Income

Gross Margin on Sales of Thompson Groceries	$50,000
Interest on U.S. Bonds	1,000
Dividends received ($100 per owner-spouse is excluded)	3,000
Net long-term capital gains before any deductions	1,000
Net short-term capital gains (100% included)	500
(Interest on State of Massachusetts Bonds is 100% excludable)	
Total Gross Income	$55,500

Schedule 2—Personal Deductions

Contributions (both apply since they do not exceed allowable limitation—all are qualifying special contributions)	$ 1,000
Interest paid on personal loans	300
Property taxes	692
Sales tax	158
Gasoline tax	100
(The $24 paid for license tags is not a deductible item in post-1963 years, and the medical expenses are not large enough to be included—only that part of the drugs that exceed $150 (1% of AGI of $15,000) would qualify as a gross medical expense and further only the medical expenses that exceed $450 (3% of AGI of $15,000) would qualify as a personal deduction.)	
Total Personal Deductions	$ 2,250

Schedule 3—Personal Exemptions

John Thompson	1
Faye Thompson	1
Mary Kay (Under a special relief provision of the tax law, she qualifies as an exemption for Thompson even though she earned over $750 income—she would have to file a return and could claim an exemption for herself; but Thompson may also claim her as an exemption)	1
John, Jr.	1
Total	4

Value of Personal Exemptions; 4 × $750 = $3,000

Schedule 4—Computations of Federal Income Tax

Referring to Rate Schedule No. 2, Figure 26–3 for married couples filing joint returns:	
Income tax on first $8,000	$ 1,380
Plus 22% × $1,750	385
Total Federal Income Tax for 1974	$ 1,765

Schedule 5—Tax Credits

Amount Paid in 1974 as a result of filing Form 1040-ES, Declaration of Estimated Income Tax for Individuals	$ 1,700

Form 1065, and the individual partners report their respective shares of operating income, net long-term and short-term capital gains, dividends received, contributions, tax-exempt income, and any other items that require special treatment on their own U. S. Individual Income Tax Returns.

Consider the partnership firm of Warren and Baker, which has an ordinary taxable income of $100,000 after salaries of $8,000 to George Warren and $10,000 to Peter Baker. Relevant items belonging to each partner are indicated in Figure 26-6.

On his U. S. Individual Income Tax Return, Warren, for example, would consolidate the following items with his own personal income and deductions: salary received from partnership, $8,000; ordinary income from partnership, $70,000; net long-term capital gains (only 50 percent included, but subject to special tax on capital gains), $700; net short-term capital gains, $700; dividends received (net of $100 exclusion, assuming that Warren is single and does not own any stocks personally), $6,900; and contributions, $1,540. The interest received on municipal bonds is tax exempt and hence would be excluded from Warren's gross income. Warren's individual Federal income tax would then be computed in the manner described in Figure 26-5.

CORPORATE INCOME TAXES

The income of business corporations is subject to a separate income tax, and the corporations are not allowed to deduct dividends paid to stockholders. Dividends are partially taxed to the individual stockholders who receive them. The special corporate tax rate schedule is a simple two-step progressive structure.

Taxable Income	Tax Rate
$0 to $25,000	22%
$25,000 and over	48%

In general, the taxable income of a corporation is computed in the same manner as the taxable income of an individual. Among the exceptions is the fact that a corporation may not take certain personal deductions allowed to individuals. For example, a corporation is not entitled to personal exemptions,

(Ch. 26)

Figure 26-6
Partnership Tax
Information

WARREN AND BAKER PARTNERSHIP
Tax Information—Taxable Year 1974

	Total	Warren's Share	Baker's Share
Partnership ordinary income	$100,000	$70,000	$30,000
Net long-term capital gains	2,000	1,400	600
Net short-term capital gains	1,000	700	300
Dividends received	10,000	7,000	3,000
Contributions	(2,200)	(1,540)	(660)
Interest received on municipal bonds	1,100	770	330
Total partnership income per books	$111,990	$78,330	$33,570

the standard deduction, or such deductions as medical expenses. Since personal deductions are not allowed, the concept of adjusted gross income would be meaningless and, therefore, is not applicable to the corporation.

The $100 dividend exclusion is not applicable to corporations. Normally, they may deduct from gross income 85 percent of dividends received from domestic corporations. Under certain conditions, when a consolidated return is filed for qualifying affiliates, the consolidated group may, in effect, deduct 100 percent of dividends received by members of the group from each other, that is, the intercompany dividend amount.

Capital losses of a corporation can be deducted only against capital gains. Capital losses may be carried back three years and forward five years and may be offset against any capital gains earned during those years, not counting the year of the loss. The unlimited carryover of losses rules included in the 1964 Revenue Act apply only to individuals; carryovers by corporations are still limited to five years.

Net long-term capital gains are 100 percent includable in taxable income of corporations, but are subject to a maximum tax rate of 30 percent. For example, if the Carter Corporation reported a taxable income in 1974 of $100,000, composed entirely of net long-term capital gains, its tax would be only $30,000; but if it reported an ordinary business income of $100,000, its tax would be $41,500.

A maximum limit of 5 percent of net income, figured without regard to the contribution deduction, for corporate contributions is imposed on corporations. Any contribution in excess of this limit may be carried over to the five succeeding years and deducted, provided the total contributions including the carried-over amounts are within the 5 percent limit of the appropriate years.

The Corporate Income Tax Return, Form 1120, must be filed two and one-half months after the end of the taxable fiscal year. Corporations are generally required to prepay their income tax.

The major features of the corporate income tax are illustrated by the tax computation for the Dickens Corporation, shown in Figure 26-7.

Figure 26-7
Corporate Income
Tax Computation

DICKENS CORPORATION		
Tax Computation—Taxable Year 1974		
Revenue		
Net Sales		$500,000
Expenses		
Cost of Goods Sold	$250,000	
Operating Expenses	100,000	350,000
Net Income per Books		$150,000
Add Items not Deductible for Tax Purposes		
Capital Losses Deducted as a Part of Operating Expenses	$ 7,200	
Charitable Contributions in Excess of 5% Limit	2,800	10,000
Net Taxable Income		$160,000
Tax Computation		
Tax on First $25,000 of Taxable Income at 22%		$ 5,500
Tax on Income over $25,000 ($135,000 × 48%)		64,800
Total Corporate Income Tax		$ 70,300

INCOME TAX PLANNING

Since 1913, the weight of the income tax has become heavier and heavier on individuals, estates, trusts, and corporations. Today, a large part of the income dollar of all taxpayers goes to various government agencies in the form of taxes, with the income tax taking one of the largest bites. Therefore, it behooves the management of taxpaying entities to plan certain controllable transactions in a manner that will minimize the tax cost in the long run. In other words, management should avoid all income taxes possible by the legal method of preventing a tax liability from coming into existence, referred to as *avoidance;* but it should never evade taxes by failure to report, by illegal reporting, or by the nonpayment of taxes.

The essence of tax planning is the predetermination of the income tax effect of transactions; with the effect thus determined, the taxpayer can make those transactions which will result in the minimization of the income tax. For example, the timing of revenue receipts and expenses is an excellent way of controlling taxable income. A few general rules illustrate this point: a taxpayer should avoid bunching taxable revenue in one year with related expenses falling in another; if he anticipates high revenue in a succeeding year, he should hold off discretionary expenses and make these in the high-revenue year in order to minimize taxable income; if a change in income tax rates is anticipated, he should accelerate or postpone revenue and expenses accordingly; and he should avoid, if possible, the offsetting of short-term capital losses against long-

FEDERAL
INCOME TAXES:
CONTEMPORARY
TOPICS

982

(Ch. 26)

term capital gains in the same year, because only 50 percent of net long-term capital gains are includable in taxable income.

There are many relief provisions in the income tax law, which should be used by taxpayers to the fullest extent possible. Some examples follow.

1. The use of LIFO in inventory valuation when prices are rising (permission must be obtained from the Internal Revenue Service for a company to switch inventory pricing methods).
2. The use of allowable accelerated depreciation methods and the use of the shorter average estimated useful lives allowed under the Asset Depreciation Range provision of the Internal Revenue Code.

In summary, these guidelines should be observed:

1. All controllable transactions should be planned in light of the tax consequences—a taxpayer may be able to do something about the tax effect before a transaction occurs; he can legally do nothing except follow the tax law after the transaction has already taken place.
2. Evidence of transactions should be preserved; in other words, a set of books should be maintained. Even a cash-basis salaried individual taxpayer should establish as a minimum a simple columnar journal of cash receipts and cash expenditures. In case of an audit by a representative of the Internal Revenue Service, this kind of record would be invaluable.

IMPACT OF INCOME TAXES ON BUSINESS DECISIONS

With the present extremely high income tax rates, it is essential for prudent business managers to consider carefully the effect of income taxes on the various alternatives under review. There is an adage among businessmen that a tax dollar saved, with a tax rate of approximately 50 percent, is as profitable as the earning of two dollars of net operating income. In the preceding section, certain suggestions were made regarding how to plan transactions so as to minimize the amount of the income tax; this planning is one aspect of decision making. In this section, however, the focus is on the impact of taxes on the choice of form of business organization, effect on financial arrangements, effect on adoption of accounting procedures, and the effect on hold-or-sell decisions.

When one or more individuals decide to establish a business, one of the first decisions that must be made is the selection of the legal form of organization—sole proprietorship, partnership, or corporation. Income taxes, along with many other factors, may help to influence the choice. Tax provisions that must be kept in mind are: (1) a sole proprietor must pay a tax on the entire taxable income of his business; (2) a partner must pay a tax on his proportionate share of the taxable partnership income whether distributed or not; (3) a corporation (unless it elects *Subchapter S* treatment) must report and pay a tax on its income, and the stockholders must include their dividend income on their individual returns. From the viewpoint of one *individual* who is to be involved in the formation of a new business, a calculation must be made to estimate how he would fare from a tax standpoint under the alternative business forms. This calculation would require anticipated after-tax net income of the corporation, the salary to be received by the major stockholder, the net income of the sole proprietorship, and a calculation of the available disposable income for the proprietor. If the calculation shows one form to yield a larger disposable net income, that business form, holding all other items constant, *may* be the one that should be used.

As indicated in Chapter 15, income taxes may influence the particular financing arrangement that a firm uses to obtain new long-term capital. The main thrust of this problem results from the fact that dividends are not deductible in arriving at taxable income, whereas interest expense is deductible. Thus, if a decision has to be made in regard to whether or not to issue bonds as compared to common or preferred stock, the calculation of taxable income and the resultant income taxes may be a deciding factor.

Certain accounting procedures may be adopted because of tax factors. For example, the LIFO inventory method may be chosen for tax purposes because it is anticipated that it will possibly yield a lower taxable income than would other inventory pricing methods. The tax law requires that LIFO be used for book purposes if it is used for tax purposes. This tax requirement thus forces firms to adopt a procedure that may not, in *most* cases, produce an income figure which is best for business decisions. Another example of possible unsound accounting procedures involves the nonrecognition of gains and losses on trade-in of plant and equipment items, discussed in Chapter 11.

Because of a difference between tax rates on ordinary income and capital gains rates on long-term capital gains, the income tax may influence a decision of an owner to hold or to sell an income-producing asset. If the present value of the future after-tax income is higher than the after-tax income resulting from a sale, then the income-producing property should be held. On the other hand, if the after-tax gain resulting from the possible sale is greater than the present value of the after-tax income, then the property should be sold.

DIFFERENCES BETWEEN BUSINESS INCOME AND TAXABLE INCOME

Taxable income should be computed in accordance with statutes and administrative regulations of the Federal government, whereas the computation of business income should be based on accepted accounting standards. Any feature of the tax law that increases taxable income also increases the amount of tax; likewise, any feature of the law that decreases the amount of taxable income decreases the amount of tax. A summary of the major differences between traditional business income and taxable income follows:

1. Some items not considered to be revenue by generally accepted accounting principles are taxed as revenue by the law.
2. Some items considered as business expenses are not deductible for tax purposes.
3. Some items generally considered to be business revenue are exempt from tax by law.

FEDERAL
INCOME TAXES:
CONTEMPORARY
TOPICS

984

(Ch. 26)

4. Some items not generally considered to be business expenses are deductible for tax purposes.

A brief discussion of each of these differences is illustrated by examples. In general, the corporate net income is the basis for the comparison; however, many of the statements apply to net income earned by a single proprietor.

Taxable Nonbusiness Revenues

The most important taxable receipts that are not generally considered to be business revenues are certain unearned revenue items, such as advance receipts of rent, interest, or royalties. The Federal government levies the tax in the year of receipt, when the cash is presumably available for payment of the tax. Sound accounting, on the other hand, recognizes these items as revenue in the year in which they are earned. An exception to the general tax rule stated is the unearned subscriptions revenue received by publishing companies. These particular entities are permitted to report taxable revenue on the basis of the earning process as opposed to the time of cash receipt.

Nondeductible Business Expenses

Representative examples of items that would normally be considered business expenses but which are not allowed for tax purposes are as follows:

1. As indicated in the discussion of corporate income tax, charitable contributions in excess of 5 percent of net income, figured without regard to the contribution deduction, are not deductible even when they are made for an ostensible business purpose.
2. Interest on money borrowed to purchase tax-exempt securities is not deductible.
3. Premiums paid on life insurance policies carried by the corporation on the lives of its key personnel are not deductible if the corporation names itself as beneficiary—sound accounting would require that the amount of the premium in excess of increases in cash surrender value (the investment in the policies) should be considered an expense.
4. The Federal income tax itself is not an expense for tax purposes.
5. Any amortization of an indefinite-life intangible fixed asset, particularly goodwill, is not deductible.

Business Revenue Items Exempt from Taxation

Several revenue items are exempt from taxation because of various reasons ranging from social desirability to administrative expediency. Representative examples of items specifically exempted by the Internal Revenue Code are as follows:

1. Interest received on state and municipal bonds and notes is specifically exempt from taxation.
2. Gains on plant assets traded in for similar assets to be held for the same purpose as the old assets are exempt; the bases of the new plant assets are reduced by the amounts of the nonrecognized gains (see page 435).

3. A portion of net long-term capital gains, in effect, is exempt, since there is a maximum tax rate on such gains.
4. Life insurance proceeds received on the death of the insured are not taxed.

Deductions Allowed by Tax Law That Are Not Generally Considered to Be Expenses

The tax law provides special relief provisions and investment incentives that are not generally deducted from business revenue to measure net income. Among these are the following:

1. The part of allowable accelerated depreciation that is in excess of sound depreciation expense.
2. The net operating loss deduction—a special feature of the tax law designed to give taxpayers who suffer a loss in a given bad year some relief from taxes paid in the three years immediately preceding, or the five years following, the year of the loss.

FEDERAL
INCOME TAXES:
CONTEMPORARY
TOPICS

986

(Ch. 26)

The differences between taxable income and business income fall into two classes: (1) those which tend to result in a near-permanent difference between taxable and business income, and (2) those for which the difference between taxable income and business income is washed out in time. The latter class has caused some financial reporting problems, which are magnified by the size of the current income tax. The controversy centers around the proper measurement of the Federal income tax expense. If the Federal income tax is a business expense, it appears that the matching concept dictates that it be computed on the basis of reported business income, taking into consideration the items in Class 2 above.

For the companies that have material differences between taxable income and reported business book income which tends to wash out in time, the Accounting Principles Board has concluded that the income tax expense must be allocated among the relevant periods and "that the deferred method of tax allocation should be followed."[1]

INTERPERIOD INCOME TAX ALLOCATION

The income tax expense for the current year under the matching concept is based on book net income. When there are differences between book net income and taxable net income, the accepted practice is to allocate income taxes between the relevant periods. The practice is referred to as interperiod income tax allocation. This procedure is made necessary because of two types of timing differences that wash out over time: (1) A difference that arises when revenue is recognized in one accounting period for book purposes but is not taxed until later periods, or when an expense is recognized on the tax return but is not recognized in the accounting records until a later period. (2) A difference that arises when revenue is recognized on the tax return before it is recognized in the books, or when expenses are recognized for book accounting purposes before they are deducted on the tax return. The first difference will give rise to a postponed income tax liability, which will be paid at a later date. The second timing difference will create prepaid income tax items, which will be deferred and allocated as income tax expense of future periods. Specific examples of the cause of these two timing differences are given in the preceding section of this chapter.

Two illustrations are given to introduce the accounting procedures involved in the deferred method of interperiod income tax allocation. First, consider an example that would create a postponed income tax liability referred to as deferred income tax liability; the classical example is the difference between book depreciation and tax depreciation. Assume, for example, that the Calgary Corporation deems that the straight-line depreciation method is appropriate for its books and hence adopts this method, but uses the sum-of-the-years'-digits

---

[1] AICPA, *APB Accounting Principles,* vol. 2 (Chicago: Commerce Clearing House, Inc., 1973), p. 6586.

(Ch. 26)

method for its tax return. Assume that the company acquired a major machine which cost $300,000 and has an estimated five-years life with no salvage value; also assume that the income tax rate is 50 percent. If the company earns $500,000 each year (before depreciation expense and income tax expense), the effect of these procedures on pretax book accounting income and taxable income is shown below:

Year	Accounting Income Before Depreciation and Income Taxes	Accounting Depreciation (Straight Line)	Tax Return Depreciation (SYD)	Pretax Book Accounting Income	Taxable Income
1	$ 500,000	$ 60,000	$100,000	$ 440,000	$ 400,000
2	500,000	60,000	80,000	440,000	420,000
3	500,000	60,000	60,000	440,000	440,000
4	500,000	60,000	40,000	440,000	460,000
5	500,000	60,000	20,000	440,000	480,000
Totals	$2,500,000	$300,000	$300,000	$2,200,000	$2,200,000

Note the total pretax accounting income and taxable income are the same for the five-year period. The journal entries to record the income tax liability and the income tax expense at the assumed rate of 50 percent are presented below:

Year 1 Income Tax Expense		220,000	
Income Tax Payable			200,000
Deferred Income Tax Liability			20,000
To record tax expense on reported net income of $440,000 at assumed rate of 50%.			
Year 2 Income Tax Expense		220,000	
Income Tax Payable			210,000
Deferred Income Tax Liability			10,000
(The explanations for years 2 to 5 are omitted, since they are essentially the same as those for year 1).			
Year 3 Income Tax Expense		220,000	
Income Tax Payable			220,000
Year 4 Income Tax Expense		220,000	
Deferred Income Tax Liability		10,000	
Income Tax Payable			230,000
Year 5 Income Tax Expense		220,000	
Deferred Income Tax Liability		20,000	
Income Tax Payable			240,000

Under the inferred assumptions that the tax law has not changed and that the Deferred Income Tax Liability account refers only to the machinery purchased in year 1, the five-year history of this account is shown below:

Deferred Income Tax Liability

Year 4	10,000	Year 1	20,000
Year 5	20,000	Year 2	10,000
	30,000		30,000

The typical statement of financial position classification of this account is as a long-term liability.

The foregoing example of a firm using one depreciation method for book purposes and another for tax purposes is only one of the many available alternative practices that cause differences between tax accounting and book accounting, which result in a temporary difference between taxable income and business income, but which wash out in time. Other cases must be considered carefully to see whether they warrant the allocation of the income tax between periods. It appears theoretically sound to make use of this practice in all relevant cases, but the deciding factors, of course, are size of the amounts involved and the complexity of the procedure in regard to a particular case. A company may use a depreciation method for tax purposes different from the theoretically appropriate book method because it has interest-free use of the funds resulting from the postponement of the tax payments.

The second illustration involves a temporary difference which creates a prepaid income tax item. Consider, for example, the advanced receipt of a three year rental revenue of $600,000 by the Guelph Company. Other book net income before taxes is $100,000 each year. The advanced receipt of rent is fully taxable in the year of receipt; for book purposes, however, $200,000 would be recognized in each of the three years. The book income and taxable income are summarized below:

Year	Book Accounting Income Other Than Rental Income	Additions to Book Accounting for Rental Revenue	Pretax Book Accounting Income	Taxable Income
1	$100,000	$200,000	$300,000	$700,000
2	100,000	200,000	300,000	100,000
3	100,000	200,000	300,000	100,000
Totals	$300,000	$600,000	$900,000	$900,000

Using the interperiod income tax allocation procedures, the Guelph Company would determine the income tax expense for each period on the basis of accounting income and would record the difference between the current income tax liability and income tax expense as prepaid income taxes. Journal entries to record income taxes at the assumed rate of 50 percent for the three years are shown on page 990:

FEDERAL
INCOME
TAXES

Year 1 Income Tax Expense (50% × $300,000)	150,000	
Prepaid Income Taxes	200,000	
Income Tax Payable		350,000
Year 2 Income Tax Expense	150,000	
Prepaid Income Taxes		100,000
Income Tax Payable		50,000
Year 3 Income Tax Expense	150,000	
Prepaid Income Taxes		100,000
Income Tax Payable		50,000

The income tax expense of $150,000 would be shown on the income statement, but the statement should include a footnote disclosing the fact that the income tax liability is different each year.

Some accountants oppose the recognition of interperiod income tax allocation. They state that the income tax is a distribution of income and not an expense and that the matching concept is therefore not involved. They also argue that the timing differences are not temporary, especially when a firm continues to replace and to add plant items each year. Where the amounts are material and the differences are expected to be reversed, it is the authors' opinion that the interperiod income tax allocation is a theoretically sound procedure and should be recorded in the accounts of the corporation.

Figure A26-1 Income Statements Showing Effect of Intraperiod Income Tax Allocation

INTRACOMPANY
Partial Income Statement
For the Year Ended December 31, 1976

Assumption I—Income Tax Is Not Allocated

Sales		$1,000,000
Net Operating Income		$ 100,000
Extraordinary Long-term Capital Gains		100,000
Net Income before Federal Income Tax		$ 200,000
Less Income Tax Expense		71,500
Net Income		$ 128,500

INTRACOMPANY
Partial Income Statement
For the Year Ended December 31, 1976

Assumption II—Income Tax Is Allocated

Sales		$1,000,000
Net Operating Income	$100,000	
Less: Federal Income Tax Applicable Thereto	41,500	
Net Operating Income after Income Tax		58,000
Extraordinary Long-Term Capital Gains	$100,000	
Less Federal Income Tax Applicable thereto	30,000	
Net Extraordinary Long-Term Capital Gains		70,000
Net Income		$ 128,500

A similar but simpler tax allocation problem exists within the different sections of an income statement when a company experiences a taxable extraordinary gain or a deductible extraordinary loss. The concept of adequate disclosure requires that these items be shown in the appropriate section of statements coupled with the income tax effect, or net after taxes. This method of disclosure is referred to as intraperiod income tax allocation.

To illustrate the problem, assume that a corporation reports in its income statement $100,000 of ordinary income and $100,000 of extraordinary net long-term capital gains. The two income statements illustrated in Figure A26-1 reveal the contrasts between not allocating income taxes and allocating income taxes. The intraperiod income tax allocation is a theoretically sound procedure under the matching concept and for purposes of full disclosure.

GLOSSARY

Adjusted Gross Income Gross income less deductions from gross for adjusted gross income, which includes business-related and revenue-producing expenses.

Avoidance of Taxes A legal method of postponing taxes, or preventing a tax liability from coming into existence.

Capital Asset Stocks, bonds, and other property which by law are specifically identified as capital assets.

Capital Gains and Losses Any excess or deficiency of cash receipts above or below the bases (usually cost) of the capital asset sold.

Evasion of Taxes Illegal tax reporting, failure to report taxes, or the nonpayment of taxes.

Exemption Deduction allowed by law, valued at $750 each for taxpayer, spouse, dependents and others; the value of the total exemptions plus standard deductions are deducted from adjusted gross income to determine taxable income.

Gross Income All revenue items and gross margin on sales that are *legally* includable in the total figure, which is the starting point for the calculation of taxable income.

Head of Household A single individual who heads a household which contains dependent persons; special tax schedules are provided for heads of household to provide an element of relief to compensate them for the additional family burden they must carry.

Interperiod Income Tax Allocation The allocation of the income tax expense among periods caused by a temporary timing difference between reported book income and taxable income.

Intraperiod Income Tax Allocation The allocation within a fiscal period of the income tax expense item between sections of statements or sometimes between statements.

Itemized Personal Deductions Personal items that are allowed by law to be deducted from adjusted gross income; these include contributions, allowable medical expenses, union dues, and others.

FEDERAL
INCOME
TAXES

Minimum Standard Deduction The minimum standard deduction is $1,300, a figure established by statute.

Percentage Standard Deduction The allowable percentage standard deduction is 15 percent of adjusted gross income; but the amount cannot be more than $2,000.

Tax Credit A credit which is allowed to be subtracted from the income tax itself; tax credits are allowed for income tax withheld or paid on a declared estimate, retirement income credit, investment credits and others.

Taxable Income Adjusted gross income less personal deductions and total value of exemptions.

Tax Rate Schedule Any one of four tax schedules (1) for separate returns for unmarried taxpayers, (2) for separate returns for married taxpayers, (3) for joint return for married taxpayers and surviving spouses, and (4) for heads of household.

Tax Table A table showing the amount of the income tax for those taxpayers with a taxable income of $10,000 or less.

QUESTIONS

Q26-1. (a) Distinguish between the *cash* and the *accrual* bases of accounting. (b) What is a modified cash basis?

Q26-2. (a) Define the term *gross income* from an individual income tax point of view. (b) List six items that must be reported as gross income. (c) List four items that are excludable from gross income.

Q26-3. (a) What is the individual income tax standard deduction? (b) State its maximum and its minimum limits.

Q26-4. Tom Jones, a bachelor, earned $40,000 in taxable income in 1974. What amount of Federal income tax could have been saved if on December 31, 1974, he had married a woman who had no taxable income in 1974?

Q26-5. (a) For tax purposes, what are capital assets? (b) Distinguish between short-term and long-term capital gains. (c) The timing of capital gains and losses is important in tax planning. Discuss.

Q26-6. Diane Bolton, aged 21, is attending Rex University. During the summer of 1974, she worked in a library and earned $850. Her parents contributed $1,850 toward her support in 1974. Can Diane's parents claim her as an exemption?

Q26-7. Ransom Suskin elected to use the cash basis for tax purposes. During 1974, he collected $24,000 from clients for services rendered in prior years, and billed clients for $60,000 for services rendered in 1974. His accounts receivable as of December 31, 1974, totaled $17,400. What is the amount of gross income he should report on his Form 1040 for 1974?

Q26-8. Samuel and Abby Washington own some shares of stock. During 1974, they received $1,400 in dividends. Of this amount, $1,305 represented dividends on stock owned by Samuel Washington only; the remainder represented dividends on stock owned by Abby Washington. What would be the dividends included in gross income on a joint return?

Q26-9. List and briefly discuss the computational differences between the individual income tax and the corporation income tax.

FEDERAL
INCOME TAXES:
CONTEMPORARY
TOPICS

992

(Ch. 26)

Q26-10. (a) State the objective of tax planning. (b) Discuss ways and means of accomplishing tax planning.

Q26-11. In outline form, state four ways that traditional business income may differ from taxable income, and under each way give two specific illustrations.

Q26-12. List some tax factors which should be considered in deciding whether to organize a new business as a corporation, a partnership, a proprietorship.

Q26-13. (Appendix). (a) What is meant by the term *income tax allocation.* (b) Discuss two concepts of income tax allocation.

E26-1. Donald F. Skakle, a bachelor, had the following cash receipts during 1974:

Salary earned as a professor	$20,500
Receipt of insurance proceeds for fire damages to personal car	1,000
Dividends from domestic companies	3,000
Interest on U. S. Government bonds	1,200
Interest on North Carolina State bonds	900
Total cash receipts	$26,600

Compute the amount of gross income subject to the individual income tax.

E26-2. Answer the following items:

1. Which of the following outlays is *not* a potential deduction from income for the computation of taxable income?
   a. Contribution to the Boy Scouts
   b. Payment of property taxes
   c. Payment of Federal income taxes
   d. Payment of bond interest charges
   e. Payment of building rental charge
2. Justice Corporation was formed late last year and started operations on January 1 of the current year. In forming the corporation, organizational expenditures of $120,000 were incurred and paid. If Justice elects to amortize these expenses, its maximum deduction for tax purposes in the current year is: (a) $120,000, (b) $24,000, (c) $12,000, (d) $ –0–, (e) none of the preceding.

(IMA adapted)

E26-3. Thomas and Barbara Kline filed a joint return in 1974. They had the following taxable income after deductions and exemptions:

Ordinary taxable income	$ 90,000
Long-term capital gains (before reduction)	20,000
Total	$110,000

Compute the 1974 Federal income tax. Remember that the income tax on net long-term capital gains cannot exceed a certain percentage of the long-term gain.

E26-4. Answer the following items:

1. Kappa Corporation carried a $500,000 insurance policy on the life of its

president with itself as the beneficiary. On August 1 of the current year, the president died. On September 1, Kappa received a check from the insurance company for $500,000. The current year's premium for this policy, up to the date of the president's death, was $15,000. In computing Kappa's taxable income for the current year:

a. The $15,000 should be deducted as an expense and the $500,000 should be included in gross income.

b. The $15,000 should not be deducted as an expense, but the $500,000 should be included in gross income.

c. The $15,000 should be deducted as an expense, but the $500,000 should not be included in gross income.

d. The $15,000 and the $500,000 should be ignored.

e. None of the above.

2. An examination of Delta Corporation, a calendar-year accrual-basis taxpayer, disclosed the following information for the current tax year:

Taxable revenues	$2,000,000
Deductible expenses, exclusive of charitable contributions and organizational expenses	1,500,000
Cash contributions to public charities—$20,000 paid in the current tax year and $20,000 paid in February of the following tax year	40,000
Organizational expenses	–0–
Domestic dividends received	–0–

Assuming that the $40,000 of charitable contributions were properly authorized by the current year's board of directors, Delta's taxable income for the current year is: (a) $498,000, (b) $480,000, (c) $475,000, (d) $460,000, (e) none of the preceding.

(IMA adapted)

E26-5. In 1974, Franklin and Betty Alexander filed a joint return on which they reported an adjusted gross income of $14,000. The couple had allowable personal deductions of $1,600; they are both under 65 and have two small children, aged six and eight.

Compute the 1974 Federal income tax.

E26-6. Answer the following items:

1. CNA Corporation bought a machine in 1968 for $30,000. The corporation used this machine in its manufacturing operation until November 1974, when it was exchanged for a similar, but larger, machine having a list price of $65,000 and which could be bought at a cash price of $60,000. At the date of the exchange, the adjusted basis of the original machine was $12,000, and CNA paid $35,000 on the exchange. The gain or loss recognized for tax purposes on the exchange by CNA Corporation and its tax basis of the new machine immediately after the exchange, are:

a. Gain recognized $13,000; basis $60,000.

b. No gain or loss recognized; basis $60,000.

c. No gain or loss recognized; basis $47,000.

d. Gain recognized $18,000; basis $65,000.

e. Loss recognized $5,000; basis $60,000.

2. An *improper* tax accounting method for a manufacturing corporation is: (a) the cash method, (b) the accrual method, (c) the hybrid method, (d) the installment method, (e) LIFO for inventories.

(IMA adapted)

FEDERAL
INCOME TAXES:
CONTEMPORARY
TOPICS

994

(Ch. 26)

E26-7. In 1974, John and Lindy Brooks filed a joint return on which they reported an adjusted gross income of $5,800. The couple's itemized deductions totaled $250; they are both under 65 and have five children, aged one, three, five, seven, and nine.

Compute the 1974 Federal income tax.

E26-8. Loren and Peggy Combs filed a joint return and reported a 1974 income tax before credits of $5,700. Includable in taxable income was $1,400 of qualifying dividends—the couple had received $1,600 on stock jointly owned. They paid $5,050 in 1974 on a declaration of estimated tax for 1974.

Compute the amount of the remaining tax liability for 1974.

E26-9. The Hightower Corporation reported a net income per books of $300,000. In addition, its records show capital losses deducted as operating expenses of $7,000 and charitable contributions in excess of the 5 percent limit of $2,000.

Compute the 1974 Federal income tax.

E26-10. (Appendix). Assume that in a given year the Interpo Company's ordinary income before income taxes is $100,000. The company is subject to an average flat-rate income tax of 40% on all income. The company allocates income taxes in its financial statements.

Each of the three independent situations below describes an item of revenue or expense that *was included* in the computation of the $100,000 reported book accounting income, but which is treated differently for income tax purposes:

1. The company reported on its tax return $24,000 of royalties received in advance; only $7,000 of this royalty income was earned during the current year.
2. The company deducted $26,000 of estimated guarantee and product warranty expense in computing book accounting income; the actual *incurred* product warranty expense which is deductible for income tax purposes was $7,500.
3. The company deducted $19,000 of research and development costs in determining taxable income; these costs are being amortized on its accounting records over a five-year period.

For each of the three independent cases described above, prepare the journal entry that should be made to record income tax expense for the current year, assuming that the company utilizes interperiod income tax procedures.

DP26-1. (*Individual income tax computation*) Allen Finner is 67 years old; his wife, Alice, is 62 years old. They have two unmarried children: John, 16 years old, and Susan, 21 years old, who is attending a university. The Finner's furnish over one-half the support for both their children, although Susan works as a salesclerk in the summer and earned $850 in 1974. Finner owns and operates a service station under the name of Finner Service Station. Mrs. Finner did not have any earned income in 1974.

Relevant business and personal information for the family is shown below:

Cash Receipts
Gross revenue from Finner Service Station $200,000

(Ch. 26)

Interest on U.S. bonds	2,000
Interest on State of Virginia bonds	6,000
Dividends on stock jointly owned	5,200
Cash proceeds from insurance policy for fire damage on non-business property which had an original cost of $3,600	3,600

Capital gains

Sale of 300 shares of United Biscuit Company common stock:

Date Acquired	Date Sold	Cost	Selling Price
3/4/72	5/2/74	$48,000	$54,000

Sale of 200 shares of National Widgets Company common stock:

Date Acquired	Date Sold	Cost	Selling Price
4/2/74	8/10/74	$15,000	$16,000

Expenditures

Cost of goods sold ($110,000) and operating expenses ($30,000) of Finner Service Station	$140,000
Contributions to church and university	4,000
Contribution to Community Chest	1,100
Interest paid on personal loans	800
Property taxes paid to town and county	1,200

State taxes paid

Sales tax	190
Automobile license tags	28
Gasoline tax	110

Family medical expenses

Doctor and hospital fees	900
Drugs and medicine	150
Blue Cross-Blue Shield Hospital Insurance	290
Amount paid in 1974 on declared estimated tax for 1974	14,000

Required: In an orderly schedule form, compute the income tax liability remaining to be paid for 1974, assuming that a joint return is filed.

DP26-2. (*Information to be reported on partnership informational return*) Flubb and Dubb are partners sharing profits 2:1, respectively. The following information has been taken from the partnership records for the year 1974:

Taxable ordinary income (less partners' salaries)	$120,000
Long-term capital gains	18,000
Short-term capital gains	7,200
Short-term capital losses	(6,000)
Dividends received	3,600
Charitable contributions	(4,200)
Interest on Orange County bonds	1,800
Salaries to partners, ($10,000 to Flubb and $8,000 to Dubb)	18,000
Net income per books before partners' salaries	$158,400

Assume that Flubb is 42 years old and single, and that he has the following tax information from sources other than the partnership:

Dividends received	$16,000
Long-term capital losses	6,000
Itemized deductions	3,000

FEDERAL
INCOME TAXES:
CONTEMPORARY
TOPICS

996

(Ch. 26)

Required:

1. Prepare a schedule showing the information that should be presented on the partnership informational return.
2. Compute the 1974 income tax for Flubb.

DP26-3. (*Corporate income tax computation*) The Dumbee Corporation reported the following information for 1974:

Sales	$1,500,000
Cost of goods sold	825,000
Operating expenses other than capital losses and charitable contributions	375,000
Capital losses	15,000
Charitable contributions	18,750
(There were no capital gains)	

Required: Compute the corporate income tax for 1974.

DP26-4. (Appendix). (*Interperiod income allocation*) In 1974, 1975 and 1976, the taxable income reported by the Mini Corporation for income tax purposes has differed from the book net income before taxes reported on its income statement. The record is as follows:

	Net Income Before Taxes	
	Income	Tax
Year	Statement	Return
1974	$225,000	$165,000
1975	135,000	157,500
1976	127,500	150,000

Included in book net income as reported on the income statement in 1974 was $22,500 of interest earned on municipal bonds that is not subject to income tax at any time. Also during 1974, $37,500 of deductions were taken for income tax purposes that will not be reported as book expenses until later years. In 1976, the company incurred a book accounting loss of $12,000, which is reflected on the income statement; for income tax purposes only $4,500 of this loss was deductible. In all other respects income reported on the income statement is ultimately subject to income taxes. Assume that the company is subject to a combined state and Federal income tax rate of 60% on all taxable income.

Required:

1. Prepare journal entries necessary to record income taxes in each of the three years and to make an interperiod allocation of income taxes on the basis of the information provided. Show supporting calculations.
2. Assuming that all income taxes due (as reported on the company's tax returns) were paid during the year following their accrual, what are the balances at the end of 1976 in the company's two tax liability accounts?

P26-1. Answer the following items:

1. The Cyclop Corporation, an accrual-basis taxpayer, was formed and began operations on May 1, 1974. The following expenses were incurred during its first tax period, May 1–December 31, 1974:

Expenses of temporary directors and of organizational meetings	$500
Fee paid to state for incorporation	100
Accounting services incident to organization	200
Legal services for drafting the corporate charter and bylaws	400
Expenses of printing bond certificates issued at date of organization	420

If Cyclop Corporation makes an appropriate and timely election, the maximum organization expense that it can properly deduct for 1974 would be: (a) $160, (b) $216, (c) $324, (d) $0, (e) none of the preceding.

2. The income tax treatment of individual and corporate taxpayers agrees in the following respect:
   a. Excess capital losses may be carried forward five years.
   b. Excess capital losses may *not* be carried back.
   c. Excess capital losses may be offset against income from other sources, but only to a limited extent.
   d. Excess capital losses retain their identity as either long-term or short-term losses in the year to which they are carried.
   e. None of the above.

3. For the taxable year ended December 31, 1974, Richards Corporation had taxable income of $100,000 before taking into account any gains or losses on the sale of assets. Information concerning its sales of assets follows:

	Type of Asset	
	Operating Equipment	Land Held as Investment
Date acquired	1/1/73	7/7/66
Date sold	12/31/74	5/4/74
Useful life	10 yrs.	n/a
Accumulated depreciation (straight line)	$10,000	n/a
Cost	50,000	$80,000
Selling price	20,000	30,000

Richard's taxable income after taking into account these two sales of property would be: (a) $100,000, (b) $99,000, (c) $80,000, (d) $30,000, (e) none of the preceding.

4. On July 17, 1974, Grover Corporation purchased a new delivery truck (list price, $4,300) for $4,000 by trading in an old truck with a fair market value of $2,500 and paying $1,500 cash. The old truck had been purchased for $3,500 cash on January 12, 1973, and had $2,100 of undepreciated cost on the date of the trade-in.
   The tax effect of this transaction to Grover Corp. would be:
   a. No recognized gain or loss and basis of new truck, $4,000.
   b. Recognized gain of $400 and basis of new truck, $4,000.
   c. No recognized gain or loss and basis of new truck, $3,600.
   d. Recognized gain of $400 and basis of new truck, $4,300.
   e. None of the above.

5. Vacconey Corporation's taxable income for 1974 was $120,000. All taxable income resulted from regular operations of the corporation. Vacconey's tax liability before credits for 1974 would be: (a) $57,600, (b) $60,000, (c) $51,100, (d) $26,400, (e) none of the preceding.

(AICPA adapted)

P26-2. Alice and Wade Council had the following income and related information for 1974:

Salary to Wade Council	$15,000
Dividends on stock owned by Wade Council	3,000
Dividends on stock owned by Alice Council	1,500
On March 16, 1974, Alice Council sold some stock she had acquired on April 1, 1966, at a gain of	6,000
On November 15, 1974, Wade Council sold some stock he had acquired on July 1, 1974, at a loss of	2,250

Required: Compute the adjusted gross income subject to tax on a joint return filed by Alice and Wade Council.

P26-3. Paton Solomons is 41 years old; his wife, Janet, is 42 years old. They have two children; a son, Peter, 9 years old, and a daughter, Sandra, 14 years old. Solomons owns and operates a furniture store under the name of the Solomons Furniture Company. Mrs. Solomons did not have any earned income in 1974.

Tax and other information for 1974 are as follows:

Cash Receipts	
Gross sales of Solomons Furniture Company	$300,000
Interest on Dare County bonds	3,000
Dividends on stock owned by Janet Solomons	9,000
Cash inherited by Janet Solomons	30,000
Capital gains on stock sold by Janet Solomons	
Long-term gains	15,000
Short-term gains	1,800
Expenditures	
Cost of goods sold of Solomons Furniture Company	150,000
Operating expenses of Solomons Furniture Company	60,000
Contribution to church	12,000
Contribution to Community Chest	1,500
Interest paid on personal loans	1,200
Personal property taxes	1,500
State taxes paid	
Sales taxes	250
Automobile license tags	46
Gasoline tax	180
Family medical expenses	
Doctor and hospital fees	1,600
Hospital insurance	340
Drugs and medicine	600
Amount paid in 1974 on declared estimated tax for 1974	29,650

Required: Compute the income tax liability remaining to be paid for 1974, assuming that a joint return is filed.

P26-4. Harrison Trembley, 66 years old, and his wife, Faye, 63 years old, file a joint return. They have two children: Harrison, Jr., who is 35 years old, and Ruth, who is 20 years old and is attending college full time. Mr. and Mrs. Trembley furnish over one-half the support for Ruth, although she earned $1,020 on a summer job in 1974. Various receipts and expenditures of Mr. and Mrs. Trembley are listed below:

Mr. Trembley

Cash Receipts	
Withdrawal by proprietor from business (sales $405,000; cost of goods sold, $231,000; operating expenses, $78,000)	$45,000

Cash dividends received	3,900
Gain on sale of stock purchased five years ago	6,000
Interest received on school district bonds	3,000
Expenditures	
Contribution to church and university	9,000
Contribution to Community Chest	300
Personal property taxes	1,500
Insurance on residence	300
Automobile license plates	36
State sales taxes	225
State gasoline tax	150
Medical expenses	
Drugs and medicines	570
Hospital insurance	420
Doctor and hospital bills	1,575
Interest on personal loans	1,050
Payment on declaration of estimated tax	30,000

Mrs. Trembley

Cash Receipts	
Rental of apartment building	$15,000
Dividends received on stock	1,275
Receipt from sale of stock purchased for $5,400 four months previously	4,350

Expenditures

Apartment building (original cost on January 1, 1966, was $94,500. Sum-of-the-years'-digits depreciation is used for tax purposes, with an assumed life of 20 years and no salvage value)

Interest on business indebtedness	$1,350
Property taxes	2,400
Insurance for 1974	315
Repairs and maintenance	2,700
Contribution to church	450

Required: Compute the remaining tax liability for 1974 for Faye and Harrison Trembley on a joint return.

P26-5. Each of the following five cases represents a possible situation with respect to capital gains and losses. Assume that Robb Adden, a bachelor, has a salary income of $12,000 in addition to the items shown below.

1. Long-term capital gains of $9,000; long-term capital losses of $5,000; short-term capital gains of $7,000; short-term capital losses of $4,000.
2. Long-term capital gains of $9,000; short-term capital losses of $17,000.
3. Long-term capital gains of $5,000; long-term capital losses of $9,000; short-term capital gains of $3,000; short-term capital losses of $8,000.
4. Long-term capital gains of $11,000; short-term capital losses of $7,000.
5. Long-term capital gains of $2,000; long-term capital losses of $600; short-term capital losses of $2,200.

Required: Compute Robb Adden's adjusted gross income in each case for the year 1974.

P26-6. John Alpha is single, aged 48; Samuel Omega is also single, aged 39; both use the standard deduction. They reported the following tax information for 1974:

Tax information for John Alpha
Ordinary income $45,000
Net long-term capital gains   1,500

Tax information for Samuel Omega
Ordinary income $ 7,500
Net long-term capital gains   50,000

Required: Compute the amount of Alpha's and Omega's income tax for 1974. (Remember that the tax on long-term capital gains cannot exceed a certain percentage of the long-term gain.)

P26-7. The following information relates to a taxpayer:

Gross revenue (including $1,500 in interest received on South Carolina bonds and $1,500 in dividends)	$20,850
Deductions to arrive at adjusted gross income	1,200
Payments made on declaration of estimated tax for 1974	1,850
Long-term capital gains	2,250
Short-term capital losses	4,350
Itemized deductions	1,260

Required:

1. Compute the remaining income tax liability, assuming that the taxpayer is married, that both he and his wife are under 65, that they have four dependent children, and that the wife did not receive any separate income.
2. Compute the remaining income tax liability, assuming that the taxpayer is single and under 65.

P26-8. Erwin and Moeller are partners; they share profits 3:1, respectively. The following information has been taken from the partnership records for the year 1974:

Taxable ordinary income (less partners' salaries)	$ 36,000
Long-term capital gains	15,000
Short-term capital losses	(6,000)
Dividends received	3,000
Charitable contributions	(1,200)
Interest on Florida State bonds	1,500
Salaries to partners ($9,000 to Erwin; $6,000 to Moeller)	15,000
Net income per books before partners' salaries	$ 63,300

Assume that Erwin is 67 years old and single, and that he has the following tax information from sources other than the partnership:

Dividends received	$9,000
Long-term capital losses	2,400
Itemized deductions	3,000

Required:

1. Prepare a schedule showing the information that should be presented on the partnership informational return.
2. Compute Erwin's 1974 income tax.

FEDERAL
INCOME
TAXES

P26-9. The Ennis Corporation reported the following information for 1974:

Sales	$3,780,000
Cost of goods sold	1,850,000
Operating expenses, other than capital losses and charitable contributions	770,000
Capital losses	35,000
Charitable contributions	30,000

Required: Compute the corporate income tax for 1974.

P26-10. (*Financial policy decision problem*) The Windham Production Company, a textile manufacturer, has recently had a change in ownership and top management. Sanders Windham, the new president, is a retired military officer and is noted for being an excellent organizer and administrator. Windham is gaining a reputation around the office for asking hard questions and for requiring complete and logical answers.

During one of the mornings that Windham is devoting to familiarizing himself with the workings of the accounting department, he reviews the latest Federal corporate tax return and the latest income statement in the corporate annual report. He immediately notices that the taxable income of $272,990 on the tax return and the net income before income taxes of $438,800 on the income statement are not the same amount. On closer examination he observes that the following items are not the same on each report:

1. Depreciation expense is $185,020 on the income statement and $294,500 on the tax return.
2. Cost of goods sold is $1,858,360 on the income statement and $1,902,400 on the tax return.
3. Interest earned is $2,400 on the income statement and $1,760 on the tax return.
4. Gain on disposal of machinery is $11,580 on the income statement and does not appear on the tax return.
5. Bad debts expense is $12,800 on the income statement and $12,700 on the tax return.
6. Amortization of organization costs does not appear on the income statement and is $170 on the tax return.

He also notes that the income tax expense on the income statement is not the same as the income tax on the tax report.

By this time he is confused and bewildered. He approaches you, an assistant accountant in the tax division, and questions the discrepancies. (He has a dual purpose in asking you questions. He wishes answers to his questions and he wishes to evaluate your knowledge of tax accounting.)

Required:

1. Reconcile the two different income amounts.
2. Identify what might be a complete and logical reason for each of the six differences. (Remember that you wish to convince the new president of your competence.)
3. (a) Why does income tax expense on the income statement differ from the income tax on the tax report? (b) What is the basis for each calculation? (c) Which would you expect to be the larger? Why?
4. What is the justification for permitting differences between business income and taxable income?
5. Identify the separate objectives of business accounting and tax accounting.

FEDERAL
INCOME TAXES:
CONTEMPORARY
TOPICS

1002

(Ch. 26)

6. How would you explain to Windham that mistakes have not been made and that everything is correct?

P26-11. (*Financial policy decision problem*) Assume that the owner of a parking garage is in the 55% tax bracket. The parking garage has a tax basis of $45,000 and a remaining useful life of four years. The net income before income tax from the garage has been averaging $33,750 a year. The garage will have no salvage value after its useful life.

   The owner receives a cash offer of $117,000 for the parking garage. Assume that any gain on the sale will be taxed at 25%.

Required:

1. Prepare a suitable analysis of the alternatives to assist the owner in deciding whether to sell or to hold the asset.
2. Mention one consideration that could influence the decision.

P26-12. (*Financial policy decision problem*) The Renegar Service Corporation has just completed its first year of operation. The income statement (on an accrual basis) for the year is as follows:

Revenues		
Sales	$125,000	
Gain on sale of land	32,000	
Interest and other revenue	1,000	$158,000
Expenses		
Materials and supplies	$ 28,000	
Wages and benefits	43,000	
Depreciation	7,000	
Bad debts	500	
Interest	5,500	
Administrative expenses	11,000	
Other expenses	5,000	$100,000
Net income		$ 58,000

You have just been hired by Renegar as accountant and office manager. Winston Renegar indicates that the company is presently in a "cash-squeeze" position. As your first task, he asks you to review the tax computation to determine if this year's tax liability might be reduced. In reviewing the firm's records, you assemble the following information:

1. Accounts receivable at year-end amount to $18,000; accounts payable and other current payables, to $4,000. (*Hint:* Consider cash versus accrual basis.)
2. There are no ending inventories.
3. New equipment costing $60,000 was purchased early in the year. Salvage value was estimated to be $4,000, and life was estimated to be 8 years. (*Hint:* Consider investment credit, additional first-year depreciation, and accelerated depreciation.)
4. Bad debts have been expensed as incurred. Similar firms in this line of business incur bad debt losses equal to 1.5% of sales.
5. A tract of land, acquired in January as a building site (at a cost of $12,000) was sold in November when a new shopping plaza was constructed on adjoining land. The land was sold for $44,000, of which $33,000 (plus interest) will be received in future years. In December, a new tract of land

was purchased for $20,000. (*Hint:* Consider installment method of reporting.)

Required: Present a revised determination of taxable income and tax computation which takes advantage of all available means to reduce this year's taxes. Explain any items for which your presentation differs from the above income statement.

(IMA adapted)

P26-13. (Appendix). The We-Deliver Company began business on January 1, 1976. Anticipating a growth in its delivery business over the next few years, the company has developed plans for the purchase of delivery equipment as shown below:

Date of Acquisition (beginning of year)	Cost of New Equipment	Salvage Value	Estimated Service Life (in years)
1976	$ 50,000	$ 5,000	5
1977	240,000	15,000	5
1978	345,000	30,000	5
1979	100,000	10,000	5
1980	75,000	15,000	5
1981	83,000	8,000	5

The head accountant of the company is studying the question of depreciation policies on the delivery equipment. He feels that the company should adopt the sum-of-the-years'-digits method of depreciation for income tax purposes but still continue to use the straight-line method for normal accounting and reporting purposes. If this policy is adopted, book net income would differ from taxable income; and this difference would require, in the head accountant's opinion, the use of interperiod income tax allocation procedures in the company's accounting records.

Required:

1. Prepare a schedule showing the difference between taxable income and book income that will result in each year of the six-year period if the head accountant adopts the policy described.
2. Determine the balance that would appear in the Deferred Income Tax Liability account at the close of 1981 if interperiod income tax allocation procedures were followed, and assuming that an income tax rate of 45% were applicable.

FEDERAL
INCOME TAXES:
CONTEMPORARY
TOPICS

1004

(Ch. 26)

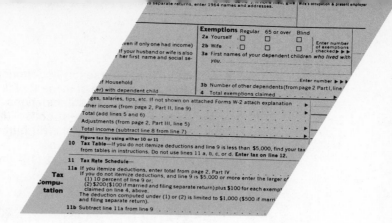

Contemporary Accounting Topics

27

In its 1973 report, *Objectives of Financial Statements,* the AICPA Accounting Objectives Study Group stated, "the basic objective of financial statements is to provide information useful for making economic decisions."[1] This statement reinforced a conclusion reached about two years earlier by a study group composed of accounting educators, who said, "The purpose of accounting is to provide information that is useful in decision making affecting resource allocation."[2] With apparent broad agreement in the profession as to the purpose of accounting, one wonders why it should be any problem to establish a set of accounting standards and to agree upon a complete package of specific procedures and practices to carry out each standard. But a commonly held basic purpose does not preclude differences of opinion about how to achieve that purpose; certainly the field of accounting is not unique in this respect. Like the other professions, accounting has a wide range of questions on which opinions vary greatly.

It is also true that as social and economic conditions change, accounting practices that were adequately serving the basic objective may be less and less able to do so. New legislation or new requirements by regulatory agencies may demand information not previously considered to be pertinent, or may shift the emphasis among or within financial statements. Accordingly, there continues to be many accounting topics on which agreement among accountants is far from universal. This chapter introduces the student to some of the major controversial accounting topics and to some specialized topics that are usually

[1] p. 13.
[2] *A New Introduction to Accounting: A Report of the Study Group Sponsored by the Price Waterhouse Foundation* (Seattle, Wash.: 1971), p. 11.

(Ch. 27)

fully developed in later courses in accounting or in the accounting literature. Included are brief discussions of these topics: (1) regulatory agencies, (2) valuation techniques, (3) business combinations, which includes brief discussions of purchase versus pooling and of consolidated statements, (4) reporting by diversified companies, (5) forecasts, (6) human resources accounting, (7) social accounting measurements, (8) not-for-profit and government accounting, (9) national income accounting, and (10) the expanding role of accounting.

UNITED STATES REGULATORY AGENCIES

Securities Exchange Commission

Several government units have had salutary influence on the development of accounting objectives and standards. One of these is the Securities Exchange Commission (SEC) created by the Securities Exchange Act of 1934. Section 13(b) of the act is quoted in part:

> The Commission may prescribe, in regard to reports made pursuant to this title, the form or forms in which the required information shall be set forth, the items or details to be shown in the balance sheet [statement of financial position] and earnings statement, and the methods to be followed in the preparation of reports, in the valuation of assets and liabilities, in the determination of depreciation and depletion, ...

The authority of the SEC to prescribe accounting principles for firms whose securities are publicly traded is quite clear, but the commission has preferred to exercise such authority through other authoritative bodies. With a strong emphasis on full disclosure to the public, SEC has usually depended upon its power to influence other authoritative bodies to develop standards acceptable to the commission.

For the protection of investors, SEC has in effect a very specific set of requirements. In its Regulation S-X, the SEC prescribes the content and form of a Registration Statement (Form S-1), which it requires to be filed prior to offering of new security issues. Regulation S-X also requires submission of an annual report to the SEC (Form 10-K) by companies whose securities are so registered. Although certain offerings are exempt, most securities traded on national exchanges or over the counter are subject to Regulation S-X reporting requirements. Both Form S-1 and Form 10-K are lengthy questionnaires in which considerable detail regarding security holders, remuneration to officers, stock option plans, and other similar information must be disclosed. It is important for the accountant to be aware of, and to insure that, the accounting system is designed to provide information for these reports.

Other Agencies

One of the most effective controls held by bodies that regulate interstate commerce is the power to prescribe accounting systems. A typical example is found in Section 407(d) of the Federal Aviation Act of 1958, which states in part: "(d) the Board [Civil Aeronautics Board] shall prescribe the forms of any and all accounts, records, and memoranda to be kept by air carriers, including the accounts, records, and memoranda of movements of traffic, as well as of the receipts and expenditures of money, ..." Similar powers reside in most other agencies with jurisdiction over interstate commerce—for example, Federal Power Commission, Interstate Commerce Commission, and others.

If a company is engaged in interstate commerce subject to regulation by a federal agency, or one engaged in intrastate business subject to a rate-setting body, its accountant should be familiar with accounting requirements of the regulatory agency.

VALUATION TECHNIQUES

Historical Cost

The value of an asset is the amount that must be paid to acquire it in the market. At the time and place of exchange, the foregoing statement is certainly factual; this fact has led to the accounting practice of recording assets in the accounts at the figure known as *historical cost*. For some assets—land, for example—the *historical cost concept* provides for no modification of the original cost figure in the accounts even when it no longer represents the economic value of the asset. A *modified historical cost* concept is applied to other plant assets; their carrying values are periodically reduced by charges to depreciation with the concomitant accumulations in the contra account. Similarly, amortization of intangible assets and depletion of natural resources modify the recorded cost, but all such adjustments tend to reduce carrying value. Modified historical cost procedures do not provide for periodic upward revisions to reflect events such as changing price levels or increases in value due to changes in environmental conditions. For this reason historical costs used to report the value of assets in the statement of financial position are inadequate.

Fair Market Value Approaches

In an effort to achieve comparability, several methods under which assets are stated at a figure more nearly approximating current economic worth are often considered under the general term *fair market value*. One such method is *replacement cost;* another is *reproduction cost*. Replacement cost is the cost of replacing one asset with another asset, probably of more modern design but of equivalent capacity. For a delivery truck, an aircraft engine, or other commonly used item of equipment, replacement cost can probably be determined with reasonable accuracy. However, for items of highly specialized equipment that are part of an industrial plant today, replacement cost is difficult to estimate. Reproduction cost is the current cost to reproduce an item exactly as it is new. A modification of this concept, called *sound value,* generally means the estimated cost to reproduce an asset in its present condition. Again, such appraisals are a matter of judgment.

One method of market value is *recoverable cost* or *exit values*. This con-

CONTEMPORARY ACCOUNTING TOPICS

cept would value an asset at its realizable value—the amount expected to be received if it were to be liquidated. Most entities do not have any means of determining exit values of plant assets except by offering them for sale (an unacceptable procedure for a going concern), thus again making valuation a matter of judgment, which is not comparable between firms. A form of exit values, *net realizable value,* is used when accounts receivable are reduced by the amount of estimated uncollectible accounts or when inventories or investments are carried at lower of cost or market. The actual market value of investments in stocks or bonds traded on the exchanges is readily available and is usually disclosed along with their cost on the statement of financial position, but there is no objective procedure to determine market value of the stock of thousands of smaller corporations not listed on the exchanges.

Discounted Cash Flow

Since the primary reason for holding assets is to produce a flow of cash into the firm at some future date, theoretically the best valuation of assets comes from the *discounted cash flow* method. This method assumes that an asset's value is equal to the present value of all cash flows it is expected to generate (including the amount to be realized on disposal) discounted at the appropriate market rate of interest. Although theoretically the best method, discounted cash flow technique suffers from several weaknesses. In many cases the amounts of future cash flows are difficult to estimate accurately; where it is possible to do so, it is sometimes impossible to attribute them to specific assets. The appropriate rate of interest to be used is another judgment, as is the useful life and disposal value of many assets. In spite of these difficulties, the Accounting Principles Board, in its *Opinion Number 21* in August 1971, ruled that receivables and payables extending over a period longer than one year should be recorded at present value if (1) they are non-interest bearing or (2) if they carry a rate of interest different from the rate in effect at the transaction date.

BUSINESS COMBINATIONS

The last two decades have witnessed a rapid acceleration in the number and size of business combinations. Companies with widely differing products and activities have been combined into new single units for a variety of reasons, but primarily to achieve certain advantages such as increased control of the market, a steady flow of raw materials from a reliable source at a favorable price, acquisition of operating companies with a minimum investment, minimization of income taxes, increased efficiency and economy in managerial operations and control, increased earnings from large-scale operations, and restriction of possible financial loss through diversification.

Business combinations may be classified either as *mergers* or as *consolidations.* A *merger* results when two or more previously separate legal entities are combined through the acquisition by one of the companies of the net assets of the other companies. In the process, the acquired companies lose their separate legal identities and are dissolved. A *consolidation* results when the net

FEDERAL
INCOME TAXES:
CONTEMPORARY
TOPICS

1008

(Ch. 27)

assets of all the previously separate legal entities are transferred to a different entity.

Some of the advantages sought through mergers and consolidations are often achieved more simply through *acquisitions,* whereby a company acquires a controlling portion of the voting stock of another company but—unlike mergers and consolidations—each component unit retains its separate legal and individual identity.

ACCOUNTING PROCEDURE—PURCHASE AND POOLING

Two concepts of accounting are applicable for the business combinations that result from either mergers or consolidations, and for business acquisitions.

Such combinations are referred to as (1) *purchase* and (2) *pooling of interests.* The differences in accounting exemplified by these two methods are not a consequence of the legal form—merger, consolidation, or acquisition—but rather arise from the point of view regarding the nature of the transaction with respect to the former ownership. The purchase viewpoint is that the former ownership is eliminated as a result of the combination, whereas the pooling viewpoint is that former ownership is continued.

Purchase versus Pooling of Interests

Under the purchase method of accounting, the valuation of the assets acquired is based on their market value. Although stock of the acquiring company is commonly issued for the stock or assets of the acquired company, the exchange is assumed to be the result of free bargaining between independent parties and is, therefore, recorded at cost as represented by the market value of the acquired stock. The value of the assets is assumed to be equal to the market value of the stock issued in the exchange. Any portion of the total purchase price not represented by specific assets acquired is assumed to represent goodwill. Under the pooling-of-interests method of accounting, the combination is viewed as a continuation of the formerly separate companies, combined into a new entity through the exchange of stock between the groups of stockholders involved. The assets and equities, including retained earnings balances, are combined and carried forward at their existing book values on the assumption that this is not a "market exchange" transaction requiring new accountability. In the typical case, accounting for the business combination using the purchase alternative resulted in higher asset values with concomitant higher depreciation charges and lower net income for a period of years following the combination. As a result, and in the absence of clear and precise guidelines, the choice of alternatives was frequently arbitrary and was influenced more by the accounting consequences than by the attendant facts. With the issuance of APB Opinion No. 16,[3] fairly explicit criteria and definitions are now

[3] AICPA, *APB Accounting Principles,* vol. 2 (Chicago: Commerce Clearing House, Inc., 1973), pp. 6637–6660.

(Ch. 27)

available for the choice of alternatives. The board concluded that "The purchase method and the pooling-of-interest method are both acceptable in accounting for business combinations, although not as alternatives in accounting for the same business combination. A business combination that meets specified conditions requires accounting by the pooling-of-interests method." All other combinations are to be accounted for as a purchase at cost.

To illustrate the accounting for the purchase and pooling alternatives in a merger, assume the following statements of financial position for Companies A and B:

	Company A	Company B	Total
Assets (net)	$650,000	$500,000	$1,150,000
Capital Stock	$500,000	$300,000	$ 800,000
Paid-In Capital in			
Excess of Par	50,000	150,000	200,000
Retained Earnings	100,000	50,000	150,000
	$650,000	$500,000	$1,150,000

Company C acquires the assets and assumes the liabilities of companies A and B. It issues 10,000 shares of its own stock to shareholders of company A and 7,500 shares to shareholders of company B. Company C stock is currently selling at $70 a share. The effects on consolidated position statements under the purchase and pooling alternatives on completion of the combination are shown below (it is assumed that the situation permits either alternative).

	Purchase	Pooling
Assets		
Assets (net) based on current market value of 17,500 shares of Company C at $70 per share	$1,225,000	
Total net assets per books of Companies A and B		$1,150,000
Equities		
Capital Stock, no par, 17,500 shares	$1,225,000	
Capital Stock, per books of Companies A and B		$ 800,000
Paid-In Capital in Excess of Par		200,000
Retained Earnings		150,000
	$1,225,000	$1,150,000

Note that accounting for the combination as a purchase resulted in $75,000 excess assets. Under pooling there is no excess, because prior book values

(Ch. 27)

are carried forward, the market value of company C's shares being ignored. If company C had issued 17,500 shares of $40 par value stock, the statements would be as follows:

	Purchase	Pooling
Net Assets	$1,225,000	$1,150,000
Capital Stock	$ 700,000	$ 700,000
Paid-In Capital in Excess of Par	525,000	300,000
Retained Earnings		150,000
	$1,225,000	$1,150,000

Under the pooling alternative in this illustration, the decrease in the capital stock account is offset by an equivalent increase in Paid-In Capital in Excess of Par. The Retained Earnings amount is unchanged.

CONSOLIDATED STATEMENTS

When a company acquires a controlling portion of the voting shares of another company, unified managerial control is achieved just as if the two companies were a single larger unit, even though each component unit retains its separate legal and individual identity. The corporation that holds the voting stock and controls the operations of other companies is known as the *parent company;* the companies controlled by the parent are called *subsidiaries.* The portion of the stock of the controlled companies held by persons outside the parent company is referred to as the *minority interest.*

> When financial and managerial control exists, the parent company may prepare consolidated financial statements.

Consolidated Statements

Consolidated statements present the financial affairs of the parent company and its subsidiaries as if they were a single economic unit. The major published financial reports for such families of corporations are in consolidated form. The terms "consolidation" and "consolidated" are commonly used, not in their legal sense denoting a form of business combination but rather to describe the accounting process of *combining* the accounts of a controlling parent company with the accounts of its subsidiary companies.

Consolidated statements should be prepared (1) when the parent company owns over 50 percent of the voting stock of the subsidiaries; (2) when the business activities of the companies are related or similar; and (3) when the financial condition of the group as a single economic unit is of greater significance than the fact of their separate existence.

(Ch. 27)

In certain instances, consolidation may be appropriate when the parent company has less than a majority of ownership. Such factors as leasehold and patent arrangements, interlocking directorates, and a satisfied group of majority stockholders create a unified managerial policy and control and provide the rationale for consolidation. Conversely, a parent company may own a majority of the voting shares, but such factors as the following may preclude consolidation: materially different business activities, differences in accounting periods, weak financial position of the subsidiary (particularly insolvency or bankruptcy), and the location of a subsidiary in a foreign country where assets may be subject to severe exchange restrictions.

Membership in a consolidated group does not eliminate the legal responsibilities of each unit to its own creditors and stockholders. Each corporation, as a separate legal entity, is responsible for its own decisions and its own obligations. Hence, even when consolidated statements are prepared, each separate legal entity prepares its own financial statements.

Typical of a corporation which prepares consolidated statements is Burlington Industries, Incorporated. With thirty-six United States divisions and eleven foreign subsidiaries consolidated into the following single set of financial statements, its 1973 Annual Report gives a picture of the total economic entity as disclosed in the financial statements shown on pages 1012–1015.

Consolidated Balance Sheet
(Dollar amounts in thousands)
Burlington Industries, Inc. and Subsidiary Companies
As of September 29, 1973 with comparative figures as of September 30, 1972

	1973	1972
Assets		
Current assets:		
Cash	$ 18,713	$ 15,483
Short-term investments, at cost, which approximates market	27,546	—
Customer accounts receivable after deduction of $17,820 (1972, $15,861) for doubtful accounts, discounts, returns and allowances	389,154	336,426
Sundry notes and accounts receivable	7,702	9,418
Inventories:		
Raw materials	93,120	60,204
Stock in process	86,582	78,243
Produced goods	215,802	204,997
Supplies, dyes and chemicals	25,710	22,546
Total inventories	421,214	365,990
Prepaid expenses	2,729	2,496
Deferred income taxes	14,277	15,074
Total current assets	881,335	744,887
Property, plant and equipment, at cost:		
Land and land improvements	31,506	30,120
Buildings	507,109	485,667
Machinery, fixtures and equipment	926,941	862,581
	1,465,556	1,378,368
Less accumulated depreciation, amortization and obsolescence	799,587	720,923
Property, plant and equipment—net	665,969	657,445
Investments and other assets:		
Investments and receivables	17,480	17,959
Deferred income taxes	4,213	5,489
Unamortized debt expense and other deferred charges	12,872	11,620
Total investments and other assets	34,565	35,068
	$1,581,869	$1,437,400

(Ch. 27)

The question of whether information about the various segments of diversified companies (conglomerates) is necessary for fair presentation in financial reports is one of the seven original agenda items established as projects by the FASB. For several years, the Securities Exchange Commission (SEC) and private groups such as security analysts have urged that financial reports carry a more detailed breakdown of results from various divisions of diversified companies. They think that shareholders can make better investment decisions if profits and losses in each segment of a diversified company are disclosed separately rather than being buried in a single set of consolidated statements. On the other hand, it is argued (1) that such detailed disclosures provide more information to a company's competitors than is in the best interest of its stockholders, (2) that there is no suitable common definition of a segment (product line, geographical division, organizational division, etc.), and (3) that strict rules for segmented disclosure would confuse rather than inform a great number of investors.

At the time of this writing the FASB has made no definitive pronouncement, but it is now common practice for diversified companies to show, in annual reports, information such as that shown on page 1016.

	1973	1972
Liabilities and Shareholders' Equity		
Current liabilities:		
Notes payable	$ 27,293	$ 46,244
Long-term debt due currently	14,042	13,454
Accounts payable—trade	116,583	97,855
Sundry accounts payable and accrued expenses	97,125	80,772
Federal and other taxes based on income	39,761	16,769
Total current liabilities	294,804	255,094
Long-term liabilities:		
Long-term debt	441,898	393,700
Other	18,827	16,644
Total long-term liabilities	460,725	410,344
Minority shareholders' interests in subsidiary companies	1,628	1,404
Shareholders' equity:		
Common stock of one dollar par value per share. Authorized, 40,000,000 shares; issued, 27,382,606 shares (1972, 26,932,781 shares)	27,383	26,933
Capital in excess of par value	193,904	186,928
Retained earnings	606,626	560,378
	827,913	774,239
Less common stock held in treasury, 120,595 shares (1972, 136,318 shares), at cost	3,201	3,681
Total shareholders' equity, 27,262,011 shares outstanding (1972, 26,796,463 shares)	824,712	770,558
	$1,581,869	$1,437,400

CONTEMPORARY
ACCOUNTING
TOPICS

(Ch. 27)

Consolidated Statement of Changes in Financial Position
(Dollar amounts in thousands)

Burlington Industries, Inc. and Subsidiary Companies
For the Period from October 1, 1972 to September 29, 1973
with comparative figures from October 3, 1971 to September 30, 1972

	1973	1972
Sources of working capital:		
From operations:		
Net earnings	$ 82,391	$ 49,607
Depreciation and amortization	90,742	87,328
Loss on retirement of property, plant and equipment	781	3,856
Deferred income taxes	981	1,319
Minority interests in earnings	147	144
	175,042	142,254
Long-term borrowings	50,199	20,589
Long-term debt increases due to changes in currency translation rates	14,791	6,593
Issuance of common stock	7,696	5,378
Sales of property, plant and equipment	16,006	14,809
Other	4,627	2,567
	268,361	192,190
Uses of working capital:		
Property, plant and equipment expenditures	98,535	114,714
Property, plant and equipment of acquired subsidiaries	722	910
Property, plant and equipment increases due to changes in currency translation rates	16,796	7,645
Repayment of long-term debt	16,792	29,196
Payment of cash dividends	37,517	37,144
Purchase of treasury shares	9	528
Other	1,252	3,701
	171,623	193,838
Increase (decrease) in working capital	$ 96,738	$ (1,648)
Increase (decrease) in working capital resulting from changes in:		
Current assets:		
Cash	$ 3,230	$ (597)
Short-term investments	27,546	—
Customer accounts receivable	52,728	24,465
Sundry notes and accounts receivable	(1,716)	3,078
Inventories	55,224	(1,413)
Prepaid expenses	233	523
Deferred income taxes	(797)	1,108
	136,448	27,164
Current liabilities:		
Notes payable	18,951	(21,769)
Long-term debt due currently	(588)	(320)
Accounts payable—trade	(18,728)	5,496
Sundry accounts payable and accrued expenses	(16,353)	(5,788)
Federal and other taxes based on income	(22,992)	(6,431)
	(39,710)	(28,812)
Increase (decrease) in working capital	$ 96,738	$ (1,648)

FEDERAL
INCOME TAXES:
CONTEMPORARY
TOPICS

1014

(Ch. 27)

Consolidated Statement of Earnings

(All amounts in thousands, except per share data)

Burlington Industries, Inc. and Subsidiary Companies
For the Period from October 1, 1972 to September 29, 1973
with comparative figures from October 3, 1971 to September 30, 1972

	1973	1972
Net sales	$2,099,801	$1,816,119
Cost of sales	1,753,083	1,552,703
Selling, administrative and general expenses	164,500	146,130
Interest charges	30,212	28,652
Total costs and expenses	1,947,795	1,727,485
	152,006	88,634
Other income—net	7,268	5,296
Earnings, before taxes based on income and minority interests	159,274	93,930
Provision for federal and other taxes based on income:		
Current	75,031	43,968
Deferred	1,705	211
	76,736	44,179
	82,538	49,751
Net earnings of subsidiary companies applicable to minority interests	147	144
Net earnings	$ 82,391	$ 49,607
Net earnings per share:		
Primary	$ 3.05	$ 1.86
Fully diluted	2.96	1.83
Cash dividends per share	1.40	1.40
Average shares outstanding during the period	27,009	26,636

Consolidated Statement of Shareholders' Equity

(All amounts in thousands, except number of shares)

Burlington Industries, Inc. and Subsidiary Companies
For the Period from October 1, 1972 to September 29, 1973
with comparative figures from October 3, 1971 to September 30, 1972

	Total Shareholders' Equity	Common Stock Issued	Capital in Excess of Par Value	Retained Earnings	Treasury Shares, at Cost	Number of Shares Issued	Number of Treasury Shares
Balance at October 2, 1971	$750,576	$26,768	$182,449	$547,942	$(6,583)	26,767,671	258,992
Shares issued for acquisition	2,669	—	(720)	(27)	3,416	—	(140,735)
Net earnings	49,607	—	—	49,607	—	—	—
Dividends paid	(37,144)	—	—	(37,144)	—	—	—
Shares issued to employees' profit sharing (retirement) plan	5,308	163	5,131	—	14	162,860	(408)
Proceeds from exercise of options	70	2	68	—	—	2,250	—
Purchase of treasury shares	(528)	—	—	—	(528)	—	18,469
Balance at September 30, 1972	770,558	26,933	186,928	560,378	(3,681)	26,932,781	136,318
Shares issued for acquisitions	1,793	210	9	1,374	200	210,008	(5,984)
Net earnings	82,391	—	—	82,391	—	—	—
Dividends paid	(37,517)	—	—	(37,517)	—	—	—
Shares issued to employees' profit sharing (retirement) plan	7,486	240	6,957	—	289	239,517	(10,000)
Proceeds from exercise of options	10	—	10	—	—	300	—
Purchase of treasury shares	(9)	—	—	—	(9)	—	261
Balance at September 29, 1973	$824,712	$27,383	$193,904	$606,626	$(3,201)	27,382,606	120,595

(Ch. 27)

1. Revenues by type of industry activity or by type of market.
2. Revenues and profits by industry segments.
3. Separate financial statements for segments of the business which represent a distinctly different capital structure, for example, the finance or insurance subsidiary of a manufacturing firm.
4. Information on profit or loss resulting from operation of a segment without revealing detailed figures thereon.

The APB in its Statement No. 2 urged diversified companies to disclose voluntarily supplemental information about industry segments of the business. It has also recognized the need for disclosure of changes in the composition of a reporting entity (APB Opinion No. 20, *Accounting Changes*) and for disclosure of separate operating results for a segment disposed of during an accounting period (APB Opinion No. 30, *Reporting the Results of Operations*).

The Financial Executives Institute (FEI) concludes that companies with activity in more than one industry to a material degree (15 percent or more of a firm's gross revenue) (1) should identify and describe the components subject to separate reporting, (2) should disclose significant changes from the previous year in those reporting components, and (3) for each reporting component, should disclose gross revenue and relative contribution made by the component to the income of the enterprise.

The SEC requires separate line-of-business reporting in Form 10-K for products or services that represent 10 percent or more of total sales or net income before taxes for the past two years. It also requires separate reporting for any line with a loss that equals or exceeds 10 percent of the foregoing net income.

FORECASTS

One of the objectives identified by the AICPA's Study Group reporting in 1973 was worded as follows: "An objective of financial statements is to provide information useful for the predictive process. Financial forecasts should be provided when they will enhance the reliability of the users' predictions."[4] Some corporations have already begun to include forecasts in their annual reports. In its 1972 annual report, for example, Fuqua Industries stated:

It has become apparent that the SEC in its continuing effort to provide better disclosure of information to stockholders will permit, and indeed at some point may require, disclosure of operating forecasts. As was said in our December preliminary report which contained 1972 estimates and 1973 forecasts of sales and earnings, if this is the music we will have to march to, we are willing to lead the band.

Forecasting of operating results raises several controversial questions. Over the period of a year, events could occur that were not considered when the forecasts were made. The AICPA Study Group, recognizing that such events could cause forecast information to be more harmful than beneficial to

[4] *Objectives of Financial Statements* (New York: AICPA, 1973), p. 46.

FEDERAL
INCOME TAXES:
CONTEMPORARY
TOPICS

1016

(Ch. 27)

an investor, suggests that forecasts be accompanied by the significant underlying assumptions used to develop them. Another problem is the amount of detail to be disclosed; a proper balance between the amount of disclosure considered to be adequate to users' needs and the amount that would be harmful to an entity's competitive position—and thus to its stockholders—must be reached. The 1973 AICPA Study Group concluded that the accuracy of forecasts themselves was not as critical a matter as the accuracy of users' predictions without forecasts compared to their predictions with forecast information available to them.

HUMAN RESOURCES ACCOUNTING

The conventional accounting model does not include in the assets of an entity the value of its human resources. Company literature and national advertising often focus on the value of loyal employees, but statements of financial position ignore them. In 1969 Professor R. Lee Brummet suggested that an outlay cost system be used as a starting point to place a valuation on human assets.[5] The R. G. Barry Corporation has actually used the historical cost approach to record human assets on the balance sheet. Other approaches have been suggested. One of these would use a technique similar to discounted cash flow—a person's worth would be recorded as the present value of the stream of future benefits he is expected to provide.[6] Another "cost-oriented" approach would value human assets as the present value of their future income streams.[7] Between these two views is one which holds that a better indicator of value of human assets is the present value of the difference between estimated benefits and estimated costs of an individual's employment.[8]

The Committee on Human Resources Accounting of the American Accounting Association is responsible for identifying, examining, and proposing alternative methods. Although the committee's 1973 report emphasized the need for continuing research, the extent of work already done in the area of human resources accounting was evidenced by its inclusion of a bibliography with more than one hundred articles and books. In decision-making situations human asset cost considerations and behavioral impact considerations are considered by many to be far too important to omit human resources accounting information from financial statements.

SOCIAL ACCOUNTING MEASUREMENTS

Each accounting entity exists in and constantly interacts with its social environment. Sacrifices may be made by the environment that benefit the entity

[5] In a speech before the annual convention of the AAA, South Bend, Indiana, August 26, 1969.

[6] Eric G. Flamholtz, "Toward a Theory of Human Resource Value in Formal Organizations," *The Accounting Review* (October 1972), p. 668.

[7] Baruch Lev, and Aba Schwartz, "On the Use of the Economic Concept of Human Capital in Financial Statements" *The Accounting Review* (January 1971), p. 103.

[8] Pekin Ogan, "A Human Resource Value Model for Professional Service Organizations," an unpublished paper prepared at the University of North Carolina at Chapel Hill.

without becoming recorded as costs thereof. Pollution of the air, the water, or the earth's surface, which must be corrected in later years, is an unrecognized current cost of business operations. At some later date corrective measures, if applied by the entity, will appear as expenses either in the period in which applied (if treated as revenue expenditures) or in a series of future periods (if capitalized and depreciated). Some expenses of corrective measures may be borne by government, and thus may fall upon all persons in the environment rather than being borne only by consumers of the entity's products or services.

Conversely, an entity may make contributions to its environment for which it does not receive any direct return. Contributions of money, time, and talents of officers and employees, or of facilities either are charged as expenses of the current period or are not recorded at all. In many cases, the benefits to the entity from such costs are felt over future years in the form of customer loyalty because of an enhanced company image.

In both the foregoing situations, the matching concept is violated by failure to associate expenses and revenues in appropriate periods. The AICPA Accounting Objectives Study Group report recognized the importance of reporting these social interactions, and stated that "An objective of financial statements is to report on those activities of the enterprise affecting society which can be determined and described or measured and which are important to the role of the enterprise in its social environment."[9] A major challenge to the accounting profession is to develop standards and procedures that will accomplish this objective.

At the present time several corporations are using narrative sections and footnotes to financial statements to report on their efforts to accept corporate social responsibility. These mostly consist of comparative statements showing expenditures to reduce air and water pollution, to recruit and train the disadvantaged, or for research and development in these areas. They also contain general statements regarding financial support given to educational, health, cultural, and community programs and the involvement of company employees in such programs. Few if any are disclosing dollar figures or narrative descriptions for additional social problems that they are creating.

Although some academic research is underway in an attempt to find meaningful ways to evaluate corporate social responsibility, there does not appear to be an immediate prospect for a set of standards or a taxonomy under which specific procedures for accounting measurements can be developed. This remains a fertile, and possibly the most important, field for accounting research.

NOT-FOR-PROFIT AND GOVERNMENT ACCOUNTING

In a sense accounting for all levels of government and accounting for not-for-profit organizations such as churches, community funds, or hospitals are similar. The basic accounting entity in each is not the organization itself; instead each organization is made up of several entities usually known as *funds*.

FEDERAL
INCOME TAXES:
CONTEMPORARY
TOPICS

9 p. 55.

1018

(Ch. 27)

A fund consists of assets—often held in the form of cash, securities, or receivables—that have been designated by the appropriate body of the organization to be used for a specific purpose. Examples of bodies that designate funds and amounts are state legislatures, city councils, or boards of directors of charitable activities. Such designation is often described as an *appropriation* and is usually available for use in one fiscal year. Each such fund is treated in accounting as a separate entity with its own assets, liabilities, and an equity or capital category known as the *fund balance*. Specific accounting procedures for such organizations are generally considered to be outside the scope of a textbook in basic accounting for the elementary level.

In recent years, a very large segment of the national expenditures have been channeled through government bodies and not-for-profit organizations. Accordingly, their financial statements have become of interest to all citizens who are making decisions regarding allocation of voluntary contributions and are seeking information on the benefits received both from their charitable contributions and their tax dollars. The AICPA Accounting Objectives Study Group report recognized this area as important enough to include in its twelve objectives of financial statements the following objective: "An objective of financial statements for governmental and not-for-profit organizations is to provide information useful for evaluating the effectiveness of the management of resources in achieving the organization's goals. Performance measures should be quantified in terms of identified goals."[10]

NATIONAL INCOME ACCOUNTING

The countless transactions of all entities in the United States are summarized annually by the Office of Business Economics, U. S. Department of Commerce. There are two basic needs for the annual summaries: (1) Managers of entities and private individuals need information on trends of economic activity on which to base decisions about their own future economic activity. (2) When the natural mechanisms of the marketplace are not adequate to sustain a healthy economy, government has a responsibility to take corrective action. A brief description of the National Income Accounting system is given here. For complete details, a book published by the U. S. Department of Commerce is recommended, *Readings in Concepts and Methods of National Income Statistics,* PB 194 900. It may be obtained from the National Technical Information Service, Springfield, Virginia.[11]

The plan of the accounting system divides the economy into four sectors—private, business, government, and foreign. One account, shown below, summarizes the output from all four sectors to obtain *gross national product* (GNP).

[10] p. 51.
[11] For a discussion of the development of national income accounts from micro data, see Chapter 5, "Social Accounting" in *Accountancy and Economic Development Policy,* by Adolf J. H. Enthoven (New York: Elsevier Publishing Company, 1973).

National Income and Product Account

Costs of GNP, such as compensation of persons, corporate profits, interest, indirect business taxes, depreciation		Payments for GNP, such as personal consumption expenditures, private investment, net foreign investment, and government expenditures	
Charges against GNP	xxx	Gross National Product	xxx

Four major accounts provide details of the National Income and Product Account. Each is balanced annually.

Personal Income and Expenditures Account

Consumption expenditures, taxes, and savings		Wages and salaries, income of proprietorships and of partnerships, rental and interest income, dividends	
Personal Outlay and Savings	xxx	Personal Income	xxx

Consolidated Business Income and Product Account

Wages, interest, taxes, depreciation		Sales and changes in inventories	
Charges against Business Gross Product	xxx	Business Gross Product	xxx

Consolidated Government Receipts and Expenditures Account

Purchases of goods and services, transfer payments, interest, subsidies		Personal taxes, corporation taxes, indirect business taxes, and contributions for social insurance	
Government Expenditures and Surplus or Deficit	xxx	Government Recipts	xxx

Rest of the World Account

Exports of goods and services		Imports of goods and services, transfer payments, foreign aid and investment	
Receipts from Foreigners	xxx	Payments to Foreigners	xxx

FEDERAL
INCOME TAXES:
CONTEMPORARY
TOPICS

1020

(Ch. 27)

The data for each of these major accounts are gathered from several subordinate accounts. The entire system enables the production of a set of interrelated tables that provide an analysis of the economy and its functioning. For example, the above system of national income accounts provides the index numbers that were used in the discussion and illustration of price-level changes in an earlier chapter. A new indicator to complement GNP called "Measure of Economic Welfare" (MEW) has recently been proposed. It would measure quality of life as well as material wealth.[12]

EXPANDING ROLE OF ACCOUNTING

In the opening sentence of this chapter, it was noted that the basic aim of accounting is to provide information useful for making economic decisions. The discussions that followed highlight only a few of the many challenges facing accountants in their pursuit of that basic aim. As changes in the structure of society occur, the role of accounting expands; basic requirements remain, and new demands are added. Referring to the AICPA's issuance of Industry Audit Guides for hospitals, colleges, and universities and for voluntary health and welfare organizations, Malvern J. Gross, Jr., has stated:

> . . . in less than 18 months, the accounting profession has laid down some very specific rules for the three most important sectors of the broad category referred to as nonprofit organizations. As a result, nonprofit organizations suddenly find themselves catapulted from an era of permissiveness to an era where the accounting and reporting requirements are spelled out in great detail."[13]

Throughout this book, the authors have attempted to integrate explanations of basic accounting standards and practices with recent developments that have changed the role of accounting—for example, the spectacular increase in the use of computers. A thorough understanding of basic accounting concepts is as essential now as ever, but the expanding role of accounting has established a need for continuing education of accountants that is greater than ever before.

GLOSSARY

Appropriation In a not-for-profit or government entity, an authorization to commit assets to achieve a stated purpose.

Conglomerates See *Diversified Companies*.

[12] For a discussion see Kenneth Stewart, "National Income Accounting and Economic Welfare: The Concepts of GNP and MEW," *Federal Reserve Bank of St. Louis Review* (April 1974), pp. 18–24.

[13] "Nonprofit Accounting: A Revolution in Process," *Price Waterhouse and Co. Review* (1973), vol. 18, no. 3, p. 43.

CONTEMPORARY
ACCOUNTING
TOPICS

(Ch. 27)

1021

Consolidated Statements A combination of the financial statements of affiliated legal entities to show, in a single set of statements, their financial condition and operating results as an economic entity.

Discounted Cash Flow The present value of a stream of cash receipts (or cost reductions) expected to occur over a finite number of future periods.

Diversified Companies Companies engaged in more than one (usually several) unrelated lines of business.

Exit Value The amount for which an asset can currently be sold. Also known as a *recoverable cost.*

Fair Market Value Recording of assets in a manner to approximate current values.

Form 10-K An annual report required by SEC from companies whose securities are traded publicly.

Fund An amount designated by an authorized governing body to be used for a specific purpose; an accounting entity in government and not-for-profit accounting.

Fund Balance The equity account or capital account of a fund.

Gross National Product (GNP) The annual sum of all expenditures in the United States for personal consumption, private investment, government purchases of goods and services, and net foreign spending.

Historical Cost The original cost of an asset including net purchase price and all other costs required to place it into service.

Human Resources Accounting A system of quantifying the value of human assets in the accounting records.

Merger Combination of one or more separate companies by an acquiring company; the companies acquired lose their identity.

Minority Interest The amount of ownership equity in a subsidiary company held by persons other than the parent company.

Modified Historical Cost Historical cost offset by a figure that recognizes the amount of original benefits already extracted from an asset.

Not-for-Profit Organization An entity whose primary aim is one other than engaging in business for profit.

Parent Company A corporation that holds a controlling share of ownership in another company.

Pooling-of-Interests Method Accounting for a merger or consolidation by combining assets at existing carrying or book values.

Purchase Method Accounting for a merger or consolidation with revaluation of assets to market prices.

Registration Statement A questionnaire-like report required by SEC prior to a new securities offering.

Regulation S-X A regulation by the SEC prescribing registration statements and other reports by companies whose stock is publicly traded.

Replacement Cost Cost of replacing an asset with another asset having the same or greater amount of future benefit.

Reproduction Cost Cost of reproducing new an existing asset in the same configuration.

FEDERAL
INCOME TAXES:
CONTEMPORARY
TOPICS

1022

(Ch. 27)

SEC Securities Exchange Commission.

Social Accounting A system which includes in the accounting records the interactions with an entity's environment that can be described and quantified.

Subsidiary Company A firm in which a controlling ownership interest is held by another company.

Q27-1. Do you consider that financial statements in annual reports of corporations are fulfilling the basic purpose of accounting? List some specific ways in which some accountants argue that they do not.

Q27-2. With regard to development of accounting standards, contrast the authority of the Financial Accounting Standards Board with that of a government regulatory agency such as the Securities Exchange Commission.

Q27-3. Describe each of the following valuation methods:
   a. modified historical cost
   b. replacement cost
   c. reproduction cost
   d. exit value
   e. discounted cash flow

Q27-4. Differentiate between the purchase and the pooling methods of business combination recording.

Q27-5. What is the purpose of consolidated financial statements?

Q27-6. In 1974, the Federal Trade Commission required that large corporations who submit certain confidential reports to FTC break down their sales and profit figures by product lines. One objection to this requirement was that it would cause companies to allocate subjectively general costs (such as advertising or research and development) to specific lines of business. Evaluate this objection.

Q27-7. In addition to forecast data per se—for example, sales and earnings for the next year—users need other information about forecasts and projections. Suggest some of this additional information and comment on the amount of detail that should be made public. (*Hint:* Consider existing shareholders.)

Q27-8. In an address before the twenty-sixth annual meeting of the Southeast Regional Group of the American Accounting Association, Professor R. Lee Brummet described human resources accounting as recording the significance of people to organizations and social accounting as recording the significance of organizations to people. Explain in more detail the meaning of his statement.

Q27-9. Contrast the concept of entity in accounting for a business firm with the concept of entity in accounting for a city government.

Q27-10. What are some of the basic uses of the national income accounting system?

E27-1. In the spring of 1974, certain regulatory agencies proposed the changes listed in column A. Match those changes with the appropriate agency in column B.

(Ch. 27)

<table>
<thead>
<tr><th>A</th><th>B</th></tr>
</thead>
<tbody>
<tr><td>a. Amendment to Rule 1-02 of Regulation S-X. _____</td><td>1. Internal Revenue Service</td></tr>
<tr><td>b. Nationally chartered banks with total assets of $100 million or more in their trust departments must make certain quarterly and annual disclosures. _____</td><td>2. National Labor Relations Board
3. Securities Exchange Commission</td></tr>
<tr><td>c. The minimum investment return for a private foundation (a basis for its tax-exempt status) was increased. _____</td><td>4. Federal Power Commission</td></tr>
<tr><td>d. Calculate overtime back pay for workers dismissed discriminatorily on the basis of overtime hours worked by employees with comparable seniority. _____</td><td>5. Comptroller of the Currency</td></tr>
<tr><td>e. Electric and natural gas companies must list their top 30 security holders instead of their top 10. _____</td><td></td></tr>
</tbody>
</table>

E27-2. A corporation engaged in production of paper products has gradually accumulated forest lands over the past thirty years and carries on its statement of financial position each parcel of land at original acquisition cost. Recently the company has received several offers for some of its lands from developers of shopping centers and suburban housing; these offers have been much higher than the original costs. The president feels that these assets should be "written up" to approximately the amounts offered for them. From the viewpoint of the basic objectives of financial statements, prepare a memorandum to the president explaining valuation approaches that could be used to accomplish his wishes and the major arguments for and against their validity as methods of valuation.

E27-3. All the capital stock of Corporations X and Y is acquired by Corporation Z. Prior to the merger, the respective statements of financial position of X and Y were:

	X	Y
Assets (net)	$250,000	$380,000
Capital Stock, $10 par value	$100,000	$200,000
Paid-in Capital in Excess of Par Value	100,000	100,000
Retained Earnings	50,000	80,000
	$250,000	$380,000

Company Z issued 10,000 shares of its own $10 par value stock to shareholders of Company X and 13,000 shares to shareholders of Company Y. Company Z's stock is currently selling on the market at $30 a share.

a. At what value would the consolidated assets of companies X and Y be recorded under the pooling method?

b. At what value would the consolidated assets be recorded under the purchase method?

E27-4. Assume that the firms described in column A decide to disclose the results of their operations by segment. Match each firm with the most suitable definition of "line of business" (or segment) in column B.

FEDERAL
INCOME TAXES:
CONTEMPORARY
TOPICS

1024

(Ch. 27)

A	B
a. A steel company that is vertically integrated (mining operations, transportation, and production of steel sheet, bar, or rolled stock) _____	**1.** Product line **2.** Organizational subdivision **3.** Geographical subdivision **4.** Type of industry
b. A decentralized automobile and truck manufacturer _____	
c. A company that manufactures tobacco products, liquor, dog food, and jewelry _____	
d. A company whose practice, as a safeguard against labor market changes, is to operate a group of plants for each product in the southeastern, midwestern, and northeastern areas of the country _____	

E27-5. Fuqua Industries, Incorporated, reported the following data in the 1973 annual report.

	(in millions)		
	1973 Forecast	1973 Actual	1974 Forecast
Total sales and revenues	$429.0	$479.2	$541.0
Pretax income	18.1	20.3	24.0

a. What arguments can you make in favor of financial forecasts in annual reports?

b. What arguments can you make opposing the publication of forecasts in annual financial reports?

(IMA adapted)

E27-6. Mary Smith is hired at the beginning of 1976 by a company whose practice is to record human assets at historical cost. It is estimated that Mary will be with the company for 20 years, and that cost of recruitment and training will amount to $5,000 in her case.

Show the summary accounting entries for the method that you would recommend to record:

a. The outlay for recruitment and training of Smith.

b. Payment of her annual salary for the first year ($10,000).

c. Amortization of her asset value at the end of the first year of service.

What was the amount of expense included in the 1976 income statement related to Smith's services?

E27-7. A plant that emits pollution into the air is faced with legislation which requires at least a 50% reduction in emissions. The following data have been developed:

Annual profits	$200,000
Cost of abatement devices	
To reduce emissions by 50%	400,000
To reduce emissions by 90%	600,000

Estimated useful life of abatement devices, 10 years

a. Using straight-line depreciation, compute the annual profits:

(1) With 50% reduction in emissions.
(2) With 90% reduction in emissions.
(3) With no reduction in emissions.
b. Which of the three foregoing courses of actions will the company choose?
c. Suppose that the Environmental Protection Agency (EPA) provides data showing that damage to the surrounding environment amounts to $300,000 a year. Develop figures to support a request to EPA for a government grant of $200,000 to this company to fund the difference between 50% reduction (minimum compliance) and 90% reduction (maximum possible). (*Hint:* Prove to the government agency, by computation, that society as a whole will benefit, and show exactly by how much.)

(*Adapted from the 1974 Report of the Committee on Measurement of Social Costs, American Accounting Association; used by permission of the American Accounting Association.*)

E27-8. The summary of financial activities of three charitable agencies engaged in similar work are shown below.

	Year Ended December 31, 1976		
	Agency A	Agency B	Agency C
Support from the public			
Contributions received	$100,000	$300,000	$ 800,000
Pledges received (less estimated uncollectibles)	40,000	80,000	200,000
Government grants	100,000	100,000	100,000
Total support received	$240,000	$480,000	$1,100,000
Expenditures			
For charitable programs	$150,000	$360,000	$700,000
Management and general	40,000	60,000	80,000
Fund raising	30,000	40,000	300,000
Total expenditures	$220,000	$460,000	$1,080,000
Excess of revenue over expenditures	$ 20,000	$ 20,000	$ 20,000

Since each agency has ended the year with $20,000, each will need to ask for contributions for 1977. On the basis of these statements, which agency appears to be most deserving of support? Why?

E27-9. Choose the best answer.

The federal income tax system acts as an automatic stabilizer of the economy, because:
a. Taxes take less from personal income during a recession.
b. Tax receipts are fixed over the business cycle.
c. Taxes automatically balance the budget at full employment.
d. Taxes provide more money to government during a recession.

(*IMA adapted*)

E27-10. Prepare a list of elements of the current role of accounting in society that would not have existed or would have been completely outside the scope of the accountant's job description at the beginning of this century.

Note: The nature of the text material in Chapter 27 does not warrant the inclusion of demonstration problems and problems.

APPENDIX
Compound
Interest
Tables

Compound Amount of 1 $a = (1 + i)^n$

	1½%	2%	3%	4%	6%	8%	10%	12%	14%	16%	20%
1	1.015000	1.020000	1.030000	1.040000	1.060000	1.080000	1.100000	1.120000	1.140000	1.160000	1.200000
2	1.030225	1.040400	1.060900	1.081600	1.123600	1.166400	1.210000	1.254400	1.299600	1.345600	1.440000
3	1.045678	1.061208	1.092727	1.124864	1.191016	1.259712	1.331000	1.404928	1.481544	1.560896	1.728000
4	1.061364	1.082432	1.125509	1.169859	1.262477	1.360489	1.464100	1.573519	1.688960	1.810639	2.073600
5	1.077284	1.104081	1.159274	1.216653	1.338226	1.469328	1.610510	1.762342	1.925415	2.100342	2.488320
6	1.093443	1.126162	1.194052	1.265319	1.418519	1.586874	1.771561	1.973823	2.194973	2.436396	2.985984
7	1.109845	1.148686	1.229874	1.315932	1.503630	1.713824	1.948717	2.210681	2.502269	2.826220	3.583181
8	1.126493	1.171659	1.266770	1.368569	1.593848	1.850930	2.143589	2.475963	2.852586	3.278415	4.299817
9	1.143390	1.195093	1.304773	1.423312	1.689479	1.999005	2.357948	2.773079	3.251949	3.802961	5.159780
10	1.160541	1.218994	1.343916	1.480244	1.790848	2.158925	2.593742	3.105848	3.707221	4.411435	6.191736
11	1.177949	1.243374	1.384234	1.539454	1.898299	2.331639	2.853117	3.478550	4.226232	5.117265	7.430084
12	1.195618	1.268242	1.425761	1.601032	2.012196	2.518170	3.138428	3.895976	4.817905	5.936027	8.916100
13	1.213553	1.293607	1.468534	1.665074	2.132928	2.719624	3.452271	4.363493	5.492411	6.885791	10.699321
14	1.231756	1.319479	1.512590	1.731676	2.260904	2.937193	3.797498	4.887112	6.261349	7.987518	12.839185
15	1.250232	1.345868	1.557967	1.800944	2.396558	3.172169	4.177248	5.473566	7.137938	9.265521	15.407022
16	1.268986	1.372786	1.604706	1.872981	2.540352	3.425942	4.594973	6.130394	8.137249	10.748004	18.488426
17	1.288021	1.400241	1.652848	1.947900	2.692773	3.700018	5.054470	6.866041	9.276464	12.467685	22.186111
18	1.307341	1.428246	1.702433	2.025817	2.854339	3.996019	5.559917	7.689966	10.575169	14.462514	26.623333
19	1.326951	1.456811	1.753506	2.106849	3.025600	4.315701	6.115909	8.612762	12.055693	16.776517	31.948000
20	1.346856	1.485947	1.806111	2.191123	3.207135	4.660957	6.727500	9.646293	13.743490	19.460759	38.337600
21	1.367058	1.515666	1.860295	2.278768	3.399563	5.033833	7.400250	10.803848	15.667578	22.574481	46.005120
22	1.387564	1.545980	1.916103	2.369919	3.603537	5.436540	8.140275	12.100310	17.861039	26.186398	55.206144
23	1.408378	1.576899	1.973587	2.464716	3.819750	5.871463	8.954302	13.552347	20.361585	30.376222	66.247373
24	1.429503	1.608437	2.032794	2.563304	4.048935	6.341180	9.849733	15.178629	23.212207	35.236417	79.496847
25	1.450946	1.640606	2.093778	2.665836	4.291871	6.848475	10.834706	17.000064	26.461916	40.874244	95.396217
26	1.472710	1.673418	2.156591	2.772470	4.549383	7.396353	11.918177	19.040072	30.166584	47.414123	114.475460
27	1.494801	1.706886	2.221289	2.883369	4.822346	7.988061	13.109994	21.324881	34.389906	55.000382	137.370552
28	1.517223	1.741024	2.287928	2.998703	5.111687	8.627106	14.420994	23.883866	39.204493	63.800444	164.844662
29	1.539981	1.775845	2.356566	3.118651	5.418388	9.317274	15.863093	26.749930	44.693122	74.008515	197.813595
30	1.563081	1.811362	2.427262	3.243398	5.743491	10.062656	17.449402	29.959922	50.950159	85.849877	237.376314
31	1.586527	1.847589	2.500080	3.373133	6.088101	10.867669	19.194342	33.555113	58.083181	99.585857	284.851577
32	1.610325	1.884541	2.575083	3.508059	6.453387	11.737082	21.113777	37.581726	66.214826	115.519594	341.821892
33	1.634480	1.922231	2.652335	3.648381	6.840590	12.676049	23.225154	42.091533	75.484902	134.002729	410.186270
34	1.658997	1.960676	2.731905	3.794316	7.251025	13.690133	25.547670	47.142517	86.052788	155.443116	492.223524
35	1.683882	1.999890	2.813662	3.946089	7.686087	14.785344	28.102437	52.799620	98.100178	180.314073	590.668229
36	1.709140	2.039887	2.898278	4.103933	8.147252	15.968171	30.912681	59.135574	111.834203	209.164324	708.801875
37	1.734777	2.080685	2.985227	4.268090	8.636087	17.245625	34.003949	66.231843	127.490092	242.630616	850.562250
38	1.760799	2.122299	3.074783	4.438813	9.154252	18.625275	37.404043	74.179664	145.339731	281.451515	1020.674700
39	1.787211	2.164745	3.167026	4.616366	9.703507	20.115297	41.144778	83.081224	165.687293	326.483757	1224.809640
40	1.814019	2.208040	3.262037	4.801021	10.285718	21.724520	45.259256	93.050970	188.883514	378.721158	1469.771568

Present Value of 1 $\quad p = \dfrac{1}{(1+i)^n}$

	1½%	2%	3%	4%	6%	8%	10%	12%	14%	16%	20%
1	.985222	.980392	.970874	.961538	.943396	.925926	.909091	.892857	.877193	.862069	.833333
2	.970662	.961169	.942596	.924556	.889996	.857339	.826446	.797194	.769468	.743163	.694444
3	.956317	.942322	.915142	.888996	.839619	.793832	.751315	.711780	.674972	.640658	.578704
4	.942184	.923845	.888487	.854804	.792094	.735030	.683013	.635518	.592080	.552291	.482253
5	.928260	.905731	.862609	.821927	.747258	.680583	.620921	.567427	.519369	.476113	.401878
6	.914542	.887971	.837484	.790315	.704961	.630170	.564474	.506631	.455587	.410442	.334898
7	.901027	.870560	.813092	.759918	.665057	.583490	.513158	.452349	.399637	.353830	.279082
8	.887711	.853490	.789409	.730690	.627412	.540269	.466507	.403883	.350559	.305025	.232568
9	.874592	.836755	.766417	.702587	.591894	.500249	.424098	.360610	.307508	.262953	.193807
10	.861667	.820348	.744094	.675564	.558395	.463193	.385543	.321973	.269744	.226684	.161506
11	.848933	.804263	.722421	.649581	.526788	.428883	.350494	.287476	.236617	.195417	.134588
12	.836387	.788493	.701380	.624597	.496969	.397114	.318631	.256675	.207559	.168463	.112157
13	.824027	.773033	.680951	.600574	.468839	.367698	.289664	.229174	.182069	.145227	.093464
14	.811849	.757875	.661118	.577475	.442301	.340461	.263331	.204620	.159710	.125195	.077887
15	.799852	.743015	.641862	.555265	.417265	.315242	.239392	.182696	.140096	.107927	.064905
16	.788031	.728446	.623167	.533908	.393646	.291890	.217629	.163122	.122892	.093041	.054088
17	.776385	.714163	.605016	.513373	.371364	.270269	.197845	.145644	.107800	.080207	.045073
18	.764912	.700159	.587395	.493628	.350344	.250249	.179859	.130040	.094561	.069144	.037561
19	.753607	.686431	.570286	.474642	.330513	.231712	.163508	.116107	.082948	.059607	.031301
20	.742470	.672971	.553676	.456387	.311805	.214548	.148644	.103667	.072762	.051385	.026084
21	.731498	.659776	.537549	.438834	.294155	.198656	.135131	.092560	.063826	.044298	.021737
22	.720688	.646839	.521893	.421955	.277505	.183941	.122846	.082643	.055988	.038188	.018114
23	.710037	.634156	.506692	.405726	.261797	.170315	.111678	.073788	.049112	.032920	.015095
24	.699544	.621722	.491934	.390121	.246979	.157699	.101526	.065882	.043081	.028380	.012579
25	.689206	.609531	.477606	.375116	.232999	.146018	.092296	.058823	.037790	.024465	.010483
26	.679021	.597579	.463695	.360689	.219810	.135202	.083905	.052521	.033149	.021091	.008735
27	.668986	.585862	.450189	.346816	.207368	.125187	.076278	.046894	.029078	.018182	.007280
28	.659099	.574375	.437077	.333477	.195630	.115914	.069343	.041869	.025507	.015674	.006066
29	.649359	.563113	.424346	.320651	.184557	.107328	.063039	.037383	.022375	.013512	.005055
30	.639762	.552071	.411987	.308318	.174110	.099377	.057309	.033378	.019627	.011648	.004213
31	.630308	.541246	.399987	.296460	.164255	.092016	.052099	.029802	.017217	.010042	.003511
32	.620993	.530633	.388337	.285058	.154957	.085200	.047362	.026609	.015102	.008657	.002926
33	.611816	.520229	.377026	.274094	.146186	.078889	.043057	.023758	.013248	.007463	.002438
34	.602774	.510028	.366045	.263552	.137912	.073045	.039143	.021212	.011621	.006433	.002032
35	.593866	.500028	.355383	.253415	.130105	.067635	.035584	.018940	.010194	.005546	.001693
36	.585090	.490223	.345032	.243669	.122741	.062625	.032349	.016910	.008942	.004781	.001411
37	.576443	.480611	.334983	.234297	.115793	.057986	.029408	.015098	.007844	.004121	.001176
38	.567924	.471187	.325226	.225285	.109239	.053690	.026735	.013481	.006880	.003553	.000980
39	.559531	.461948	.315753	.216620	.103056	.049713	.024304	.012036	.006035	.003063	.000816
40	.551262	.452891	.306557	.208289	.097222	.046031	.022095	.010747	.005294	.002640	.000680

Amount of an Annuity of 1

$$A \frac{(1+i)^n - 1}{i}$$

n	1½%	2%	3%	4%	6%	8%	10%	12%	14%	16%	20%
1	1.000000	1.000000	1.000000	1.000000	1.000000	1.000000	1.000000	1.000000	1.000000	1.000000	1.000000
2	2.015000	2.020000	2.030000	2.040000	2.060000	2.080000	2.100000	2.120000	2.140000	2.160000	2.200000
3	3.045225	3.060400	3.090900	3.121600	3.183600	3.246400	3.310000	3.374400	3.439600	3.505600	3.640000
4	4.090903	4.121608	4.183627	4.246464	4.374616	4.506112	4.641000	4.779328	4.921144	5.066496	5.368000
5	5.152267	5.204040	5.309136	5.416323	5.637093	5.866601	6.105100	6.352847	6.610104	6.877135	7.441600
6	6.229551	6.388121	6.468410	6.632975	6.975319	7.335929	7.715610	8.115189	8.535519	8.977477	9.929920
7	7.322994	7.434283	7.662462	7.898294	8.393838	8.922803	9.487171	10.089012	10.730491	11.413873	12.915904
8	8.432839	8.582969	8.892336	9.214226	9.897468	10.636628	11.435888	12.299693	13.232760	14.240093	16.499085
9	9.559332	9.754628	10.159106	10.582795	11.491316	12.487558	13.579477	14.775656	16.085347	17.518508	20.798902
10	10.702722	10.949721	11.463879	12.006107	13.180795	14.486562	15.937425	17.548735	19.337295	21.321469	25.958682
11	11.863263	12.168715	12.807796	13.486351	14.971643	16.645487	18.531167	20.654583	23.044516	25.732904	32.150419
12	13.041211	13.412090	14.192030	15.025805	16.869941	18.977126	21.384284	24.133133	27.270749	30.850169	39.580502
13	14.236830	14.680332	15.617790	16.626838	18.882138	21.495297	24.522712	28.029109	32.088654	36.786196	48.496603
14	15.450382	15.973938	17.086324	18.291911	21.015066	24.214920	27.974983	32.392602	37.581065	43.671987	59.195923
15	16.682138	17.293417	18.598914	20.023588	23.275970	27.152114	31.772482	37.279715	43.842414	51.659505	72.035108
16	17.932370	18.639285	20.156881	21.824531	25.672528	30.324283	35.949730	42.753280	50.980352	60.925026	87.442129
17	19.201355	20.012071	21.761588	23.697512	28.212880	33.750226	40.544703	48.883674	59.117601	71.673030	105.930555
18	20.489376	21.412312	23.414435	25.645413	30.905653	37.450244	45.599173	55.749715	68.394066	84.140715	128.116666
19	21.796716	22.840559	25.116868	27.671229	33.759992	41.446263	51.159090	63.439681	78.969235	98.603230	154.740000
20	23.123667	24.297370	26.870374	29.778079	36.785591	45.761964	57.274999	72.052442	91.024928	115.379747	186.688000
21	24.470522	25.783317	28.676486	31.969202	39.992727	50.422921	64.002499	81.698736	104.768417	134.840506	225.025600
22	25.837580	27.298984	30.536780	34.247970	43.392290	55.456755	71.402749	92.502584	120.435996	157.414987	271.030719
23	27.225143	28.844963	32.452884	36.617889	46.995828	60.893296	79.543024	104.602894	138.297035	183.601385	326.236863
24	28.633521	30.421862	34.426470	39.082604	50.815577	66.764759	88.497327	118.155241	158.658620	213.977606	392.484236
25	30.063023	32.030300	36.459264	41.645908	54.864512	73.105940	98.347059	133.333870	181.870827	249.214024	471.981083
26	31.513969	33.670906	38.553042	44.311745	59.156383	79.954415	109.181765	150.333934	208.332743	290.088267	567.377300
27	32.986678	35.344324	40.709634	47.084214	63.705766	87.350768	121.099942	169.374007	238.499327	337.502390	681.852760
28	34.481479	37.051210	42.930923	49.967583	68.528112	95.338830	134.209936	190.698887	272.889233	392.502772	819.223312
29	35.998701	38.792235	45.218850	52.966286	73.639798	103.965936	148.630930	214.582754	312.093725	456.303216	984.067974
30	37.538681	40.568079	47.575416	56.084938	79.058186	113.283211	164.494023	241.332684	356.786847	530.311731	1181.881569
31	39.101761	42.379441	50.002678	59.328335	84.801677	123.345868	181.943425	271.292606	407.737005	616.161608	1419.257883
32	40.688288	44.227030	52.502759	62.701469	90.889778	134.213537	201.137767	304.847719	465.820186	715.747465	1704.109459
33	42.298612	46.111570	55.077841	66.209527	97.343165	145.950620	222.251544	342.429446	532.035012	831.267059	2045.931351
34	43.933091	48.033602	57.730177	69.857909	104.183755	158.626804	245.476699	384.520979	607.519914	965.269789	2456.117621
35	45.592088	49.994478	60.462082	73.652225	111.434780	172.316804	271.024368	431.663496	693.572702	1120.712955	2948.341146
36	47.275969	51.994367	63.275944	77.598314	119.120867	187.102148	299.126805	484.463116	791.672880	1301.027027	3539.009375
37	48.985109	54.034255	66.174223	81.702246	127.268119	203.070320	330.039486	543.598690	903.507083	1510.191352	4247.811250
38	50.789885	56.114940	69.159449	85.970336	135.904206	220.315945	364.043434	609.830533	1030.998075	1752.821968	5098.373500
39	52.480683	58.237238	72.234233	90.409150	145.058458	238.941221	401.447778	684.010197	1176.337806	2034.273483	6119.048200
40	54.267894	60.401983	75.401260	95.025516	154.761966	259.056519	442.592556	767.091420	1342.025098	2360.757240	7343.857840

Present Value of an Annuity of 1

$$P = \left[\frac{1 - \frac{1}{(1+i)^n}}{i} \right]$$

	1½%	2%	3%	4%	6%	8%	10%	12%	14%	16%	20%
1	.985222	.980392	.970874	.961538	.943396	.925926	.909091	.892857	.877193	.862069	.833333
2	1.955883	1.941561	1.913470	1.886095	1.833393	1.783265	1.735537	1.690051	1.646660	1.605232	1.527779
3	2.912200	2.883883	2.828611	2.775091	2.673012	2.577097	2.486852	2.401831	2.321631	2.245890	2.106482
4	3.854385	3.807729	3.717098	3.629895	3.465106	3.312127	3.169865	3.037349	2.913712	2.798181	2.588735
5	4.782645	4.713460	4.579707	4.451822	4.212364	3.992710	3.790787	3.604776	3.433080	3.274294	2.990613
6	5.697187	5.601431	5.417191	5.242137	4.917324	4.622880	4.355261	4.111407	3.888667	3.684736	3.325511
7	6.598214	6.471991	6.230283	6.002055	5.582381	5.206370	4.868419	4.563757	4.288304	4.038565	3.604592
8	7.485925	7.325481	7.019692	6.732745	6.209794	5.746639	5.334926	4.967640	4.638864	4.343590	3.837160
9	8.360517	8.162237	7.786109	7.435332	6.801692	6.246888	5.759024	5.328250	4.946372	4.606543	4.030967
10	9.222185	8.982585	8.530203	8.110896	7.360087	6.710081	6.144567	5.650223	5.216115	4.833227	4.192472
11	10.171118	9.786848	9.252624	8.760477	7.886875	7.138964	6.495061	5.937699	5.452733	5.028644	4.327060
12	10.907505	10.575341	9.954004	9.385074	8.383844	7.536078	6.813692	6.194374	5.660292	5.197107	4.439217
13	11.731532	11.348374	10.634955	9.985648	8.852683	7.903776	7.103356	6.423548	5.842361	5.342334	4.532681
14	12.543382	12.106249	11.296073	10.563123	9.294984	8.244237	7.366687	6.628168	6.002071	5.467529	4.610567
15	13.343233	12.849264	11.937935	11.118387	9.712249	8.559479	7.606080	6.810864	6.142168	5.575456	4.675473
16	14.131264	13.577709	12.561102	11.652296	10.105895	8.851369	7.823709	6.973986	6.265060	5.668497	4.729561
17	14.907649	14.291872	13.166118	12.165669	10.477260	9.121638	8.021553	7.119630	6.372859	5.748704	4.774634
18	15.672561	14.992031	13.753513	12.659297	10.827603	9.371887	8.201412	7.249670	6.467420	5.817848	4.812195
19	16.426168	15.678462	14.323799	13.133939	11.158116	9.603599	8.364920	7.365777	6.550369	5.877455	4.843496
20	17.168639	16.351433	14.877475	13.590326	11.469921	9.818147	8.513564	7.469444	6.623130	5.928841	4.869580
21	17.900137	17.011209	15.415024	14.029160	11.764077	10.016803	8.648694	7.562003	6.686957	5.973139	4.891316
22	18.620824	17.658048	15.936917	14.451115	12.041582	10.200744	8.771540	7.644646	6.742944	6.011326	4.909430
23	19.330862	18.292204	16.443608	14.856842	12.303379	10.371059	8.883218	7.718434	6.792056	6.044247	4.924525
24	20.030405	18.913926	16.935542	15.246963	12.550358	10.528758	8.984744	7.784316	6.835137	6.072627	4.937104
25	20.719611	19.523457	17.413148	15.622080	12.783356	10.674776	9.077040	7.843139	6.872927	6.097092	4.947587
26	21.398632	20.121036	17.876842	15.982769	13.003166	10.809978	9.160945	7.895660	6.906077	6.118183	4.956323
27	22.067618	20.706898	18.327031	16.329586	13.210534	10.935165	9.237223	7.942553	6.935155	6.136364	4.963602
28	22.726717	21.281272	18.764108	16.663063	13.406164	11.051078	9.306567	7.984423	6.960662	6.152038	4.969668
29	23.376076	21.844385	19.188455	16.983715	13.590721	11.158406	9.369606	8.021806	6.983037	6.165550	4.974724
30	24.015838	22.396456	19.600441	17.292033	13.764831	11.257783	9.426914	8.055184	7.002664	6.177198	4.978936
31	24.646146	22.937702	20.000429	17.588494	13.929086	11.349799	9.479013	8.084986	7.019881	6.187240	4.982447
32	25.267139	23.468335	20.388766	17.873551	14.084043	11.434999	9.526376	8.111594	7.034983	6.195897	4.985373
33	25.878955	23.988564	20.765792	18.147646	14.230230	11.513888	9.569432	8.135352	7.048231	6.203359	4.987810
34	26.481729	24.498592	21.131837	18.411198	14.368141	11.586934	9.608575	8.156564	7.059852	6.209792	4.989842
35	27.075595	24.998619	21.487220	18.664613	14.498246	11.654568	9.644159	8.175504	7.070045	6.215338	4.991535
36	27.660684	25.488843	21.832253	18.908282	14.620987	11.717193	9.676508	8.192414	7.078987	6.220119	4.992946
37	28.237127	25.969453	22.167235	19.142579	14.736780	11.775179	9.705917	8.207513	7.086831	6.224241	4.994122
38	28.805052	26.440641	22.492462	19.367864	14.846019	11.828869	9.732651	8.220993	7.093711	6.227794	4.995101
39	29.364583	26.902589	22.808215	19.584485	14.949075	11.878582	9.756956	8.233030	7.099747	6.230857	4.995918
40	29.915845	27.355479	23.114772	19.792774	15.046297	11.924613	9.779051	8.243777	7.105041	6.233497	4.996598

Index

American Accounting Association (AAA)
248, 251
American Institute of Certified Public
Accountants, 247
comments and quotations concerning
accounting changes, 661
business combinations, 1009–1010
comparative financial statements, 663
cost, defined, 379
current assets, defined, 653
current liabilities, defined, 29–30
earnings per share, 525–526
extraordinary items, 658–659
financial statement objectives, 251–252
funds statement, 718–720
intangible assets, 442
lower of cost or market, 390
price-level statements, 763
statement of changes in financial
position, 697–698
statement of financial activities,
727–728
stock dividends, 514
value, defined, 379
Amortization, 419
bond investment, 621, 630–634, 637–638
bonds payable, 591–599, 605–606
intangible assets, 442
organization costs, 478
patents, 777
Analog computer,
Analysis of financial statements, see
Financial statement analysis
Analyzing transactions, 87–89
Annuities, 282–284, 285–288
Articles of copartnership, 465
Articles of incorporation, 477
Asset valuation account, defined, 136
Assets, 24
capital, see Plant and equipment
carrying value, 430–432
current, 28–29, 653–654
fixed, see Plant and equipment
gift of, 25, 504–505
intangible, 417, 442–444
amortization, 442
on position statement, 29, 654–655
net, 25
plant and equipment, see Plant and
equipment
quick, 55, 654
revaluations, 505
trading, 654
valuation, 379–380
Auditor's opinion, 657
Authoritative bodies, 247–251
Average attainable standards, 847
Average collection period, 360–361
Average inventory costing, 386–387

Bad debts, 349–359
adjustment, 349–350, 786
comparison of methods, 357–358, 359
errors in allowance account, 356–359
estimating, 350–354, 359
on position statement, 351–354
recovery, 355–356
writing off, 357, 359
Balance sheet, see Position statement
Balance-form ledger account, 45, 245
Balancing accounts, 43, 102–106
Bank, notes payable to, 30, 550–553
Bank charges
protest fee, 564
service charge, 298
Bank reconciliation, 299–305
Bank statement, 298–299
Batch totals, 244
Bearer bonds, 584
Bill of lading, order, 568
Blank endorsement, 546
Blue-chip stocks, 620
Board of directors, 478, 587
Bond indenture, 583, 584
Bonds, 28, 582
classifications, 583–584
compared with capital stock, 583
long-term investment in, 29, 630–634,
637–638
temporary investment in, 620–622
times interest earned ratio, 635
yield table, 591
see also Bonds payable
Bonds payable, 30, 582–583
accounting for, 587–599
adjustments, 596–599
amortization
compound-interest method, 605–606
straight-line method, 591–596
authorizing, 586–587
conversion, 600
issued at discount, 589–590, 594–596
issued at face value, 588–589
issued at premium, 589–590, 591–594
reasons for issuing, 585–586
refunding, 599–603
retained earnings restriction, 602–603
retirement, 588, 599–603
sinking fund, 600–602
Book of final entry, defined, 48
Book of original entry, defined, 48
Book value, 483, 519–521
Bookkeeping, defined, 26
Bookkeeping machines, 244–246
Break-even analysis, 882–888
margin of safety, 889–890
marginal income statement, 888–889
Break-even chart, 885–888
limitations, 888
Break-even point, 666, 882–885
computation, 883–885